兎用心棒

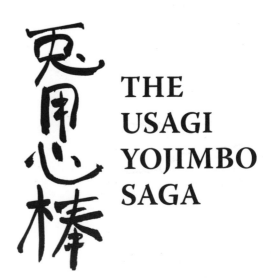

# THE USAGI YOJIMBO SAGA

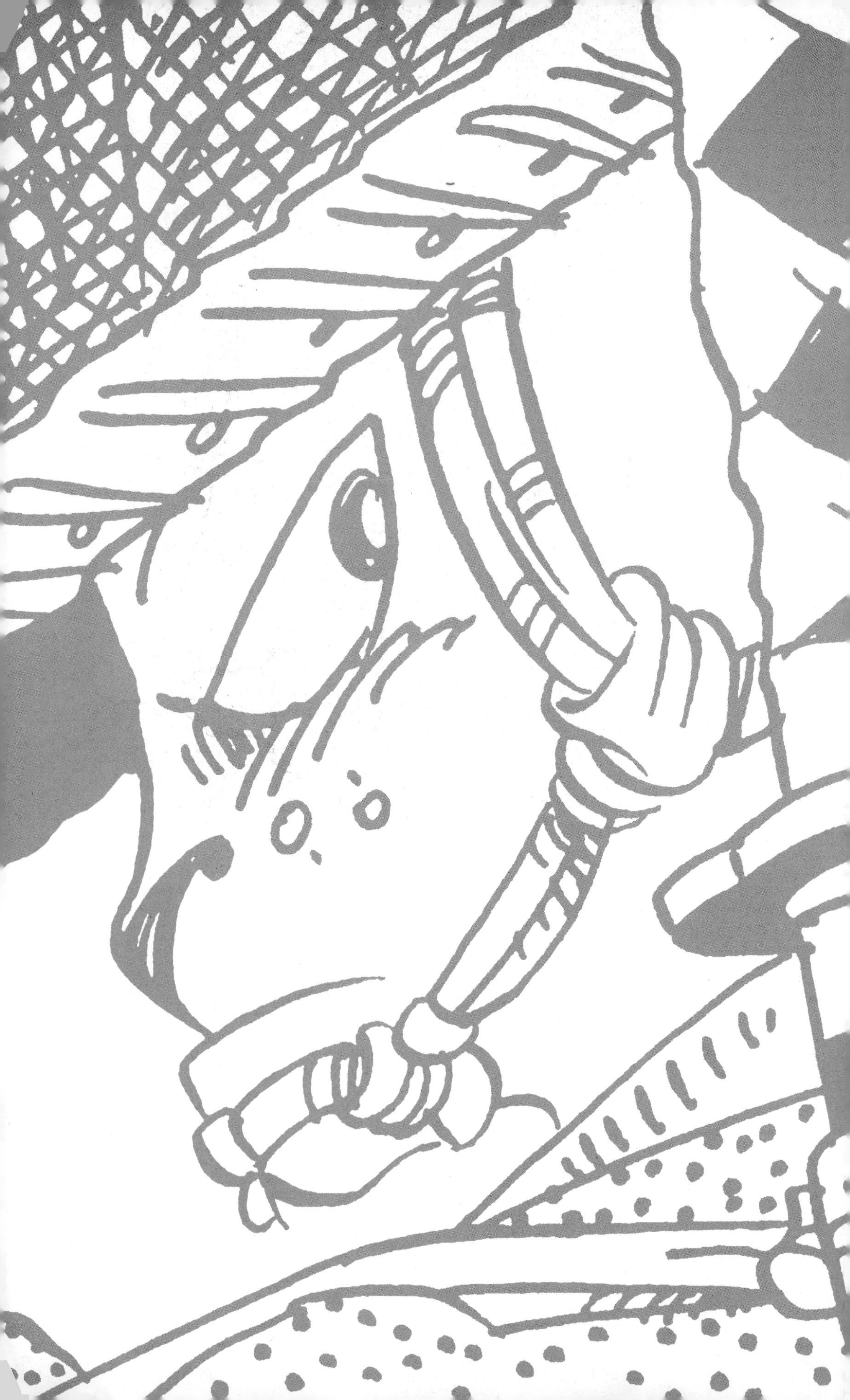

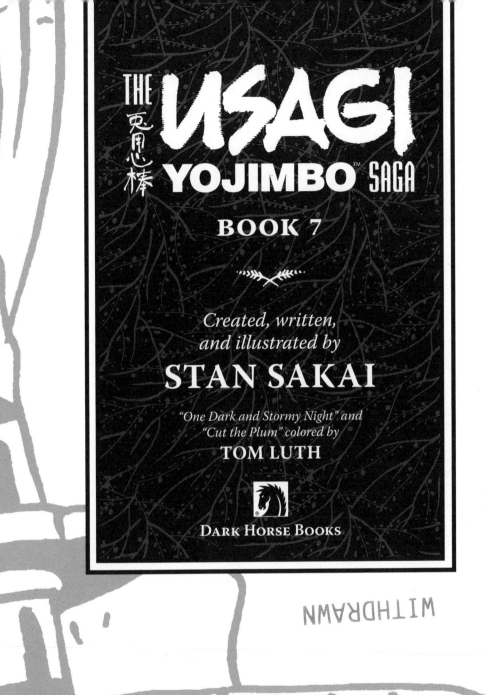

THE 兎恩忠棒 USAGI YOJIMBO™ SAGA

# BOOK 7

*Created, written,
and illustrated by*

# STAN SAKAI

*"One Dark and Stormy Night" and
"Cut the Plum" colored by*
**TOM LUTH**

**DARK HORSE BOOKS**

WITHDRAWN

*Publisher*
**MIKE RICHARDSON**

*Series Editor*
**DIANA SCHUTZ**

*Series Assistant Editors*
**BRENDAN WRIGHT** *and* **AARON WALKER**

*Collection Editor*
**AARON WALKER**

*Assistant Editor*
**RACHEL ROBERTS**

*Designer and Digital Art Technician*
**CARY GRAZZINI**

THE USAGI YOJIMBO™ SAGA Book 7


This volume collects issues #117–#138 of the Dark Horse comic book series *Usagi Yojimbo Volume Three*,
"One Dark and Stormy Night" from *Free Comic Book Day 2009*, and "Cut the Plum" from *Usagi Yojimbo Color Special* #5.

StanSakai.com
UsagiYojimbo.com

Published by Dark Horse Books
A division of Dark Horse Comics, Inc.
10956 SE Main Street
Milwaukie, OR 97222
DarkHorse.com

To find a comics shop in your area, call the Comic Shop Locator Service toll-free at (888) 266-4226.
International Licensing: (503) 905-2377

Library of Congress Cataloging-in-Publication Data

Names: Sakai, Stan, author, illustrator. | Luth, Tom, illustrator.
Title: The Usagi Yojimbo saga. Book 7 / created, written, and illustrated by Stan Sakai ; "One Dark and Stormy Night" and "Cut the Plum" colored by Tom Luth.
Description: First edition. | Limited edition. | Milwaukie, OR : Dark Horse Books, 2016. | "This volume collects issues #117/#138 of the Dark Horse comic book series Usagi Yojimbo Volume Three, "One Dark and Stormy Night" from Free Comic Book Day 2009, and "Cut the Plum" from Usagi Yojimbo Color Special #5." | Summary: "In this volume, a new love tempts Usagi to abandon his wandering lifestyle, the origin of the demon Jei is revealed at last, and Frank Miller, Jeff Smith, Sergio Aragones and more contribute to the landmark issue #100!"-- Provided by publisher.
Identifiers: LCCN 2016016170| ISBN 9781506700465 (hardback) | ISBN 9781616556150 (paperback)
Subjects: LCSH: Graphic novels. | CYAC: Graphic novels. | Samurai--Fiction. | BISAC: COMICS & GRAPHIC NOVELS / Fantasy.
Classification: LCC PZ7.7.S138 Us 2016 | DDC 741.5/973--dc23
LC record available at https://lccn.loc.gov/2016016170

First edition: September 2016
ISBN 978-1-61655-615-0

Limited edition: September 2016
ISBN 978-1-50670-046-5

10 9 8 7 6 5 4 3 2 1

PRINTED IN CHINA

To Daniel Fujii, a great stepson
and even better friend.

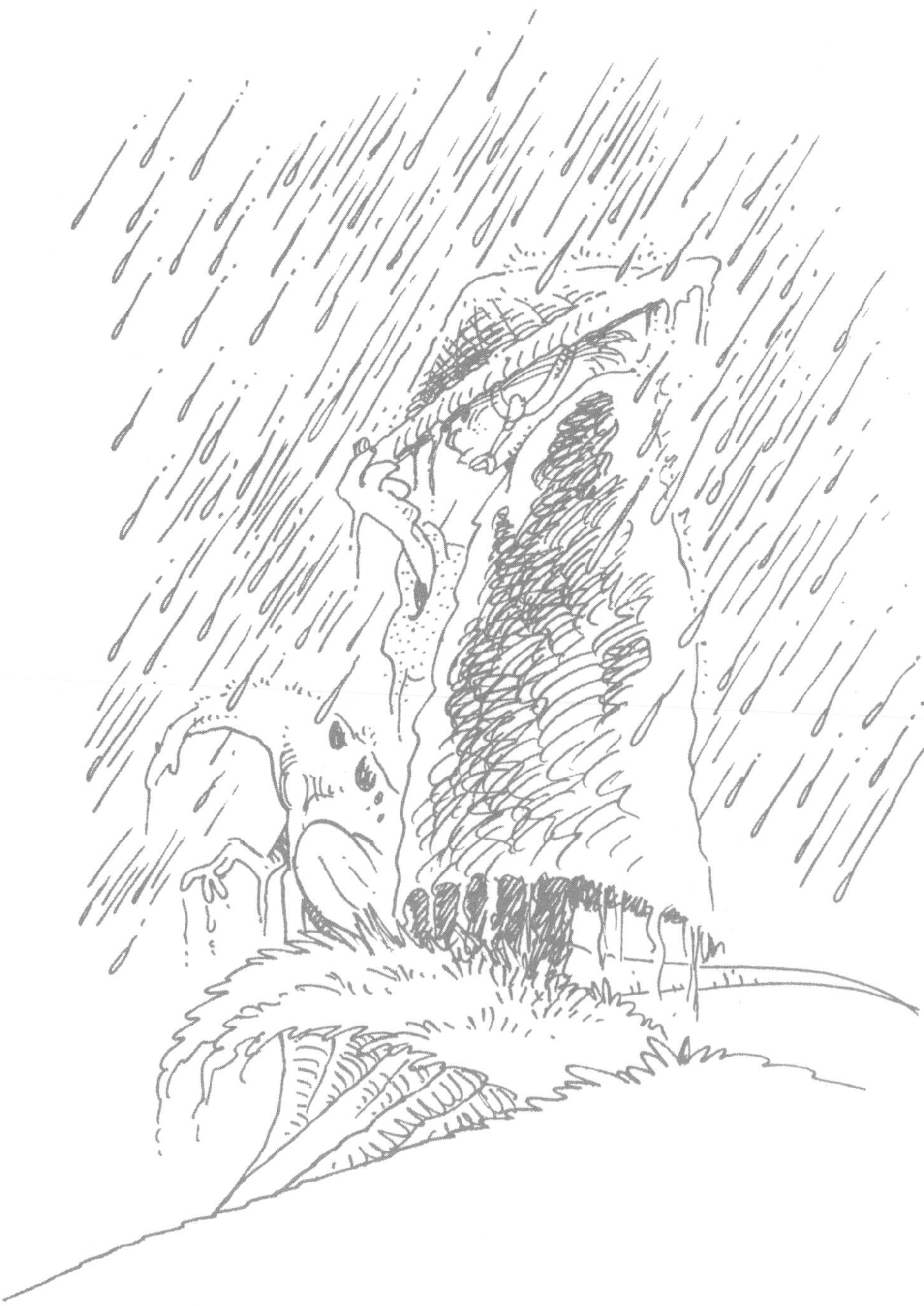

Cast of Characters . . . . . . . . . . . . . . . . . . . . . . . . . . . . . . . . . . . . . . . . . . . . 8

# TRAITORS OF THE EARTH

Introduction by Walter Simonson . . . . . . . . . . . . . . . . . . . . . . . . . . 10

Traitors of the Earth . . . . . . . . . . . . . . . . . . . . . . . . . . . . . . . . . . . . 11

What the Little Thief Heard . . . . . . . . . . . . . . . . . . . . . . . . . . . . . . 85

One Dark and Stormy Night . . . . . . . . . . . . . . . . . . . . . . . . . . . . . . 109

The Hidden Fortress . . . . . . . . . . . . . . . . . . . . . . . . . . . . . . . . . . . 115

A Place to Stay . . . . . . . . . . . . . . . . . . . . . . . . . . . . . . . . . . . . . . . . . . 139

The Death of Lord Hikiji . . . . . . . . . . . . . . . . . . . . . . . . . . . . . . . . . 163

# A TOWN CALLED HELL

Introduction by Geof Darrow . . . . . . . . . . . . . . . . . . . . . . . . . . . . . . 188

A Town Called Hell! . . . . . . . . . . . . . . . . . . . . . . . . . . . . . . . . . . . . . 191

Nukekubi . . . . . . . . . . . . . . . . . . . . . . . . . . . . . . . . . . . . . . . . . . . . . . 239

The Sword of Narukami . . . . . . . . . . . . . . . . . . . . . . . . . . . . . . . . . . 263

Teru Teru Bozu . . . . . . . . . . . . . . . . . . . . . . . . . . . . . . . . . . . . . . . . . 287

Encounter at Blood Tree Pass . . . . . . . . . . . . . . . . . . . . . . . . . . . . . 311

Return to Hell . . . . . . . . . . . . . . . . . . . . . . . . . . . . . . . . . . . . . . . . . 335

# RED SCORPION

Introduction by George Takei . . . . . . . . . . . . . . . . . . . . . . . . . . . . . . 386

*Taiko* . . . . . . . . . . . . . . . . . . . . . . . . . . . . . . . . . . . . . . . . . . . . . 387

Toad Oil . . . . . . . . . . . . . . . . . . . . . . . . . . . . . . . . . . . . . . . . . . . . 437

The Return of the Lord of Owls . . . . . . . . . . . . . . . . . . . . . . . . . 461

Those Who Tread on the Scorpion's Tail . . . . . . . . . . . . . . . . . . . 485

Cut the Plum . . . . . . . . . . . . . . . . . . . . . . . . . . . . . . . . . . . . . . . . 557


Story Notes . . . . . . . . . . . . . . . . . . . . . . . . . . . . . . . . . . . . . . . . . . 559

Gallery . . . . . . . . . . . . . . . . . . . . . . . . . . . . . . . . . . . . . . . . . . . . . 564

Extras . . . . . . . . . . . . . . . . . . . . . . . . . . . . . . . . . . . . . . . . . . . . . . 593

Pinup . . . . . . . . . . . . . . . . . . . . . . . . . . . . . . . . . . . . . . . . . . . . . . 597

# CAST OF CHARACTERS

After the death of Lord Mifune in the battle of Adachi Plain, retainer **MIYAMOTO USAGI** chose the warrior's pilgrimage, becoming a wandering *ronin* in search of peace. Practicing the warrior code of *bushido*, Usagi avoids conflict whenever possible, but when called upon, his bravery and fighting prowess are unsurpassed.

A street performer who believes "a girl has to do what she can to get by," **KITSUNE** makes extra money as a pickpocket, but steals only from those who deserve it. She and Usagi have been friends for many years, since the day she stole his purse and he stole it back.

Apprentice and sidekick to the wily Kitsune, young **KIYOKO** is every bit as enterprising, mischievous, and cunning as her mentor. Kiyoko is one of a very few whom Kitsune calls friend, and their bond is as strong as that of a big and a little sister.

Ceaselessly called to slay dangerous *yokai*, **SASUKÉ THE DEMON QUELLER** is the strangest and most mysterious of Usagi's allies. Sasuké is tight lipped about his origins and mission, and he often unsettles Usagi as much as whatever supernatural force they are facing.

In the midst of a gang war brewing between two rival crime bosses, Usagi encounters **KATO**, one of the most lethal killers the rabbit *ronin* has ever faced. Kato sells his services to the highest bidder and is a master swordsman—perhaps even better than Usagi himself.

Like his namesake, **THE LORD OF OWLS** is a harbinger of death. This enigmatic samurai can see death in a person's eyes . . . and the first time he and Usagi crossed paths, he made a dire prediction: one day the two of them will meet as adversaries, and one will surely kill the other.

# TRAITORS OF THE EARTH

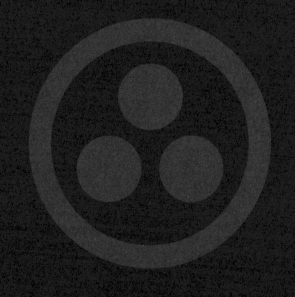

STAN SAKAI'S *USAGI YOJIMBO* has been my favorite comic book, like . . . forever.

It's the one comic I have read regularly for years. But be warned. I haven't memorized it; I would fail a Usagi Yojimbo Trivial Pursuit contest. I don't have that much unused memory storage left anyway. But I have read this comic book, since its beginning, for all the right reasons. Regularly, like clockwork, it brings me the unalloyed joy of reading a well-told, well-drawn story, about characters I have come to care about. For me, that's the highest praise I can give any comic book.

In some ways, I am transported back to the comics of my youth when I read the adventures of Usagi. Stan eschews bombast, the use of elaborate panel layouts, black gutters, or artwork extended beyond the edge of the page and trimmed. Any given issue is liable to contain thought balloons and sound effects. He fashions his stories using all the classic tools that comic books have used for years. In other words, Stan fills his comic book, every month, with straightforward storytelling that is by turns lyrical, direct, subtle, engaging, funny, and occasionally tragic. Stan's art, in every sense, is always at the service of his story.

I keep a copy of a quotation taped on the bookshelf to my right in my studio. It is there to remind me, lest I forget, of the nature of the business in which I am engaged, both as an artist and as a storyteller. It is a quote from C. S. Lewis, from his book *The Great Divorce*:

"Every poet and musician and artist, but for Grace, is drawn away from love of the thing he tells, to love of the telling till, down in Deep Hell, they cannot be interested in God at all but only in what they say about Him."

I do not work thinking that the Eye of God is looking over my shoulder and prodding me to do His will, or anything else for that matter. I fervently hope He has more important things to worry about. Mostly, I try to keep in mind the old quotation, sometimes erroneously ascribed to the Bible, that "God helps those who help themselves."

For me, the meaning of Lewis's quotation is that I do not want to be caught and seduced by the cleverness of my own storytelling. I want whatever words and pictures I put down on paper to be at the service of my story. I will do things sometimes that are less than straightforward, but always with the thought that I am trying to make my story better.

Stan Sakai's *Usagi Yojimbo* is the complete exemplar of that idea. Stan never wastes a panel; he never throws away a moment or a word balloon, and his stories are fashioned with craft, care, devotion, and a deep respect for history. With every issue, Stan creates a comic that is a story for an audience of every age, in the best sense of that expression. Perhaps that is why these books transport me back to the days of my youth. That was when I read the stories of another writer/artist about whose work I feel the same way: a Mr. Carl Barks, purveyor of duck stories for about a quarter-century.

The biography of the masterless *ronin*, Usagi Yojimbo, continues. I invite the reader to join me, and accompany Usagi on his marvelous journey.

WALTER SIMONSON
NEW YORK
JANUARY 2012

THREE HUNDRED YEARS AGO, THERE WAS AN UPRISING WITHIN THE OTOMO CLAN WHEN LORD HAYASHI TOOK UP ARMS AGAINST HIS LORD MIYAKE.

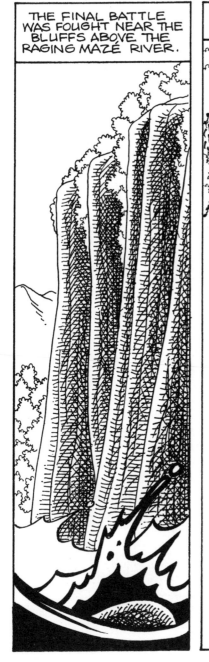

THE FINAL BATTLE WAS FOUGHT NEAR THE BLUFFS ABOVE THE RAGING MAZE RIVER.

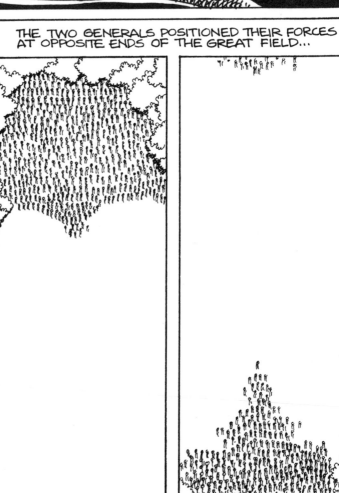

THE TWO GENERALS POSITIONED THEIR FORCES AT OPPOSITE ENDS OF THE GREAT FIELD...

...LORD MIYAKE TO THE EAST...

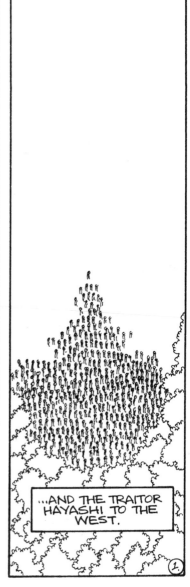

...AND THE TRAITOR HAYASHI TO THE WEST.

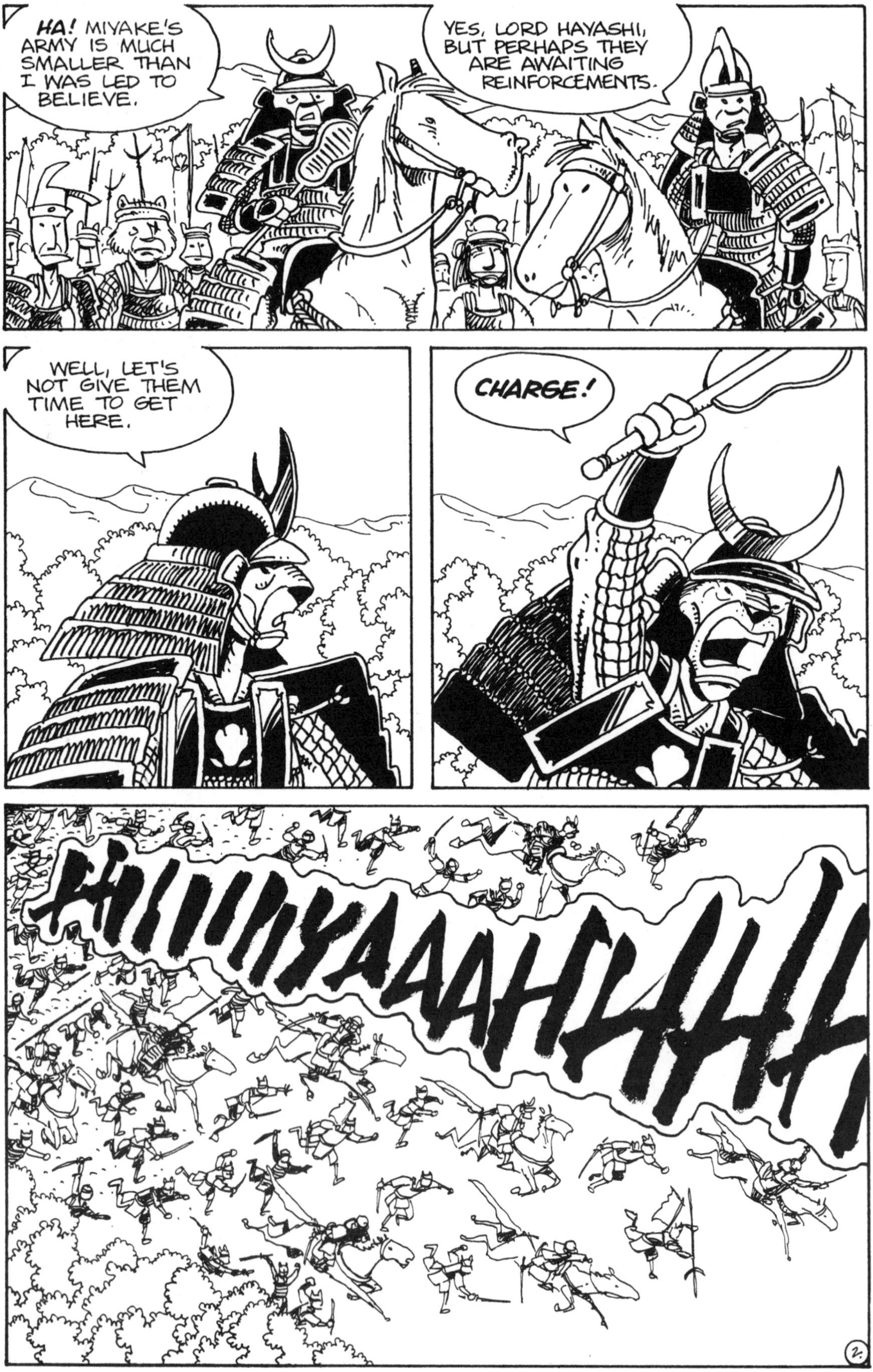

HA! MIYAKE'S ARMY IS MUCH SMALLER THAN I WAS LED TO BELIEVE.
YES, LORD HAYASHI, BUT PERHAPS THEY ARE AWAITING REINFORCEMENTS.
WELL, LET'S NOT GIVE THEM TIME TO GET HERE.
CHARGE!
HIIIIIYAAAHHHH

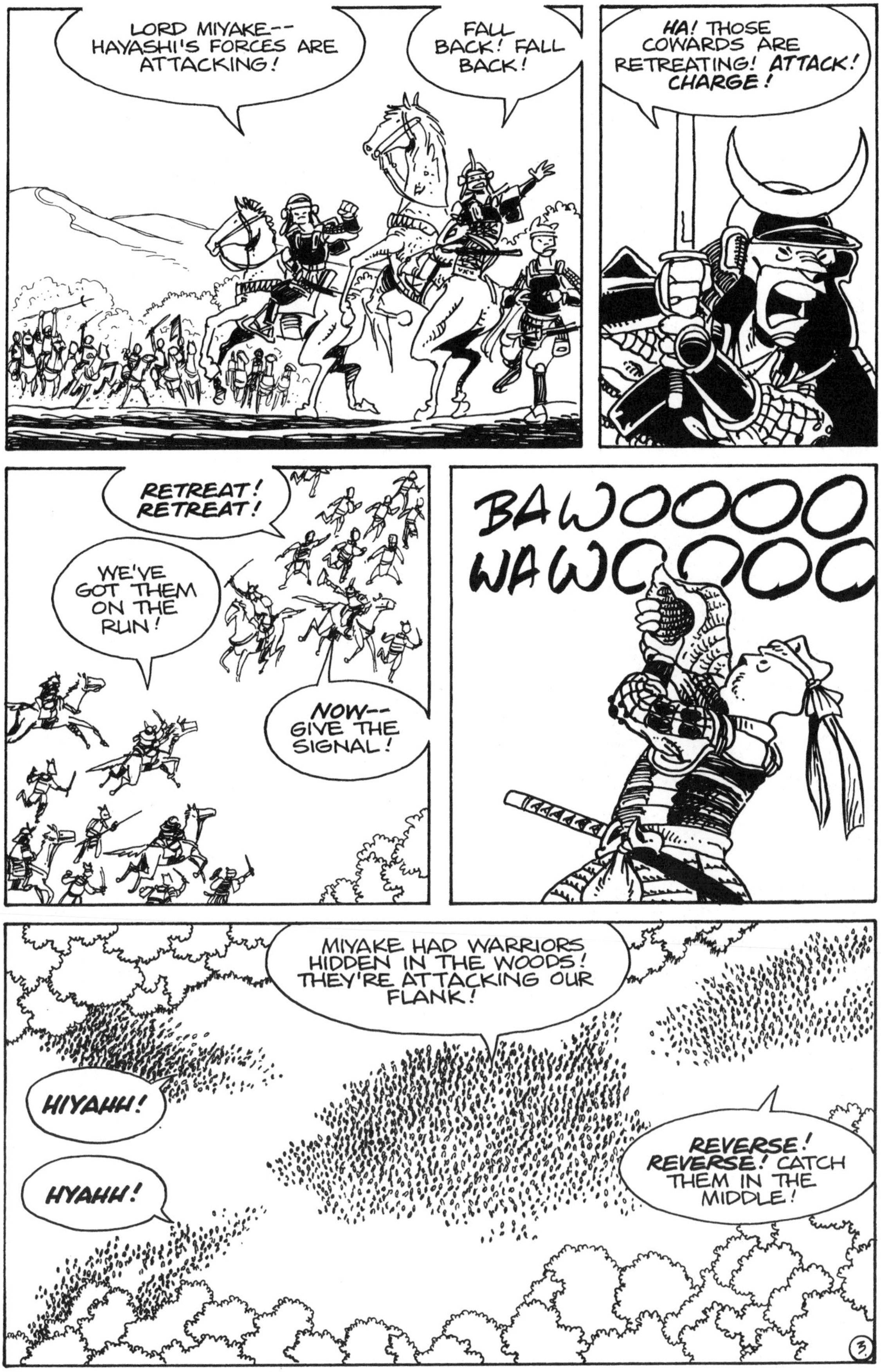
LORD MIYAKE-- HAYASHI'S FORCES ARE ATTACKING!
FALL BACK! FALL BACK!
HA! THOSE COWARDS ARE RETREATING! ATTACK! CHARGE!
RETREAT! RETREAT!
WE'VE GOT THEM ON THE RUN!
NOW-- GIVE THE SIGNAL!
BAWOOOOO WAWOOOOO
MIYAKE HAD WARRIORS HIDDEN IN THE WOODS! THEY'RE ATTACKING OUR FLANK!
HIYAHH!
HYAHH!
REVERSE! REVERSE! CATCH THEM IN THE MIDDLE!
3.

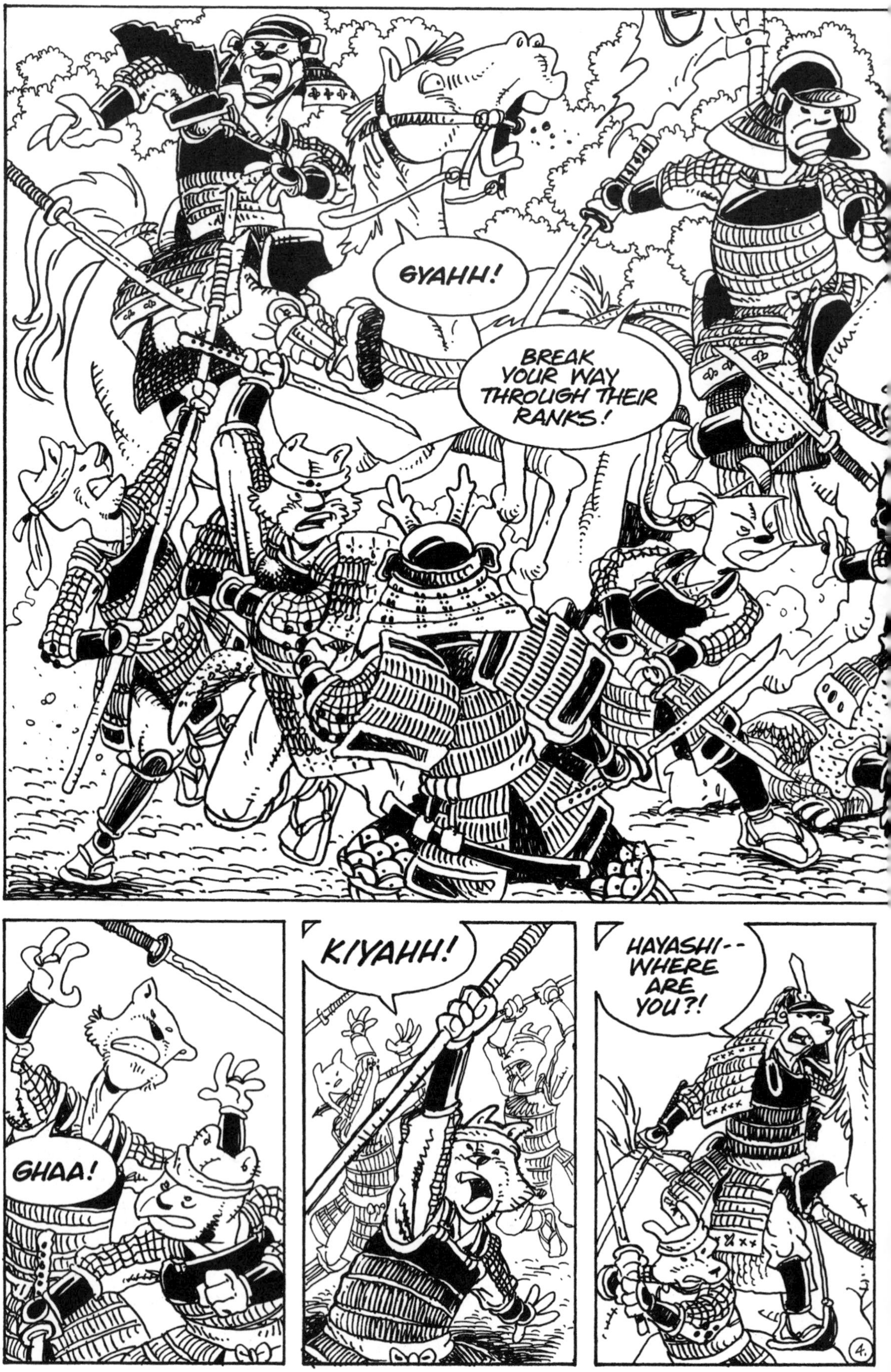
GYAHH!
BREAK YOUR WAY THROUGH THEIR RANKS!
GHAA!
KIYAHH!
HAYASHI-- WHERE ARE YOU?!
4.

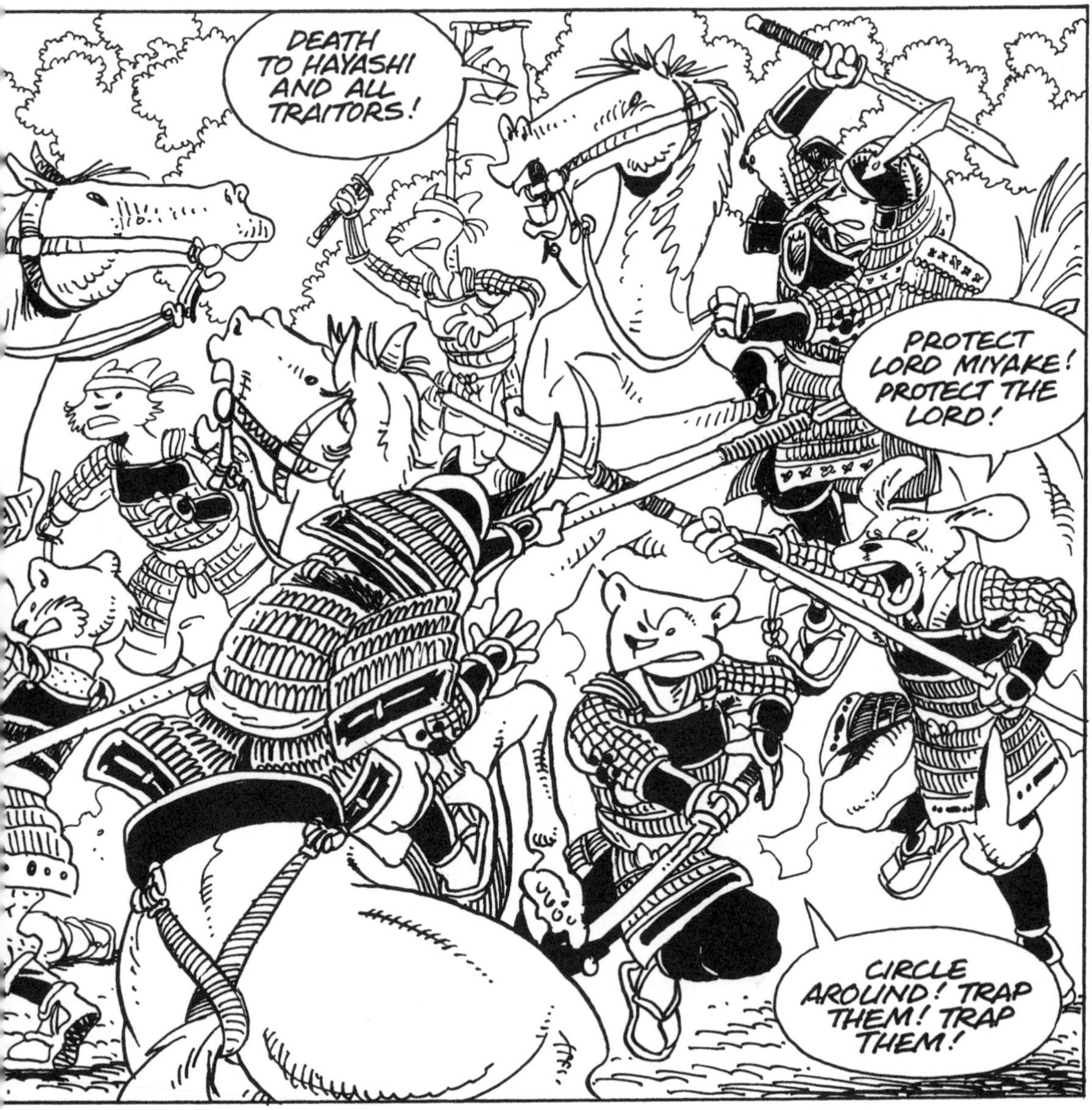
DEATH TO HAYASHI AND ALL TRAITORS!
PROTECT LORD MIYAKE! PROTECT THE LORD!
CIRCLE AROUND! TRAP THEM! TRAP THEM!
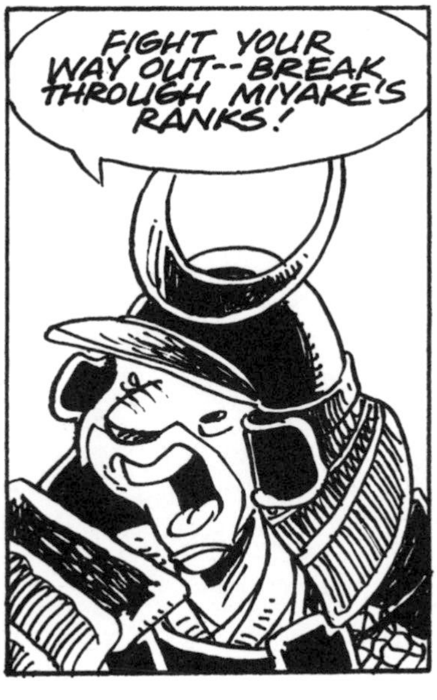
FIGHT YOUR WAY OUT--BREAK THROUGH MIYAKE'S RANKS!
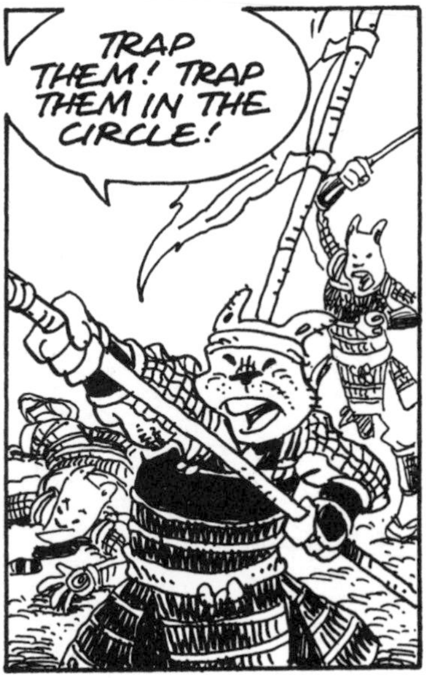
TRAP THEM! TRAP THEM IN THE CIRCLE!
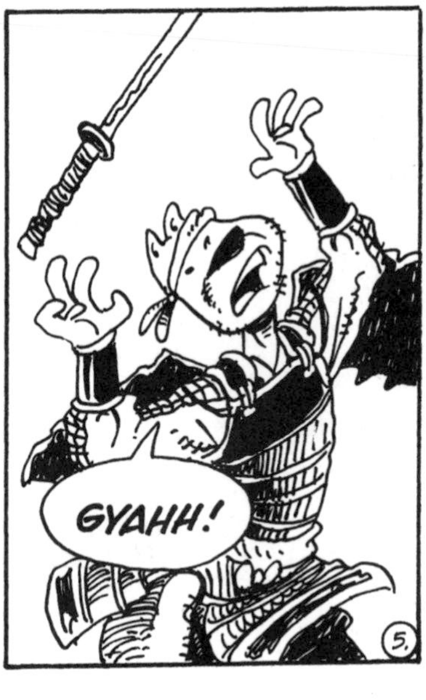
GYAHH!
5.

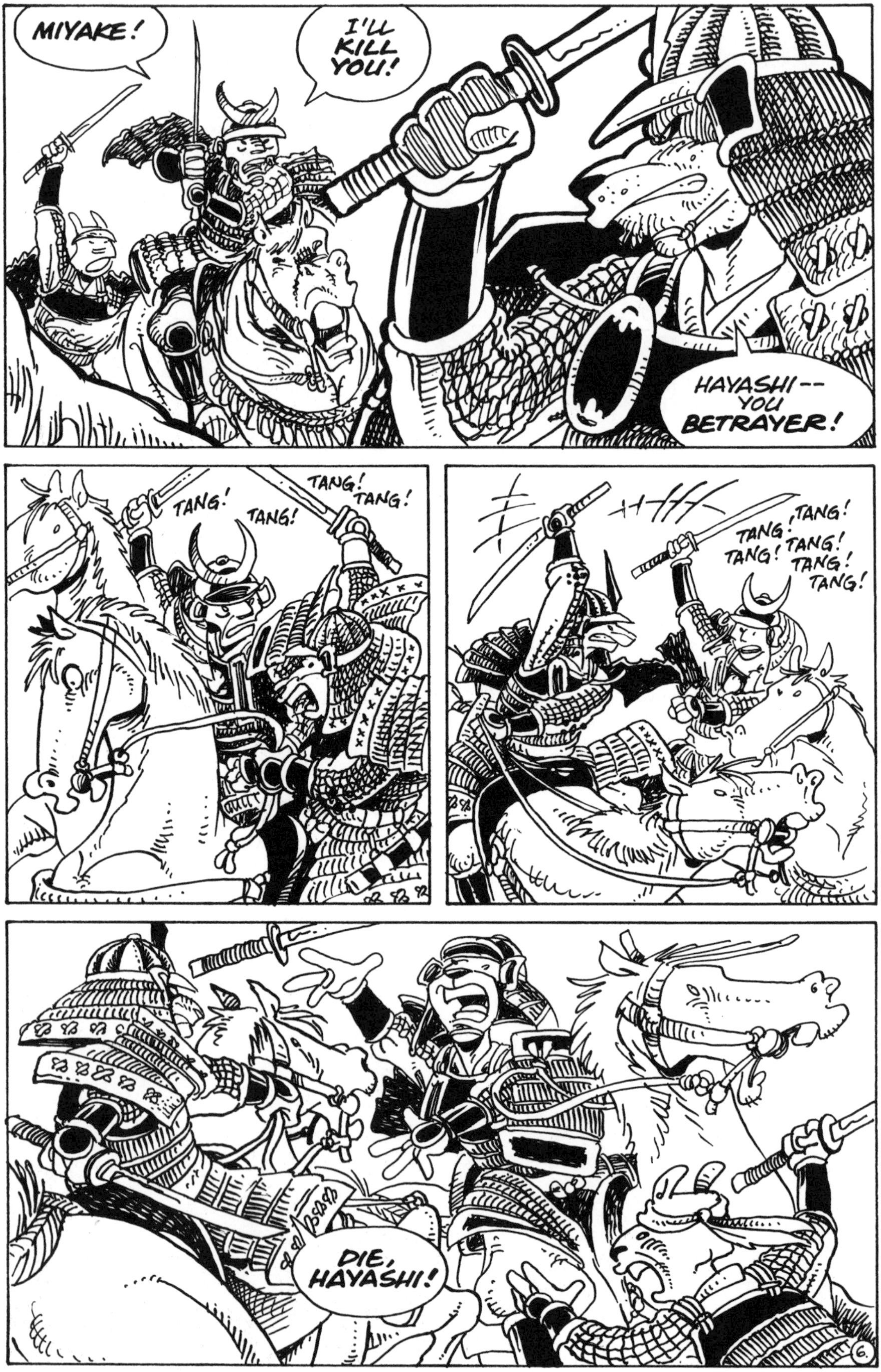
MIYAKE!
I'LL KILL YOU!
HAYASHI -- YOU BETRAYER!
TANG!
TANG!
TANG! TANG!
TANG! TANG! TANG! TANG! TANG! TANG!
DIE, HAYASHI!

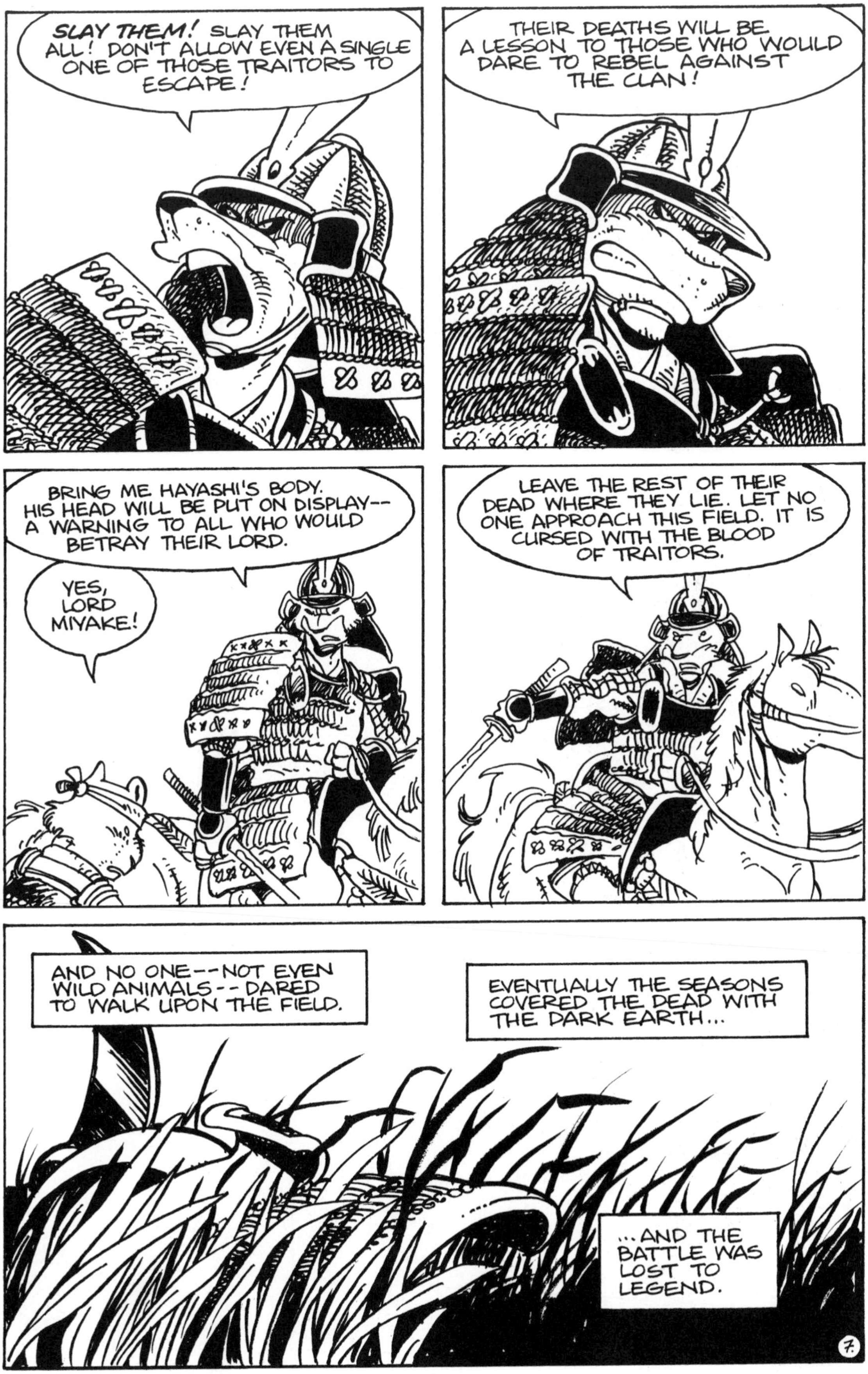
SLAY THEM! SLAY THEM ALL! DON'T ALLOW EVEN A SINGLE ONE OF THOSE TRAITORS TO ESCAPE!
THEIR DEATHS WILL BE A LESSON TO THOSE WHO WOULD DARE TO REBEL AGAINST THE CLAN!
BRING ME HAYASHI'S BODY. HIS HEAD WILL BE PUT ON DISPLAY-- A WARNING TO ALL WHO WOULD BETRAY THEIR LORD.
YES, LORD MIYAKE!
LEAVE THE REST OF THEIR DEAD WHERE THEY LIE. LET NO ONE APPROACH THIS FIELD. IT IS CURSED WITH THE BLOOD OF TRAITORS.
AND NO ONE--NOT EVEN WILD ANIMALS--DARED TO WALK UPON THE FIELD.
EVENTUALLY THE SEASONS COVERED THE DEAD WITH THE DARK EARTH...
...AND THE BATTLE WAS LOST TO LEGEND.
7.

# TRAITORS OF THE EARTH PART ONE

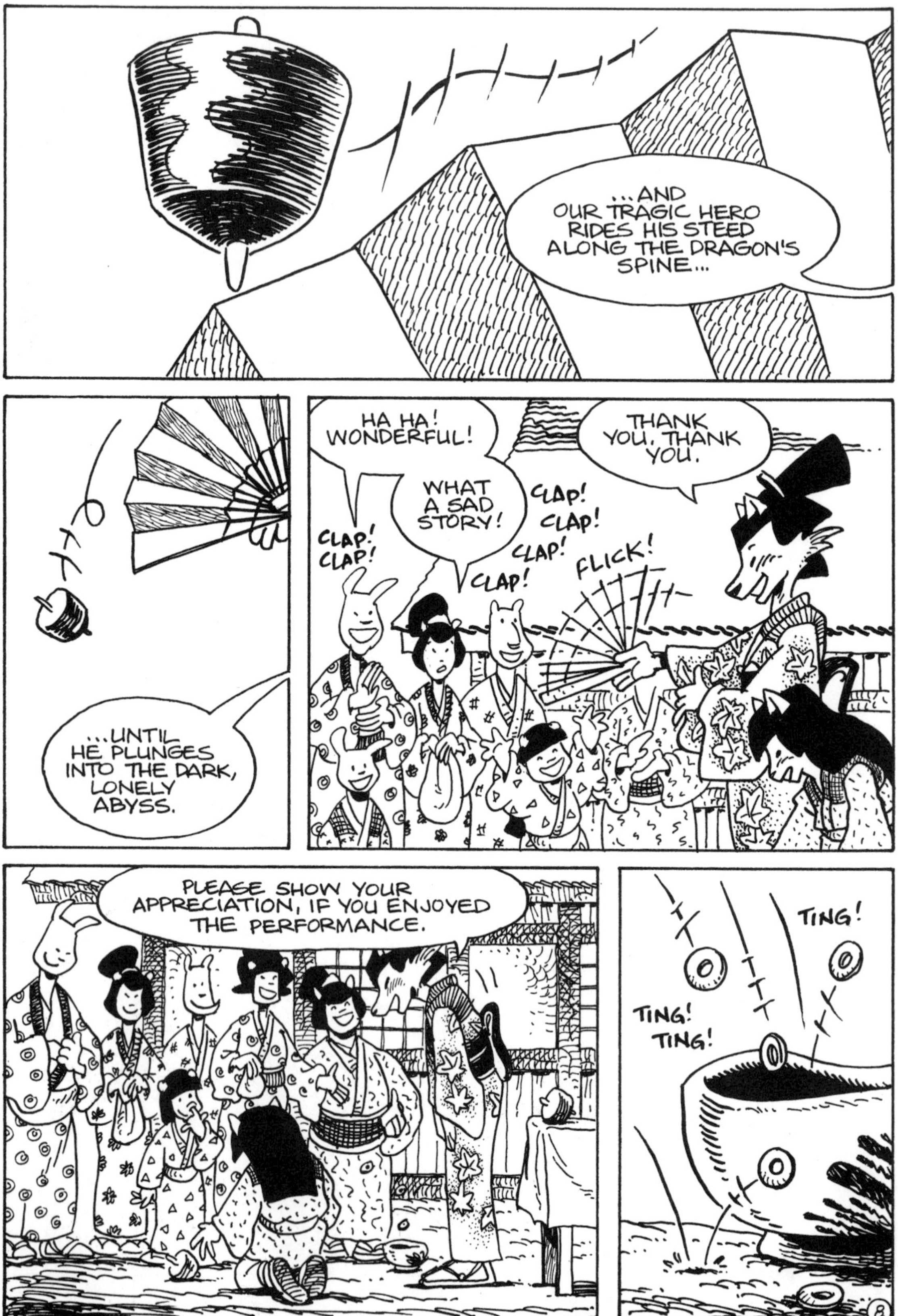
...AND OUR TRAGIC HERO RIDES HIS STEED ALONG THE DRAGON'S SPINE...
...UNTIL HE PLUNGES INTO THE DARK, LONELY ABYSS.
HA HA! WONDERFUL!
WHAT A SAD STORY!
CLAP! CLAP!
CLAP!
CLAP! CLAP!
CLAP!
FLICK!
THANK YOU, THANK YOU.
PLEASE SHOW YOUR APPRECIATION, IF YOU ENJOYED THE PERFORMANCE.
TING!
TING! TING!
8

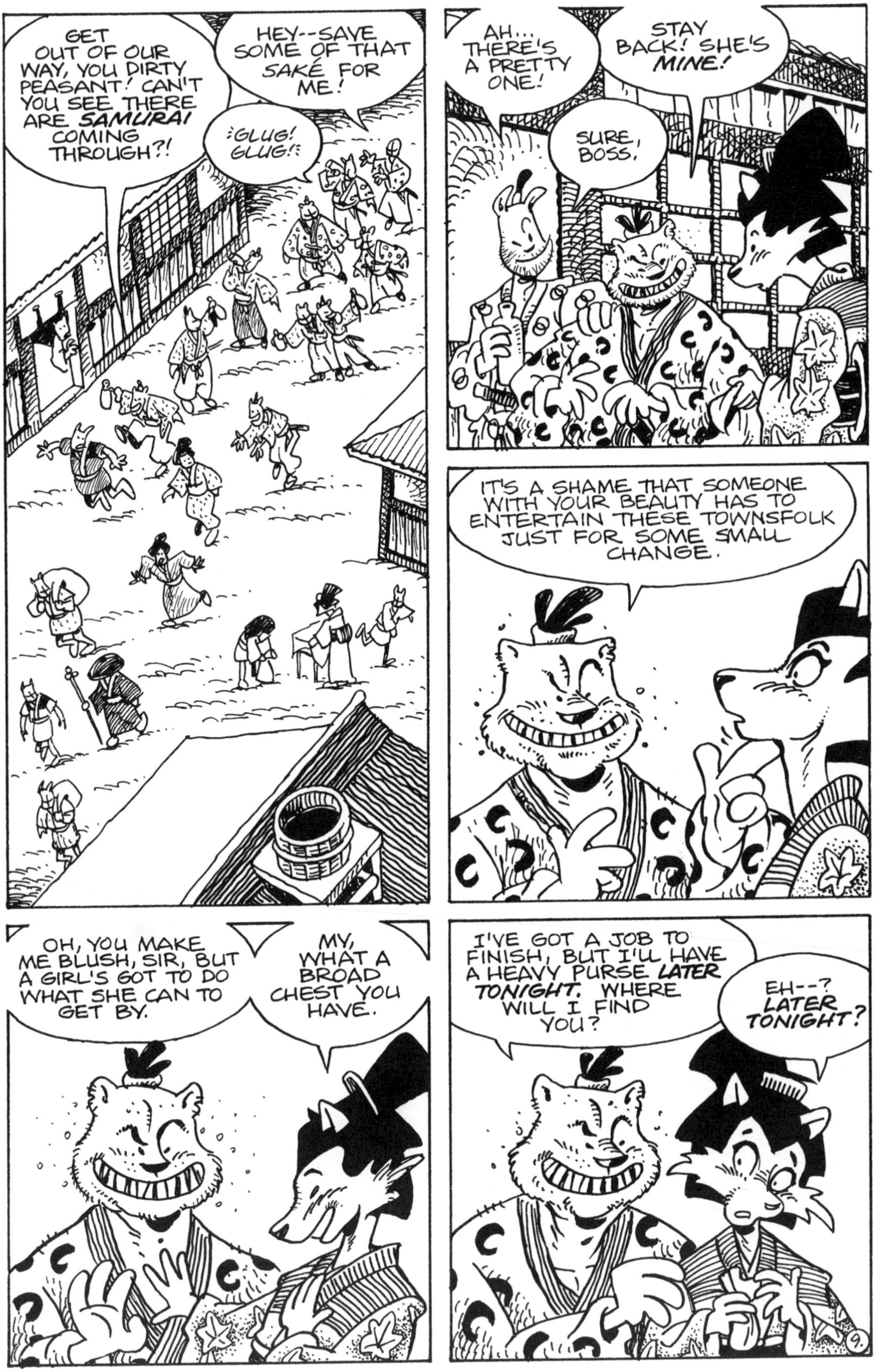
GET OUT OF OUR WAY, YOU DIRTY PEASANT! CAN'T YOU SEE THERE ARE *SAMURAI* COMING THROUGH?!
HEY--SAVE SOME OF THAT *SAKÉ* FOR ME!
GLUG! GLUG!
AH... THERE'S A PRETTY ONE!
STAY BACK! SHE'S *MINE!*
SURE, BOSS.
IT'S A SHAME THAT SOMEONE WITH YOUR BEAUTY HAS TO ENTERTAIN THESE TOWNSFOLK JUST FOR SOME SMALL CHANGE.
OH, YOU MAKE ME BLUSH, SIR, BUT A GIRL'S GOT TO DO WHAT SHE CAN TO GET BY.
MY, WHAT A BROAD CHEST YOU HAVE.
I'VE GOT A JOB TO FINISH, BUT I'LL HAVE A HEAVY PURSE *LATER TONIGHT.* WHERE WILL I FIND YOU?
EH--? *LATER TONIGHT?*
9.

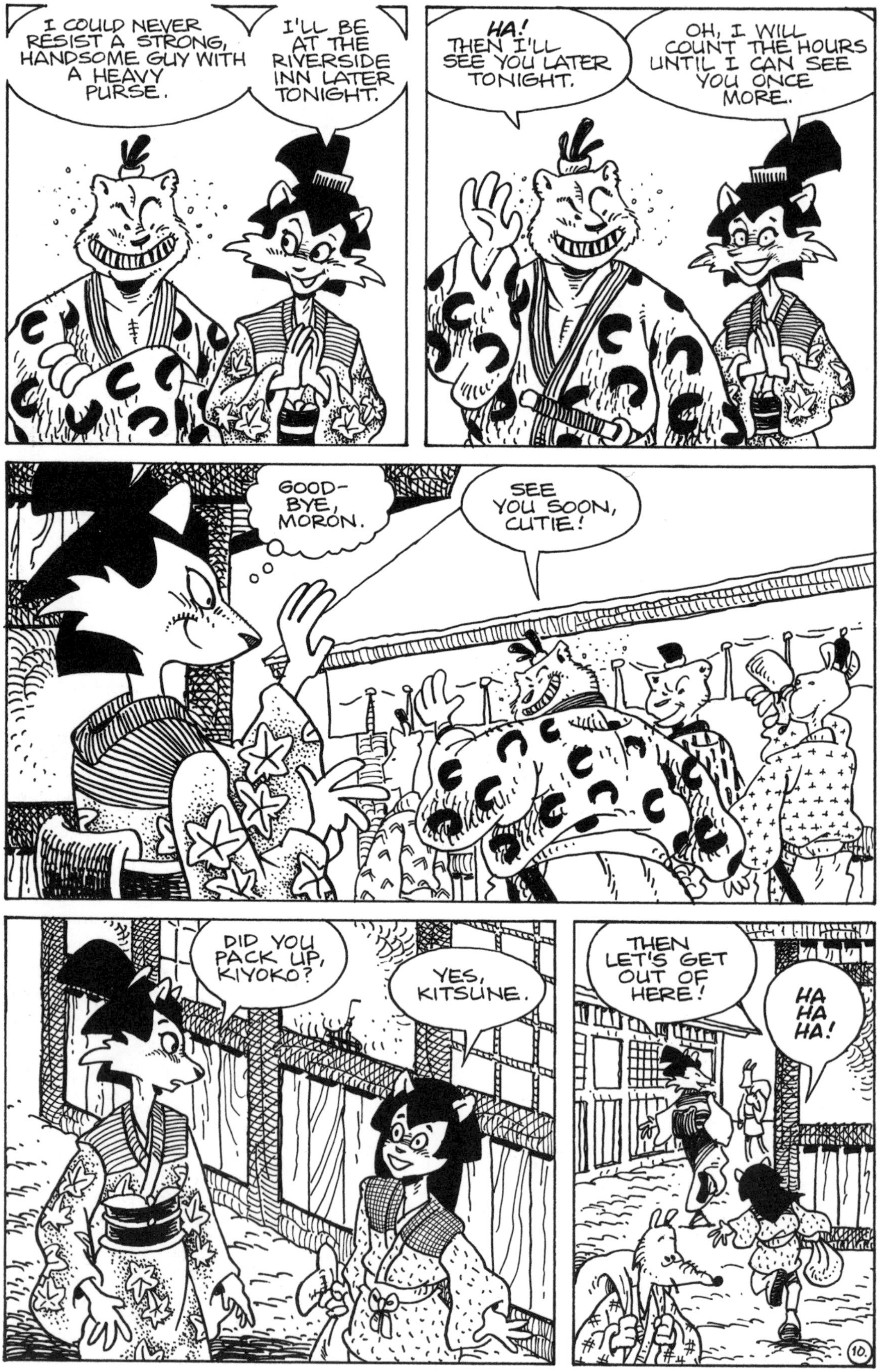
I COULD NEVER RESIST A STRONG, HANDSOME GUY WITH A HEAVY PURSE.
I'LL BE AT THE RIVERSIDE INN LATER TONIGHT.
HA! THEN I'LL SEE YOU LATER TONIGHT.
OH, I WILL COUNT THE HOURS UNTIL I CAN SEE YOU ONCE MORE.
GOOD-BYE, MORON.
SEE YOU SOON, CUTIE!
DID YOU PACK UP, KIYOKO?
YES, KITSUNE.
THEN LET'S GET OUT OF HERE!
HA HA HA!
10.

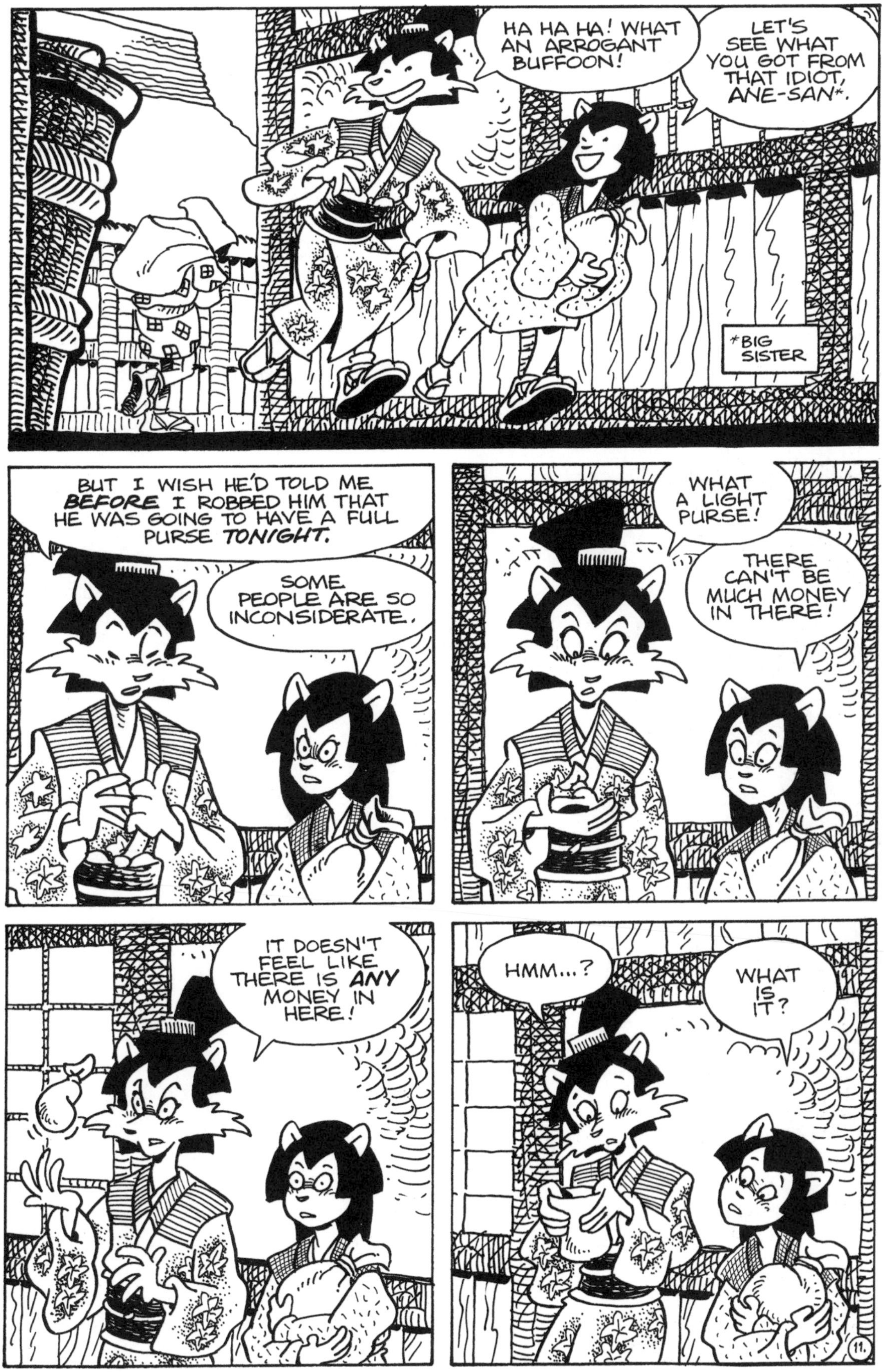
HA HA HA! WHAT AN ARROGANT BUFFOON!
LET'S SEE WHAT YOU GOT FROM THAT IDIOT, ANE-SAN*.
*BIG SISTER
BUT I WISH HE'D TOLD ME **BEFORE** I ROBBED HIM THAT HE WAS GOING TO HAVE A FULL PURSE **TONIGHT.**
SOME PEOPLE ARE SO INCONSIDERATE.
WHAT A LIGHT PURSE!
THERE CAN'T BE MUCH MONEY IN THERE!
IT DOESN'T FEEL LIKE THERE IS **ANY** MONEY IN HERE!
HMM...?
WHAT IS IT?
11.

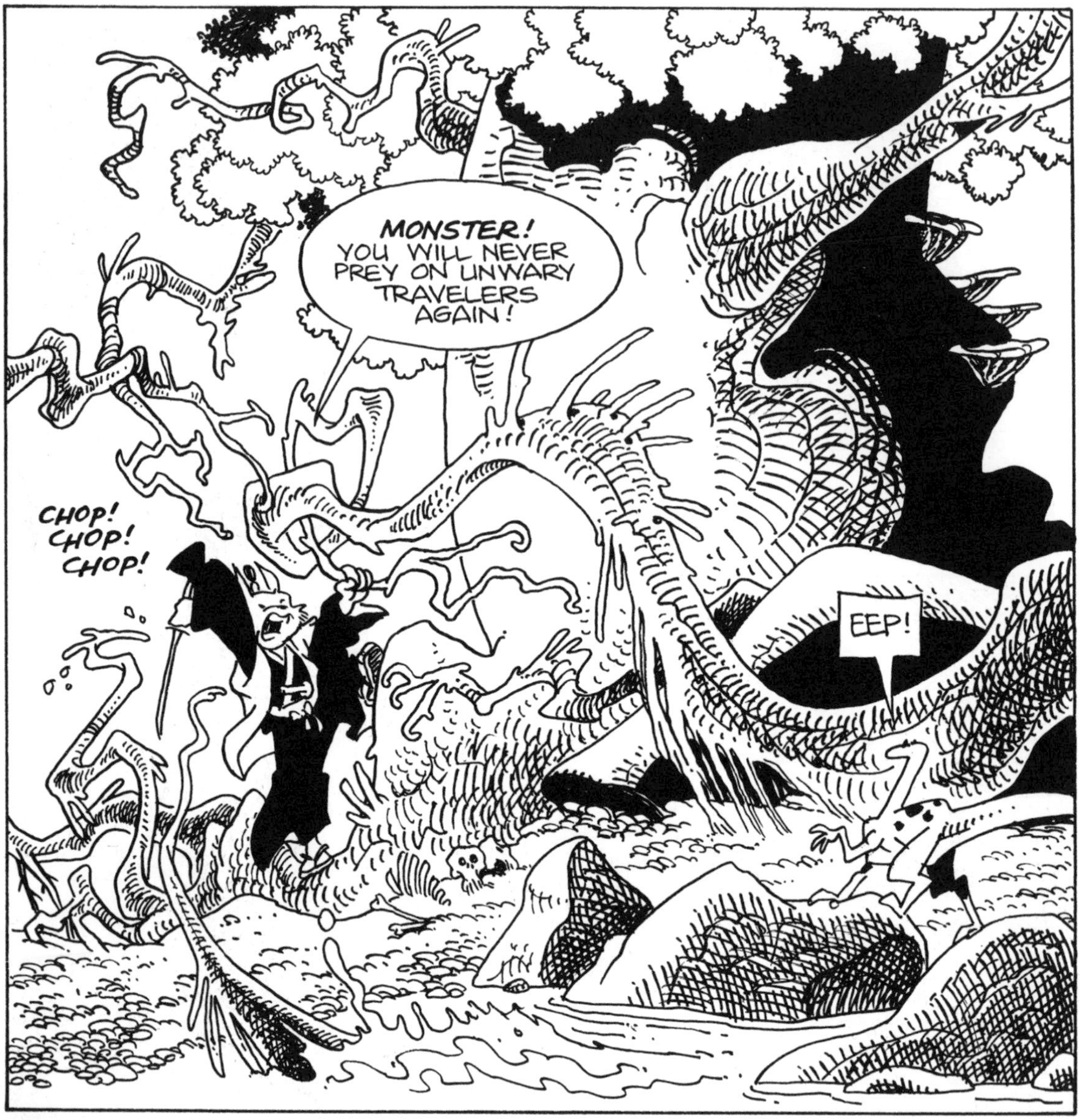
MONSTER! YOU WILL NEVER PREY ON UNWARY TRAVELERS AGAIN!
CHOP! CHOP! CHOP!
EEP!

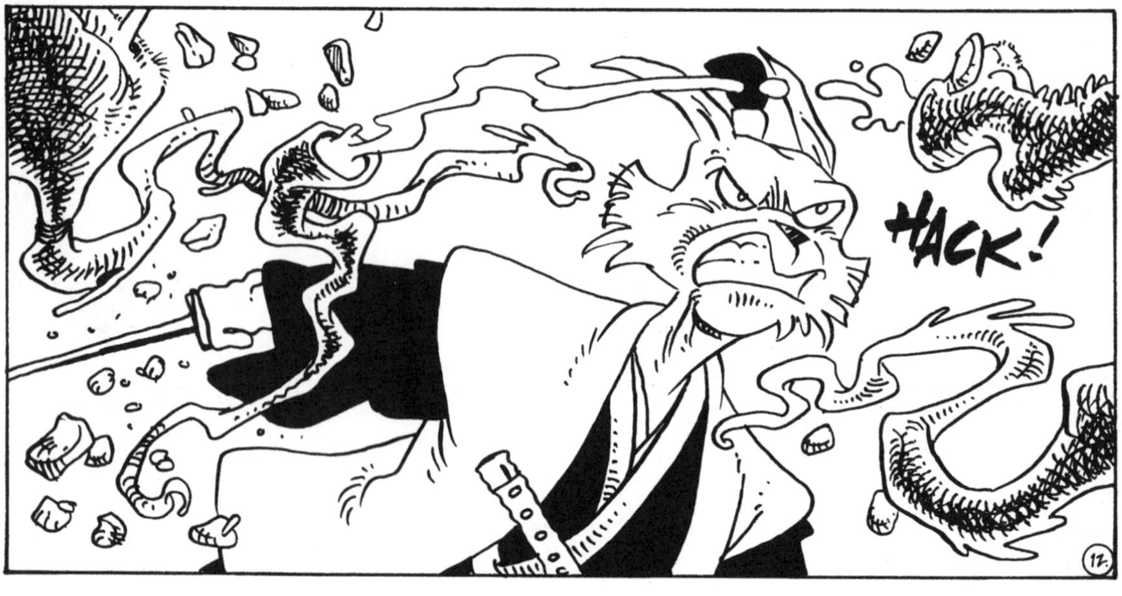
HACK!
17.

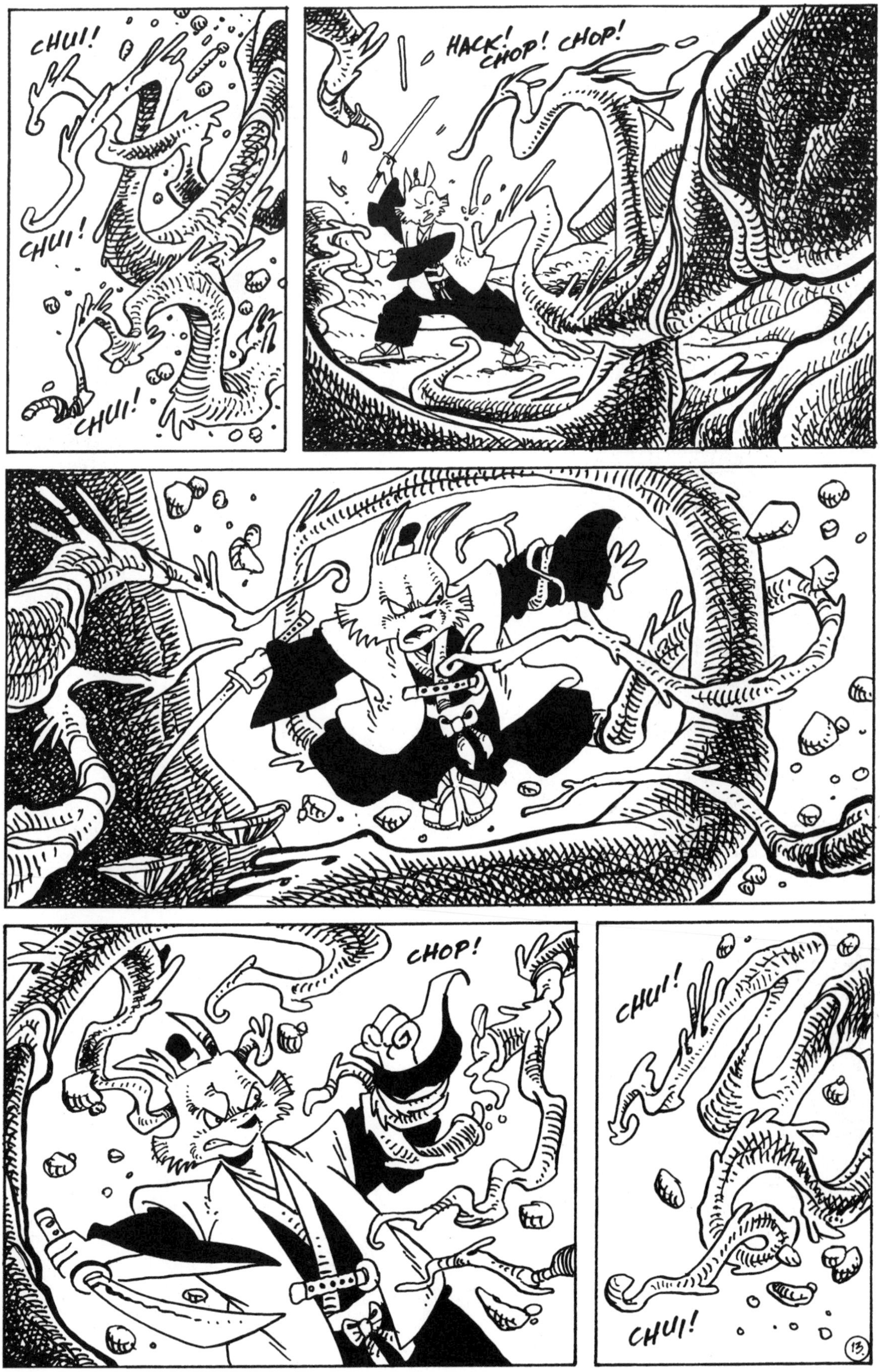
CHUI!
CHUI!
CHUI!
HACK! CHOP! CHOP!
CHOP!
CHUI!
CHUI!
13.

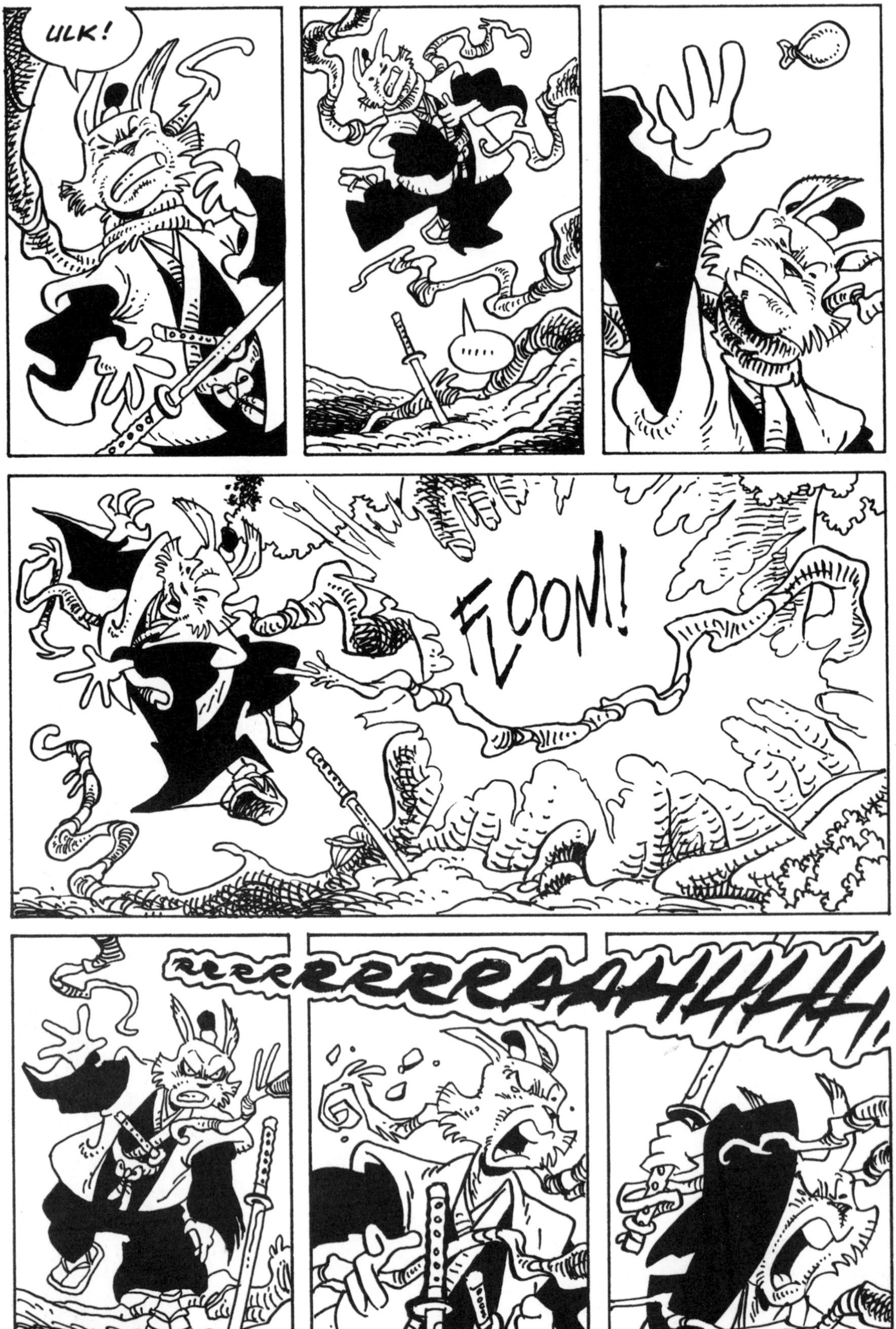
ULK!
.....
FLOOM!
RRRRRRRRRRRAAHHHH!
14

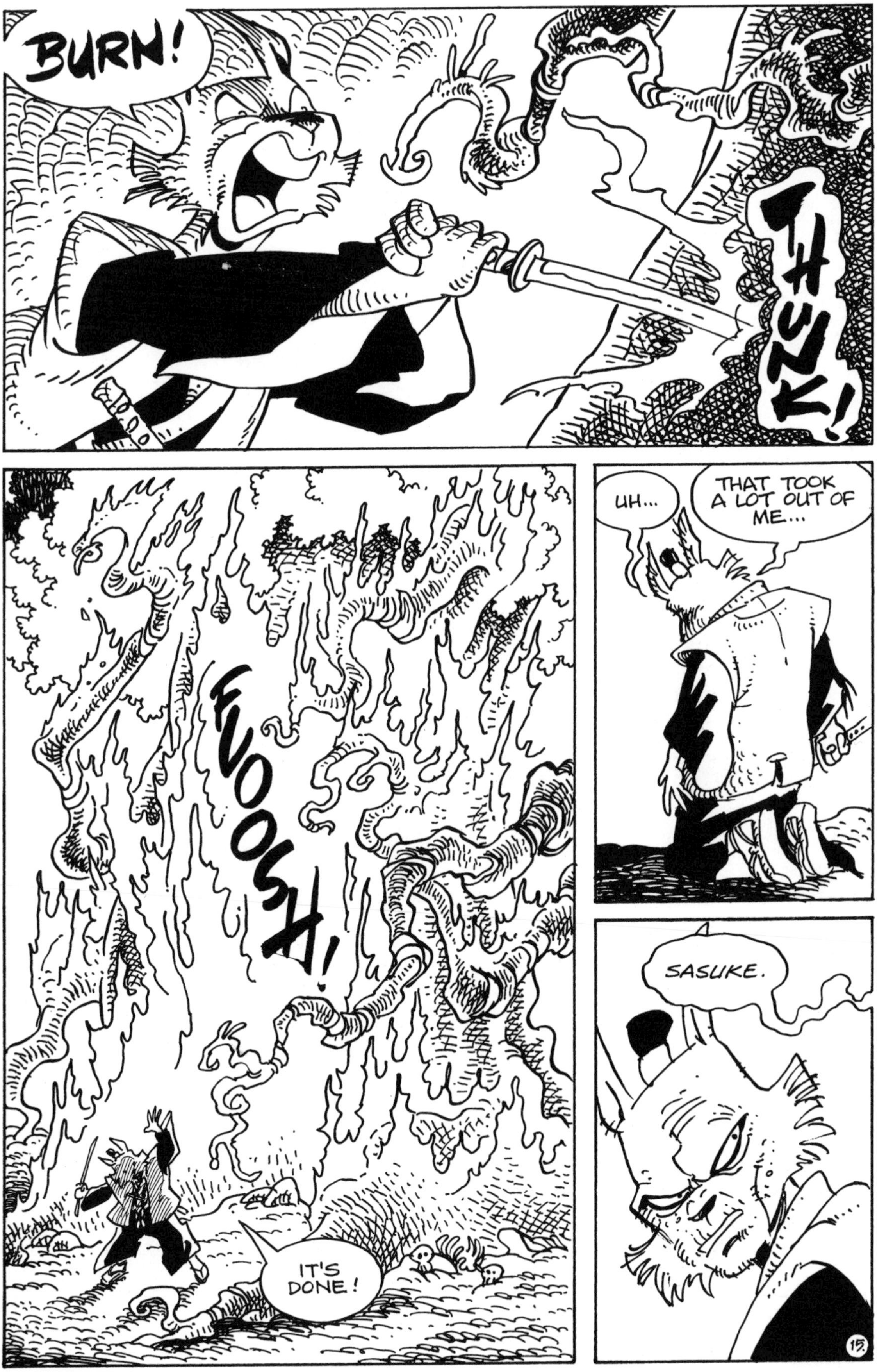
BURN!
THUNK!
FWOOSH!
IT'S DONE!
UH...
THAT TOOK A LOT OUT OF ME...
SASUKE.
15.

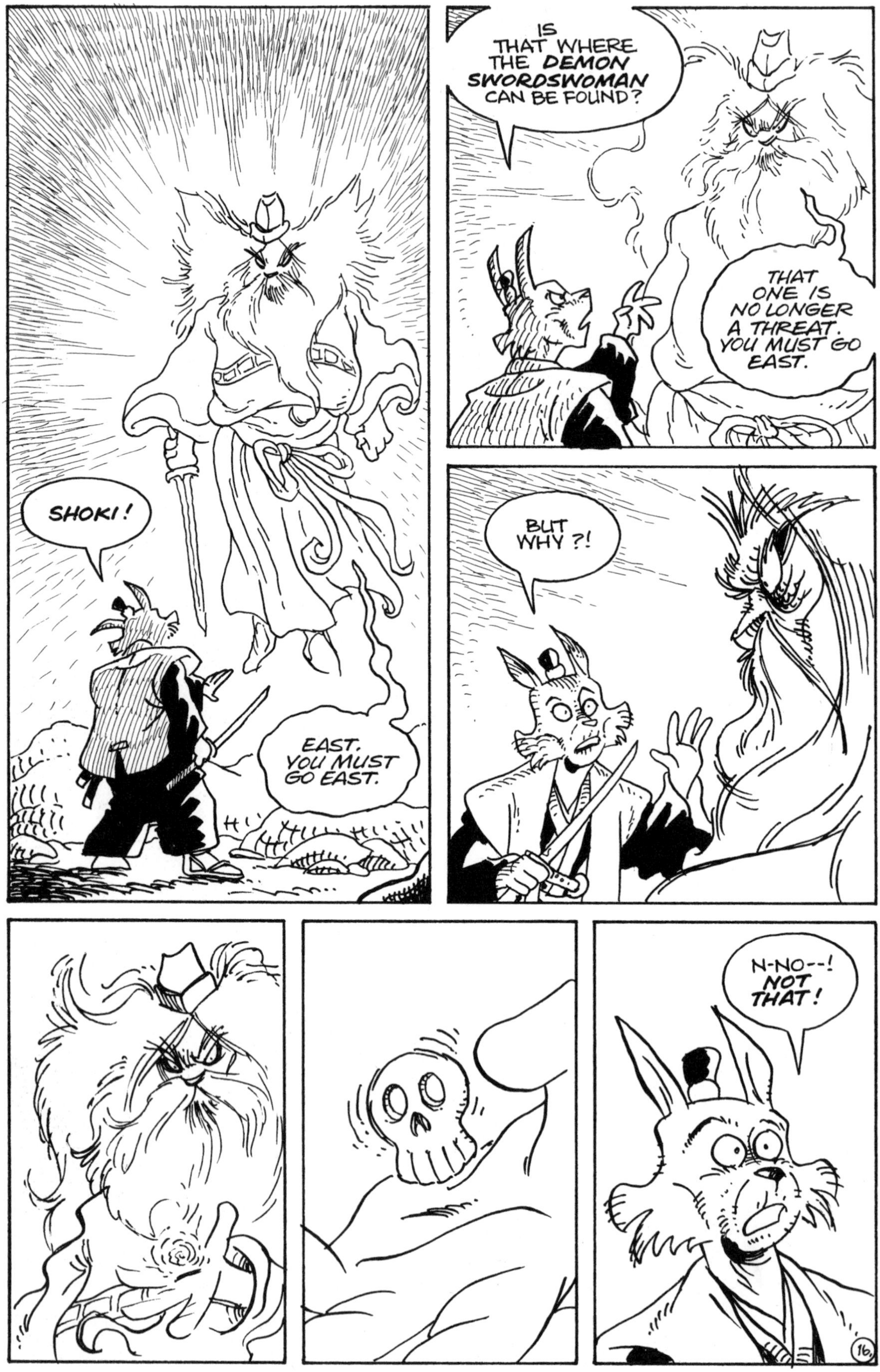
SHOKI!
EAST. YOU MUST GO EAST.
IS THAT WHERE THE DEMON SWORDSWOMAN CAN BE FOUND?
THAT ONE IS NO LONGER A THREAT. YOU MUST GO EAST.
BUT WHY?!
N-NO--! NOT THAT!
16

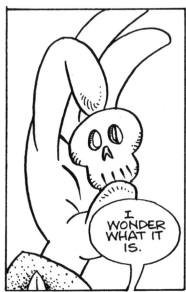

I WONDER WHAT IT IS.

IT'S JUST A *CHEAP* TRINKET!

IT COULD BE A *NETSUKE*--A TINY FIGURE CARVED FROM BONE OR IVORY. IT DOES NOT LOOK LIKE IVORY. I WONDER WHAT KIND OF BONE IT IS.

IT CERTAINLY LOOKS OLD!

THEN WE MIGHT BE ABLE TO GET A FEW COINS FOR IT.

YEAH. BUT FOR NOW, WE'VE MADE ENOUGH FOR A DECENT MEAL. WE'LL SELL THIS LITTLE TRINKET LATER.

WHAT DO YOU SAY TO THAT?

LET'S GO. I'M HUNGRY!

PLOP!

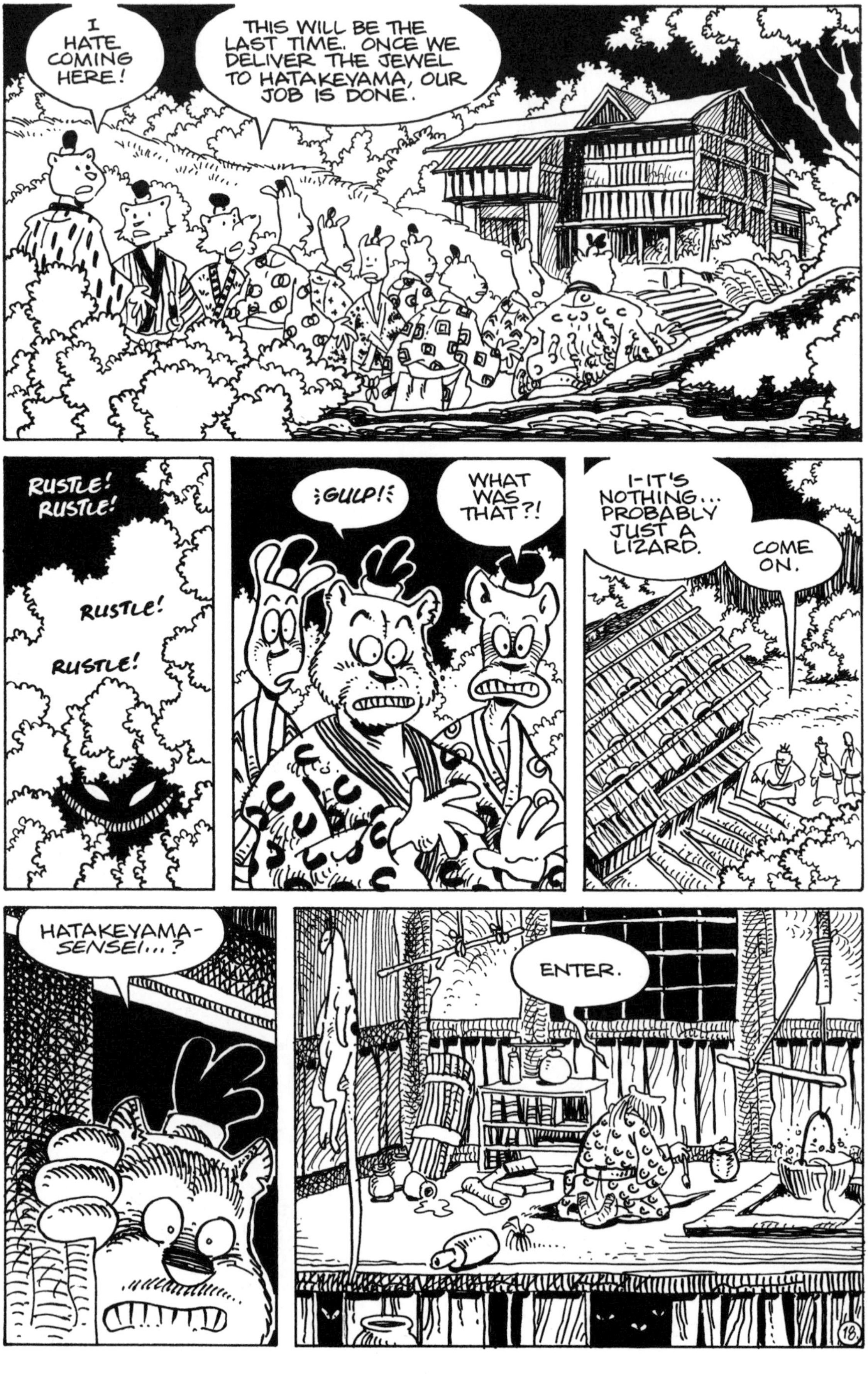
I HATE COMING HERE!
THIS WILL BE THE LAST TIME. ONCE WE DELIVER THE JEWEL TO HATAKEYAMA, OUR JOB IS DONE.
RUSTLE! RUSTLE!
RUSTLE!
RUSTLE!
GULP!
WHAT WAS THAT?!
I-IT'S NOTHING... PROBABLY JUST A LIZARD.
COME ON.
HATAKEYAMA-SENSEI...?
ENTER.
18

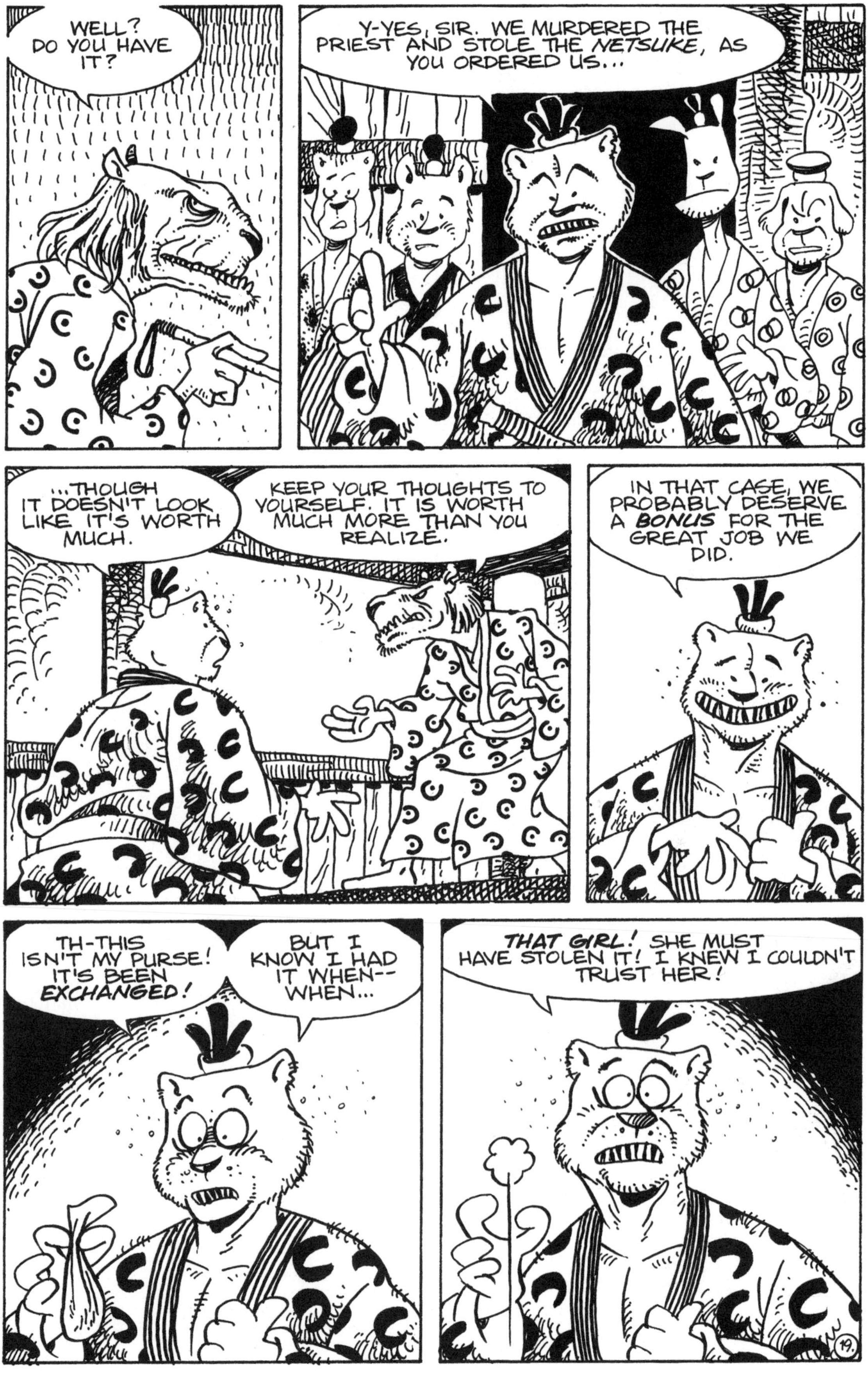
WELL? DO YOU HAVE IT?
Y-YES, SIR. WE MURDERED THE PRIEST AND STOLE THE *NETSUKE*, AS YOU ORDERED US...
...THOUGH IT DOESN'T LOOK LIKE IT'S WORTH MUCH.
KEEP YOUR THOUGHTS TO YOURSELF. IT IS WORTH MUCH MORE THAN YOU REALIZE.
IN THAT CASE, WE PROBABLY DESERVE A **BONUS** FOR THE GREAT JOB WE DID.
TH-THIS ISN'T MY PURSE! IT'S BEEN **EXCHANGED**!
BUT I KNOW I HAD IT WHEN-- WHEN...
**THAT GIRL!** SHE MUST HAVE STOLEN IT! I KNEW I COULDN'T TRUST HER!
19.

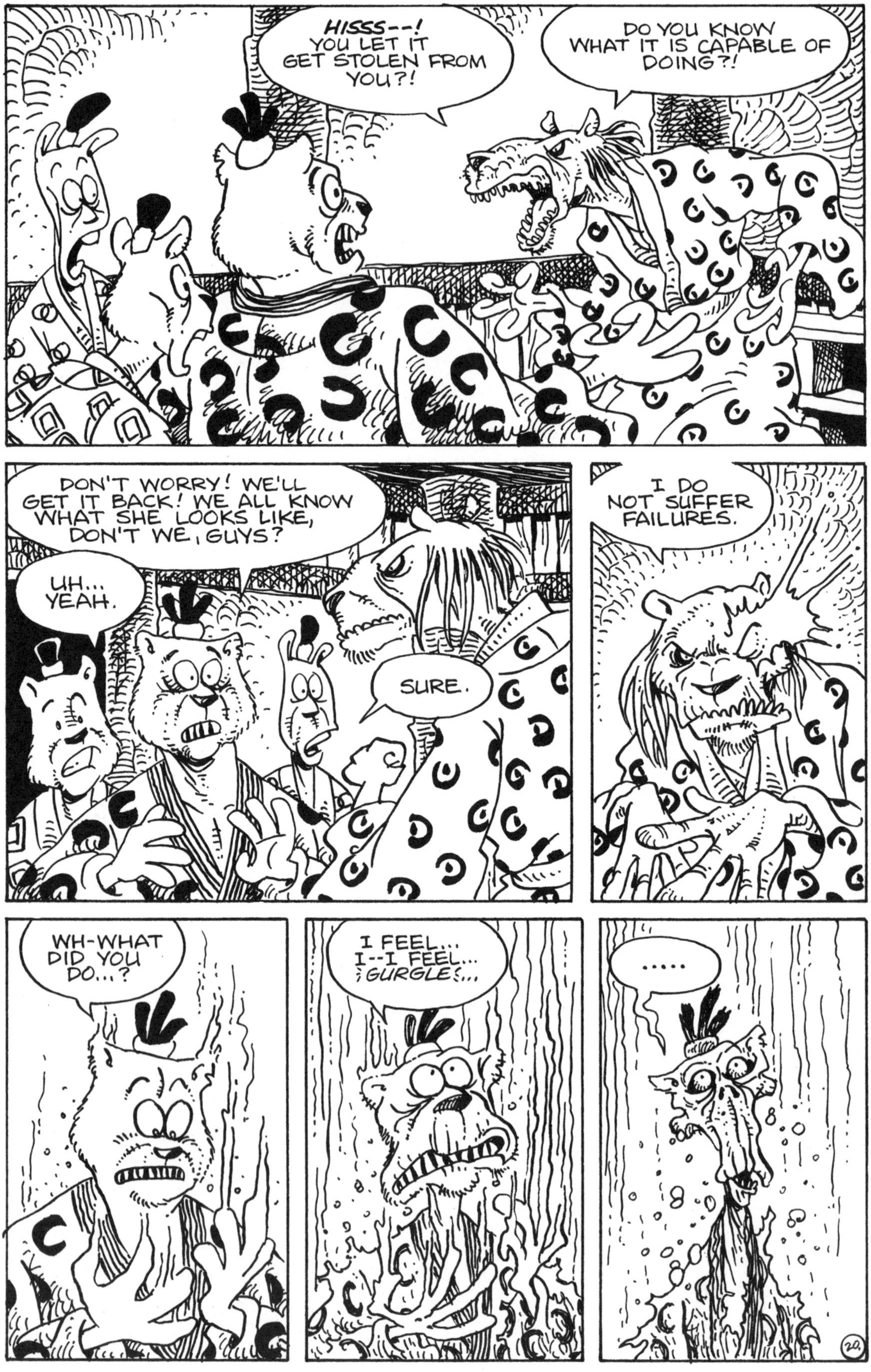
HISSS--! YOU LET IT GET STOLEN FROM YOU?!
DO YOU KNOW WHAT IT IS CAPABLE OF DOING?!
DON'T WORRY! WE'LL GET IT BACK! WE ALL KNOW WHAT SHE LOOKS LIKE, DON'T WE, GUYS?
UH... YEAH.
SURE.
I DO NOT SUFFER FAILURES.
WH-WHAT DID YOU DO...?
I FEEL... I--I FEEL... ¡GURGLE¡...
.....
20

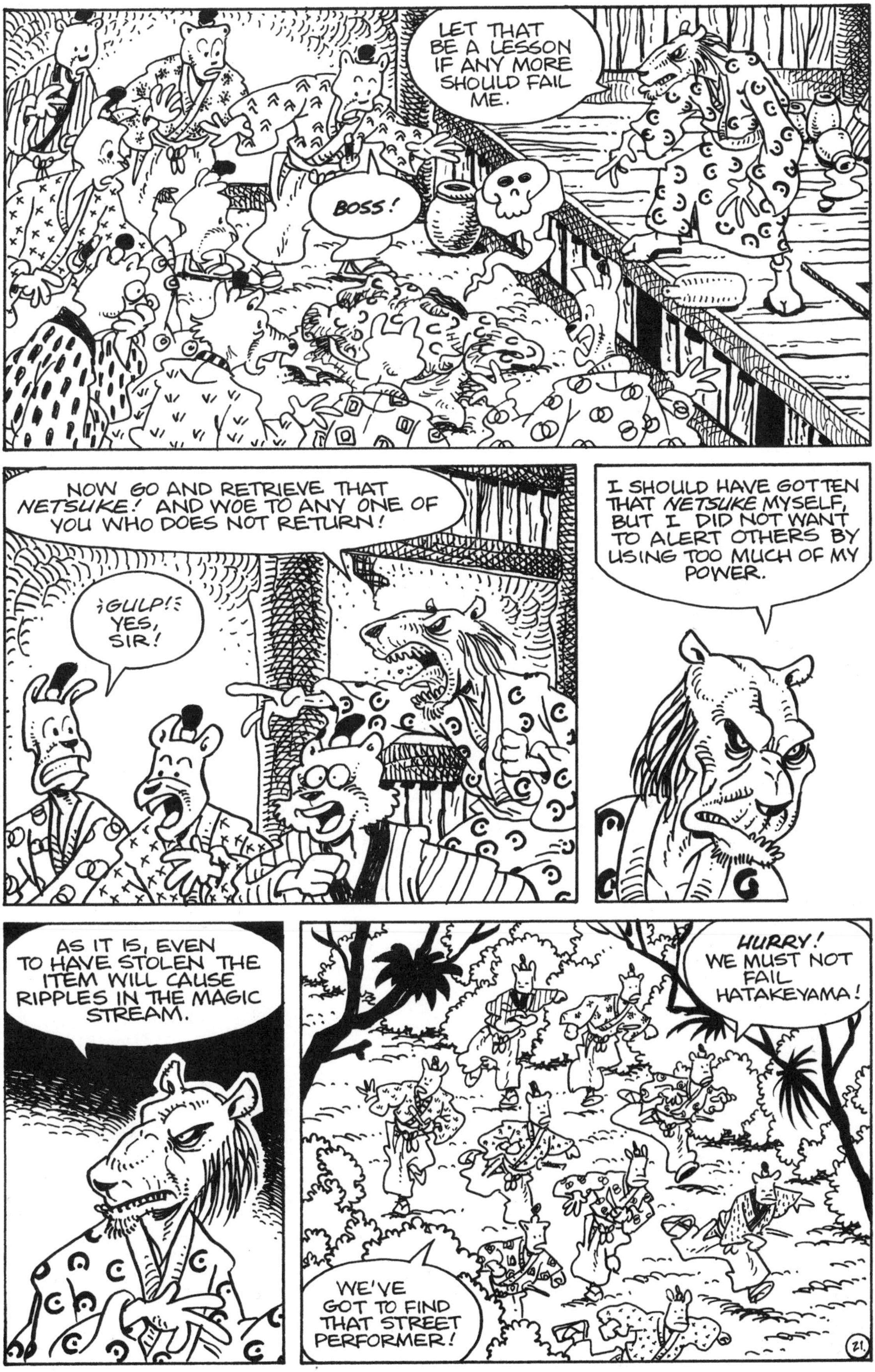
LET THAT BE A LESSON IF ANY MORE SHOULD FAIL ME.
BOSS!
NOW GO AND RETRIEVE THAT *NETSUKE*! AND WOE TO ANY ONE OF YOU WHO DOES NOT RETURN!
¡GULP!¡ YES, SIR!
I SHOULD HAVE GOTTEN THAT *NETSUKE* MYSELF, BUT I DID NOT WANT TO ALERT OTHERS BY USING TOO MUCH OF MY POWER.
AS IT IS, EVEN TO HAVE STOLEN THE ITEM WILL CAUSE RIPPLES IN THE MAGIC STREAM.
*HURRY*! WE MUST NOT FAIL HATAKEYAMA!
WE'VE GOT TO FIND THAT STREET PERFORMER!
21.

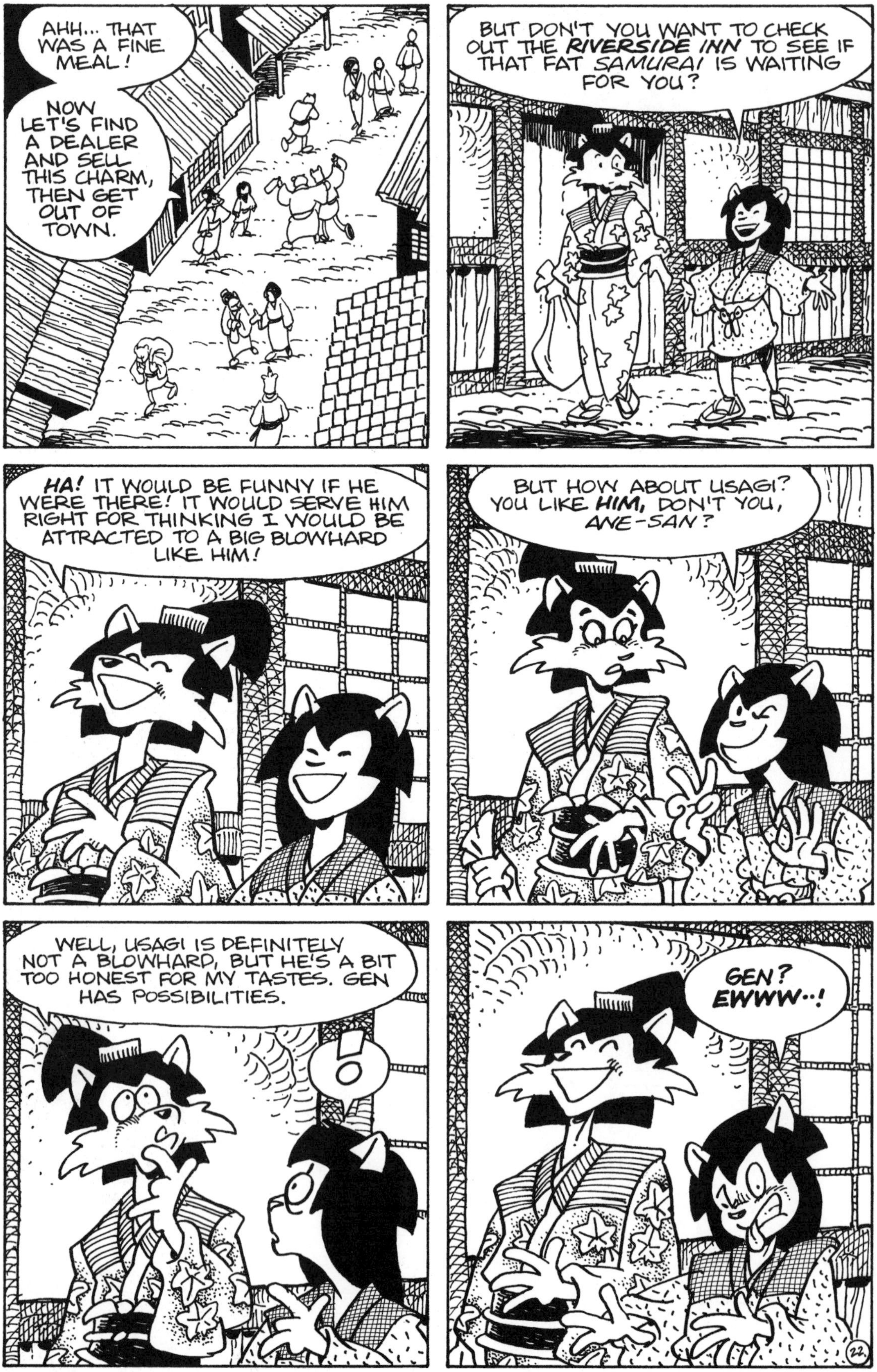

AHH... THAT WAS A FINE MEAL!
NOW LET'S FIND A DEALER AND SELL THIS CHARM, THEN GET OUT OF TOWN.
BUT DON'T YOU WANT TO CHECK OUT THE **RIVERSIDE INN** TO SEE IF THAT FAT *SAMURAI* IS WAITING FOR YOU?
**HA!** IT WOULD BE FUNNY IF HE WERE THERE! IT WOULD SERVE HIM RIGHT FOR THINKING I WOULD BE ATTRACTED TO A BIG BLOWHARD LIKE HIM!
BUT HOW ABOUT USAGI? YOU LIKE **HIM,** DON'T YOU, *ANE-SAN?*
WELL, USAGI IS DEFINITELY NOT A BLOWHARD, BUT HE'S A BIT TOO HONEST FOR MY TASTES. GEN HAS POSSIBILITIES.
!
**GEN? EWWW..!**
22.

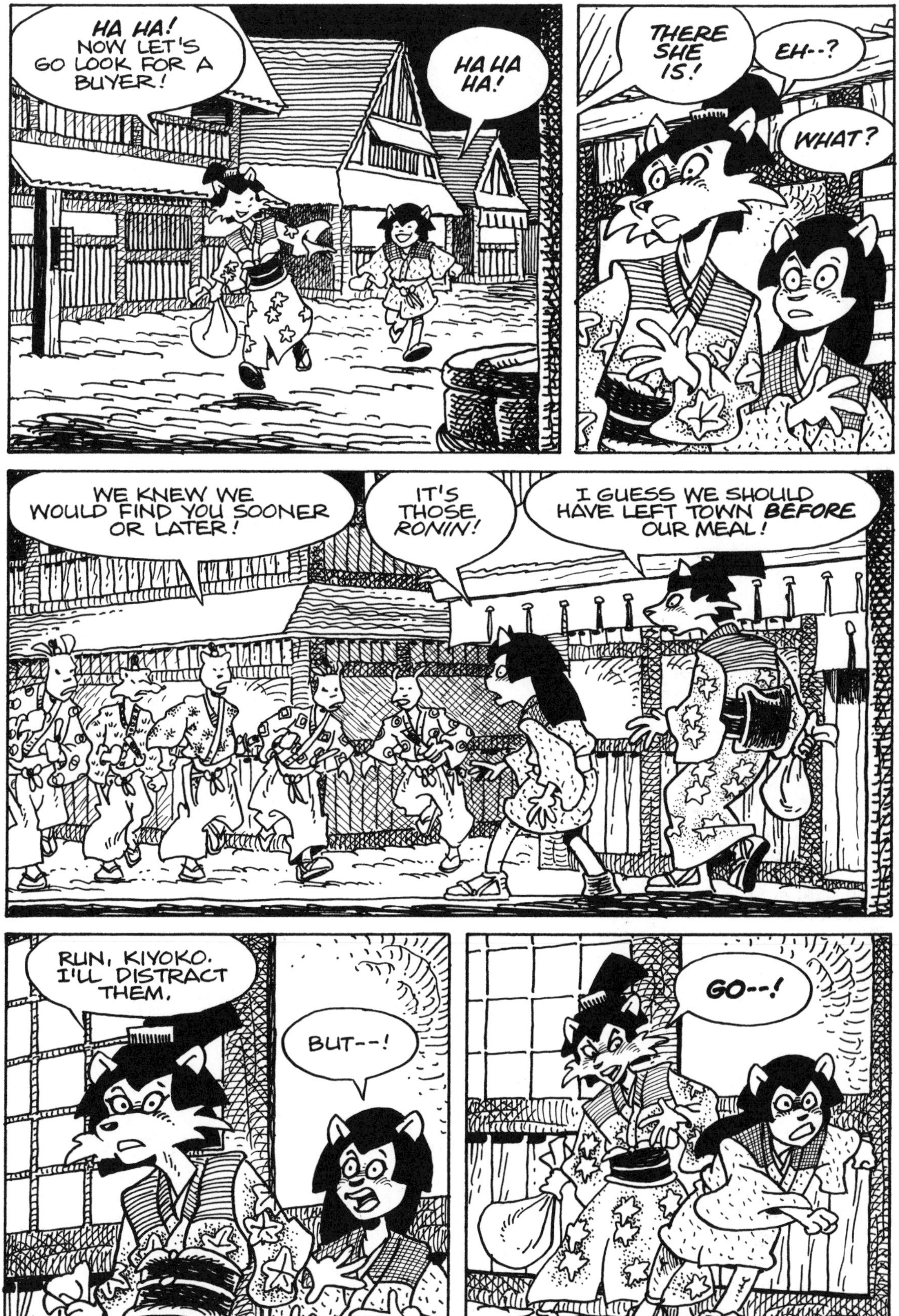
HA HA! NOW LET'S GO LOOK FOR A BUYER!
HA HA HA!
THERE SHE IS!
EH--?
WHAT?
WE KNEW WE WOULD FIND YOU SOONER OR LATER!
IT'S THOSE RONIN!
I GUESS WE SHOULD HAVE LEFT TOWN BEFORE OUR MEAL!
RUN, KIYOKO. I'LL DISTRACT THEM.
BUT--!
GO--!
23.

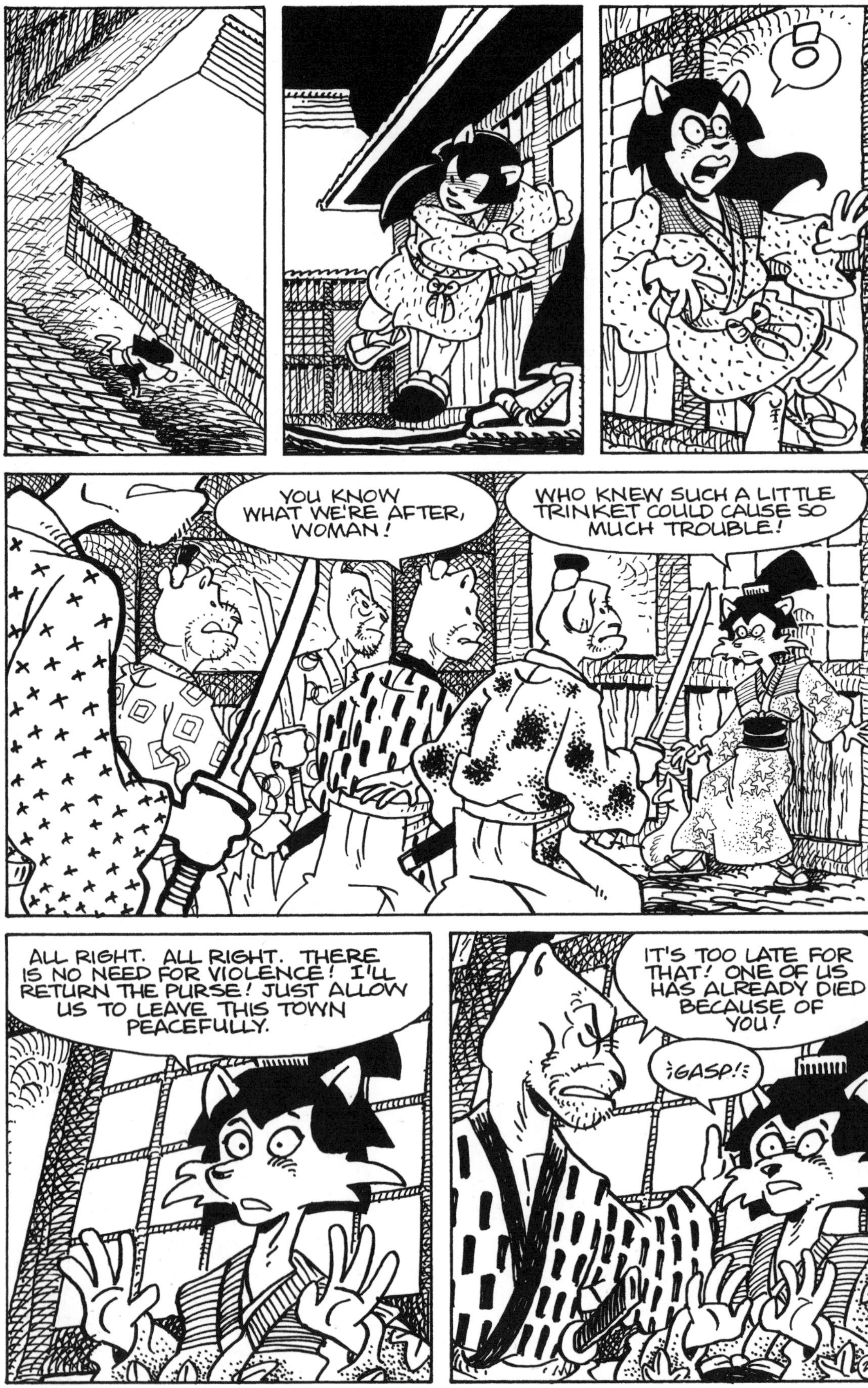
!
YOU KNOW WHAT WE'RE AFTER, WOMAN!
WHO KNEW SUCH A LITTLE TRINKET COULD CAUSE SO MUCH TROUBLE!
ALL RIGHT. ALL RIGHT. THERE IS NO NEED FOR VIOLENCE! I'LL RETURN THE PURSE! JUST ALLOW US TO LEAVE THIS TOWN PEACEFULLY.
IT'S TOO LATE FOR THAT! ONE OF US HAS ALREADY DIED BECAUSE OF YOU!
¡GASP!¡
24

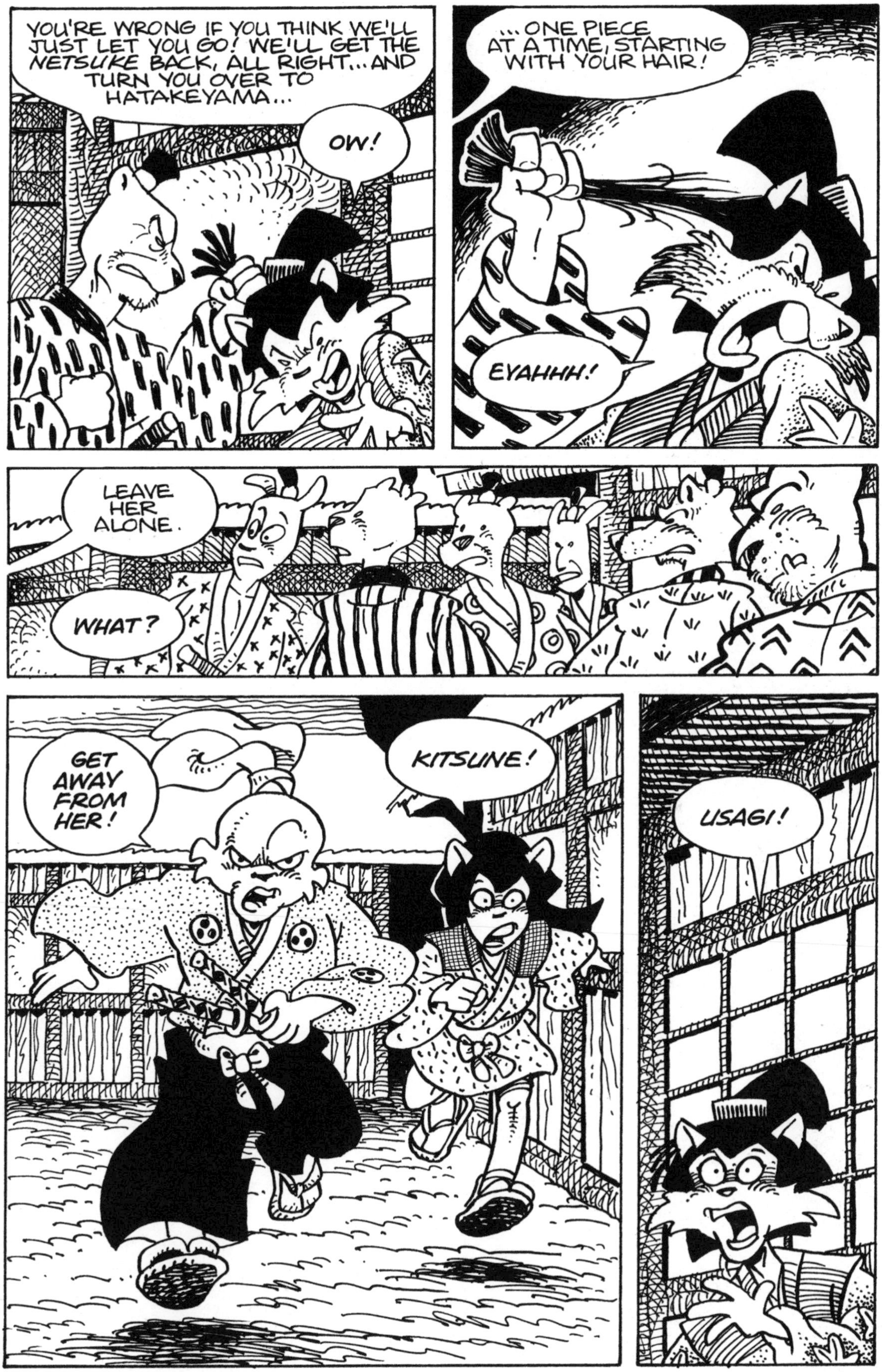
YOU'RE WRONG IF YOU THINK WE'LL JUST LET YOU GO! WE'LL GET THE NETSUKE BACK, ALL RIGHT... AND TURN YOU OVER TO HATAKEYAMA...
OW!
...ONE PIECE AT A TIME, STARTING WITH YOUR HAIR!
EYAHHH!
LEAVE HER ALONE.
WHAT?
GET AWAY FROM HER!
KITSUNE!
USAGI!

# TRAITORS OF THE EARTH PART TWO

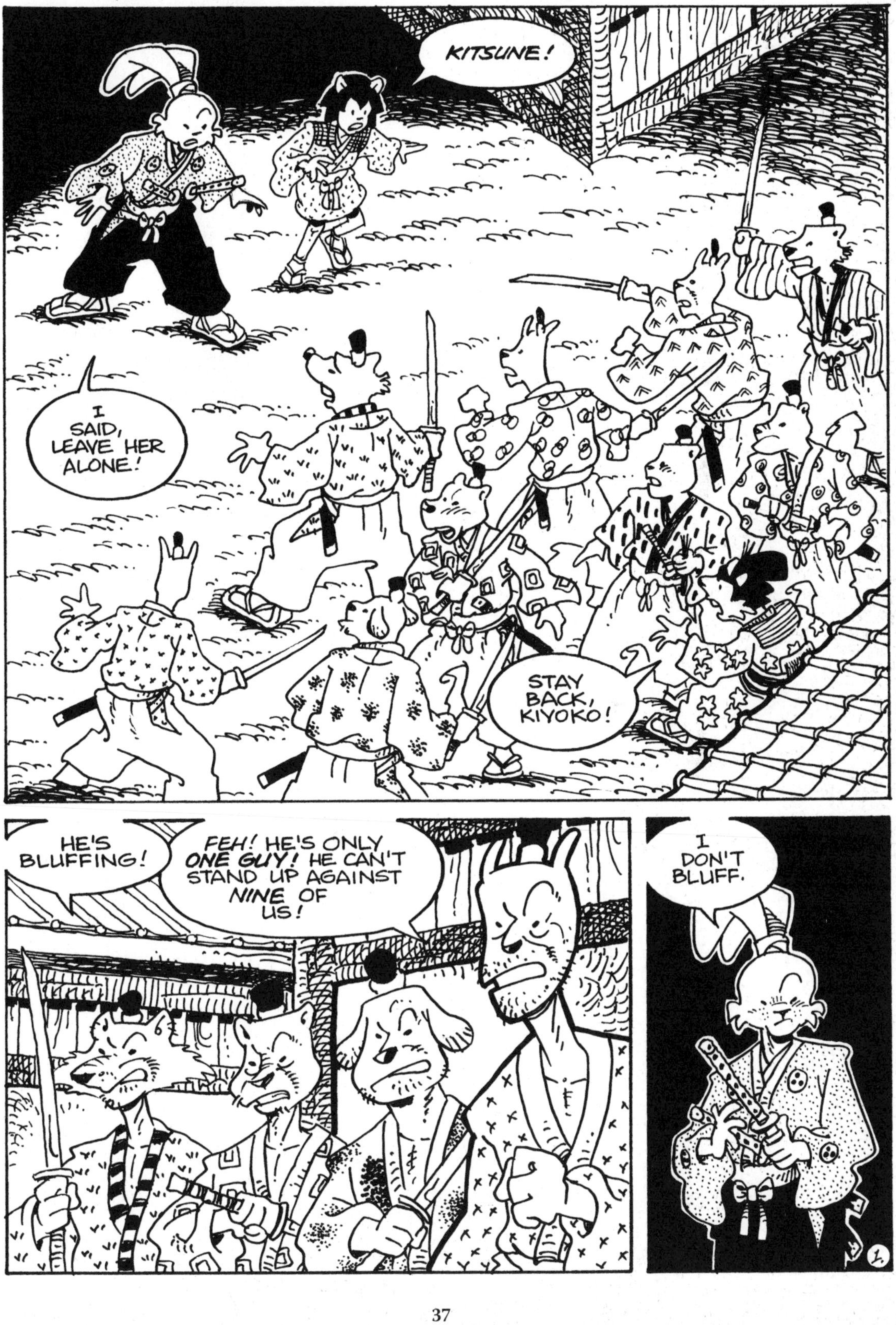
KITSUNE!
I SAID, LEAVE HER ALONE!
STAY BACK, KIYOKO!
HE'S BLUFFING!
FEH! HE'S ONLY ONE GUY! HE CAN'T STAND UP AGAINST NINE OF US!
I DON'T BLUFF.

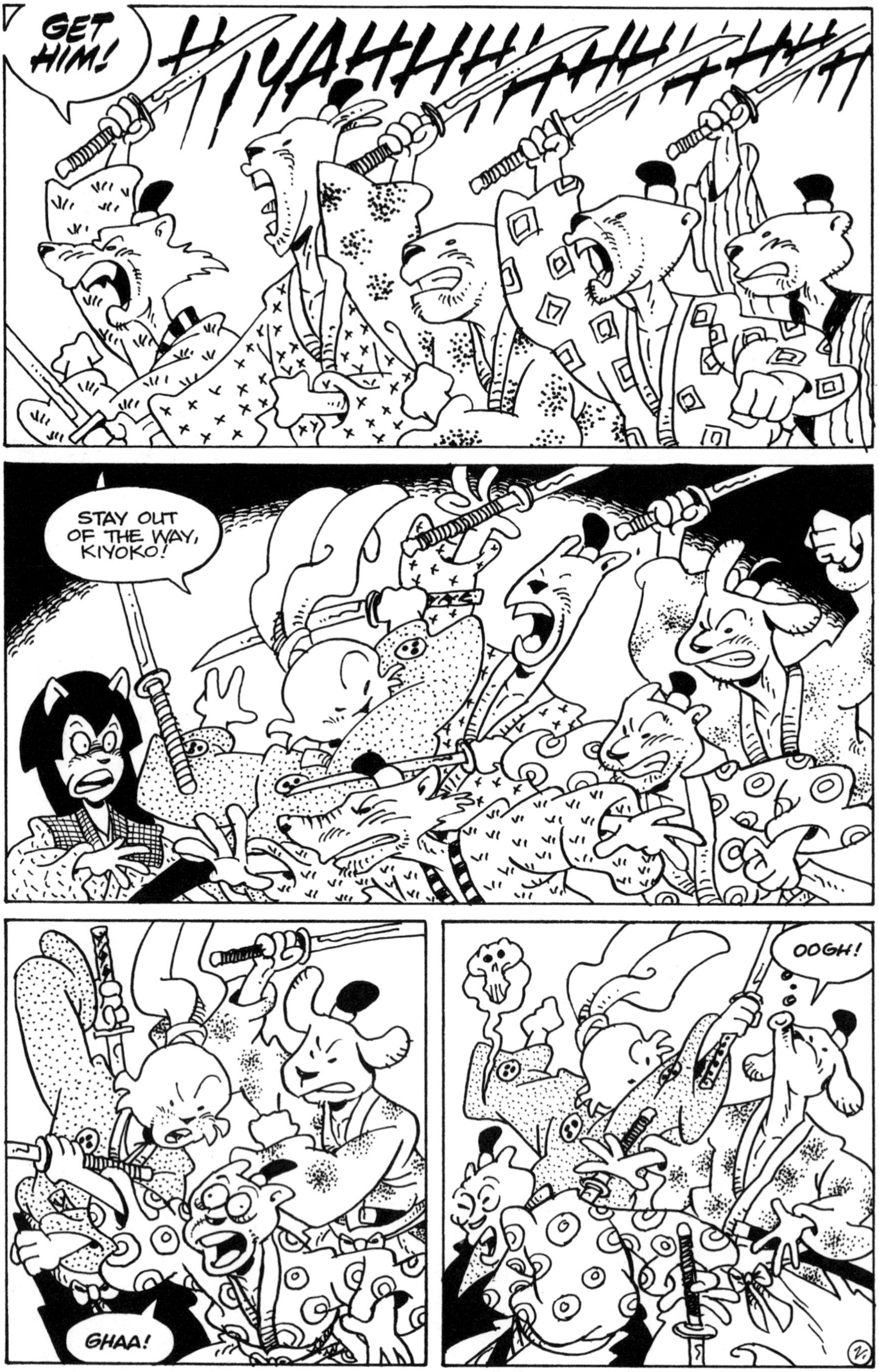
GET HIM!
HIYAHHHHHHHHHHHH
STAY OUT OF THE WAY, KIYOKO!
GHAA!
OOGH!

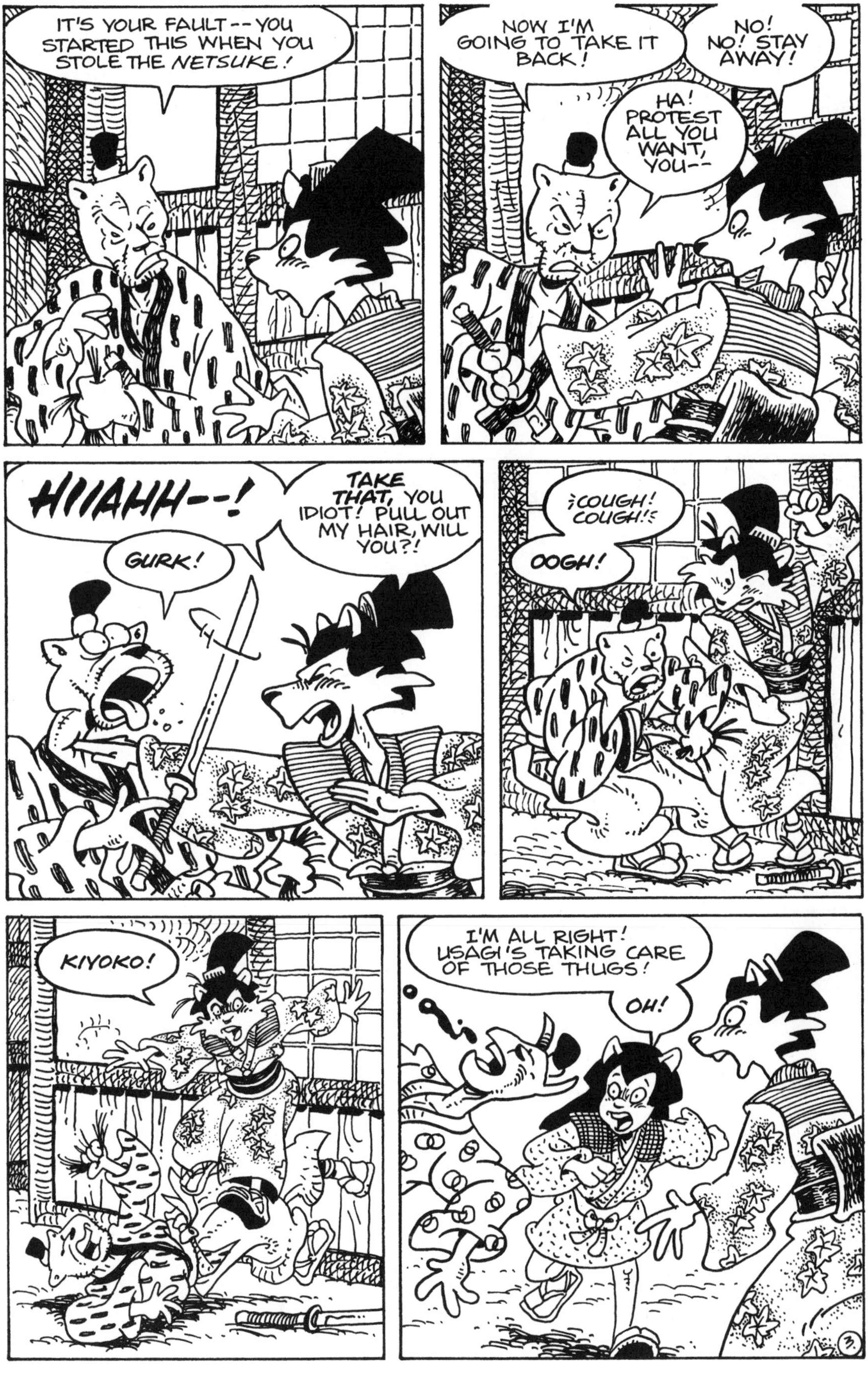
IT'S YOUR FAULT--YOU STARTED THIS WHEN YOU STOLE THE *NETSUKE*!
NOW I'M GOING TO TAKE IT BACK!
NO! NO! STAY AWAY!
HA! PROTEST ALL YOU WANT, YOU--
HIIAHH--!
GURK!
TAKE THAT, YOU IDIOT! PULL OUT MY HAIR, WILL YOU?!
COUGH! COUGH!
OOGH!
KIYOKO!
I'M ALL RIGHT! USAGI'S TAKING CARE OF THOSE THUGS!
OH!
3.

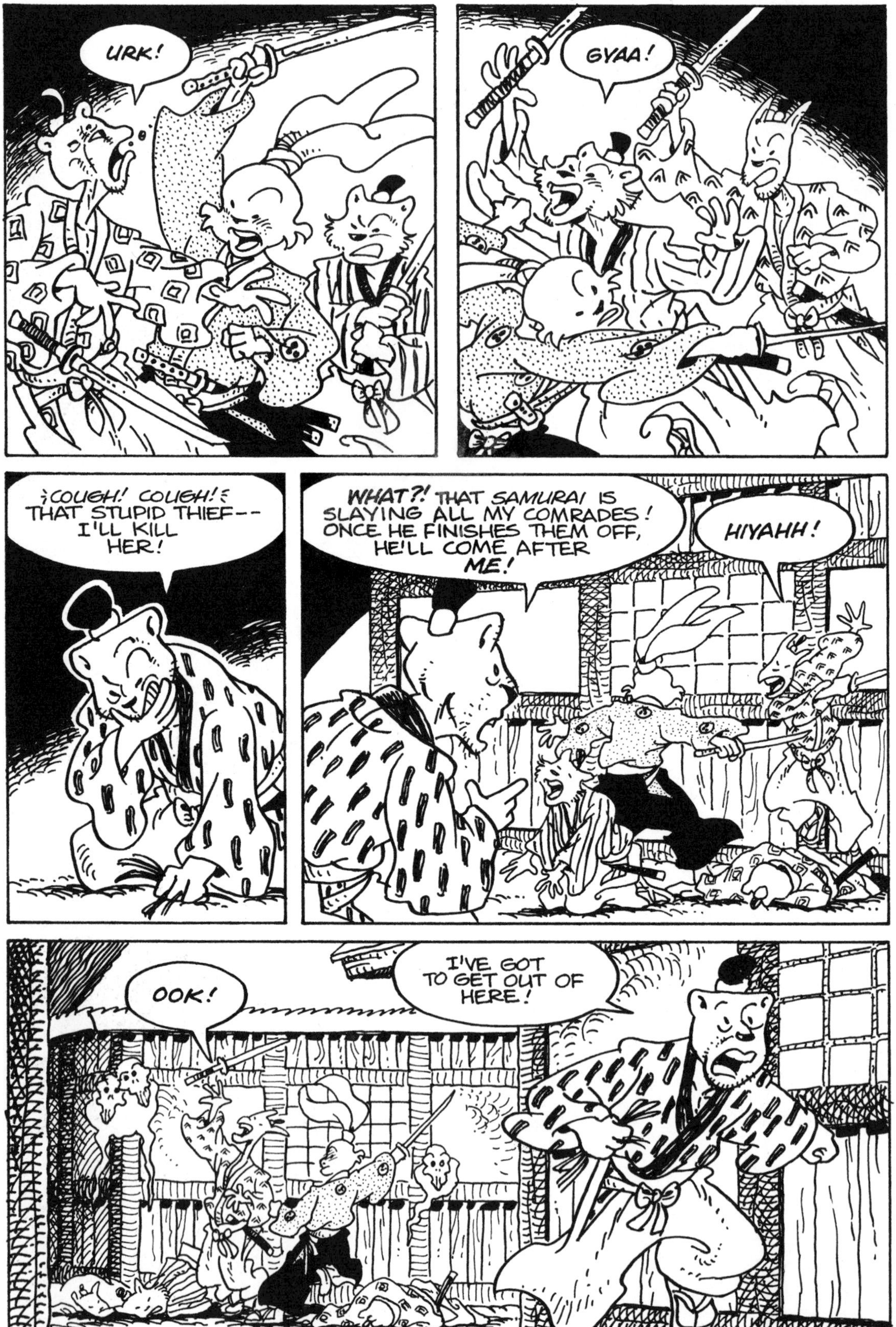
URK!
GYAA!
¡COUGH! COUGH!¡ THAT STUPID THIEF-- I'LL KILL HER!
WHAT?! THAT SAMURAI IS SLAYING ALL MY COMRADES! ONCE HE FINISHES THEM OFF, HE'LL COME AFTER ME!
HIYAHH!
OOK!
I'VE GOT TO GET OUT OF HERE!
4.

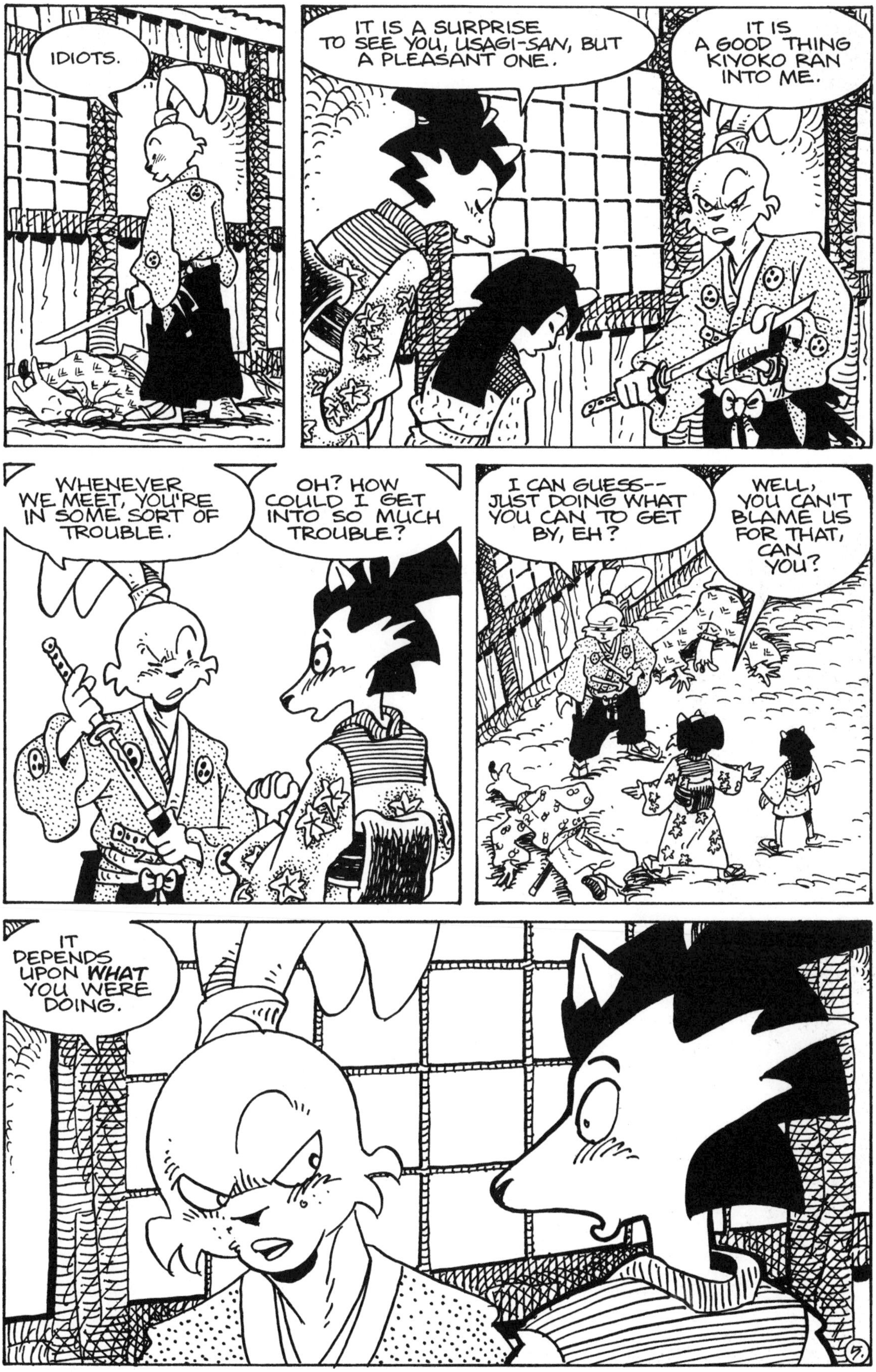
IDIOTS.
IT IS A SURPRISE TO SEE YOU, USAGI-SAN, BUT A PLEASANT ONE.
IT IS A GOOD THING KIYOKO RAN INTO ME.
WHENEVER WE MEET, YOU'RE IN SOME SORT OF TROUBLE.
OH? HOW COULD I GET INTO SO MUCH TROUBLE?
I CAN GUESS-- JUST DOING WHAT YOU CAN TO GET BY, EH?
WELL, YOU CAN'T BLAME US FOR THAT, CAN YOU?
IT DEPENDS UPON **WHAT** YOU WERE DOING.

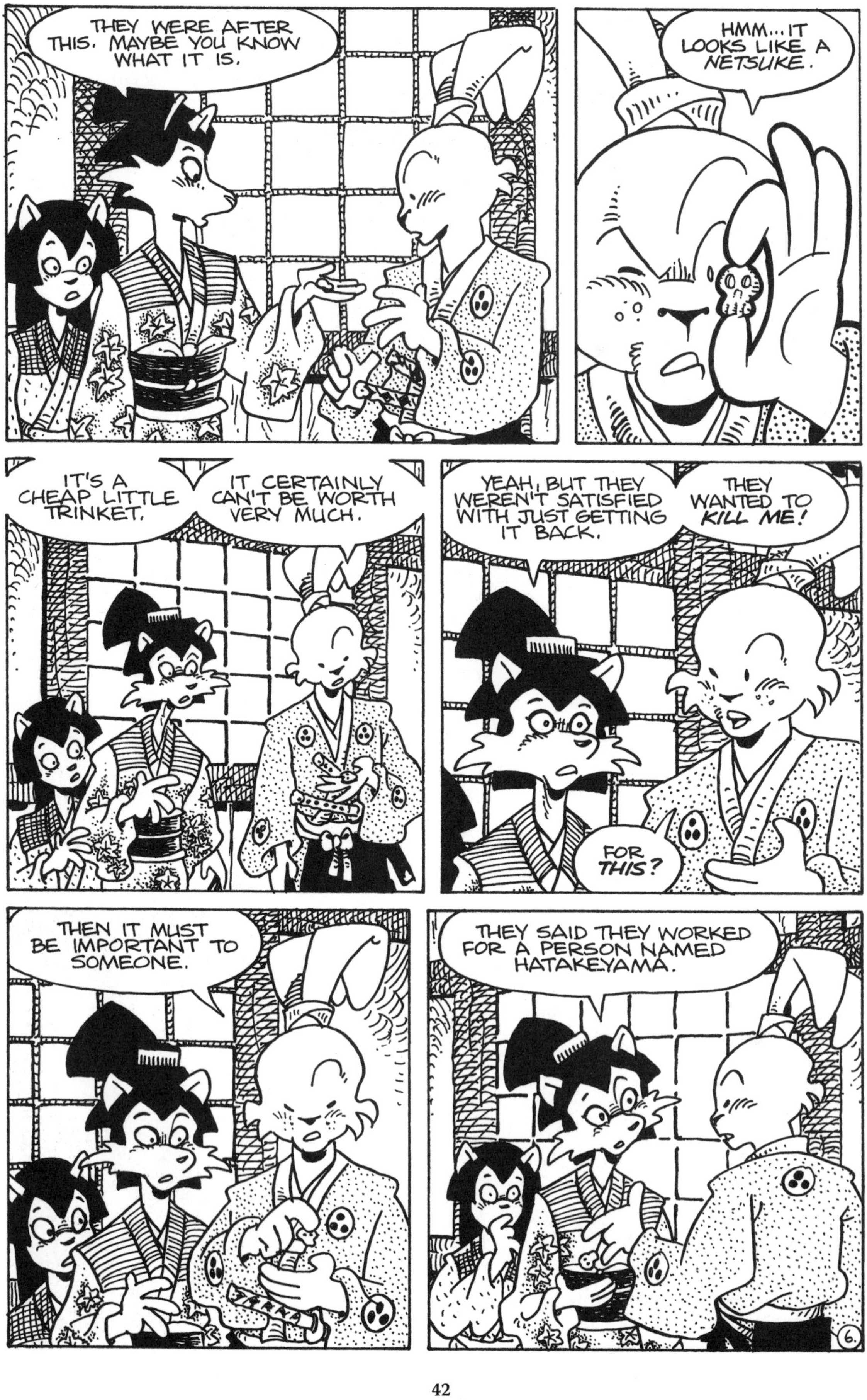
THEY WERE AFTER THIS. MAYBE YOU KNOW WHAT IT IS.
HMM... IT LOOKS LIKE A NETSUKE.
IT'S A CHEAP LITTLE TRINKET.
IT CERTAINLY CAN'T BE WORTH VERY MUCH.
YEAH, BUT THEY WEREN'T SATISFIED WITH JUST GETTING IT BACK.
THEY WANTED TO KILL ME!
FOR THIS?
THEN IT MUST BE IMPORTANT TO SOMEONE.
THEY SAID THEY WORKED FOR A PERSON NAMED HATAKEYAMA.
6.

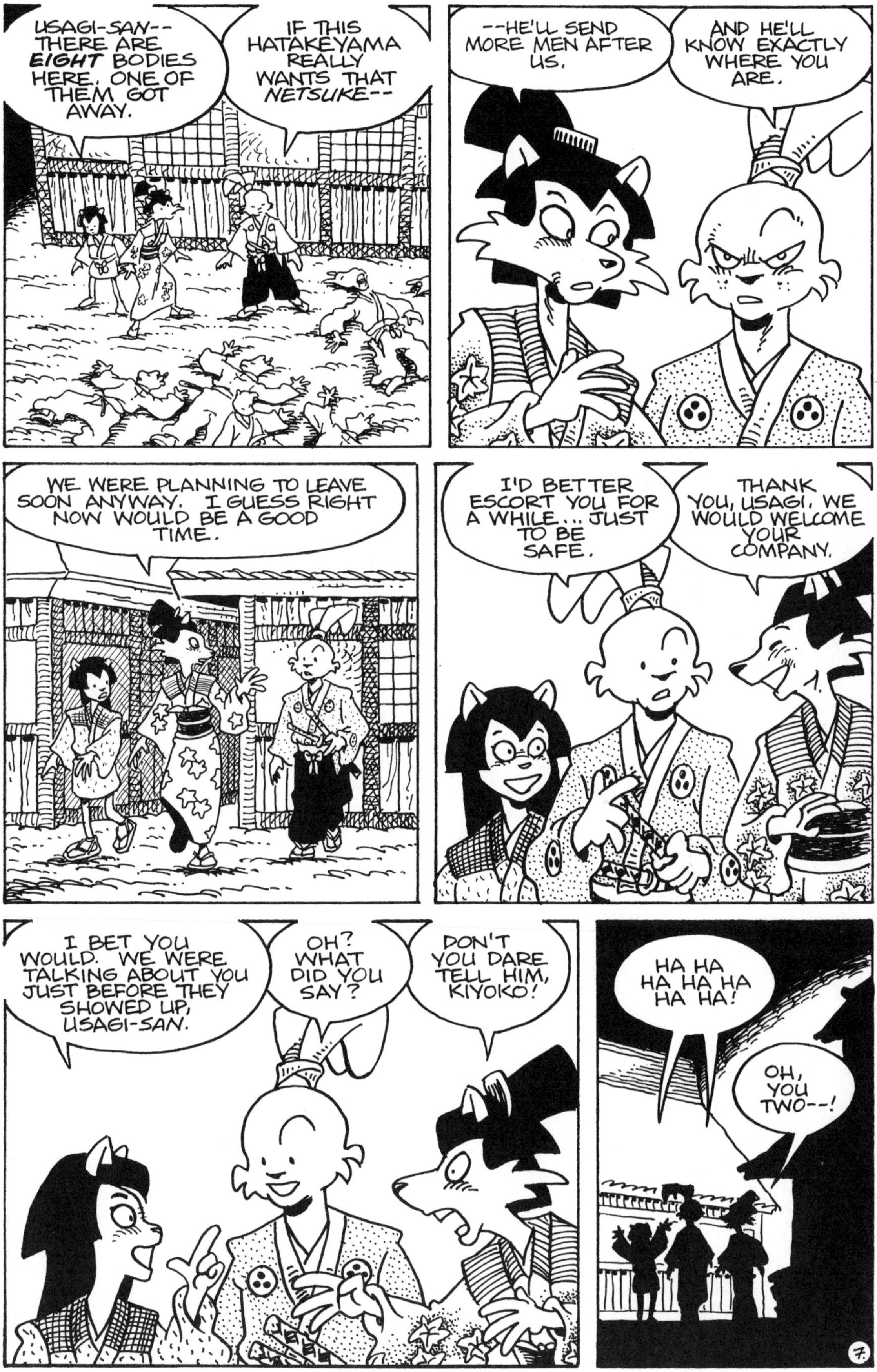
USAGI-SAN-- THERE ARE **EIGHT** BODIES HERE. ONE OF THEM GOT AWAY.
IF THIS HATAKEYAMA REALLY WANTS THAT *NETSUKE*--
--HE'LL SEND MORE MEN AFTER US.
AND HE'LL KNOW EXACTLY WHERE YOU ARE.
WE WERE PLANNING TO LEAVE SOON ANYWAY. I GUESS RIGHT NOW WOULD BE A GOOD TIME.
I'D BETTER ESCORT YOU FOR A WHILE... JUST TO BE SAFE.
THANK YOU, USAGI. WE WOULD WELCOME YOUR COMPANY.
I BET YOU WOULD. WE WERE TALKING ABOUT YOU JUST BEFORE THEY SHOWED UP, USAGI-SAN.
OH? WHAT DID YOU SAY?
DON'T YOU DARE TELL HIM, KIYOKO!
HA HA HA HA HA HA HA!
OH, YOU TWO--!
7.

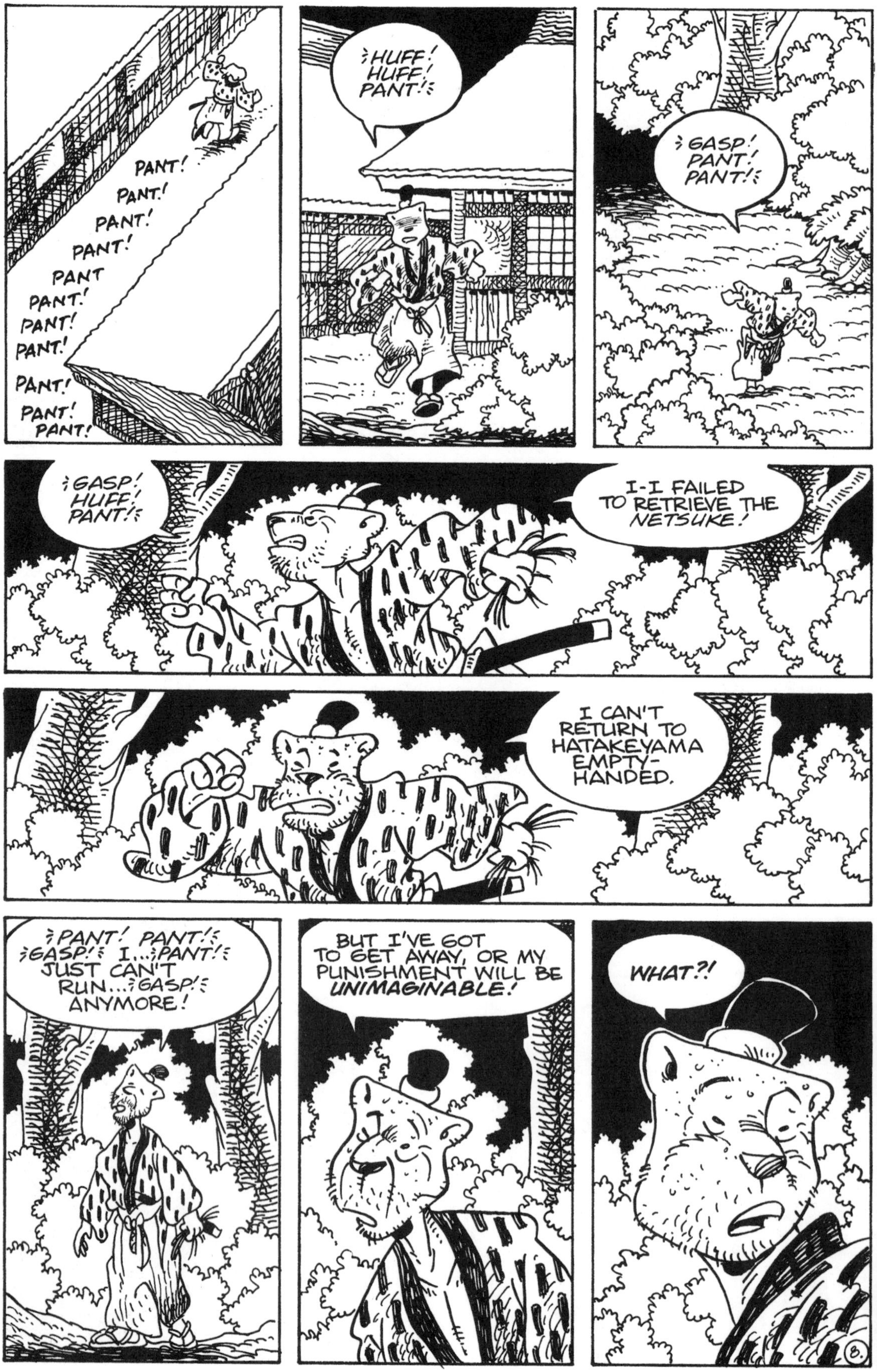
PANT! PANT! PANT! PANT! PANT PANT! PANT! PANT! PANT! PANT! PANT!
HUFF! HUFF! PANT!
GASP! PANT! PANT!
GASP! HUFF! PANT!
I-I FAILED TO RETRIEVE THE NETSUKE!
I CAN'T RETURN TO HATAKEYAMA EMPTY-HANDED.
PANT! PANT! GASP! I... PANT! JUST CAN'T RUN... GASP! ANYMORE!
BUT I'VE GOT TO GET AWAY, OR MY PUNISHMENT WILL BE UNIMAGINABLE!
WHAT?!
8.

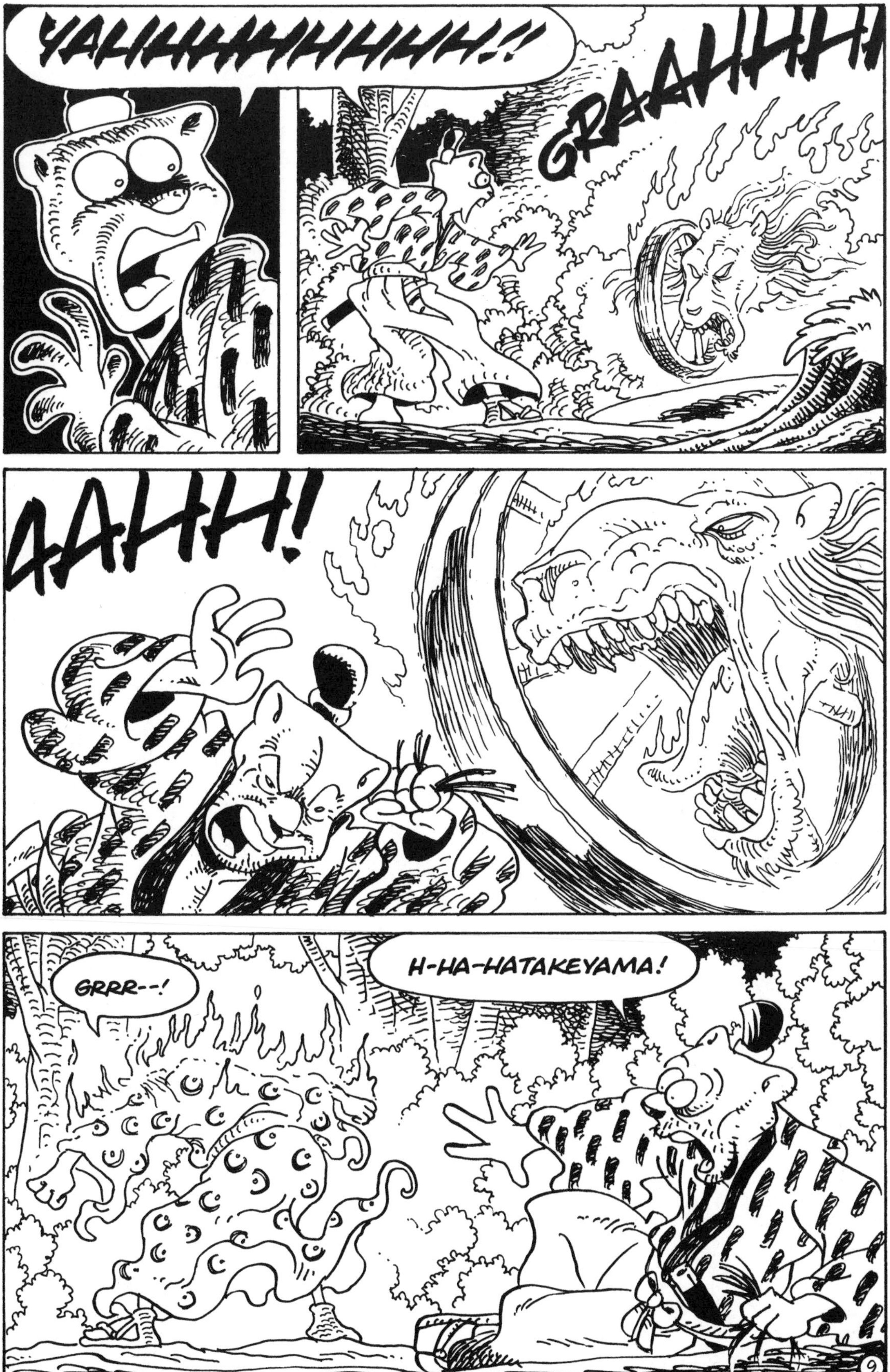
YAHHHHHHHHHHH!?!
GRAAHHHH
AAHH!
GRRR--!
H-HA-HATAKEYAMA!
9.

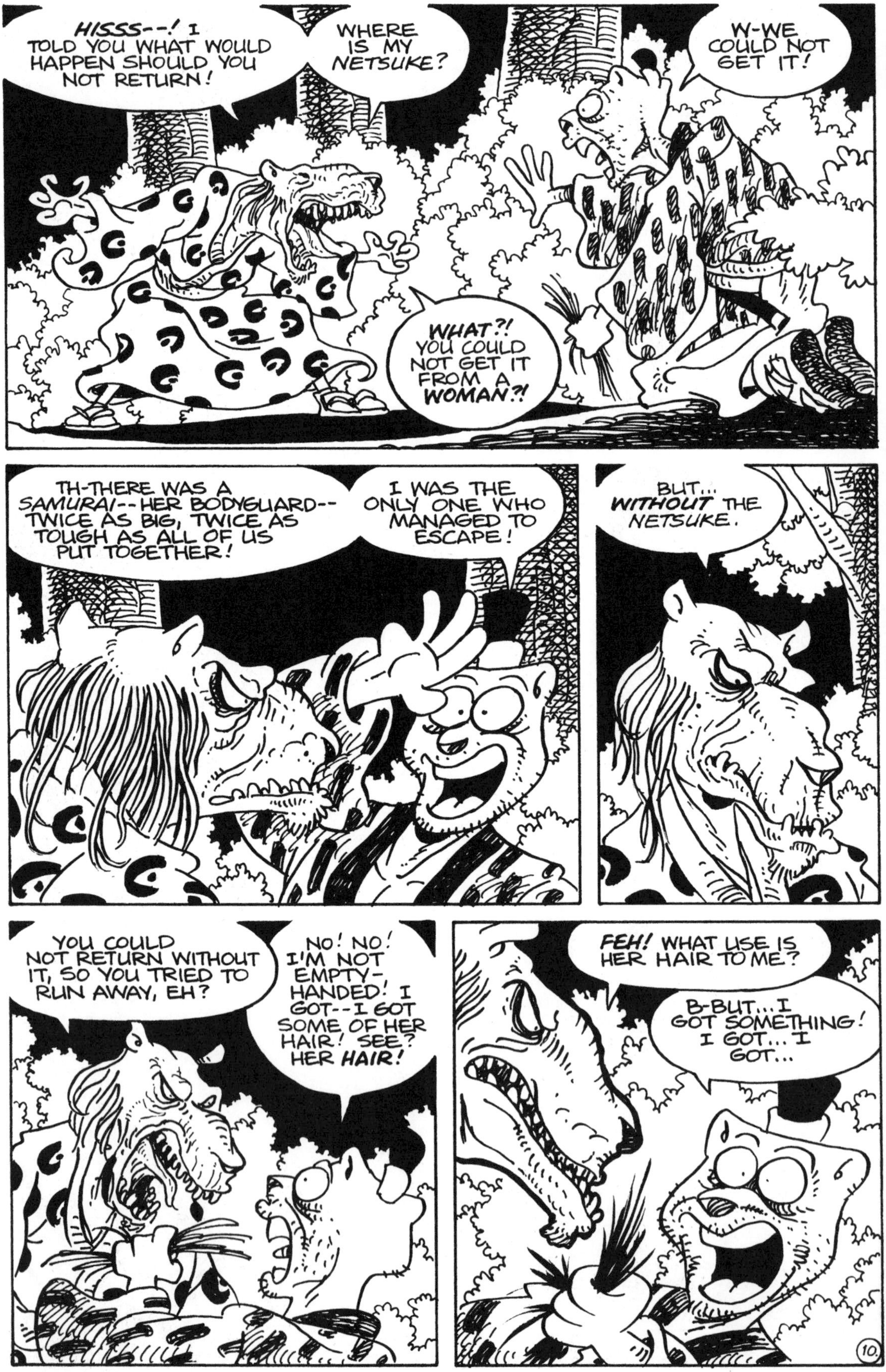
HISSS--! I TOLD YOU WHAT WOULD HAPPEN SHOULD YOU NOT RETURN!
WHERE IS MY NETSUKE?
W-WE COULD NOT GET IT!
WHAT?! YOU COULD NOT GET IT FROM A WOMAN?!
TH-THERE WAS A SAMURAI--HER BODYGUARD--TWICE AS BIG, TWICE AS TOUGH AS ALL OF US PUT TOGETHER!
I WAS THE ONLY ONE WHO MANAGED TO ESCAPE!
BUT... WITHOUT THE NETSUKE.
YOU COULD NOT RETURN WITHOUT IT, SO YOU TRIED TO RUN AWAY, EH?
NO! NO! I'M NOT EMPTY-HANDED! I GOT--I GOT SOME OF HER HAIR! SEE? HER HAIR!
FEH! WHAT USE IS HER HAIR TO ME?
B-BUT... I GOT SOMETHING! I GOT... I GOT...
10

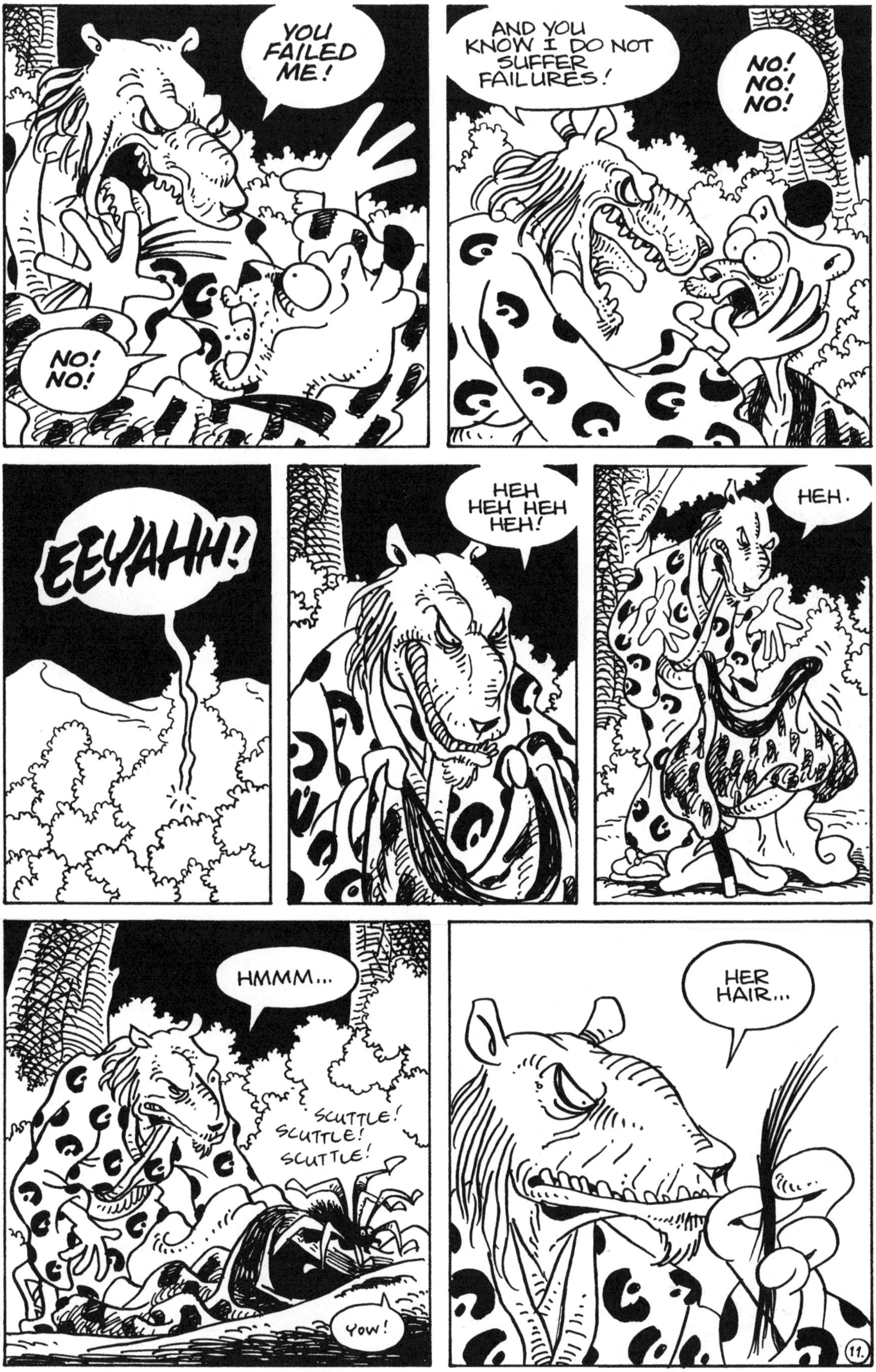
YOU FAILED ME!
NO! NO!
AND YOU KNOW I DO NOT SUFFER FAILURES!
NO! NO! NO!
EEYAHH!
HEH HEH HEH HEH!
HEH.
HMMM...
SCUTTLE! SCUTTLE! SCUTTLE!
YOW!
HER HAIR...
11.

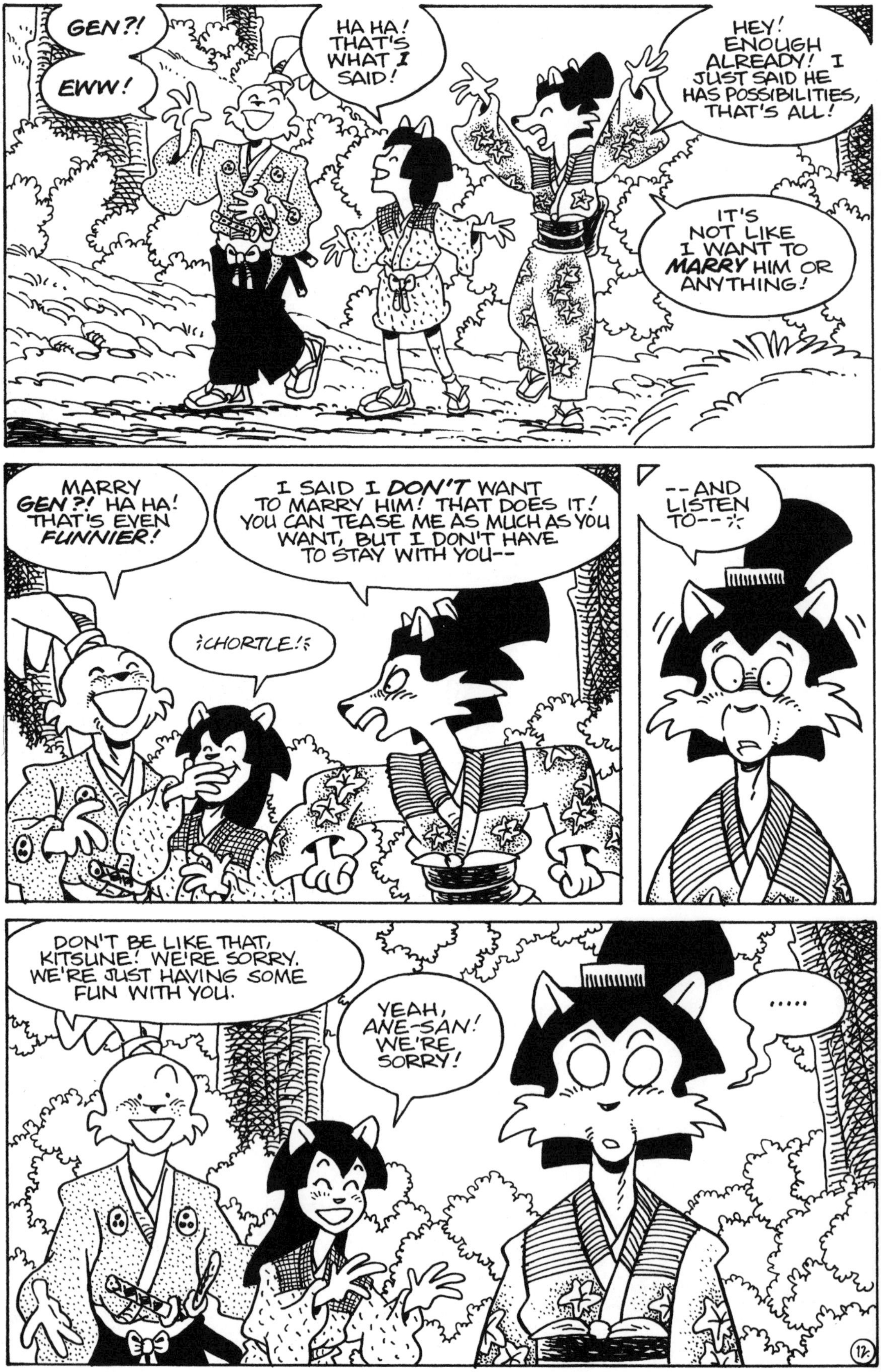

GEN?!
EWW!
HA HA! THAT'S WHAT I SAID!
HEY! ENOUGH ALREADY! I JUST SAID HE HAS POSSIBILITIES, THAT'S ALL!
IT'S NOT LIKE I WANT TO MARRY HIM OR ANYTHING!
MARRY GEN?! HA HA! THAT'S EVEN FUNNIER!
CHORTLE!
I SAID I DON'T WANT TO MARRY HIM! THAT DOES IT! YOU CAN TEASE ME AS MUCH AS YOU WANT, BUT I DON'T HAVE TO STAY WITH YOU--
--AND LISTEN TO--
DON'T BE LIKE THAT, KITSUNE! WE'RE SORRY. WE'RE JUST HAVING SOME FUN WITH YOU.
YEAH, ANE-SAN! WE'RE SORRY!
.....
12.

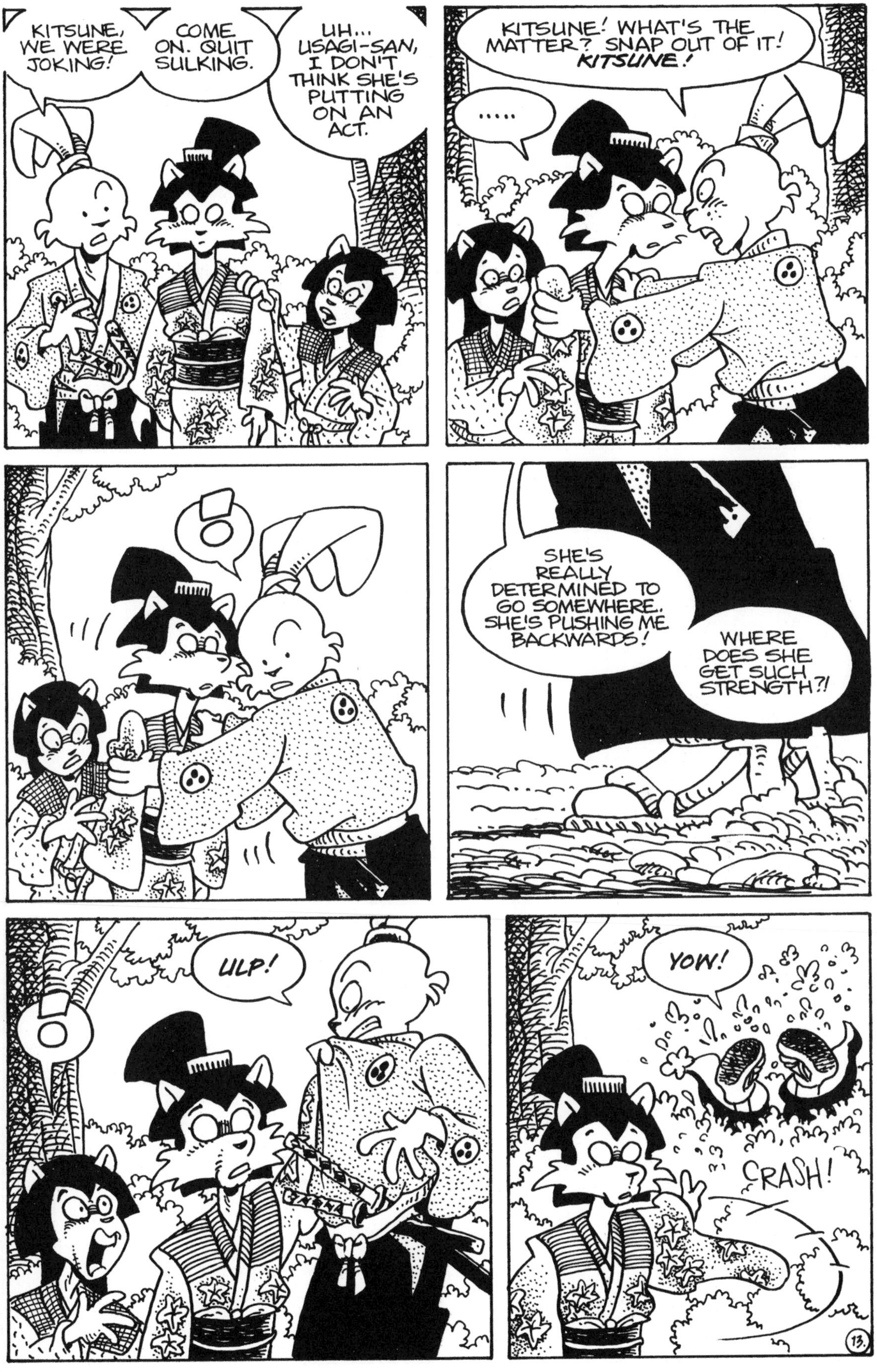
KITSUNE, WE WERE JOKING!
COME ON. QUIT SULKING.
UH... USAGI-SAN, I DON'T THINK SHE'S PUTTING ON AN ACT.
KITSUNE! WHAT'S THE MATTER? SNAP OUT OF IT! KITSUNE!
.....
SHE'S REALLY DETERMINED TO GO SOMEWHERE. SHE'S PUSHING ME BACKWARDS!
WHERE DOES SHE GET SUCH STRENGTH?!
ULP!
YOW!
CRASH!
13.

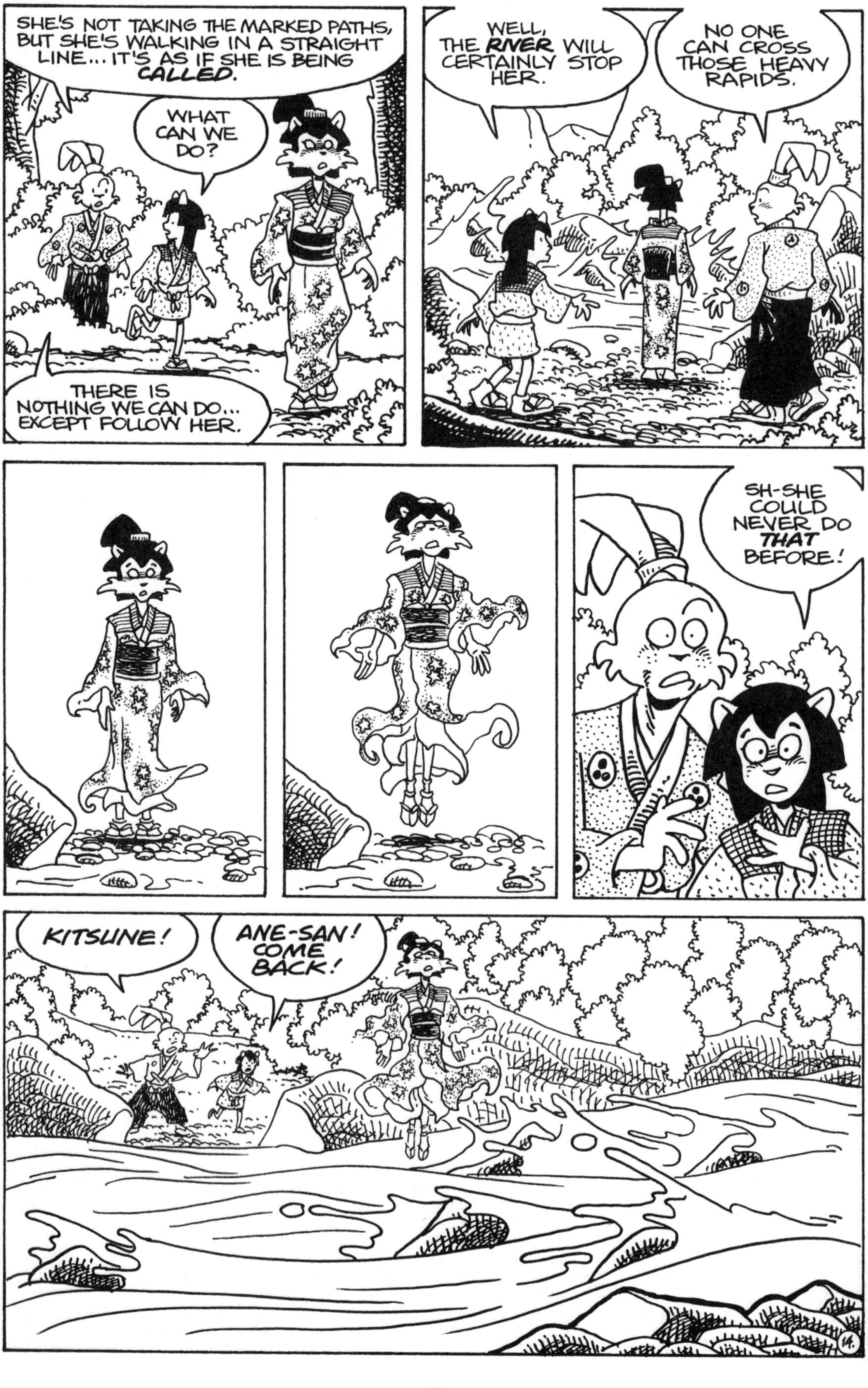
SHE'S NOT TAKING THE MARKED PATHS, BUT SHE'S WALKING IN A STRAIGHT LINE... IT'S AS IF SHE IS BEING CALLED.
WHAT CAN WE DO?
THERE IS NOTHING WE CAN DO... EXCEPT FOLLOW HER.
WELL, THE RIVER WILL CERTAINLY STOP HER.
NO ONE CAN CROSS THOSE HEAVY RAPIDS.
SH-SHE COULD NEVER DO THAT BEFORE!
KITSUNE!
ANE-SAN! COME BACK!
14.

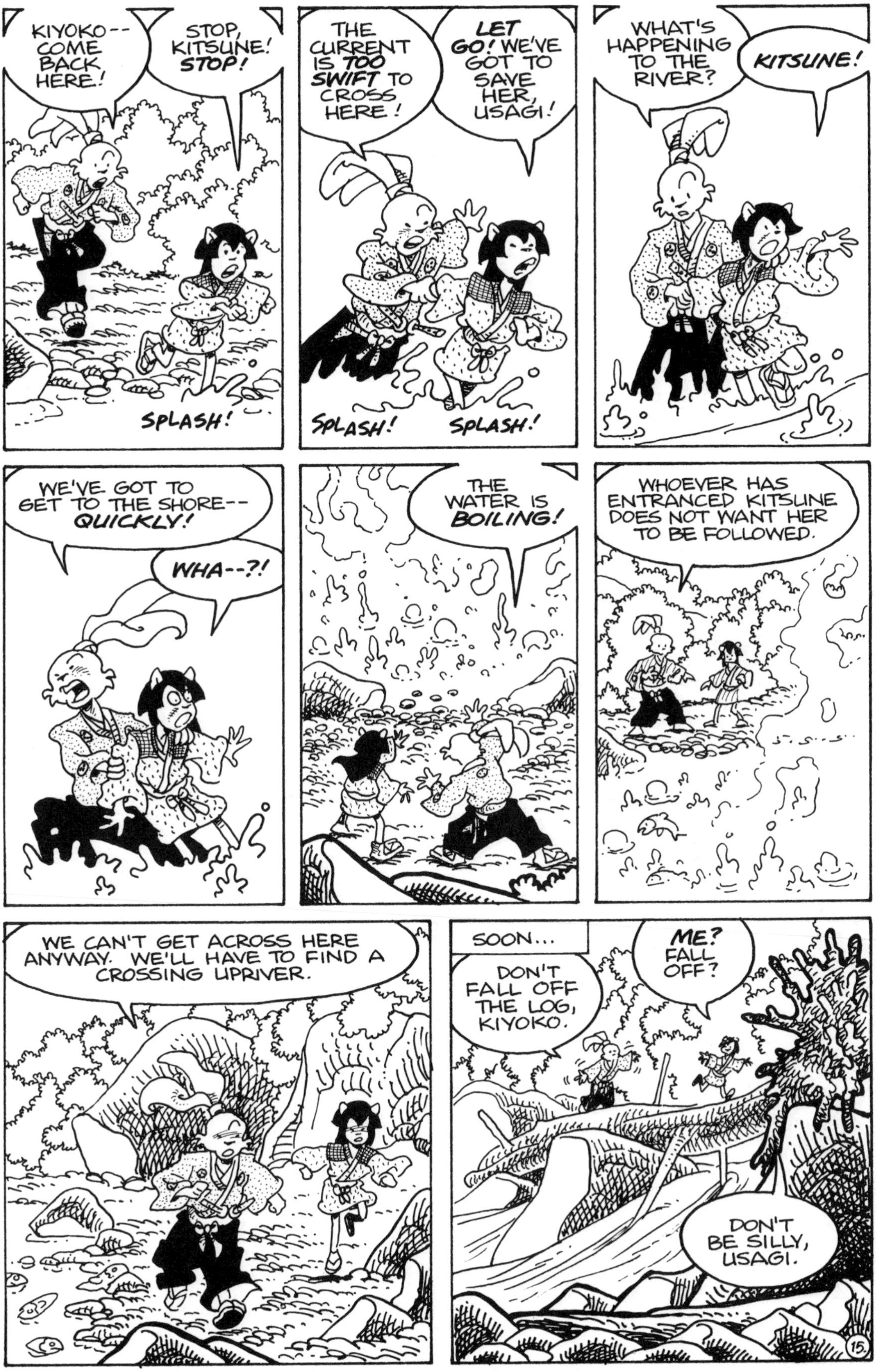
KIYOKO-- COME BACK HERE!
STOP, KITSUNE! **STOP!**
SPLASH!
THE CURRENT IS **TOO SWIFT** TO CROSS HERE!
**LET GO!** WE'VE GOT TO SAVE HER, USAGI!
SPLASH!
SPLASH!
WHAT'S HAPPENING TO THE RIVER?
**KITSUNE!**
WE'VE GOT TO GET TO THE SHORE-- **QUICKLY!**
**WHA--?!**
THE WATER IS **BOILING!**
WHOEVER HAS ENTRANCED KITSUNE DOES NOT WANT HER TO BE FOLLOWED.
WE CAN'T GET ACROSS HERE ANYWAY. WE'LL HAVE TO FIND A CROSSING UPRIVER.
SOON...
DON'T FALL OFF THE LOG, KIYOKO.
**ME?** FALL OFF?
DON'T BE SILLY, USAGI.
15.

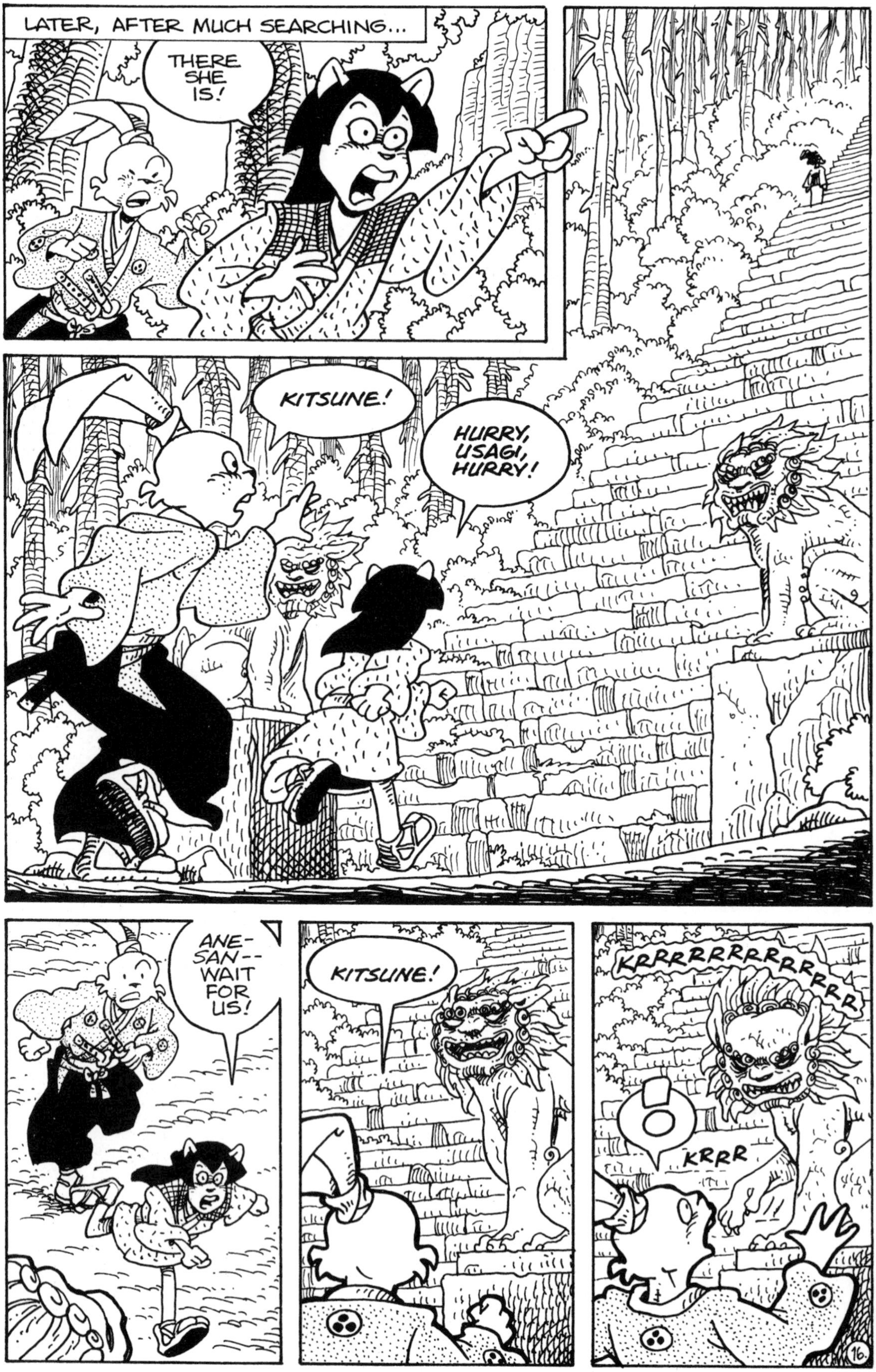
LATER, AFTER MUCH SEARCHING...
THERE SHE IS!
KITSUNE!
HURRY, USAGI, HURRY!
ANE-SAN-- WAIT FOR US!
KITSUNE!
KRRRRRRRRRRRRRR
!
KRRR
16.

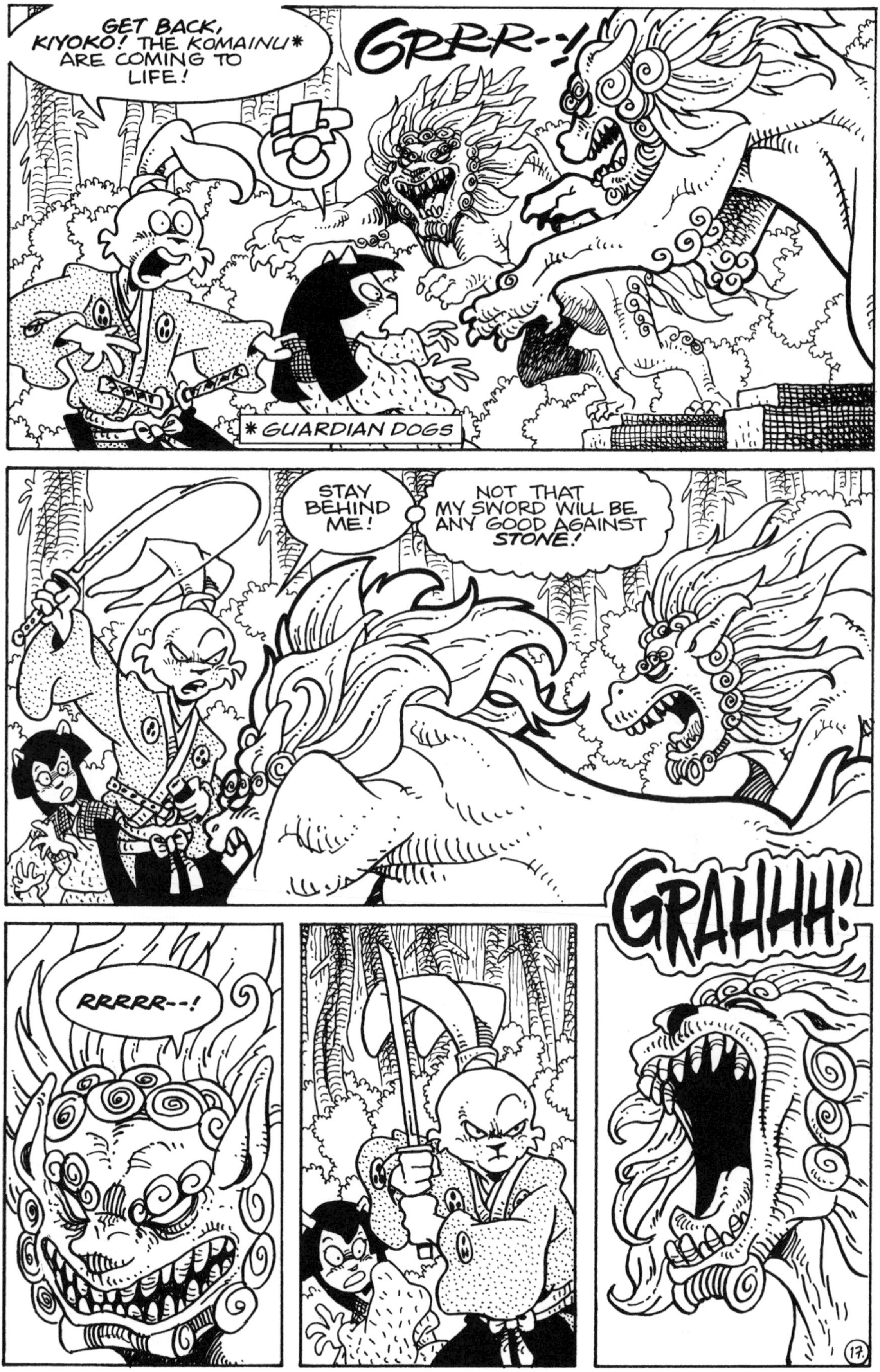
GET BACK, KIYOKO! THE KOMAINU* ARE COMING TO LIFE!
GRRR--!
*GUARDIAN DOGS
STAY BEHIND ME!
NOT THAT MY SWORD WILL BE ANY GOOD AGAINST STONE!
RRRRR--!
GRAHHH!
17.

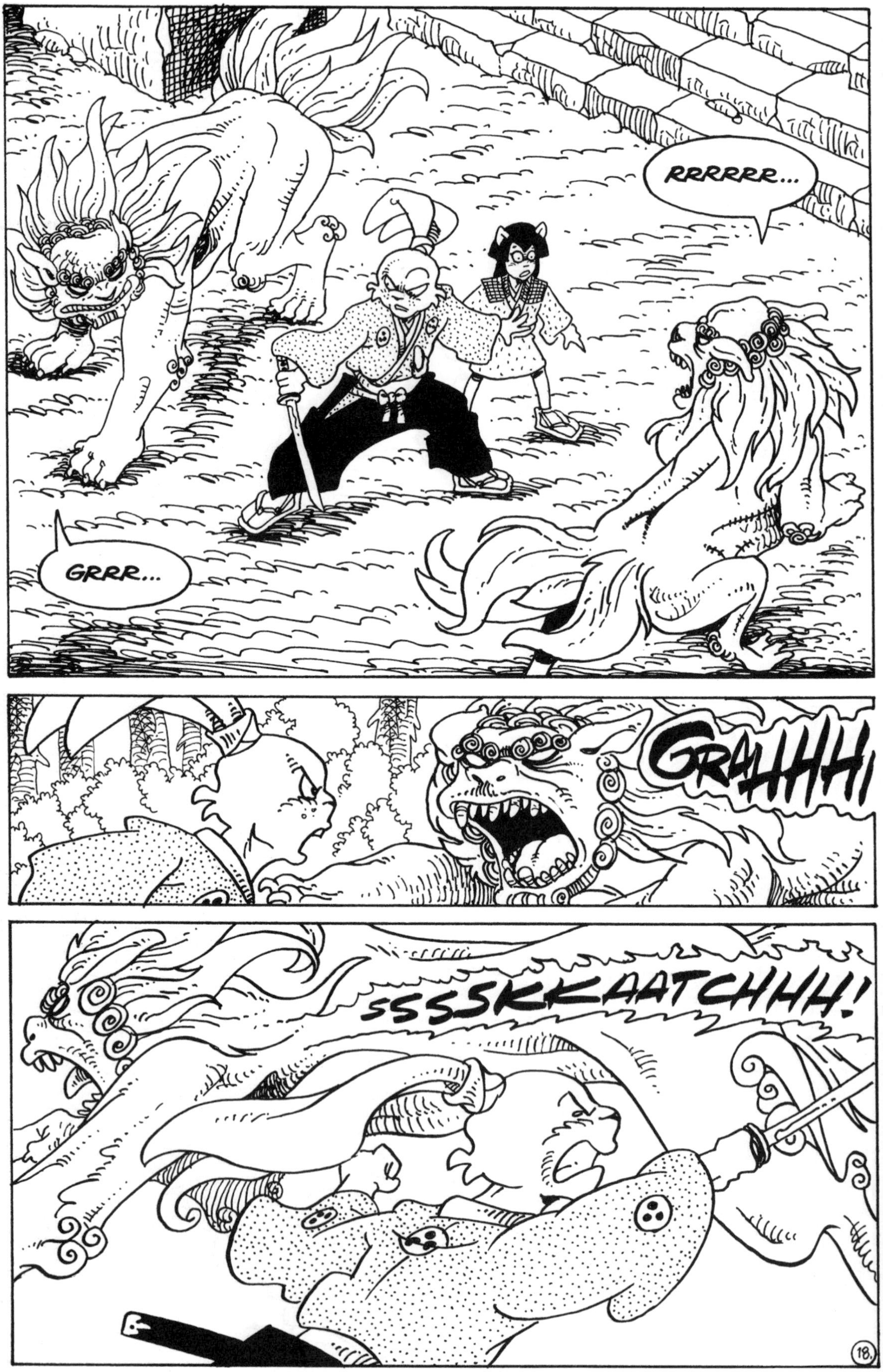
RRRRRR...
GRRR...
GRAHHH
SSSSKKAATCHHH!
18

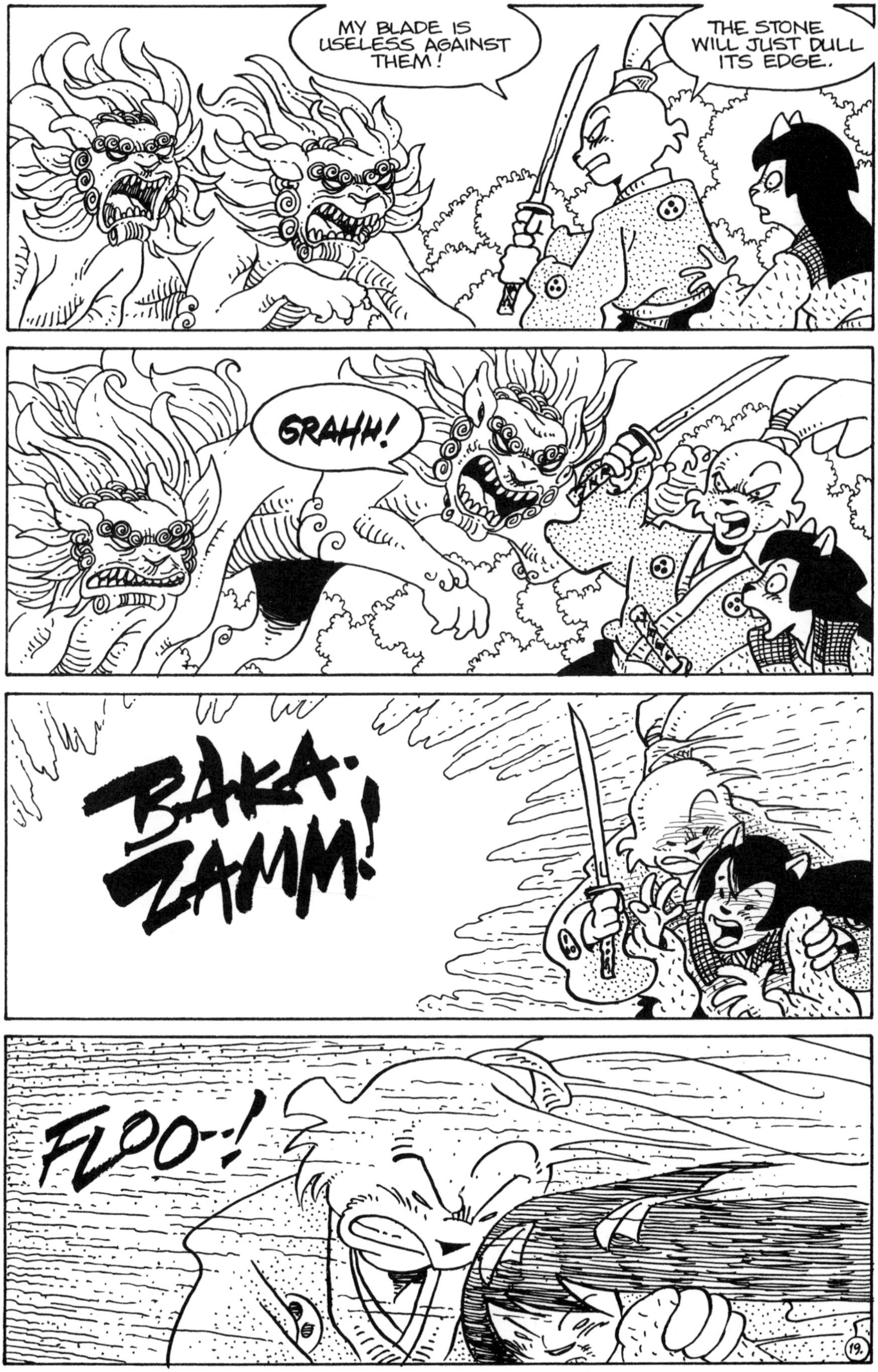
MY BLADE IS USELESS AGAINST THEM!
THE STONE WILL JUST DULL ITS EDGE.
GRAHH!
BAKA-ZAMM!
FLOO--!
19.

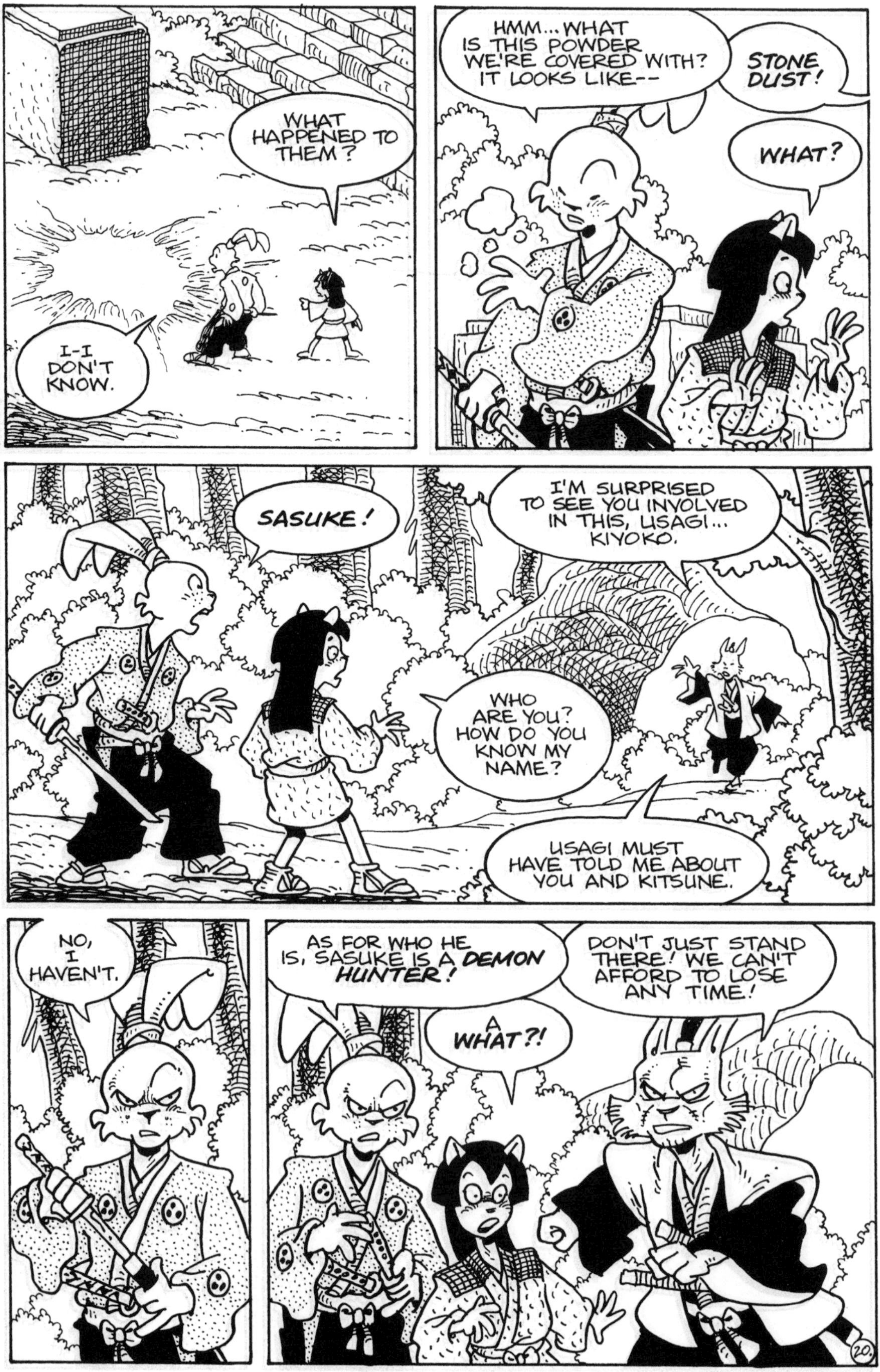
WHAT HAPPENED TO THEM?
I-I DON'T KNOW.
HMM... WHAT IS THIS POWDER WE'RE COVERED WITH? IT LOOKS LIKE--
STONE DUST!
WHAT?
SASUKE!
I'M SURPRISED TO SEE YOU INVOLVED IN THIS, USAGI... KIYOKO.
WHO ARE YOU? HOW DO YOU KNOW MY NAME?
USAGI MUST HAVE TOLD ME ABOUT YOU AND KITSUNE.
NO, I HAVEN'T.
AS FOR WHO HE IS, SASUKE IS A **DEMON HUNTER!**
A **WHAT?!**
DON'T JUST STAND THERE! WE CAN'T AFFORD TO LOSE ANY TIME!
20.

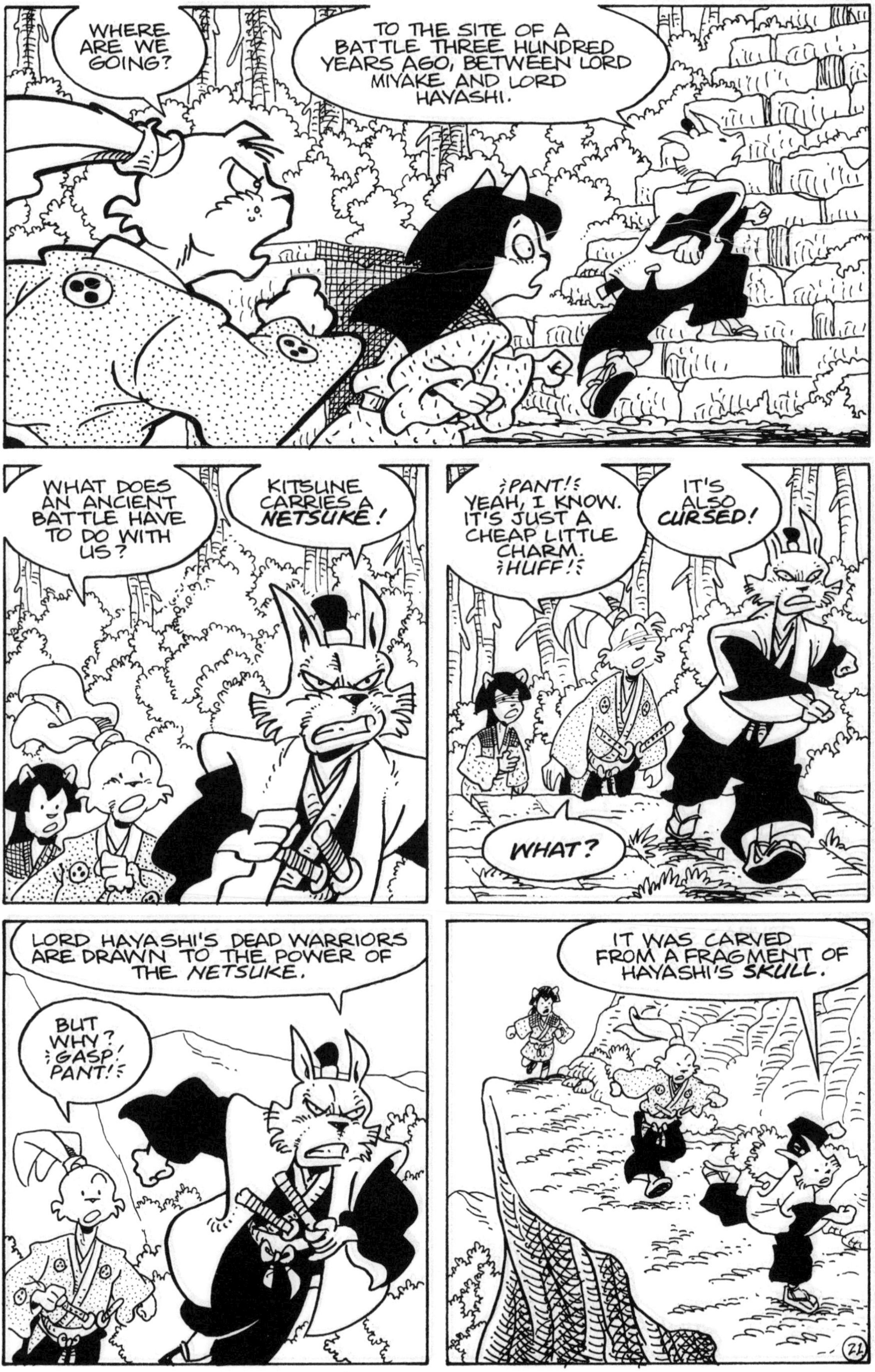
WHERE ARE WE GOING?
TO THE SITE OF A BATTLE THREE HUNDRED YEARS AGO, BETWEEN LORD MIYAKE AND LORD HAYASHI.
WHAT DOES AN ANCIENT BATTLE HAVE TO DO WITH US?
KITSUNE CARRIES A NETSUKE!
PANT! YEAH, I KNOW. IT'S JUST A CHEAP LITTLE CHARM. HUFF!
IT'S ALSO CURSED!
WHAT?
LORD HAYASHI'S DEAD WARRIORS ARE DRAWN TO THE POWER OF THE NETSUKE.
BUT WHY? GASP PANT!
IT WAS CARVED FROM A FRAGMENT OF HAYASHI'S SKULL.
21

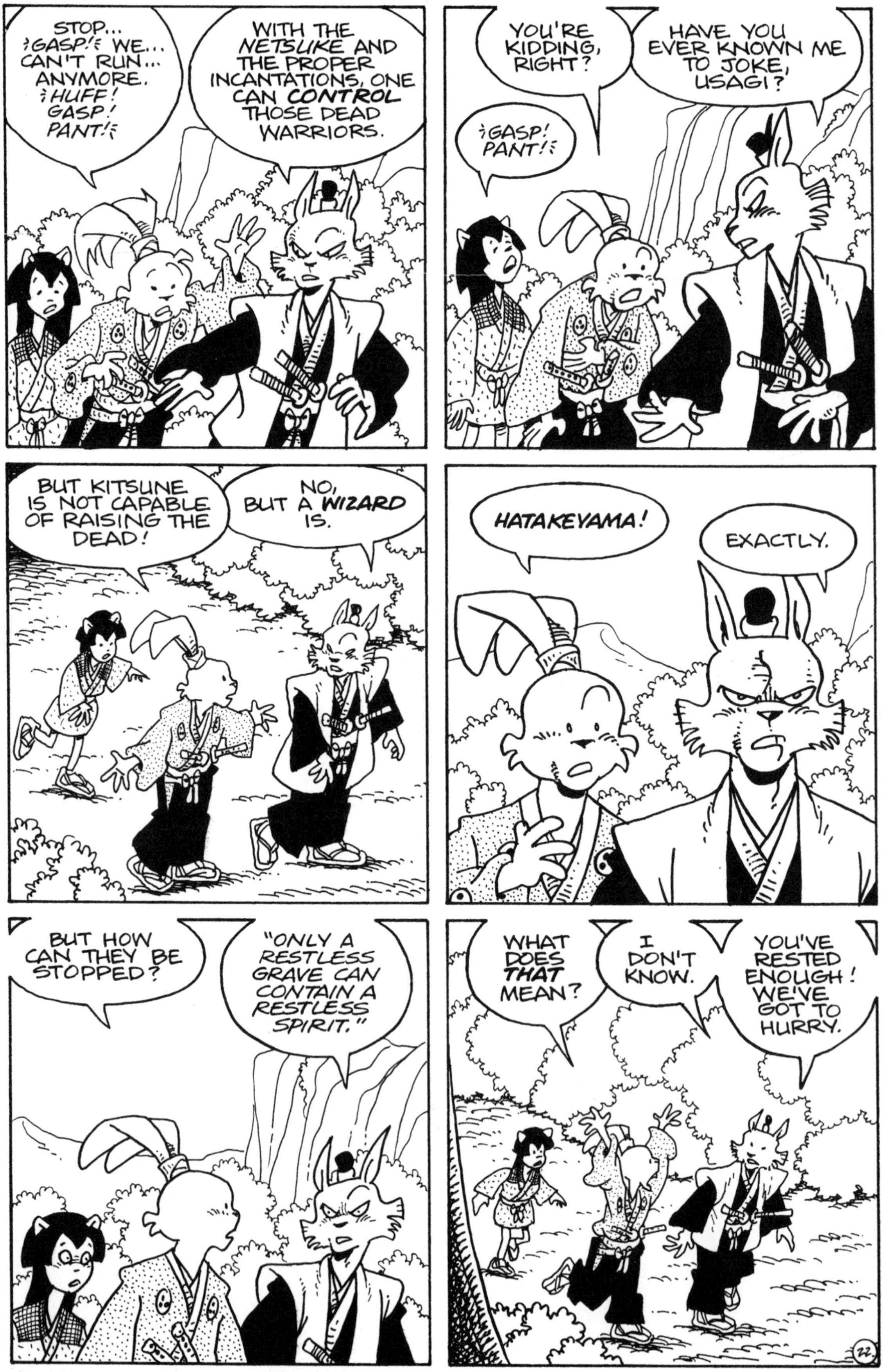
STOP... ¡GASP!¡ WE... CAN'T RUN... ANYMORE. ¡HUFF! GASP! PANT!¡
WITH THE *NETSUKE* AND THE PROPER INCANTATIONS, ONE CAN **CONTROL** THOSE DEAD WARRIORS.
YOU'RE KIDDING, RIGHT?
¡GASP! PANT!¡
HAVE YOU EVER KNOWN ME TO JOKE, USAGI?
BUT KITSUNE IS NOT CAPABLE OF RAISING THE DEAD!
NO, BUT A ***WIZARD*** IS.
***HATAKEYAMA!***
EXACTLY.
BUT HOW CAN THEY BE STOPPED?
*"ONLY A RESTLESS GRAVE CAN CONTAIN A RESTLESS SPIRIT."*
WHAT DOES ***THAT*** MEAN?
I DON'T KNOW.
YOU'VE RESTED ENOUGH! WE'VE GOT TO HURRY.
22

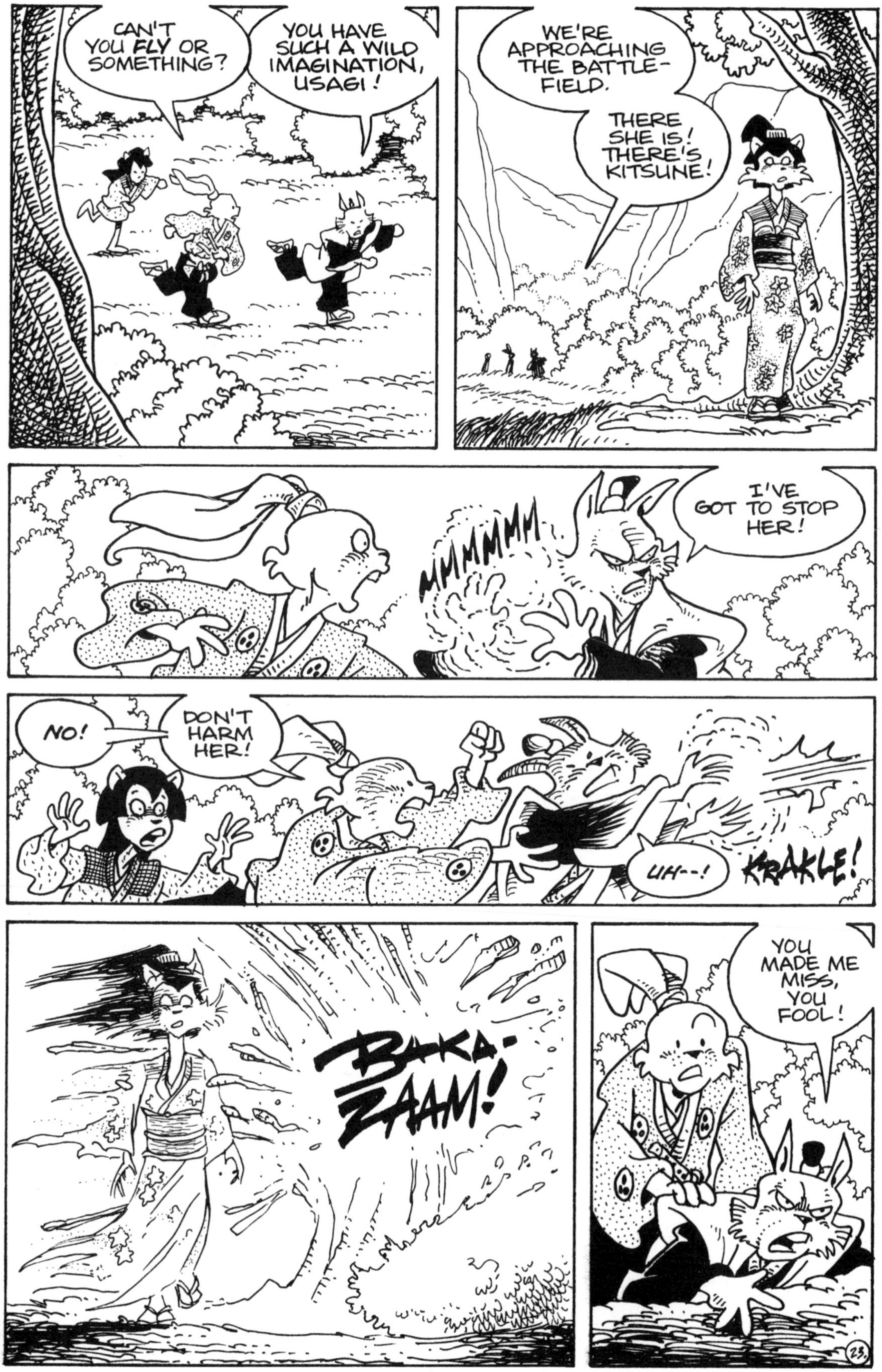
CAN'T YOU FLY OR SOMETHING?
YOU HAVE SUCH A WILD IMAGINATION, USAGI!
WE'RE APPROACHING THE BATTLE-FIELD.
THERE SHE IS! THERE'S KITSUNE!
MMMMMM
I'VE GOT TO STOP HER!
NO!
DON'T HARM HER!
UH--!
KRAKLE!
BAKA-ZAAM!
YOU MADE ME MISS, YOU FOOL!
23

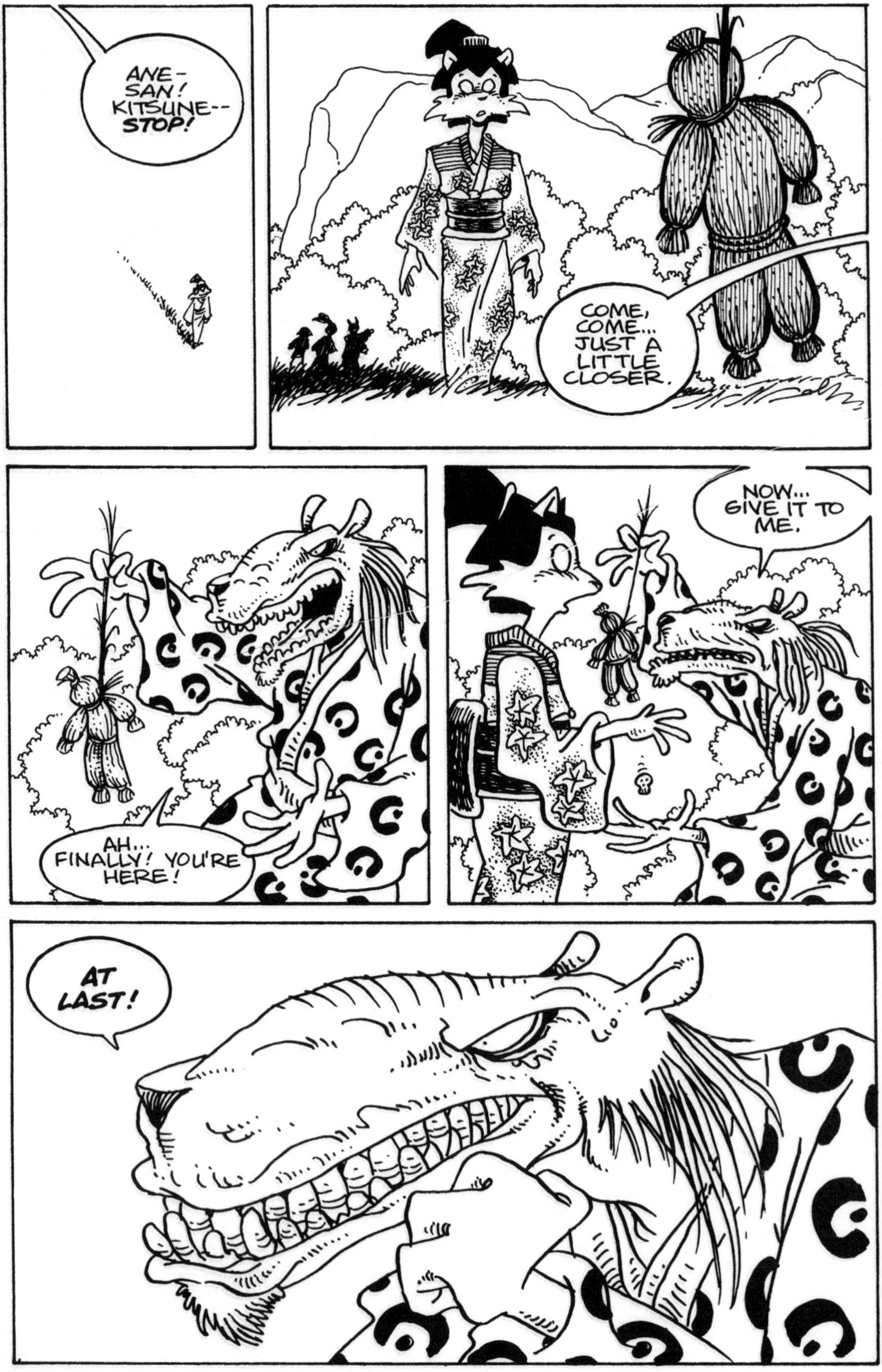
ANE-SAN! KITSUNE-- STOP!
COME, COME... JUST A LITTLE CLOSER.
AH... FINALLY! YOU'RE HERE!
NOW... GIVE IT TO ME.
AT LAST!

# TRAITORS OF THE EARTH PART THREE

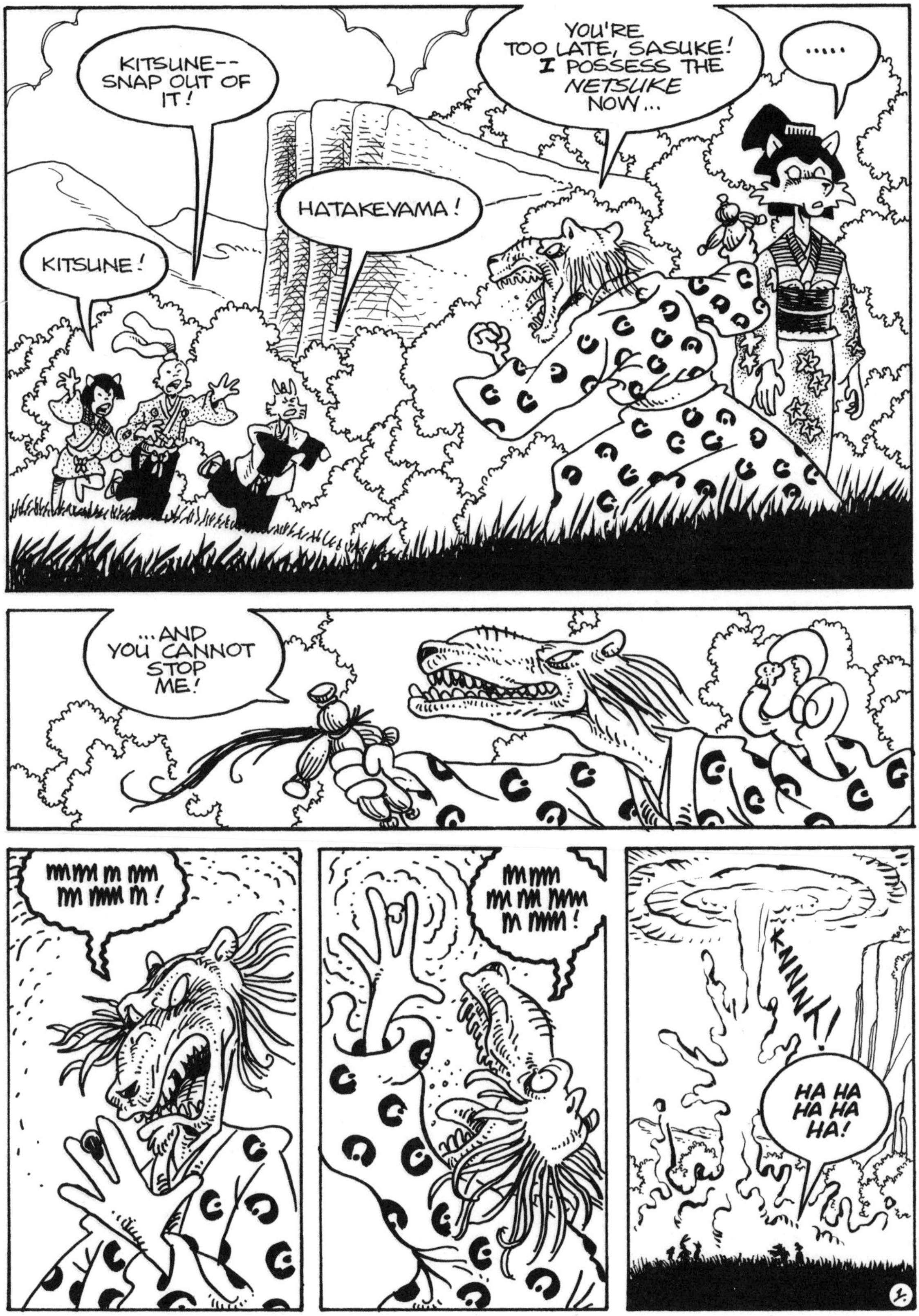

KITSUNE-- SNAP OUT OF IT!
YOU'RE TOO LATE, SASUKE! I POSSESS THE *NETSUKE* NOW...
.....
HATAKEYAMA!
KITSUNE!
...AND YOU CANNOT STOP ME!
MMMM M MM MM MMM M!
MMM MM MM MMM M MMM!
KNNNT!
HA HA HA HA HA!

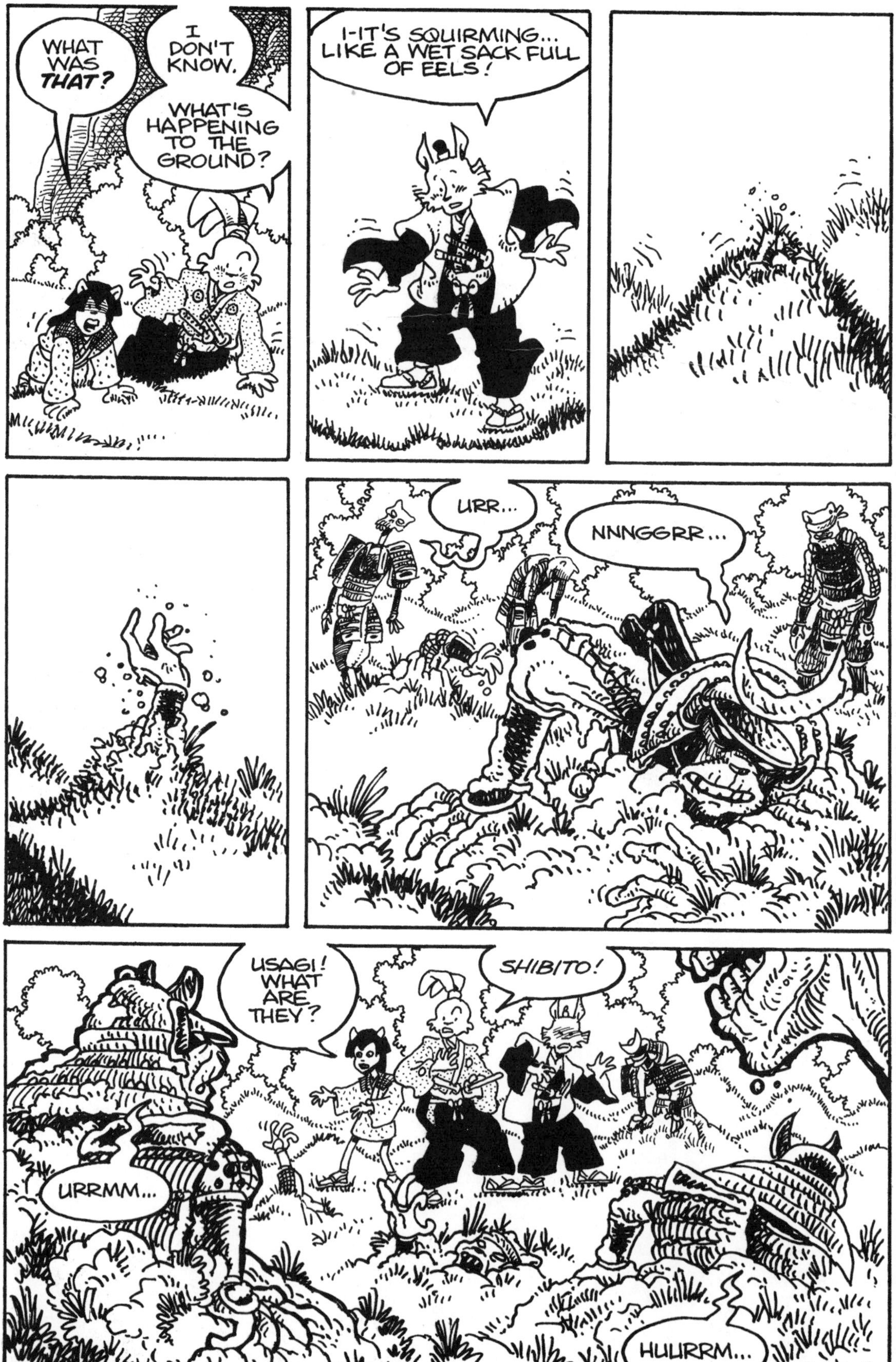
WHAT WAS *THAT*?
I DON'T KNOW.
WHAT'S HAPPENING TO THE GROUND?
I-IT'S SQUIRMING... LIKE A WET SACK FULL OF EELS!
URR...
NNNGGRR...
USAGI! WHAT ARE THEY?
SHIBITO!
URRMM...
HUURRM...

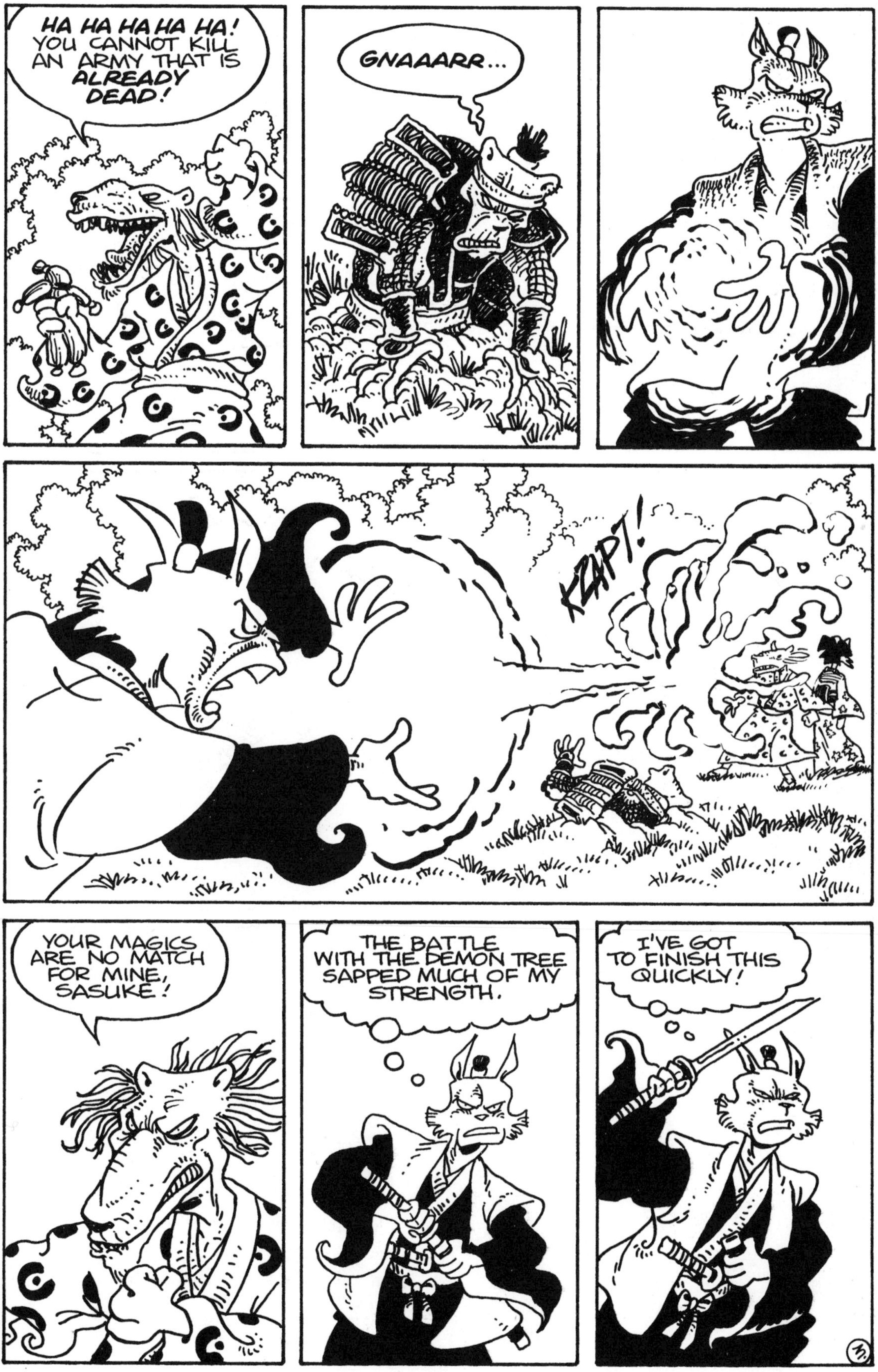
HA HA HA HA HA! YOU CANNOT KILL AN ARMY THAT IS ALREADY DEAD!
GNAAARR...
KZAPT!
YOUR MAGICS ARE NO MATCH FOR MINE, SASUKE!
THE BATTLE WITH THE DEMON TREE SAPPED MUCH OF MY STRENGTH.
I'VE GOT TO FINISH THIS QUICKLY!

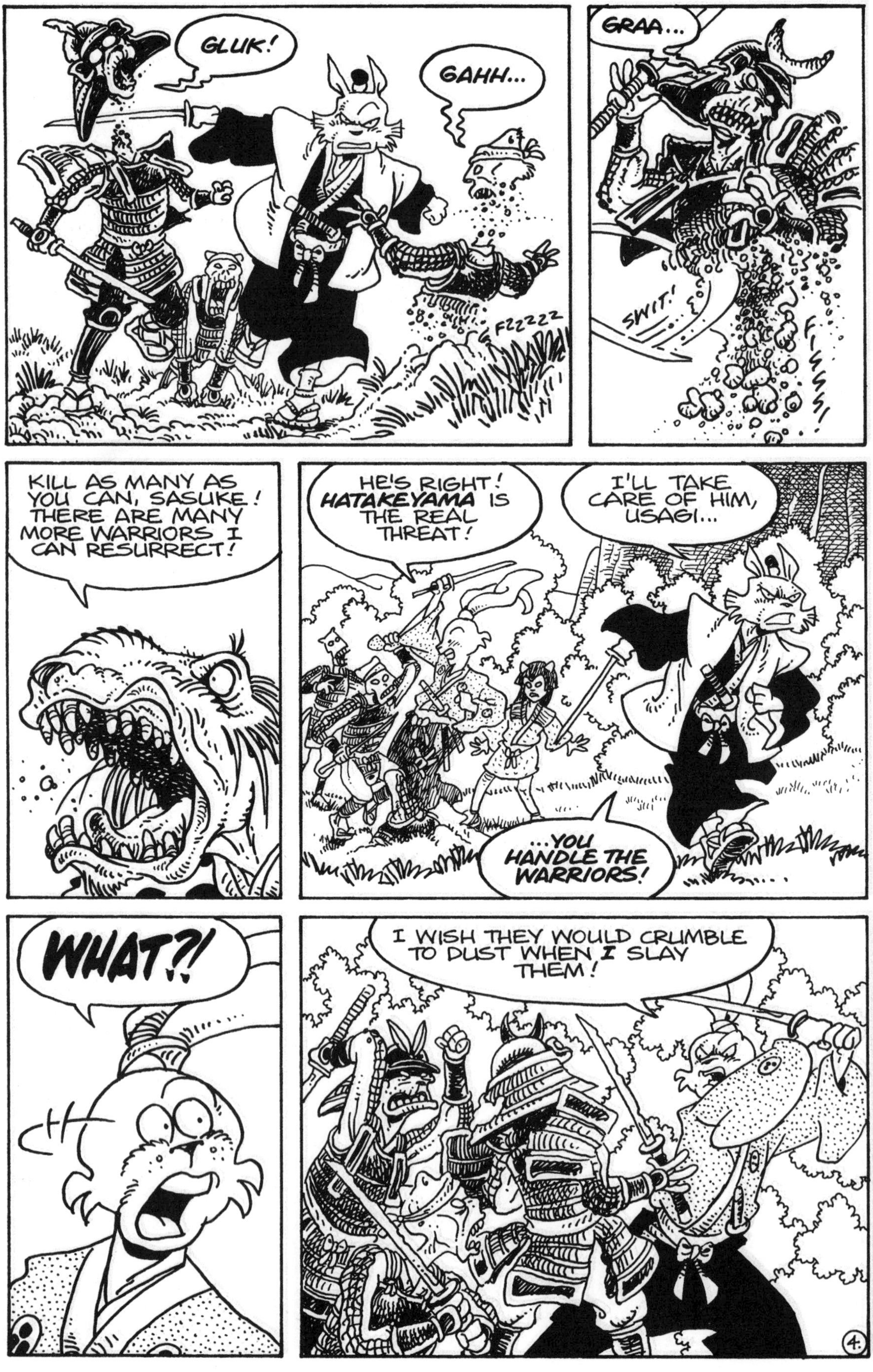
GLUK!
GAHH...
FZZZZZ
GRAA...
SWIT!
KILL AS MANY AS YOU CAN, SASUKE! THERE ARE MANY MORE WARRIORS I CAN RESURRECT!
HE'S RIGHT! **HATAKEYAMA** IS THE REAL THREAT!
I'LL TAKE CARE OF HIM, USAGI...
**...YOU HANDLE THE WARRIORS!**
**WHAT?!**
I WISH THEY WOULD CRUMBLE TO DUST WHEN **I** SLAY THEM!
4.

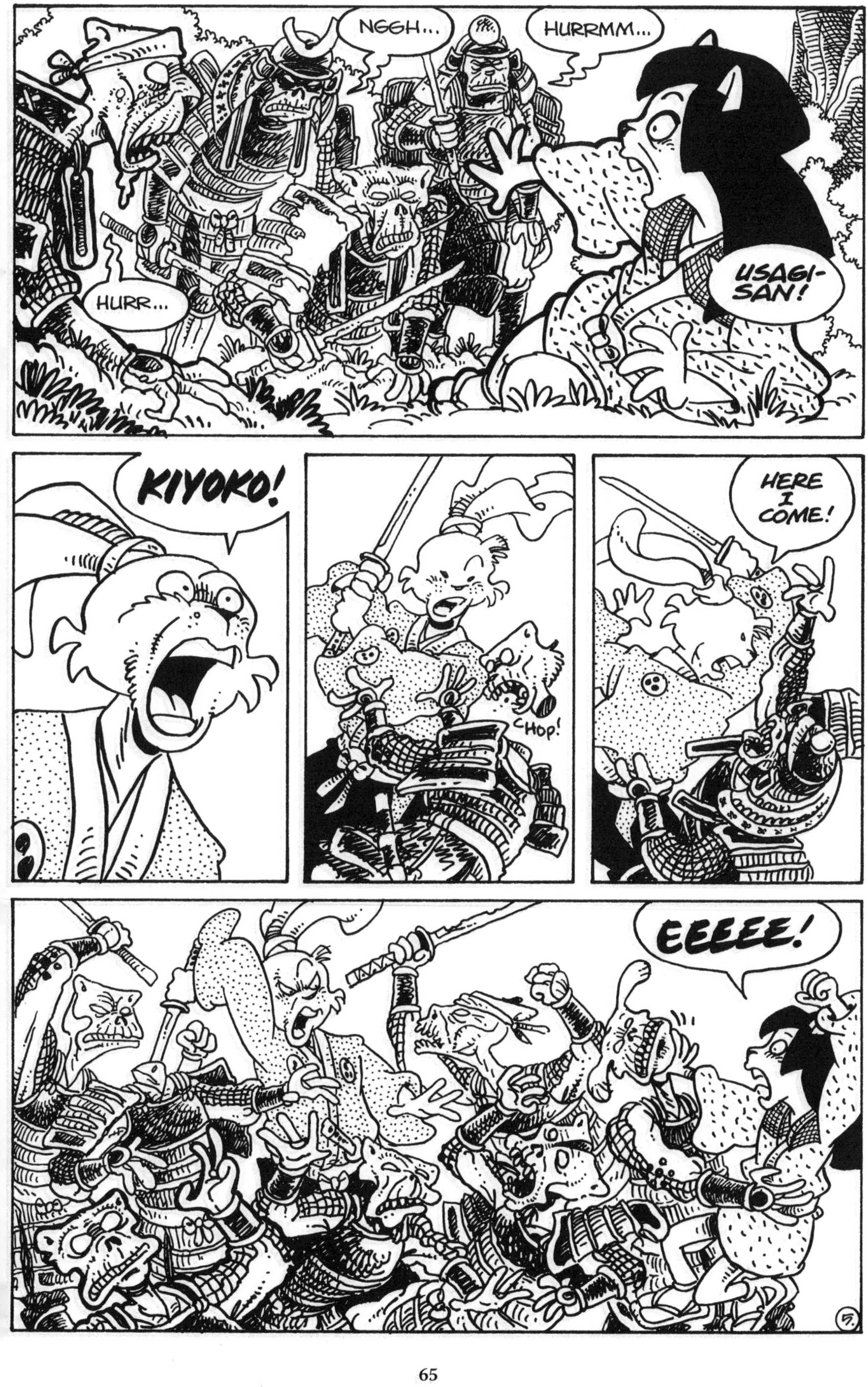
NGGH...
HURRMM...
HURR...
USAGI-SAN!
KIYOKO!
CHOP!
HERE I COME!
EEEEE!
5.

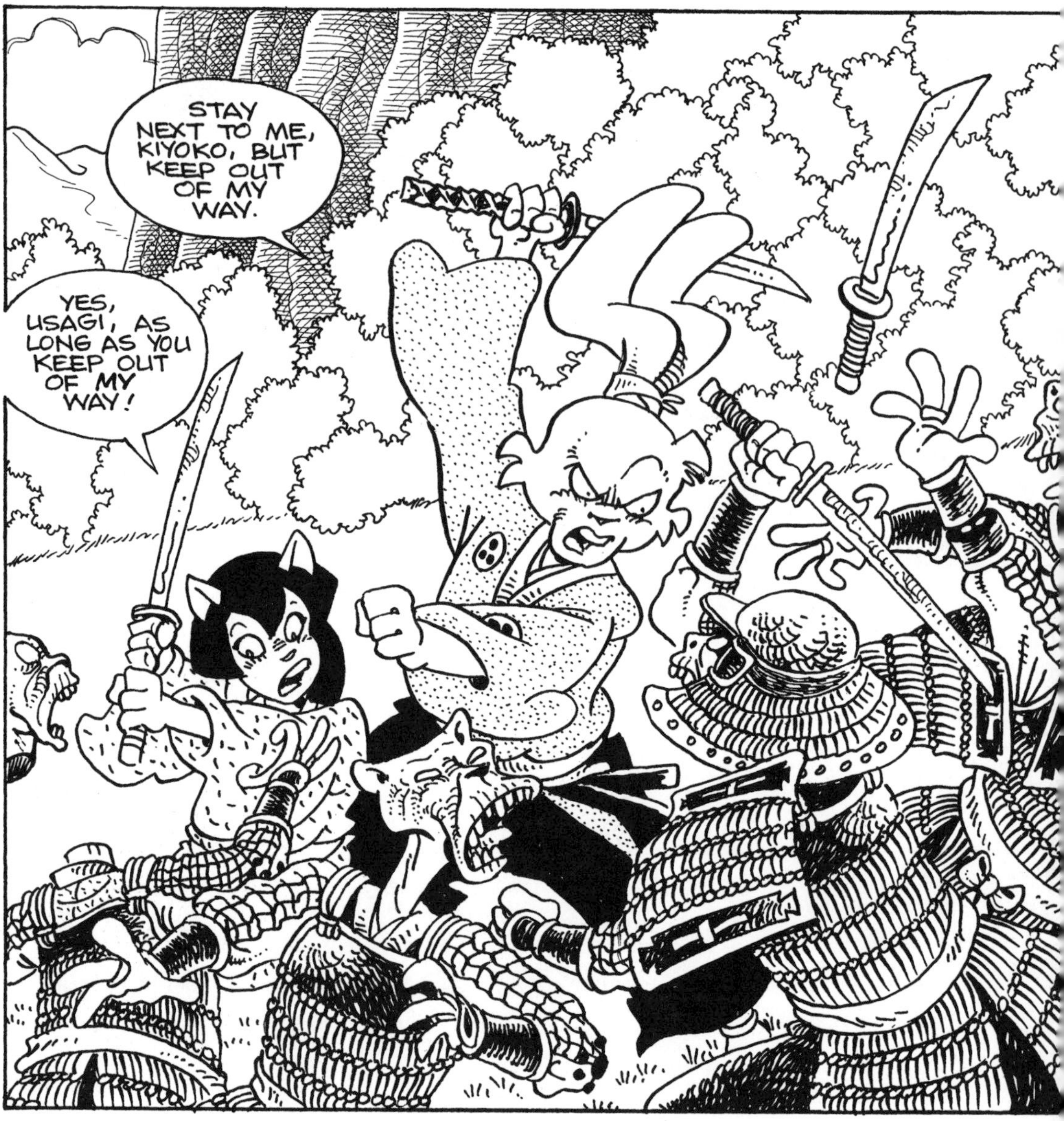
STAY NEXT TO ME, KIYOKO, BUT KEEP OUT OF MY WAY.
YES, USAGI, AS LONG AS YOU KEEP OUT OF MY WAY!

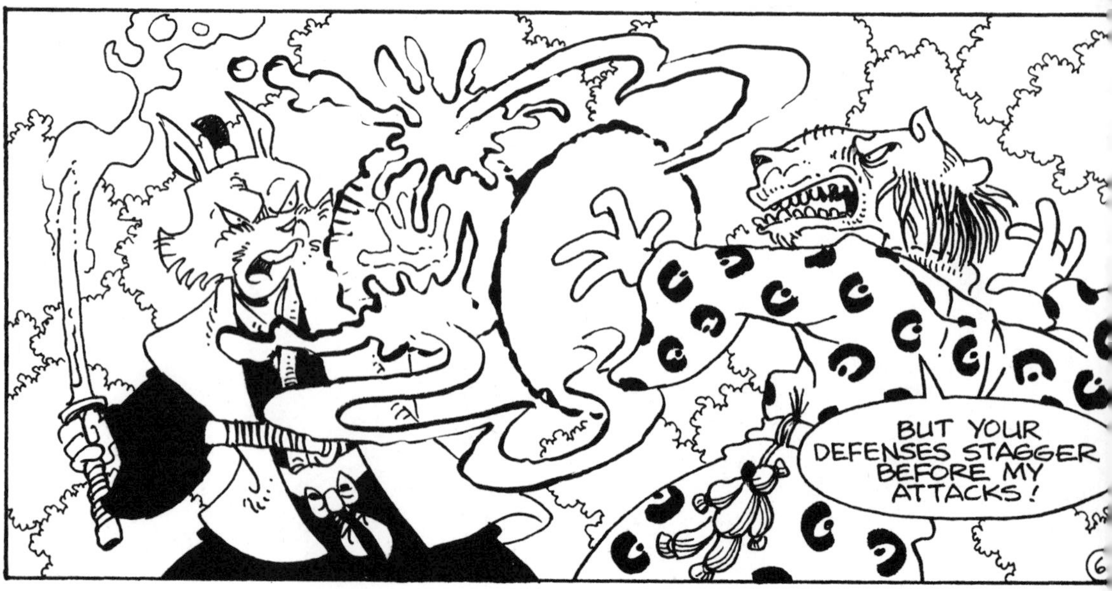
BUT YOUR DEFENSES STAGGER BEFORE MY ATTACKS!

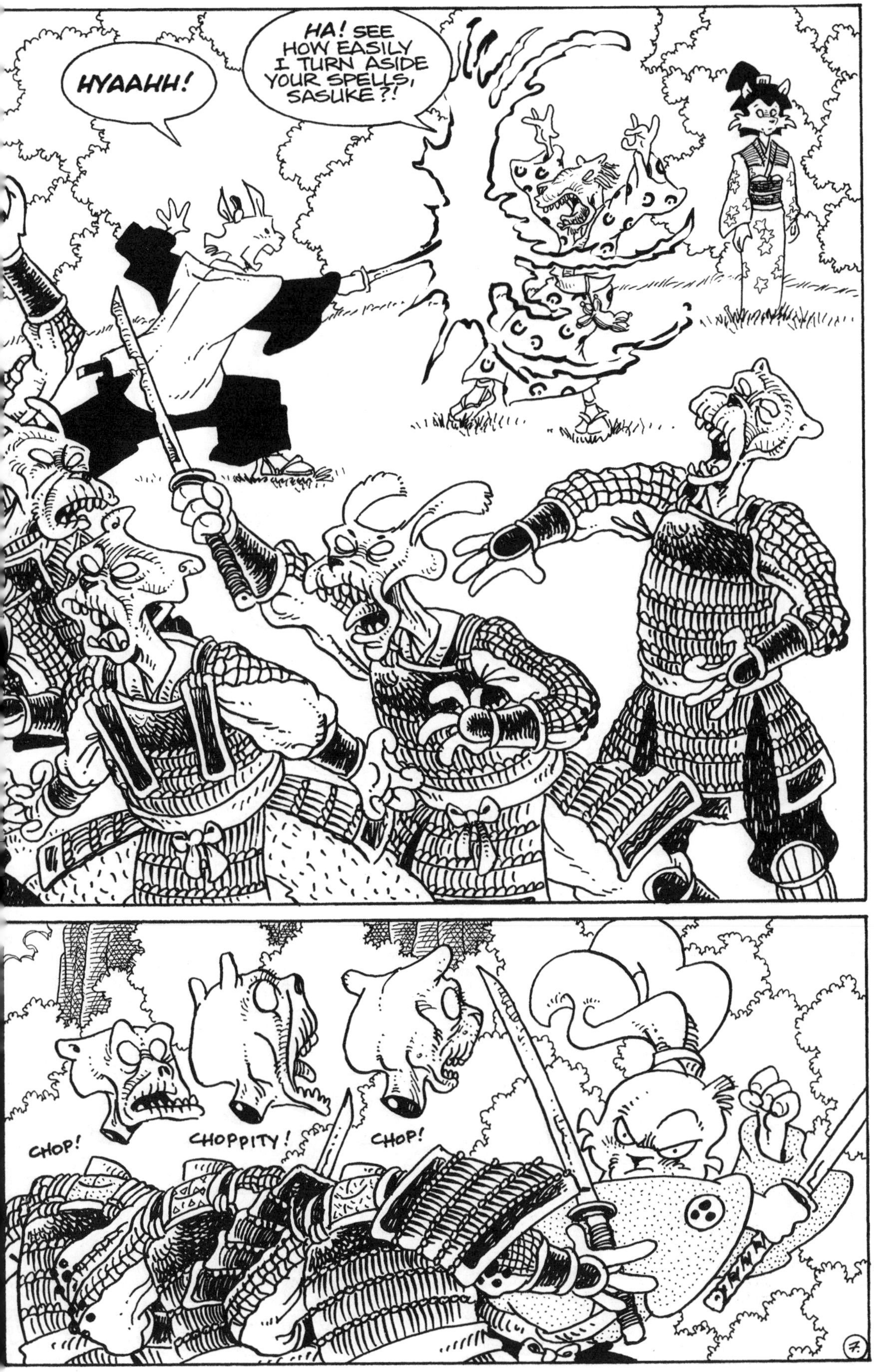
HYAAHH!
HA! SEE HOW EASILY I TURN ASIDE YOUR SPELLS, SASUKE?!
CHOP!
CHOPPITY!
CHOP!
7

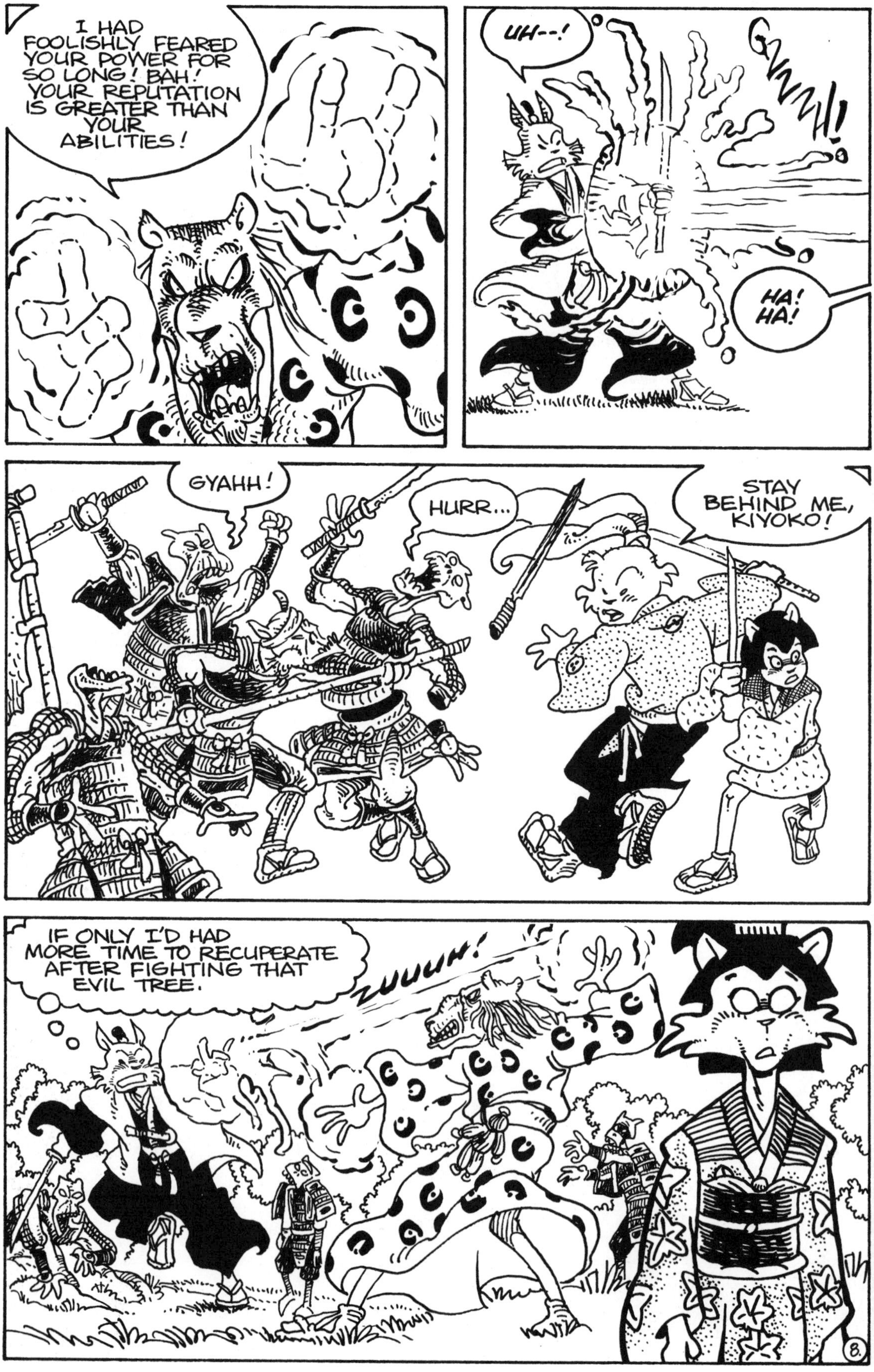
I HAD FOOLISHLY FEARED YOUR POWER FOR SO LONG! BAH! YOUR REPUTATION IS GREATER THAN YOUR ABILITIES!
UH--!
HA! HA!
GYAHH!
HURR...
STAY BEHIND ME, KIYOKO!
IF ONLY I'D HAD MORE TIME TO RECUPERATE AFTER FIGHTING THAT EVIL TREE.
ZUUUH!
8.

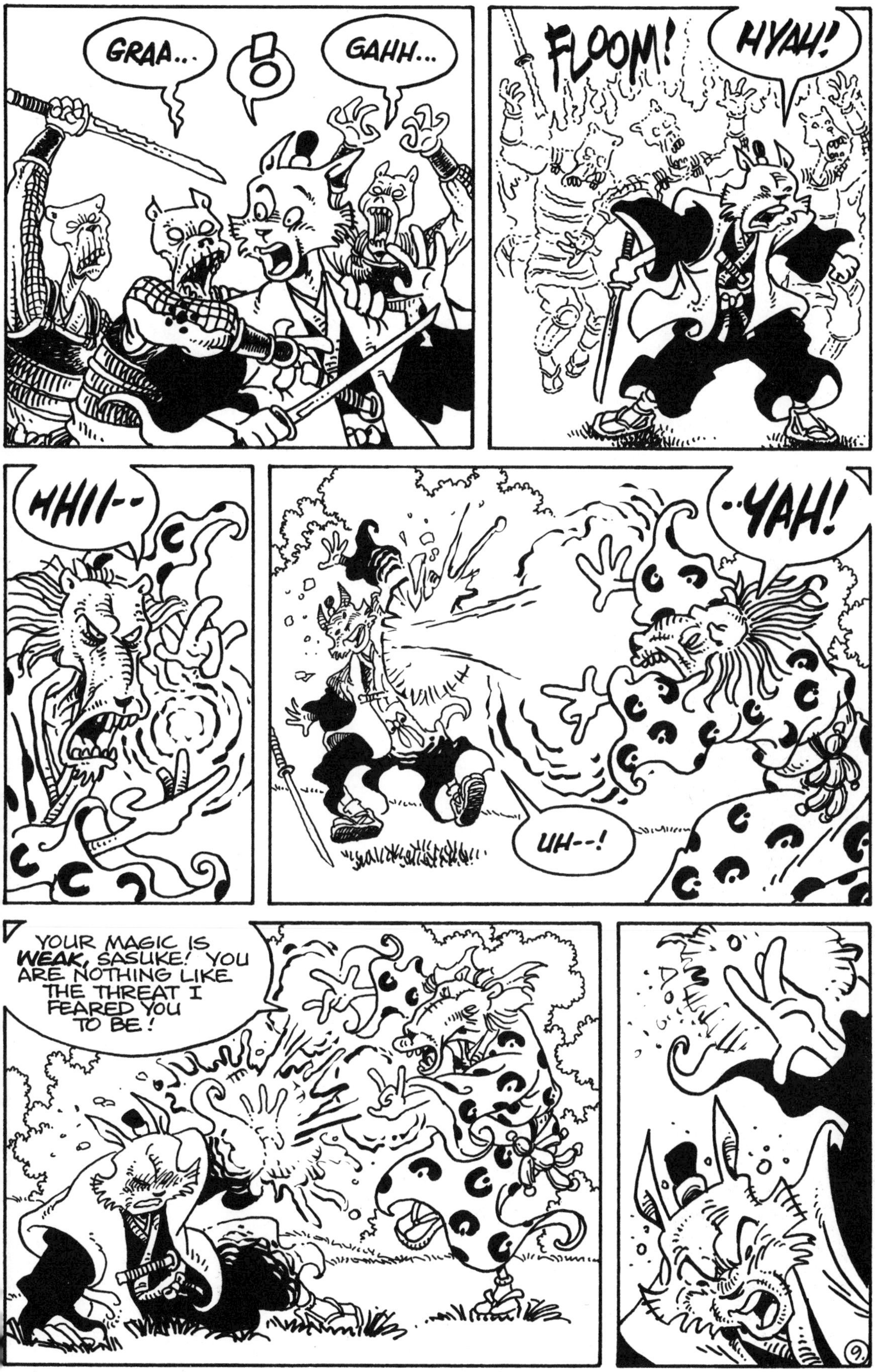
GRAA...
!?
GAHH...
FLOOM!
HYAH!
HHII--
--YAH!
UH--!
YOUR MAGIC IS WEAK, SASUKE! YOU ARE NOTHING LIKE THE THREAT I FEARED YOU TO BE!
9.

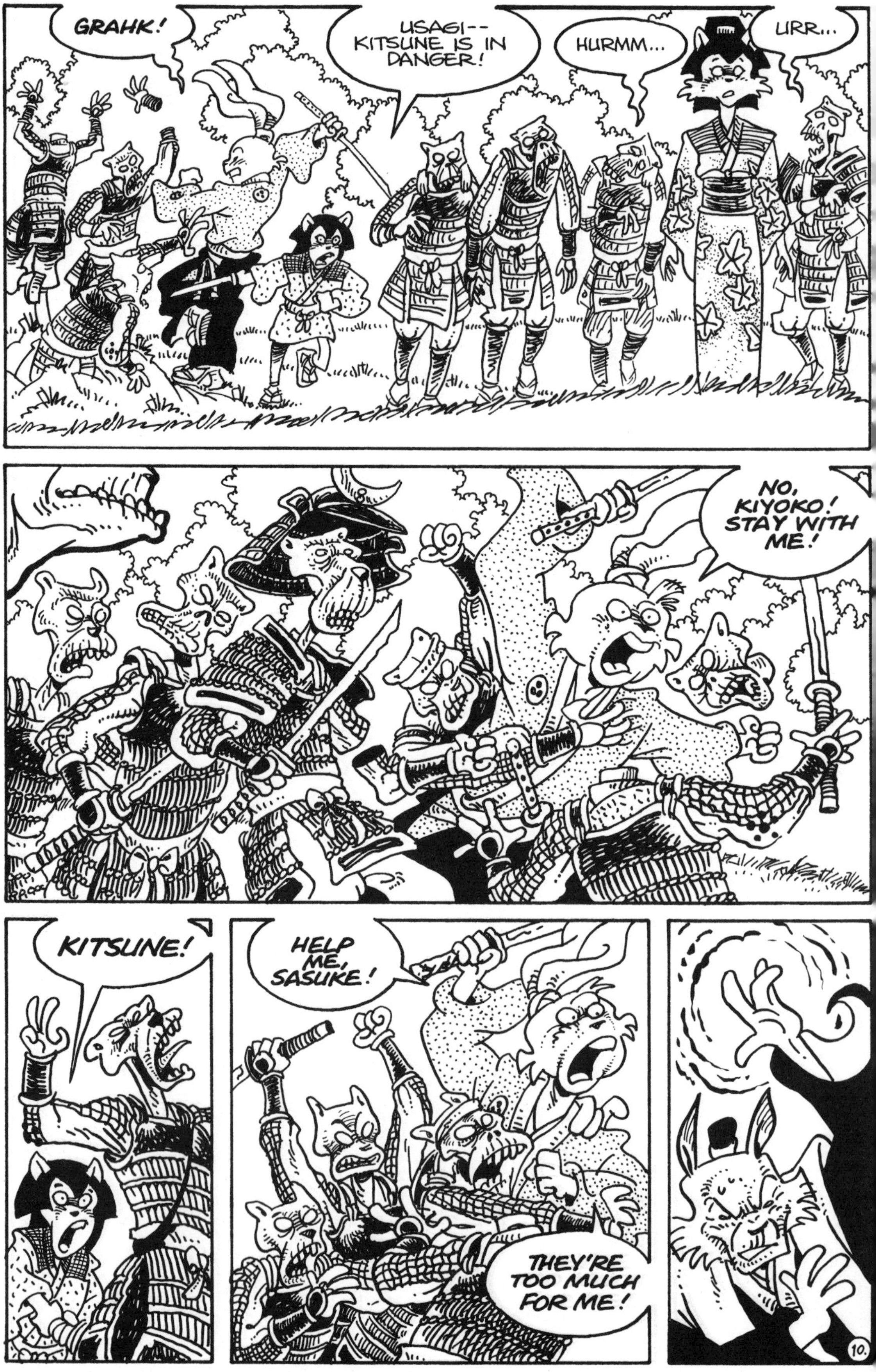
GRAHK!
USAGI-- KITSUNE IS IN DANGER!
HURMM...
URR...
NO, KIYOKO! STAY WITH ME!
KITSUNE!
HELP ME, SASUKE!
THEY'RE TOO MUCH FOR ME!
10.

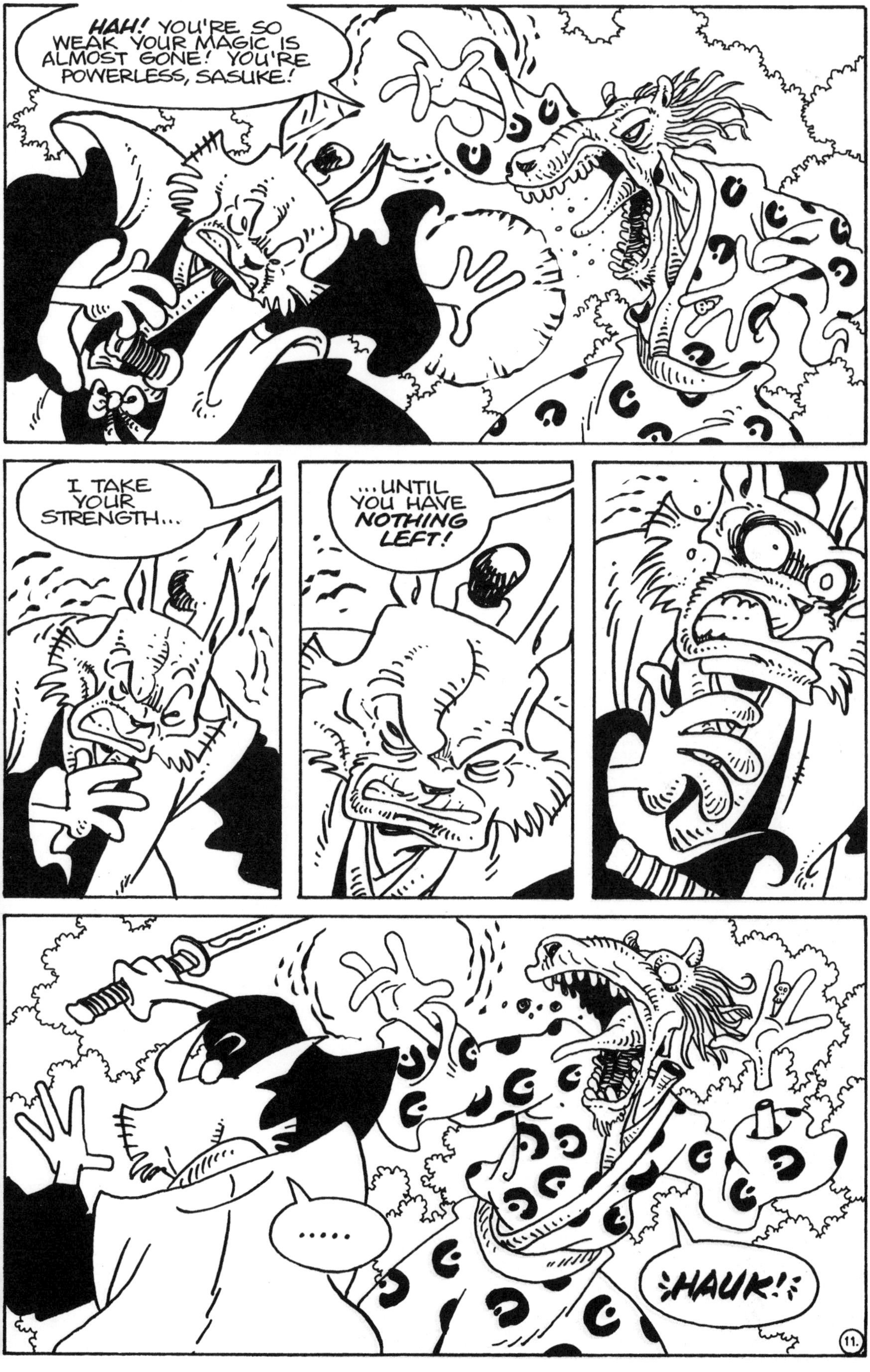
HAH! YOU'RE SO WEAK YOUR MAGIC IS ALMOST GONE! YOU'RE POWERLESS, SASUKE!
I TAKE YOUR STRENGTH...
...UNTIL YOU HAVE NOTHING LEFT!
.....
HAUK!
11.

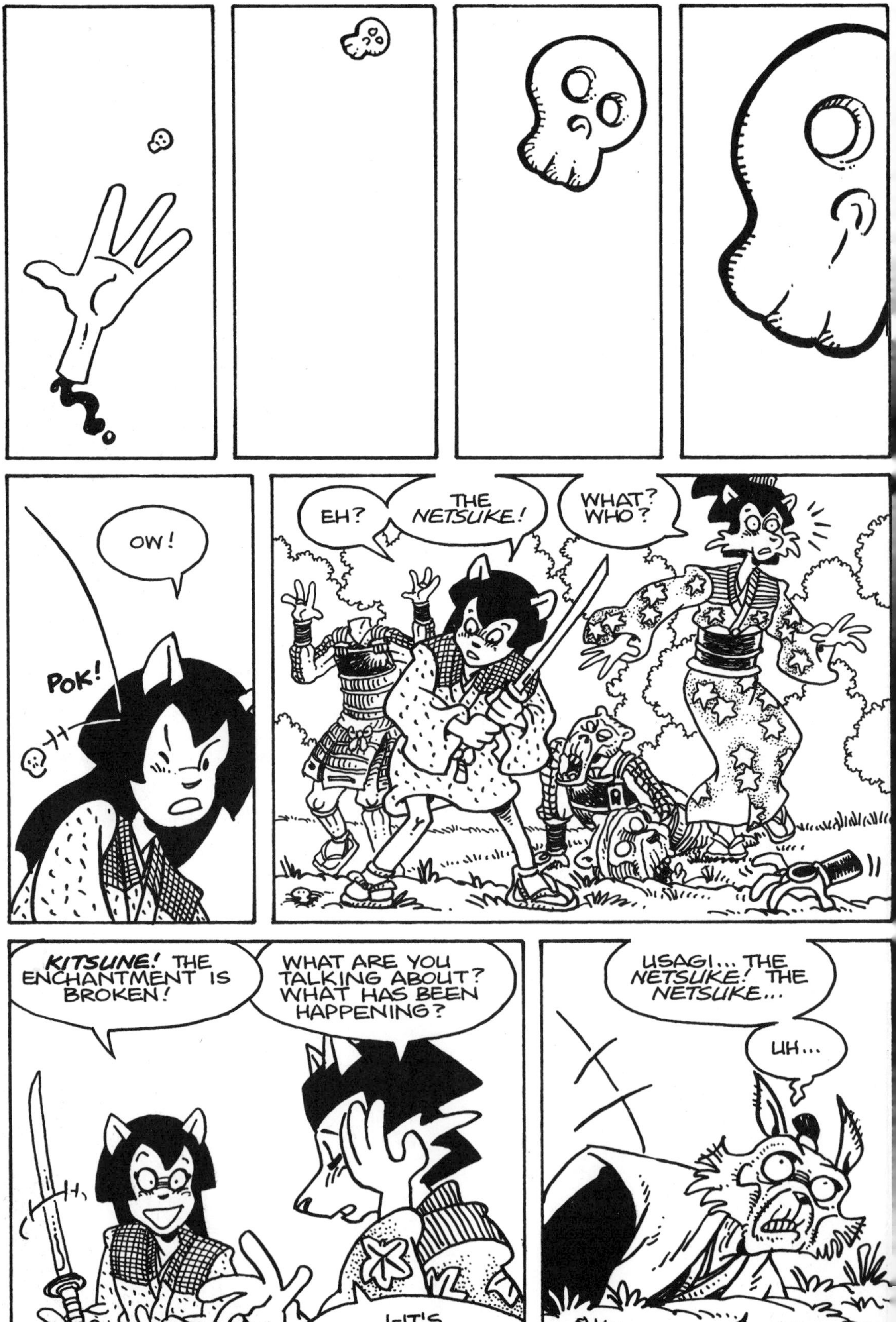
OW!
POK!
EH?
THE NETSUKE!
WHAT? WHO?
KITSUNE! THE ENCHANTMENT IS BROKEN!
WHAT ARE YOU TALKING ABOUT? WHAT HAS BEEN HAPPENING?
I-IT'S LIKE I'M WALKING THROUGH A THICK FOG.
USAGI... THE NETSUKE! THE NETSUKE...
UH...
.....
12

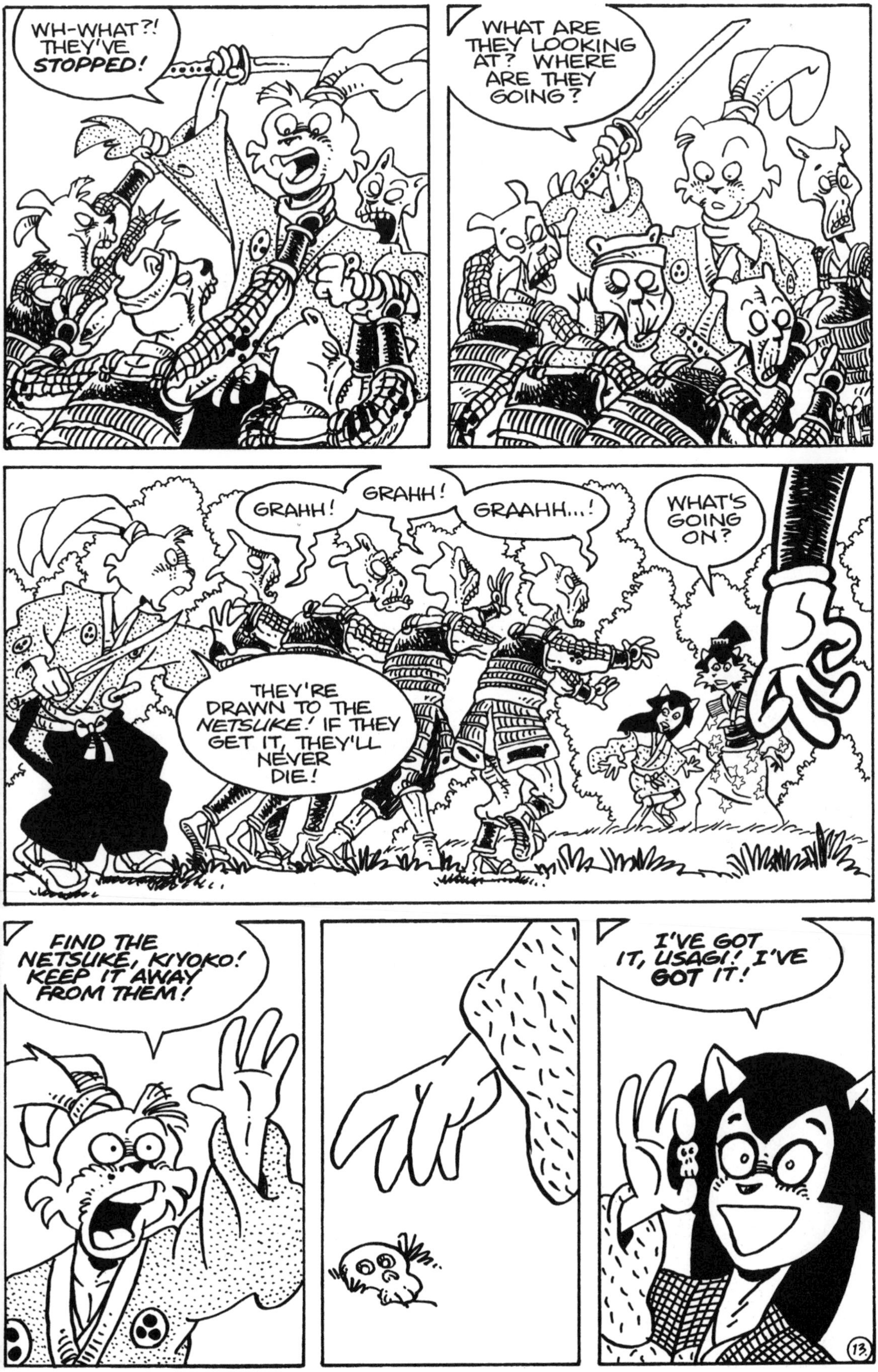
WH-WHAT?! THEY'VE STOPPED!
WHAT ARE THEY LOOKING AT? WHERE ARE THEY GOING?
GRAHH!
GRAHH!
GRAAHH...!
WHAT'S GOING ON?
THEY'RE DRAWN TO THE NETSUKE! IF THEY GET IT, THEY'LL NEVER DIE!
FIND THE NETSUKE, KIYOKO! KEEP IT AWAY FROM THEM!
I'VE GOT IT, USAGI! I'VE GOT IT!
13

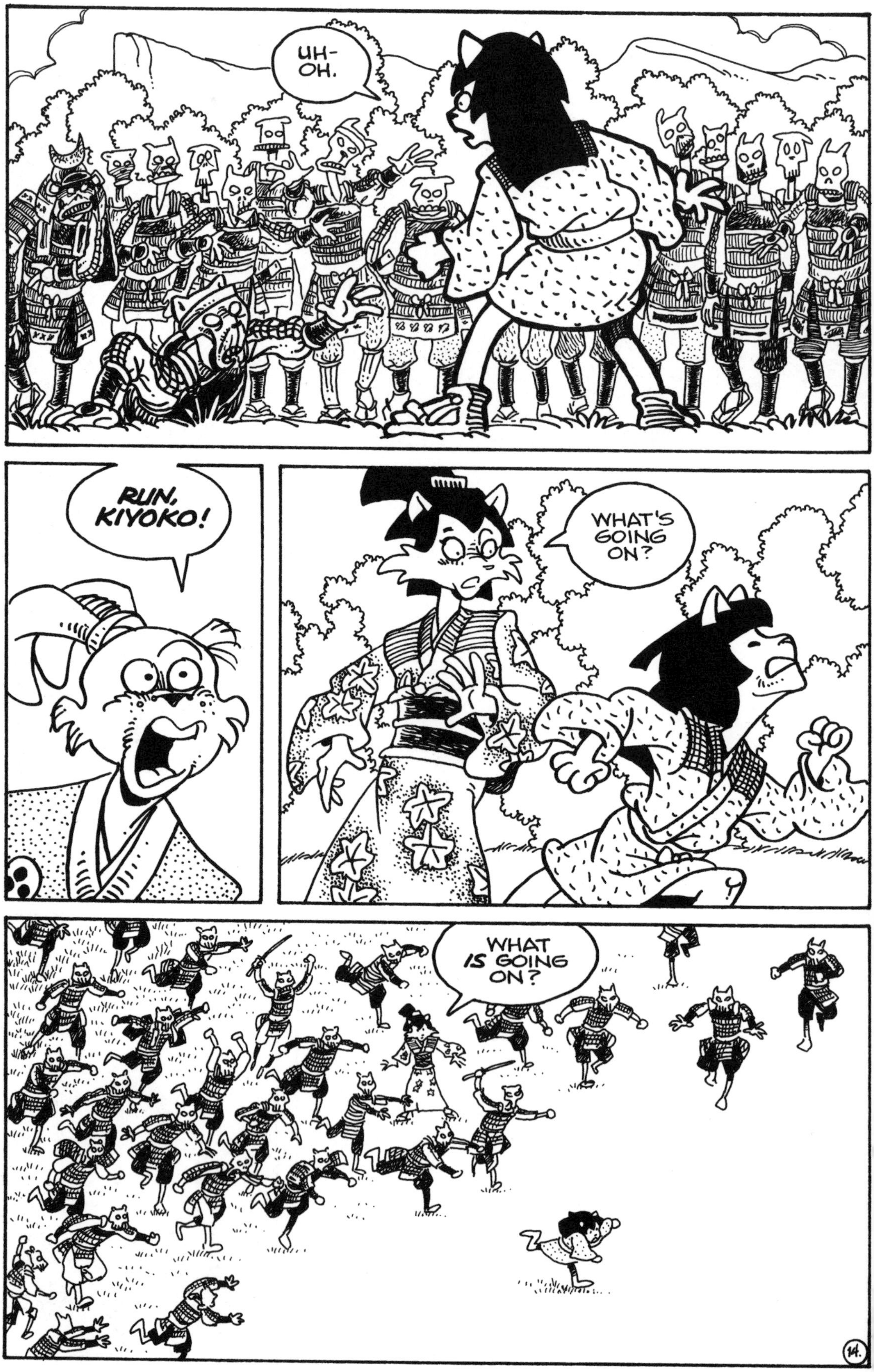
UH-OH.
RUN, KIYOKO!
WHAT'S GOING ON?
WHAT IS GOING ON?
14.

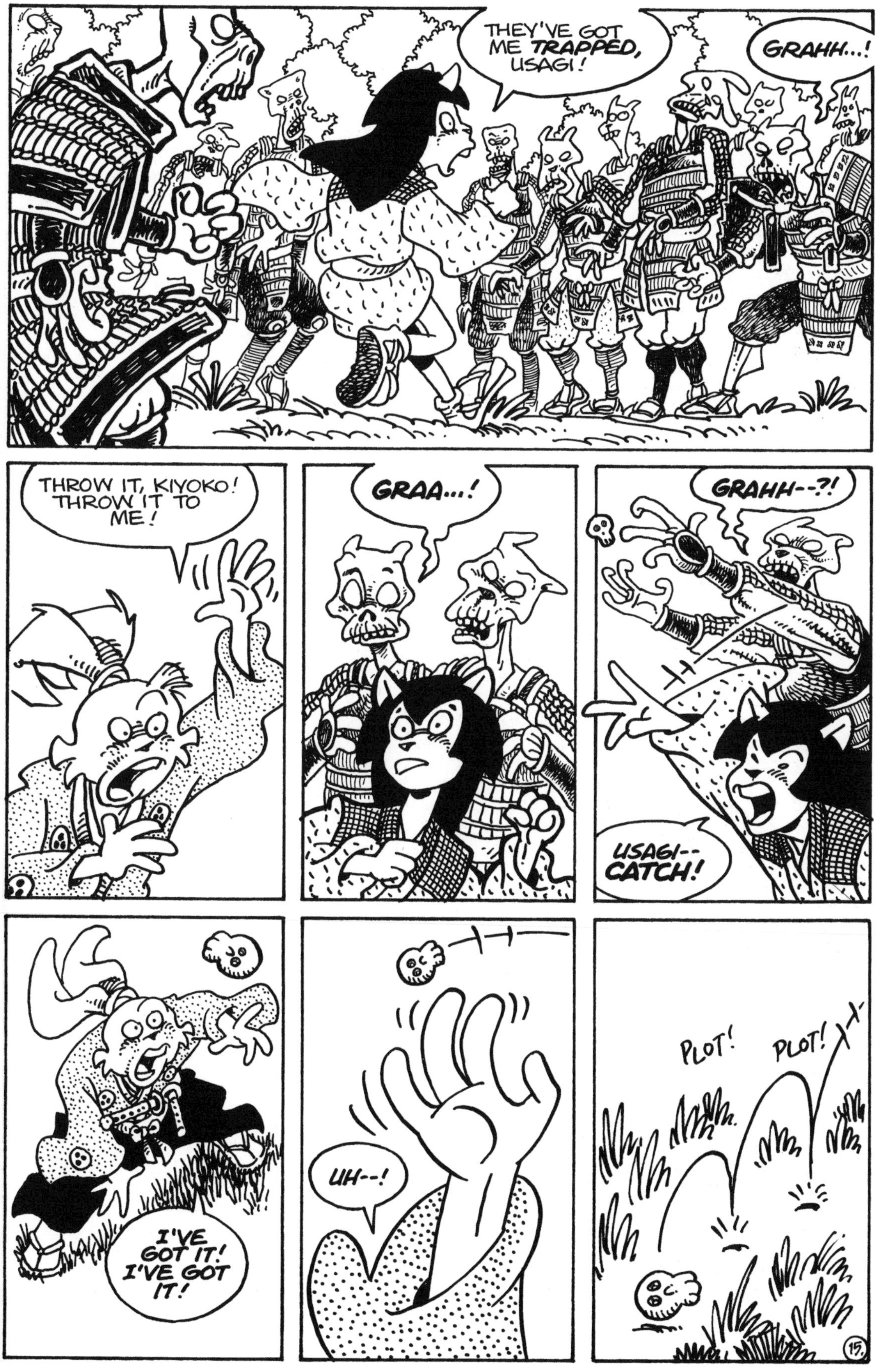
THEY'VE GOT ME TRAPPED, USAGI!
GRAHH...!
THROW IT, KIYOKO! THROW IT TO ME!
GRAA...!
GRAHH--?!
USAGI-- CATCH!
I'VE GOT IT! I'VE GOT IT!
UH--!
PLOT!
PLOT!
15.

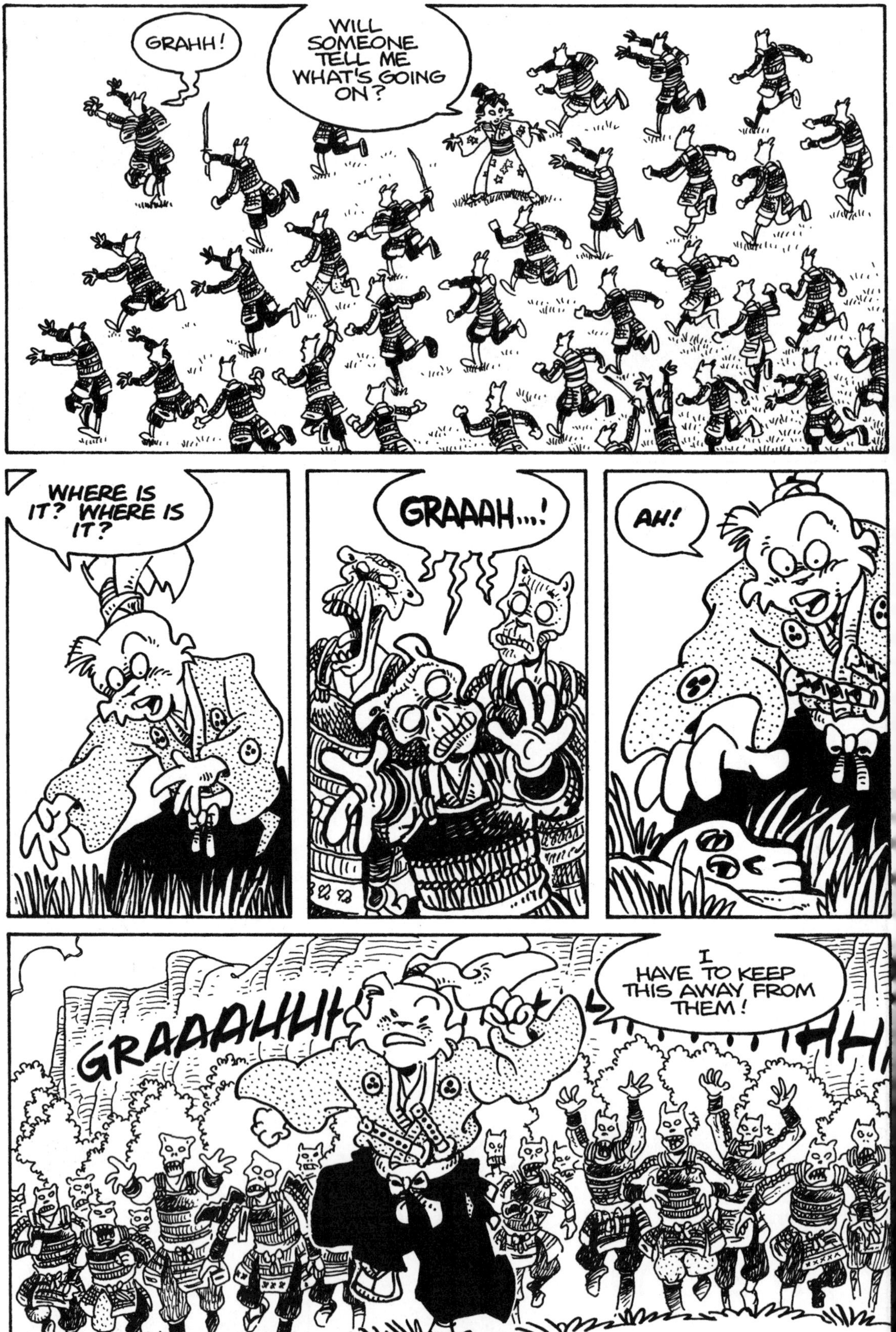
GRAHH!
WILL SOMEONE TELL ME WHAT'S GOING ON?
WHERE IS IT? WHERE IS IT?
GRAAAH...!
AH!
GRAAAHHHHHH
I HAVE TO KEEP THIS AWAY FROM THEM!
16.

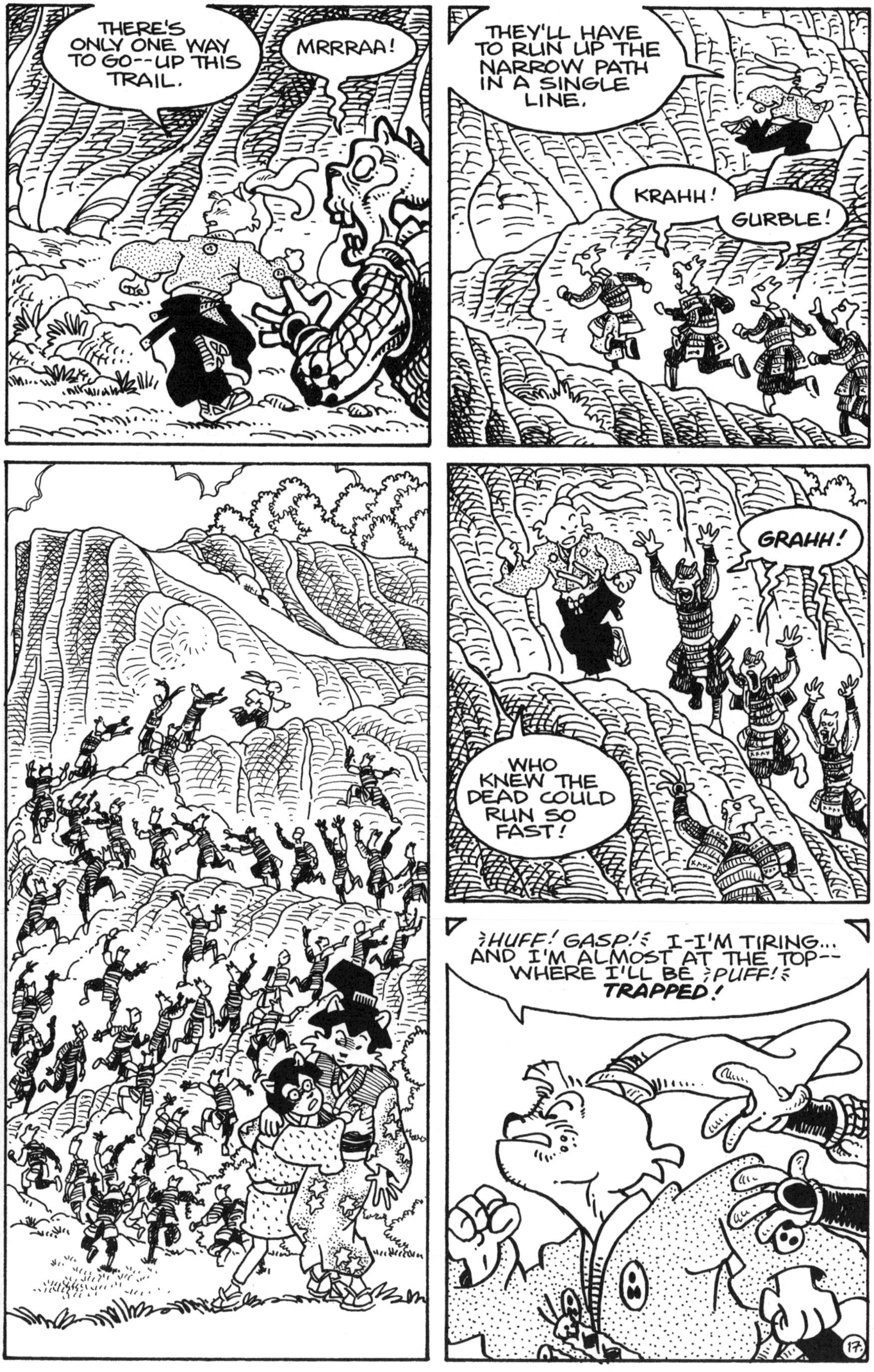
THERE'S ONLY ONE WAY TO GO--UP THIS TRAIL.
MRRRAA!
THEY'LL HAVE TO RUN UP THE NARROW PATH IN A SINGLE LINE.
KRAHH!
GURBLE!
GRAHH!
WHO KNEW THE DEAD COULD RUN SO FAST!
HUFF! GASP! I-I'M TIRING... AND I'M ALMOST AT THE TOP--WHERE I'LL BE PUFF! TRAPPED!
17

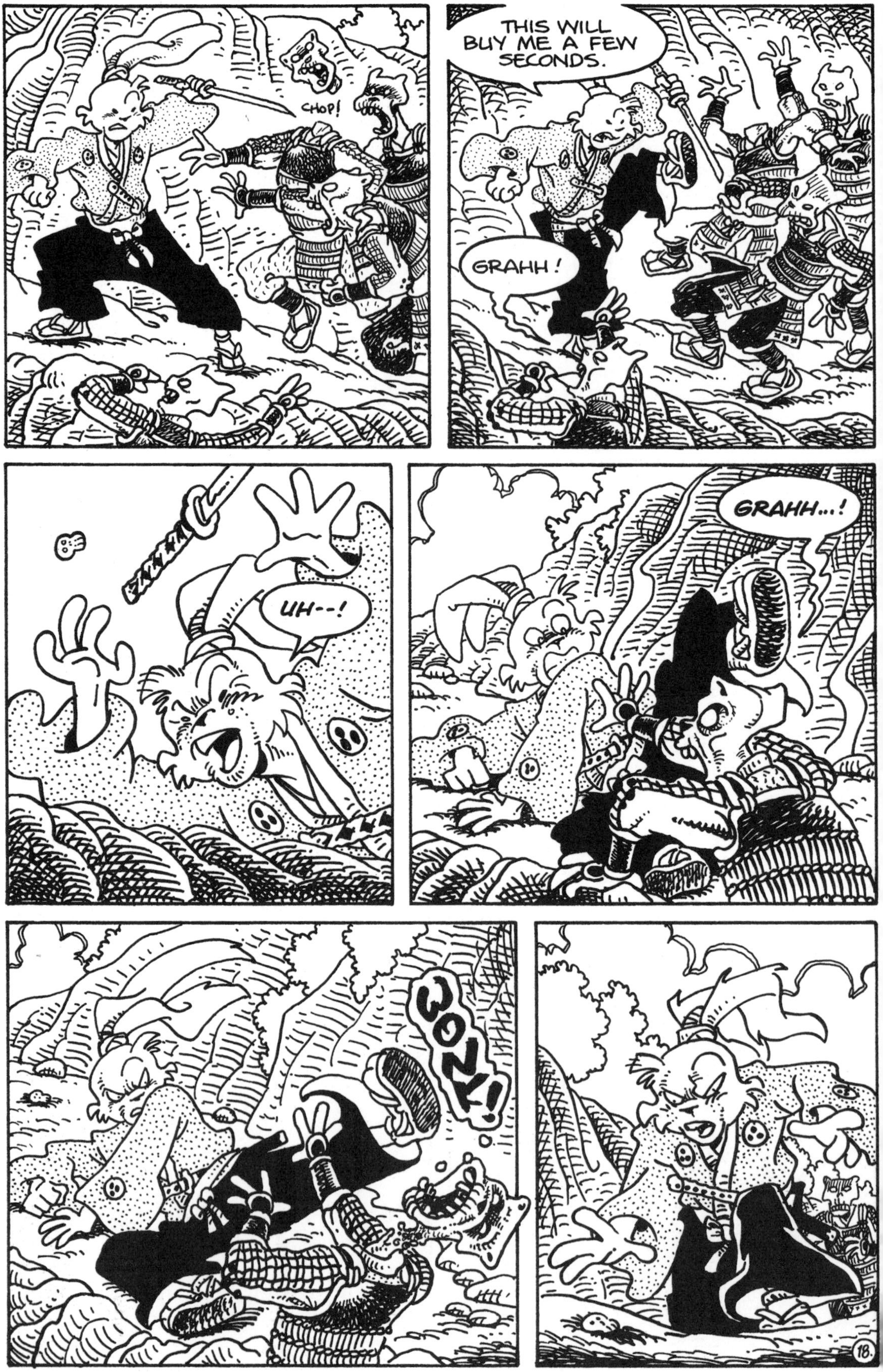
CHOP!
THIS WILL BUY ME A FEW SECONDS.
GRAHH!
UH--!
GRAHH...!
WONK!
18.

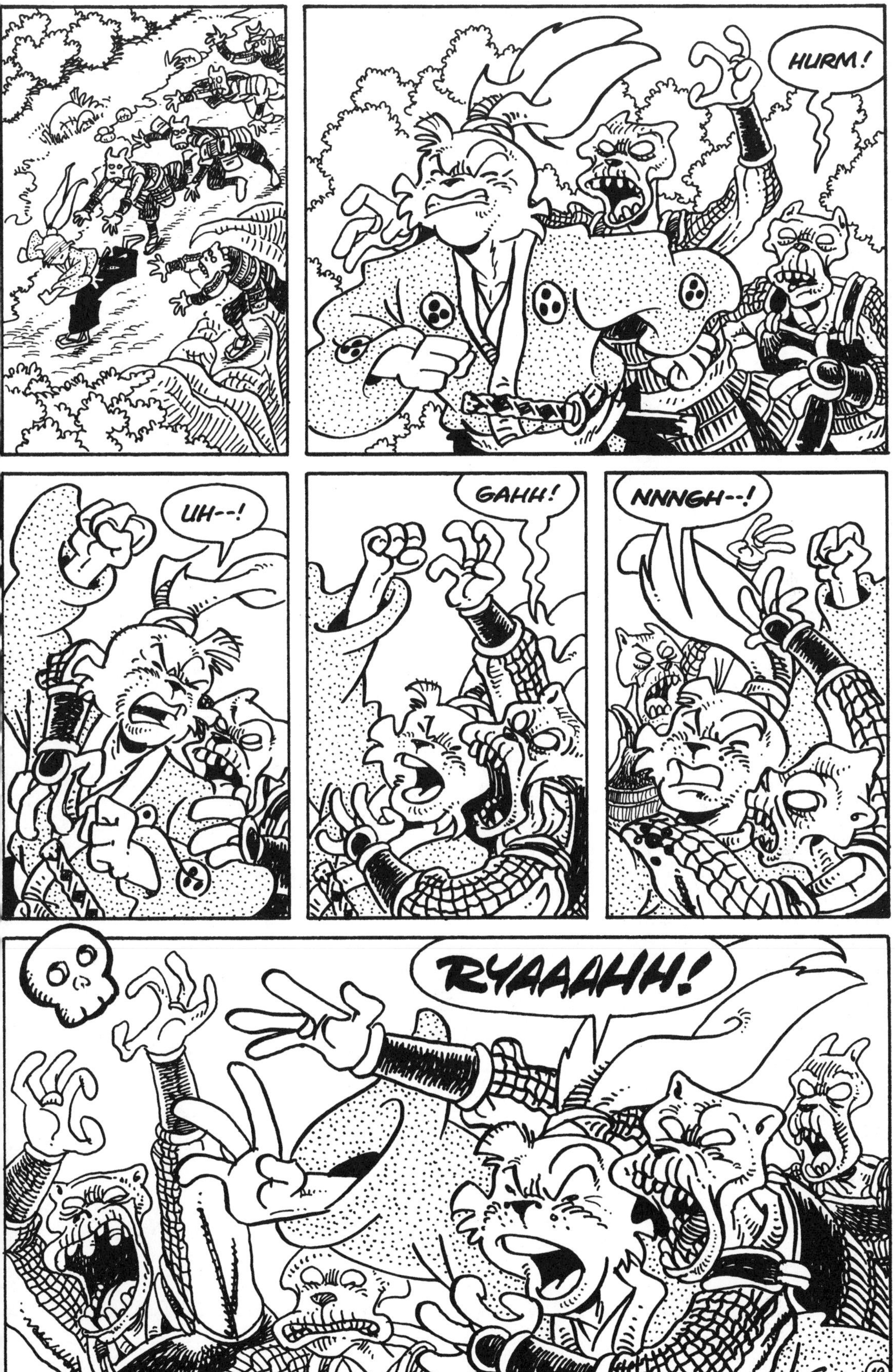
HURM!
UH--!
GAHH!
NNNGH--!
RYAAAHH!
19.

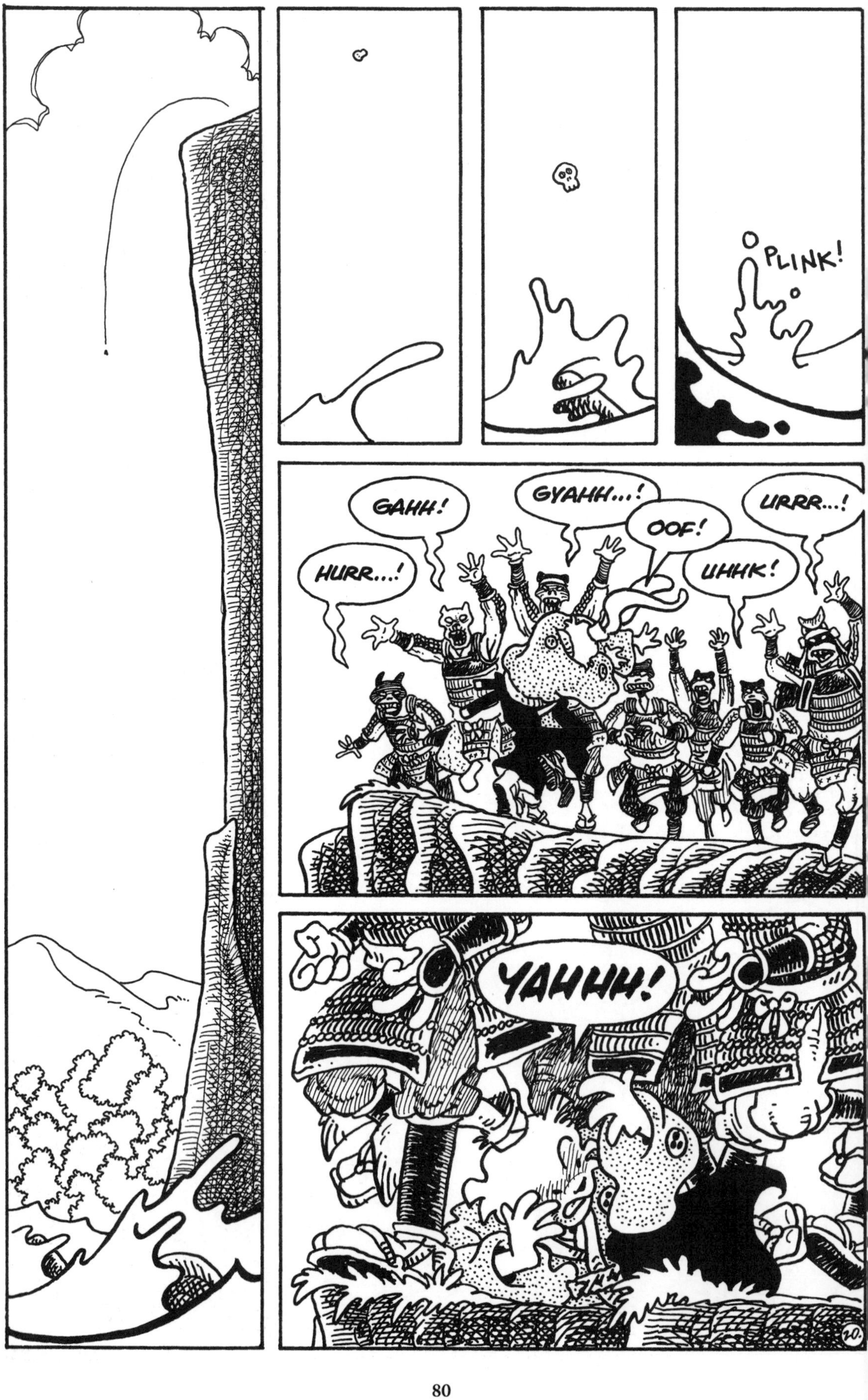
PLINK!
HURR....!
GAHH!
GYAHH...!
OOF!
UHHK!
URRR...!
YAHHH!

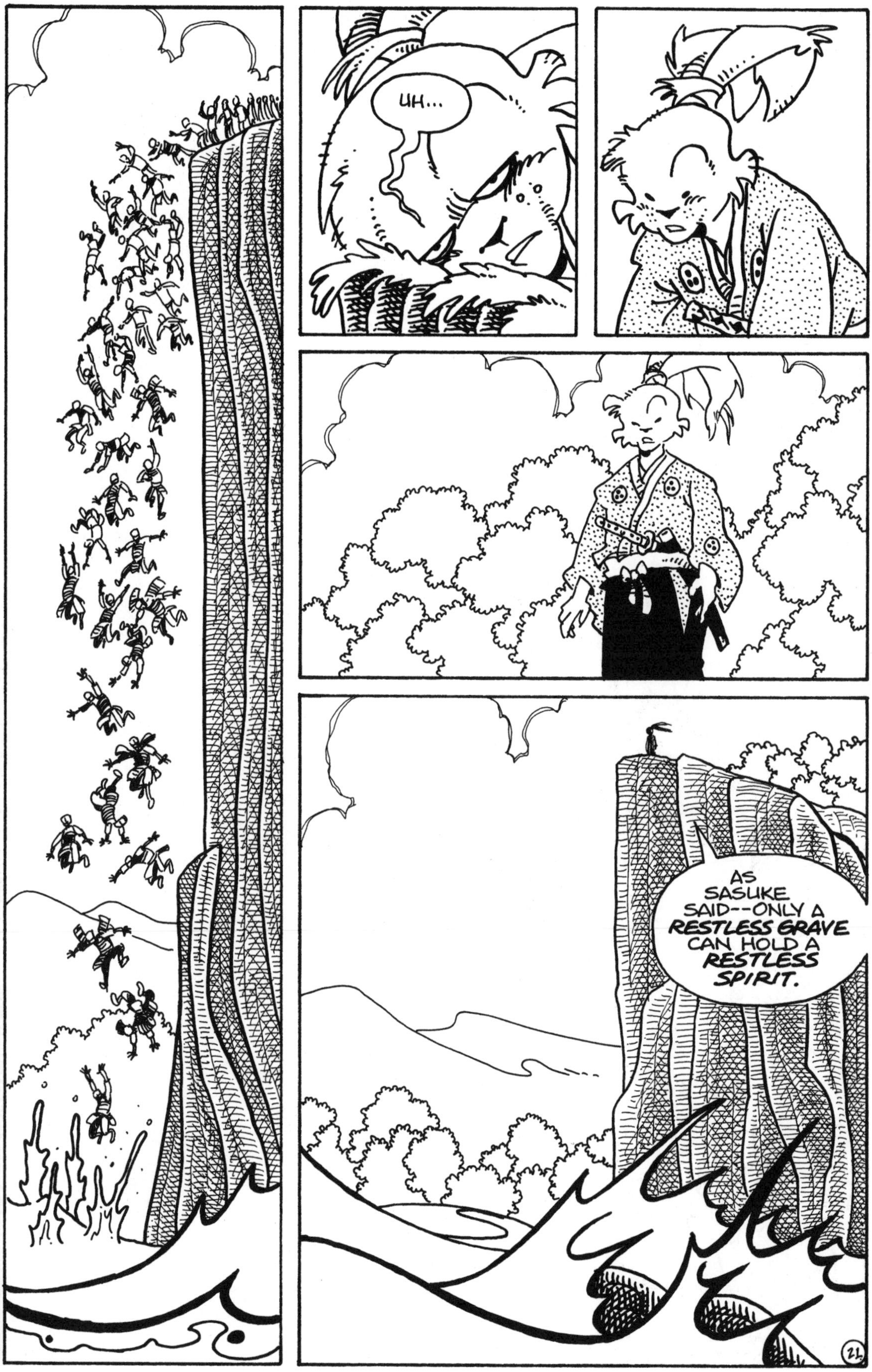
UH...
AS SASUKE SAID--ONLY A RESTLESS GRAVE CAN HOLD A RESTLESS SPIRIT.
21

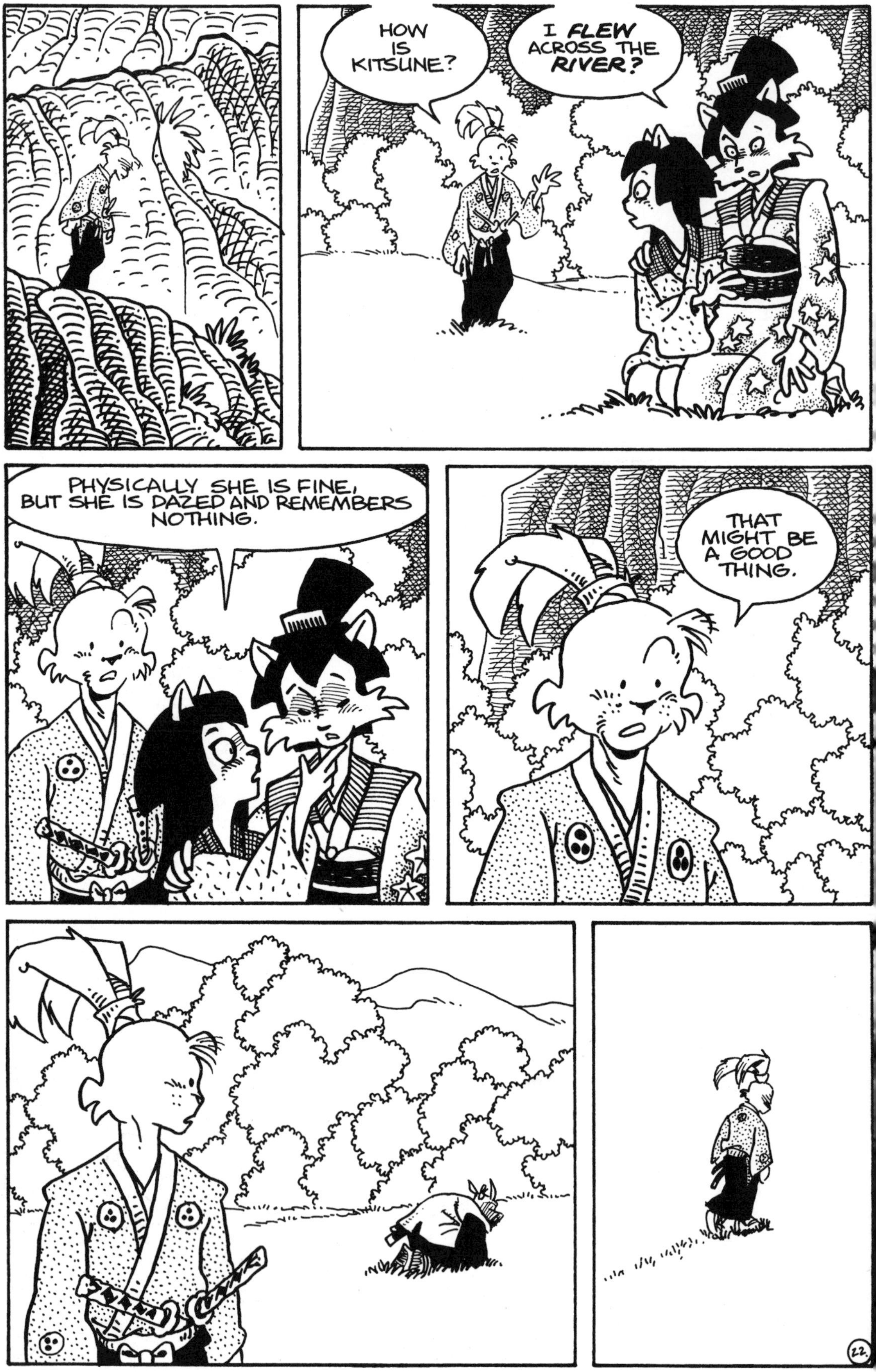

HOW IS KITSUNE?
I FLEW ACROSS THE RIVER?
PHYSICALLY SHE IS FINE, BUT SHE IS DAZED AND REMEMBERS NOTHING.
THAT MIGHT BE A GOOD THING.
22.

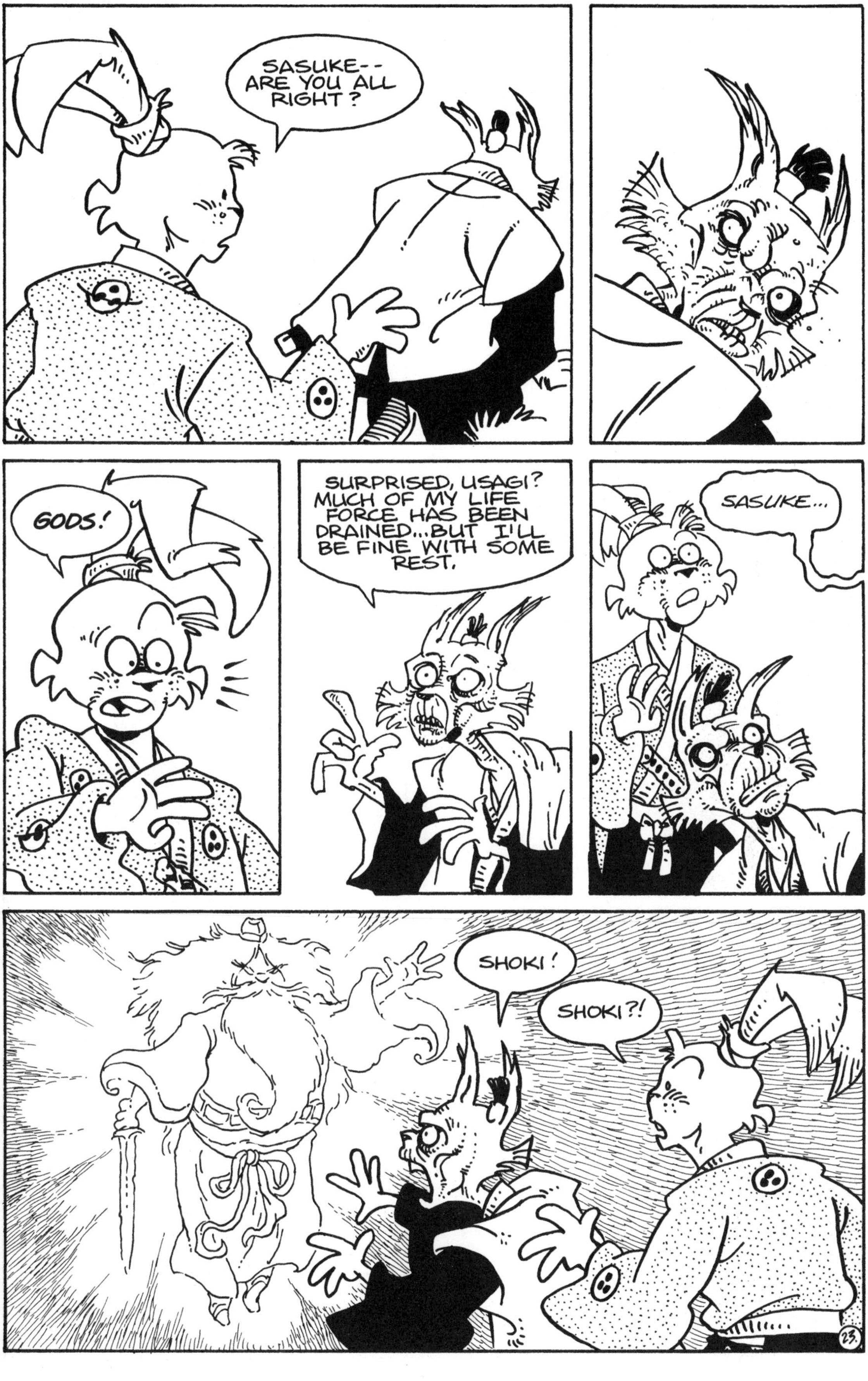
SASUKE-- ARE YOU ALL RIGHT?
GODS!
SURPRISED, USAGI? MUCH OF MY LIFE FORCE HAS BEEN DRAINED...BUT I'LL BE FINE WITH SOME REST.
SASUKE...
SHOKI!
SHOKI?!
23.

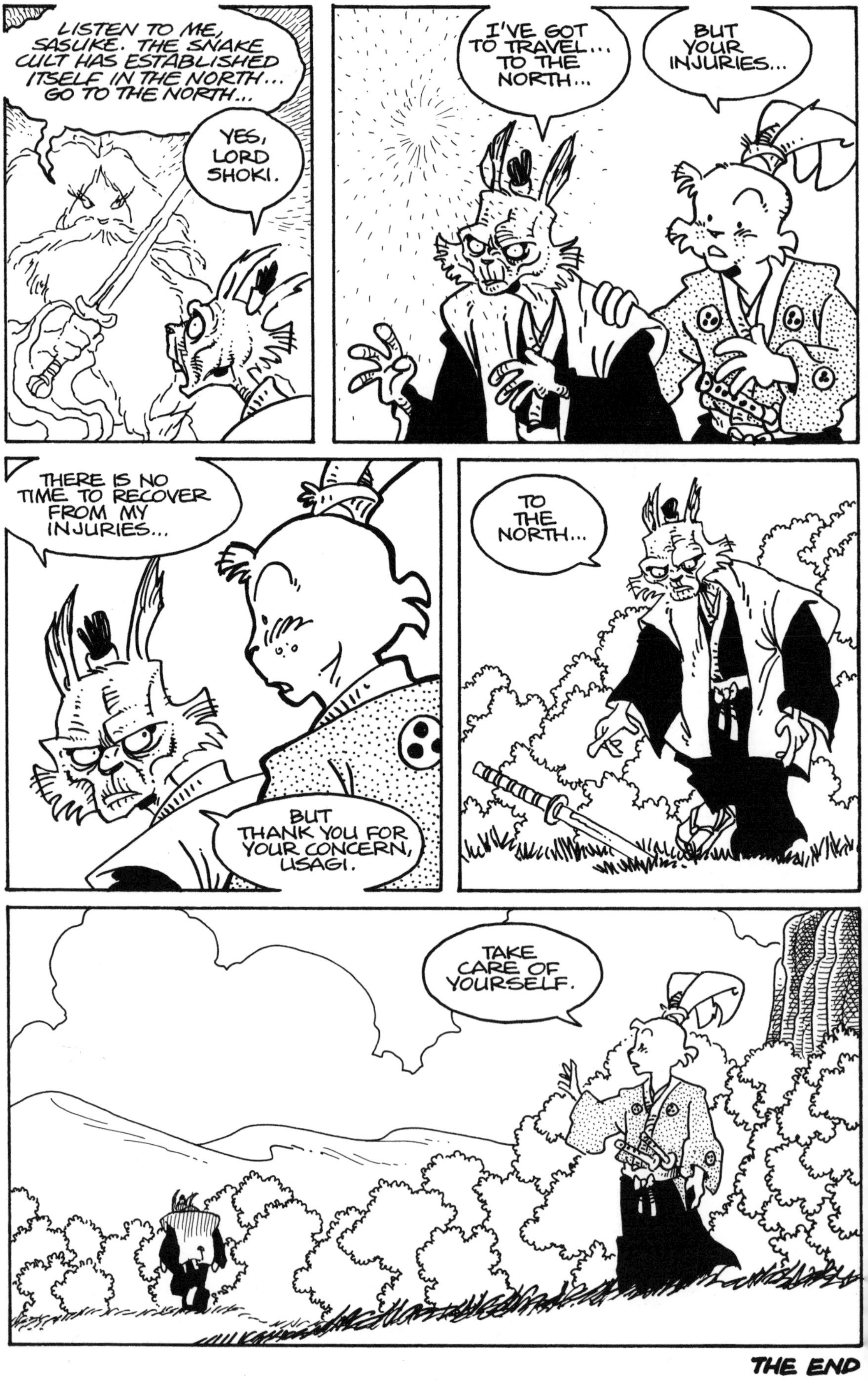
LISTEN TO ME, SASUKE. THE SNAKE CULT HAS ESTABLISHED ITSELF IN THE NORTH... GO TO THE NORTH...
YES, LORD SHOKI.
I'VE GOT TO TRAVEL... TO THE NORTH...
BUT YOUR INJURIES...
THERE IS NO TIME TO RECOVER FROM MY INJURIES...
BUT THANK YOU FOR YOUR CONCERN, USAGI.
TO THE NORTH...
TAKE CARE OF YOURSELF.
THE END

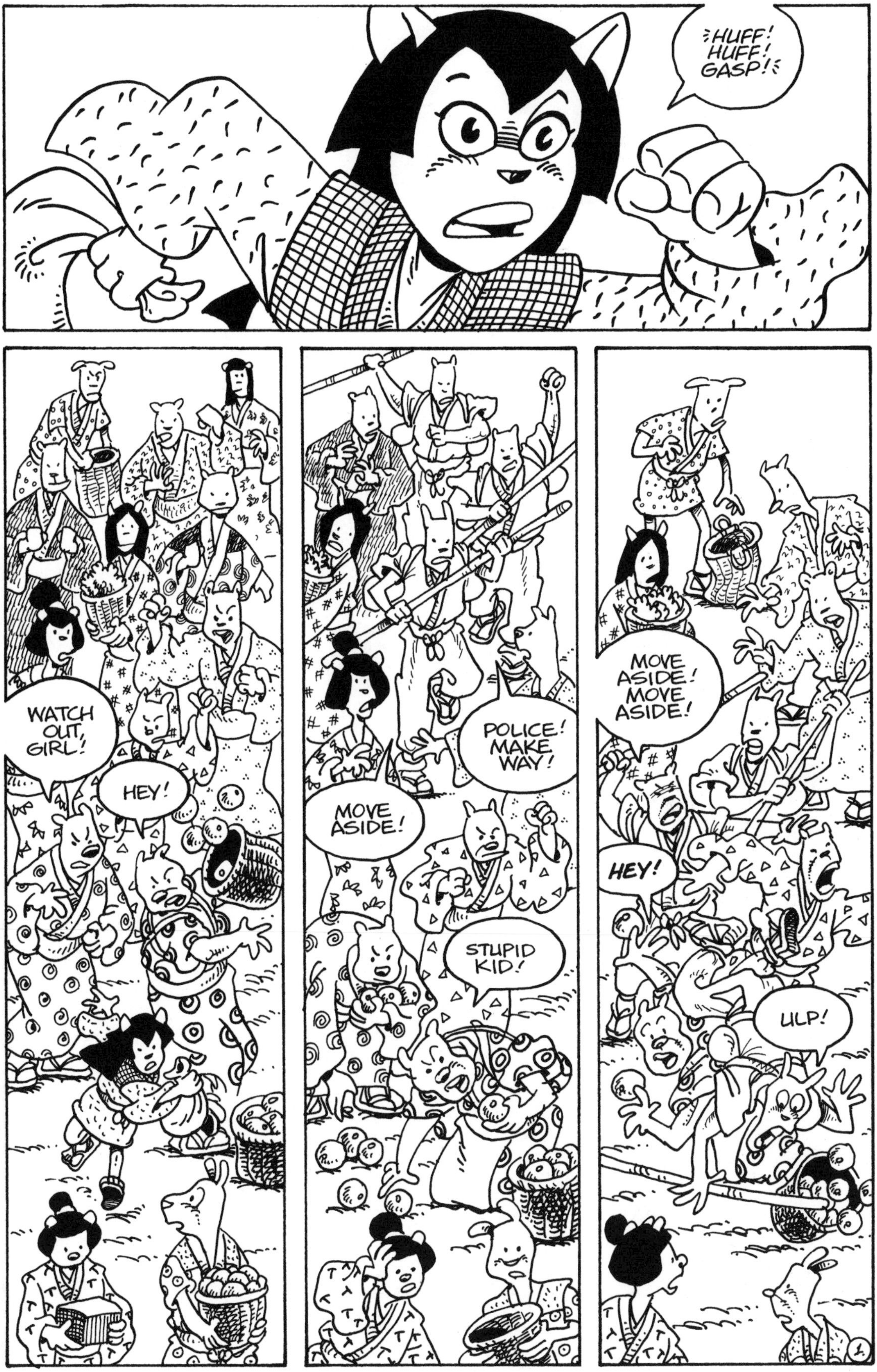

HUFF! HUFF! GASP!
WATCH OUT, GIRL!
HEY!
POLICE! MAKE WAY!
MOVE ASIDE!
STUPID KID!
MOVE ASIDE! MOVE ASIDE!
HEY!
ULP!

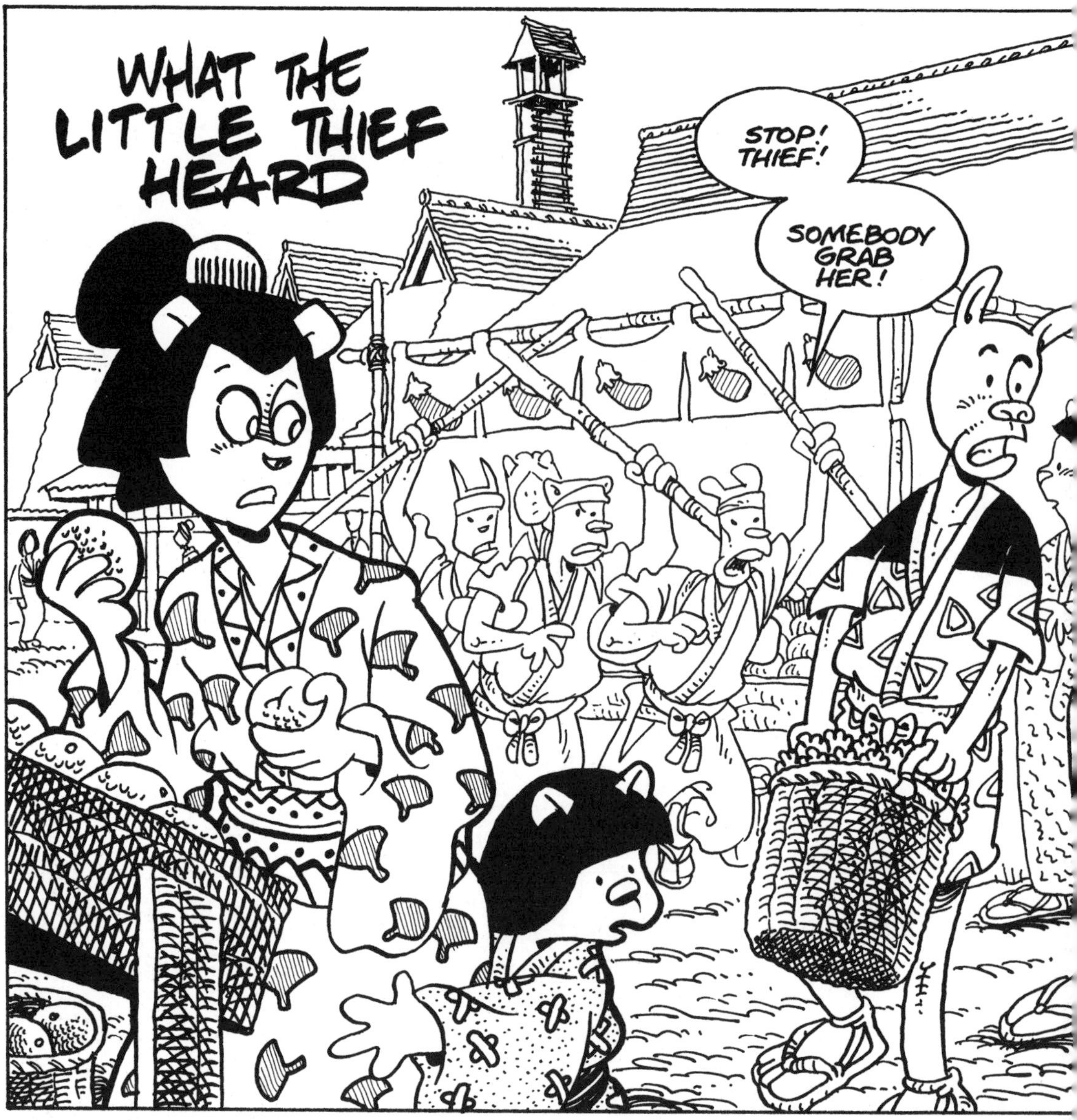
WHAT THE LITTLE THIEF HEARD
STOP! THIEF!
SOMEBODY GRAB HER!

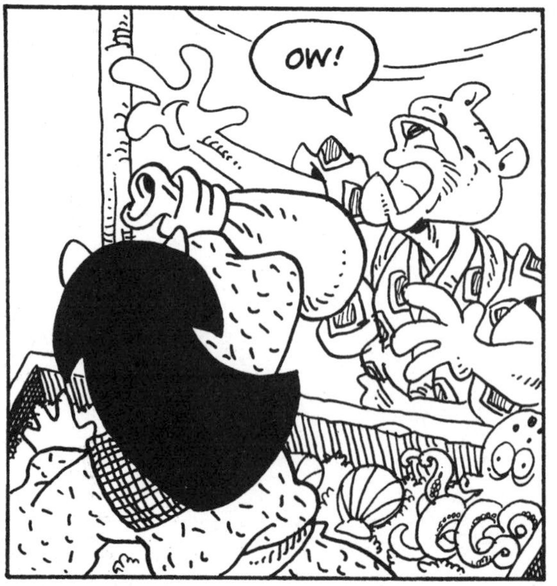
OW!

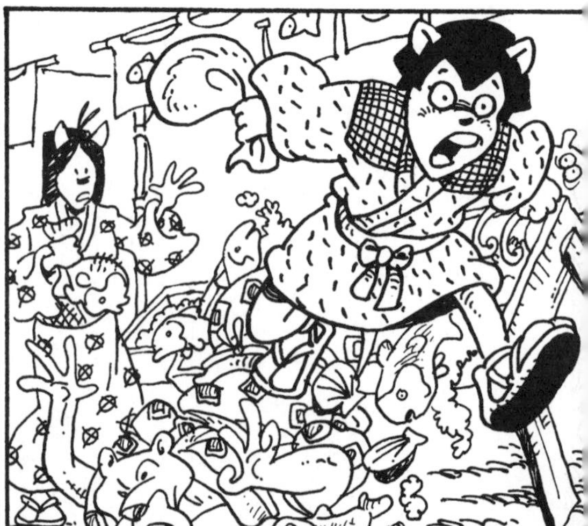

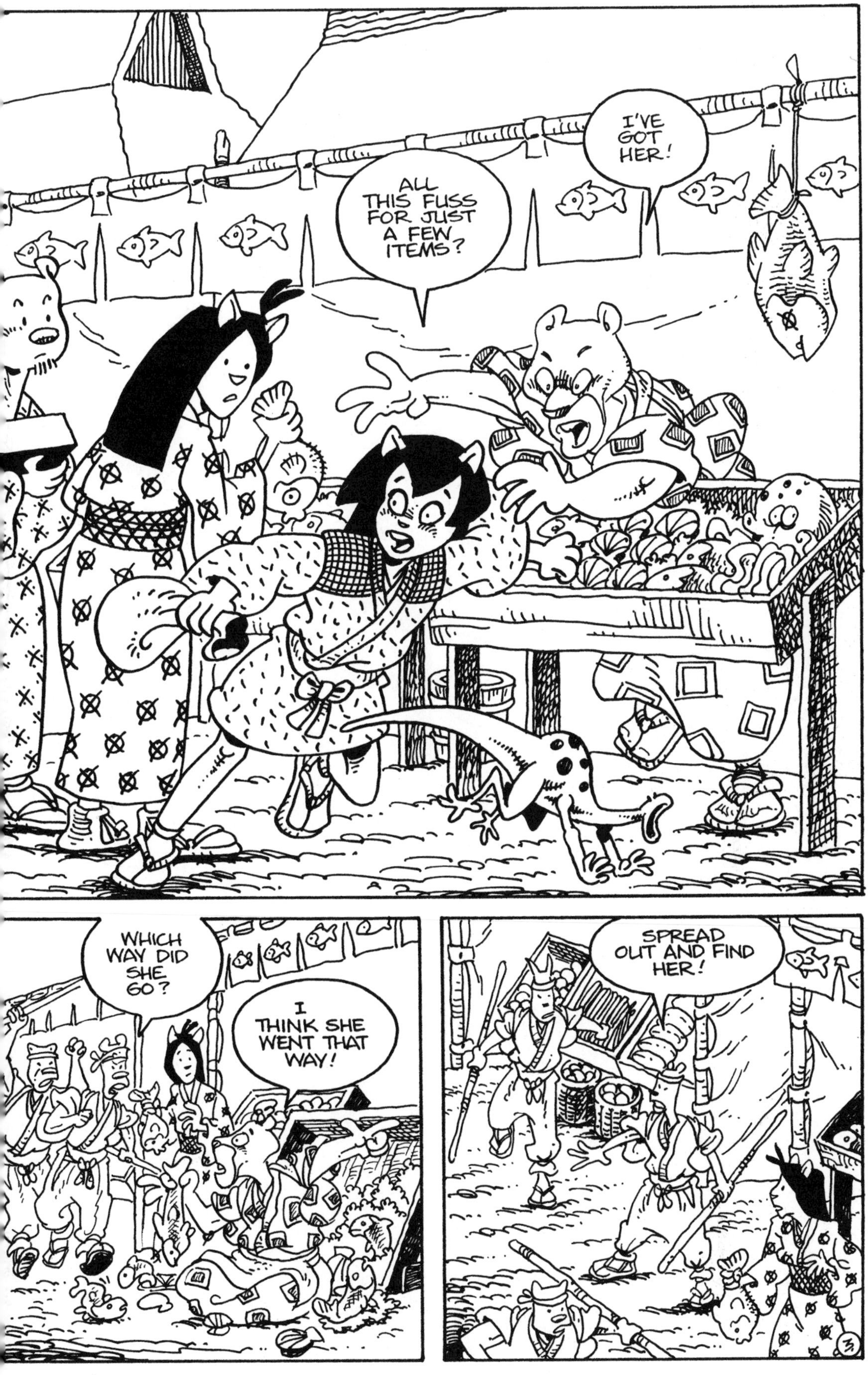

ALL THIS FUSS FOR JUST A FEW ITEMS?
I'VE GOT HER!
WHICH WAY DID SHE GO?
I THINK SHE WENT THAT WAY!
SPREAD OUT AND FIND HER!

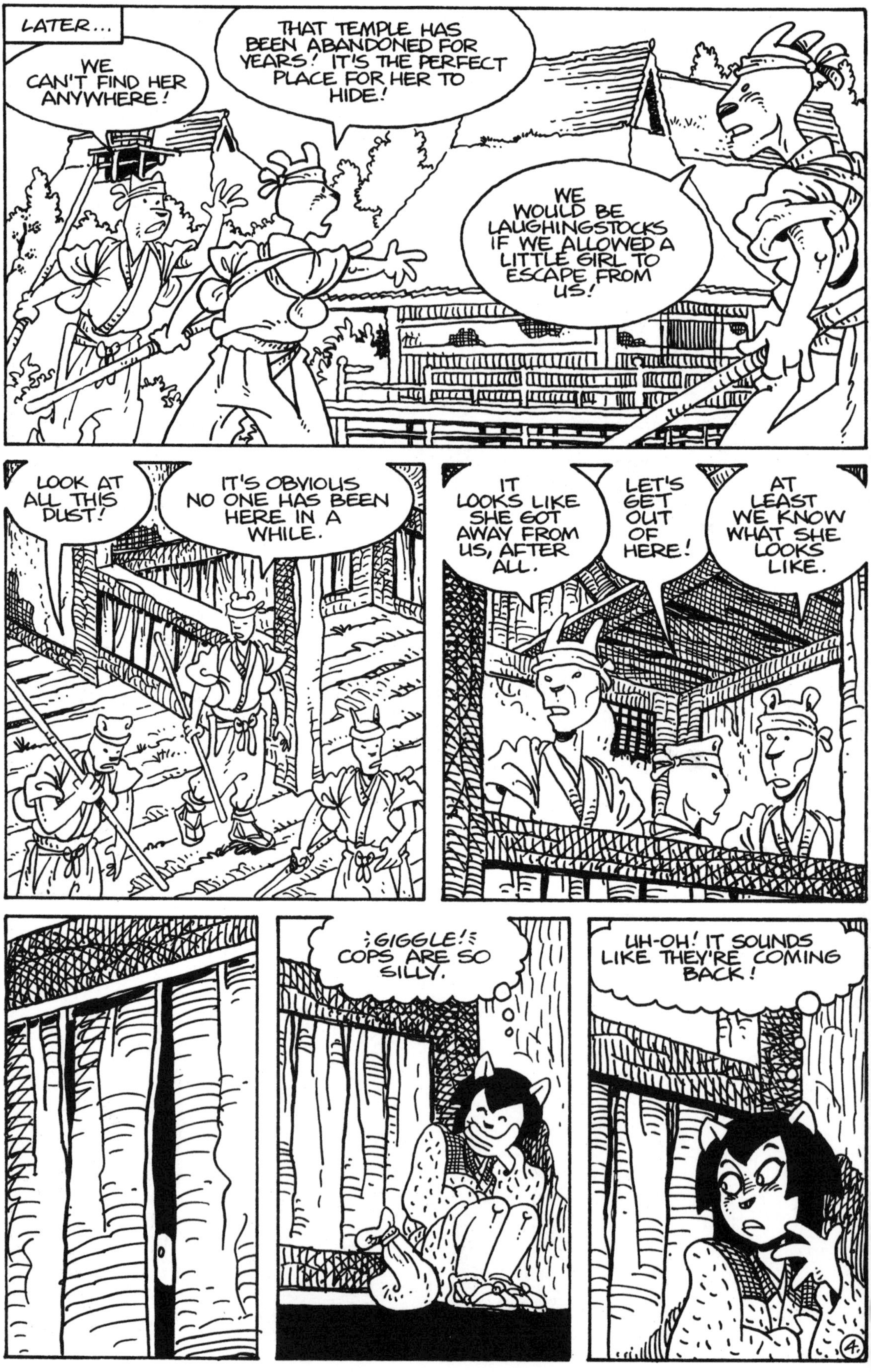
LATER...
WE CAN'T FIND HER ANYWHERE!
THAT TEMPLE HAS BEEN ABANDONED FOR YEARS! IT'S THE PERFECT PLACE FOR HER TO HIDE!
WE WOULD BE LAUGHINGSTOCKS IF WE ALLOWED A LITTLE GIRL TO ESCAPE FROM US!
LOOK AT ALL THIS DUST!
IT'S OBVIOUS NO ONE HAS BEEN HERE IN A WHILE.
IT LOOKS LIKE SHE GOT AWAY FROM US, AFTER ALL.
LET'S GET OUT OF HERE!
AT LEAST WE KNOW WHAT SHE LOOKS LIKE.
GIGGLE! COPS ARE SO SILLY.
UH-OH! IT SOUNDS LIKE THEY'RE COMING BACK!
4.

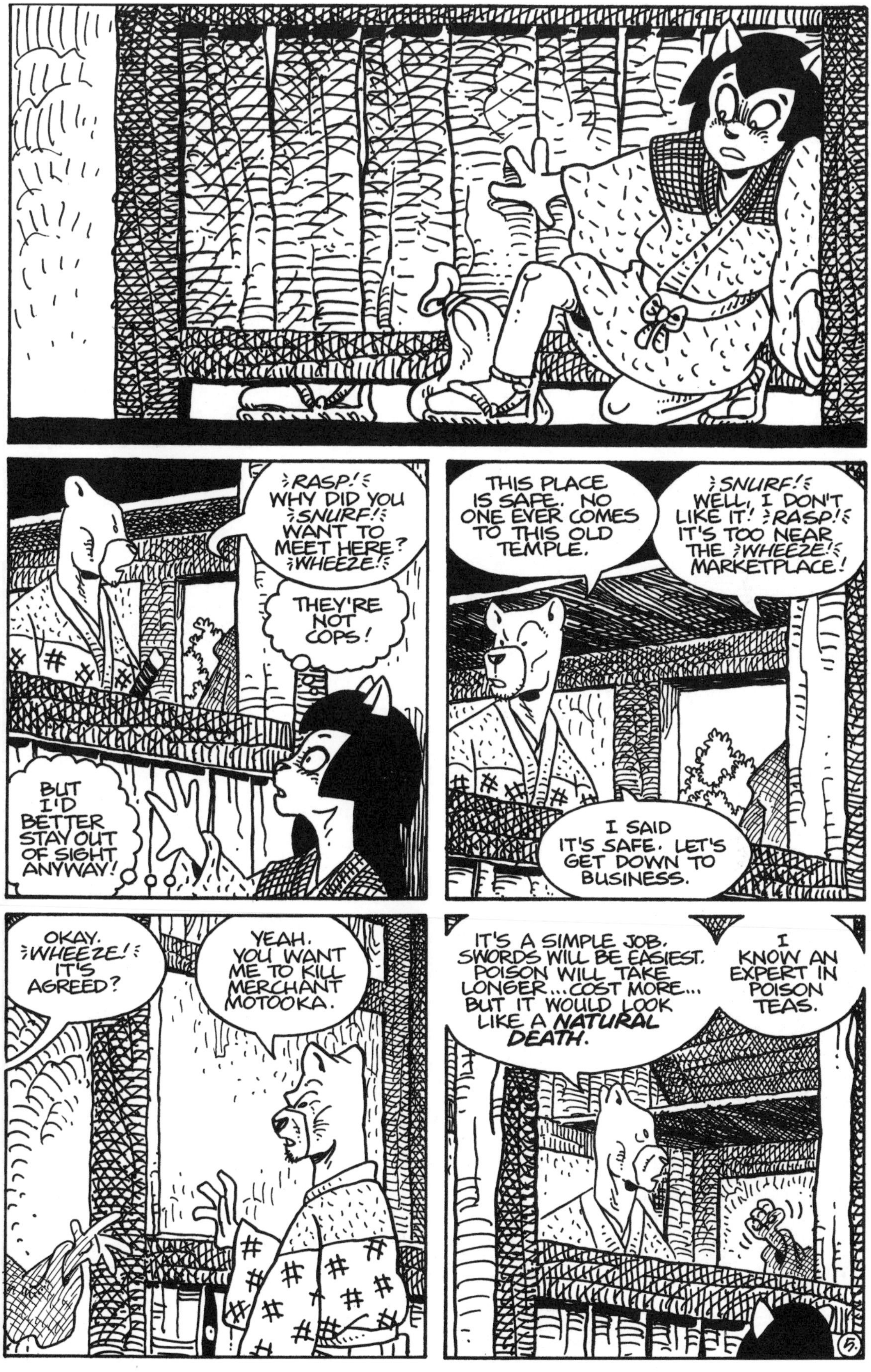

RASP! WHY DID YOU SNURF! WANT TO MEET HERE? WHEEZE!
THEY'RE NOT COPS!
BUT I'D BETTER STAY OUT OF SIGHT ANYWAY!
THIS PLACE IS SAFE. NO ONE EVER COMES TO THIS OLD TEMPLE.
SNURF! WELL, I DON'T LIKE IT! RASP! IT'S TOO NEAR THE WHEEZE! MARKETPLACE!
I SAID IT'S SAFE. LET'S GET DOWN TO BUSINESS.
OKAY. WHEEZE! IT'S AGREED?
YEAH. YOU WANT ME TO KILL MERCHANT MOTOOKA.
IT'S A SIMPLE JOB. SWORDS WILL BE EASIEST. POISON WILL TAKE LONGER...COST MORE... BUT IT WOULD LOOK LIKE A ***NATURAL DEATH***.
I KNOW AN EXPERT IN POISON TEAS.
5.

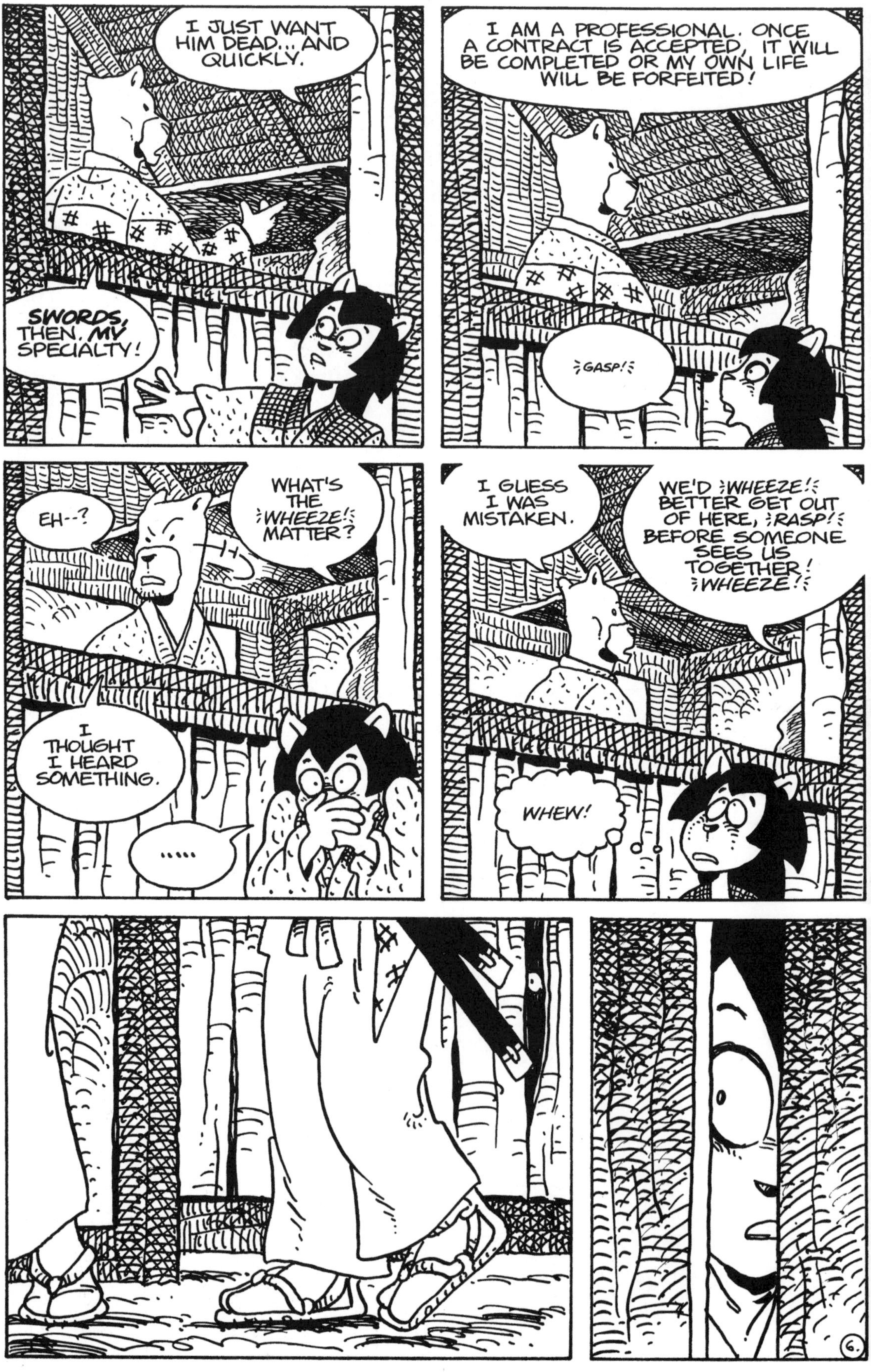
I JUST WANT HIM DEAD... AND QUICKLY.
SWORDS, THEN. MY SPECIALTY!
I AM A PROFESSIONAL. ONCE A CONTRACT IS ACCEPTED, IT WILL BE COMPLETED OR MY OWN LIFE WILL BE FORFEITED!
GASP!
EH--?
WHAT'S THE WHEEZE! MATTER?
I THOUGHT I HEARD SOMETHING.
.....
I GUESS I WAS MISTAKEN.
WE'D WHEEZE! BETTER GET OUT OF HERE, RASP! BEFORE SOMEONE SEES US TOGETHER! WHEEZE!
WHEW!
6.

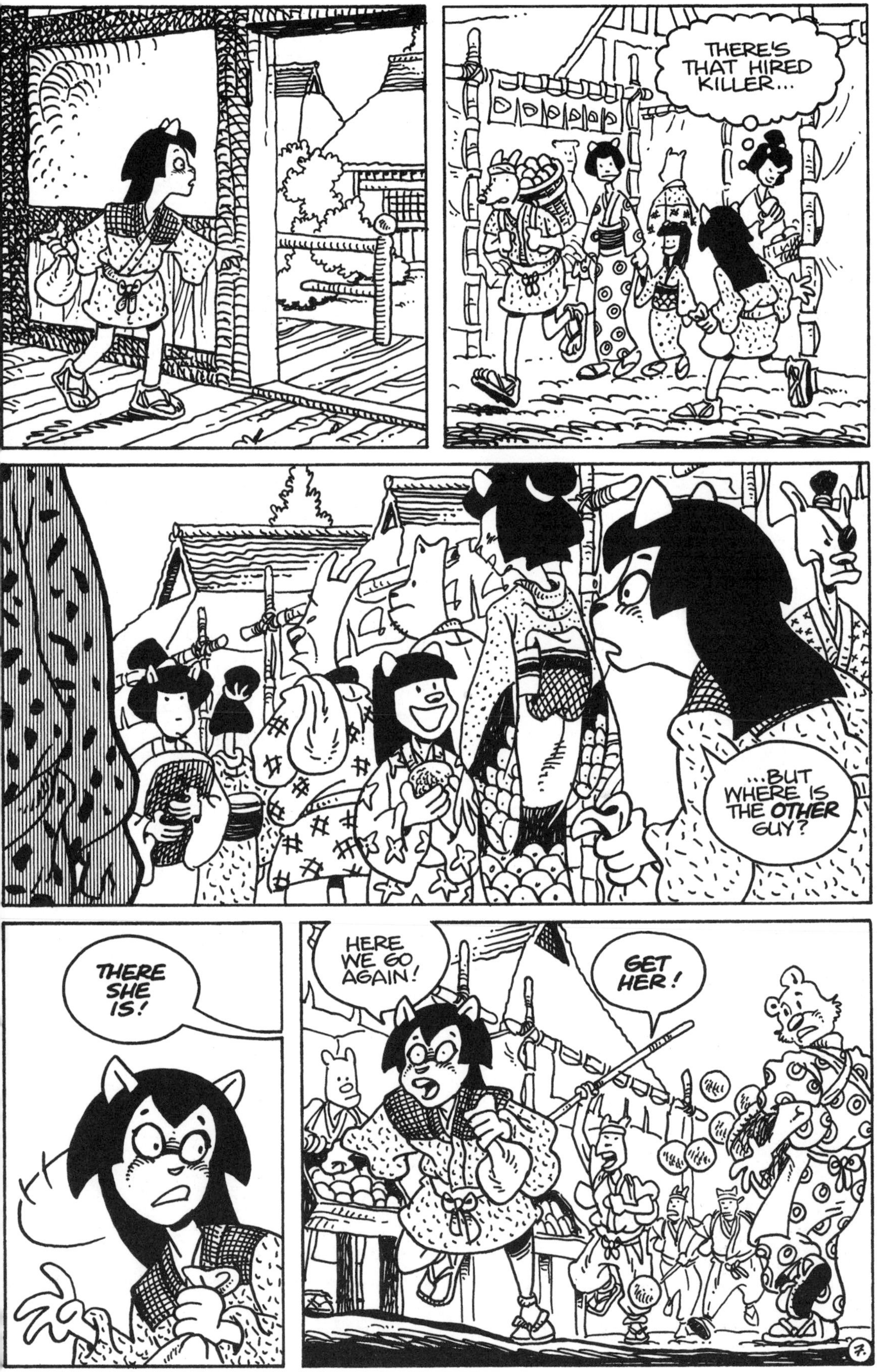
THERE'S THAT HIRED KILLER...
...BUT WHERE IS THE **OTHER** GUY?
THERE SHE IS!
HERE WE GO AGAIN!
GET HER!
7.

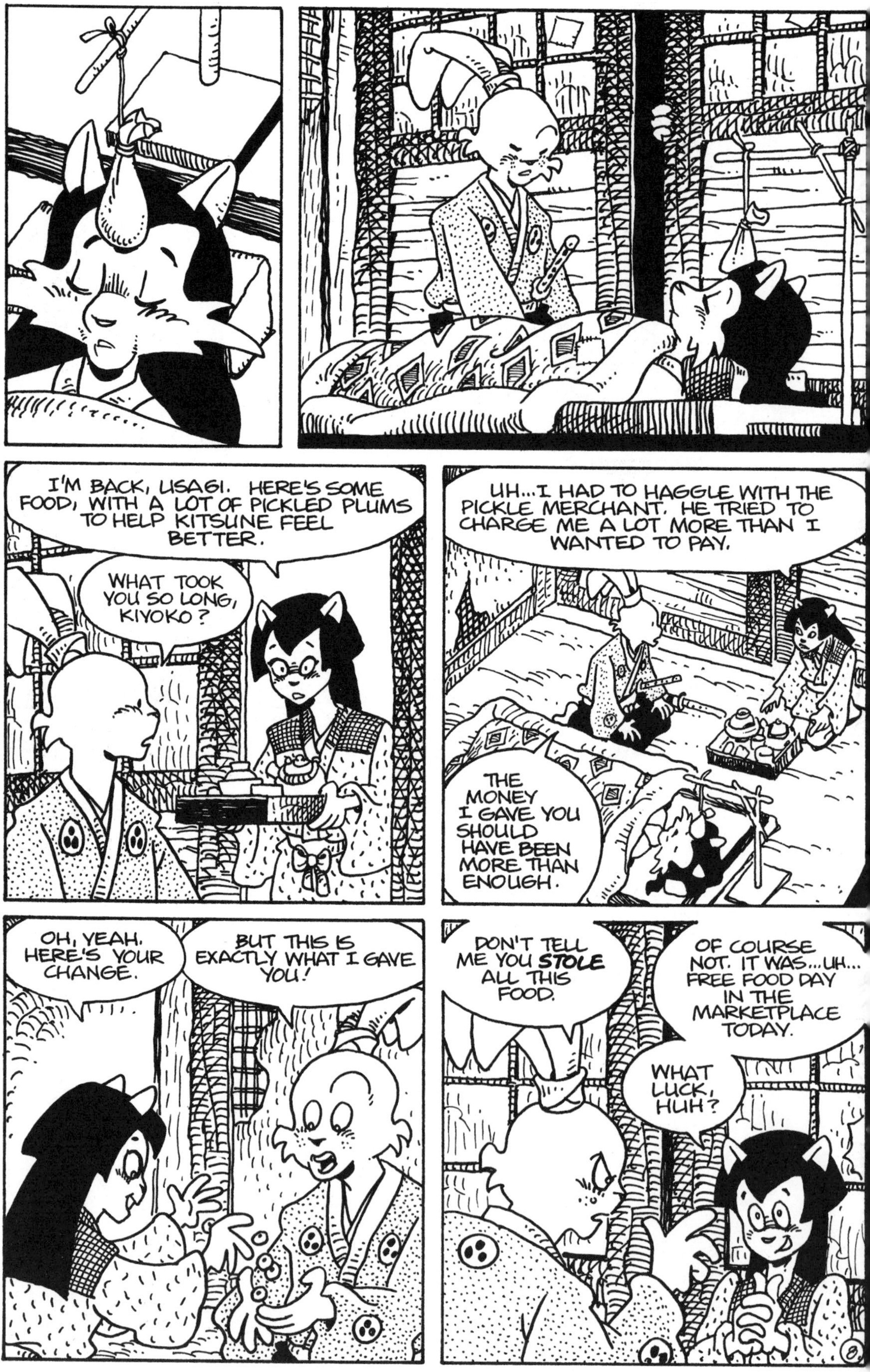

I'M BACK, USAGI. HERE'S SOME FOOD, WITH A LOT OF PICKLED PLUMS TO HELP KITSUNE FEEL BETTER.
WHAT TOOK YOU SO LONG, KIYOKO?
UH...I HAD TO HAGGLE WITH THE PICKLE MERCHANT. HE TRIED TO CHARGE ME A LOT MORE THAN I WANTED TO PAY.
THE MONEY I GAVE YOU SHOULD HAVE BEEN MORE THAN ENOUGH.
OH, YEAH. HERE'S YOUR CHANGE.
BUT THIS IS EXACTLY WHAT I GAVE YOU!
DON'T TELL ME YOU **STOLE** ALL THIS FOOD.
OF COURSE NOT. IT WAS...UH... FREE FOOD DAY IN THE MARKETPLACE TODAY.
WHAT LUCK, HUH?
8

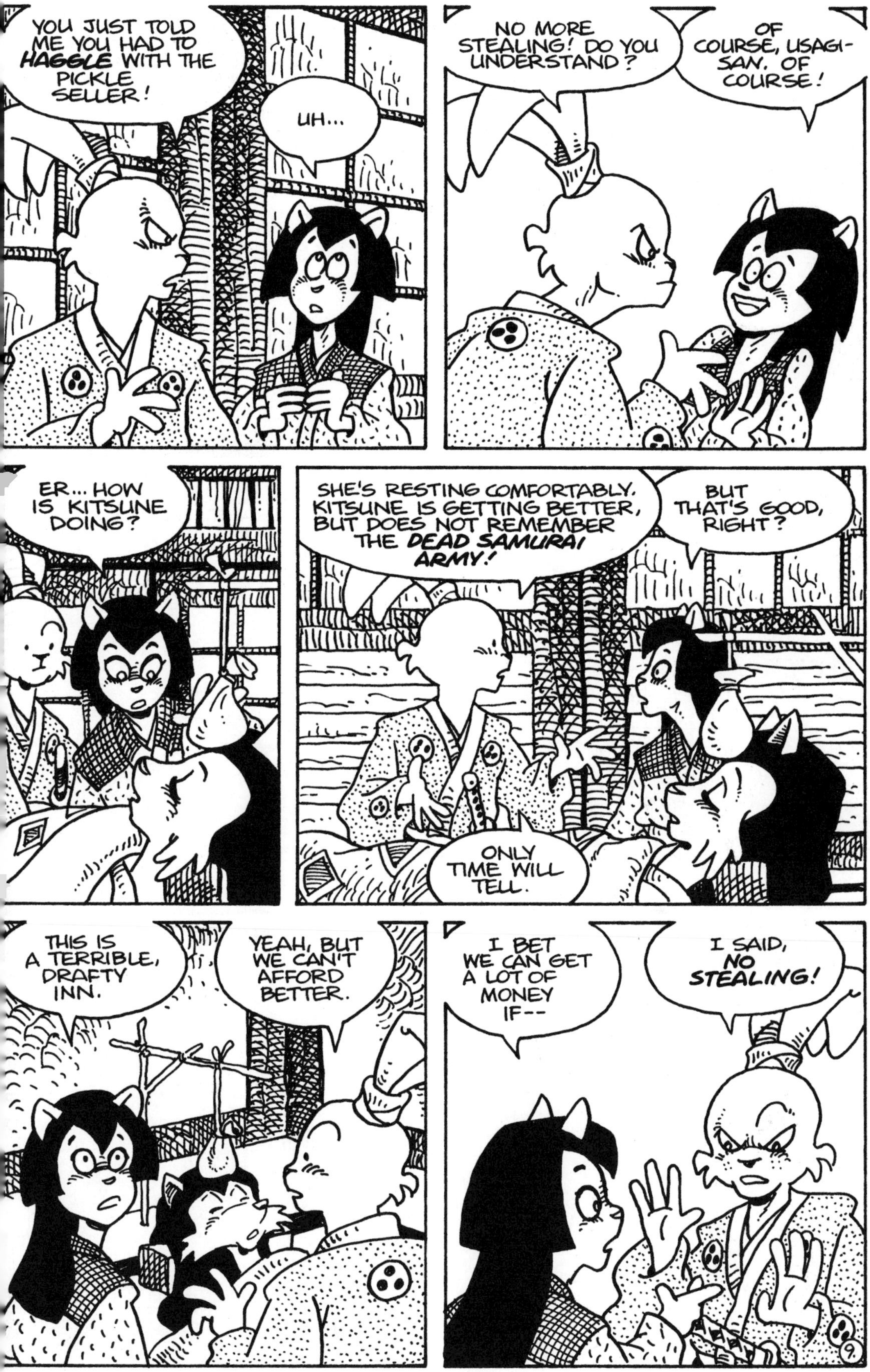
YOU JUST TOLD ME YOU HAD TO HAGGLE WITH THE PICKLE SELLER!
UH...
NO MORE STEALING! DO YOU UNDERSTAND?
OF COURSE, USAGI-SAN. OF COURSE!
ER... HOW IS KITSUNE DOING?
SHE'S RESTING COMFORTABLY. KITSUNE IS GETTING BETTER, BUT DOES NOT REMEMBER THE DEAD SAMURAI ARMY!
BUT THAT'S GOOD, RIGHT?
ONLY TIME WILL TELL.
THIS IS A TERRIBLE, DRAFTY INN.
YEAH, BUT WE CAN'T AFFORD BETTER.
I BET WE CAN GET A LOT OF MONEY IF--
I SAID, NO STEALING!
9

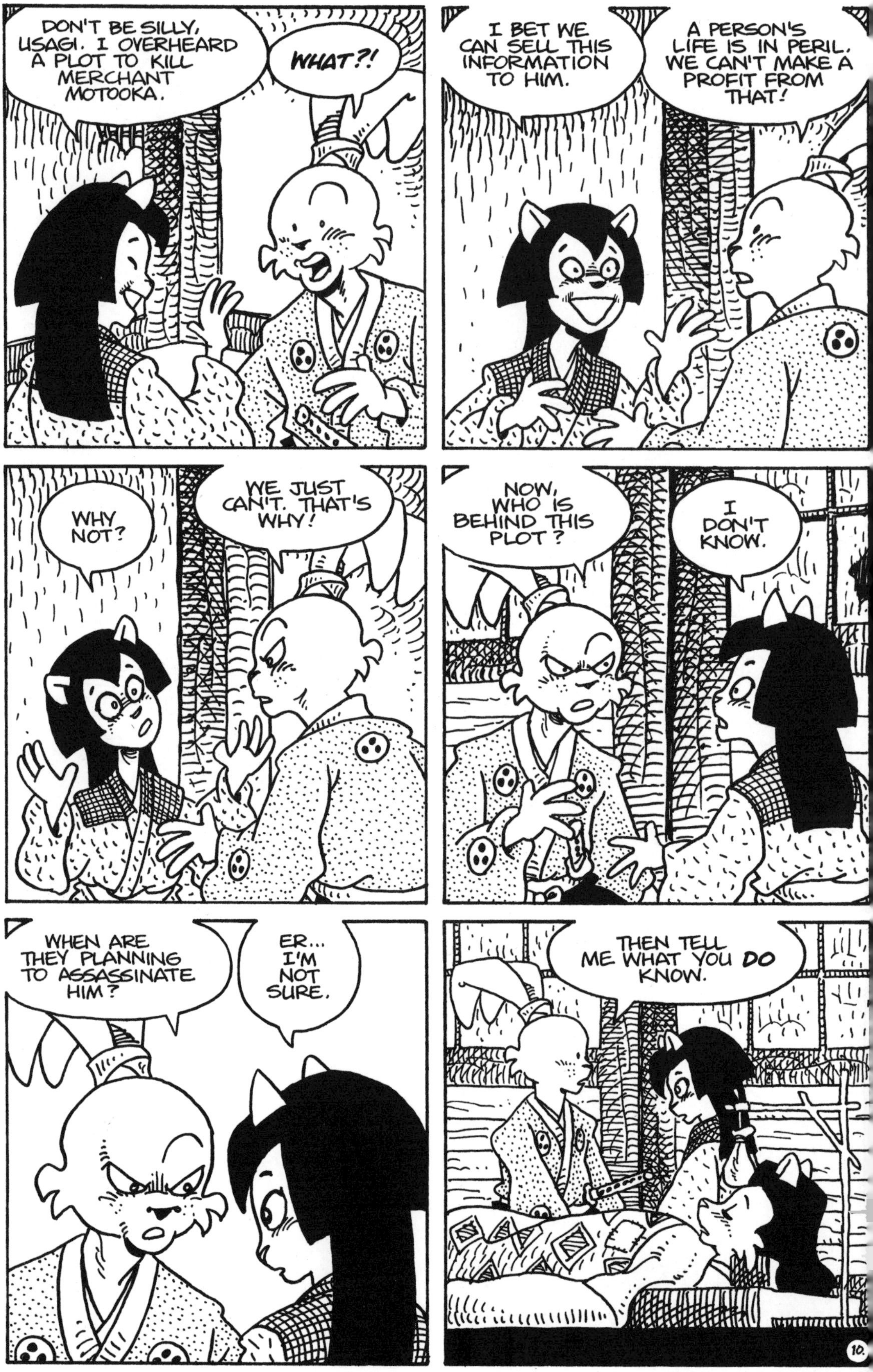

DON'T BE SILLY, USAGI. I OVERHEARD A PLOT TO KILL MERCHANT MOTOOKA.
WHAT?!
I BET WE CAN SELL THIS INFORMATION TO HIM.
A PERSON'S LIFE IS IN PERIL. WE CAN'T MAKE A PROFIT FROM THAT!
WHY NOT?
WE JUST CAN'T. THAT'S WHY!
NOW, WHO IS BEHIND THIS PLOT?
I DON'T KNOW.
WHEN ARE THEY PLANNING TO ASSASSINATE HIM?
ER... I'M NOT SURE.
THEN TELL ME WHAT YOU DO KNOW.
10.

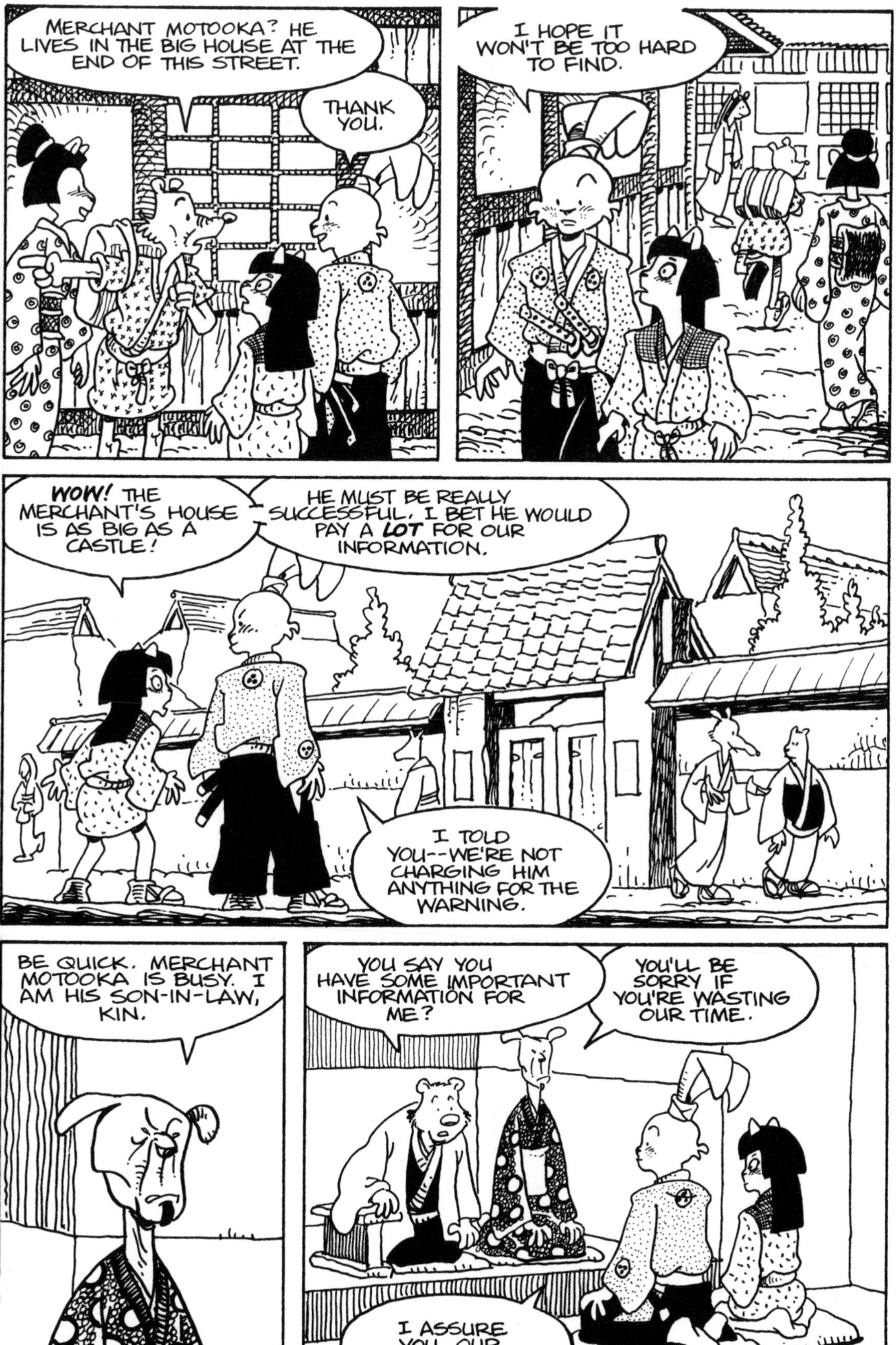
MERCHANT MOTOOKA? HE LIVES IN THE BIG HOUSE AT THE END OF THIS STREET.
THANK YOU.
I HOPE IT WON'T BE TOO HARD TO FIND.
**WOW!** THE MERCHANT'S HOUSE IS AS BIG AS A CASTLE!
HE MUST BE REALLY SUCCESSFUL. I BET HE WOULD PAY A **LOT** FOR OUR INFORMATION.
I TOLD YOU--WE'RE NOT CHARGING HIM ANYTHING FOR THE WARNING.
BE QUICK. MERCHANT MOTOOKA IS BUSY. I AM HIS SON-IN-LAW, KIN.
YOU SAY YOU HAVE SOME IMPORTANT INFORMATION FOR ME?
YOU'LL BE SORRY IF YOU'RE WASTING OUR TIME.
I ASSURE YOU, OUR INFORMATION IS VITAL.
11.

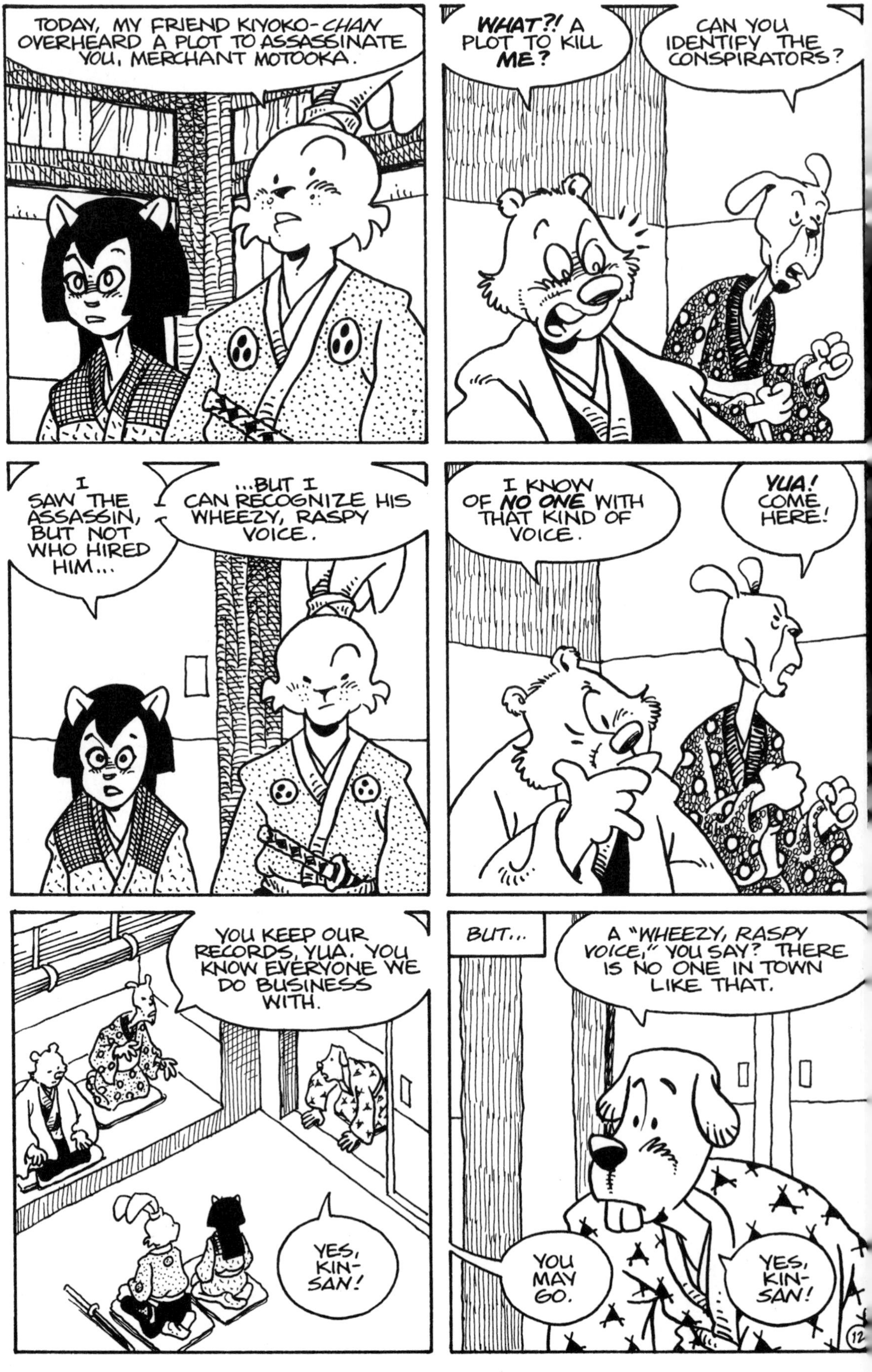
TODAY, MY FRIEND KIYOKO-*CHAN* OVERHEARD A PLOT TO ASSASSINATE YOU, MERCHANT MOTOOKA.
***WHAT?!*** A PLOT TO KILL ***ME***?
CAN YOU IDENTIFY THE CONSPIRATORS?
I SAW THE ASSASSIN, BUT NOT WHO HIRED HIM...
...BUT I CAN RECOGNIZE HIS WHEEZY, RASPY VOICE.
I KNOW OF ***NO ONE*** WITH THAT KIND OF VOICE.
***YUA!*** COME HERE!
YOU KEEP OUR RECORDS, YUA. YOU KNOW EVERYONE WE DO BUSINESS WITH.
YES, KIN-SAN!
*BUT...*
A "*WHEEZY, RASPY VOICE*," YOU SAY? THERE IS NO ONE IN TOWN LIKE THAT.
YOU MAY GO.
YES, KIN-SAN!
12

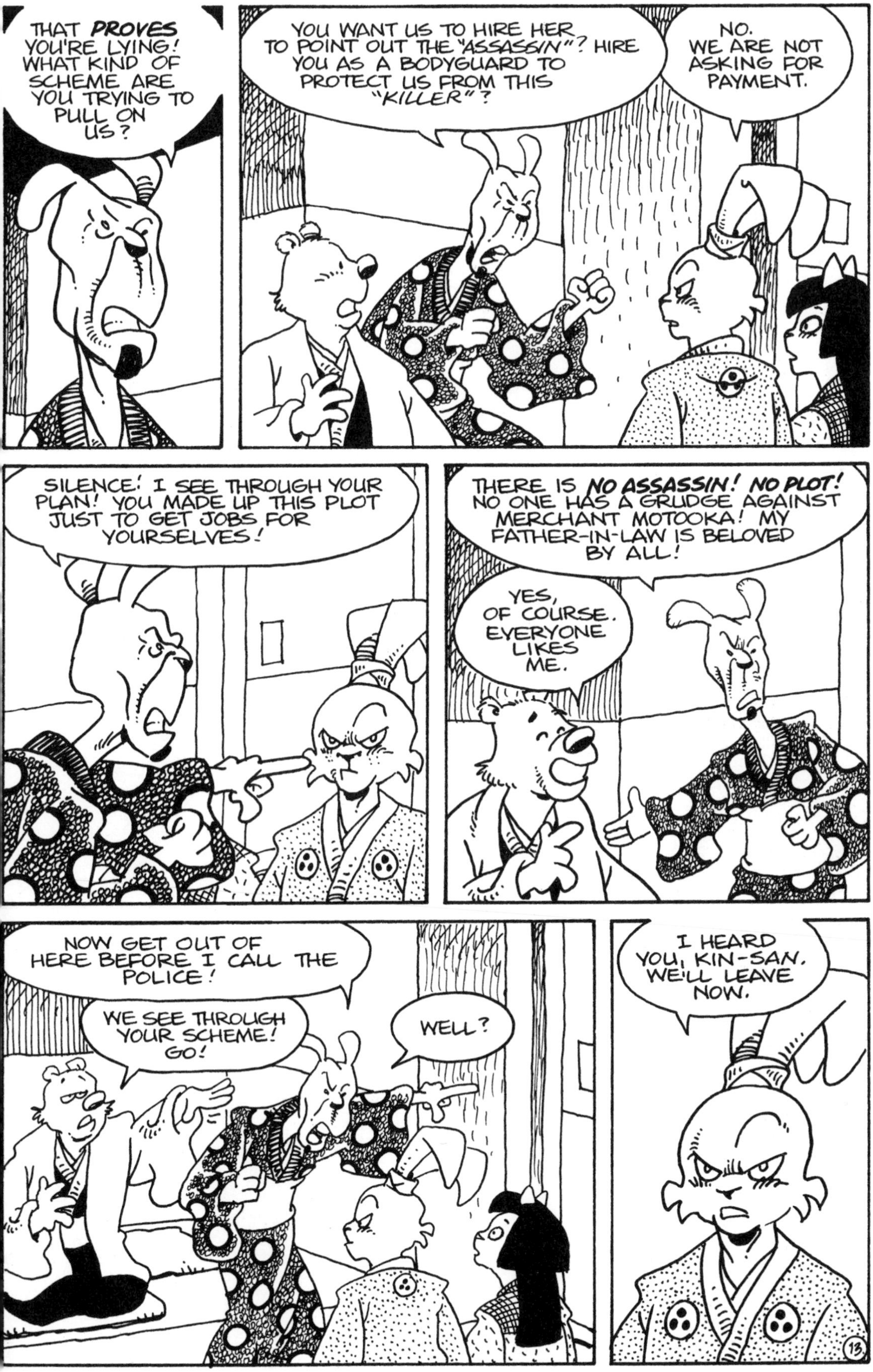
THAT **PROVES** YOU'RE LYING! WHAT KIND OF SCHEME ARE YOU TRYING TO PULL ON US?
YOU WANT US TO HIRE HER TO POINT OUT THE "ASSASSIN"? HIRE YOU AS A BODYGUARD TO PROTECT US FROM THIS "KILLER"?
NO. WE ARE NOT ASKING FOR PAYMENT.
SILENCE! I SEE THROUGH YOUR PLAN! YOU MADE UP THIS PLOT JUST TO GET JOBS FOR YOURSELVES!
THERE IS **NO ASSASSIN! NO PLOT!** NO ONE HAS A GRUDGE AGAINST MERCHANT MOTOOKA! MY FATHER-IN-LAW IS BELOVED BY ALL!
YES, OF COURSE. EVERYONE LIKES ME.
NOW GET OUT OF HERE BEFORE I CALL THE POLICE!
WE SEE THROUGH YOUR SCHEME! GO!
WELL?
I HEARD YOU, KIN-SAN. WE'LL LEAVE NOW.
13

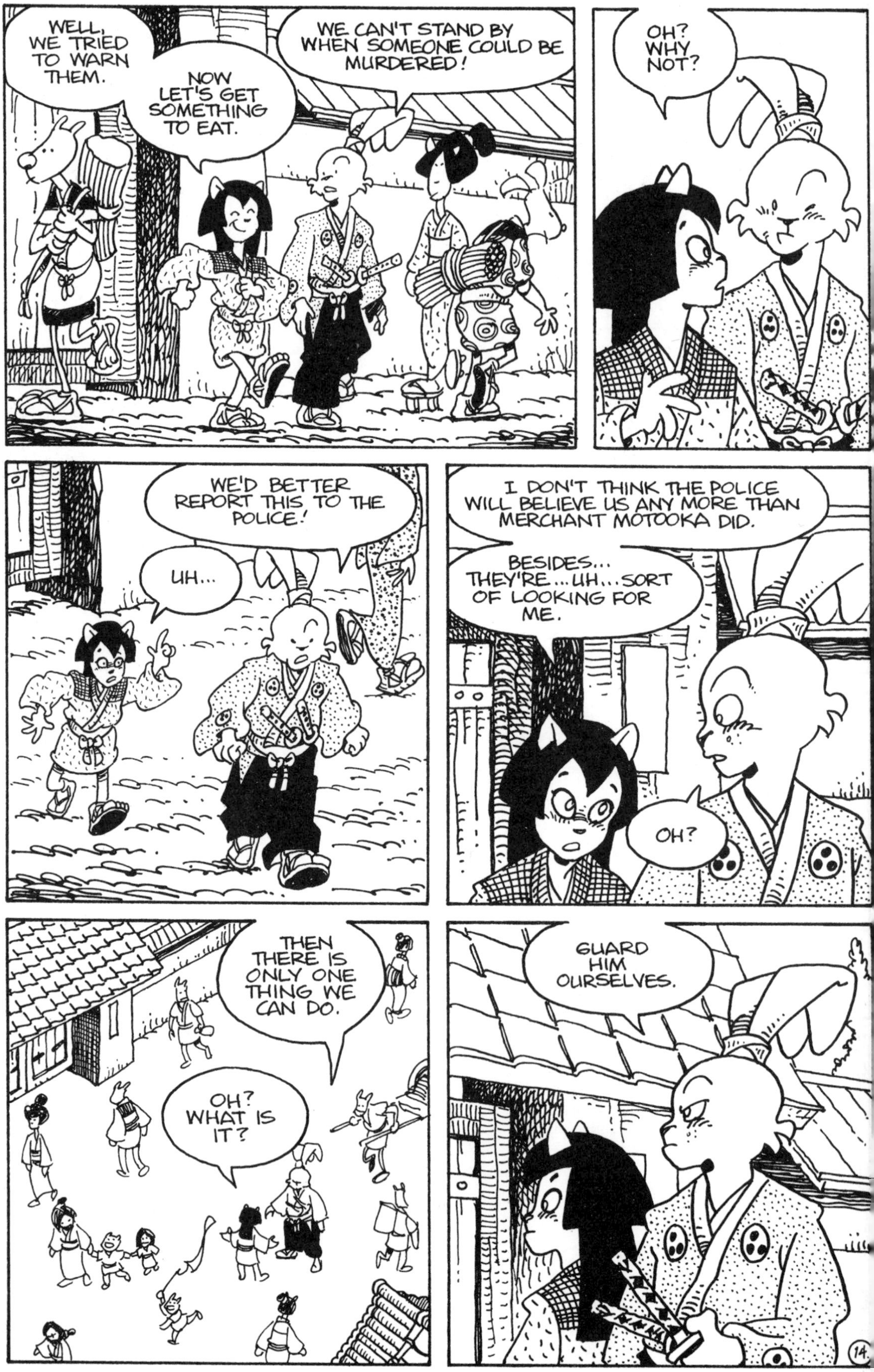
WELL, WE TRIED TO WARN THEM.
NOW LET'S GET SOMETHING TO EAT.
WE CAN'T STAND BY WHEN SOMEONE COULD BE MURDERED!
OH? WHY NOT?
WE'D BETTER REPORT THIS TO THE POLICE!
UH...
I DON'T THINK THE POLICE WILL BELIEVE US ANY MORE THAN MERCHANT MOTOOKA DID.
BESIDES... THEY'RE...UH...SORT OF LOOKING FOR ME.
OH?
THEN THERE IS ONLY ONE THING WE CAN DO.
OH? WHAT IS IT?
GUARD HIM OURSELVES.
14

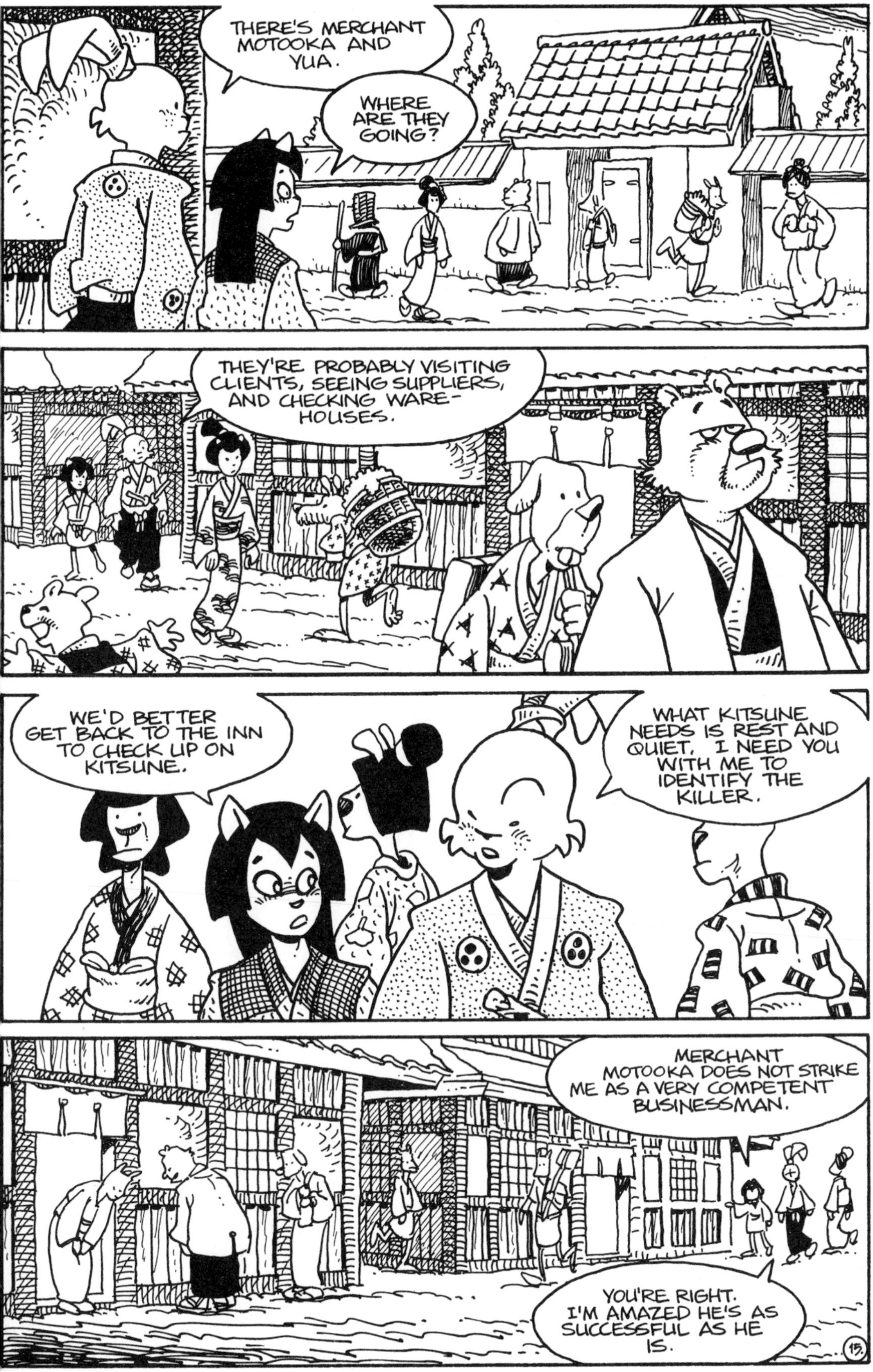
THERE'S MERCHANT MOTOOKA AND YUA.
WHERE ARE THEY GOING?
THEY'RE PROBABLY VISITING CLIENTS, SEEING SUPPLIERS, AND CHECKING WARE-HOUSES.
WE'D BETTER GET BACK TO THE INN TO CHECK UP ON KITSUNE.
WHAT KITSUNE NEEDS IS REST AND QUIET. I NEED YOU WITH ME TO IDENTIFY THE KILLER.
MERCHANT MOTOOKA DOES NOT STRIKE ME AS A VERY COMPETENT BUSINESSMAN.
YOU'RE RIGHT. I'M AMAZED HE'S AS SUCCESSFUL AS HE IS.
15.

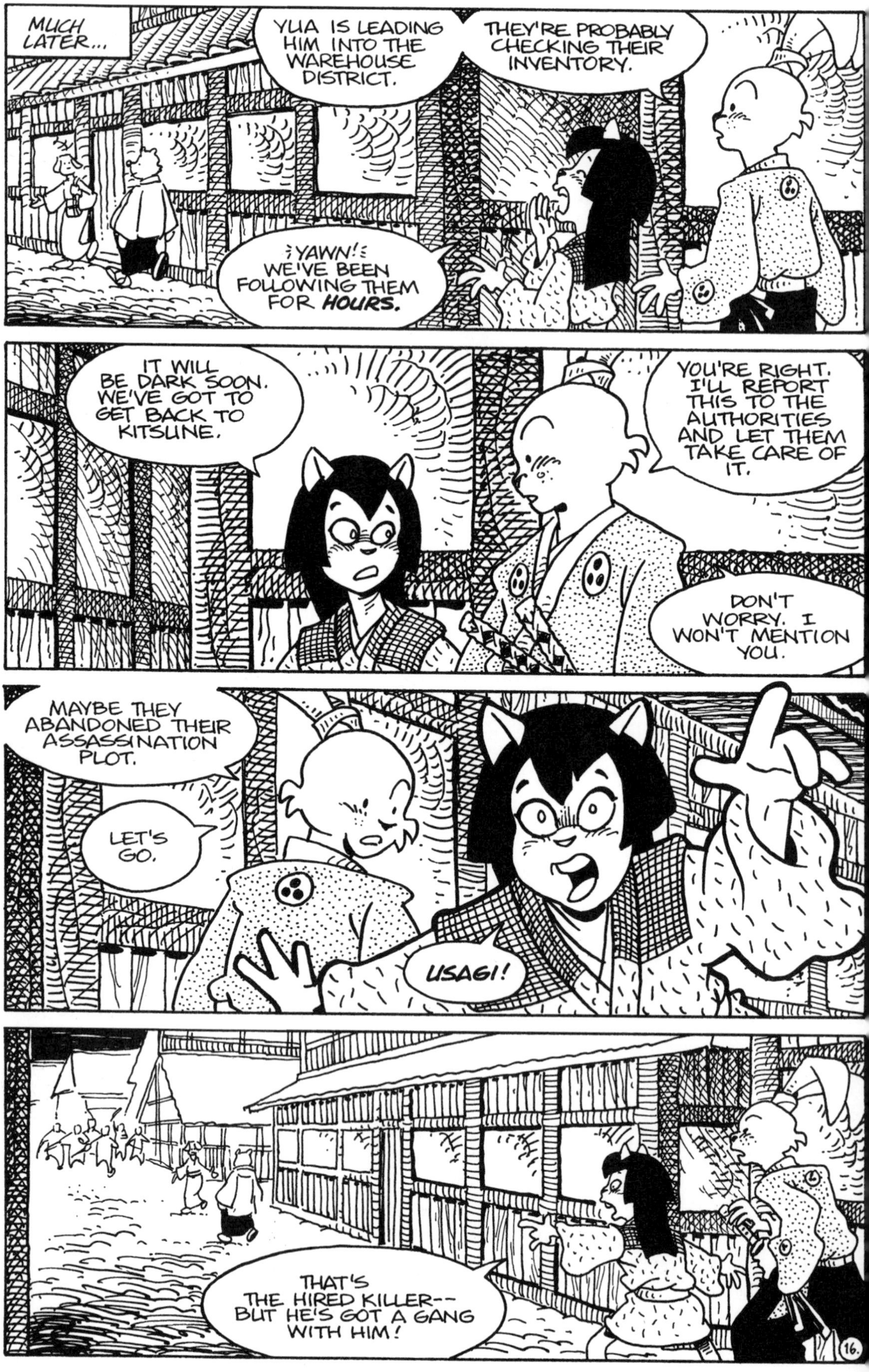
MUCH LATER...
YUA IS LEADING HIM INTO THE WAREHOUSE DISTRICT.
THEY'RE PROBABLY CHECKING THEIR INVENTORY.
YAWN! WE'VE BEEN FOLLOWING THEM FOR HOURS.
IT WILL BE DARK SOON. WE'VE GOT TO GET BACK TO KITSUNE.
YOU'RE RIGHT. I'LL REPORT THIS TO THE AUTHORITIES AND LET THEM TAKE CARE OF IT.
DON'T WORRY. I WON'T MENTION YOU.
MAYBE THEY ABANDONED THEIR ASSASSINATION PLOT.
LET'S GO.
USAGI!
THAT'S THE HIRED KILLER-- BUT HE'S GOT A GANG WITH HIM!
16.

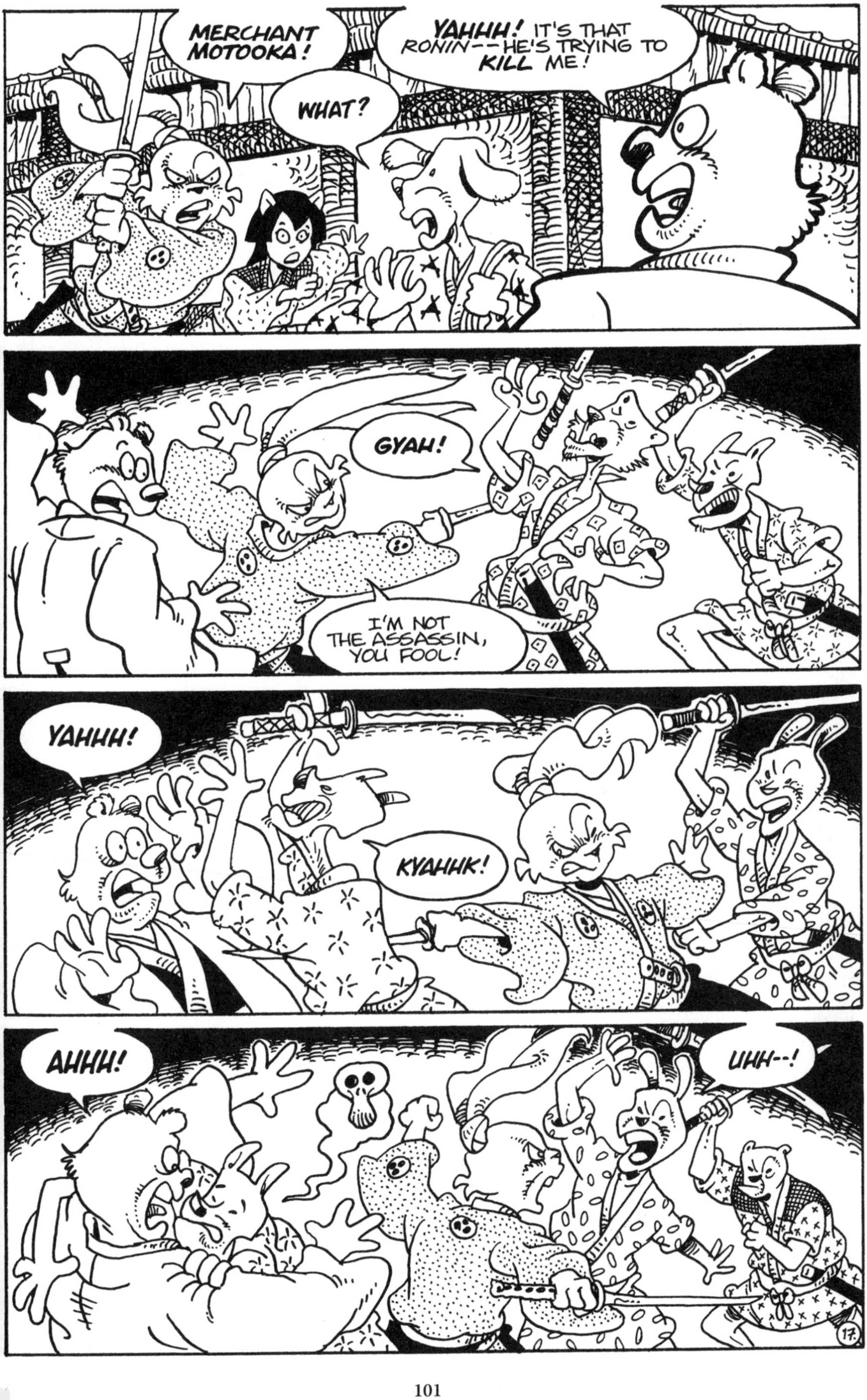
MERCHANT MOTOOKA!
WHAT?
YAHHH! IT'S THAT RONIN--HE'S TRYING TO KILL ME!
GYAH!
I'M NOT THE ASSASSIN, YOU FOOL!
YAHHH!
KYAHHK!
AHHH!
UHH--!
17.

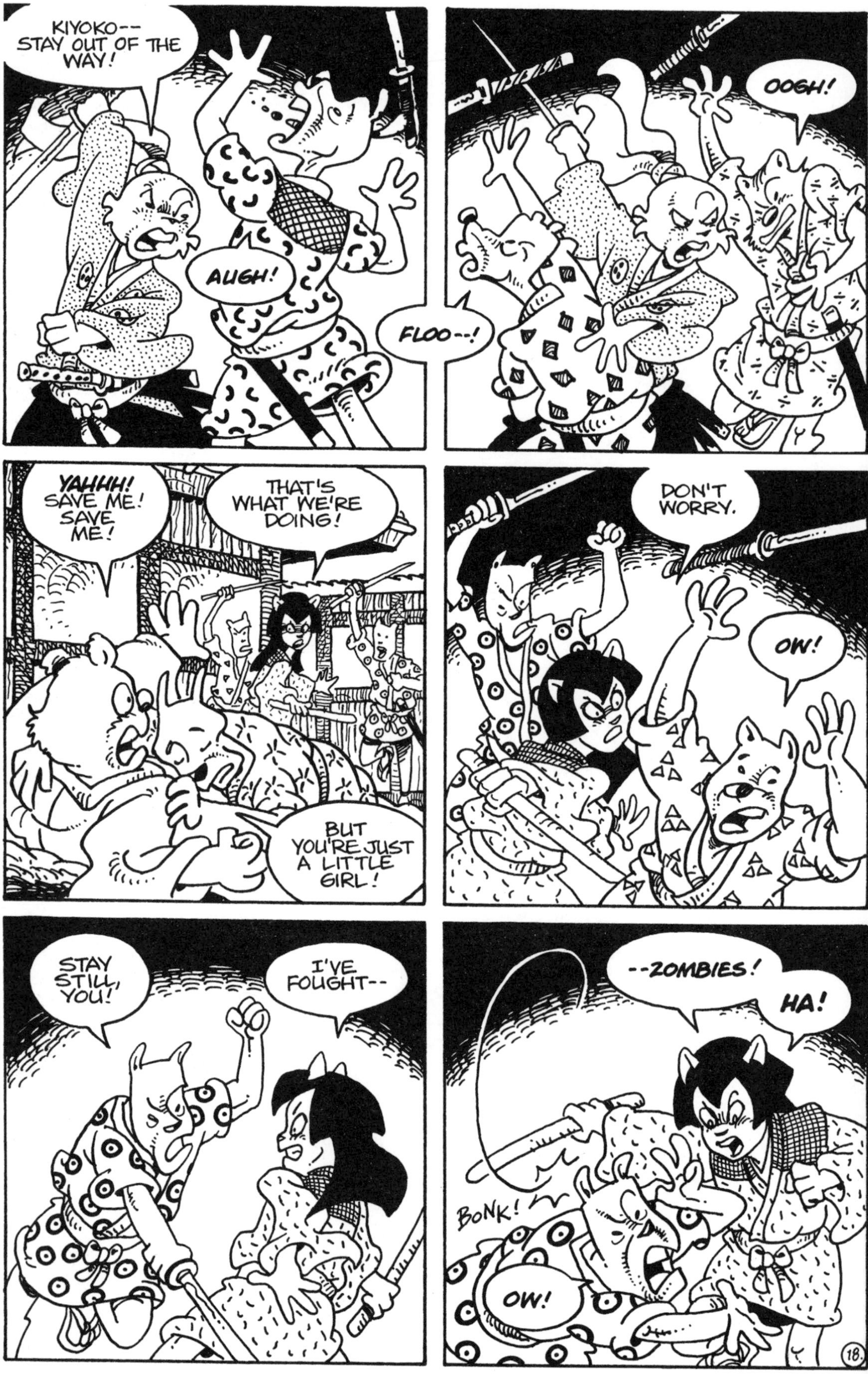
KIYOKO--
STAY OUT OF THE
WAY!
AUGH!
FLOO--!
OOGH!
YAHHH!
SAVE ME!
SAVE
ME!
THAT'S
WHAT WE'RE
DOING!
BUT
YOU'RE JUST
A LITTLE
GIRL!
DON'T
WORRY.
OW!
STAY
STILL,
YOU!
I'VE
FOUGHT--
--ZOMBIES!
HA!
BONK!
OW!
18.

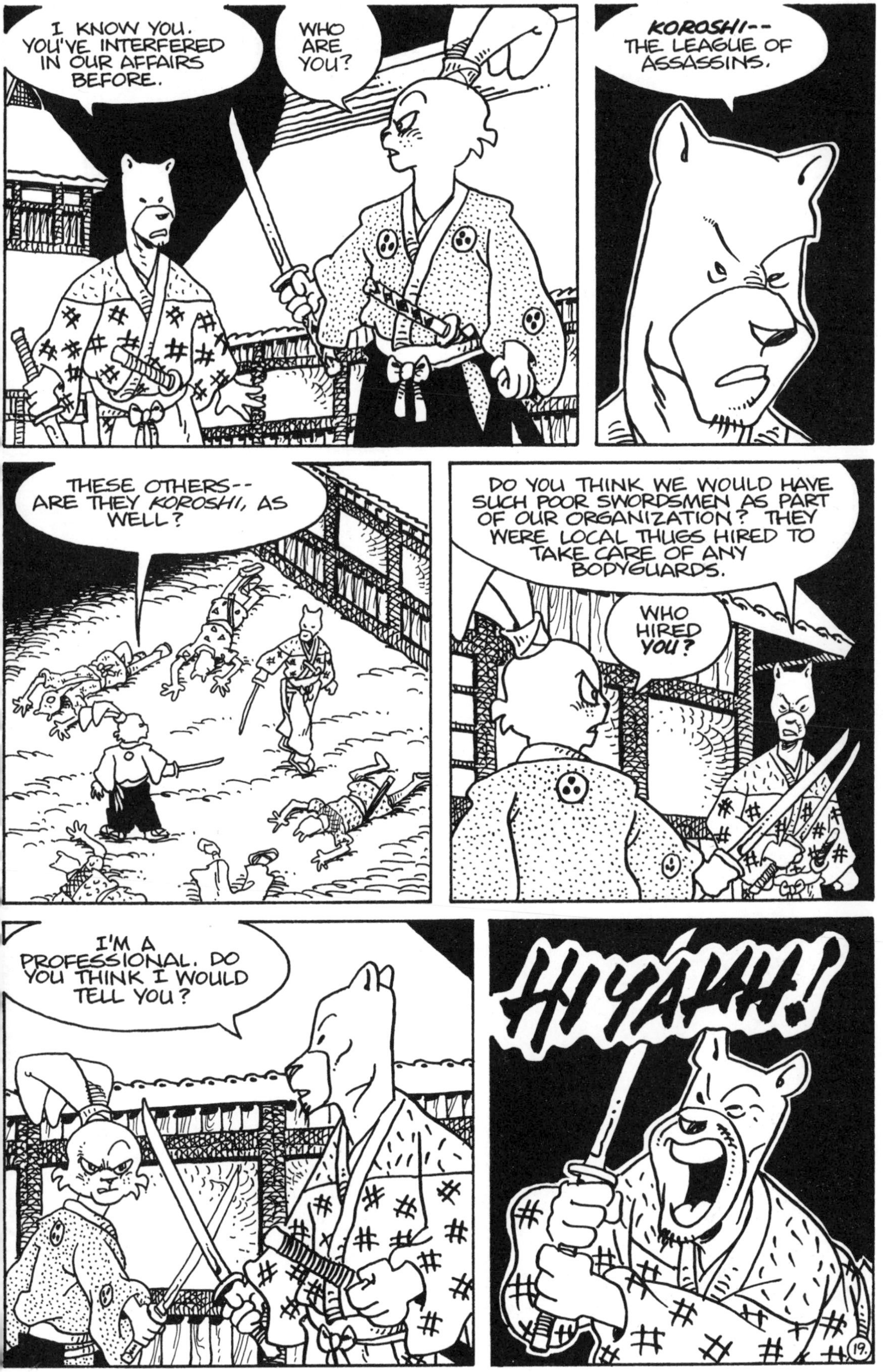
I KNOW YOU. YOU'VE INTERFERED IN OUR AFFAIRS BEFORE.
WHO ARE YOU?
*KOROSHI*-- THE LEAGUE OF ASSASSINS.
THESE OTHERS-- ARE THEY *KOROSHI*, AS WELL?
DO YOU THINK WE WOULD HAVE SUCH POOR SWORDSMEN AS PART OF OUR ORGANIZATION? THEY WERE LOCAL THUGS HIRED TO TAKE CARE OF ANY BODYGUARDS.
WHO HIRED *YOU*?
I'M A PROFESSIONAL. DO YOU THINK I WOULD TELL YOU?
HIYAAH!
19.

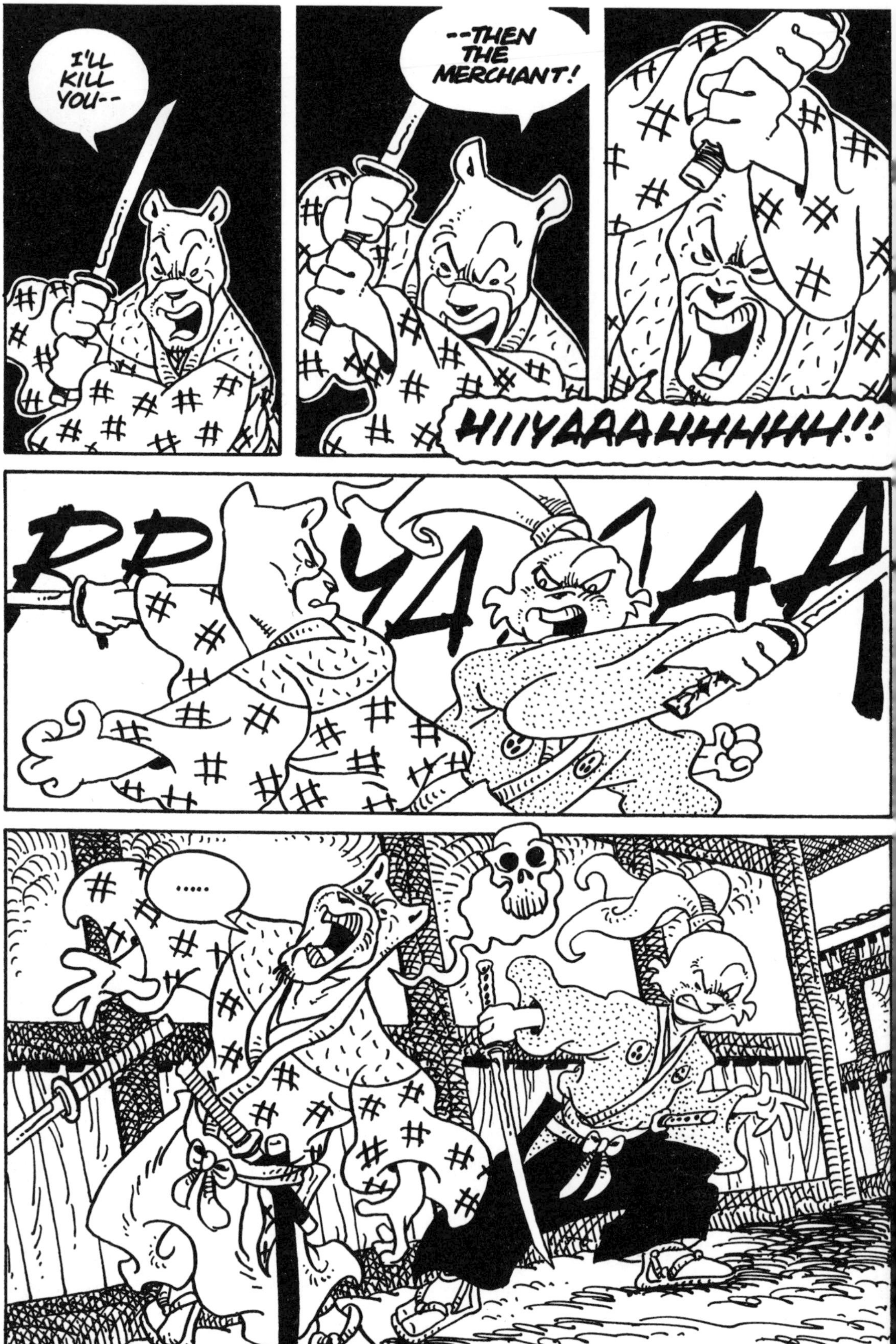
I'LL KILL YOU--
--THEN THE MERCHANT!
HIIYAAAAHHHHH!!
RRYAAAA
.....
2a

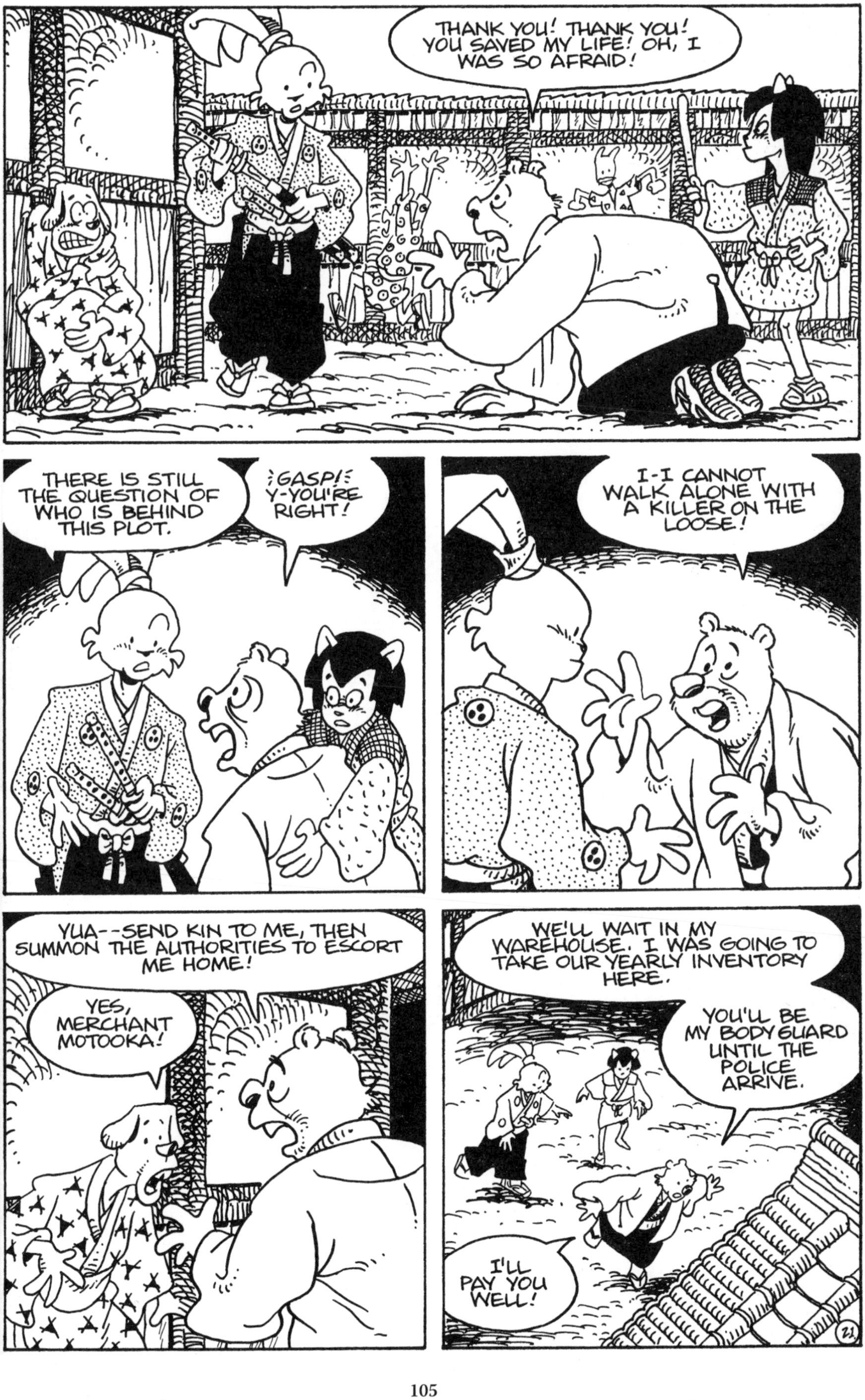
THANK YOU! THANK YOU! YOU SAVED MY LIFE! OH, I WAS SO AFRAID!
THERE IS STILL THE QUESTION OF WHO IS BEHIND THIS PLOT.
GASP! Y-YOU'RE RIGHT!
I-I CANNOT WALK ALONE WITH A KILLER ON THE LOOSE!
YUA--SEND KIN TO ME, THEN SUMMON THE AUTHORITIES TO ESCORT ME HOME!
YES, MERCHANT MOTOOKA!
WE'LL WAIT IN MY WAREHOUSE. I WAS GOING TO TAKE OUR YEARLY INVENTORY HERE.
YOU'LL BE MY BODYGUARD UNTIL THE POLICE ARRIVE.
I'LL PAY YOU WELL!
21

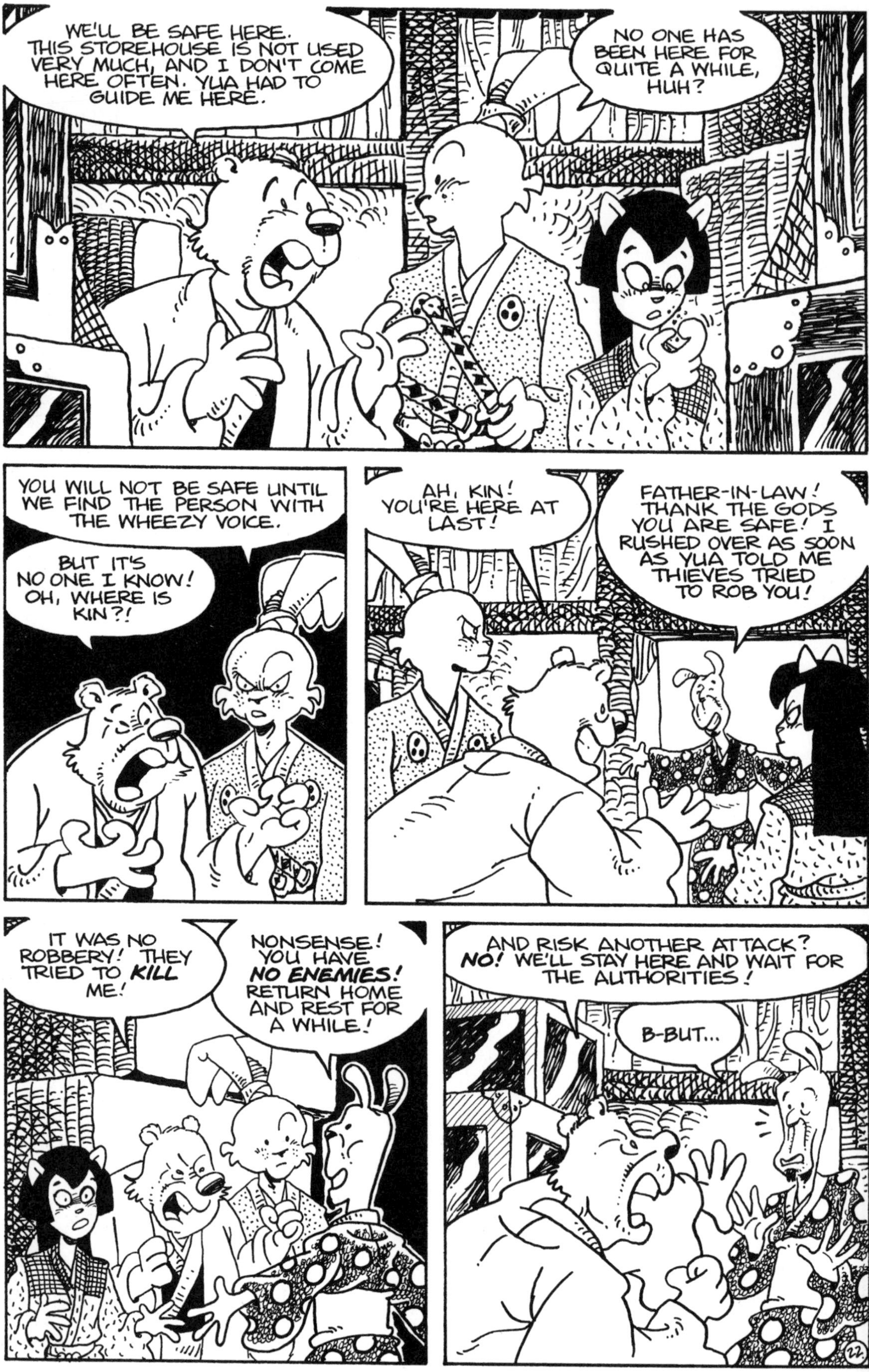
WE'LL BE SAFE HERE. THIS STOREHOUSE IS NOT USED VERY MUCH, AND I DON'T COME HERE OFTEN. YUA HAD TO GUIDE ME HERE.
NO ONE HAS BEEN HERE FOR QUITE A WHILE, HUH?
YOU WILL NOT BE SAFE UNTIL WE FIND THE PERSON WITH THE WHEEZY VOICE.
BUT IT'S NO ONE I KNOW! OH, WHERE IS KIN?!
AH, KIN! YOU'RE HERE AT LAST!
FATHER-IN-LAW! THANK THE GODS YOU ARE SAFE! I RUSHED OVER AS SOON AS YUA TOLD ME THIEVES TRIED TO ROB YOU!
IT WAS NO ROBBERY! THEY TRIED TO **KILL** ME!
NONSENSE! YOU HAVE **NO ENEMIES!** RETURN HOME AND REST FOR A WHILE!
AND RISK ANOTHER ATTACK? **NO!** WE'LL STAY HERE AND WAIT FOR THE AUTHORITIES!
B-BUT...
22.

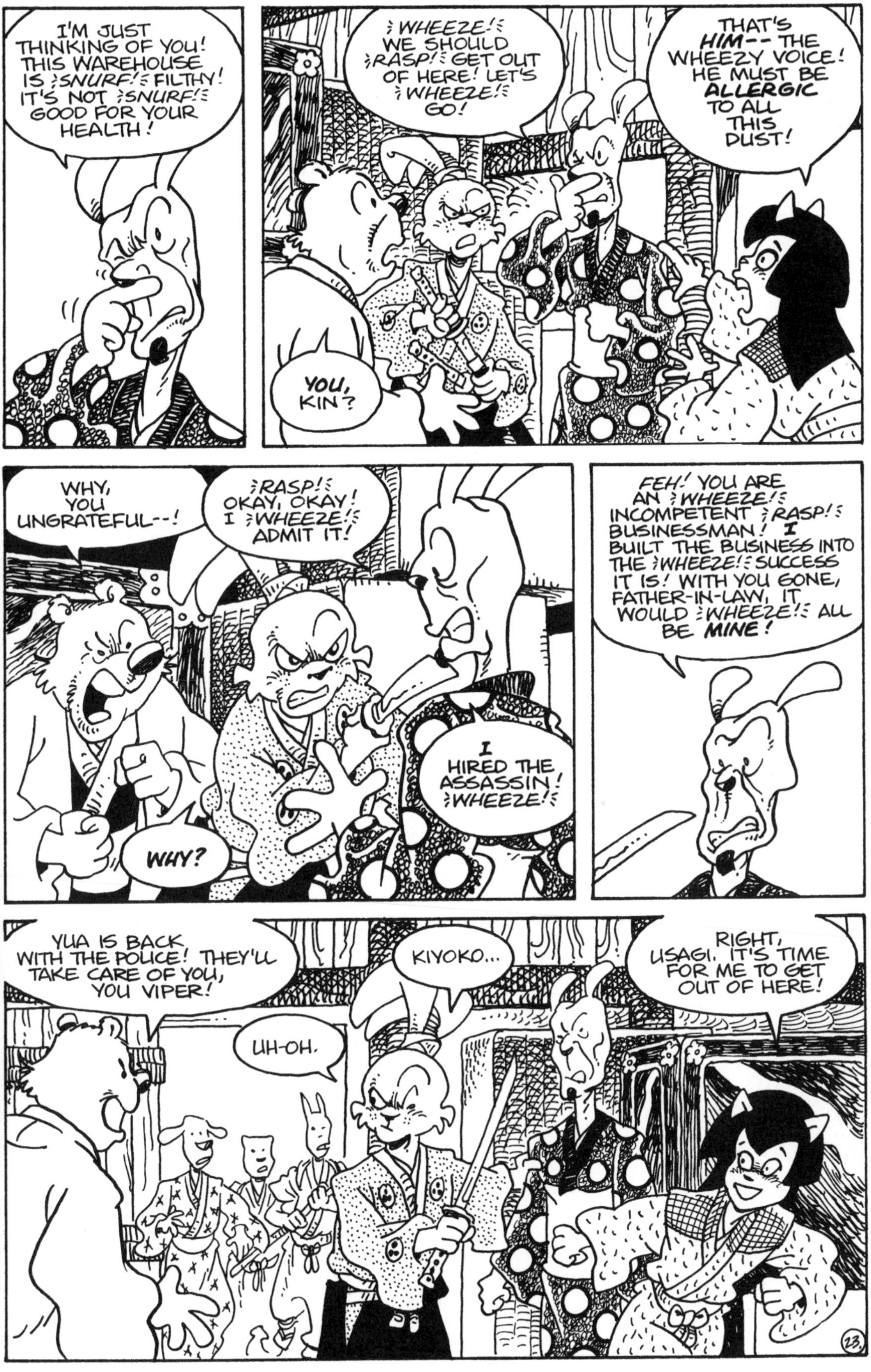
I'M JUST THINKING OF YOU! THIS WAREHOUSE IS ;SNURF!; FILTHY! IT'S NOT ;SNURF!; GOOD FOR YOUR HEALTH!
;WHEEZE!; WE SHOULD ;RASP!; GET OUT OF HERE! LET'S ;WHEEZE!; GO!
YOU, KIN?
THAT'S HIM-- THE WHEEZY VOICE! HE MUST BE ALLERGIC TO ALL THIS DUST!
WHY, YOU UNGRATEFUL--!
;RASP!; OKAY, OKAY! I ;WHEEZE!; ADMIT IT!
I HIRED THE ASSASSIN! ;WHEEZE!;
WHY?
FEH! YOU ARE AN ;WHEEZE!; INCOMPETENT ;RASP!; BUSINESSMAN! I BUILT THE BUSINESS INTO THE ;WHEEZE!; SUCCESS IT IS! WITH YOU GONE, FATHER-IN-LAW, IT WOULD ;WHEEZE!; ALL BE MINE!
YUA IS BACK WITH THE POLICE! THEY'LL TAKE CARE OF YOU, YOU VIPER!
UH-OH.
KIYOKO...
RIGHT, USAGI. IT'S TIME FOR ME TO GET OUT OF HERE!
23

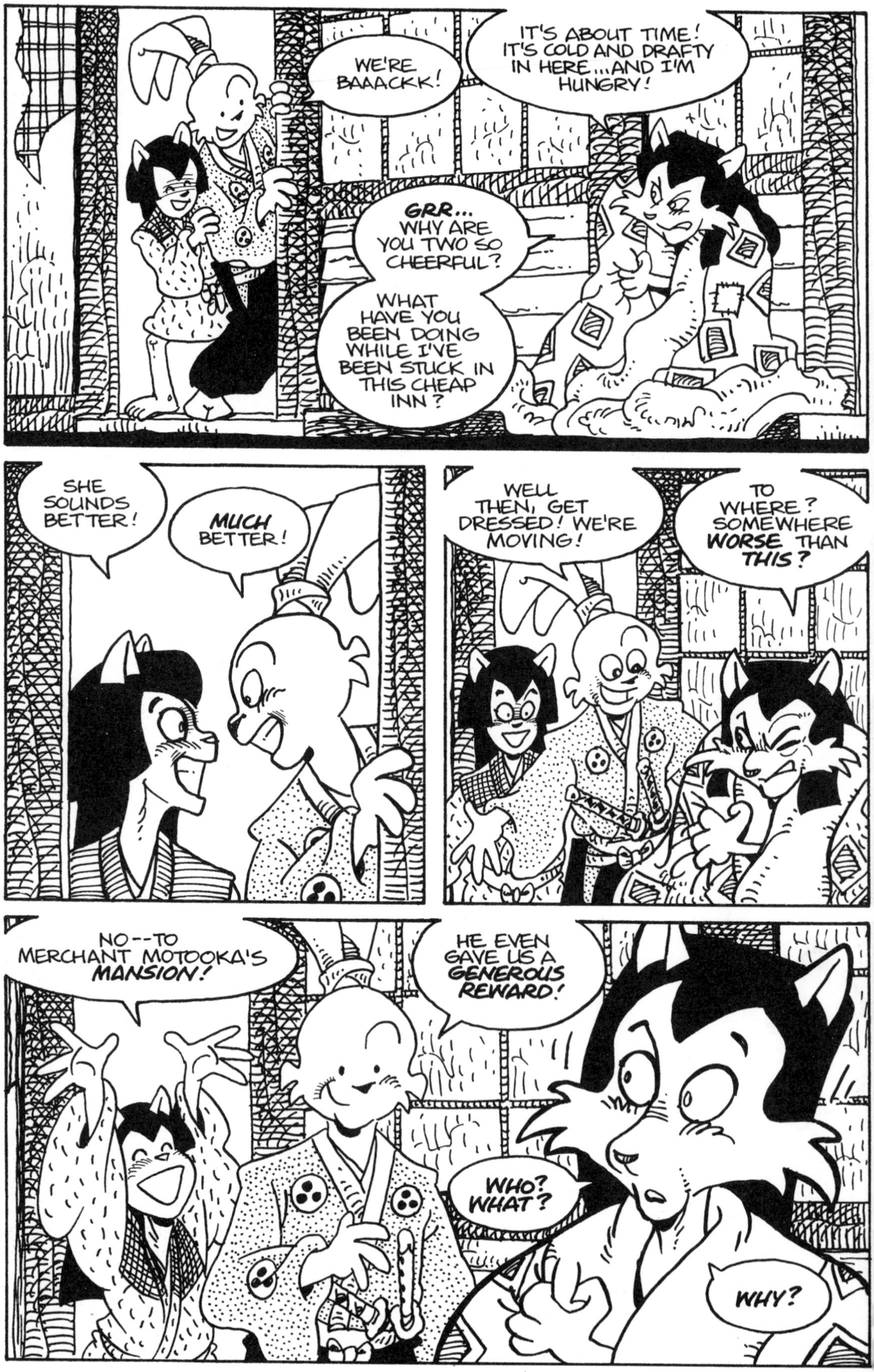
WE'RE BAAACKK!
IT'S ABOUT TIME! IT'S COLD AND DRAFTY IN HERE...AND I'M HUNGRY!
GRR... WHY ARE YOU TWO SO CHEERFUL?
WHAT HAVE YOU BEEN DOING WHILE I'VE BEEN STUCK IN THIS CHEAP INN?
SHE SOUNDS BETTER!
MUCH BETTER!
WELL THEN, GET DRESSED! WE'RE MOVING!
TO WHERE? SOMEWHERE WORSE THAN THIS?
NO--TO MERCHANT MOTOOKA'S MANSION!
HE EVEN GAVE US A GENEROUS REWARD!
WHO? WHAT?
WHY?

THE END

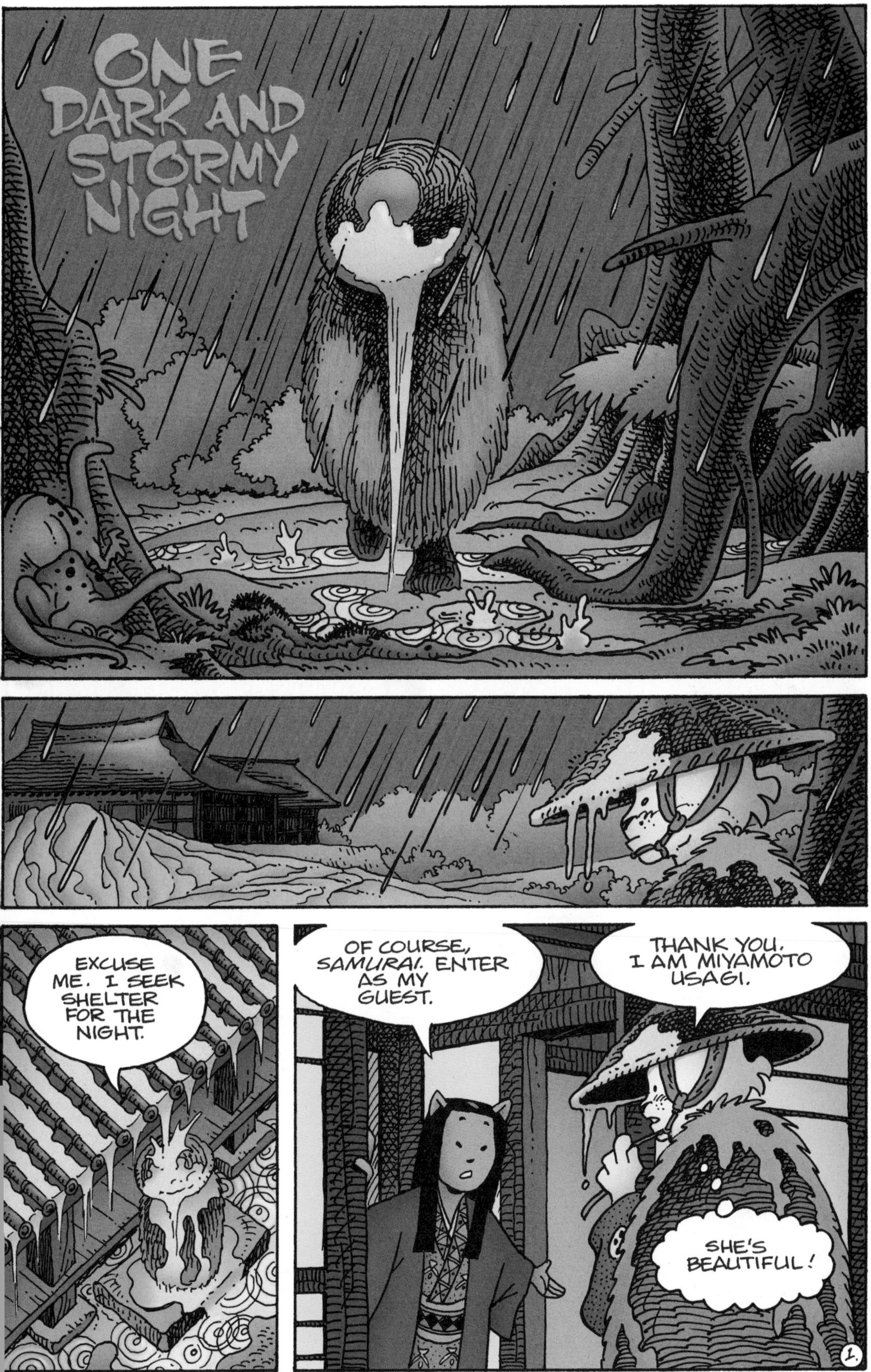
ONE DARK AND STORMY NIGHT
EXCUSE ME. I SEEK SHELTER FOR THE NIGHT.
OF COURSE, SAMURAI. ENTER AS MY GUEST.
THANK YOU. I AM MIYAMOTO USAGI.
SHE'S BEAUTIFUL!
1.

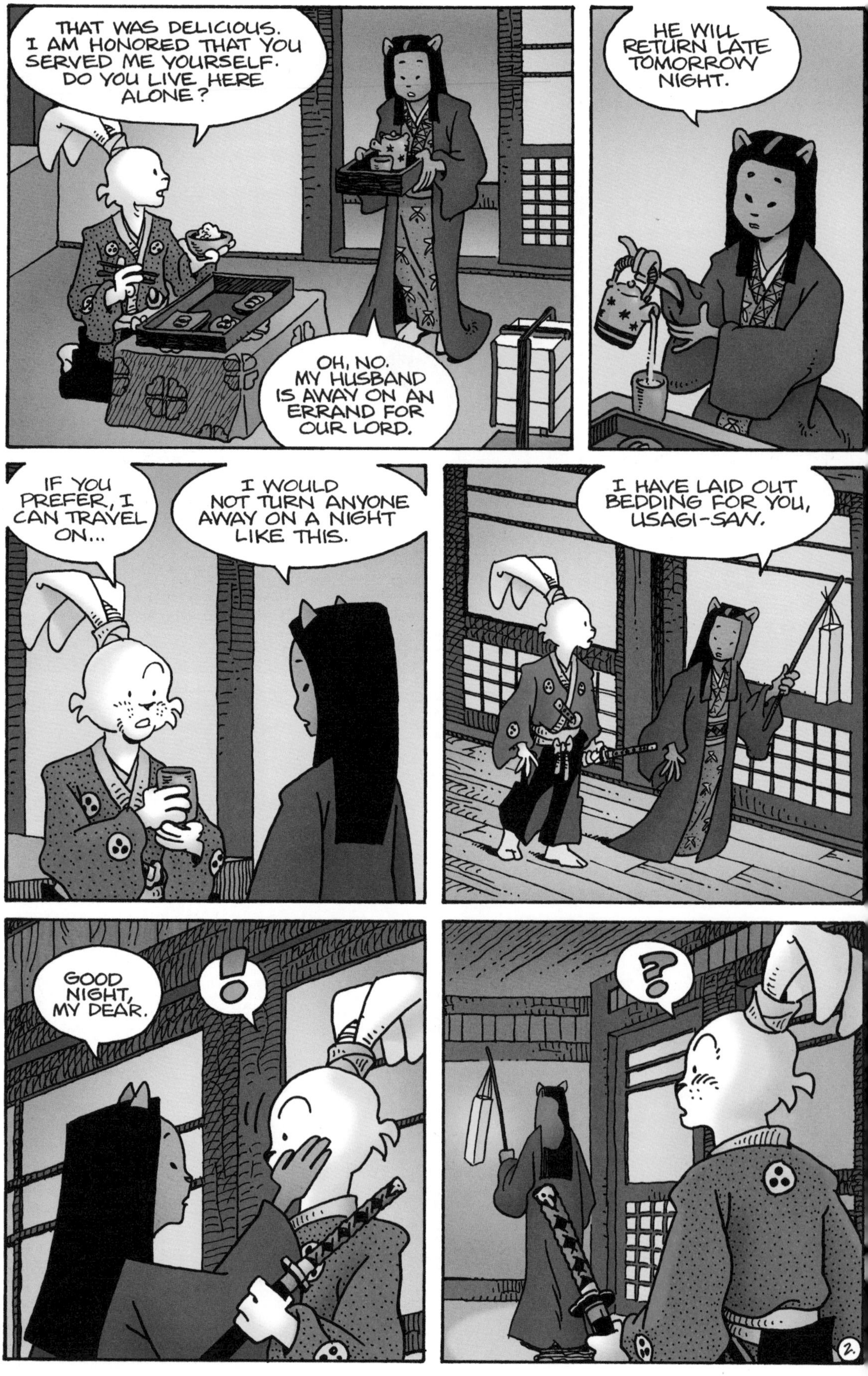
THAT WAS DELICIOUS. I AM HONORED THAT YOU SERVED ME YOURSELF. DO YOU LIVE HERE ALONE?
OH, NO. MY HUSBAND IS AWAY ON AN ERRAND FOR OUR LORD.
HE WILL RETURN LATE TOMORROW NIGHT.
IF YOU PREFER, I CAN TRAVEL ON...
I WOULD NOT TURN ANYONE AWAY ON A NIGHT LIKE THIS.
I HAVE LAID OUT BEDDING FOR YOU, USAGI-SAN.
GOOD NIGHT, MY DEAR.
!
?
2.

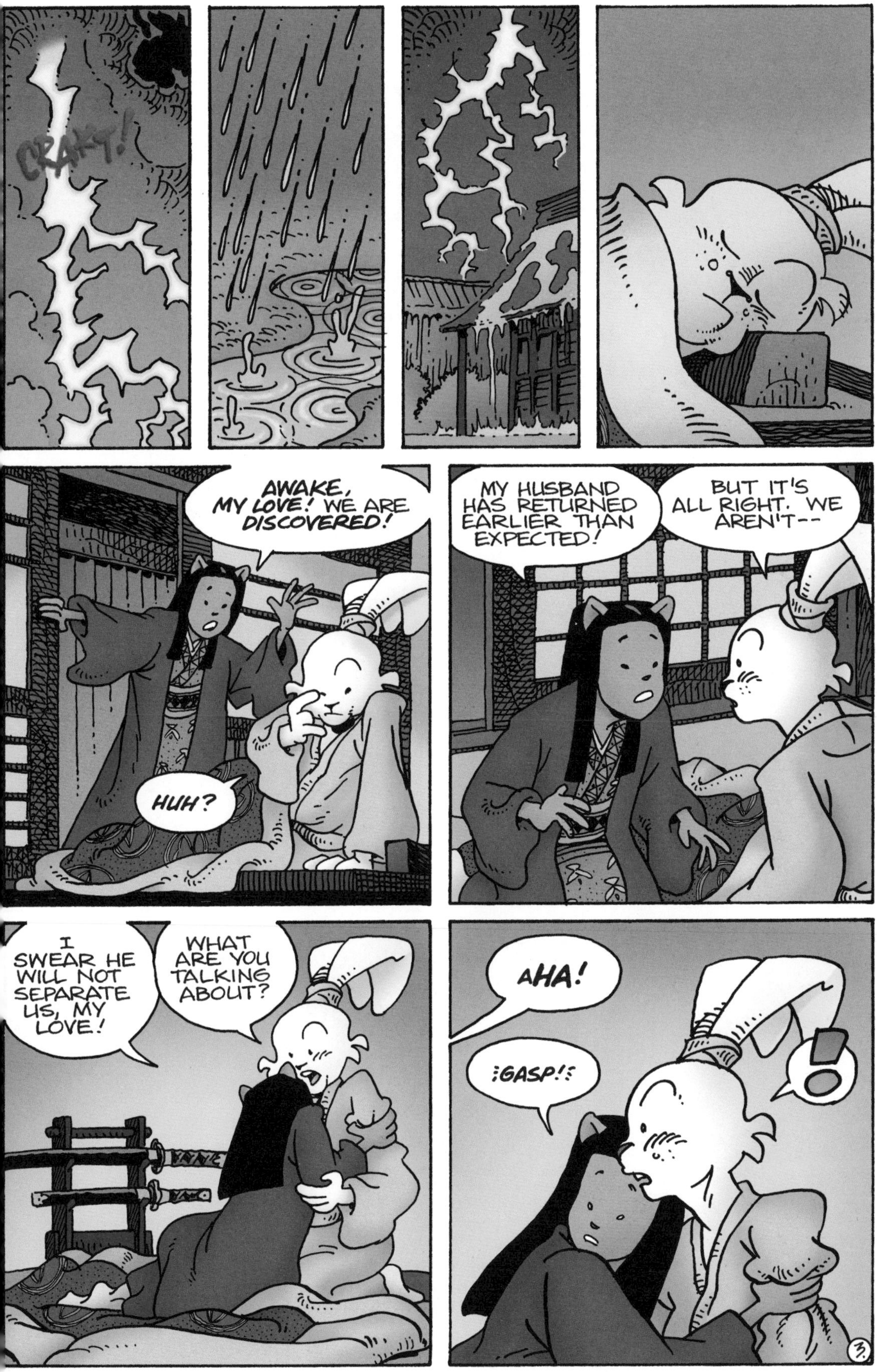
CRAKT!
AWAKE, MY LOVE! WE ARE DISCOVERED!
HUH?
MY HUSBAND HAS RETURNED EARLIER THAN EXPECTED!
BUT IT'S ALL RIGHT. WE AREN'T--
I SWEAR HE WILL NOT SEPARATE US, MY LOVE!
WHAT ARE YOU TALKING ABOUT?
AHA!
GASP!
!
3.

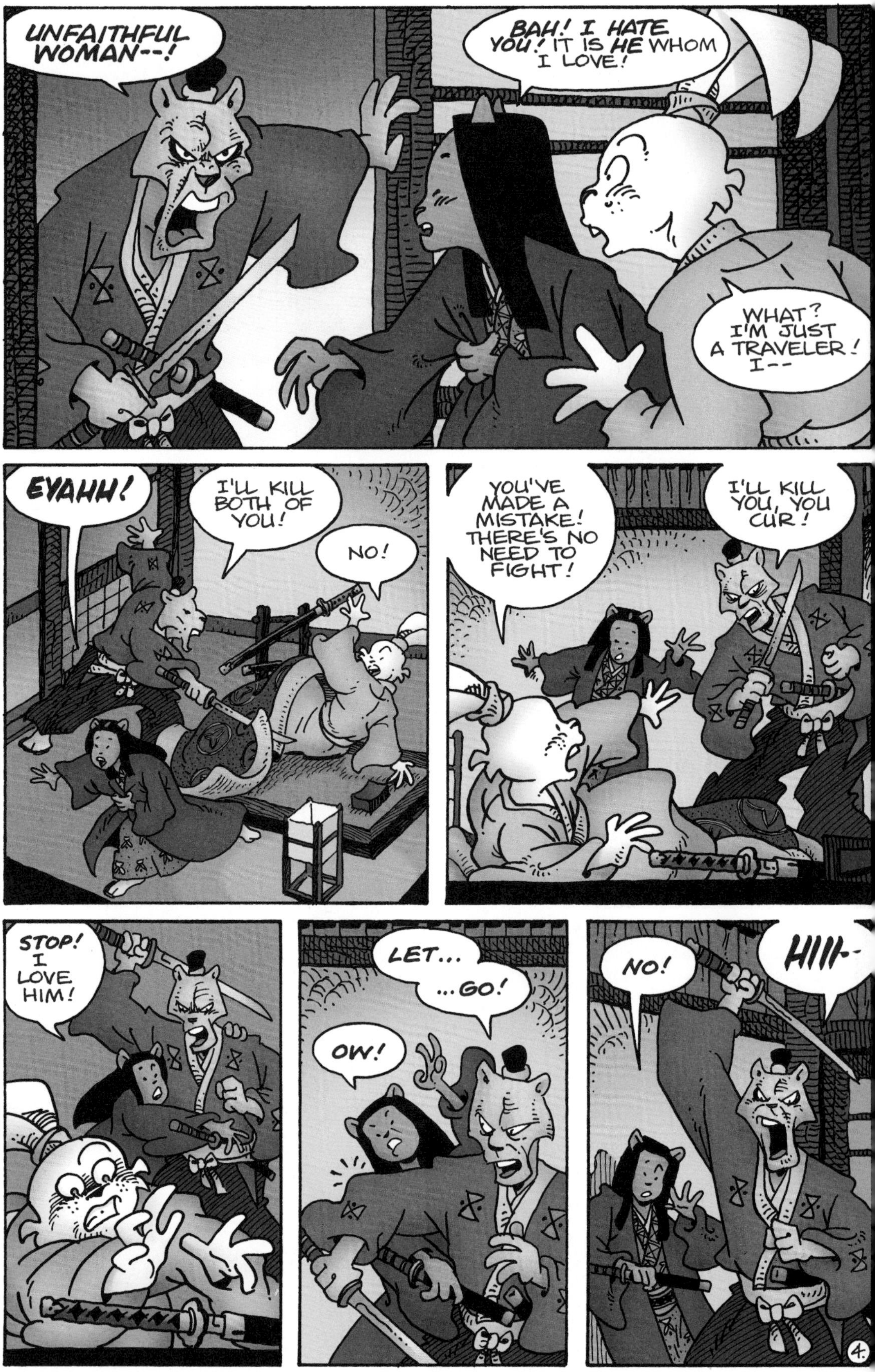
UNFAITHFUL WOMAN--!
BAH! I HATE YOU! IT IS HE WHOM I LOVE!
WHAT? I'M JUST A TRAVELER! I--
EYAHH!
I'LL KILL BOTH OF YOU!
NO!
YOU'VE MADE A MISTAKE! THERE'S NO NEED TO FIGHT!
I'LL KILL YOU, YOU CUR!
STOP! I LOVE HIM!
LET...
...GO!
OW!
NO!
HIII-
4.

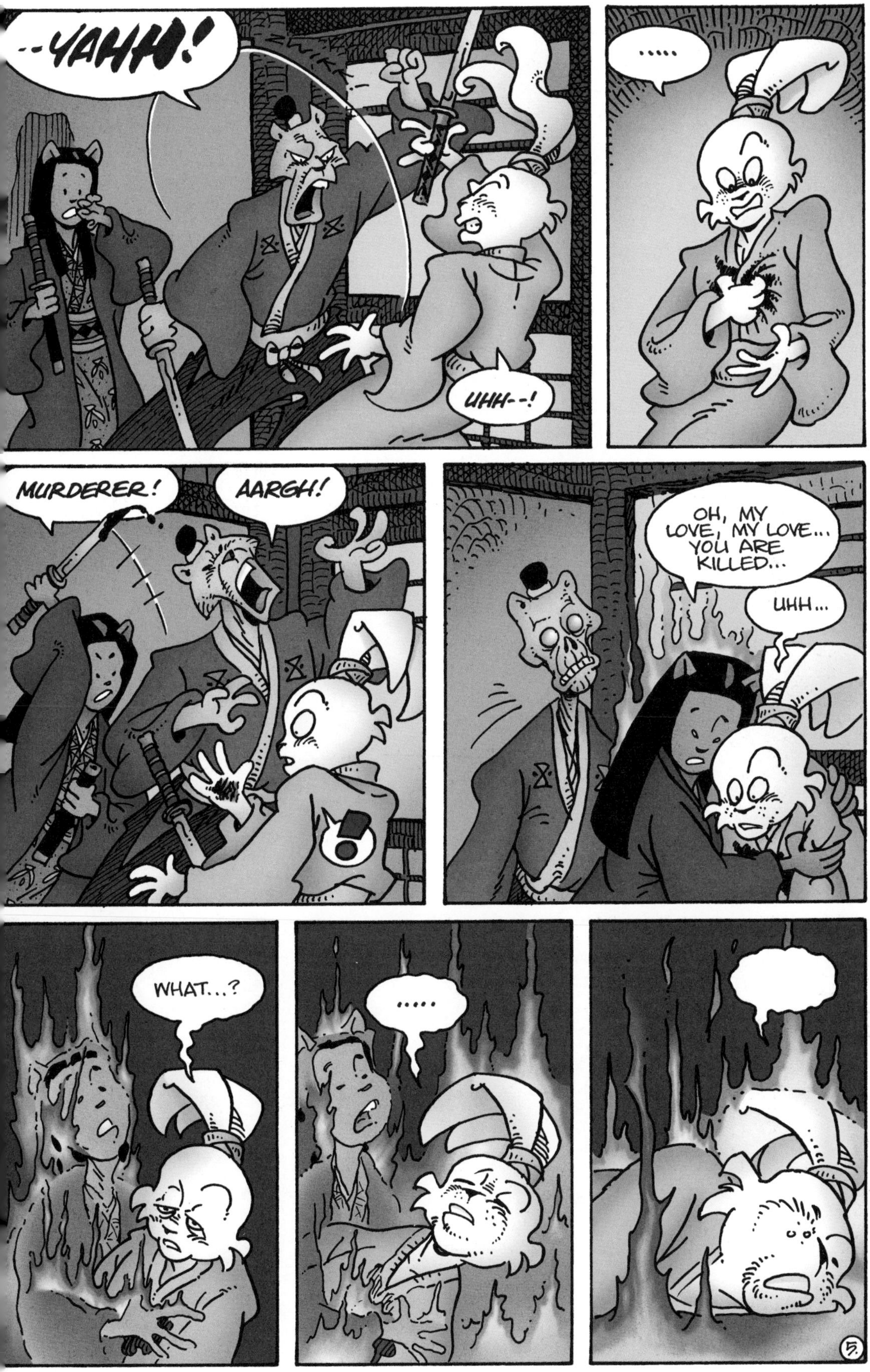

--YAHH!
UHH--!
.....
MURDERER!
AARGH!
OH, MY LOVE, MY LOVE... YOU ARE KILLED...
UHH...
WHAT...?
.....
5.

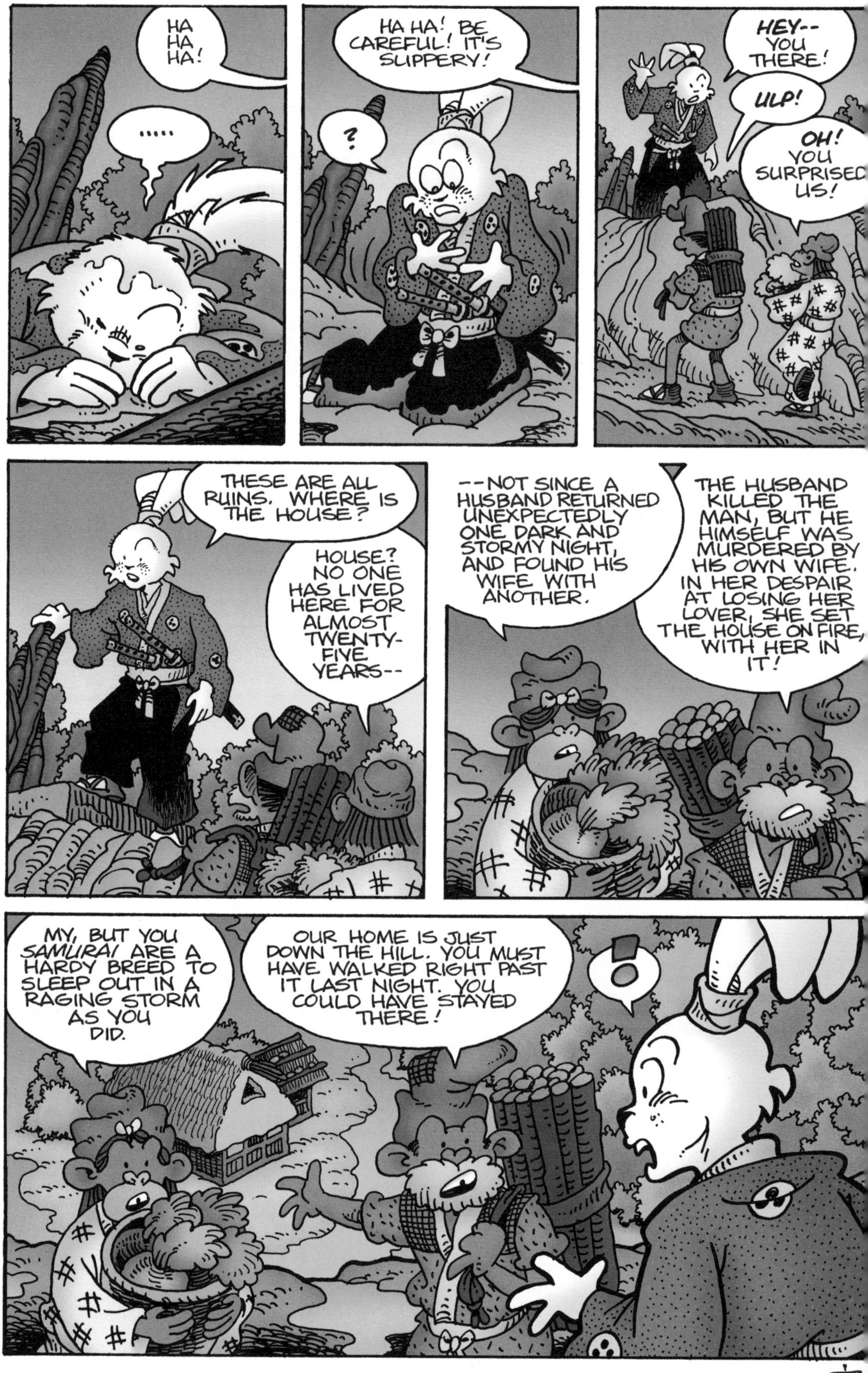
HA HA HA!
.....
HA HA! BE CAREFUL! IT'S SLIPPERY!
?
HEY-- YOU THERE!
ULP!
OH! YOU SURPRISED US!
THESE ARE ALL RUINS. WHERE IS THE HOUSE?
HOUSE? NO ONE HAS LIVED HERE FOR ALMOST TWENTY-FIVE YEARS--
--NOT SINCE A HUSBAND RETURNED UNEXPECTEDLY ONE DARK AND STORMY NIGHT, AND FOUND HIS WIFE WITH ANOTHER.
THE HUSBAND KILLED THE MAN, BUT HE HIMSELF WAS MURDERED BY HIS OWN WIFE. IN HER DESPAIR AT LOSING HER LOVER, SHE SET THE HOUSE ON FIRE, WITH HER IN IT!
MY, BUT YOU *SAMURAI* ARE A HARDY BREED TO SLEEP OUT IN A RAGING STORM AS YOU DID.
OUR HOME IS JUST DOWN THE HILL. YOU MUST HAVE WALKED RIGHT PAST IT LAST NIGHT. YOU COULD HAVE STAYED THERE!
!

完

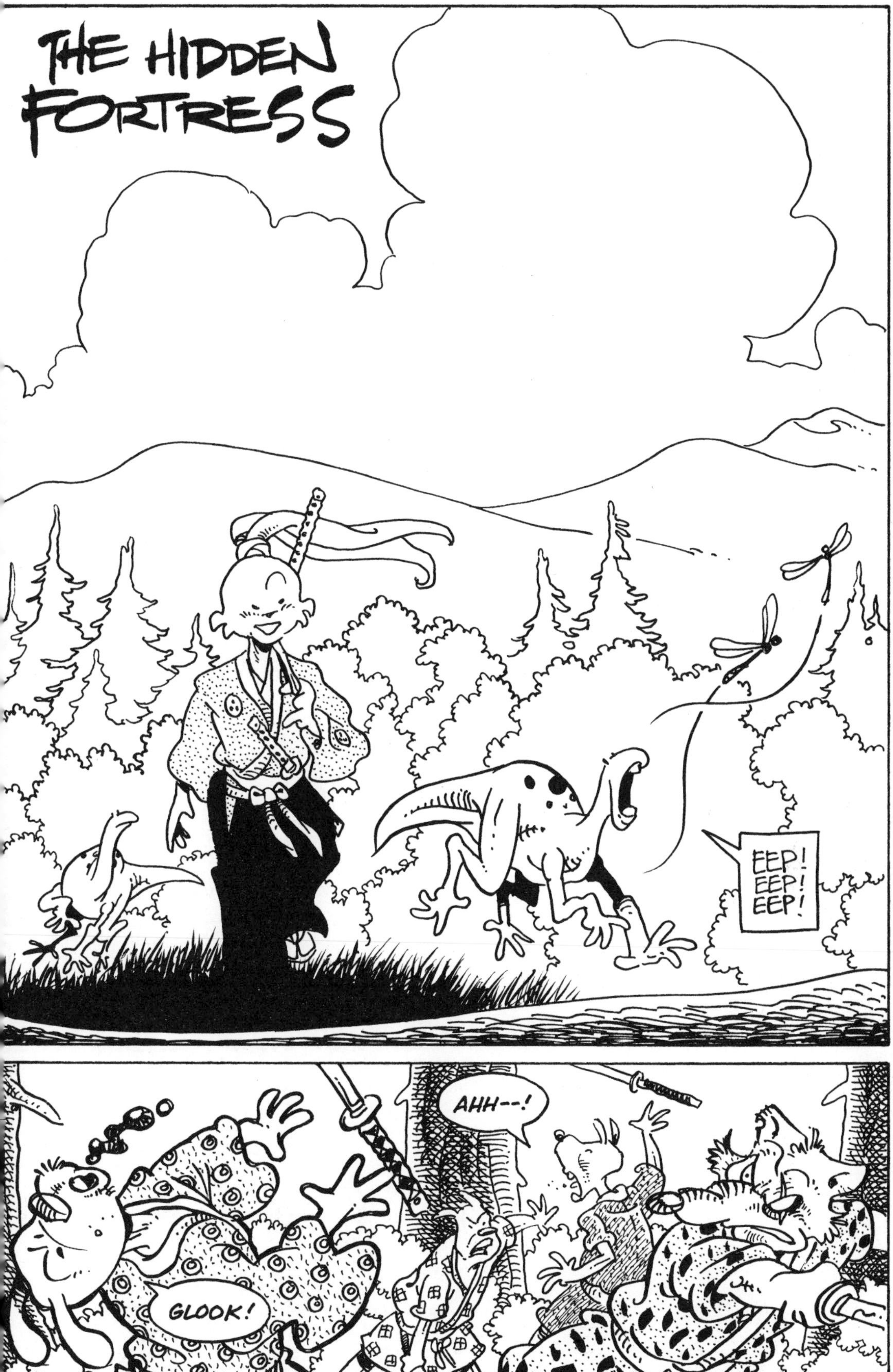
THE HIDDEN FORTRESS
EEP! EEP! EEP!
GLOOK!
AHH--!
1.

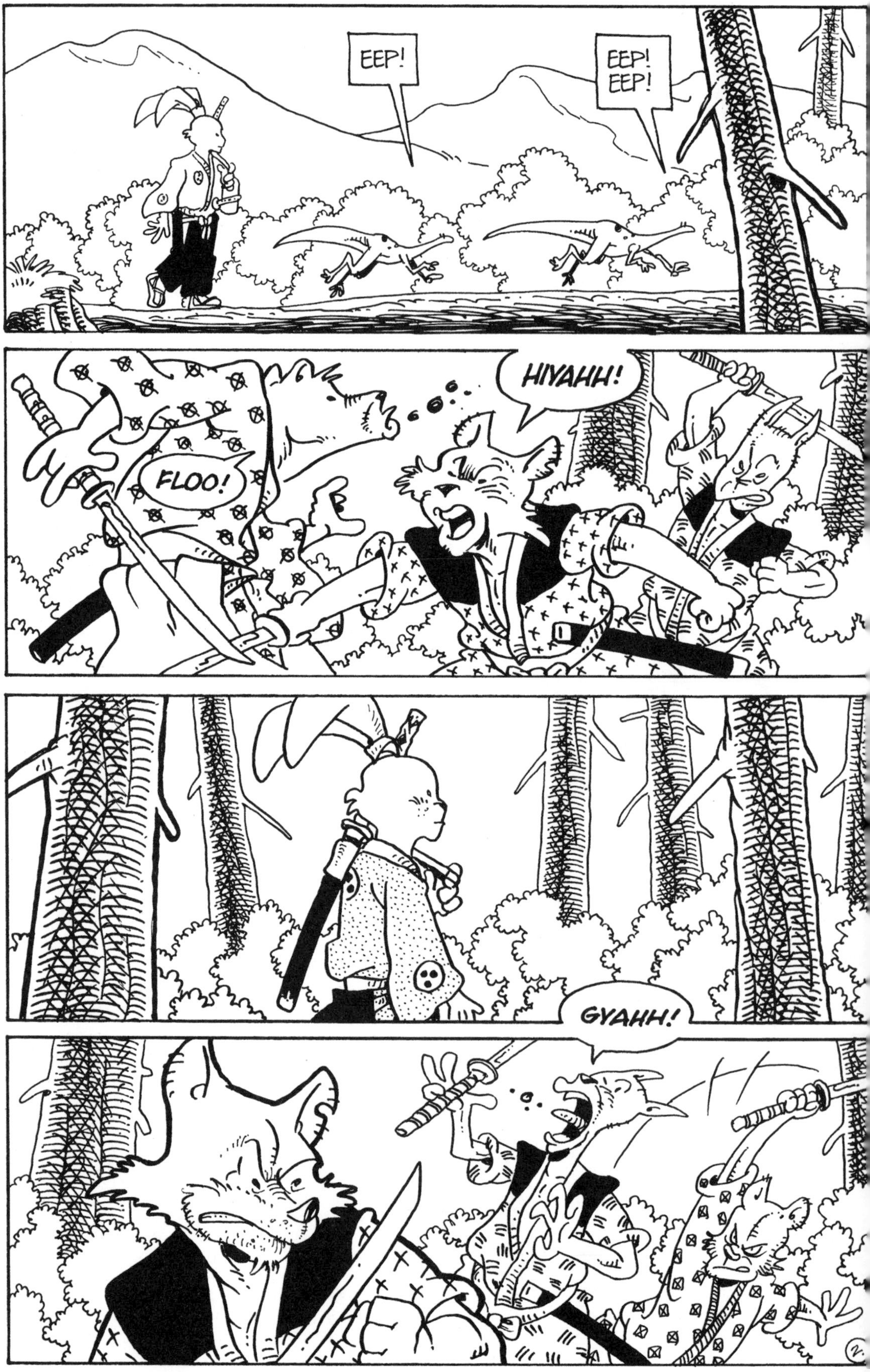
EEP!
EEP! EEP!
HIYAHH!
FLOO!
GYAHH!

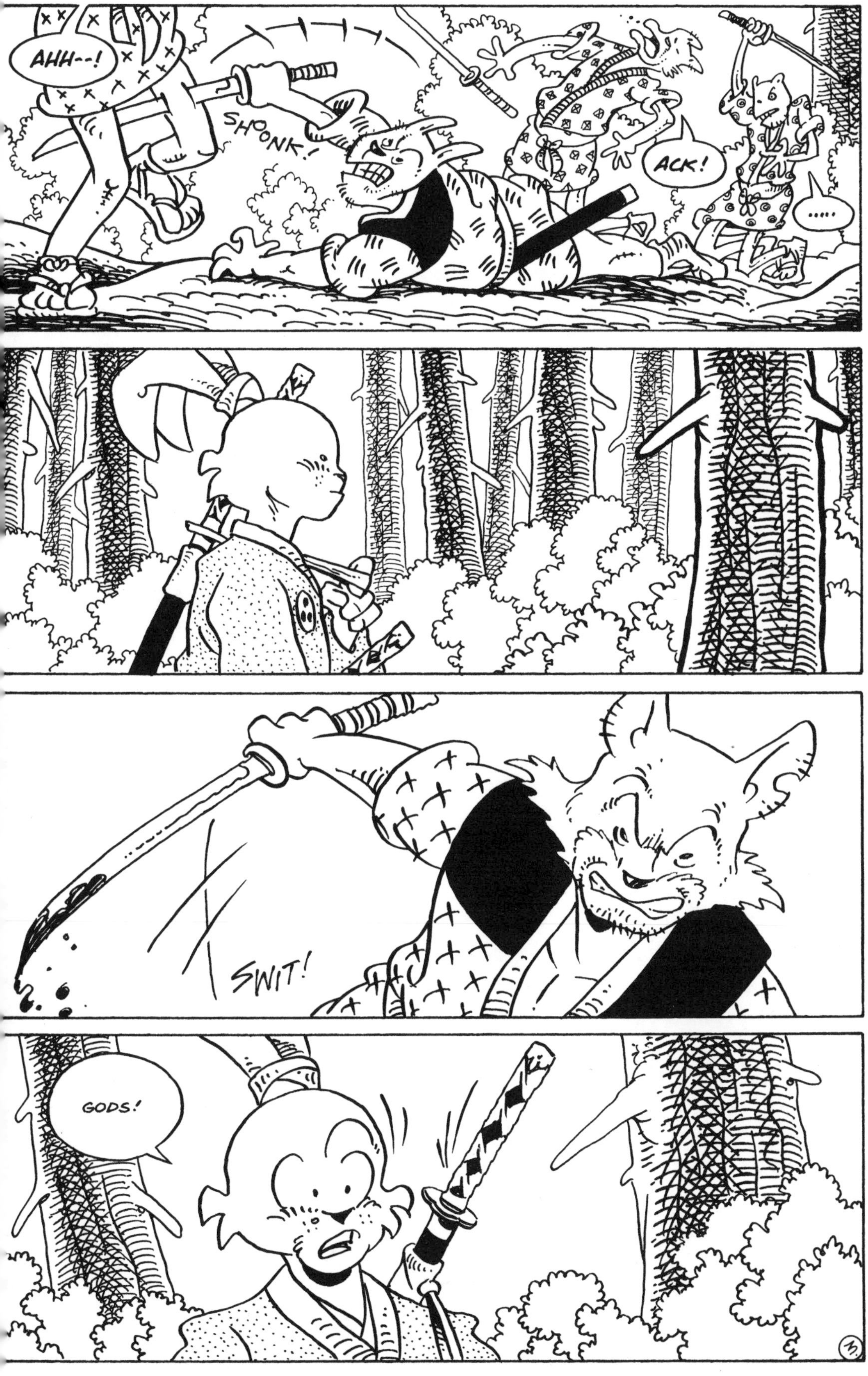
AHH--!
SHOONK!
ACK!
.....
SWIT!
GODS!
3.

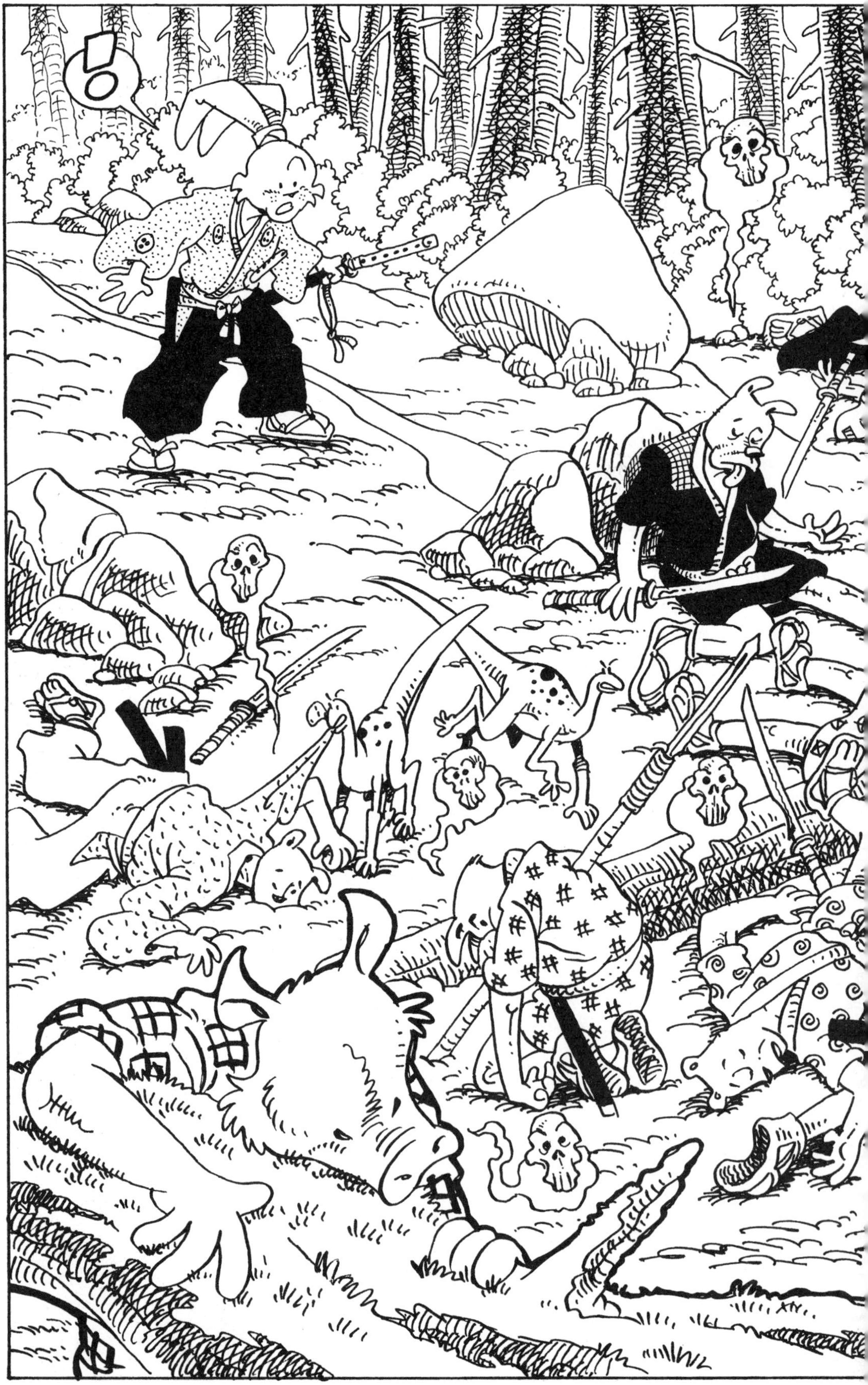
!?

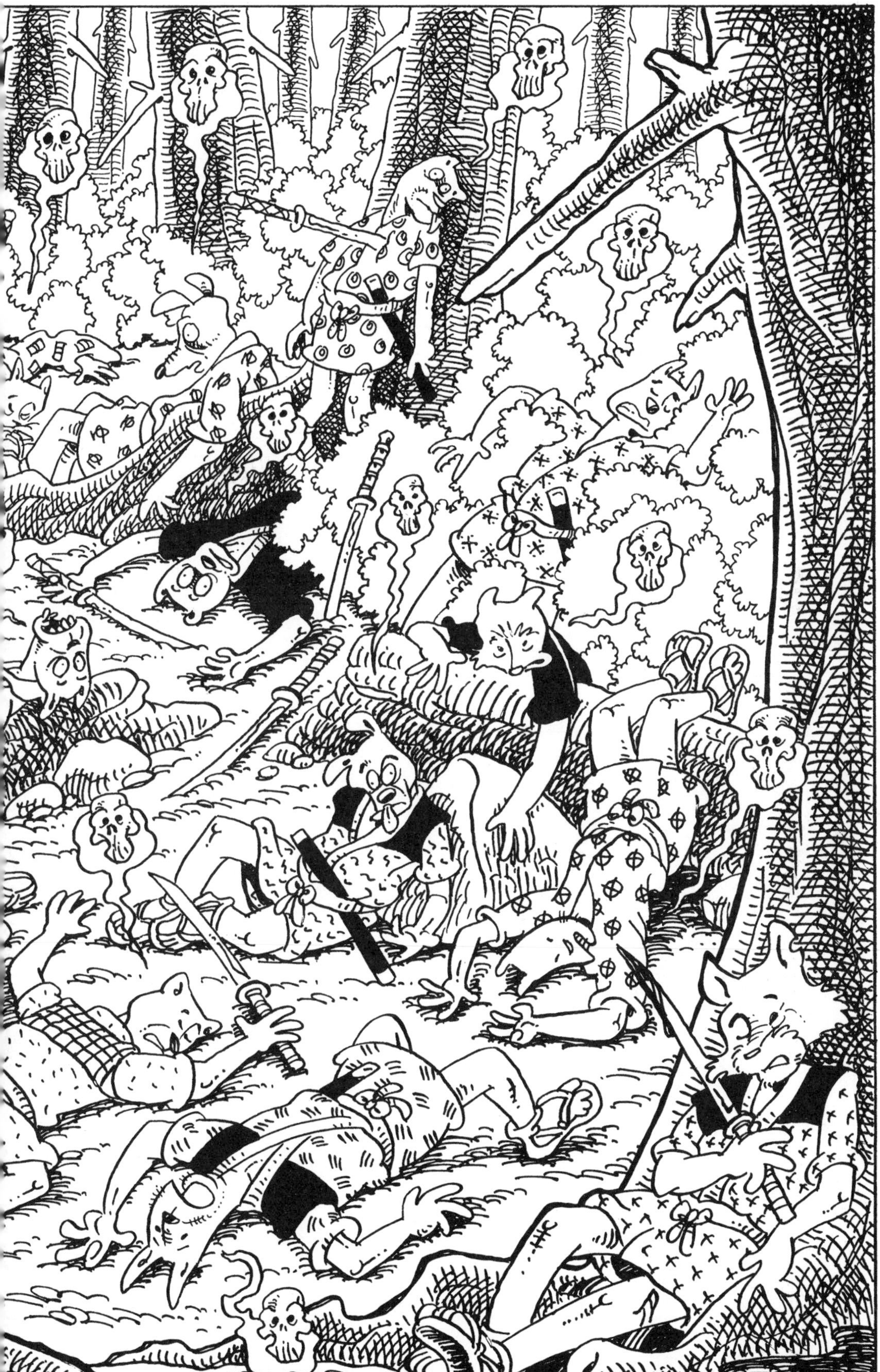

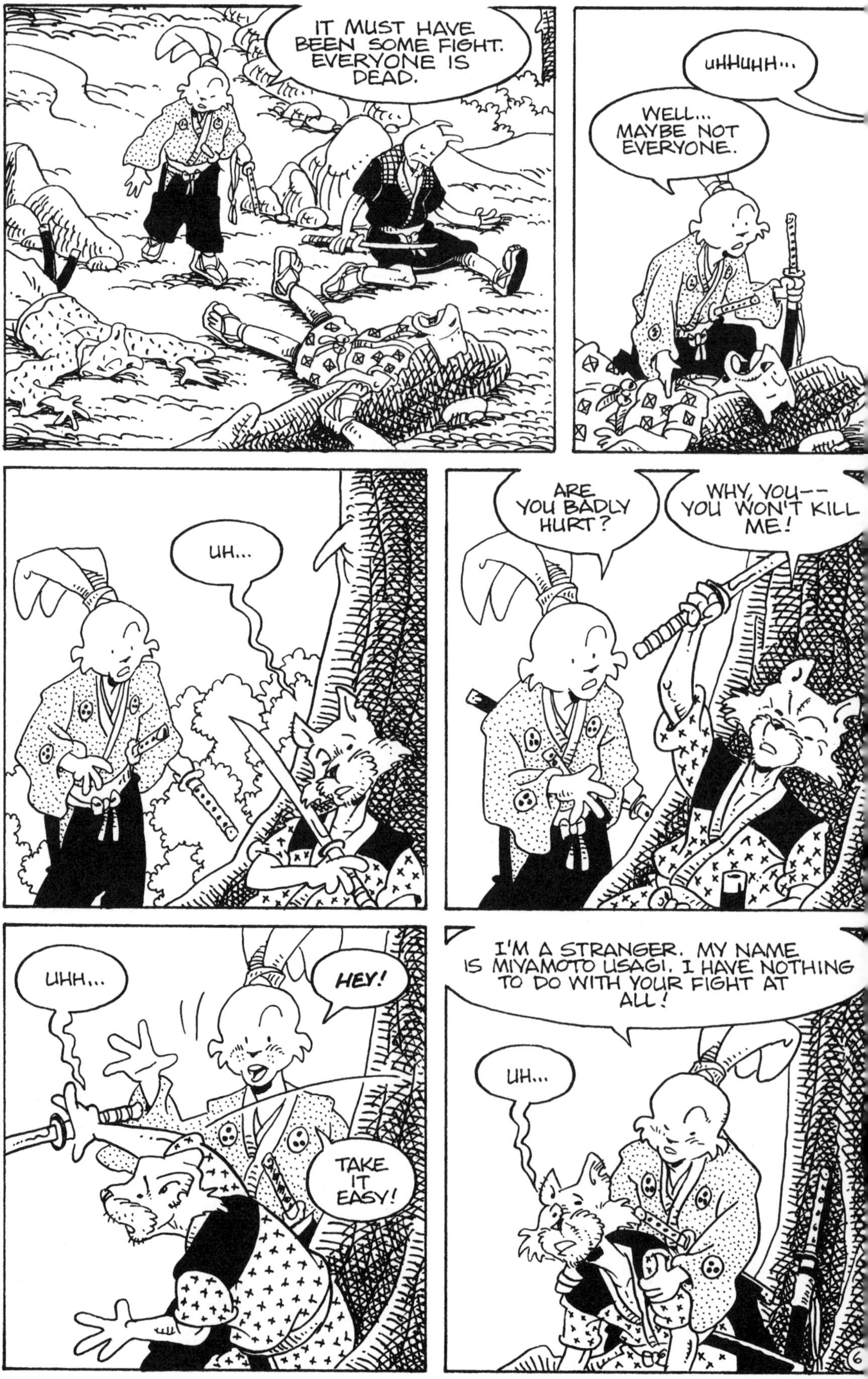
IT MUST HAVE BEEN SOME FIGHT. EVERYONE IS DEAD.
WELL... MAYBE NOT EVERYONE.
uHHuHH...
uH...
ARE YOU BADLY HURT?
WHY, YOU-- YOU WON'T KILL ME!
uHH...
HEY!
TAKE IT EASY!
I'M A STRANGER. MY NAME IS MIYAMOTO USAGI. I HAVE NOTHING TO DO WITH YOUR FIGHT AT ALL!
uH...
6

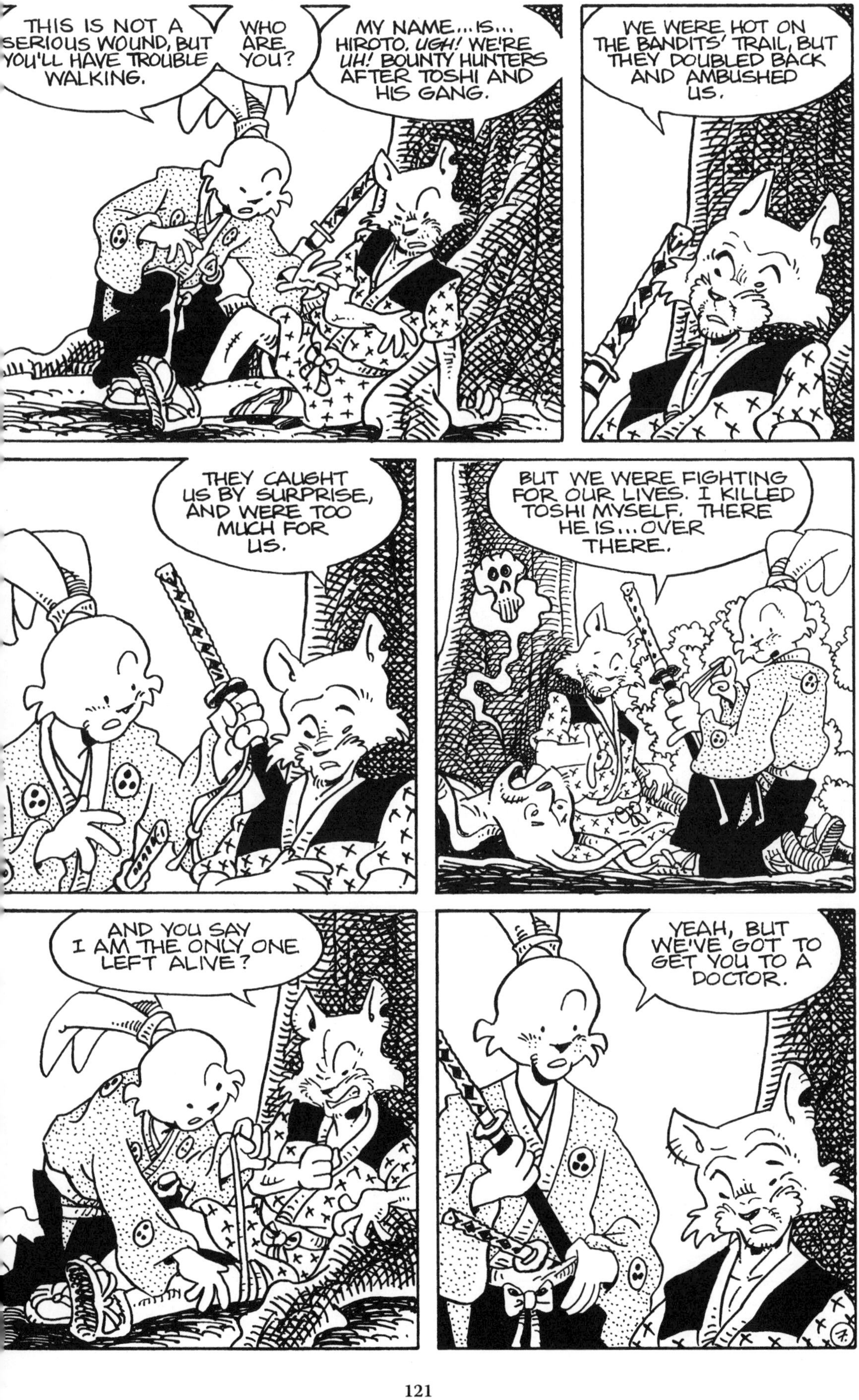
THIS IS NOT A SERIOUS WOUND, BUT YOU'LL HAVE TROUBLE WALKING.
WHO ARE YOU?
MY NAME... IS... HIROTO. *UGH!* WE'RE *UH!* BOUNTY HUNTERS AFTER TOSHI AND HIS GANG.
WE WERE HOT ON THE BANDITS' TRAIL, BUT THEY DOUBLED BACK AND AMBUSHED US.
THEY CAUGHT US BY SURPRISE, AND WERE TOO MUCH FOR US.
BUT WE WERE FIGHTING FOR OUR LIVES. I KILLED TOSHI MYSELF. THERE HE IS... OVER THERE.
AND YOU SAY I AM THE ONLY ONE LEFT ALIVE?
YEAH, BUT WE'VE GOT TO GET YOU TO A DOCTOR.

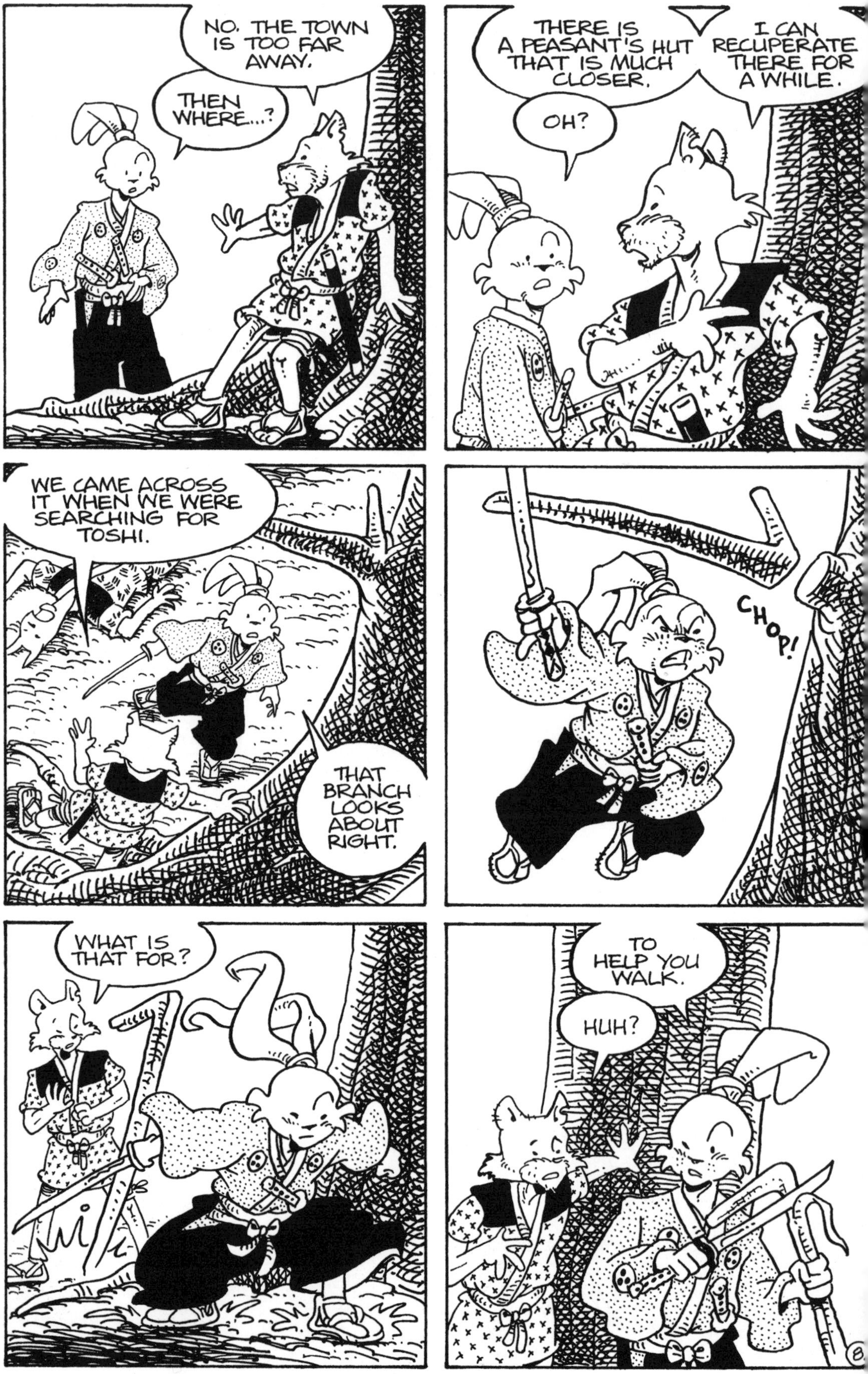
NO. THE TOWN IS TOO FAR AWAY.
THEN WHERE...?
THERE IS A PEASANT'S HUT THAT IS MUCH CLOSER.
I CAN RECUPERATE THERE FOR A WHILE.
OH?
WE CAME ACROSS IT WHEN WE WERE SEARCHING FOR TOSHI.
THAT BRANCH LOOKS ABOUT RIGHT.
CHOP!
WHAT IS THAT FOR?
TO HELP YOU WALK.
HUH?
8

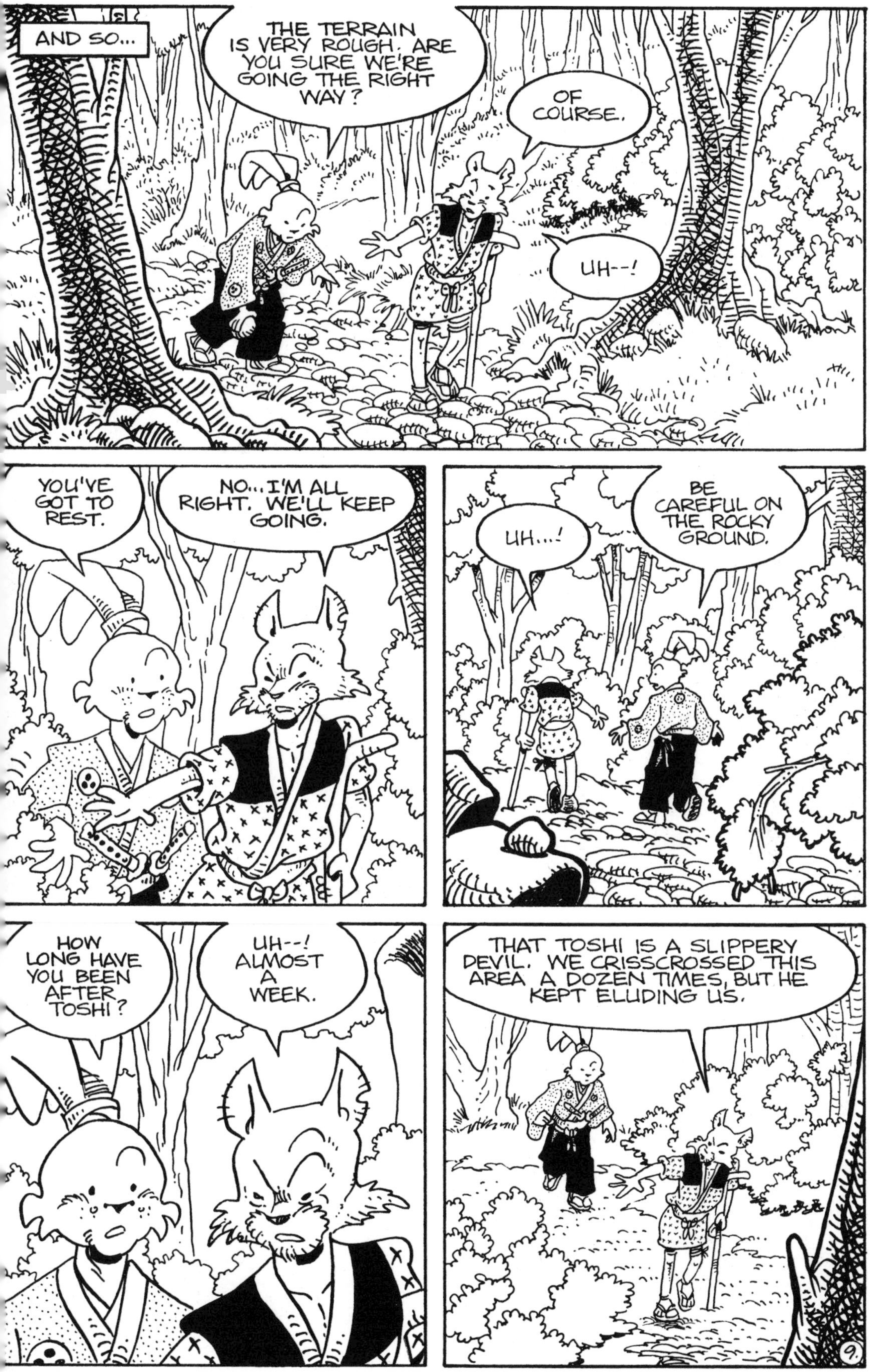
AND SO...
THE TERRAIN IS VERY ROUGH. ARE YOU SURE WE'RE GOING THE RIGHT WAY?
OF COURSE.
UH--!
YOU'VE GOT TO REST.
NO...I'M ALL RIGHT. WE'LL KEEP GOING.
UH...!
BE CAREFUL ON THE ROCKY GROUND.
HOW LONG HAVE YOU BEEN AFTER TOSHI?
UH--! ALMOST A WEEK.
THAT TOSHI IS A SLIPPERY DEVIL. WE CRISSCROSSED THIS AREA A DOZEN TIMES, BUT HE KEPT ELUDING US.
9.

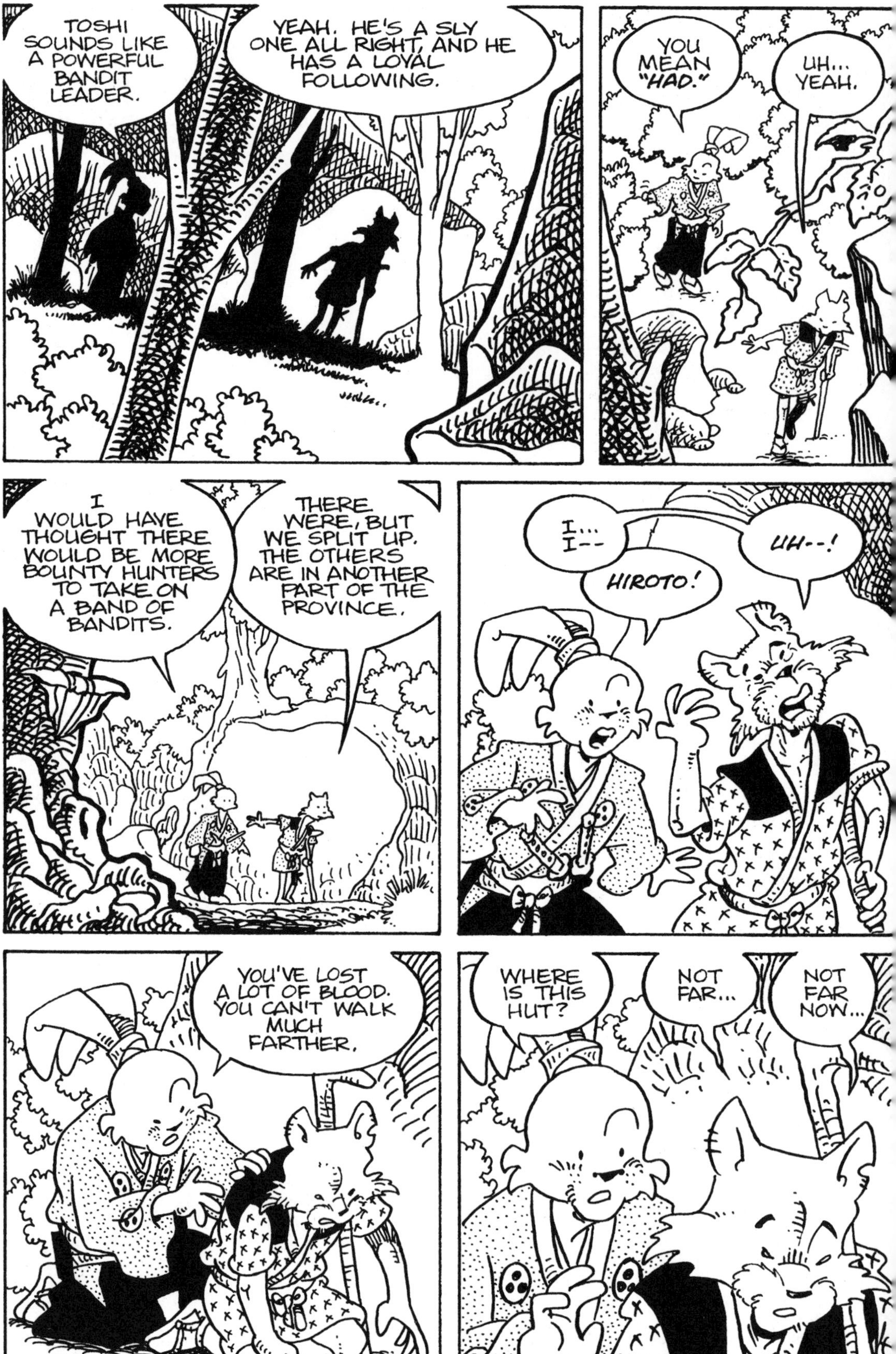
TOSHI SOUNDS LIKE A POWERFUL BANDIT LEADER.
YEAH. HE'S A SLY ONE ALL RIGHT, AND HE HAS A LOYAL FOLLOWING.
YOU MEAN "*HAD.*"
UH... YEAH.
I WOULD HAVE THOUGHT THERE WOULD BE MORE BOUNTY HUNTERS TO TAKE ON A BAND OF BANDITS.
THERE WERE, BUT WE SPLIT UP. THE OTHERS ARE IN ANOTHER PART OF THE PROVINCE.
I... I--
HIROTO!
UH--!
YOU'VE LOST A LOT OF BLOOD. YOU CAN'T WALK MUCH FARTHER.
WHERE IS THIS HUT?
NOT FAR...
NOT FAR NOW...
10

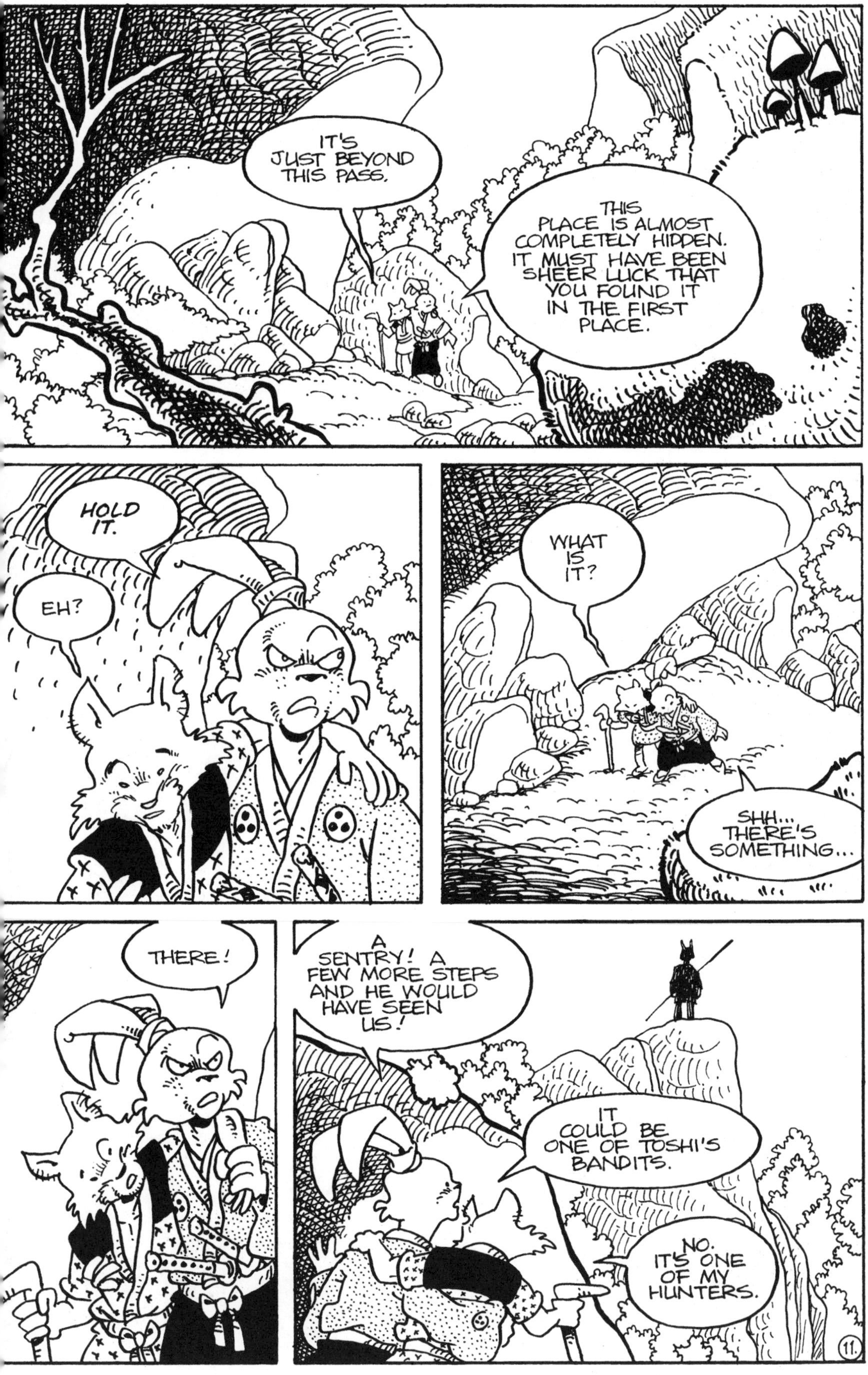
IT'S JUST BEYOND THIS PASS.
THIS PLACE IS ALMOST COMPLETELY HIDDEN. IT MUST HAVE BEEN SHEER LUCK THAT YOU FOUND IT IN THE FIRST PLACE.
HOLD IT.
EH?
WHAT IS IT?
SHH... THERE'S SOMETHING...
THERE!
A SENTRY! A FEW MORE STEPS AND HE WOULD HAVE SEEN US!
IT COULD BE ONE OF TOSHI'S BANDITS.
NO. IT'S ONE OF MY HUNTERS.
11.

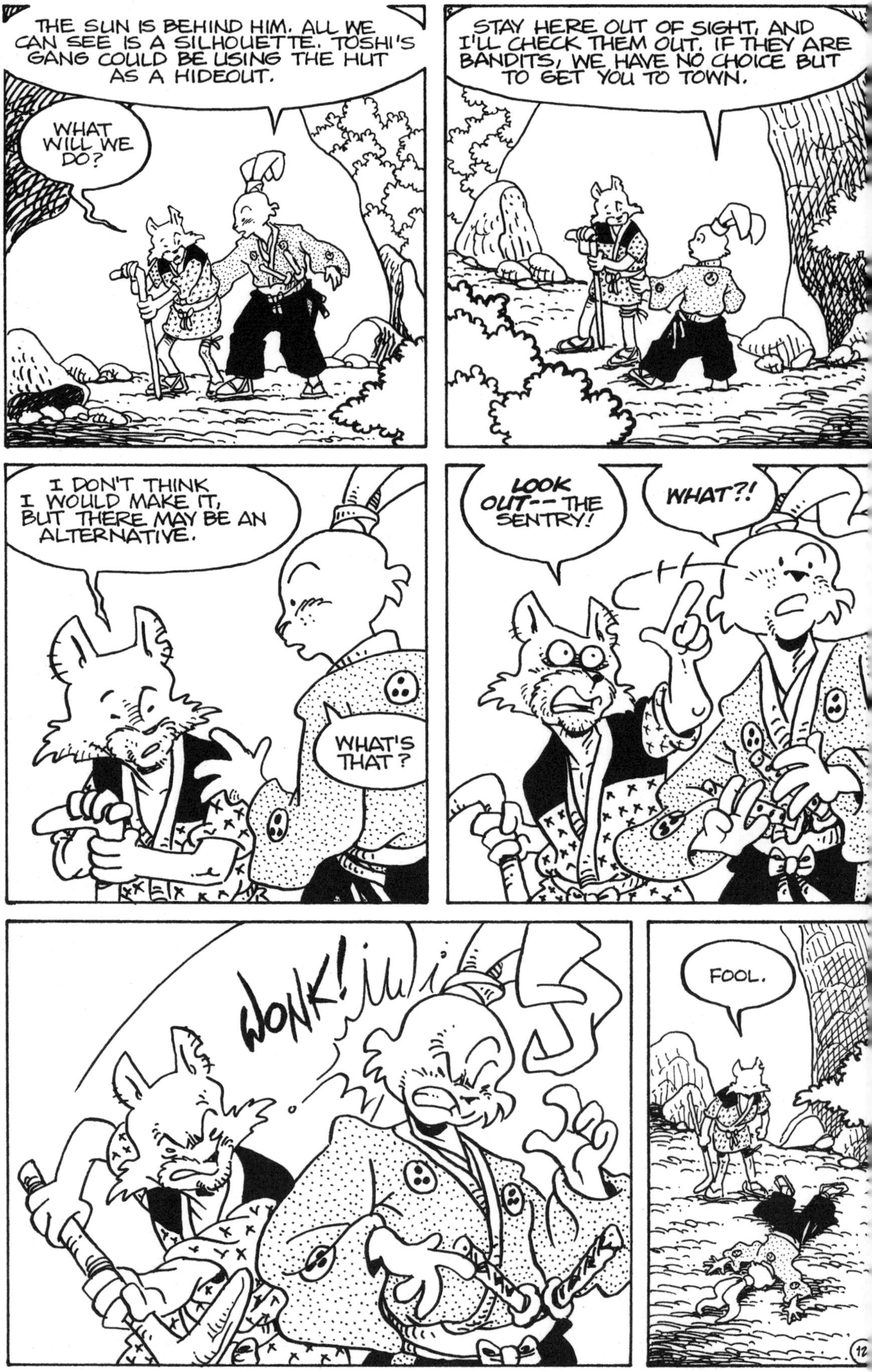
THE SUN IS BEHIND HIM. ALL WE CAN SEE IS A SILHOUETTE. TOSHI'S GANG COULD BE USING THE HUT AS A HIDEOUT.
WHAT WILL WE DO?
STAY HERE OUT OF SIGHT, AND I'LL CHECK THEM OUT. IF THEY ARE BANDITS, WE HAVE NO CHOICE BUT TO GET YOU TO TOWN.
I DON'T THINK I WOULD MAKE IT, BUT THERE MAY BE AN ALTERNATIVE.
WHAT'S THAT?
LOOK OUT-- THE SENTRY!
WHAT?!
WONK!
FOOL.
12

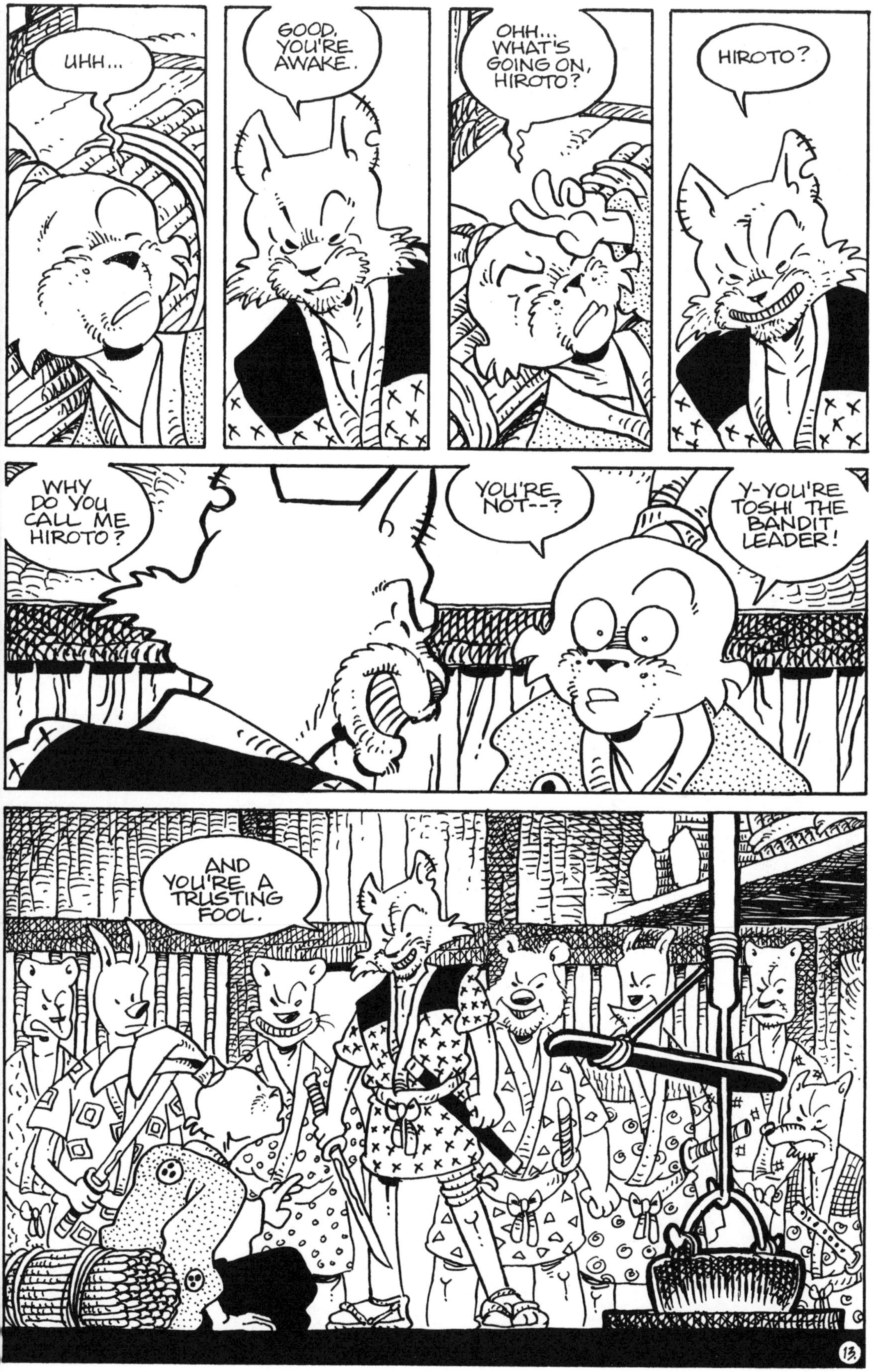
UHH...
GOOD, YOU'RE AWAKE.
OHH... WHAT'S GOING ON, HIROTO?
HIROTO?
WHY DO YOU CALL ME HIROTO?
YOU'RE NOT--?
Y-YOU'RE TOSHI THE BANDIT LEADER!
AND YOU'RE A TRUSTING FOOL.
13

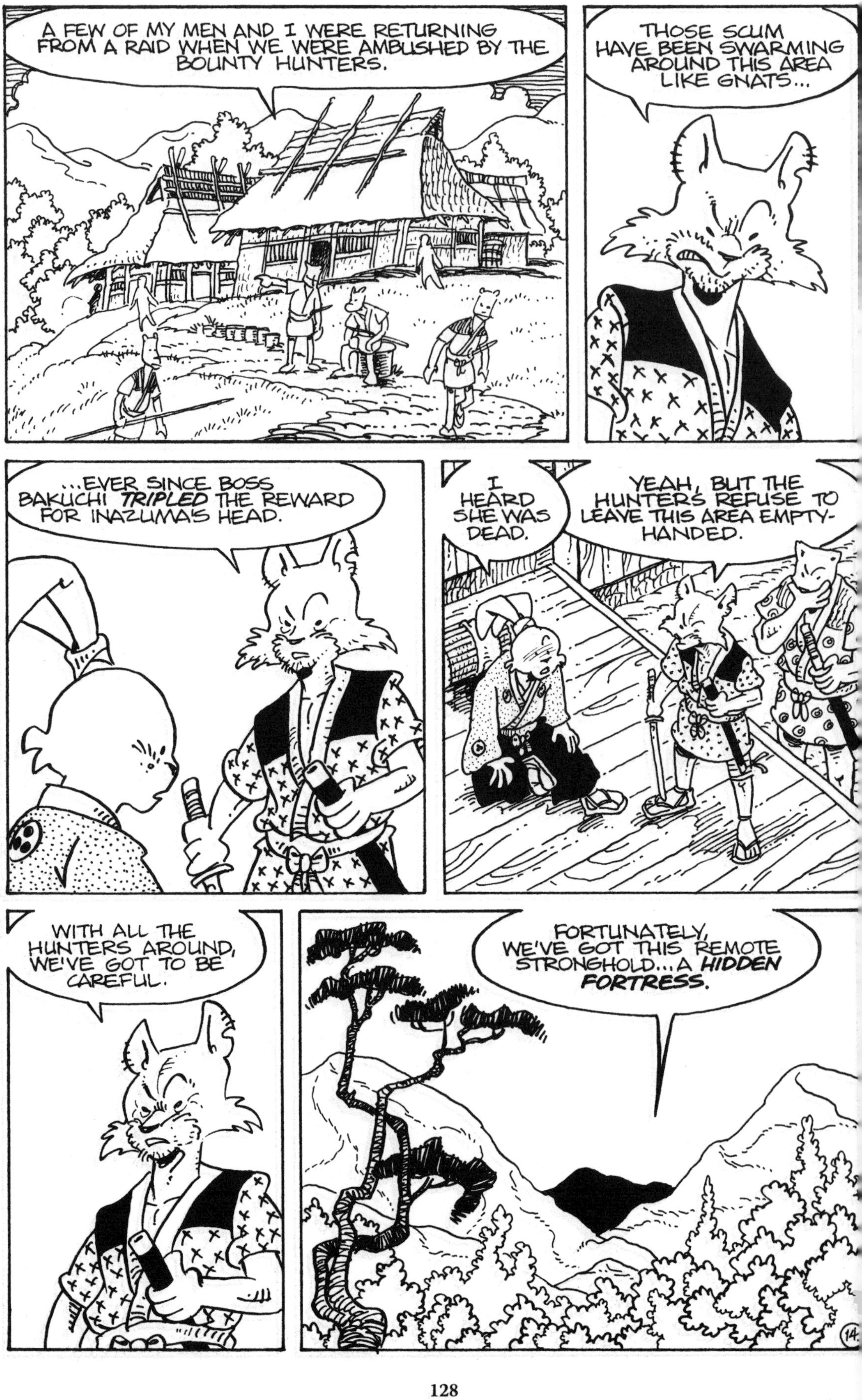
A FEW OF MY MEN AND I WERE RETURNING FROM A RAID WHEN WE WERE AMBUSHED BY THE BOUNTY HUNTERS.
THOSE SCUM HAVE BEEN SWARMING AROUND THIS AREA LIKE GNATS...
...EVER SINCE BOSS BAKUCHI *TRIPLED* THE REWARD FOR INAZUMA'S HEAD.
I HEARD SHE WAS DEAD.
YEAH, BUT THE HUNTERS REFUSE TO LEAVE THIS AREA EMPTY-HANDED.
WITH ALL THE HUNTERS AROUND, WE'VE GOT TO BE CAREFUL.
FORTUNATELY, WE'VE GOT THIS REMOTE STRONGHOLD...A ***HIDDEN FORTRESS***.
14

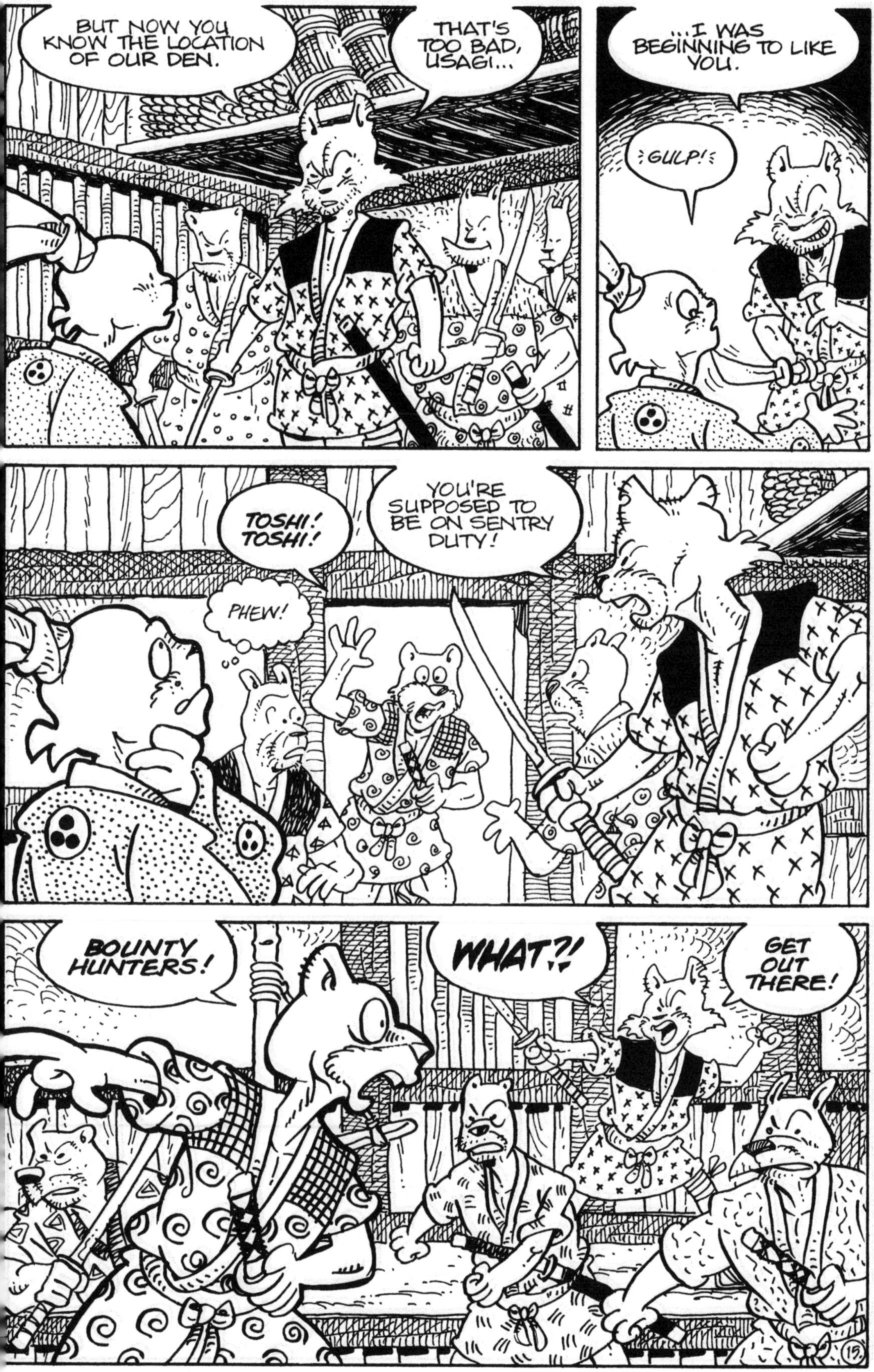
BUT NOW YOU KNOW THE LOCATION OF OUR DEN.
THAT'S TOO BAD, USAGI...
...I WAS BEGINNING TO LIKE YOU.
GULP!
TOSHI! TOSHI!
YOU'RE SUPPOSED TO BE ON SENTRY DUTY!
PHEW!
BOUNTY HUNTERS!
WHAT?!
GET OUT THERE!
15

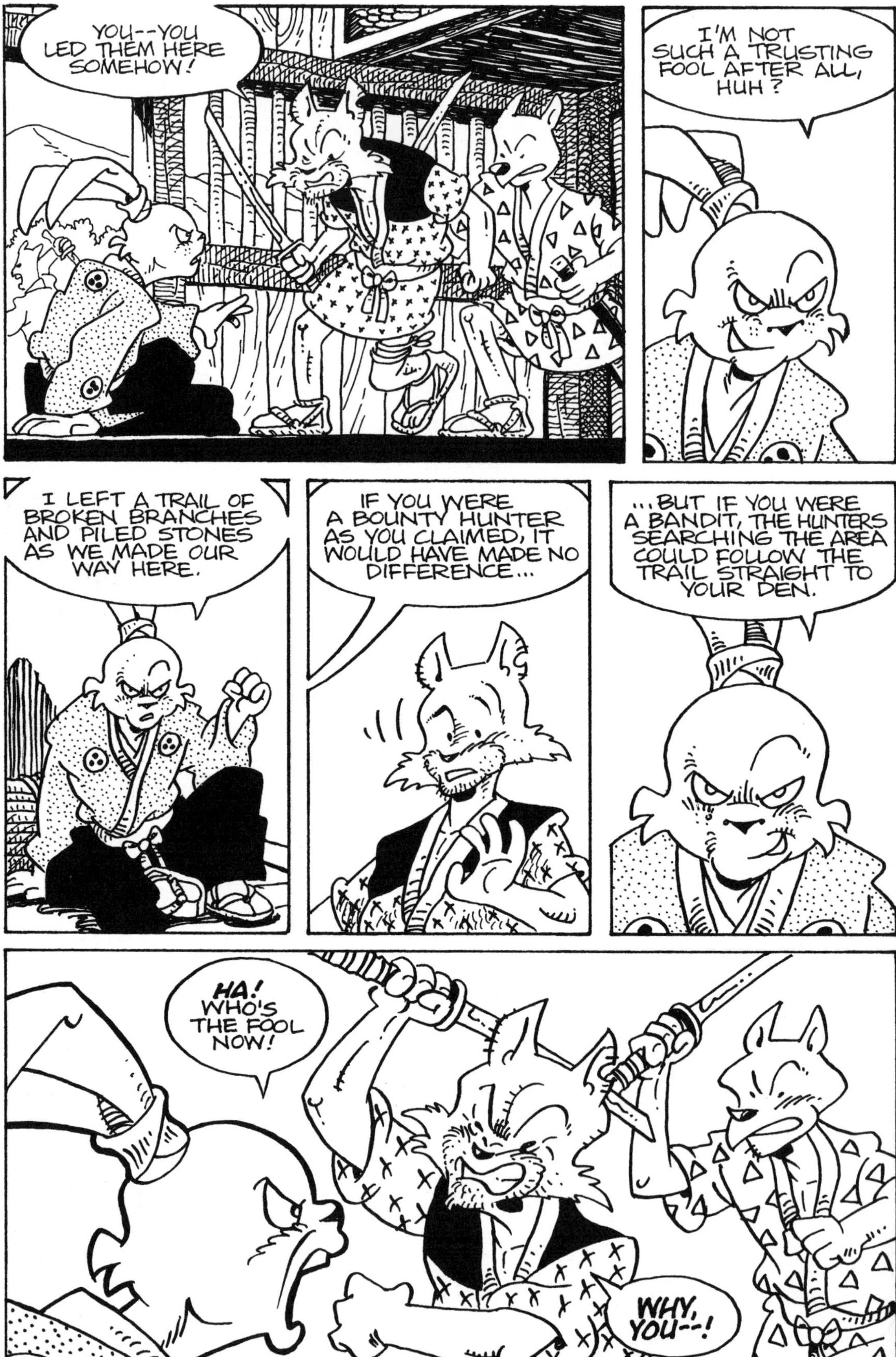
YOU--YOU LED THEM HERE SOMEHOW!
I'M NOT SUCH A TRUSTING FOOL AFTER ALL, HUH?
I LEFT A TRAIL OF BROKEN BRANCHES AND PILED STONES AS WE MADE OUR WAY HERE.
IF YOU WERE A BOUNTY HUNTER AS YOU CLAIMED, IT WOULD HAVE MADE NO DIFFERENCE...
...BUT IF YOU WERE A BANDIT, THE HUNTERS SEARCHING THE AREA COULD FOLLOW THE TRAIL STRAIGHT TO YOUR DEN.
HA! WHO'S THE FOOL NOW!
WHY, YOU--!
16

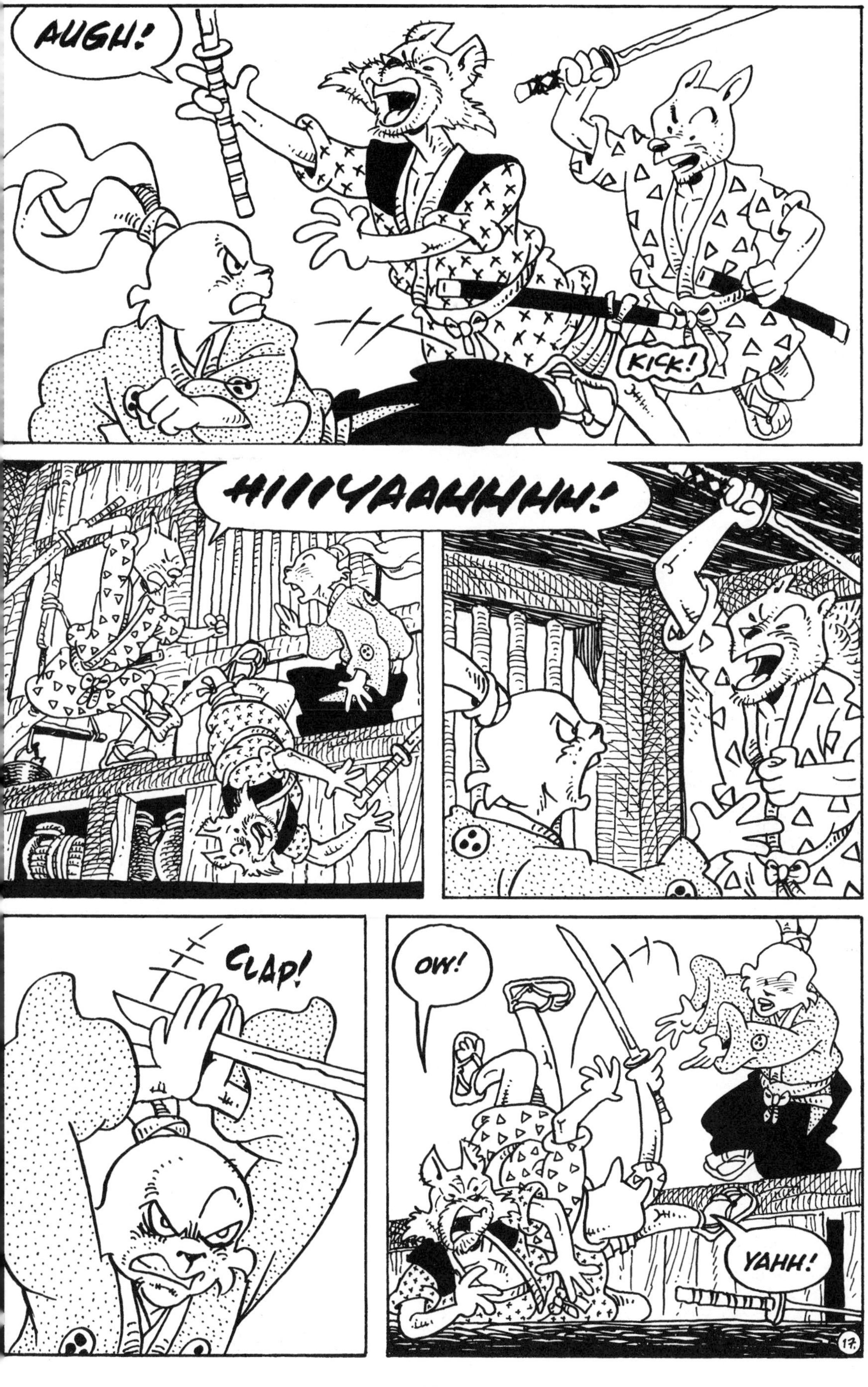

AUGH!
KICK!
HIIIYAAHHHH!
CLAP!
OW!
YAHH!
17

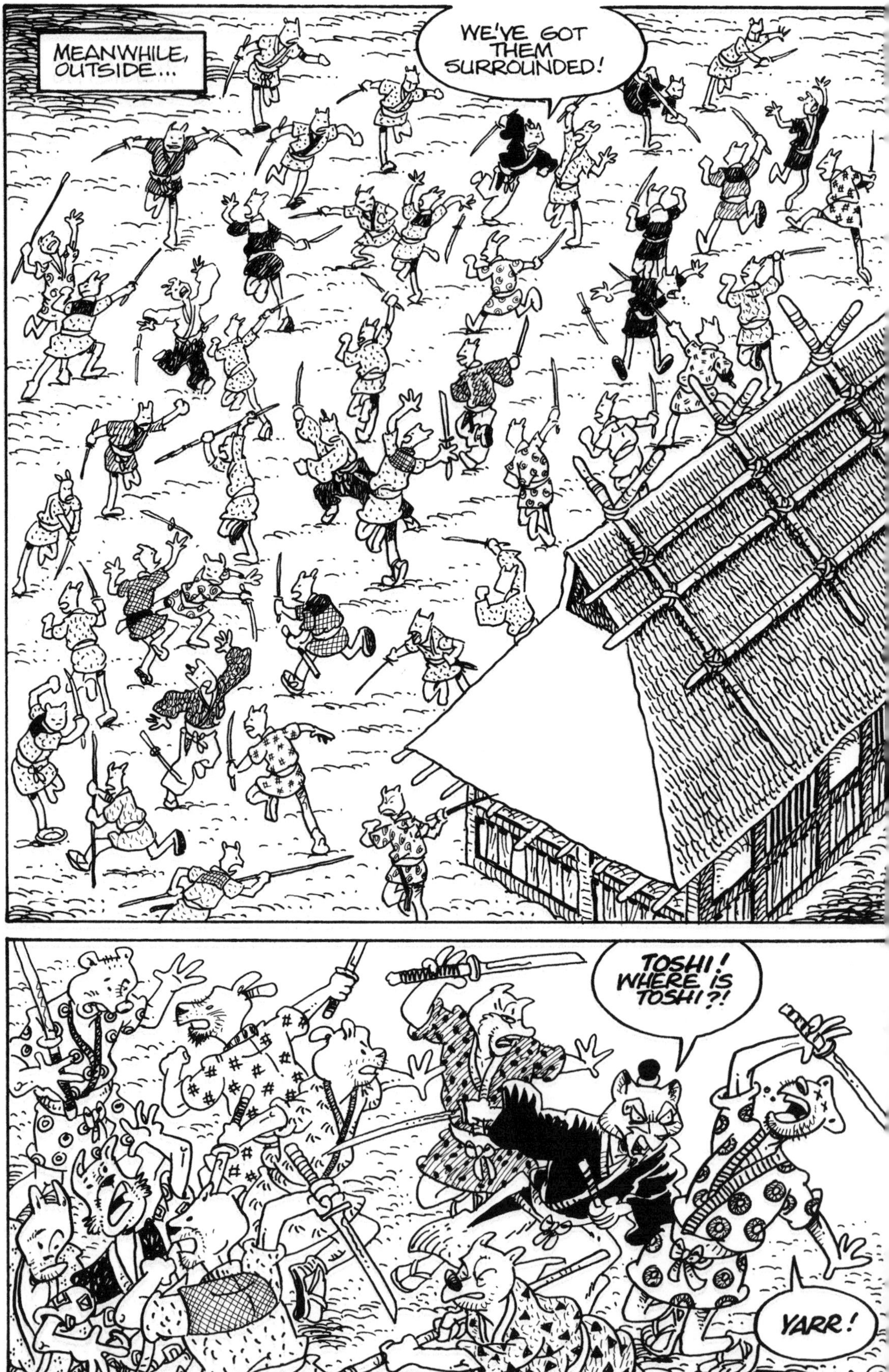
MEANWHILE, OUTSIDE...
WE'VE GOT THEM SURROUNDED!
TOSHI! WHERE IS TOSHI?!
YARR!

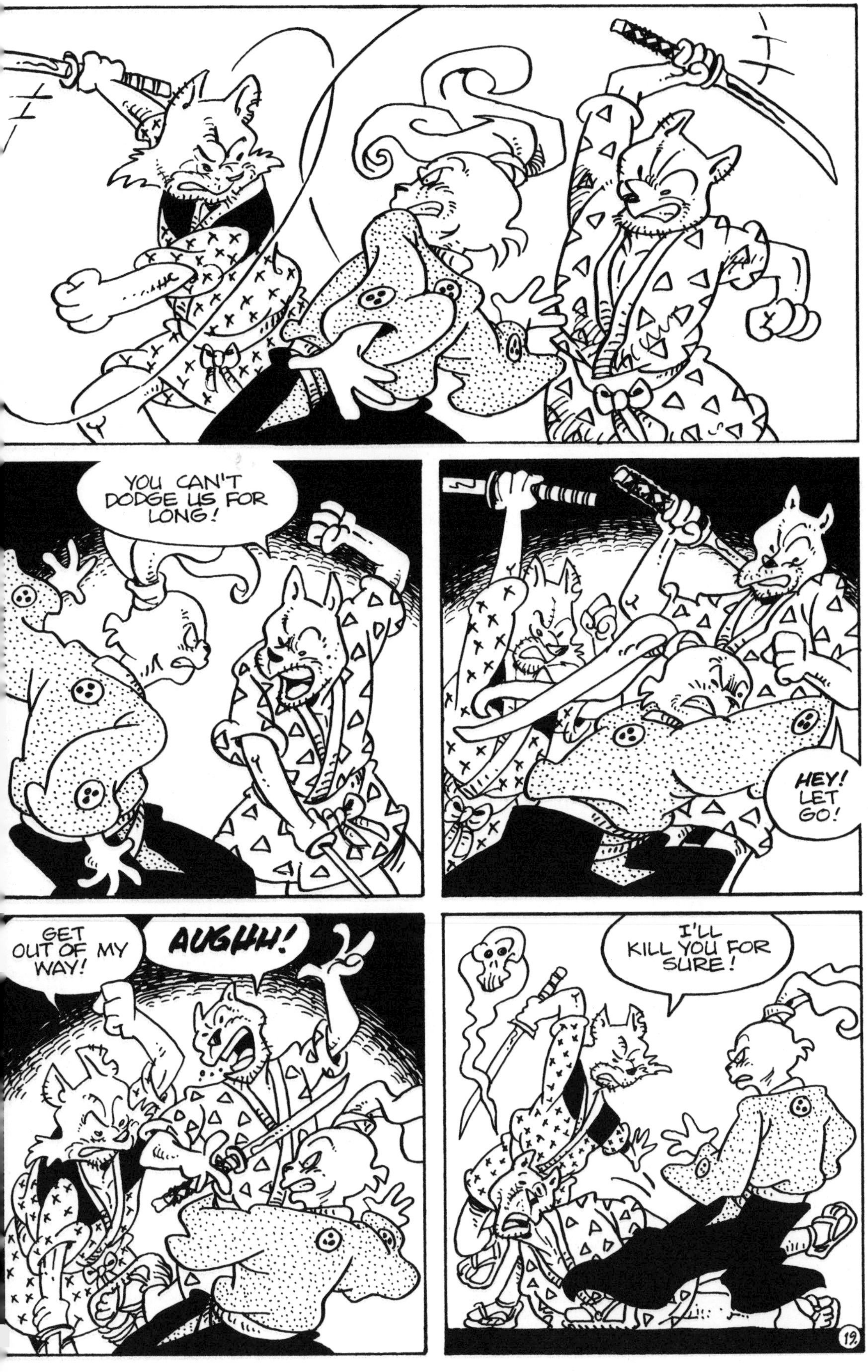
YOU CAN'T DODGE US FOR LONG!
HEY! LET GO!
GET OUT OF MY WAY!
AUGHH!
I'LL KILL YOU FOR SURE!
19

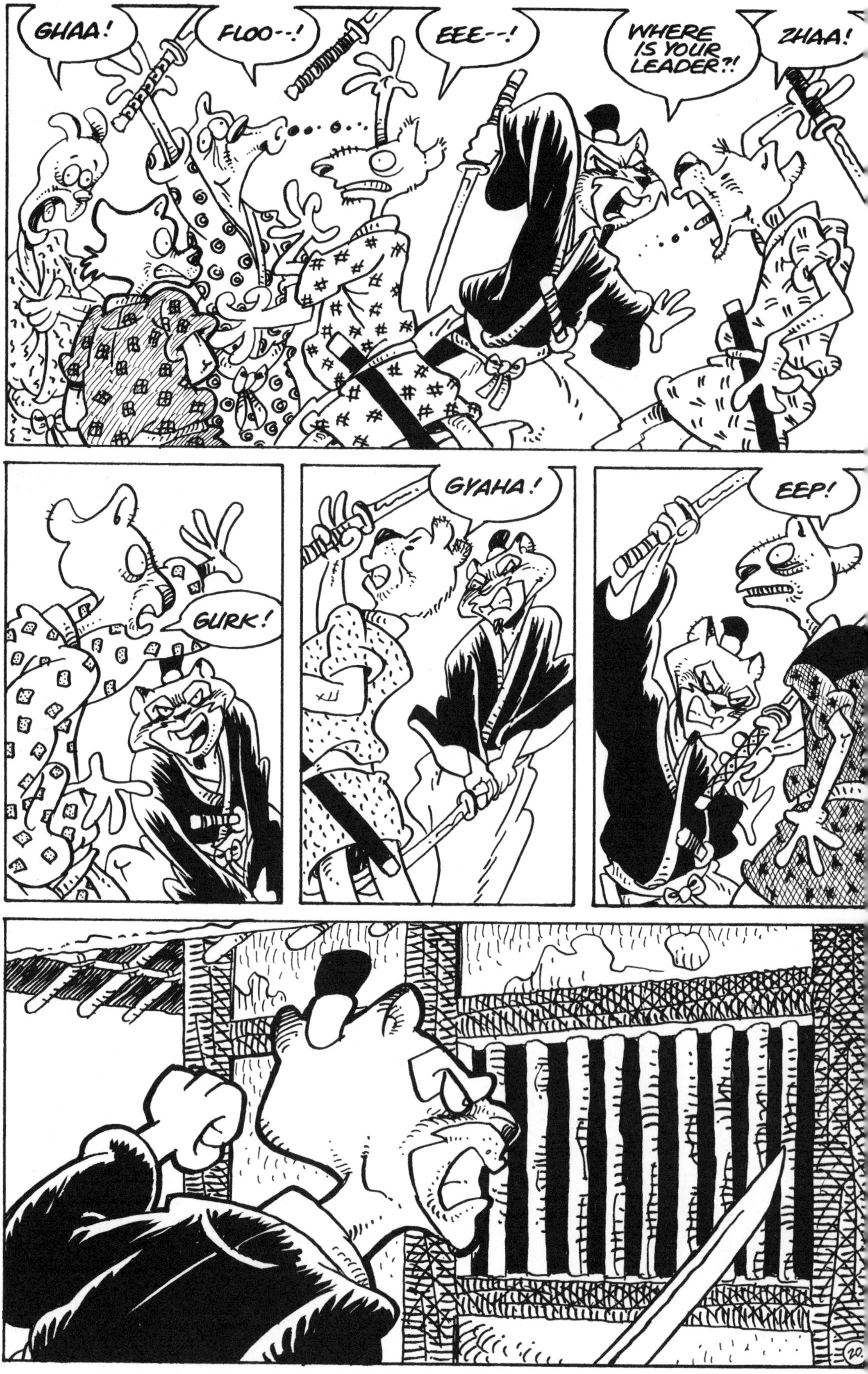
GHAA!
FLOO--!
EEE--!
WHERE IS YOUR LEADER?!
ZHAA!
GURK!
GYAHA!
EEP!
20

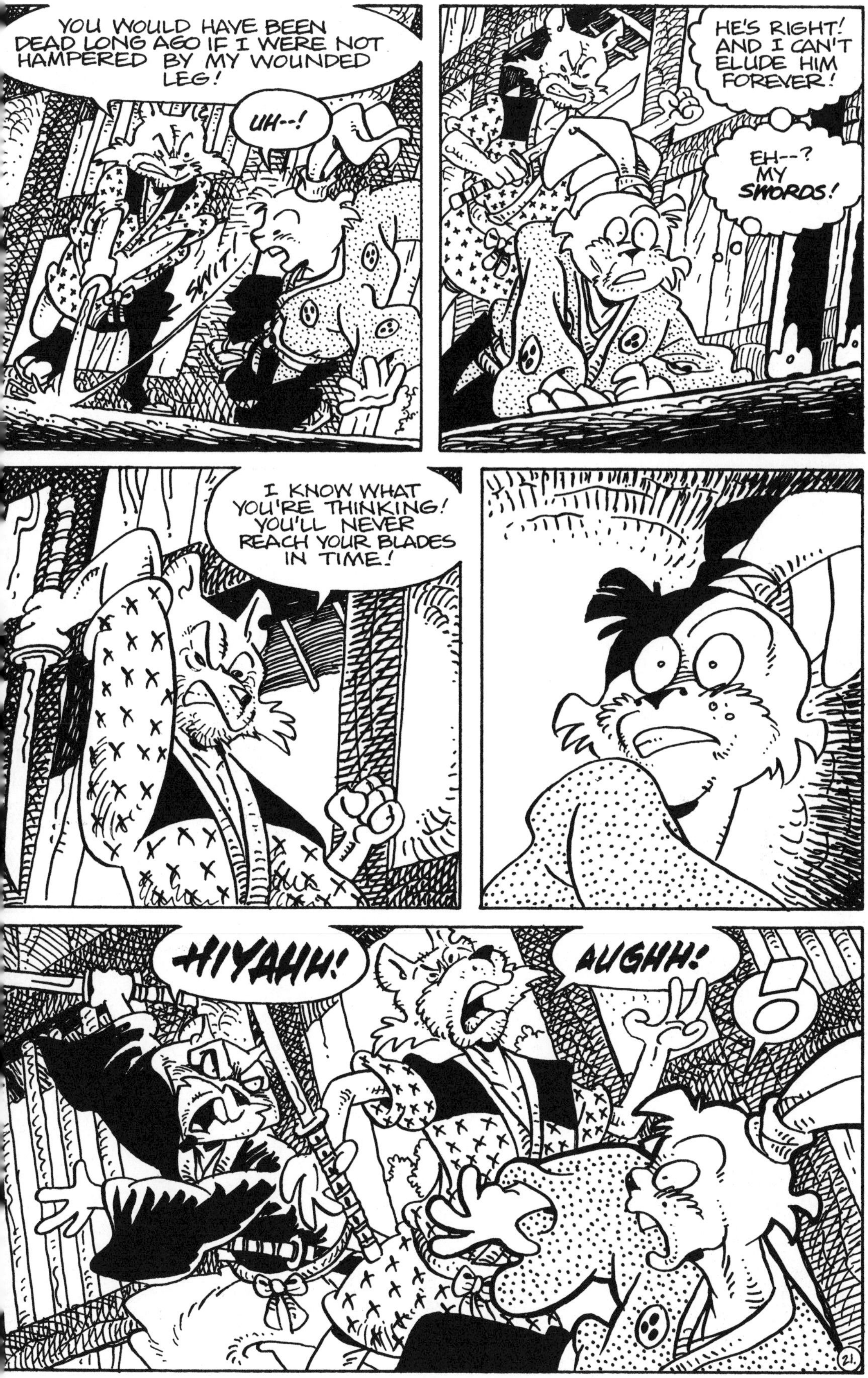
YOU WOULD HAVE BEEN DEAD LONG AGO IF I WERE NOT HAMPERED BY MY WOUNDED LEG!
UH--!
SWIT!
HE'S RIGHT! AND I CAN'T ELUDE HIM FOREVER!
EH--? MY SWORDS!
I KNOW WHAT YOU'RE THINKING! YOU'LL NEVER REACH YOUR BLADES IN TIME!
HIYAHH!
AUGHH!
21.

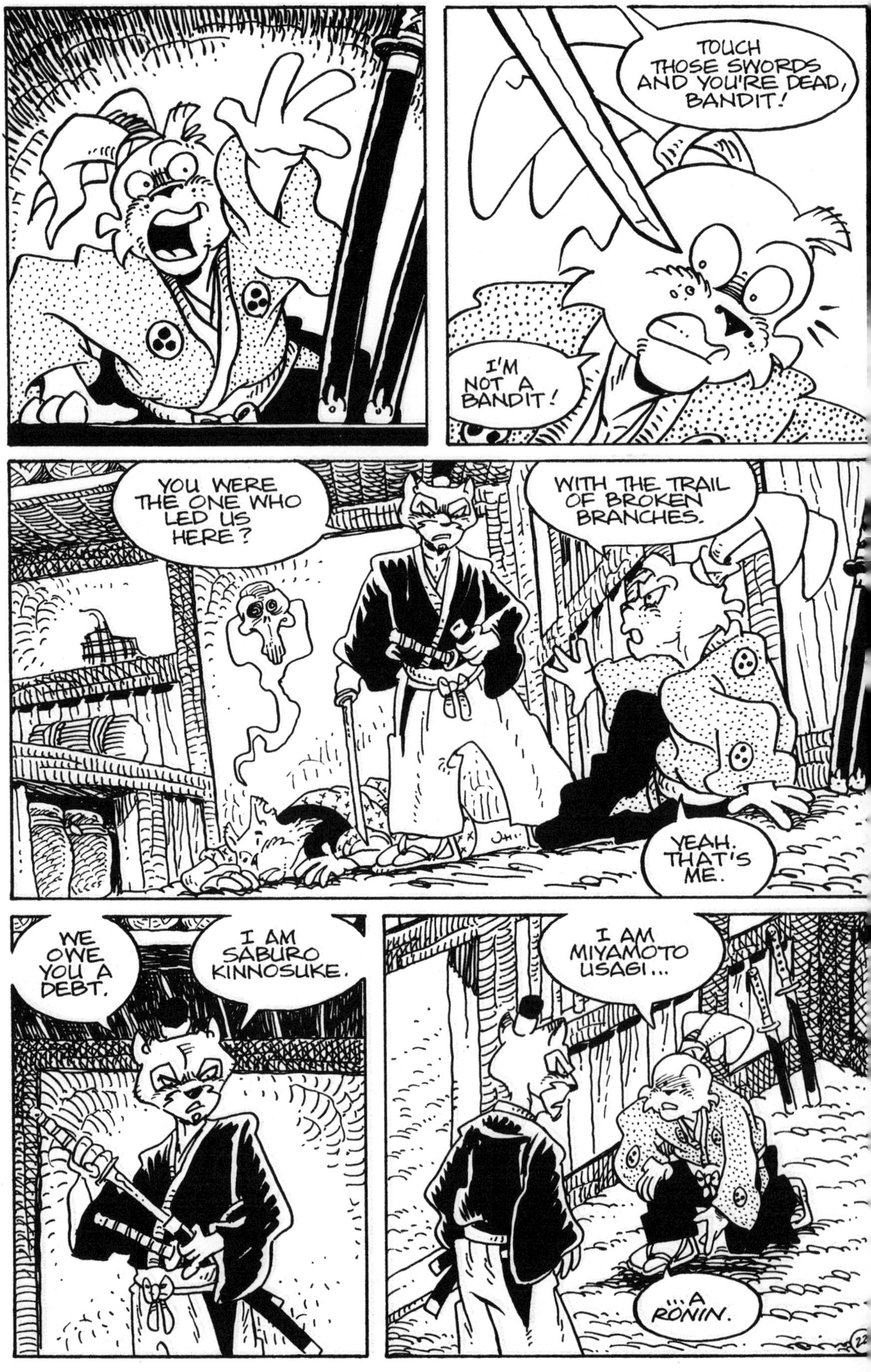
TOUCH THOSE SWORDS AND YOU'RE DEAD, BANDIT!
I'M NOT A BANDIT!
YOU WERE THE ONE WHO LED US HERE?
WITH THE TRAIL OF BROKEN BRANCHES.
YEAH. THAT'S ME.
WE OWE YOU A DEBT.
I AM SABURO KINNOSUKE.
I AM MIYAMOTO USAGI...
...A RONIN.

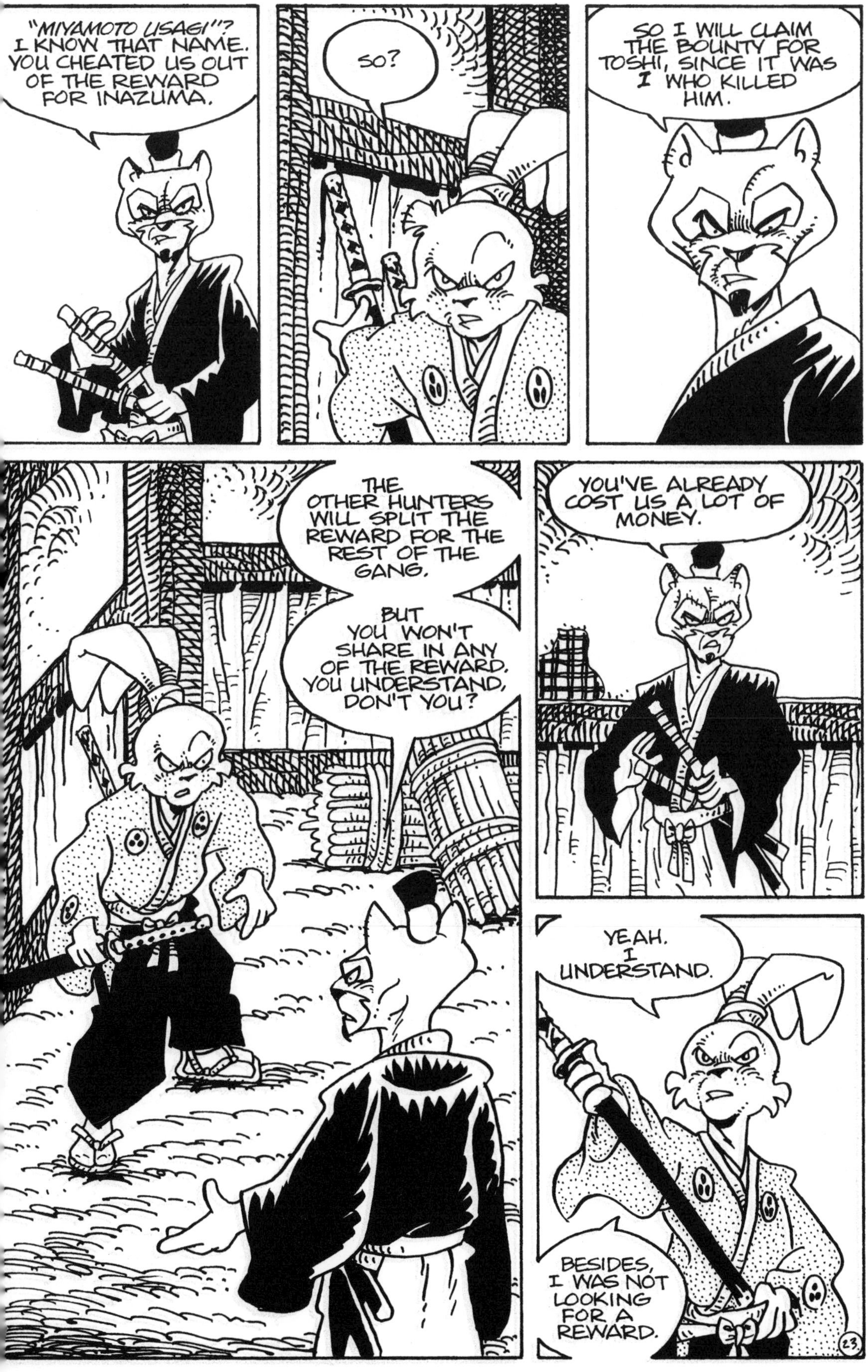
"MIYAMOTO USAGI"? I KNOW THAT NAME. YOU CHEATED US OUT OF THE REWARD FOR INAZUMA.
SO?
SO I WILL CLAIM THE BOUNTY FOR TOSHI, SINCE IT WAS I WHO KILLED HIM.
THE OTHER HUNTERS WILL SPLIT THE REWARD FOR THE REST OF THE GANG.
BUT YOU WON'T SHARE IN ANY OF THE REWARD. YOU UNDERSTAND, DON'T YOU?
YOU'VE ALREADY COST US A LOT OF MONEY.
YEAH. I UNDERSTAND.
BESIDES, I WAS NOT LOOKING FOR A REWARD.
23

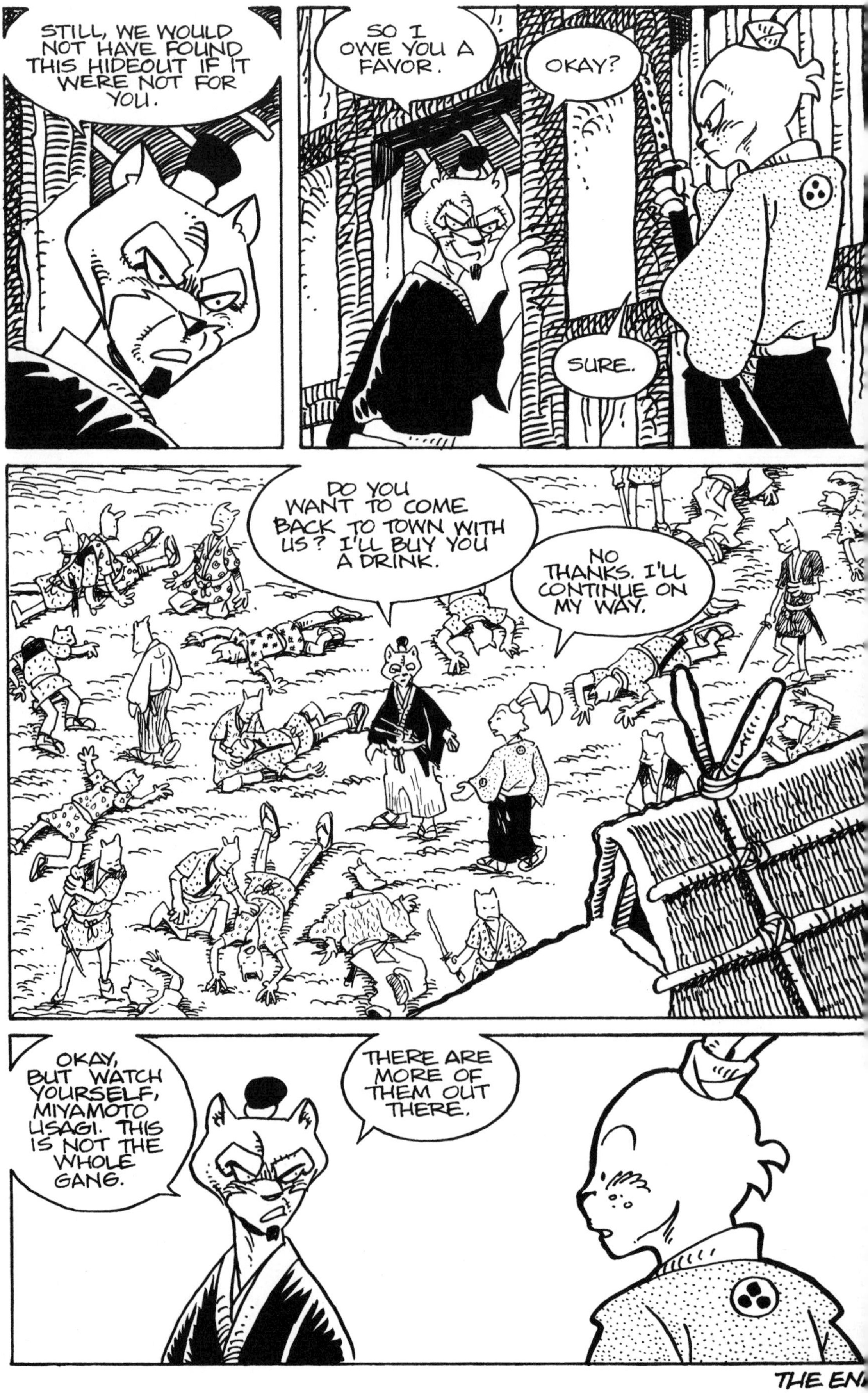
STILL, WE WOULD NOT HAVE FOUND THIS HIDEOUT IF IT WERE NOT FOR YOU.
SO I OWE YOU A FAVOR.
OKAY?
SURE.
DO YOU WANT TO COME BACK TO TOWN WITH US? I'LL BUY YOU A DRINK.
NO THANKS. I'LL CONTINUE ON MY WAY.
OKAY, BUT WATCH YOURSELF, MIYAMOTO USAGI. THIS IS NOT THE WHOLE GANG.
THERE ARE MORE OF THEM OUT THERE.
THE EN

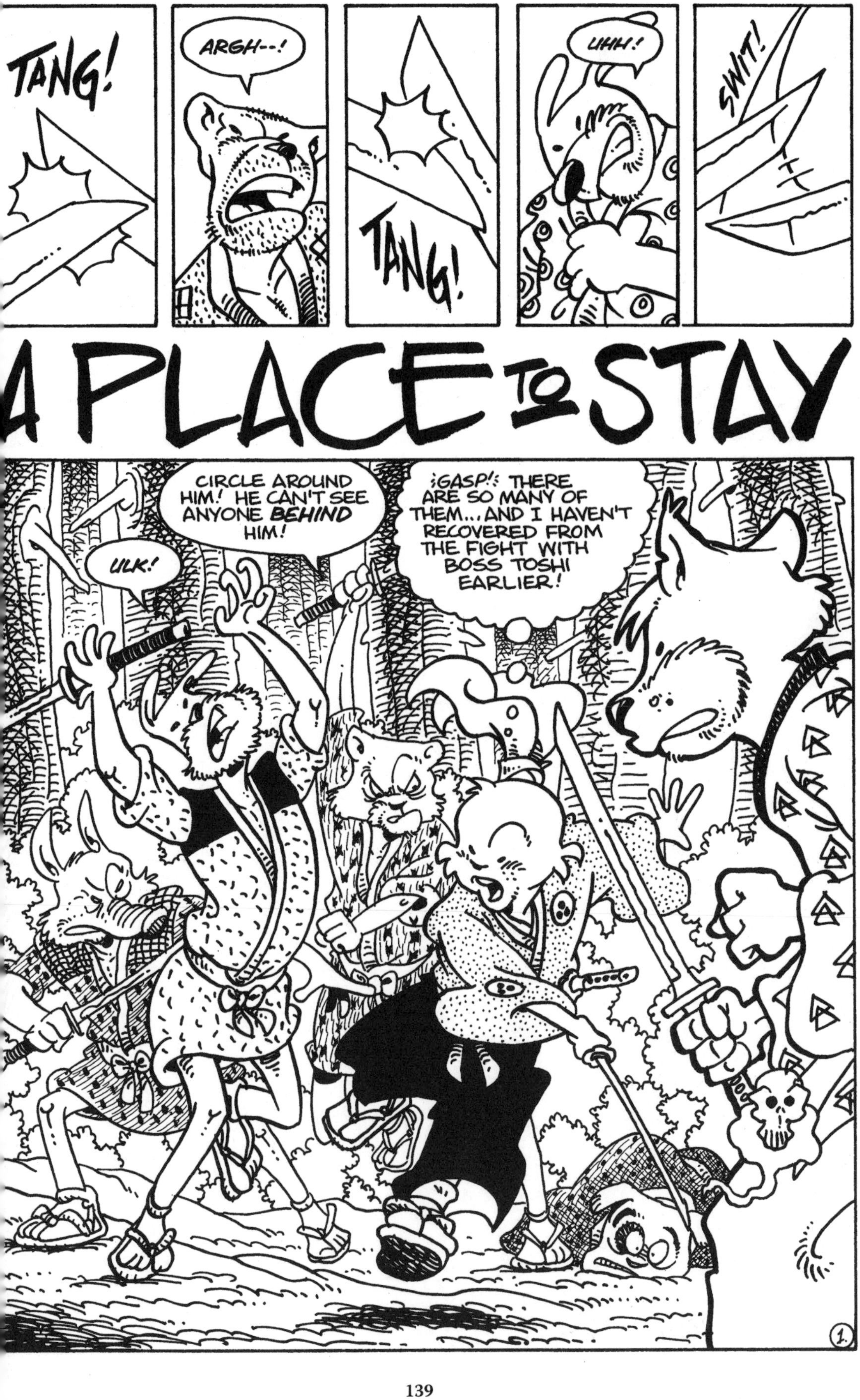
TANG!
ARGH--!
TANG!
UHH!
SWIT!
A PLACE TO STAY
ULK!
CIRCLE AROUND HIM! HE CAN'T SEE ANYONE BEHIND HIM!
¡GASP!¡ THERE ARE SO MANY OF THEM... AND I HAVEN'T RECOVERED FROM THE FIGHT WITH BOSS TOSHI EARLIER!
1.

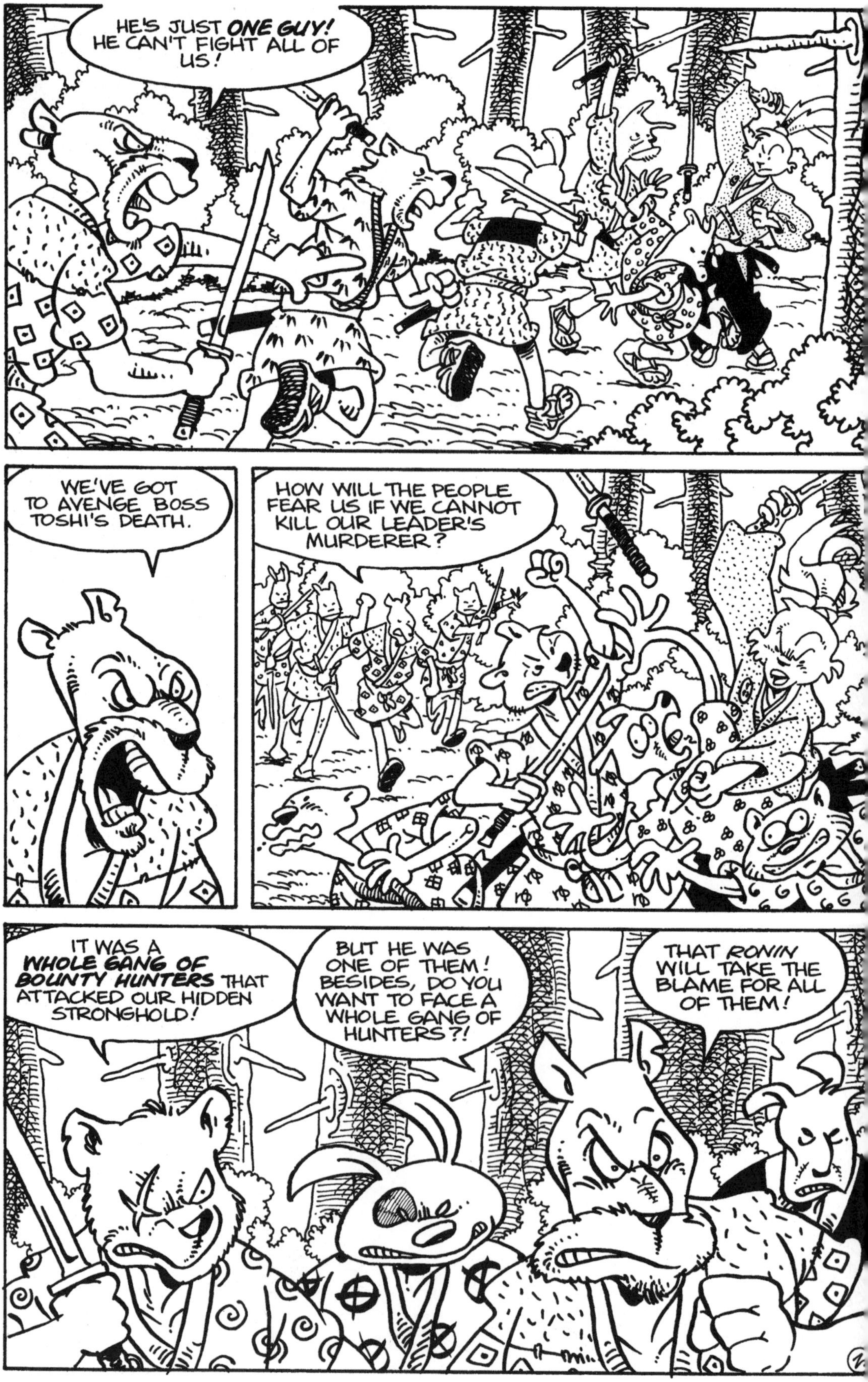
HE'S JUST ONE GUY! HE CAN'T FIGHT ALL OF US!
WE'VE GOT TO AVENGE BOSS TOSHI'S DEATH.
HOW WILL THE PEOPLE FEAR US IF WE CANNOT KILL OUR LEADER'S MURDERER?
IT WAS A WHOLE GANG OF BOUNTY HUNTERS THAT ATTACKED OUR HIDDEN STRONGHOLD!
BUT HE WAS ONE OF THEM! BESIDES, DO YOU WANT TO FACE A WHOLE GANG OF HUNTERS?!
THAT RONIN WILL TAKE THE BLAME FOR ALL OF THEM!

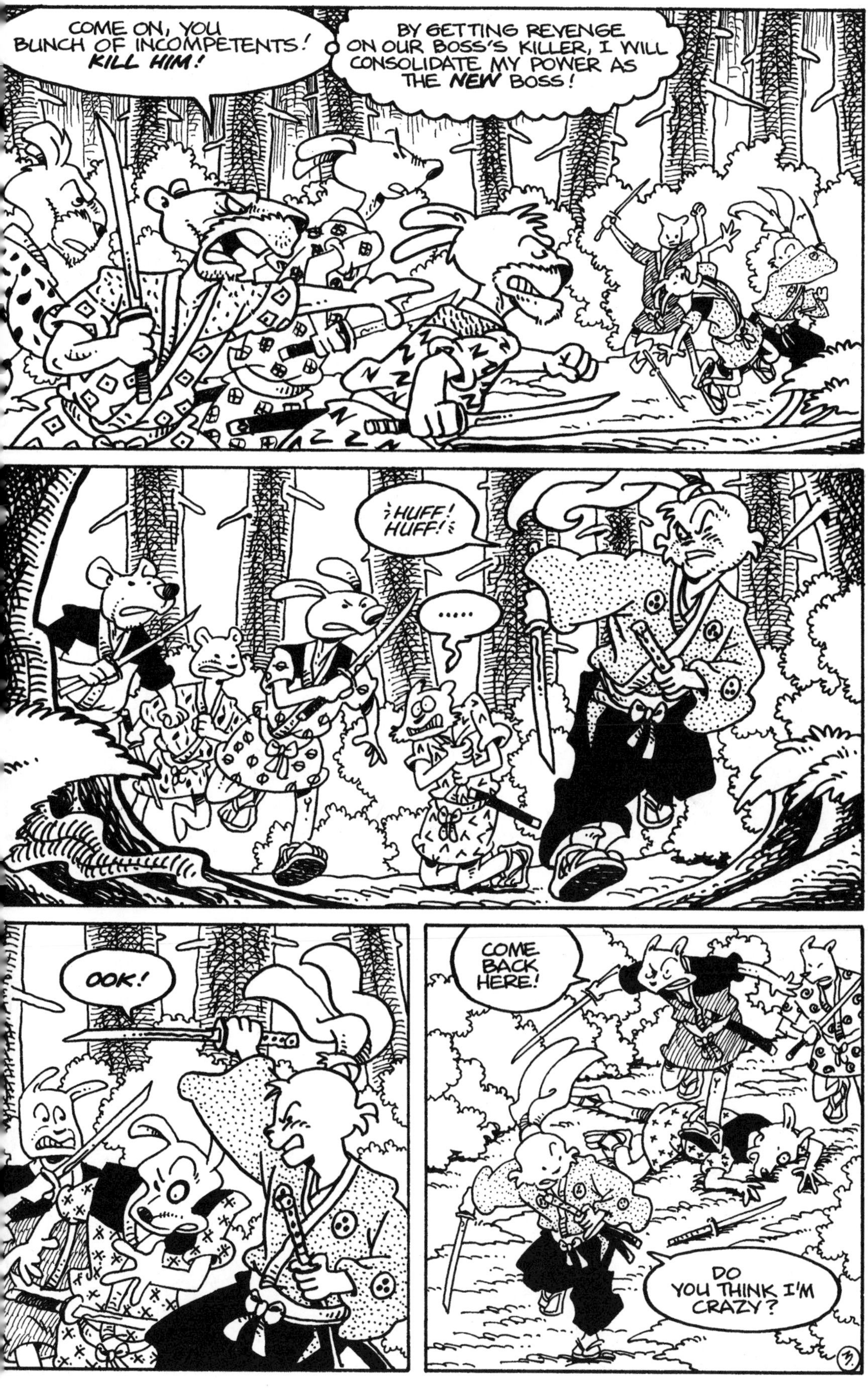
COME ON, YOU BUNCH OF INCOMPETENTS! KILL HIM!
BY GETTING REVENGE ON OUR BOSS'S KILLER, I WILL CONSOLIDATE MY POWER AS THE NEW BOSS!
HUFF! HUFF!
.....
OOK!
COME BACK HERE!
DO YOU THINK I'M CRAZY?

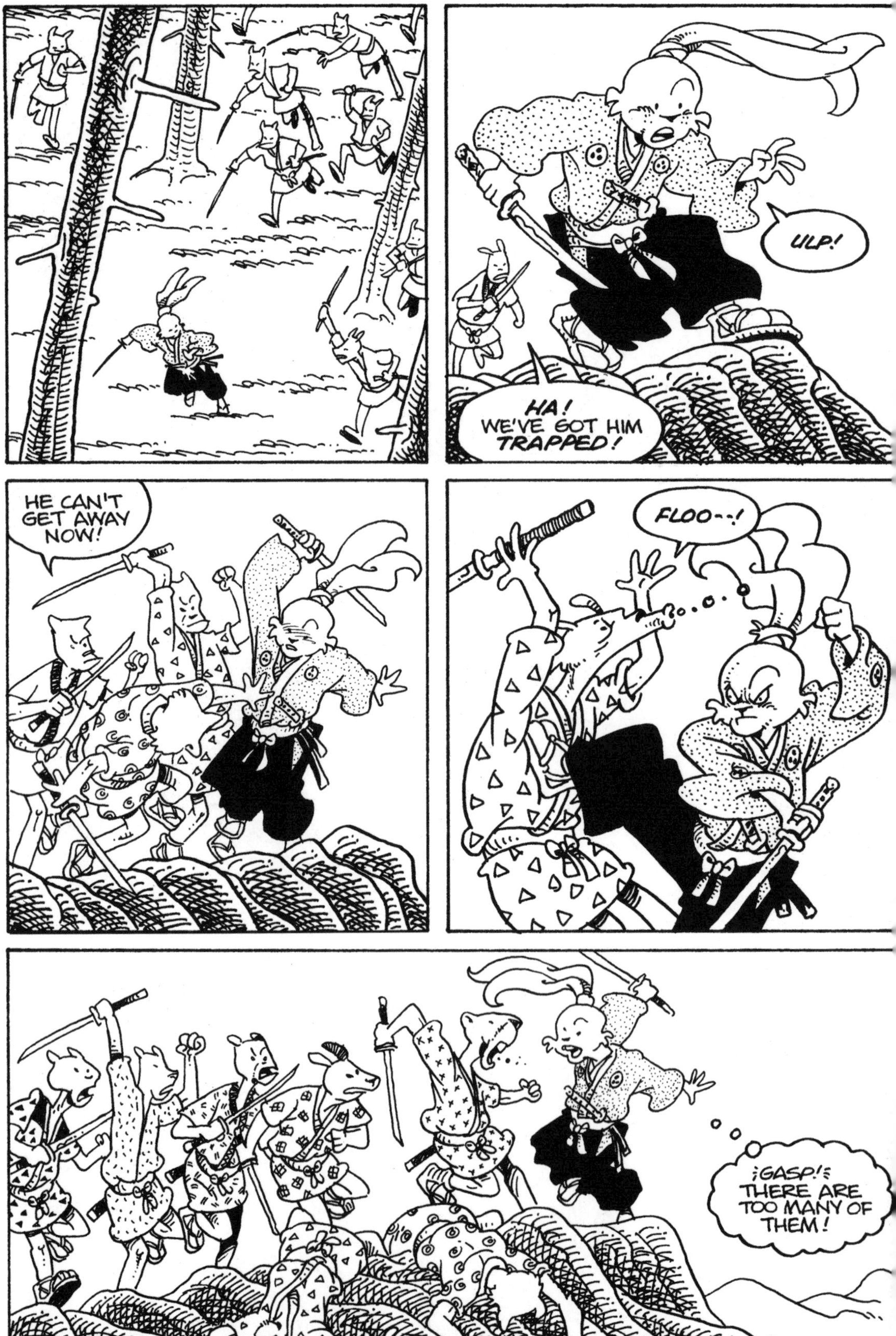

ULP!
HA! WE'VE GOT HIM TRAPPED!
HE CAN'T GET AWAY NOW!
FLOO--!
¡GASP!¡ THERE ARE TOO MANY OF THEM!

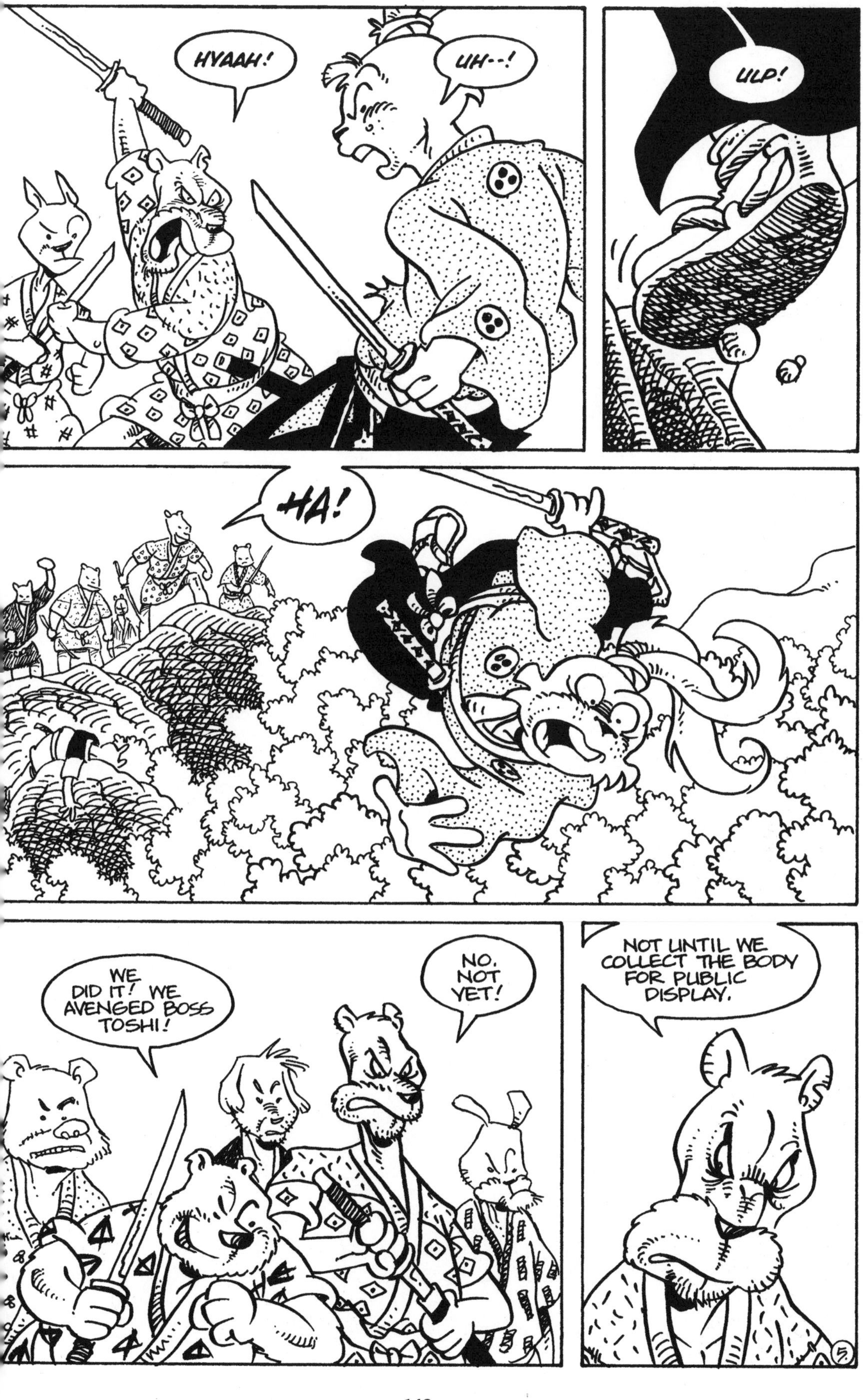
HYAAH!
UH--!
ULP!
HA!
WE DID IT! WE AVENGED BOSS TOSHI!
NO. NOT YET!
NOT UNTIL WE COLLECT THE BODY FOR PUBLIC DISPLAY.
5

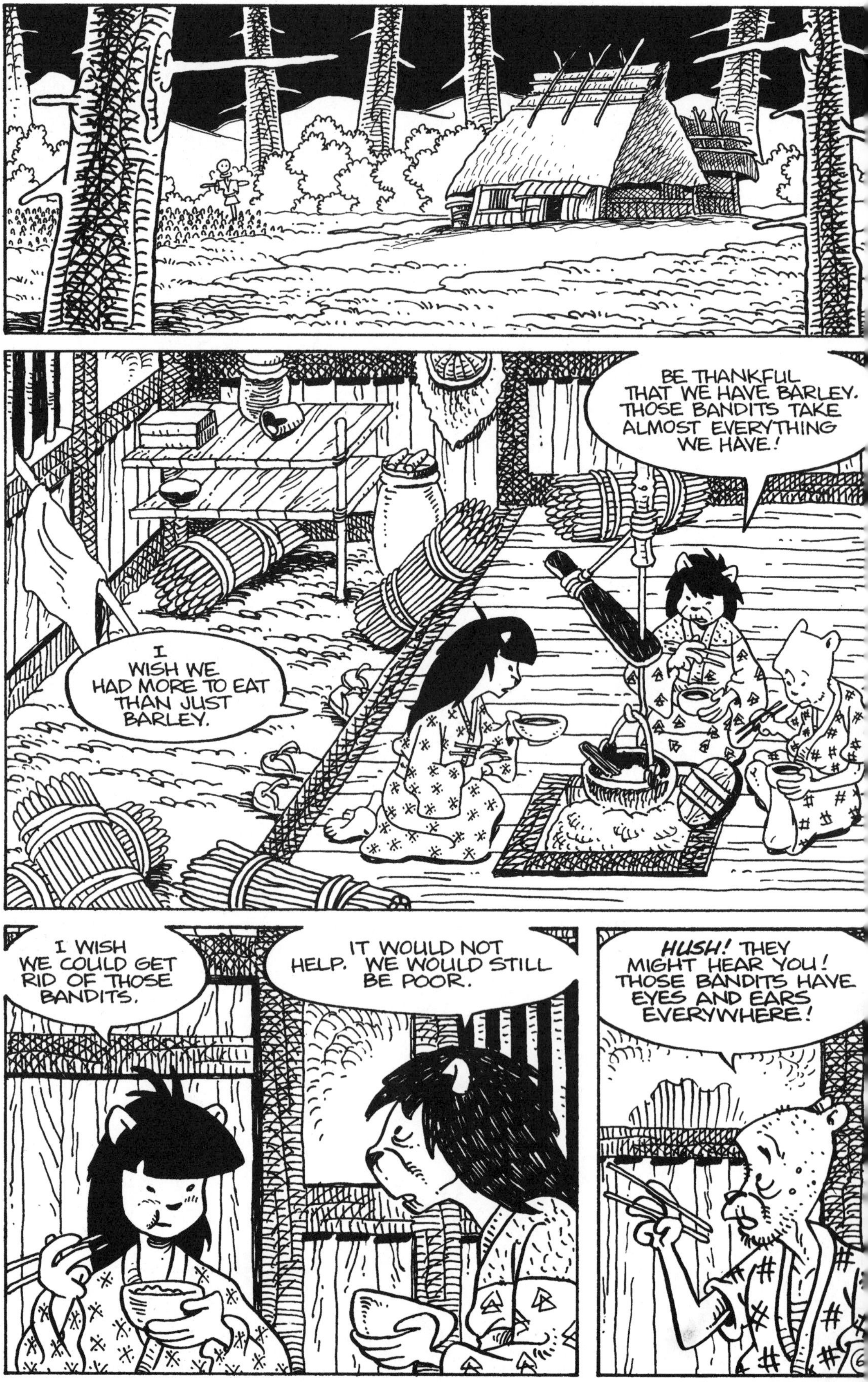
I WISH WE HAD MORE TO EAT THAN JUST BARLEY.
BE THANKFUL THAT WE HAVE BARLEY. THOSE BANDITS TAKE ALMOST EVERYTHING WE HAVE!
I WISH WE COULD GET RID OF THOSE BANDITS.
IT WOULD NOT HELP. WE WOULD STILL BE POOR.
*HUSH!* THEY MIGHT HEAR YOU! THOSE BANDITS HAVE EYES AND EARS EVERYWHERE!

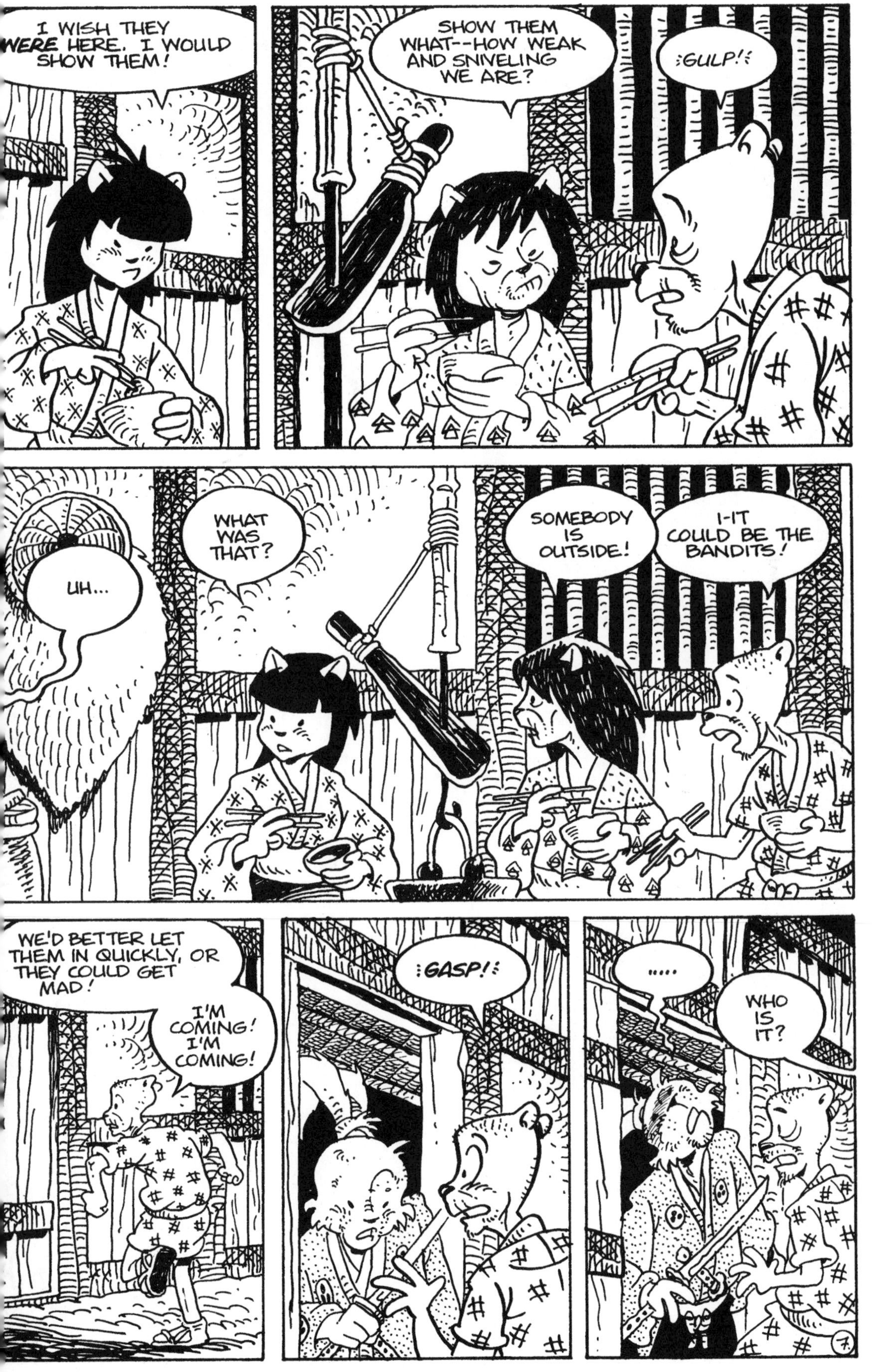
I WISH THEY *WERE* HERE. I WOULD SHOW THEM!
SHOW THEM WHAT--HOW WEAK AND SNIVELING WE ARE?
GULP!
UH...
WHAT WAS THAT?
SOMEBODY IS OUTSIDE!
I-IT COULD BE THE BANDITS!
WE'D BETTER LET THEM IN QUICKLY, OR THEY COULD GET MAD!
I'M COMING! I'M COMING!
GASP!
.....
WHO IS IT?
7.

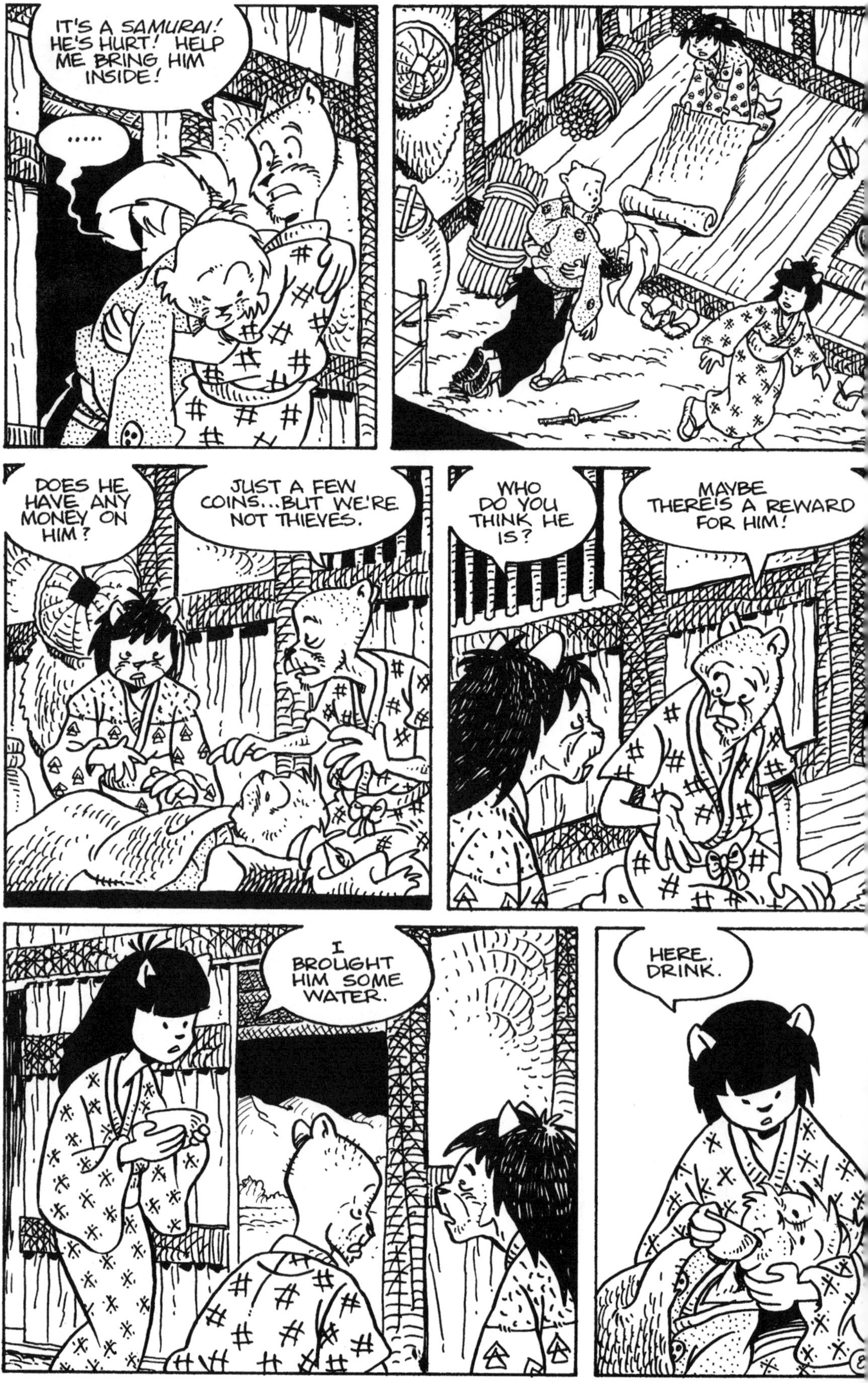
IT'S A SAMURAI! HE'S HURT! HELP ME BRING HIM INSIDE!
.....
DOES HE HAVE ANY MONEY ON HIM?
JUST A FEW COINS...BUT WE'RE NOT THIEVES.
WHO DO YOU THINK HE IS?
MAYBE THERE'S A REWARD FOR HIM!
I BROUGHT HIM SOME WATER.
HERE. DRINK.

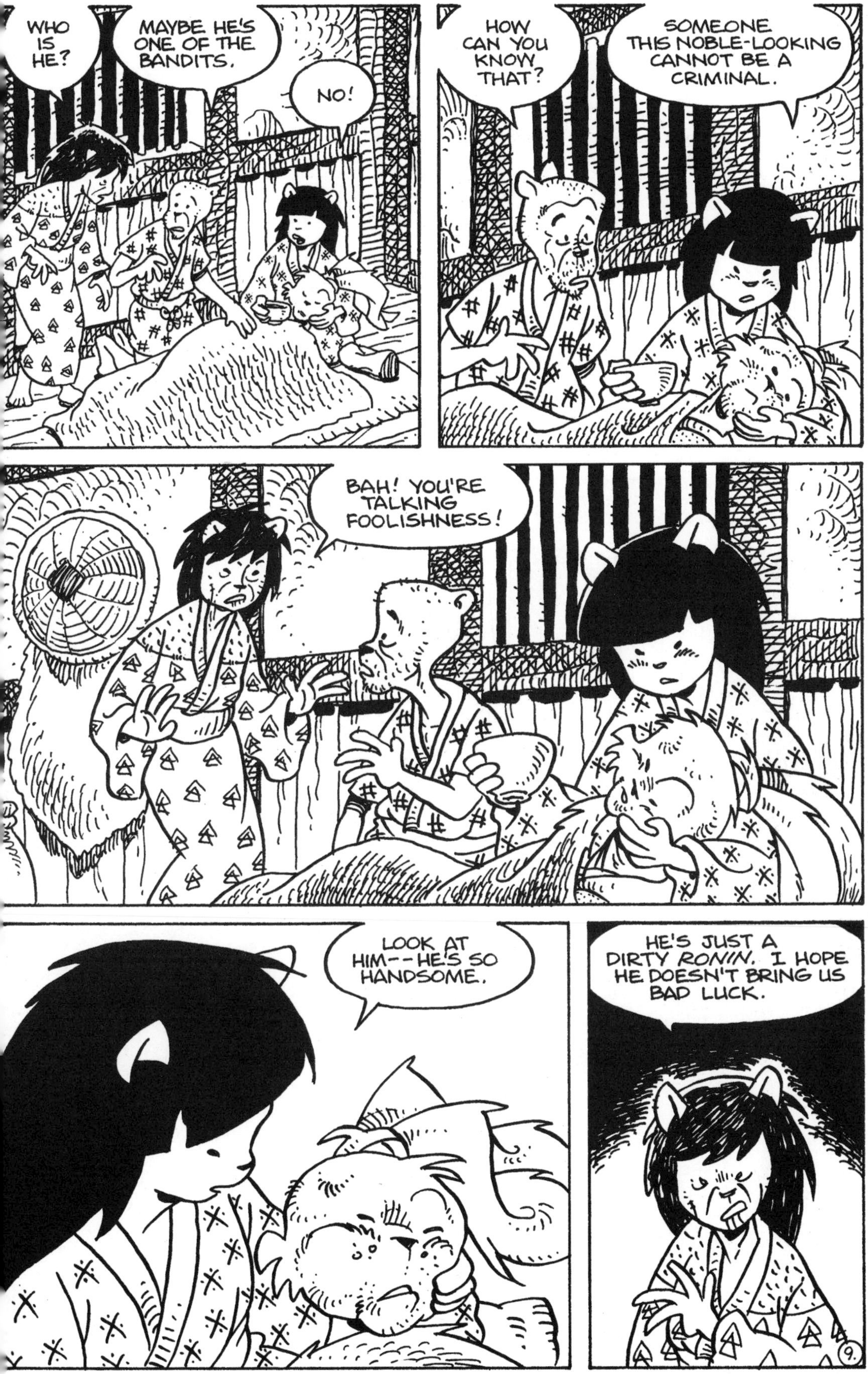
WHO IS HE?
MAYBE HE'S ONE OF THE BANDITS.
NO!
HOW CAN YOU KNOW THAT?
SOMEONE THIS NOBLE-LOOKING CANNOT BE A CRIMINAL.
BAH! YOU'RE TALKING FOOLISHNESS!
LOOK AT HIM--HE'S SO HANDSOME.
HE'S JUST A DIRTY *RONIN*. I HOPE HE DOESN'T BRING US BAD LUCK.
9.

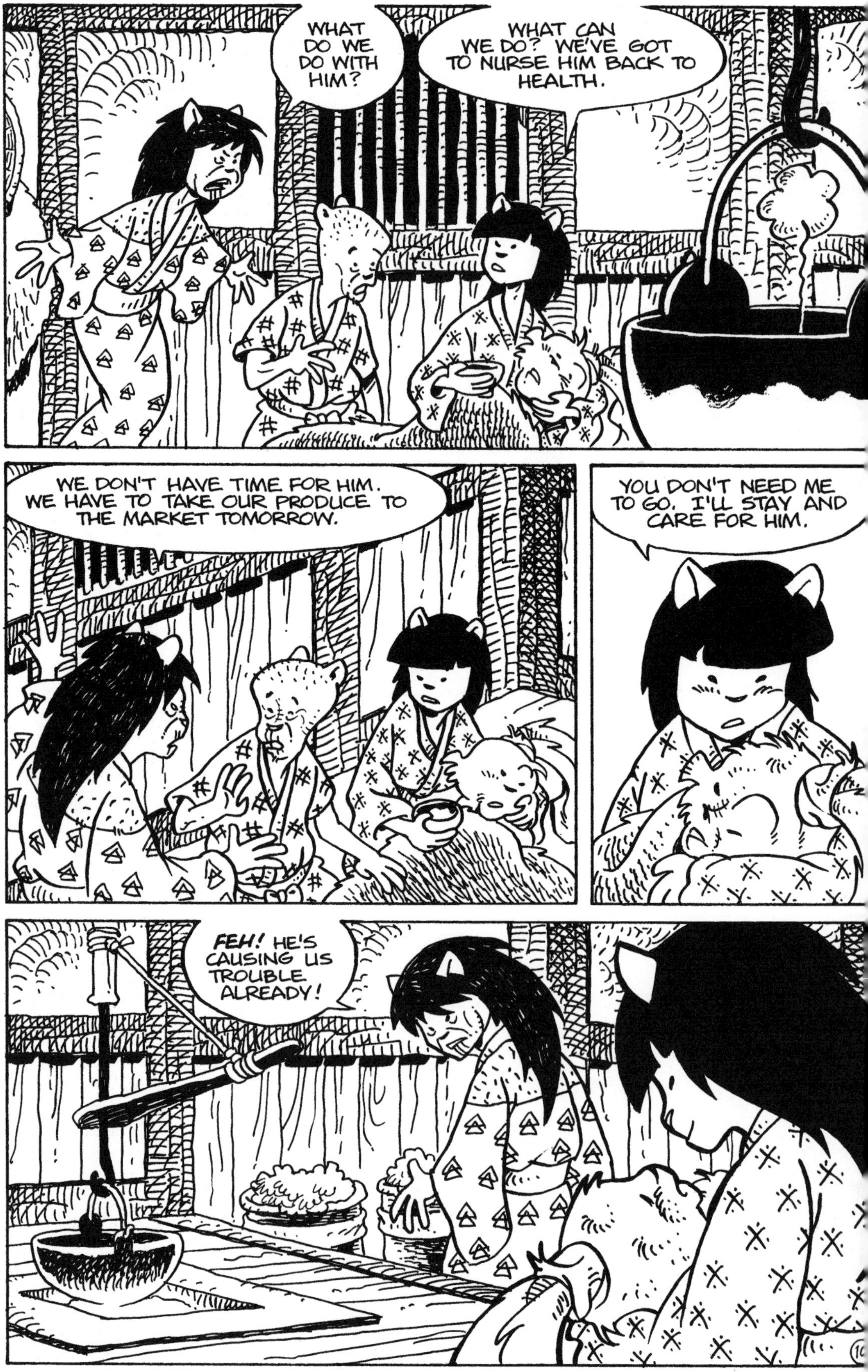
WHAT DO WE DO WITH HIM?
WHAT CAN WE DO? WE'VE GOT TO NURSE HIM BACK TO HEALTH.
WE DON'T HAVE TIME FOR HIM. WE HAVE TO TAKE OUR PRODUCE TO THE MARKET TOMORROW.
YOU DON'T NEED ME TO GO. I'LL STAY AND CARE FOR HIM.
FEH! HE'S CAUSING US TROUBLE ALREADY!

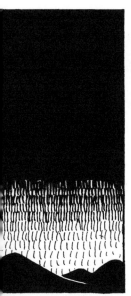

UHH...

OH, YOU'RE AWAKE. I WAS GETTING WORRIED. YOU HAVEN'T MOVED SINCE YOU GOT HERE.

WHO...?

I AM YOKO. YOU STUMBLED INTO OUR HOME LAST NIGHT.

I REMEMBER-- I FELL OFF THAT CLIFF.

YOU SHOULD BE MORE CAREFUL WHERE YOU WALK.

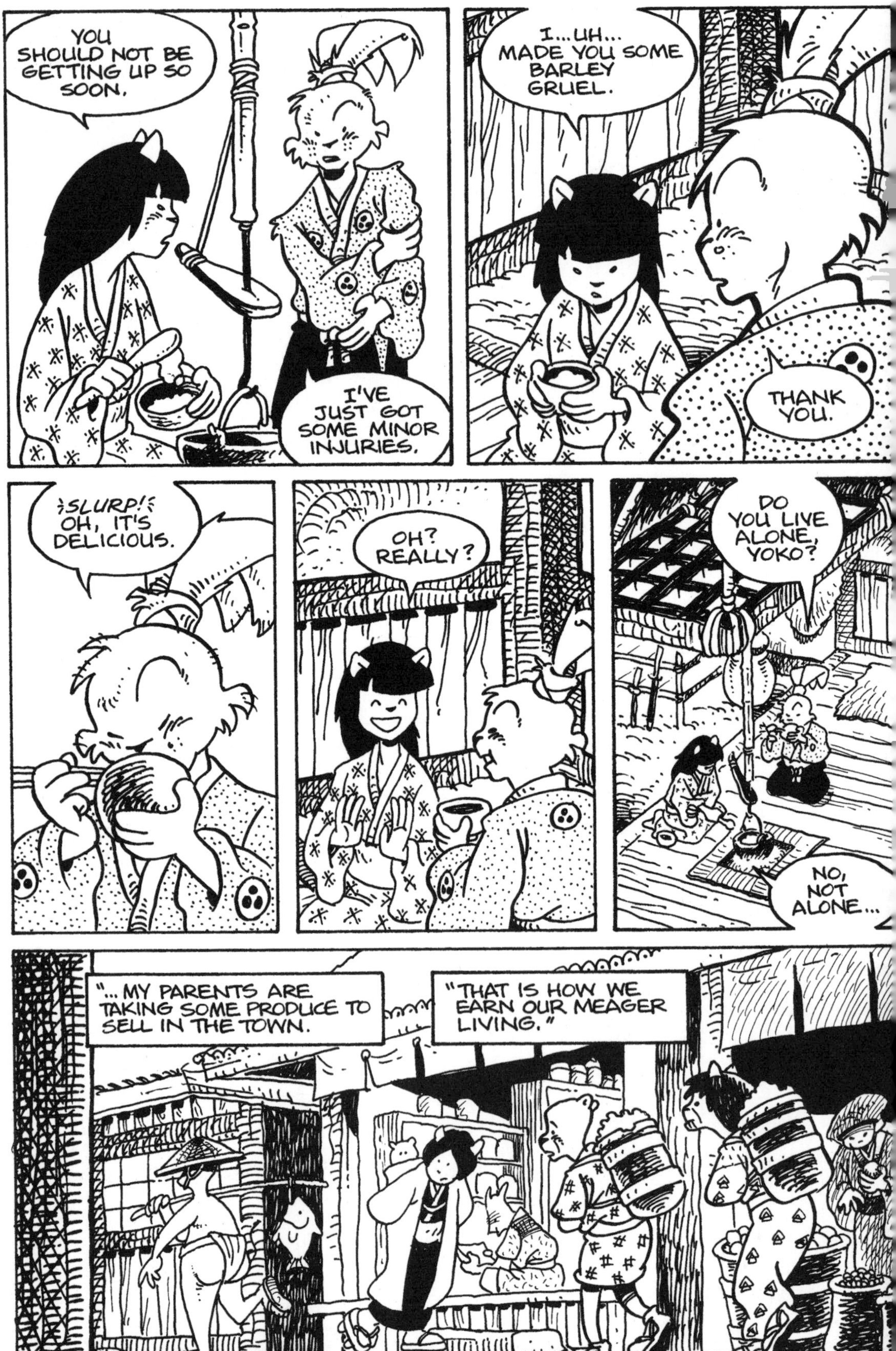

YOU SHOULD NOT BE GETTING UP SO SOON.
I'VE JUST GOT SOME MINOR INJURIES.
I...UH... MADE YOU SOME BARLEY GRUEL.
THANK YOU.
SLURP! OH, IT'S DELICIOUS.
OH? REALLY?
DO YOU LIVE ALONE, YOKO?
NO, NOT ALONE...
"...MY PARENTS ARE TAKING SOME PRODUCE TO SELL IN THE TOWN.
"THAT IS HOW WE EARN OUR MEAGER LIVING."

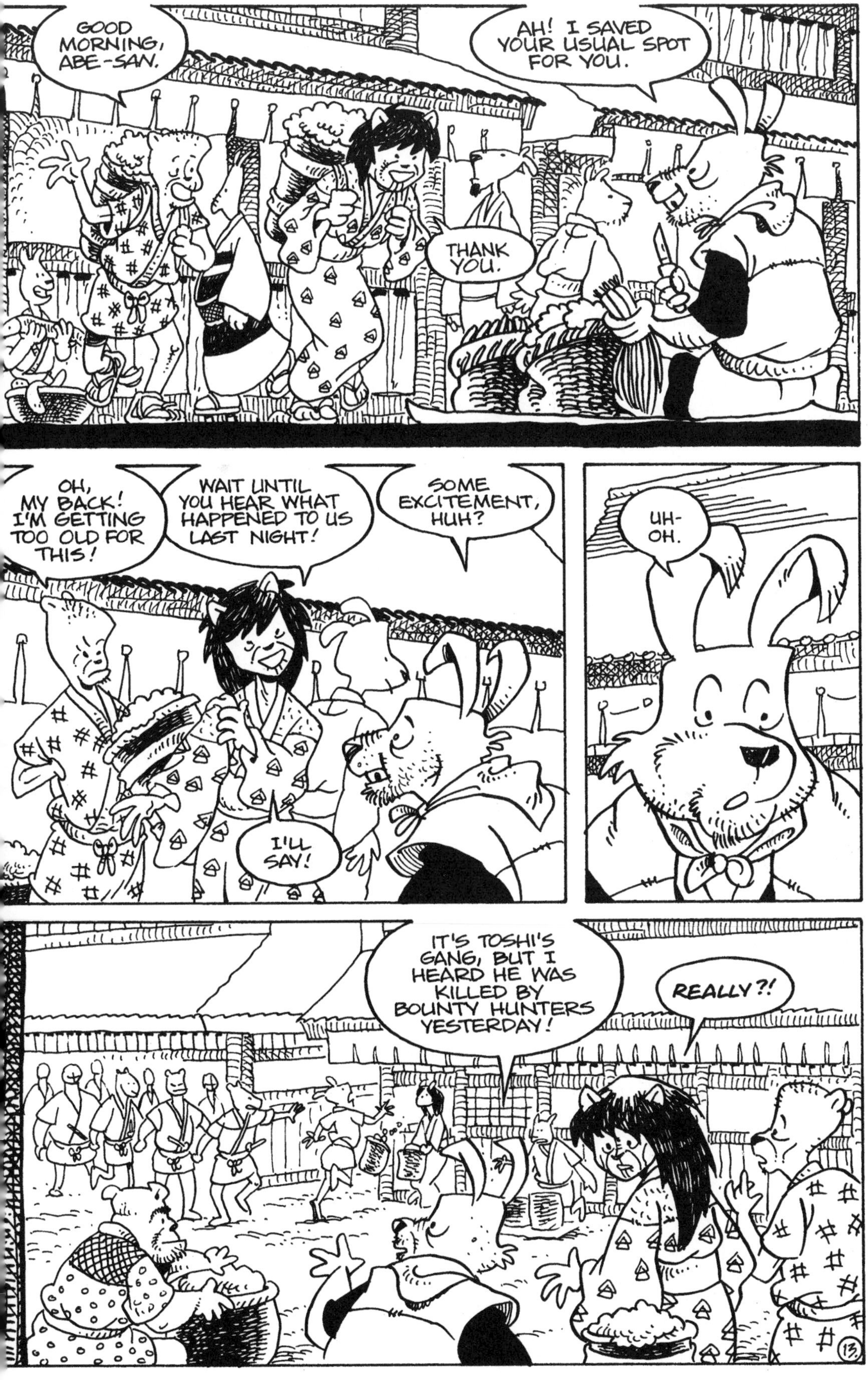
GOOD MORNING, ABE-SAN.
AH! I SAVED YOUR USUAL SPOT FOR YOU.
THANK YOU.
OH, MY BACK! I'M GETTING TOO OLD FOR THIS!
WAIT UNTIL YOU HEAR WHAT HAPPENED TO US LAST NIGHT!
SOME EXCITEMENT, HUH?
I'LL SAY!
UH-OH.
IT'S TOSHI'S GANG, BUT I HEARD HE WAS KILLED BY BOUNTY HUNTERS YESTERDAY!
REALLY?!
13

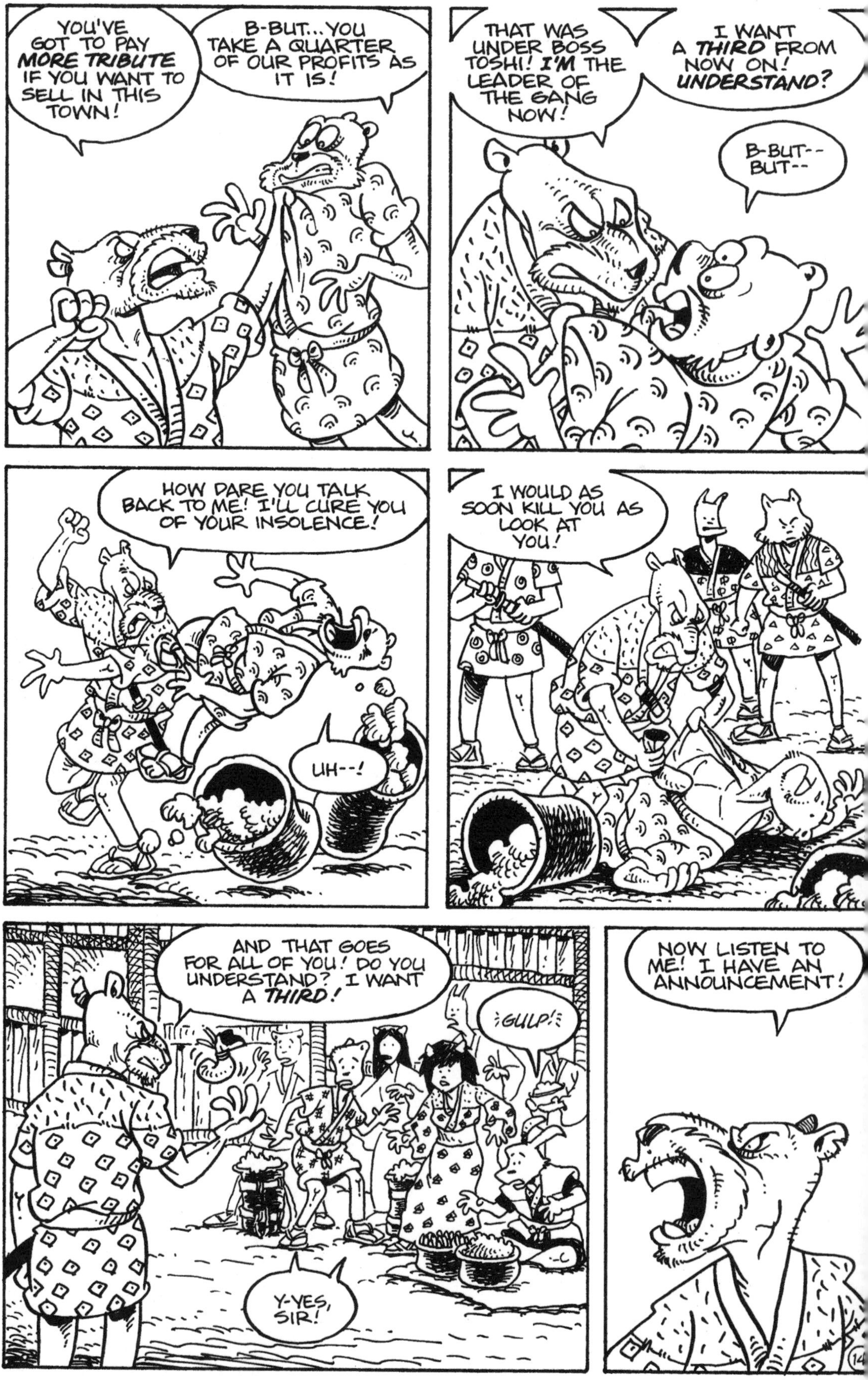
YOU'VE GOT TO PAY MORE TRIBUTE IF YOU WANT TO SELL IN THIS TOWN!
B-BUT...YOU TAKE A QUARTER OF OUR PROFITS AS IT IS!
THAT WAS UNDER BOSS TOSHI! I'M THE LEADER OF THE GANG NOW!
I WANT A THIRD FROM NOW ON! UNDERSTAND?
B-BUT-- BUT--
HOW DARE YOU TALK BACK TO ME! I'LL CURE YOU OF YOUR INSOLENCE!
UH--!
I WOULD AS SOON KILL YOU AS LOOK AT YOU!
AND THAT GOES FOR ALL OF YOU! DO YOU UNDERSTAND? I WANT A THIRD!
GULP!
Y-YES, SIR!
NOW LISTEN TO ME! I HAVE AN ANNOUNCEMENT!

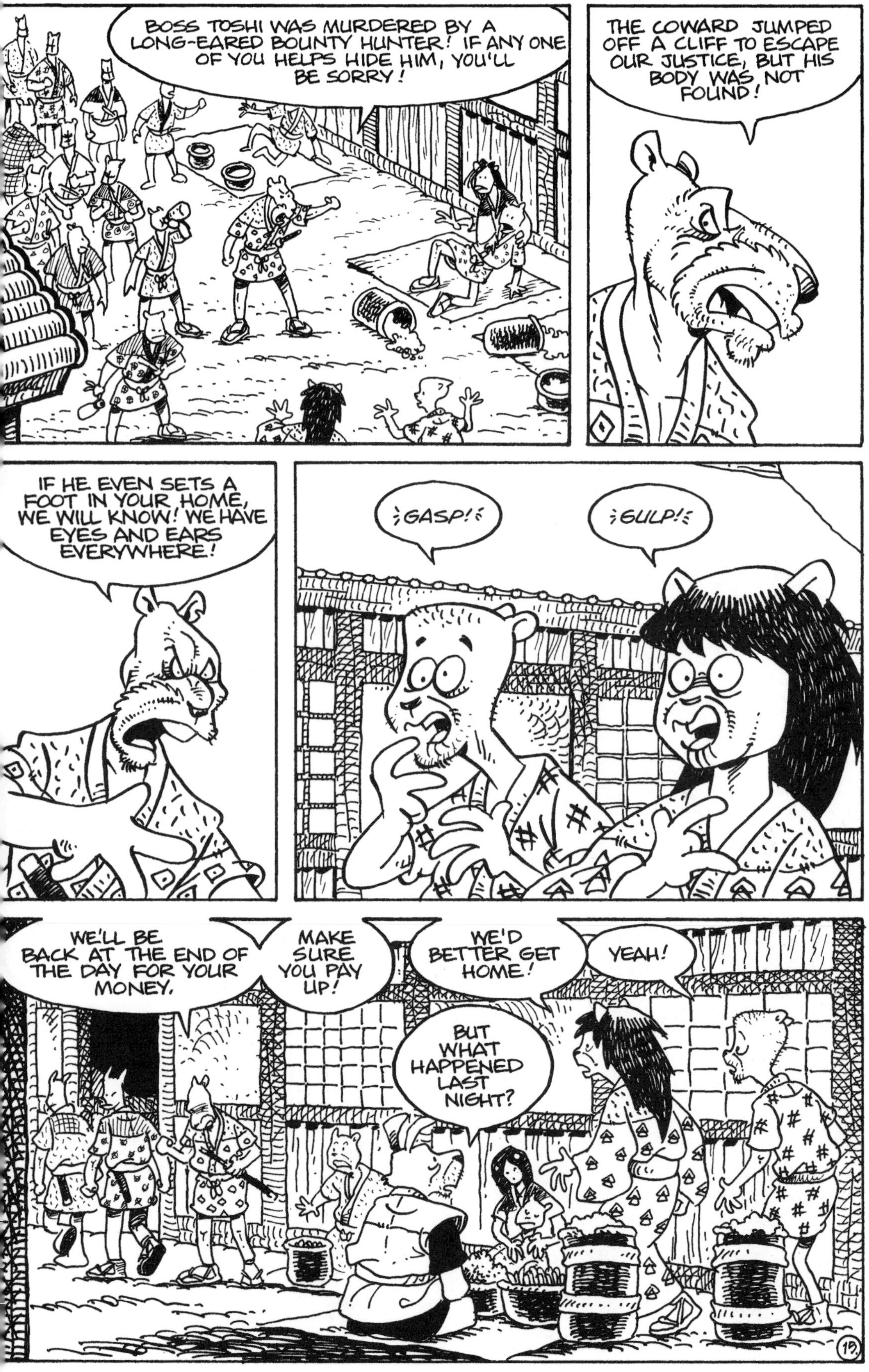
BOSS TOSHI WAS MURDERED BY A LONG-EARED BOUNTY HUNTER! IF ANY ONE OF YOU HELPS HIDE HIM, YOU'LL BE SORRY!
THE COWARD JUMPED OFF A CLIFF TO ESCAPE OUR JUSTICE, BUT HIS BODY WAS NOT FOUND!
IF HE EVEN SETS A FOOT IN YOUR HOME, WE WILL KNOW! WE HAVE EYES AND EARS EVERYWHERE!
GASP!
GULP!
WE'LL BE BACK AT THE END OF THE DAY FOR YOUR MONEY.
MAKE SURE YOU PAY UP!
WE'D BETTER GET HOME!
YEAH!
BUT WHAT HAPPENED LAST NIGHT?
13

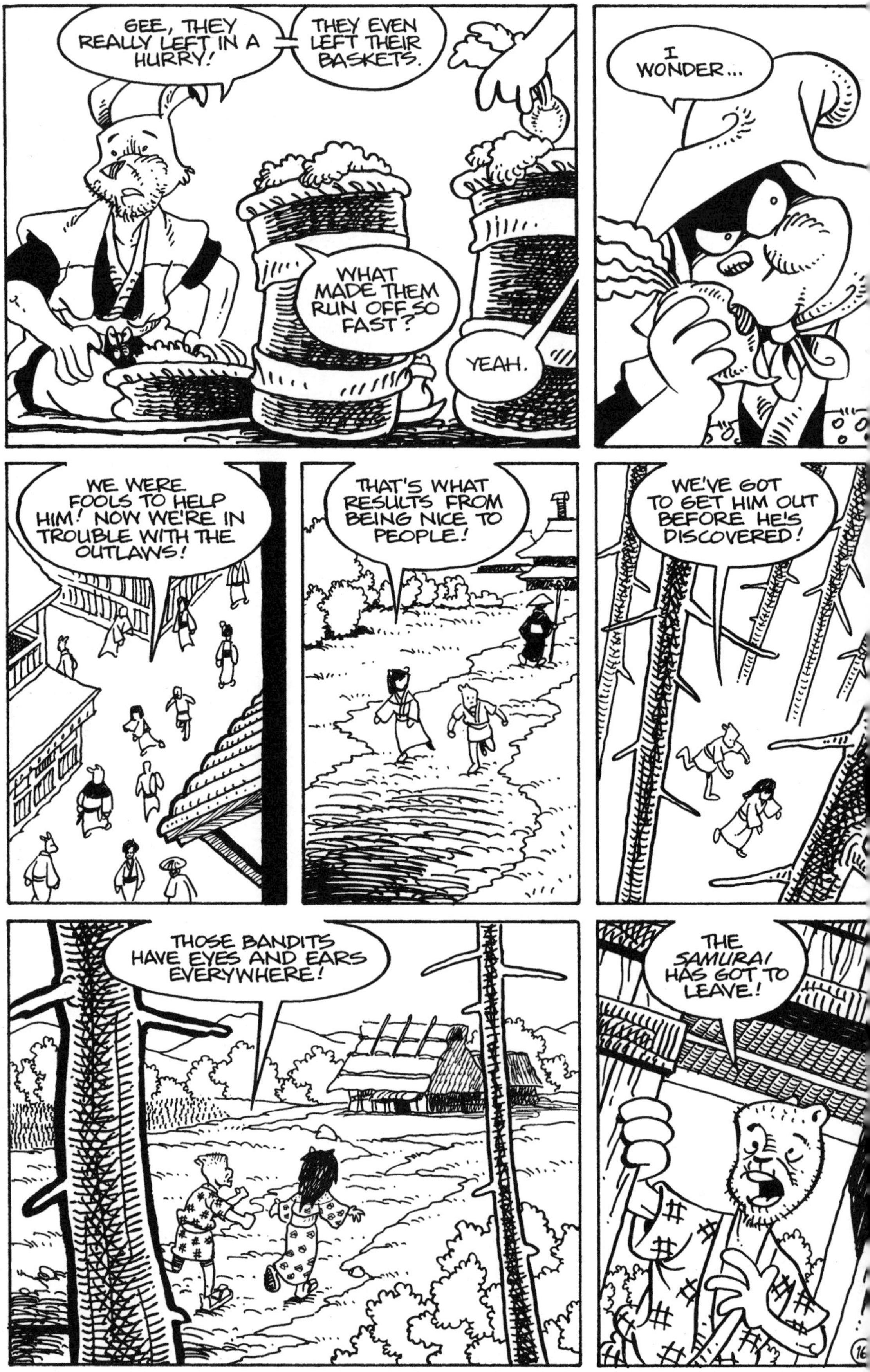
GEE, THEY REALLY LEFT IN A HURRY!
THEY EVEN LEFT THEIR BASKETS.
WHAT MADE THEM RUN OFF SO FAST?
YEAH.
I WONDER...
WE WERE FOOLS TO HELP HIM! NOW WE'RE IN TROUBLE WITH THE OUTLAWS!
THAT'S WHAT RESULTS FROM BEING NICE TO PEOPLE!
WE'VE GOT TO GET HIM OUT BEFORE HE'S DISCOVERED!
THOSE BANDITS HAVE EYES AND EARS EVERYWHERE!
THE SAMURAI HAS GOT TO LEAVE!
16

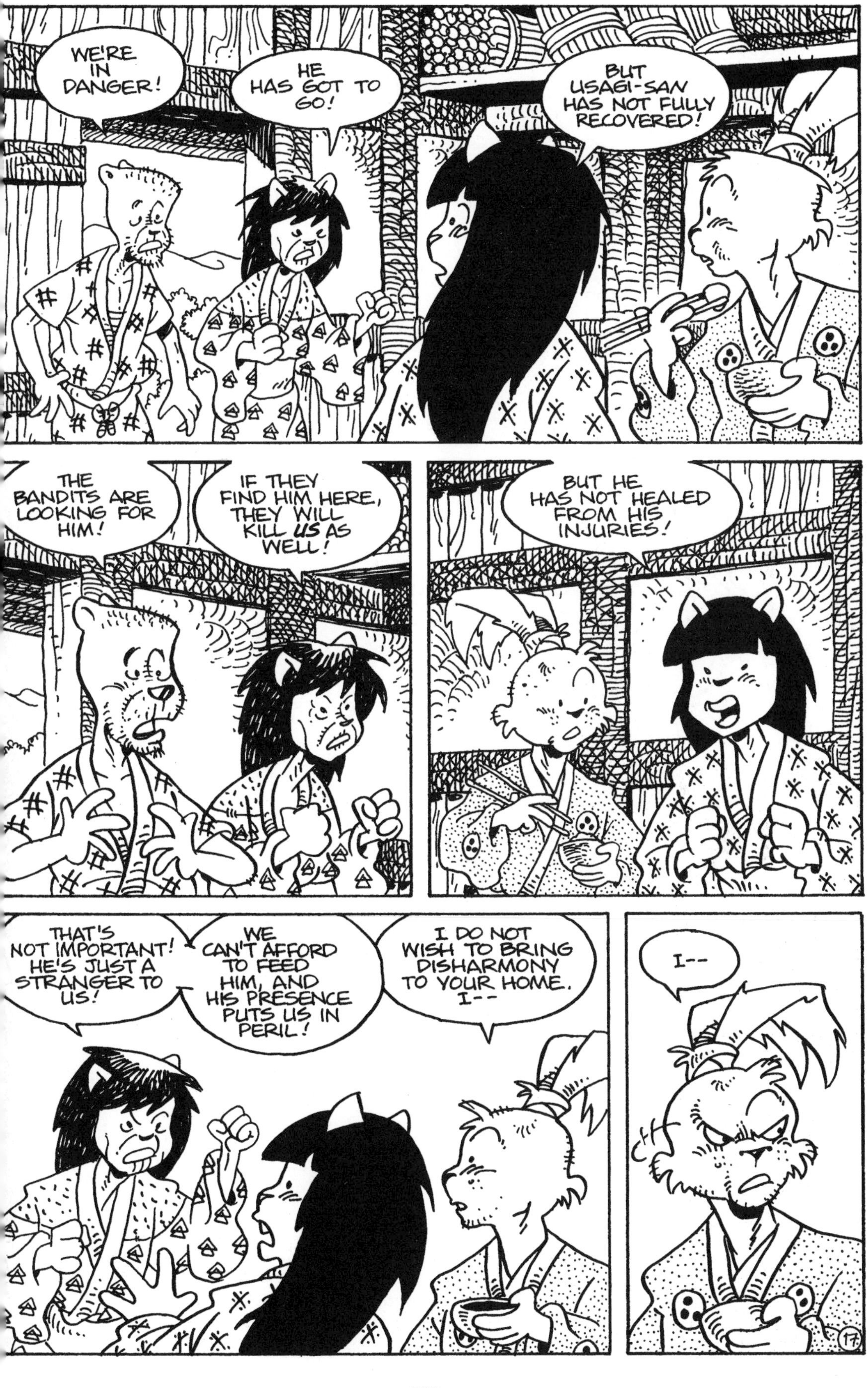
WE'RE IN DANGER!
HE HAS GOT TO GO!
BUT USAGI-SAN HAS NOT FULLY RECOVERED!
THE BANDITS ARE LOOKING FOR HIM!
IF THEY FIND HIM HERE, THEY WILL KILL *US* AS WELL!
BUT HE HAS NOT HEALED FROM HIS INJURIES!
THAT'S NOT IMPORTANT! HE'S JUST A STRANGER TO US!
WE CAN'T AFFORD TO FEED HIM, AND HIS PRESENCE PUTS US IN PERIL!
I DO NOT WISH TO BRING DISHARMONY TO YOUR HOME. I--
I--
17

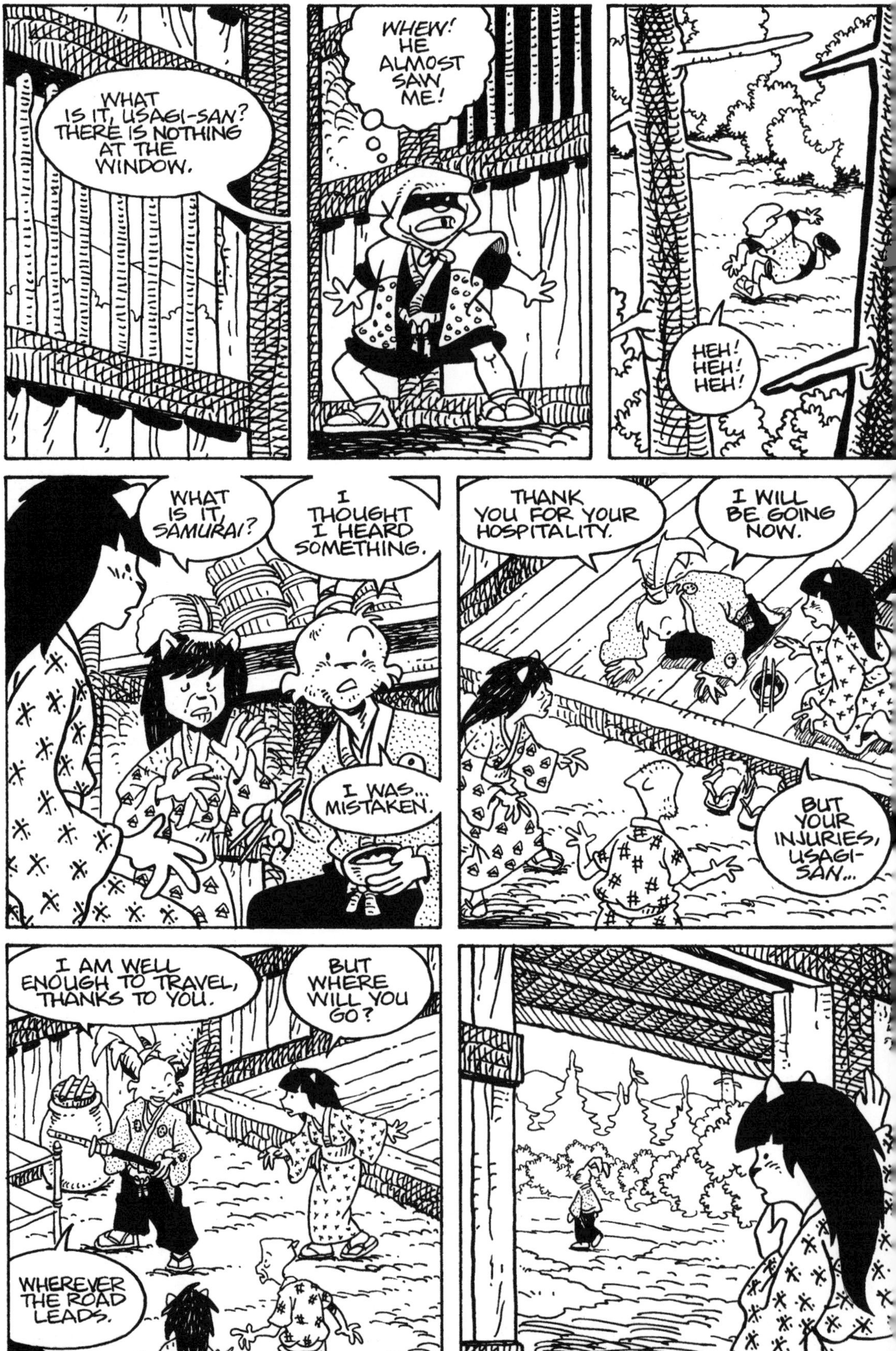
WHAT IS IT, USAGI-SAN? THERE IS NOTHING AT THE WINDOW.
WHEW! HE ALMOST SAW ME!
HEH! HEH! HEH!
WHAT IS IT, SAMURAI?
I THOUGHT I HEARD SOMETHING.
I WAS... MISTAKEN.
THANK YOU FOR YOUR HOSPITALITY.
I WILL BE GOING NOW.
BUT YOUR INJURIES, USAGI-SAN...
I AM WELL ENOUGH TO TRAVEL, THANKS TO YOU.
BUT WHERE WILL YOU GO?
WHEREVER THE ROAD LEADS.

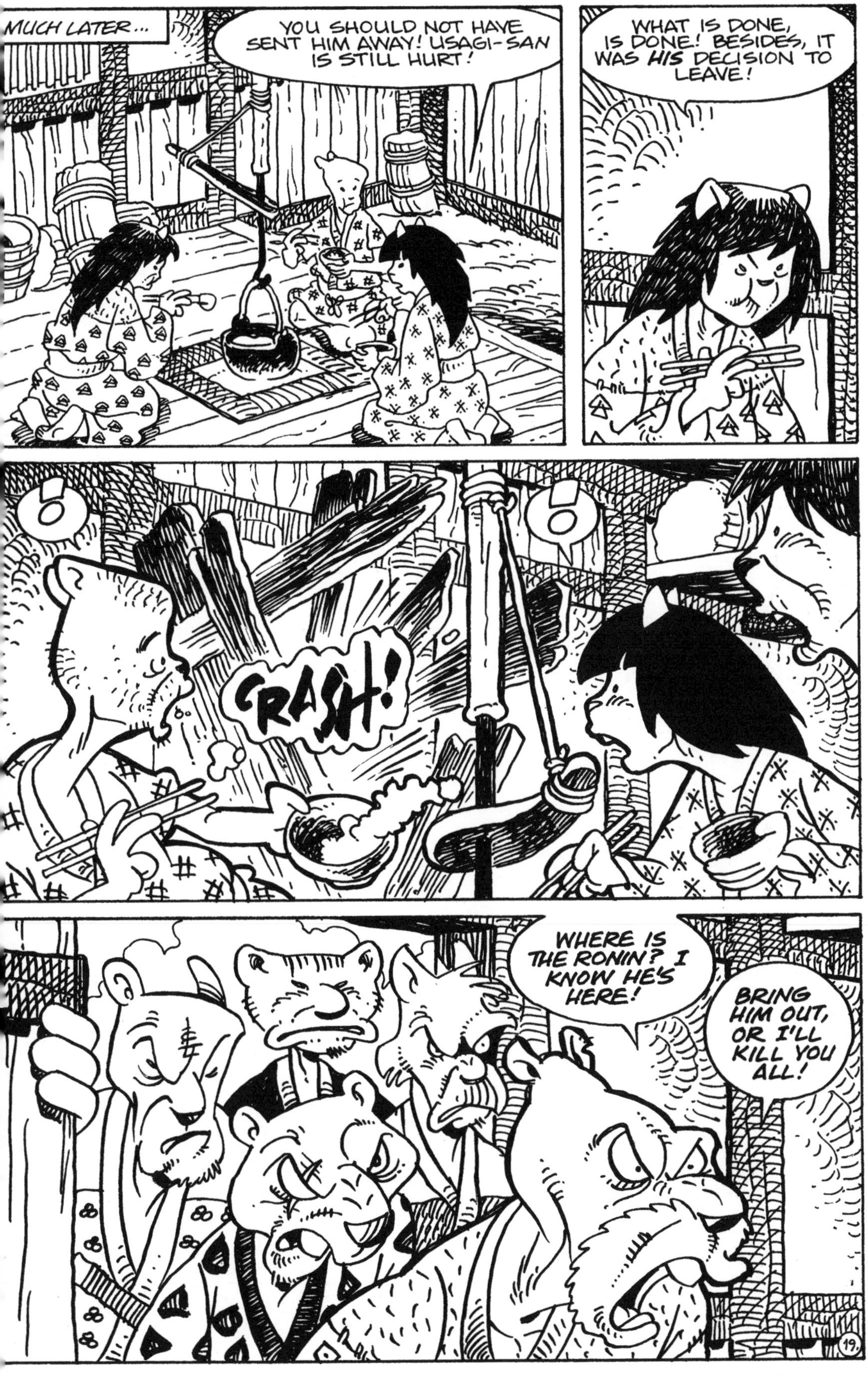
MUCH LATER...
YOU SHOULD NOT HAVE SENT HIM AWAY! USAGI-SAN IS STILL HURT!
WHAT IS DONE, IS DONE! BESIDES, IT WAS HIS DECISION TO LEAVE!
!
CRASH!
!
WHERE IS THE RONIN? I KNOW HE'S HERE!
BRING HIM OUT, OR I'LL KILL YOU ALL!
19.

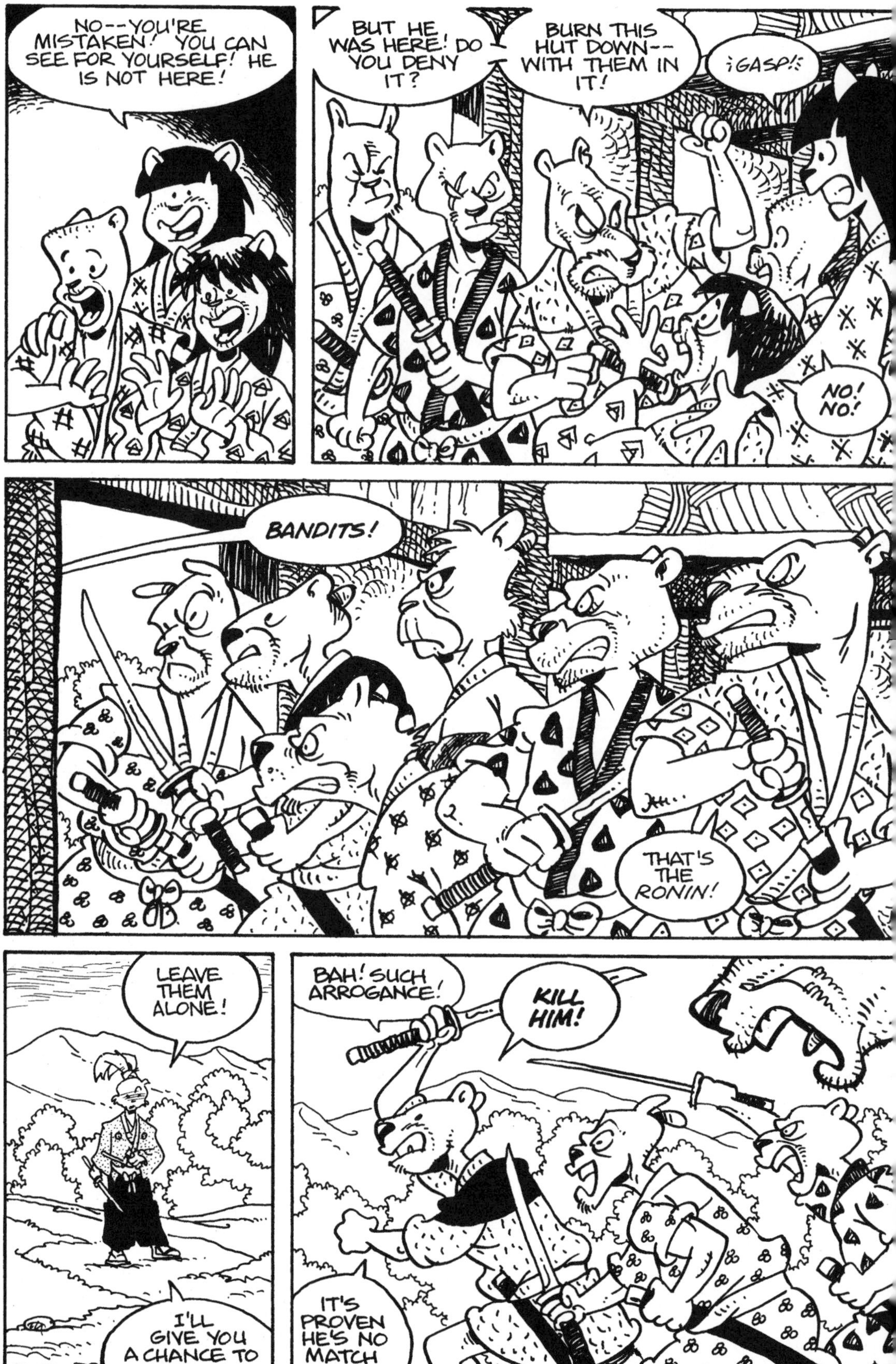
NO--YOU'RE MISTAKEN! YOU CAN SEE FOR YOURSELF! HE IS NOT HERE!
BUT HE WAS HERE! DO YOU DENY IT?
BURN THIS HUT DOWN-- WITH THEM IN IT!
¡GASP!
NO! NO!
BANDITS!
THAT'S THE RONIN!
LEAVE THEM ALONE!
I'LL GIVE YOU A CHANCE TO DEPART QUIETLY.
BAH! SUCH ARROGANCE!
KILL HIM!
IT'S PROVEN HE'S NO MATCH FOR US!

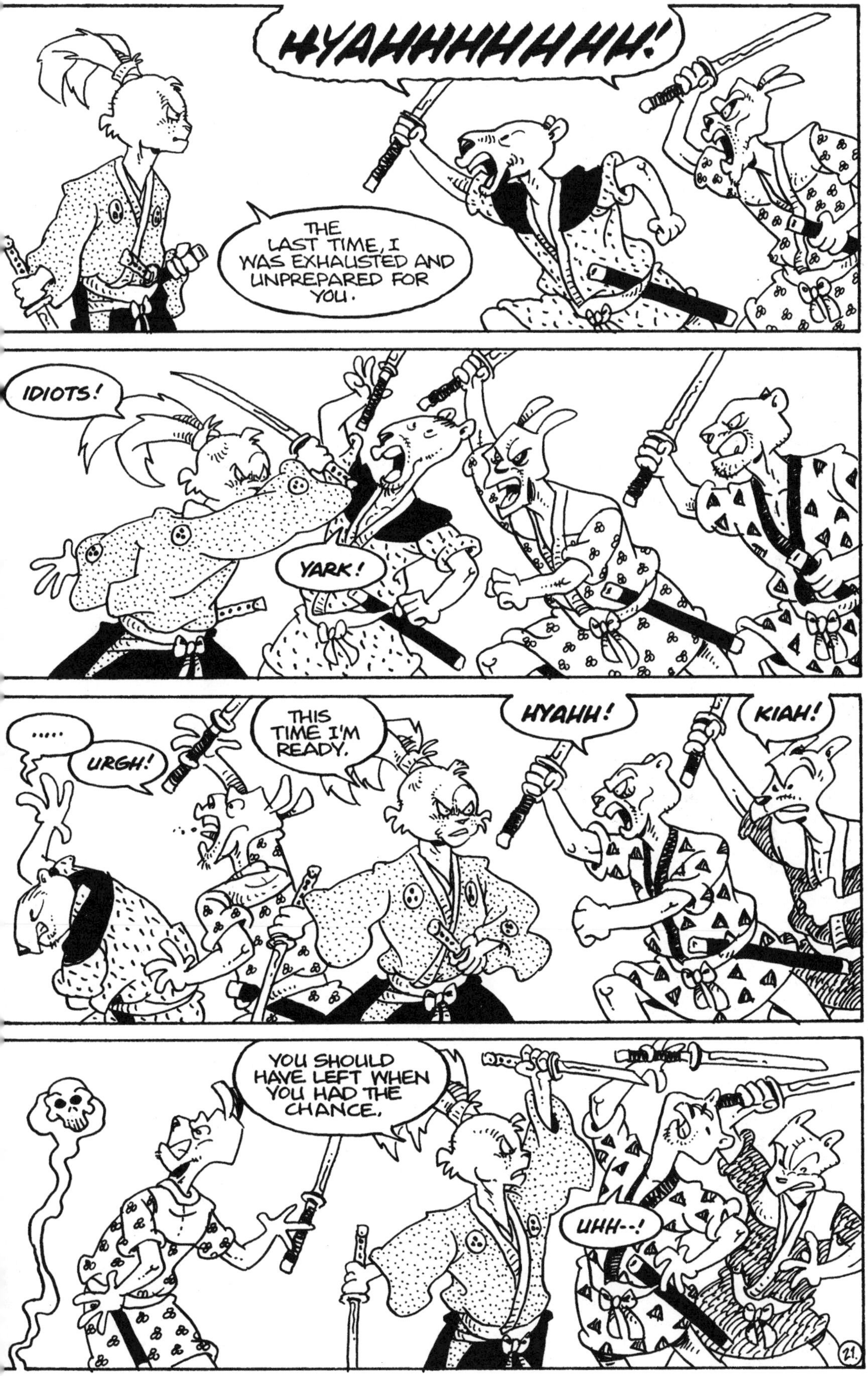
HYAHHHHHHHH!
THE LAST TIME, I WAS EXHAUSTED AND UNPREPARED FOR YOU.
IDIOTS!
YARK!
.....
URGH!
THIS TIME I'M READY.
HYAHH!
KIAH!
YOU SHOULD HAVE LEFT WHEN YOU HAD THE CHANCE.
UHH--!
21.

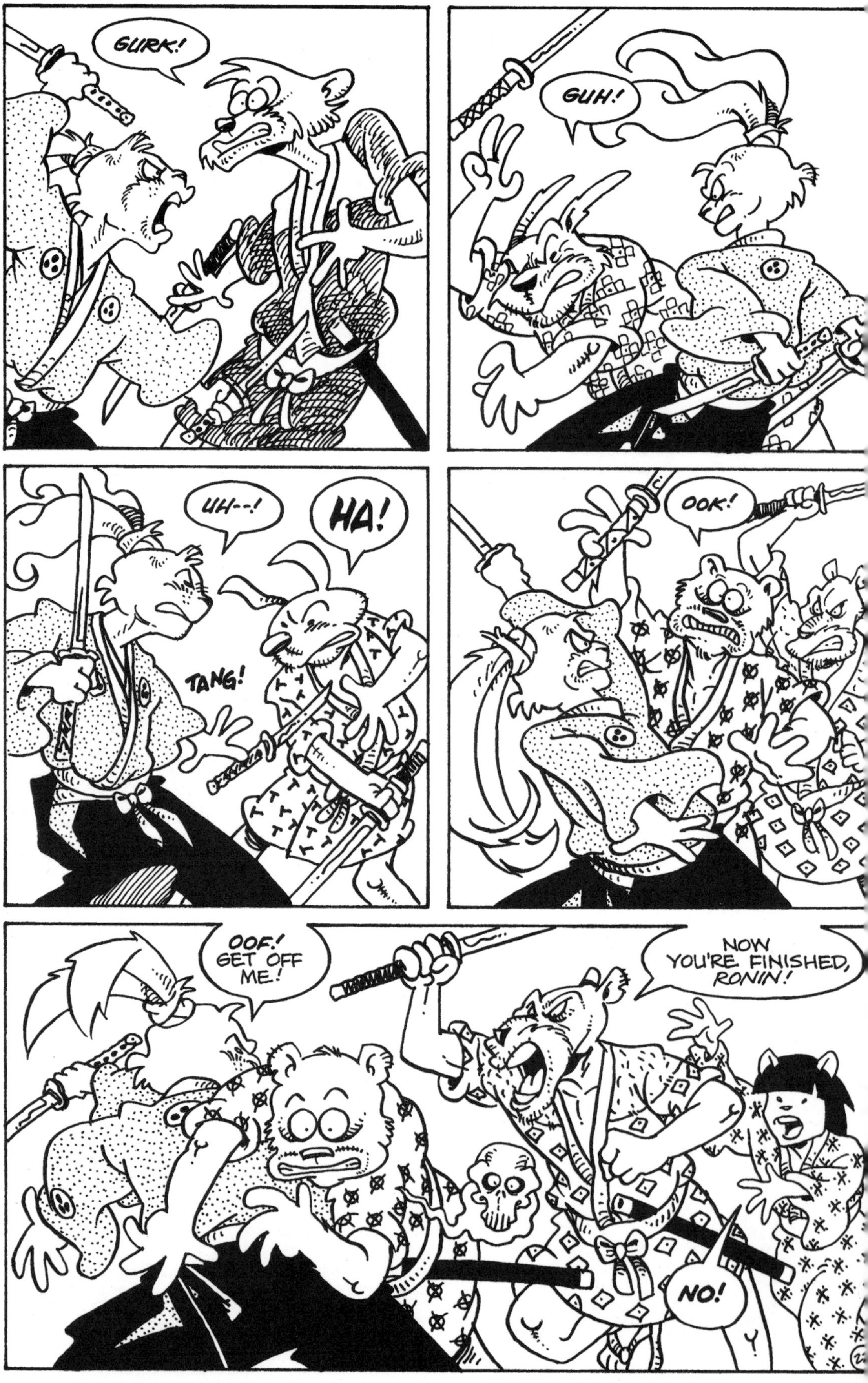
GURK!
GUH!
UH--!
HA!
TANG!
OOK!
OOF! GET OFF ME!
NOW YOU'RE FINISHED, RONIN!
NO!

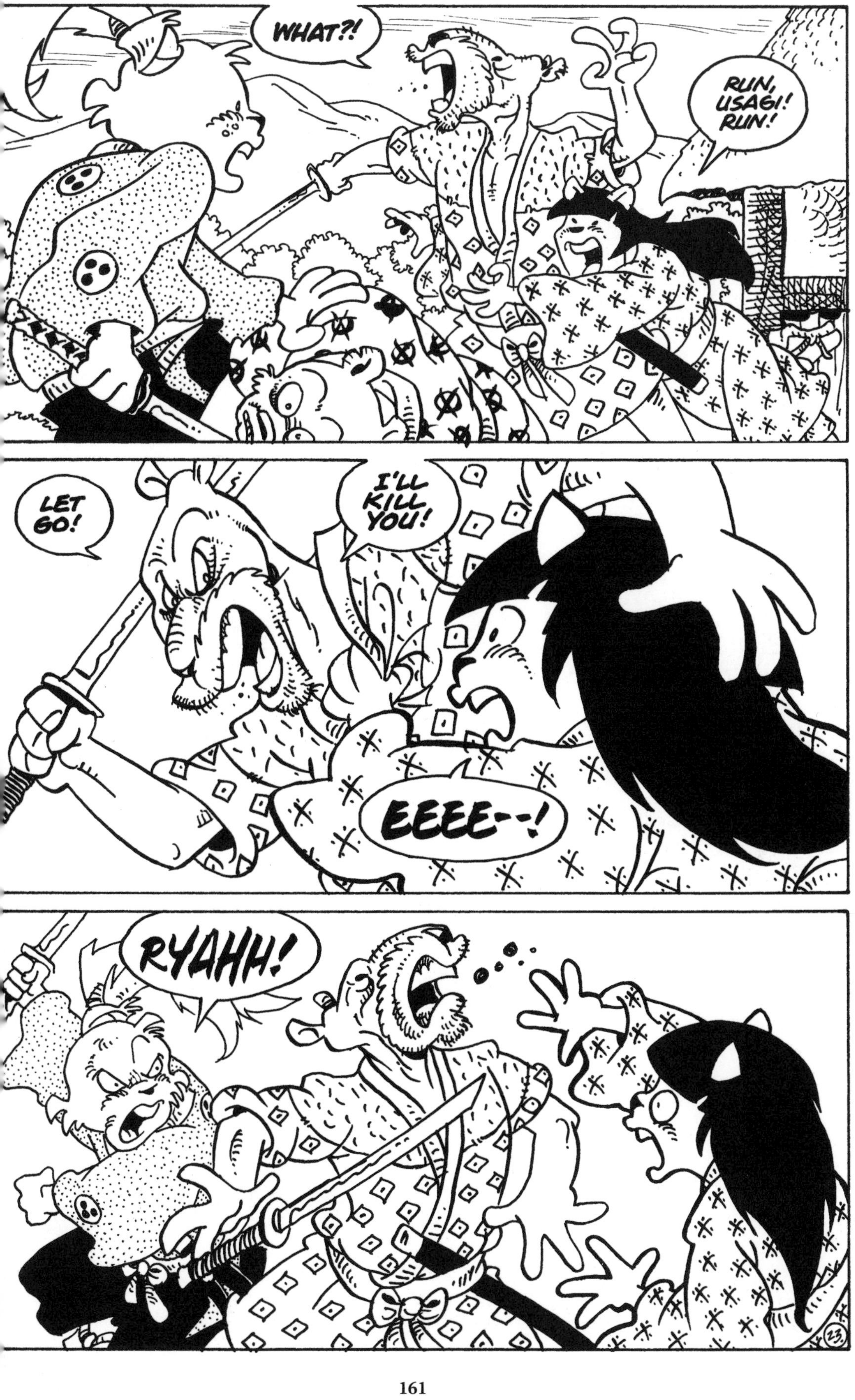
WHAT?!
RUN, USAGI! RUN!
LET GO!
I'LL KILL YOU!
EEEE--!
RYAHH!
23

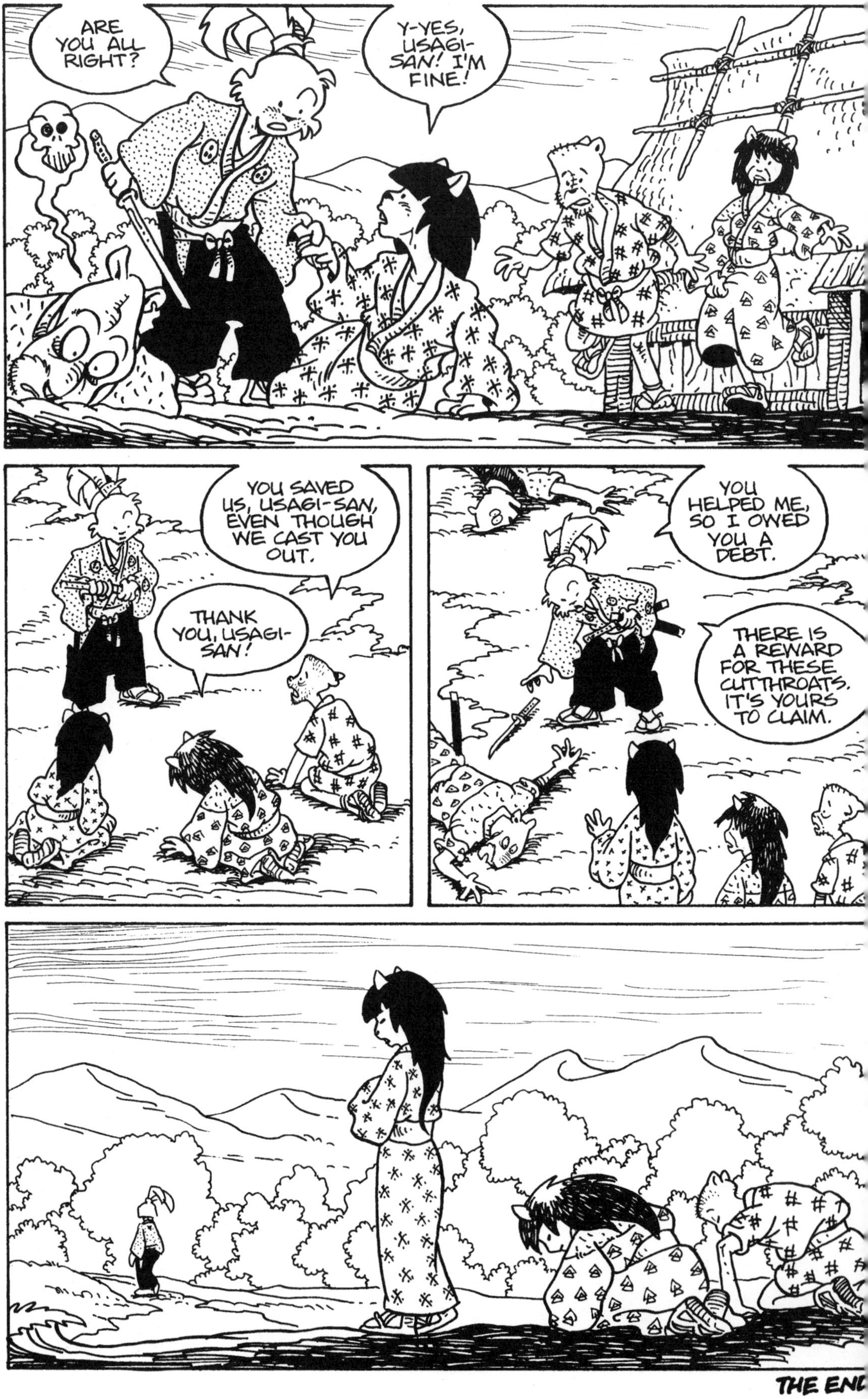
ARE YOU ALL RIGHT?
Y-YES, USAGI-SAN! I'M FINE!
YOU SAVED US, USAGI-SAN, EVEN THOUGH WE CAST YOU OUT.
THANK YOU, USAGI-SAN!
YOU HELPED ME, SO I OWED YOU A DEBT.
THERE IS A REWARD FOR THESE CUTTHROATS. IT'S YOURS TO CLAIM.

THE END

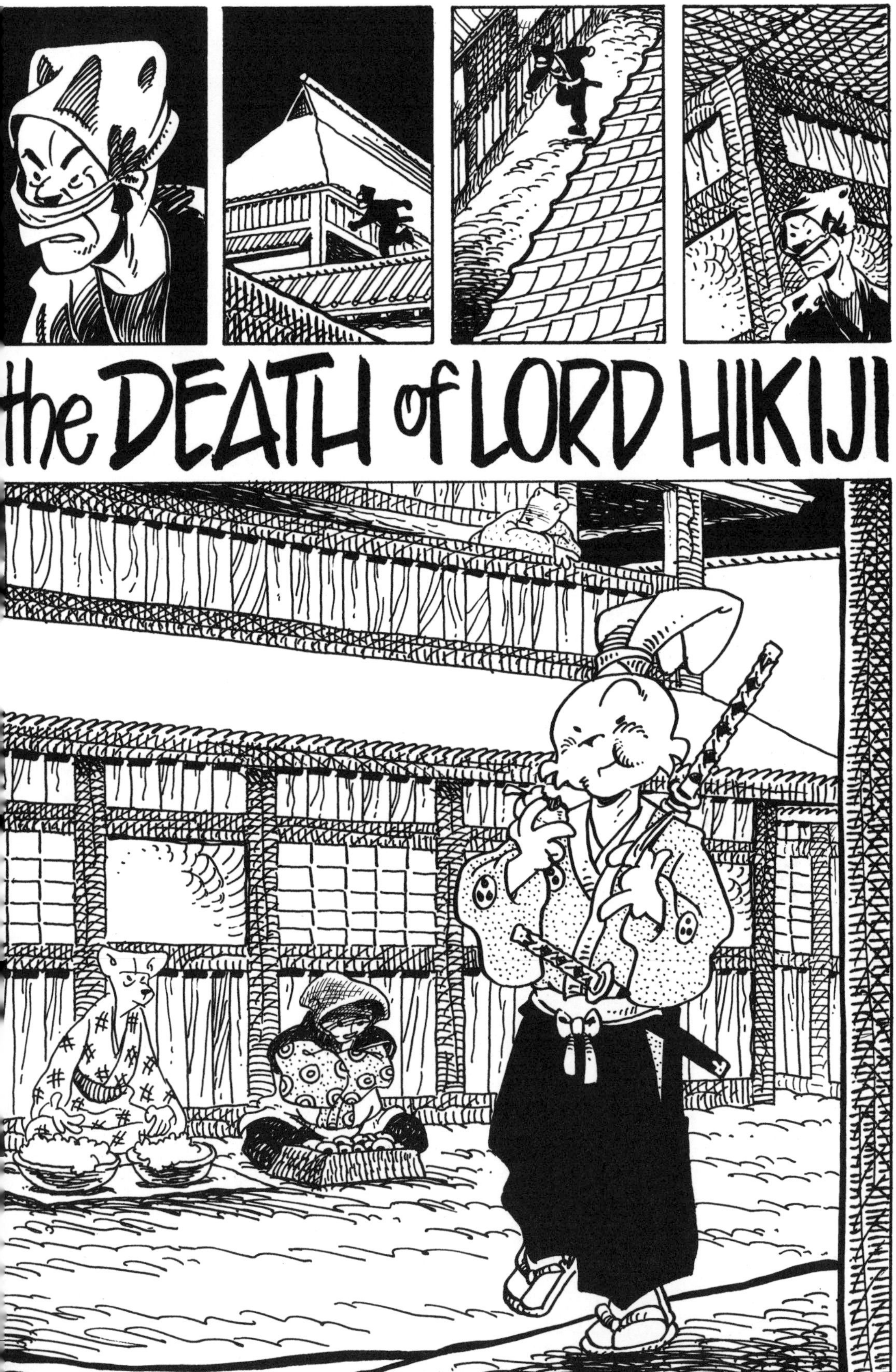
the DEATH of LORD HIKIJI

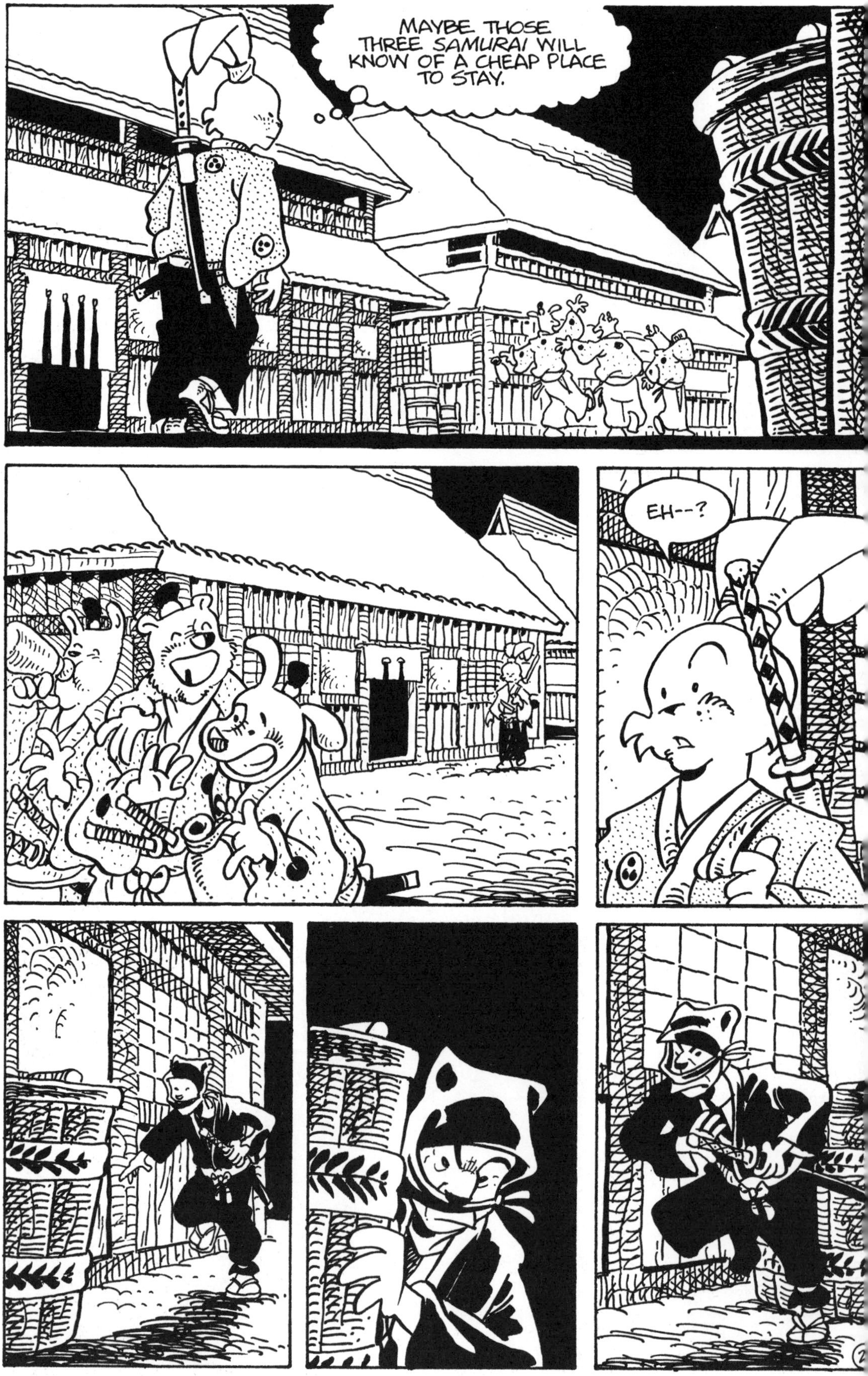
MAYBE THOSE THREE SAMURAI WILL KNOW OF A CHEAP PLACE TO STAY.
EH--?

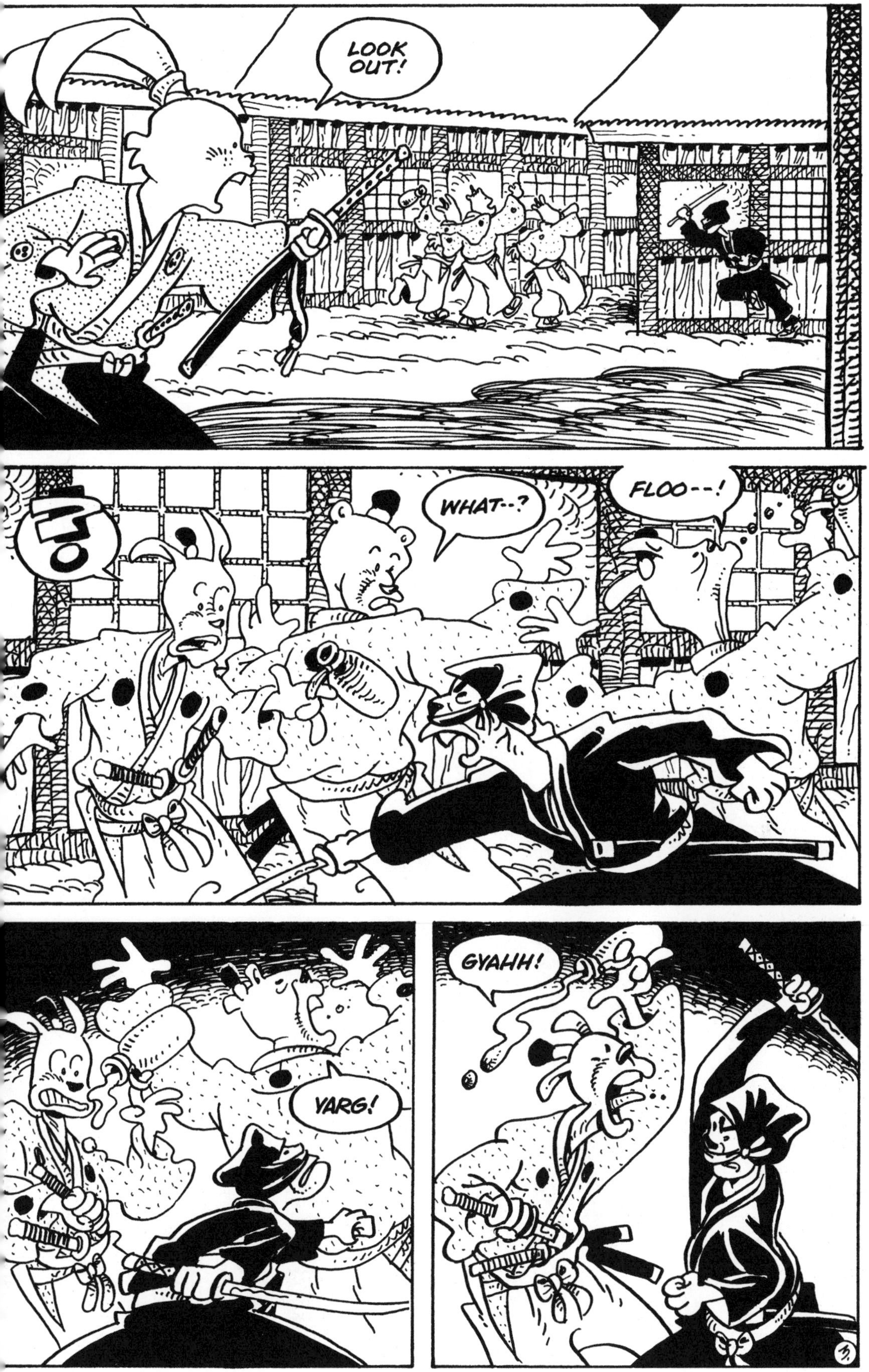
LOOK OUT!
WHAT--?
FLOO--!
YARG!
GYAHH!

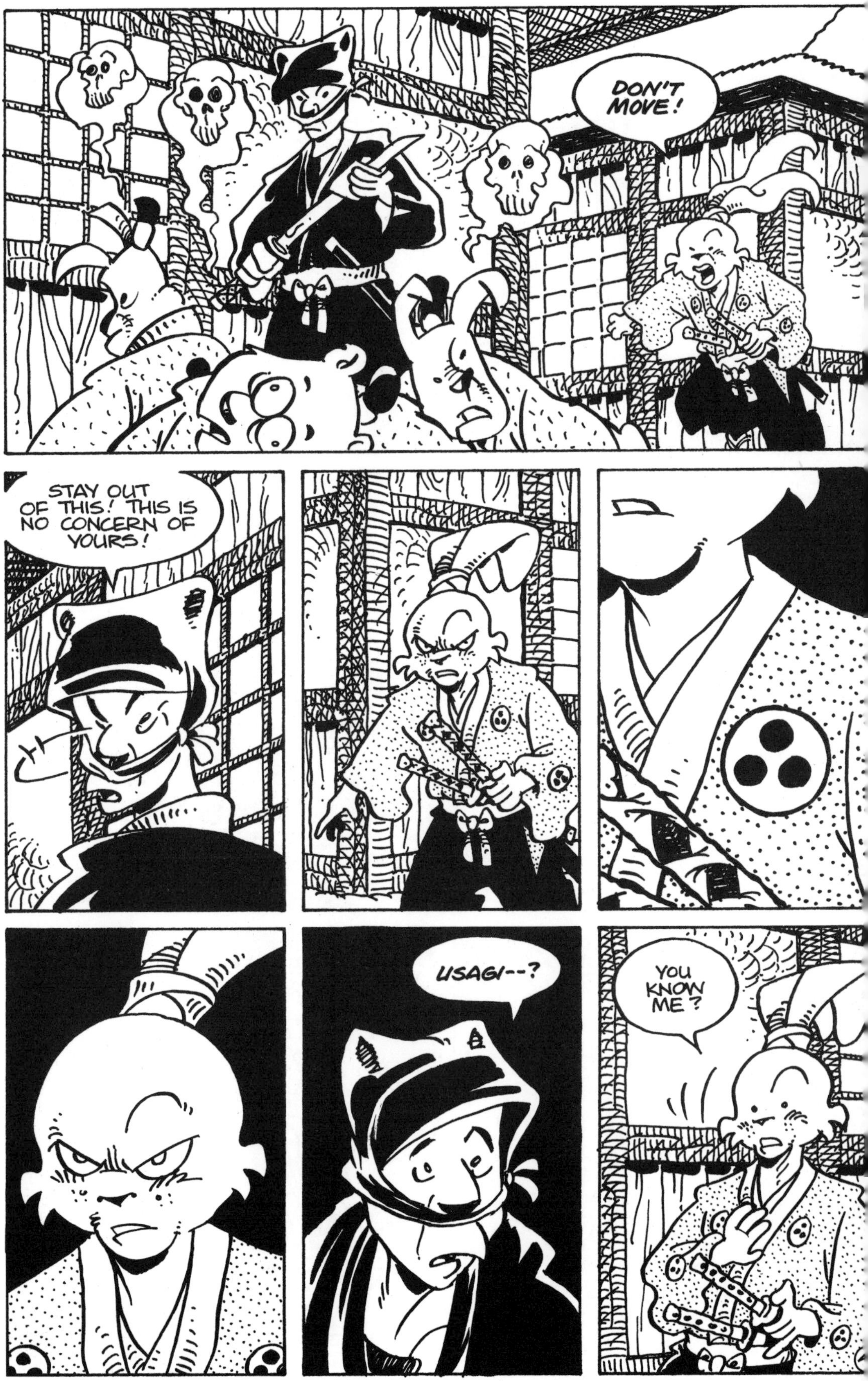
DON'T MOVE!
STAY OUT OF THIS! THIS IS NO CONCERN OF YOURS!
USAGI--?
YOU KNOW ME?

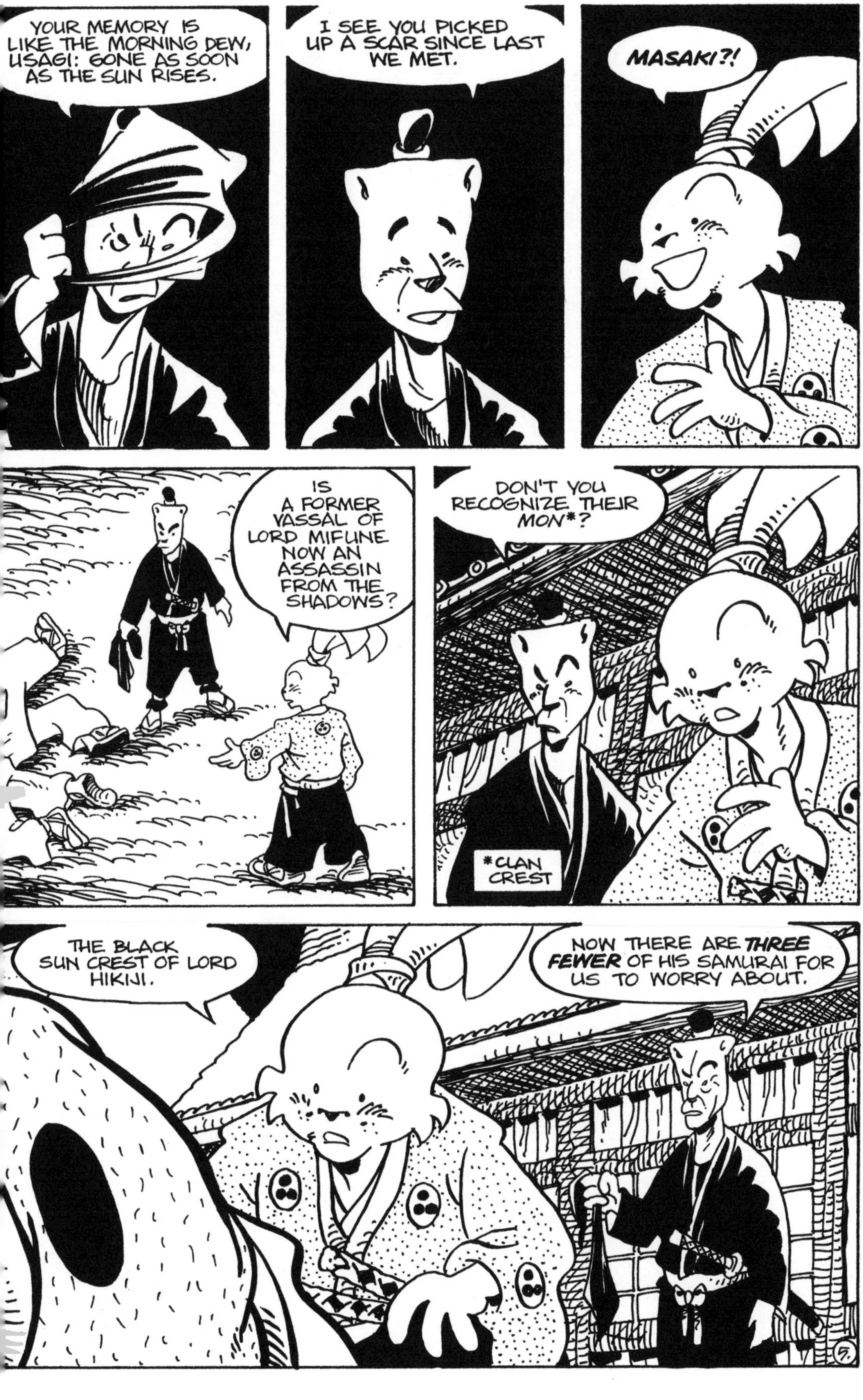
YOUR MEMORY IS LIKE THE MORNING DEW, USAGI: GONE AS SOON AS THE SUN RISES.
I SEE YOU PICKED UP A SCAR SINCE LAST WE MET.
MASAKI?!
IS A FORMER VASSAL OF LORD MIFUNE NOW AN ASSASSIN FROM THE SHADOWS?
DON'T YOU RECOGNIZE THEIR MON*?
*CLAN CREST
THE BLACK SUN CREST OF LORD HIKIJI.
NOW THERE ARE THREE FEWER OF HIS SAMURAI FOR US TO WORRY ABOUT.
7

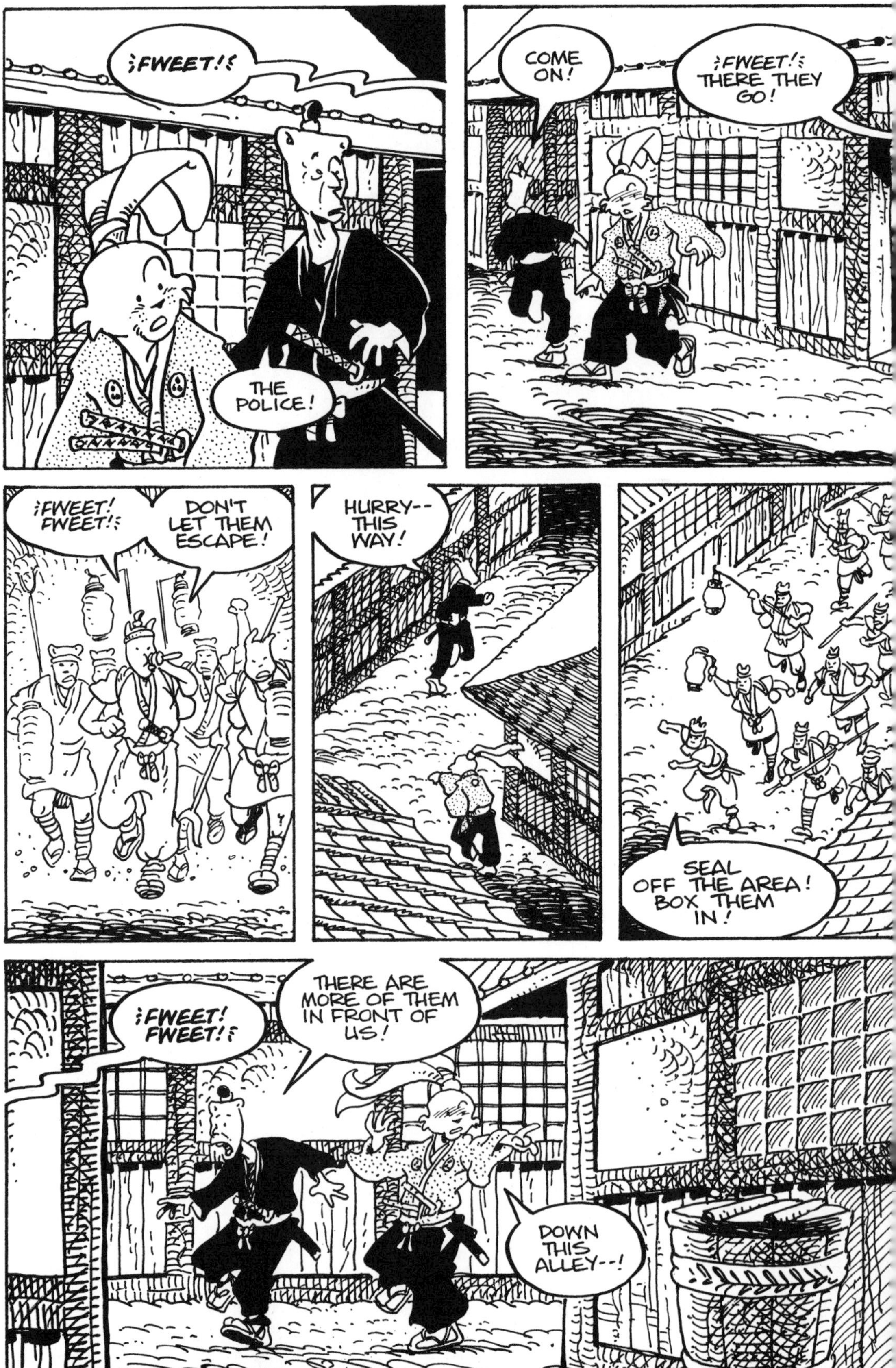
FWEET!
THE POLICE!
COME ON!
FWEET! THERE THEY GO!
FWEET! FWEET!
DON'T LET THEM ESCAPE!
HURRY-- THIS WAY!
SEAL OFF THE AREA! BOX THEM IN!
FWEET! FWEET!
THERE ARE MORE OF THEM IN FRONT OF US!
DOWN THIS ALLEY--!

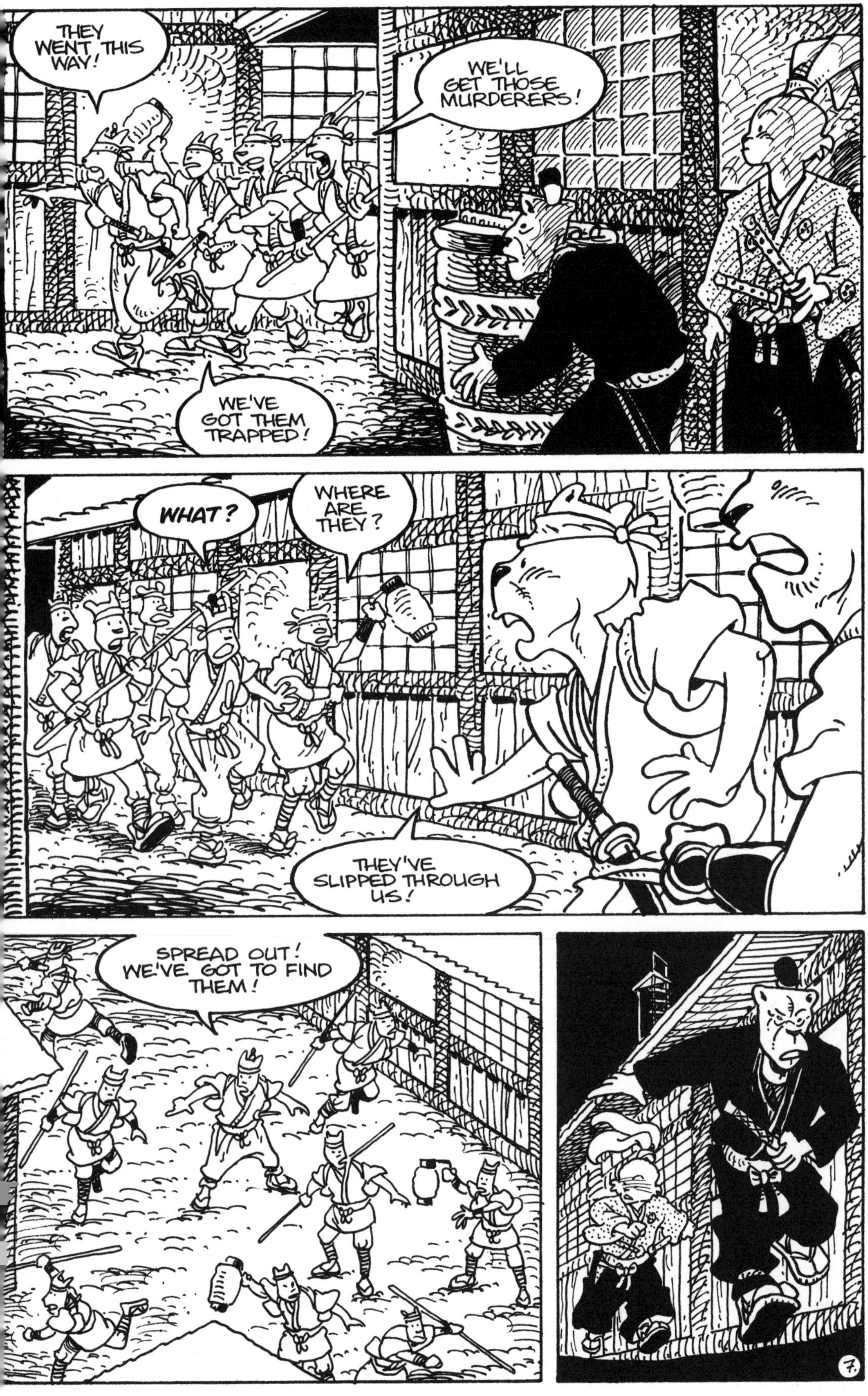
THEY WENT THIS WAY!
WE'LL GET THOSE MURDERERS!
WE'VE GOT THEM TRAPPED!
WHAT?
WHERE ARE THEY?
THEY'VE SLIPPED THROUGH US!
SPREAD OUT! WE'VE GOT TO FIND THEM!
7.

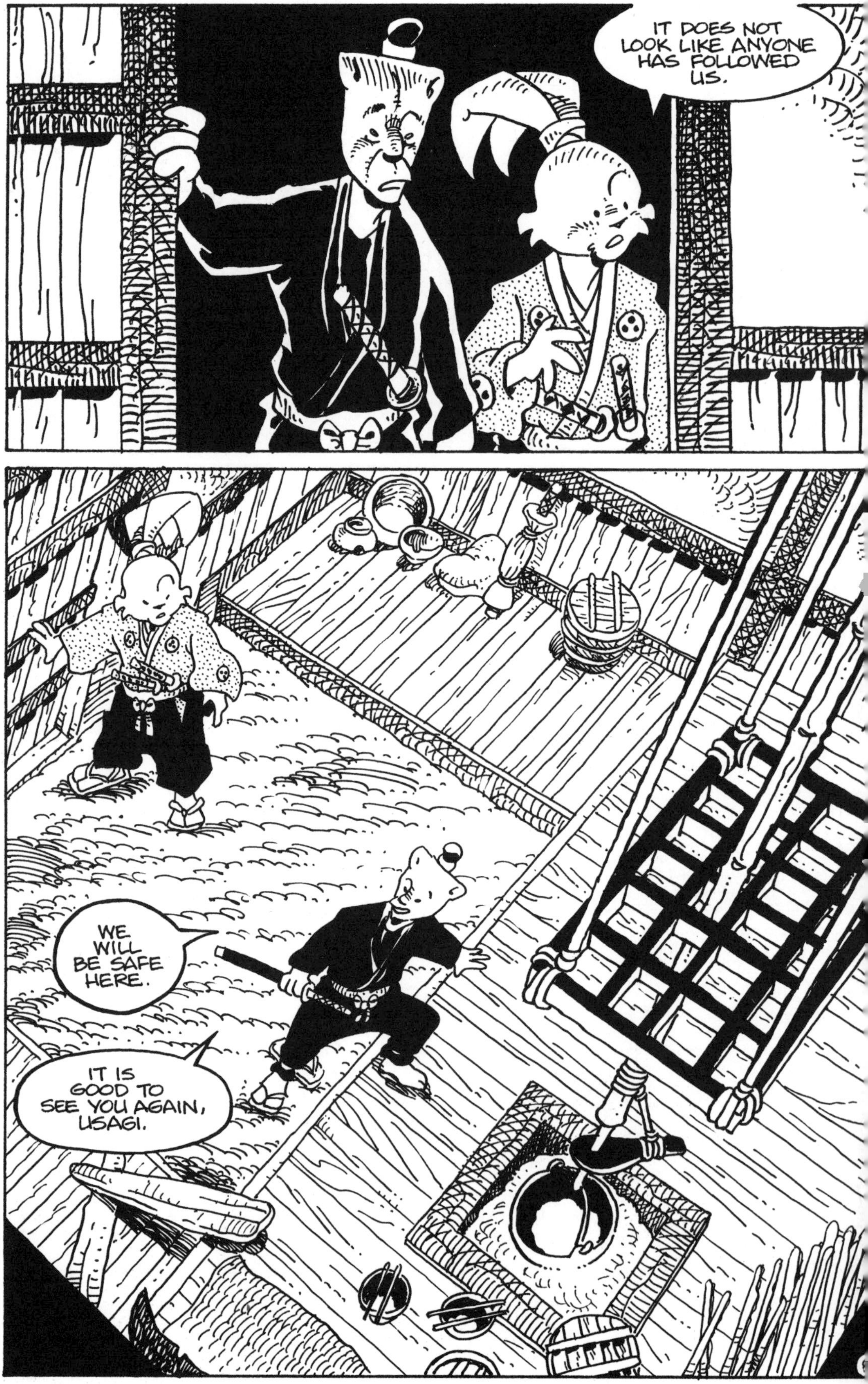
IT DOES NOT LOOK LIKE ANYONE HAS FOLLOWED US.
WE WILL BE SAFE HERE.
IT IS GOOD TO SEE YOU AGAIN, USAGI.

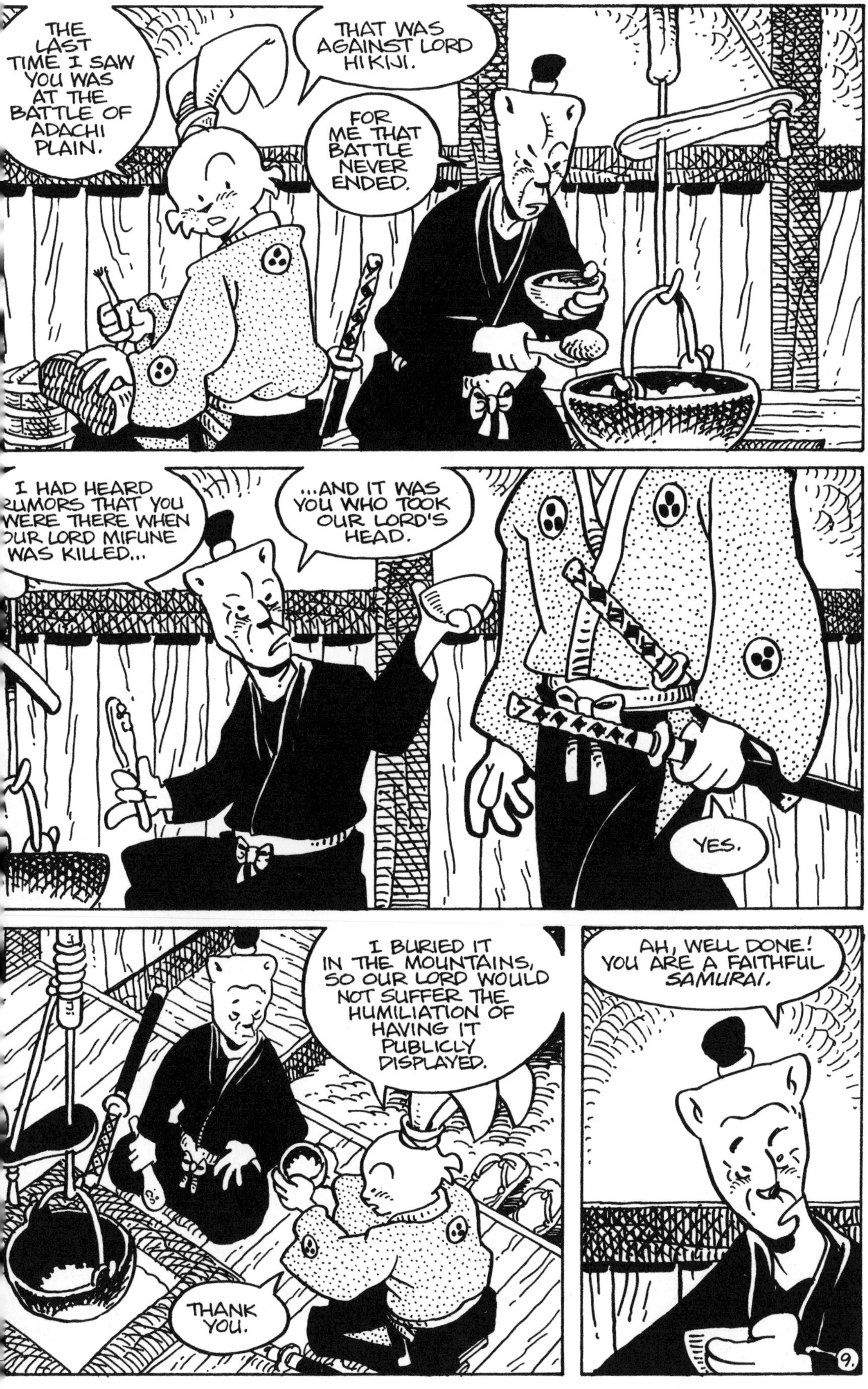
THE LAST TIME I SAW YOU WAS AT THE BATTLE OF ADACHI PLAIN.
THAT WAS AGAINST LORD HIKIJI.
FOR ME THAT BATTLE NEVER ENDED.
I HAD HEARD RUMORS THAT YOU WERE THERE WHEN OUR LORD MIFUNE WAS KILLED...
...AND IT WAS YOU WHO TOOK OUR LORD'S HEAD.
YES.
I BURIED IT IN THE MOUNTAINS, SO OUR LORD WOULD NOT SUFFER THE HUMILIATION OF HAVING IT PUBLICLY DISPLAYED.
THANK YOU.
AH, WELL DONE! YOU ARE A FAITHFUL *SAMURAI*.
9.

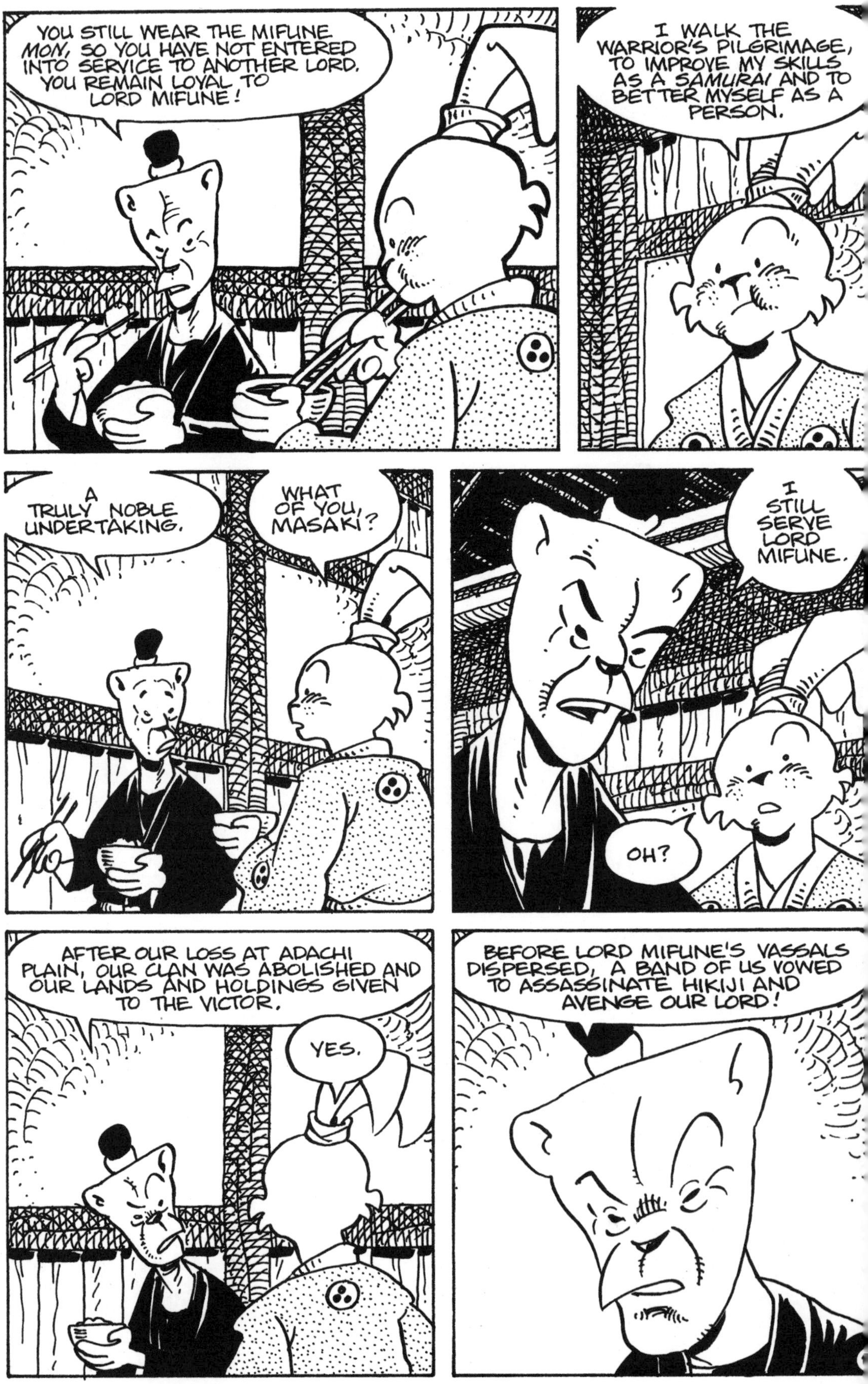
YOU STILL WEAR THE MIFUNE *MON*, SO YOU HAVE NOT ENTERED INTO SERVICE TO ANOTHER LORD. YOU REMAIN LOYAL TO LORD MIFUNE!
I WALK THE WARRIOR'S PILGRIMAGE, TO IMPROVE MY SKILLS AS A *SAMURAI* AND TO BETTER MYSELF AS A PERSON.
A TRULY NOBLE UNDERTAKING.
WHAT OF YOU, MASAKI?
I STILL SERVE LORD MIFUNE.
OH?
AFTER OUR LOSS AT ADACHI PLAIN, OUR CLAN WAS ABOLISHED AND OUR LANDS AND HOLDINGS GIVEN TO THE VICTOR.
YES.
BEFORE LORD MIFUNE'S VASSALS DISPERSED, A BAND OF US VOWED TO ASSASSINATE HIKIJI AND AVENGE OUR LORD!

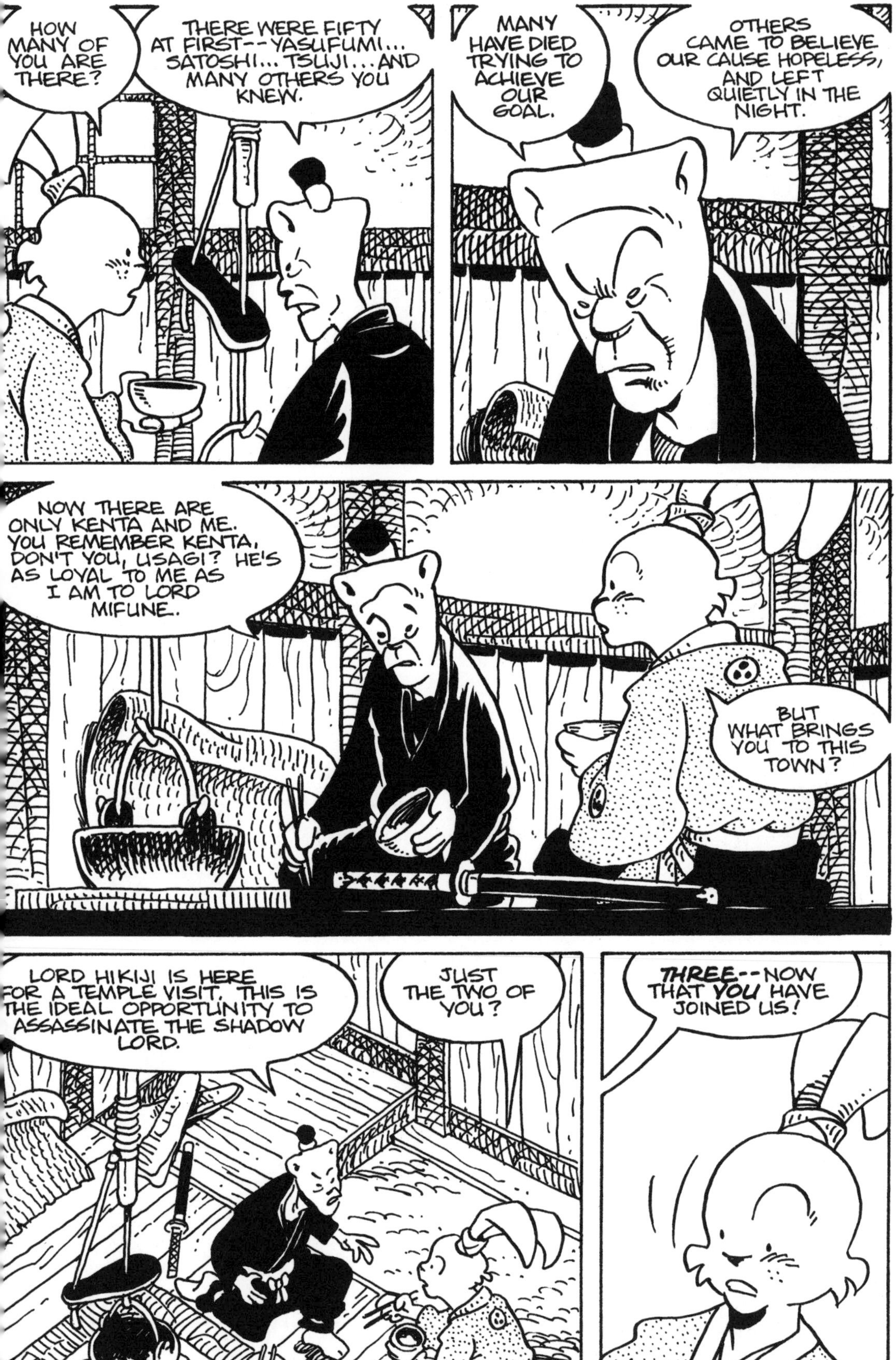
HOW MANY OF YOU ARE THERE?
THERE WERE FIFTY AT FIRST--YASUFUMI... SATOSHI... TSUJI... AND MANY OTHERS YOU KNEW.
MANY HAVE DIED TRYING TO ACHIEVE OUR GOAL.
OTHERS CAME TO BELIEVE OUR CAUSE HOPELESS, AND LEFT QUIETLY IN THE NIGHT.
NOW THERE ARE ONLY KENTA AND ME. YOU REMEMBER KENTA, DON'T YOU, USAGI? HE'S AS LOYAL TO ME AS I AM TO LORD MIFUNE.
BUT WHAT BRINGS YOU TO THIS TOWN?
LORD HIKIJI IS HERE FOR A TEMPLE VISIT. THIS IS THE IDEAL OPPORTUNITY TO ASSASSINATE THE SHADOW LORD.
JUST THE TWO OF YOU?
*THREE*--NOW THAT *YOU* HAVE JOINED US!
11.

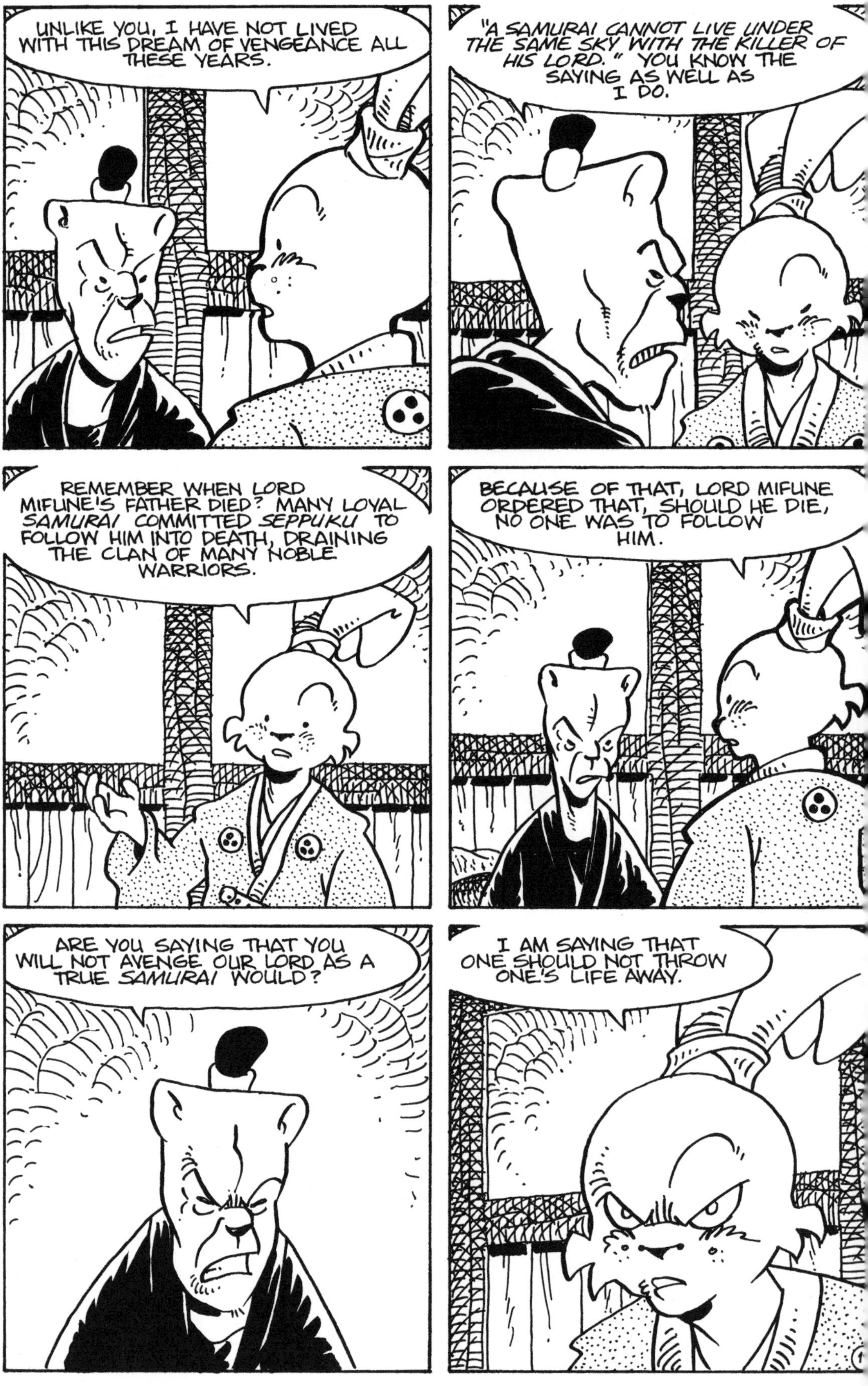
UNLIKE YOU, I HAVE NOT LIVED WITH THIS DREAM OF VENGEANCE ALL THESE YEARS.
"A SAMURAI CANNOT LIVE UNDER THE SAME SKY WITH THE KILLER OF HIS LORD." YOU KNOW THE SAYING AS WELL AS I DO.
REMEMBER WHEN LORD MIFUNE'S FATHER DIED? MANY LOYAL SAMURAI COMMITTED SEPPUKU TO FOLLOW HIM INTO DEATH, DRAINING THE CLAN OF MANY NOBLE WARRIORS.
BECAUSE OF THAT, LORD MIFUNE ORDERED THAT, SHOULD HE DIE, NO ONE WAS TO FOLLOW HIM.
ARE YOU SAYING THAT YOU WILL NOT AVENGE OUR LORD AS A TRUE SAMURAI WOULD?
I AM SAYING THAT ONE SHOULD NOT THROW ONE'S LIFE AWAY.

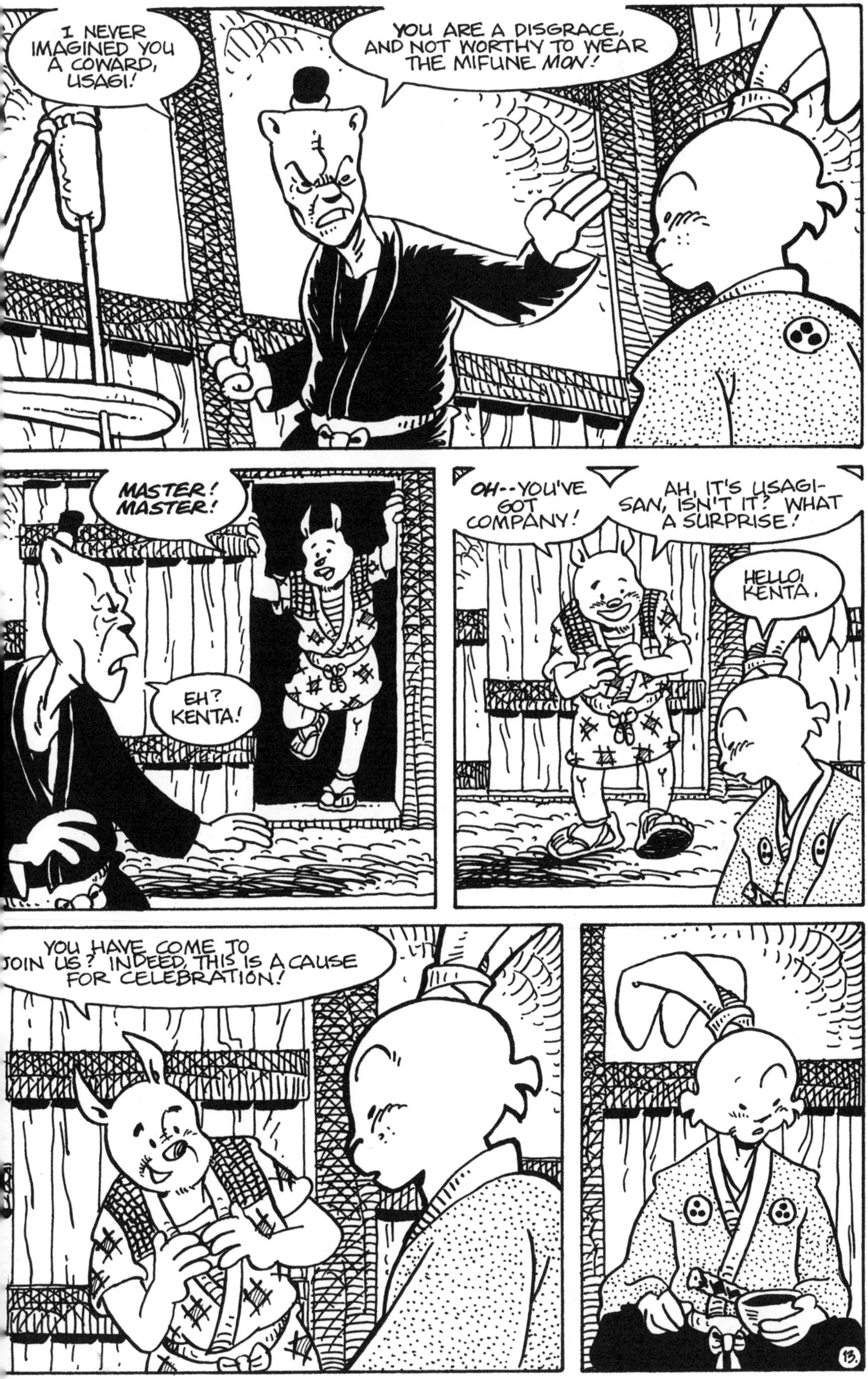
I NEVER IMAGINED YOU A COWARD, USAGI!
YOU ARE A DISGRACE, AND NOT WORTHY TO WEAR THE MIFUNE *MON*!
*MASTER! MASTER!*
EH? KENTA!
*OH*--YOU'VE GOT COMPANY!
AH, IT'S USAGI-SAN, ISN'T IT? WHAT A SURPRISE!
HELLO, KENTA.
YOU HAVE COME TO JOIN US? INDEED, THIS IS A CAUSE FOR CELEBRATION!
13.

WHAT DID YOU RUSH IN HERE TO TELL ME?

YES, OF COURSE. I WAS DISGUISED AS A COMMON LABORER, AND HUNG AROUND LORD HIKIJI'S MANSION.

I OVERHEARD THE GUARDS SAY THAT THE SHADOW LORD IS TRAVELING TO THE TEMPLE VERY EARLY TOMORROW MORNING, BEFORE THE PUBLIC ARRIVES.

AT LAST! THIS WILL BE OUR CHANCE-- TOMORROW!

YOU DID WELL, KENTA.

WHAT OF YOU, USAGI? ARE YOU WITH US, OR NOT?

WELL?

I'M WITH YOU!

176

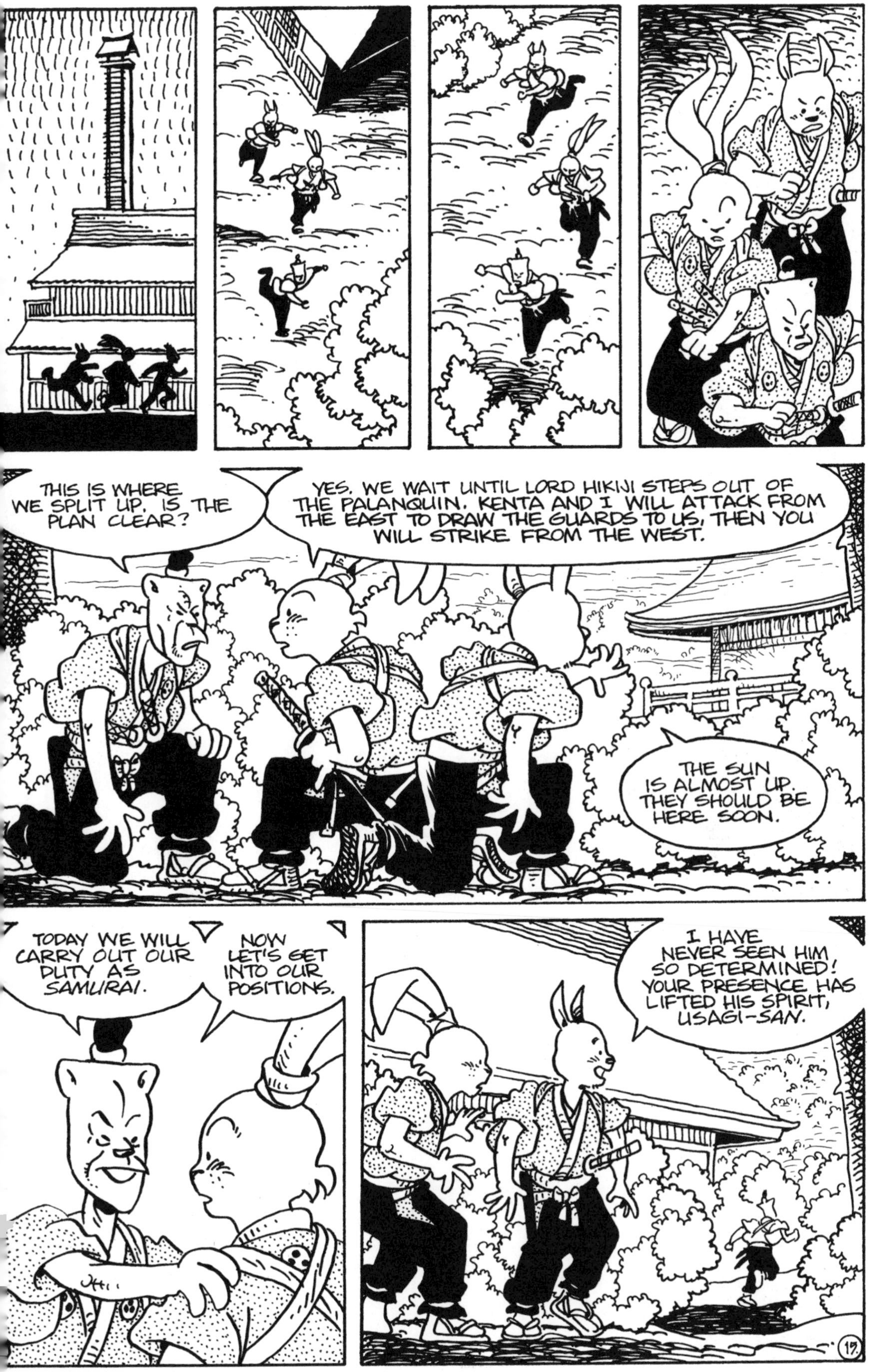

THIS IS WHERE WE SPLIT UP. IS THE PLAN CLEAR?
YES. WE WAIT UNTIL LORD HIKIJI STEPS OUT OF THE PALANQUIN. KENTA AND I WILL ATTACK FROM THE EAST TO DRAW THE GUARDS TO US, THEN YOU WILL STRIKE FROM THE WEST.
THE SUN IS ALMOST UP. THEY SHOULD BE HERE SOON.
TODAY WE WILL CARRY OUT OUR DUTY AS SAMURAI.
NOW LET'S GET INTO OUR POSITIONS.
I HAVE NEVER SEEN HIM SO DETERMINED! YOUR PRESENCE HAS LIFTED HIS SPIRIT, USAGI-SAN.
19

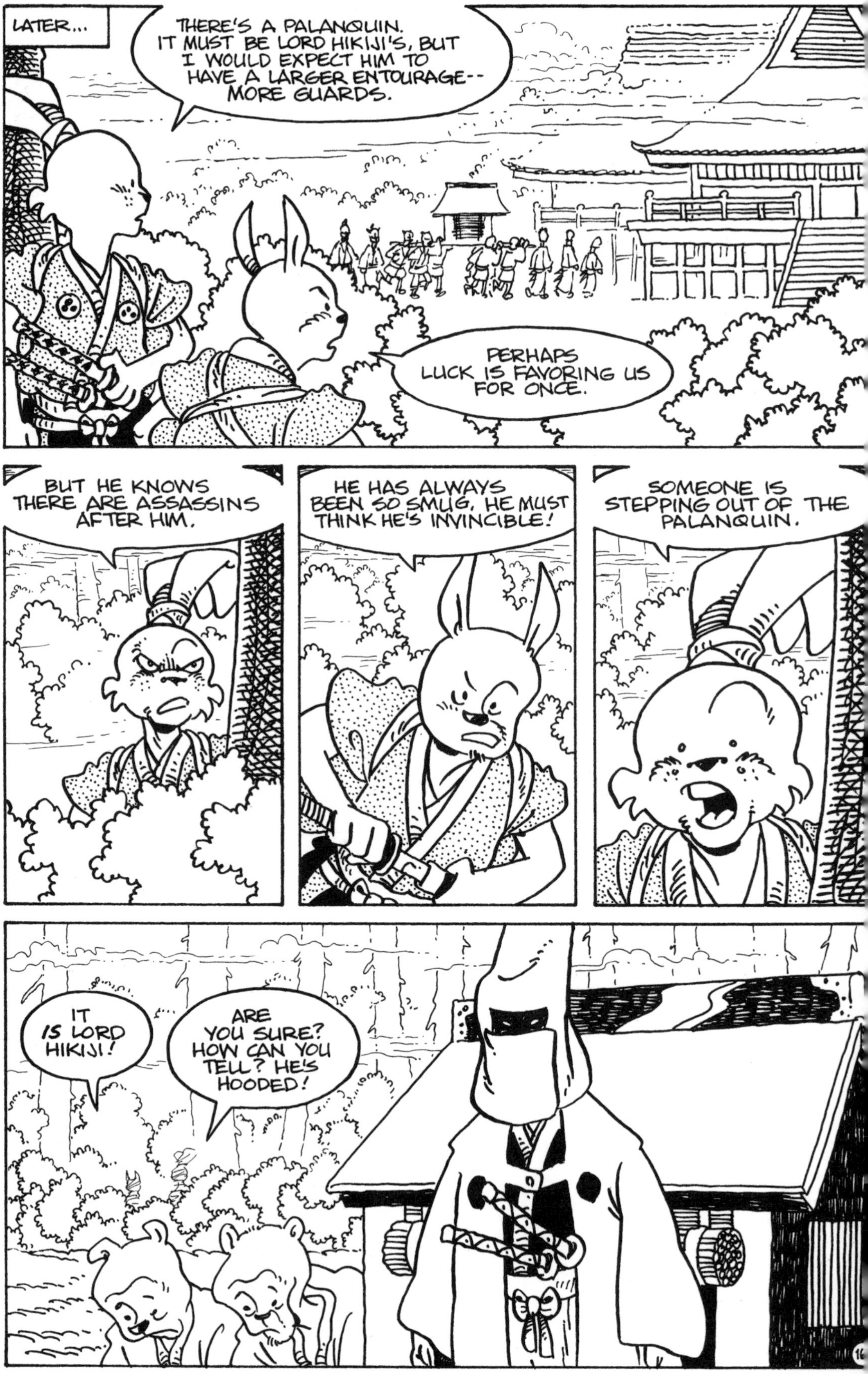
LATER...
THERE'S A PALANQUIN. IT MUST BE LORD HIKIJI'S, BUT I WOULD EXPECT HIM TO HAVE A LARGER ENTOURAGE-- MORE GUARDS.
PERHAPS LUCK IS FAVORING US FOR ONCE.
BUT HE KNOWS THERE ARE ASSASSINS AFTER HIM.
HE HAS ALWAYS BEEN SO SMUG, HE MUST THINK HE'S INVINCIBLE!
SOMEONE IS STEPPING OUT OF THE PALANQUIN.
IT *IS* LORD HIKIJI!
ARE YOU SURE? HOW CAN YOU TELL? HE'S HOODED!

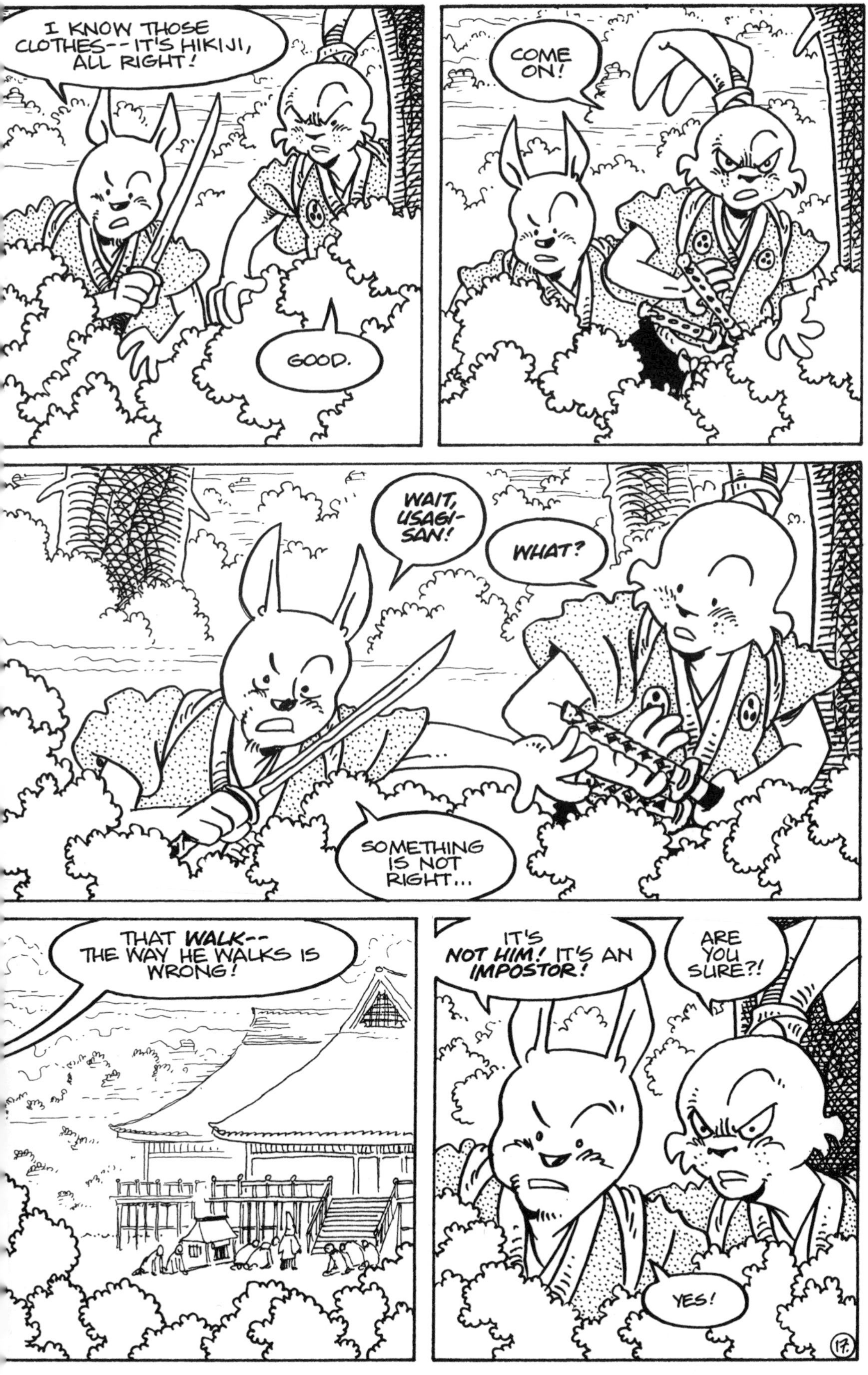

I KNOW THOSE CLOTHES--IT'S HIKIJI, ALL RIGHT!
GOOD.
COME ON!
WAIT, USAGI-SAN!
WHAT?
SOMETHING IS NOT RIGHT...
THAT **WALK**-- THE WAY HE WALKS IS WRONG!
IT'S **NOT HIM!** IT'S AN **IMPOSTOR**!
ARE YOU SURE?!
YES!
17.

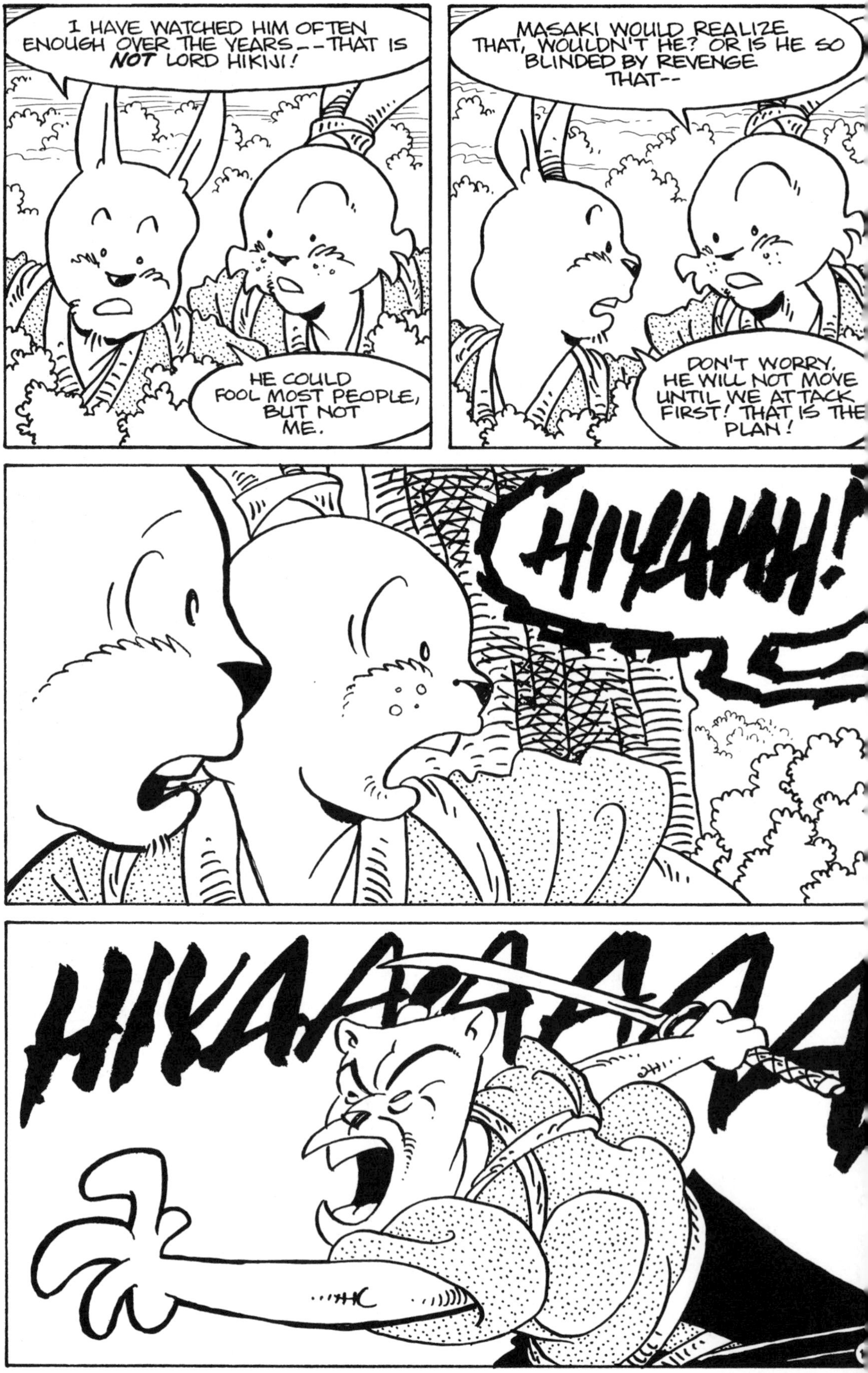
I HAVE WATCHED HIM OFTEN ENOUGH OVER THE YEARS--THAT IS ***NOT*** LORD HIKIJI!
HE COULD FOOL MOST PEOPLE, BUT NOT ME.
MASAKI WOULD REALIZE THAT, WOULDN'T HE? OR IS HE SO BLINDED BY REVENGE THAT--
DON'T WORRY. HE WILL NOT MOVE UNTIL WE ATTACK FIRST! THAT IS THE PLAN!
HIYAHH!
HIYAAAAAAA

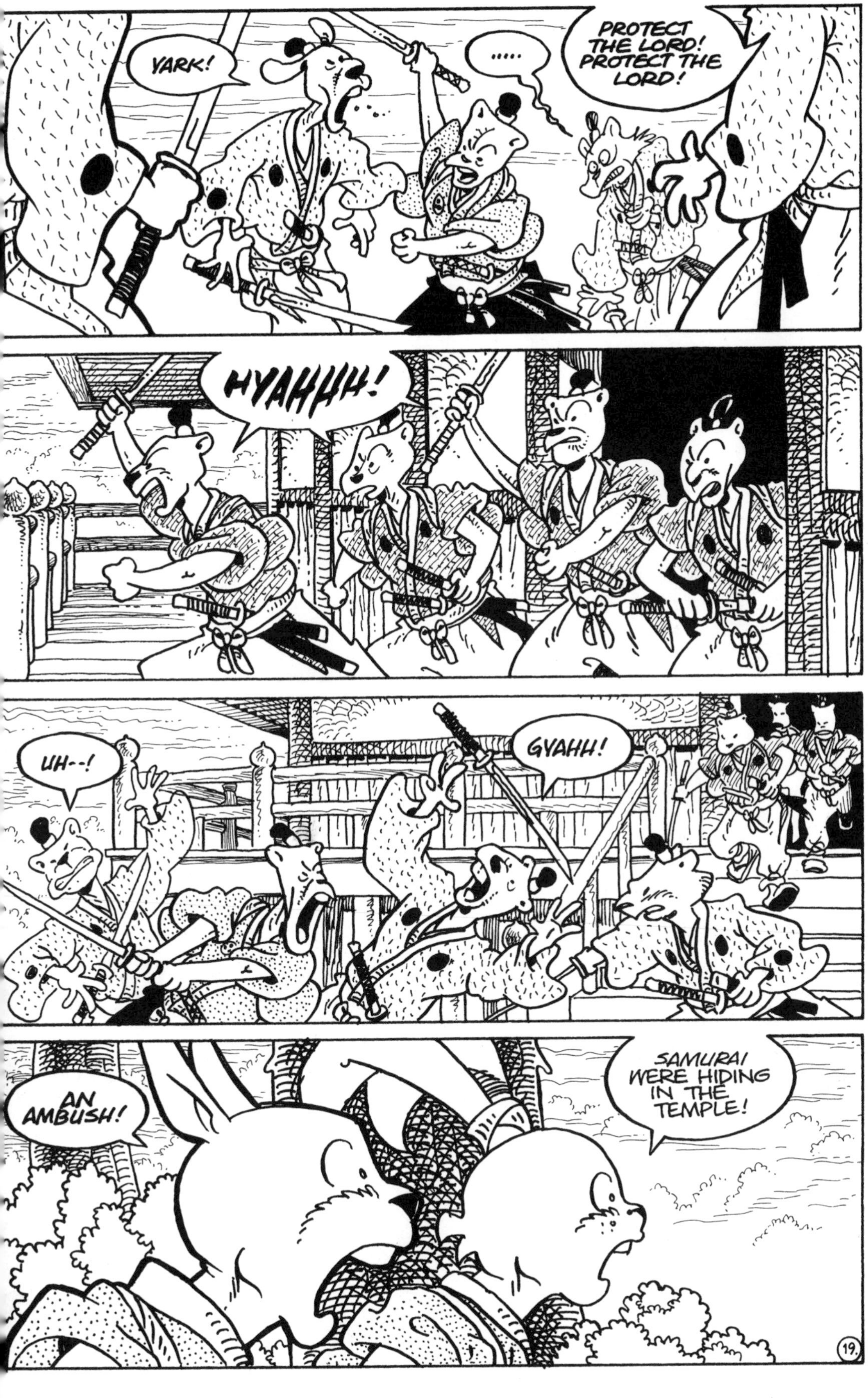
YARK!
.....
PROTECT THE LORD! PROTECT THE LORD!
HYAHHH!
UH--!
GYAHH!
AN AMBUSH!
SAMURAI WERE HIDING IN THE TEMPLE!
19.

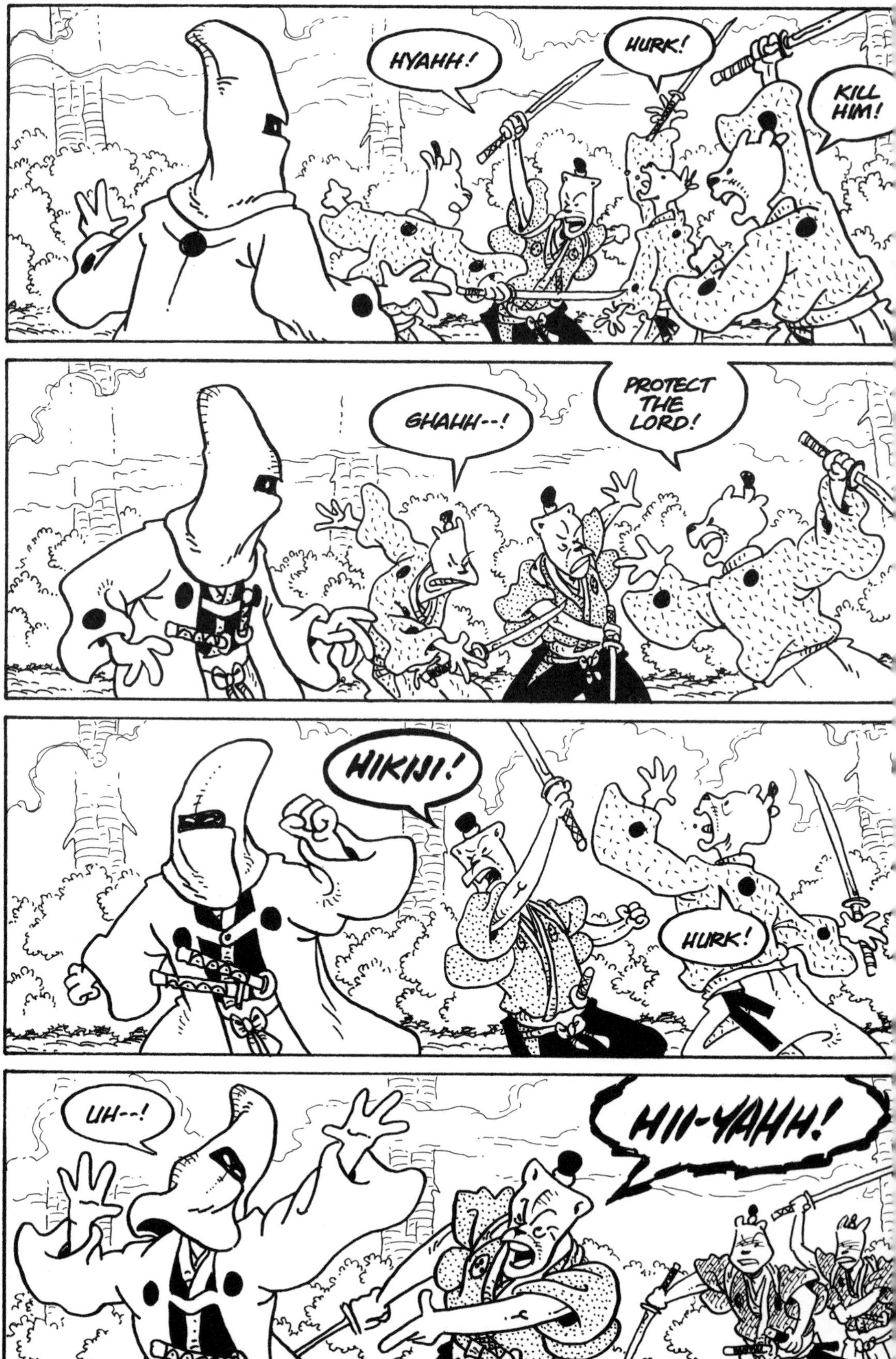
HYAHH!
HURK!
KILL HIM!
GHAHH--!
PROTECT THE LORD!
HIKIJI!
HURK!
UH--!
HII-YAHH!

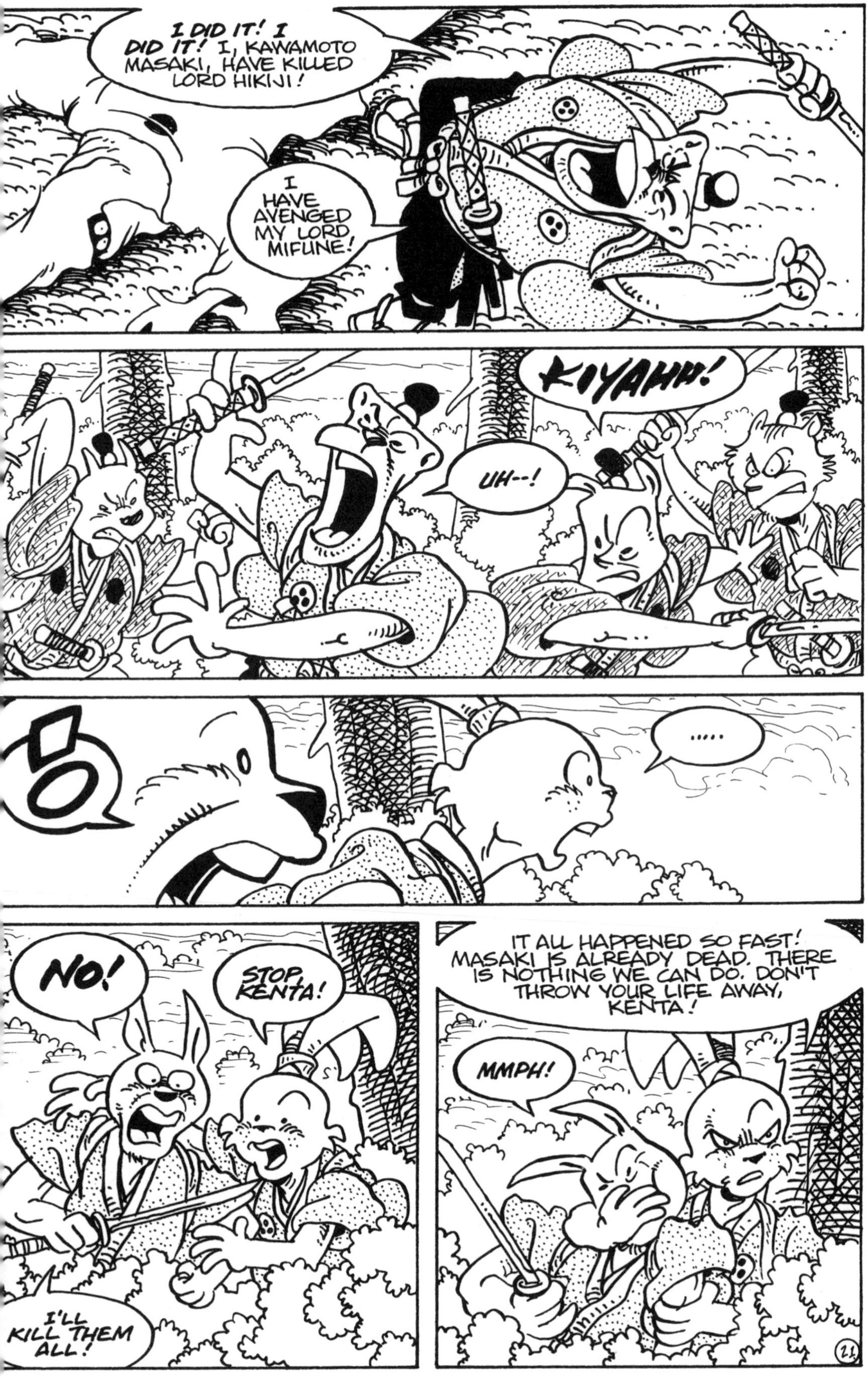

I DID IT! I DID IT! I, KAWAMOTO MASAKI, HAVE KILLED LORD HIKIJI!
I HAVE AVENGED MY LORD MIFUNE!
KIYAHH!
UH--!
!?
.....
NO!
STOP, KENTA!
I'LL KILL THEM ALL!
IT ALL HAPPENED SO FAST! MASAKI IS ALREADY DEAD. THERE IS NOTHING WE CAN DO. DON'T THROW YOUR LIFE AWAY, KENTA!
MMPH!
21

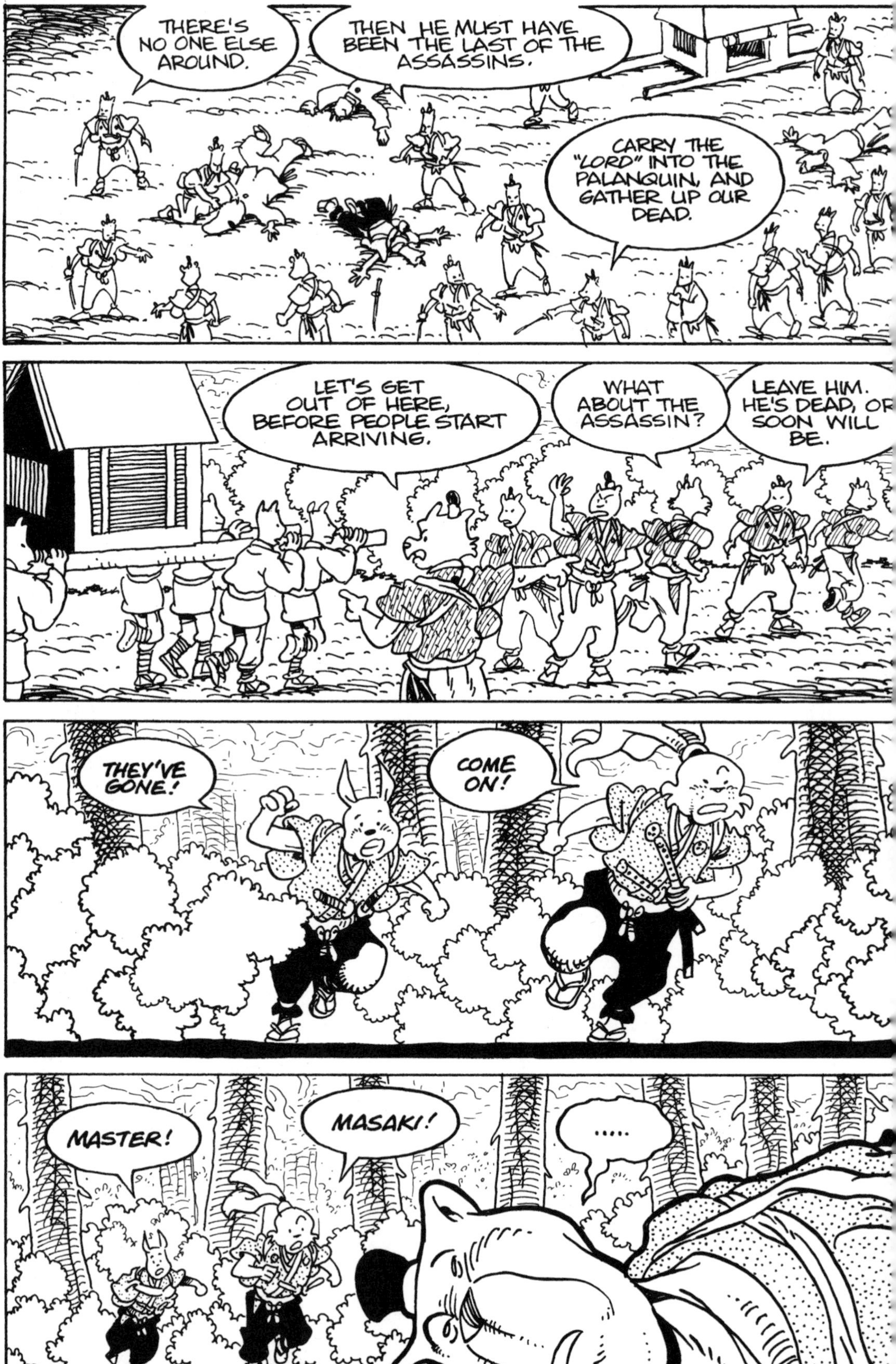
THERE'S NO ONE ELSE AROUND.
THEN HE MUST HAVE BEEN THE LAST OF THE ASSASSINS.
CARRY THE "LORD" INTO THE PALANQUIN, AND GATHER UP OUR DEAD.
LET'S GET OUT OF HERE, BEFORE PEOPLE START ARRIVING.
WHAT ABOUT THE ASSASSIN?
LEAVE HIM. HE'S DEAD, OR SOON WILL BE.
THEY'VE GONE!
COME ON!
MASTER!
MASAKI!
.....

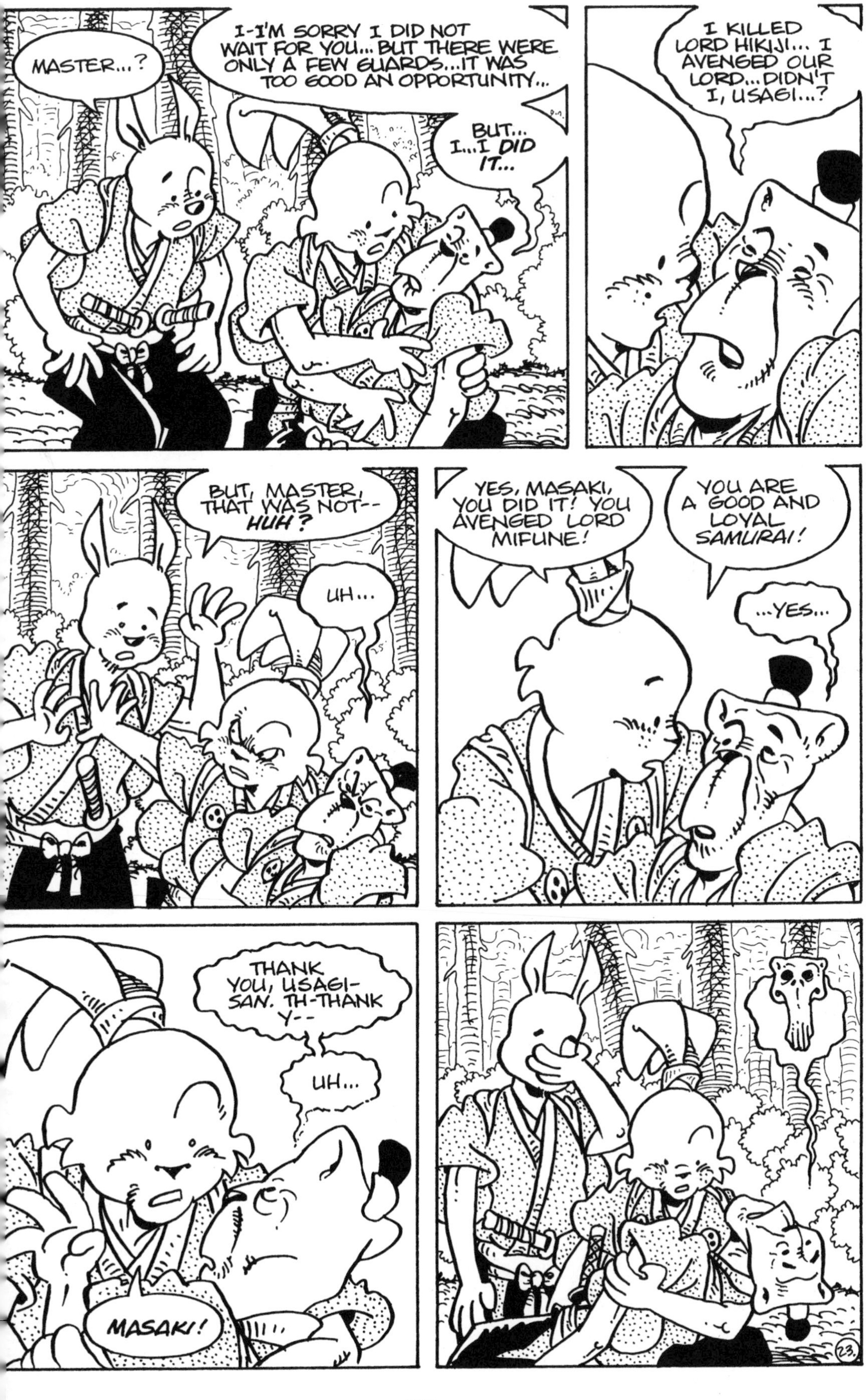

MASTER...?
I-I'M SORRY I DID NOT WAIT FOR YOU... BUT THERE WERE ONLY A FEW GUARDS...IT WAS TOO GOOD AN OPPORTUNITY...
BUT... I...I DID IT...
I KILLED LORD HIKIJI... I AVENGED OUR LORD...DIDN'T I, USAGI...?
BUT, MASTER, THAT WAS NOT--HUH?
UH...
YES, MASAKI, YOU DID IT! YOU AVENGED LORD MIFUNE!
YOU ARE A GOOD AND LOYAL SAMURAI!
...YES...
THANK YOU, USAGI-SAN. TH-THANK Y--
UH...
MASAKI!
23.

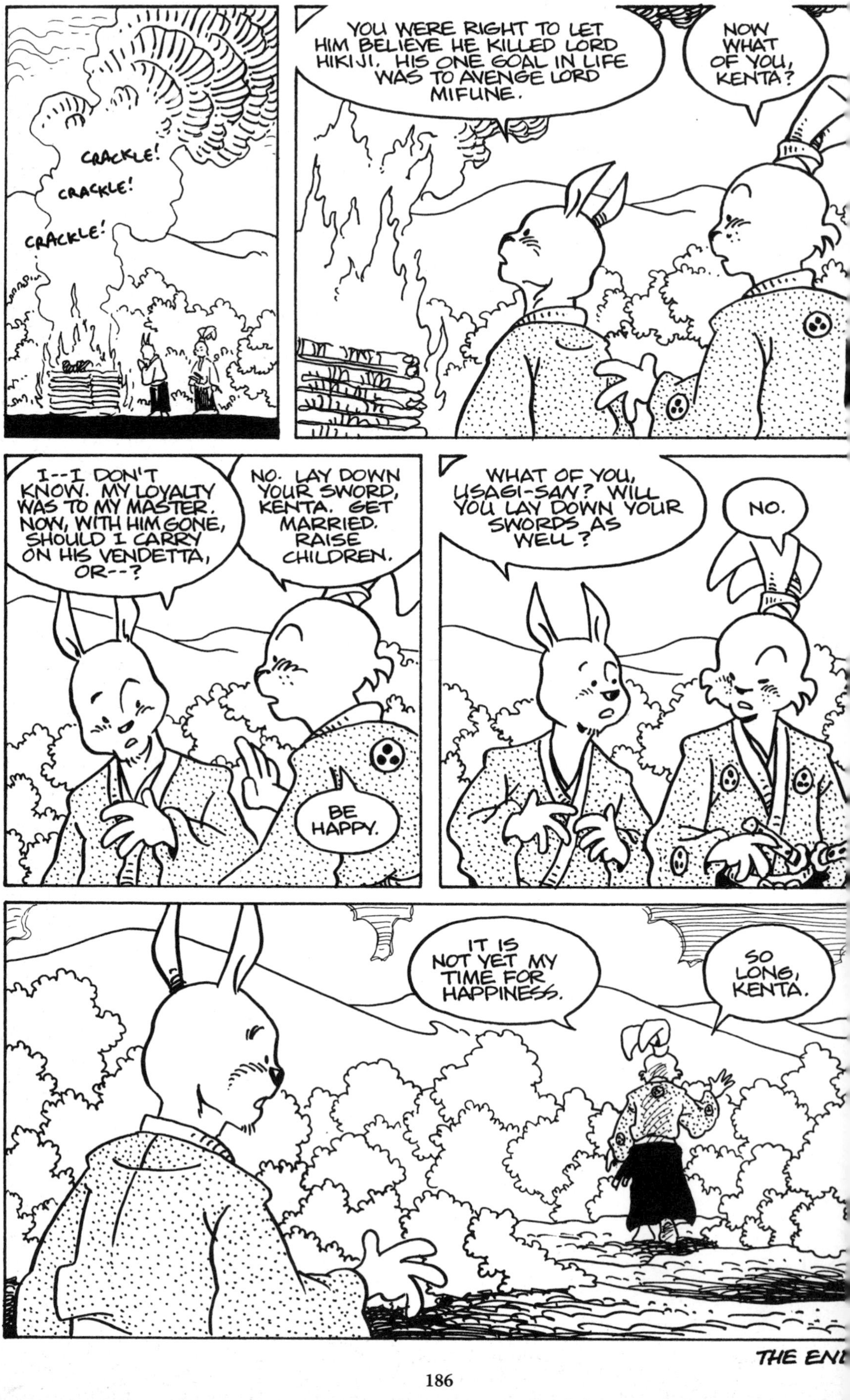
CRACKLE!
CRACKLE!
CRACKLE!
YOU WERE RIGHT TO LET HIM BELIEVE HE KILLED LORD HIKIJI. HIS ONE GOAL IN LIFE WAS TO AVENGE LORD MIFUNE.
NOW WHAT OF YOU, KENTA?
I--I DON'T KNOW. MY LOYALTY WAS TO MY MASTER. NOW, WITH HIM GONE, SHOULD I CARRY ON HIS VENDETTA, OR--?
NO. LAY DOWN YOUR SWORD, KENTA. GET MARRIED. RAISE CHILDREN.
BE HAPPY.
WHAT OF YOU, USAGI-SAN? WILL YOU LAY DOWN YOUR SWORDS AS WELL?
NO.
IT IS NOT YET MY TIME FOR HAPPINESS.
SO LONG, KENTA.
THE END

# A TOWN CALLED HELL

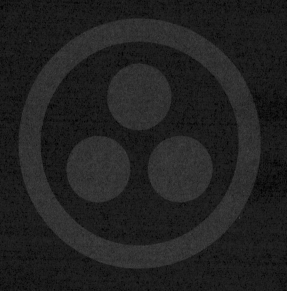

# INTRODUCTION

**I CAN'T TELL YOU** how pleasantly surprised I was when Diana Schutz rang me up on my new iPhone 5—*Time* magazine's gadget of the year, by the way—and asked if I would be interested in writing an introduction to Stan's latest collection. First off, I was saddened to hear that Stan had left Marvel—Disney must have found someone cheaper to put on his soapbox—but I was glad that Mike Richardson had given him a chance to work at Dark Horse. Diana quickly pointed out that it was the *other* Stan—Stan Sakai—and would I still be interested in doing an introduction to his latest collection? I think my robust laugh let her know I knew who it was she was talking about, and again I expressed how saddened I was that Fantagraphics had let Stan go, but glad that Mike Richardson had given him a chance to work at Dark Horse.

That being said, and given the long list of luminaries who have been put to task writing introductions for Stan's *Usagi Yojimbo* volumes, I wondered why Diana would have thought of me. So I asked, and she said that she'd wanted a philosophic bent, but Jean-Paul Sartre, Arthur Schopenhauer, and Friedrich Nietzsche were not returning her calls, and I was fourth on the list. I was flattered, to say the least, for although I have never read any of those fellows' comics, I know people who have, and I knew I was in good company.

Diana said she would need five hundred words, give or take, and I was a bit reluctant at first, given the recent difficulty I had even coming up with a combination of eight letters, numbers, or symbols for my eBay account, but this was for Stan Sakai—and, besides, I am considered Iowa's reigning *poet lariat.* So, for inspiration I trotted over to my Jewel-Osco, where I do my best thinking (in your region, it might be a Winn-Dixie, Piggly Wiggly, Albertsons . . . well, I'd better stop there before you get the idea I am padding out my word count—I think you get the idea), and began strolling up and down the cereal aisle, looking for inspiration as well as the evening's menu. There was so much to choose from, but so little with much real taste or nutritional substance. Sure, Count Chocula is pretty cool and turns your milk into chocolate milk, but then so do Cocoa Puffs. Frosted Flakes are great, but Honey Nut Cheerios are, too, and they are supposed to help lower cholesterol. Then it hit me. *Usagi Yojimbo* is like the greatest breakfast cereal in the world!!!!!!! And unlike many of the other cereals you find in your comics store, or comics you find in your cereal store—er, comics store—*Usagi Yojimbo* is not only great, but it helps lower cholesterol . . . well, not cholesterol, but it does something for your heart, and for your mind, to boot.

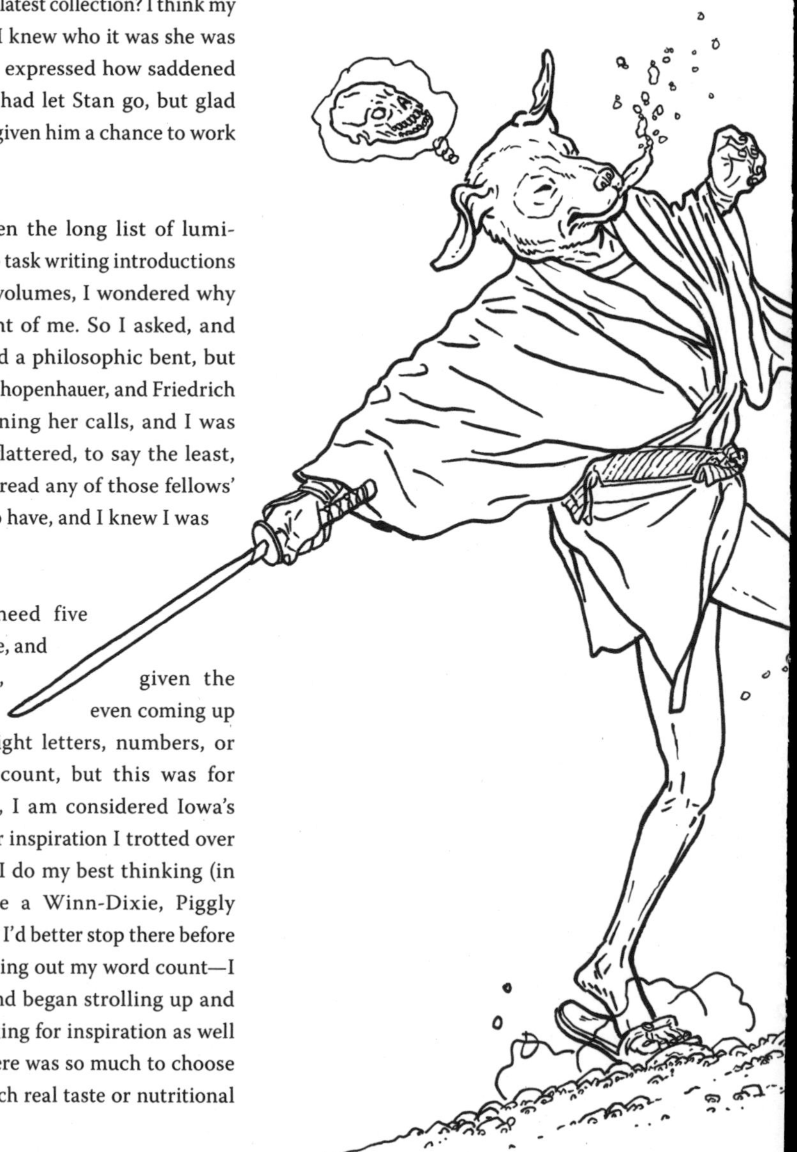

How often can you say *that* about a comic book—or anything, for that matter? It is a heart-friendly brain food that makes you feel good about yourself whenever you eat it. I mean, read it.

And if you are reading this volume of *Usagi Yojimbo* for the first time . . . brother or sister, are you lucky, because there are twenty-six volumes before this one, and by the time you finish reading this one, or all of them, you'll feel good about yourself, about comics, and about the choices that led you to buy these *awesome* (I only used the word "awesome" because I wanted to include some vernacular kids could relate to) books to begin with, because it means you care about great art, great story, and great nutrition . . .

I hope that's five hundred words. If it is, then that's *awesome*!

geof darrow
AWESOME LAND, USA

P.S. I drew Zato-Ino the Blind Swordspig, because I love that character and his movie counterpart Zatoichi so much, and I love Stan so much, and I am very selfish and wanted to have one of my drawings in his *awesome* books. Sorry. Is that five hundred words?

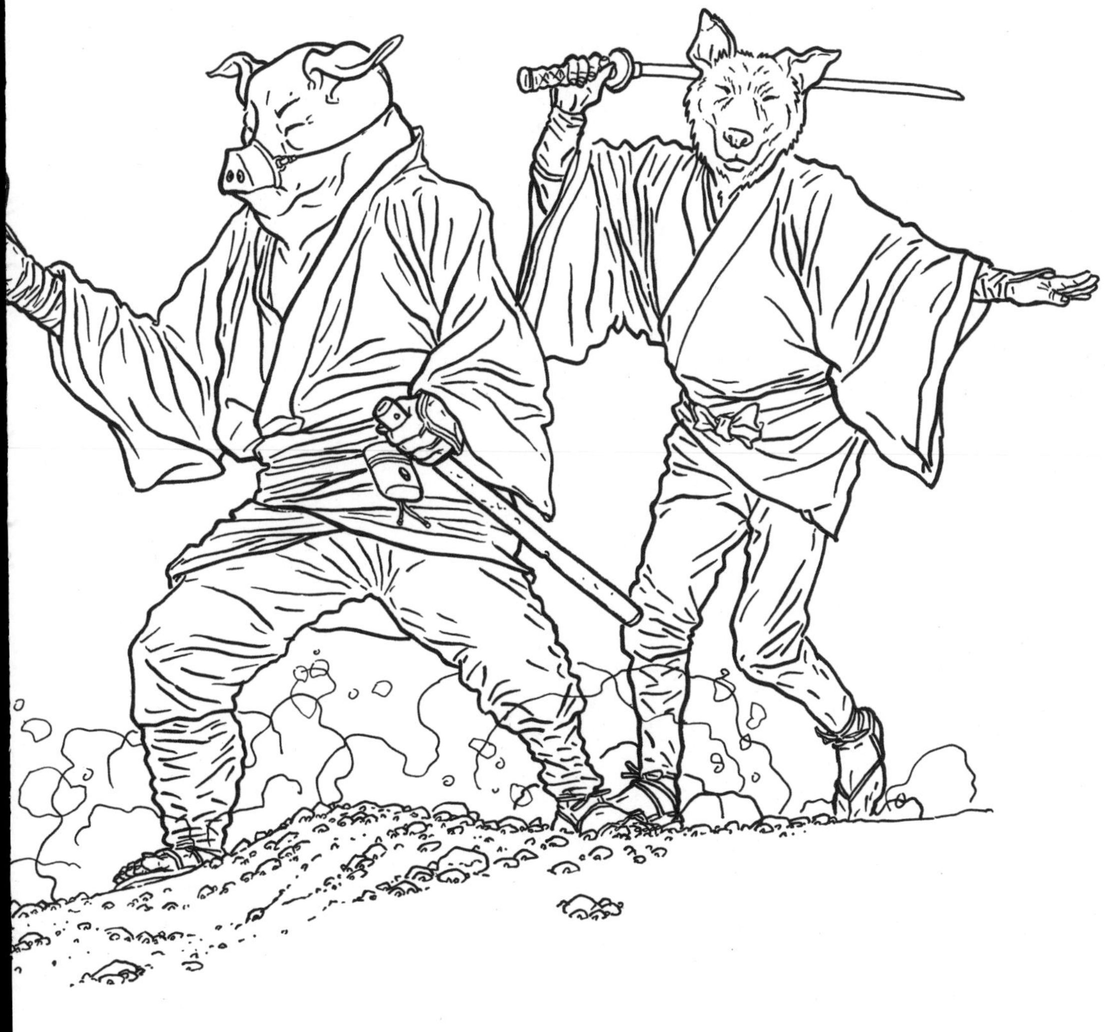

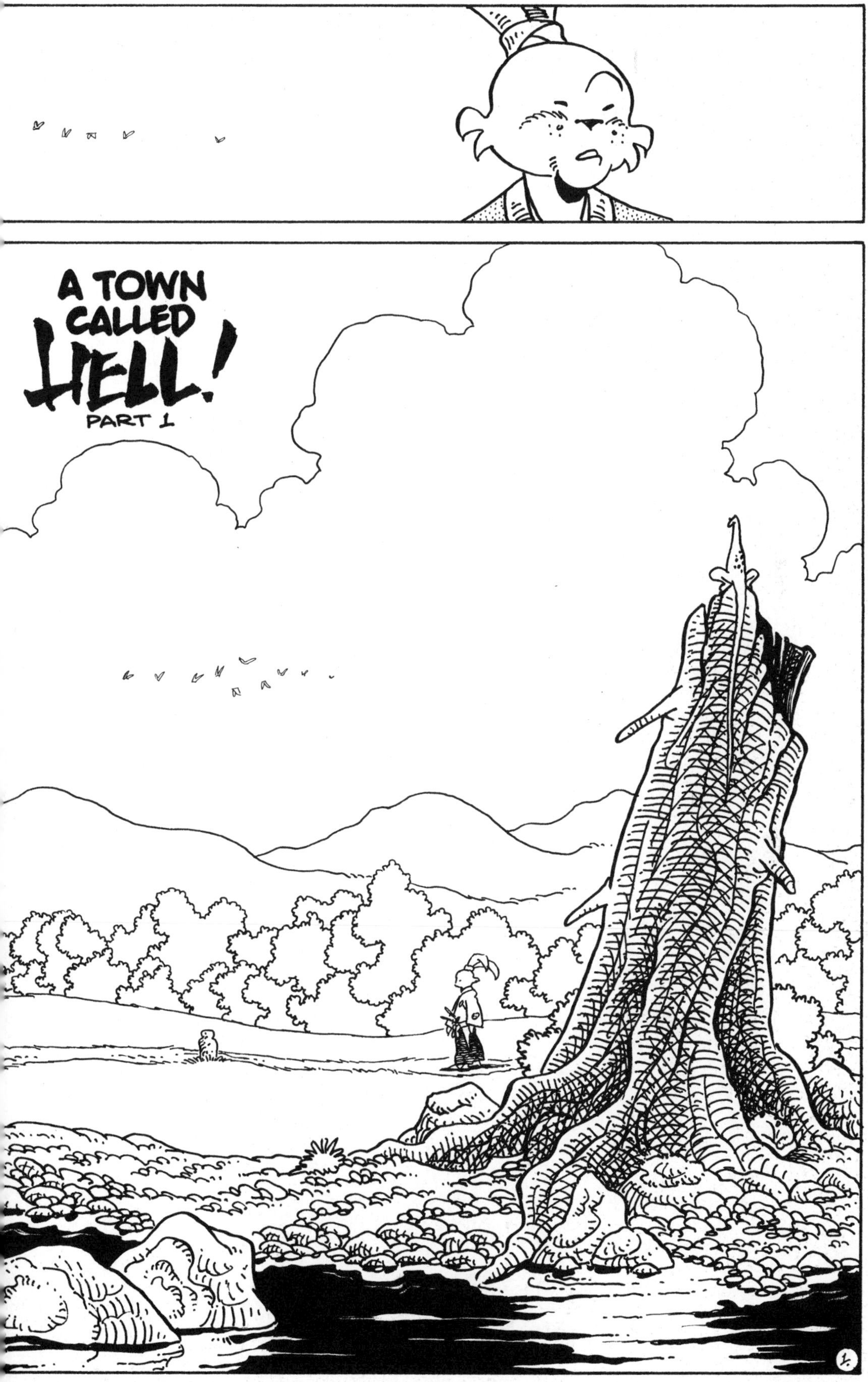
A TOWN CALLED HELL!
PART 1

IT LOOKS LIKE THEY'RE CARRYING EVERYTHING THEY OWN ON THEIR BACKS.

EXCUSE ME. HOW FAR IS IT TO THE NEXT TOWN?

GEH?

*TCH!* IT'S NOT FAR ENOUGH... AND WE WOULD NOT GO BACK THERE FOR ALL THE MONEY IN THE WORLD, EVEN POOR AS WE ARE! IF YOU HAD ANY SENSE, YOU WOULD BYPASS IT ALTOGETHER.

OH?

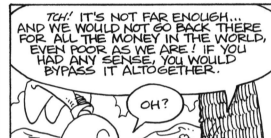

BOSS HIGA USED TO CONTROL THE TOWN. SURE, IT WAS TOUGH ON US, BUT AT LEAST THERE WAS NO VIOLENCE.

LAST WEEK, A NEW GANG CAME IN, LED BY BOSS KOMO. HE'S INTENT ON DRIVING OUT BOSS HIGA.

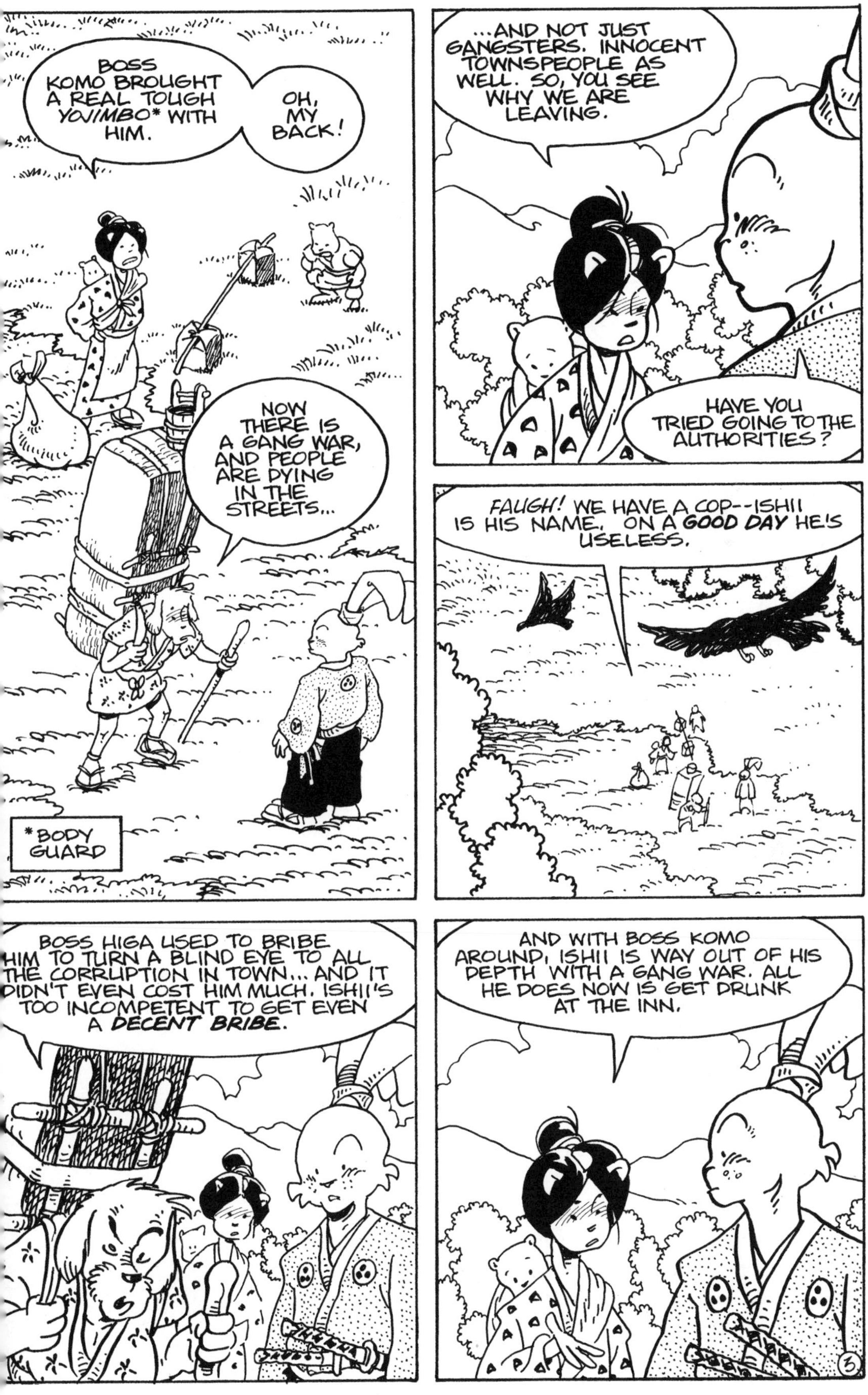
BOSS KOMO BROUGHT A REAL TOUGH YOJIMBO* WITH HIM.
OH, MY BACK!
NOW THERE IS A GANG WAR, AND PEOPLE ARE DYING IN THE STREETS...
*BODY GUARD
...AND NOT JUST GANGSTERS. INNOCENT TOWNSPEOPLE AS WELL. SO, YOU SEE WHY WE ARE LEAVING.
HAVE YOU TRIED GOING TO THE AUTHORITIES?
FAUGH! WE HAVE A COP--ISHII IS HIS NAME. ON A GOOD DAY HE'S USELESS.
BOSS HIGA USED TO BRIBE HIM TO TURN A BLIND EYE TO ALL THE CORRUPTION IN TOWN... AND IT DIDN'T EVEN COST HIM MUCH. ISHII'S TOO INCOMPETENT TO GET EVEN A DECENT BRIBE.
AND WITH BOSS KOMO AROUND, ISHII IS WAY OUT OF HIS DEPTH WITH A GANG WAR. ALL HE DOES NOW IS GET DRUNK AT THE INN.
3

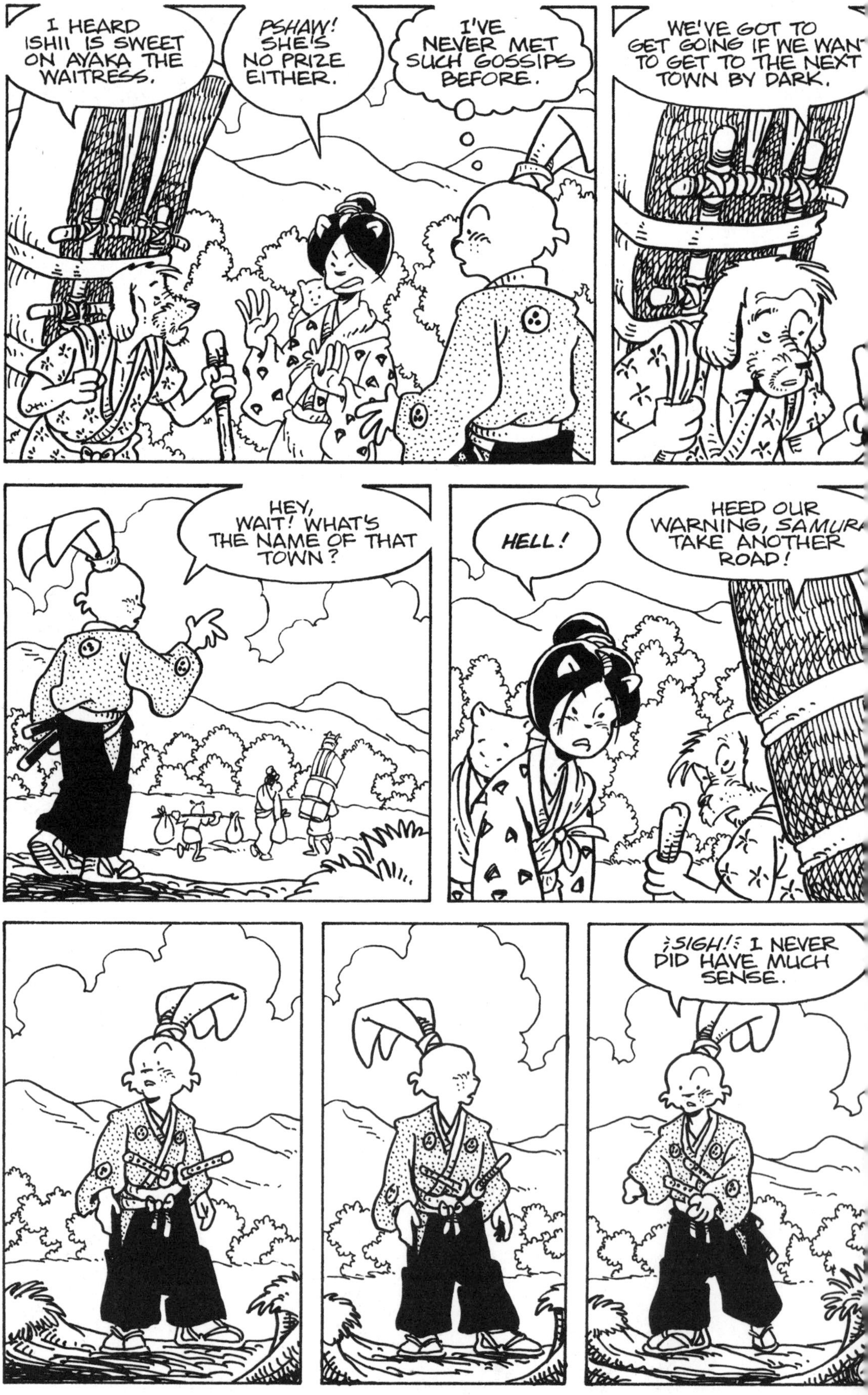
I HEARD ISHII IS SWEET ON AYAKA THE WAITRESS.
PSHAW! SHE'S NO PRIZE EITHER.
I'VE NEVER MET SUCH GOSSIPS BEFORE.
WE'VE GOT TO GET GOING IF WE WANT TO GET TO THE NEXT TOWN BY DARK.
HEY, WAIT! WHAT'S THE NAME OF THAT TOWN?
HELL!
HEED OUR WARNING, SAMURAI TAKE ANOTHER ROAD!
SIGH! I NEVER DID HAVE MUCH SENSE.

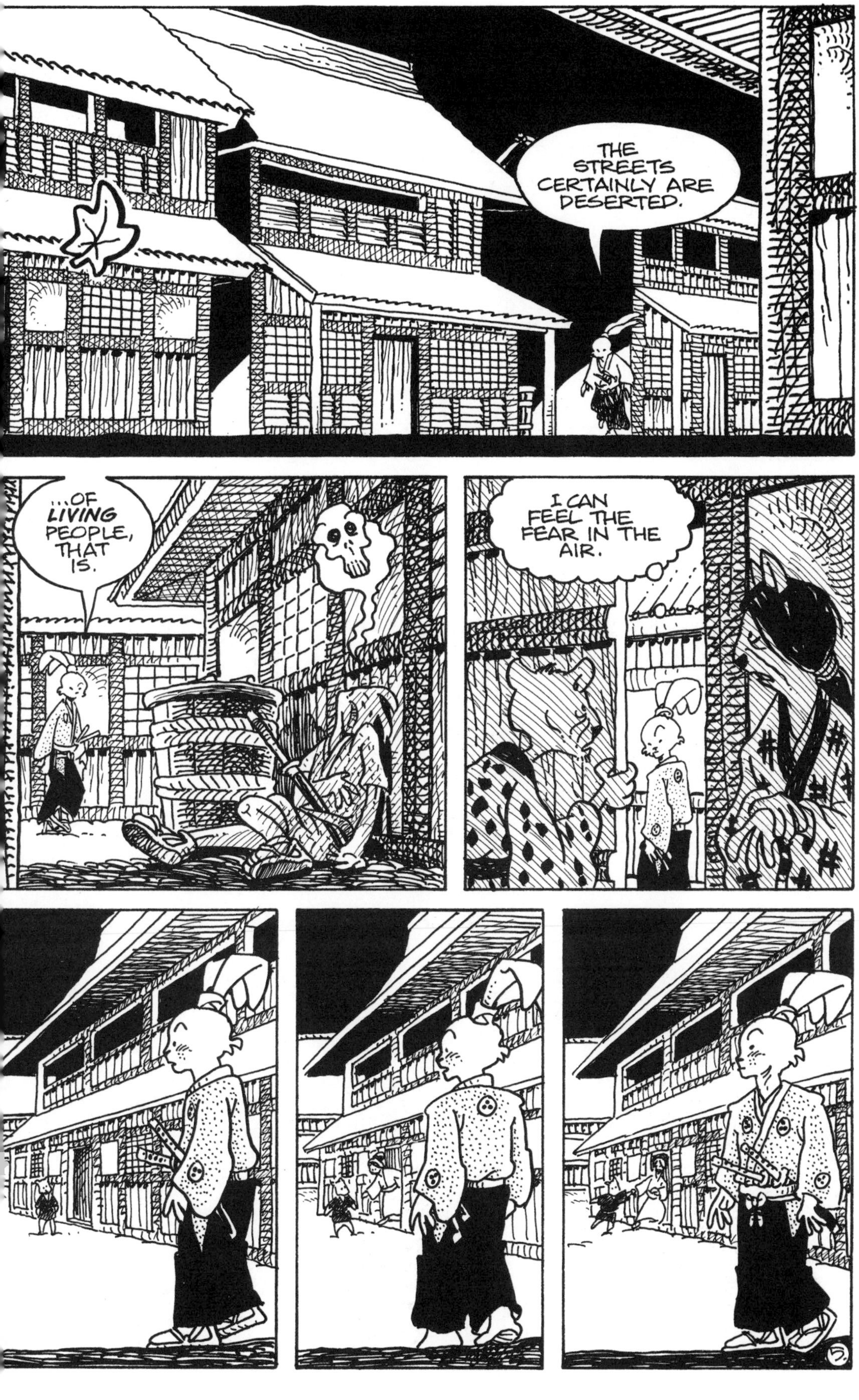
THE STREETS CERTAINLY ARE DESERTED.
...OF **LIVING** PEOPLE, THAT IS.
I CAN FEEL THE FEAR IN THE AIR.

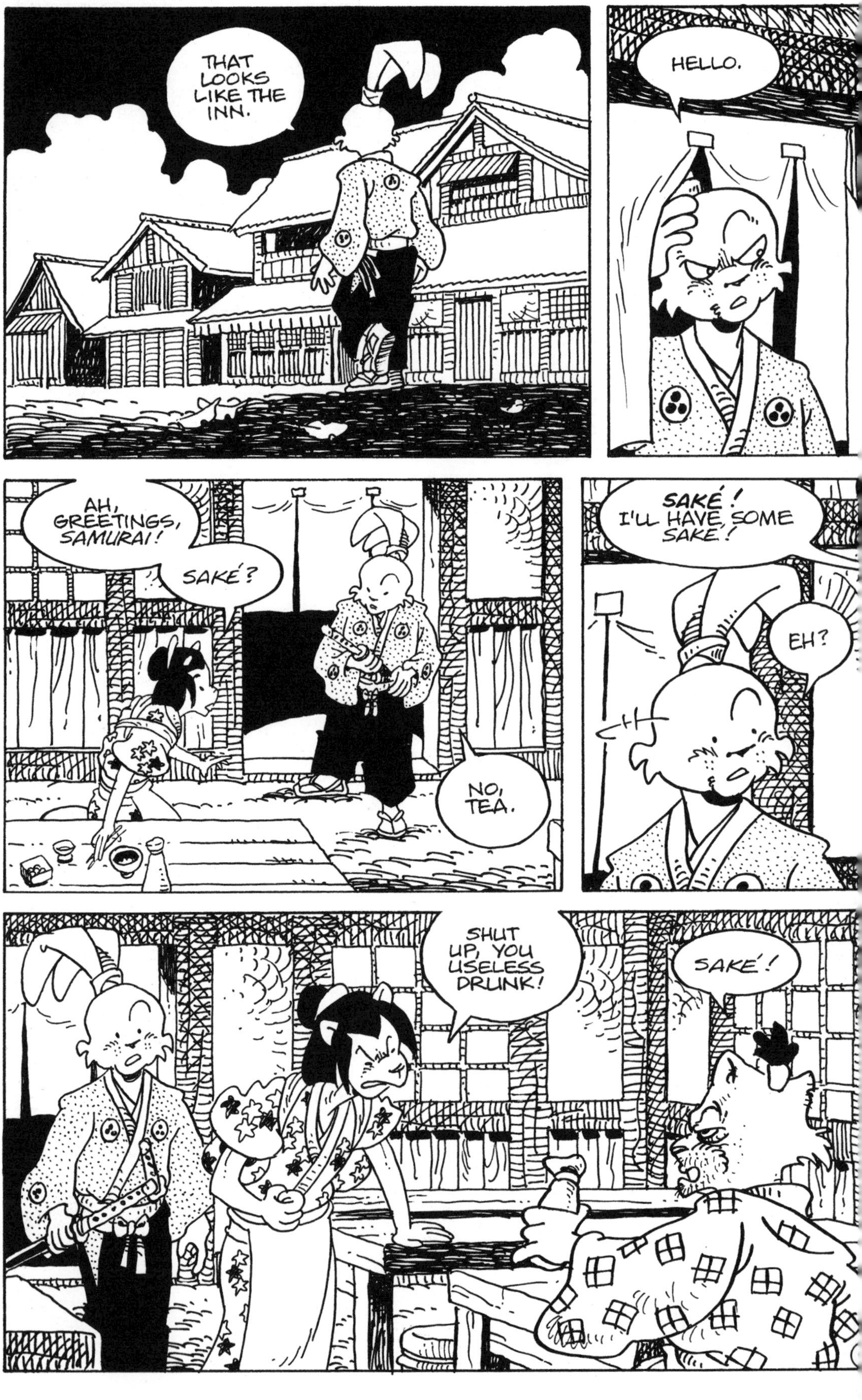

THAT LOOKS LIKE THE INN.
HELLO.
AH, GREETINGS, SAMURAI!
SAKÉ?
NO, TEA.
SAKÉ! I'LL HAVE SOME SAKÉ!
EH?
SHUT UP, YOU USELESS DRUNK!
SAKÉ!

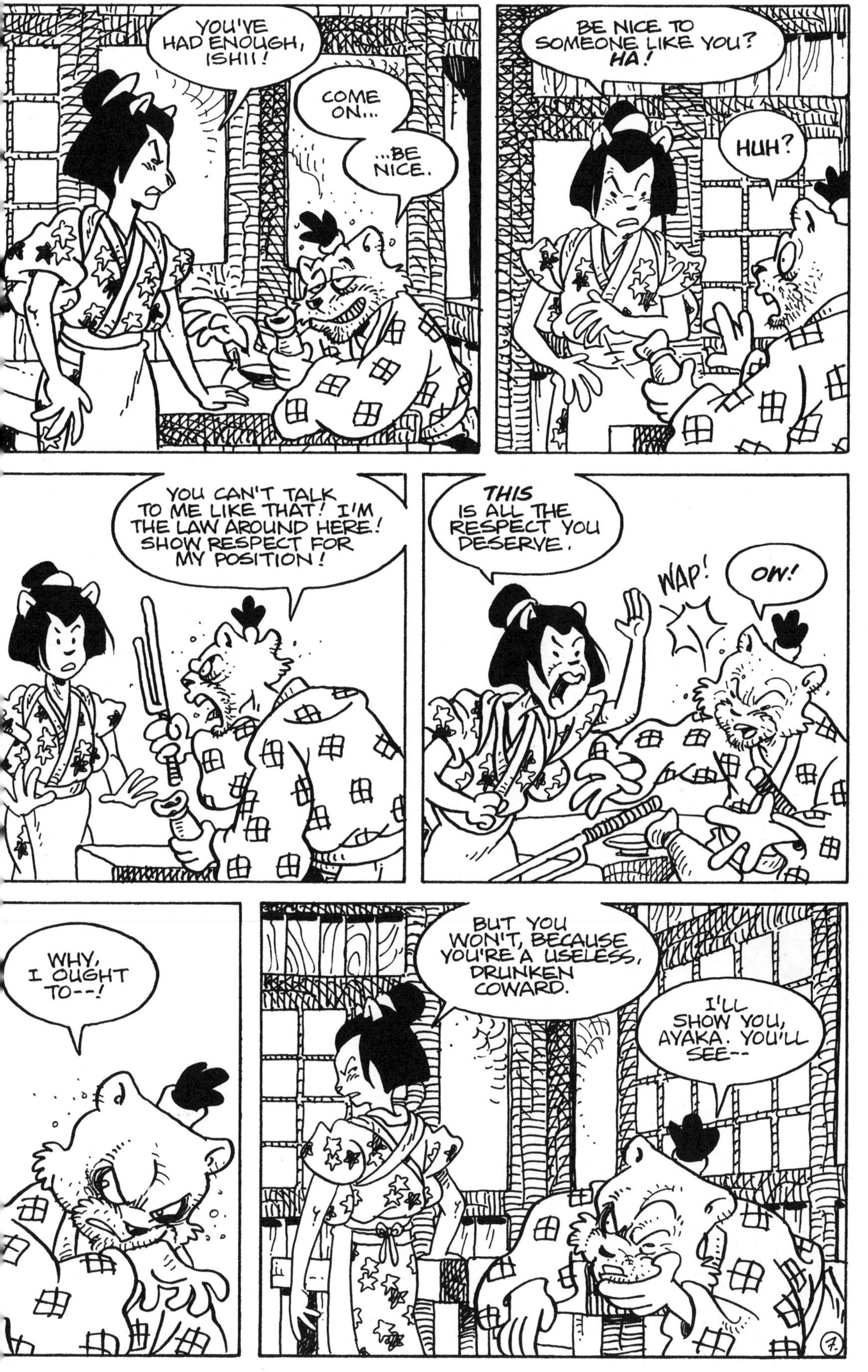
YOU'VE HAD ENOUGH, ISHII!
COME ON...
...BE NICE.
BE NICE TO SOMEONE LIKE YOU? HA!
HUH?
YOU CAN'T TALK TO ME LIKE THAT! I'M THE LAW AROUND HERE! SHOW RESPECT FOR MY POSITION!
THIS IS ALL THE RESPECT YOU DESERVE.
WAP!
OW!
WHY, I OUGHT TO--!
BUT YOU WON'T, BECAUSE YOU'RE A USELESS, DRUNKEN COWARD.
I'LL SHOW YOU, AYAKA. YOU'LL SEE--
7.

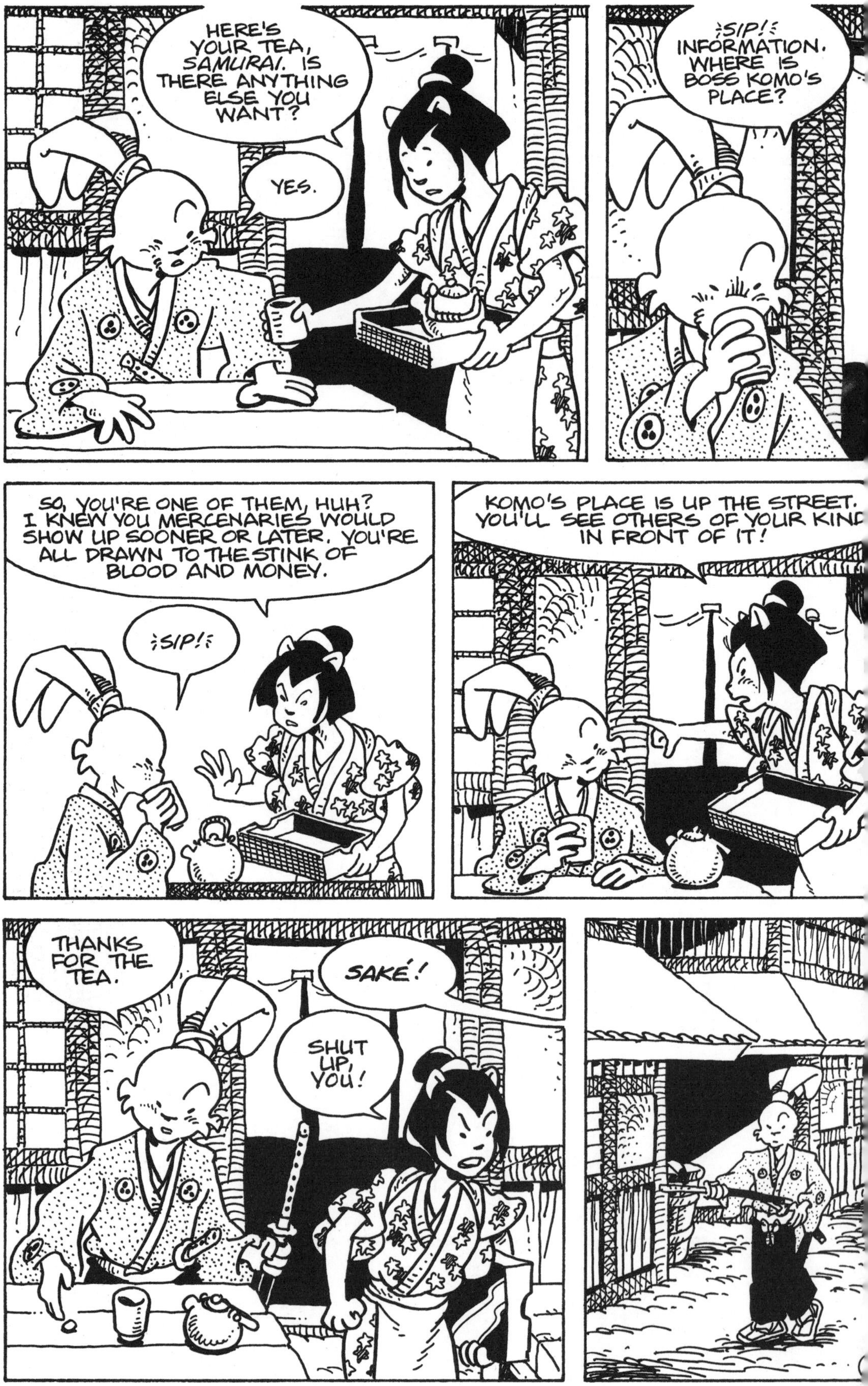
HERE'S YOUR TEA, SAMURAI. IS THERE ANYTHING ELSE YOU WANT?
YES.
¡SIP!¡ INFORMATION. WHERE IS BOSS KOMO'S PLACE?
SO, YOU'RE ONE OF THEM, HUH? I KNEW YOU MERCENARIES WOULD SHOW UP SOONER OR LATER. YOU'RE ALL DRAWN TO THE STINK OF BLOOD AND MONEY.
¡SIP!¡
KOMO'S PLACE IS UP THE STREET. YOU'LL SEE OTHERS OF YOUR KIND IN FRONT OF IT!
THANKS FOR THE TEA.
SAKÉ!
SHUT UP, YOU!

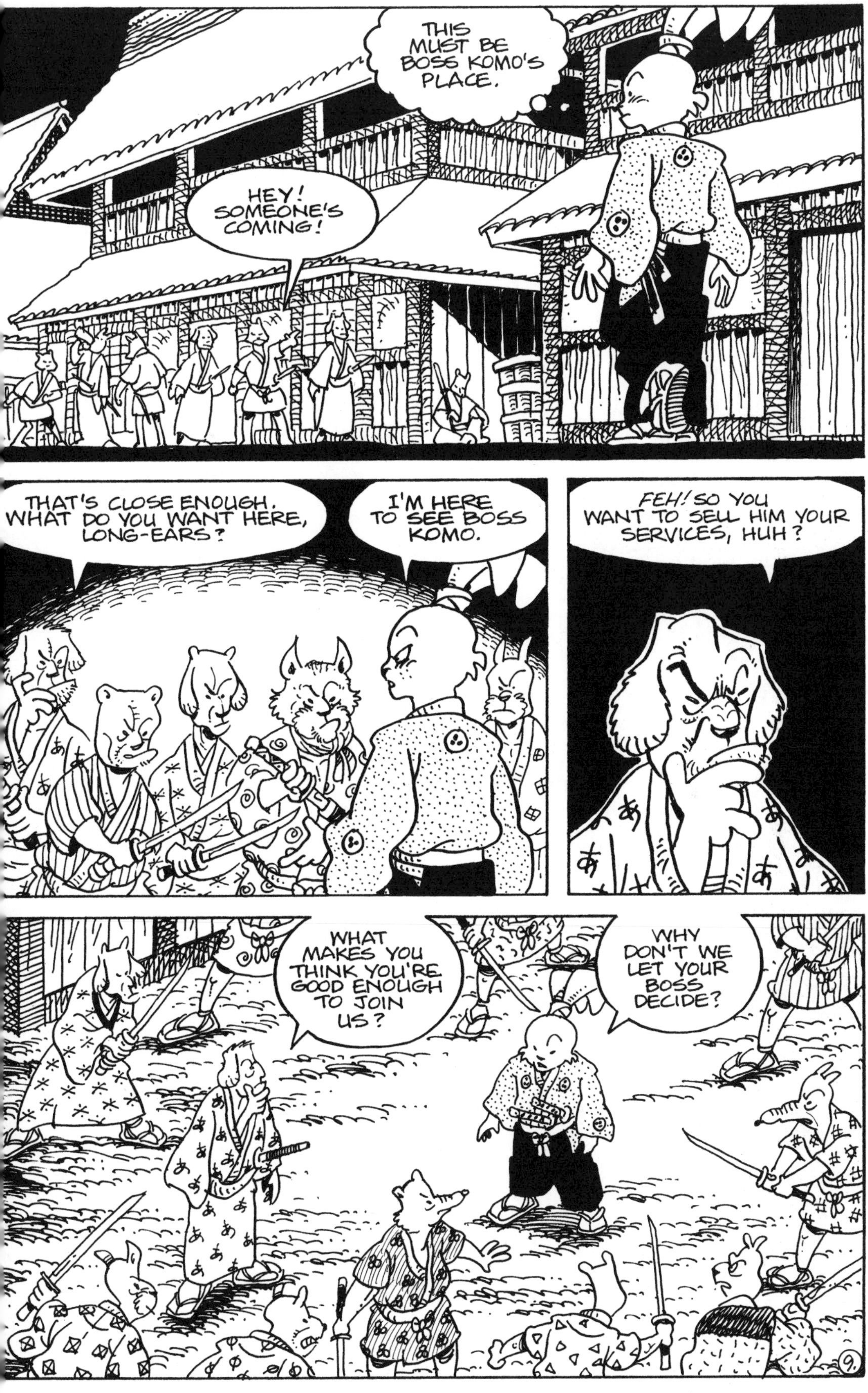
THIS MUST BE BOSS KOMO'S PLACE.
HEY! SOMEONE'S COMING!
THAT'S CLOSE ENOUGH. WHAT DO YOU WANT HERE, LONG-EARS?
I'M HERE TO SEE BOSS KOMO.
FEH! SO YOU WANT TO SELL HIM YOUR SERVICES, HUH?
WHAT MAKES YOU THINK YOU'RE GOOD ENOUGH TO JOIN US?
WHY DON'T WE LET YOUR BOSS DECIDE?
9.

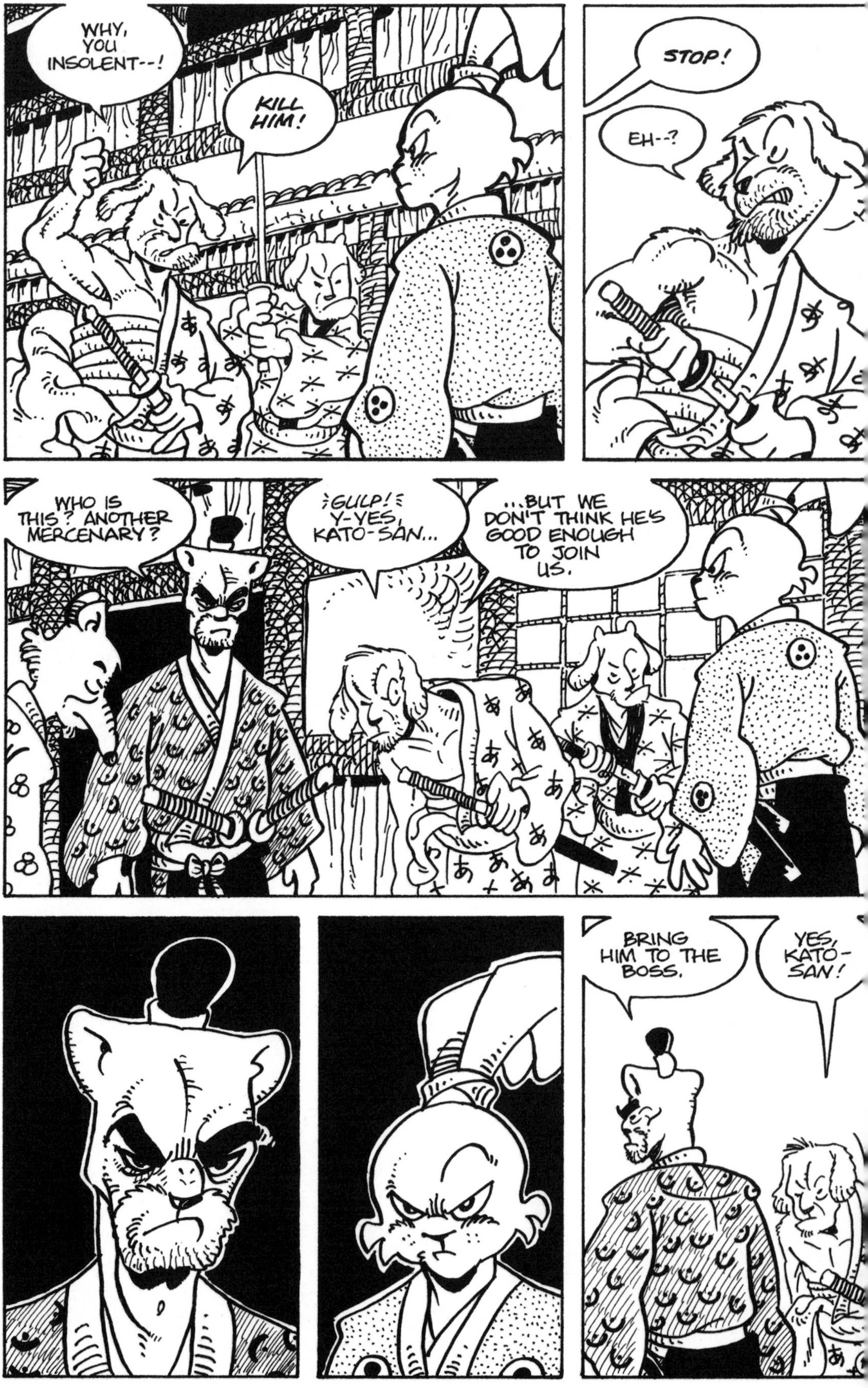
WHY, YOU INSOLENT--!
KILL HIM!
STOP!
EH--?
WHO IS THIS? ANOTHER MERCENARY?
GULP! Y-YES, KATO-SAN...
...BUT WE DON'T THINK HE'S GOOD ENOUGH TO JOIN US.
BRING HIM TO THE BOSS.
YES, KATO-SAN!

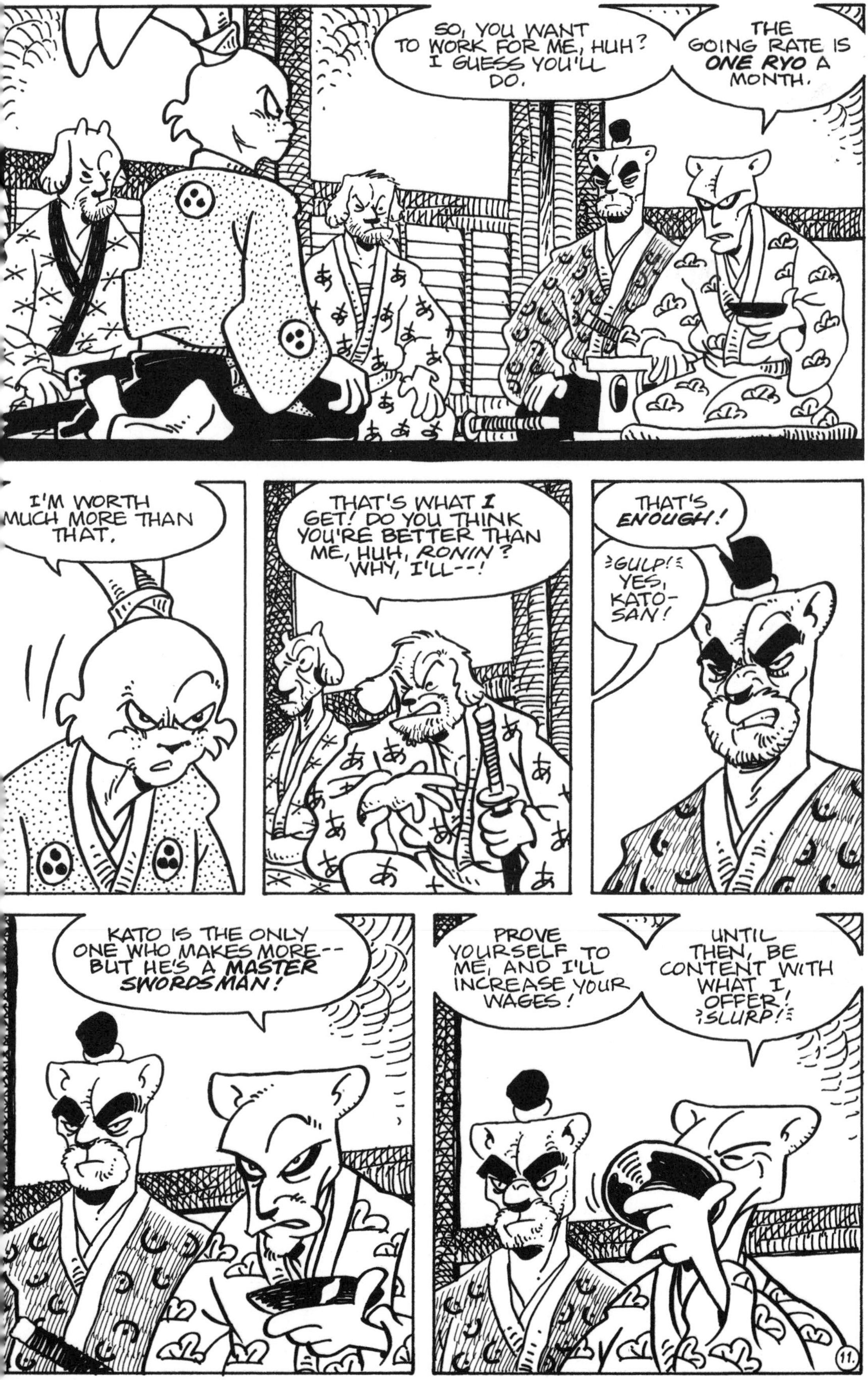
SO, YOU WANT TO WORK FOR ME, HUH? I GUESS YOU'LL DO.
THE GOING RATE IS ONE RYO A MONTH.
I'M WORTH MUCH MORE THAN THAT.
THAT'S WHAT I GET! DO YOU THINK YOU'RE BETTER THAN ME, HUH, RONIN? WHY, I'LL--!
THAT'S ENOUGH!
GULP! YES, KATO-SAN!
KATO IS THE ONLY ONE WHO MAKES MORE-- BUT HE'S A MASTER SWORDSMAN!
PROVE YOURSELF TO ME, AND I'LL INCREASE YOUR WAGES!
UNTIL THEN, BE CONTENT WITH WHAT I OFFER!
SLURP!
11.

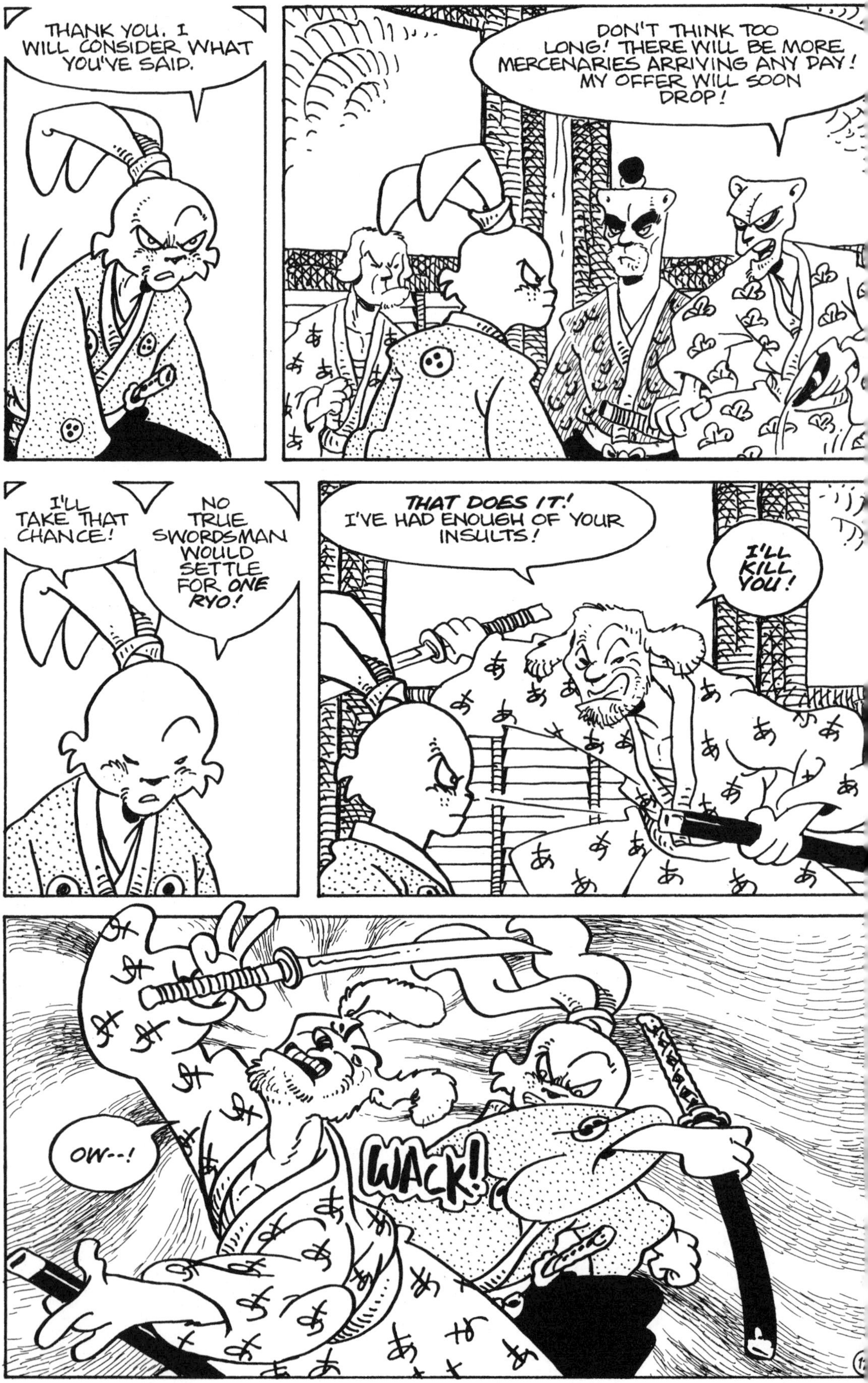
THANK YOU. I WILL CONSIDER WHAT YOU'VE SAID.
DON'T THINK TOO LONG! THERE WILL BE MORE MERCENARIES ARRIVING ANY DAY! MY OFFER WILL SOON DROP!
I'LL TAKE THAT CHANCE!
NO TRUE SWORDSMAN WOULD SETTLE FOR *ONE RYO*!
*THAT DOES IT!* I'VE HAD ENOUGH OF YOUR INSULTS!
*I'LL KILL YOU!*
OW--!
WACK!

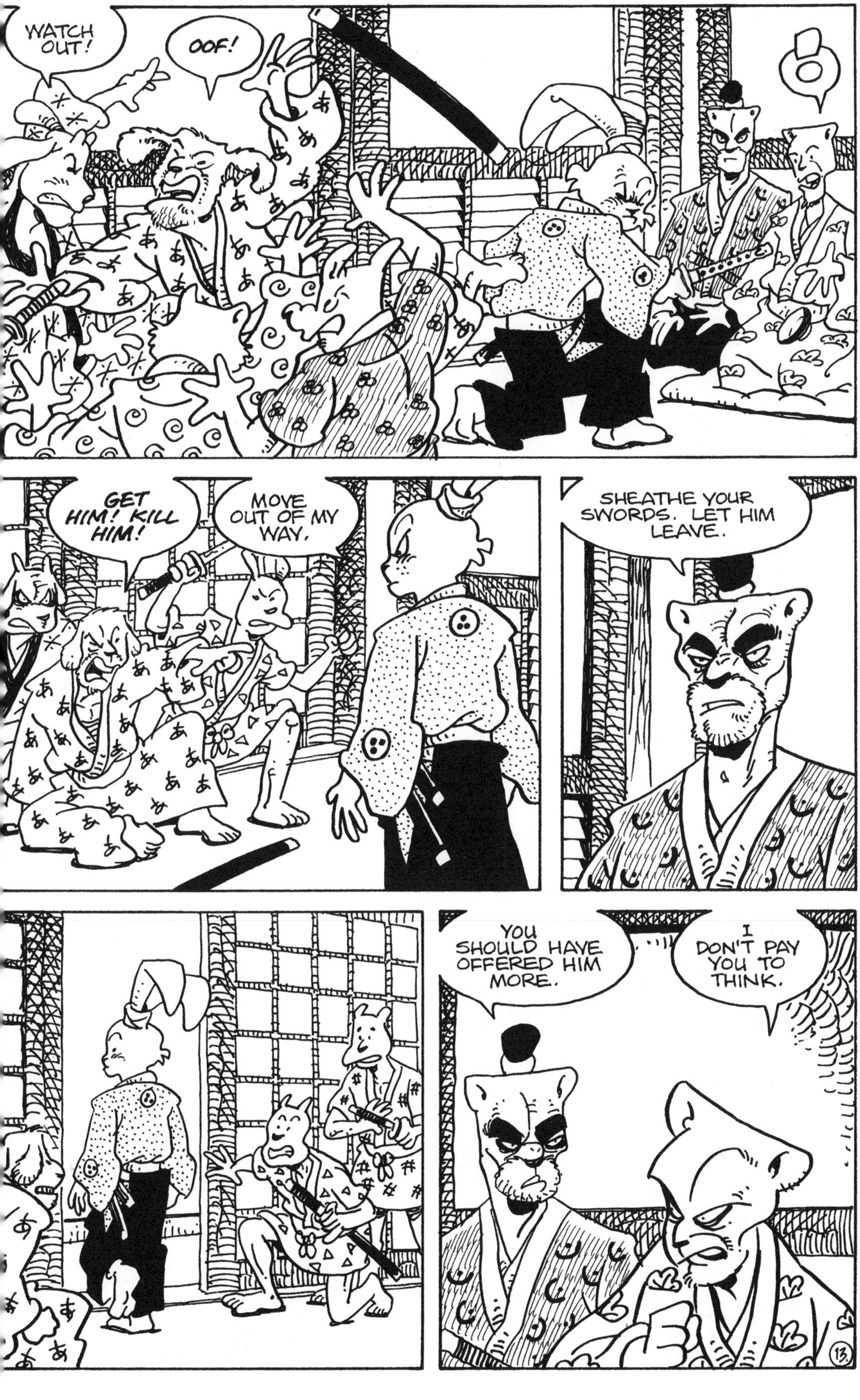
WATCH OUT!
OOF!
GET HIM! KILL HIM!
MOVE OUT OF MY WAY.
SHEATHE YOUR SWORDS. LET HIM LEAVE.
YOU SHOULD HAVE OFFERED HIM MORE.
I DON'T PAY YOU TO THINK.
13

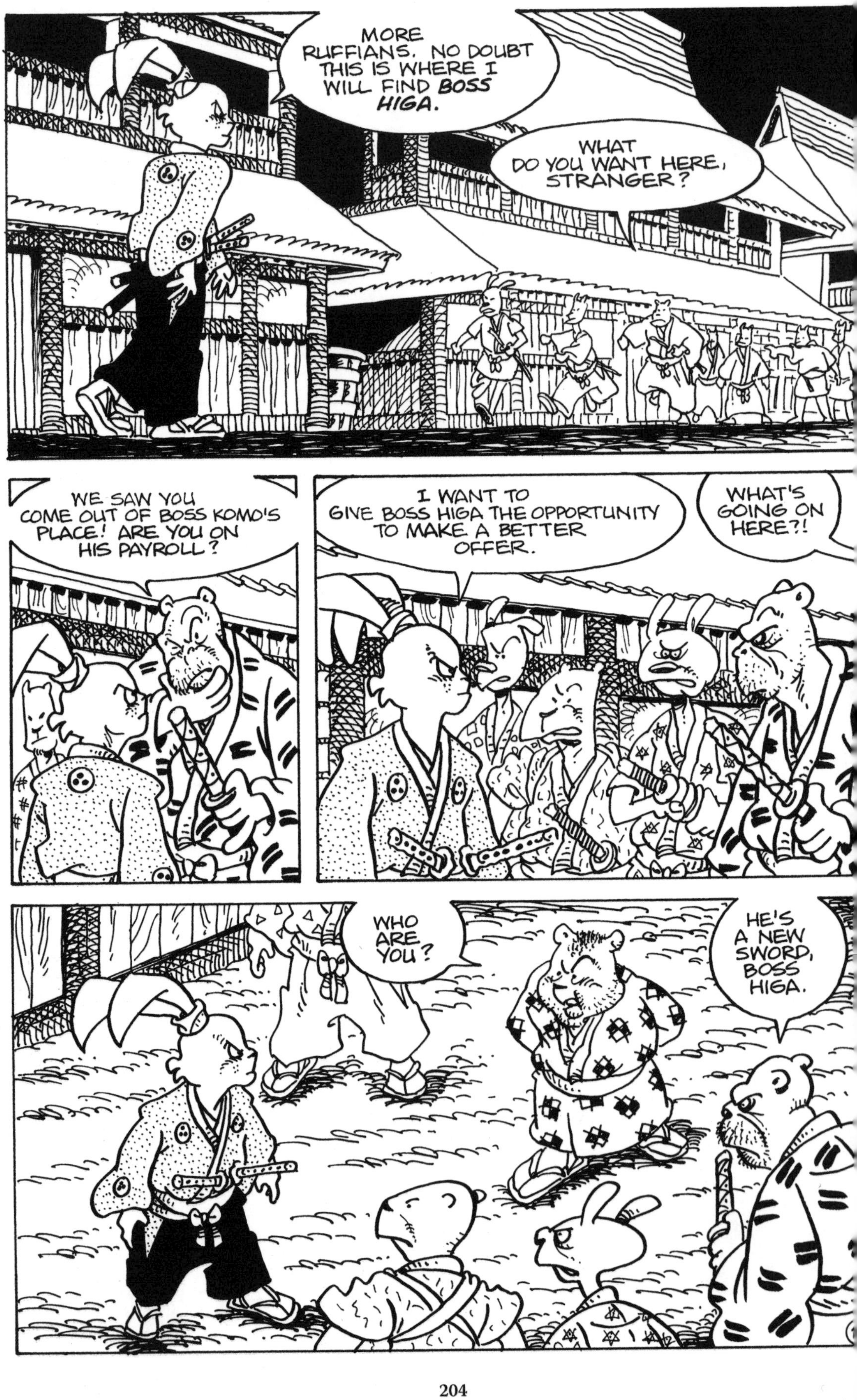
MORE RUFFIANS. NO DOUBT THIS IS WHERE I WILL FIND **BOSS HIGA**.
WHAT DO YOU WANT HERE, STRANGER?
WE SAW YOU COME OUT OF BOSS KOMO'S PLACE! ARE YOU ON HIS PAYROLL?
I WANT TO GIVE BOSS HIGA THE OPPORTUNITY TO MAKE A BETTER OFFER.
WHAT'S GOING ON HERE?!
WHO ARE YOU?
HE'S A NEW SWORD, BOSS HIGA.

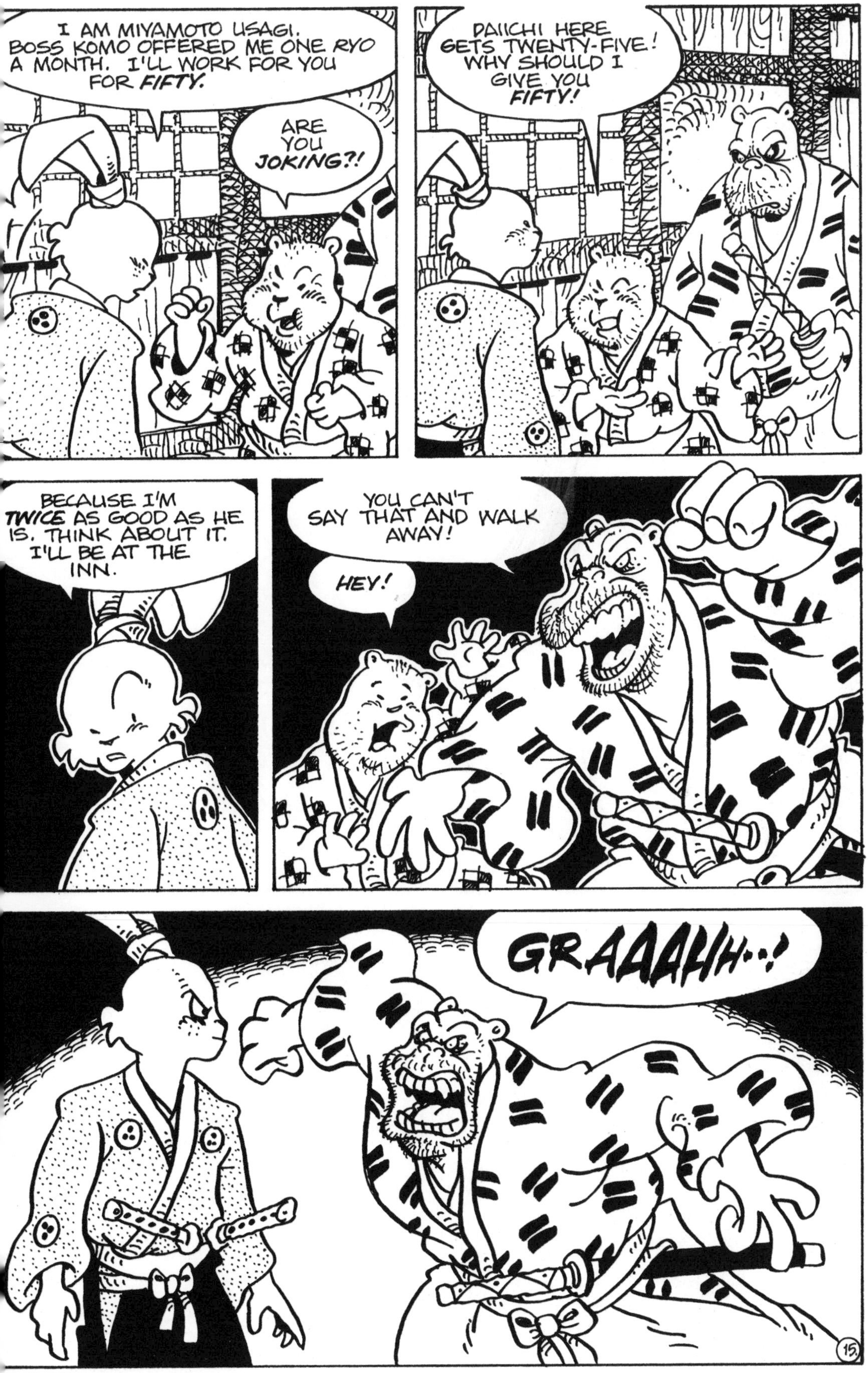
I AM MIYAMOTO USAGI. BOSS KOMO OFFERED ME ONE RYO A MONTH. I'LL WORK FOR YOU FOR FIFTY.
ARE YOU JOKING?!
DAIICHI HERE GETS TWENTY-FIVE! WHY SHOULD I GIVE YOU FIFTY!
BECAUSE I'M TWICE AS GOOD AS HE IS. THINK ABOUT IT. I'LL BE AT THE INN.
YOU CAN'T SAY THAT AND WALK AWAY!
HEY!
GRAAAHH..!
15

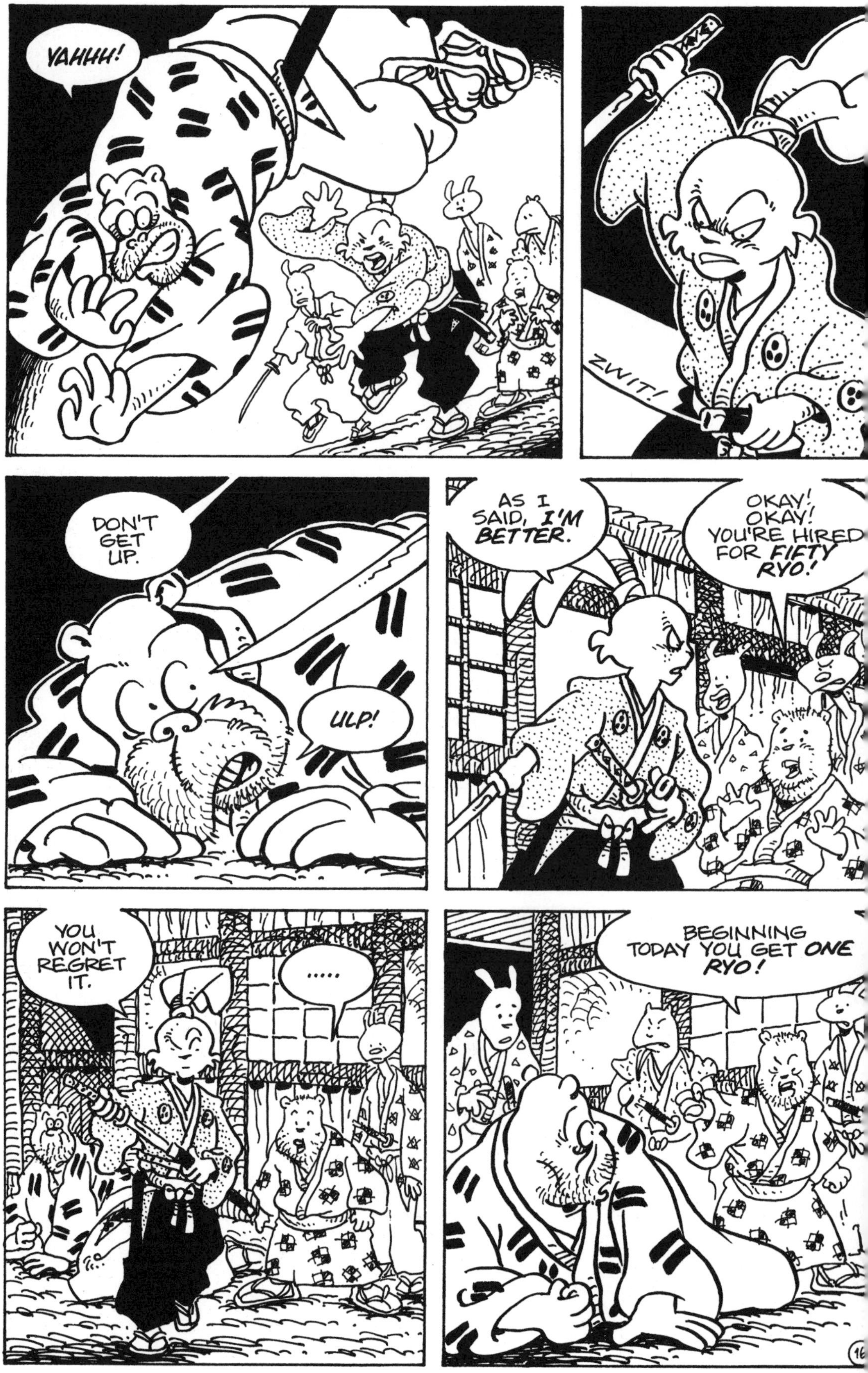
YAHHH!
ZWIT!
DON'T GET UP.
ULP!
AS I SAID, I'M BETTER.
OKAY! OKAY! YOU'RE HIRED FOR FIFTY RYO!
YOU WON'T REGRET IT.
.....
BEGINNING TODAY YOU GET ONE RYO!
16

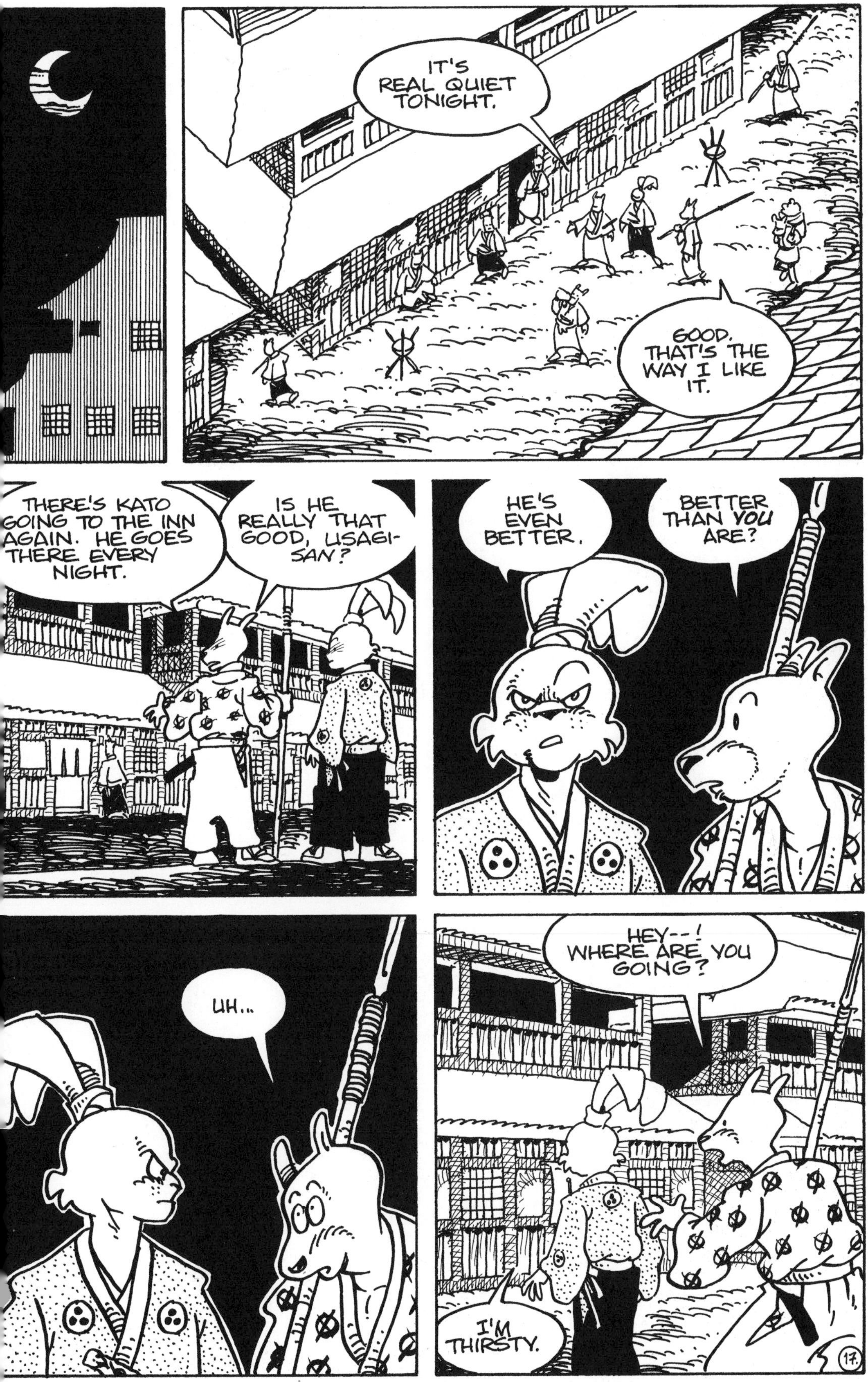
IT'S REAL QUIET TONIGHT.
GOOD. THAT'S THE WAY I LIKE IT.
THERE'S KATO GOING TO THE INN AGAIN. HE GOES THERE EVERY NIGHT.
IS HE REALLY THAT GOOD, USAGI-SAN?
HE'S EVEN BETTER.
BETTER THAN YOU ARE?
UH...
HEY--! WHERE ARE YOU GOING?
I'M THIRSTY.
17.

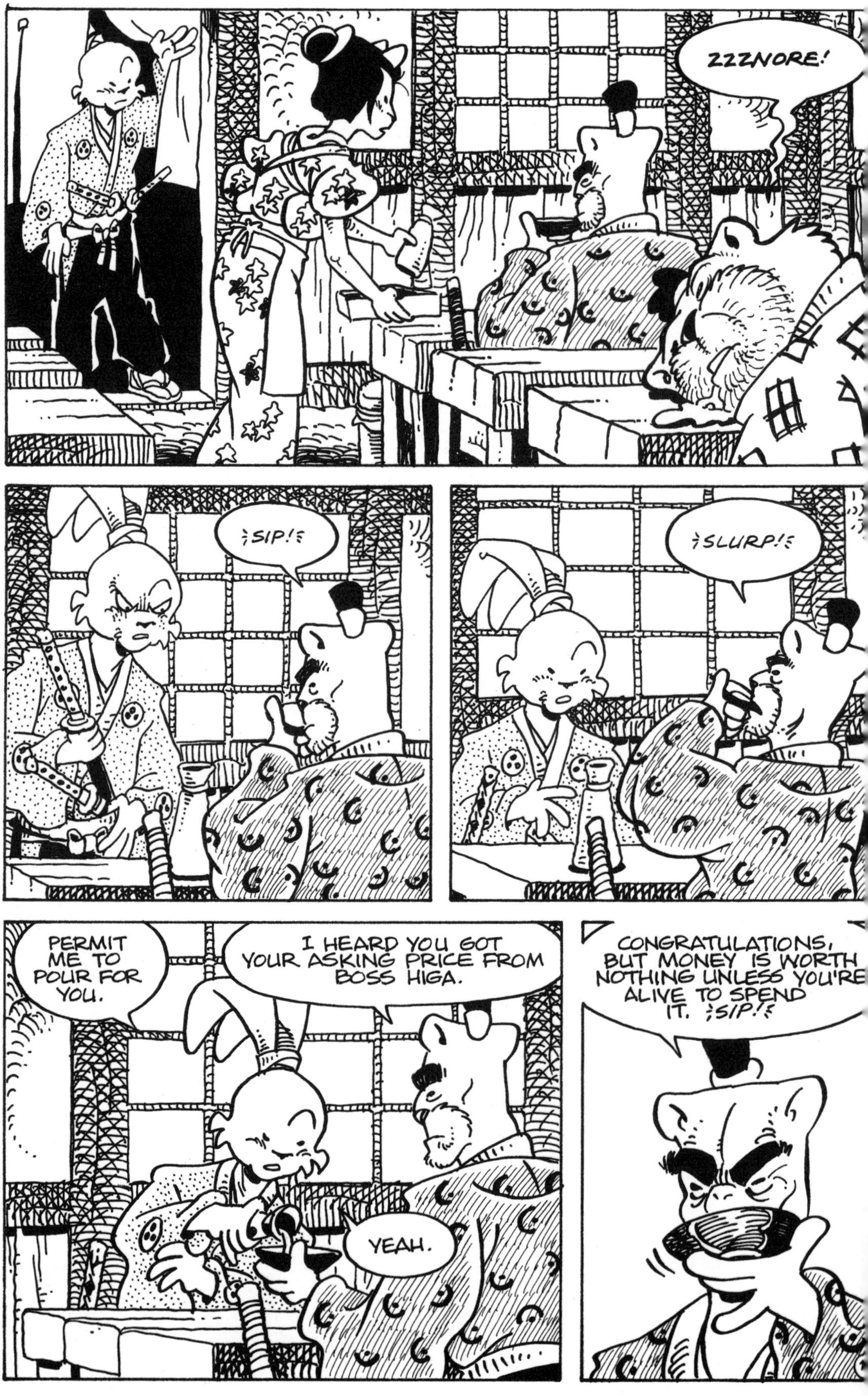
ZZZNORE!
SIP!
SLURP!
PERMIT ME TO POUR FOR YOU.
I HEARD YOU GOT YOUR ASKING PRICE FROM BOSS HIGA.
YEAH.
CONGRATULATIONS, BUT MONEY IS WORTH NOTHING UNLESS YOU'RE ALIVE TO SPEND IT. SIP!

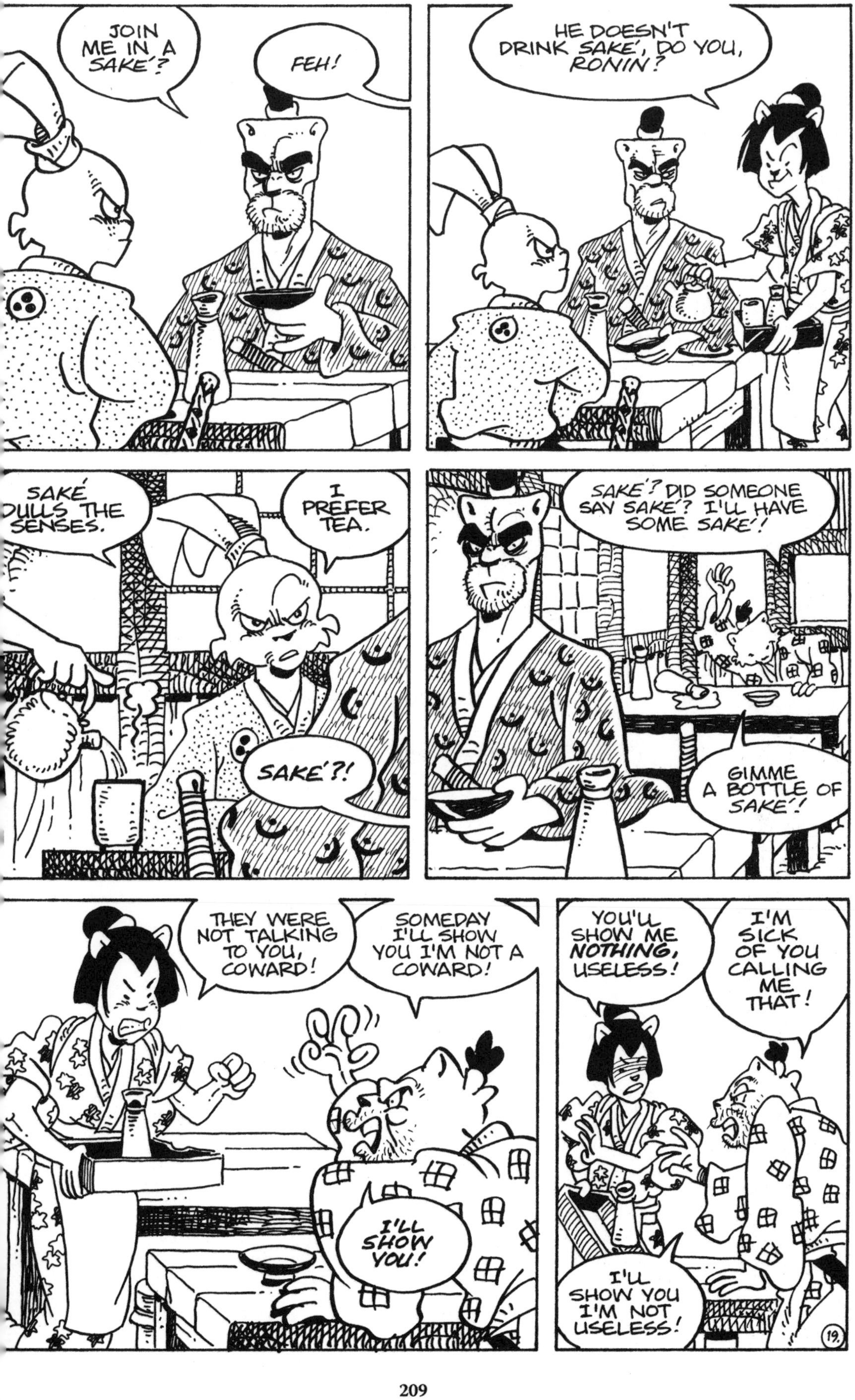
JOIN ME IN A SAKE´?
FEH!
HE DOESN'T DRINK SAKE´, DO YOU, RONIN?
SAKÉ DULLS THE SENSES.
I PREFER TEA.
SAKE´?!
SAKE´? DID SOMEONE SAY SAKE´? I'LL HAVE SOME SAKE´!
GIMME A BOTTLE OF SAKE´!
THEY WERE NOT TALKING TO YOU, COWARD!
SOMEDAY I'LL SHOW YOU I'M NOT A COWARD!
I'LL SHOW YOU!
YOU'LL SHOW ME NOTHING, USELESS!
I'M SICK OF YOU CALLING ME THAT!
I'LL SHOW YOU I'M NOT USELESS!
19.

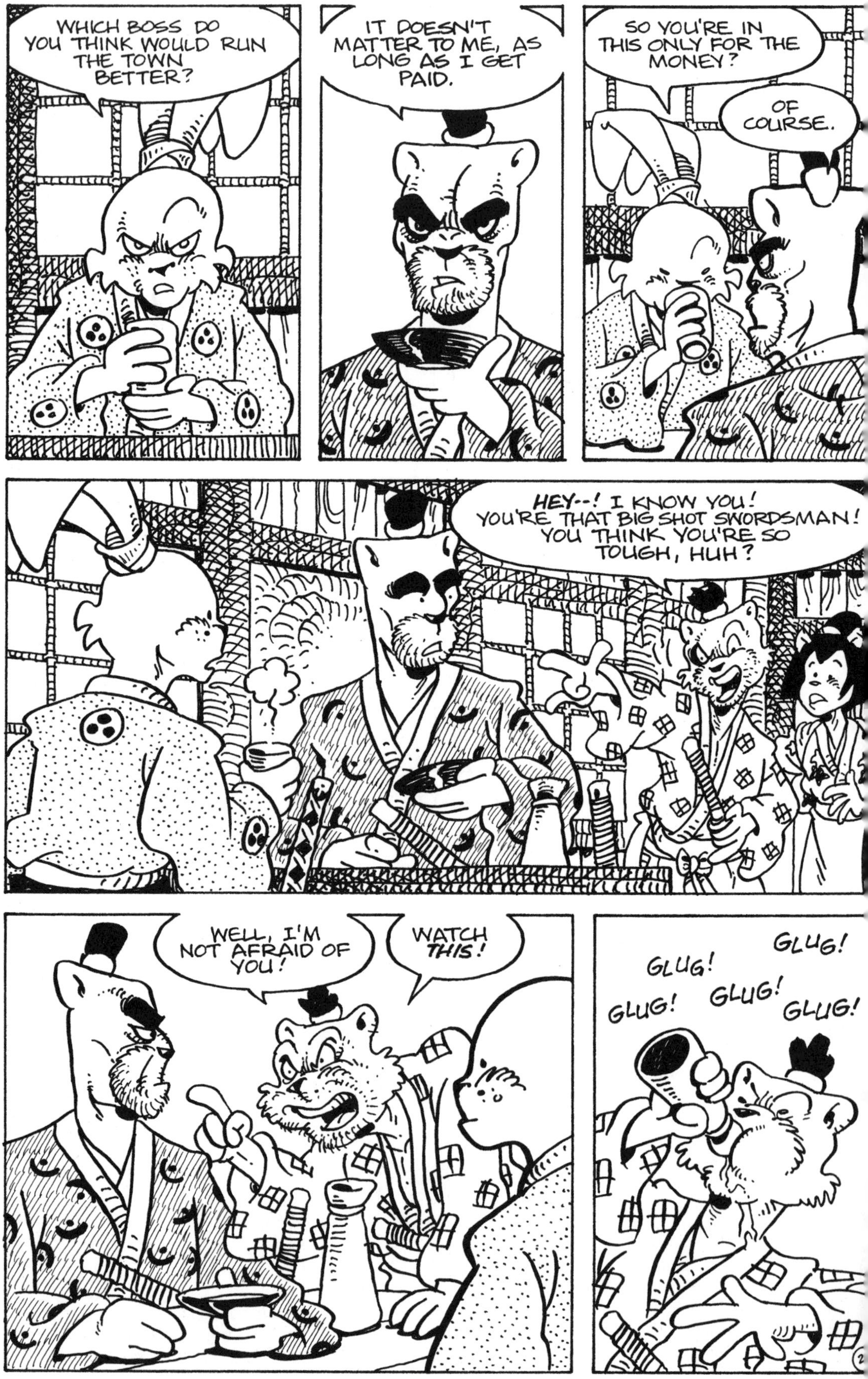
WHICH BOSS DO YOU THINK WOULD RUN THE TOWN BETTER?
IT DOESN'T MATTER TO ME, AS LONG AS I GET PAID.
SO YOU'RE IN THIS ONLY FOR THE MONEY?
OF COURSE.
HEY--! I KNOW YOU! YOU'RE THAT BIG SHOT SWORDSMAN! YOU THINK YOU'RE SO TOUGH, HUH?
WELL, I'M NOT AFRAID OF YOU!
WATCH THIS!
GLUG! GLUG! GLUG! GLUG! GLUG!

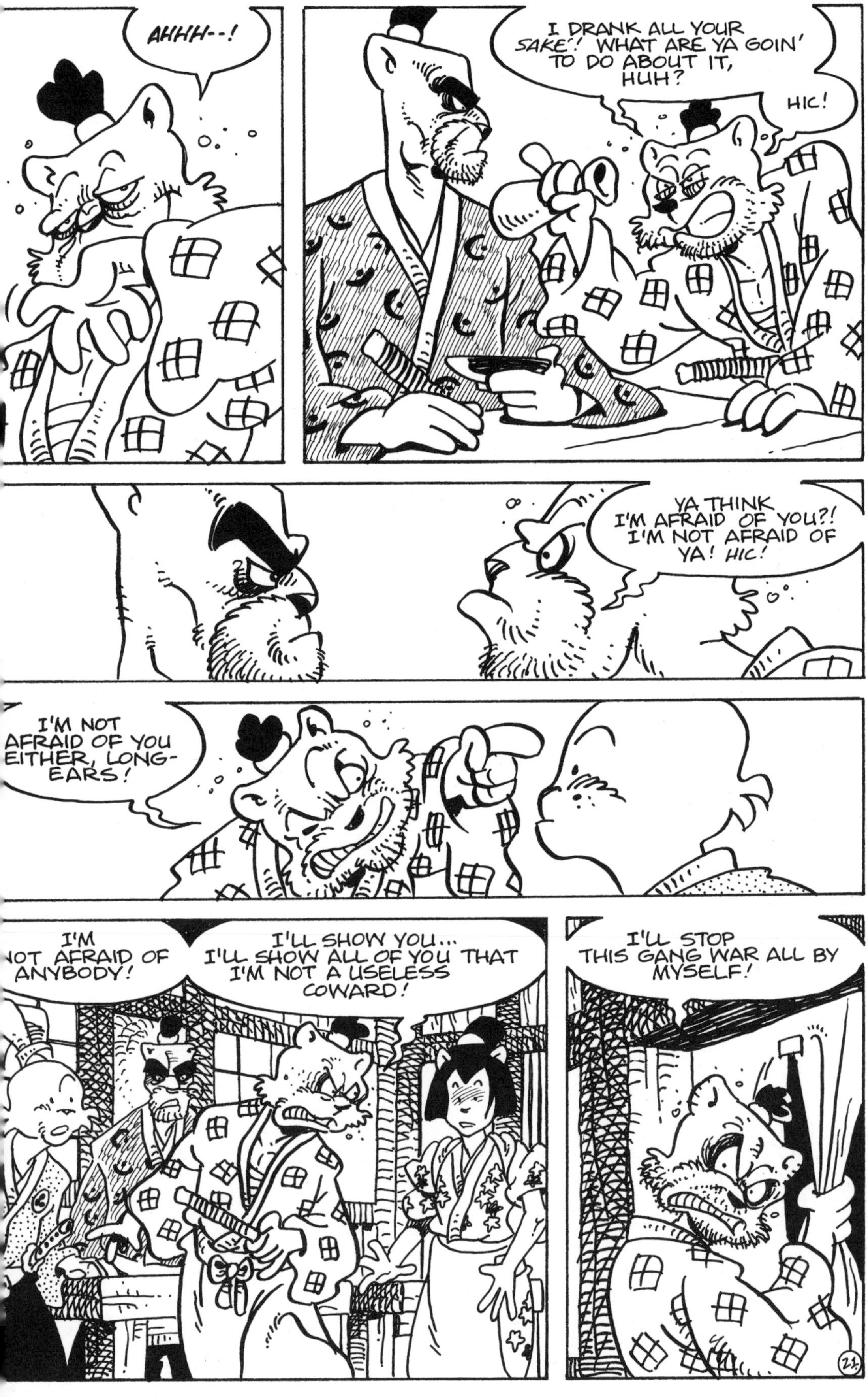
AHHH--!
I DRANK ALL YOUR SAKE! WHAT ARE YA GOIN' TO DO ABOUT IT, HUH?
HIC!
YA THINK I'M AFRAID OF YOU?! I'M NOT AFRAID OF YA! HIC!
I'M NOT AFRAID OF YOU EITHER, LONG-EARS!
I'M NOT AFRAID OF ANYBODY!
I'LL SHOW YOU... I'LL SHOW ALL OF YOU THAT I'M NOT A USELESS COWARD!
I'LL STOP THIS GANG WAR ALL BY MYSELF!
21

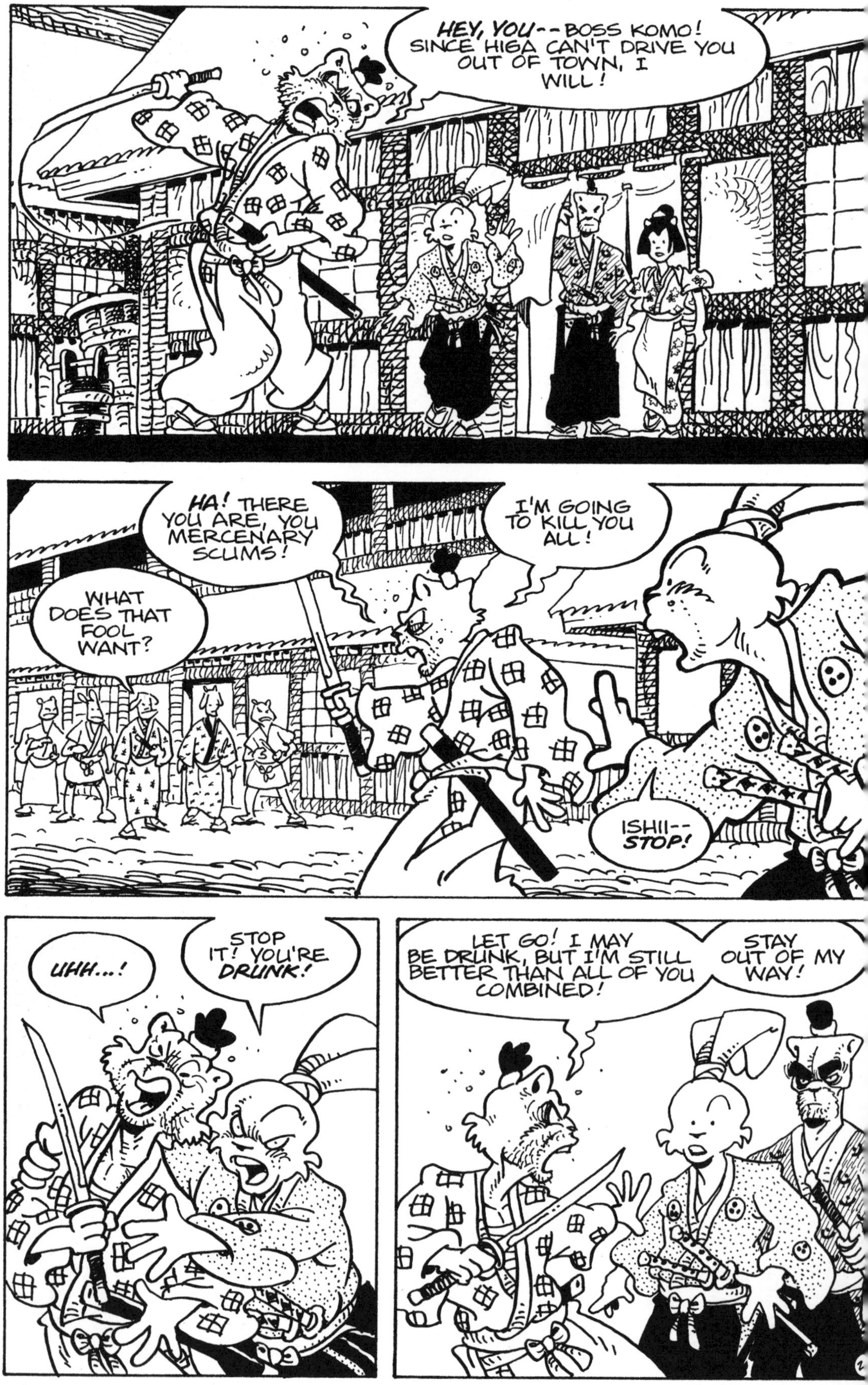
HEY, YOU--BOSS KOMO! SINCE HIGA CAN'T DRIVE YOU OUT OF TOWN, I WILL!
HA! THERE YOU ARE, YOU MERCENARY SCUMS!
I'M GOING TO KILL YOU ALL!
WHAT DOES THAT FOOL WANT?
ISHII-- STOP!
UHH...!
STOP IT! YOU'RE DRUNK!
LET GO! I MAY BE DRUNK, BUT I'M STILL BETTER THAN ALL OF YOU COMBINED!
STAY OUT OF MY WAY!

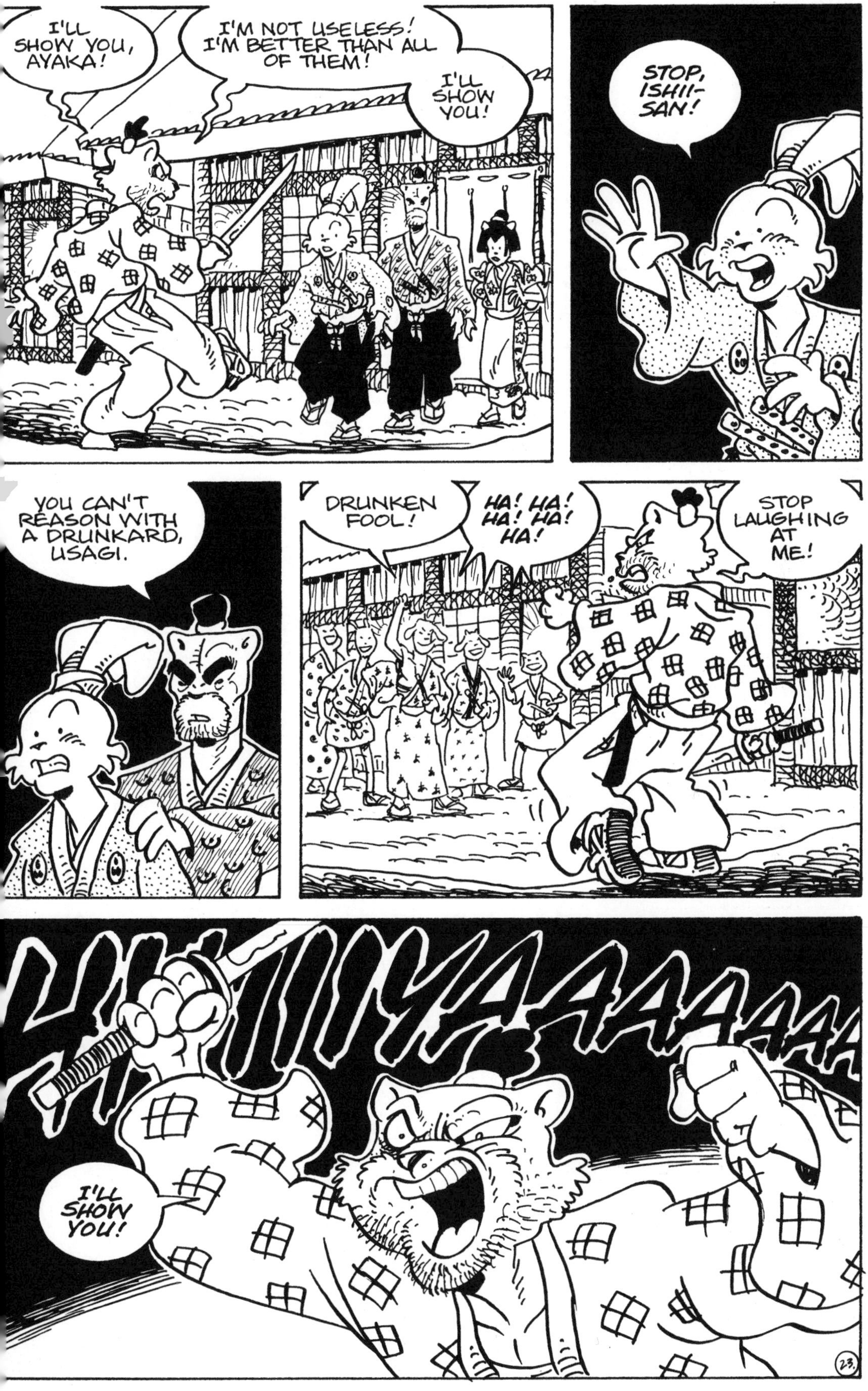
I'LL SHOW YOU, AYAKA!
I'M NOT USELESS! I'M BETTER THAN ALL OF THEM!
I'LL SHOW YOU!
STOP, ISHII-SAN!
YOU CAN'T REASON WITH A DRUNKARD, USAGI.
DRUNKEN FOOL!
HA! HA! HA! HA! HA!
STOP LAUGHING AT ME!
HIIIIIYAAAAAAA
I'LL SHOW YOU!
23.

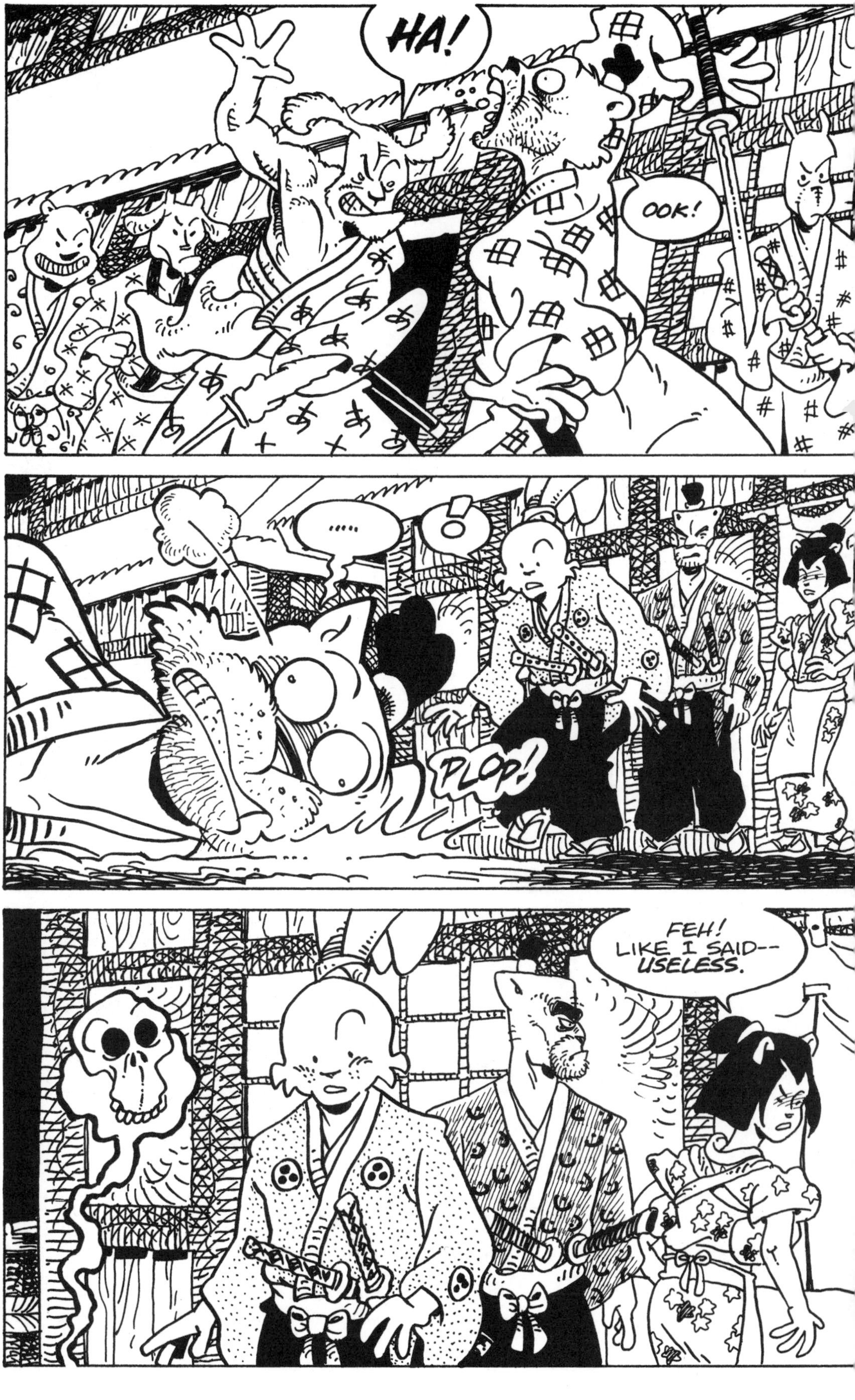
HA!
OOK!
.....
!
PLOP!
FEH! LIKE I SAID-- USELESS.

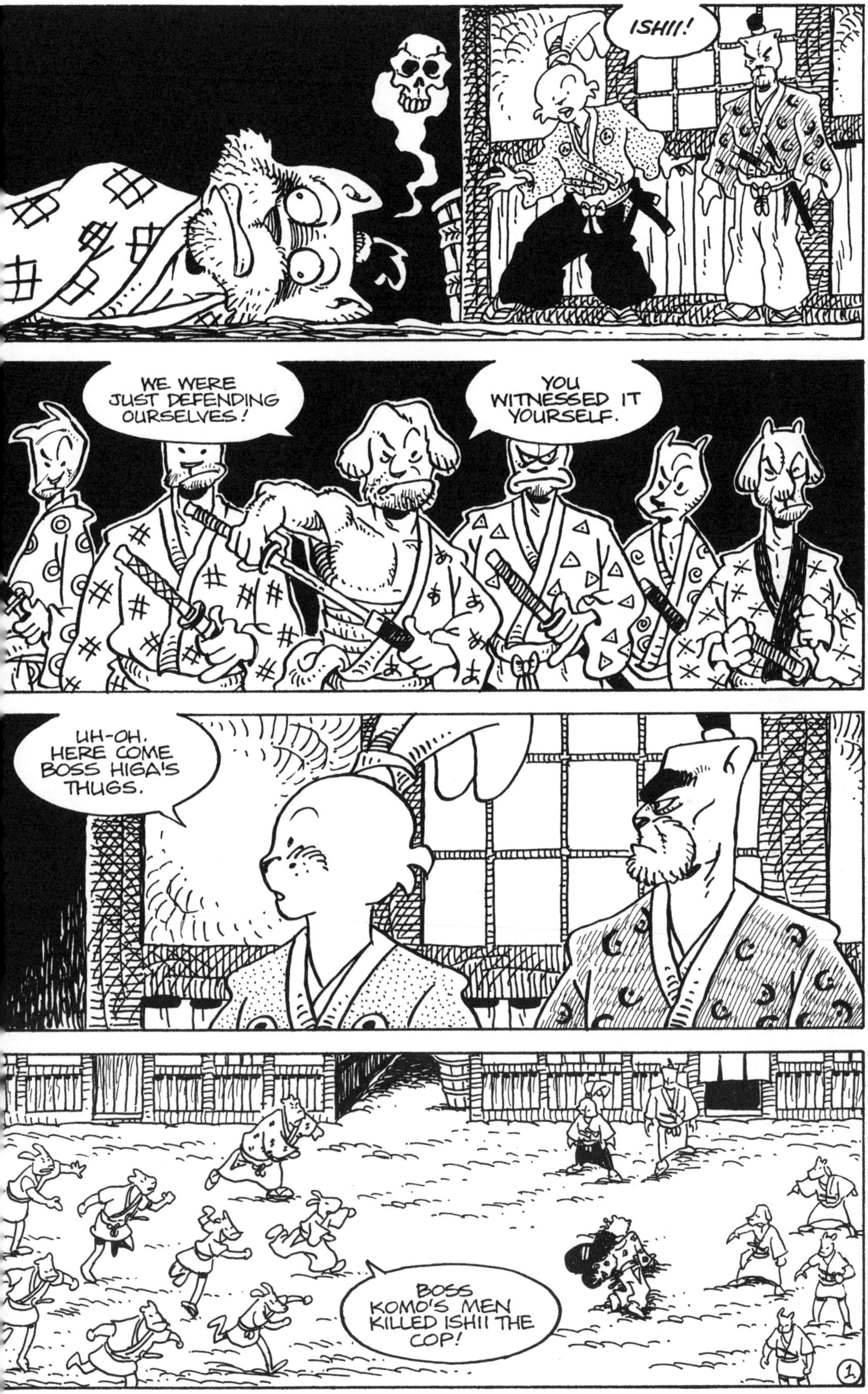
ISHII!
WE WERE JUST DEFENDING OURSELVES!
YOU WITNESSED IT YOURSELF.
UH-OH. HERE COME BOSS HIGA'S THUGS.
BOSS KOMO'S MEN KILLED ISHII THE COP!
1

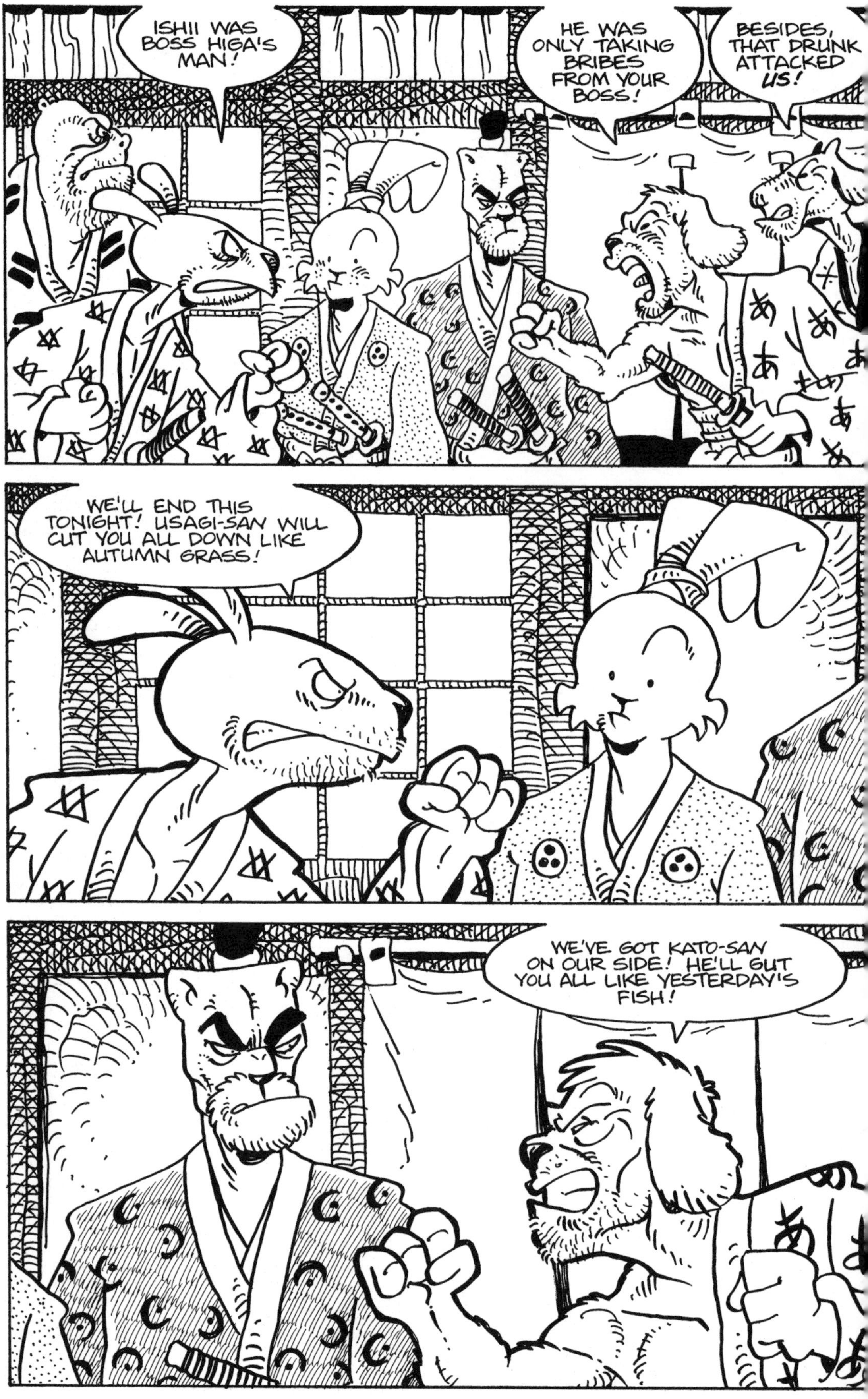
ISHII WAS BOSS HIGA'S MAN!
HE WAS ONLY TAKING BRIBES FROM YOUR BOSS!
BESIDES, THAT DRUNK ATTACKED *US*!
WE'LL END THIS TONIGHT! USAGI-SAN WILL CUT YOU ALL DOWN LIKE AUTUMN GRASS!
WE'VE GOT KATO-SAN ON OUR SIDE! HE'LL GUT YOU ALL LIKE YESTERDAY'S FISH!

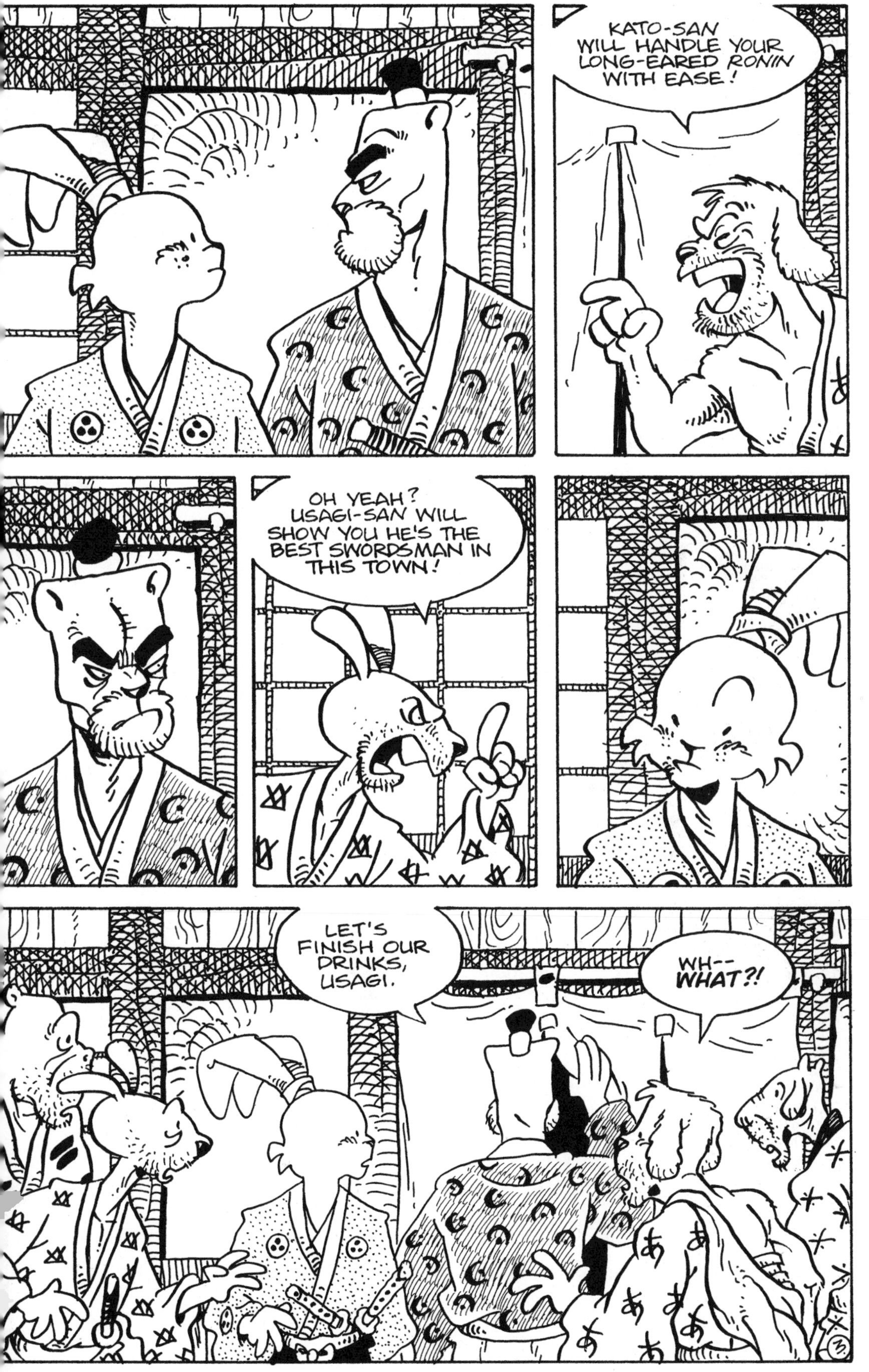
KATO-SAN WILL HANDLE YOUR LONG-EARED RONIN WITH EASE!
OH YEAH? USAGI-SAN WILL SHOW YOU HE'S THE BEST SWORDSMAN IN THIS TOWN!
LET'S FINISH OUR DRINKS, USAGI.
WH-- WHAT?!

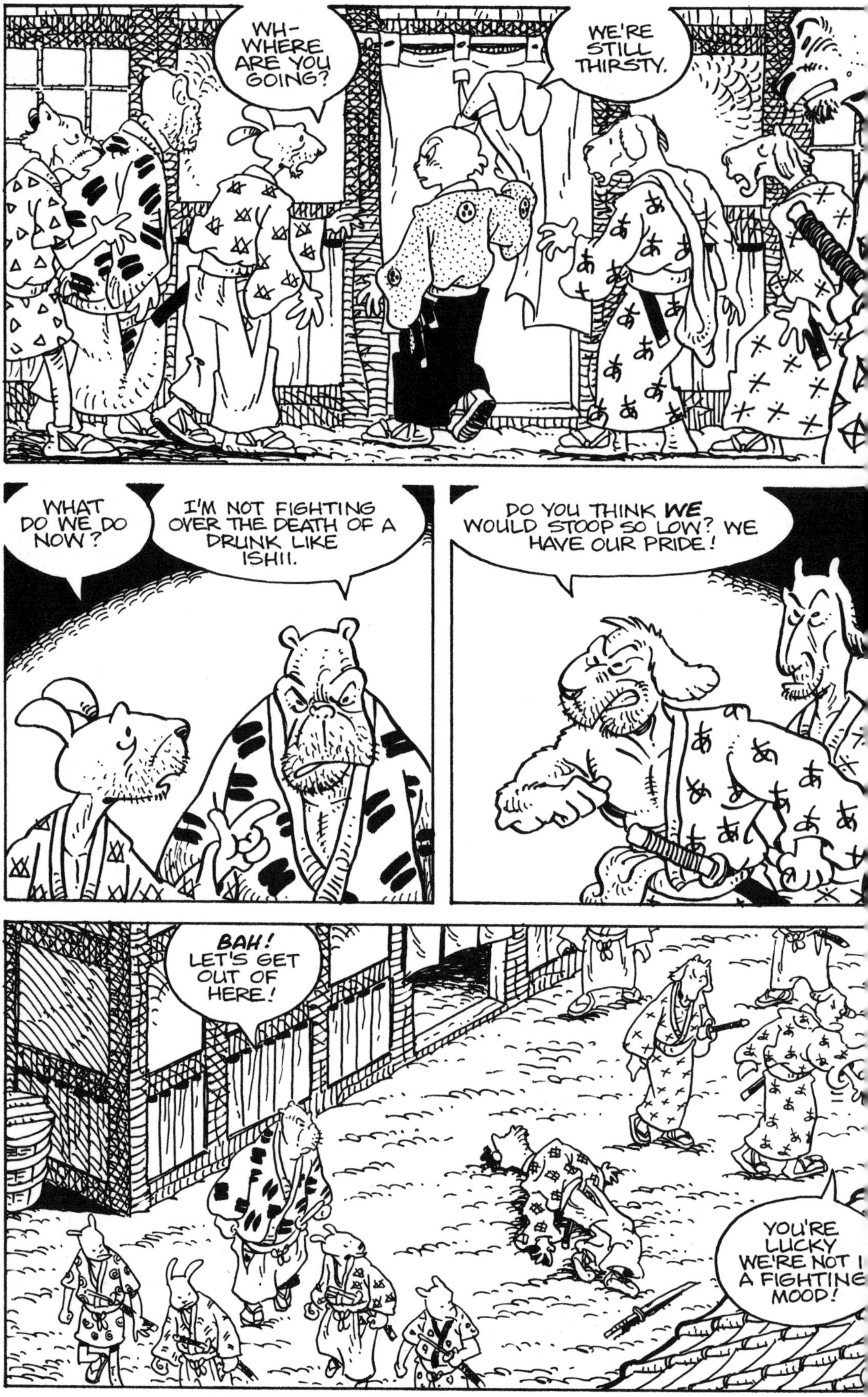

WH-WHERE ARE YOU GOING?
WE'RE STILL THIRSTY.
WHAT DO WE DO NOW?
I'M NOT FIGHTING OVER THE DEATH OF A DRUNK LIKE ISHII.
DO YOU THINK WE WOULD STOOP SO LOW? WE HAVE OUR PRIDE!
BAH! LET'S GET OUT OF HERE!
YOU'RE LUCKY WE'RE NOT I A FIGHTING MOOD!

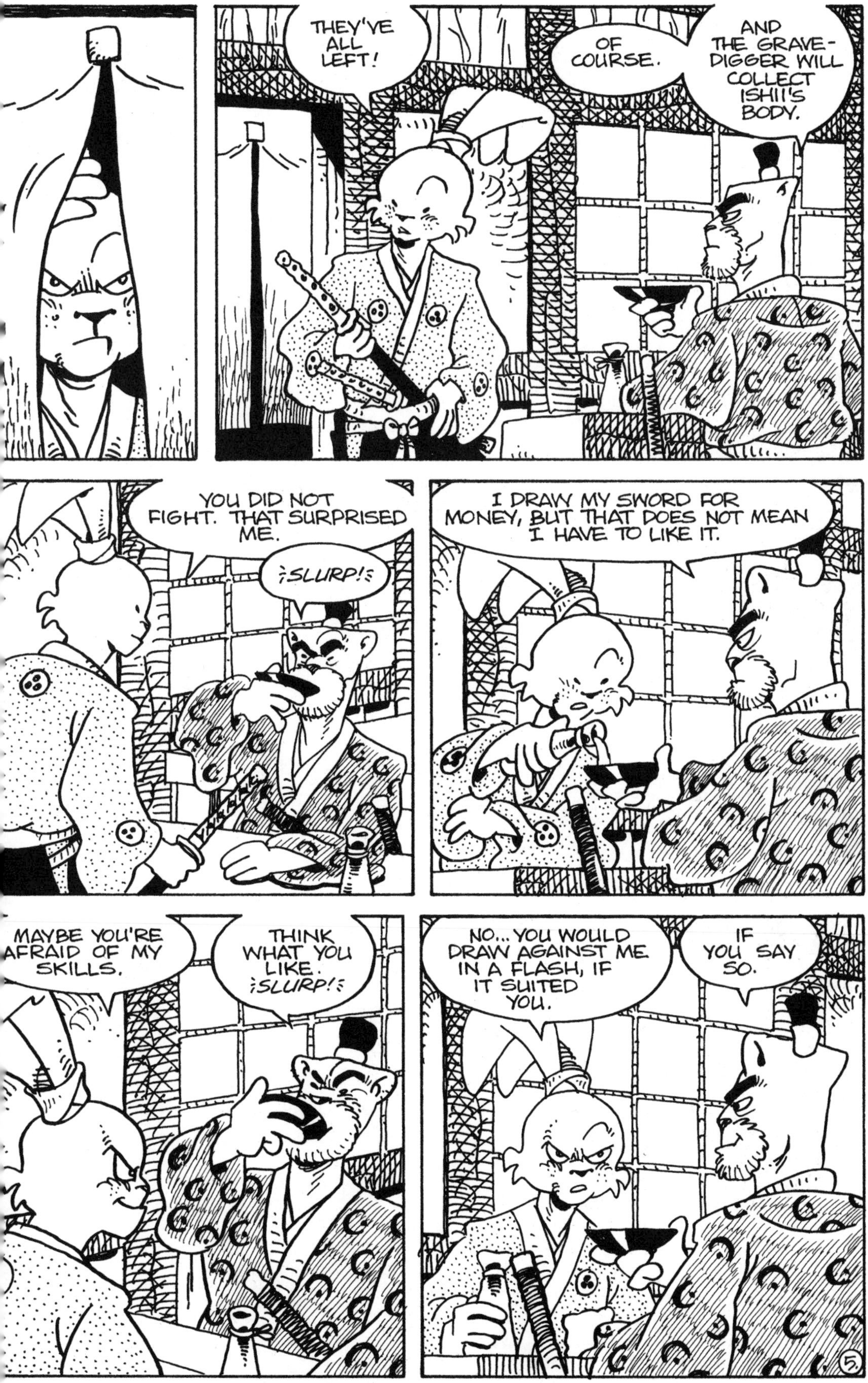
THEY'VE ALL LEFT!
OF COURSE.
AND THE GRAVE-DIGGER WILL COLLECT ISHII'S BODY.
YOU DID NOT FIGHT. THAT SURPRISED ME.
¡SLURP!¡
I DRAW MY SWORD FOR MONEY, BUT THAT DOES NOT MEAN I HAVE TO LIKE IT.
MAYBE YOU'RE AFRAID OF MY SKILLS.
THINK WHAT YOU LIKE. ¡SLURP!¡
NO... YOU WOULD DRAW AGAINST ME IN A FLASH, IF IT SUITED YOU.
IF YOU SAY SO.
5

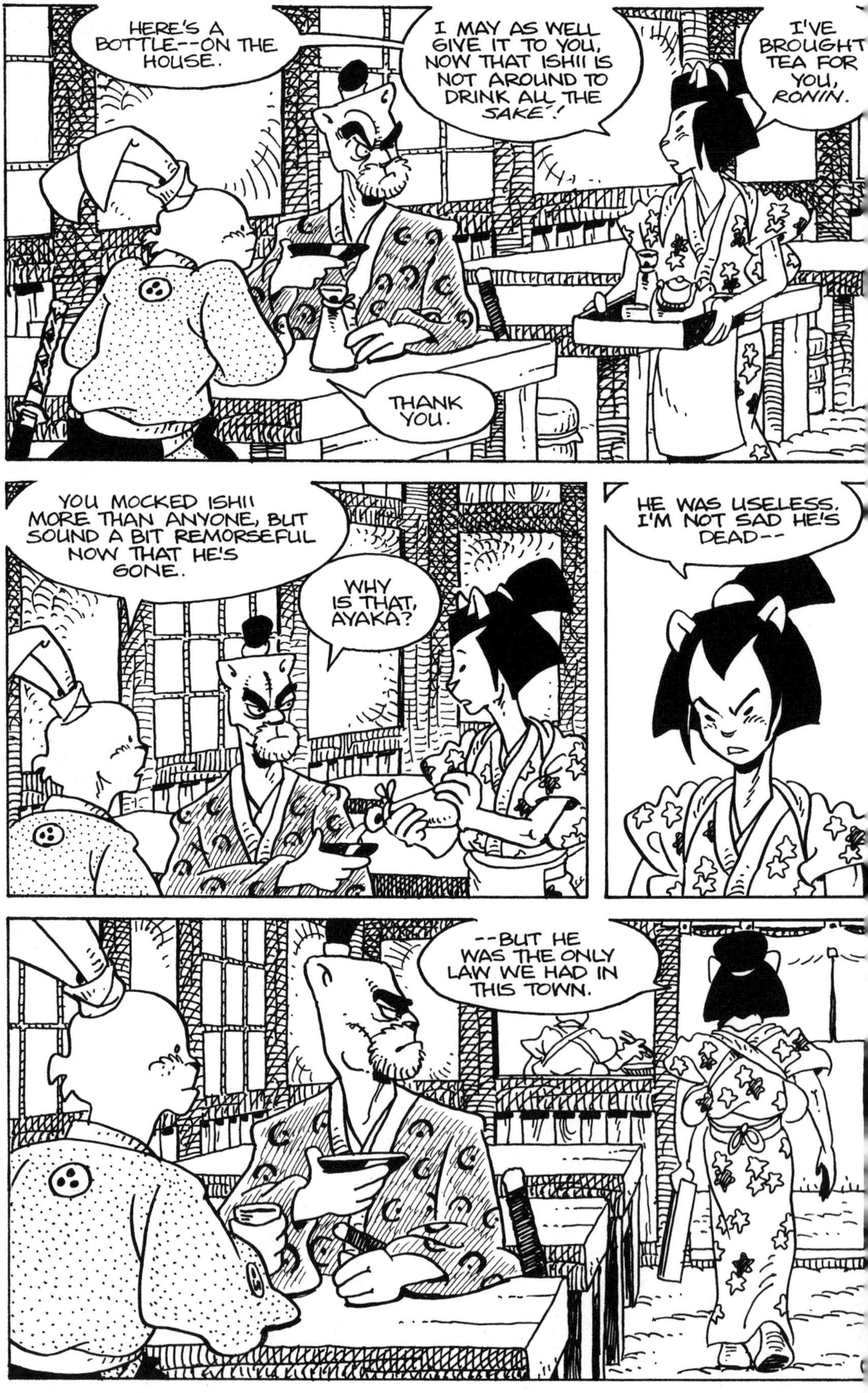
HERE'S A BOTTLE--ON THE HOUSE.
I MAY AS WELL GIVE IT TO YOU, NOW THAT ISHII IS NOT AROUND TO DRINK ALL THE SAKE!
I'VE BROUGHT TEA FOR YOU, RONIN.
THANK YOU.
YOU MOCKED ISHII MORE THAN ANYONE, BUT SOUND A BIT REMORSEFUL NOW THAT HE'S GONE.
WHY IS THAT, AYAKA?
HE WAS USELESS. I'M NOT SAD HE'S DEAD--
--BUT HE WAS THE ONLY LAW WE HAD IN THIS TOWN.

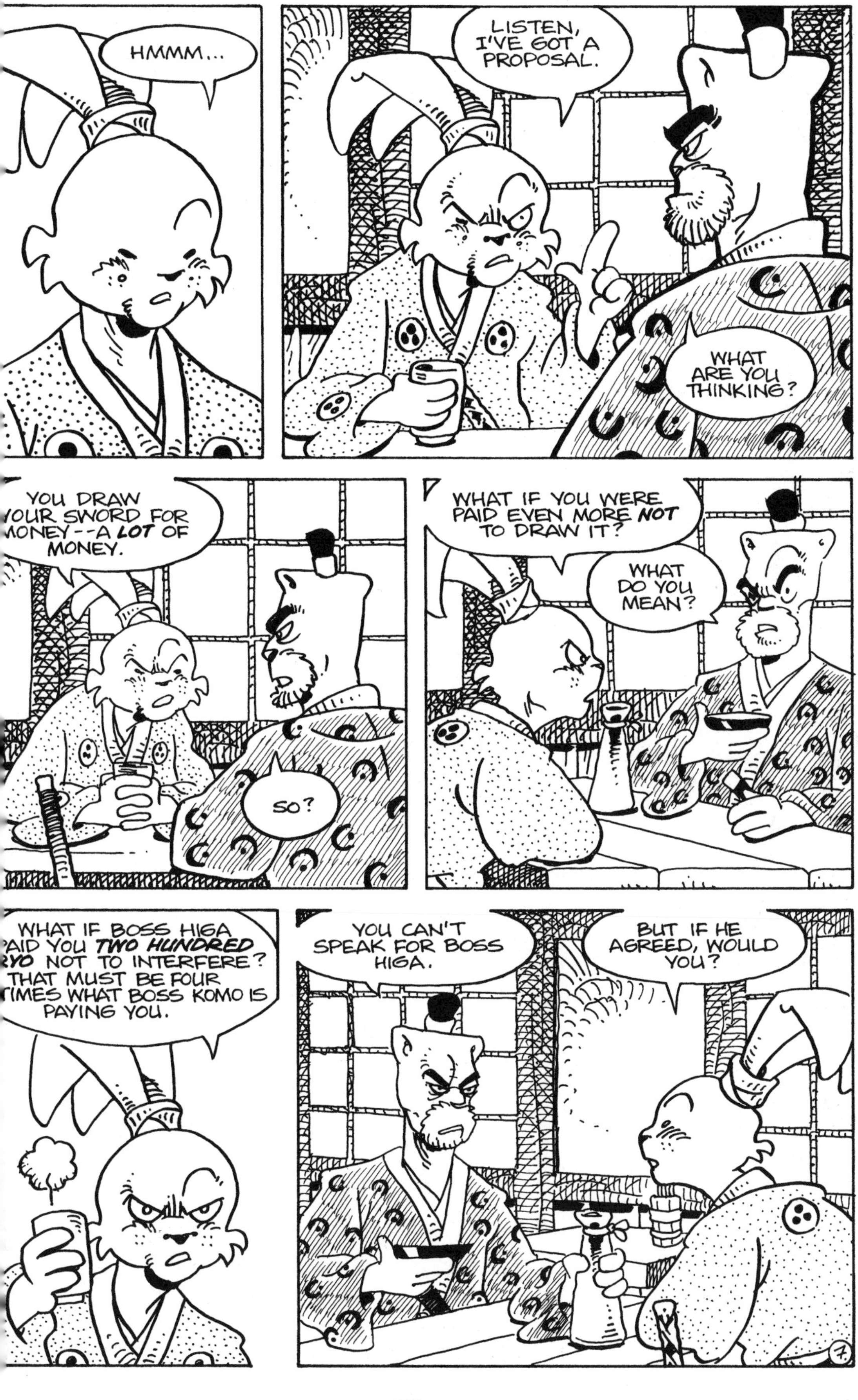
HMMM...
LISTEN, I'VE GOT A PROPOSAL.
WHAT ARE YOU THINKING?
YOU DRAW YOUR SWORD FOR MONEY--A **LOT** OF MONEY.
SO?
WHAT IF YOU WERE PAID EVEN MORE **NOT** TO DRAW IT?
WHAT DO YOU MEAN?
WHAT IF BOSS HIGA PAID YOU **TWO HUNDRED RYO** NOT TO INTERFERE? THAT MUST BE FOUR TIMES WHAT BOSS KOMO IS PAYING YOU.
YOU CAN'T SPEAK FOR BOSS HIGA.
BUT IF HE AGREED, WOULD YOU?
7.

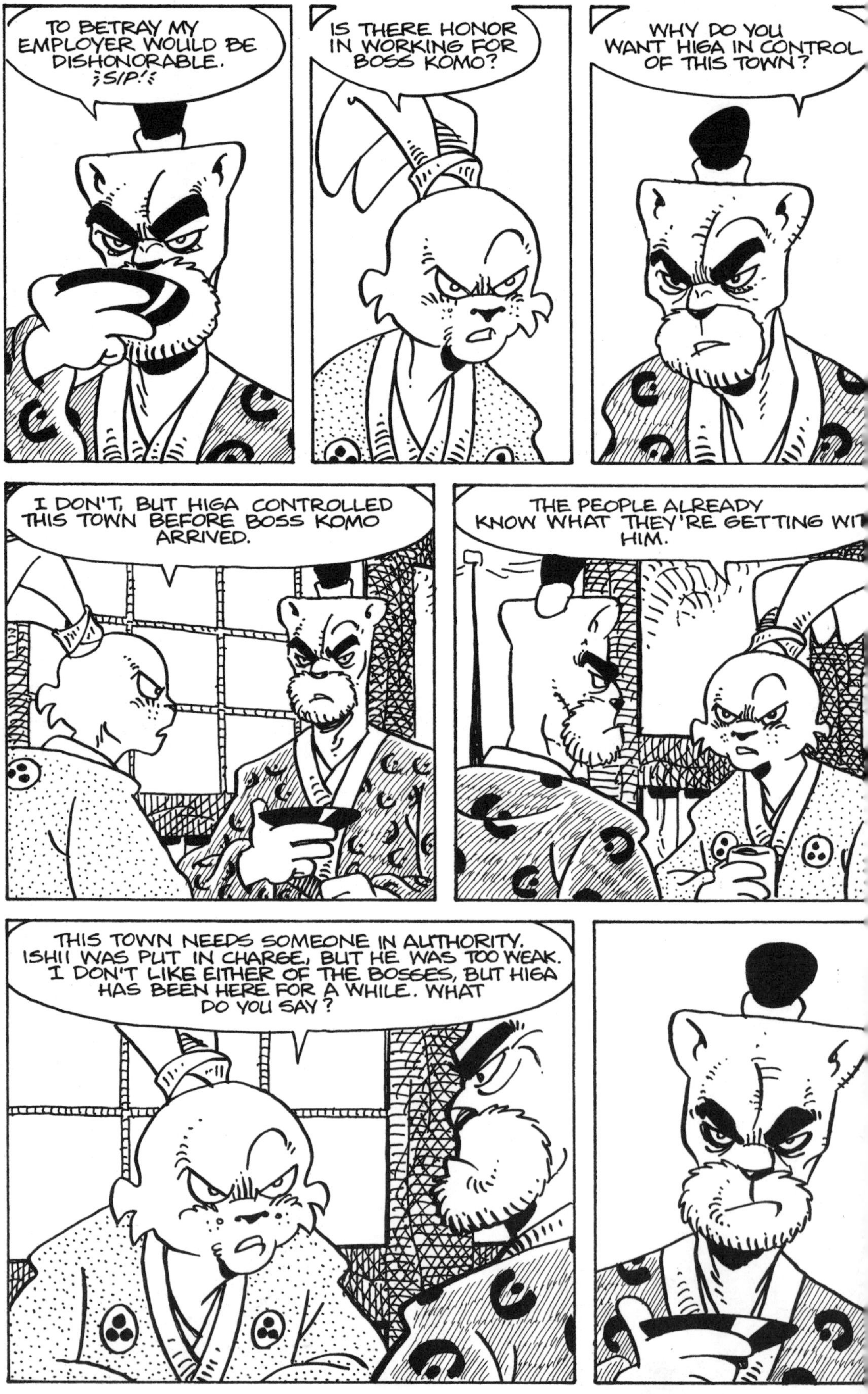
TO BETRAY MY EMPLOYER WOULD BE DISHONORABLE.
SIP!
IS THERE HONOR IN WORKING FOR BOSS KOMO?
WHY DO YOU WANT HIGA IN CONTROL OF THIS TOWN?
I DON'T, BUT HIGA CONTROLLED THIS TOWN BEFORE BOSS KOMO ARRIVED.
THE PEOPLE ALREADY KNOW WHAT THEY'RE GETTING WIT HIM.
THIS TOWN NEEDS SOMEONE IN AUTHORITY. ISHII WAS PUT IN CHARGE, BUT HE WAS TOO WEAK. I DON'T LIKE EITHER OF THE BOSSES, BUT HIGA HAS BEEN HERE FOR A WHILE. WHAT DO YOU SAY?

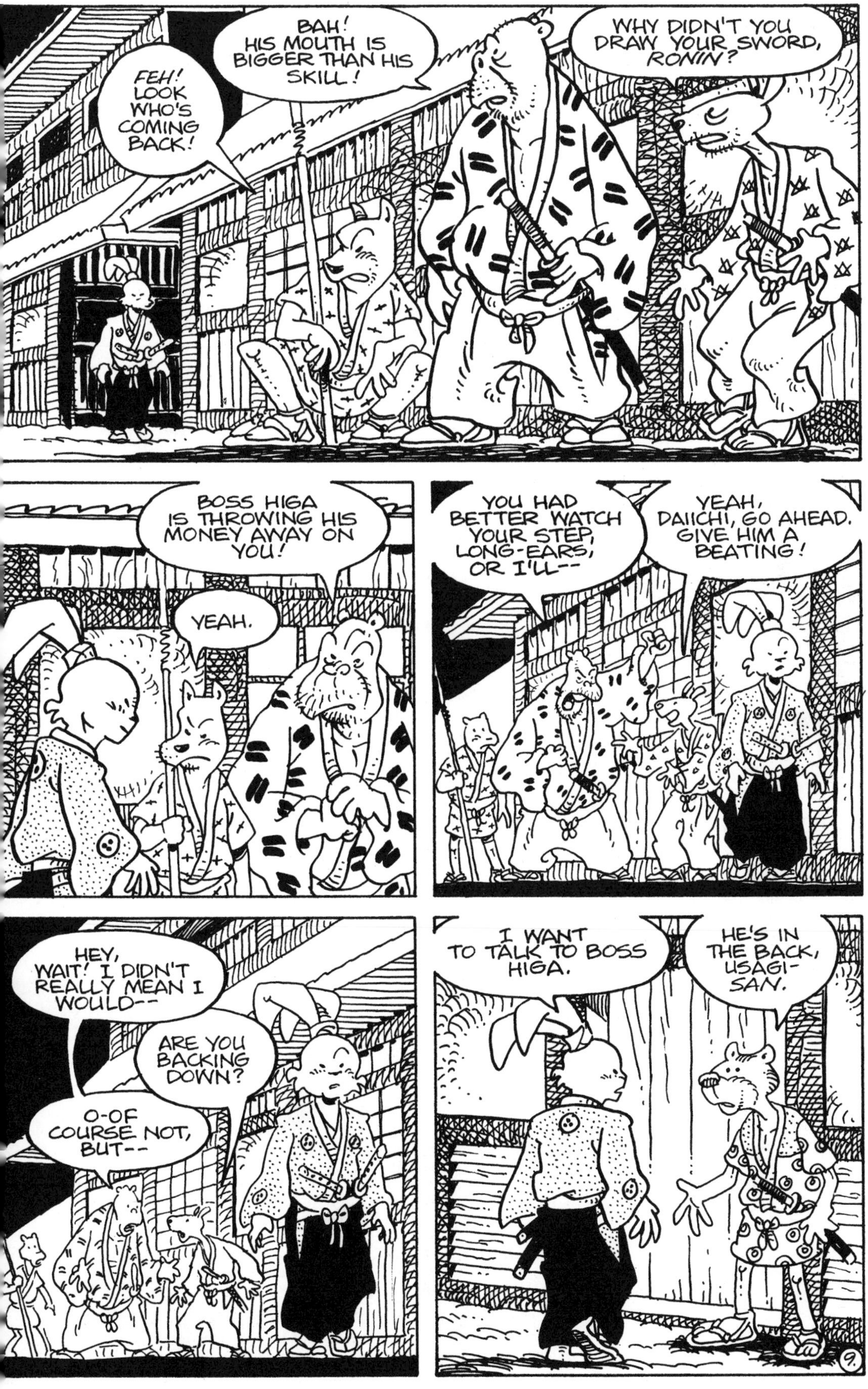
FEH! LOOK WHO'S COMING BACK!
BAH! HIS MOUTH IS BIGGER THAN HIS SKILL!
WHY DIDN'T YOU DRAW YOUR SWORD, RONIN?
BOSS HIGA IS THROWING HIS MONEY AWAY ON YOU!
YEAH.
YOU HAD BETTER WATCH YOUR STEP, LONG-EARS, OR I'LL--
YEAH, DAIICHI, GO AHEAD. GIVE HIM A BEATING!
HEY, WAIT! I DIDN'T REALLY MEAN I WOULD--
ARE YOU BACKING DOWN?
O-OF COURSE NOT, BUT--
I WANT TO TALK TO BOSS HIGA.
HE'S IN THE BACK, USAGI-SAN.
9.

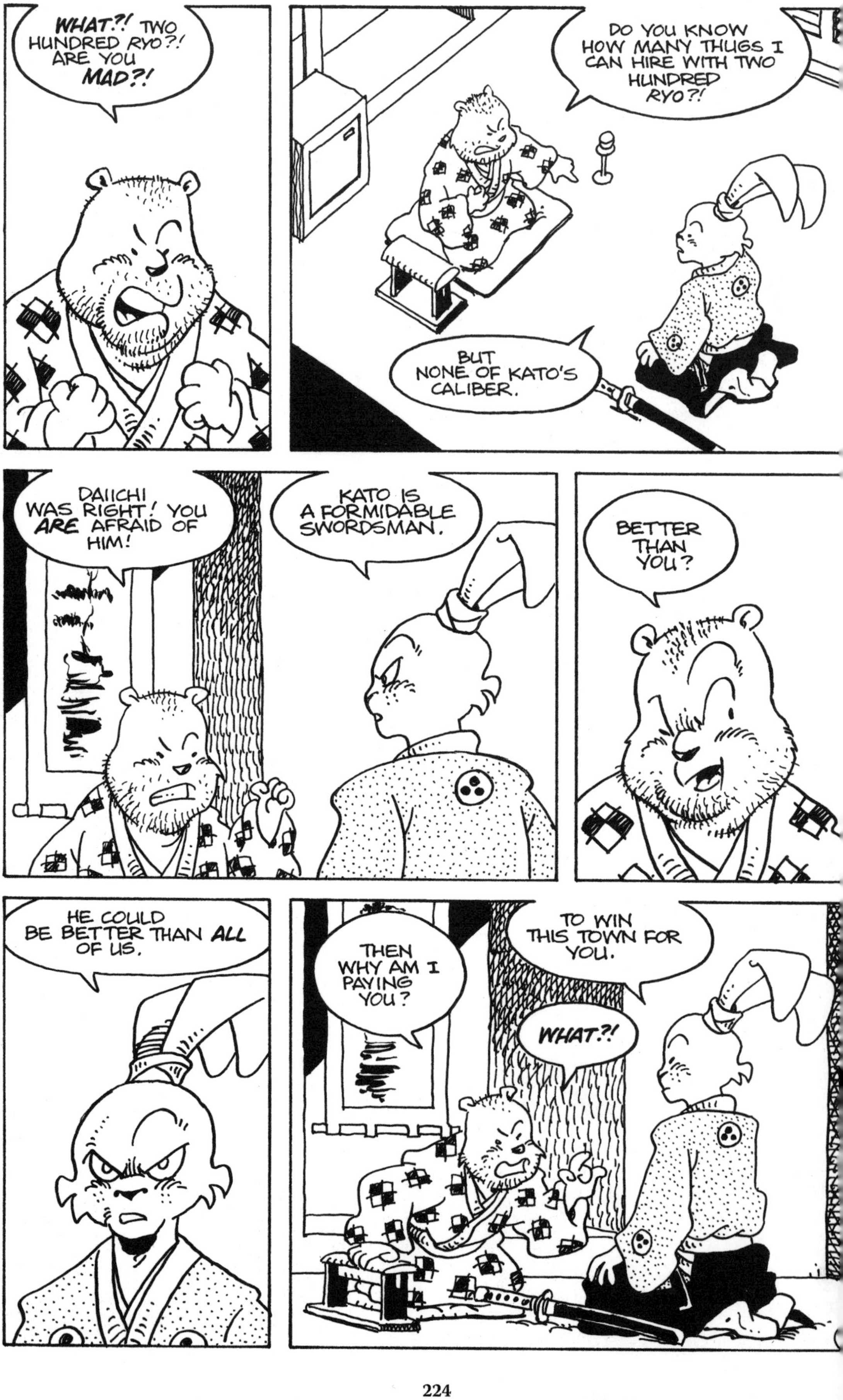
WHAT?! TWO HUNDRED RYO?! ARE YOU MAD?!
DO YOU KNOW HOW MANY THUGS I CAN HIRE WITH TWO HUNDRED RYO?!
BUT NONE OF KATO'S CALIBER.
DAIICHI WAS RIGHT! YOU ARE AFRAID OF HIM!
KATO IS A FORMIDABLE SWORDSMAN.
BETTER THAN YOU?
HE COULD BE BETTER THAN ALL OF US.
THEN WHY AM I PAYING YOU?
TO WIN THIS TOWN FOR YOU.
WHAT?!

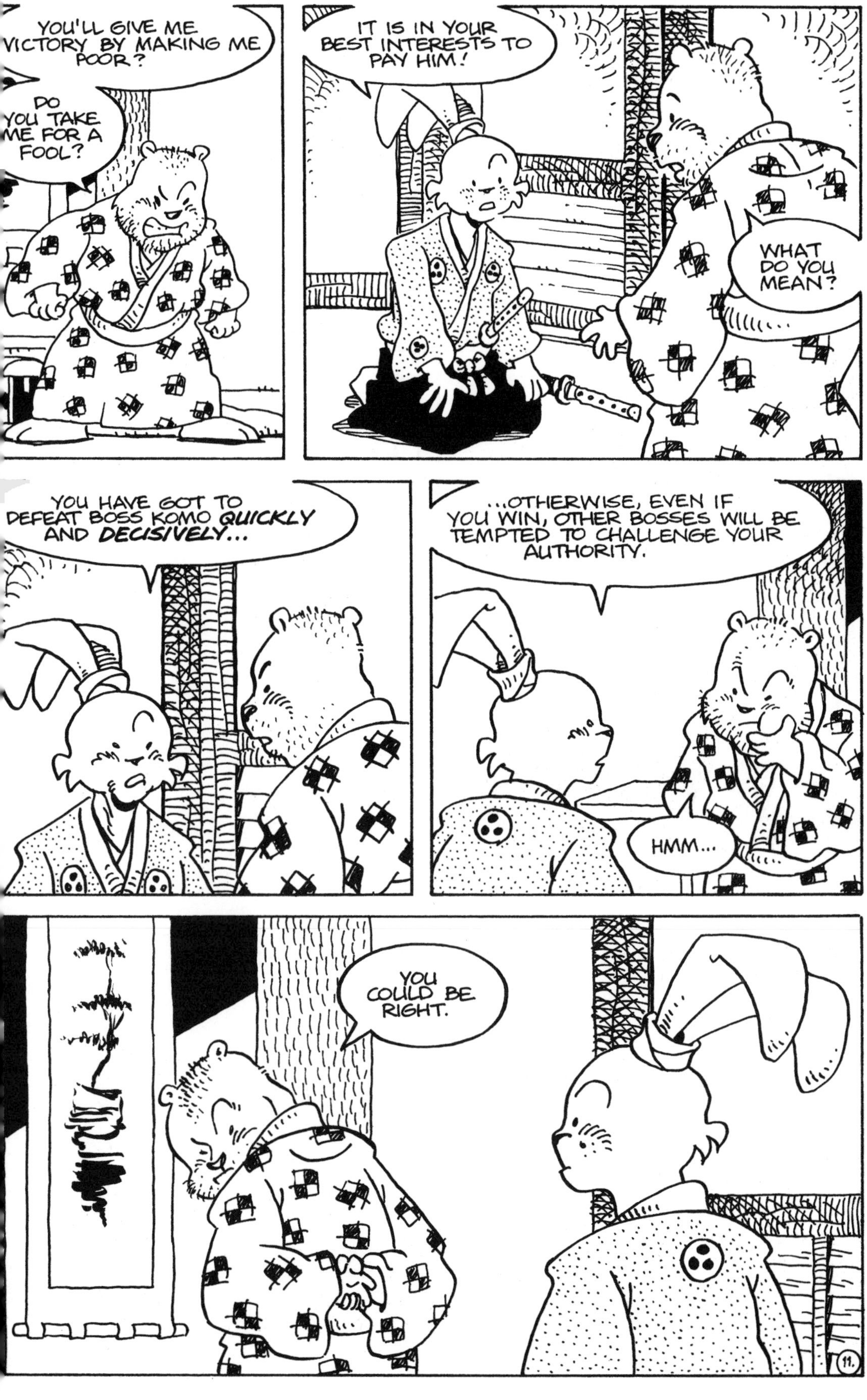
YOU'LL GIVE ME VICTORY BY MAKING ME POOR?
DO YOU TAKE ME FOR A FOOL?
IT IS IN YOUR BEST INTERESTS TO PAY HIM!
WHAT DO YOU MEAN?
YOU HAVE GOT TO DEFEAT BOSS KOMO QUICKLY AND DECISIVELY...
...OTHERWISE, EVEN IF YOU WIN, OTHER BOSSES WILL BE TEMPTED TO CHALLENGE YOUR AUTHORITY.
HMM...
YOU COULD BE RIGHT.
11.

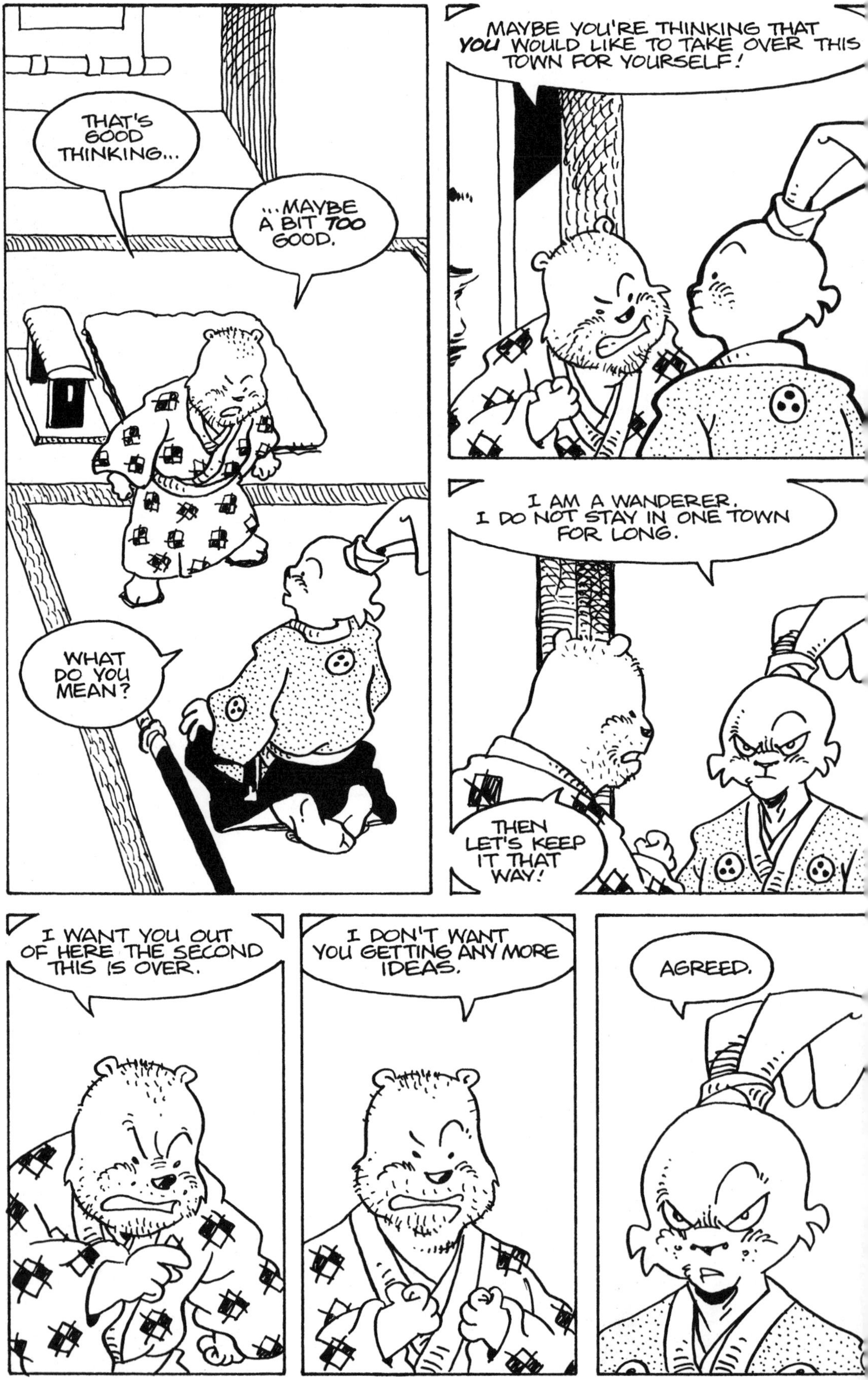
THAT'S GOOD THINKING...
...MAYBE A BIT TOO GOOD.
WHAT DO YOU MEAN?
MAYBE YOU'RE THINKING THAT YOU WOULD LIKE TO TAKE OVER THIS TOWN FOR YOURSELF!
I AM A WANDERER. I DO NOT STAY IN ONE TOWN FOR LONG.
THEN LET'S KEEP IT THAT WAY!
I WANT YOU OUT OF HERE THE SECOND THIS IS OVER.
I DON'T WANT YOU GETTING ANY MORE IDEAS.
AGREED.

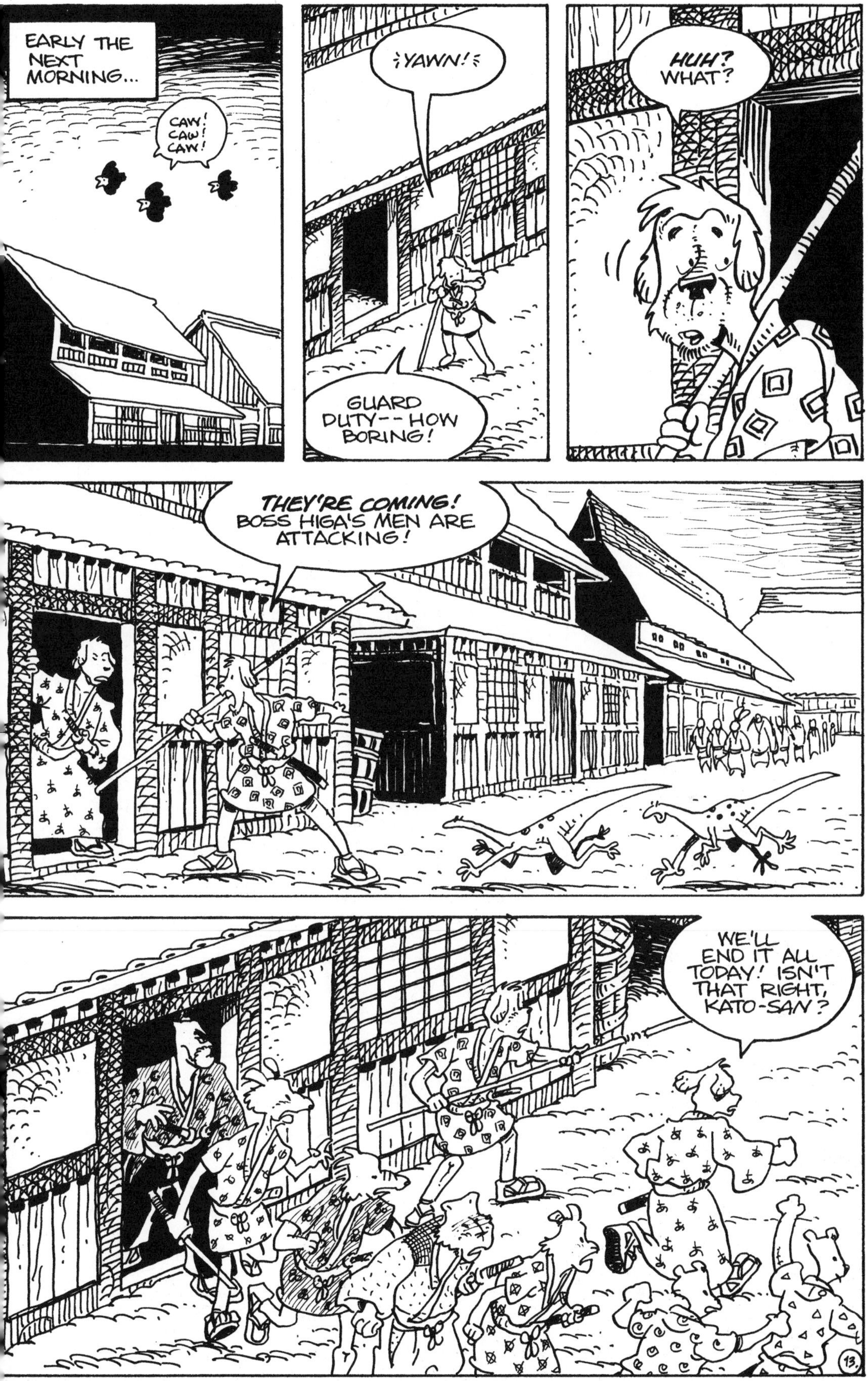

EARLY THE NEXT MORNING...
CAW! CAW! CAW!
¡YAWN!
GUARD DUTY--HOW BORING!
HUH? WHAT?
THEY'RE COMING! BOSS HIGA'S MEN ARE ATTACKING!
WE'LL END IT ALL TODAY! ISN'T THAT RIGHT, KATO-SAN?
13.

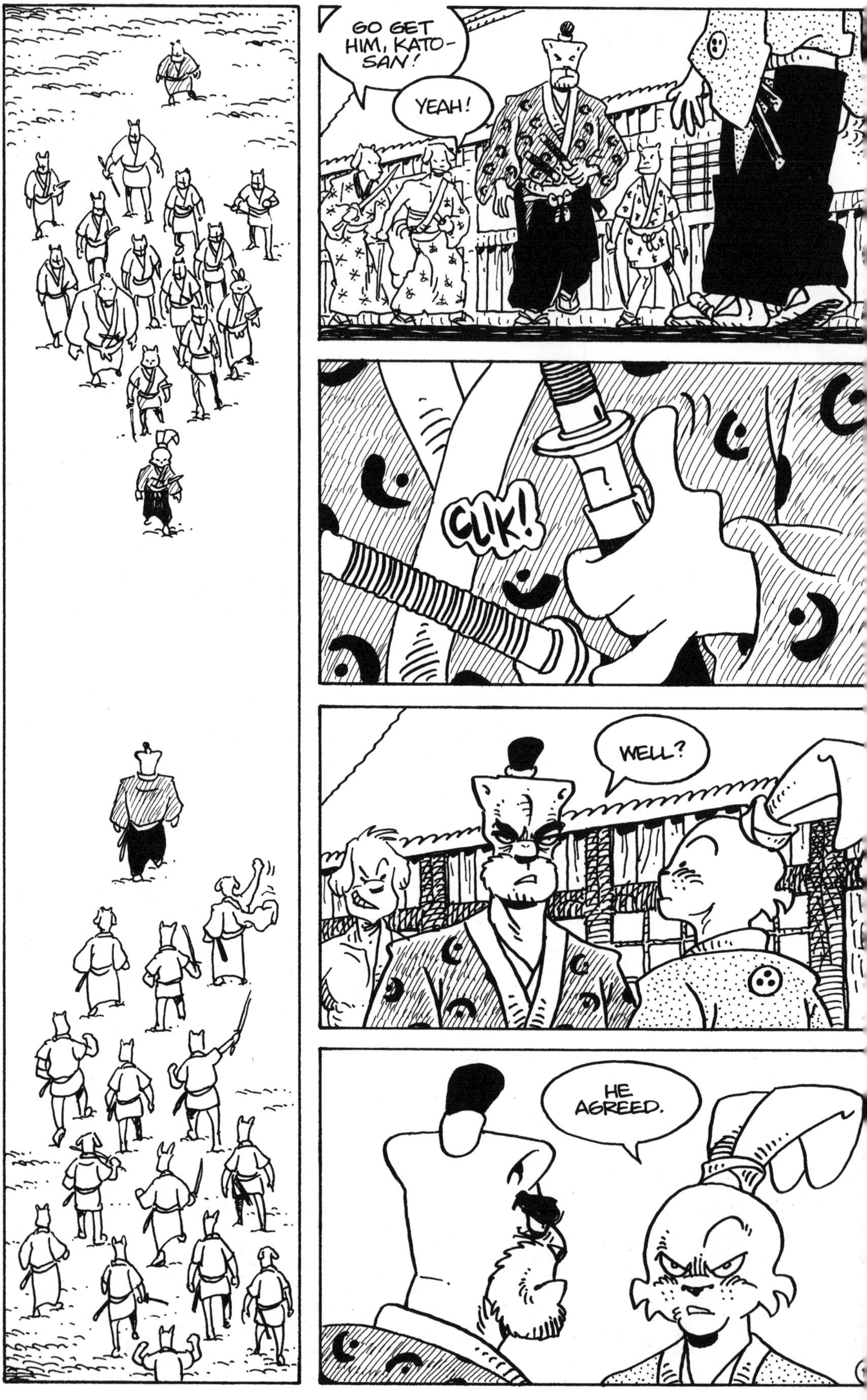
GO GET HIM, KATO-SAN!
YEAH!
GLIK!
WELL?
HE AGREED.

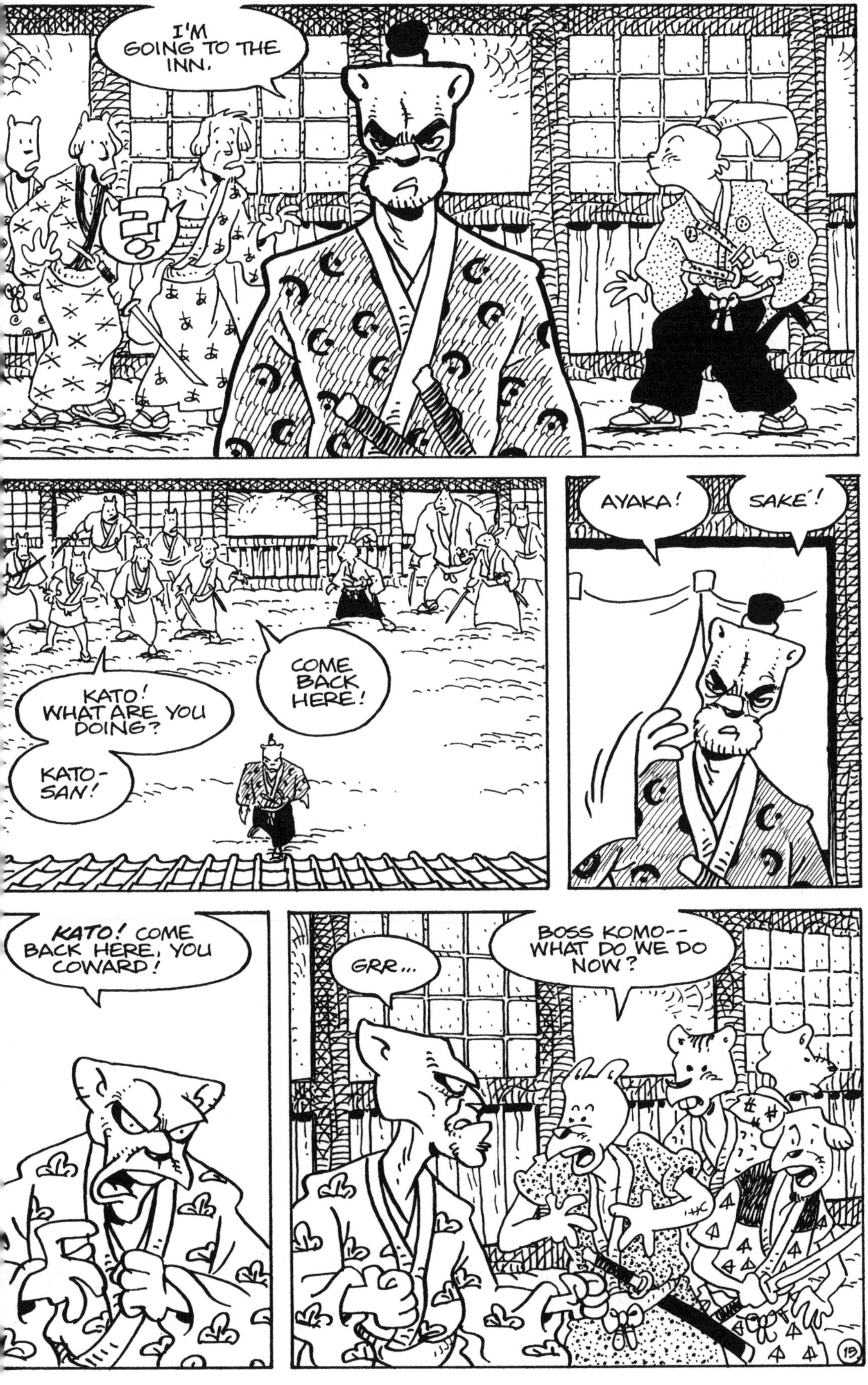
I'M GOING TO THE INN.
KATO! WHAT ARE YOU DOING?
KATO-SAN!
COME BACK HERE!
AYAKA!
SAKE!
KATO! COME BACK HERE, YOU COWARD!
GRR...
BOSS KOMO-- WHAT DO WE DO NOW?
13

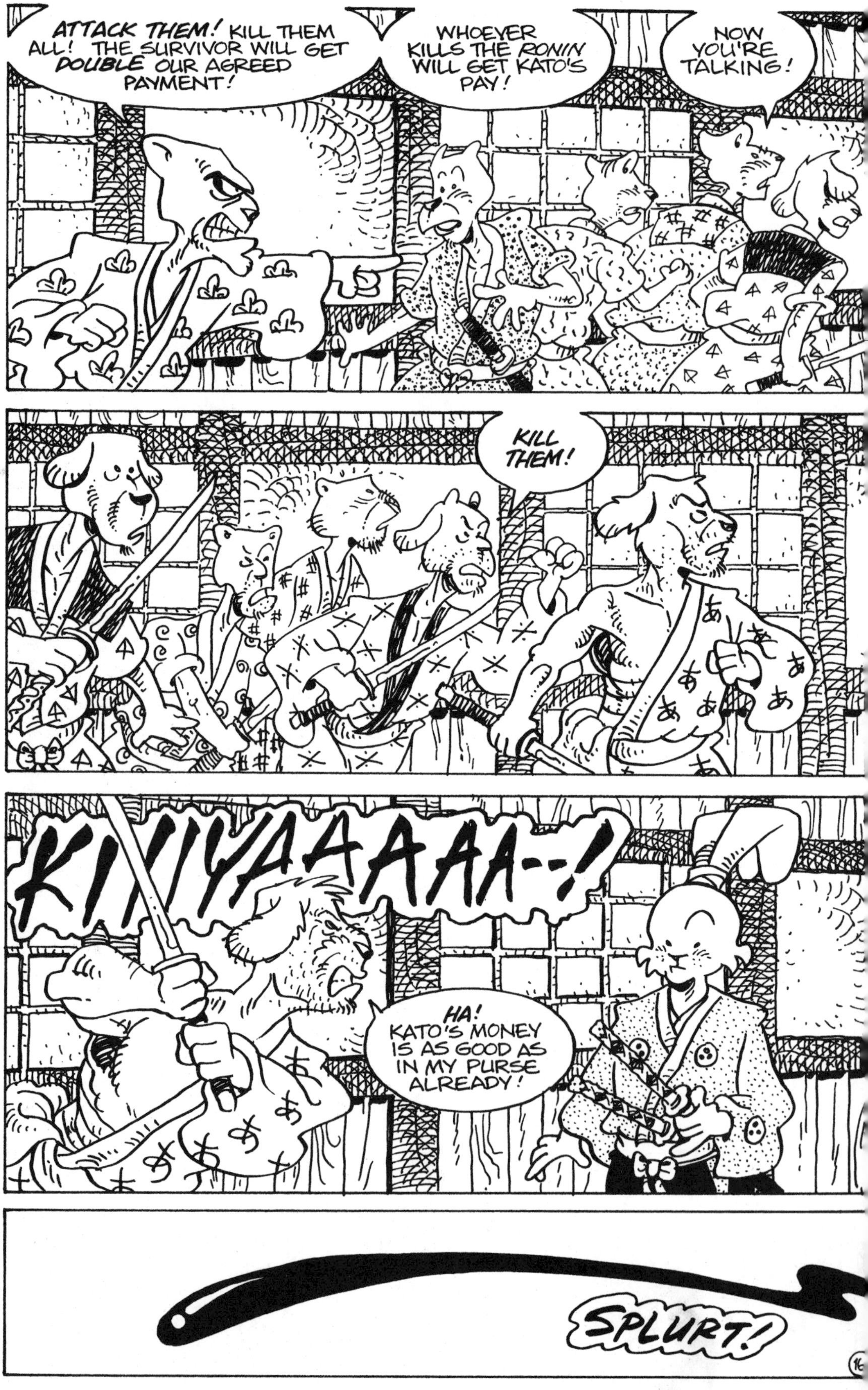
ATTACK THEM! KILL THEM ALL! THE SURVIVOR WILL GET DOUBLE OUR AGREED PAYMENT!
WHOEVER KILLS THE RONIN WILL GET KATO'S PAY!
NOW YOU'RE TALKING!
KILL THEM!
KIIIYAAAAAA--!
HA! KATO'S MONEY IS AS GOOD AS IN MY PURSE ALREADY!
SPLURT!
16

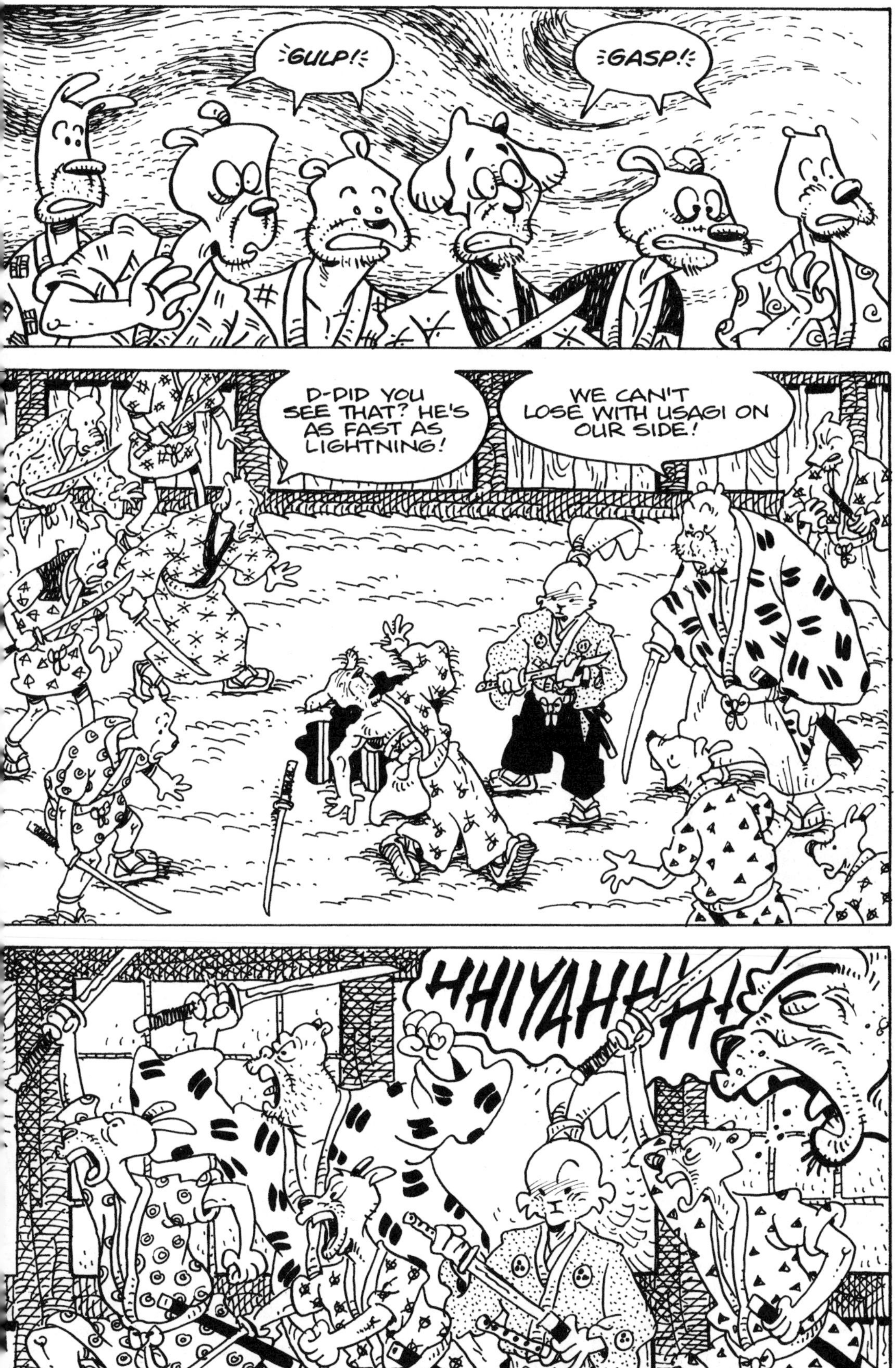
GULP!
GASP!
D-DID YOU SEE THAT? HE'S AS FAST AS LIGHTNING!
WE CAN'T LOSE WITH USAGI ON OUR SIDE!
HHIYAHHH!
17

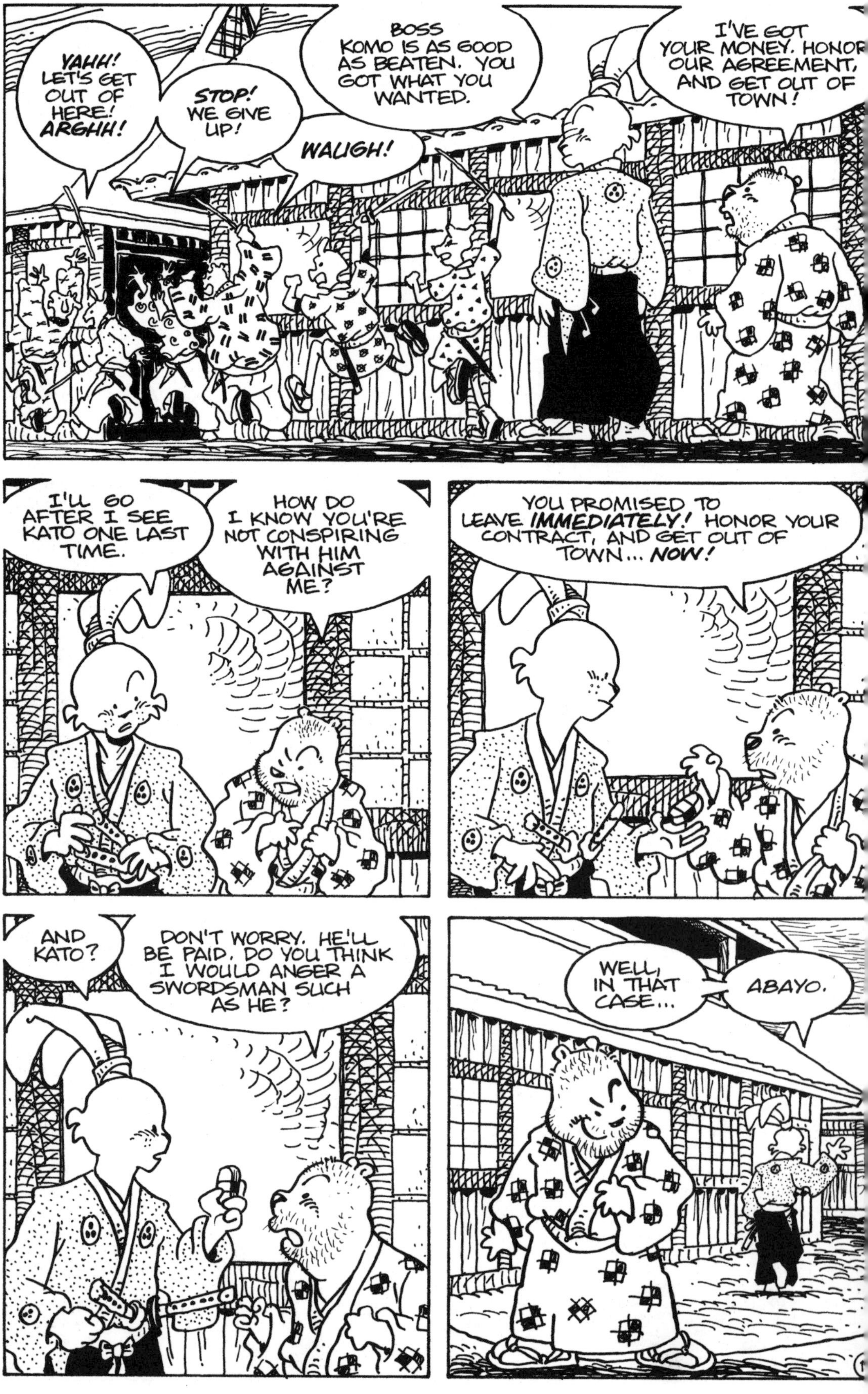

YAHH! LET'S GET OUT OF HERE! ARGHH!
STOP! WE GIVE UP!
WAUGH!
BOSS KOMO IS AS GOOD AS BEATEN. YOU GOT WHAT YOU WANTED.
I'VE GOT YOUR MONEY. HONOR OUR AGREEMENT, AND GET OUT OF TOWN!
I'LL GO AFTER I SEE KATO ONE LAST TIME.
HOW DO I KNOW YOU'RE NOT CONSPIRING WITH HIM AGAINST ME?
YOU PROMISED TO LEAVE IMMEDIATELY! HONOR YOUR CONTRACT, AND GET OUT OF TOWN... NOW!
AND KATO?
DON'T WORRY. HE'LL BE PAID. DO YOU THINK I WOULD ANGER A SWORDSMAN SUCH AS HE?
WELL, IN THAT CASE...
ABAYO.

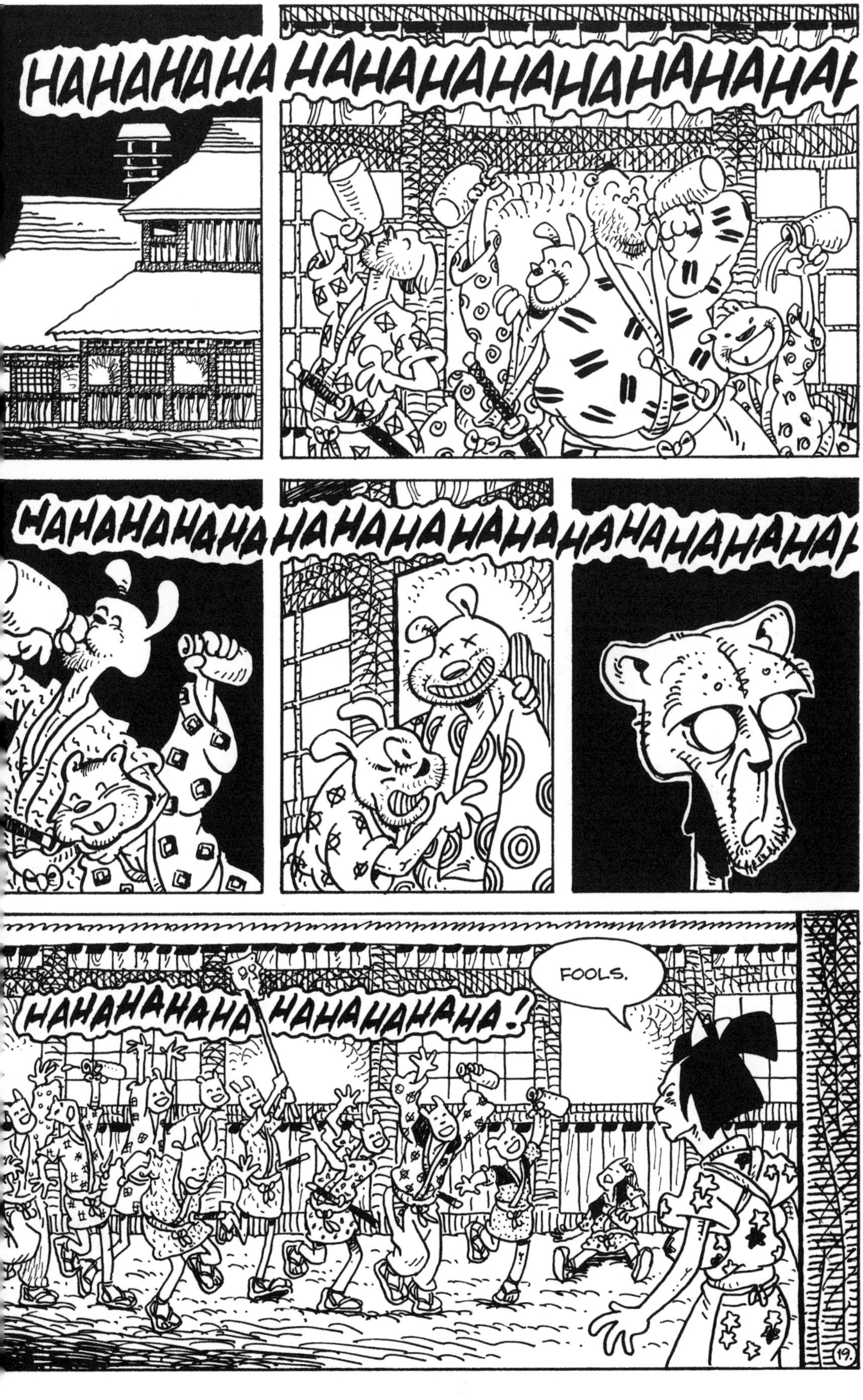
HAHAHAHA HAHAHAHAHAHAHAHAHA
HAHAHAHAHA HAHAHAHAHAHAHAHAHAHAHA
HAHAHAHAHA HAHAHAHAHA!
FOOLS.
19.

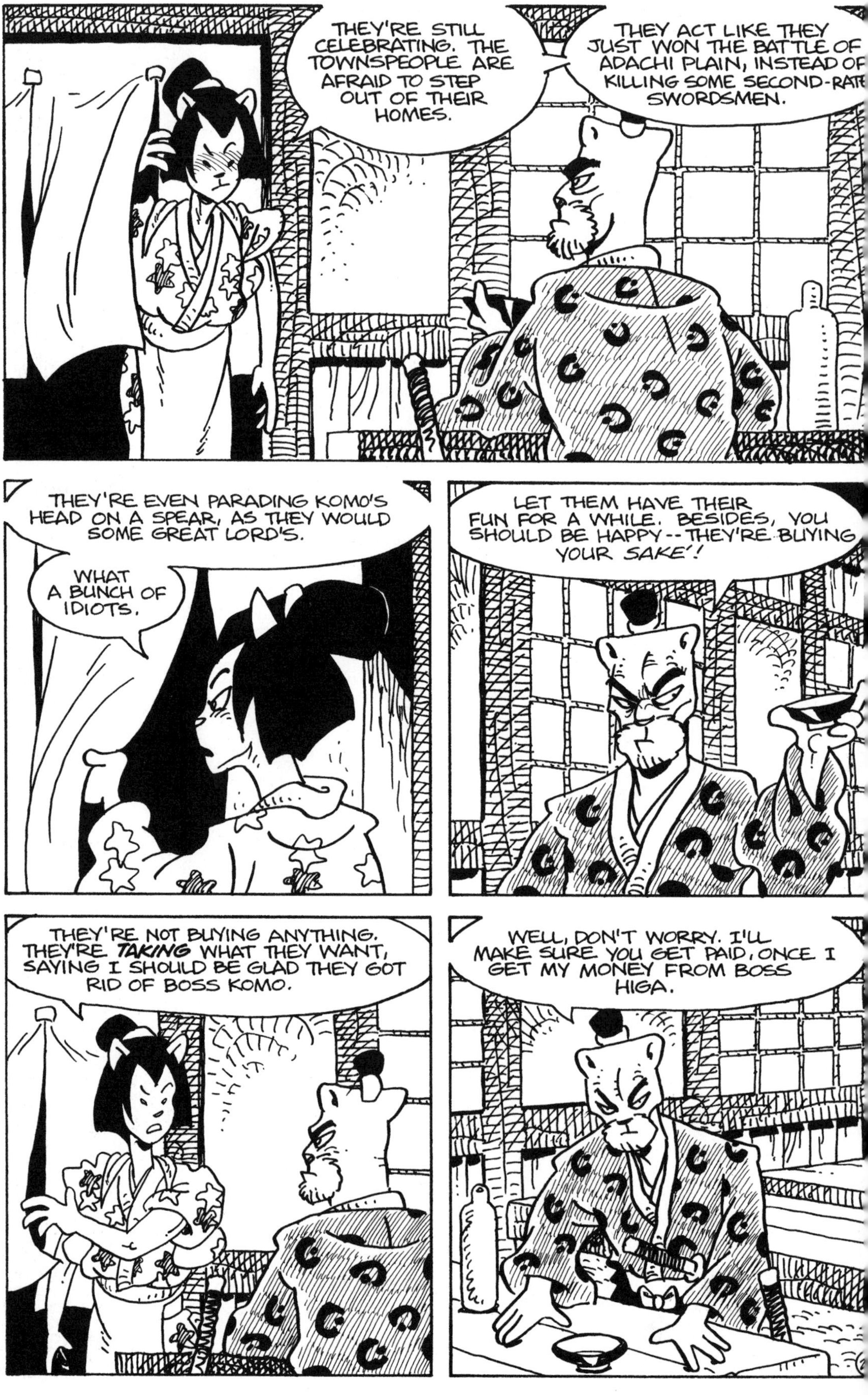
THEY'RE STILL CELEBRATING. THE TOWNSPEOPLE ARE AFRAID TO STEP OUT OF THEIR HOMES.
THEY ACT LIKE THEY JUST WON THE BATTLE OF ADACHI PLAIN, INSTEAD OF KILLING SOME SECOND-RATE SWORDSMEN.
THEY'RE EVEN PARADING KOMO'S HEAD ON A SPEAR, AS THEY WOULD SOME GREAT LORD'S.
WHAT A BUNCH OF IDIOTS.
LET THEM HAVE THEIR FUN FOR A WHILE. BESIDES, YOU SHOULD BE HAPPY -- THEY'RE BUYING YOUR SAKE'!
THEY'RE NOT BUYING ANYTHING. THEY'RE TAKING WHAT THEY WANT, SAYING I SHOULD BE GLAD THEY GOT RID OF BOSS KOMO.
WELL, DON'T WORRY. I'LL MAKE SURE YOU GET PAID, ONCE I GET MY MONEY FROM BOSS HIGA.

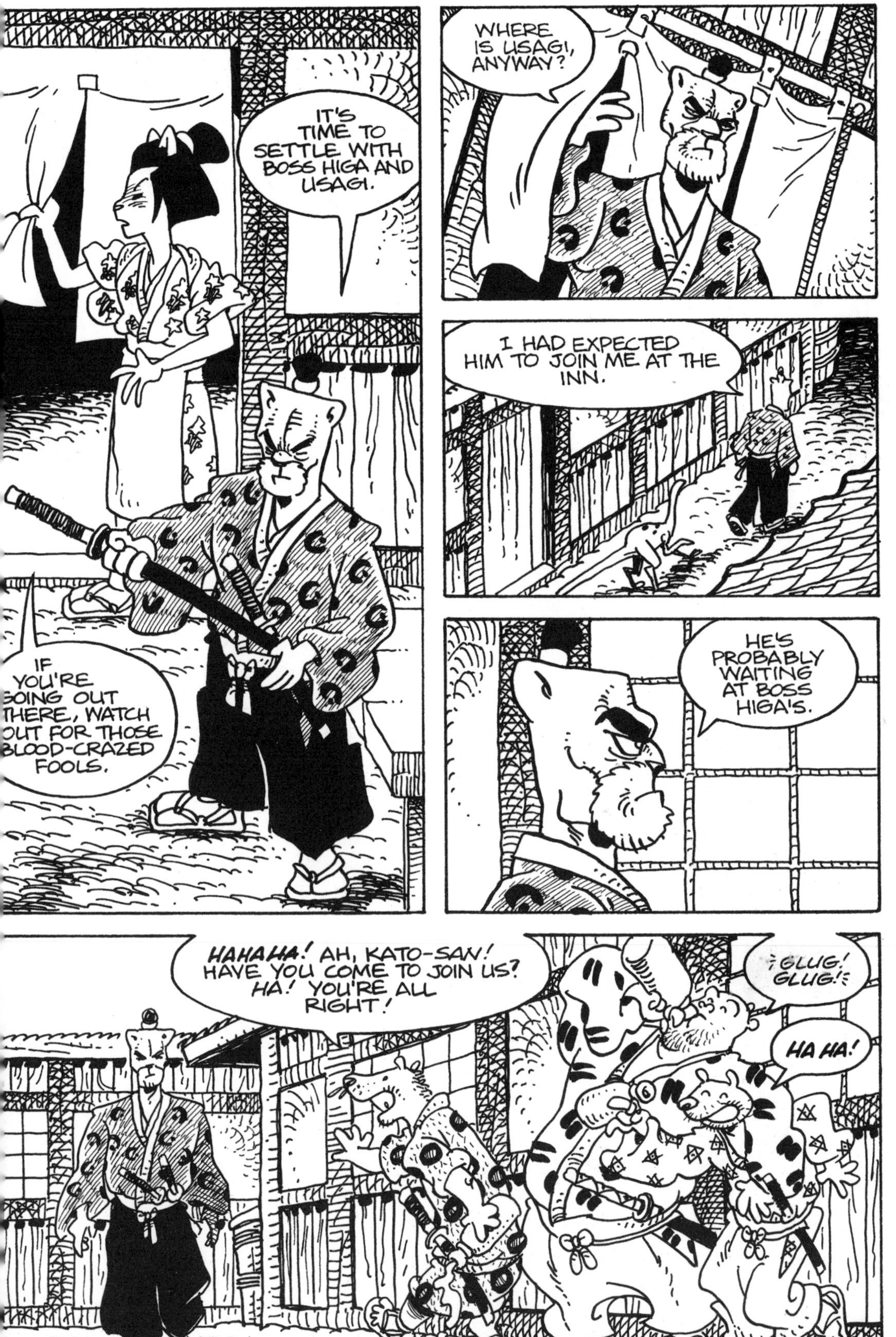
IT'S TIME TO SETTLE WITH BOSS HIGA AND USAGI.
IF YOU'RE GOING OUT THERE, WATCH OUT FOR THOSE BLOOD-CRAZED FOOLS.
WHERE IS USAGI, ANYWAY?
I HAD EXPECTED HIM TO JOIN ME AT THE INN.
HE'S PROBABLY WAITING AT BOSS HIGA'S.
HAHAHA! AH, KATO-SAN! HAVE YOU COME TO JOIN US? HA! YOU'RE ALL RIGHT!
GLUG! GLUG!
HA HA!
21

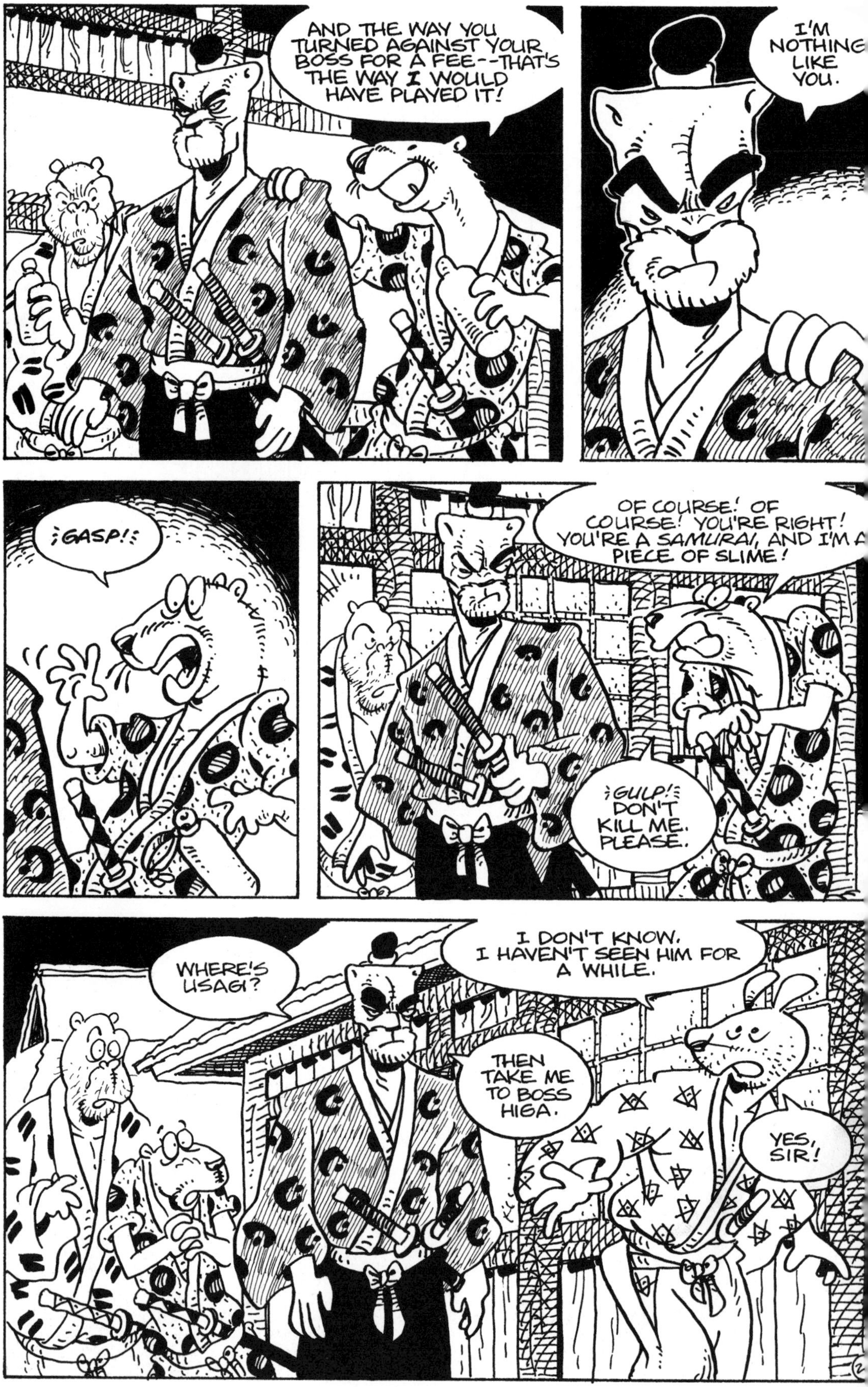
AND THE WAY YOU TURNED AGAINST YOUR BOSS FOR A FEE--THAT'S THE WAY *I* WOULD HAVE PLAYED IT!
I'M NOTHING LIKE YOU.
¡GASP!¡
OF COURSE! OF COURSE! YOU'RE RIGHT! YOU'RE A *SAMURAI*, AND I'M A PIECE OF SLIME!
¡GULP!¡ DON'T KILL ME. PLEASE.
WHERE'S USAGI?
I DON'T KNOW. I HAVEN'T SEEN HIM FOR A WHILE.
THEN TAKE ME TO BOSS HIGA.
YES, SIR!

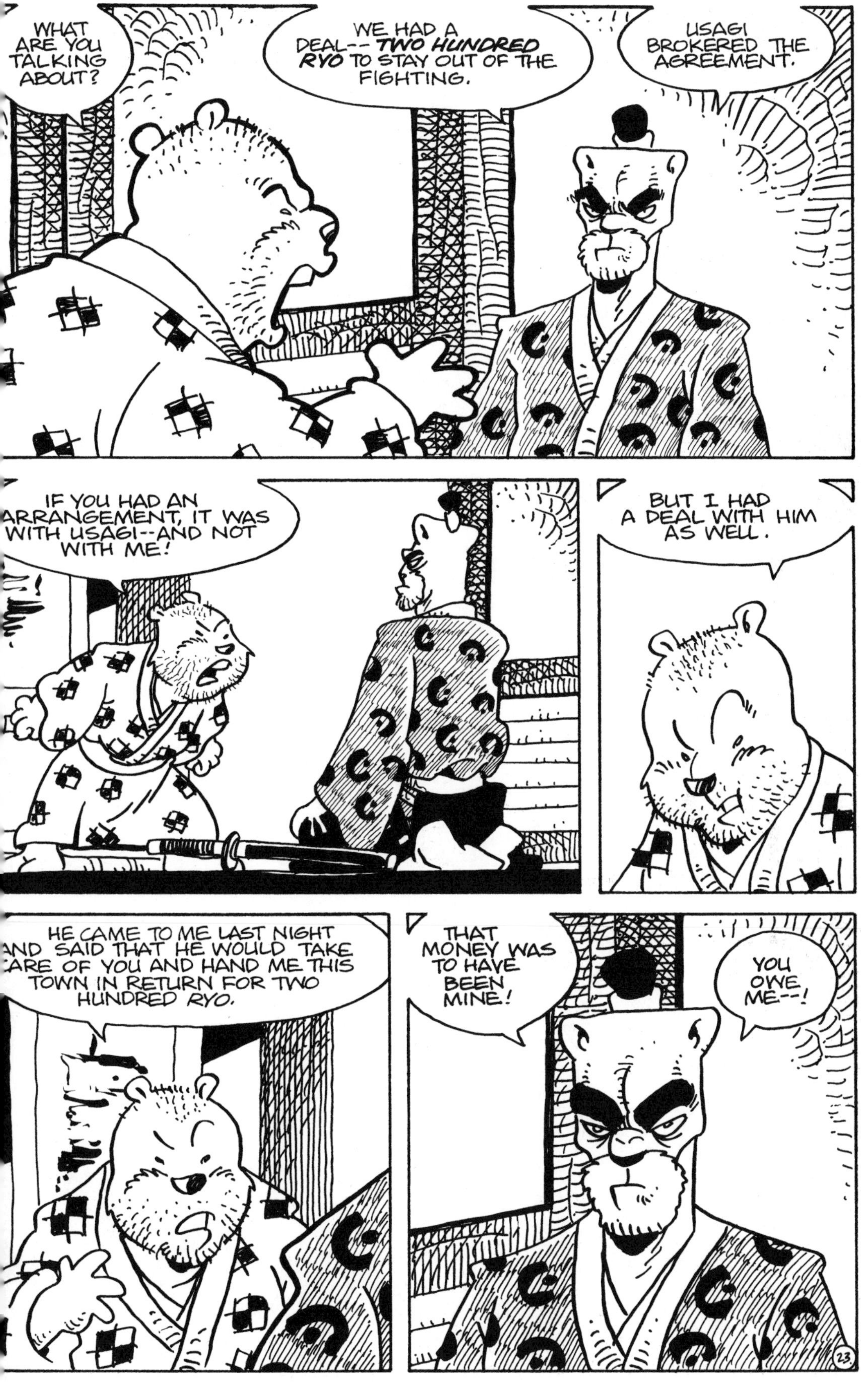
WHAT ARE YOU TALKING ABOUT?
WE HAD A DEAL-- TWO HUNDRED RYO TO STAY OUT OF THE FIGHTING.
USAGI BROKERED THE AGREEMENT.
IF YOU HAD AN ARRANGEMENT, IT WAS WITH USAGI--AND NOT WITH ME!
BUT I HAD A DEAL WITH HIM AS WELL.
HE CAME TO ME LAST NIGHT AND SAID THAT HE WOULD TAKE CARE OF YOU AND HAND ME THIS TOWN IN RETURN FOR TWO HUNDRED RYO.
THAT MONEY WAS TO HAVE BEEN MINE!
YOU OWE ME--!
23

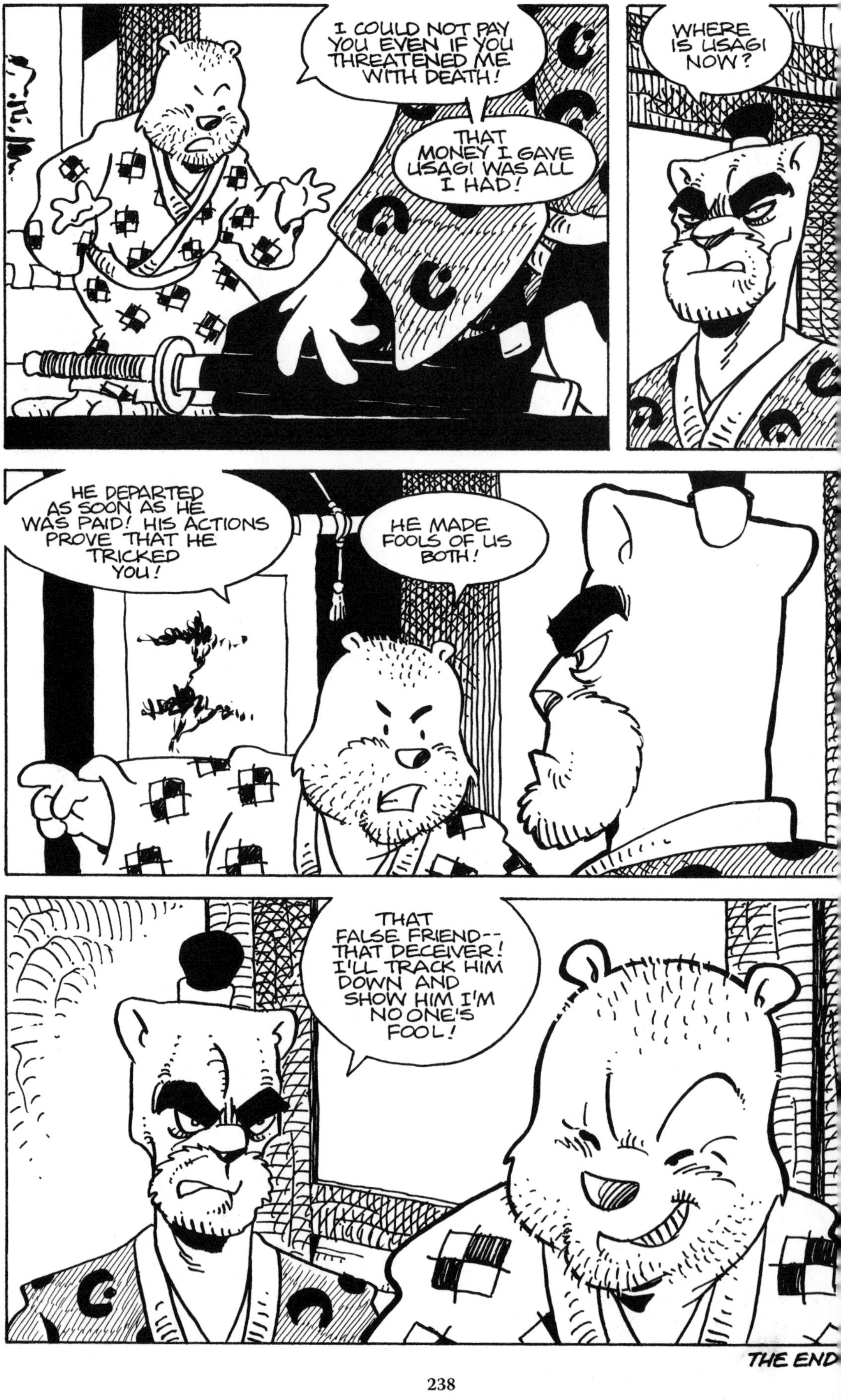
I COULD NOT PAY YOU EVEN IF YOU THREATENED ME WITH DEATH!
THAT MONEY I GAVE USAGI WAS ALL I HAD!
WHERE IS USAGI NOW?
HE DEPARTED AS SOON AS HE WAS PAID! HIS ACTIONS PROVE THAT HE TRICKED YOU!
HE MADE FOOLS OF US BOTH!
THAT FALSE FRIEND-- THAT DECEIVER! I'LL TRACK HIM DOWN AND SHOW HIM I'M NO ONE'S FOOL!
THE END

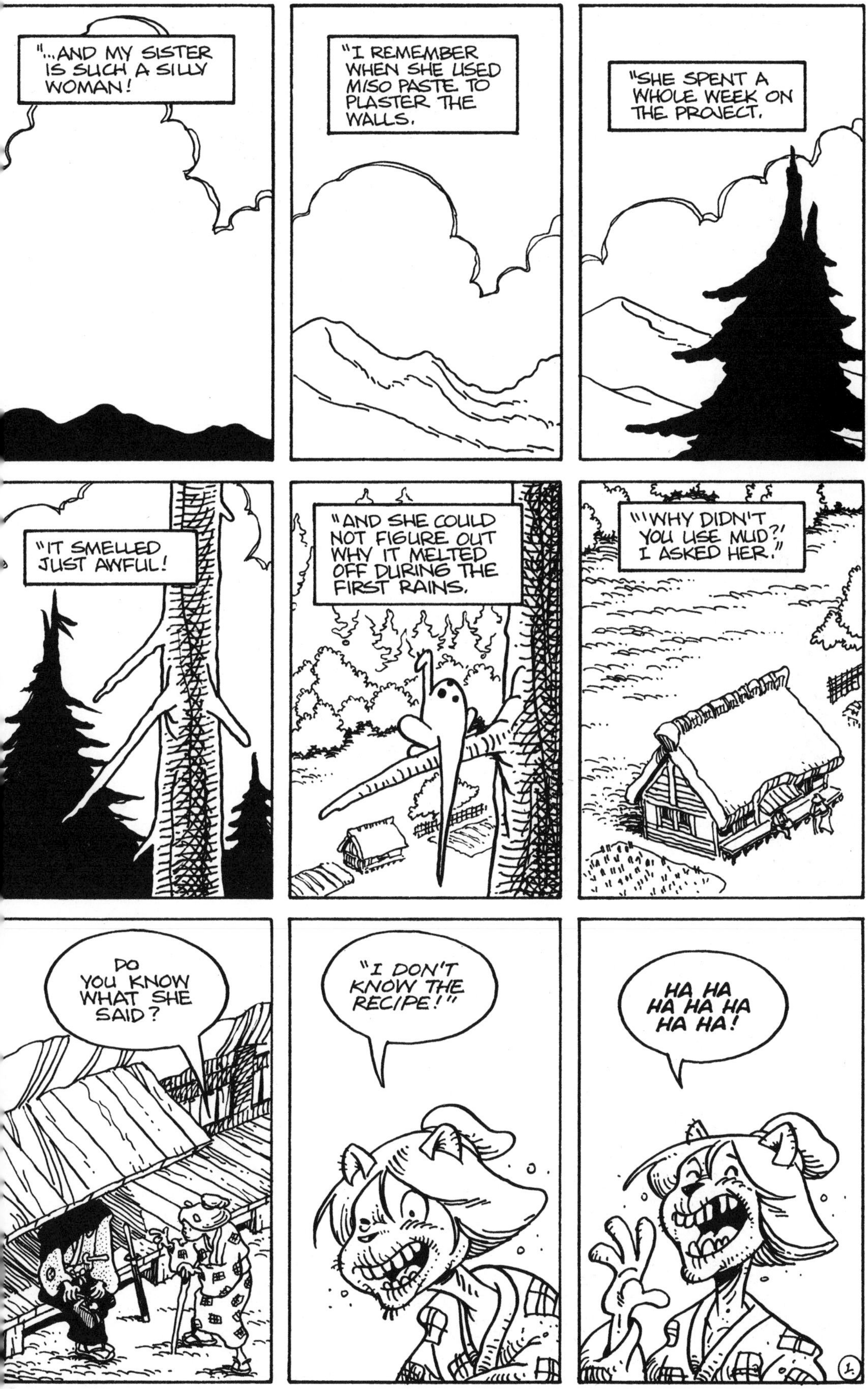
"...AND MY SISTER IS SUCH A SILLY WOMAN!
"I REMEMBER WHEN SHE USED MISO PASTE TO PLASTER THE WALLS.
"SHE SPENT A WHOLE WEEK ON THE PROJECT.
"IT SMELLED JUST AWFUL!
"AND SHE COULD NOT FIGURE OUT WHY IT MELTED OFF DURING THE FIRST RAINS.
"'WHY DIDN'T YOU USE MUD?' I ASKED HER."
DO YOU KNOW WHAT SHE SAID?
"I DON'T KNOW THE RECIPE!"
HA HA HA HA HA HA HA!

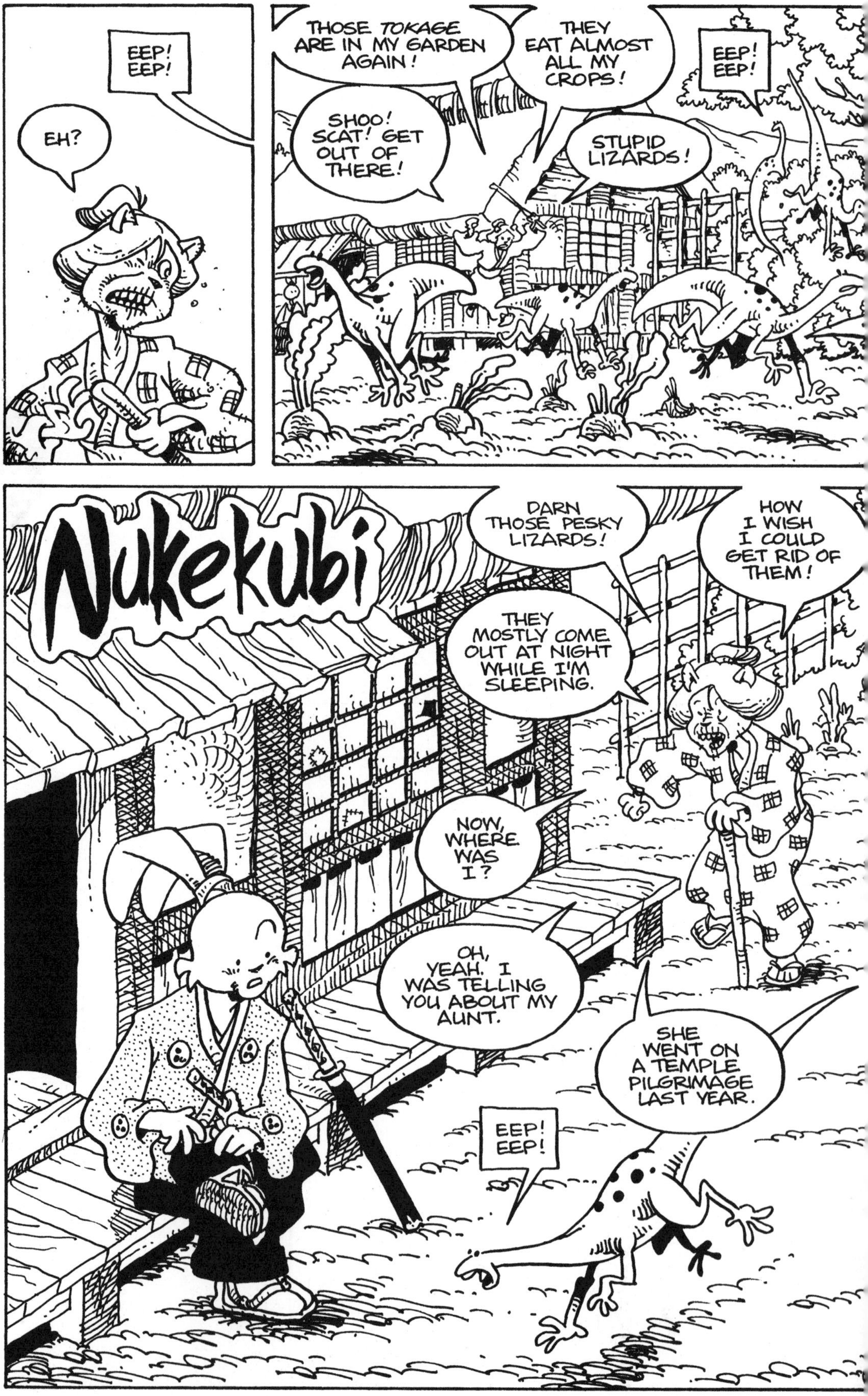
EEP! EEP!
EH?
THOSE *TOKAGE* ARE IN MY GARDEN AGAIN!
THEY EAT ALMOST ALL MY CROPS!
EEP! EEP!
SHOO! SCAT! GET OUT OF THERE!
STUPID LIZARDS!
Nukekubi
DARN THOSE PESKY LIZARDS!
HOW I WISH I COULD GET RID OF THEM!
THEY MOSTLY COME OUT AT NIGHT WHILE I'M SLEEPING.
NOW, WHERE WAS I?
OH, YEAH. I WAS TELLING YOU ABOUT MY AUNT.
SHE WENT ON A TEMPLE PILGRIMAGE LAST YEAR.
EEP! EEP!

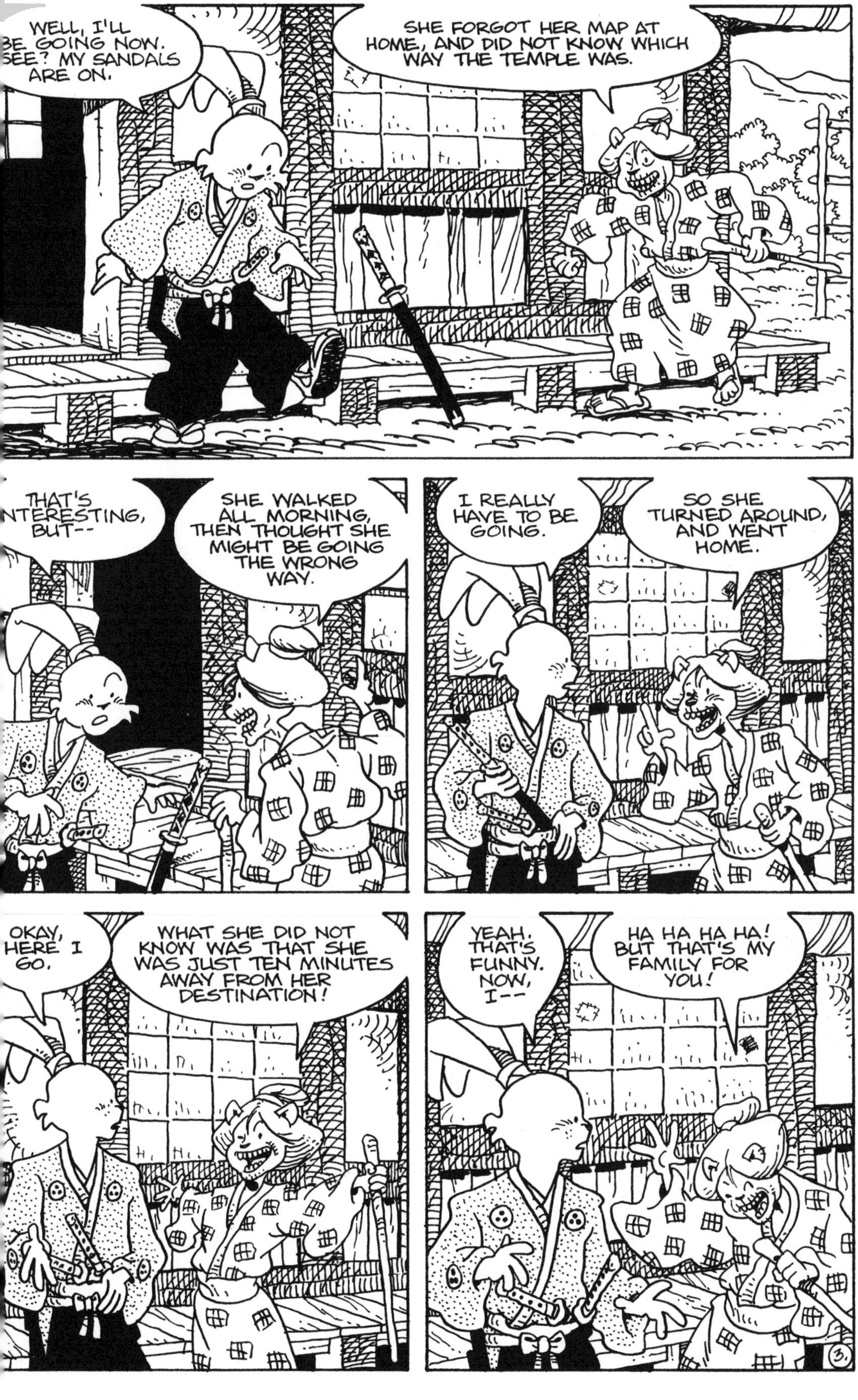

WELL, I'LL BE GOING NOW. SEE? MY SANDALS ARE ON.
SHE FORGOT HER MAP AT HOME, AND DID NOT KNOW WHICH WAY THE TEMPLE WAS.
THAT'S INTERESTING, BUT--
SHE WALKED ALL MORNING, THEN THOUGHT SHE MIGHT BE GOING THE WRONG WAY.
I REALLY HAVE TO BE GOING.
SO SHE TURNED AROUND, AND WENT HOME.
OKAY, HERE I GO.
WHAT SHE DID NOT KNOW WAS THAT SHE WAS JUST TEN MINUTES AWAY FROM HER DESTINATION!
YEAH. THAT'S FUNNY. NOW, I--
HA HA HA HA! BUT THAT'S MY FAMILY FOR YOU!
3.

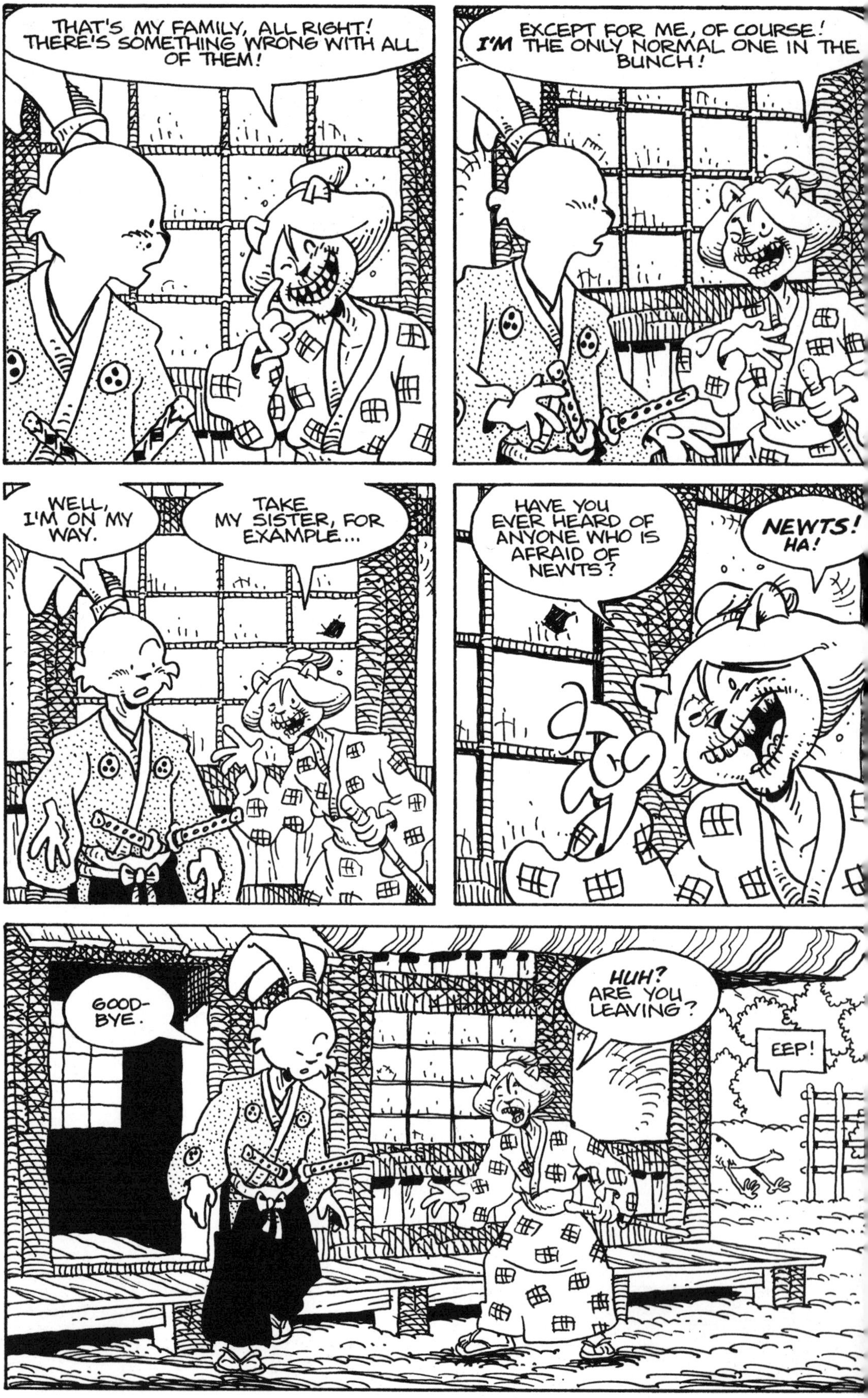
THAT'S MY FAMILY, ALL RIGHT! THERE'S SOMETHING WRONG WITH ALL OF THEM!
EXCEPT FOR ME, OF COURSE! I'M THE ONLY NORMAL ONE IN THE BUNCH!
WELL, I'M ON MY WAY.
TAKE MY SISTER, FOR EXAMPLE...
HAVE YOU EVER HEARD OF ANYONE WHO IS AFRAID OF NEWTS?
NEWTS! HA!
GOOD-BYE.
HUH? ARE YOU LEAVING?
EEP!

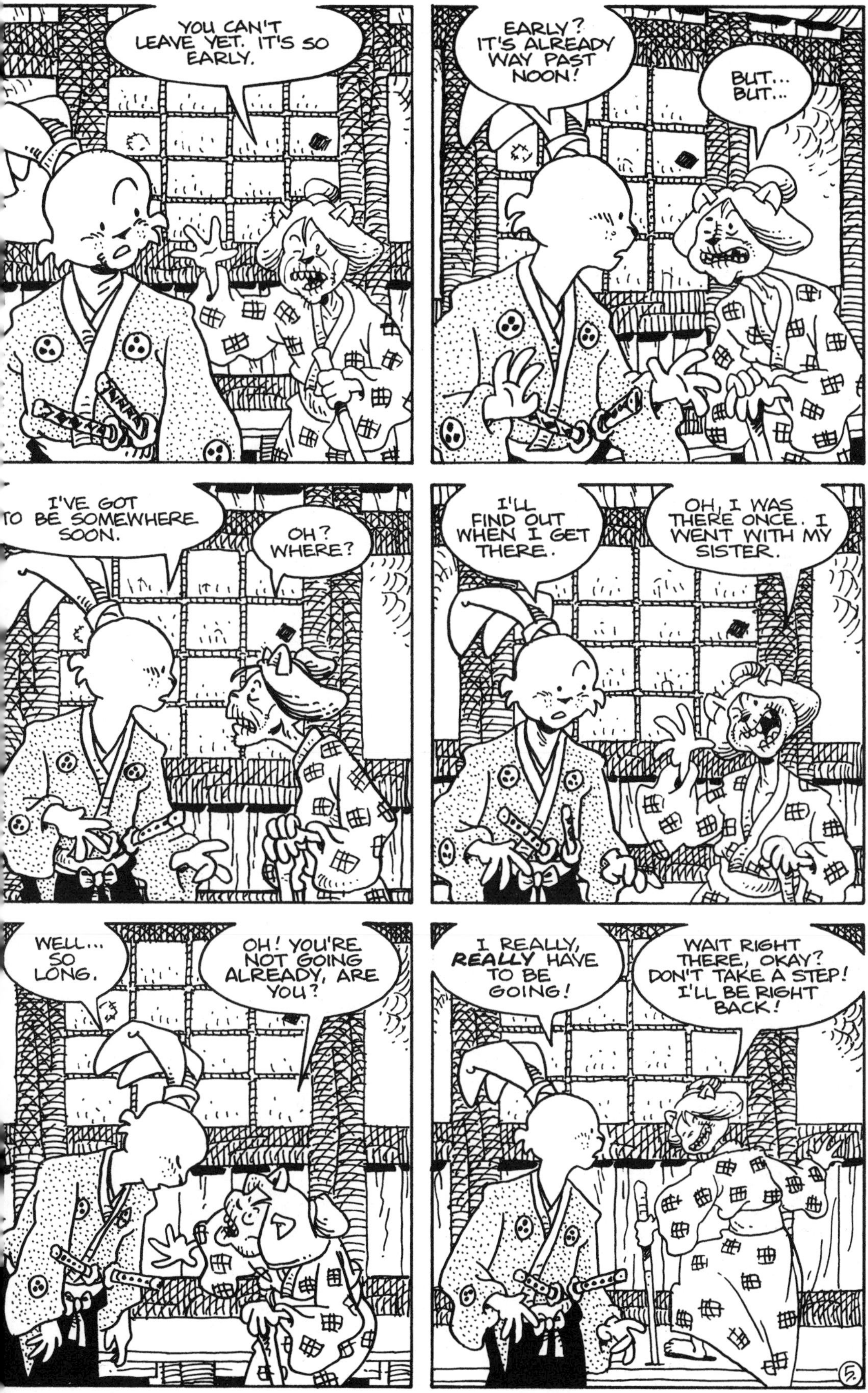
YOU CAN'T LEAVE YET. IT'S SO EARLY.
EARLY? IT'S ALREADY WAY PAST NOON!
BUT... BUT...
I'VE GOT TO BE SOMEWHERE SOON.
OH? WHERE?
I'LL FIND OUT WHEN I GET THERE.
OH, I WAS THERE ONCE. I WENT WITH MY SISTER.
WELL... SO LONG.
OH! YOU'RE NOT GOING ALREADY, ARE YOU?
I REALLY, **REALLY** HAVE TO BE GOING!
WAIT RIGHT THERE, OKAY? DON'T TAKE A STEP! I'LL BE RIGHT BACK!
5

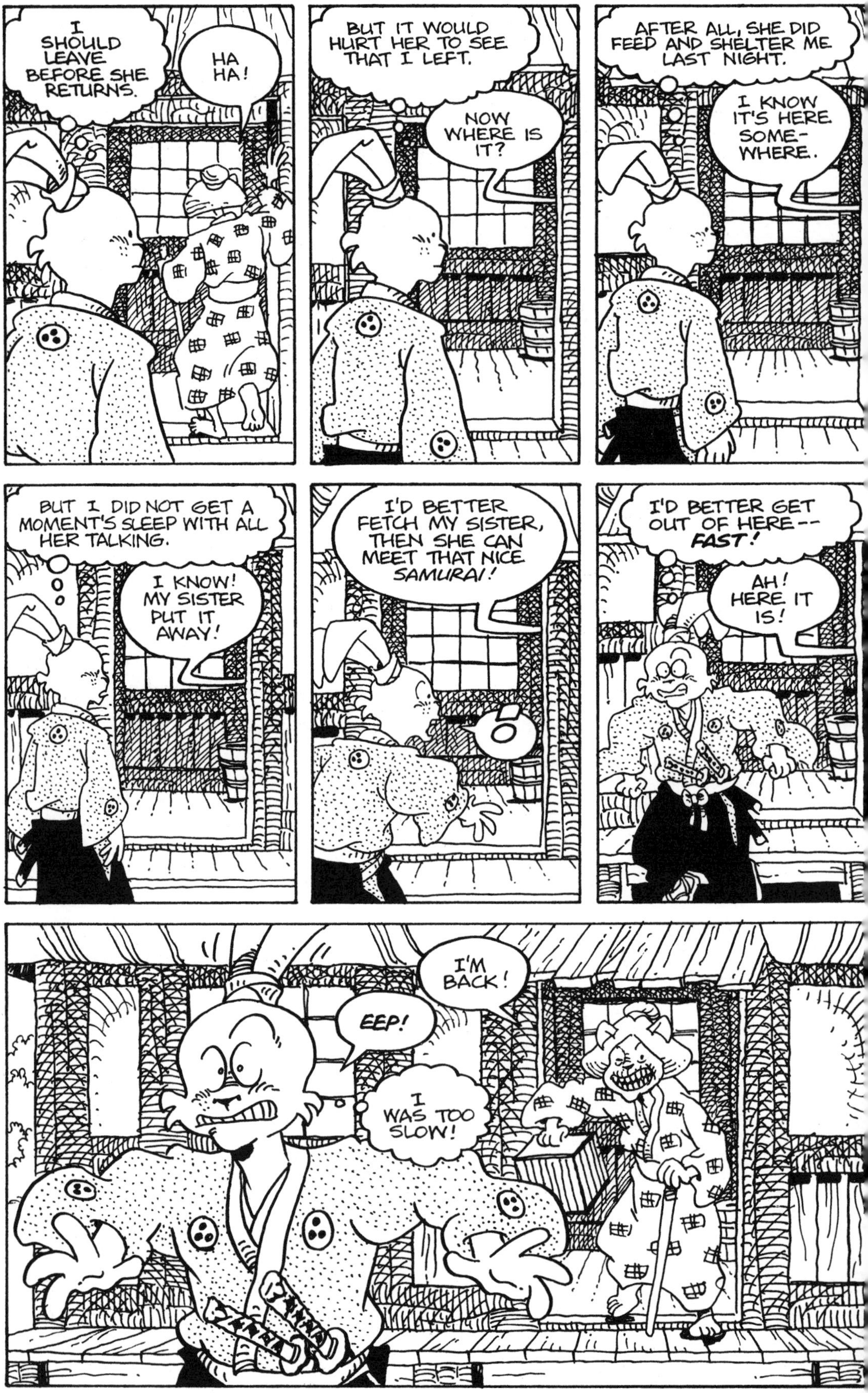
I SHOULD LEAVE BEFORE SHE RETURNS.
HA HA!
BUT IT WOULD HURT HER TO SEE THAT I LEFT.
NOW WHERE IS IT?
AFTER ALL, SHE DID FEED AND SHELTER ME LAST NIGHT.
I KNOW IT'S HERE SOME-WHERE.
BUT I DID NOT GET A MOMENT'S SLEEP WITH ALL HER TALKING.
I KNOW! MY SISTER PUT IT AWAY!
I'D BETTER FETCH MY SISTER, THEN SHE CAN MEET THAT NICE SAMURAI!
I'D BETTER GET OUT OF HERE-- FAST!
AH! HERE IT IS!
I'M BACK!
EEP!
I WAS TOO SLOW!

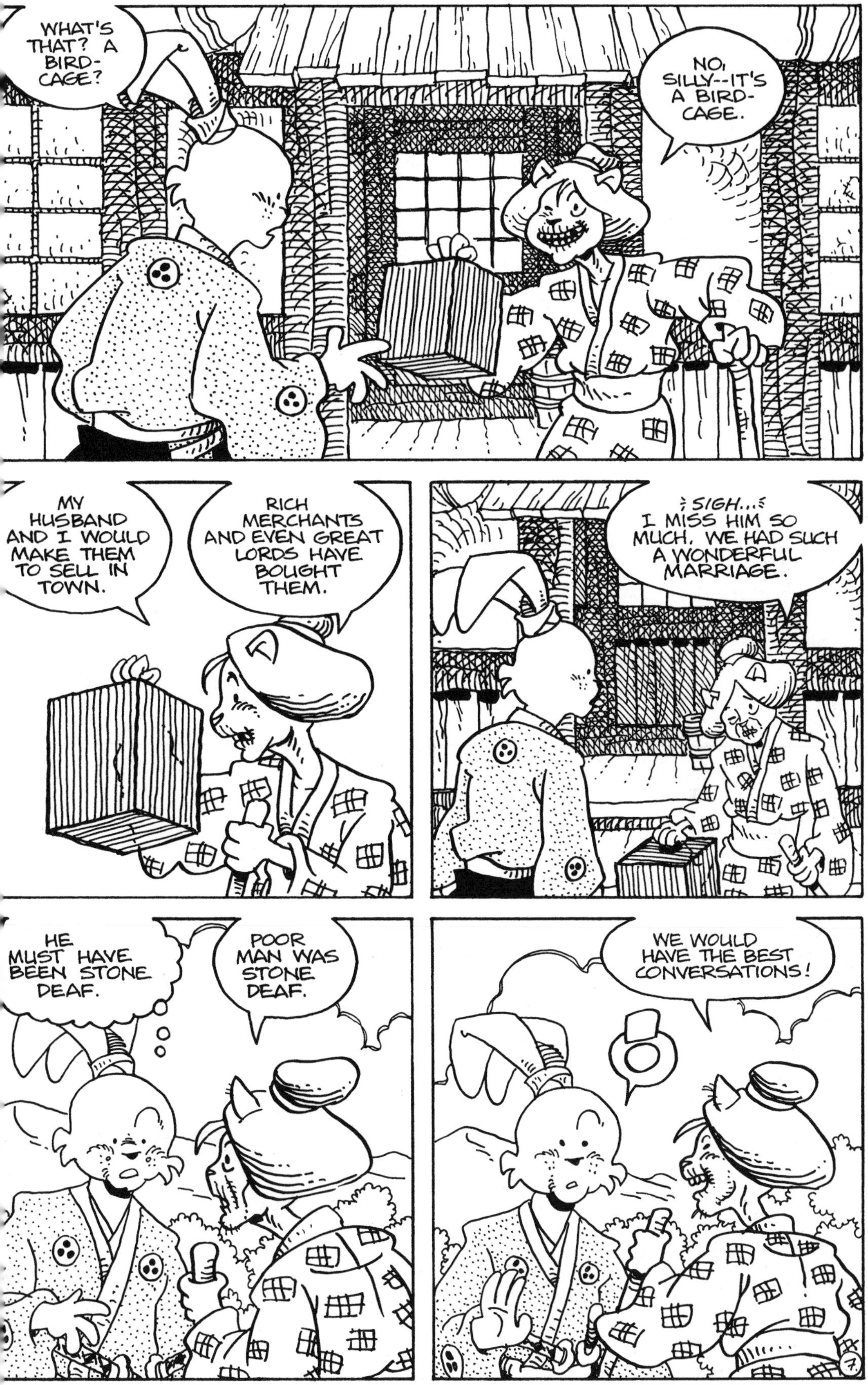
WHAT'S THAT? A BIRD-CAGE?
NO, SILLY--IT'S A BIRD-CAGE.
MY HUSBAND AND I WOULD MAKE THEM TO SELL IN TOWN.
RICH MERCHANTS AND EVEN GREAT LORDS HAVE BOUGHT THEM.
SIGH... I MISS HIM SO MUCH. WE HAD SUCH A WONDERFUL MARRIAGE.
HE MUST HAVE BEEN STONE DEAF.
POOR MAN WAS STONE DEAF.
WE WOULD HAVE THE BEST CONVERSATIONS!
7

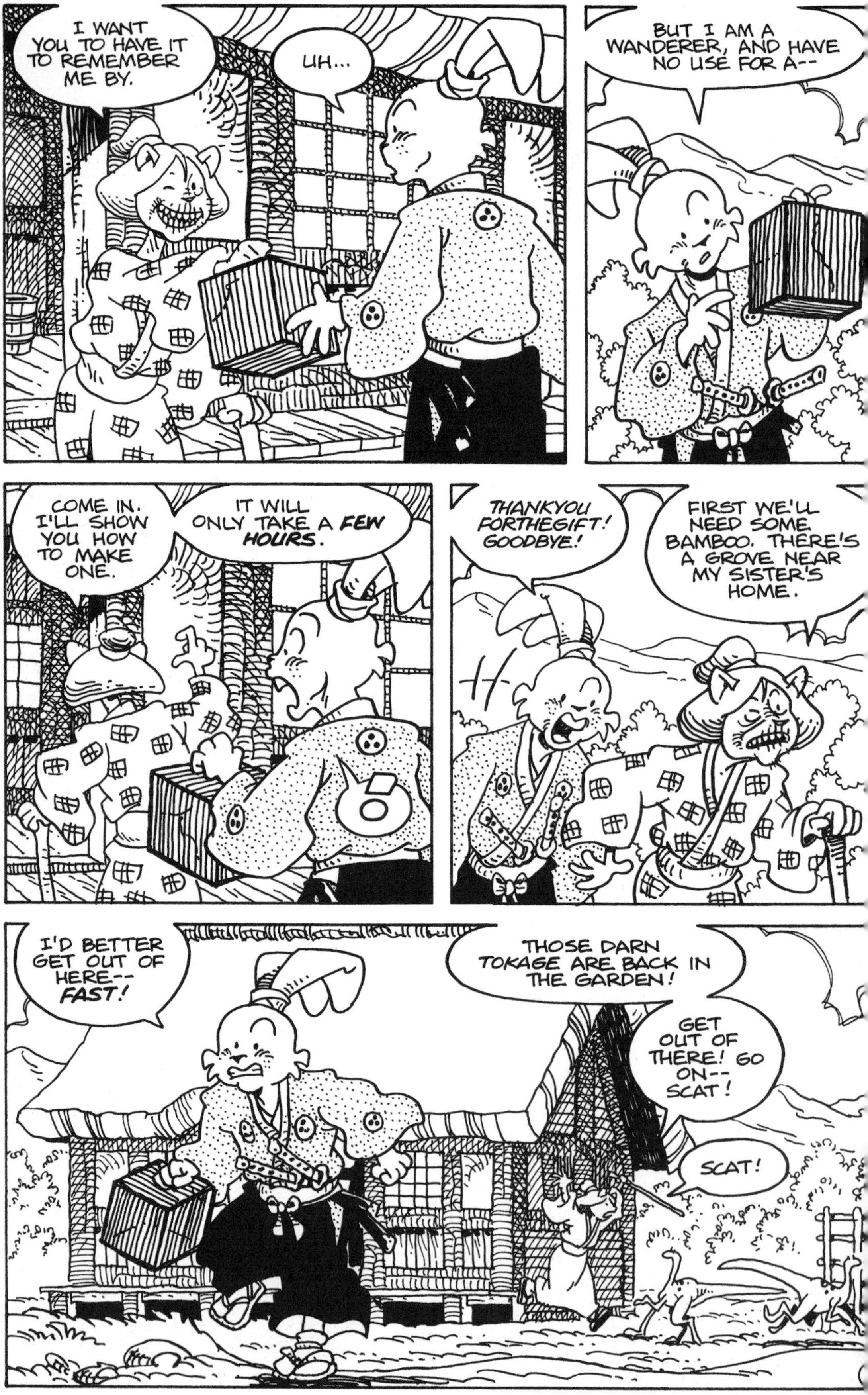

I WANT YOU TO HAVE IT TO REMEMBER ME BY.
UH...
BUT I AM A WANDERER, AND HAVE NO USE FOR A--
COME IN. I'LL SHOW YOU HOW TO MAKE ONE.
IT WILL ONLY TAKE A *FEW HOURS*.
*THANKYOU FORTHEGIFT! GOODBYE!*
FIRST WE'LL NEED SOME BAMBOO. THERE'S A GROVE NEAR MY SISTER'S HOME.
I'D BETTER GET OUT OF HERE-- *FAST!*
THOSE DARN *TOKAGE* ARE BACK IN THE GARDEN!
GET OUT OF THERE! GO ON-- SCAT!
SCAT!

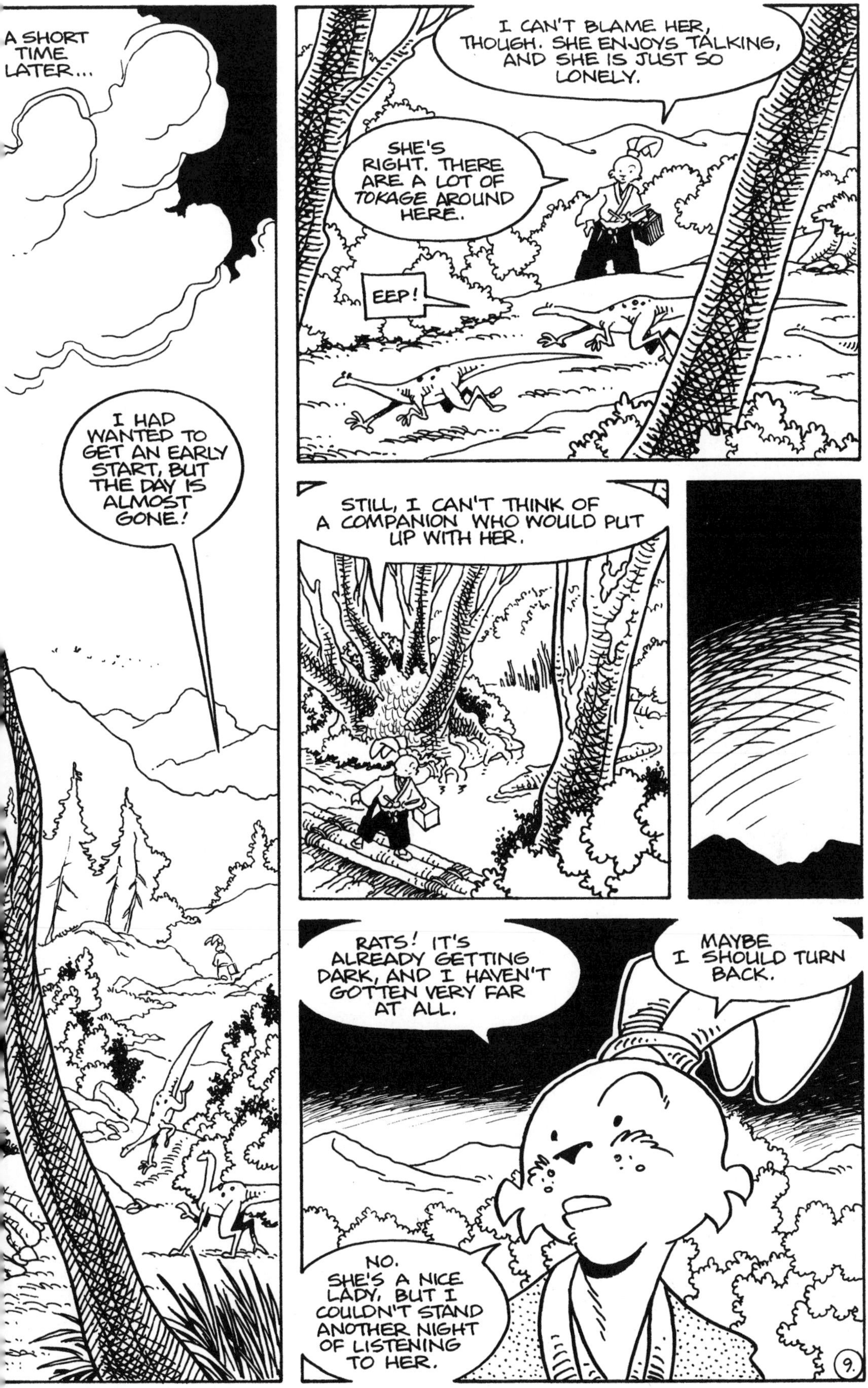
A SHORT TIME LATER...
I HAD WANTED TO GET AN EARLY START, BUT THE DAY IS ALMOST GONE!
I CAN'T BLAME HER, THOUGH. SHE ENJOYS TALKING, AND SHE IS JUST SO LONELY.
SHE'S RIGHT. THERE ARE A LOT OF *TOKAGE* AROUND HERE.
EEP!
STILL, I CAN'T THINK OF A COMPANION WHO WOULD PUT UP WITH HER.
RATS! IT'S ALREADY GETTING DARK, AND I HAVEN'T GOTTEN VERY FAR AT ALL.
MAYBE I SHOULD TURN BACK.
NO. SHE'S A NICE LADY, BUT I COULDN'T STAND ANOTHER NIGHT OF LISTENING TO HER.
9.

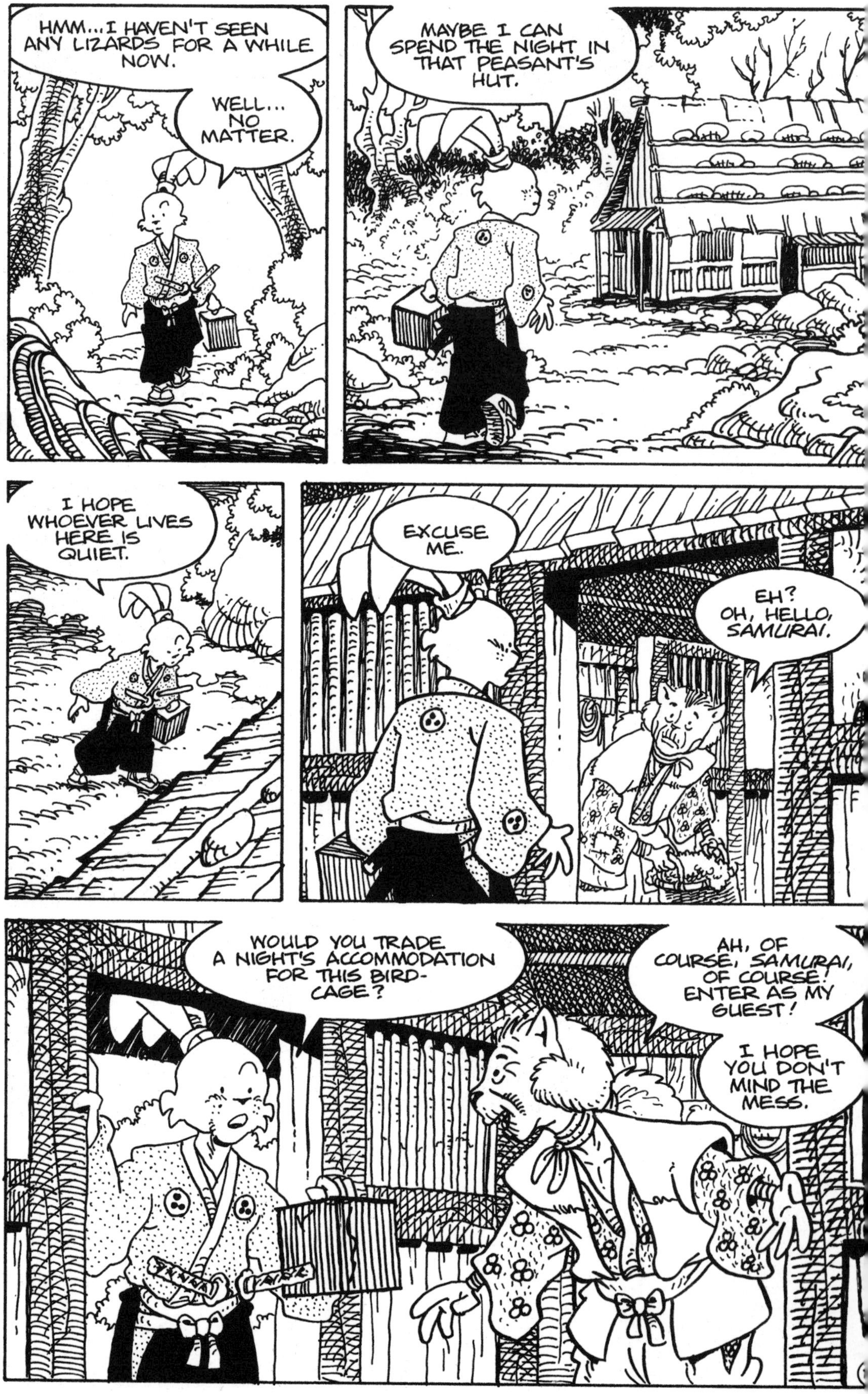
HMM...I HAVEN'T SEEN ANY LIZARDS FOR A WHILE NOW.
WELL... NO MATTER.
MAYBE I CAN SPEND THE NIGHT IN THAT PEASANT'S HUT.
I HOPE WHOEVER LIVES HERE IS QUIET.
EXCUSE ME.
EH? OH, HELLO, SAMURAI.
WOULD YOU TRADE A NIGHT'S ACCOMMODATION FOR THIS BIRD-CAGE?
AH, OF COURSE, SAMURAI, OF COURSE! ENTER AS MY GUEST!
I HOPE YOU DON'T MIND THE MESS.

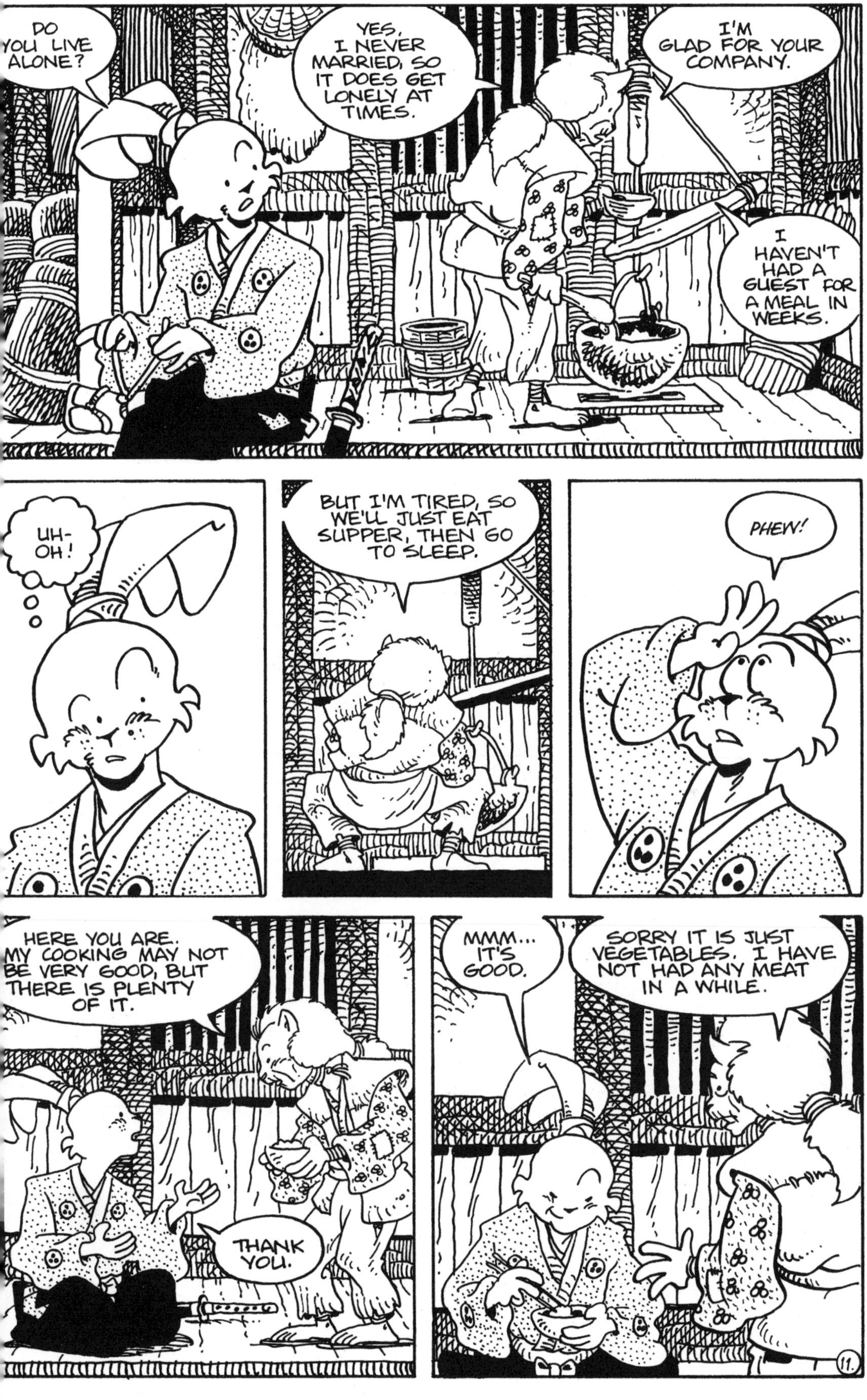

DO YOU LIVE ALONE?
YES, I NEVER MARRIED, SO IT DOES GET LONELY AT TIMES.
I'M GLAD FOR YOUR COMPANY.
I HAVEN'T HAD A GUEST FOR A MEAL IN WEEKS.
UH-OH!
BUT I'M TIRED, SO WE'LL JUST EAT SUPPER, THEN GO TO SLEEP.
PHEW!
HERE YOU ARE. MY COOKING MAY NOT BE VERY GOOD, BUT THERE IS PLENTY OF IT.
THANK YOU.
MMM... IT'S GOOD.
SORRY IT IS JUST VEGETABLES. I HAVE NOT HAD ANY MEAT IN A WHILE.
11.

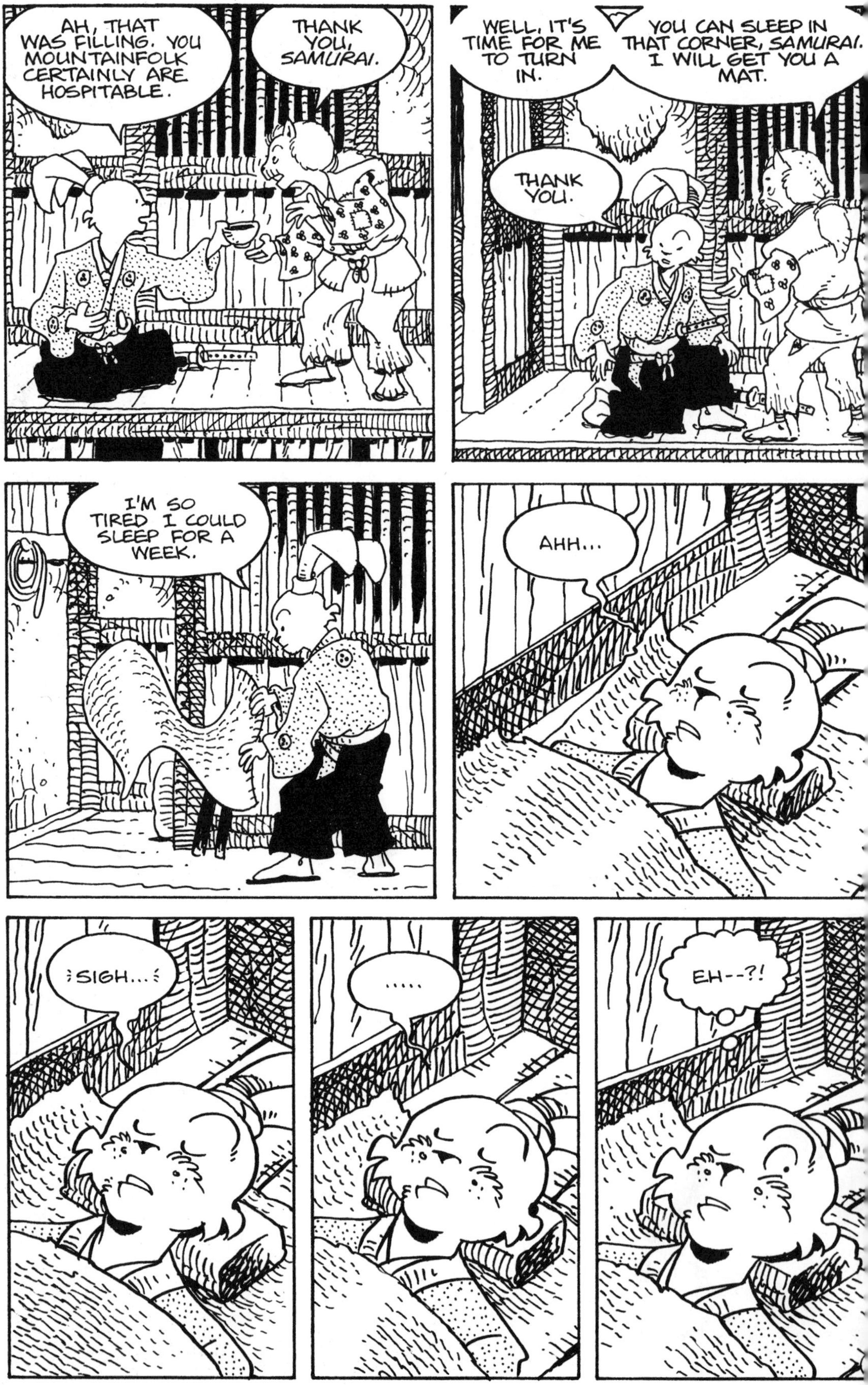
AH, THAT WAS FILLING. YOU MOUNTAINFOLK CERTAINLY ARE HOSPITABLE.
THANK YOU, SAMURAI.
WELL, IT'S TIME FOR ME TO TURN IN.
YOU CAN SLEEP IN THAT CORNER, SAMURAI. I WILL GET YOU A MAT.
THANK YOU.
I'M SO TIRED I COULD SLEEP FOR A WEEK.
AHH...
SIGH...
.....
EH--?!

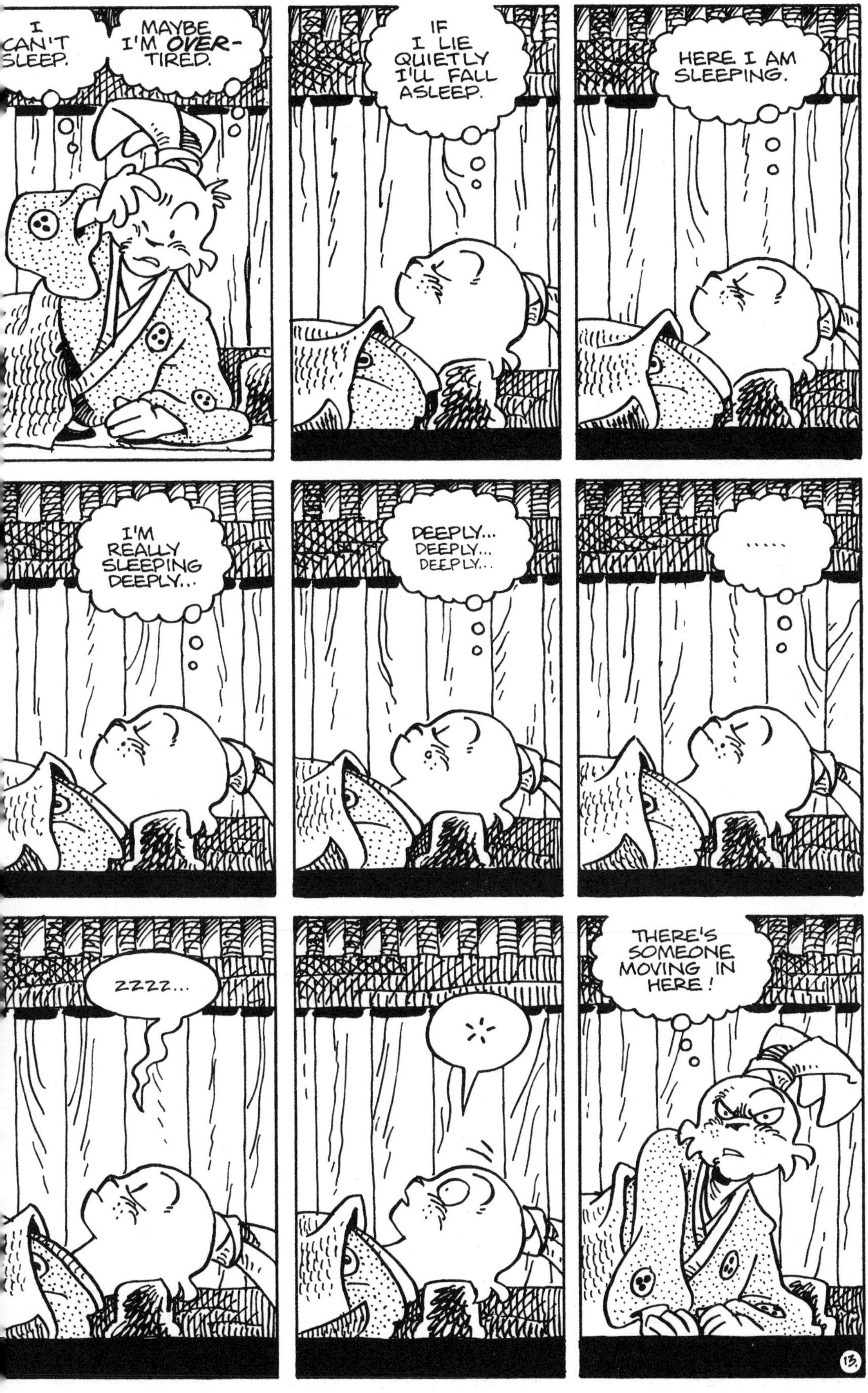
I CAN'T SLEEP.
MAYBE I'M OVER-TIRED.
IF I LIE QUIETLY I'LL FALL ASLEEP.
HERE I AM SLEEPING.
I'M REALLY SLEEPING DEEPLY...
DEEPLY... DEEPLY... DEEPLY...
.....
ZZZZ...
THERE'S SOMEONE MOVING IN HERE!
13

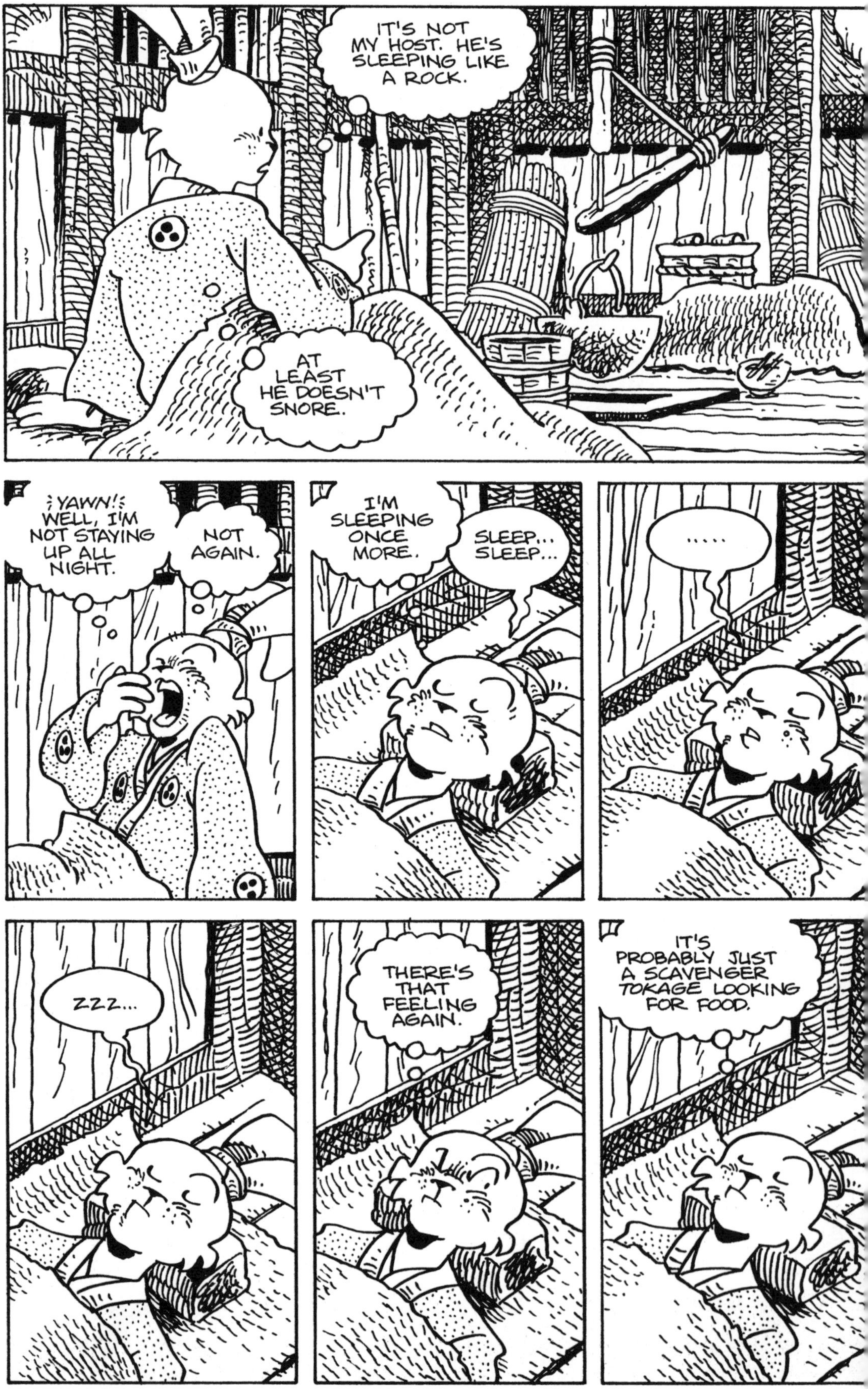
IT'S NOT MY HOST. HE'S SLEEPING LIKE A ROCK.
AT LEAST HE DOESN'T SNORE.
YAWN! WELL, I'M NOT STAYING UP ALL NIGHT.
NOT AGAIN.
I'M SLEEPING ONCE MORE.
SLEEP... SLEEP...
.....
ZZZ...
THERE'S THAT FEELING AGAIN.
IT'S PROBABLY JUST A SCAVENGER *TOKAGE* LOOKING FOR FOOD.

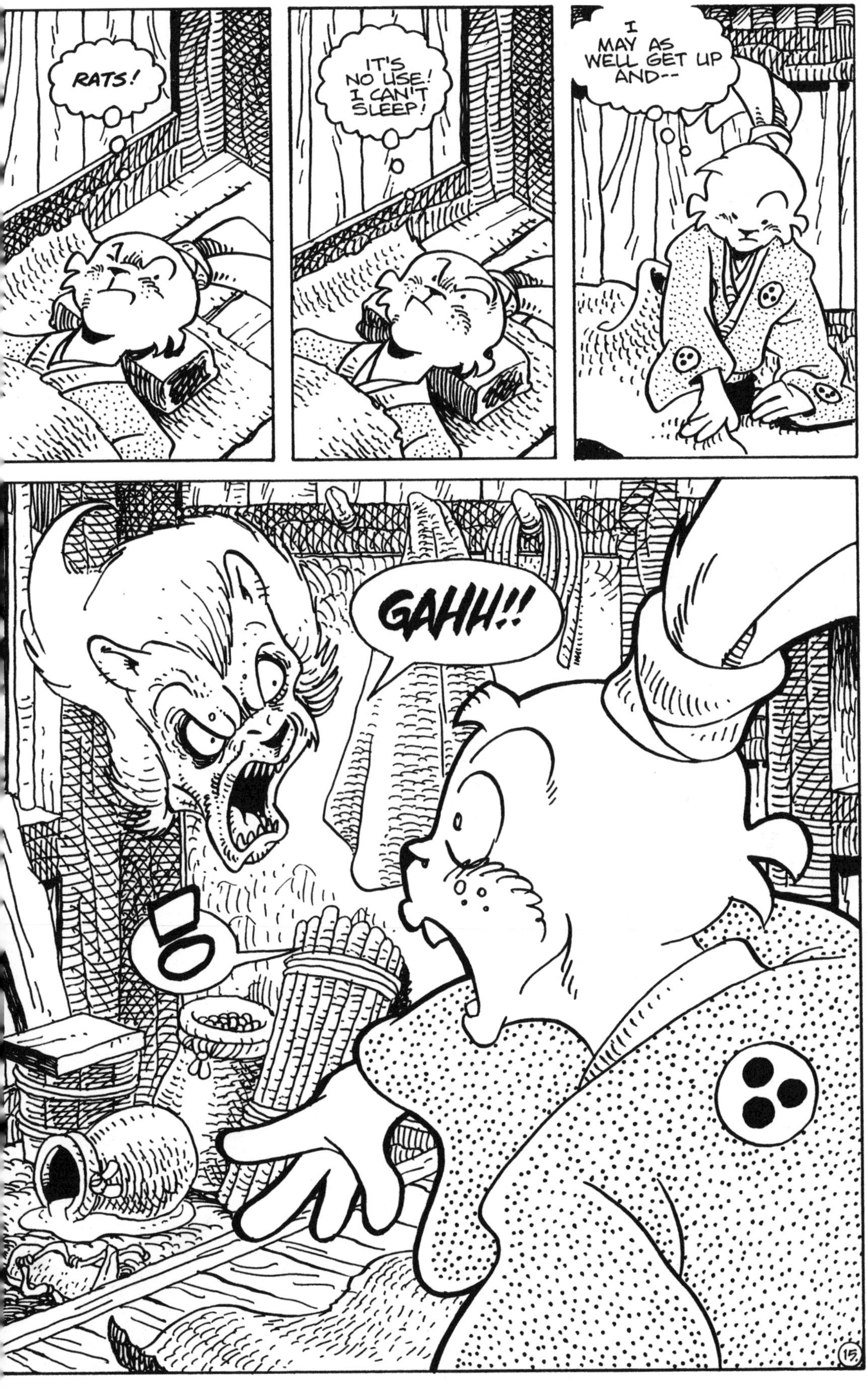

RATS!
IT'S NO USE! I CAN'T SLEEP!
I MAY AS WELL GET UP AND--
GAHH!!
!
15

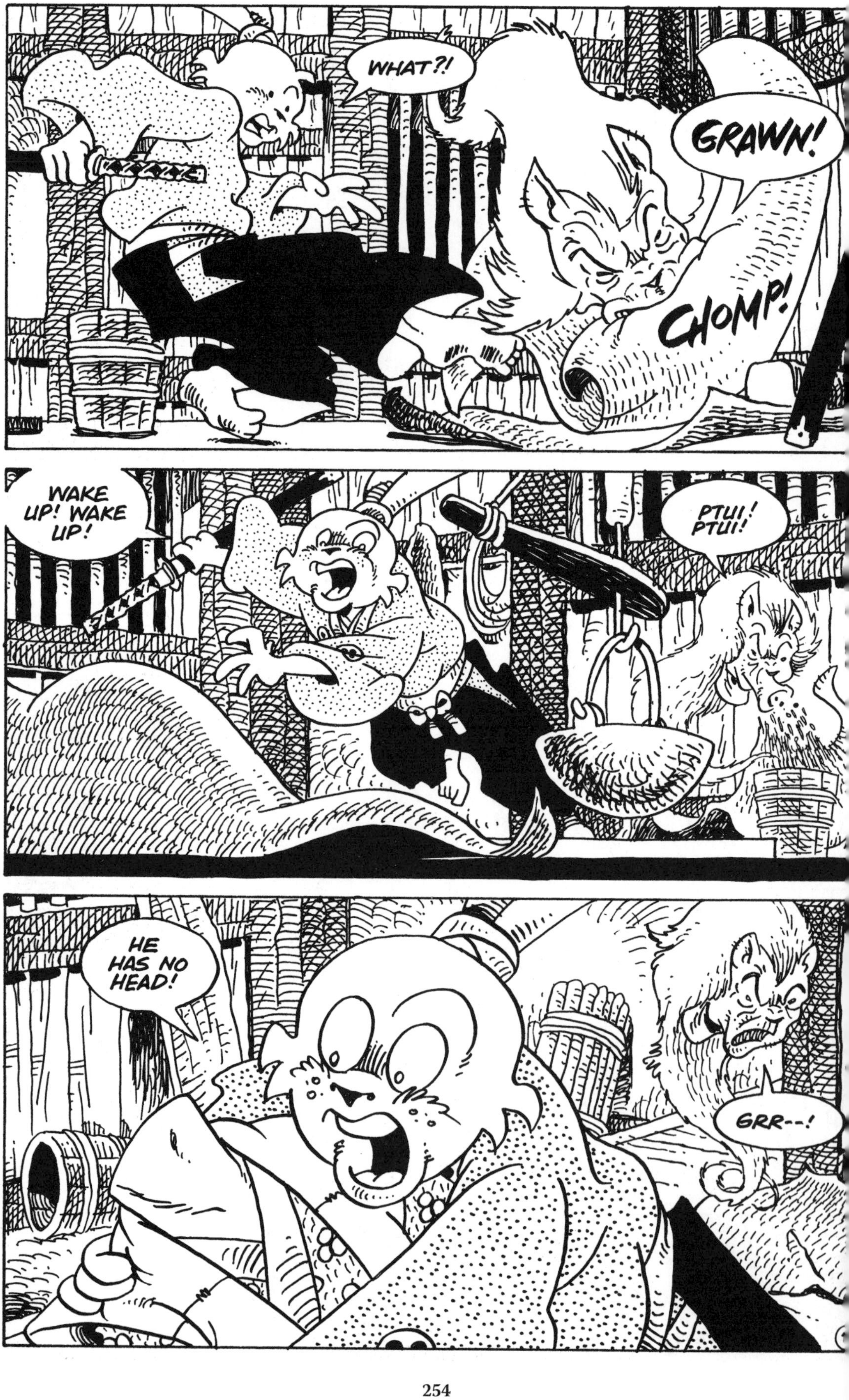
WHAT?!
GRAWN!
CHOMP!
WAKE UP! WAKE UP!
PTUI! PTUI!
HE HAS NO HEAD!
GRR--!

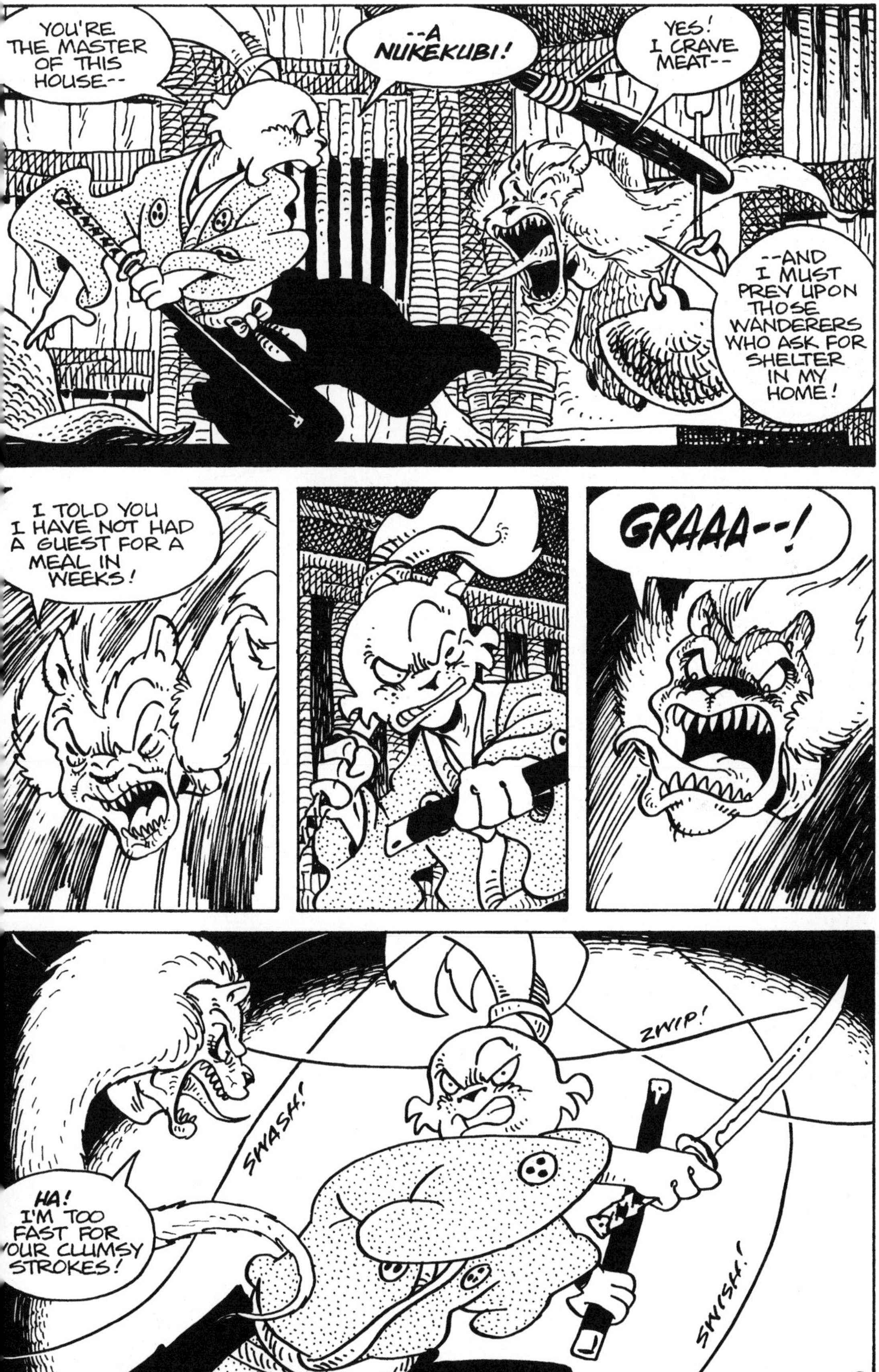

YOU'RE THE MASTER OF THIS HOUSE--
--A NUKEKUBI!
YES! I CRAVE MEAT--
--AND I MUST PREY UPON THOSE WANDERERS WHO ASK FOR SHELTER IN MY HOME!
I TOLD YOU I HAVE NOT HAD A GUEST FOR A MEAL IN WEEKS!
GRAAA--!
ZWIP!
SWASH!
HA! I'M TOO FAST FOR YOUR CLUMSY STROKES!
SWISH!
17

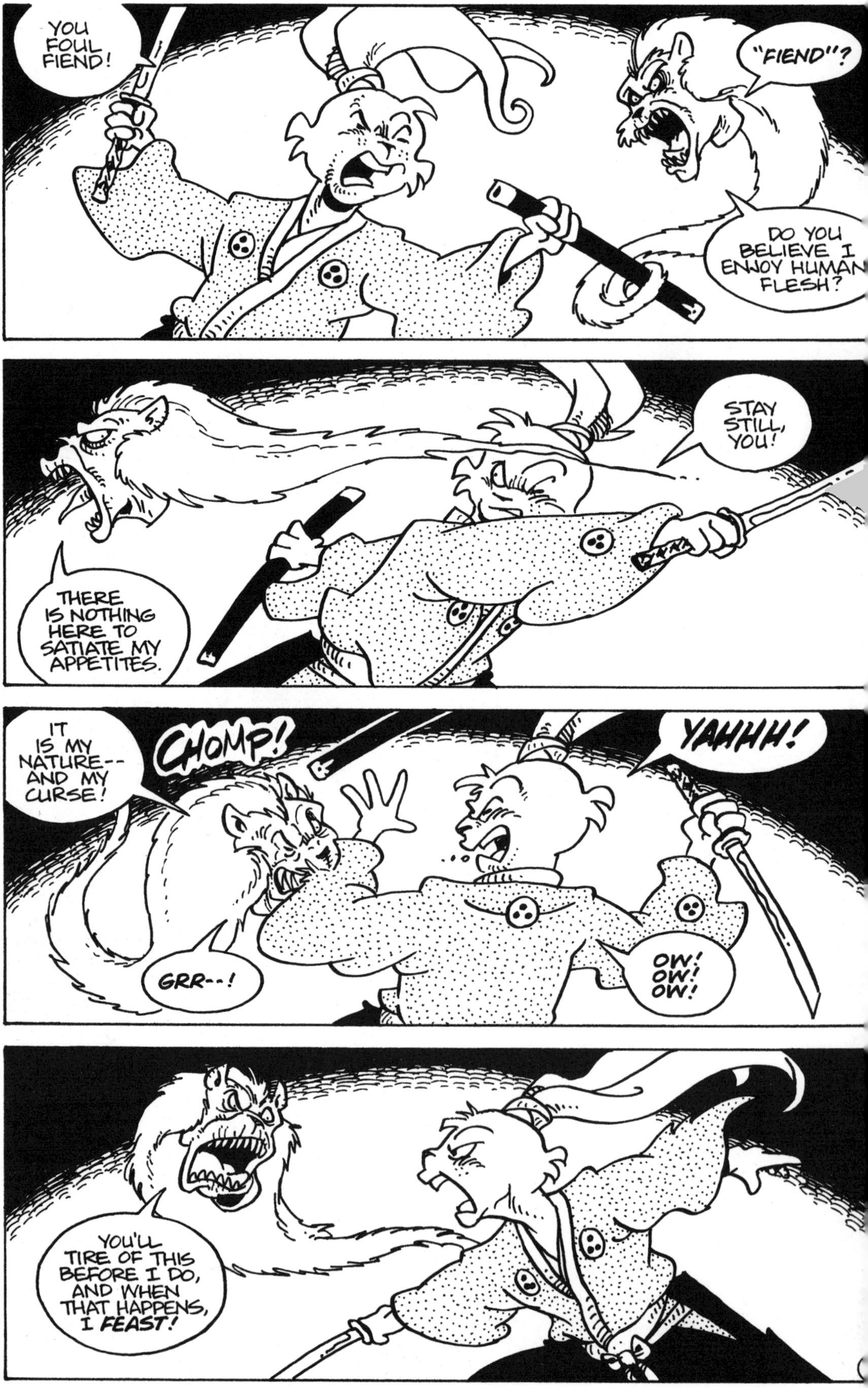

YOU FOUL FIEND!
"FIEND"?
DO YOU BELIEVE I ENJOY HUMAN FLESH?
STAY STILL, YOU!
THERE IS NOTHING HERE TO SATIATE MY APPETITES.
IT IS MY NATURE-- AND MY CURSE!
CHOMP!
YAHHH!
GRR--!
OW! OW! OW!
YOU'LL TIRE OF THIS BEFORE I DO, AND WHEN THAT HAPPENS, I FEAST!

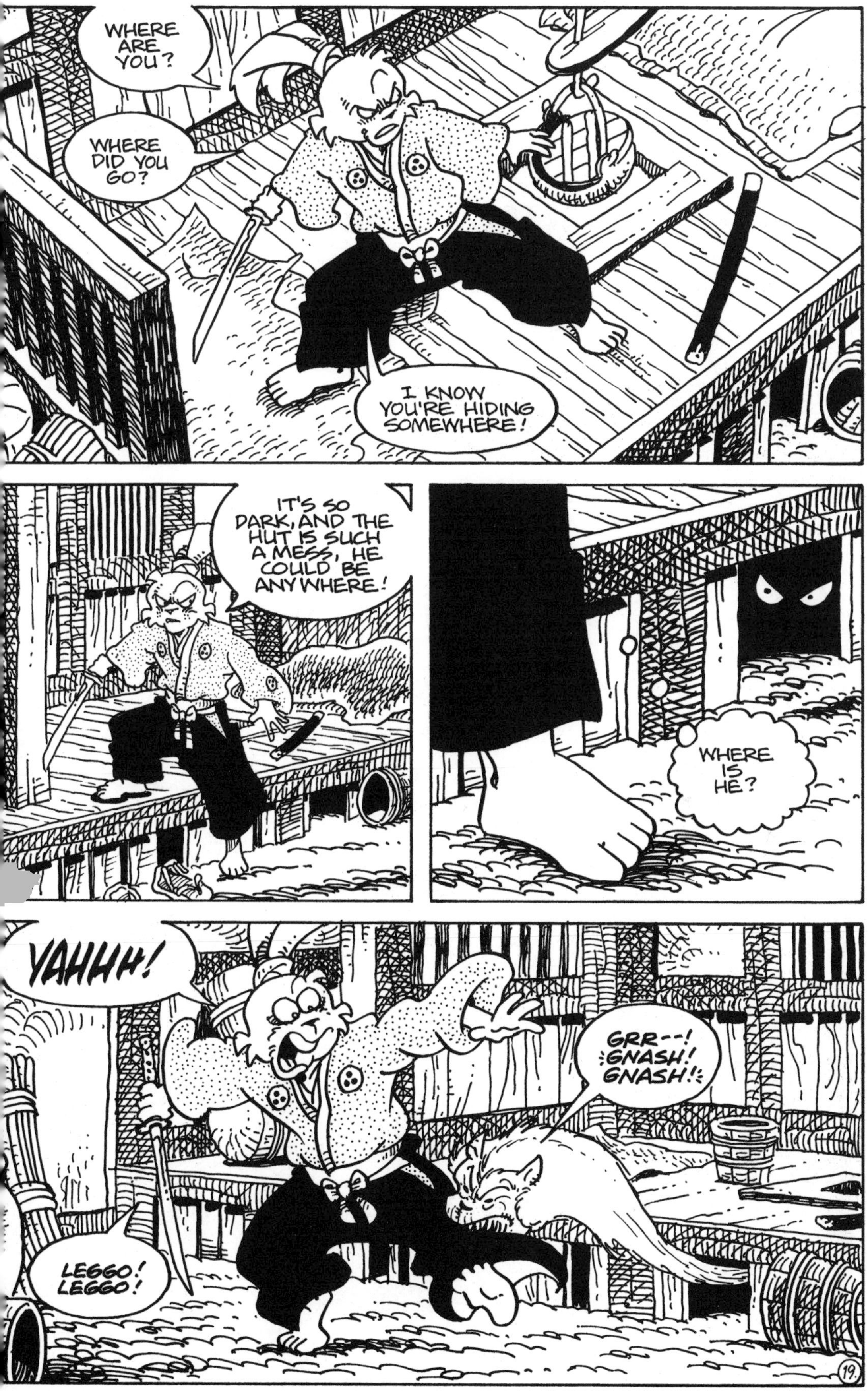
WHERE ARE YOU?
WHERE DID YOU GO?
I KNOW YOU'RE HIDING SOMEWHERE!
IT'S SO DARK, AND THE HUT IS SUCH A MESS, HE COULD BE ANYWHERE!
WHERE IS HE?
YAHHH!
GRR--! GNASH! GNASH!
LEGGO! LEGGO!
19.

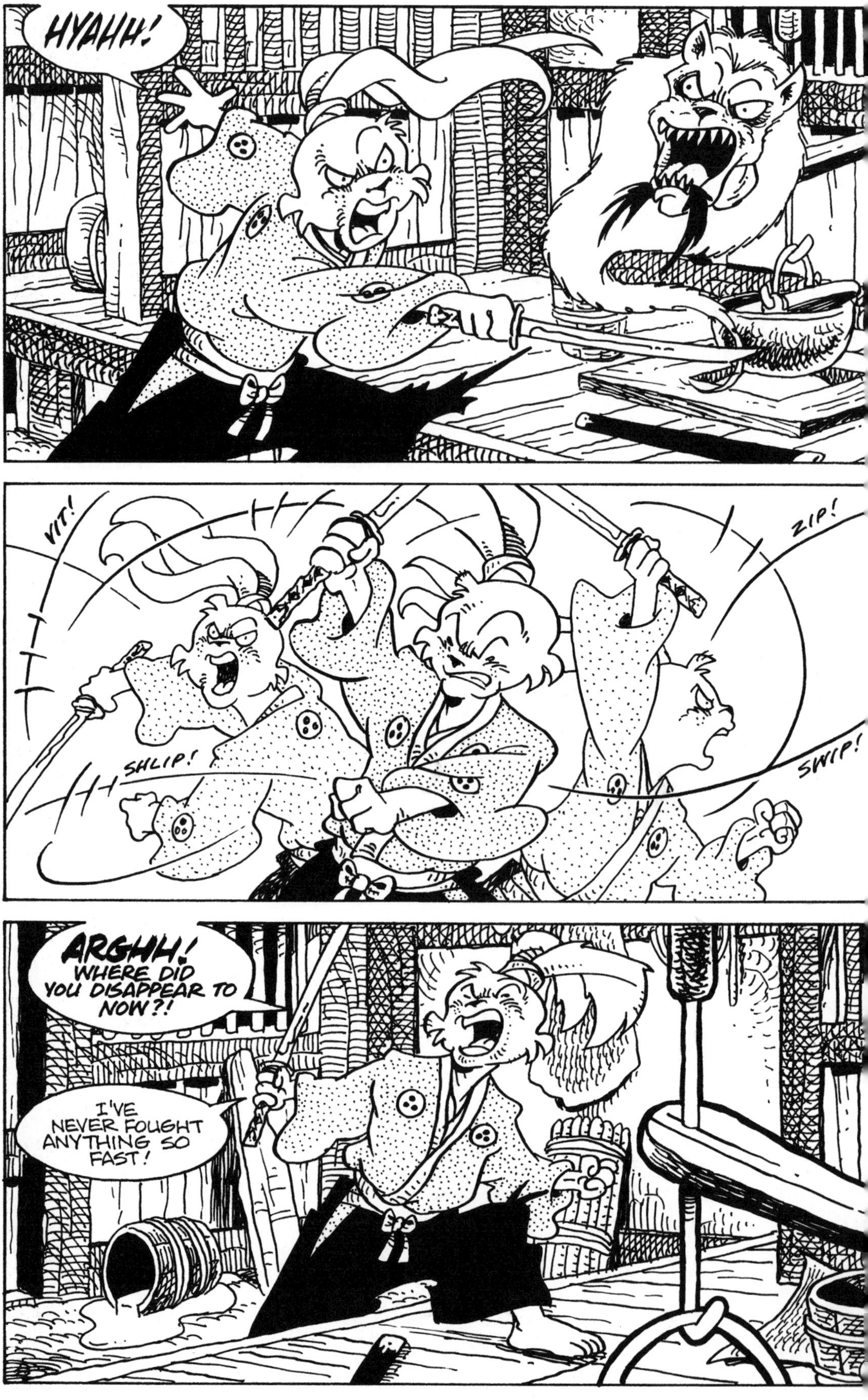
HYAHH!
VIT!
ZIP!
SHLIP!
SWIP!
ARGHH! WHERE DID YOU DISAPPEAR TO NOW?!
I'VE NEVER FOUGHT ANYTHING SO FAST!

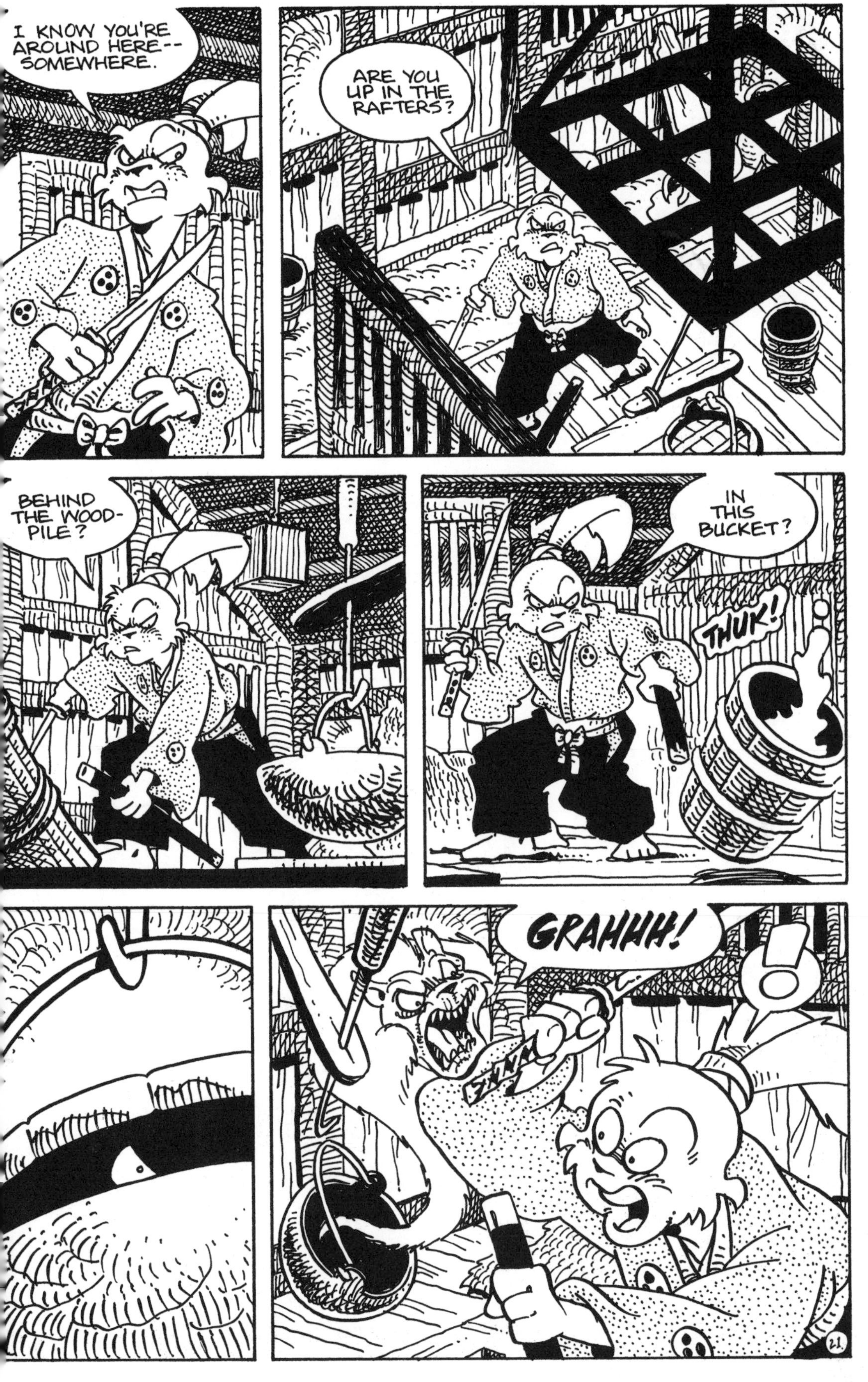
I KNOW YOU'RE AROUND HERE-- SOMEWHERE.
ARE YOU UP IN THE RAFTERS?
BEHIND THE WOOD-PILE?
IN THIS BUCKET?
THUK!
GRAHHH!
!
21.

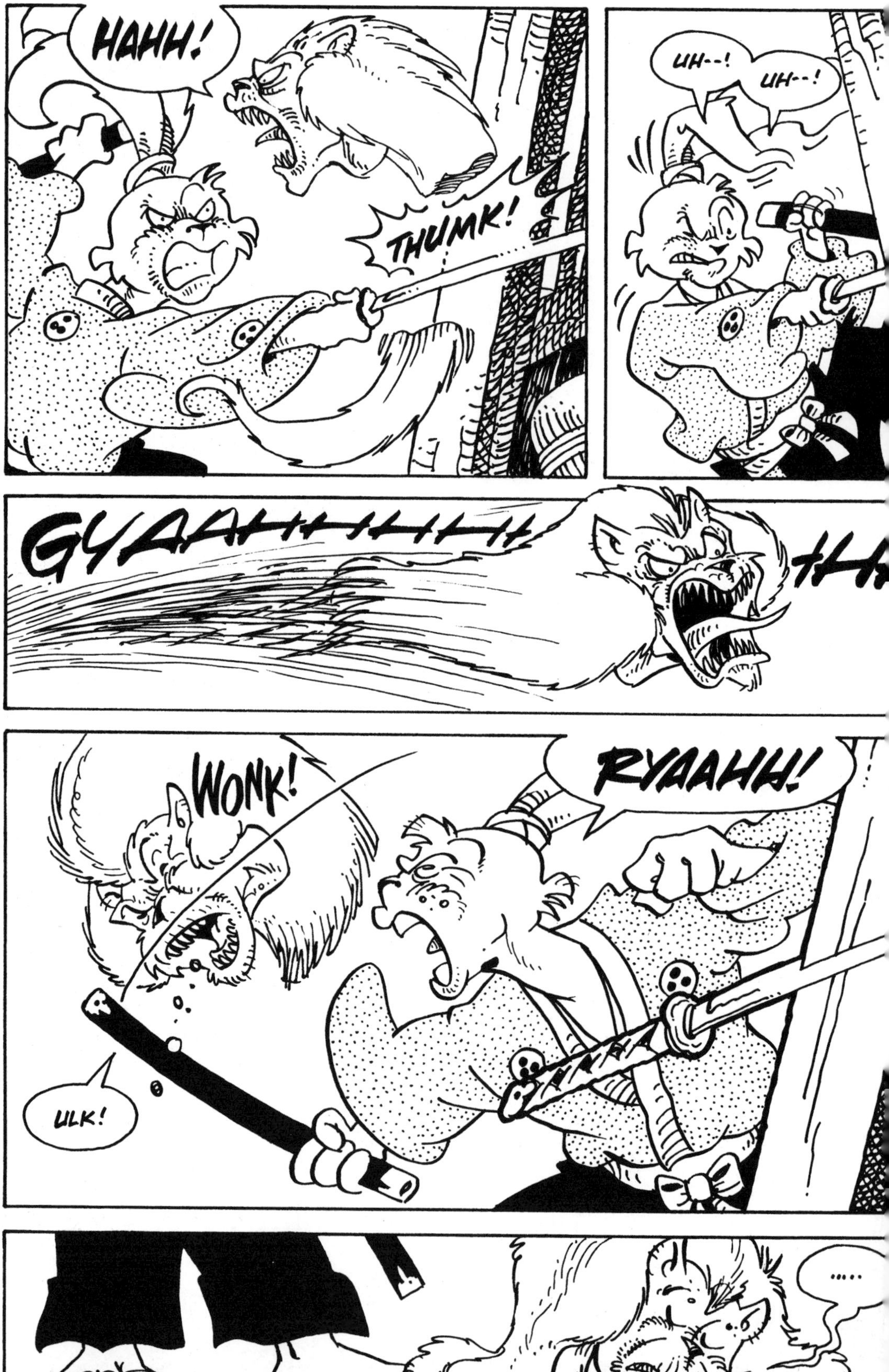
HAHH!
THUMK!
UH--!
UH--!
GYAHHHHHHHHH
WONK!
RYAAHH!
ULK!
.....

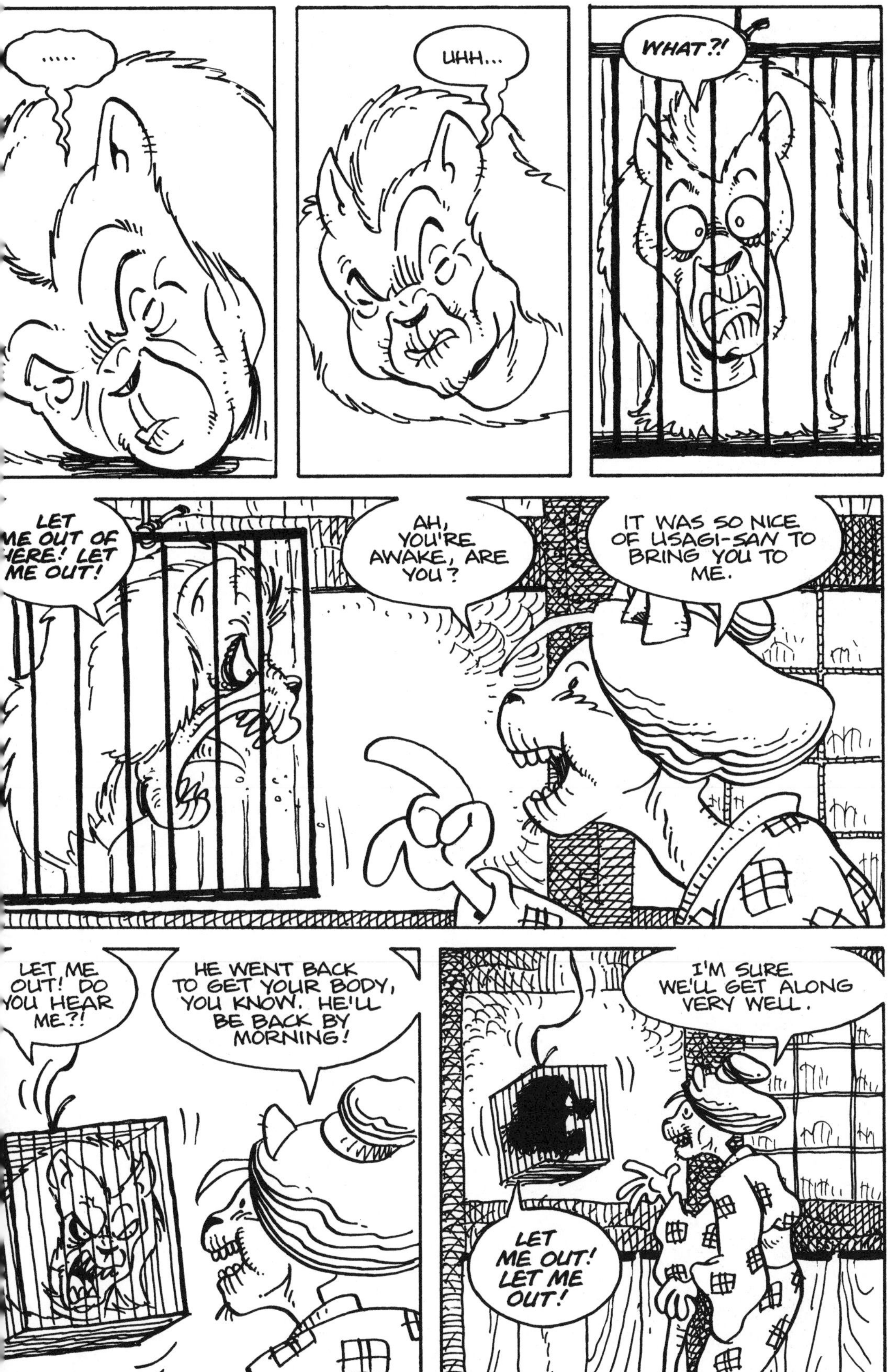
.....
UHH...
WHAT?!
LET ME OUT OF HERE! LET ME OUT!
AH, YOU'RE AWAKE, ARE YOU?
IT WAS SO NICE OF USAGI-SAN TO BRING YOU TO ME.
LET ME OUT! DO YOU HEAR ME?!
HE WENT BACK TO GET YOUR BODY, YOU KNOW. HE'LL BE BACK BY MORNING!
I'M SURE WE'LL GET ALONG VERY WELL.
LET ME OUT! LET ME OUT!
23.

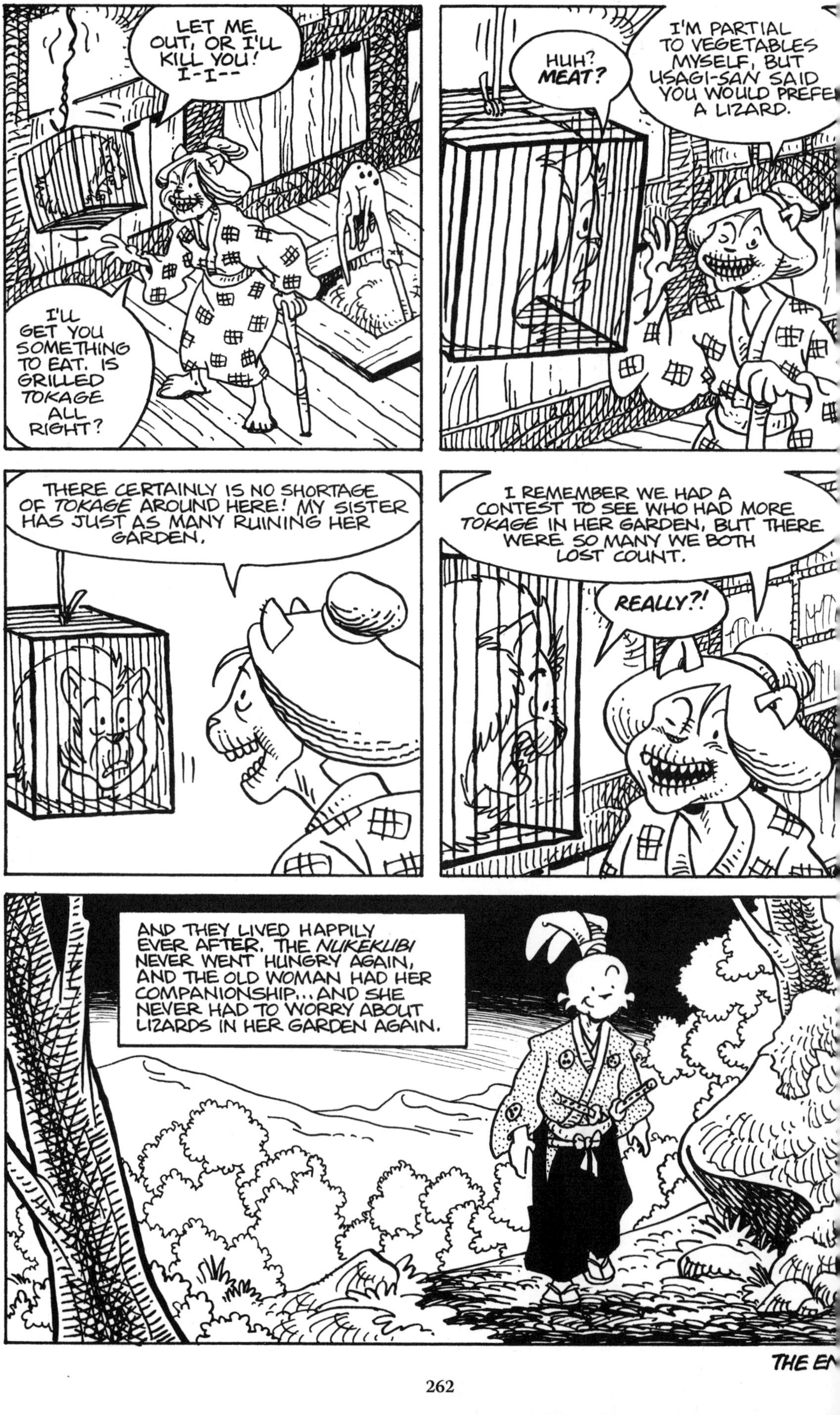
LET ME OUT, OR I'LL KILL YOU! I-I--
I'LL GET YOU SOMETHING TO EAT. IS GRILLED *TOKAGE* ALL RIGHT?
HUH? *MEAT?*
I'M PARTIAL TO VEGETABLES MYSELF, BUT USAGI-SAN SAID YOU WOULD PREFE A LIZARD.
THERE CERTAINLY IS NO SHORTAGE OF *TOKAGE* AROUND HERE! MY SISTER HAS JUST AS MANY RUINING HER GARDEN.
I REMEMBER WE HAD A CONTEST TO SEE WHO HAD MORE *TOKAGE* IN HER GARDEN, BUT THERE WERE SO MANY WE BOTH LOST COUNT.
*REALLY?!*
AND THEY LIVED HAPPILY EVER AFTER. THE *NUKEKUBI* NEVER WENT HUNGRY AGAIN, AND THE OLD WOMAN HAD HER COMPANIONSHIP...AND SHE NEVER HAD TO WORRY ABOUT LIZARDS IN HER GARDEN AGAIN.
THE EN

# THE SWORD of NARUKAMI

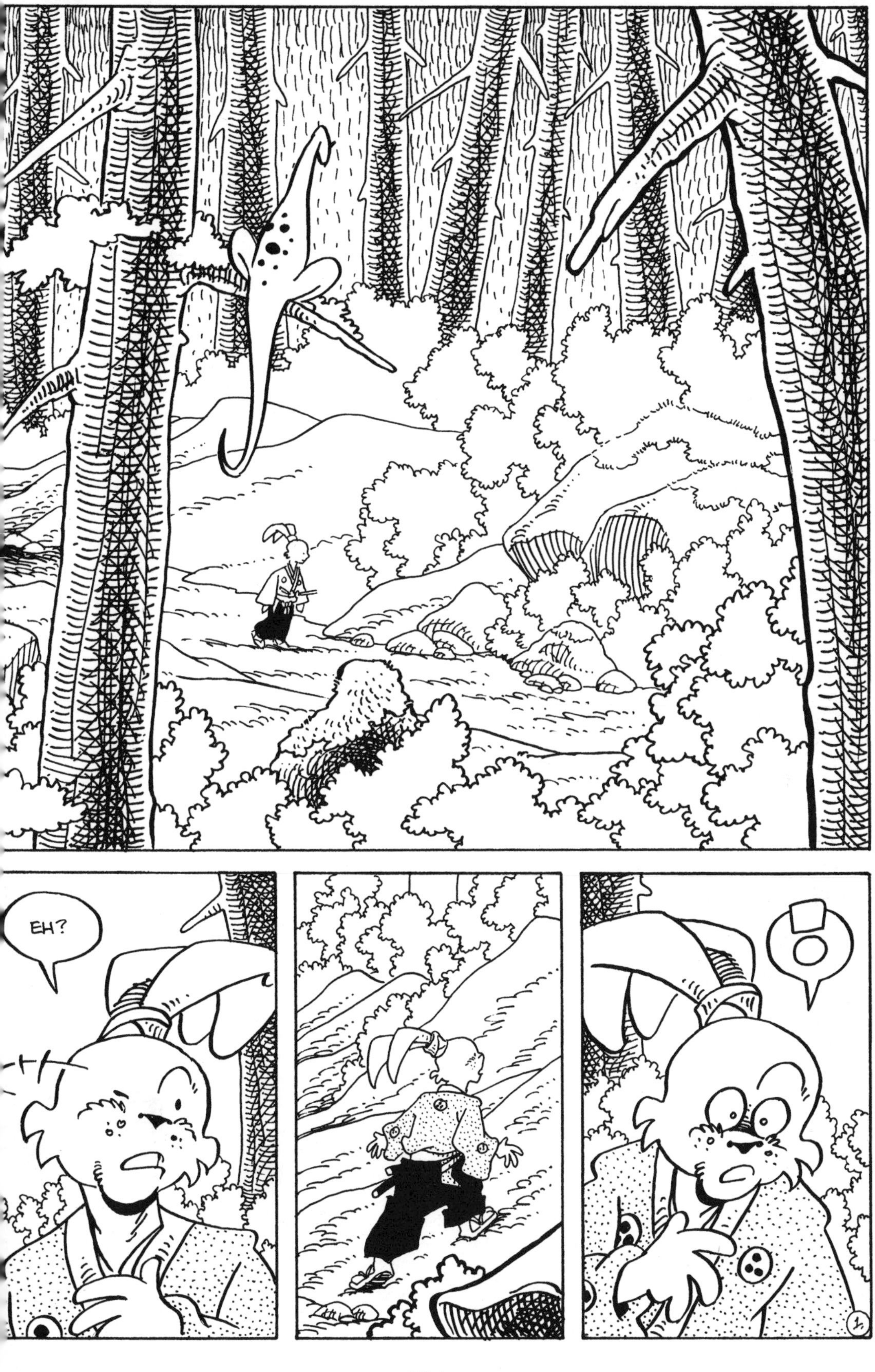
EH?

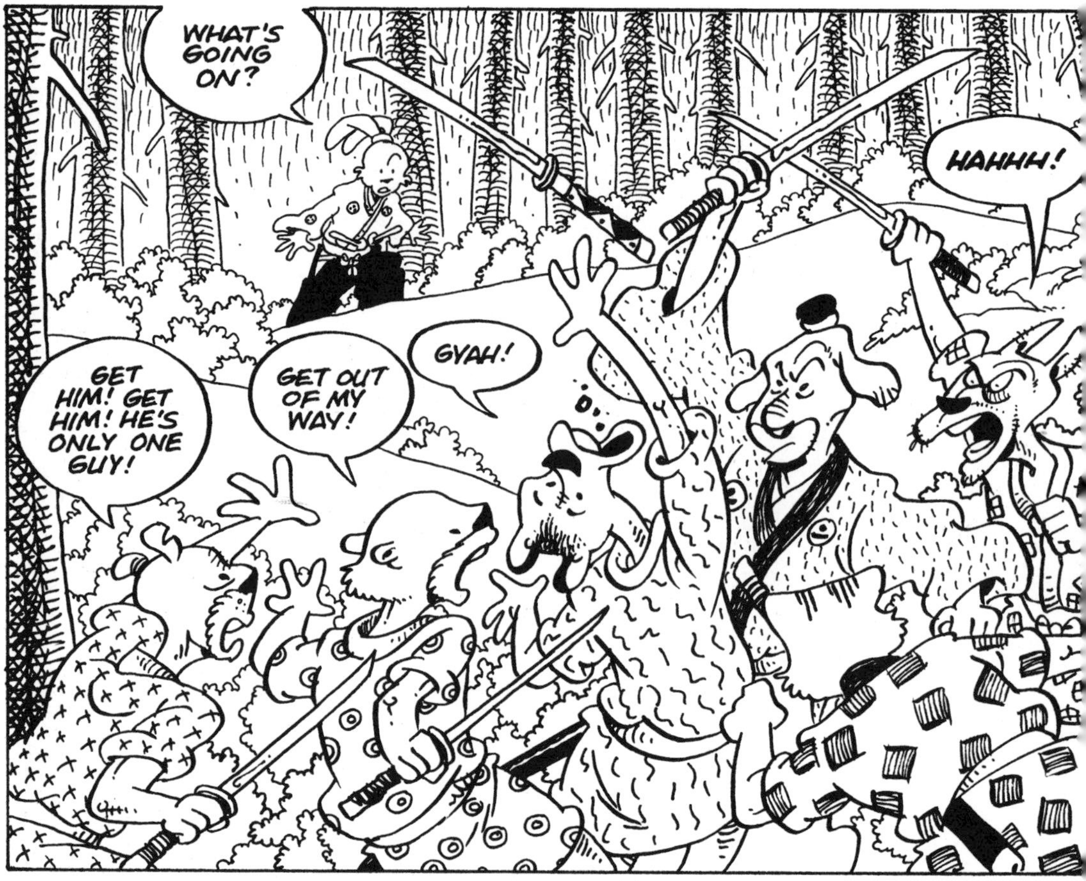
WHAT'S GOING ON?
HAHHH!
GET HIM! GET HIM! HE'S ONLY ONE GUY!
GET OUT OF MY WAY!
GYAH!

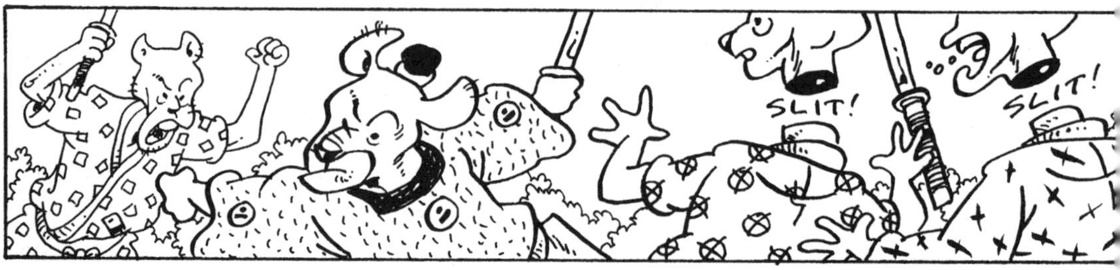
SLIT!
SLIT!

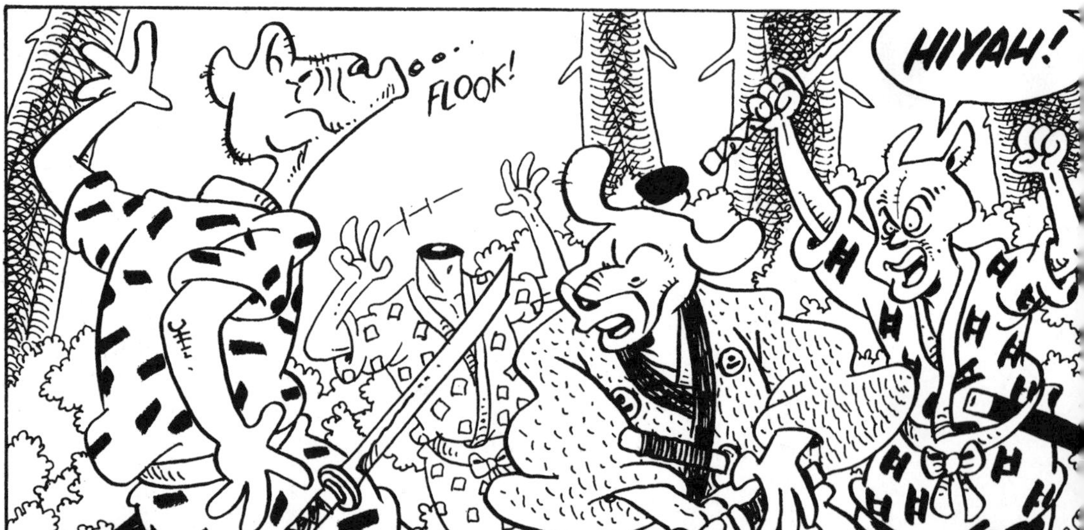
FLOOK!
HIYAH!

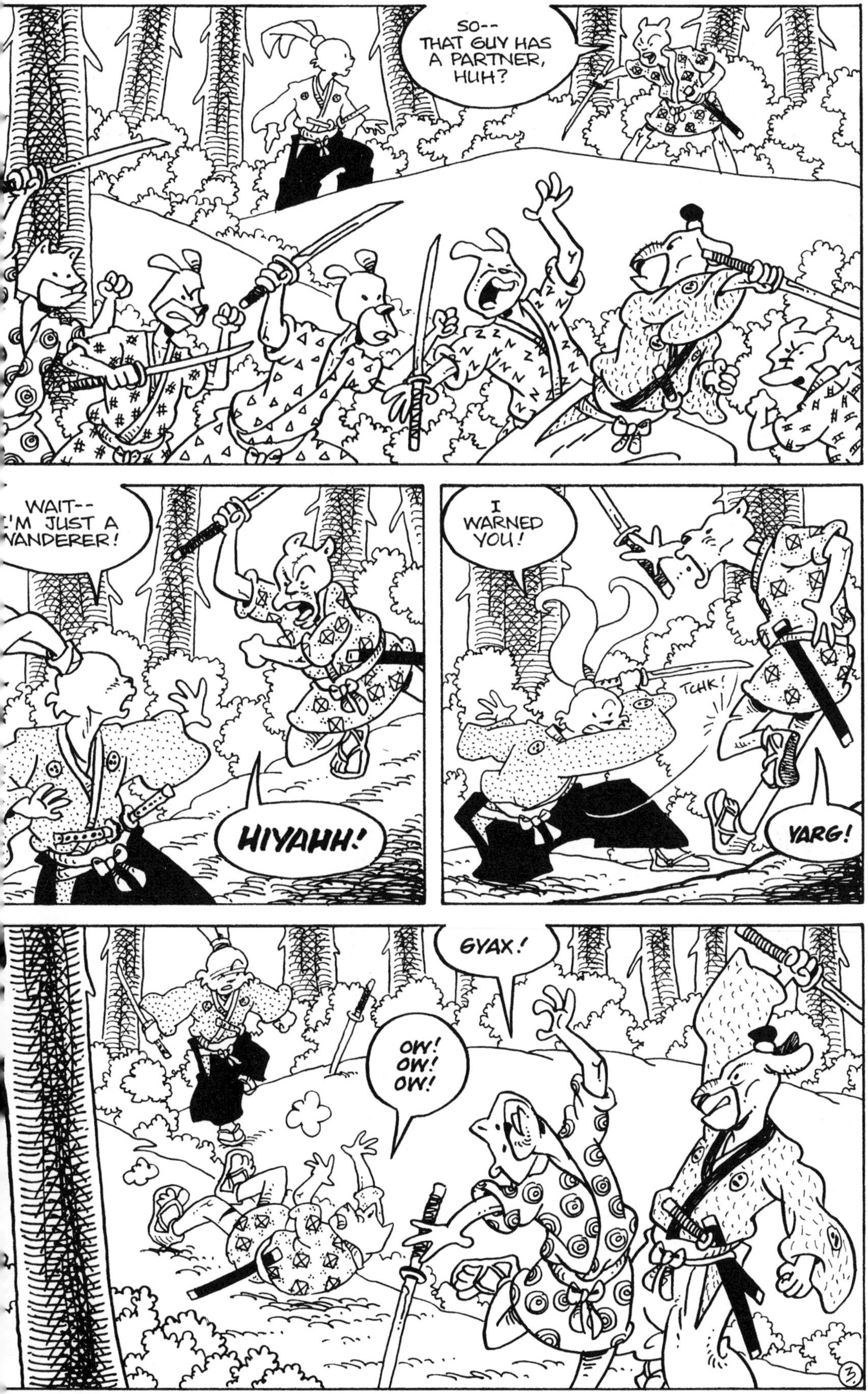

SO--
THAT GUY HAS
A PARTNER,
HUH?
WAIT--
I'M JUST A
WANDERER!
HIYAHH!
I
WARNED
YOU!
TCHK!
YARG!
GYAX!
OW!
OW!
OW!

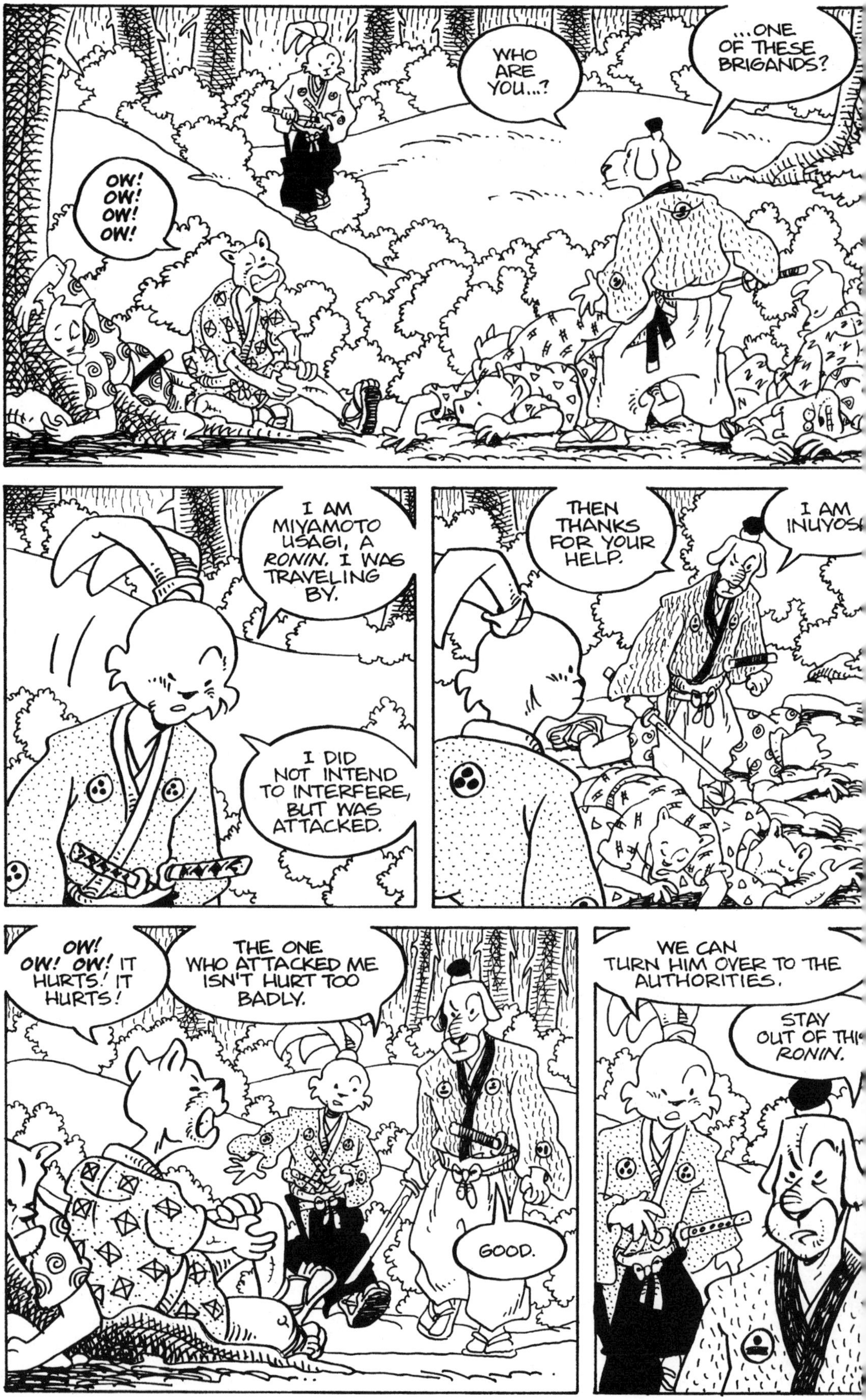
OW! OW! OW! OW!
WHO ARE YOU...?
...ONE OF THESE BRIGANDS?
I AM MIYAMOTO USAGI, A *RONIN.* I WAS TRAVELING BY.
I DID NOT INTEND TO INTERFERE, BUT WAS ATTACKED.
THEN THANKS FOR YOUR HELP.
I AM INUYOS
OW! OW! OW! IT HURTS! IT HURTS!
THE ONE WHO ATTACKED ME ISN'T HURT TOO BADLY.
GOOD.
WE CAN TURN HIM OVER TO THE AUTHORITIES.
STAY OUT OF THI *RONIN.*

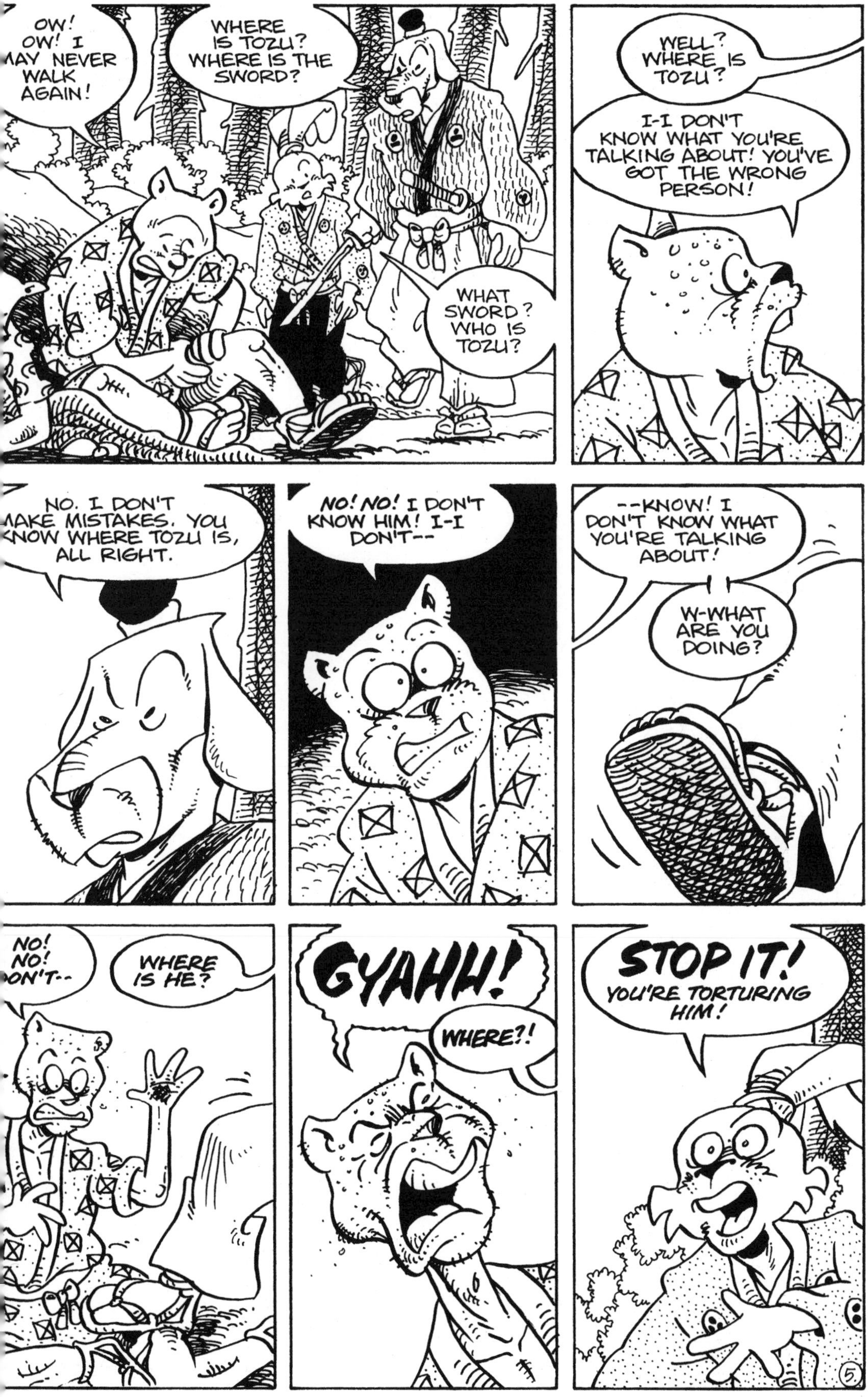
OW! OW! I MAY NEVER WALK AGAIN!
WHERE IS TOZU? WHERE IS THE SWORD?
WHAT SWORD? WHO IS TOZU?
WELL? WHERE IS TOZU?
I-I DON'T KNOW WHAT YOU'RE TALKING ABOUT! YOU'VE GOT THE WRONG PERSON!
NO. I DON'T MAKE MISTAKES. YOU KNOW WHERE TOZU IS, ALL RIGHT.
NO! NO! I DON'T KNOW HIM! I-I DON'T--
--KNOW! I DON'T KNOW WHAT YOU'RE TALKING ABOUT!
W-WHAT ARE YOU DOING?
NO! NO! DON'T--
WHERE IS HE?
GYAHH!
WHERE?!
STOP IT! YOU'RE TORTURING HIM!
5

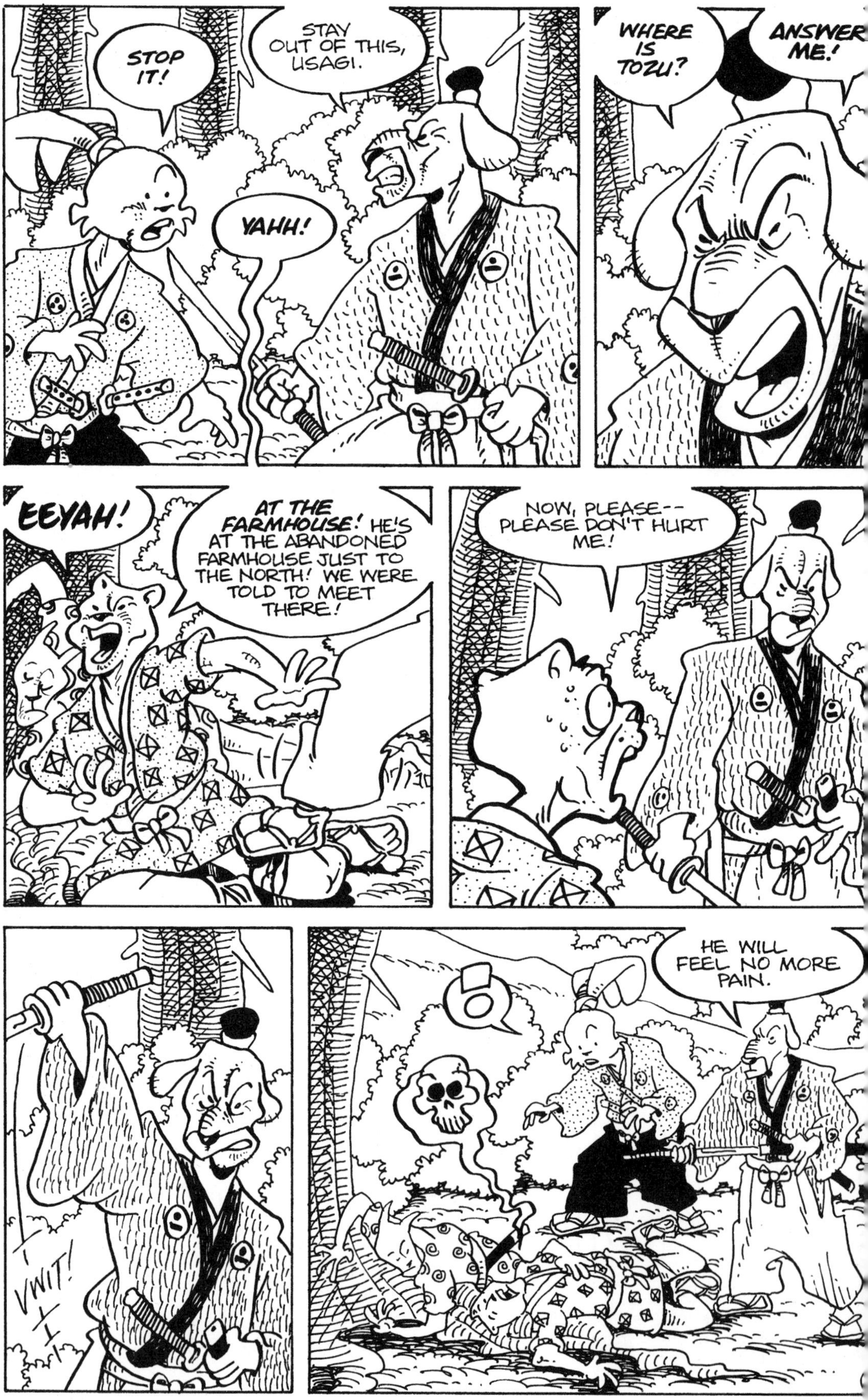
STOP IT!
STAY OUT OF THIS, USAGI.
YAHH!
WHERE IS TOZU?
ANSWER ME!
EEYAH!
AT THE FARMHOUSE! HE'S AT THE ABANDONED FARMHOUSE JUST TO THE NORTH! WE WERE TOLD TO MEET THERE!
NOW, PLEASE-- PLEASE DON'T HURT ME!
VWIT!
HE WILL FEEL NO MORE PAIN.

YOU KILLED HIM IN COLD BLOOD!

I APOLOGIZE THAT YOU HAD TO WITNESS THAT, USAGI-SAN! I AM NOT USUALLY SO CRUEL.

YOU MAY UNDERSTAND WHEN YOU HEAR MY STORY.

I WAS THE CHIEF RETAINER TO LORD MASAKI. HE WAS A FINE MASTER, EXCEPT WHEN IT CAME TO HIS SON, YAKICHI.

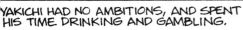

YAKICHI HAD NO AMBITIONS, AND SPENT HIS TIME DRINKING AND GAMBLING.

"ONE NIGHT, WHILE RETURNING HOME FROM THE GAMING DENS, YAKICHI'S GUARDS WERE OVERPOWERED AND HE WAS KIDNAPPED.

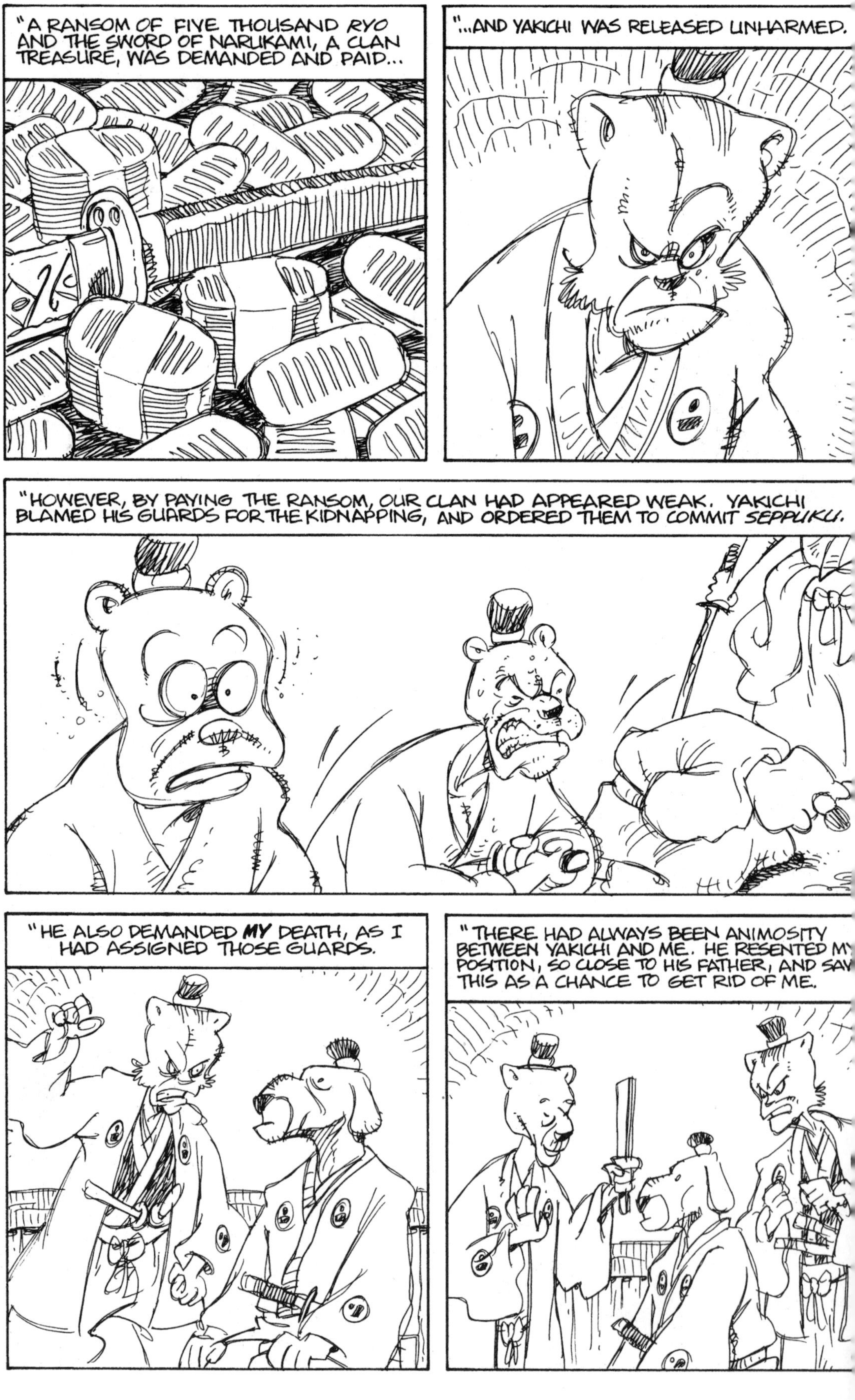
"A RANSOM OF FIVE THOUSAND *RYO* AND THE SWORD OF NARUKAMI, A CLAN TREASURE, WAS DEMANDED AND PAID...
"...AND YAKICHI WAS RELEASED UNHARMED.
"HOWEVER, BY PAYING THE RANSOM, OUR CLAN HAD APPEARED WEAK. YAKICHI BLAMED HIS GUARDS FOR THE KIDNAPPING, AND ORDERED THEM TO COMMIT *SEPPUKU*.
"HE ALSO DEMANDED **MY** DEATH, AS I HAD ASSIGNED THOSE GUARDS.
"THERE HAD ALWAYS BEEN ANIMOSITY BETWEEN YAKICHI AND ME. HE RESENTED MY POSITION, SO CLOSE TO HIS FATHER, AND SAW THIS AS A CHANCE TO GET RID OF ME.

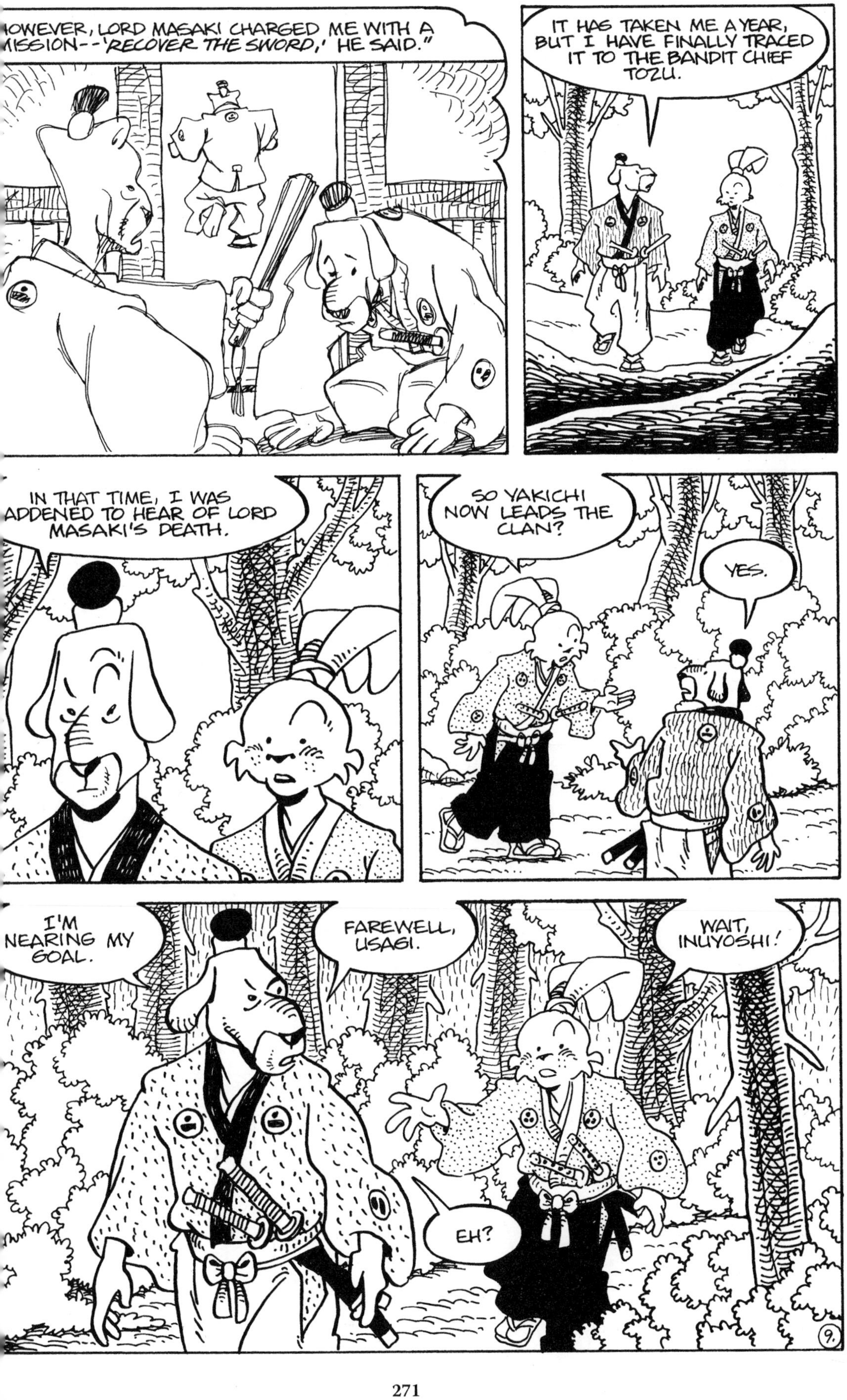

HOWEVER, LORD MASAKI CHARGED ME WITH A MISSION--'RECOVER THE SWORD,' HE SAID."
IT HAS TAKEN ME A YEAR, BUT I HAVE FINALLY TRACED IT TO THE BANDIT CHIEF TOZU.
IN THAT TIME, I WAS SADDENED TO HEAR OF LORD MASAKI'S DEATH.
SO YAKICHI NOW LEADS THE CLAN?
YES.
I'M NEARING MY GOAL.
FAREWELL, USAGI.
WAIT, INUYOSHI!
EH?
9.

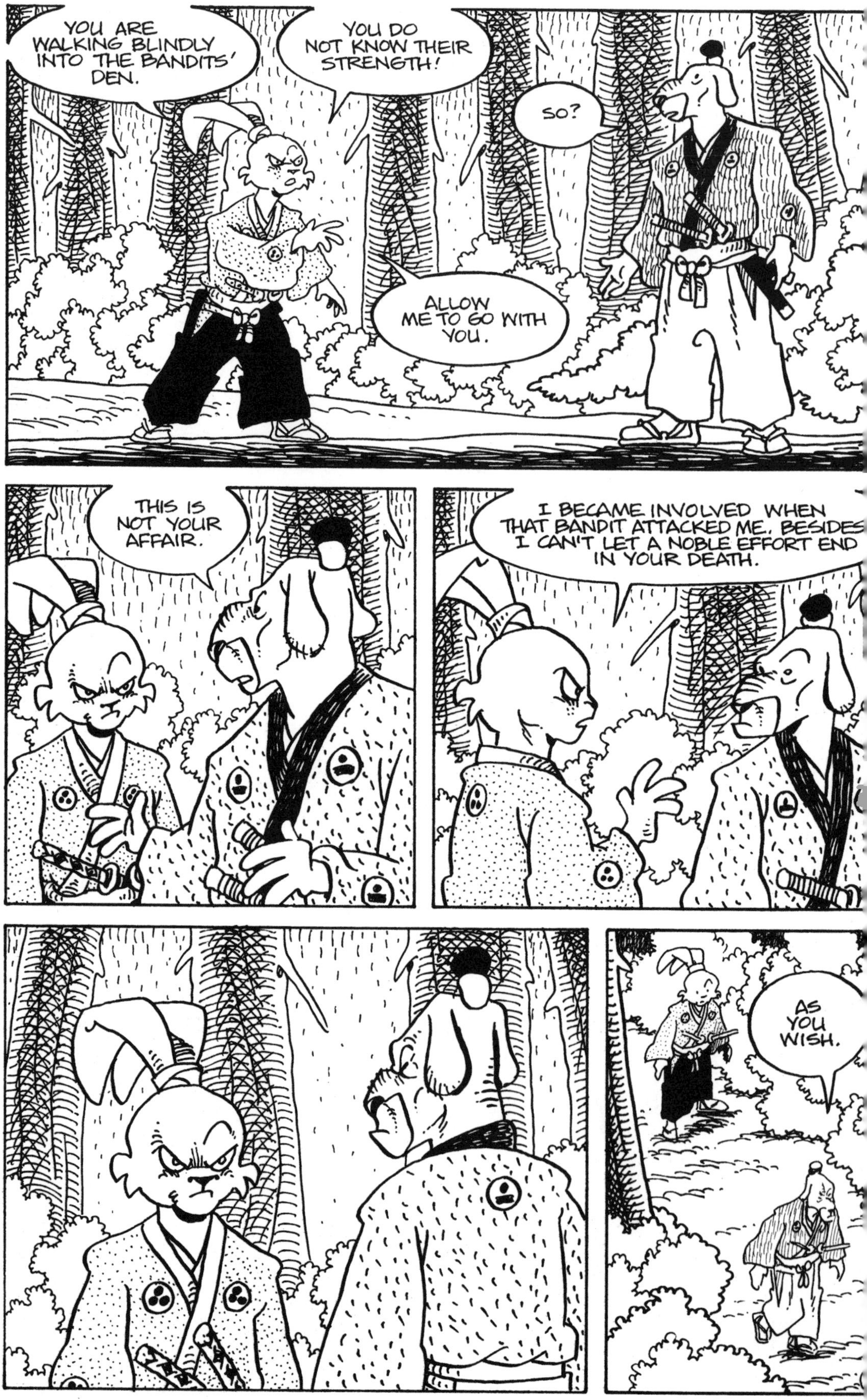
YOU ARE WALKING BLINDLY INTO THE BANDITS' DEN.
YOU DO NOT KNOW THEIR STRENGTH!
SO?
ALLOW ME TO GO WITH YOU.
THIS IS NOT YOUR AFFAIR.
I BECAME INVOLVED WHEN THAT BANDIT ATTACKED ME. BESIDES I CAN'T LET A NOBLE EFFORT END IN YOUR DEATH.
AS YOU WISH.

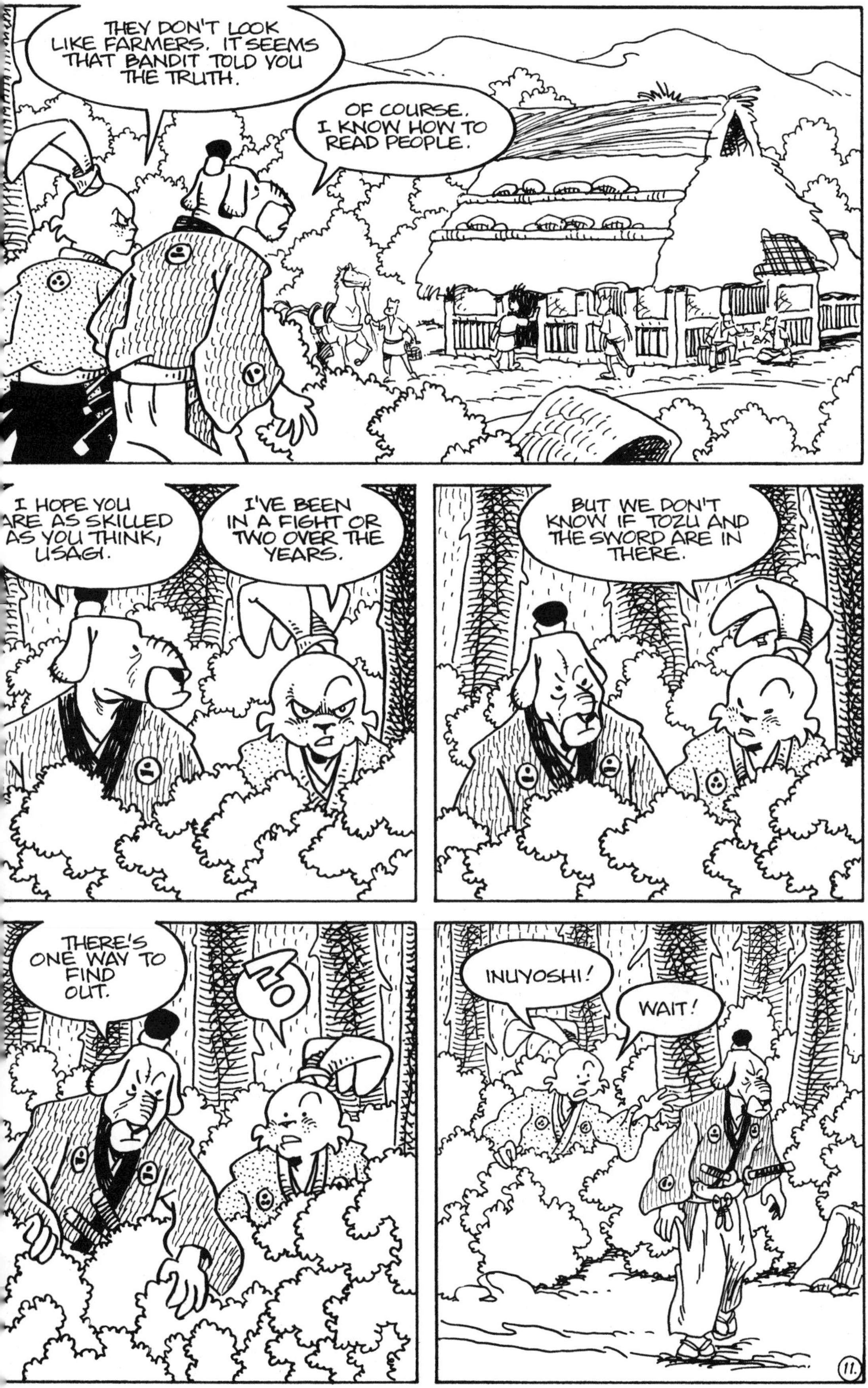

THEY DON'T LOOK LIKE FARMERS. IT SEEMS THAT BANDIT TOLD YOU THE TRUTH.
OF COURSE. I KNOW HOW TO READ PEOPLE.
I HOPE YOU ARE AS SKILLED AS YOU THINK, USAGI.
I'VE BEEN IN A FIGHT OR TWO OVER THE YEARS.
BUT WE DON'T KNOW IF TOZU AND THE SWORD ARE IN THERE.
THERE'S ONE WAY TO FIND OUT.
MO
INUYOSHI!
WAIT!
11.

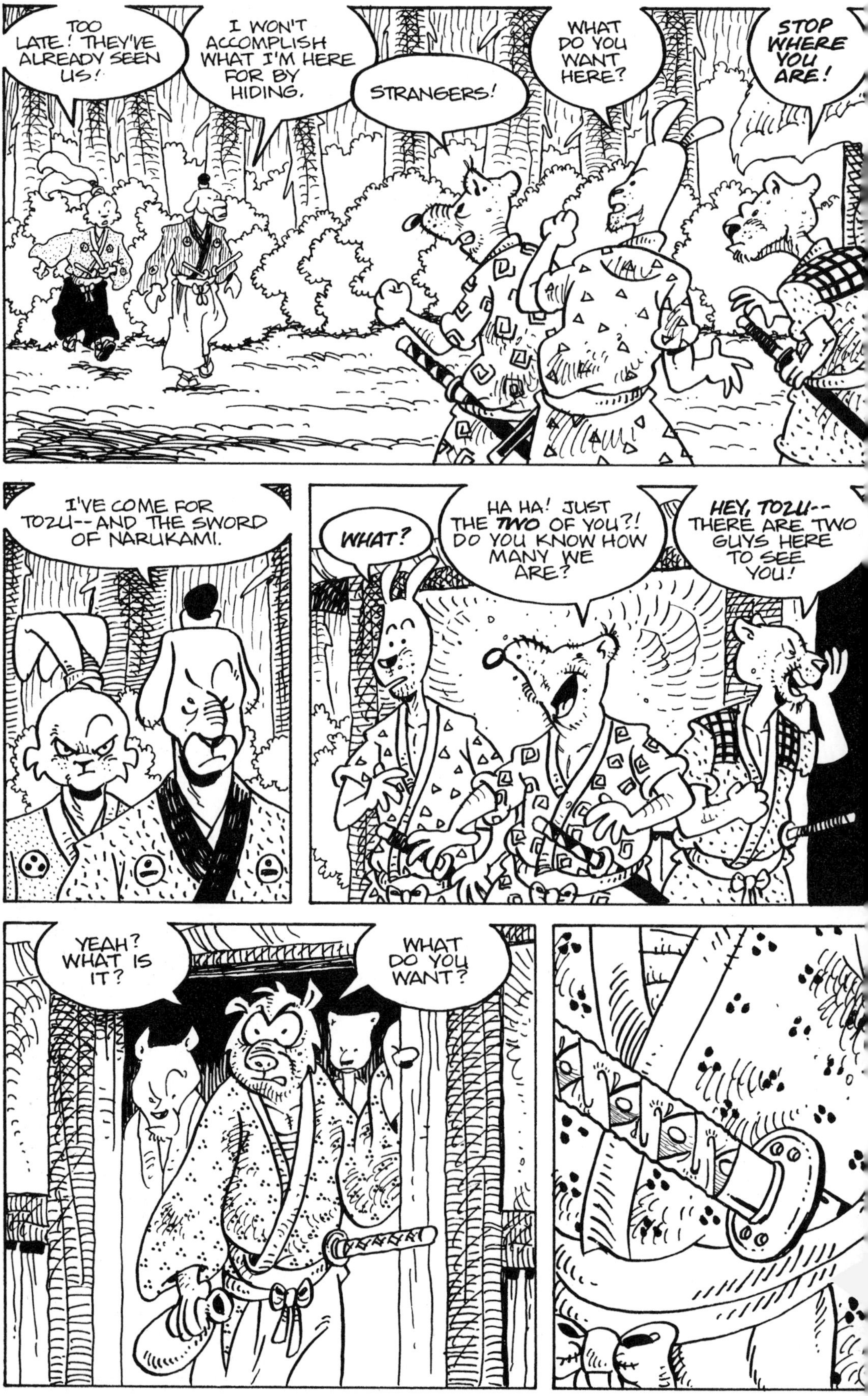
TOO LATE! THEY'VE ALREADY SEEN US!
I WON'T ACCOMPLISH WHAT I'M HERE FOR BY HIDING.
STRANGERS!
WHAT DO YOU WANT HERE?
STOP WHERE YOU ARE!
I'VE COME FOR TOZU--AND THE SWORD OF NARUKAMI.
WHAT?
HA HA! JUST THE TWO OF YOU?! DO YOU KNOW HOW MANY WE ARE?
HEY, TOZU-- THERE ARE TWO GUYS HERE TO SEE YOU!
YEAH? WHAT IS IT?
WHAT DO YOU WANT?

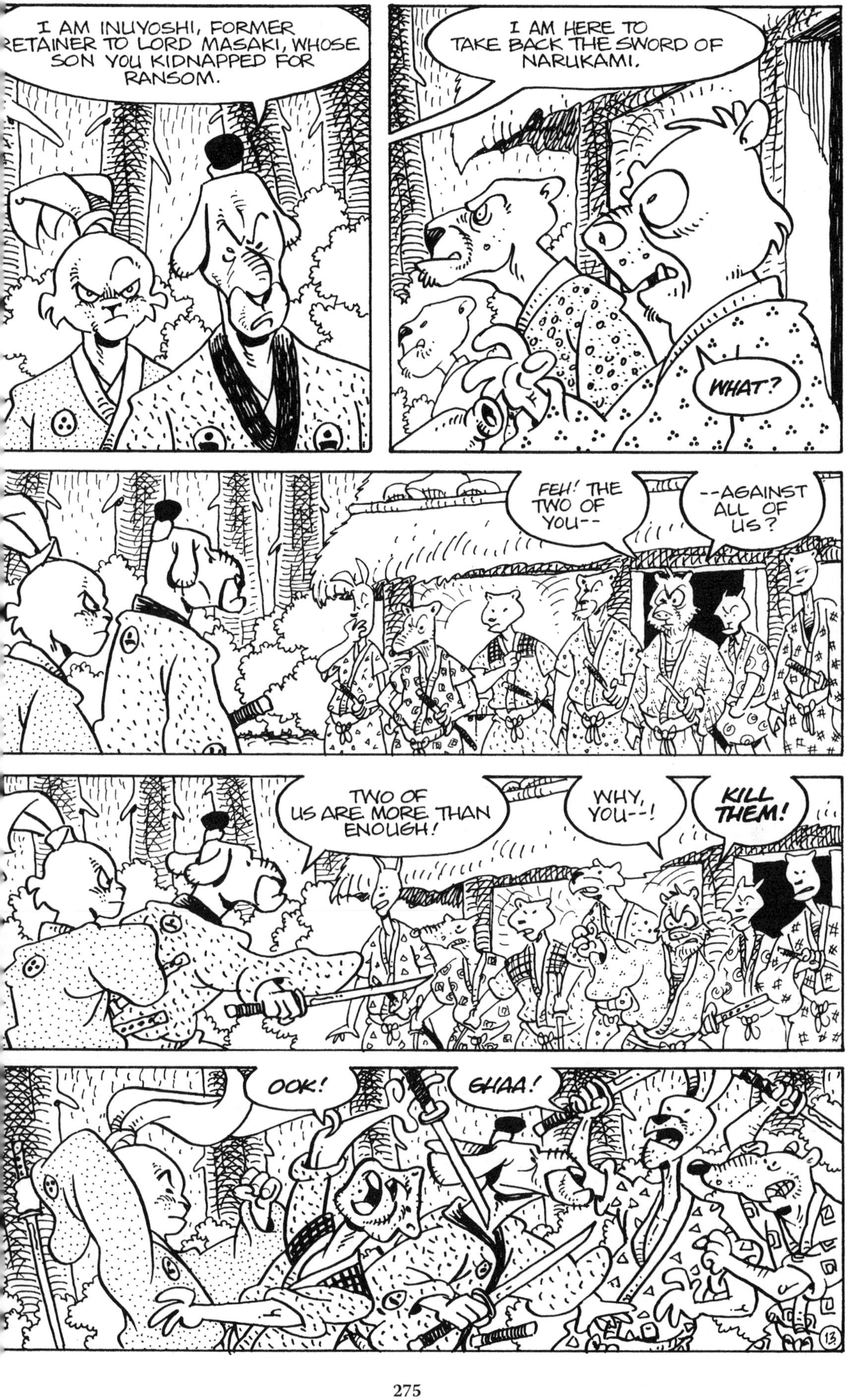
I AM INUYOSHI, FORMER RETAINER TO LORD MASAKI, WHOSE SON YOU KIDNAPPED FOR RANSOM.
I AM HERE TO TAKE BACK THE SWORD OF NARUKAMI.
WHAT?
FEH! THE TWO OF YOU--
--AGAINST ALL OF US?
TWO OF US ARE MORE THAN ENOUGH!
WHY, YOU--!
KILL THEM!
OOK!
GHAA!
13

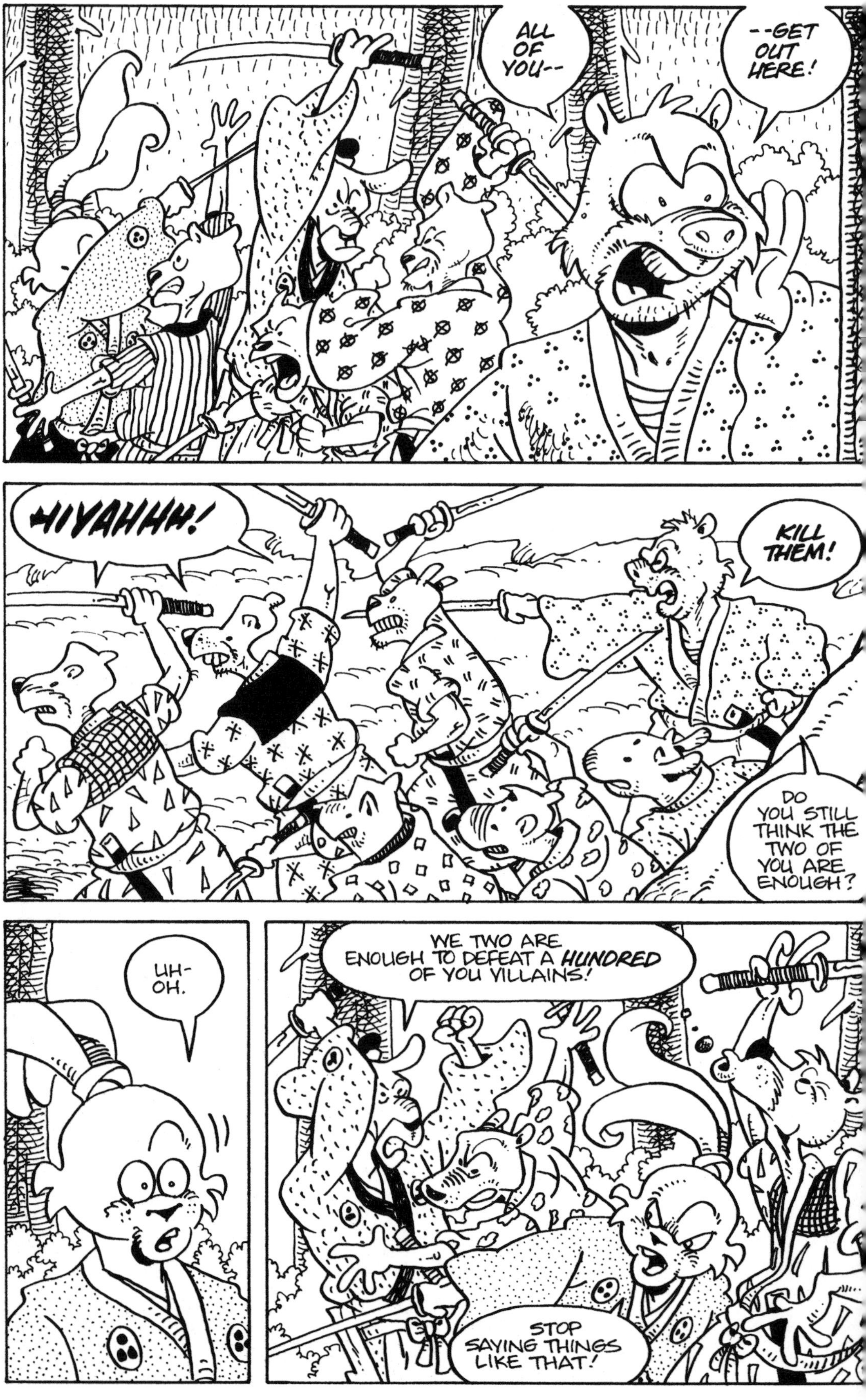
ALL OF YOU--
--GET OUT HERE!
HIYAHHH!
KILL THEM!
DO YOU STILL THINK THE TWO OF YOU ARE ENOUGH?
UH-OH.
WE TWO ARE ENOUGH TO DEFEAT A *HUNDRED* OF YOU VILLAINS!
STOP SAYING THINGS LIKE THAT!

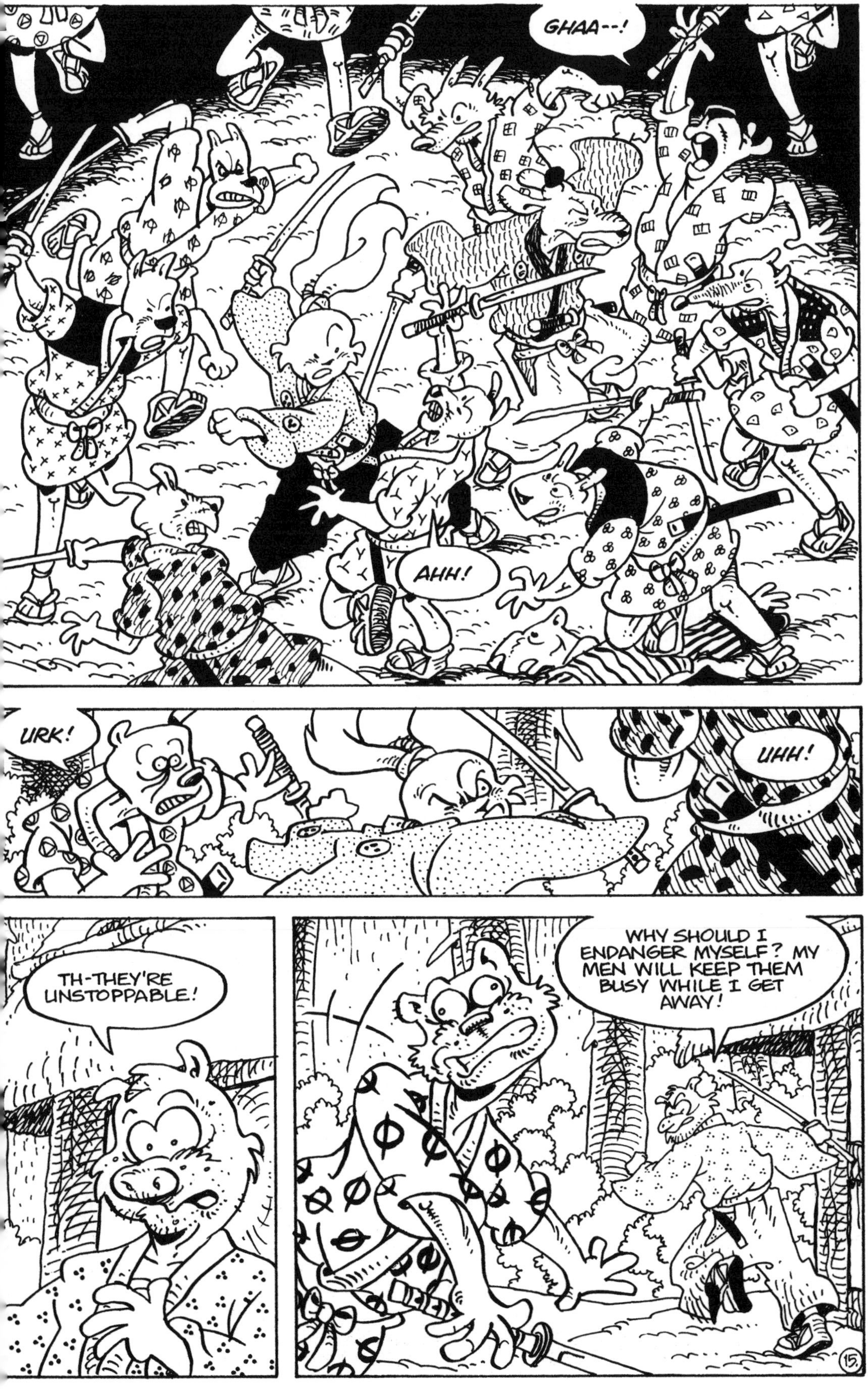
GHAA--!
AHH!
URK!
UHH!
TH-THEY'RE UNSTOPPABLE!
WHY SHOULD I ENDANGER MYSELF? MY MEN WILL KEEP THEM BUSY WHILE I GET AWAY!
15

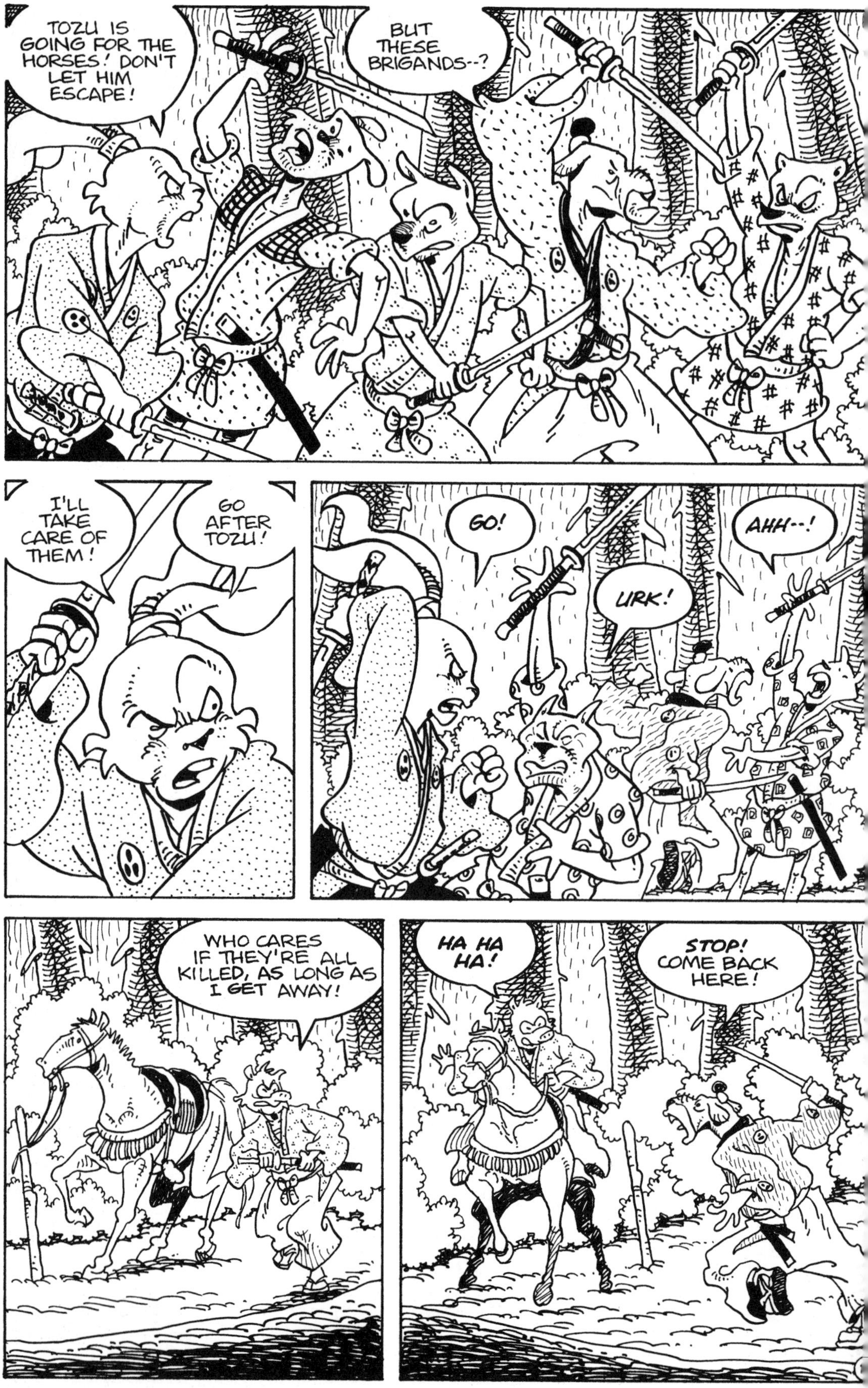
TOZU IS GOING FOR THE HORSES! DON'T LET HIM ESCAPE!
BUT THESE BRIGANDS--?
I'LL TAKE CARE OF THEM!
GO AFTER TOZU!
GO!
URK!
AHH--!
WHO CARES IF THEY'RE ALL KILLED, AS LONG AS I GET AWAY!
HA HA HA!
STOP! COME BACK HERE!

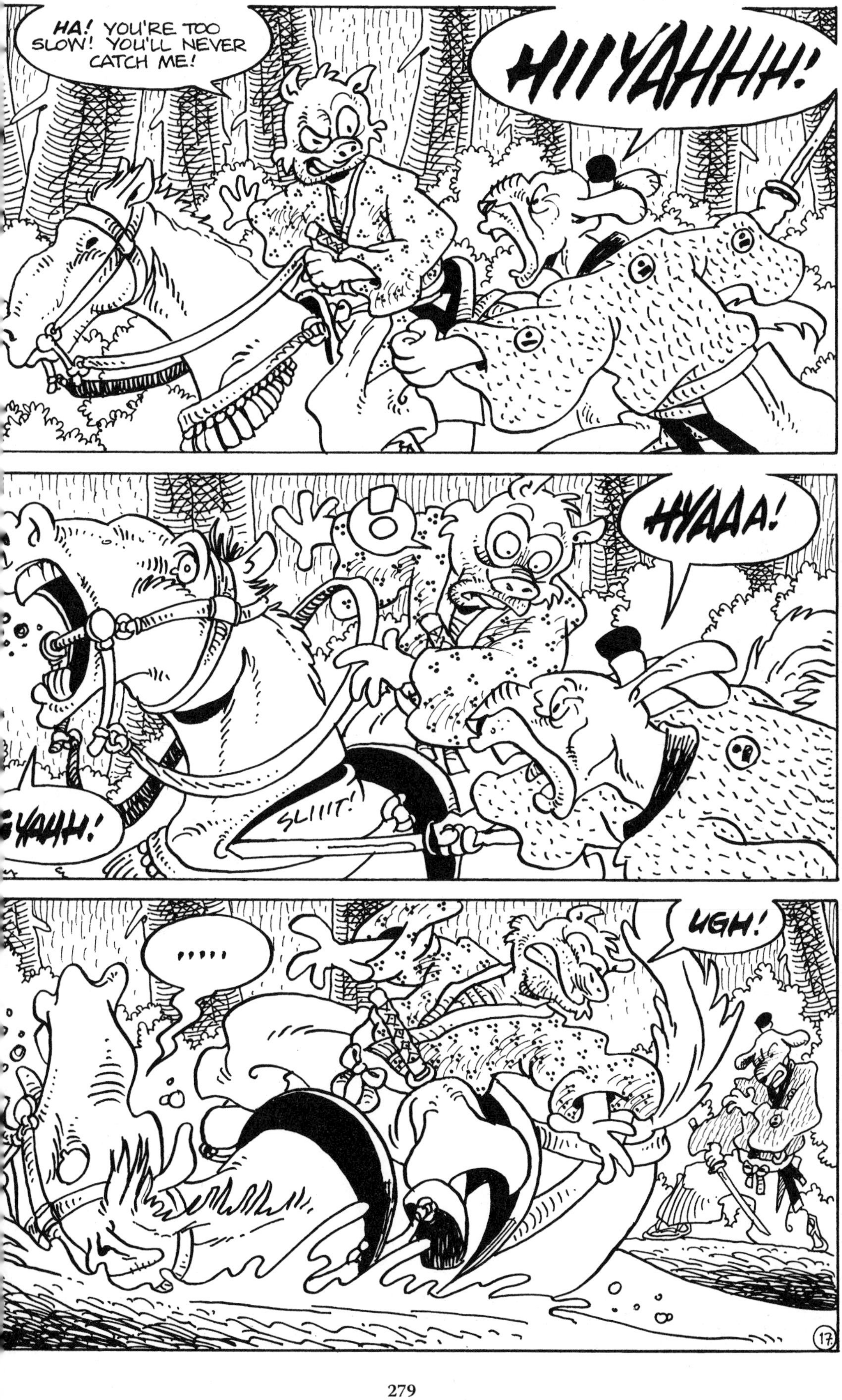
HA! YOU'RE TOO SLOW! YOU'LL NEVER CATCH ME!
HIIYAHHH!
HYAAA!
GYAHH!
SLIIIT!
.....
UGH!
17

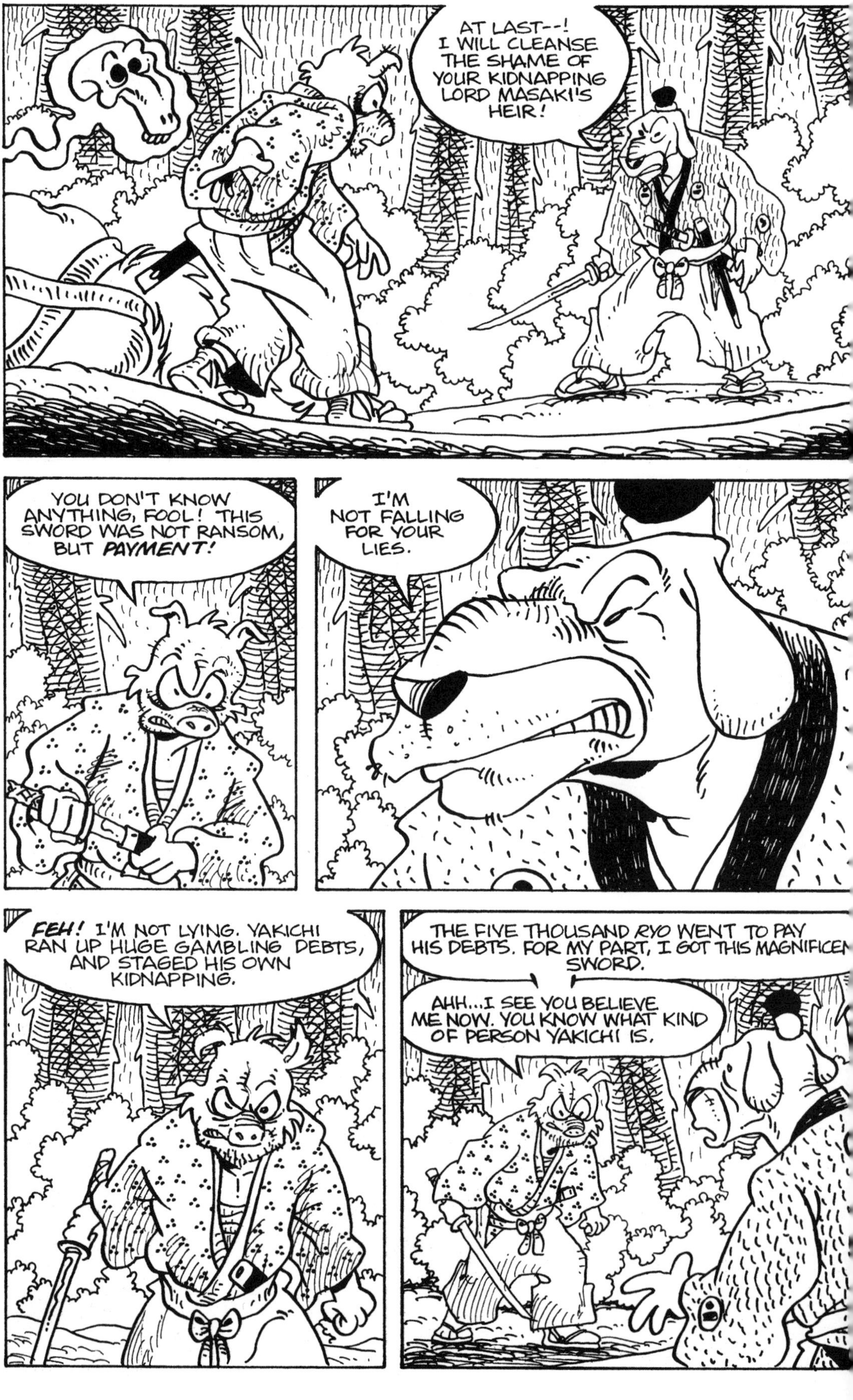
AT LAST--! I WILL CLEANSE THE SHAME OF YOUR KIDNAPPING LORD MASAKI'S HEIR!
YOU DON'T KNOW ANYTHING, FOOL! THIS SWORD WAS NOT RANSOM, BUT *PAYMENT!*
I'M NOT FALLING FOR YOUR LIES.
*FEH!* I'M NOT LYING. YAKICHI RAN UP HUGE GAMBLING DEBTS, AND STAGED HIS OWN KIDNAPPING.
THE FIVE THOUSAND *RYO* WENT TO PAY HIS DEBTS. FOR MY PART, I GOT THIS MAGNIFICEN SWORD.
AHH...I SEE YOU BELIEVE ME NOW. YOU KNOW WHAT KIND OF PERSON YAKICHI IS.

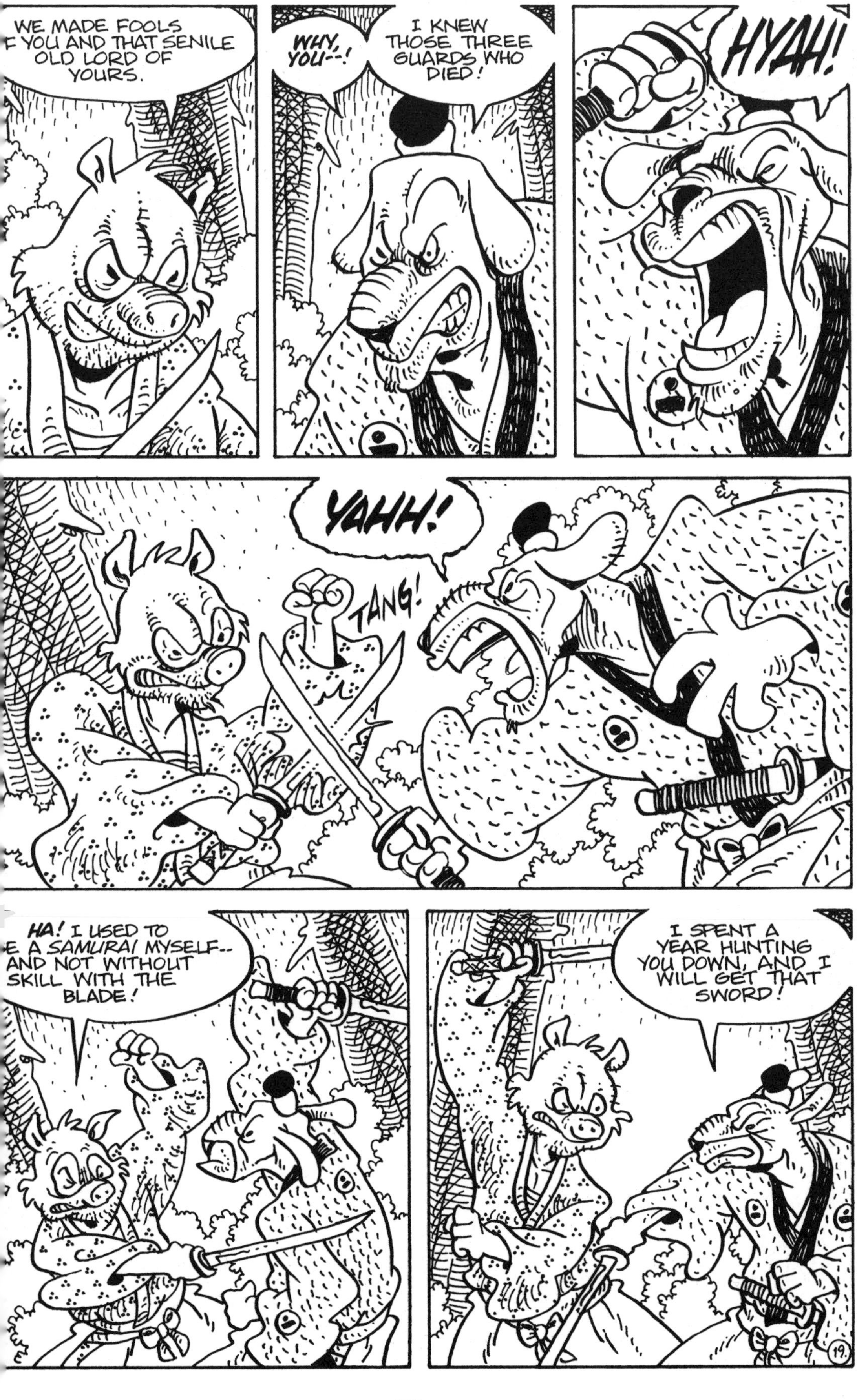

WE MADE FOOLS F YOU AND THAT SENILE OLD LORD OF YOURS.
WHY, YOU--!
I KNEW THOSE THREE GUARDS WHO DIED!
HYAH!
YAHH!
TANG!
HA! I USED TO E A SAMURAI MYSELF-- AND NOT WITHOUT SKILL WITH THE BLADE!
I SPENT A YEAR HUNTING YOU DOWN, AND I WILL GET THAT SWORD!
19.

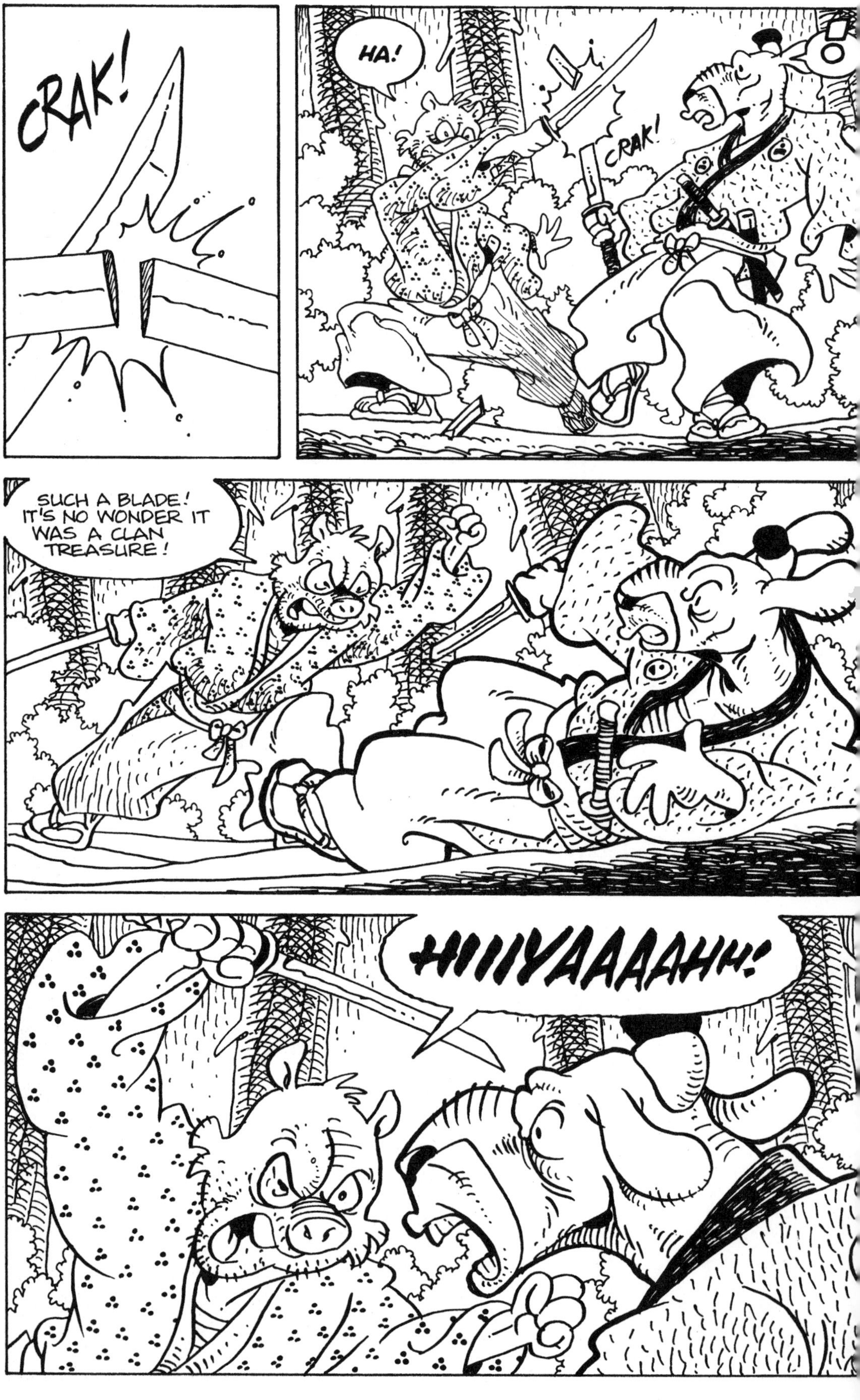
CRAK!
HA!
CRAK!
SUCH A BLADE! IT'S NO WONDER IT WAS A CLAN TREASURE!
HIIIYAAAAAHH!

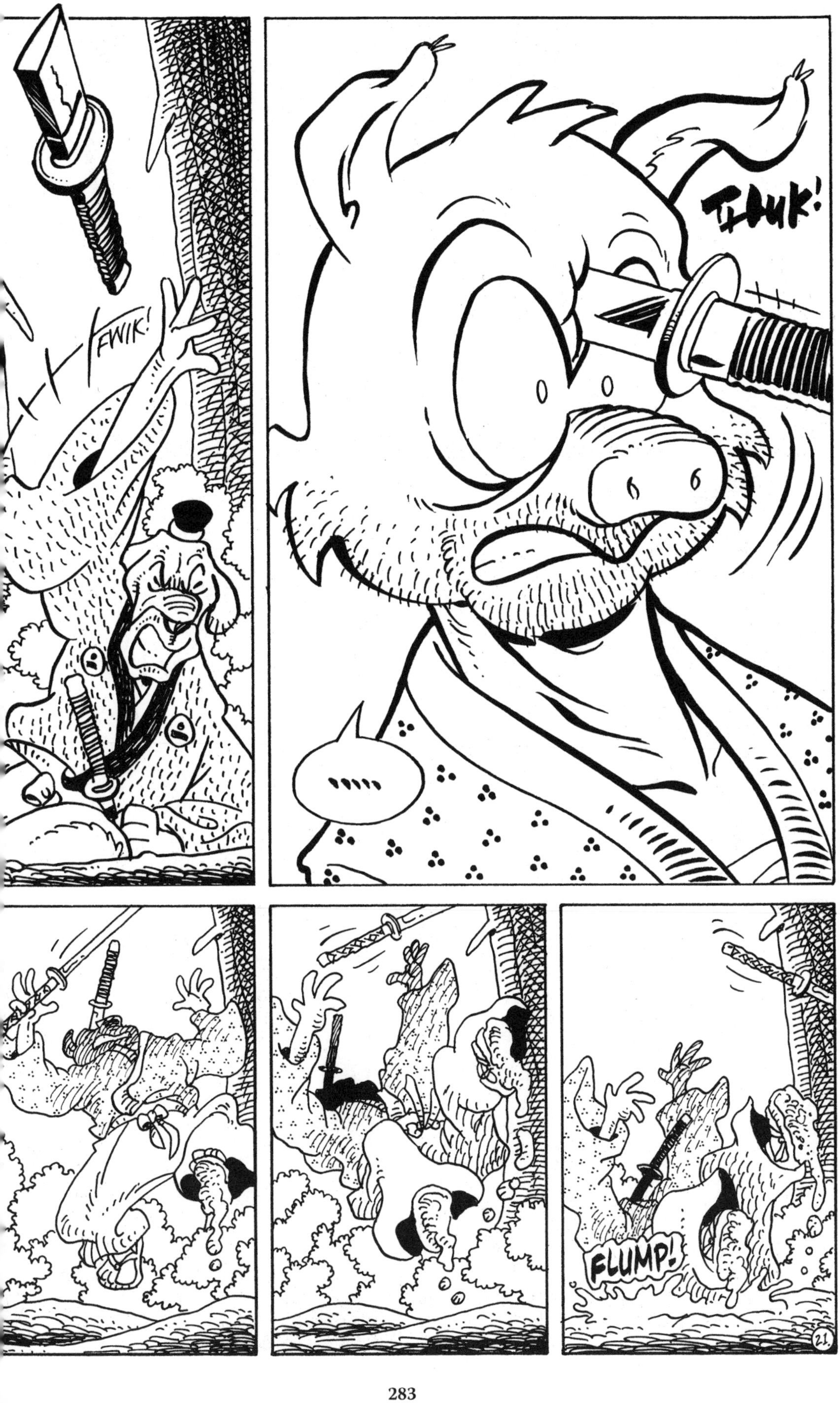
FWIK!
THUK!
.....
FLUMP!
21.

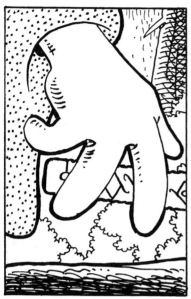

A TRULY MAGNIFICENT BLADE!

YOU HANDLED THE REST OF THE GANG ON YOUR OWN. I GUESS YOU *ARE* AS GOOD A YOU THINK, USAGI.

BUT I DON'T THINK VERY HIGHLY OF MYSELF.

HA HA HA!

HERE.

YOUR QUEST IS COMPLETED.

YES, BUT NOT AS I EXPECTED. I HAVE BEEN TOLD OF A BETRAYAL.

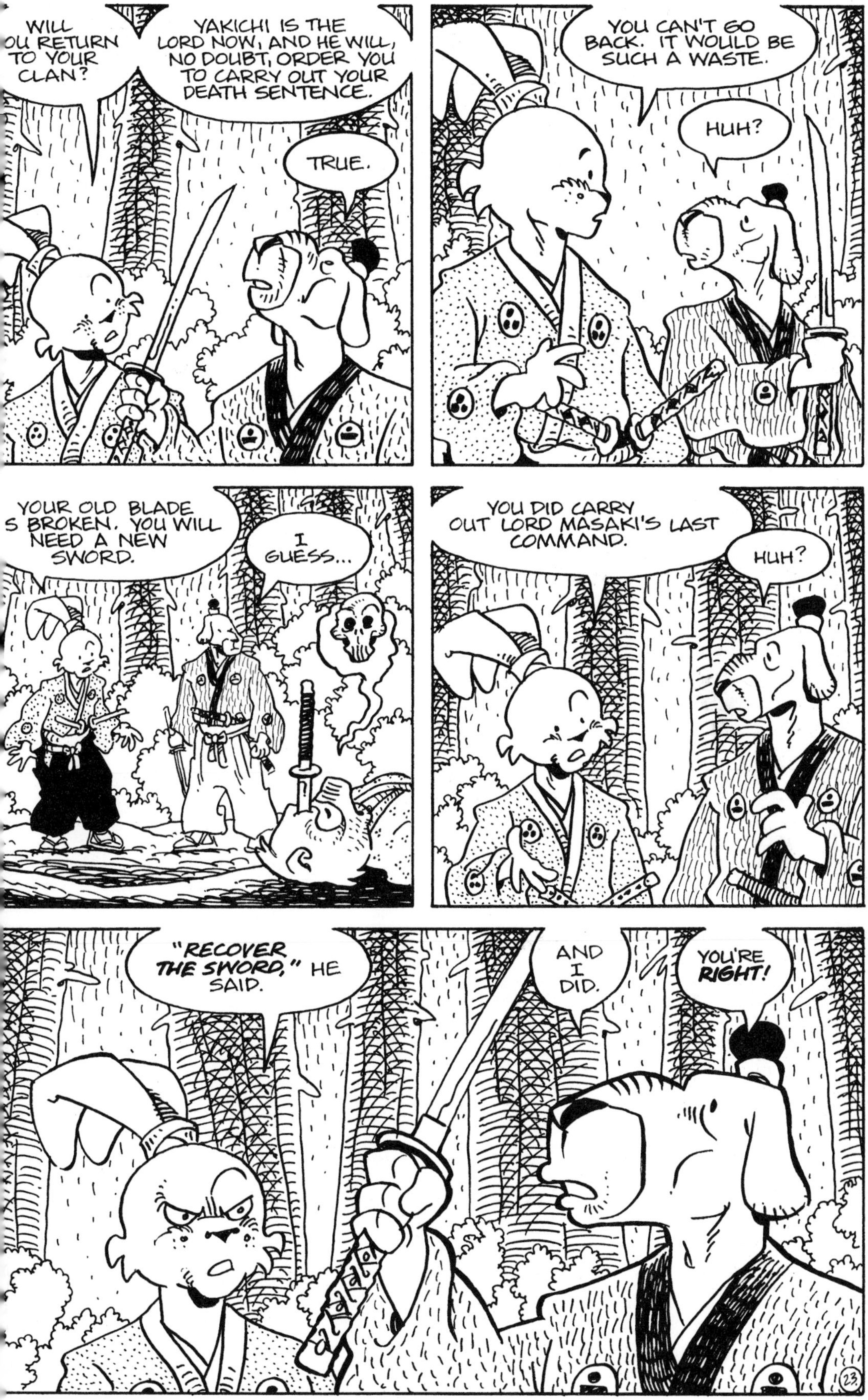
WILL OU RETURN TO YOUR CLAN?
YAKICHI IS THE LORD NOW, AND HE WILL, NO DOUBT, ORDER YOU TO CARRY OUT YOUR DEATH SENTENCE.
TRUE.
YOU CAN'T GO BACK. IT WOULD BE SUCH A WASTE.
HUH?
YOUR OLD BLADE S BROKEN. YOU WILL NEED A NEW SWORD.
I GUESS...
YOU DID CARRY OUT LORD MASAKI'S LAST COMMAND.
HUH?
"**RECOVER THE SWORD,**" HE SAID.
AND I DID.
YOU'RE **RIGHT!**
23

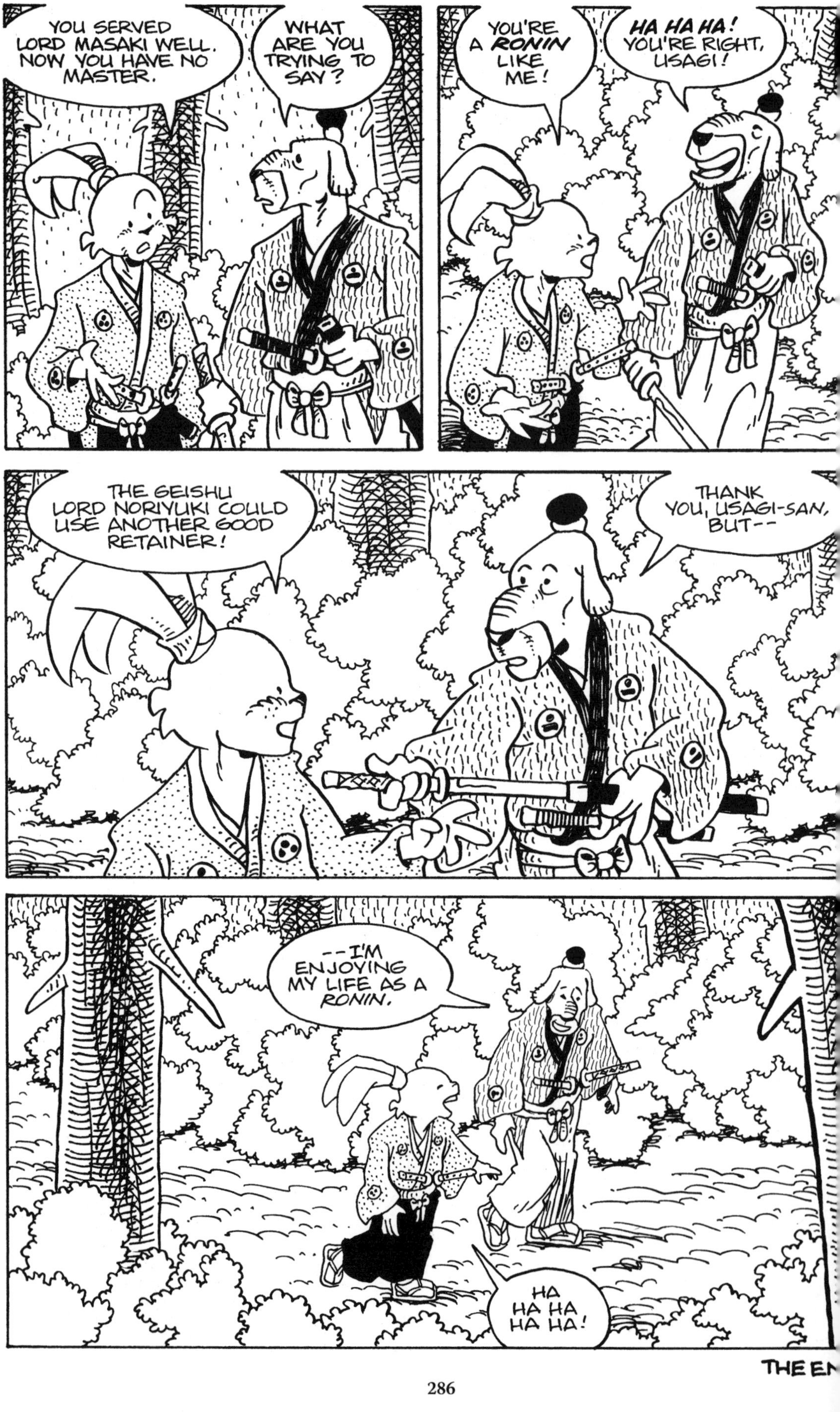
YOU SERVED LORD MASAKI WELL. NOW YOU HAVE NO MASTER.
WHAT ARE YOU TRYING TO SAY?
YOU'RE A *RONIN* LIKE ME!
*HA HA HA!* YOU'RE RIGHT, USAGI!
THE GEISHU LORD NORIYUKI COULD USE ANOTHER GOOD RETAINER!
THANK YOU, USAGI-SAN, BUT--
--I'M ENJOYING MY LIFE AS A *RONIN*.
HA HA HA HA HA!
THE EN

KUSHA
KUSHA

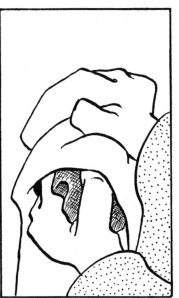

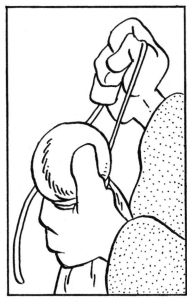

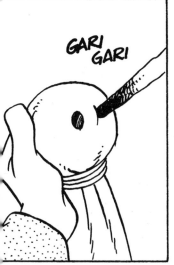

GARI
GARI

AH...
IT'S
DONE!

GAA~RI

TERU TERU BOZU!

I GUESS
IT LOOKS
OKAY!

THIS
BURNT STICK
DRAWS PRETTY
WELL!

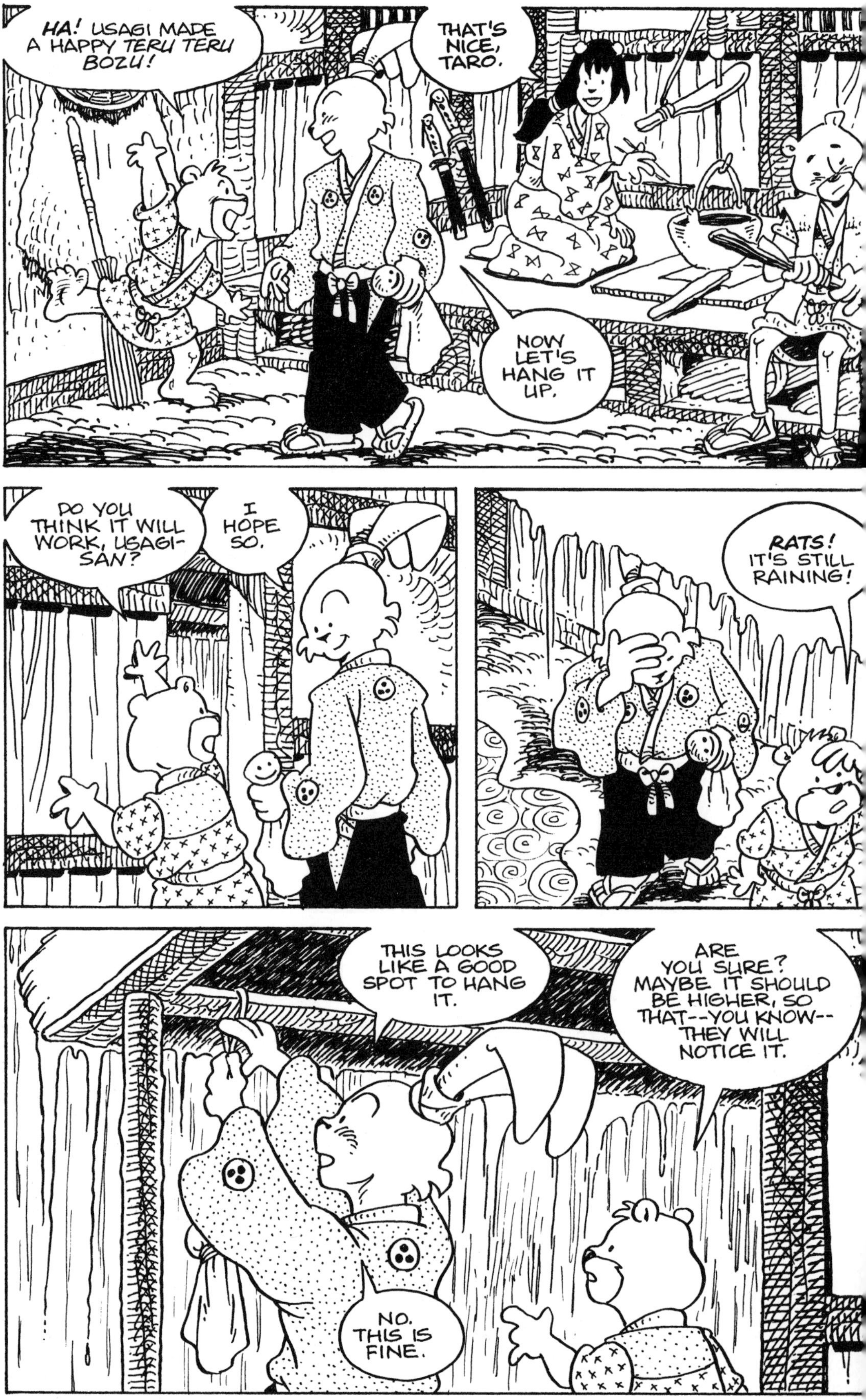
HA! USAGI MADE A HAPPY TERU TERU BOZU!
THAT'S NICE, TARO.
NOW LET'S HANG IT UP.
DO YOU THINK IT WILL WORK, USAGI-SAN?
I HOPE SO.
RATS! IT'S STILL RAINING!
THIS LOOKS LIKE A GOOD SPOT TO HANG IT.
ARE YOU SURE? MAYBE IT SHOULD BE HIGHER, SO THAT--YOU KNOW--THEY WILL NOTICE IT.
NO. THIS IS FINE.

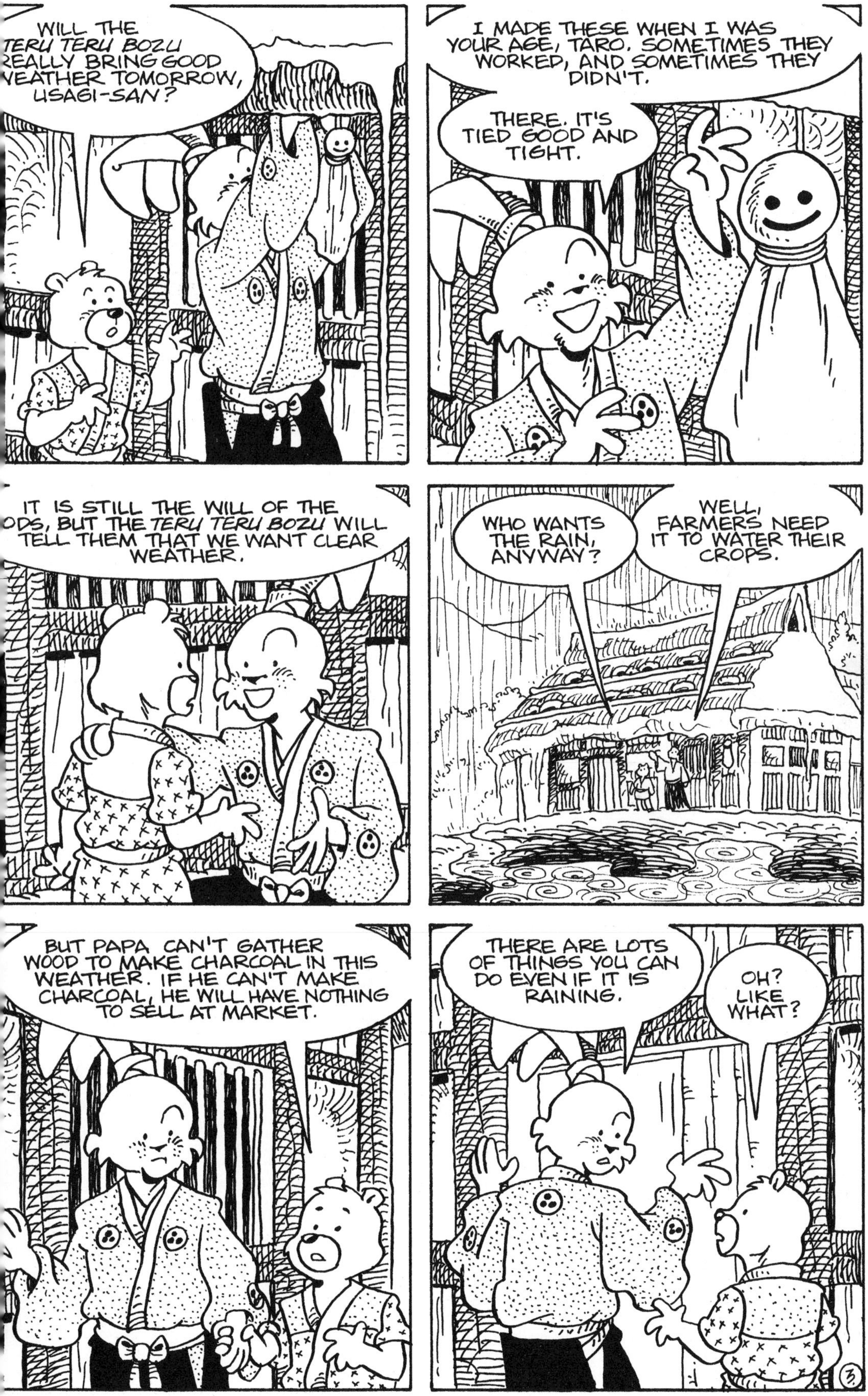
WILL THE TERU TERU BOZU REALLY BRING GOOD WEATHER TOMORROW, USAGI-SAN?
I MADE THESE WHEN I WAS YOUR AGE, TARO. SOMETIMES THEY WORKED, AND SOMETIMES THEY DIDN'T.
THERE. IT'S TIED GOOD AND TIGHT.
IT IS STILL THE WILL OF THE GODS, BUT THE TERU TERU BOZU WILL TELL THEM THAT WE WANT CLEAR WEATHER.
WHO WANTS THE RAIN, ANYWAY?
WELL, FARMERS NEED IT TO WATER THEIR CROPS.
BUT PAPA CAN'T GATHER WOOD TO MAKE CHARCOAL IN THIS WEATHER. IF HE CAN'T MAKE CHARCOAL, HE WILL HAVE NOTHING TO SELL AT MARKET.
THERE ARE LOTS OF THINGS YOU CAN DO EVEN IF IT IS RAINING.
OH? LIKE WHAT?
3

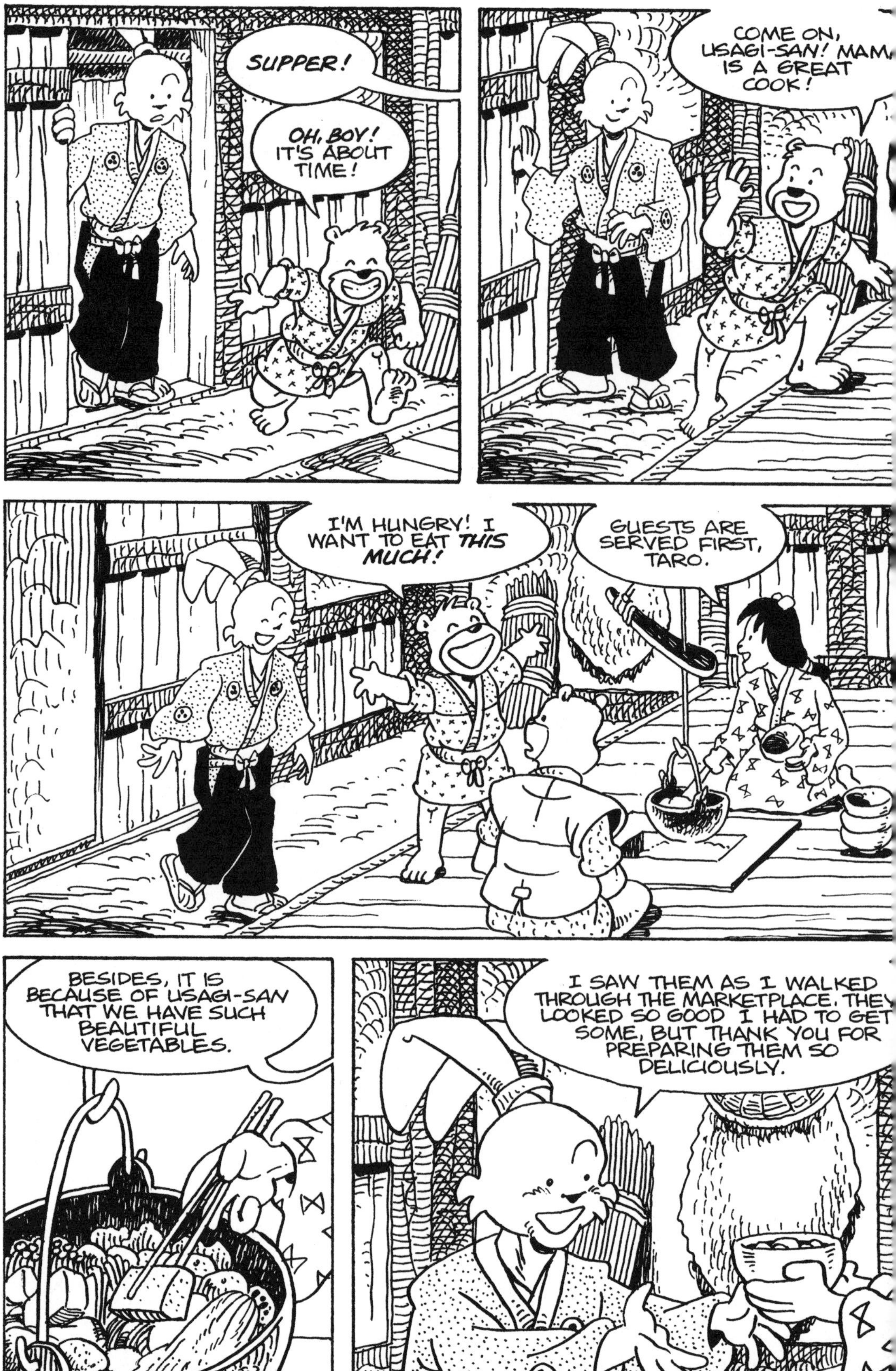
SUPPER!
OH, BOY! IT'S ABOUT TIME!
COME ON, USAGI-SAN! MAMA IS A GREAT COOK!
I'M HUNGRY! I WANT TO EAT THIS MUCH!
GUESTS ARE SERVED FIRST, TARO.
BESIDES, IT IS BECAUSE OF USAGI-SAN THAT WE HAVE SUCH BEAUTIFUL VEGETABLES.
I SAW THEM AS I WALKED THROUGH THE MARKETPLACE. THEY LOOKED SO GOOD I HAD TO GET SOME, BUT THANK YOU FOR PREPARING THEM SO DELICIOUSLY.

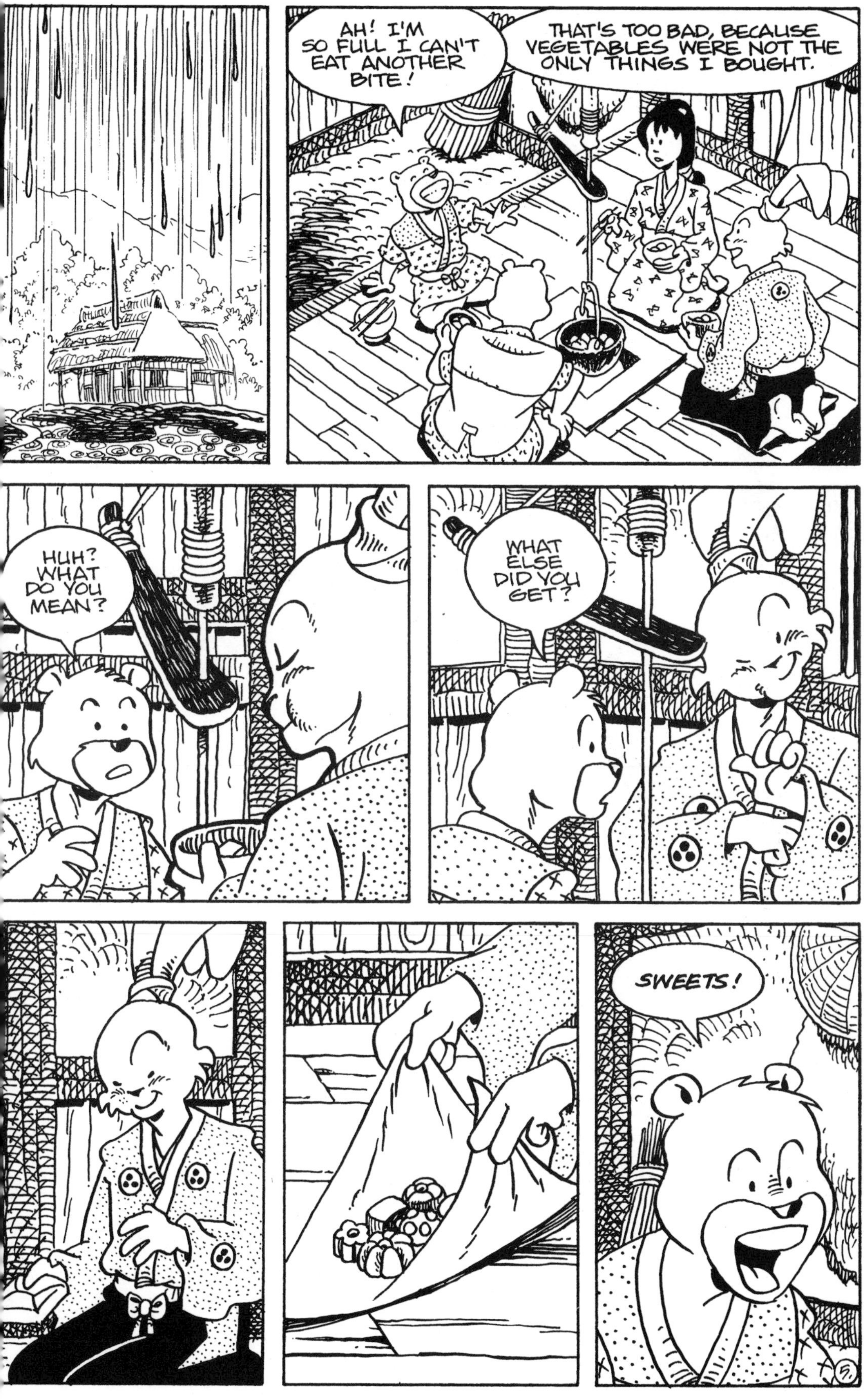
AH! I'M SO FULL I CAN'T EAT ANOTHER BITE!
THAT'S TOO BAD, BECAUSE VEGETABLES WERE NOT THE ONLY THINGS I BOUGHT.
HUH? WHAT DO YOU MEAN?
WHAT ELSE DID YOU GET?
SWEETS!
5

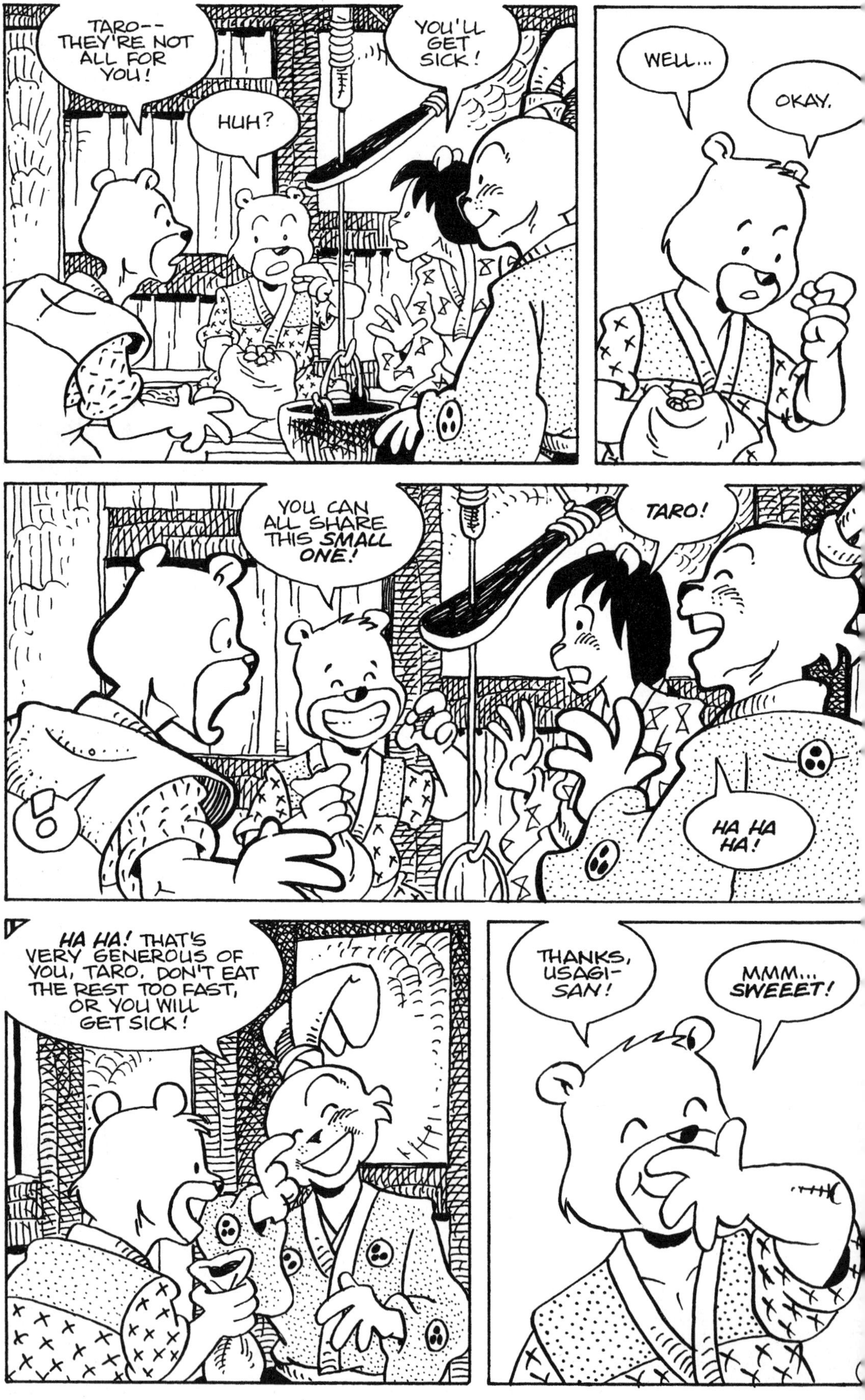
TARO-- THEY'RE NOT ALL FOR YOU!
HUH?
YOU'LL GET SICK!
WELL...
OKAY.
YOU CAN ALL SHARE THIS *SMALL ONE!*
*TARO!*
*HA HA HA!*
*HA HA!* THAT'S VERY GENEROUS OF YOU, TARO. DON'T EAT THE REST TOO FAST, OR YOU WILL GET SICK!
THANKS, USAGI-SAN!
MMM... *SWEEET!*

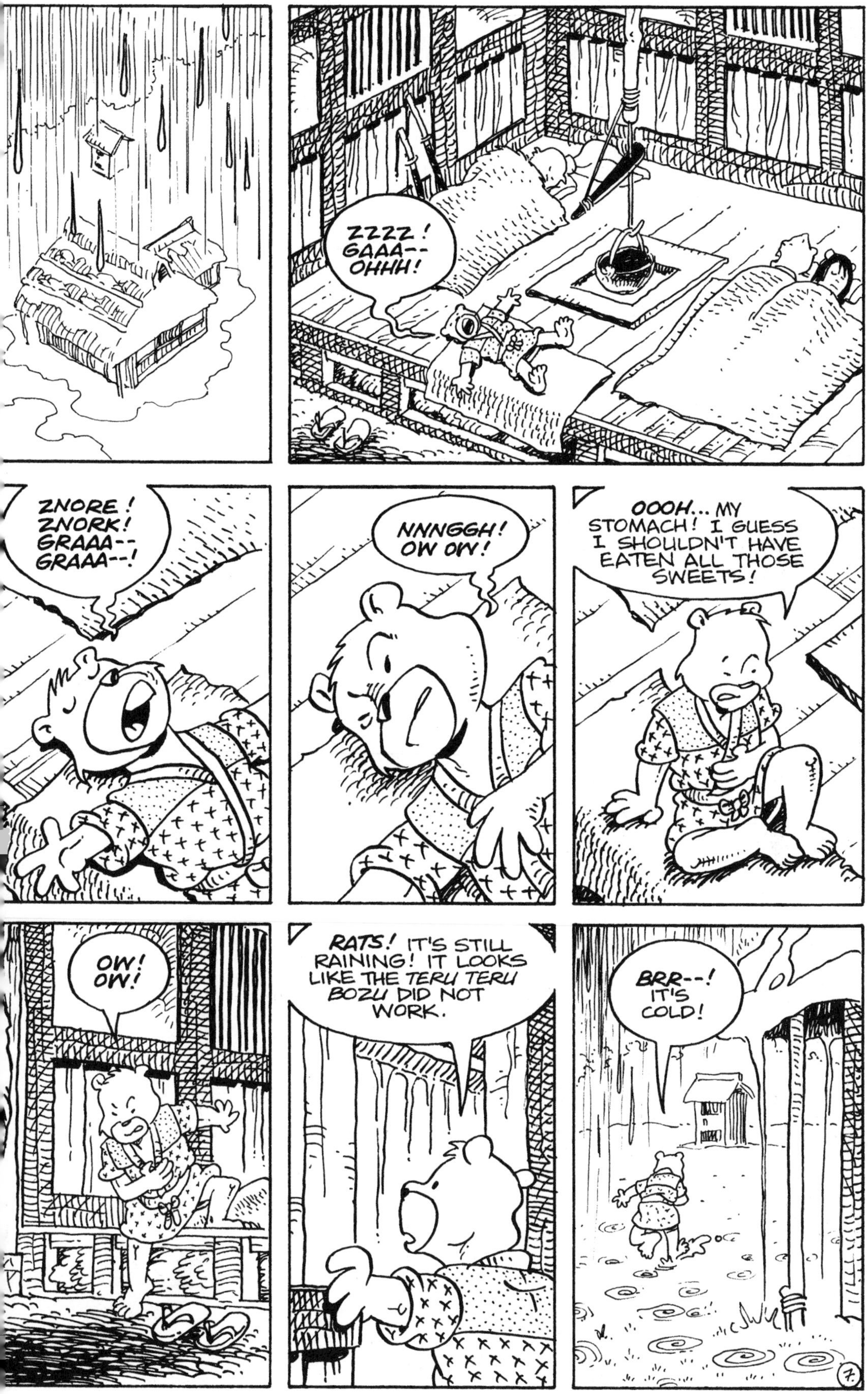
ZZZZ! GAAA--OHHH!
ZNORE! ZNORK! GRAAA--GRAAA--!
NNNGGH! OW OW!
OOOH... MY STOMACH! I GUESS I SHOULDN'T HAVE EATEN ALL THOSE SWEETS!
OW! OW!
RATS! IT'S STILL RAINING! IT LOOKS LIKE THE TERU TERU BOZU DID NOT WORK.
BRR--! IT'S COLD!
7.

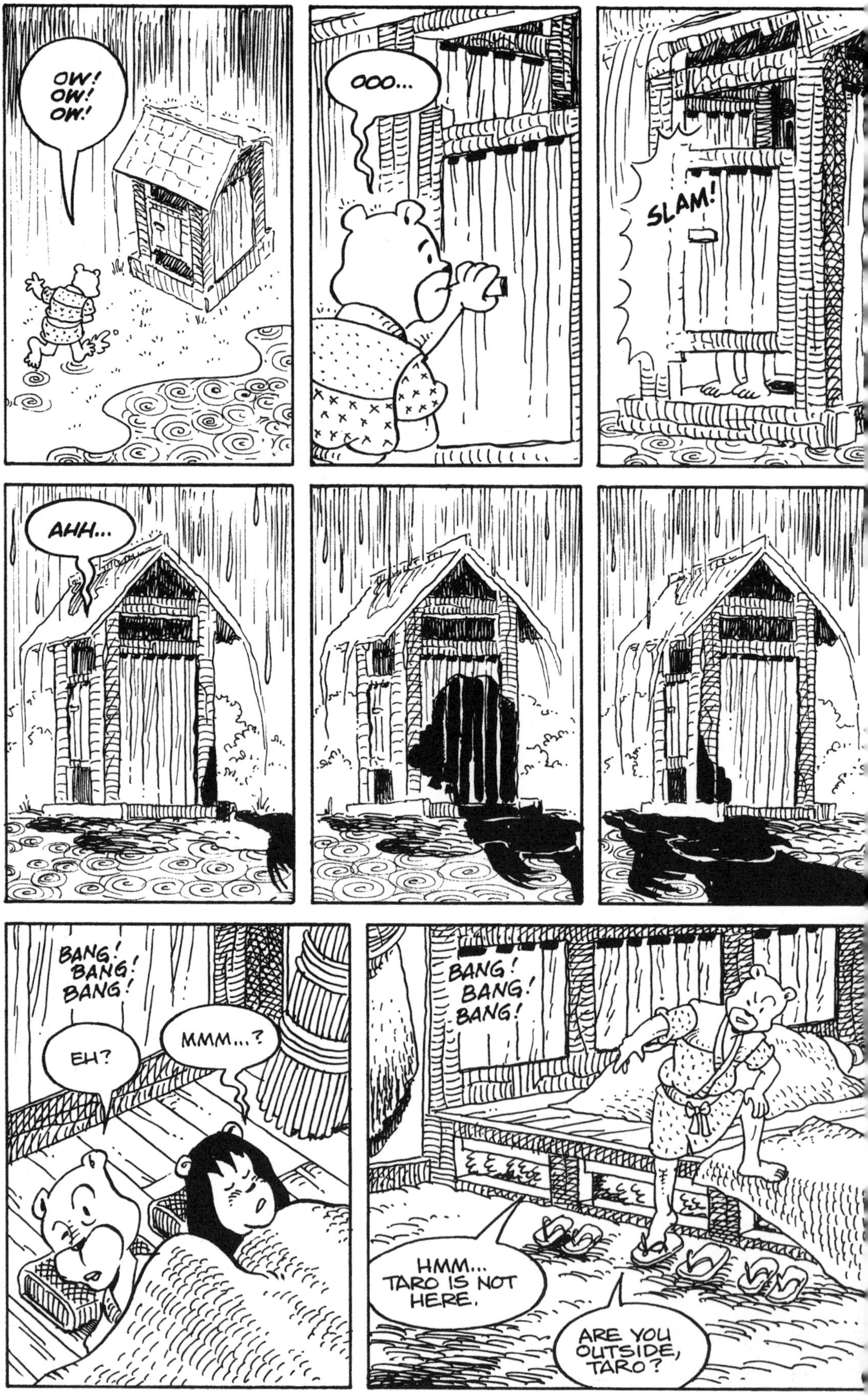
OW! OW! OW!
OOO...
SLAM!
AHH...
BANG! BANG! BANG!
EH?
MMM...?
BANG! BANG! BANG!
HMM... TARO IS NOT HERE.
ARE YOU OUTSIDE, TARO?

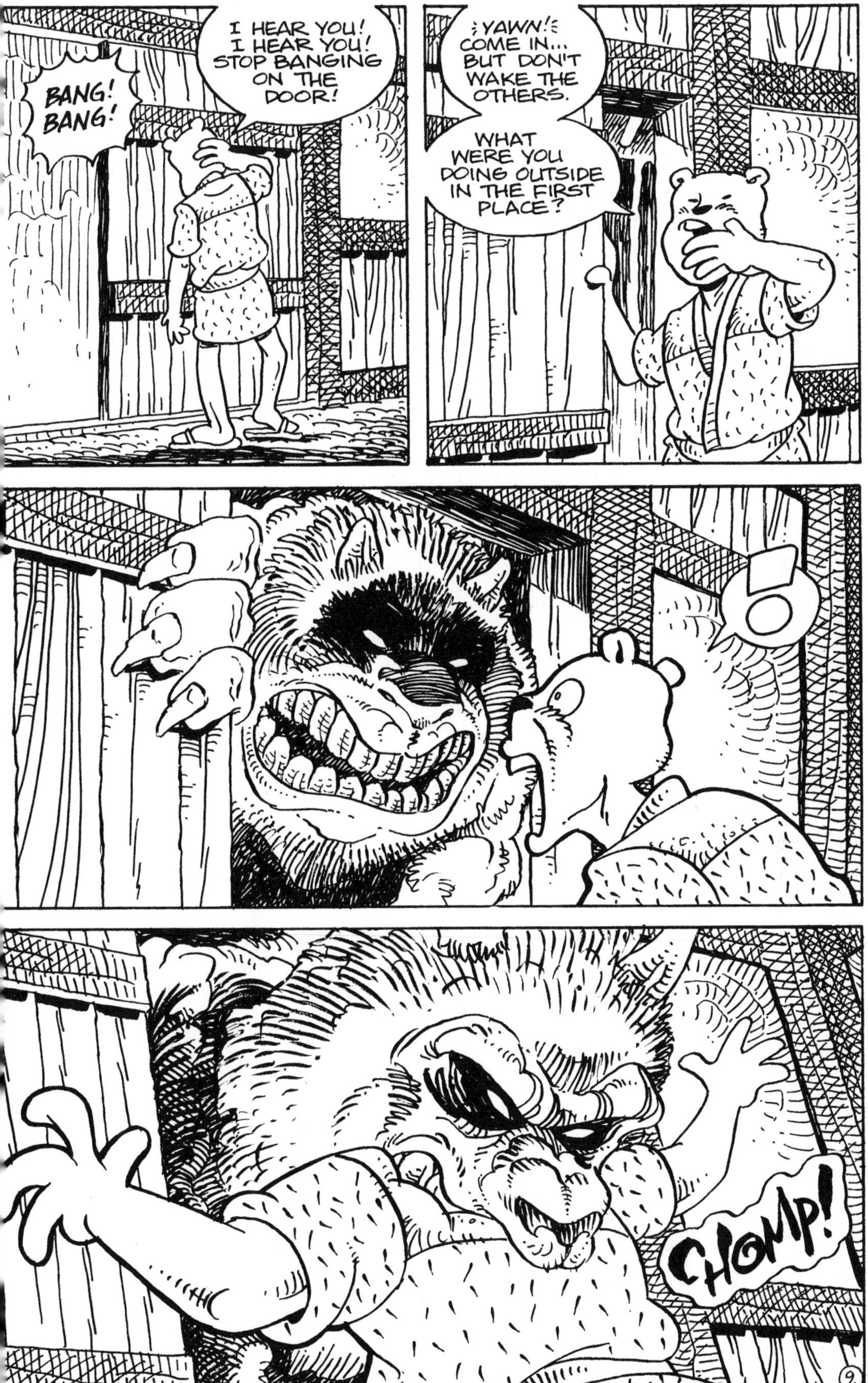
BANG! BANG!
I HEAR YOU! I HEAR YOU! STOP BANGING ON THE DOOR!
¡YAWN¡ COME IN... BUT DON'T WAKE THE OTHERS.
WHAT WERE YOU DOING OUTSIDE IN THE FIRST PLACE?
!
CHOMP!
9.

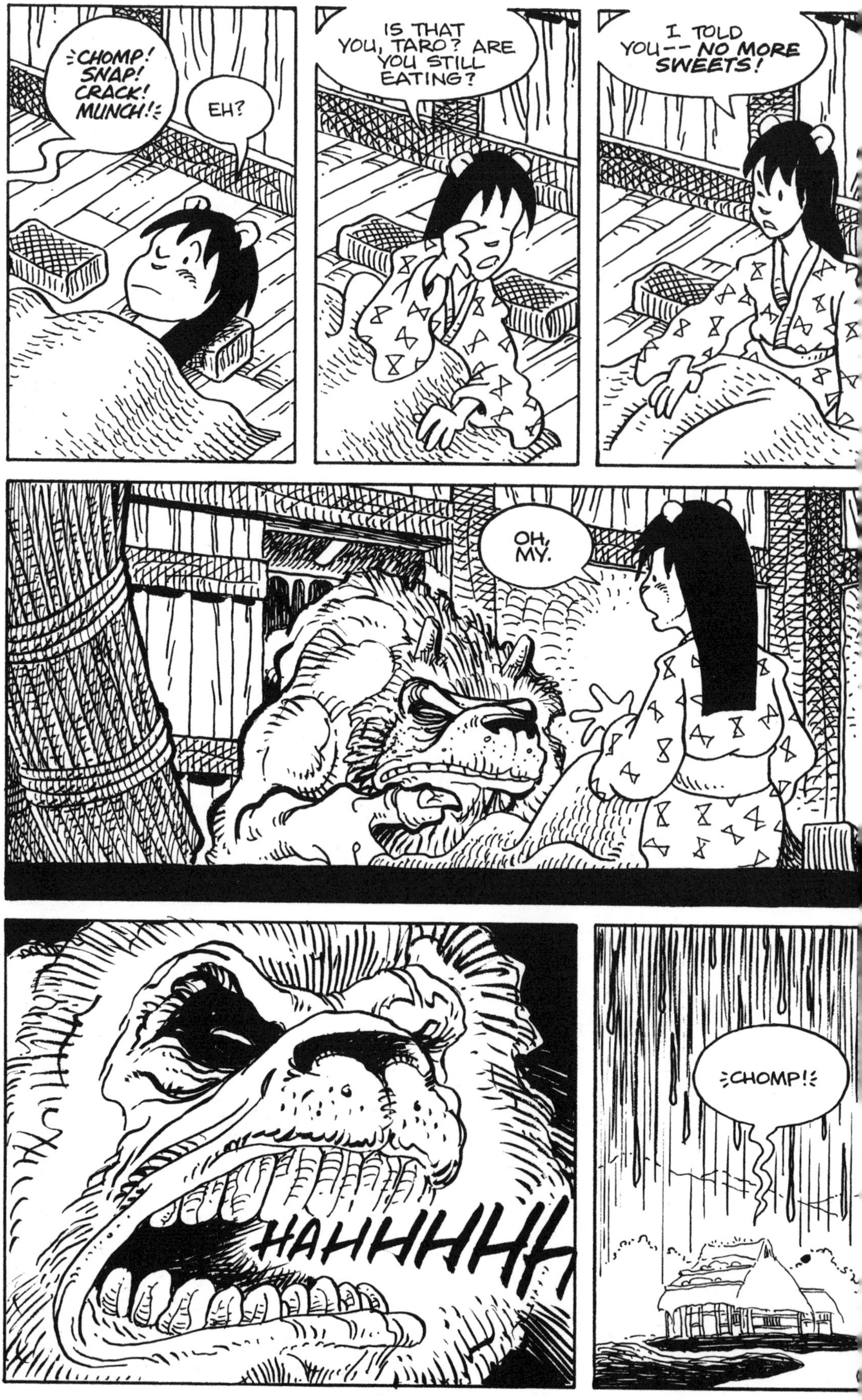
CHOMP! SNAP! CRACK! MUNCH!
EH?
IS THAT YOU, TARO? ARE YOU STILL EATING?
I TOLD YOU-- NO MORE SWEETS!
OH, MY.
HAHHHHH
CHOMP!

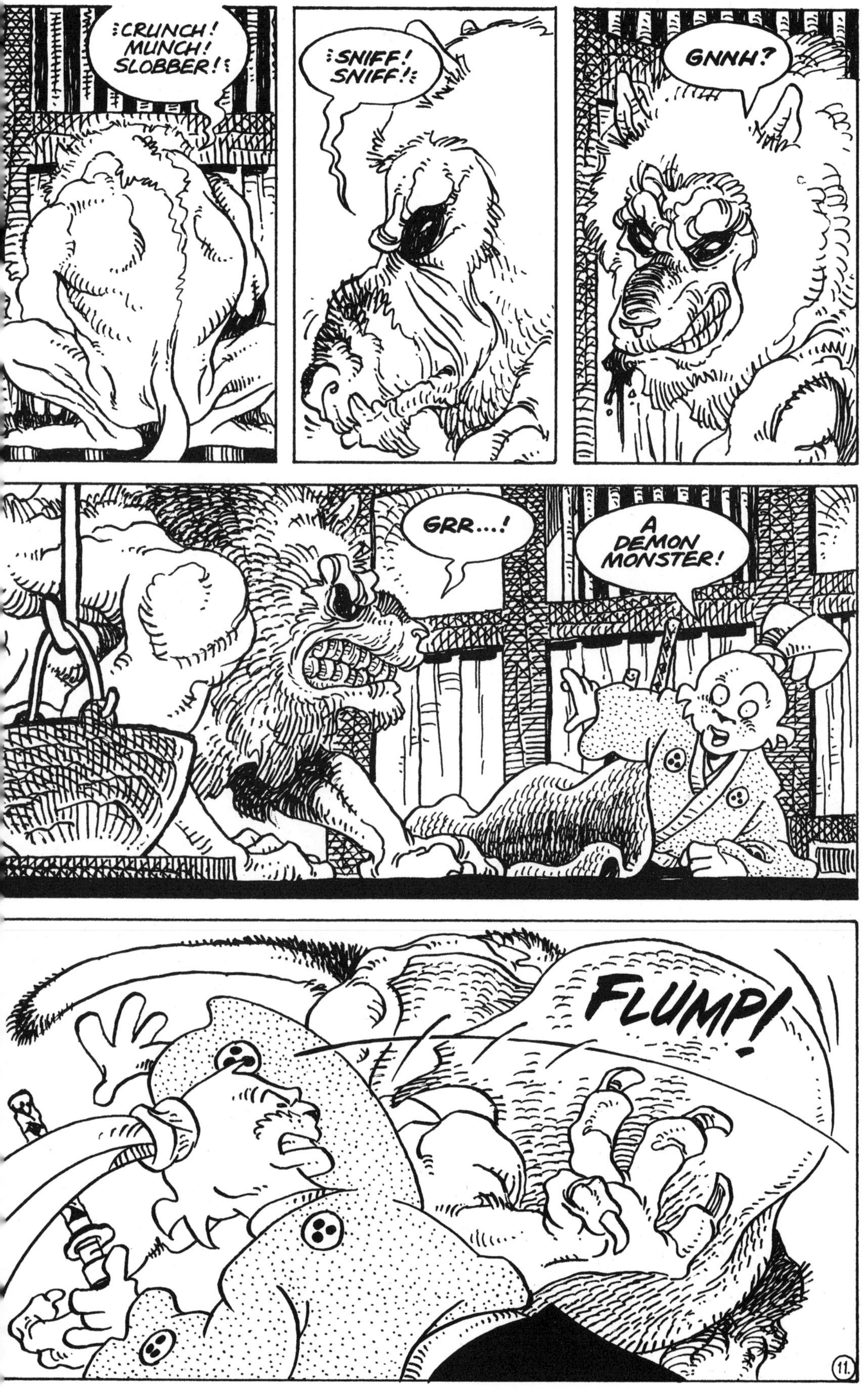
CRUNCH! MUNCH! SLOBBER!
SNIFF! SNIFF!
GNNH?
GRR...!
A DEMON MONSTER!
FLUMP!
11.

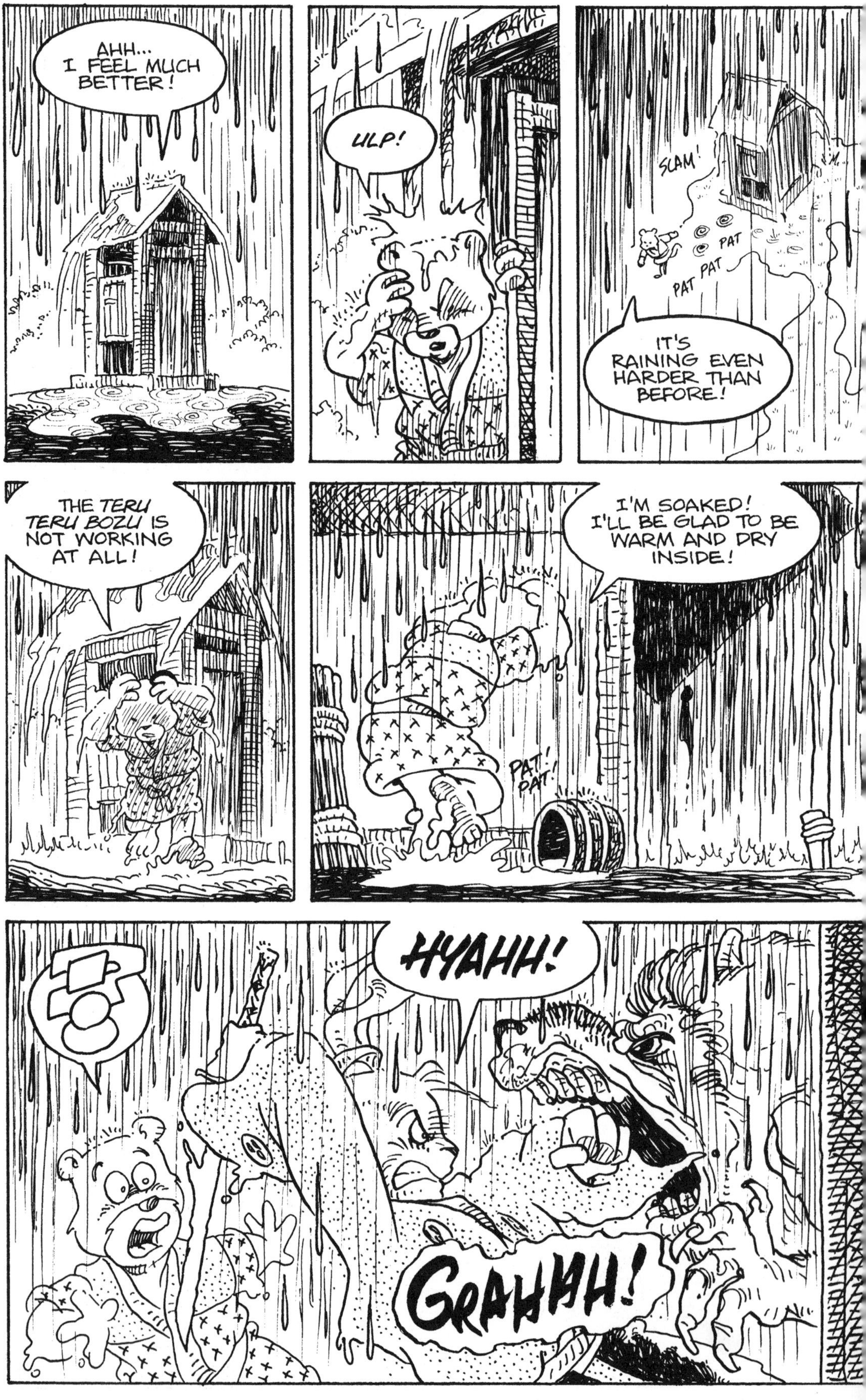
AHH... I FEEL MUCH BETTER!
ULP!
SLAM!
PAT PAT PAT
IT'S RAINING EVEN HARDER THAN BEFORE!
THE TERU TERU BOZU IS NOT WORKING AT ALL!
I'M SOAKED! I'LL BE GLAD TO BE WARM AND DRY INSIDE!
PAT! PAT!
HYAHH!
GRAHHH!

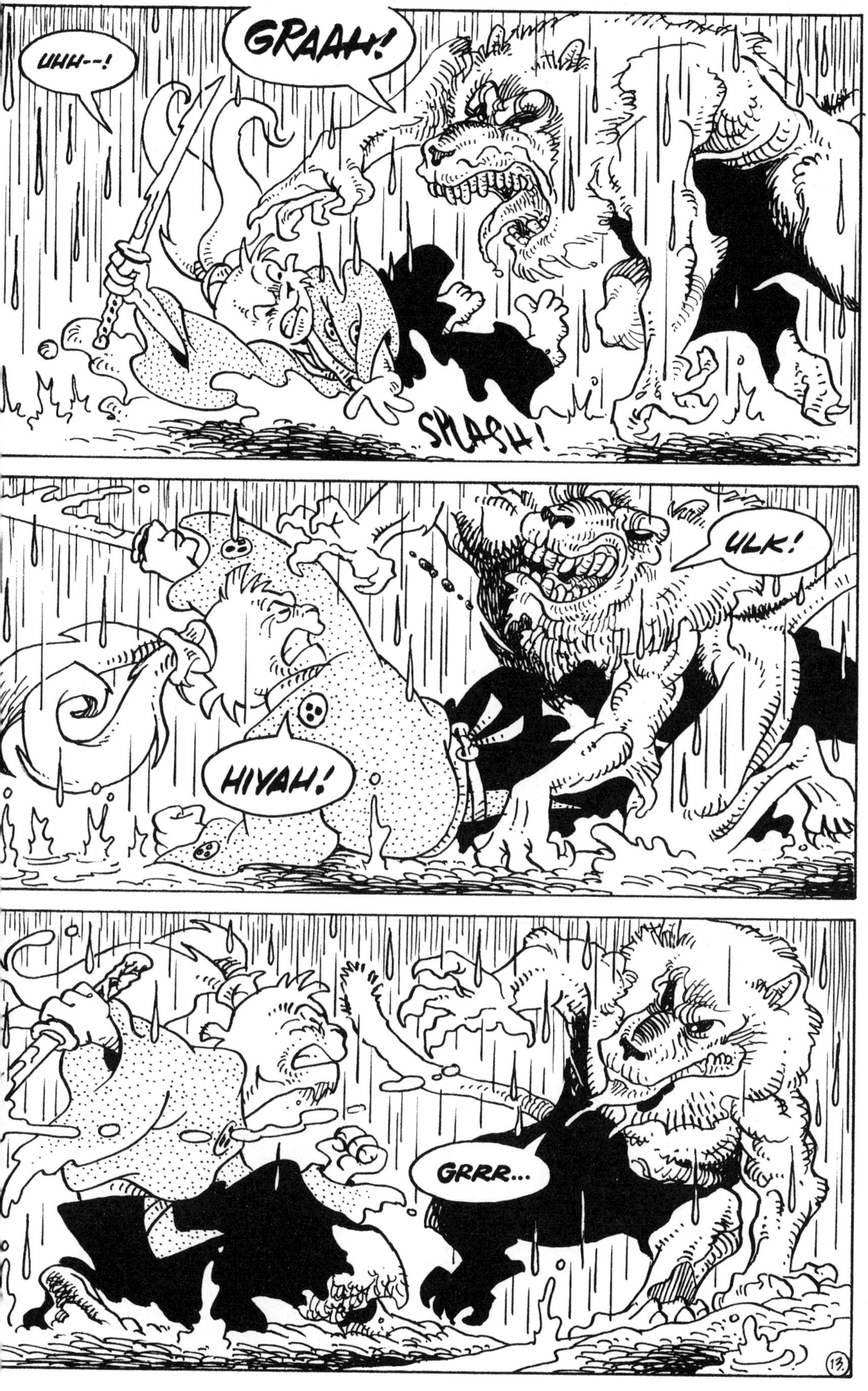
UHH--!
GRAAH!
SMASH!
ULK!
HIYAH!
GRRR...
13.

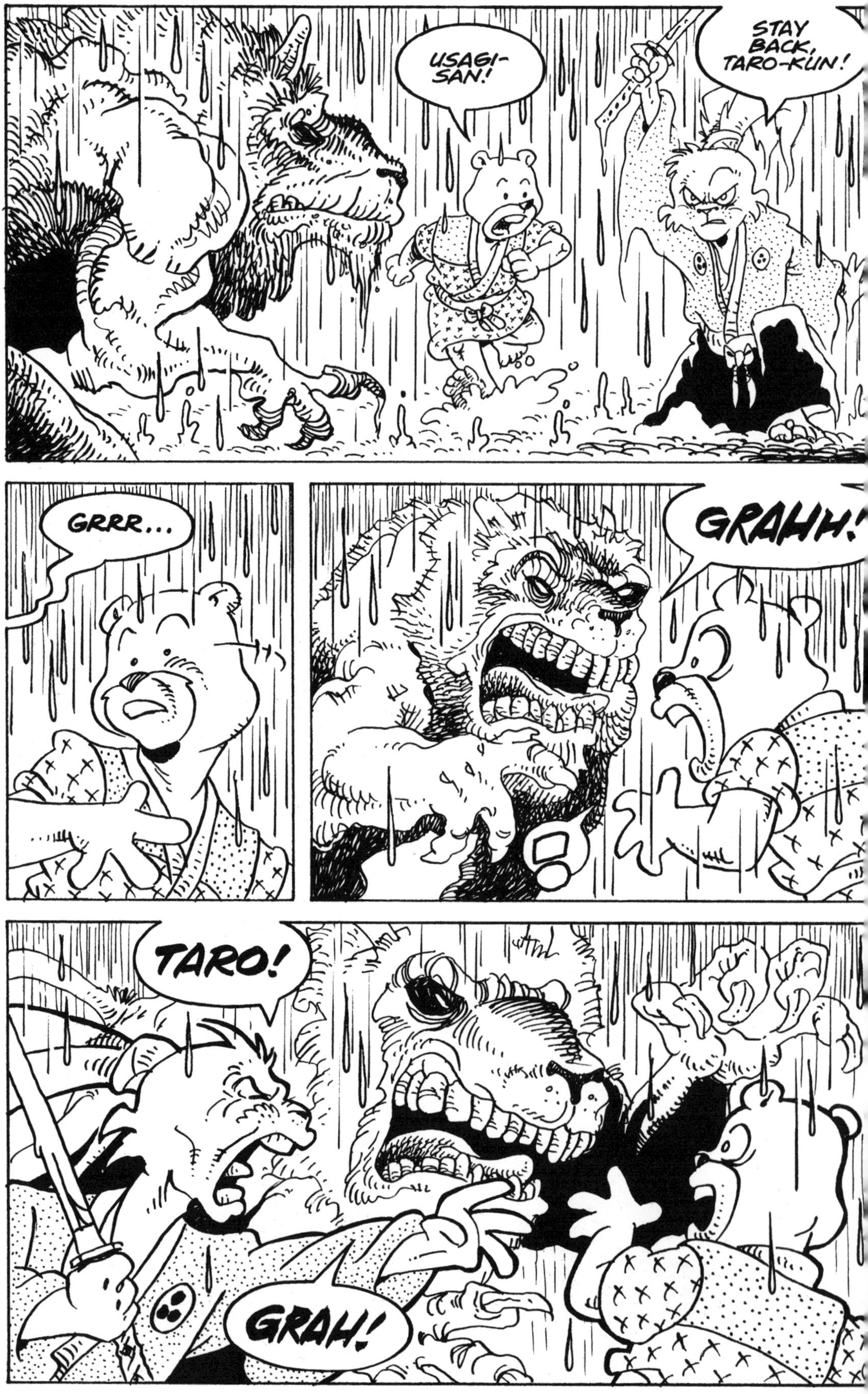
USAGI-SAN!
STAY BACK, TARO-KUN!
GRRR...
GRAHH!
TARO!
GRAH!

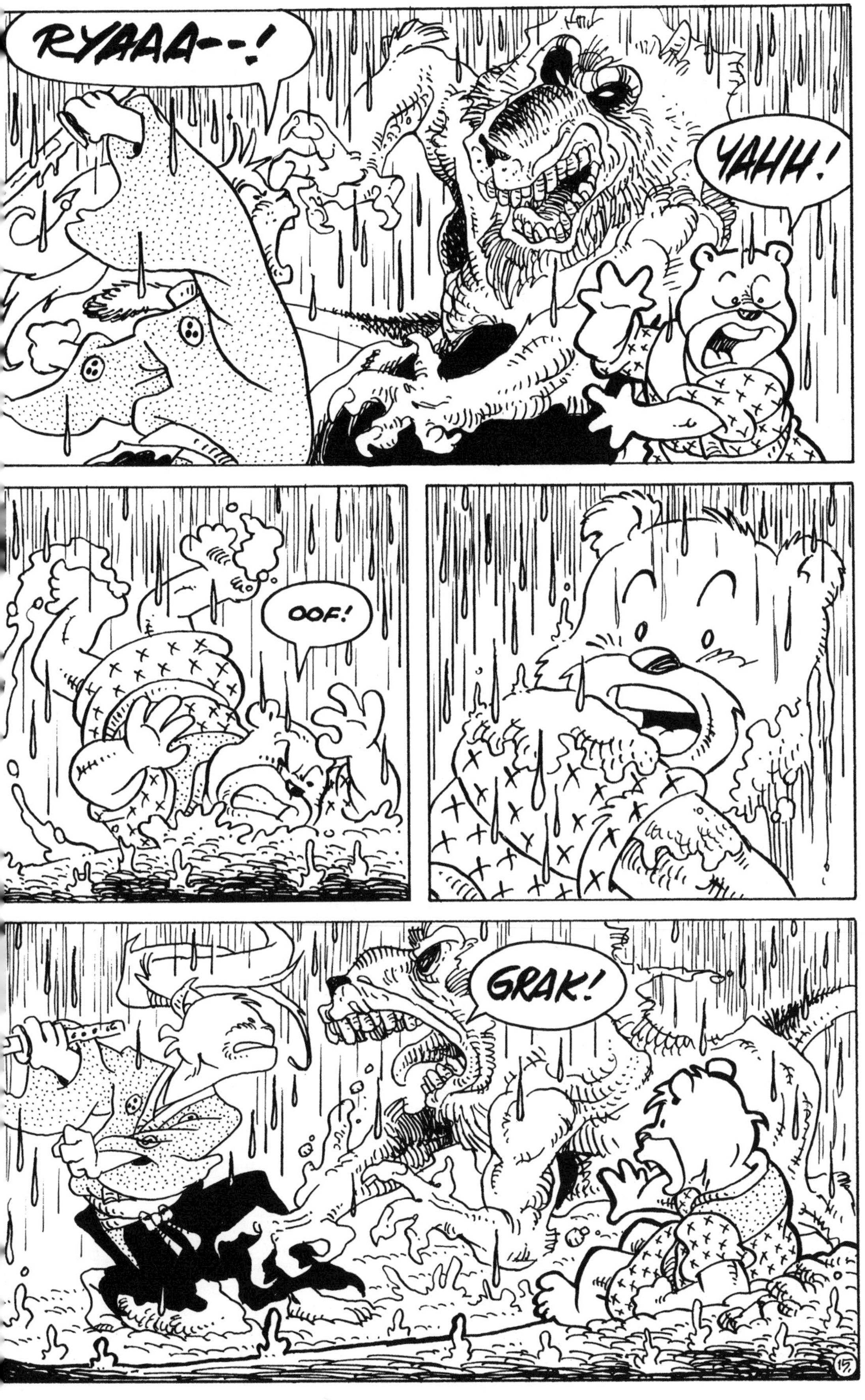
RYAAA--!
YAHH!
OOF!
GRAK!
15

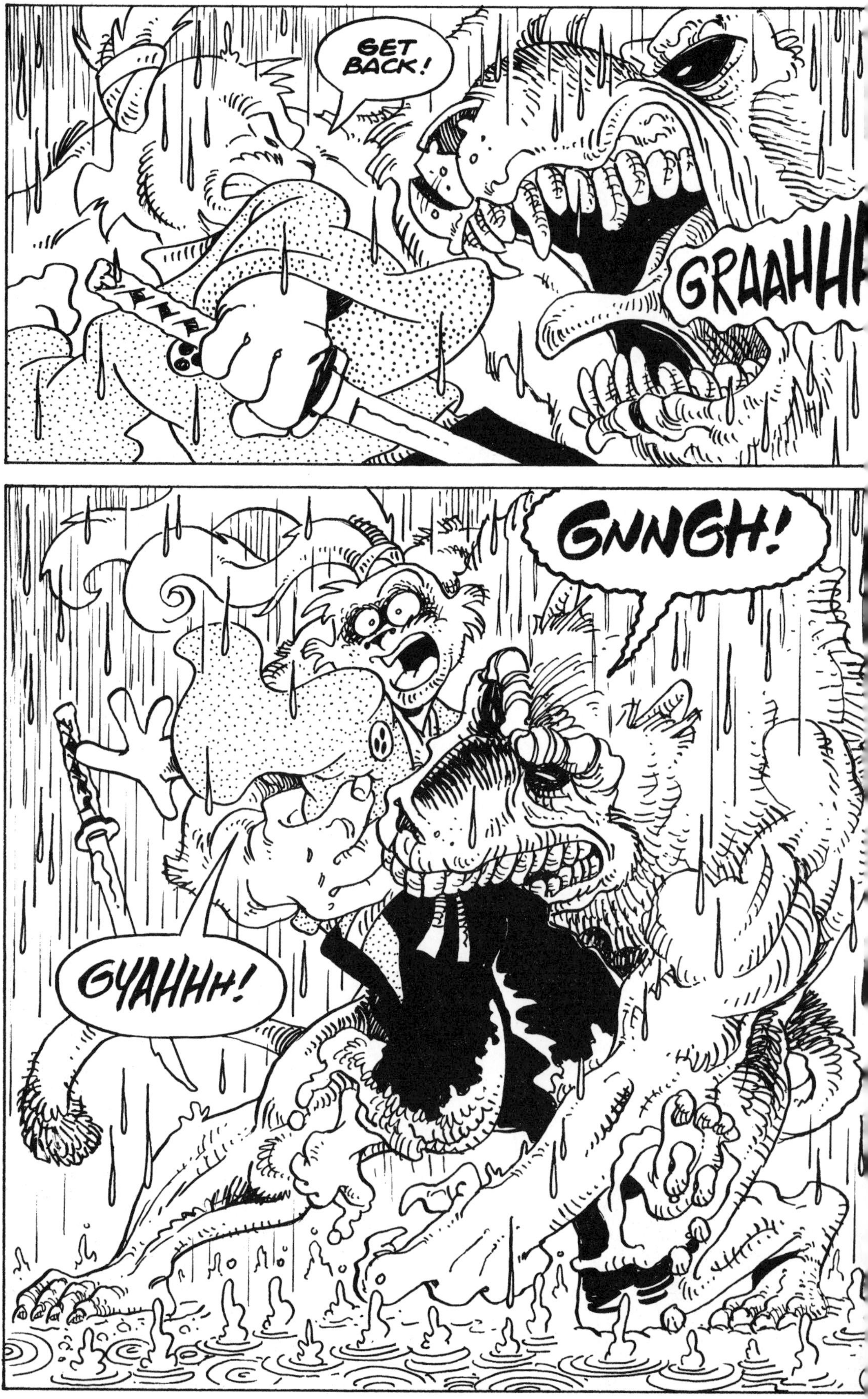
GET BACK!
GRAAHHH
GNNGH!
GYAHHH!

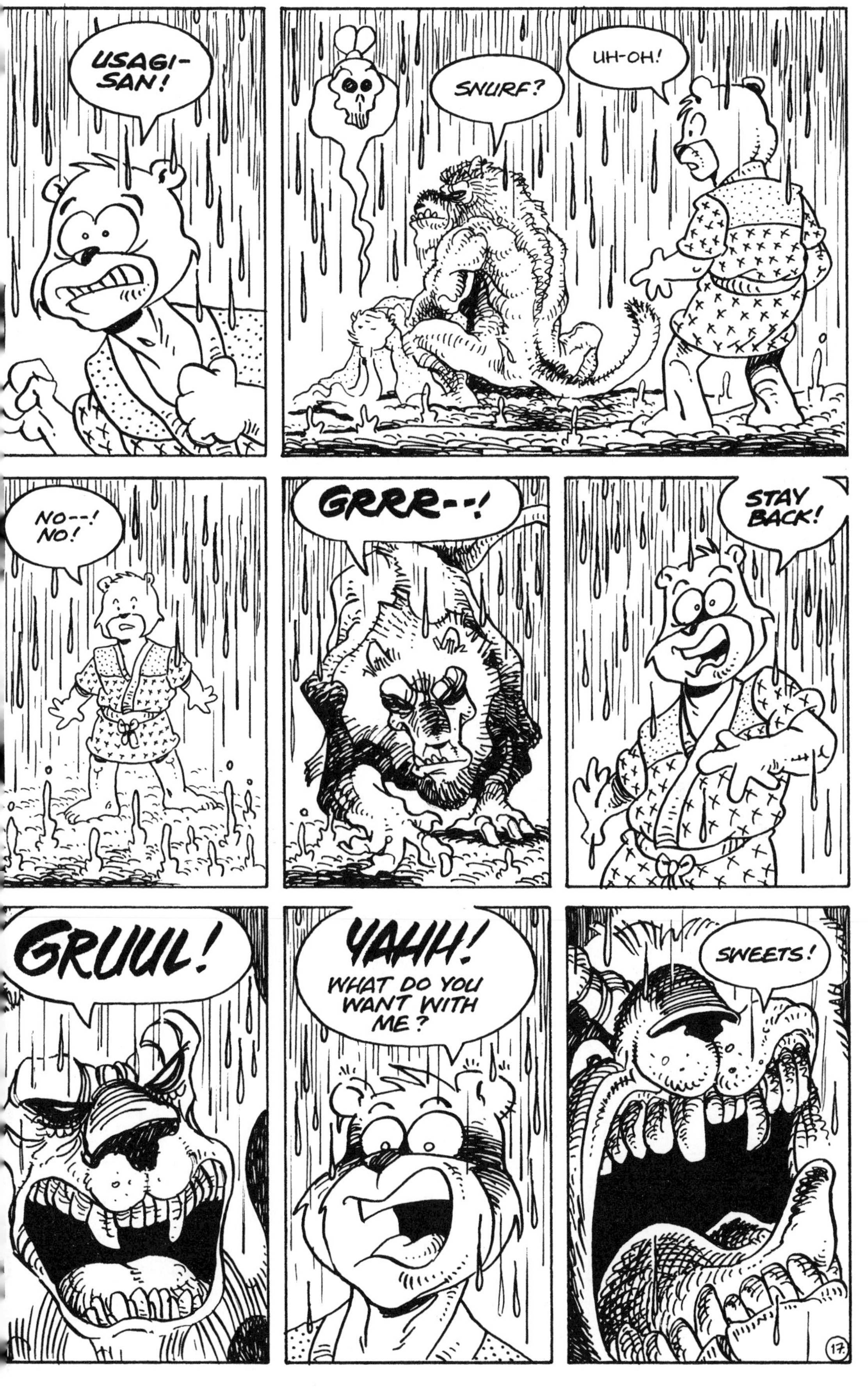
USAGI-SAN!
SNURF?
UH-OH!
NO--! NO!
GRRR--!
STAY BACK!
GRUUL!
YAHH! WHAT DO YOU WANT WITH ME?
SWEETS!
17.

**YAHH**
·Q·O·O·

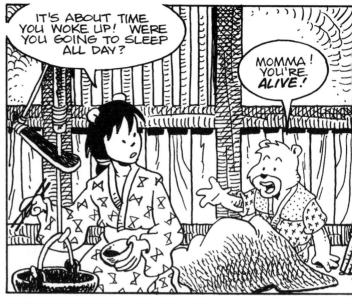
IT'S ABOUT TIME YOU WOKE UP! WERE YOU GOING TO SLEEP ALL DAY?

MOMMA! YOU'RE *ALIVE!*

OF COURSE I'M ALIVE! WHAT ARE YOU TALKING ABOUT? DID EATING ALL THOSE SWEETS GIVE YOU NIGHTMARES?

YOUR FATHER AND USAGI-SAN ARE OUTSIDE. THEY'VE BEEN WAITING FOR YOU ALL MORNING.

*USAGI-SAN!* I HAD FORGOTTEN HE'S HERE!

OH-- IT'S *BRIGHT!*

GOOD MORNING, SLEEPY-HEAD!

I-IT STOPPED RAINING.

304

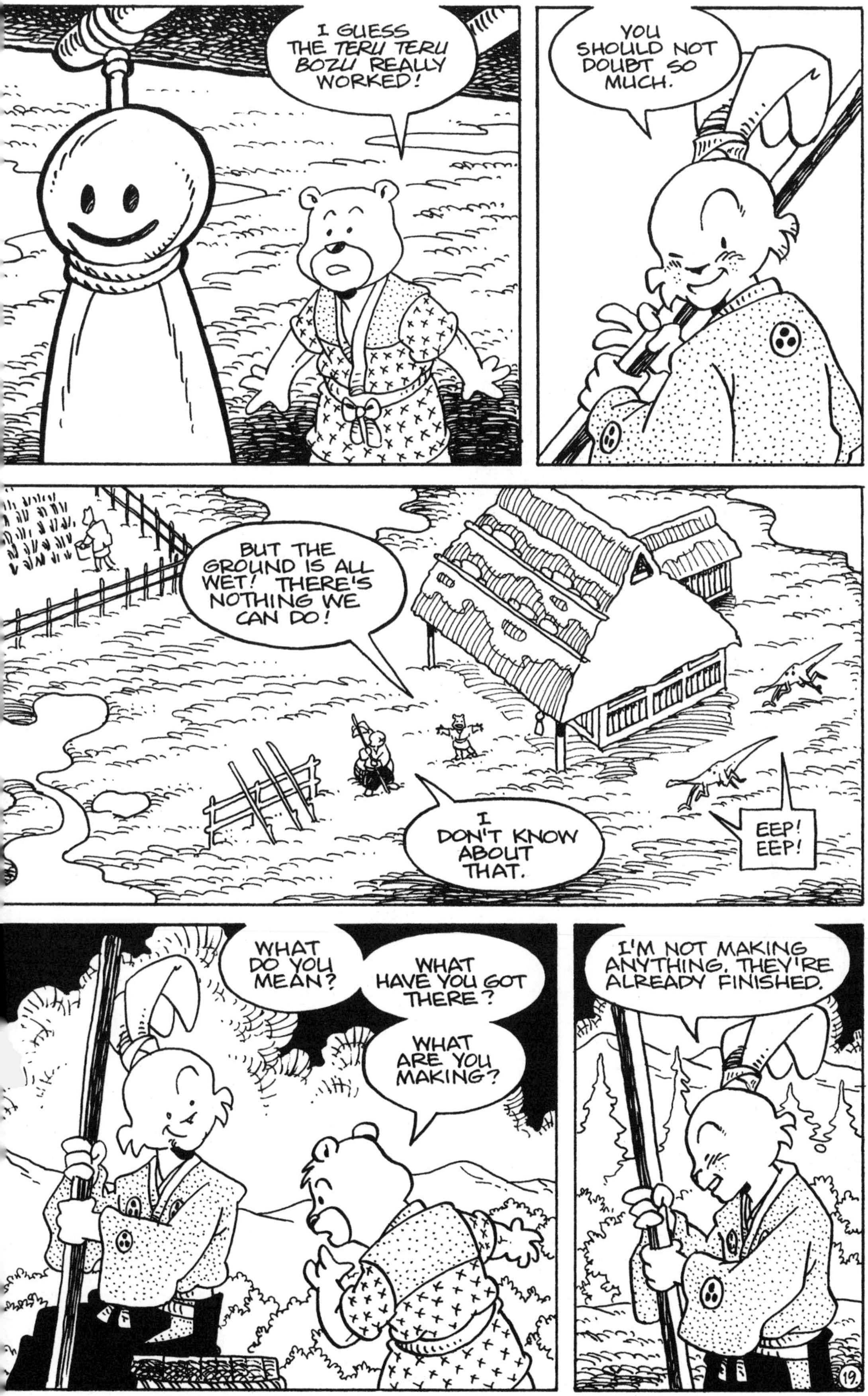
I GUESS THE *TERU TERU BOZU* REALLY WORKED!
YOU SHOULD NOT DOUBT SO MUCH.
BUT THE GROUND IS ALL WET! THERE'S NOTHING WE CAN DO!
I DON'T KNOW ABOUT THAT.
EEP! EEP!
WHAT DO YOU MEAN?
WHAT HAVE YOU GOT THERE?
WHAT ARE YOU MAKING?
I'M NOT MAKING ANYTHING. THEY'RE ALREADY FINISHED.
19.

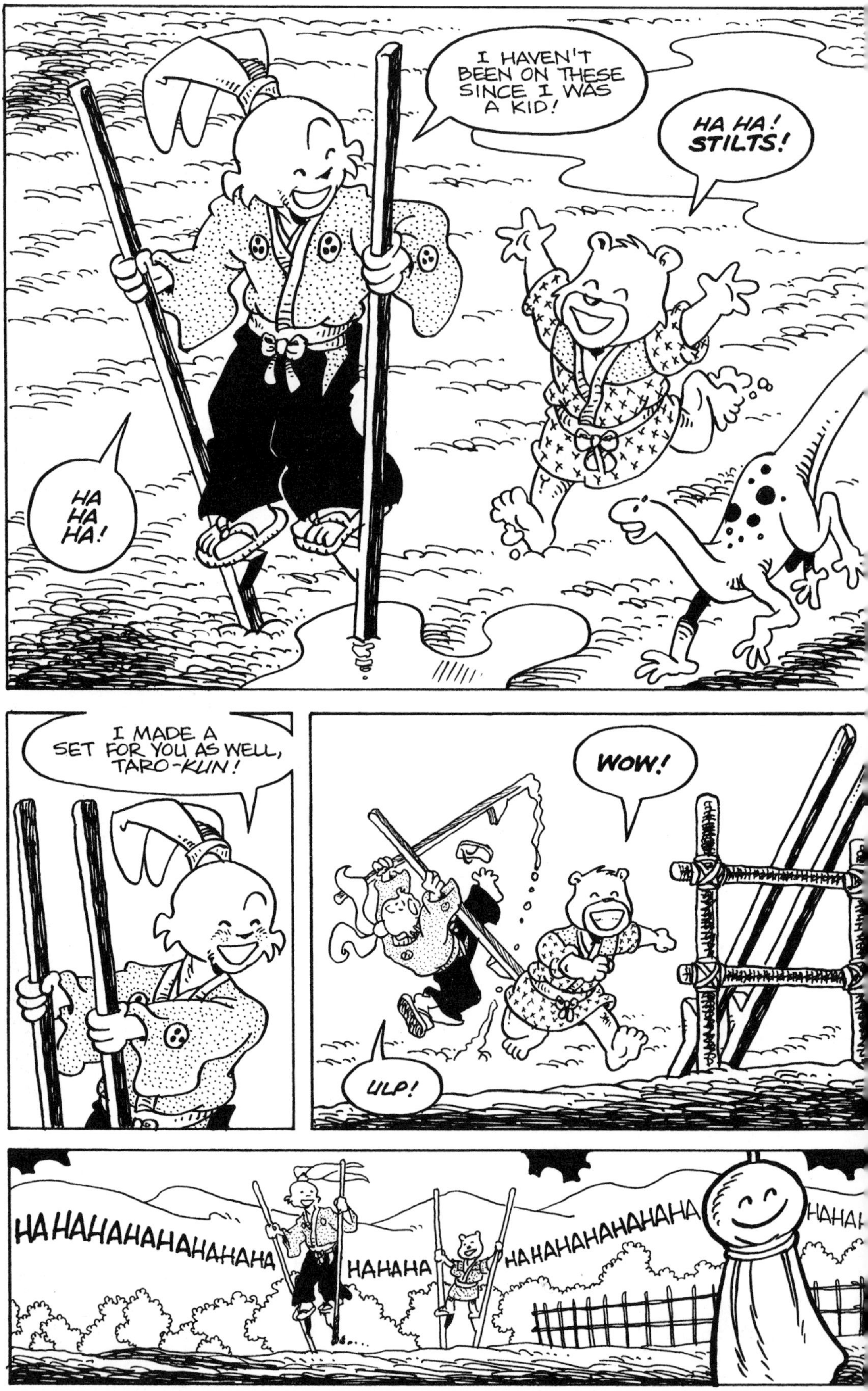
I HAVEN'T BEEN ON THESE SINCE I WAS A KID!
HA HA! STILTS!
HA HA HA!
I MADE A SET FOR YOU AS WELL, TARO-KUN!
WOW!
ULP!
HAHAHAHAHAHAHAHAHA
HAHAHA
HAHAHAHAHAHAHAHAHA
HAHAH

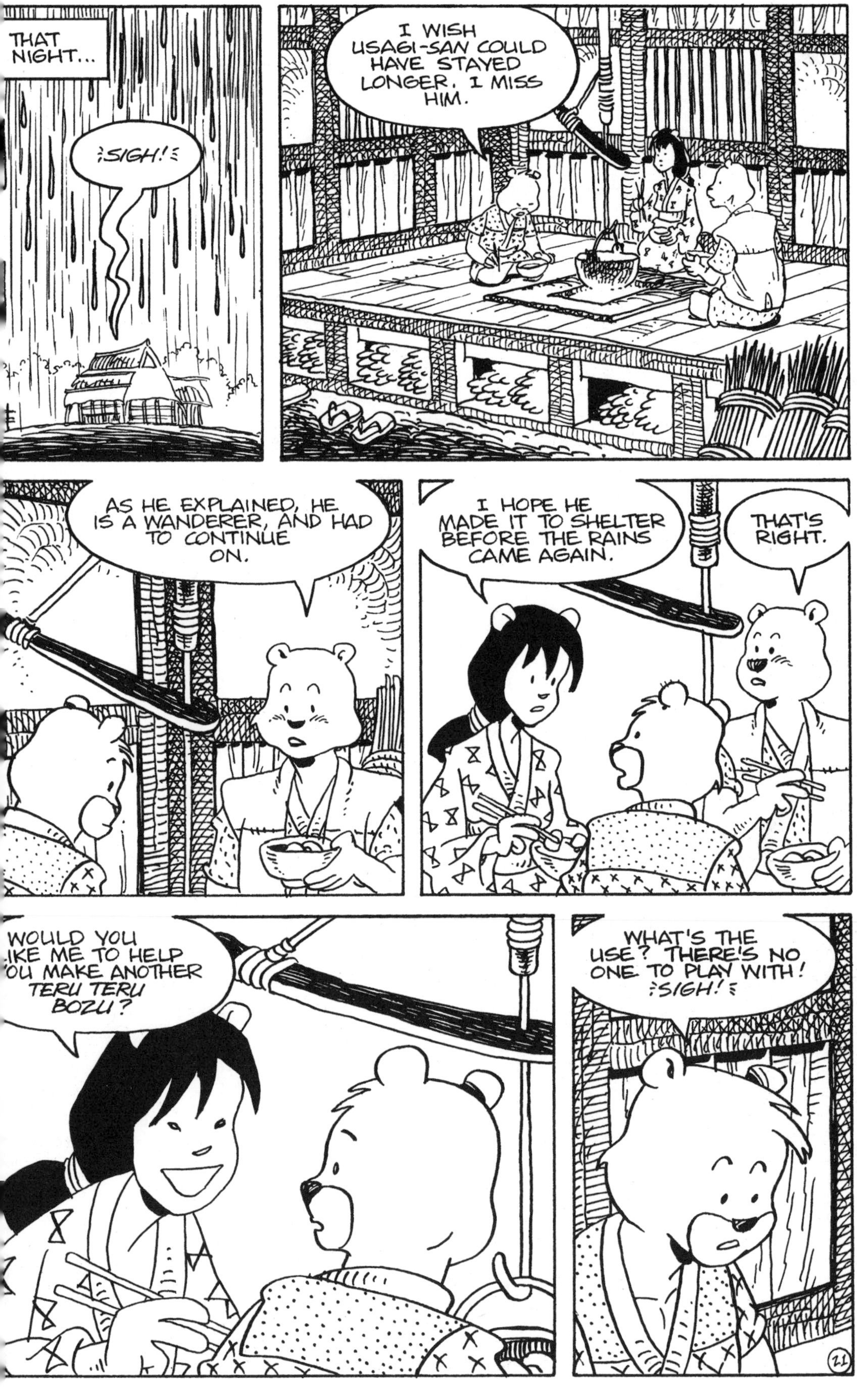
THAT NIGHT...
¡SIGH!
I WISH USAGI-SAN COULD HAVE STAYED LONGER. I MISS HIM.
AS HE EXPLAINED, HE IS A WANDERER, AND HAD TO CONTINUE ON.
I HOPE HE MADE IT TO SHELTER BEFORE THE RAINS CAME AGAIN.
THAT'S RIGHT.
WOULD YOU LIKE ME TO HELP YOU MAKE ANOTHER *TERU TERU BOZU*?
WHAT'S THE USE? THERE'S NO ONE TO PLAY WITH! ¡SIGH!
21

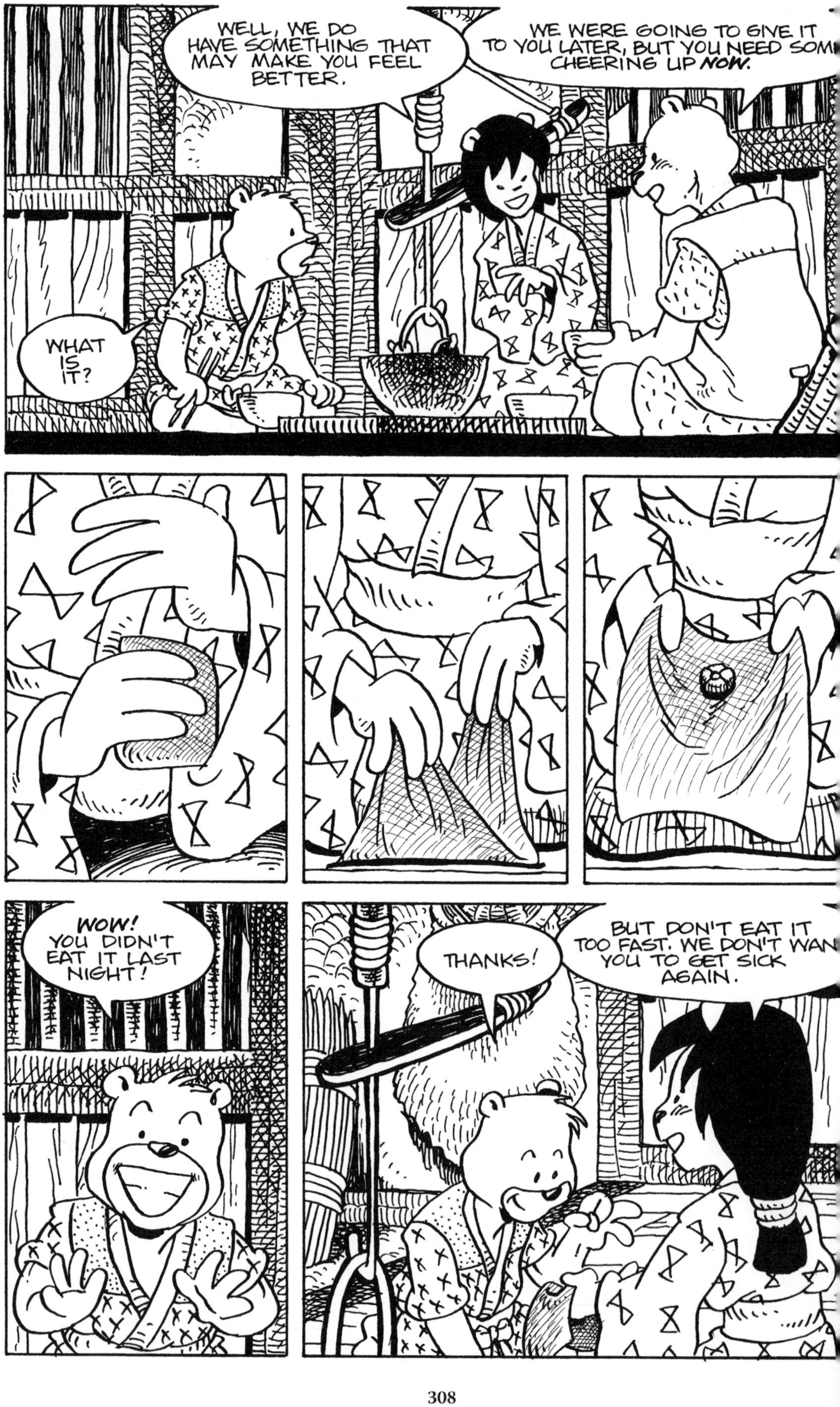
WELL, WE DO HAVE SOMETHING THAT MAY MAKE YOU FEEL BETTER.
WE WERE GOING TO GIVE IT TO YOU LATER, BUT YOU NEED SOM CHEERING UP **NOW**.
WHAT IS IT?
**WOW!** YOU DIDN'T EAT IT LAST NIGHT!
THANKS!
BUT DON'T EAT IT TOO FAST. WE DON'T WAN YOU TO GET SICK AGAIN.

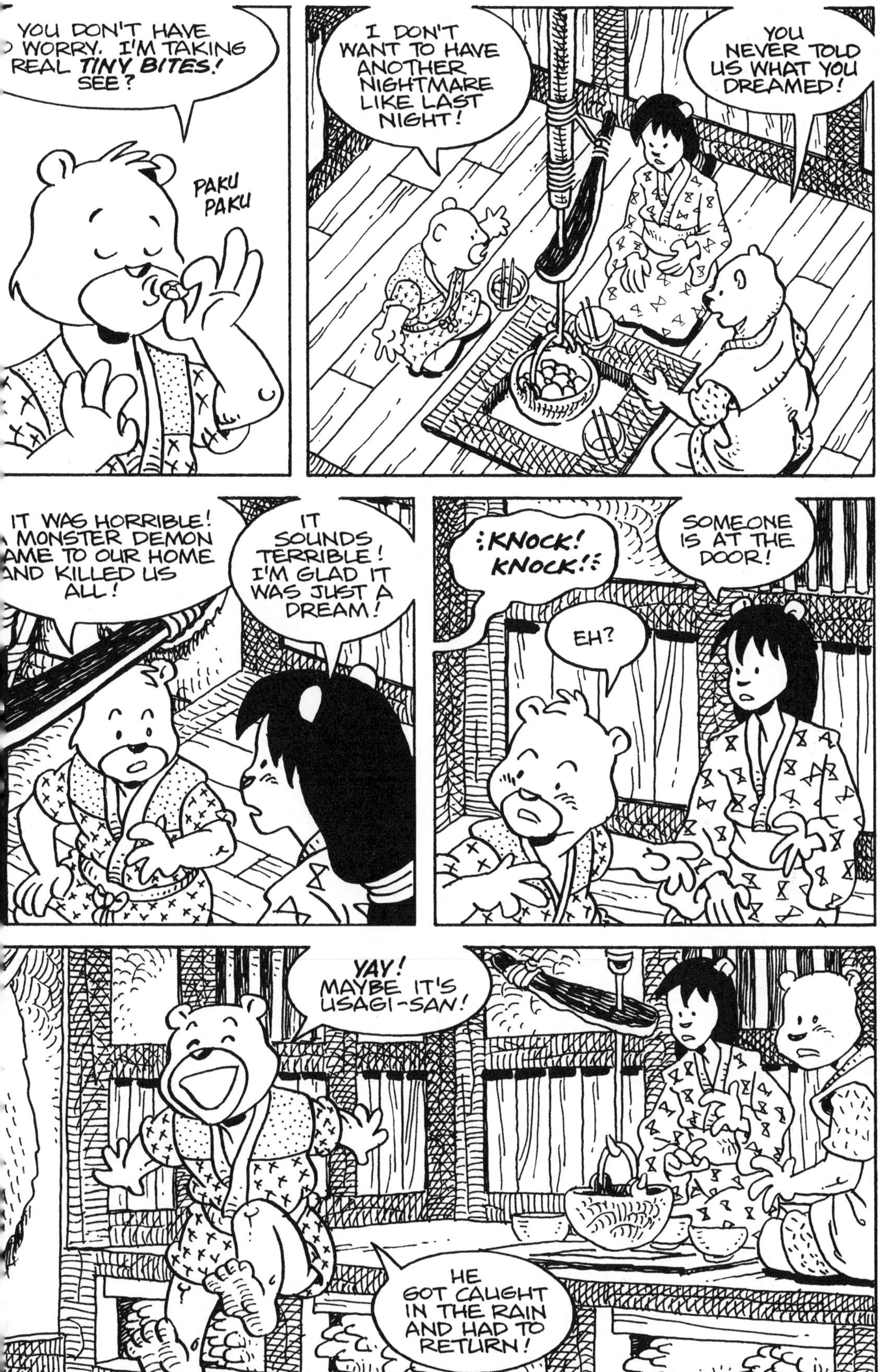
YOU DON'T HAVE
O WORRY. I'M TAKING
REAL TINY BITES!
SEE?
PAKU
PAKU
I DON'T
WANT TO HAVE
ANOTHER
NIGHTMARE
LIKE LAST
NIGHT!
YOU
NEVER TOLD
US WHAT YOU
DREAMED!
IT WAS HORRIBLE!
MONSTER DEMON
AME TO OUR HOME
AND KILLED US
ALL!
IT
SOUNDS
TERRIBLE!
I'M GLAD IT
WAS JUST A
DREAM!
KNOCK!
KNOCK!
SOMEONE
IS AT THE
DOOR!
EH?
YAY!
MAYBE IT'S
USAGI-SAN!
HE
GOT CAUGHT
IN THE RAIN
AND HAD TO
RETURN!
23

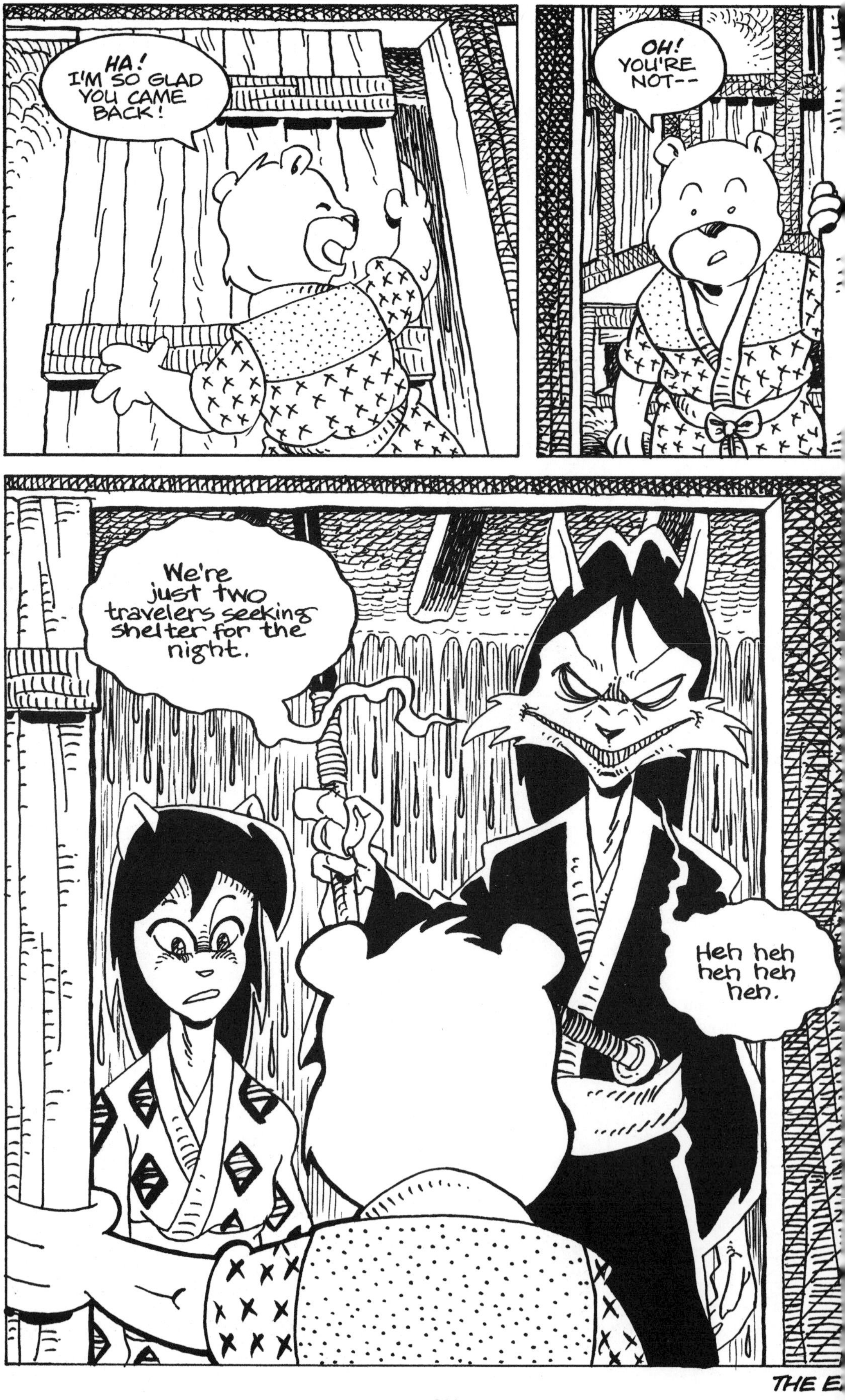
HA! I'M SO GLAD YOU CAME BACK!
OH! YOU'RE NOT--
We're just two travelers seeking shelter for the night.
Heh heh heh heh heh.
THE E

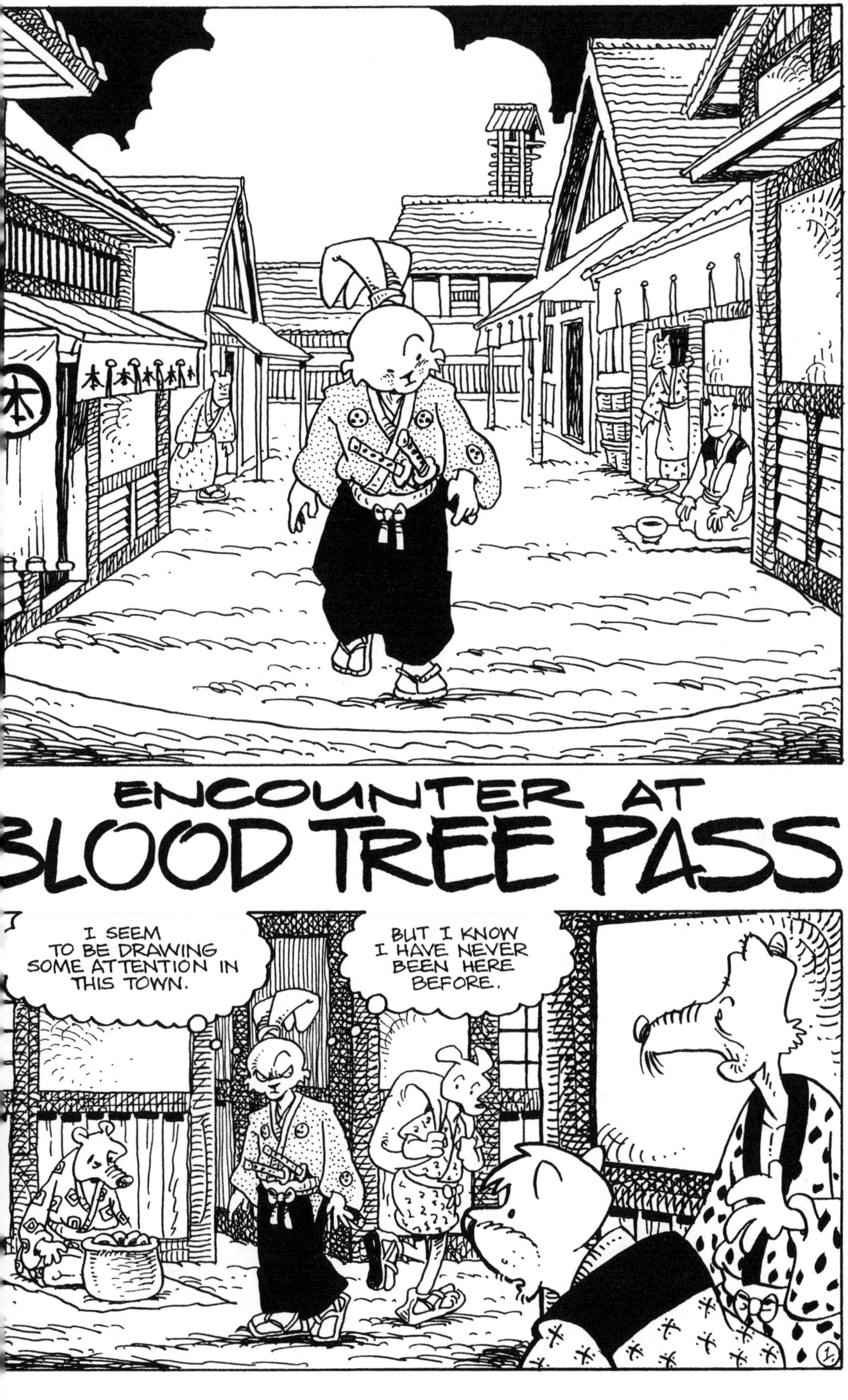
ENCOUNTER AT
BLOOD TREE PASS
I SEEM TO BE DRAWING SOME ATTENTION IN THIS TOWN.
BUT I KNOW I HAVE NEVER BEEN HERE BEFORE.

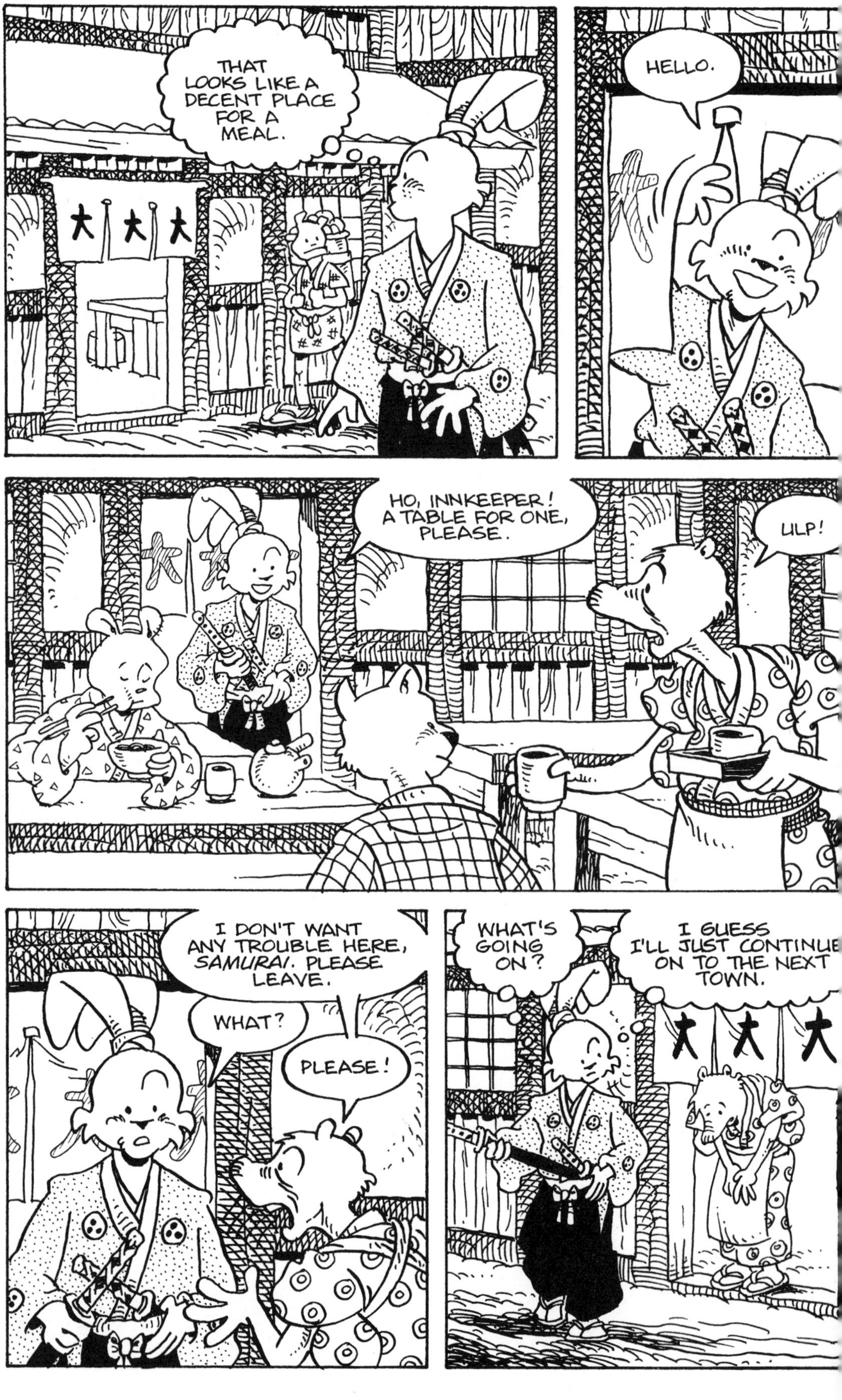
THAT LOOKS LIKE A DECENT PLACE FOR A MEAL.
HELLO.
HO, INNKEEPER! A TABLE FOR ONE, PLEASE.
ULP!
I DON'T WANT ANY TROUBLE HERE, SAMURAI. PLEASE LEAVE.
WHAT?
PLEASE!
WHAT'S GOING ON?
I GUESS I'LL JUST CONTINUE ON TO THE NEXT TOWN.

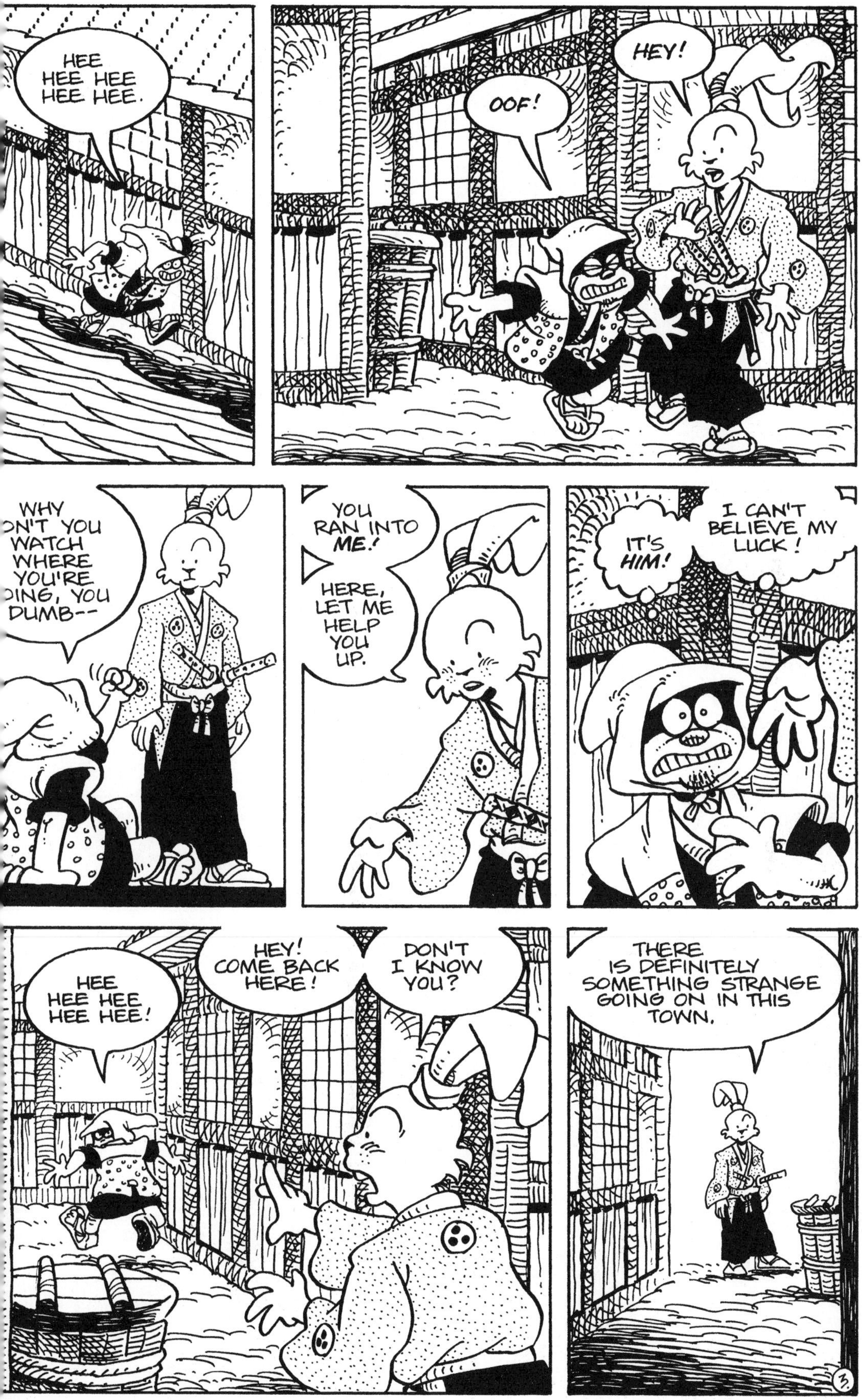
HEE HEE HEE HEE HEE.
OOF!
HEY!
WHY DON'T YOU WATCH WHERE YOU'RE GOING, YOU DUMB--
YOU RAN INTO ME!
HERE, LET ME HELP YOU UP.
IT'S HIM!
I CAN'T BELIEVE MY LUCK!
HEE HEE HEE HEE HEE!
HEY! COME BACK HERE!
DON'T I KNOW YOU?
THERE IS DEFINITELY SOMETHING STRANGE GOING ON IN THIS TOWN.
3

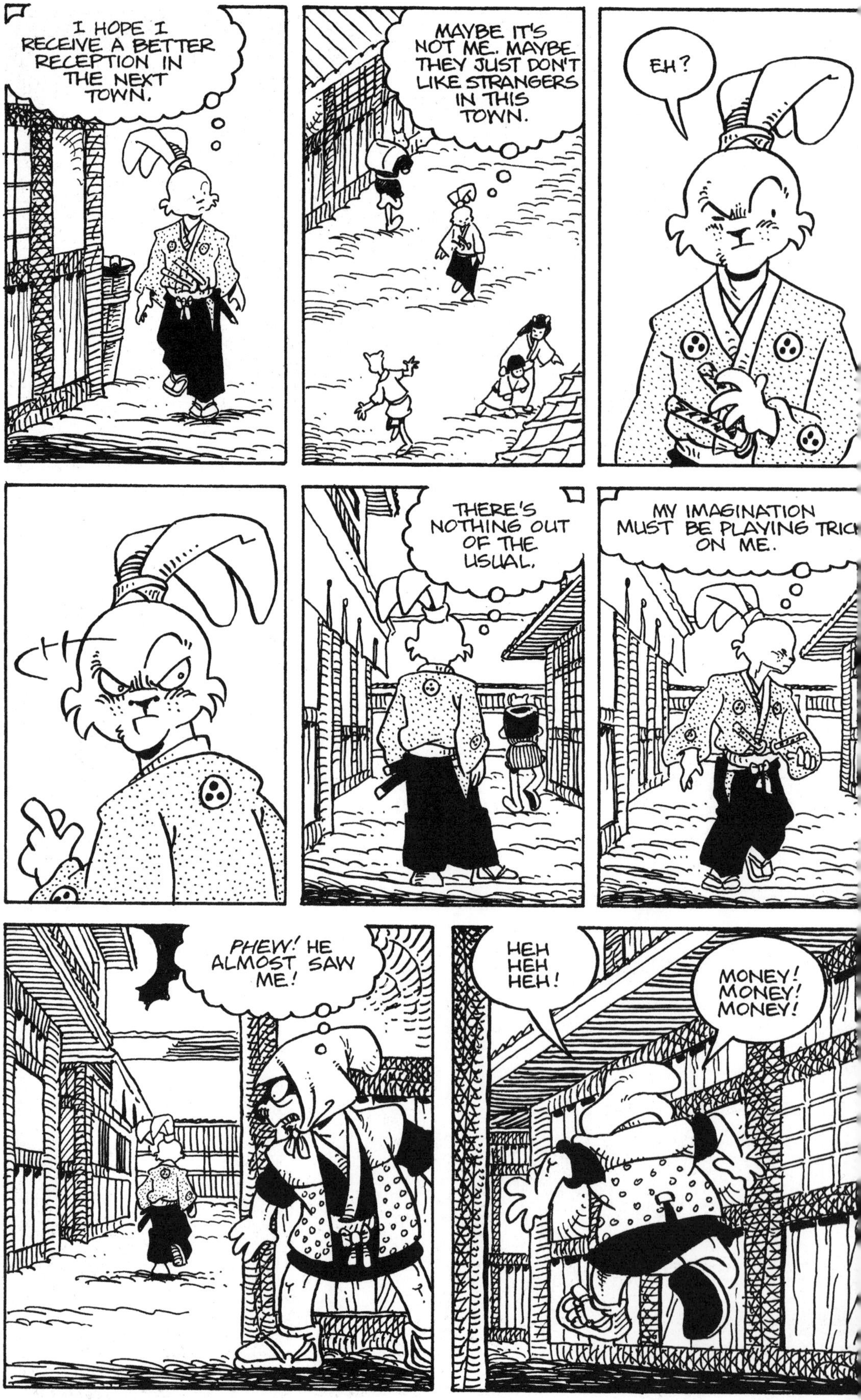
I HOPE I RECEIVE A BETTER RECEPTION IN THE NEXT TOWN.
MAYBE IT'S NOT ME. MAYBE THEY JUST DON'T LIKE STRANGERS IN THIS TOWN.
EH?
THERE'S NOTHING OUT OF THE USUAL.
MY IMAGINATION MUST BE PLAYING TRIC
ON ME.
PHEW! HE ALMOST SAW ME!
HEH HEH HEH!
MONEY! MONEY! MONEY!

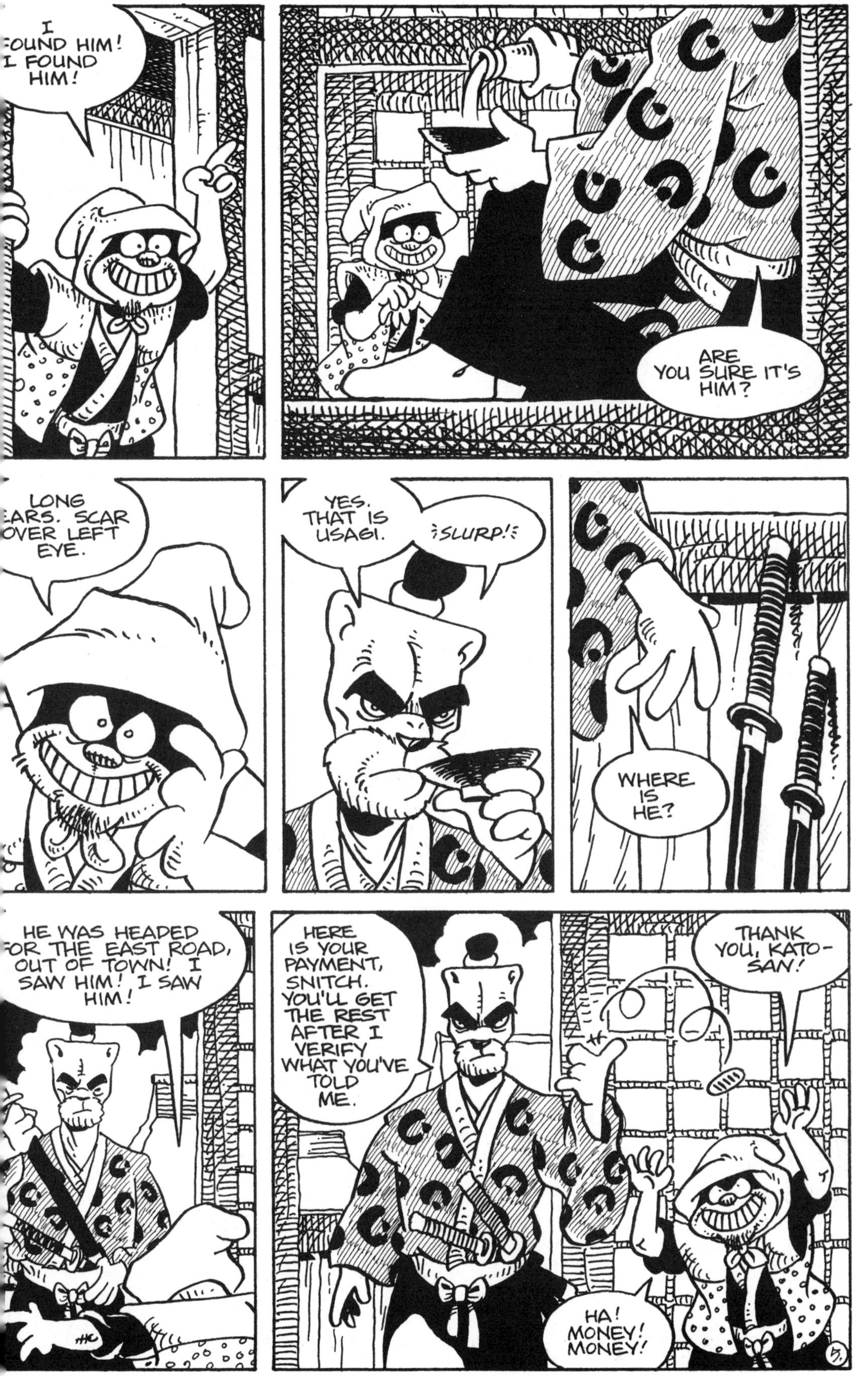

I FOUND HIM! I FOUND HIM!
ARE YOU SURE IT'S HIM?
LONG EARS. SCAR OVER LEFT EYE.
YES. THAT IS USAGI.
SLURP!
WHERE IS HE?
HE WAS HEADED FOR THE EAST ROAD, OUT OF TOWN! I SAW HIM! I SAW HIM!
HERE IS YOUR PAYMENT, SNITCH. YOU'LL GET THE REST AFTER I VERIFY WHAT YOU'VE TOLD ME.
THANK YOU, KATO-SAN!
HA! MONEY! MONEY!

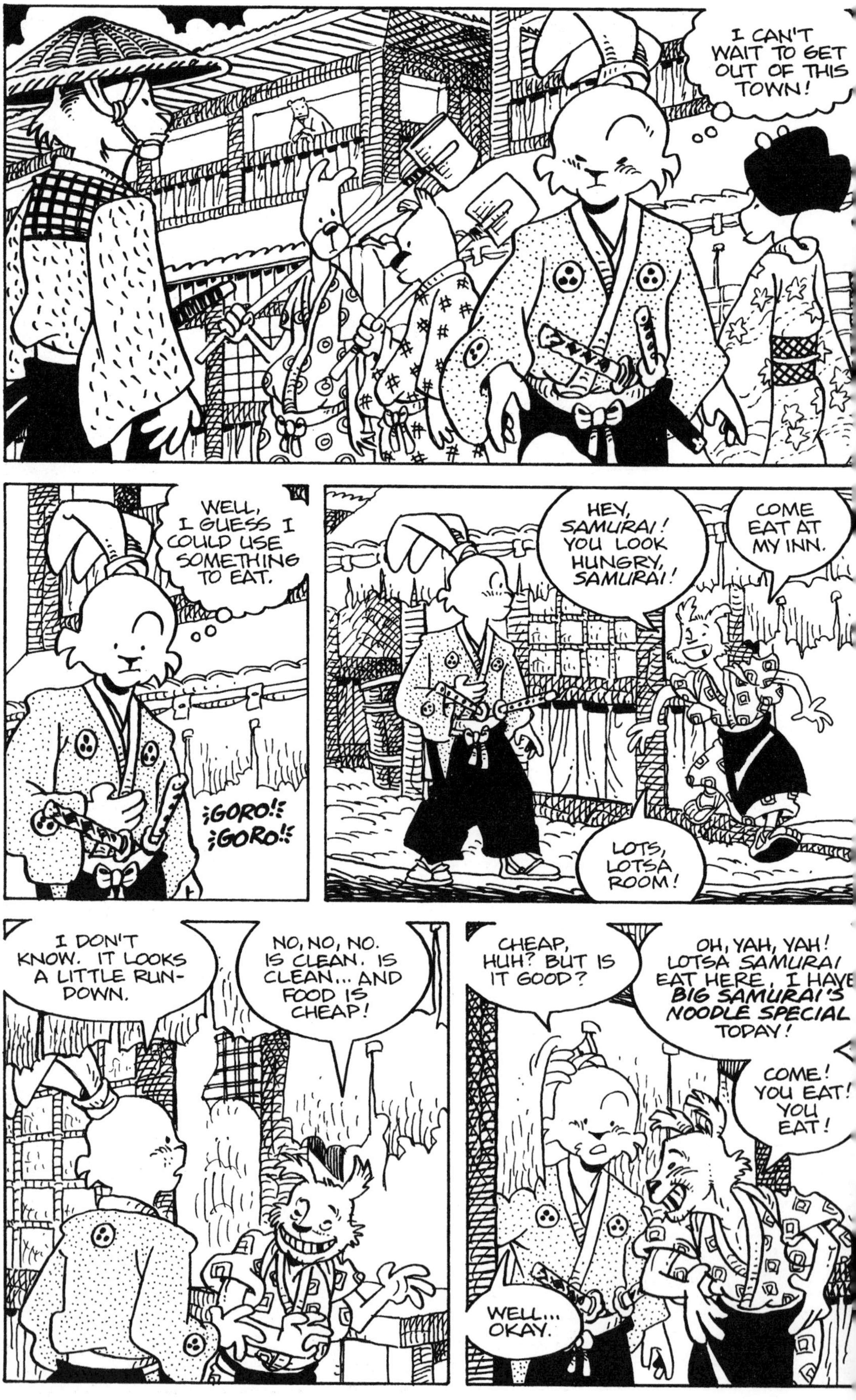

I CAN'T WAIT TO GET OUT OF THIS TOWN!
WELL, I GUESS I COULD USE SOMETHING TO EAT.
¡GORO!¡ ¡GORO!¡
HEY, SAMURAI! YOU LOOK HUNGRY, SAMURAI!
COME EAT AT MY INN.
LOTS, LOTSA ROOM!
I DON'T KNOW. IT LOOKS A LITTLE RUN-DOWN.
NO, NO, NO. IS CLEAN. IS CLEAN... AND FOOD IS CHEAP!
CHEAP, HUH? BUT IS IT GOOD?
OH, YAH, YAH! LOTSA SAMURAI EAT HERE, I HAVE BIG SAMURAI'S NOODLE SPECIAL TODAY!
COME! YOU EAT! YOU EAT!
WELL... OKAY.

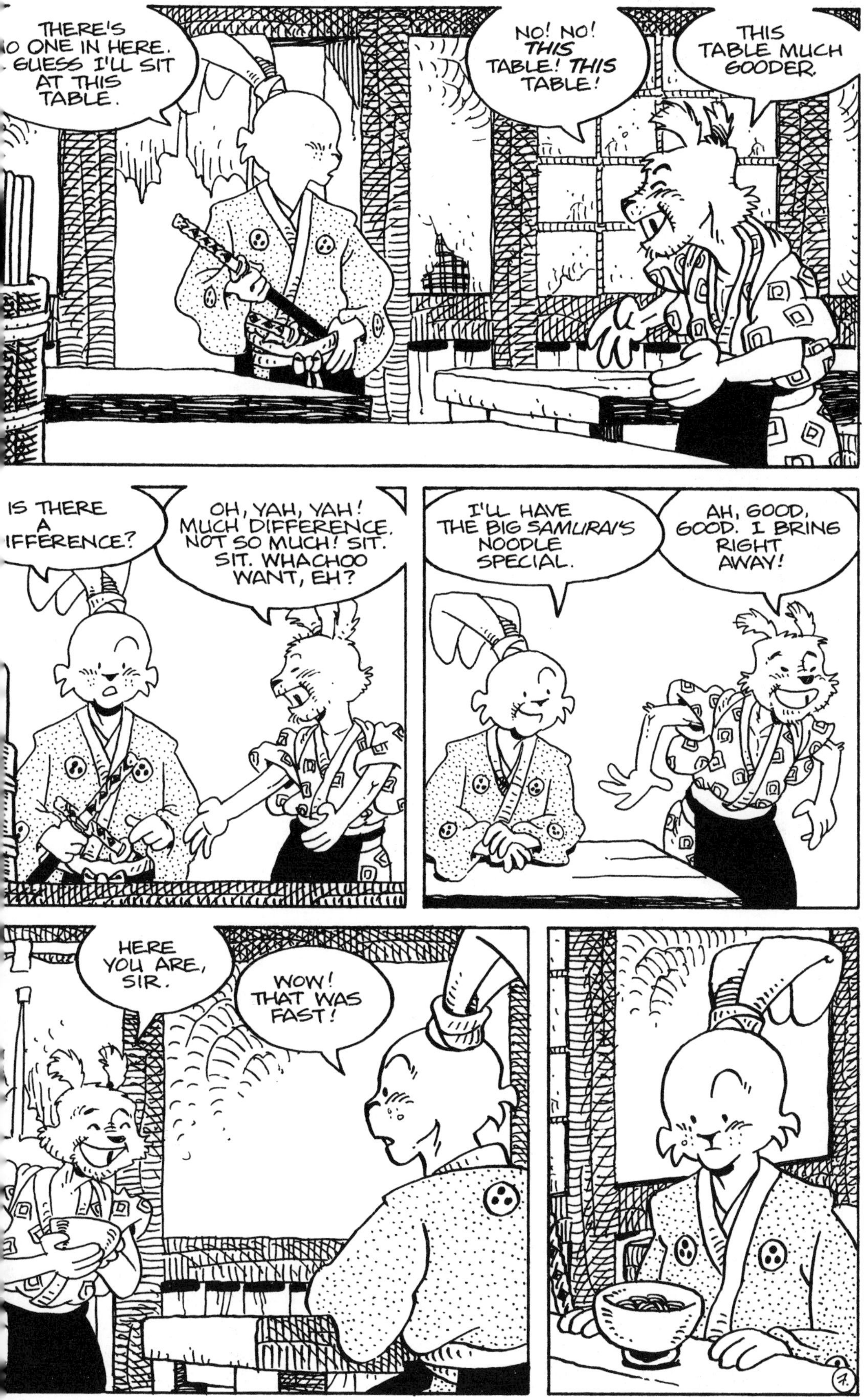
THERE'S
O ONE IN HERE. GUESS I'LL SIT AT THIS TABLE.
NO! NO! *THIS* TABLE! *THIS* TABLE!
THIS TABLE MUCH GOODER.
IS THERE A IFFERENCE?
OH, YAH, YAH! MUCH DIFFERENCE. NOT SO MUCH! SIT. SIT. WHACHOO WANT, EH?
I'LL HAVE THE BIG *SAMURAI'S* NOODLE SPECIAL.
AH, GOOD, GOOD. I BRING RIGHT AWAY!
HERE YOU ARE, SIR.
WOW! THAT WAS FAST!

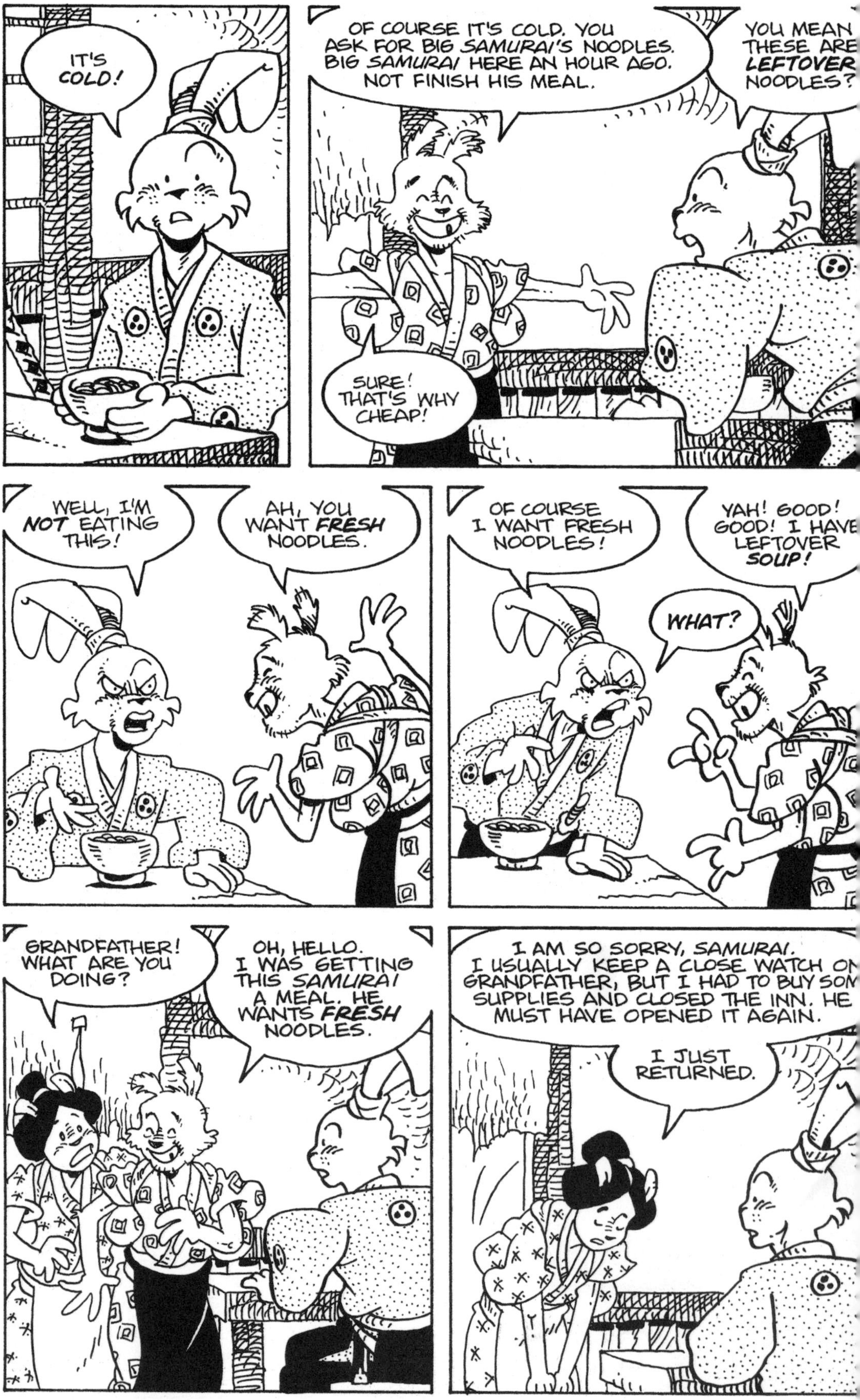
IT'S COLD!
OF COURSE IT'S COLD. YOU ASK FOR BIG SAMURAI'S NOODLES. BIG SAMURAI HERE AN HOUR AGO. NOT FINISH HIS MEAL.
YOU MEAN THESE ARE LEFTOVER NOODLES?
SURE! THAT'S WHY CHEAP!
WELL, I'M NOT EATING THIS!
AH, YOU WANT FRESH NOODLES.
OF COURSE I WANT FRESH NOODLES!
YAH! GOOD! GOOD! I HAVE LEFTOVER SOUP!
WHAT?
GRANDFATHER! WHAT ARE YOU DOING?
OH, HELLO. I WAS GETTING THIS SAMURAI A MEAL. HE WANTS FRESH NOODLES.
I AM SO SORRY, SAMURAI. I USUALLY KEEP A CLOSE WATCH ON GRANDFATHER, BUT I HAD TO BUY SOME SUPPLIES AND CLOSED THE INN. HE MUST HAVE OPENED IT AGAIN.
I JUST RETURNED.

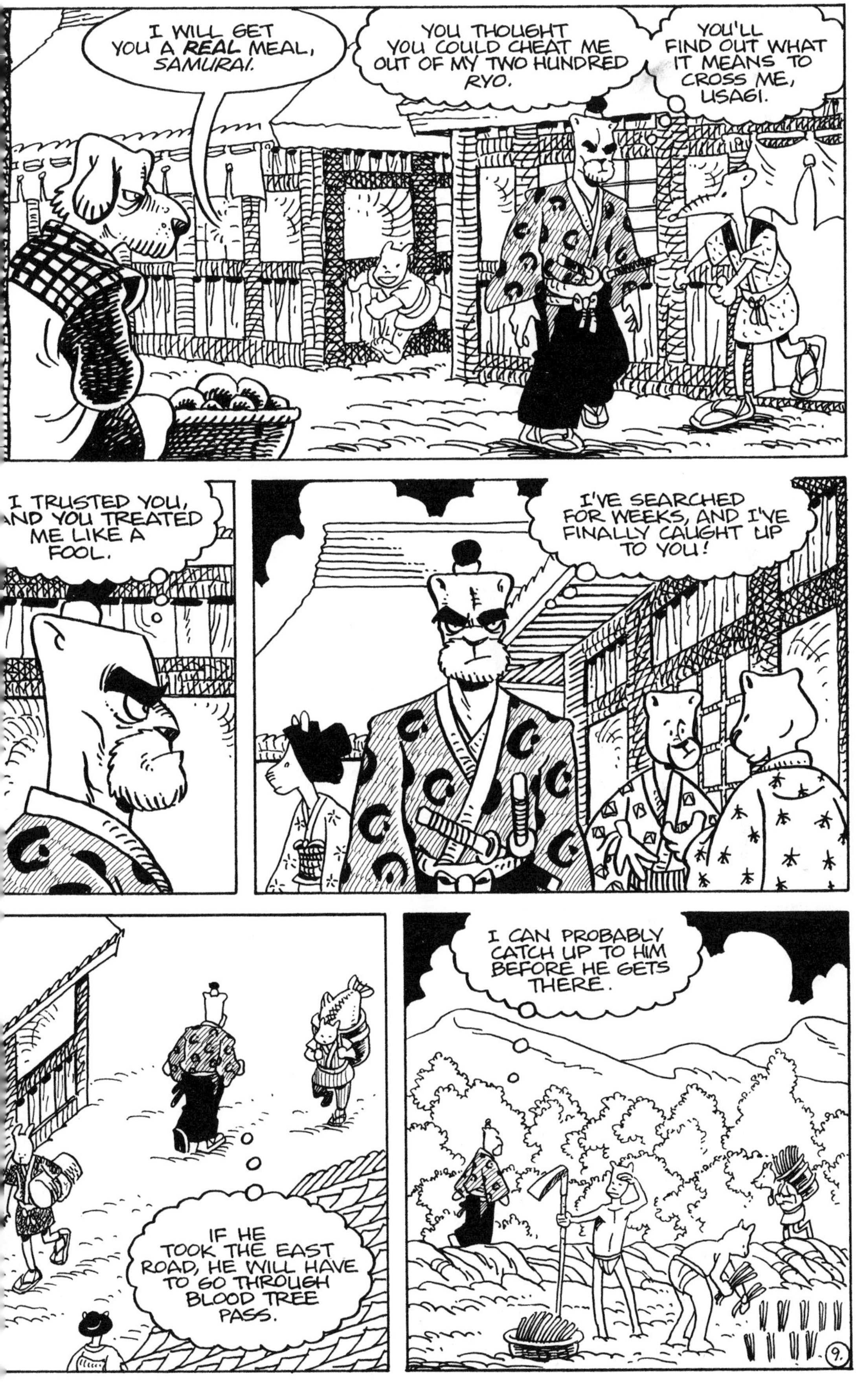
I WILL GET YOU A **REAL** MEAL, SAMURAI.
YOU THOUGHT YOU COULD CHEAT ME OUT OF MY TWO HUNDRED RYO.
YOU'LL FIND OUT WHAT IT MEANS TO CROSS ME, USAGI.
I TRUSTED YOU, AND YOU TREATED ME LIKE A FOOL.
I'VE SEARCHED FOR WEEKS, AND I'VE FINALLY CAUGHT UP TO YOU!
IF HE TOOK THE EAST ROAD, HE WILL HAVE TO GO THROUGH BLOOD TREE PASS.
I CAN PROBABLY CATCH UP TO HIM BEFORE HE GETS THERE.
9.

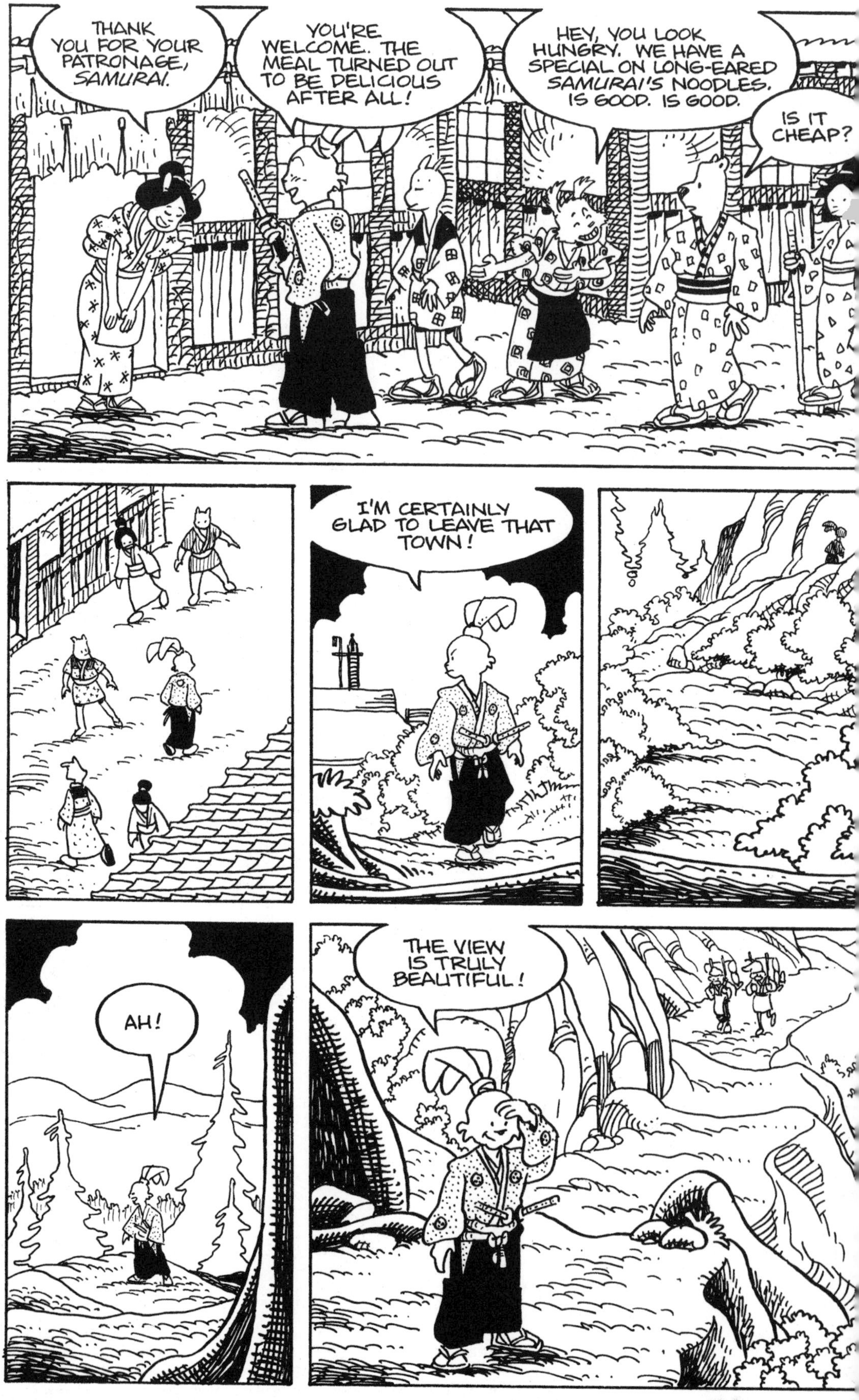
THANK YOU FOR YOUR PATRONAGE, SAMURAI.
YOU'RE WELCOME. THE MEAL TURNED OUT TO BE DELICIOUS AFTER ALL!
HEY, YOU LOOK HUNGRY. WE HAVE A SPECIAL ON LONG-EARED SAMURAI'S NOODLES. IS GOOD. IS GOOD.
IS IT CHEAP?
I'M CERTAINLY GLAD TO LEAVE THAT TOWN!
AH!
THE VIEW IS TRULY BEAUTIFUL!

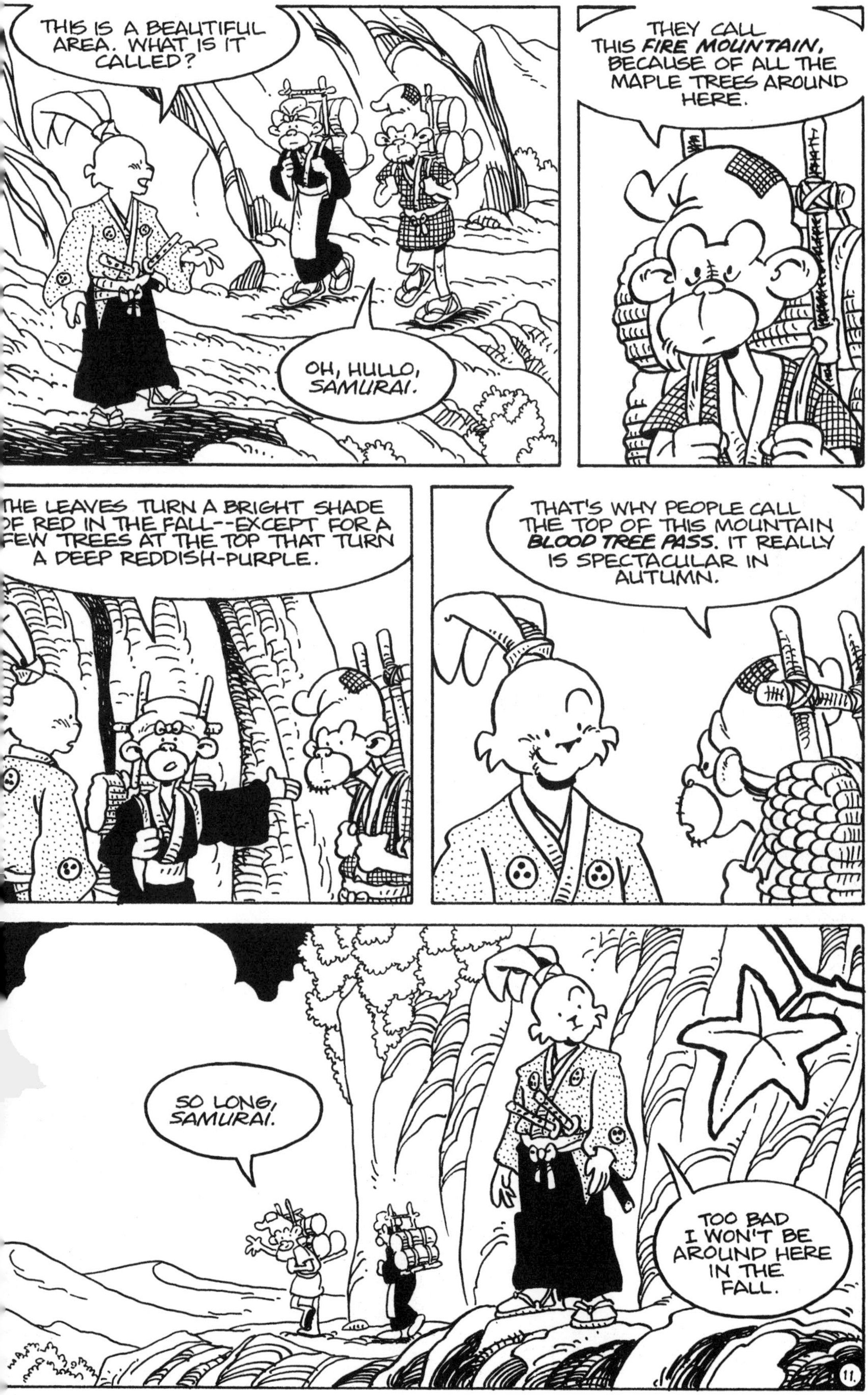
THIS IS A BEAUTIFUL AREA. WHAT IS IT CALLED?
OH, HULLO, SAMURAI.
THEY CALL THIS FIRE MOUNTAIN, BECAUSE OF ALL THE MAPLE TREES AROUND HERE.
THE LEAVES TURN A BRIGHT SHADE OF RED IN THE FALL--EXCEPT FOR A FEW TREES AT THE TOP THAT TURN A DEEP REDDISH-PURPLE.
THAT'S WHY PEOPLE CALL THE TOP OF THIS MOUNTAIN BLOOD TREE PASS. IT REALLY IS SPECTACULAR IN AUTUMN.
SO LONG, SAMURAI.
TOO BAD I WON'T BE AROUND HERE IN THE FALL.
11.

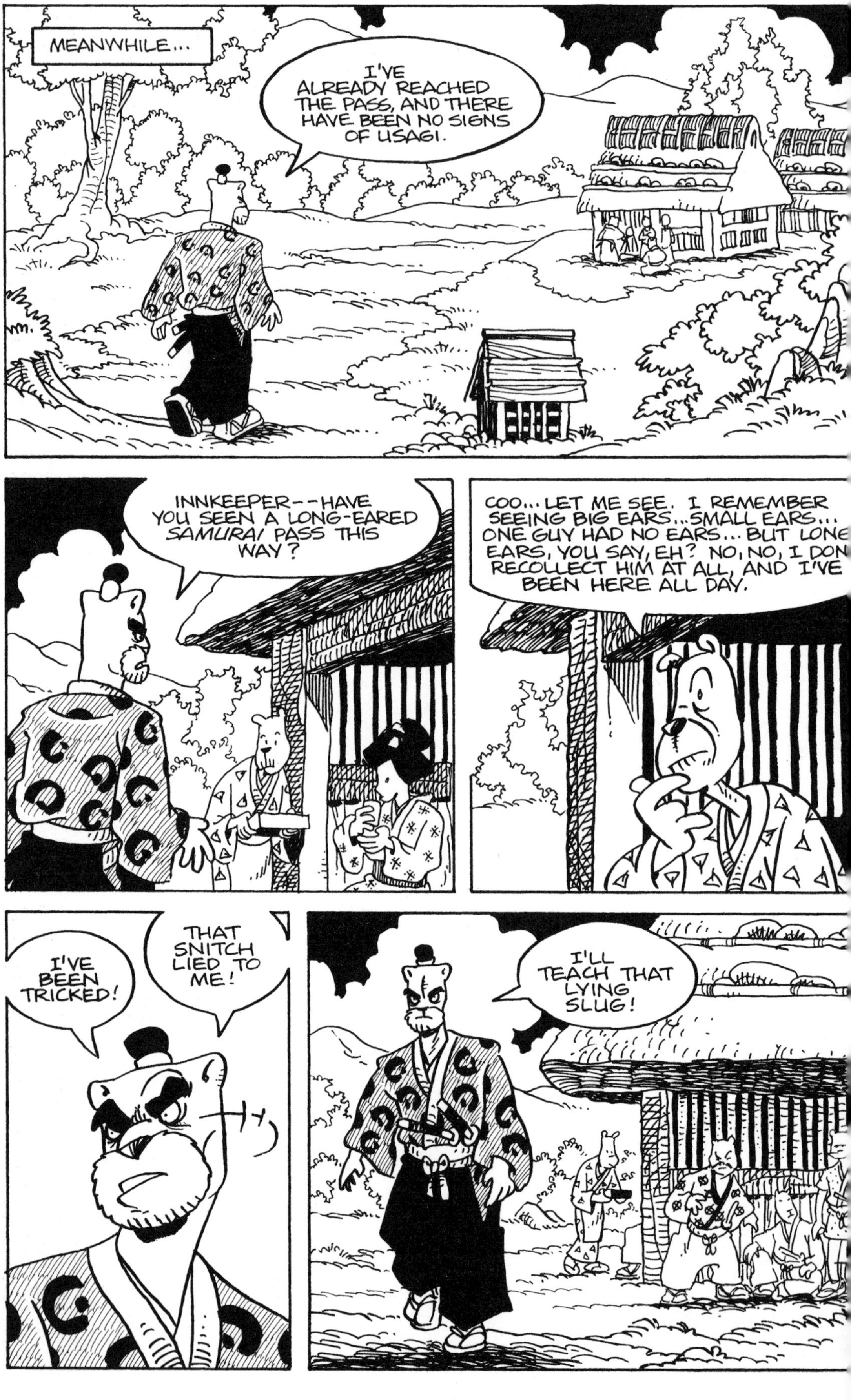
MEANWHILE...
I'VE ALREADY REACHED THE PASS, AND THERE HAVE BEEN NO SIGNS OF USAGI.
INNKEEPER--HAVE YOU SEEN A LONG-EARED *SAMURAI* PASS THIS WAY?
COO... LET ME SEE. I REMEMBER SEEING BIG EARS...SMALL EARS... ONE GUY HAD NO EARS... BUT LONG EARS, YOU SAY, EH? NO, NO, I DON RECOLLECT HIM AT ALL, AND I'VE BEEN HERE ALL DAY.
I'VE BEEN TRICKED!
THAT SNITCH LIED TO ME!
I'LL TEACH THAT LYING SLUG!

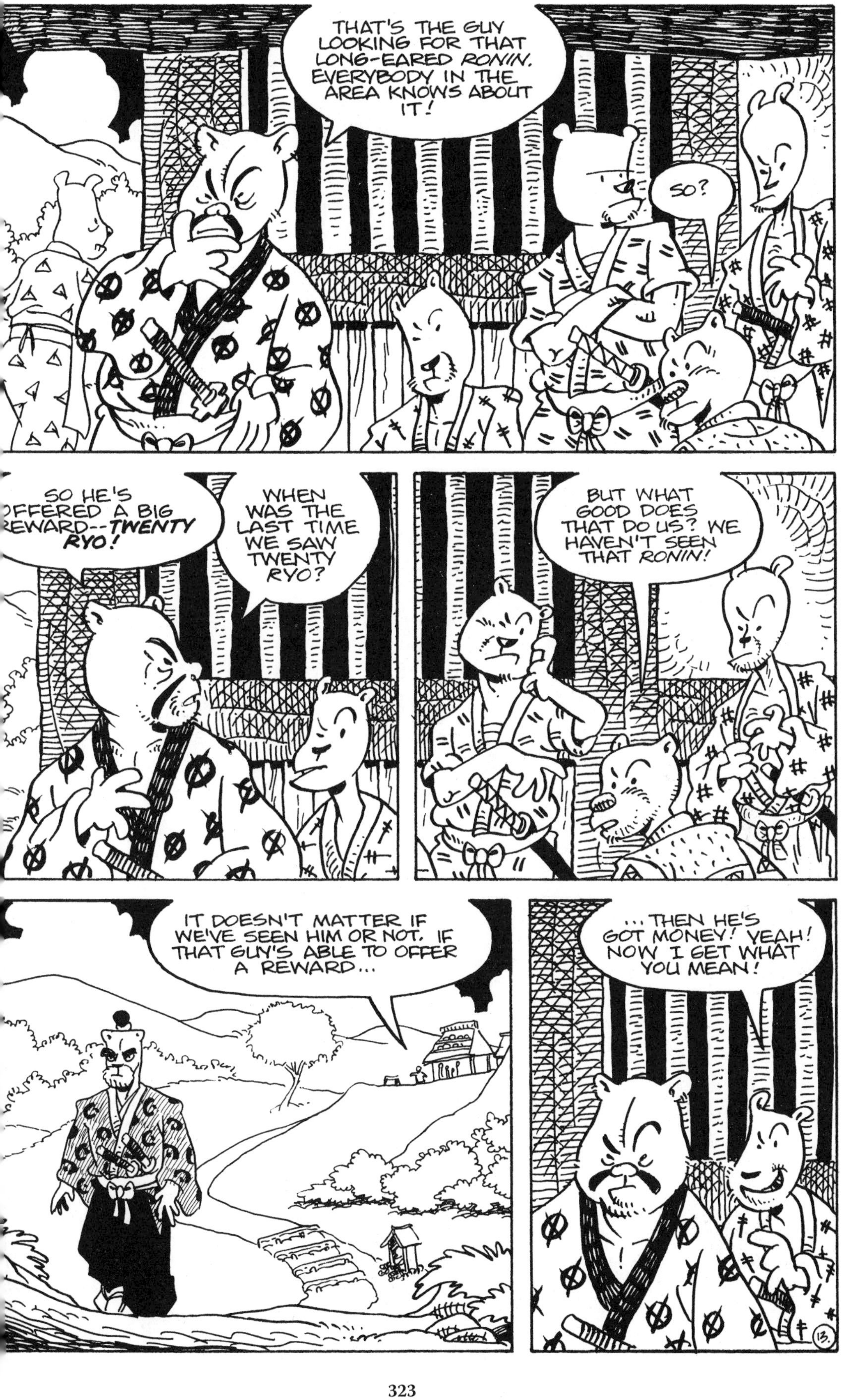
THAT'S THE GUY LOOKING FOR THAT LONG-EARED *RONIN*. EVERYBODY IN THE AREA KNOWS ABOUT IT!
SO?
SO HE'S OFFERED A BIG REWARD--***TWENTY RYO!***
WHEN WAS THE LAST TIME WE SAW TWENTY *RYO*?
BUT WHAT GOOD DOES THAT DO US? WE HAVEN'T SEEN THAT *RONIN*!
IT DOESN'T MATTER IF WE'VE SEEN HIM OR NOT. IF THAT GUY'S ABLE TO OFFER A REWARD...
...THEN HE'S GOT MONEY! YEAH! NOW I GET WHAT YOU MEAN!
13.

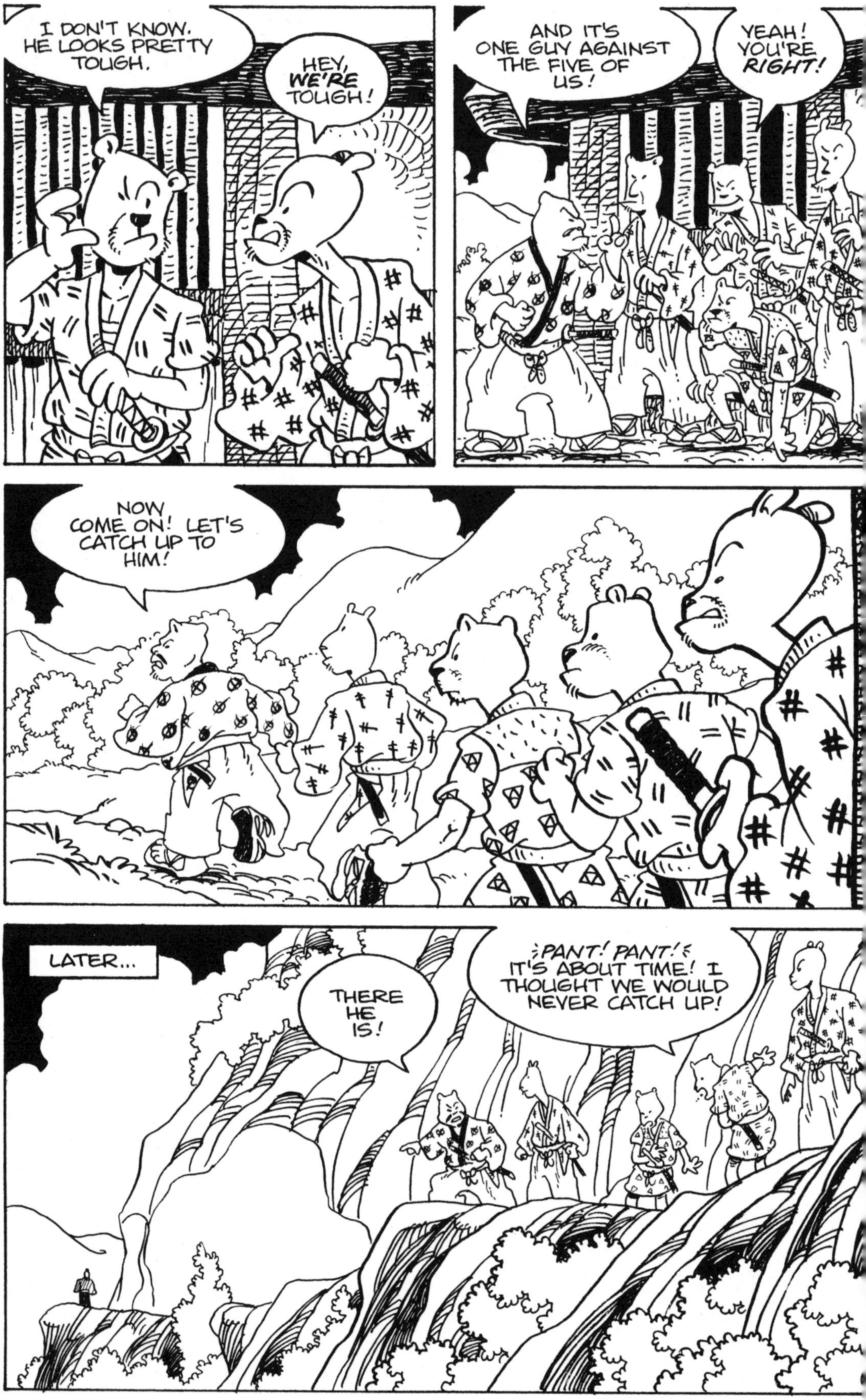

I DON'T KNOW. HE LOOKS PRETTY TOUGH.
HEY, WE'RE TOUGH!
AND IT'S ONE GUY AGAINST THE FIVE OF US!
YEAH! YOU'RE RIGHT!
NOW COME ON! LET'S CATCH UP TO HIM!
LATER...
THERE HE IS!
PANT! PANT! IT'S ABOUT TIME! I THOUGHT WE WOULD NEVER CATCH UP!

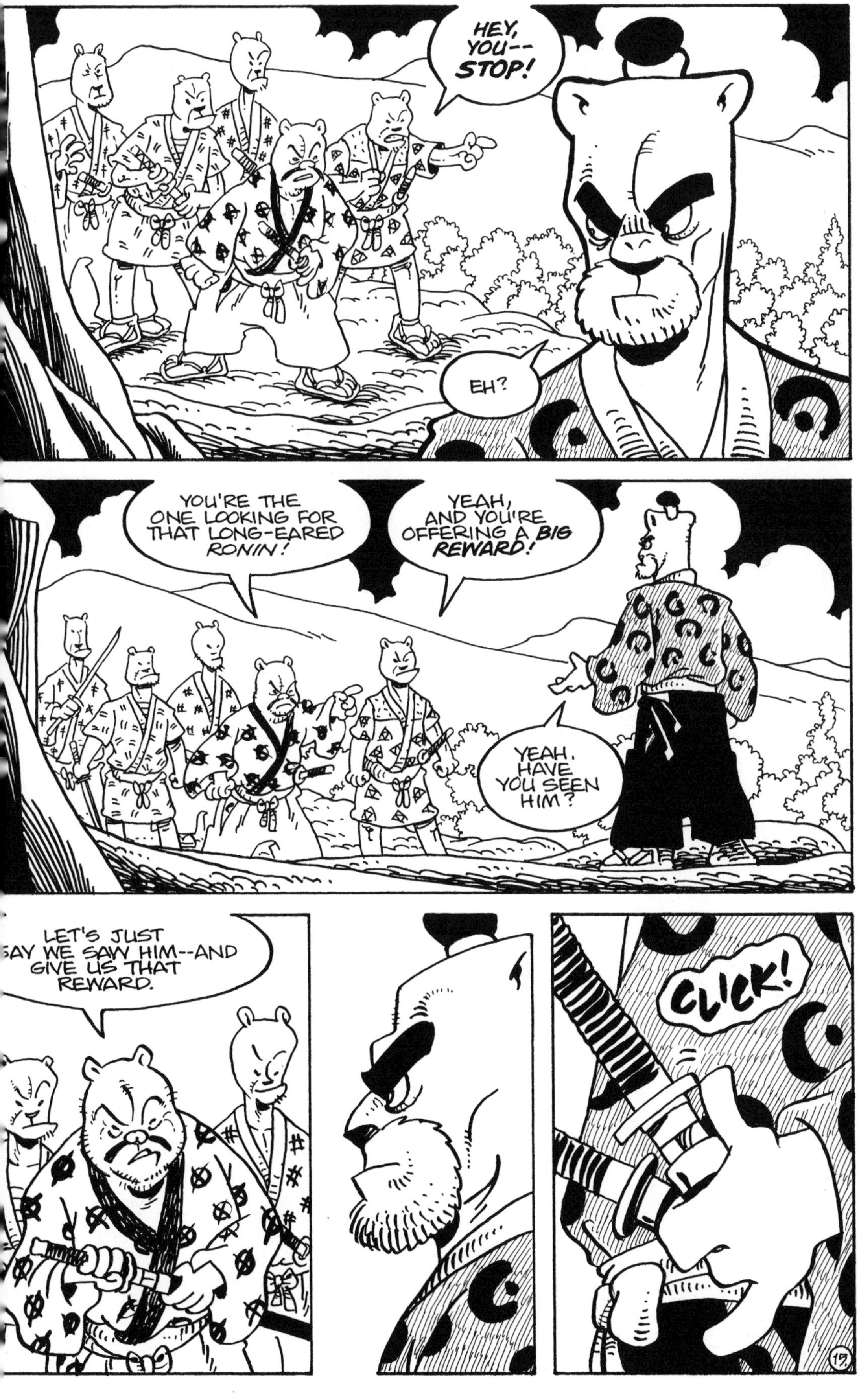
HEY, YOU-- STOP!
EH?
YOU'RE THE ONE LOOKING FOR THAT LONG-EARED RONIN!
YEAH, AND YOU'RE OFFERING A BIG REWARD!
YEAH. HAVE YOU SEEN HIM?
LET'S JUST SAY WE SAW HIM--AND GIVE US THAT REWARD.
CLICK!
15

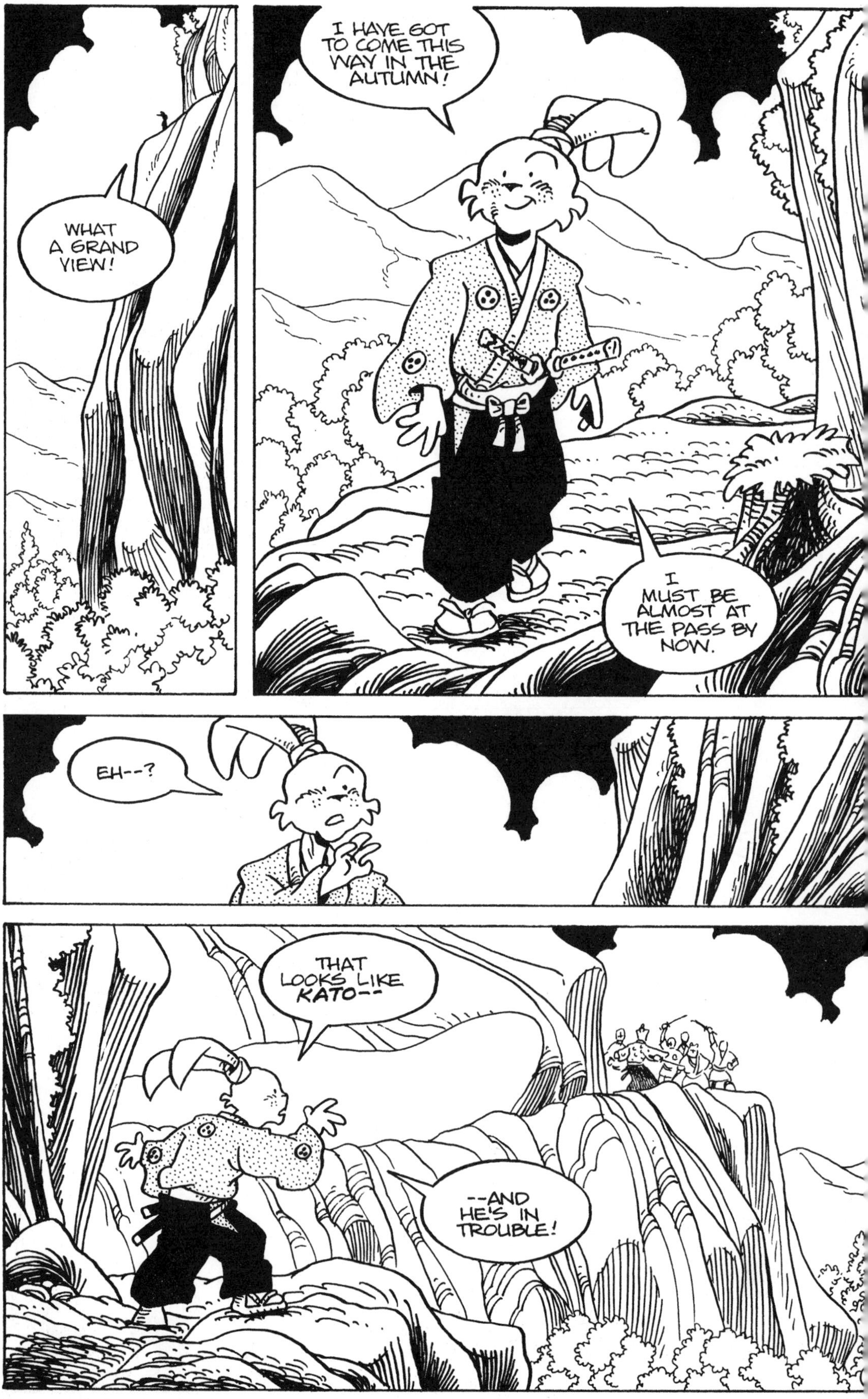
WHAT A GRAND VIEW!
I HAVE GOT TO COME THIS WAY IN THE AUTUMN!
I MUST BE ALMOST AT THE PASS BY NOW.
EH--?
THAT LOOKS LIKE KATO--
--AND HE'S IN TROUBLE!

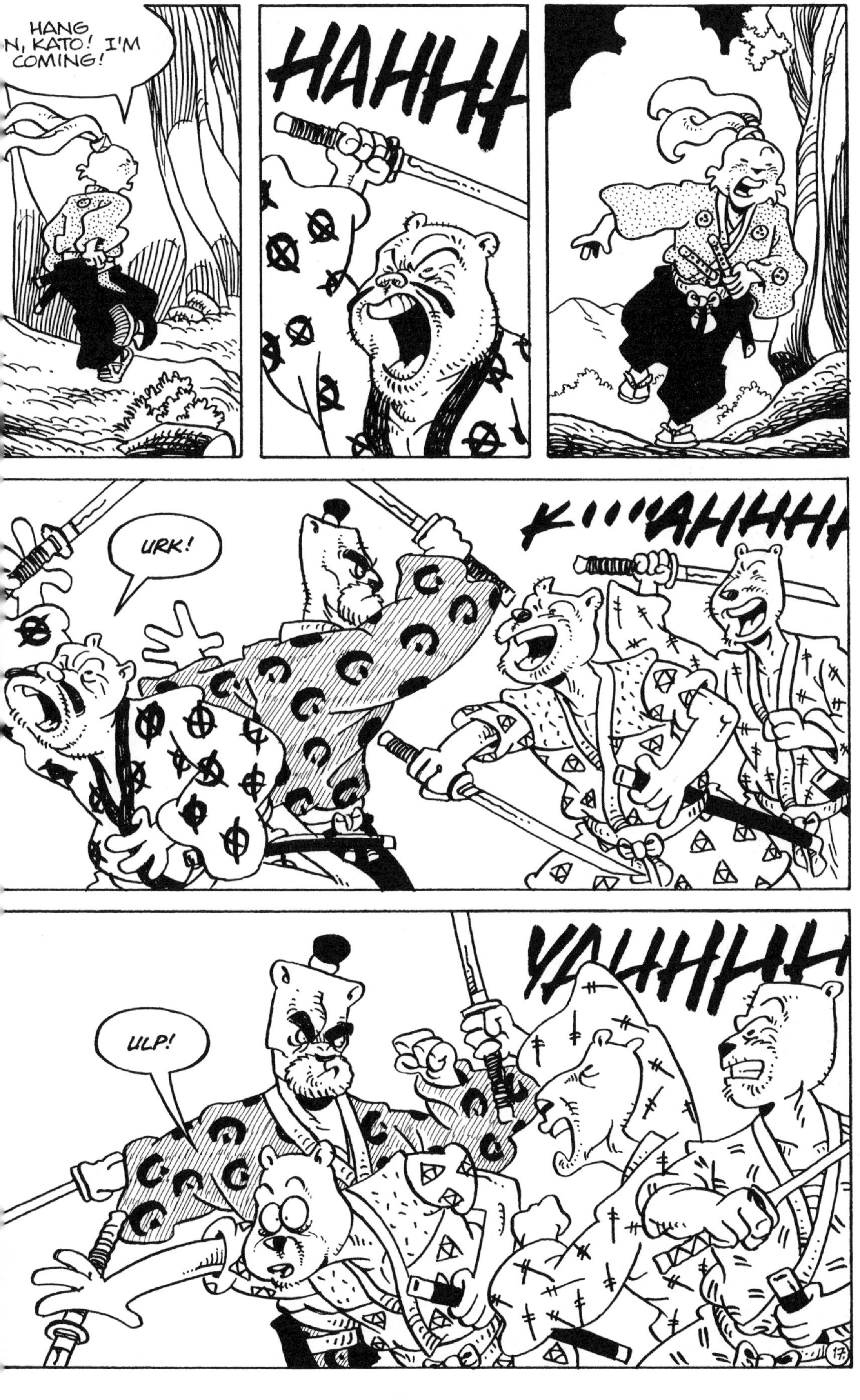
HANG
N, KATO! I'M
COMING!
HAHHH
URK!
K'''AHHHH
ULP!
YAHHHH
17.

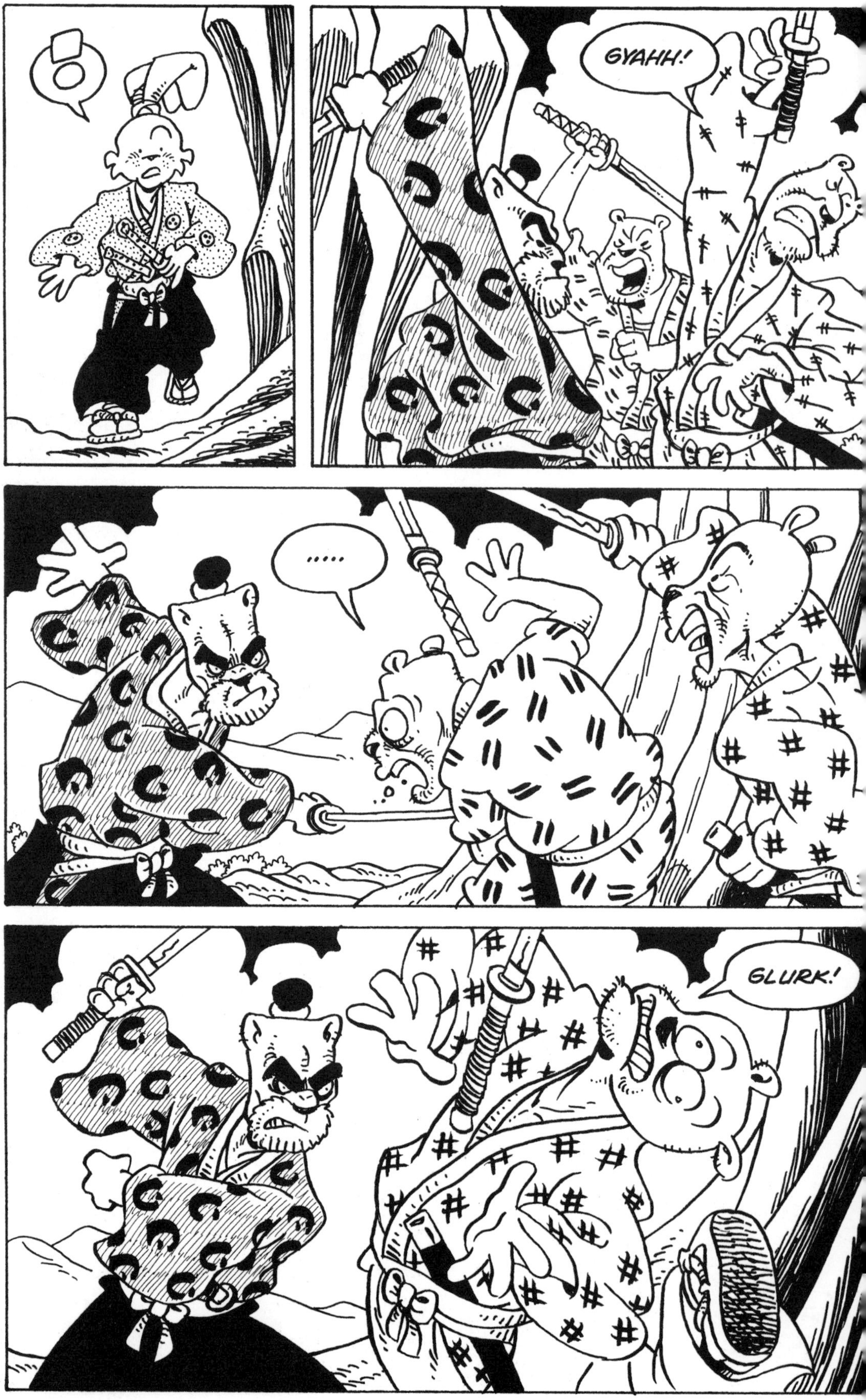
GYAHH!
.....
GLURK!

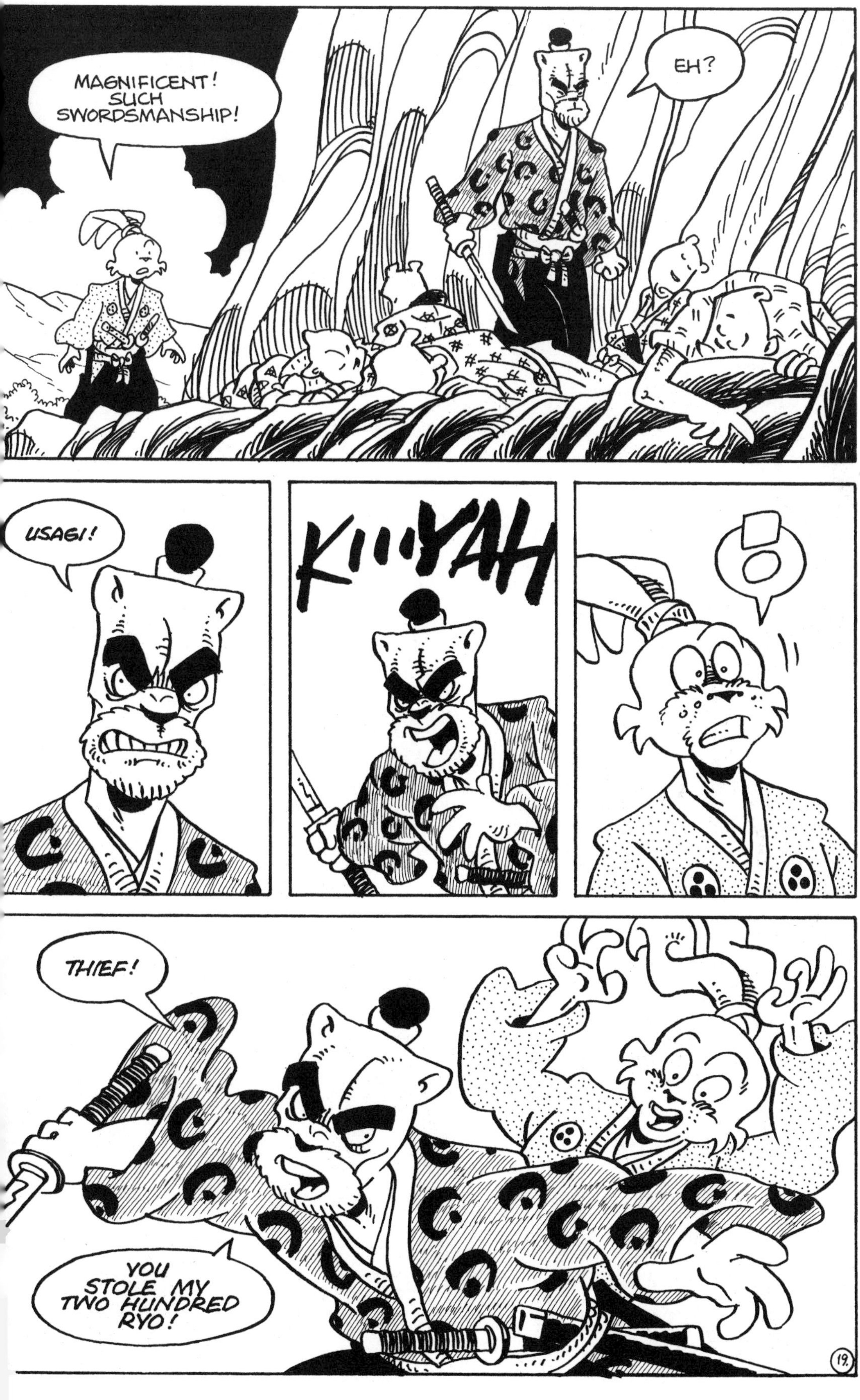
MAGNIFICENT! SUCH SWORDSMANSHIP!
EH?
USAGI!
KIIIYAH
!
THIEF!
YOU STOLE MY TWO HUNDRED RYO!
19

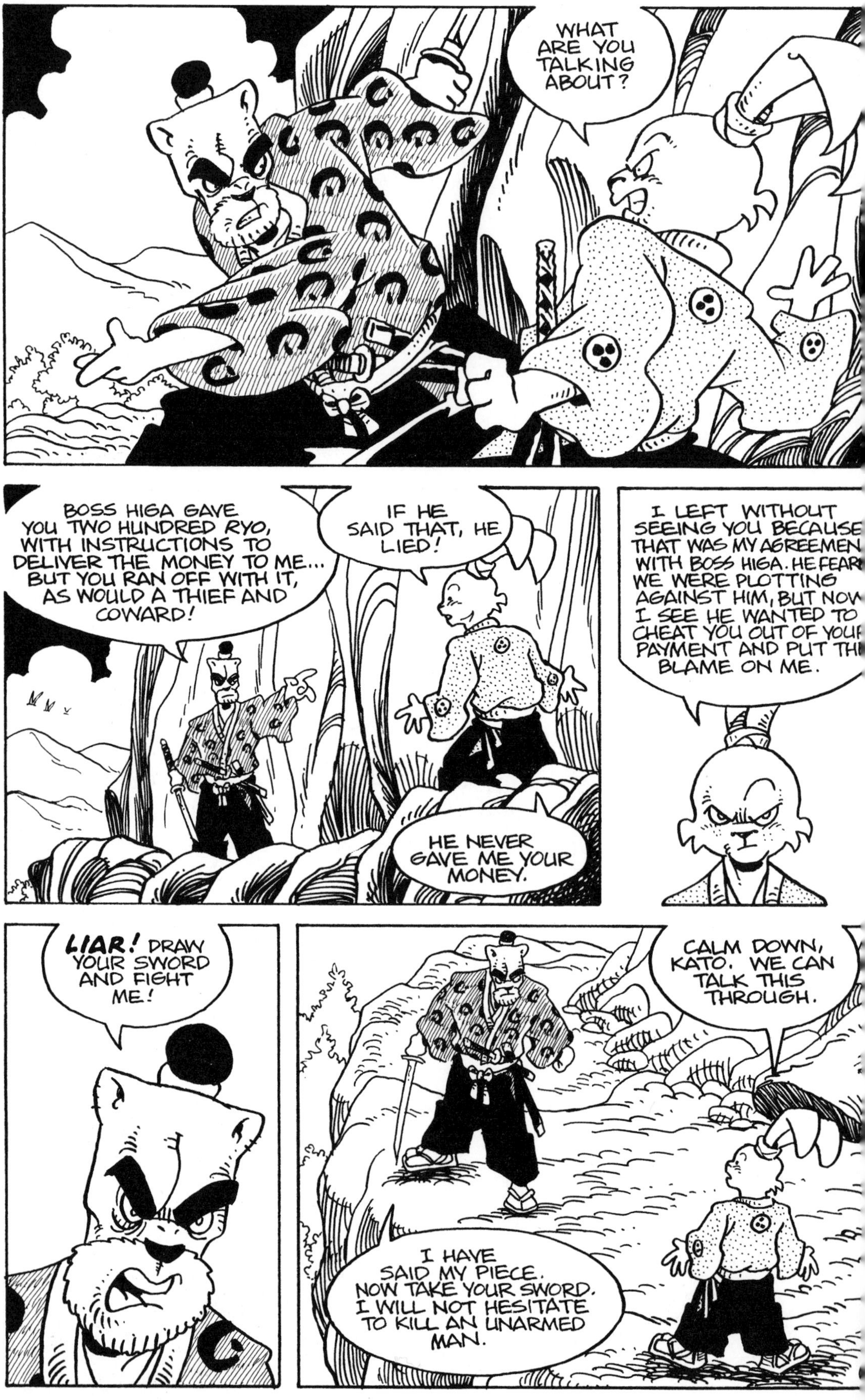
WHAT ARE YOU TALKING ABOUT?
BOSS HIGA GAVE YOU TWO HUNDRED RYO, WITH INSTRUCTIONS TO DELIVER THE MONEY TO ME... BUT YOU RAN OFF WITH IT, AS WOULD A THIEF AND COWARD!
IF HE SAID THAT, HE LIED!
HE NEVER GAVE ME YOUR MONEY.
I LEFT WITHOUT SEEING YOU BECAUSE THAT WAS MY AGREEMEN WITH BOSS HIGA. HE FEAR WE WERE PLOTTING AGAINST HIM, BUT NOW I SEE HE WANTED TO CHEAT YOU OUT OF YOU PAYMENT AND PUT TH BLAME ON ME.
LIAR! DRAW YOUR SWORD AND FIGHT ME!
CALM DOWN, KATO. WE CAN TALK THIS THROUGH.
I HAVE SAID MY PIECE. NOW TAKE YOUR SWORD. I WILL NOT HESITATE TO KILL AN UNARMED MAN.

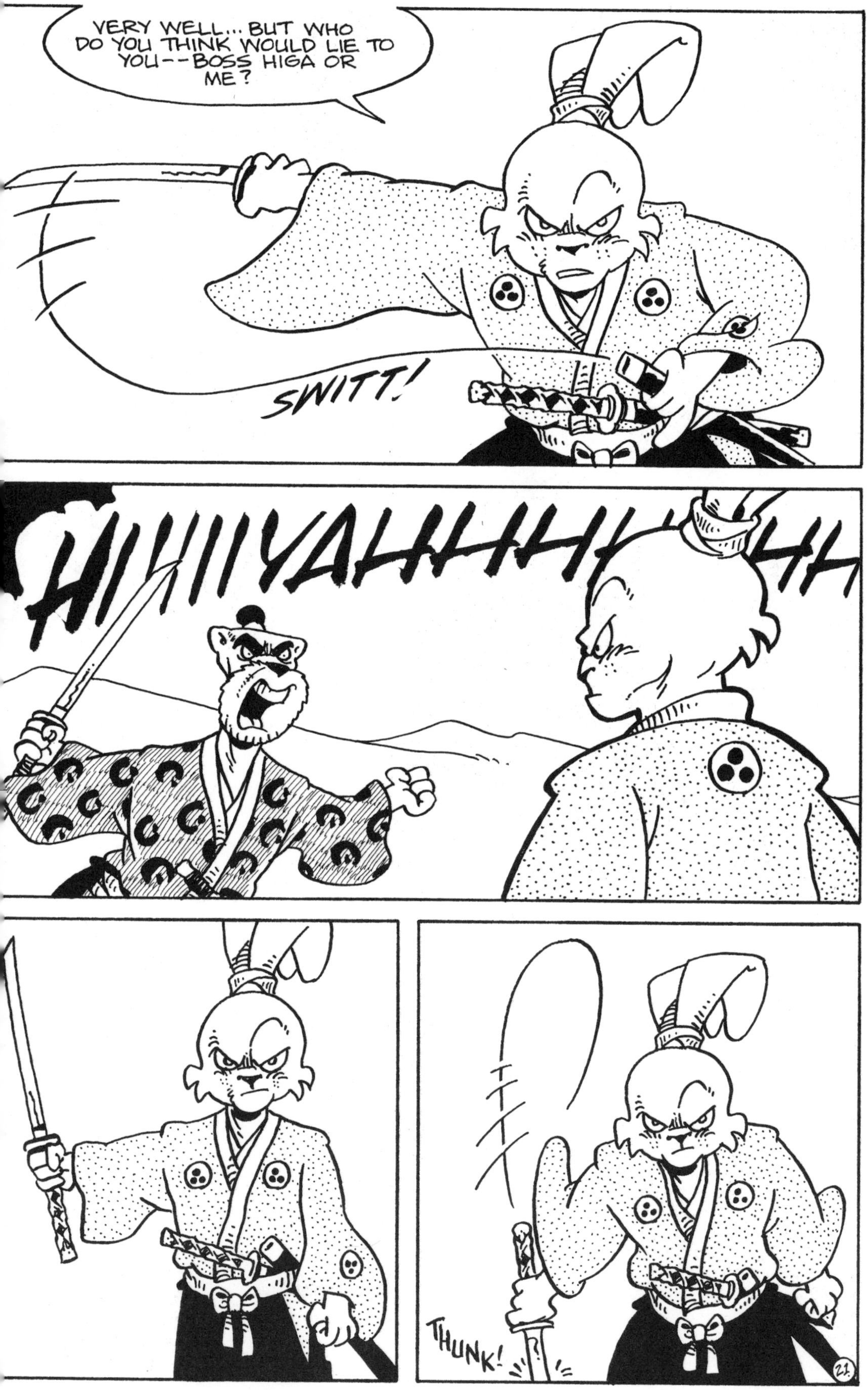

VERY WELL... BUT WHO DO YOU THINK WOULD LIE TO YOU--BOSS HIGA OR ME?
SWITT!
HIIIIYAHHHHHHHHH
THUNK!
21.

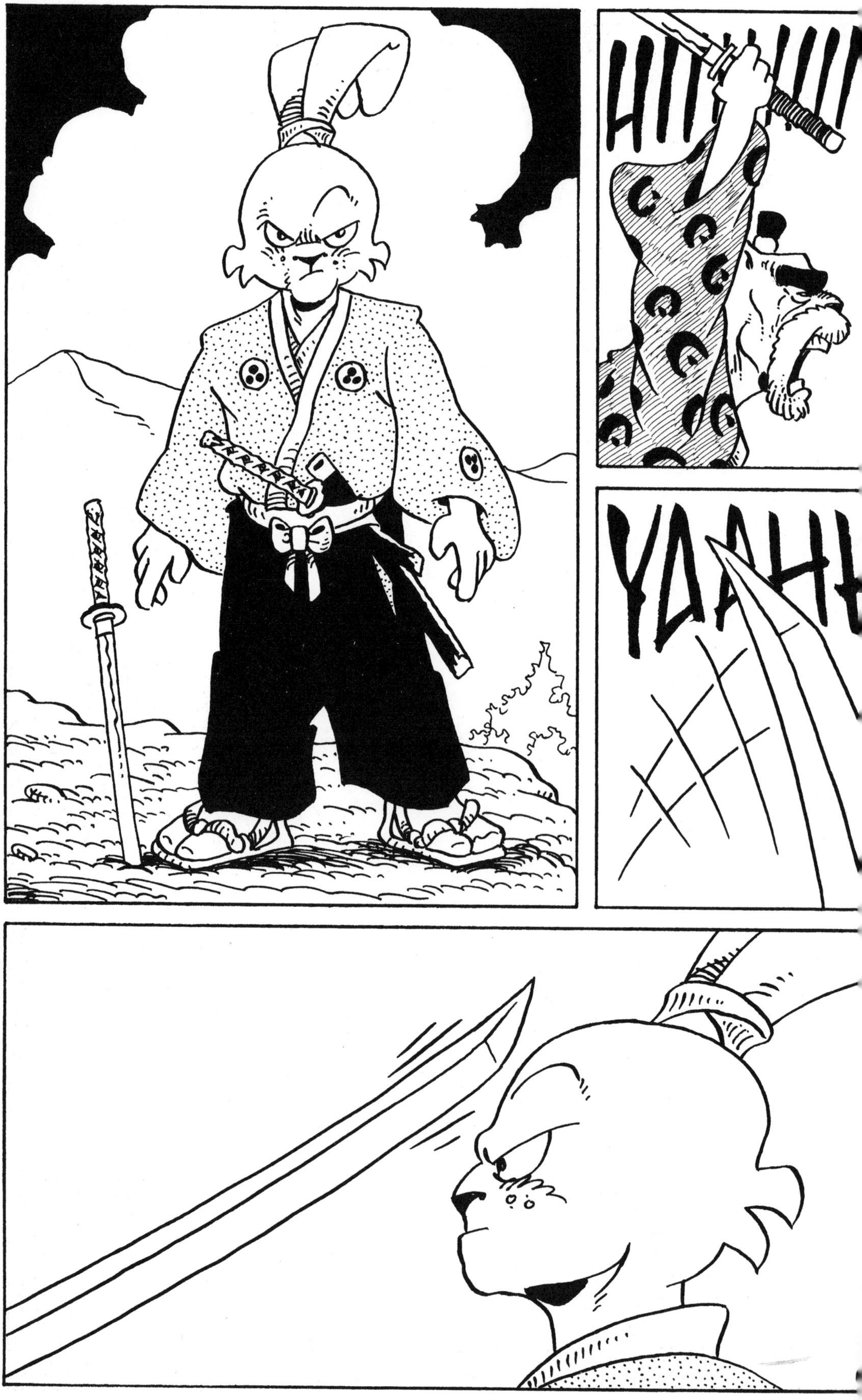
YAAH

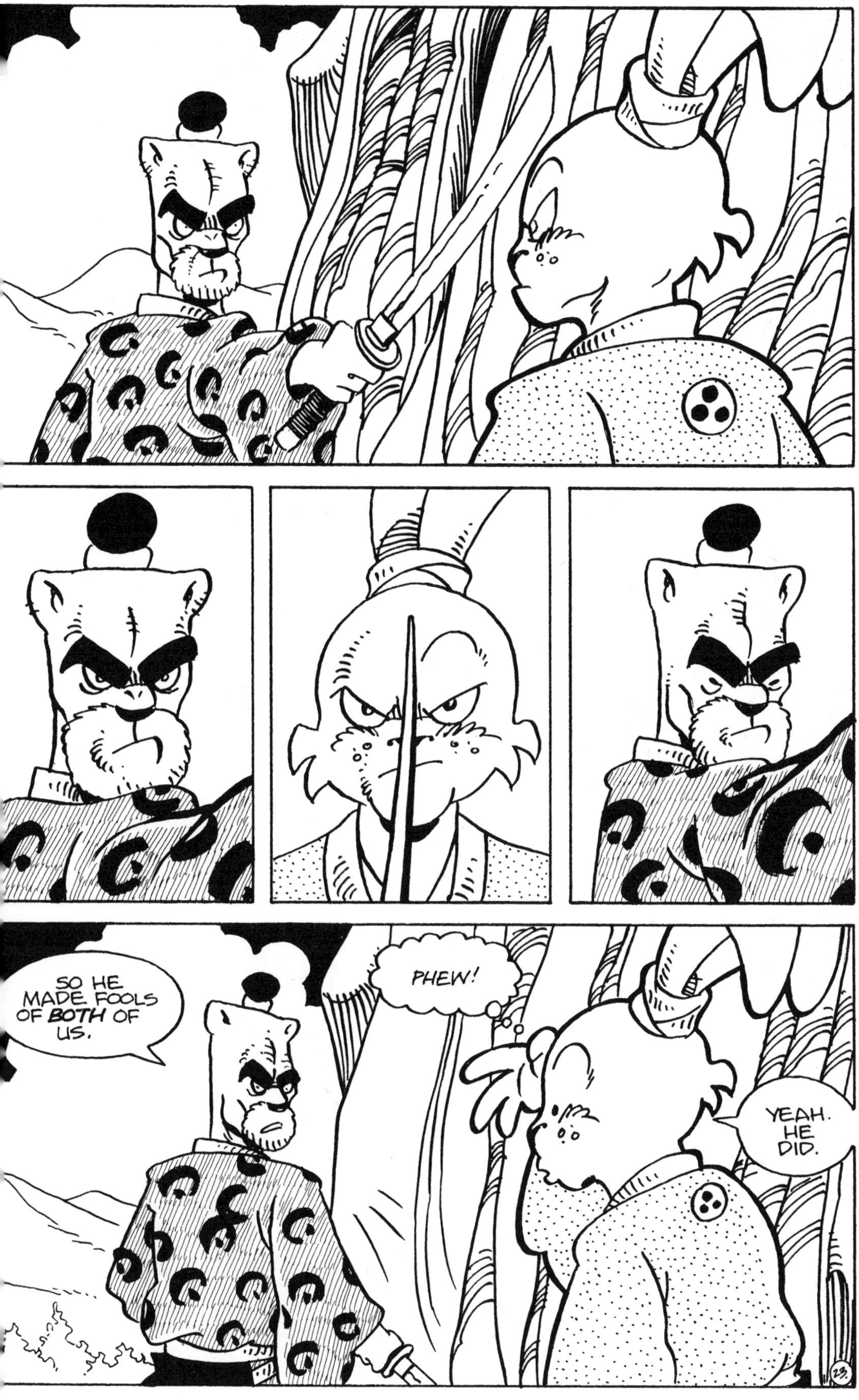
SO HE MADE FOOLS OF BOTH OF US.
PHEW!
YEAH. HE DID.
23

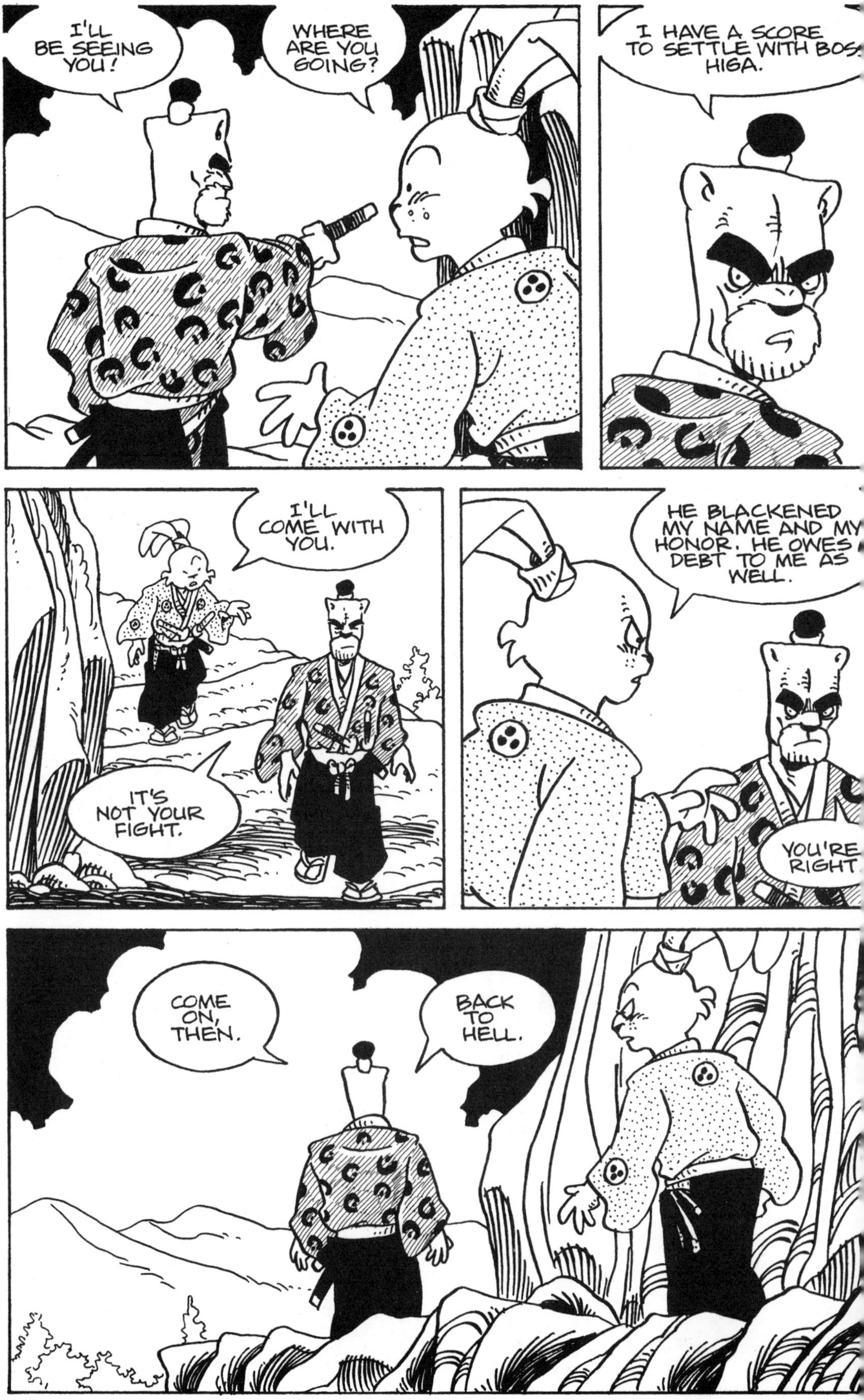
I'LL BE SEEING YOU!
WHERE ARE YOU GOING?
I HAVE A SCORE TO SETTLE WITH BOSS HIGA.
I'LL COME WITH YOU.
IT'S NOT YOUR FIGHT.
HE BLACKENED MY NAME AND MY HONOR. HE OWES A DEBT TO ME AS WELL.
YOU'RE RIGHT.
COME ON, THEN.
BACK TO HELL.

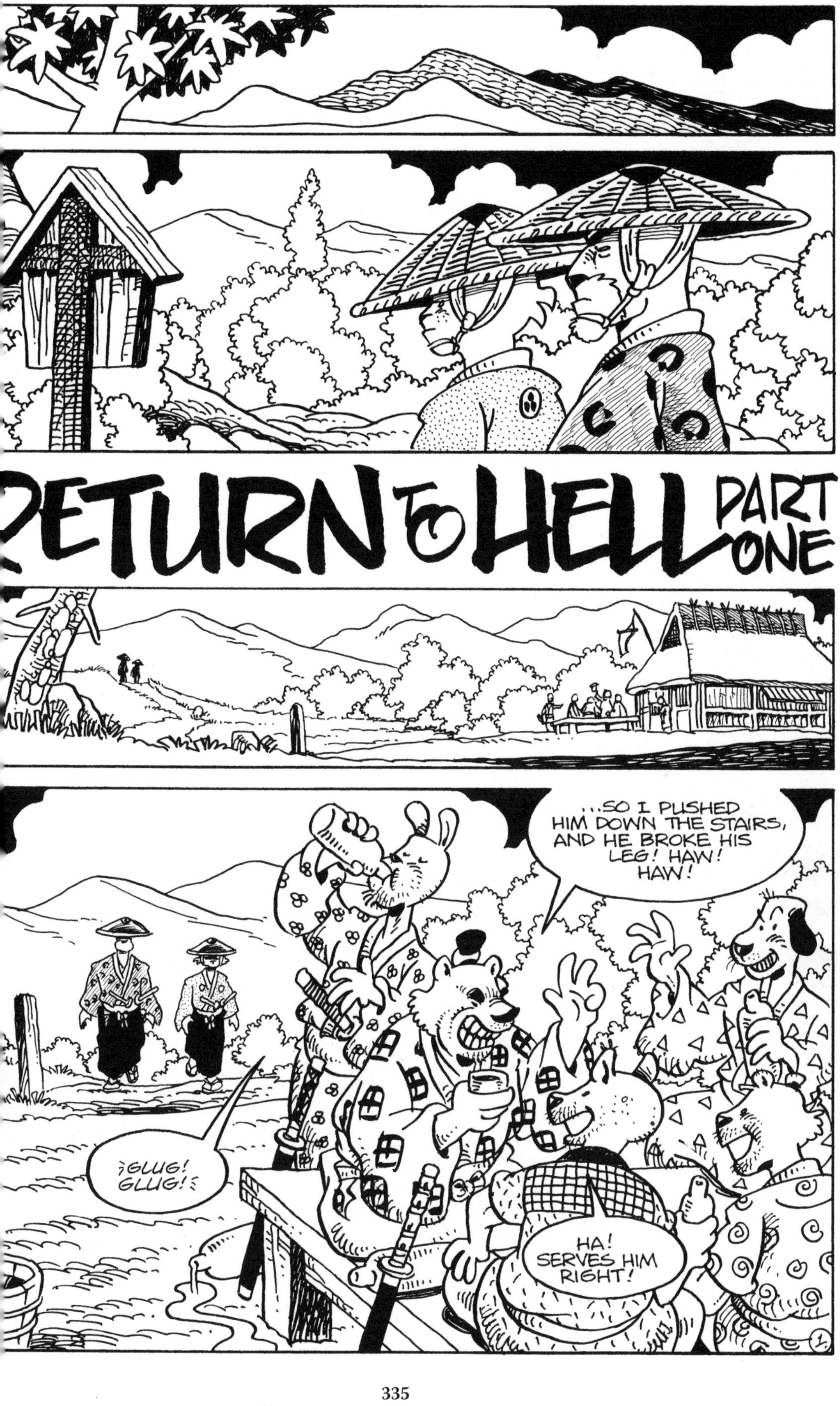
RETURN TO HELL PART ONE
...SO I PUSHED HIM DOWN THE STAIRS, AND HE BROKE HIS LEG! HAW! HAW!
¡GLUG! GLUG!
HA! SERVES HIM RIGHT!
1.

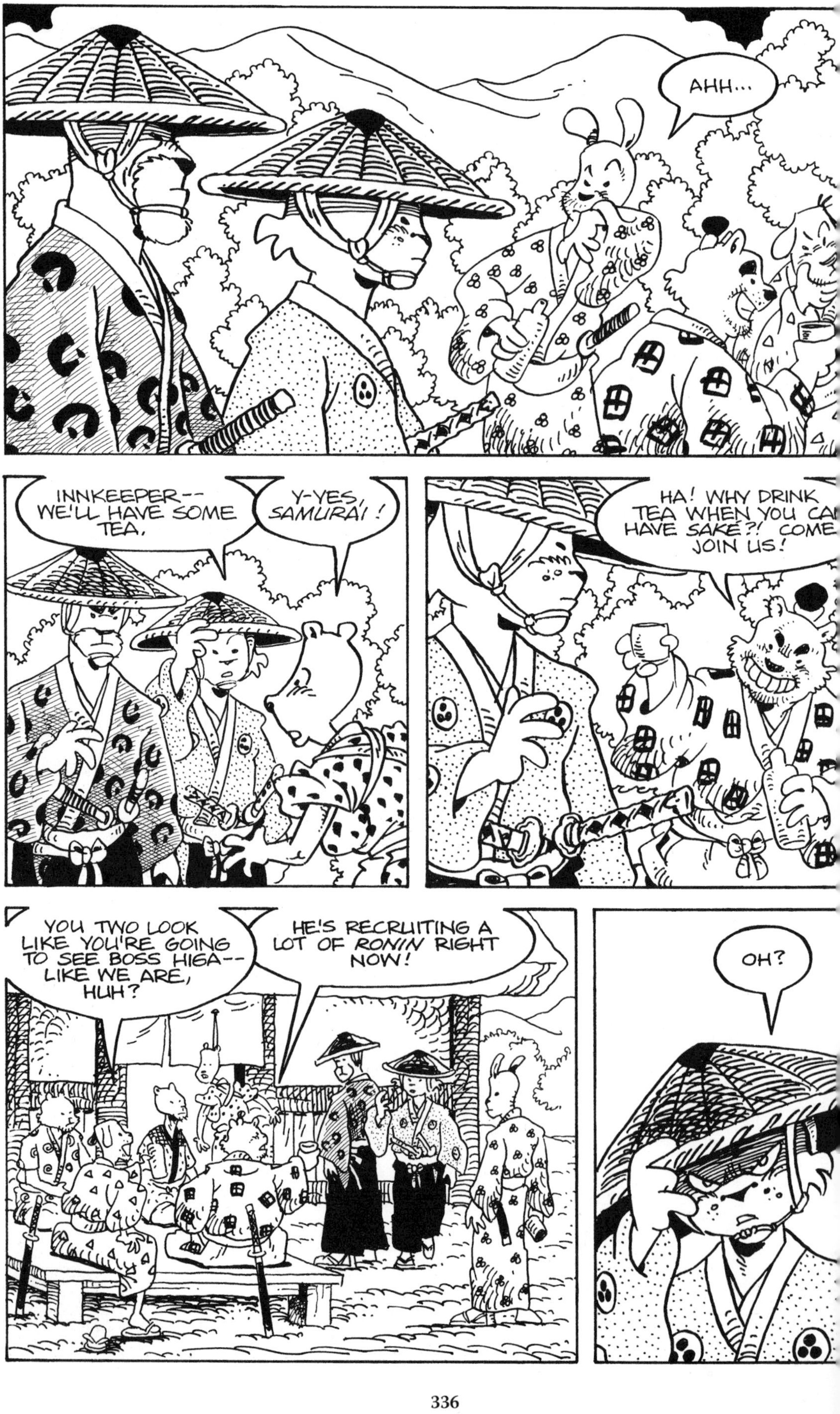
AHH...
INNKEEPER-- WE'LL HAVE SOME TEA.
Y-YES, *SAMURAI*!
HA! WHY DRINK TEA WHEN YOU CA HAVE *SAKE*?! COME JOIN US!
YOU TWO LOOK LIKE YOU'RE GOING TO SEE BOSS HIGA-- LIKE WE ARE, HUH?
HE'S RECRUITING A LOT OF *RONIN* RIGHT NOW!
OH?

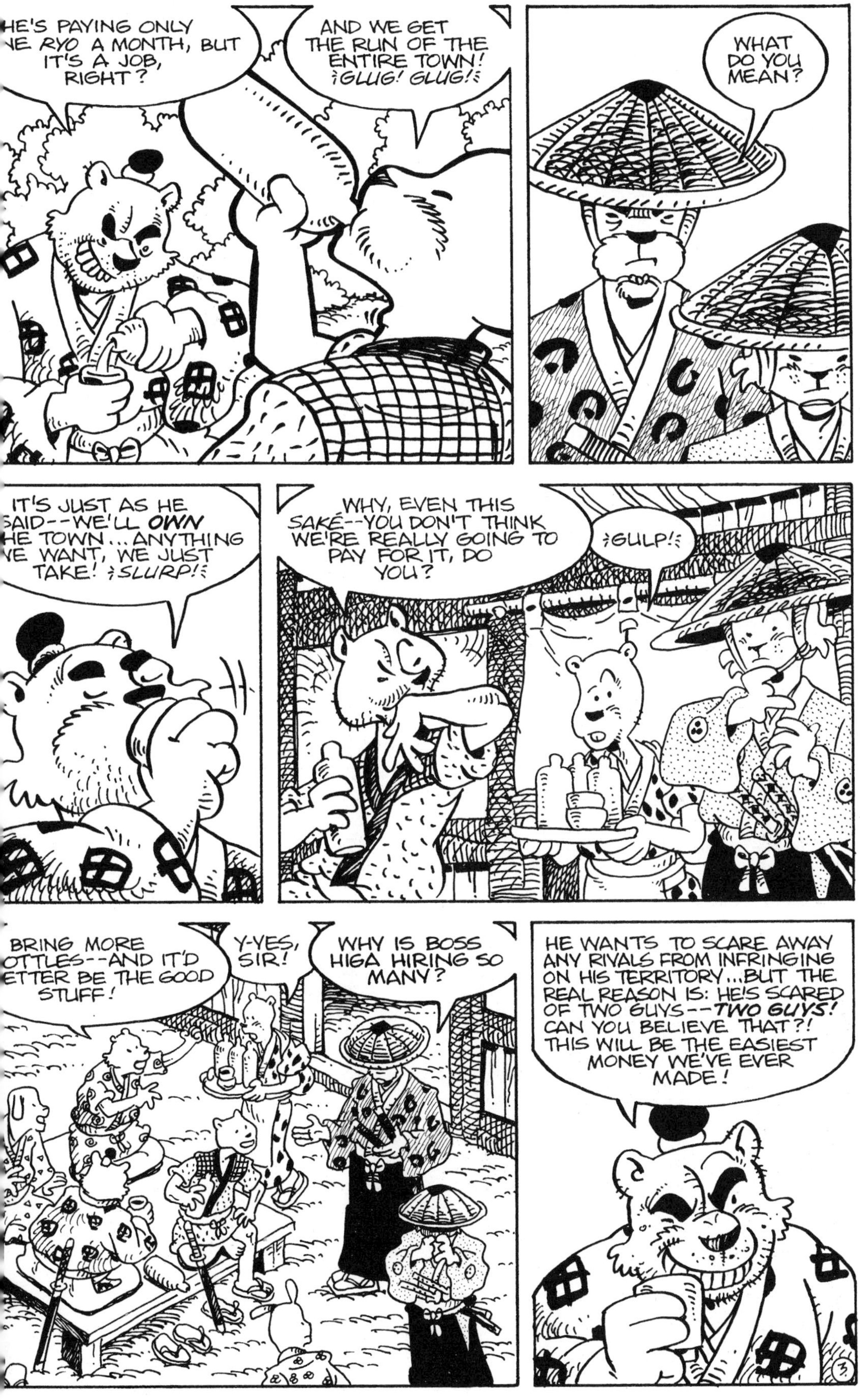
HE'S PAYING ONLY ONE RYO A MONTH, BUT IT'S A JOB, RIGHT?
AND WE GET THE RUN OF THE ENTIRE TOWN! ¡GLUG! GLUG!¡
WHAT DO YOU MEAN?
IT'S JUST AS HE SAID--WE'LL OWN THE TOWN... ANYTHING WE WANT, WE JUST TAKE! ¡SLURP!¡
WHY, EVEN THIS SAKÉ--YOU DON'T THINK WE'RE REALLY GOING TO PAY FOR IT, DO YOU?
¡GULP!¡
BRING MORE BOTTLES--AND IT'D BETTER BE THE GOOD STUFF!
Y-YES, SIR!
WHY IS BOSS HIGA HIRING SO MANY?
HE WANTS TO SCARE AWAY ANY RIVALS FROM INFRINGING ON HIS TERRITORY...BUT THE REAL REASON IS: HE'S SCARED OF TWO GUYS--TWO GUYS! CAN YOU BELIEVE THAT?! THIS WILL BE THE EASIEST MONEY WE'VE EVER MADE!
3

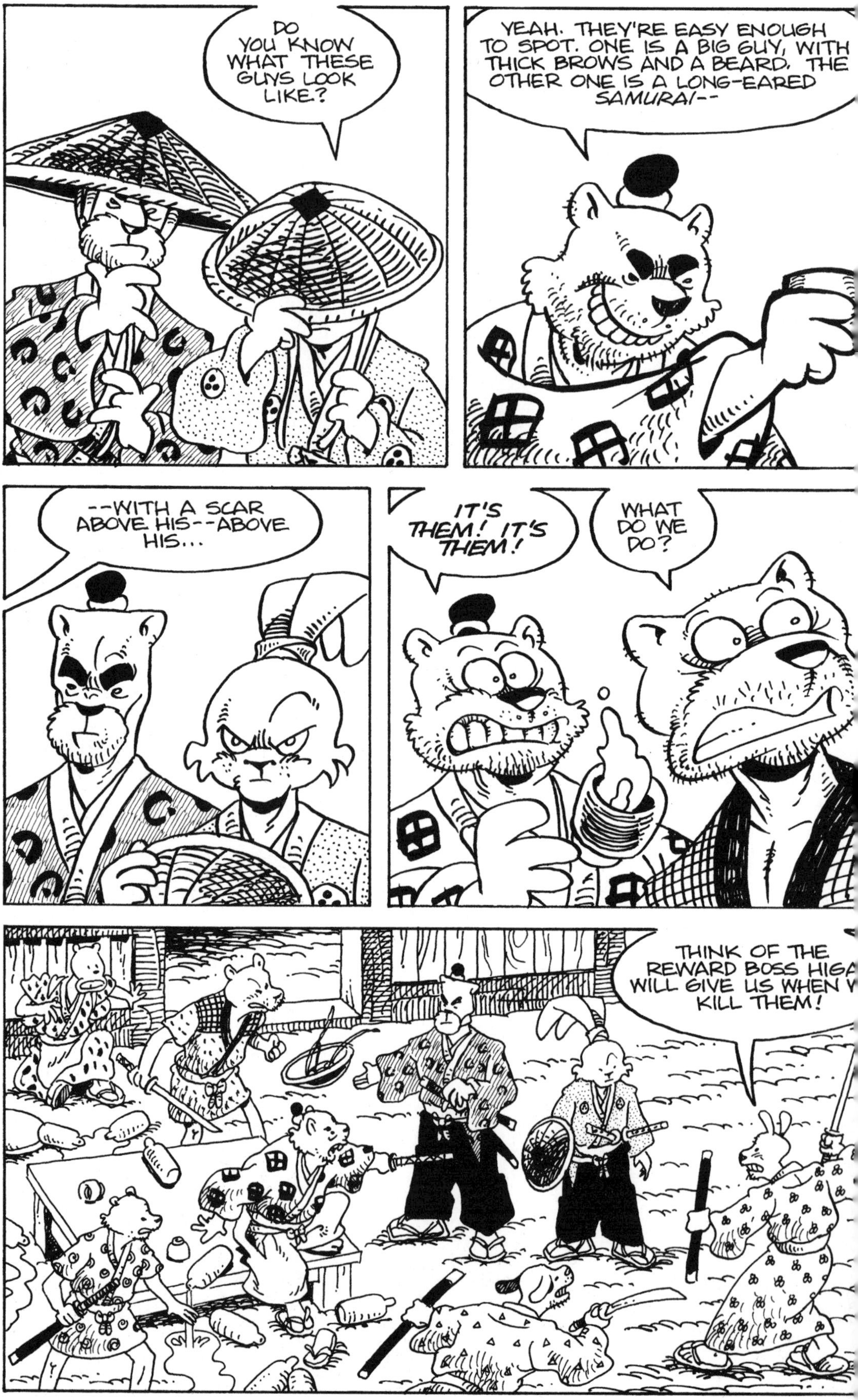

DO YOU KNOW WHAT THESE GUYS LOOK LIKE?
YEAH. THEY'RE EASY ENOUGH TO SPOT. ONE IS A BIG GUY, WITH THICK BROWS AND A BEARD. THE OTHER ONE IS A LONG-EARED SAMURAI--
--WITH A SCAR ABOVE HIS--ABOVE HIS...
IT'S THEM! IT'S THEM!
WHAT DO WE DO?

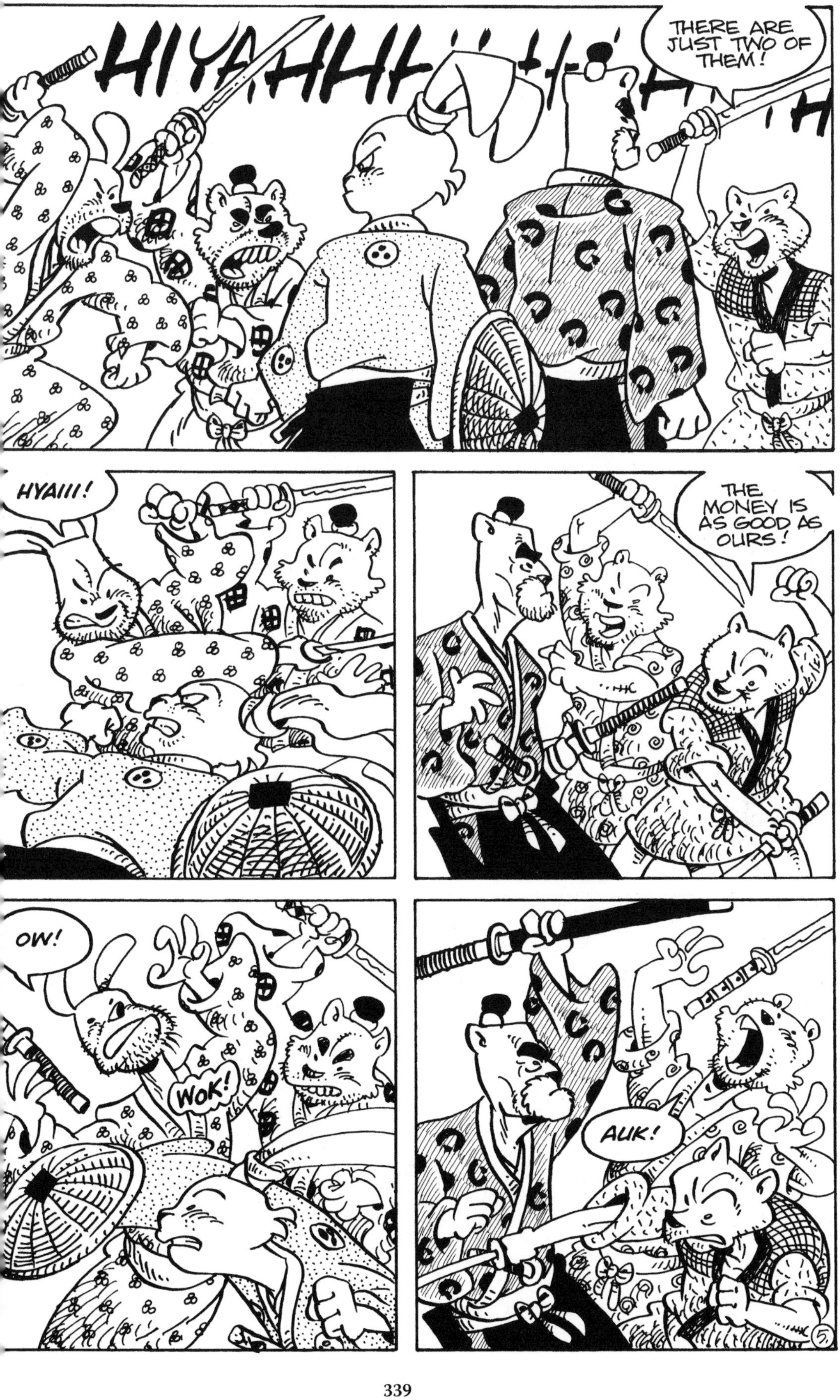
HIYAHHHHHH
THERE ARE JUST TWO OF THEM!
HYAIII!
THE MONEY IS AS GOOD AS OURS!
OW!
WOK!
AUK!
5

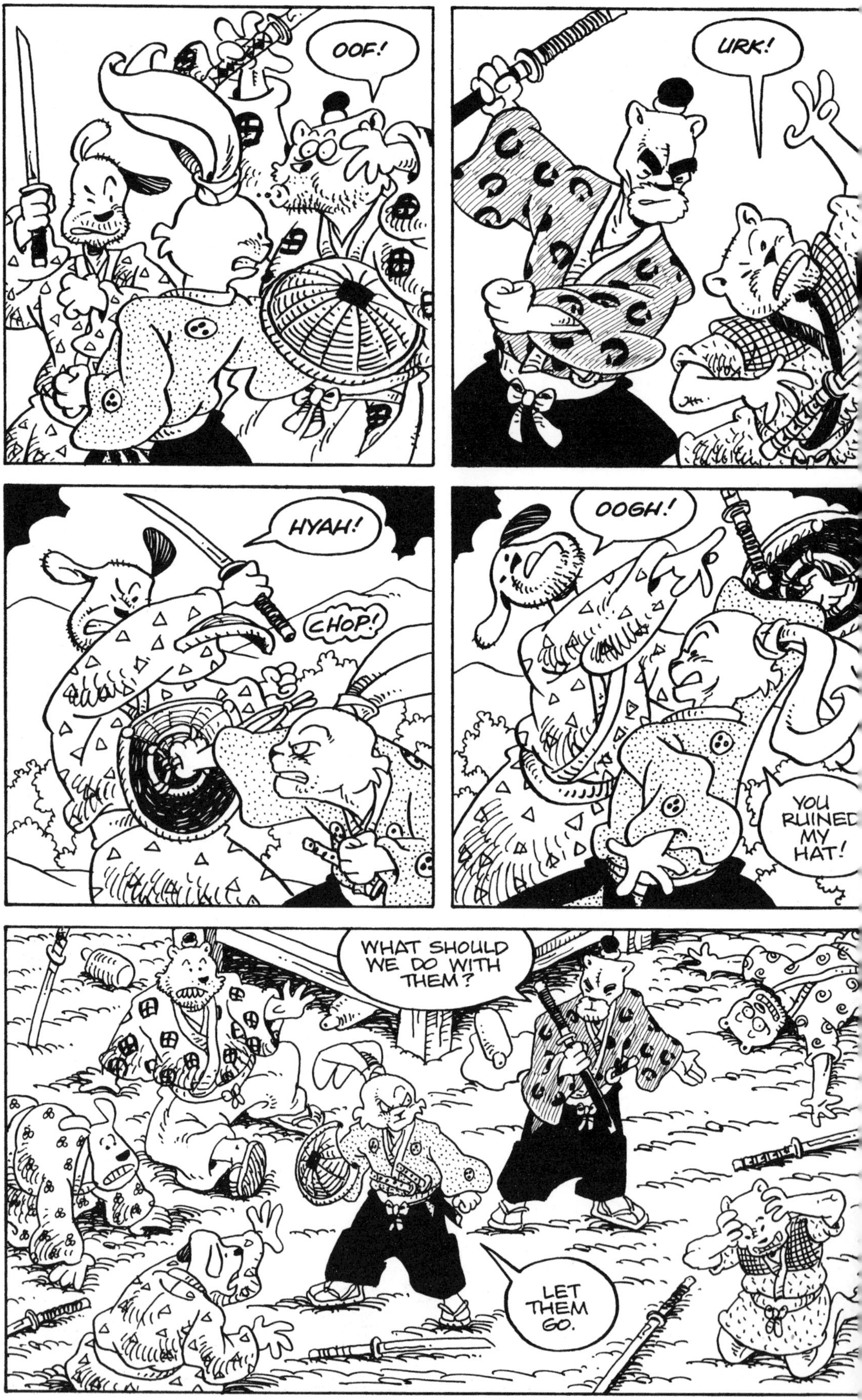
OOF!
URK!
HYAH!
CHOP!
OOGH!
YOU RUINED MY HAT!
WHAT SHOULD WE DO WITH THEM?
LET THEM GO.

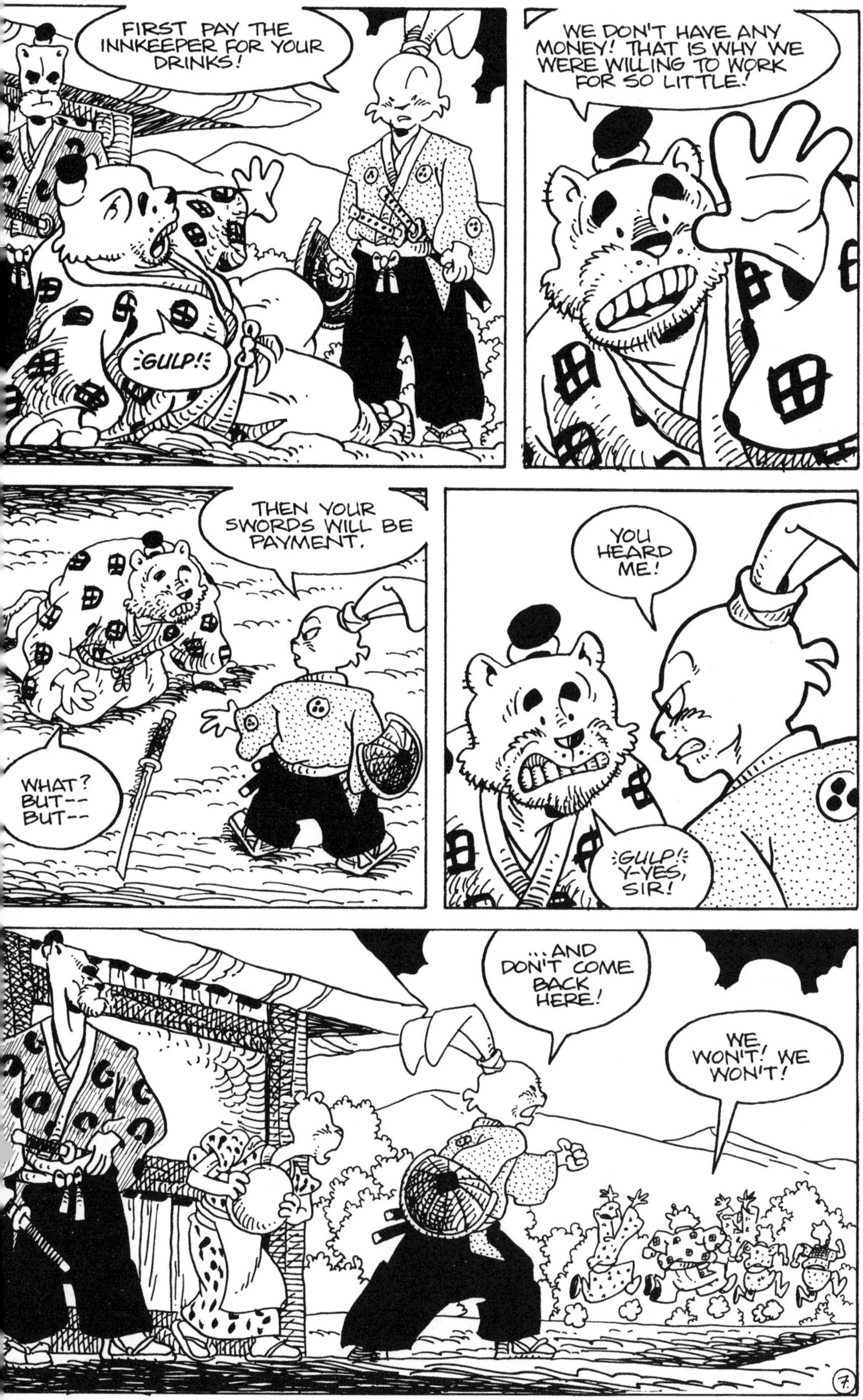
FIRST PAY THE INNKEEPER FOR YOUR DRINKS!
GULP!
WE DON'T HAVE ANY MONEY! THAT IS WHY WE WERE WILLING TO WORK FOR SO LITTLE!
THEN YOUR SWORDS WILL BE PAYMENT.
WHAT? BUT-- BUT--
YOU HEARD ME!
GULP! Y-YES, SIR!
...AND DON'T COME BACK HERE!
WE WON'T! WE WON'T!
7.

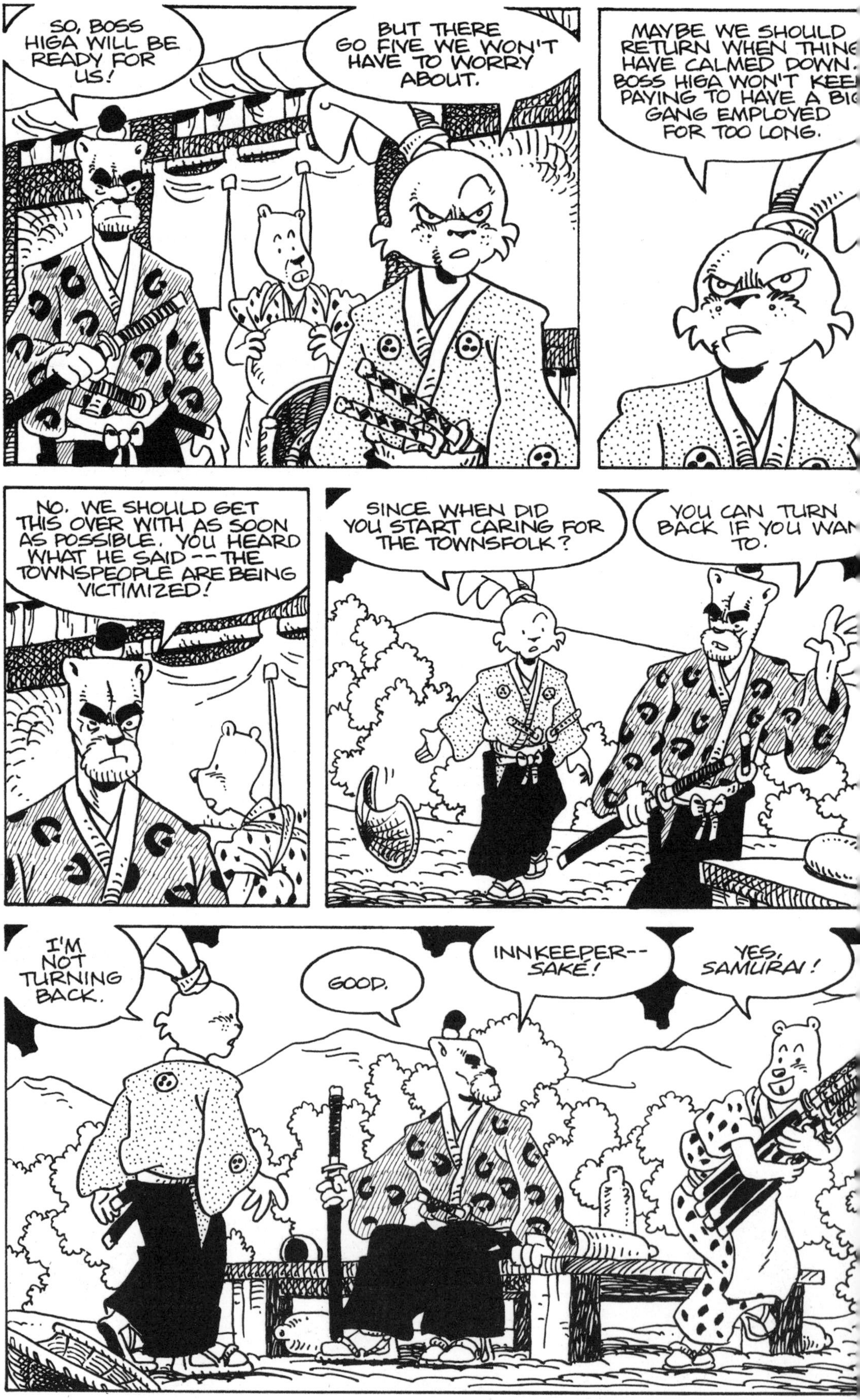
SO, BOSS HIGA WILL BE READY FOR US!
BUT THERE GO FIVE WE WON'T HAVE TO WORRY ABOUT.
MAYBE WE SHOULD RETURN WHEN THING HAVE CALMED DOWN. BOSS HIGA WON'T KEE PAYING TO HAVE A BIG GANG EMPLOYED FOR TOO LONG.
NO. WE SHOULD GET THIS OVER WITH AS SOON AS POSSIBLE. YOU HEARD WHAT HE SAID -- THE TOWNSPEOPLE ARE BEING VICTIMIZED!
SINCE WHEN DID YOU START CARING FOR THE TOWNSFOLK?
YOU CAN TURN BACK IF YOU WAN TO.
I'M NOT TURNING BACK.
GOOD.
INNKEEPER-- SAKE!
YES, SAMURAI!

LATER...

HOW EMPTY THE STREETS ARE!

I THOUGHT WE DID THIS TOWN A FAVOR WHEN WE GOT RID OF BOSS KOMO.

BOSS HIGA REALLY CLAMPED DOWN AN IRON HAND AFTER WE LEFT.

THIS PLACE IS IN WORSE SHAPE THAN WHEN THERE WERE TWO BOSSES FIGHTING OVER IT.

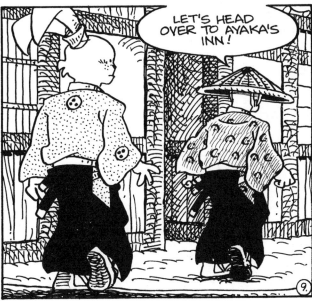

LET'S HEAD OVER TO AYAKA'S INN!

9.

343

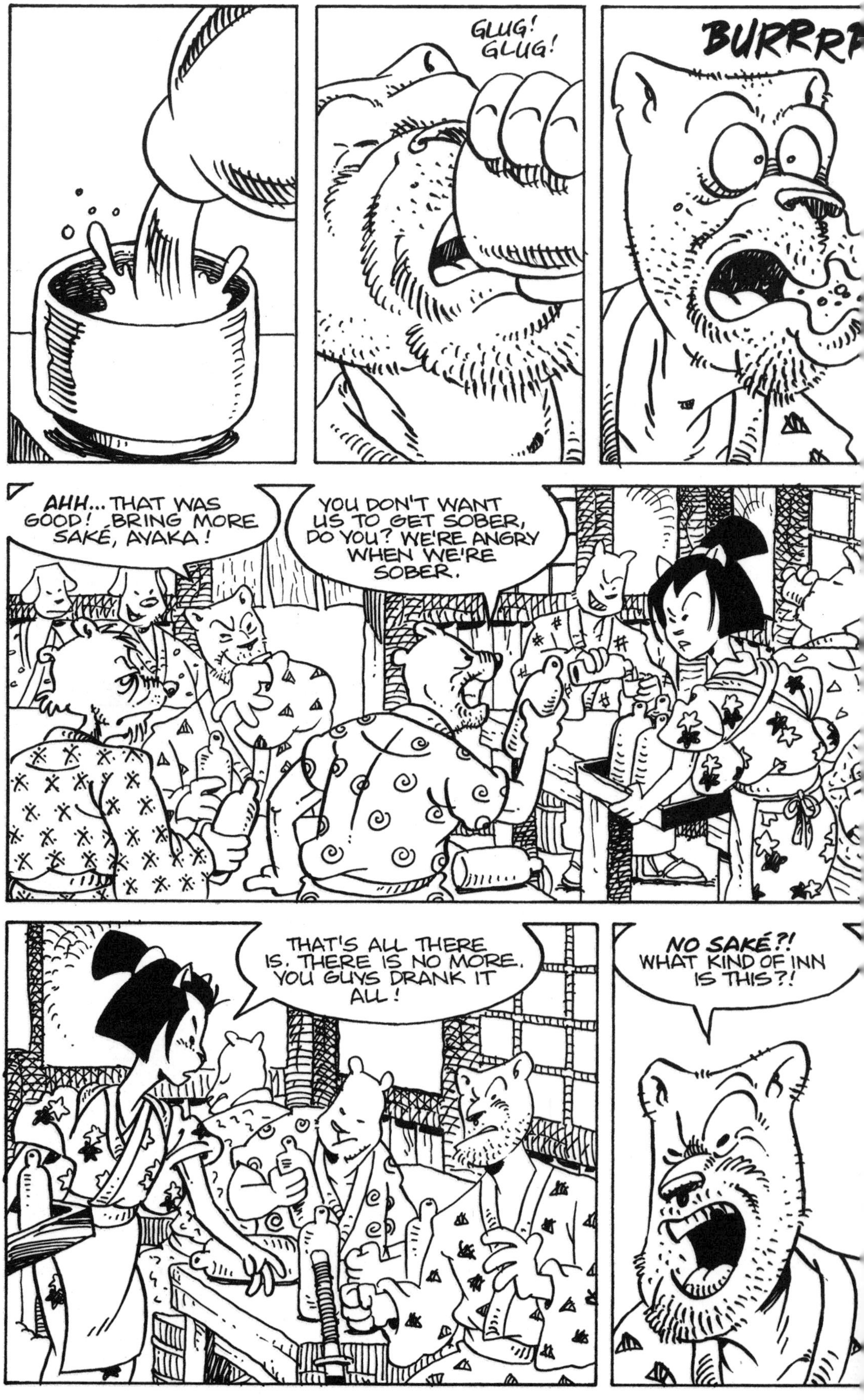
GLUG! GLUG!
BURRRP
AHH... THAT WAS GOOD! BRING MORE SAKÉ, AYAKA!
YOU DON'T WANT US TO GET SOBER, DO YOU? WE'RE ANGRY WHEN WE'RE SOBER.
THAT'S ALL THERE IS. THERE IS NO MORE. YOU GUYS DRANK IT ALL!
NO SAKÉ?! WHAT KIND OF INN IS THIS?!

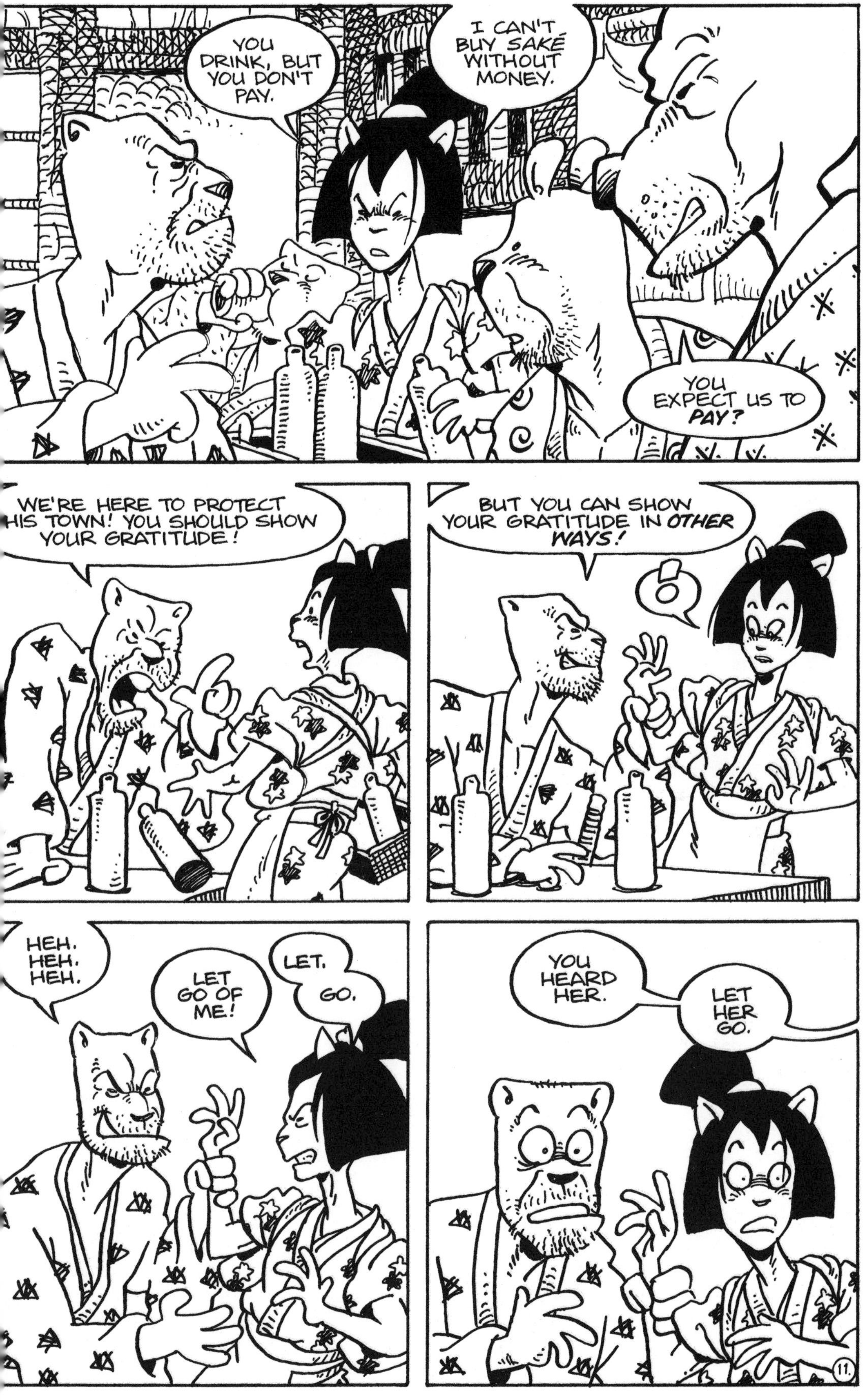
YOU DRINK, BUT YOU DON'T PAY.
I CAN'T BUY SAKE WITHOUT MONEY.
YOU EXPECT US TO *PAY?*
WE'RE HERE TO PROTECT HIS TOWN! YOU SHOULD SHOW YOUR GRATITUDE!
BUT YOU CAN SHOW YOUR GRATITUDE IN *OTHER WAYS!*
HEH. HEH. HEH.
LET GO OF ME!
LET. GO.
YOU HEARD HER.
LET HER GO.
11.

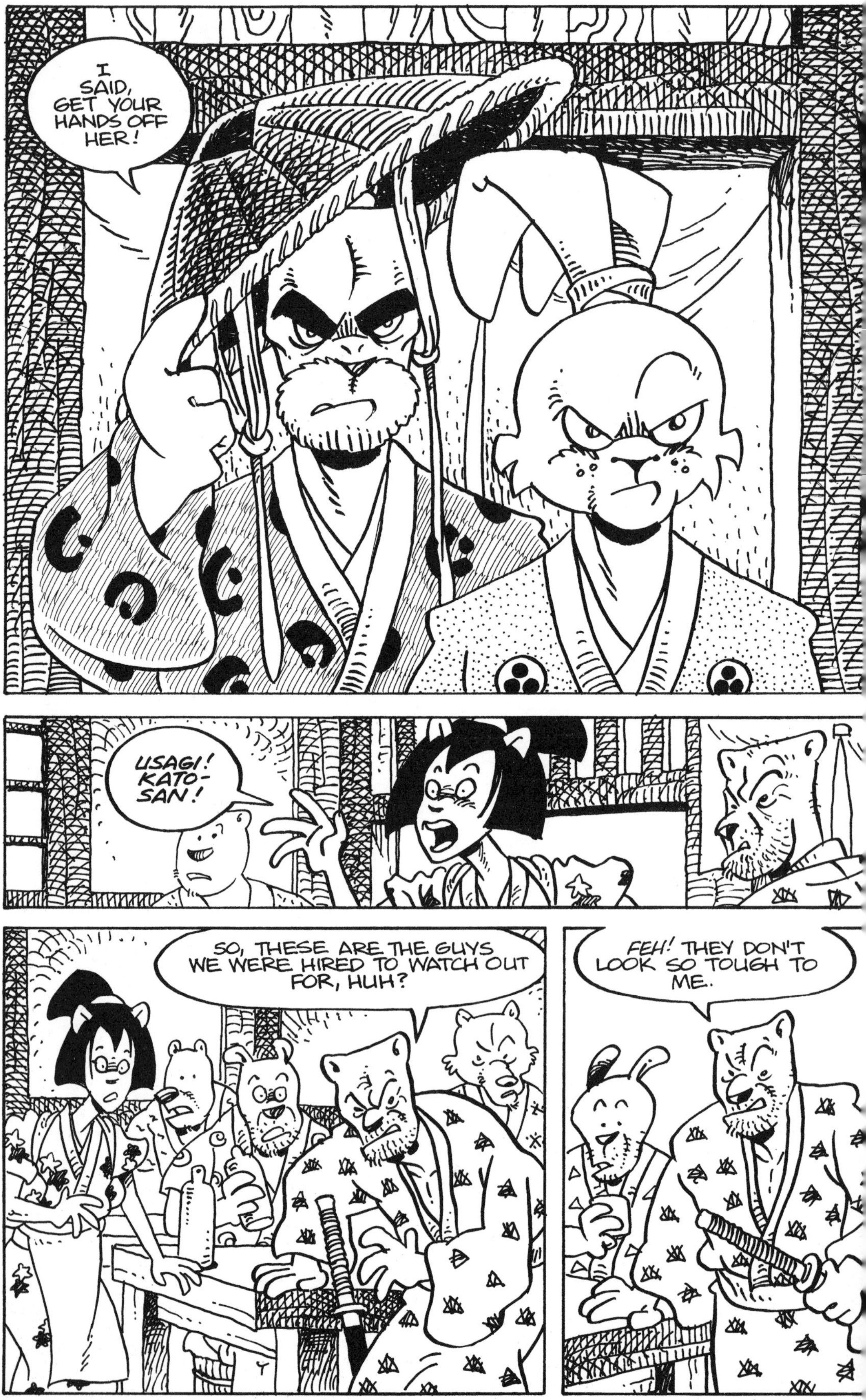
I SAID, GET YOUR HANDS OFF HER!
USAGI! KATO-SAN!
SO, THESE ARE THE GUYS WE WERE HIRED TO WATCH OUT FOR, HUH?
FEH! THEY DON'T LOOK SO TOUGH TO ME.

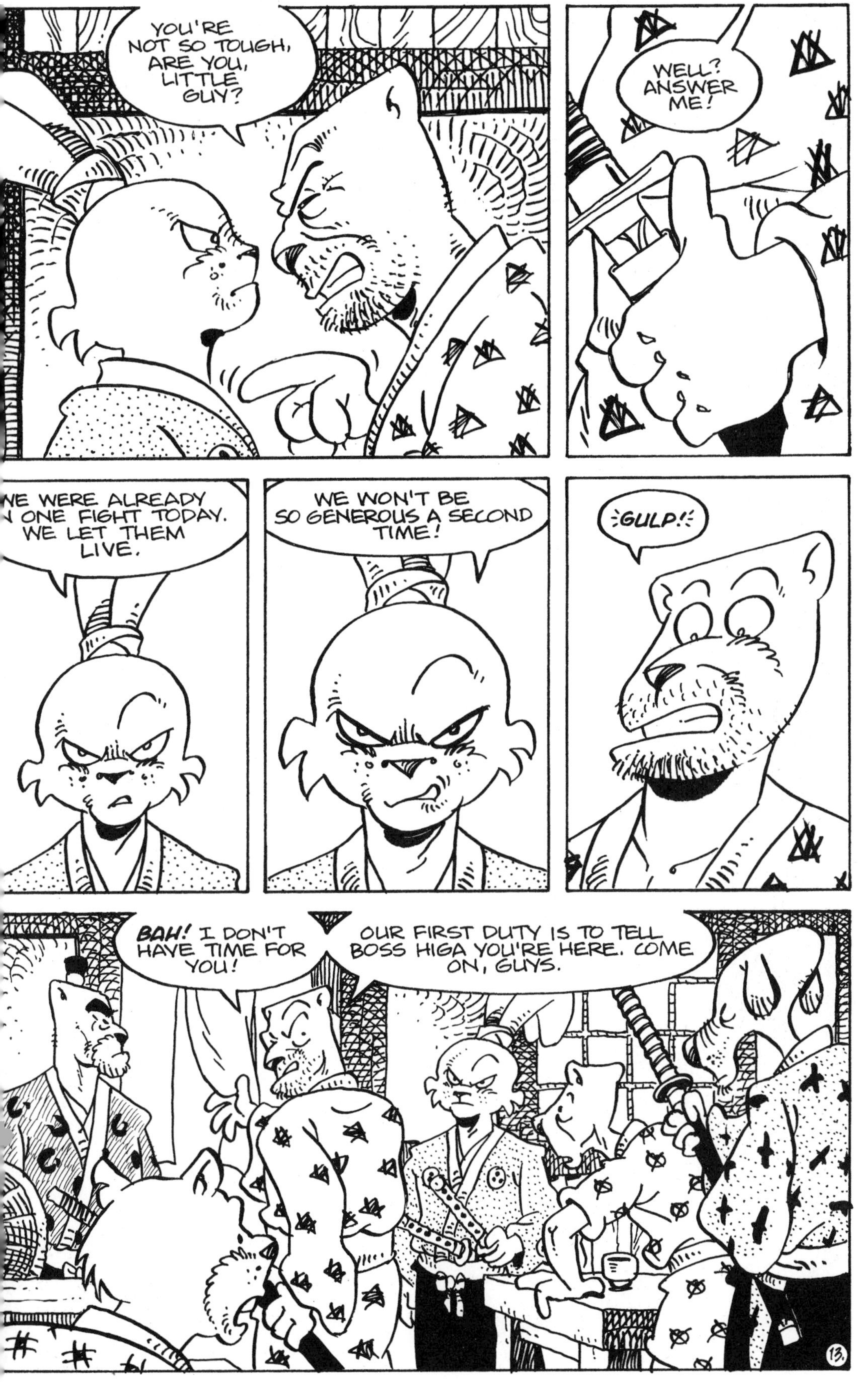

YOU'RE NOT SO TOUGH, ARE YOU, LITTLE GUY?
WELL? ANSWER ME!
WE WERE ALREADY IN ONE FIGHT TODAY. WE LET THEM LIVE.
WE WON'T BE SO GENEROUS A SECOND TIME!
GULP!
BAH! I DON'T HAVE TIME FOR YOU!
OUR FIRST DUTY IS TO TELL BOSS HIGA YOU'RE HERE. COME ON, GUYS.
13

WOW. LOOK AT THEM GO.

I DID NOT THINK YOU TWO WOULD BE BACK.

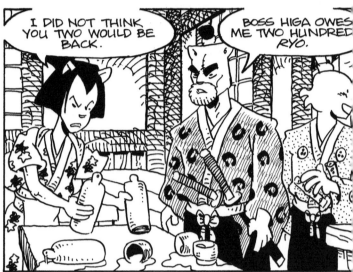

BOSS HIGA OWES ME TWO HUNDRED RYO.

THE MONEY? YEAH, THAT WOULD BE THE REASON FOR YOU TO RETURN.

IT WAS YOUR FAULT THAT THINGS GOT AS BAD AS THEY DID, BUT YOU SAMURAI STILL JUST THINK OF YOURSELVES.

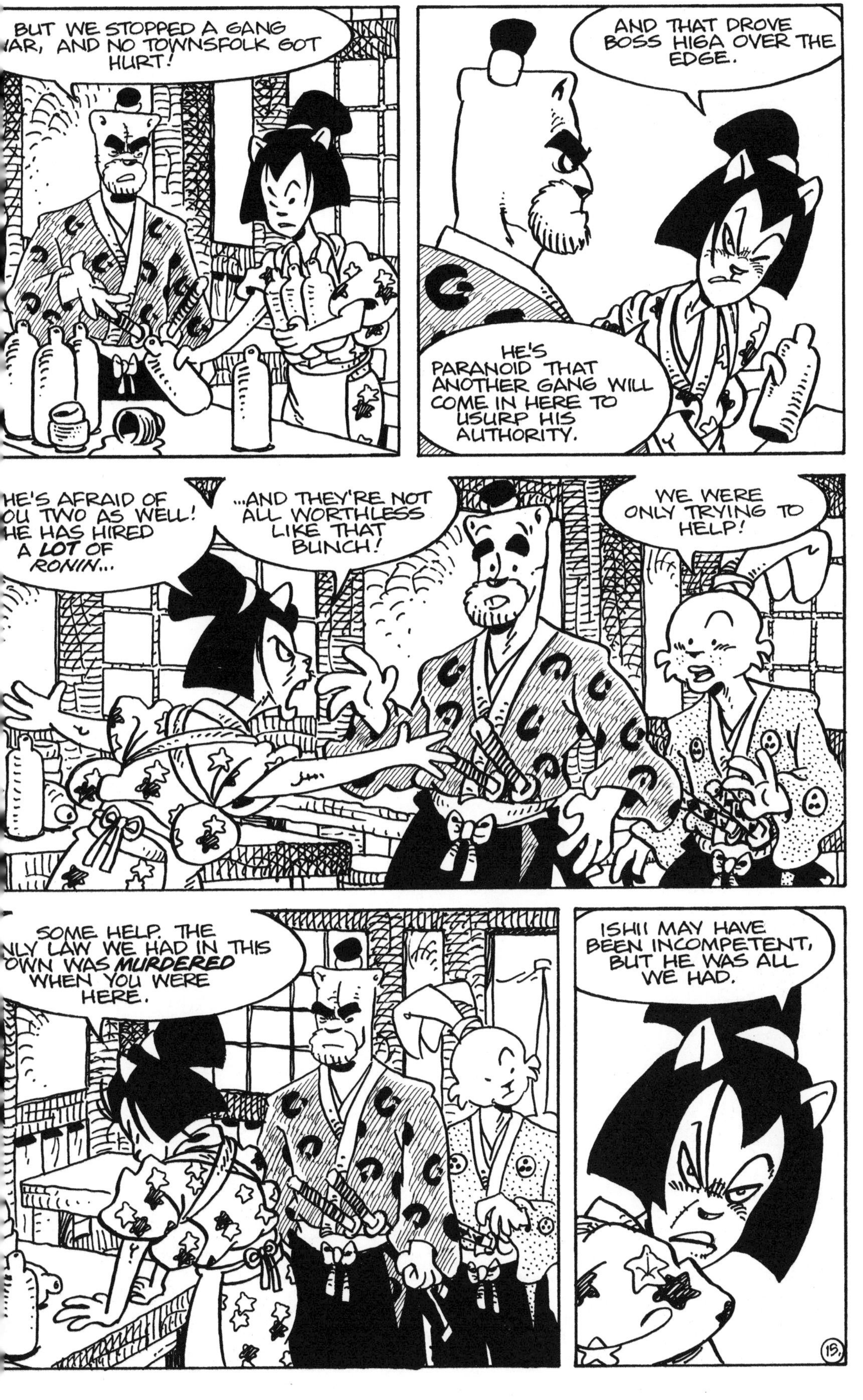
BUT WE STOPPED A GANG AR, AND NO TOWNSFOLK GOT HURT!
AND THAT DROVE BOSS HIGA OVER THE EDGE.
HE'S PARANOID THAT ANOTHER GANG WILL COME IN HERE TO USURP HIS AUTHORITY.
HE'S AFRAID OF OU TWO AS WELL! HE HAS HIRED A LOT OF RONIN...
...AND THEY'RE NOT ALL WORTHLESS LIKE THAT BUNCH!
WE WERE ONLY TRYING TO HELP!
SOME HELP. THE NLY LAW WE HAD IN THIS OWN WAS MURDERED WHEN YOU WERE HERE.
ISHII MAY HAVE BEEN INCOMPETENT, BUT HE WAS ALL WE HAD.
15

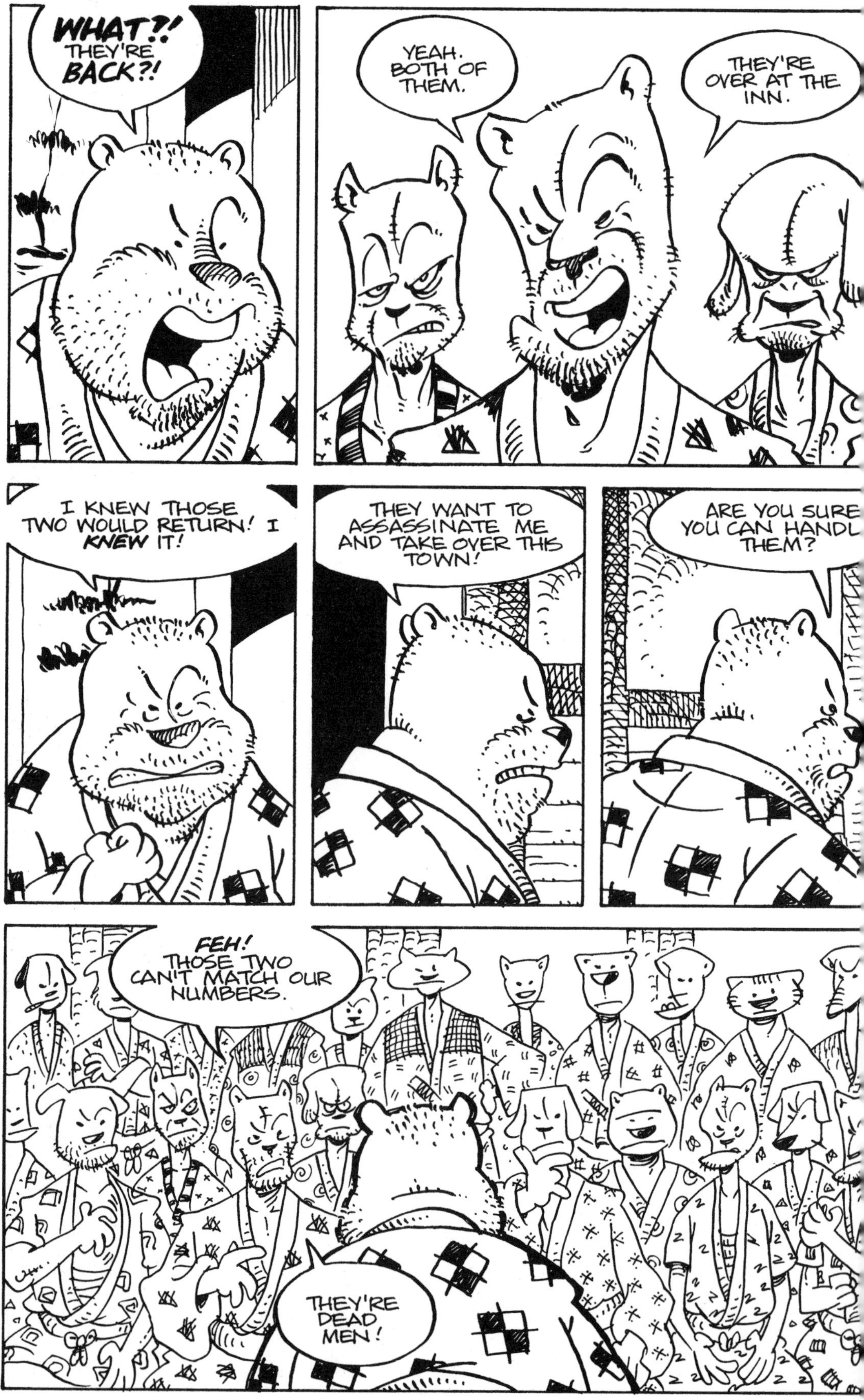
WHAT?! THEY'RE BACK?!
YEAH. BOTH OF THEM.
THEY'RE OVER AT THE INN.
I KNEW THOSE TWO WOULD RETURN! I KNEW IT!
THEY WANT TO ASSASSINATE ME AND TAKE OVER THIS TOWN!
ARE YOU SURE YOU CAN HANDL THEM?
FEH! THOSE TWO CAN'T MATCH OUR NUMBERS.
THEY'RE DEAD MEN!

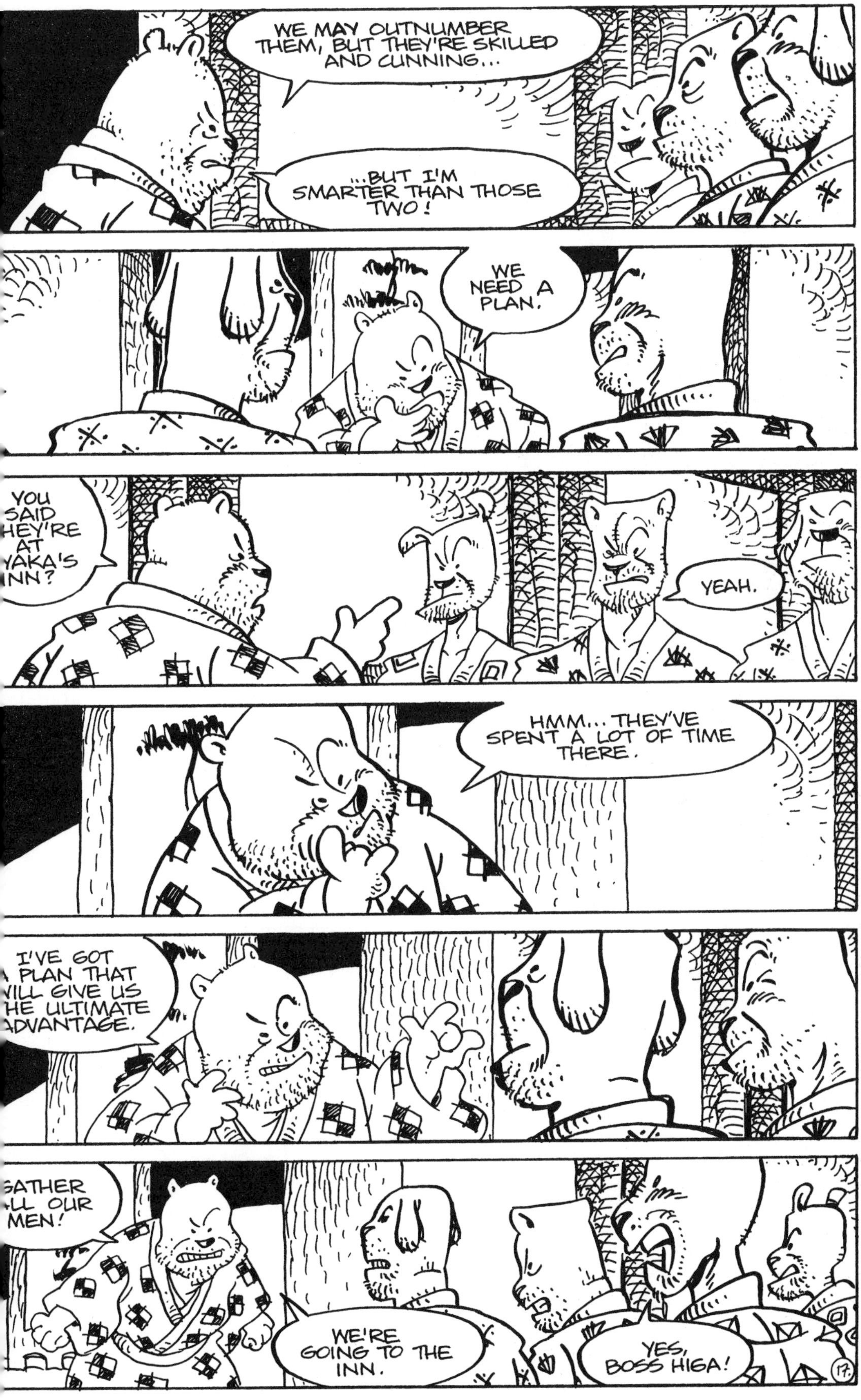
WE MAY OUTNUMBER THEM, BUT THEY'RE SKILLED AND CUNNING...
...BUT I'M SMARTER THAN THOSE TWO!
WE NEED A PLAN.
YOU SAID HEY'RE AT YAKA'S INN?
YEAH.
HMM... THEY'VE SPENT A LOT OF TIME THERE.
I'VE GOT A PLAN THAT VILL GIVE US HE ULTIMATE ADVANTAGE.
GATHER LL OUR MEN!
WE'RE GOING TO THE INN.
YES, BOSS HIGA!
17

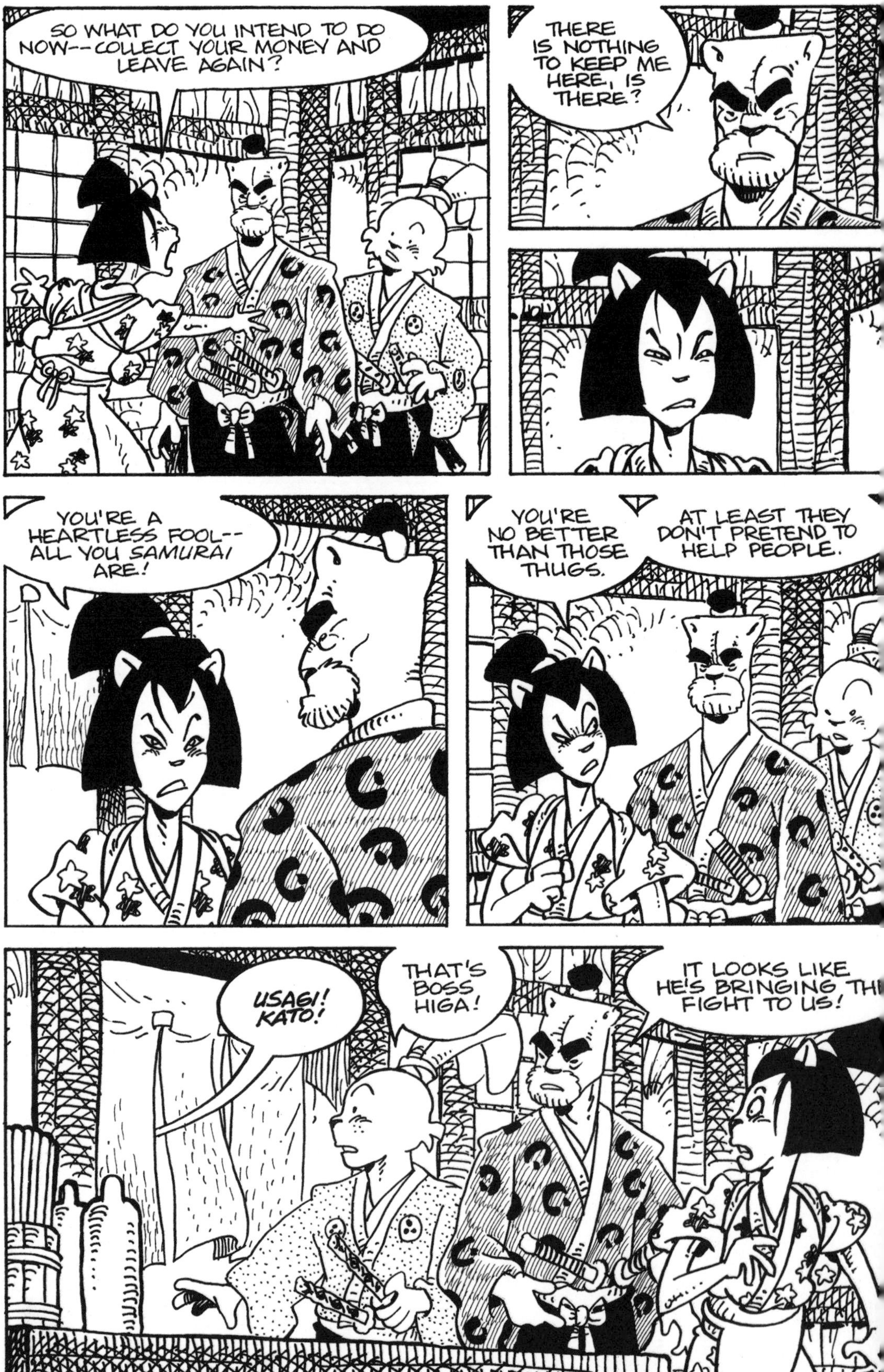
SO WHAT DO YOU INTEND TO DO NOW--COLLECT YOUR MONEY AND LEAVE AGAIN?
THERE IS NOTHING TO KEEP ME HERE, IS THERE?
YOU'RE A HEARTLESS FOOL--ALL YOU SAMURAI ARE!
YOU'RE NO BETTER THAN THOSE THUGS.
AT LEAST THEY DON'T PRETEND TO HELP PEOPLE.
USAGI! KATO!
THAT'S BOSS HIGA!
IT LOOKS LIKE HE'S BRINGING TH
FIGHT TO US!

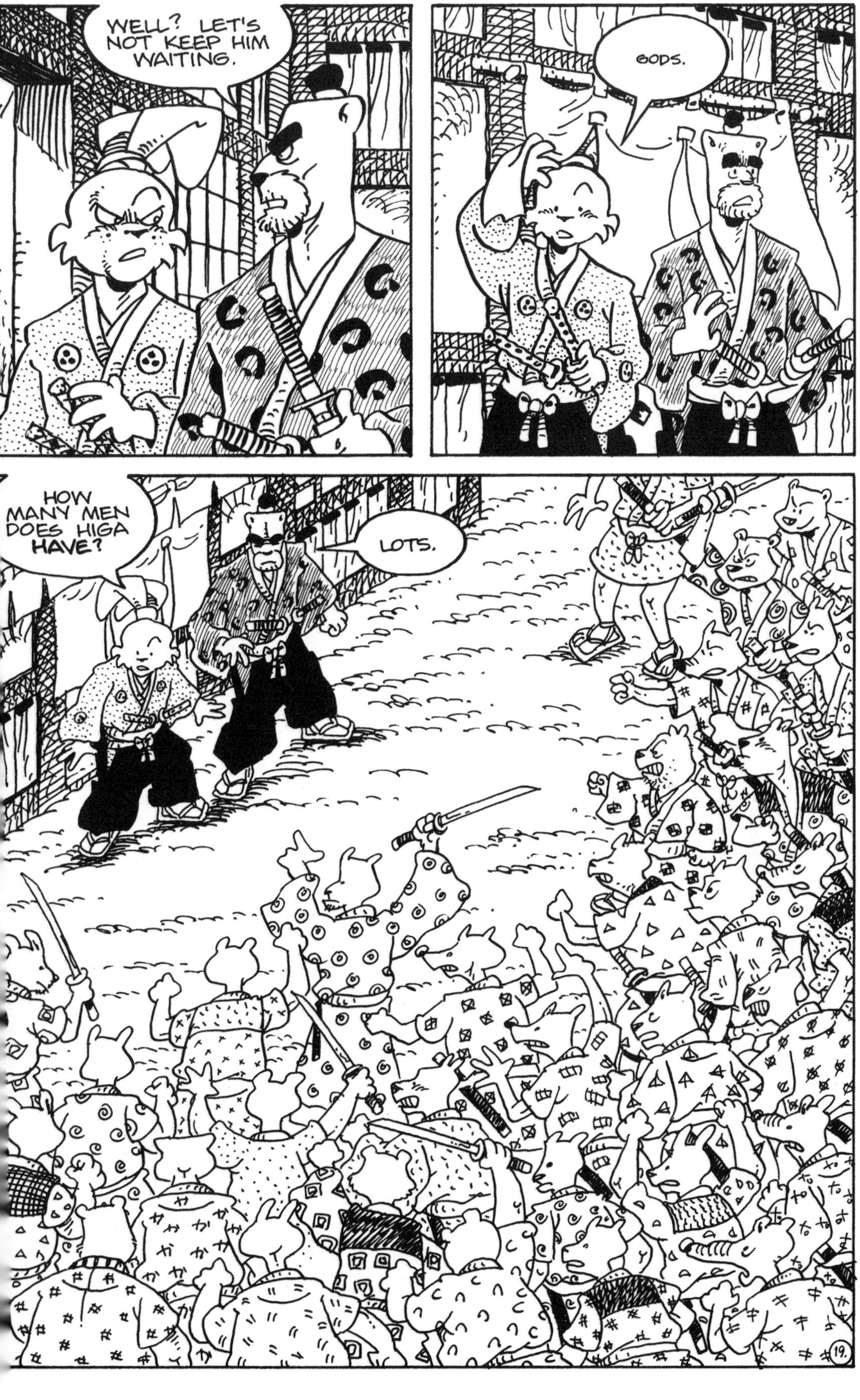
WELL? LET'S NOT KEEP HIM WAITING.
GODS.
HOW MANY MEN DOES HIGA **HAVE?**
LOTS.
19.

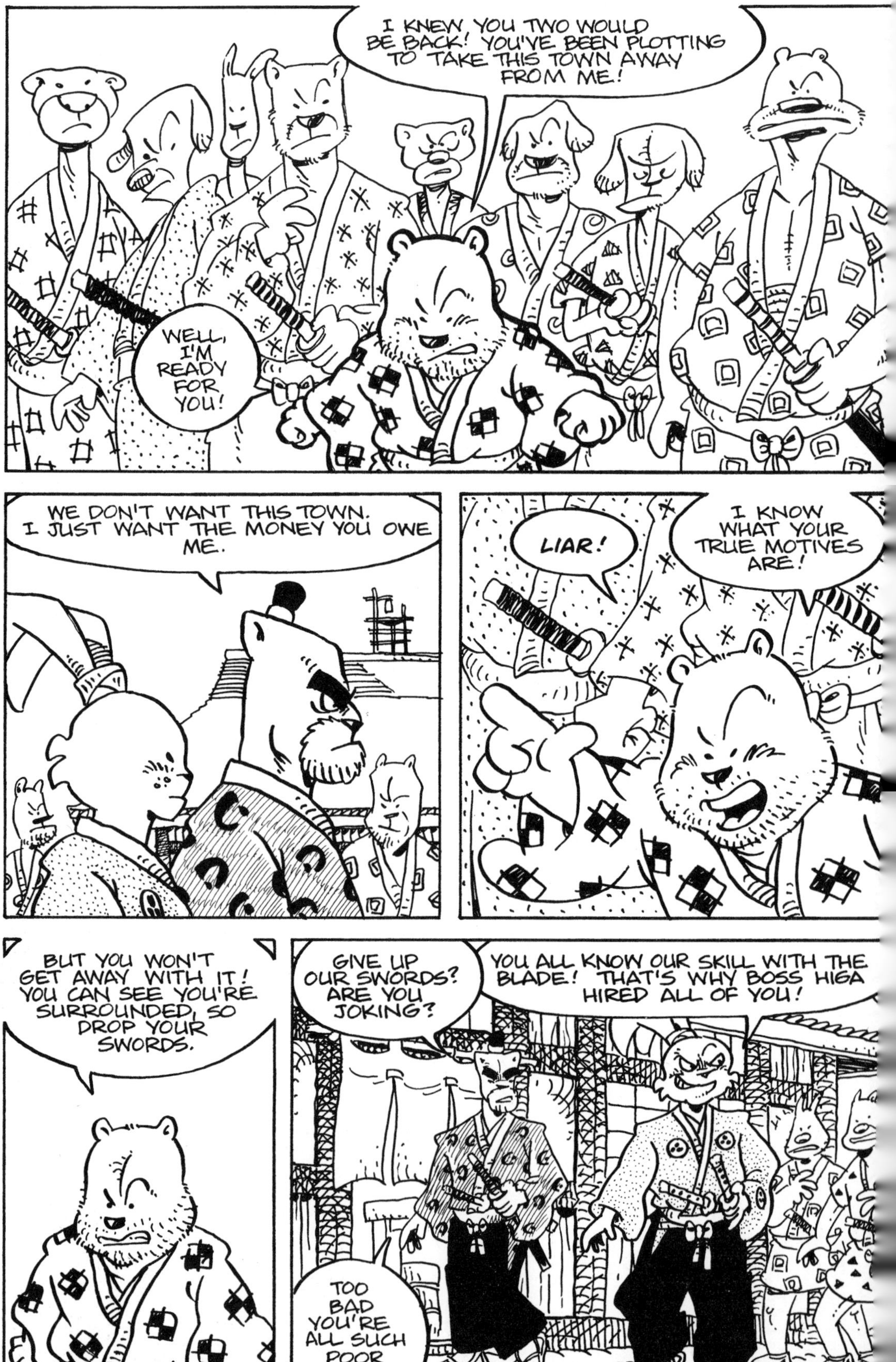
I KNEW, YOU TWO WOULD BE BACK! YOU'VE BEEN PLOTTING TO TAKE THIS TOWN AWAY FROM ME!
WELL, I'M READY FOR YOU!
WE DON'T WANT THIS TOWN. I JUST WANT THE MONEY YOU OWE ME.
LIAR!
I KNOW WHAT YOUR TRUE MOTIVES ARE!
BUT YOU WON'T GET AWAY WITH IT! YOU CAN SEE YOU'RE SURROUNDED, SO DROP YOUR SWORDS.
GIVE UP OUR SWORDS? ARE YOU JOKING?
YOU ALL KNOW OUR SKILL WITH THE BLADE! THAT'S WHY BOSS HIGA HIRED ALL OF YOU!
TOO BAD YOU'RE ALL SUCH POOR SWORDS-MEN.

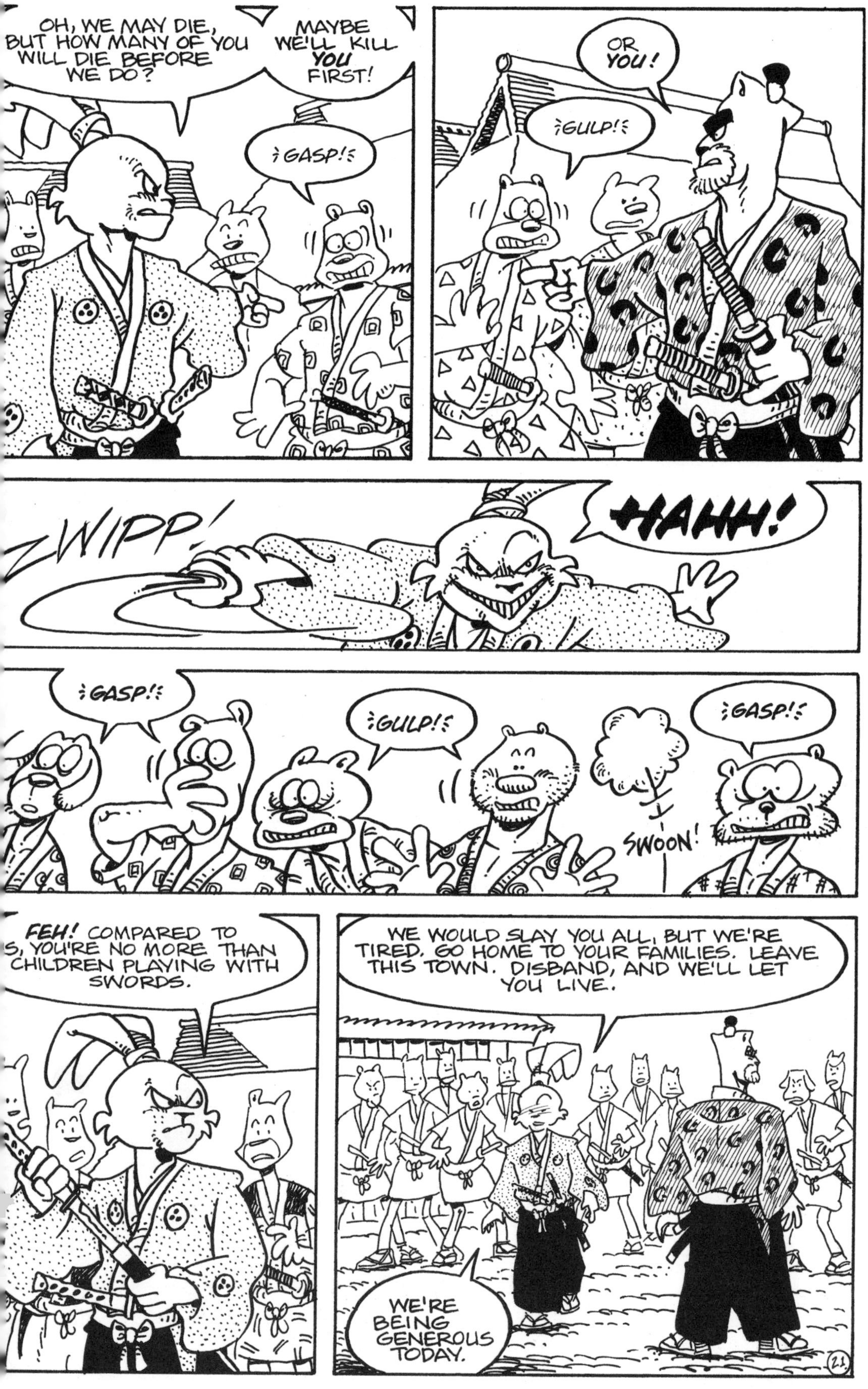

OH, WE MAY DIE, BUT HOW MANY OF YOU WILL DIE BEFORE WE DO?
MAYBE WE'LL KILL YOU FIRST!
¡GASP!¡
OR YOU!
¡GULP!¡
ZWIPP!
HAHH!
¡GASP!¡
¡GULP!¡
SWOON!
¡GASP!¡
FEH! COMPARED TO
S, YOU'RE NO MORE THAN CHILDREN PLAYING WITH SWORDS.
WE WOULD SLAY YOU ALL, BUT WE'RE TIRED. GO HOME TO YOUR FAMILIES. LEAVE THIS TOWN. DISBAND, AND WE'LL LET YOU LIVE.
WE'RE BEING GENEROUS TODAY.
21

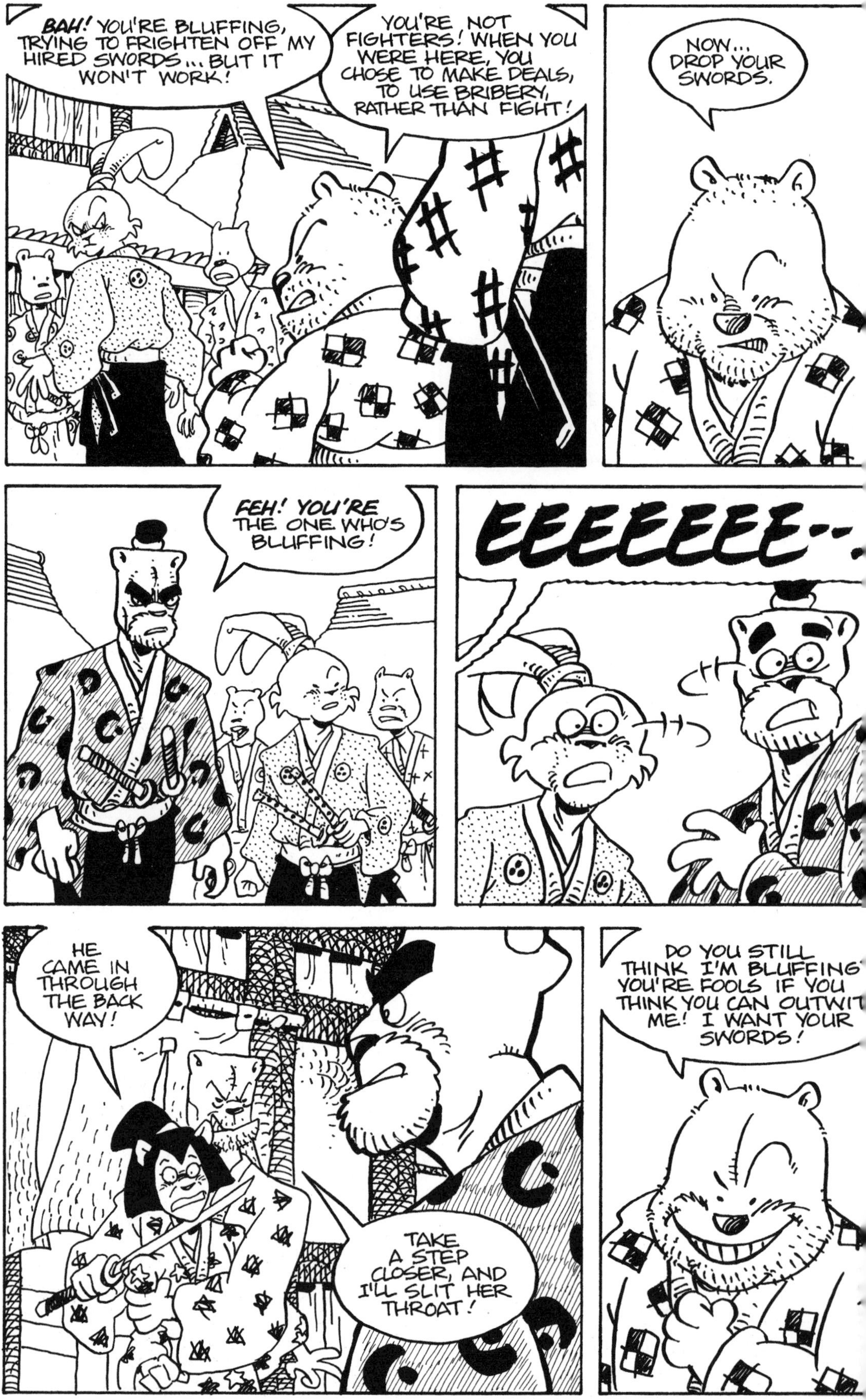
BAH! YOU'RE BLUFFING, TRYING TO FRIGHTEN OFF MY HIRED SWORDS... BUT IT WON'T WORK!
YOU'RE NOT FIGHTERS! WHEN YOU WERE HERE, YOU CHOSE TO MAKE DEALS, TO USE BRIBERY, RATHER THAN FIGHT!
NOW... DROP YOUR SWORDS.
FEH! YOU'RE THE ONE WHO'S BLUFFING!
EEEEEEEE--
HE CAME IN THROUGH THE BACK WAY!
TAKE A STEP CLOSER, AND I'LL SLIT HER THROAT!
DO YOU STILL THINK I'M BLUFFING? YOU'RE FOOLS IF YOU THINK YOU CAN OUTWIT ME! I WANT YOUR SWORDS!

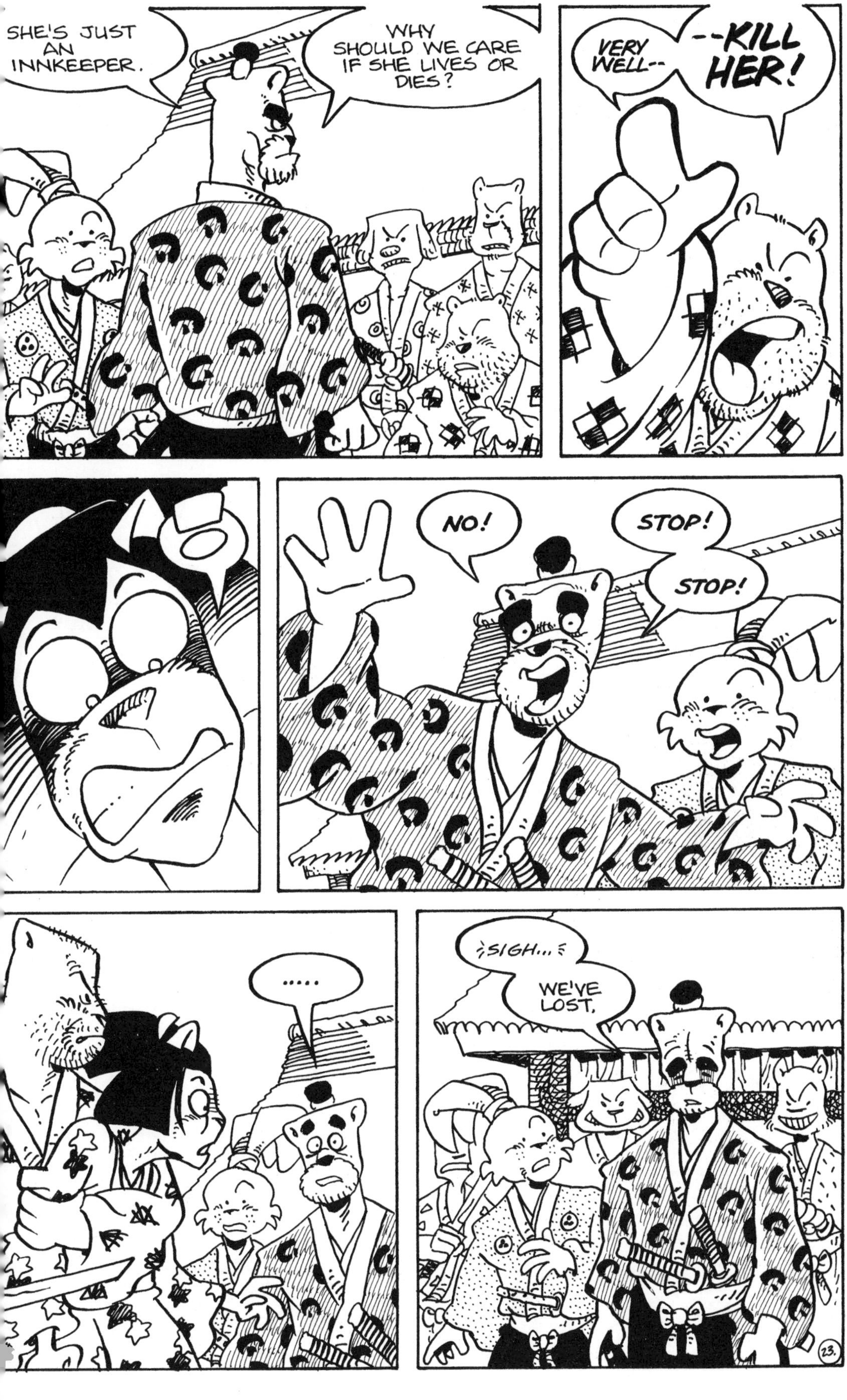

SHE'S JUST AN INNKEEPER.
WHY SHOULD WE CARE IF SHE LIVES OR DIES?
VERY WELL--
--KILL HER!
NO!
STOP!
STOP!
.....
SIGH...
WE'VE LOST.
23.

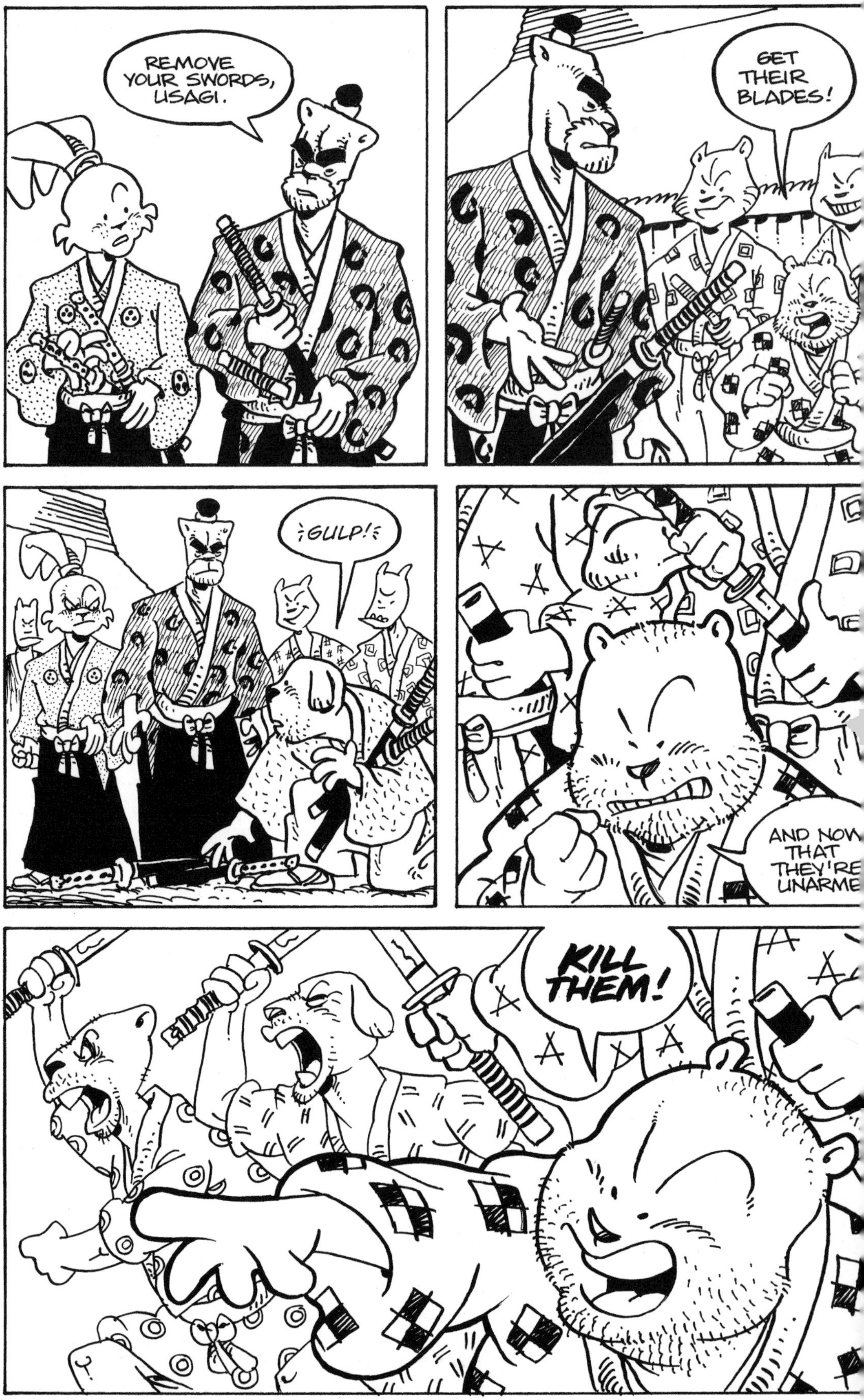
REMOVE YOUR SWORDS, USAGI.
GET THEIR BLADES!
GULP!
AND NOW THAT THEY'RE UNARME
KILL THEM!

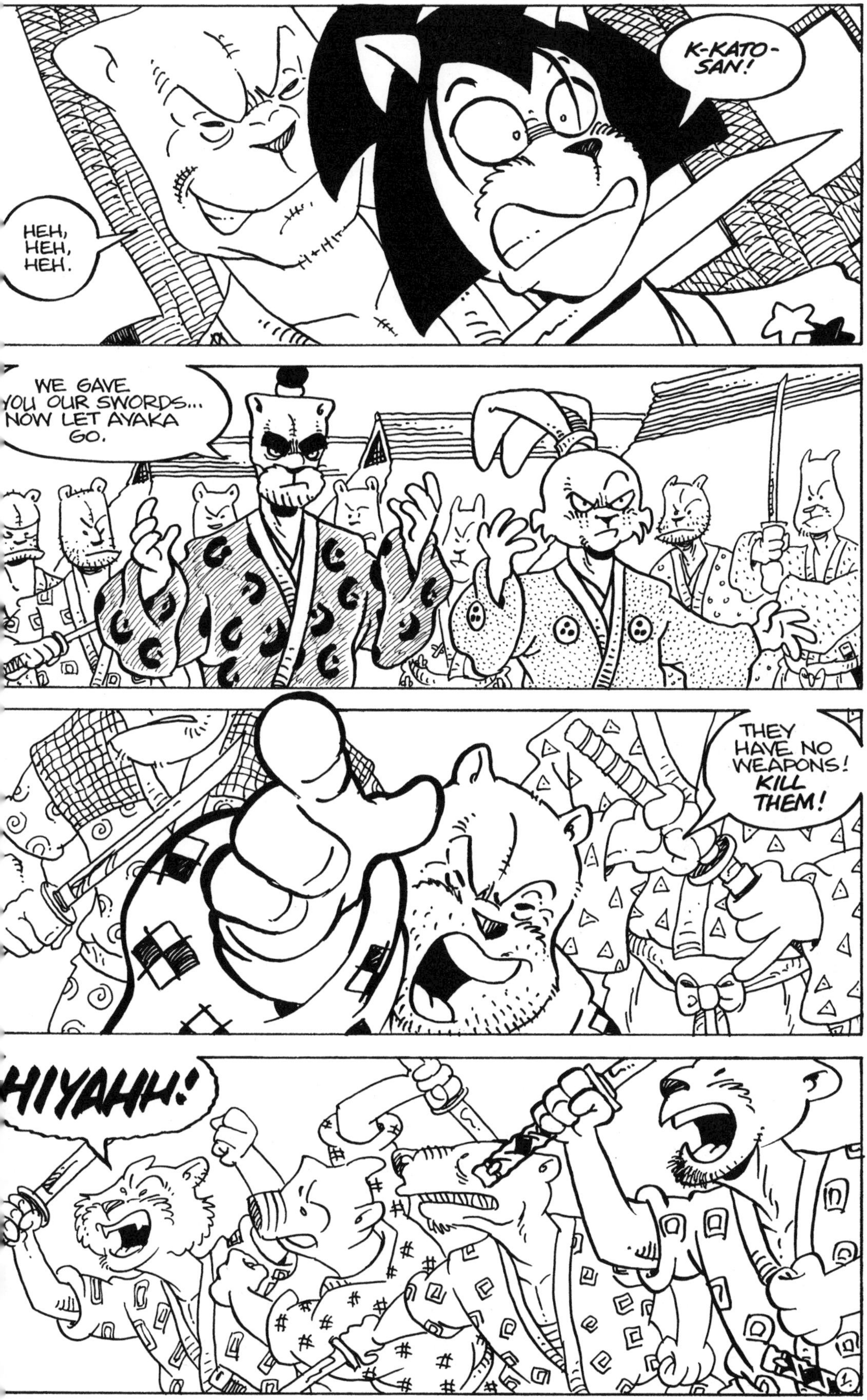
K-KATO-SAN!
HEH, HEH, HEH.
WE GAVE YOU OUR SWORDS... NOW LET AYAKA GO.
THEY HAVE NO WEAPONS! **KILL THEM!**
HIYAHH!

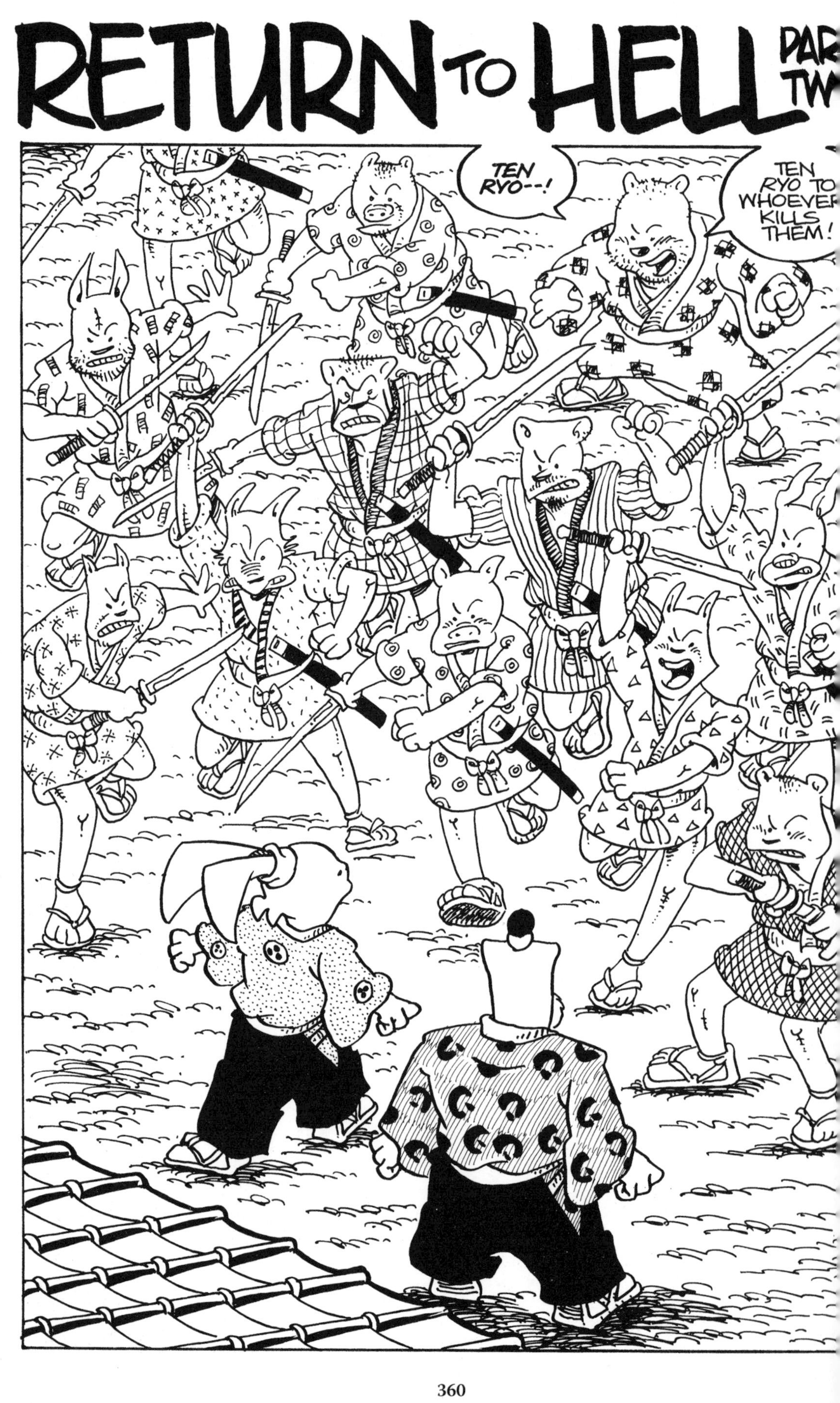
RETURN TO HELL PAR TW
TEN RYO--!
TEN RYO TO WHOEVER KILLS THEM!

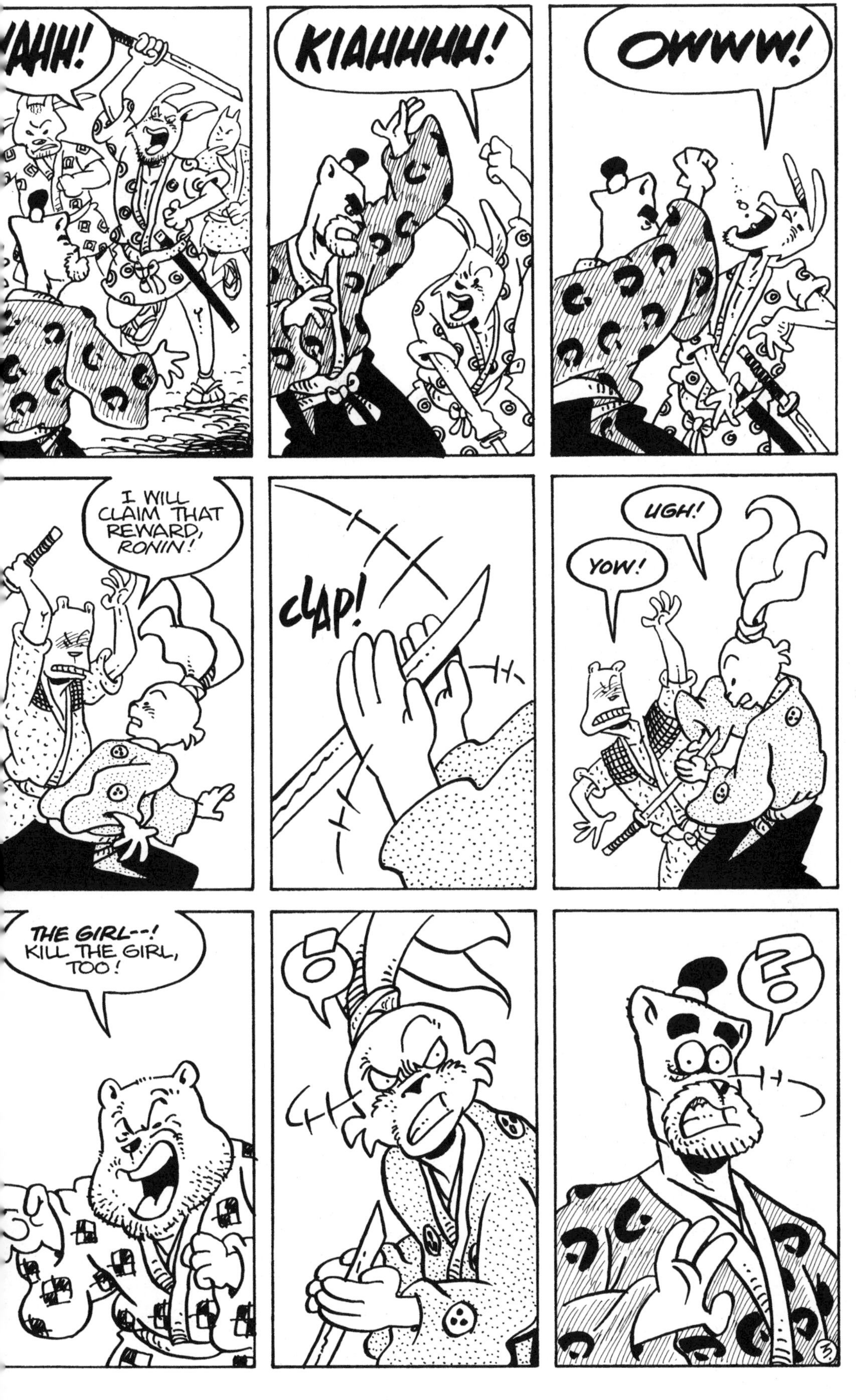
AHH!
KIAHHHH!
OWWW!
I WILL CLAIM THAT REWARD, RONIN!
CLAP!
YOW!
UGH!
THE GIRL--! KILL THE GIRL, TOO!

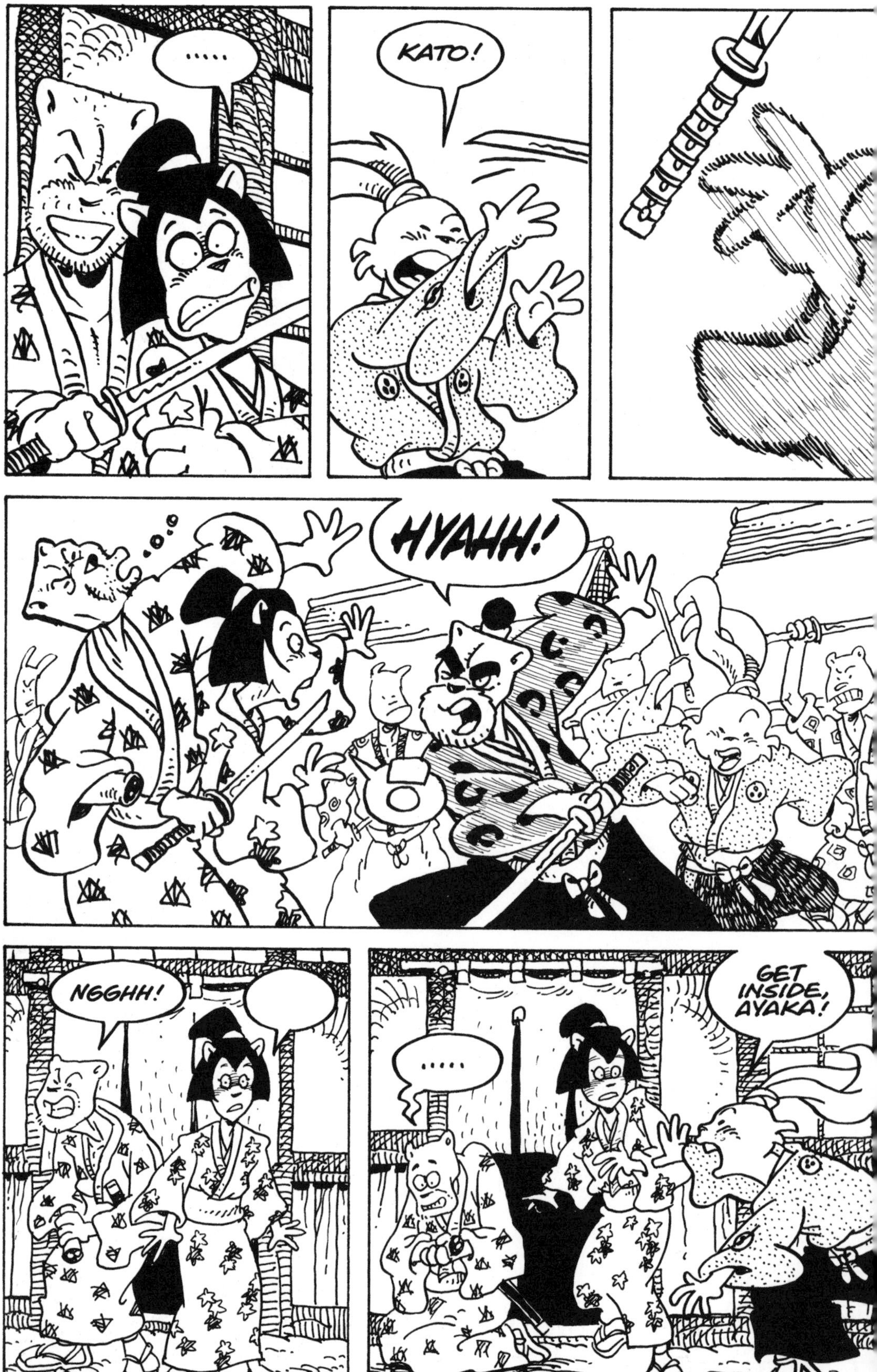
.....
KATO!
HYAHH!
NGGHH!
.....
GET INSIDE, AYAKA!

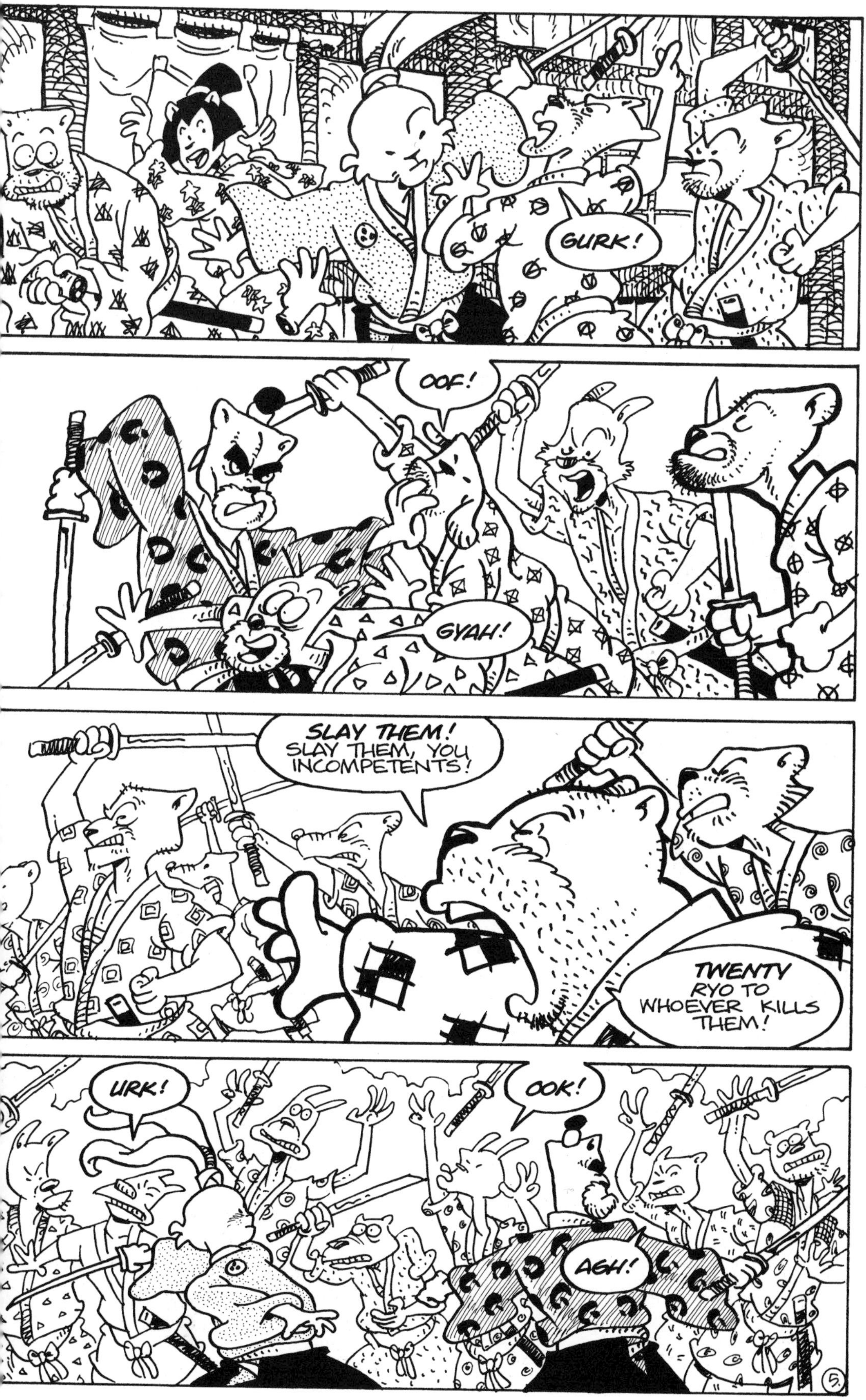
GURK!
OOF!
GYAH!
SLAY THEM! SLAY THEM, YOU INCOMPETENTS!
TWENTY RYO TO WHOEVER KILLS THEM!
URK!
OOK!
AGH!
5

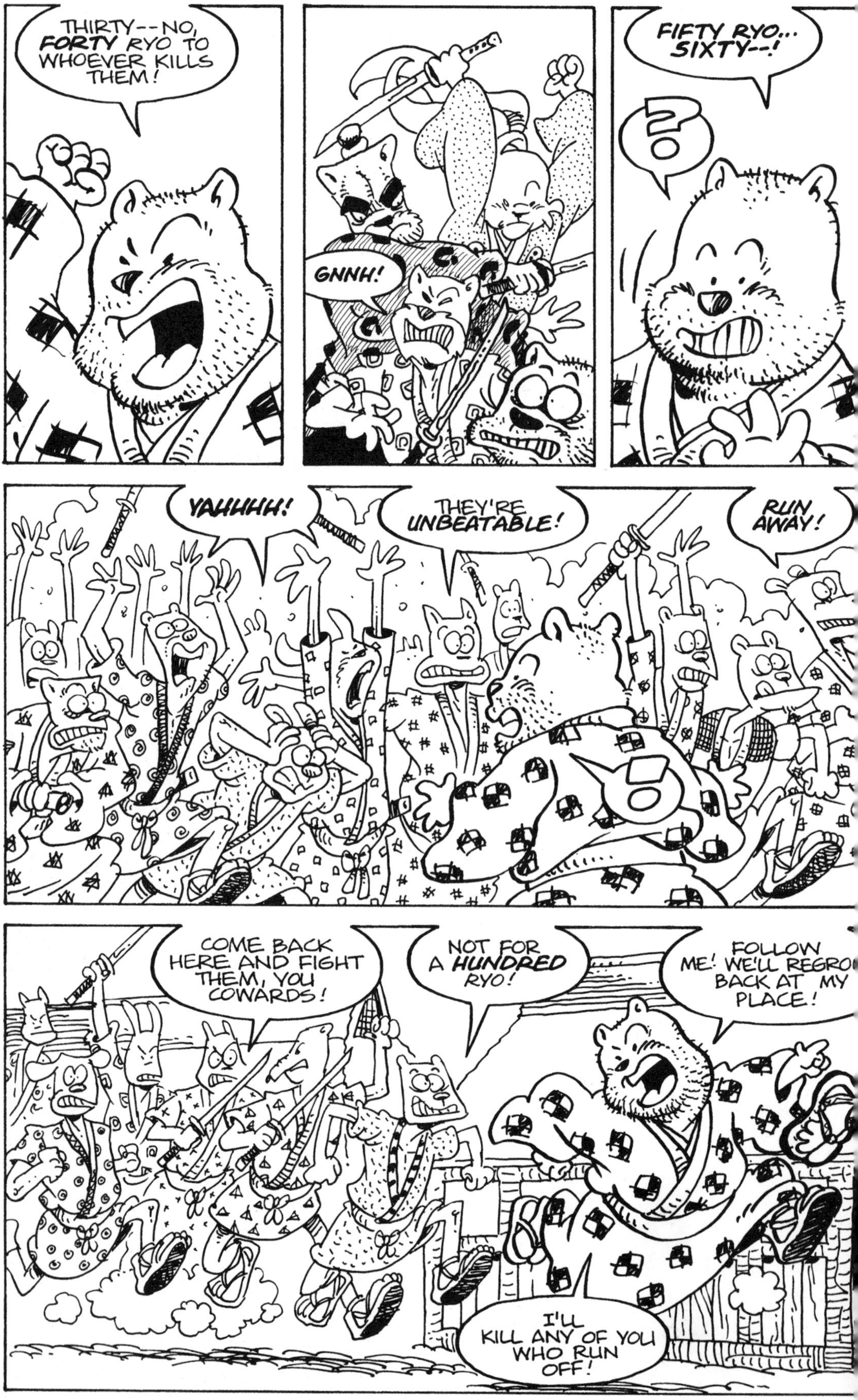
THIRTY--NO, FORTY RYO TO WHOEVER KILLS THEM!
GNNH!
FIFTY RYO... SIXTY--!
?
YAHHHH!
THEY'RE UNBEATABLE!
RUN AWAY!
COME BACK HERE AND FIGHT THEM, YOU COWARDS!
NOT FOR A HUNDRED RYO!
FOLLOW ME! WE'LL REGRO BACK AT MY PLACE!
I'LL KILL ANY OF YOU WHO RUN OFF!

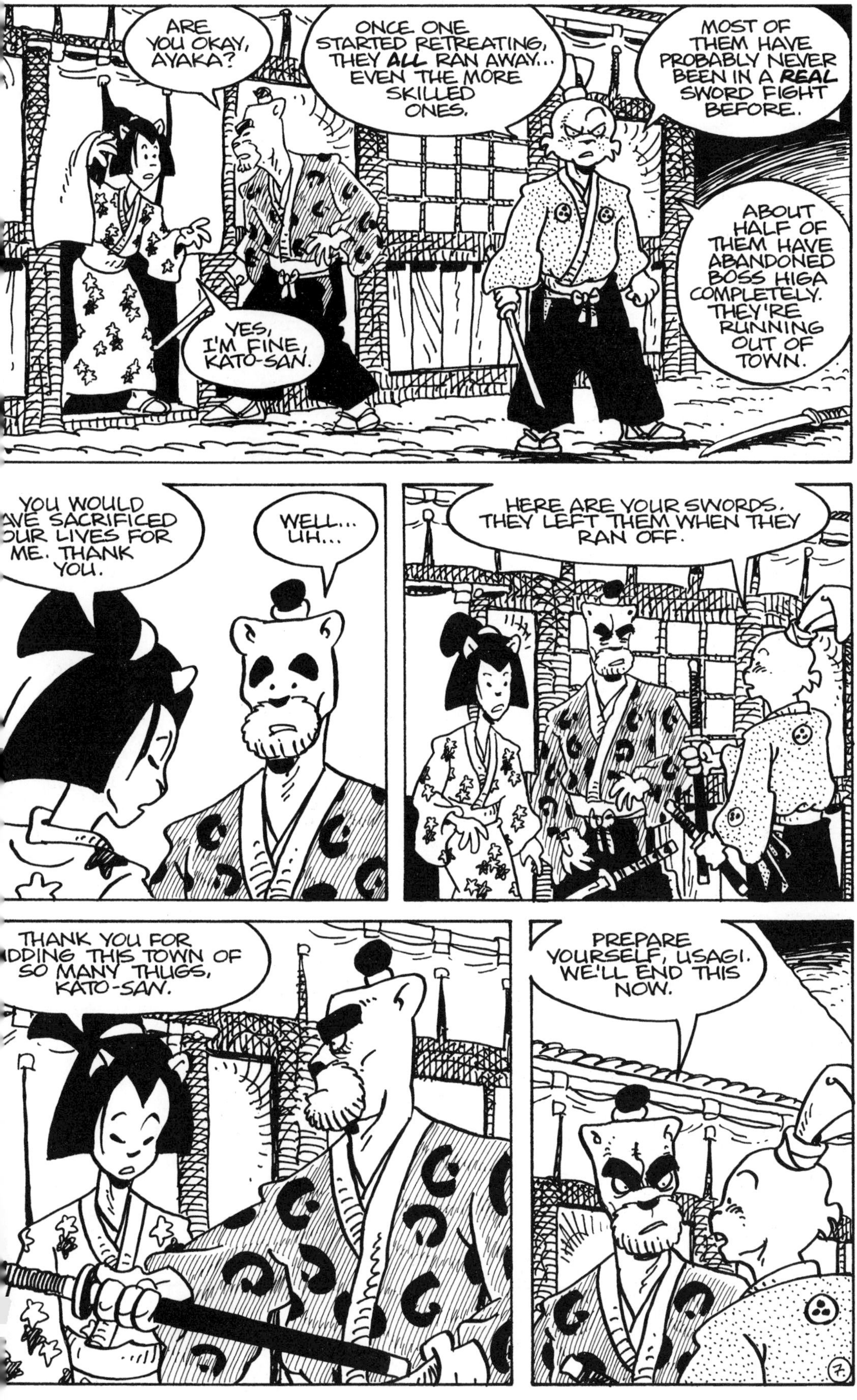
ARE YOU OKAY, AYAKA?
YES, I'M FINE, KATO-SAN.
ONCE ONE STARTED RETREATING, THEY ALL RAN AWAY... EVEN THE MORE SKILLED ONES.
MOST OF THEM HAVE PROBABLY NEVER BEEN IN A REAL SWORD FIGHT BEFORE.
ABOUT HALF OF THEM HAVE ABANDONED BOSS HIGA COMPLETELY. THEY'RE RUNNING OUT OF TOWN.
YOU WOULD AVE SACRIFICED OUR LIVES FOR ME. THANK YOU.
WELL... UH...
HERE ARE YOUR SWORDS. THEY LEFT THEM WHEN THEY RAN OFF.
THANK YOU FOR IDDING THIS TOWN OF SO MANY THUGS, KATO-SAN.
PREPARE YOURSELF, USAGI. WE'LL END THIS NOW.
7.

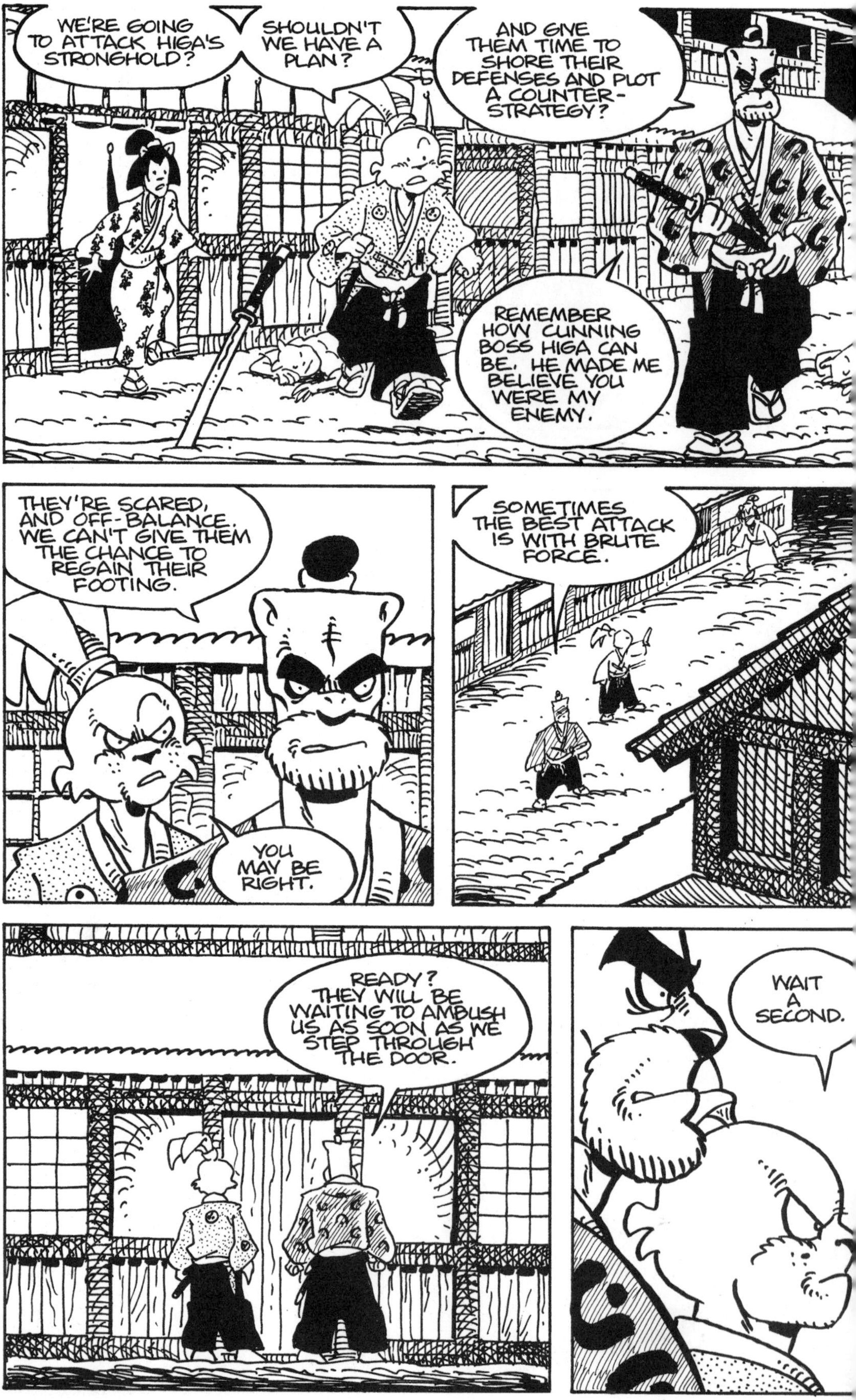
WE'RE GOING TO ATTACK HIGA'S STRONGHOLD?
SHOULDN'T WE HAVE A PLAN?
AND GIVE THEM TIME TO SHORE THEIR DEFENSES AND PLOT A COUNTER-STRATEGY?
REMEMBER HOW CUNNING BOSS HIGA CAN BE. HE MADE ME BELIEVE YOU WERE MY ENEMY.
THEY'RE SCARED, AND OFF-BALANCE. WE CAN'T GIVE THEM THE CHANCE TO REGAIN THEIR FOOTING.
YOU MAY BE RIGHT.
SOMETIMES THE BEST ATTACK IS WITH BRUTE FORCE.
READY? THEY WILL BE WAITING TO AMBUSH US AS SOON AS WE STEP THROUGH THE DOOR.
WAIT A SECOND.

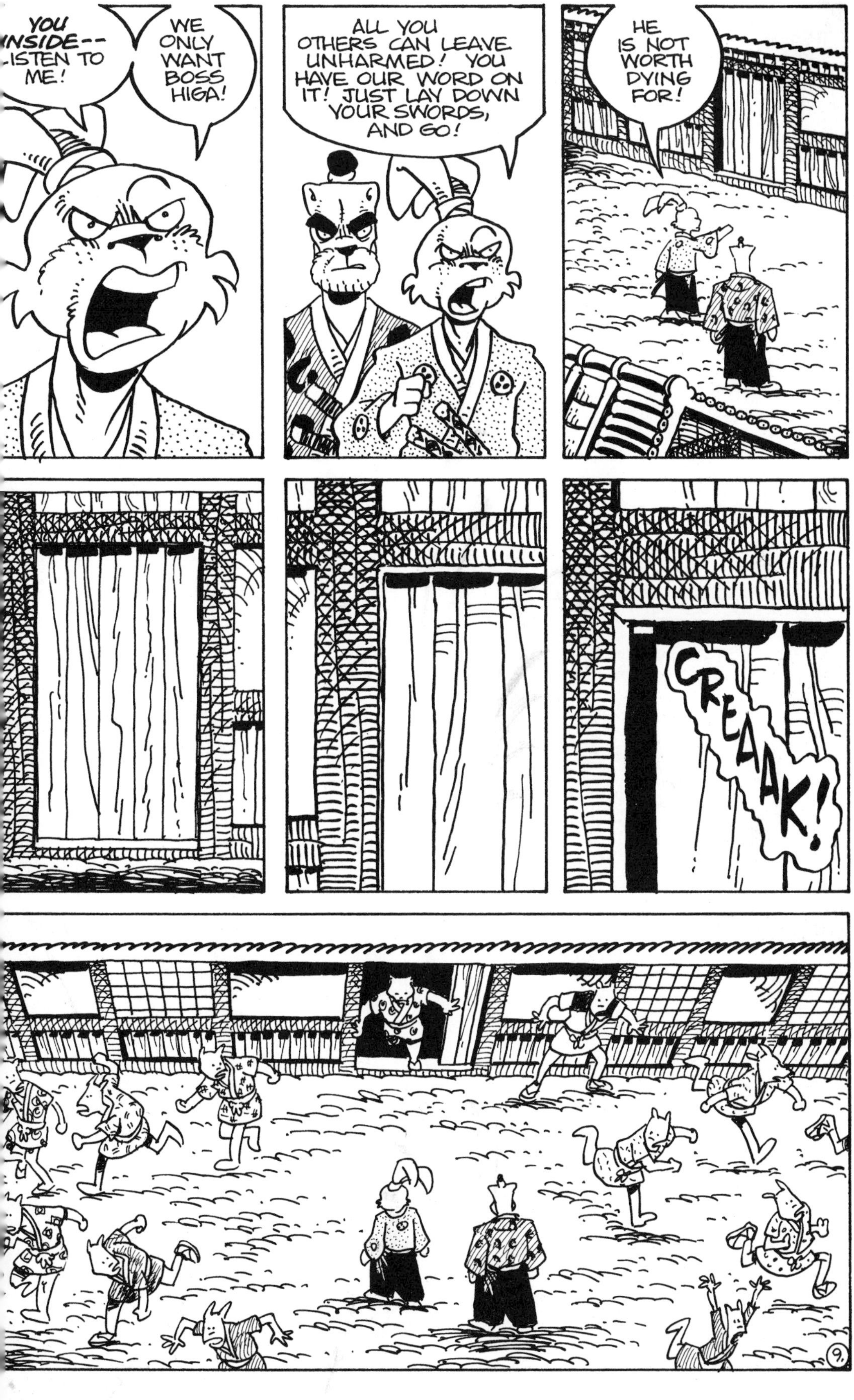
YOU INSIDE-- LISTEN TO ME!
WE ONLY WANT BOSS HIGA!
ALL YOU OTHERS CAN LEAVE UNHARMED! YOU HAVE OUR WORD ON IT! JUST LAY DOWN YOUR SWORDS, AND GO!
HE IS NOT WORTH DYING FOR!
CREAAAK!
9

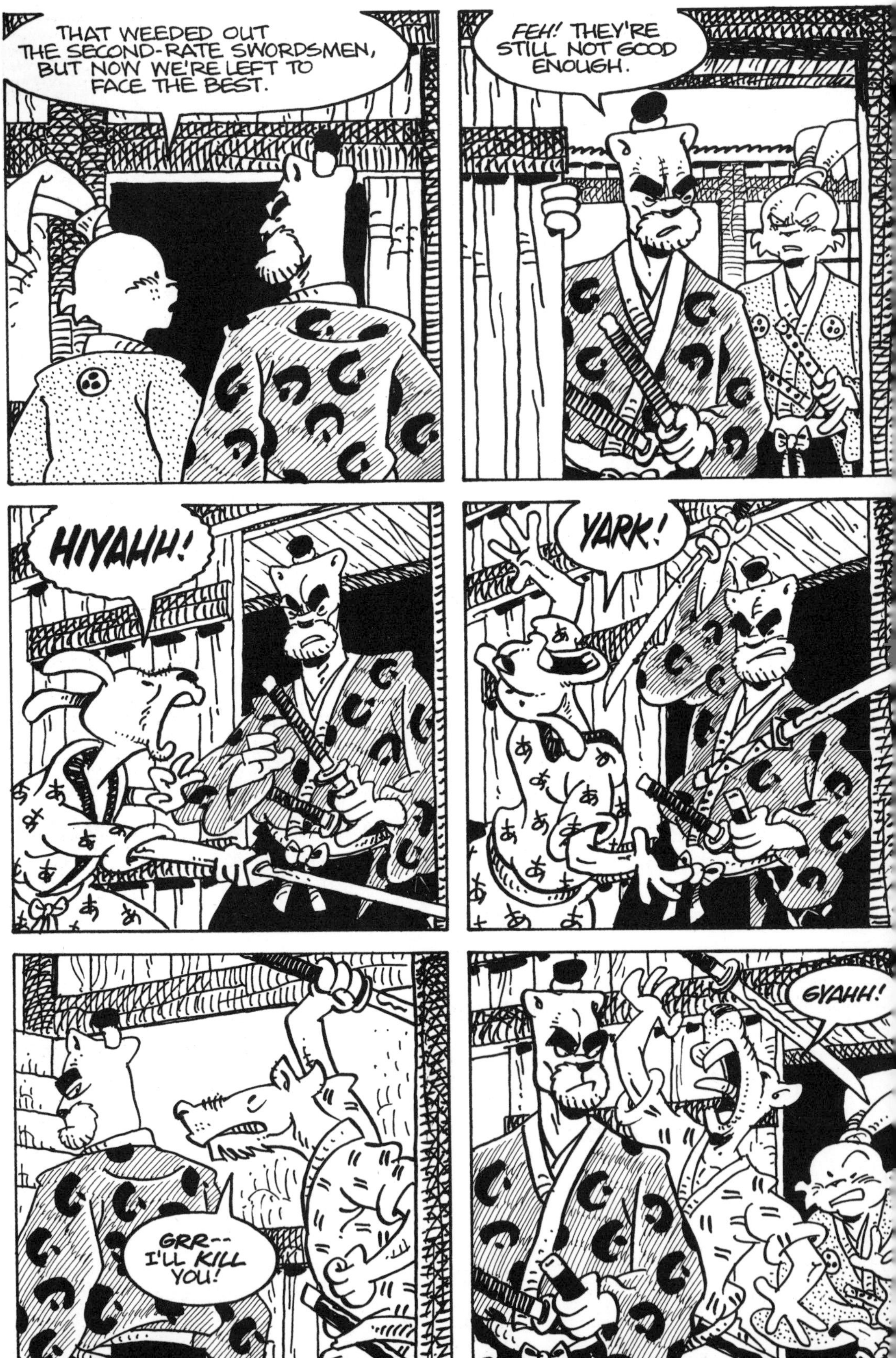
THAT WEEDED OUT THE SECOND-RATE SWORDSMEN, BUT NOW WE'RE LEFT TO FACE THE BEST.
FEH! THEY'RE STILL NOT GOOD ENOUGH.
HIYAHH!
YARK!
GRR-- I'LL KILL YOU!
GYAHH!

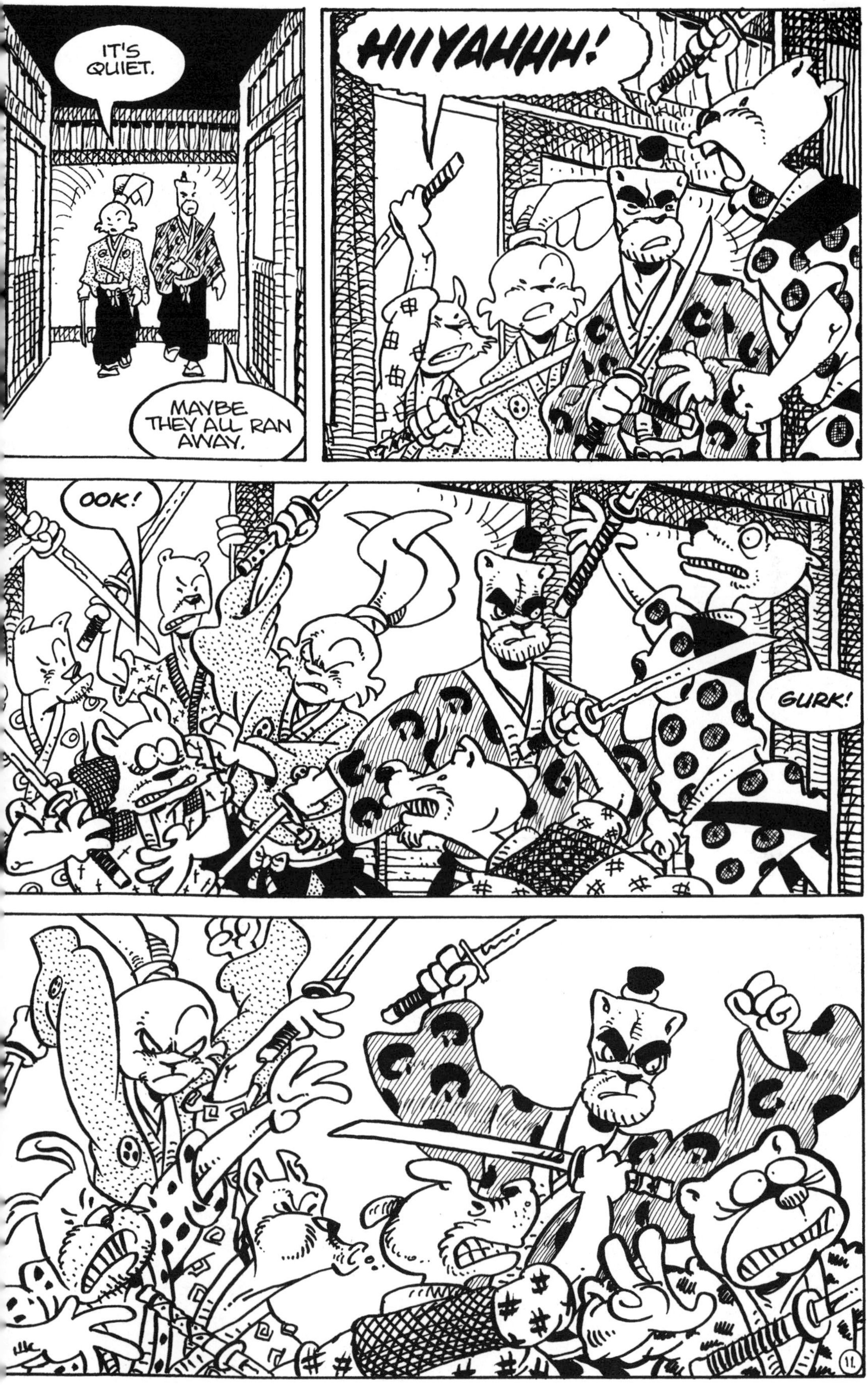
IT'S QUIET.
MAYBE THEY ALL RAN AWAY.
HIIYAHHH!
OOK!
GURK!

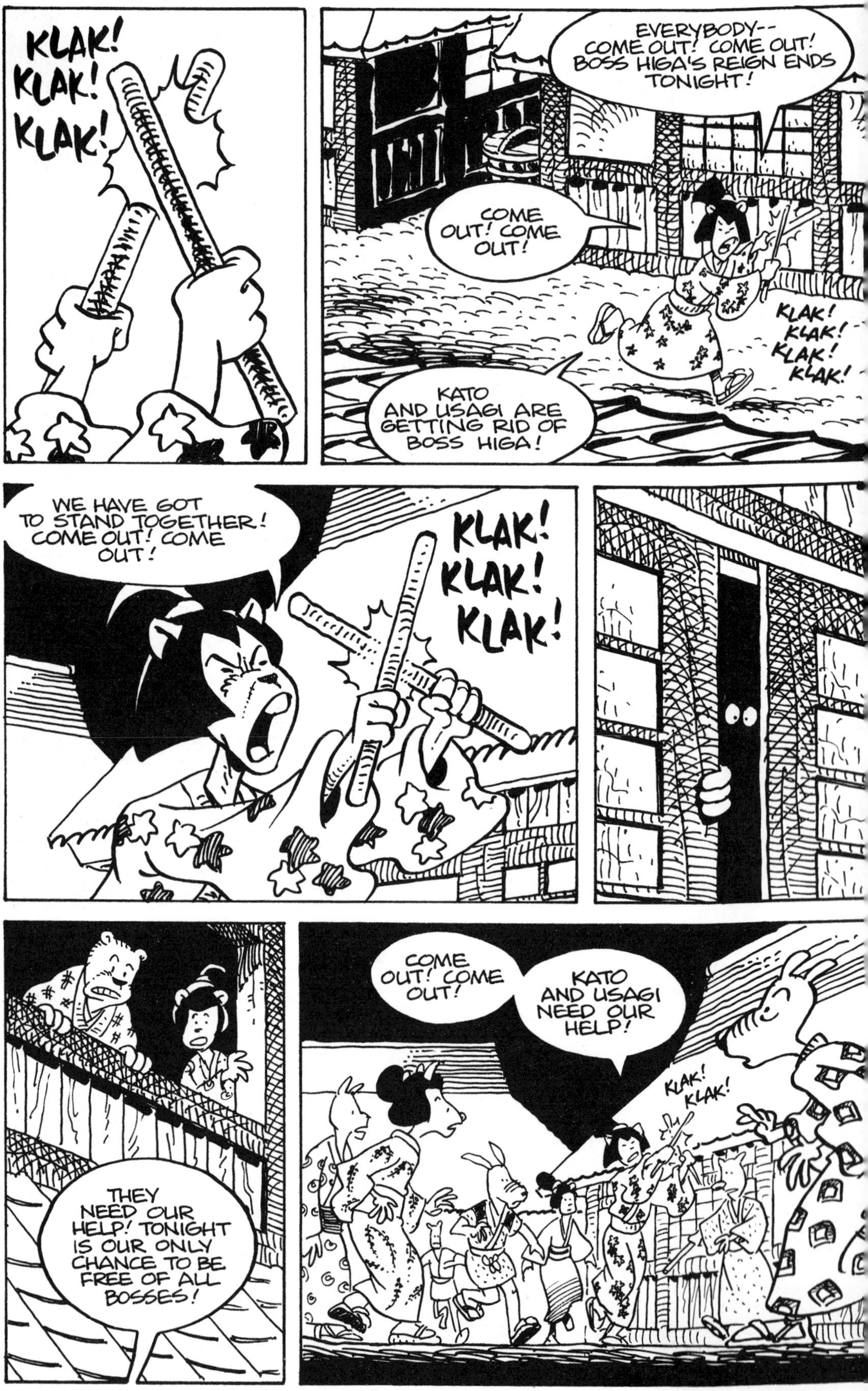
KLAK! KLAK! KLAK!
EVERYBODY-- COME OUT! COME OUT! BOSS HIGA'S REIGN ENDS TONIGHT!
COME OUT! COME OUT!
KLAK! KLAK! KLAK! KLAK!
KATO AND USAGI ARE GETTING RID OF BOSS HIGA!
WE HAVE GOT TO STAND TOGETHER! COME OUT! COME OUT!
KLAK! KLAK! KLAK!
THEY NEED OUR HELP! TONIGHT IS OUR ONLY CHANCE TO BE FREE OF ALL BOSSES!
COME OUT! COME OUT!
KATO AND USAGI NEED OUR HELP!
KLAK! KLAK!

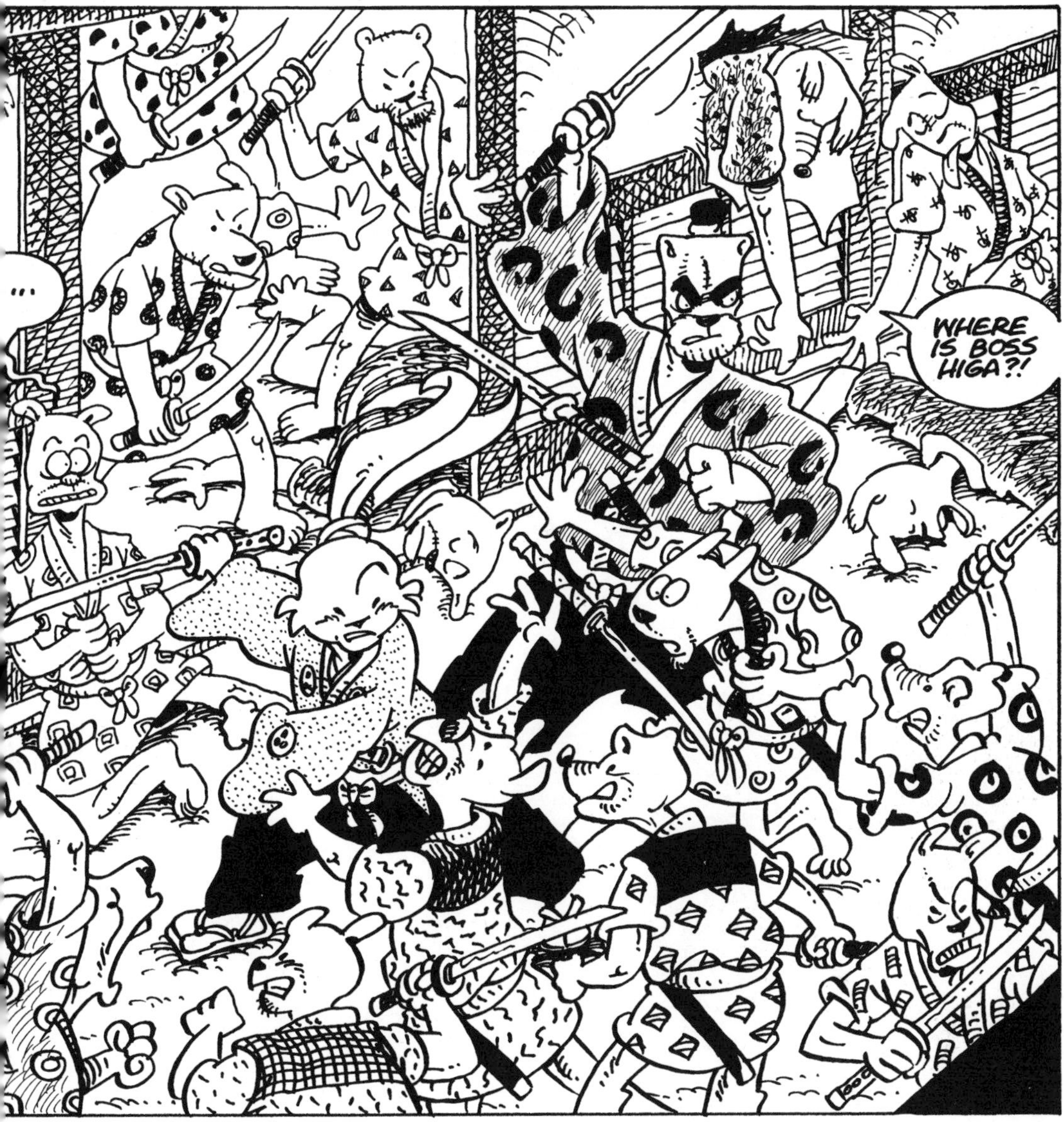
...
WHERE IS BOSS HIGA?!

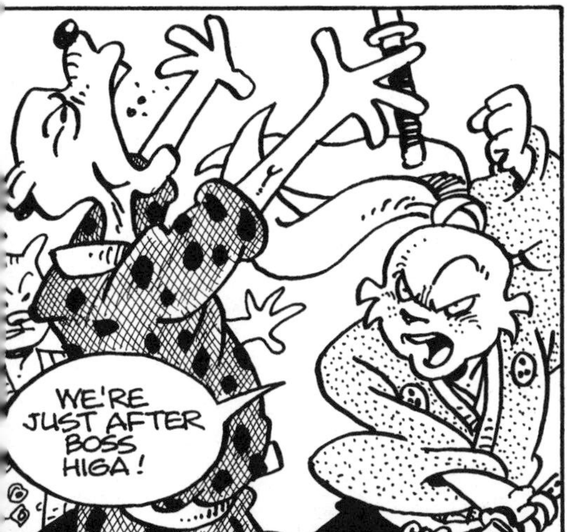
WE'RE JUST AFTER BOSS HIGA!

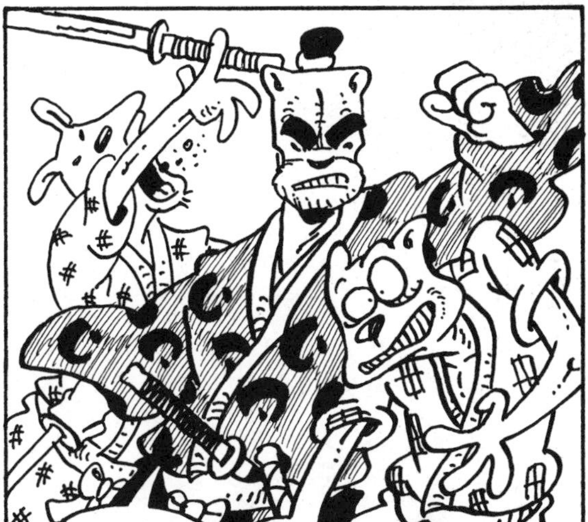
WHERE IS HE HIDING?
13.

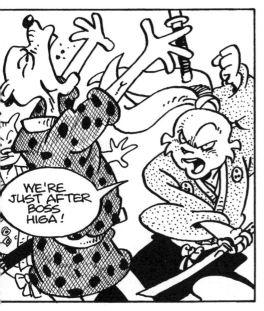

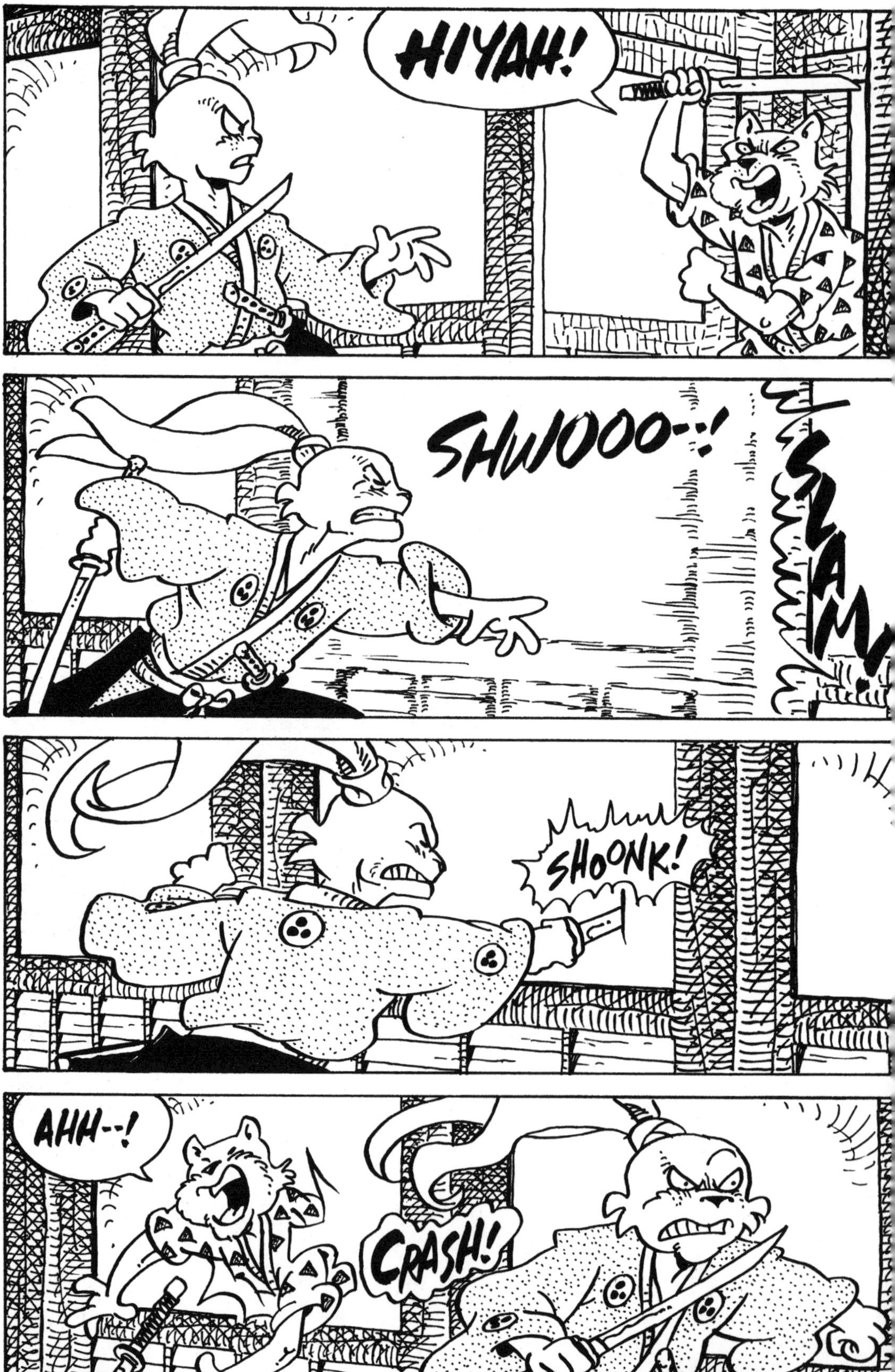
HIYAH!
SHWOOO--!
SLAM!
SHOONK!
AHH--!
CRASH!

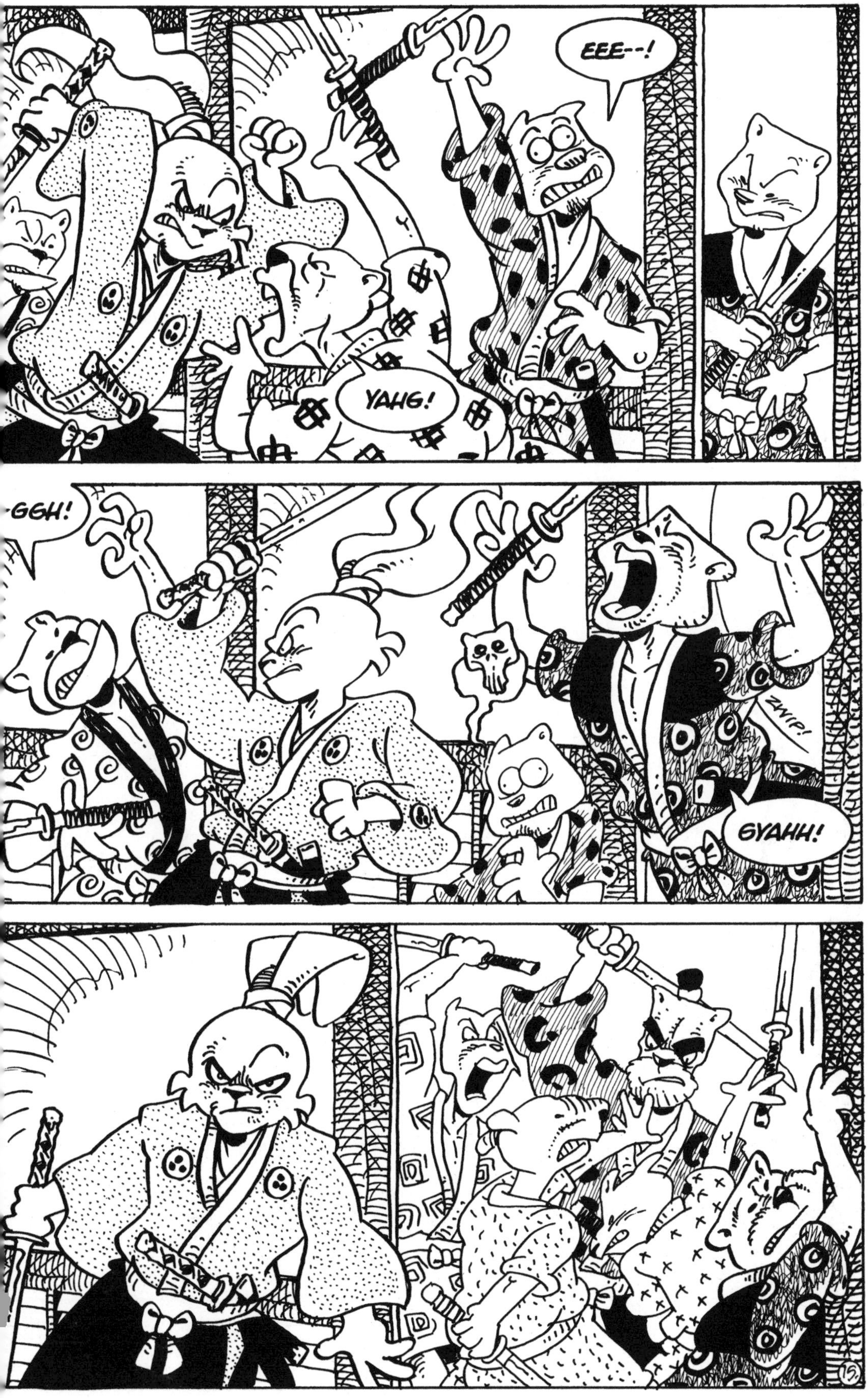
EEE--!
YAHG!
-GGH!
ZWIP!
GYAHH!
15

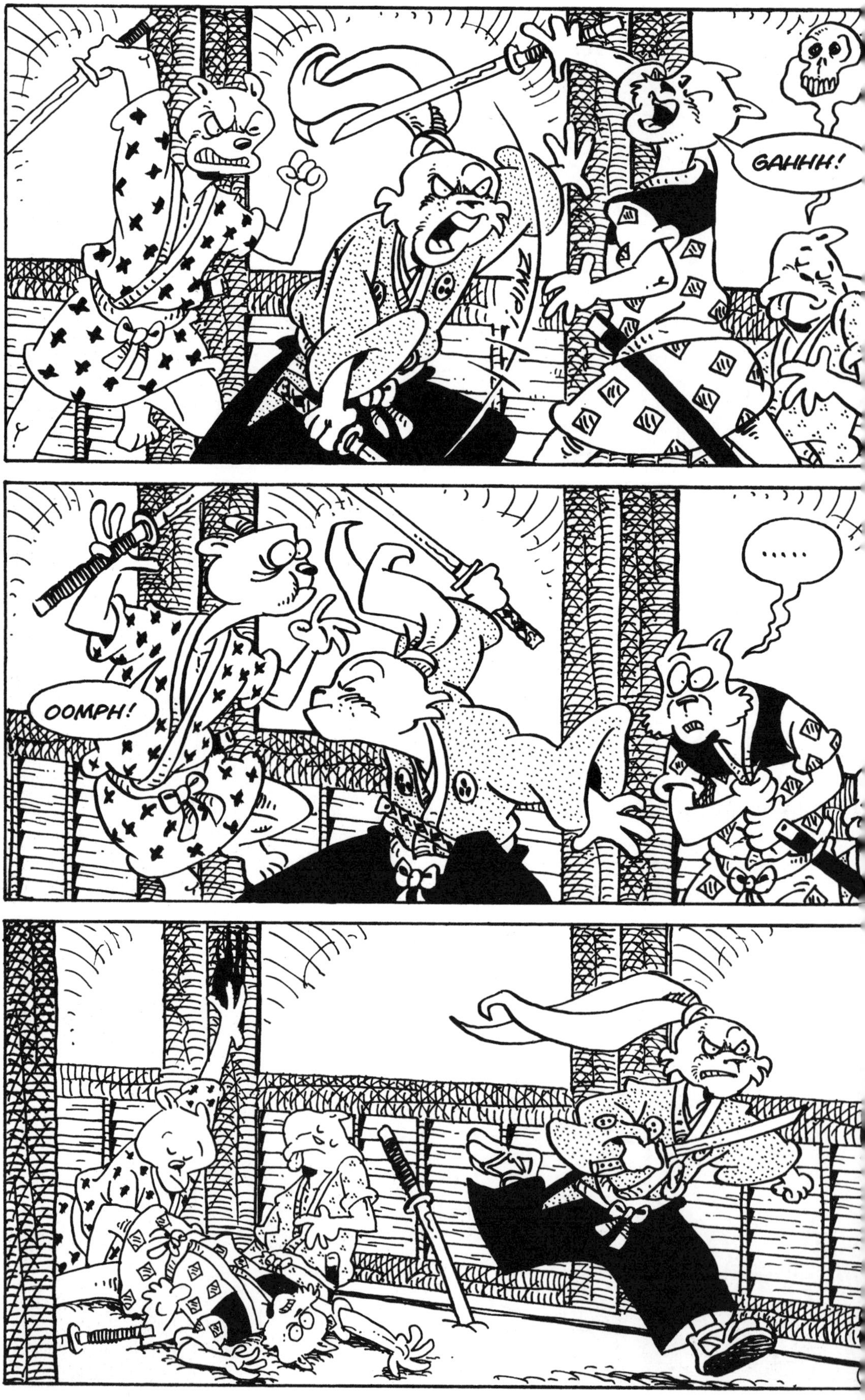
GAHHH!
ZWIP!
OOMPH!
.....

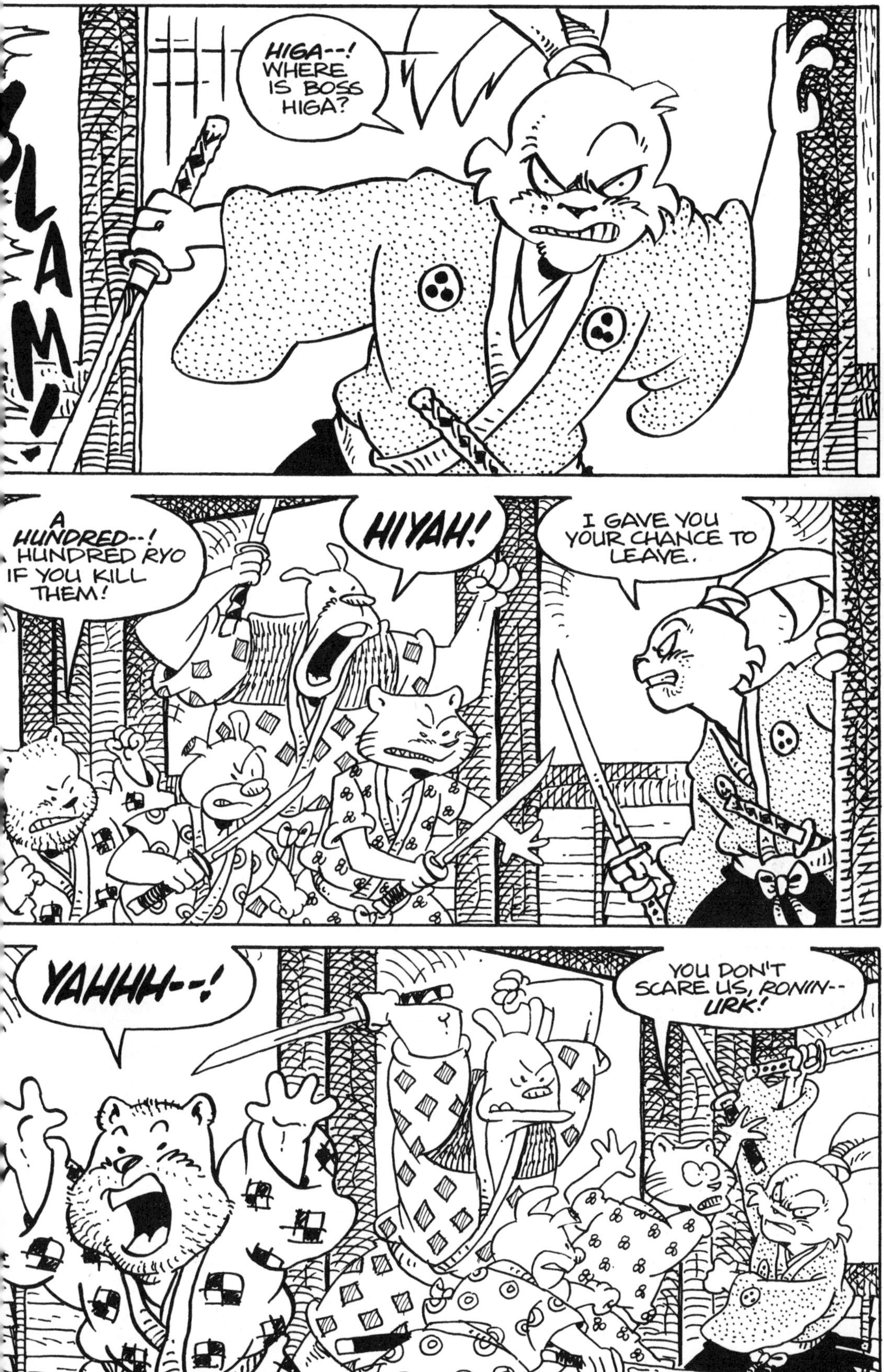
SLAM!
HIGA--! WHERE IS BOSS HIGA?
A HUNDRED--! HUNDRED RYO IF YOU KILL THEM!
HIYAH!
I GAVE YOU YOUR CHANCE TO LEAVE.
YAHHH--!
YOU DON'T SCARE US, RONIN-- URK!
17.

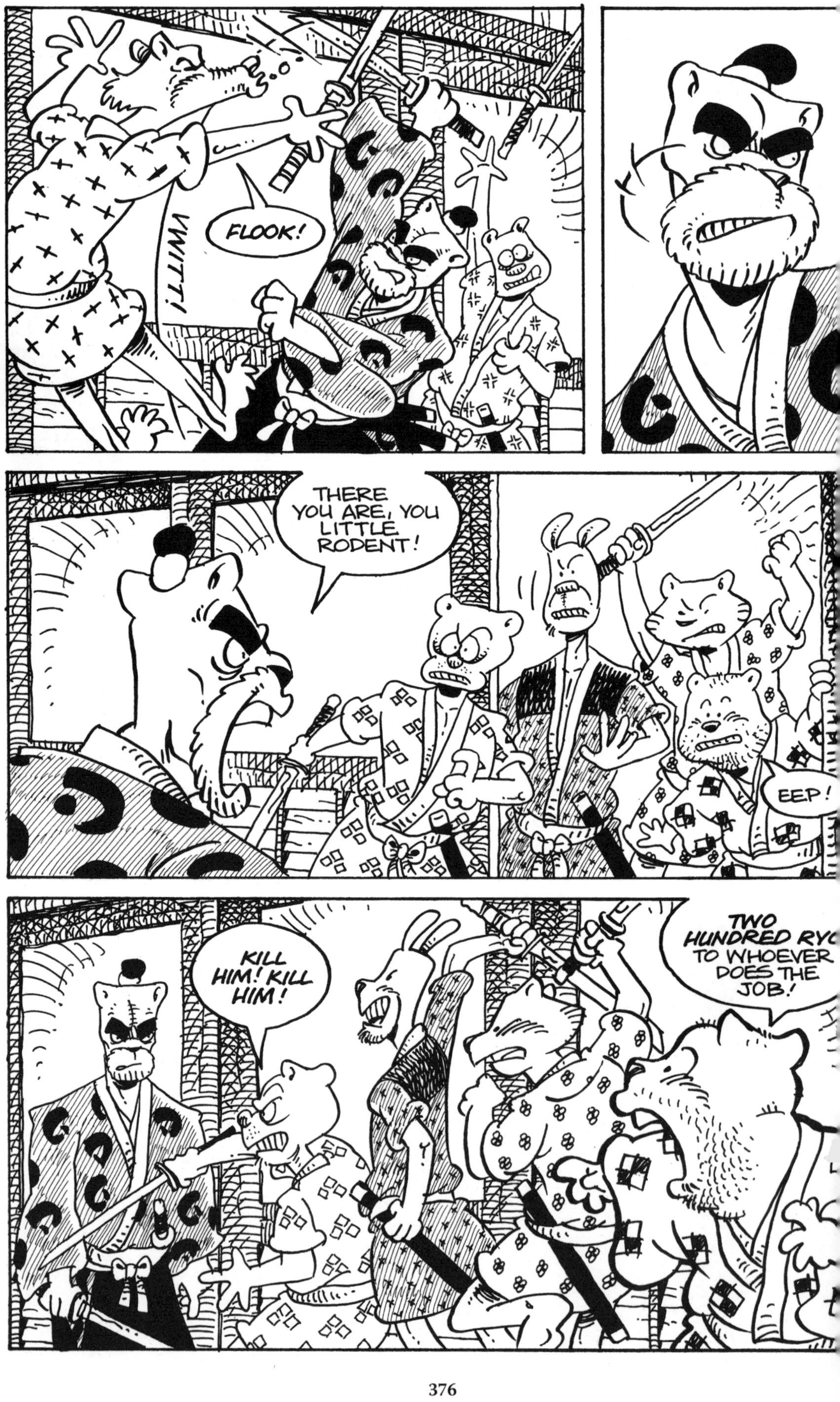
FLOOK!
VWITT!
THERE YOU ARE, YOU LITTLE RODENT!
EEP!
KILL HIM! KILL HIM!
TWO HUNDRED RY
TO WHOEVER DOES THE JOB!

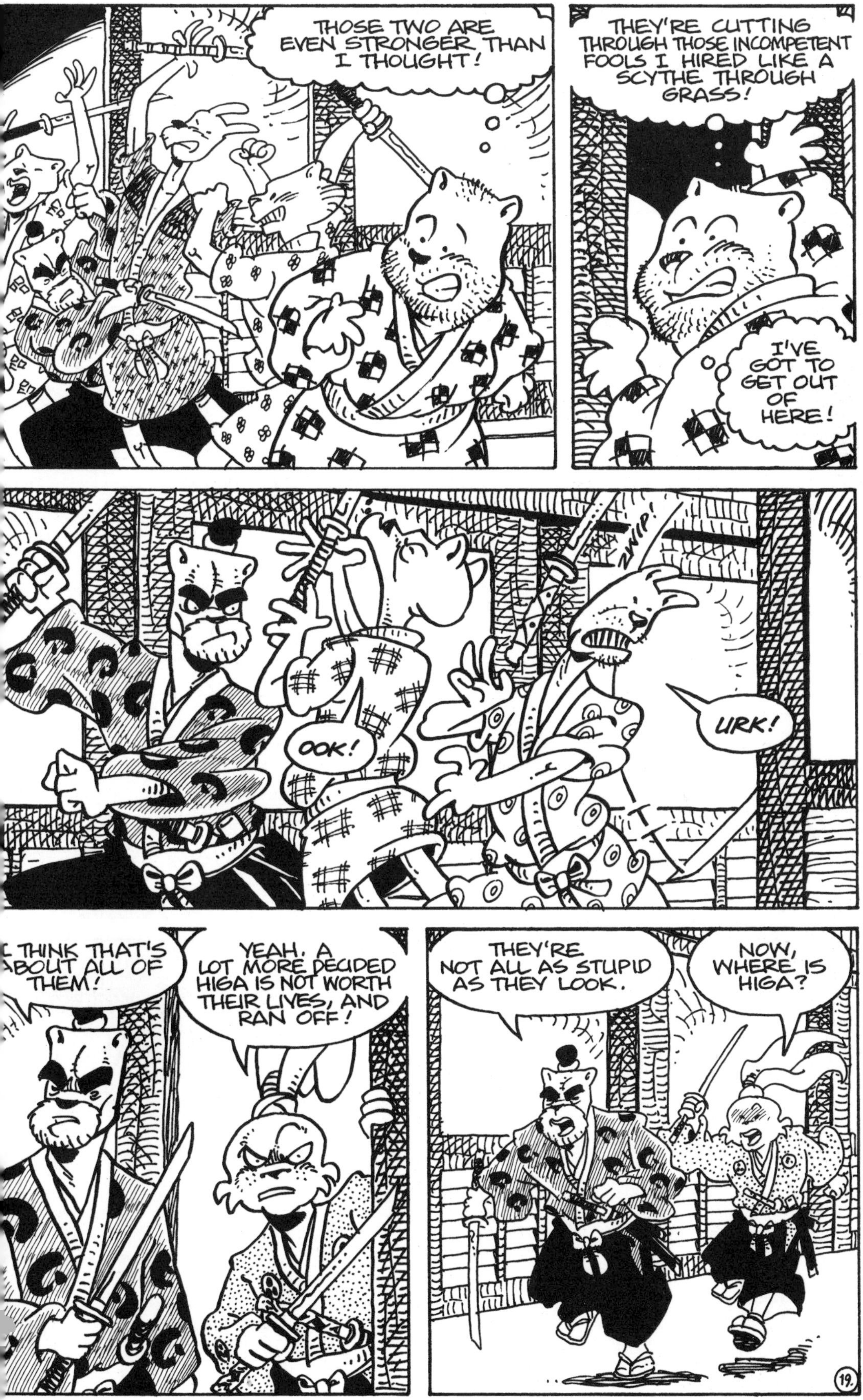
THOSE TWO ARE EVEN STRONGER THAN I THOUGHT!
THEY'RE CUTTING THROUGH THOSE INCOMPETENT FOOLS I HIRED LIKE A SCYTHE THROUGH GRASS!
I'VE GOT TO GET OUT OF HERE!
ZWIP!
OOK!
URK!
I THINK THAT'S ABOUT ALL OF THEM!
YEAH. A LOT MORE DECIDED HIGA IS NOT WORTH THEIR LIVES, AND RAN OFF!
THEY'RE NOT ALL AS STUPID AS THEY LOOK.
NOW, WHERE IS HIGA?
19.

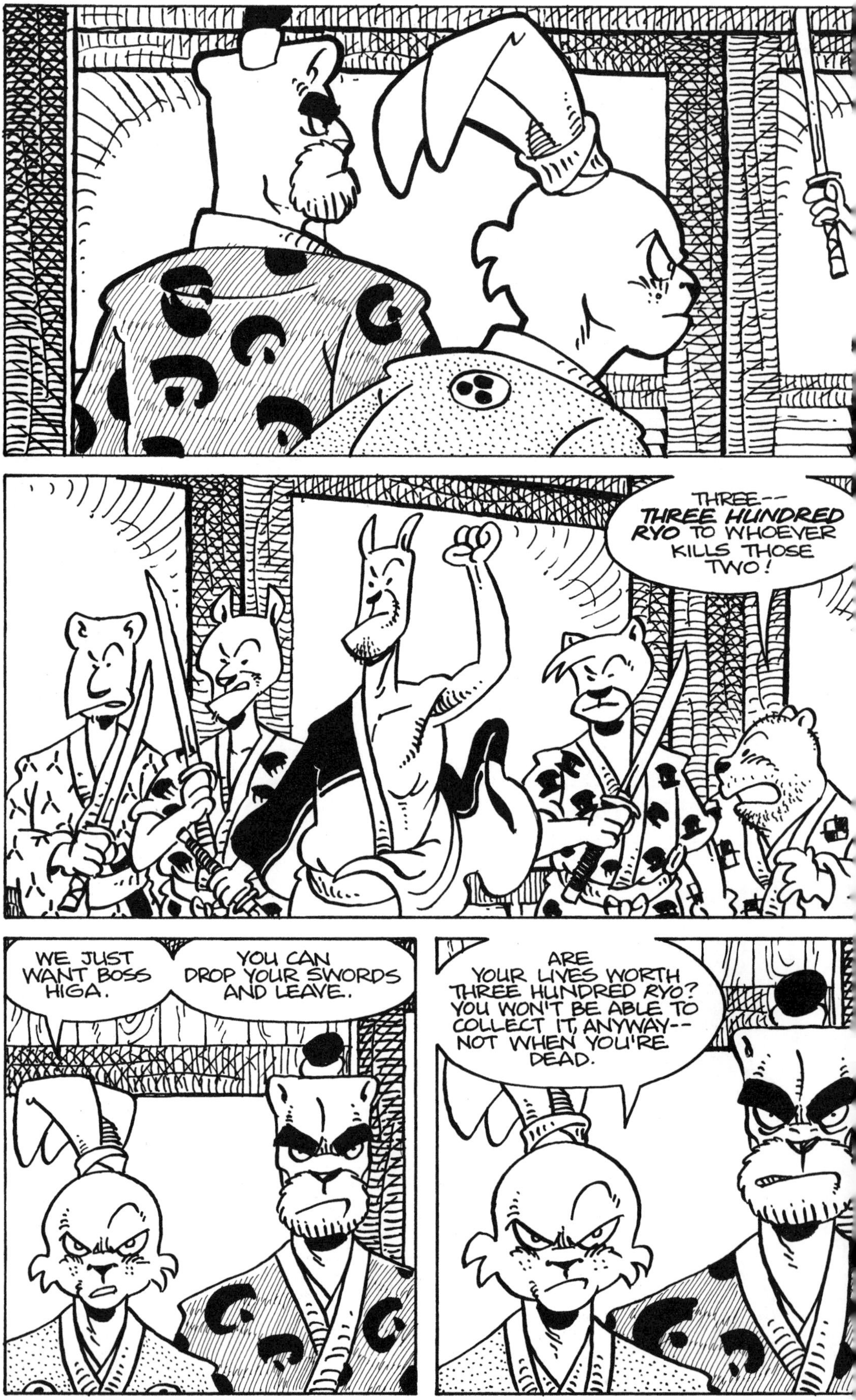
THREE-- THREE HUNDRED RYO TO WHOEVER KILLS THOSE TWO!
WE JUST WANT BOSS HIGA.
YOU CAN DROP YOUR SWORDS AND LEAVE.
ARE YOUR LIVES WORTH THREE HUNDRED RYO? YOU WON'T BE ABLE TO COLLECT IT, ANYWAY-- NOT WHEN YOU'RE DEAD.

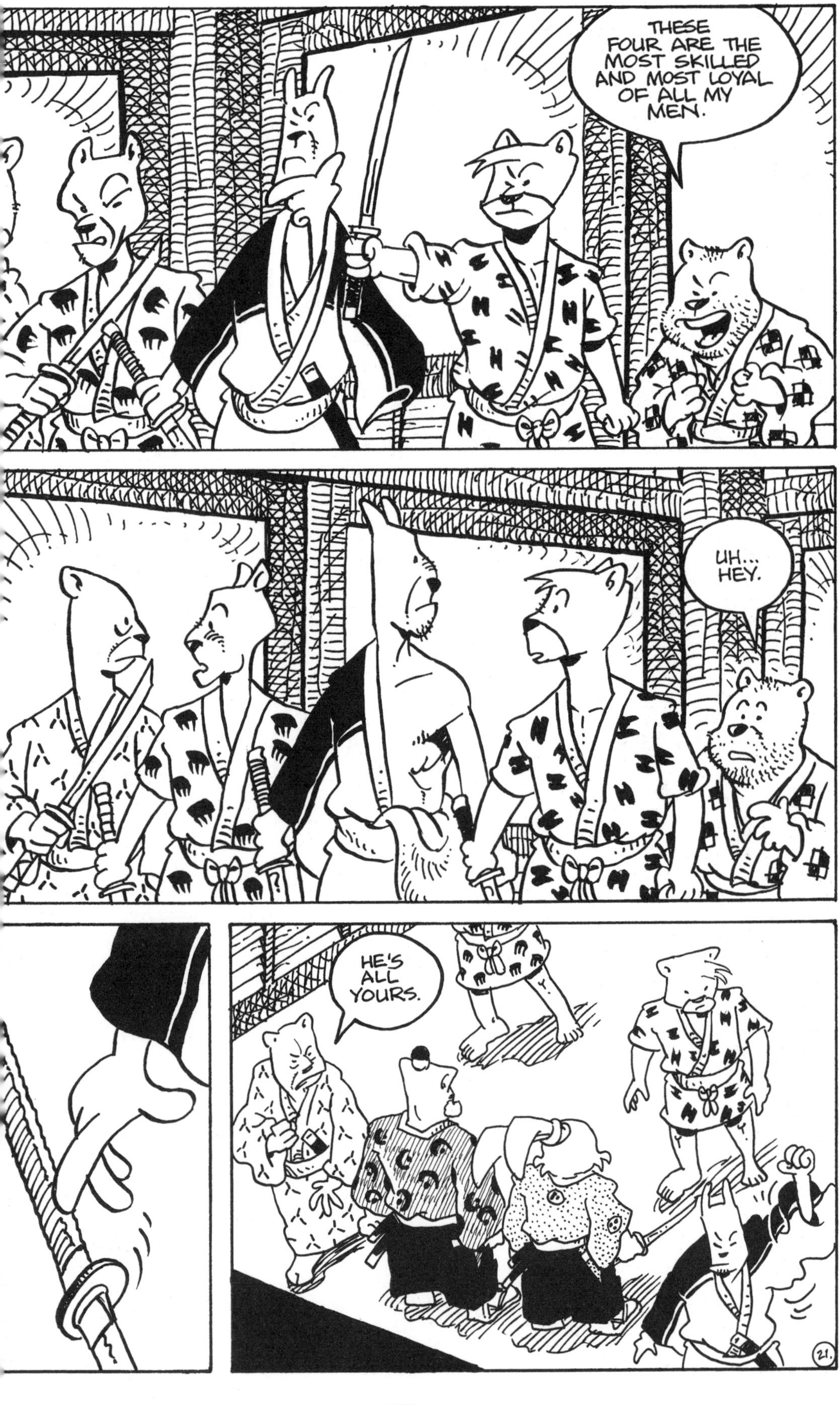
THESE FOUR ARE THE MOST SKILLED AND MOST LOYAL OF ALL MY MEN.
UH... HEY.
HE'S ALL YOURS.
21.

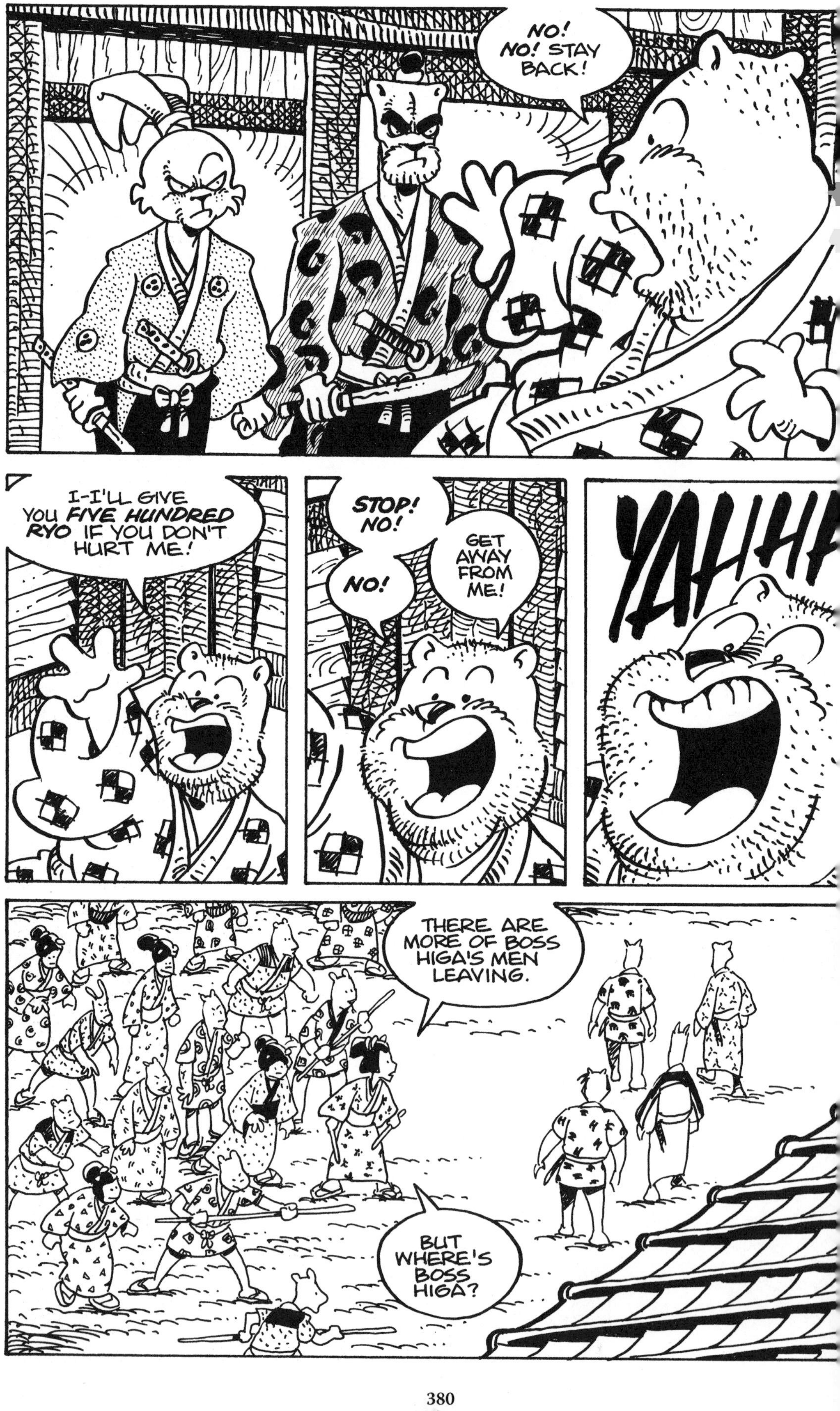
NO! NO! STAY BACK!
I-I'LL GIVE YOU FIVE HUNDRED RYO IF YOU DON'T HURT ME!
STOP! NO!
NO!
GET AWAY FROM ME!
YAHHH
THERE ARE MORE OF BOSS HIGA'S MEN LEAVING.
BUT WHERE'S BOSS HIGA?

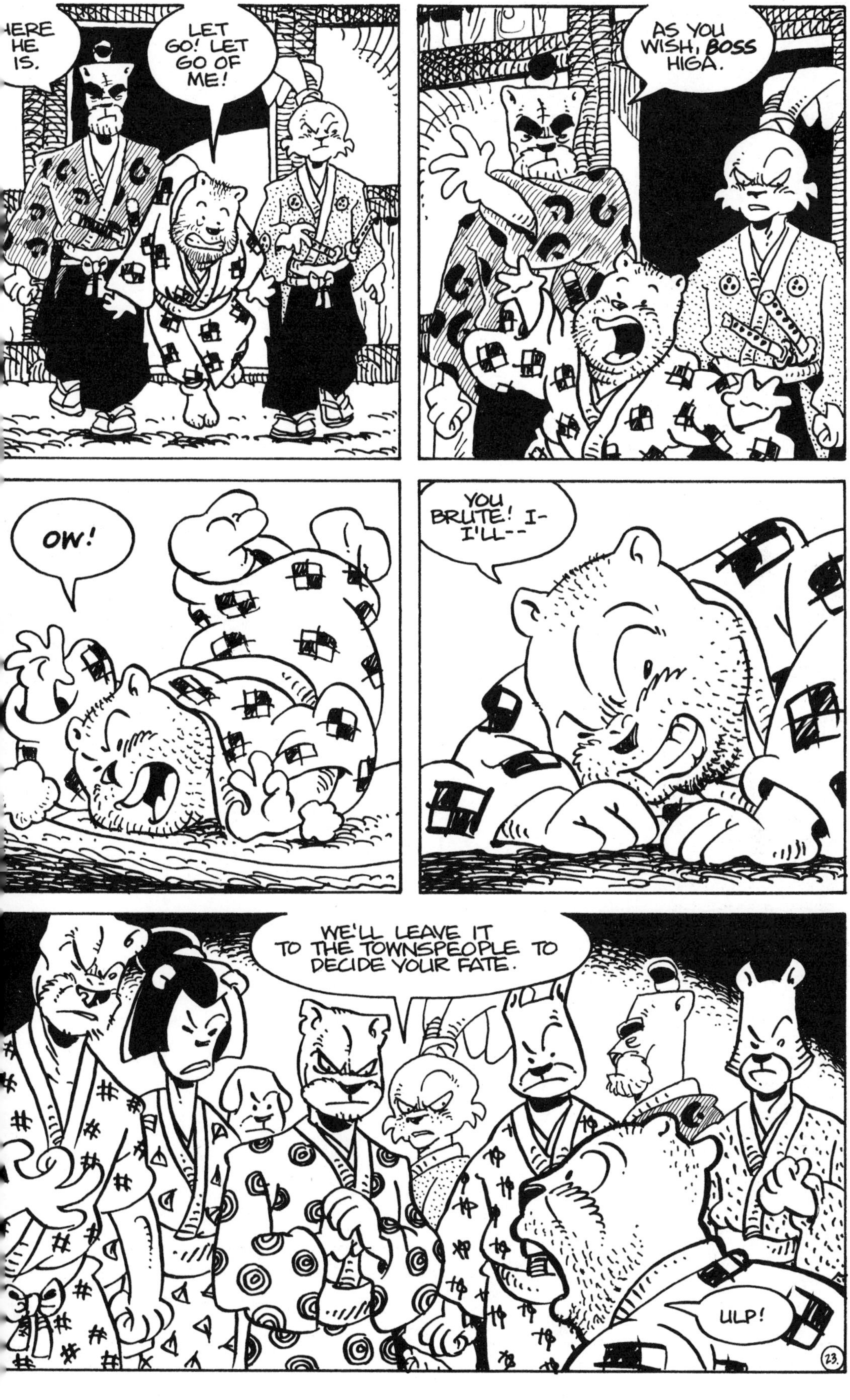
HERE HE IS.
LET GO! LET GO OF ME!
AS YOU WISH, BOSS HIGA.
OW!
YOU BRUTE! I- I'LL--
WE'LL LEAVE IT TO THE TOWNSPEOPLE TO DECIDE YOUR FATE.
ULP!
23.

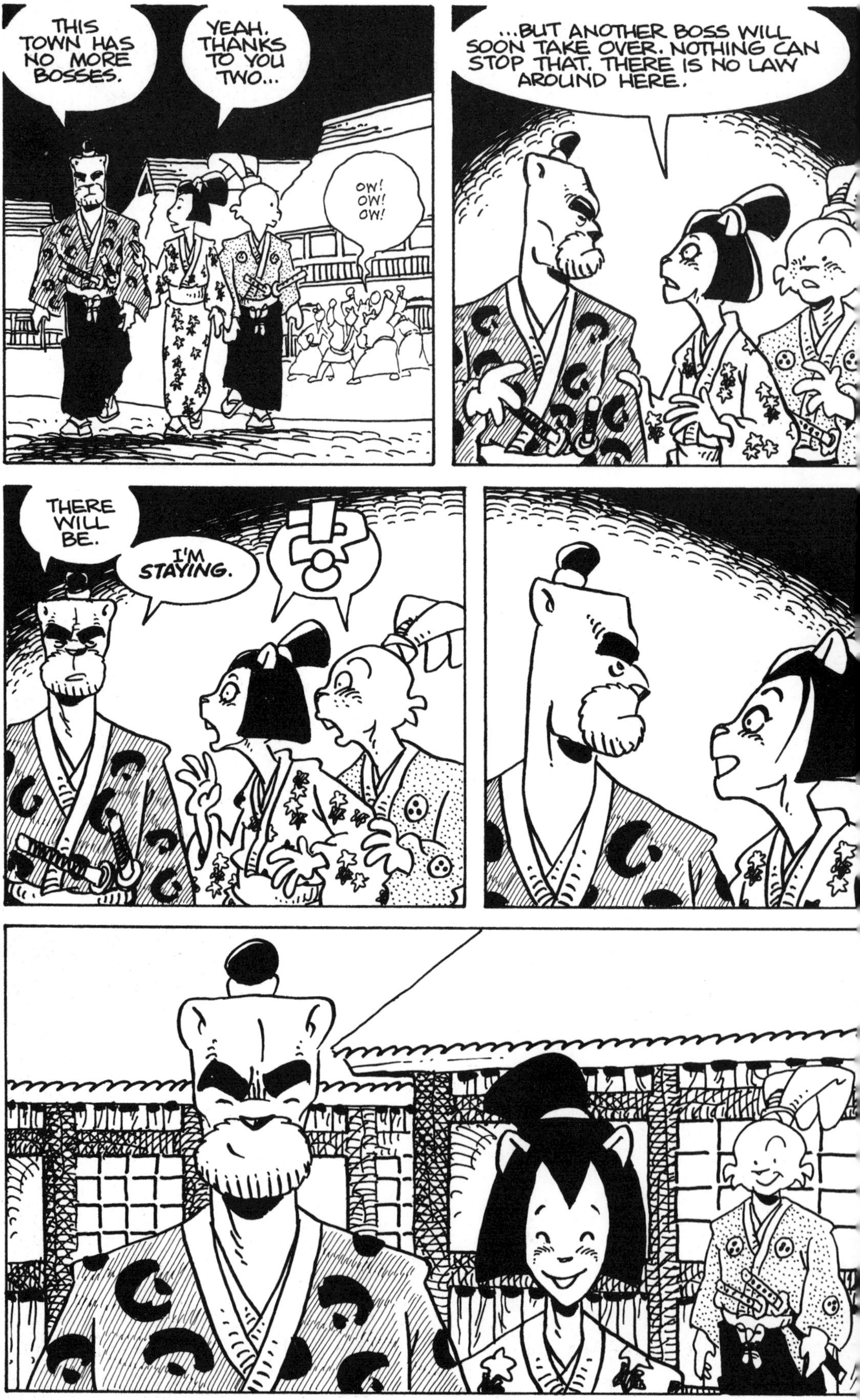
THIS TOWN HAS NO MORE BOSSES.
YEAH. THANKS TO YOU TWO...
OW! OW! OW!
...BUT ANOTHER BOSS WILL SOON TAKE OVER. NOTHING CAN STOP THAT. THERE IS NO LAW AROUND HERE.
THERE WILL BE.
I'M *STAYING*.
!?

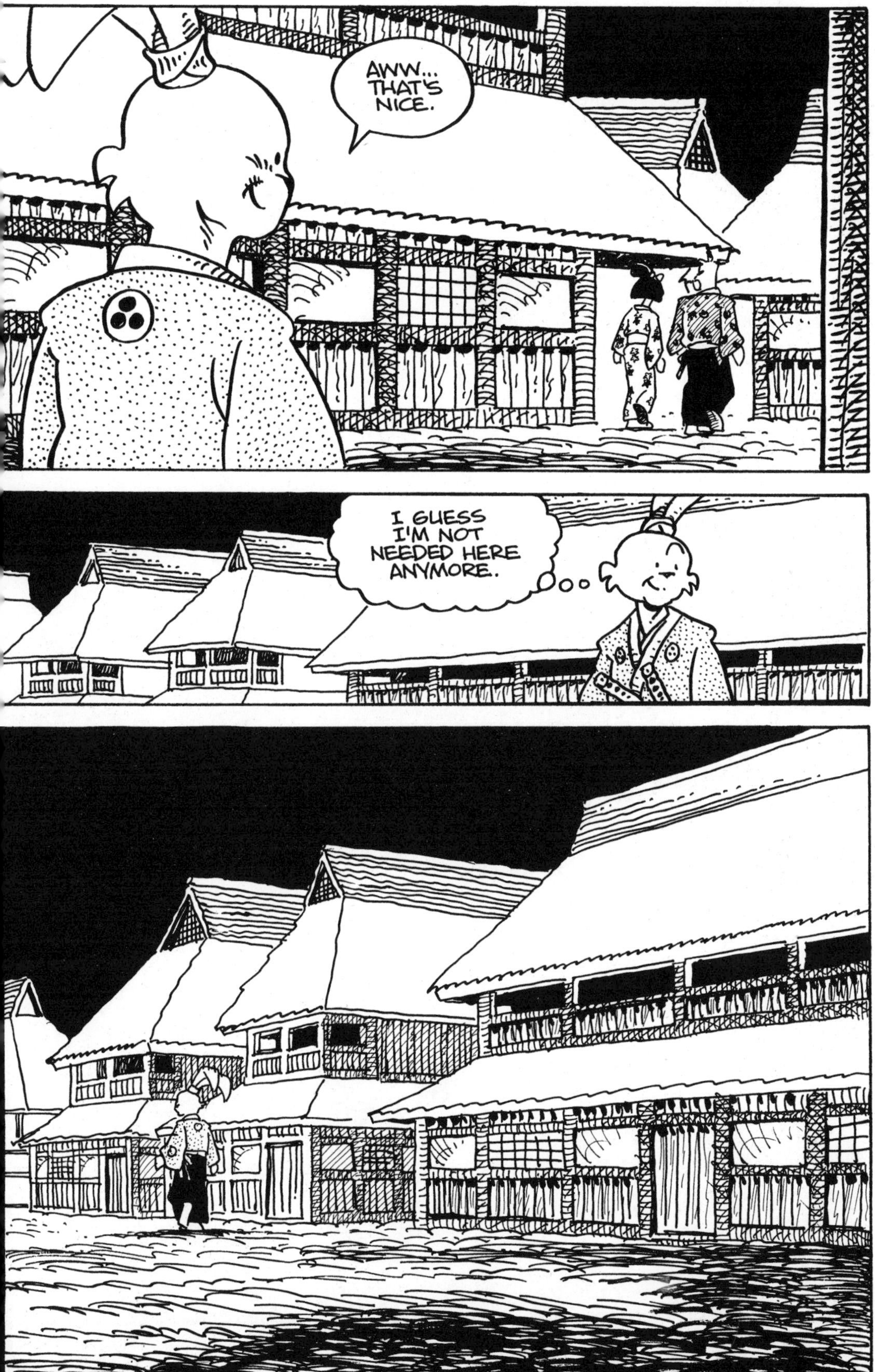
AWW... THAT'S NICE.
I GUESS I'M NOT NEEDED HERE ANYMORE.
THE END

# RED SCORPION

A S A KID, I LISTENED with bated breath to the exploits of the Lone Ranger on our radio. I was captivated by the adventures of good guys who fought for the underdog.

When I was a preteen, I went to the movies and saw Errol Flynn in *The Adventures of Robin Hood*. It was fantastic. I was transported to Sherwood Forest and the swashbuckling derring-do of Robin Hood. He took from the rich and gave to the poor. And I loved the sword fights up and down the castle stairs.

As a teenager, I had an absolutely unforgettable experience at the movies. I saw *Yojimbo* by the great Japanese director, Akira Kurosawa. It was mind-blowing. A ragged, flea-bitten, lone samurai with no master, a "ronin," roams the countryside fighting to bring justice to the downtrodden. He risks his life for no payment, no glory—only for his code of honor as a samurai. And he is a terrific swordsman. He can wipe out a couple dozen enemy samurai in one spectacular, bloody combat.

In 2011, the Japanese American National Museum, of which I am Chairman Emeritus and a Trustee, put on an exhibit of Stan Sakai's *Usagi Yojimbo*. It was a retrospective of the twenty-five-year scope of his graphic novel series about a "ronin," a vagabond samurai just like the one played by the incomparable Toshiro Mifune in the movie *Yojimbo*—but, of all things, in the form of a rabbit! A "ronin" rabbit in a world inhabited by comic anthropomorphic animals. What a deliciously whimsical notion. It was a world I had never heard of. Where had I been for twenty-five years? *Usagi Yojimbo* was enthrallingly engaging. Since my boyhood, the demands of life and career had drawn me away from my love of fantasy heroes. The Stan Sakai exhibit took me back to a fantastical place that was yet so familiar.

The hero is a rabbit samurai dressed in well-worn "hakama" pantaloons and swords, with his ears gathered up on his head like a "chonmage," the samurai topknot. He has a strong sense of decency and empathy for the common people—a rabbit Lone Ranger. And he is a magnificent swordsman.

Every frame of Stan Sakai's fight scenes captures with ferocious cinematic rhythm the rabbit samurai's amazing swordsmanship.

The villains are equally fully developed animal baddies. They are as powerful as hippos and as devious as foxes can be. They are as dangerous as wolves. They are shysters and gangsters. They are human animals in an imaginatively detailed universe. And the exploits of our rabbit "yojimbo" are all watched by cute little lizards and observant newts. There are witnesses.

This, however, is not mere whimsy. Stan Sakai places our rabbit in the authentic world of seventeenth-century feudal Japan. The details of culture and history are finely researched. Every frame has the look and smell of reality. This specificity of detail in customs and time transforms our rabbit into a very human animal. He becomes the hero that we all would like to be, whether we live in Buenos Aires or Berlin, Osaka or Omaha. Usagi Yojimbo becomes as timeless and as mythic as the lone good guy roaming the Wild West or Sherwood Forest, coming to the aid of the oppressed. The "ronin" rabbit's stories become universal.

Congratulations, Stan, on your thirtieth anniversary! *Usagi Yojimbo* transports me at once to a fantastical world and to my long-ago boyhood.

GEORGE TAKEI

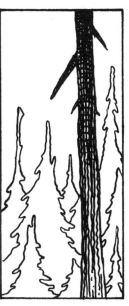

HMM...

THIS AREA CERTAINLY LOOKS FAMILIAR.

I'M SURE I HAVE TRAVELED THIS WAY BEFORE.

THE KEYAKI* STUMP!

TAIKO

*ZELKOVA TREE

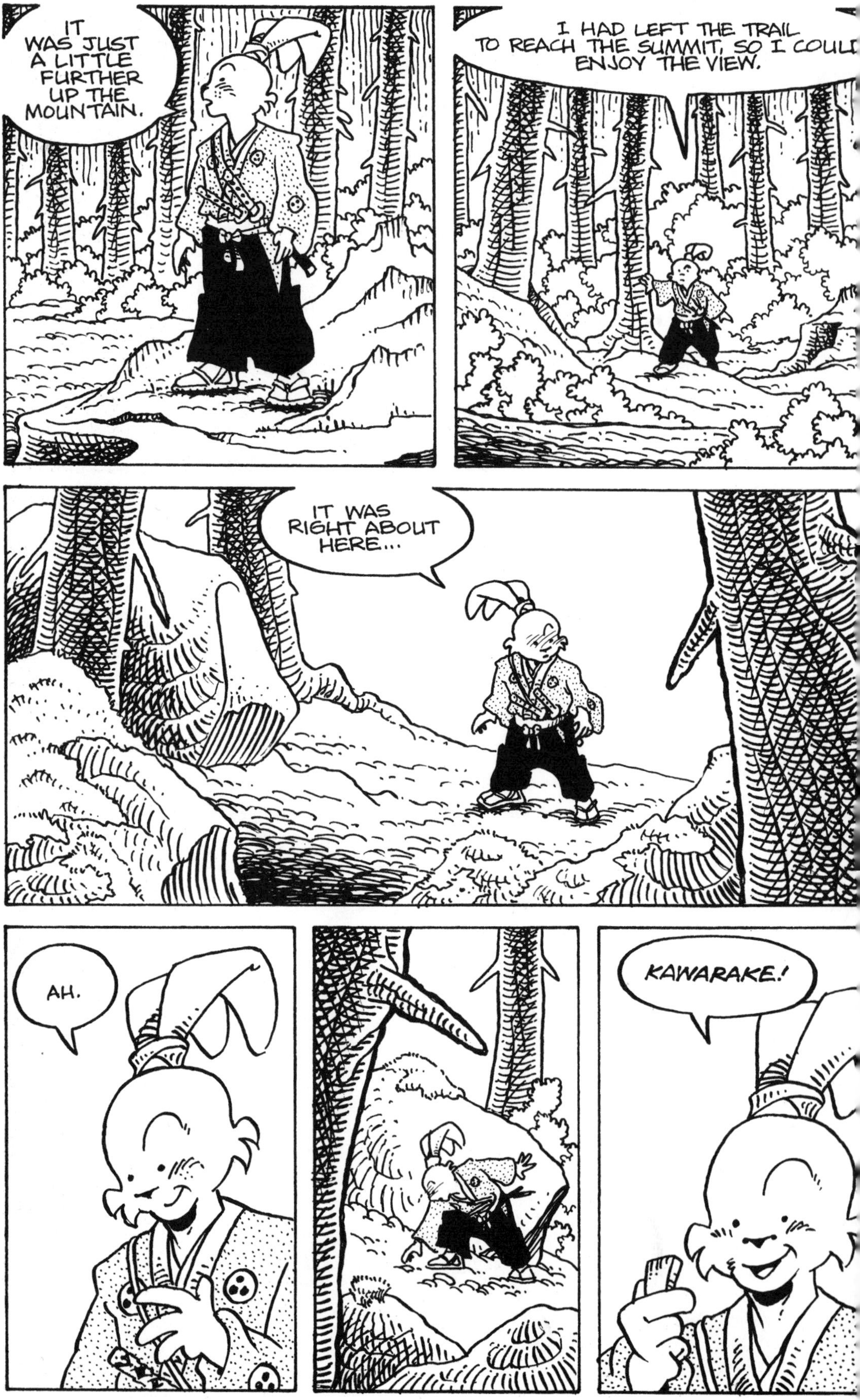
IT WAS JUST A LITTLE FURTHER UP THE MOUNTAIN.
I HAD LEFT THE TRAIL TO REACH THE SUMMIT, SO I COULD ENJOY THE VIEW.
IT WAS RIGHT ABOUT HERE...
AH.
KAWARAKE!

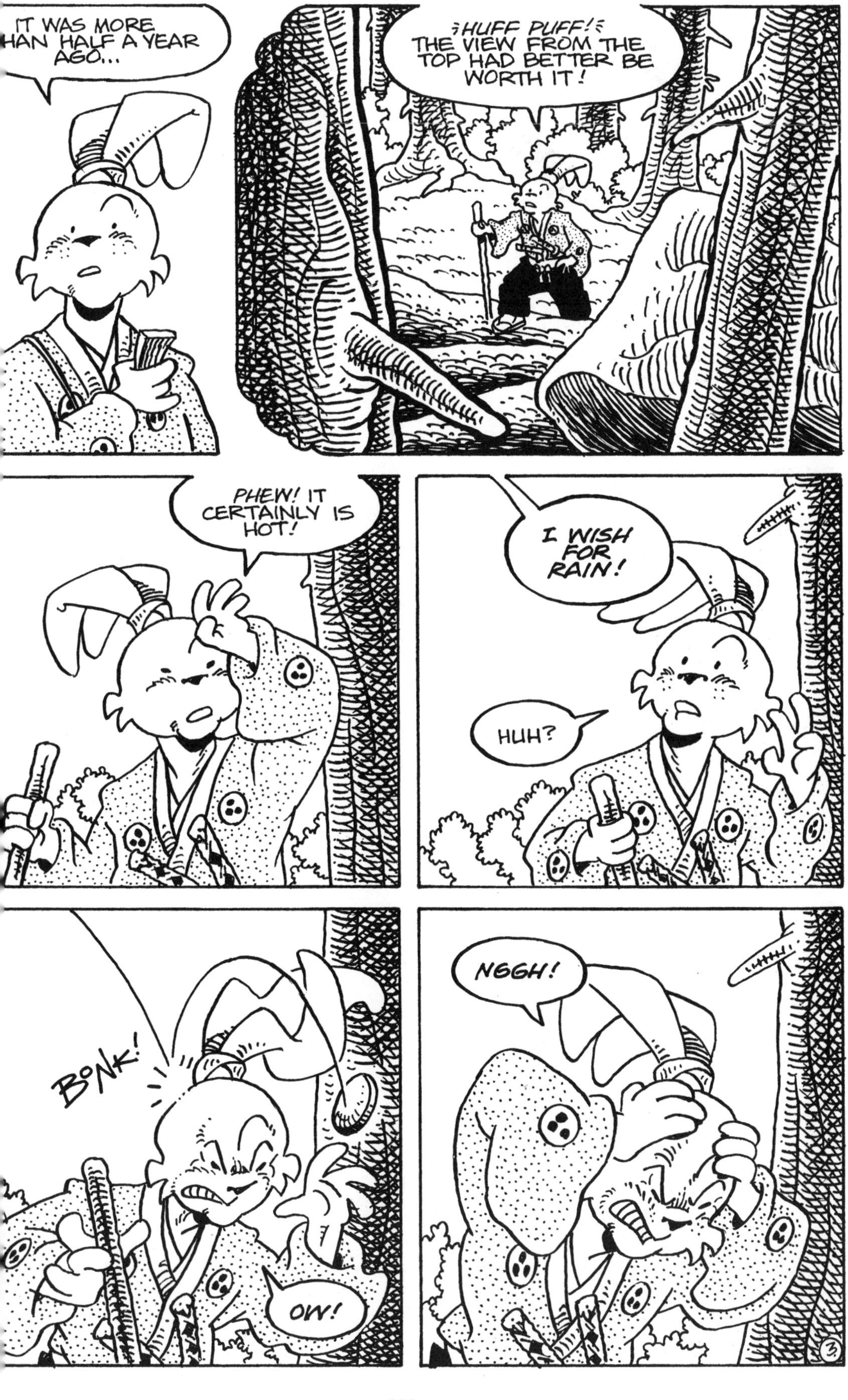
IT WAS MORE THAN HALF A YEAR AGO...
HUFF PUFF! THE VIEW FROM THE TOP HAD BETTER BE WORTH IT!
PHEW! IT CERTAINLY IS HOT!
I WISH FOR RAIN!
HUH?
BONK!
OW!
NGGH!

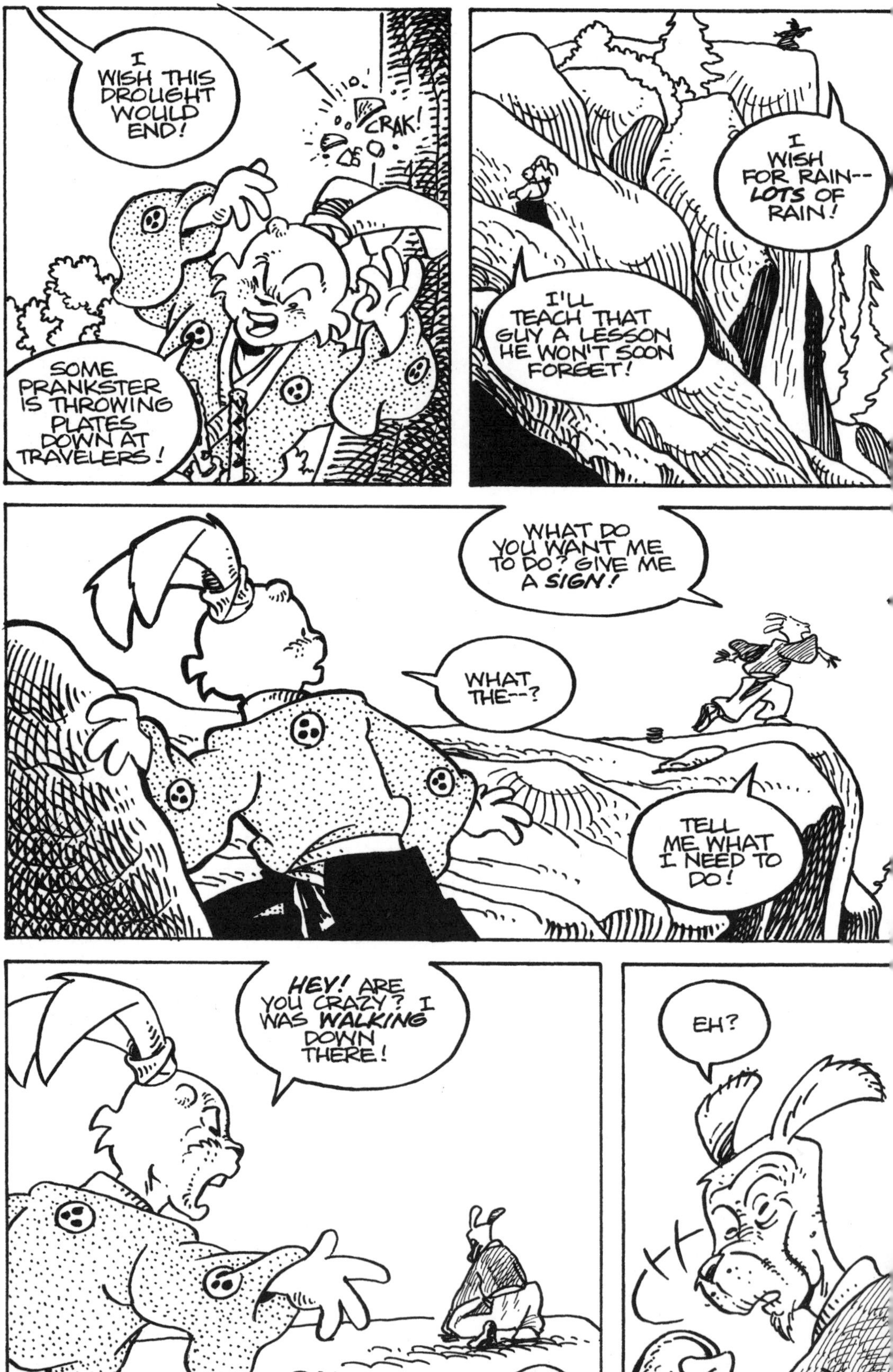
I WISH THIS DROUGHT WOULD END!
CRAK!
SOME PRANKSTER IS THROWING PLATES DOWN AT TRAVELERS!
I WISH FOR RAIN-- LOTS OF RAIN!
I'LL TEACH THAT GUY A LESSON HE WON'T SOON FORGET!
WHAT DO YOU WANT ME TO DO? GIVE ME A SIGN!
WHAT THE--?
TELL ME WHAT I NEED TO DO!
HEY! ARE YOU CRAZY? I WAS WALKING DOWN THERE!
EH?

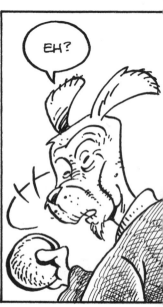

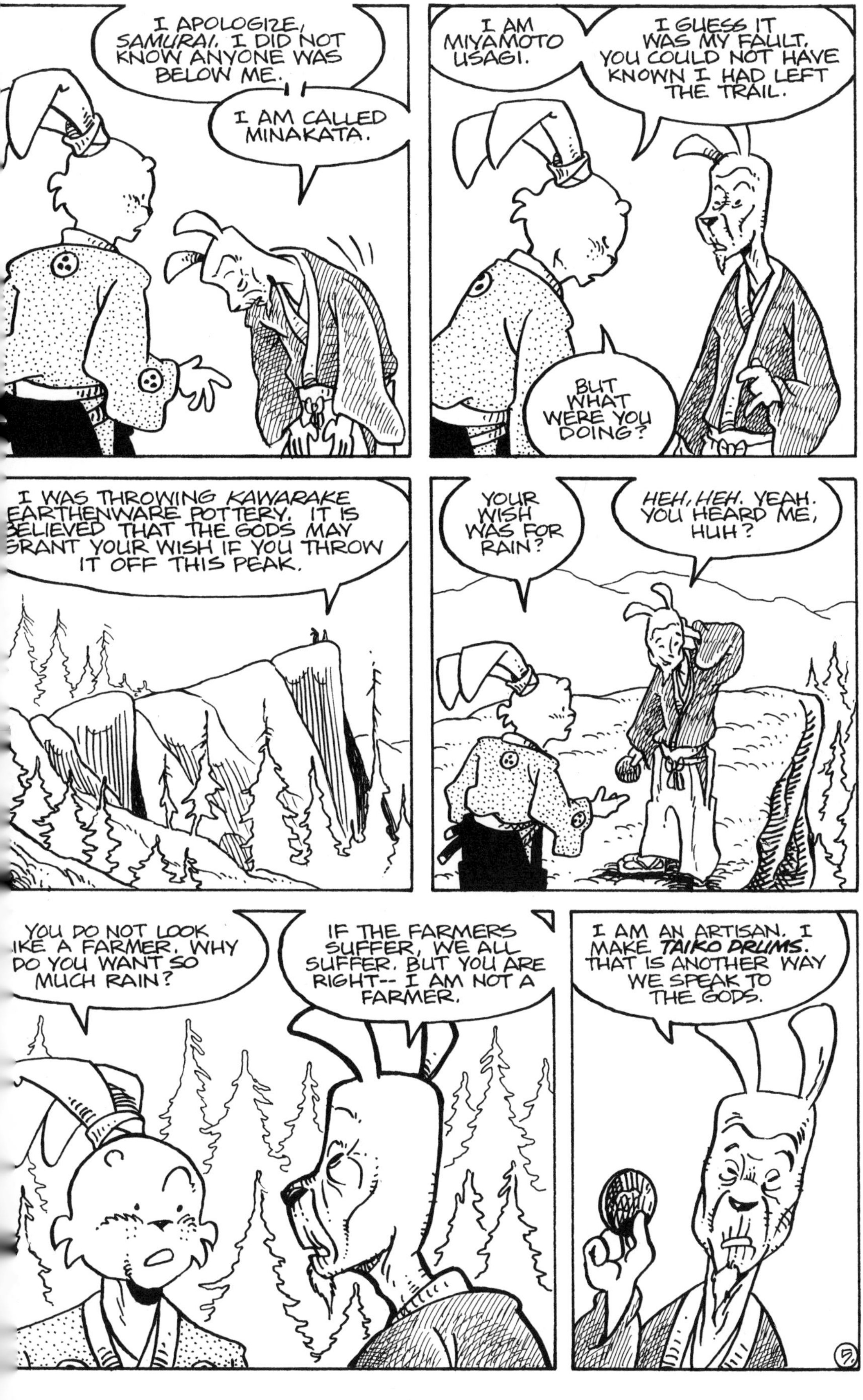
I APOLOGIZE, SAMURAI. I DID NOT KNOW ANYONE WAS BELOW ME.
I AM CALLED MINAKATA.
I AM MIYAMOTO USAGI.
I GUESS IT WAS MY FAULT. YOU COULD NOT HAVE KNOWN I HAD LEFT THE TRAIL.
BUT WHAT WERE YOU DOING?
I WAS THROWING *KAWARAKE* EARTHENWARE POTTERY. IT IS BELIEVED THAT THE GODS MAY GRANT YOUR WISH IF YOU THROW IT OFF THIS PEAK.
YOUR WISH WAS FOR RAIN?
*HEH, HEH.* YEAH. YOU HEARD ME, HUH?
YOU DO NOT LOOK LIKE A FARMER. WHY DO YOU WANT SO MUCH RAIN?
IF THE FARMERS SUFFER, WE ALL SUFFER. BUT YOU ARE RIGHT-- I AM NOT A FARMER.
I AM AN ARTISAN. I MAKE ***TAIKO DRUMS***. THAT IS ANOTHER WAY WE SPEAK TO THE GODS.
5

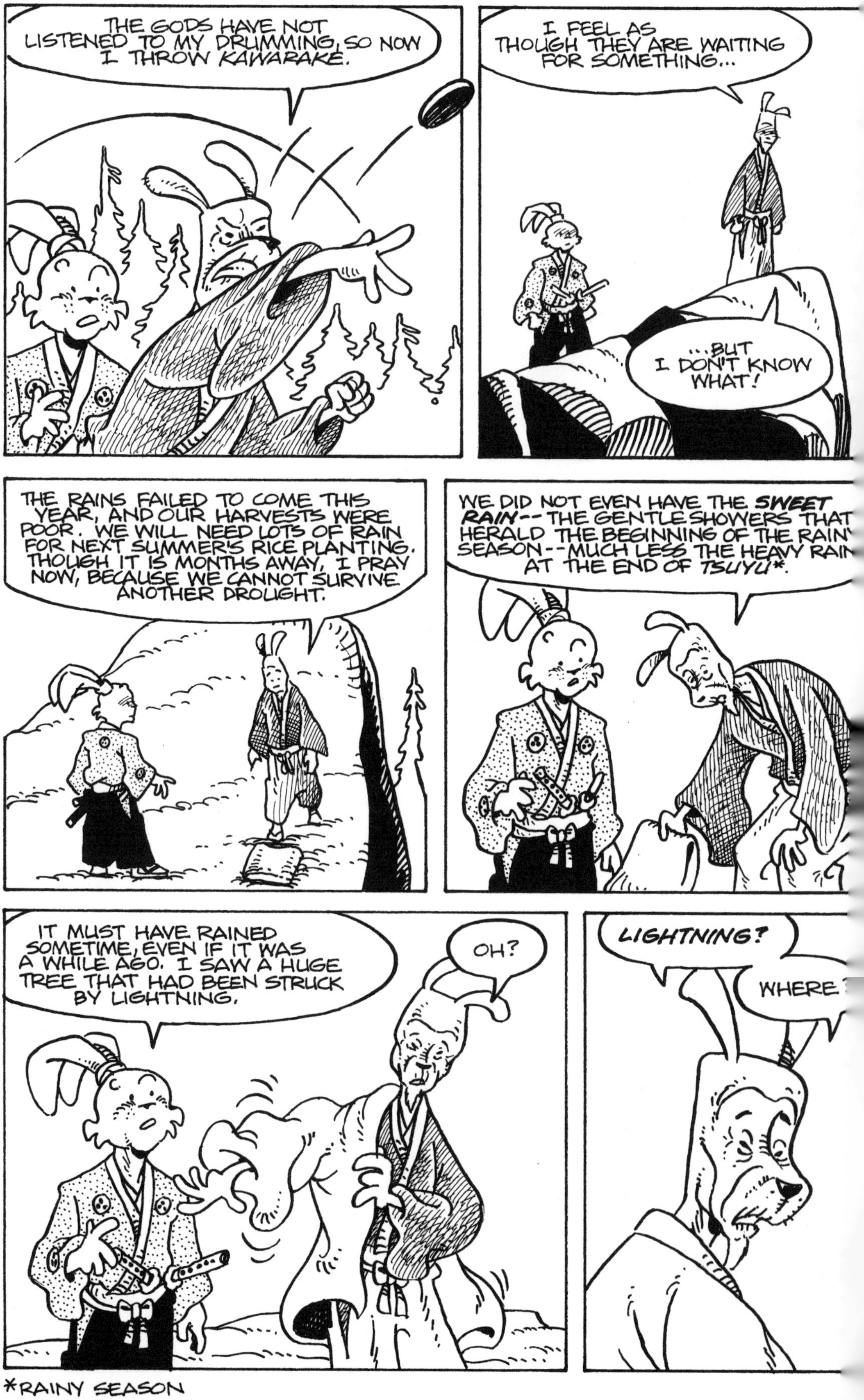
THE GODS HAVE NOT LISTENED TO MY DRUMMING, SO NOW I THROW KAWARAKE.
I FEEL AS THOUGH THEY ARE WAITING FOR SOMETHING...
...BUT I DON'T KNOW WHAT!
THE RAINS FAILED TO COME THIS YEAR, AND OUR HARVESTS WERE POOR. WE WILL NEED LOTS OF RAIN FOR NEXT SUMMER'S RICE PLANTING. THOUGH IT IS MONTHS AWAY, I PRAY NOW, BECAUSE WE CANNOT SURVIVE ANOTHER DROUGHT.
WE DID NOT EVEN HAVE THE SWEET RAIN--THE GENTLE SHOWERS THAT HERALD THE BEGINNING OF THE RAINY SEASON--MUCH LESS THE HEAVY RAIN AT THE END OF TSUYU*.
IT MUST HAVE RAINED SOMETIME, EVEN IF IT WAS A WHILE AGO. I SAW A HUGE TREE THAT HAD BEEN STRUCK BY LIGHTNING.
OH?
LIGHTNING?
WHERE

*RAINY SEASON

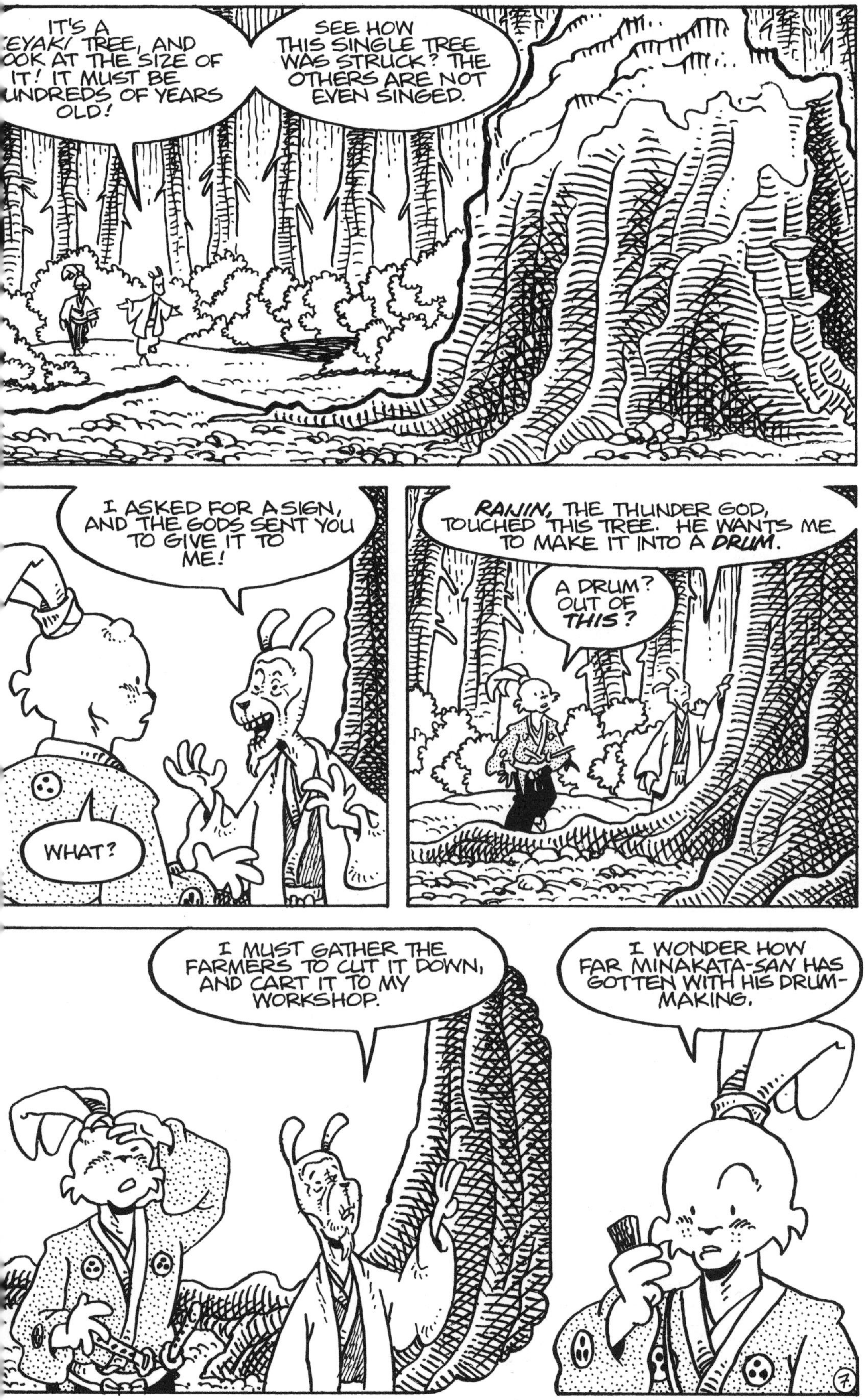
IT'S A EYAKI TREE, AND OOK AT THE SIZE OF IT! IT MUST BE UNDREDS OF YEARS OLD!
SEE HOW THIS SINGLE TREE WAS STRUCK? THE OTHERS ARE NOT EVEN SINGED.
I ASKED FOR A SIGN, AND THE GODS SENT YOU TO GIVE IT TO ME!
WHAT?
RAIJIN, THE THUNDER GOD, TOUCHED THIS TREE. HE WANTS ME TO MAKE IT INTO A DRUM.
A DRUM? OUT OF THIS?
I MUST GATHER THE FARMERS TO CUT IT DOWN, AND CART IT TO MY WORKSHOP.
I WONDER HOW FAR MINAKATA-SAN HAS GOTTEN WITH HIS DRUM-MAKING.
7.

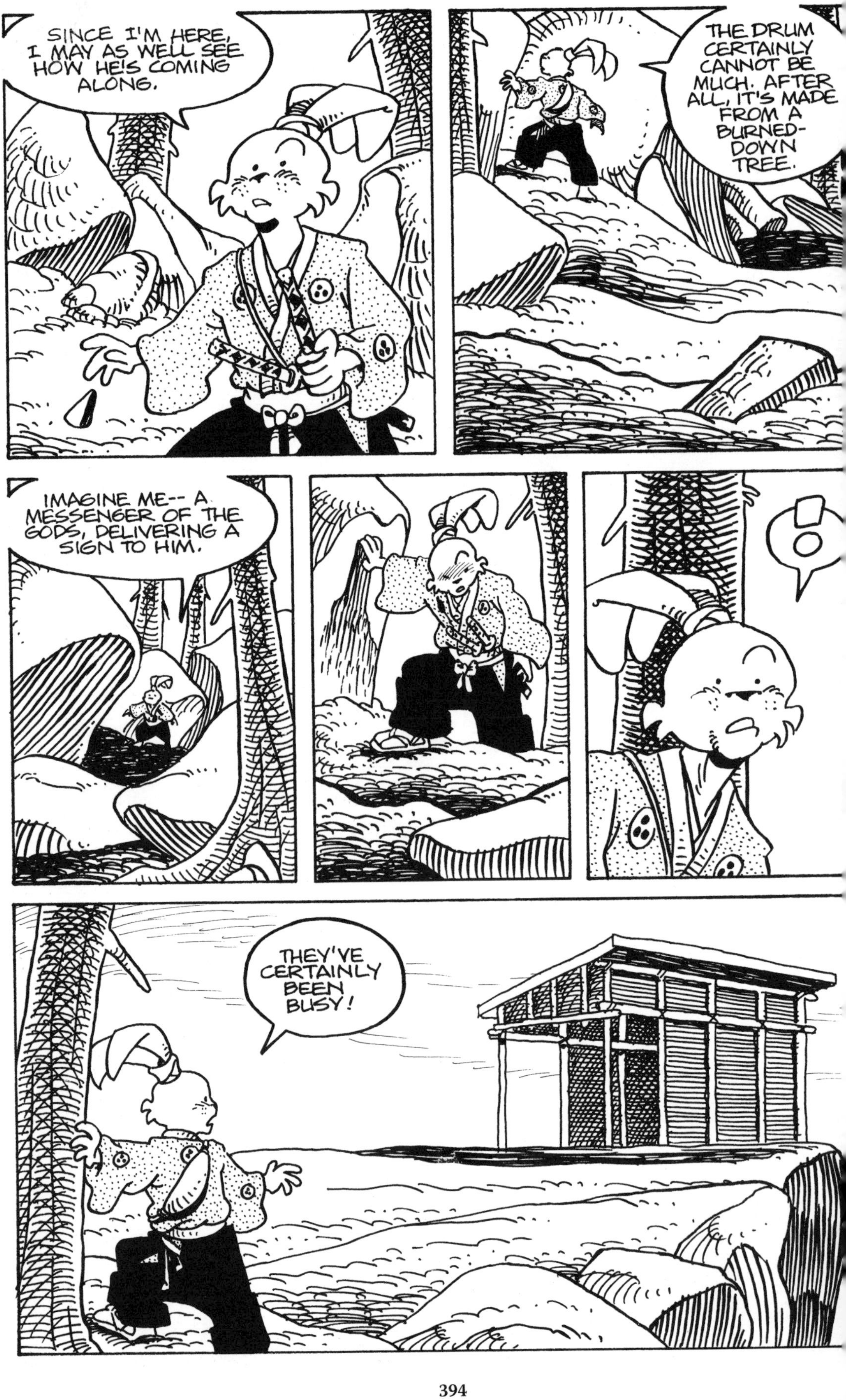

SINCE I'M HERE, I MAY AS WELL SEE HOW HE'S COMING ALONG.
THE DRUM CERTAINLY CANNOT BE MUCH. AFTER ALL, IT'S MADE FROM A BURNED-DOWN TREE.
IMAGINE ME-- A MESSENGER OF THE GODS, DELIVERING A SIGN TO HIM.
!
THEY'VE CERTAINLY BEEN BUSY!

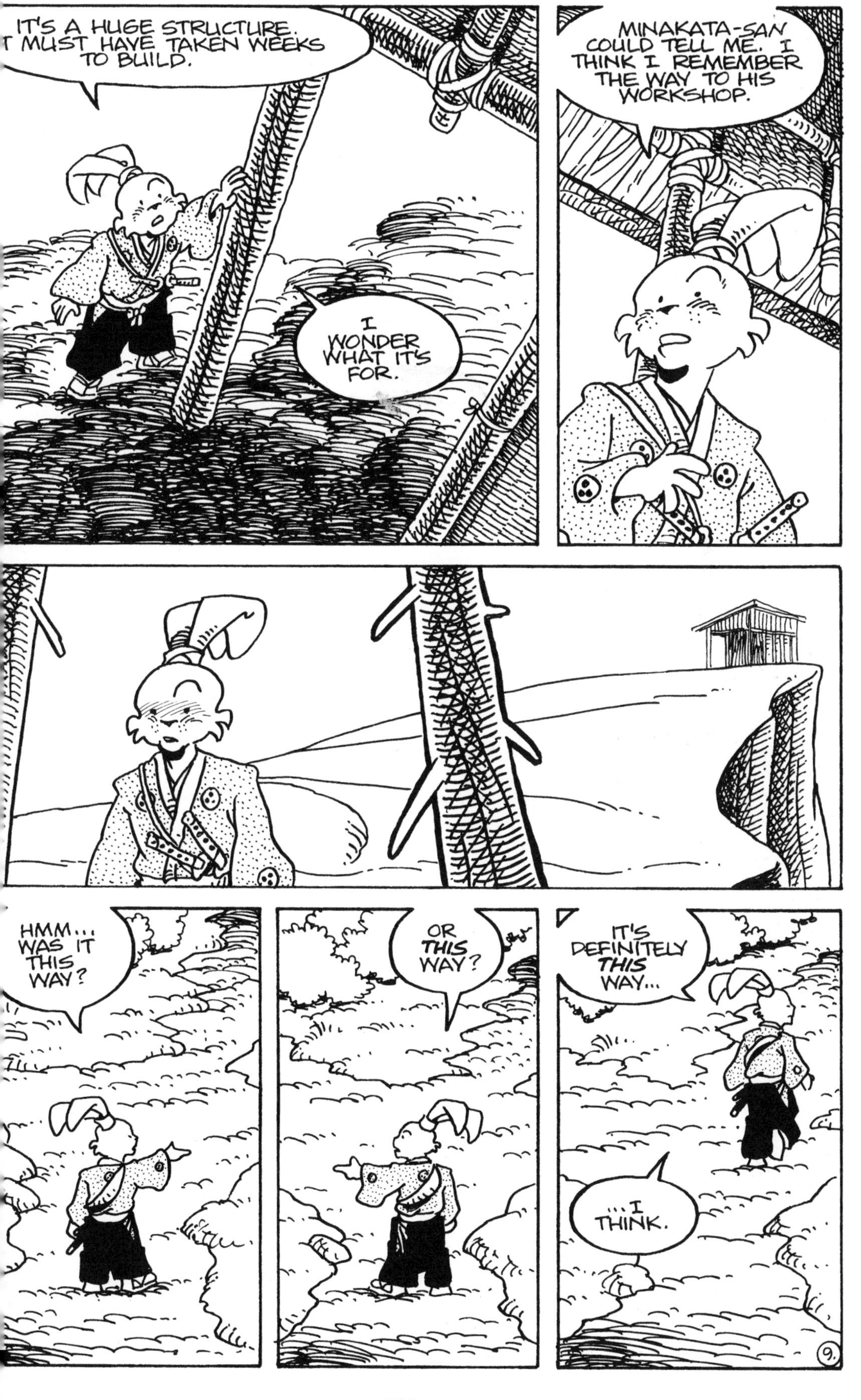
IT'S A HUGE STRUCTURE. IT MUST HAVE TAKEN WEEKS TO BUILD.
I WONDER WHAT IT'S FOR.
MINAKATA-SAN COULD TELL ME. I THINK I REMEMBER THE WAY TO HIS WORKSHOP.
HMM... WAS IT THIS WAY?
OR *THIS* WAY?
IT'S DEFINITELY *THIS* WAY...
...I THINK.
9.

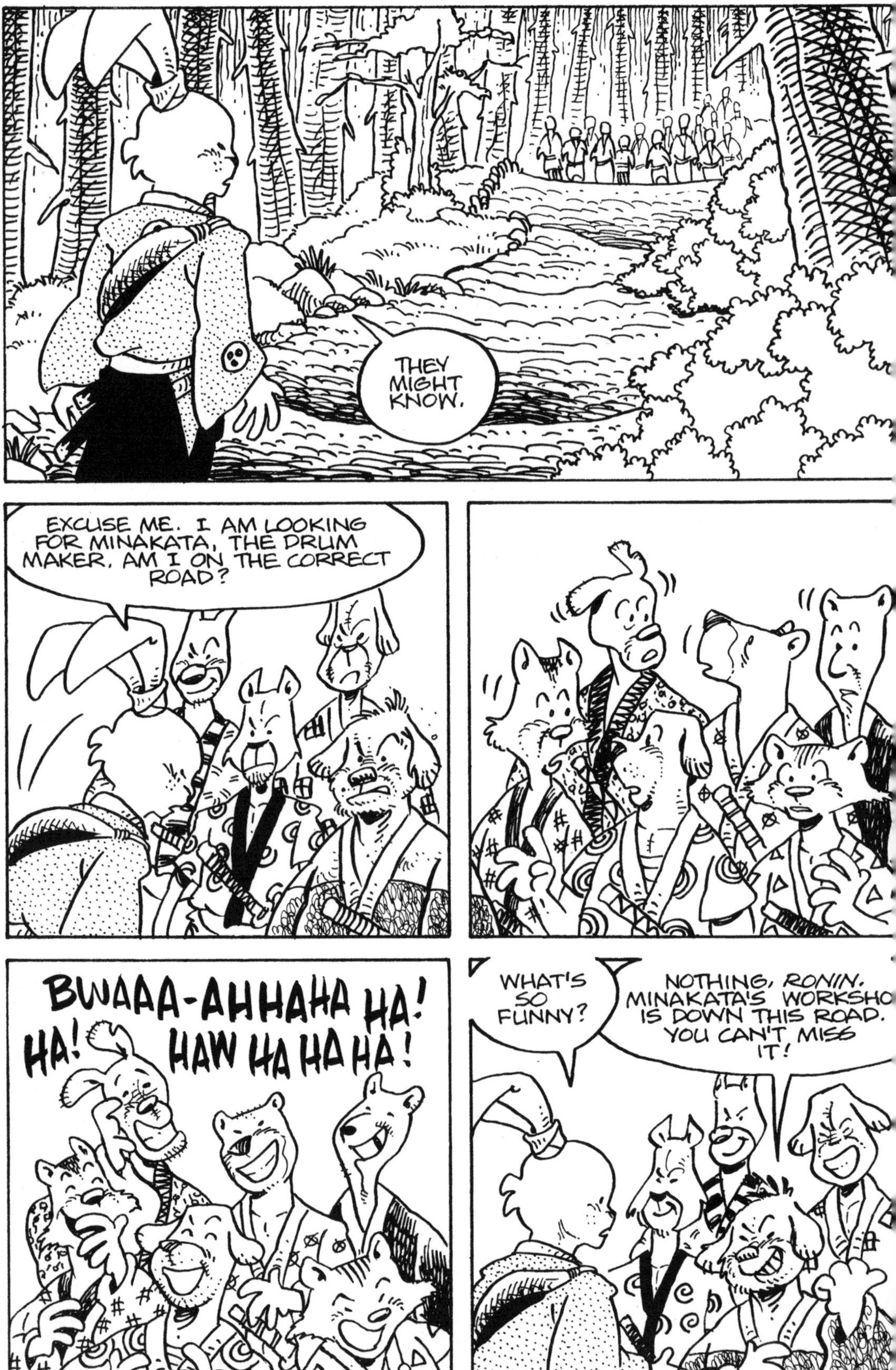

THEY MIGHT KNOW.
EXCUSE ME. I AM LOOKING FOR MINAKATA, THE DRUM MAKER. AM I ON THE CORRECT ROAD?
BWAAA-AHHAHA HA! HA! HAW HA HA HA!
WHAT'S SO FUNNY?
NOTHING, *RONIN*. MINAKATA'S WORKSHO IS DOWN THIS ROAD. YOU CAN'T MISS IT!

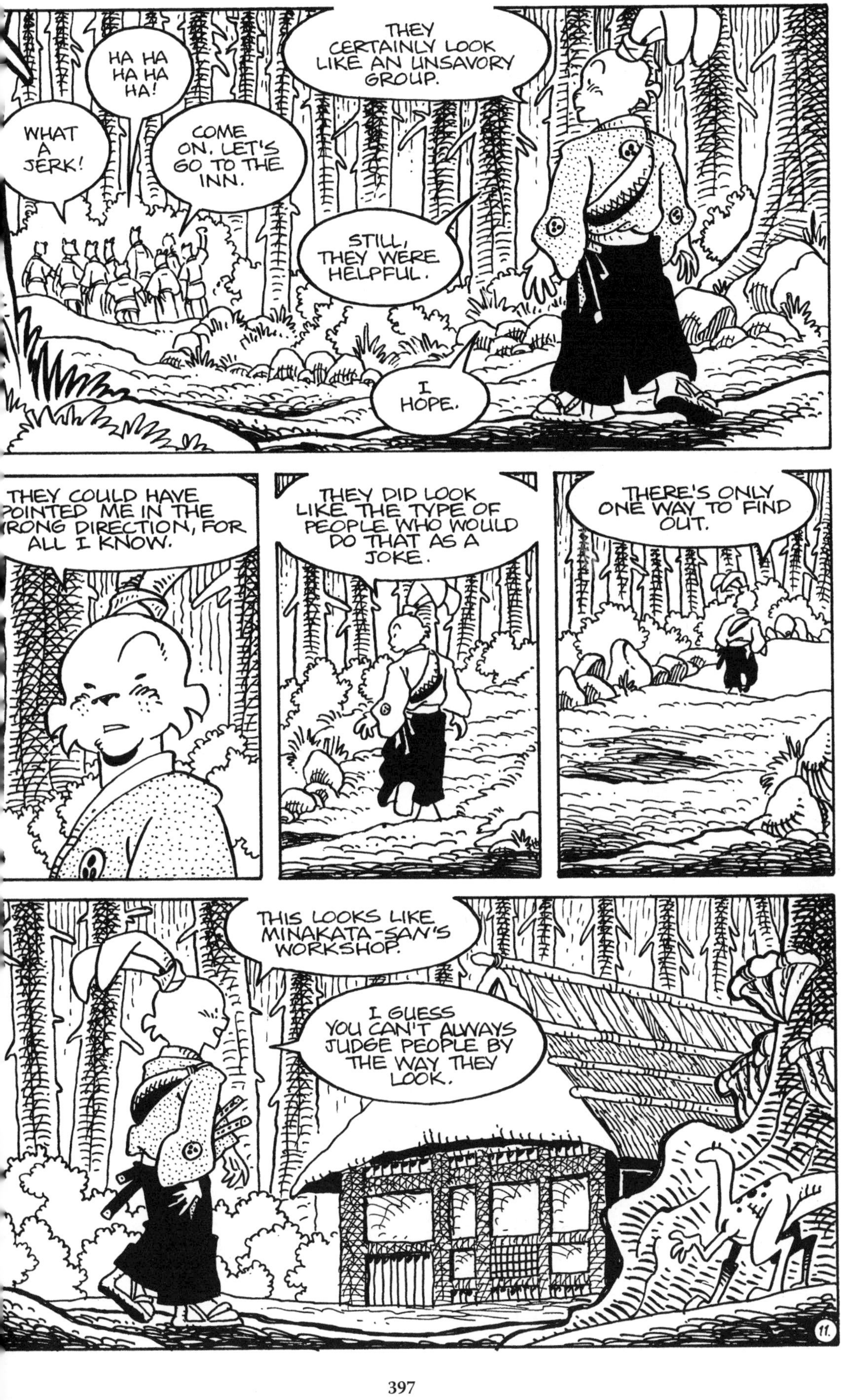
WHAT A JERK!
HA HA HA HA HA!
COME ON. LET'S GO TO THE INN.
THEY CERTAINLY LOOK LIKE AN UNSAVORY GROUP.
STILL, THEY WERE HELPFUL.
I HOPE.
THEY COULD HAVE POINTED ME IN THE WRONG DIRECTION, FOR ALL I KNOW.
THEY DID LOOK LIKE THE TYPE OF PEOPLE WHO WOULD DO THAT AS A JOKE.
THERE'S ONLY ONE WAY TO FIND OUT.
THIS LOOKS LIKE MINAKATA-SAN'S WORKSHOP.
I GUESS YOU CAN'T ALWAYS JUDGE PEOPLE BY THE WAY THEY LOOK.
11.

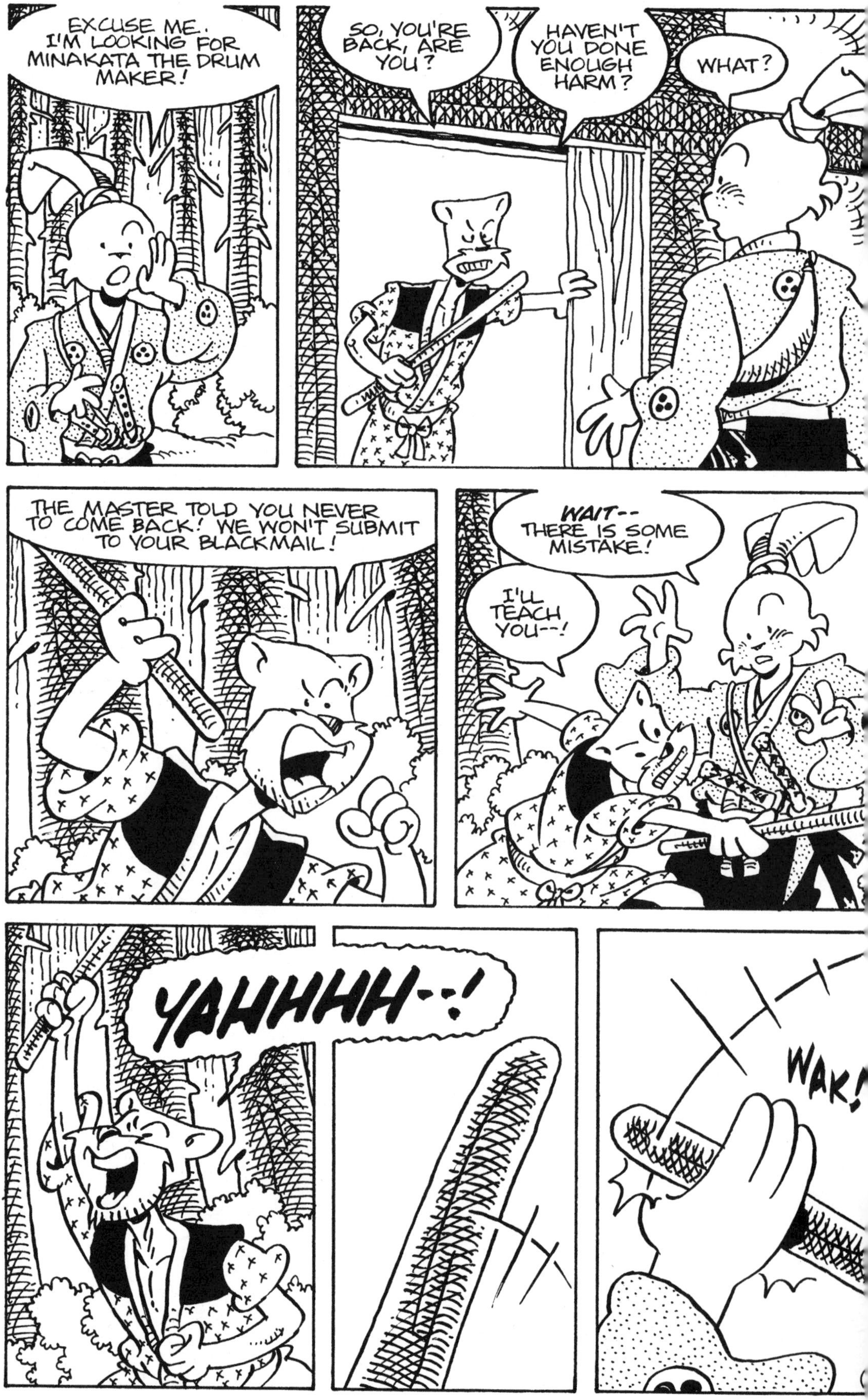
EXCUSE ME. I'M LOOKING FOR MINAKATA THE DRUM MAKER!
SO, YOU'RE BACK, ARE YOU?
HAVEN'T YOU DONE ENOUGH HARM?
WHAT?
THE MASTER TOLD YOU NEVER TO COME BACK! WE WON'T SUBMIT TO YOUR BLACKMAIL!
WAIT-- THERE IS SOME MISTAKE!
I'LL TEACH YOU--!
YAHHHH--!
WAK!

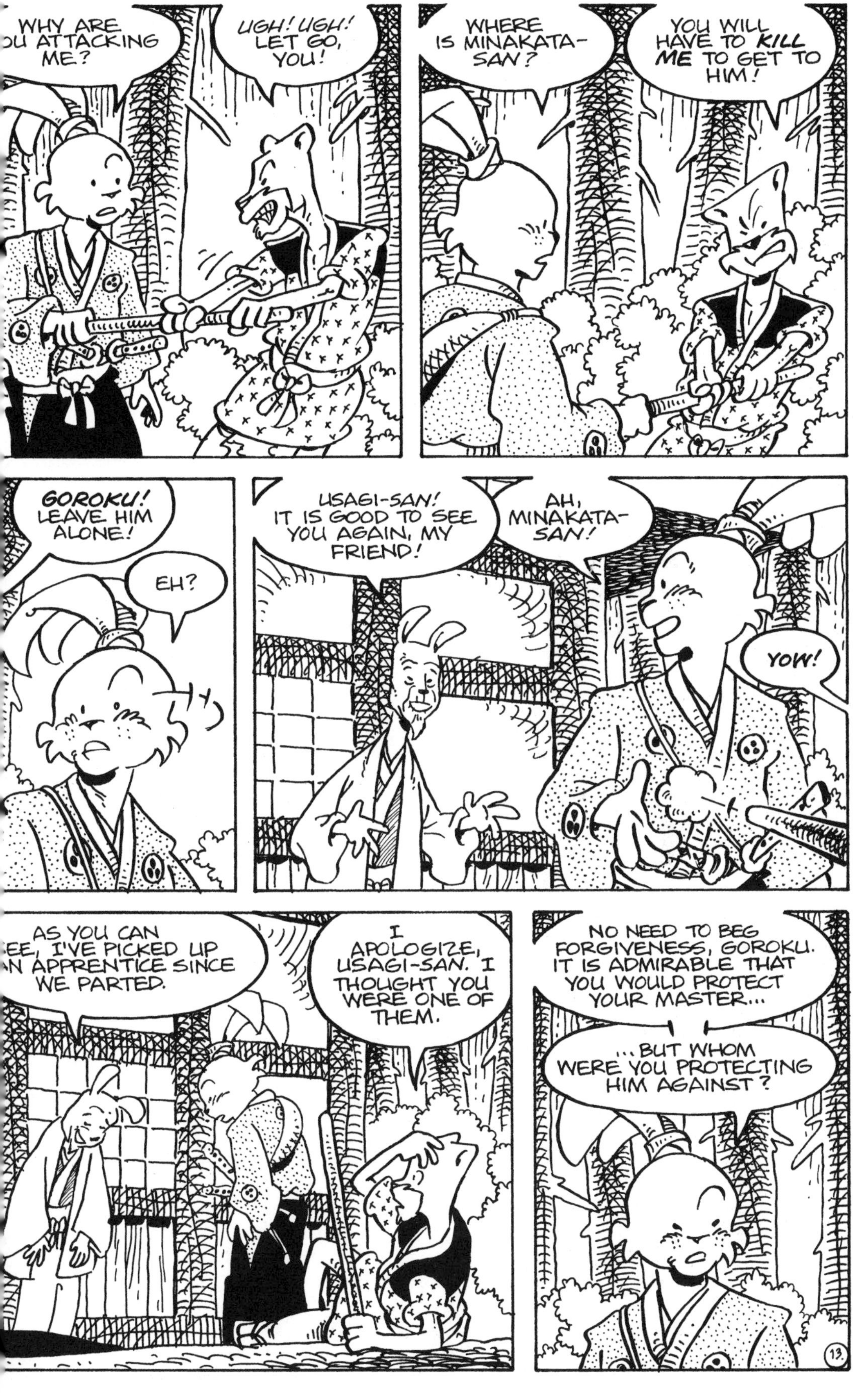

WHY ARE OU ATTACKING ME?
UGH! UGH! LET GO, YOU!
WHERE IS MINAKATA-SAN?
YOU WILL HAVE TO KILL ME TO GET TO HIM!
GOROKU! LEAVE HIM ALONE!
EH?
USAGI-SAN! IT IS GOOD TO SEE YOU AGAIN, MY FRIEND!
AH, MINAKATA-SAN!
YOW!
AS YOU CAN EE, I'VE PICKED UP N APPRENTICE SINCE WE PARTED.
I APOLOGIZE, USAGI-SAN. I THOUGHT YOU WERE ONE OF THEM.
NO NEED TO BEG FORGIVENESS, GOROKU. IT IS ADMIRABLE THAT YOU WOULD PROTECT YOUR MASTER...
...BUT WHOM WERE YOU PROTECTING HIM AGAINST?
13

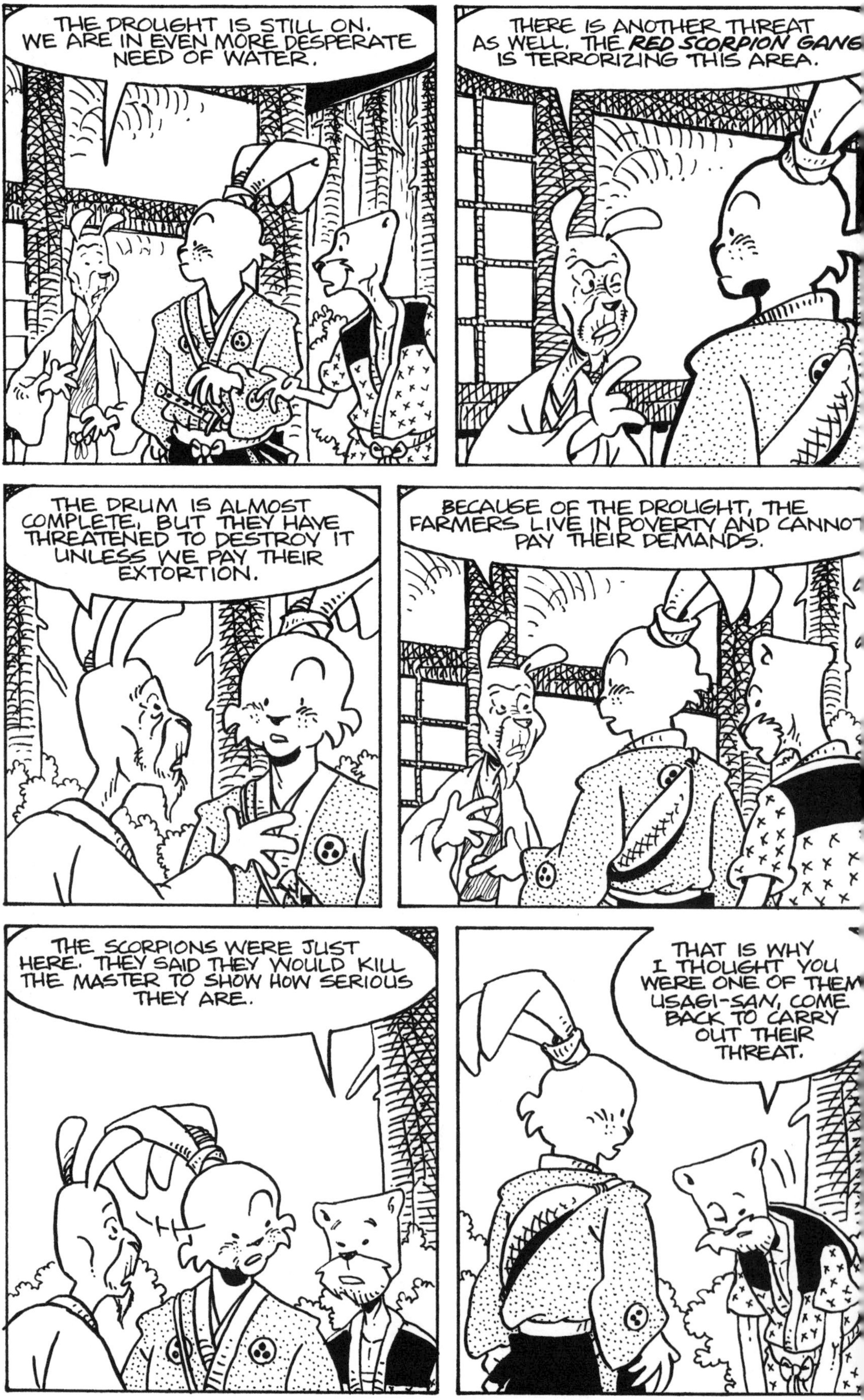
THE DROUGHT IS STILL ON. WE ARE IN EVEN MORE DESPERATE NEED OF WATER.
THERE IS ANOTHER THREAT AS WELL. THE ***RED SCORPION GANG*** IS TERRORIZING THIS AREA.
THE DRUM IS ALMOST COMPLETE, BUT THEY HAVE THREATENED TO DESTROY IT UNLESS WE PAY THEIR EXTORTION.
BECAUSE OF THE DROUGHT, THE FARMERS LIVE IN POVERTY AND CANNOT PAY THEIR DEMANDS.
THE SCORPIONS WERE JUST HERE. THEY SAID THEY WOULD KILL THE MASTER TO SHOW HOW SERIOUS THEY ARE.
THAT IS WHY I THOUGHT YOU WERE ONE OF THEM, USAGI-SAN, COME BACK TO CARRY OUT THEIR THREAT.

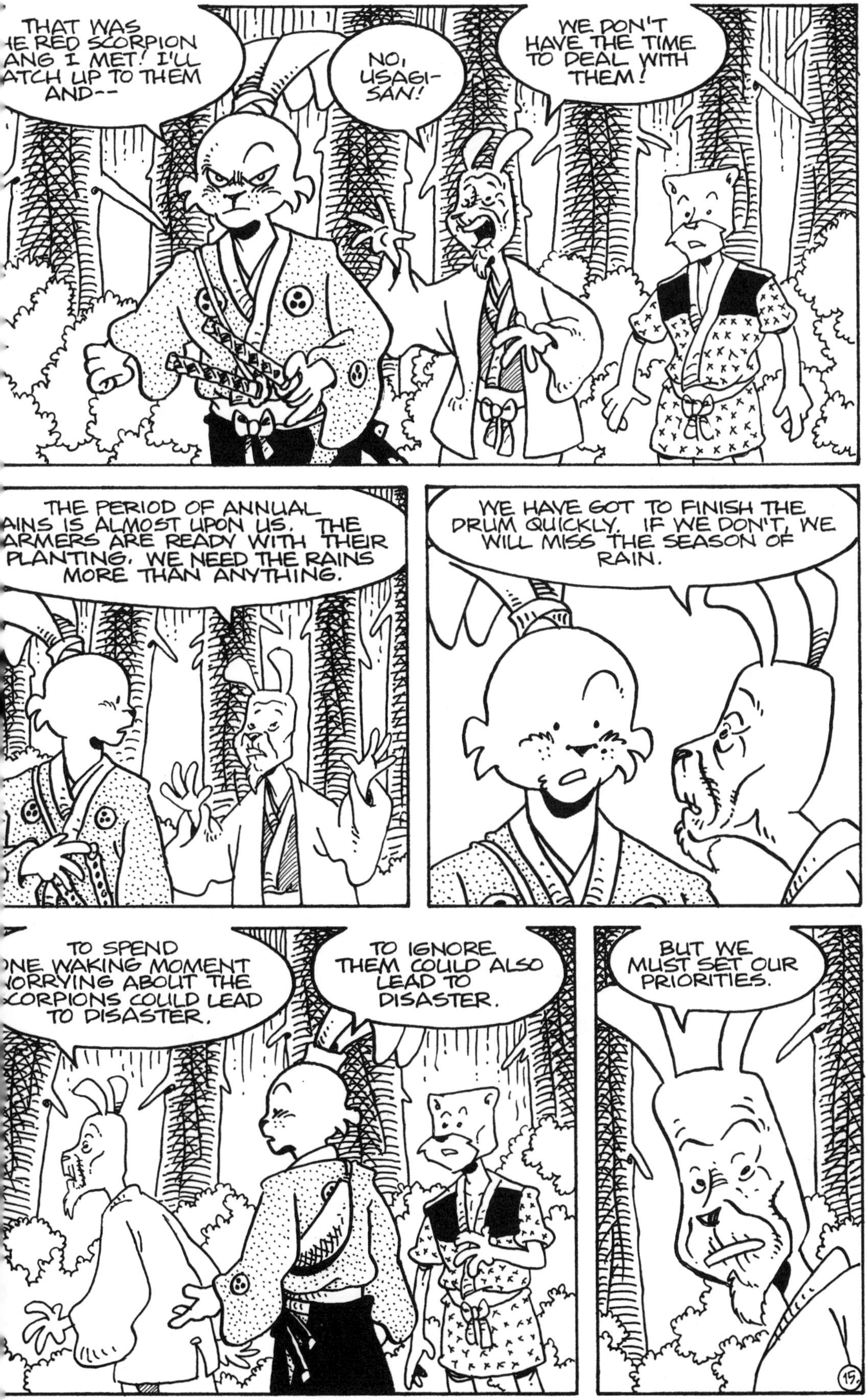
THAT WAS
E RED SCORPION
ANG I MET! I'LL
ATCH UP TO THEM
AND--
NO, USAGI-SAN!
WE DON'T HAVE THE TIME TO DEAL WITH THEM!
THE PERIOD OF ANNUAL
AINS IS ALMOST UPON US. THE
ARMERS ARE READY WITH THEIR
PLANTING. WE NEED THE RAINS
MORE THAN ANYTHING.
WE HAVE GOT TO FINISH THE DRUM QUICKLY. IF WE DON'T, WE WILL MISS THE SEASON OF RAIN.
TO SPEND
NE WAKING MOMENT
ORRYING ABOUT THE
CORPIONS COULD LEAD
TO DISASTER.
TO IGNORE THEM COULD ALSO LEAD TO DISASTER.
BUT WE MUST SET OUR PRIORITIES.
15

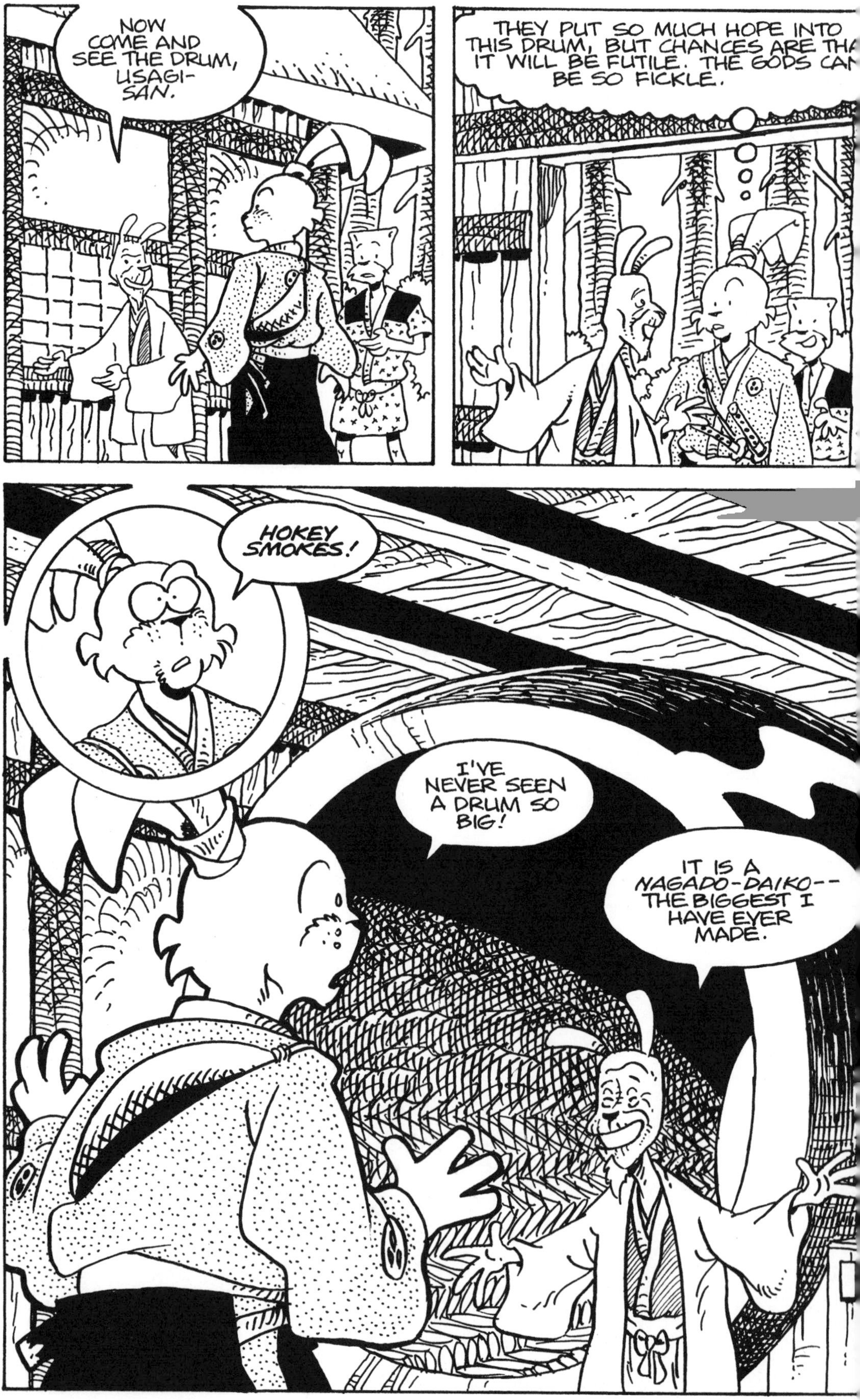
NOW COME AND SEE THE DRUM, USAGI-SAN.
THEY PUT SO MUCH HOPE INTO THIS DRUM, BUT CHANCES ARE THA IT WILL BE FUTILE. THE GODS CAN BE SO FICKLE.
HOKEY SMOKES!
I'VE NEVER SEEN A DRUM SO BIG!
IT IS A *NAGADO-DAIKO*-- THE BIGGEST I HAVE EVER MADE.

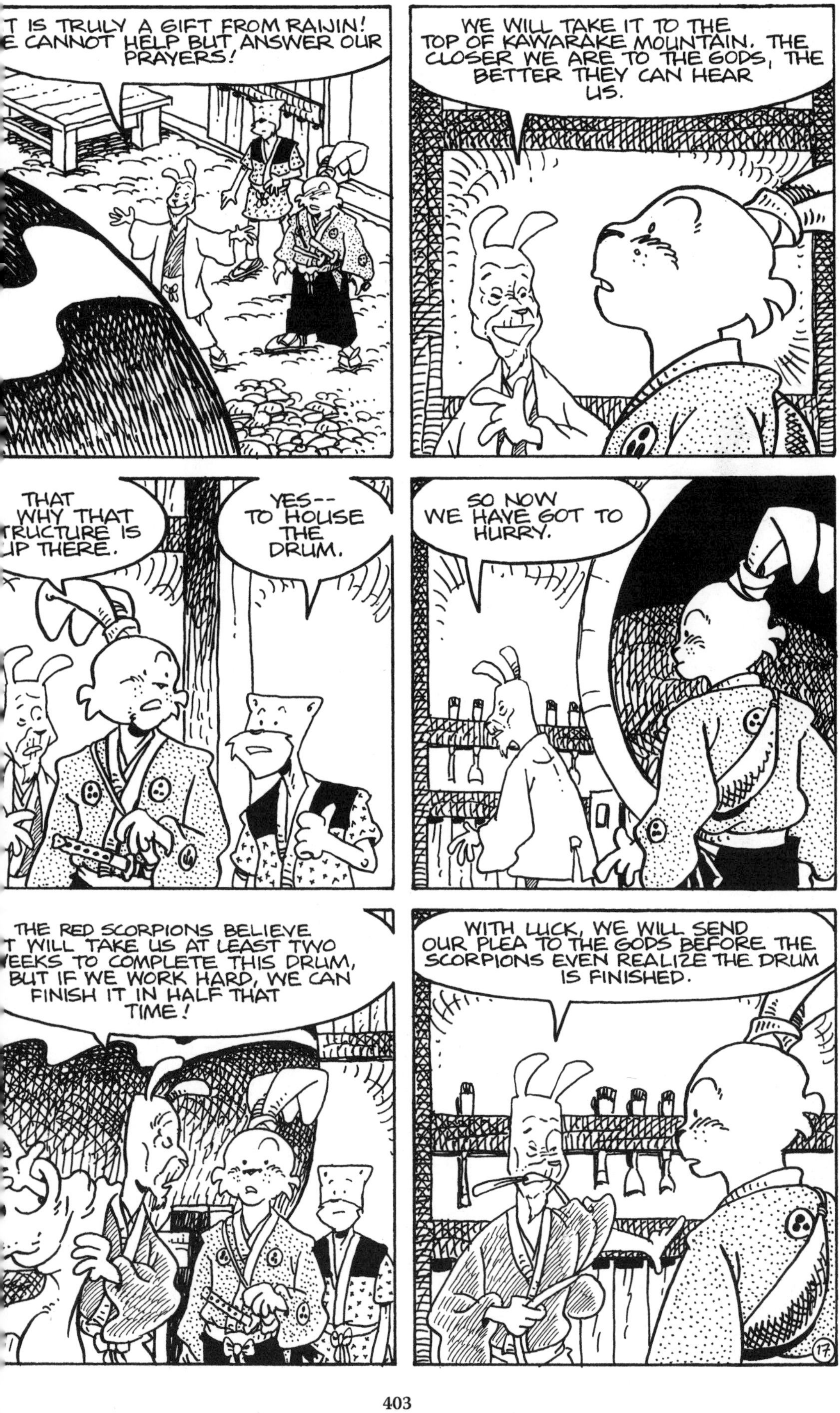
T IS TRULY A GIFT FROM RAIJIN! E CANNOT HELP BUT ANSWER OUR PRAYERS!
WE WILL TAKE IT TO THE TOP OF KAWARAKE MOUNTAIN. THE CLOSER WE ARE TO THE GODS, THE BETTER THEY CAN HEAR US.
THAT WHY THAT TRUCTURE IS UP THERE.
YES-- TO HOUSE THE DRUM.
SO NOW WE HAVE GOT TO HURRY.
THE RED SCORPIONS BELIEVE T WILL TAKE US AT LEAST TWO EEKS TO COMPLETE THIS DRUM, BUT IF WE WORK HARD, WE CAN FINISH IT IN HALF THAT TIME!
WITH LUCK, WE WILL SEND OUR PLEA TO THE GODS BEFORE THE SCORPIONS EVEN REALIZE THE DRUM IS FINISHED.
17

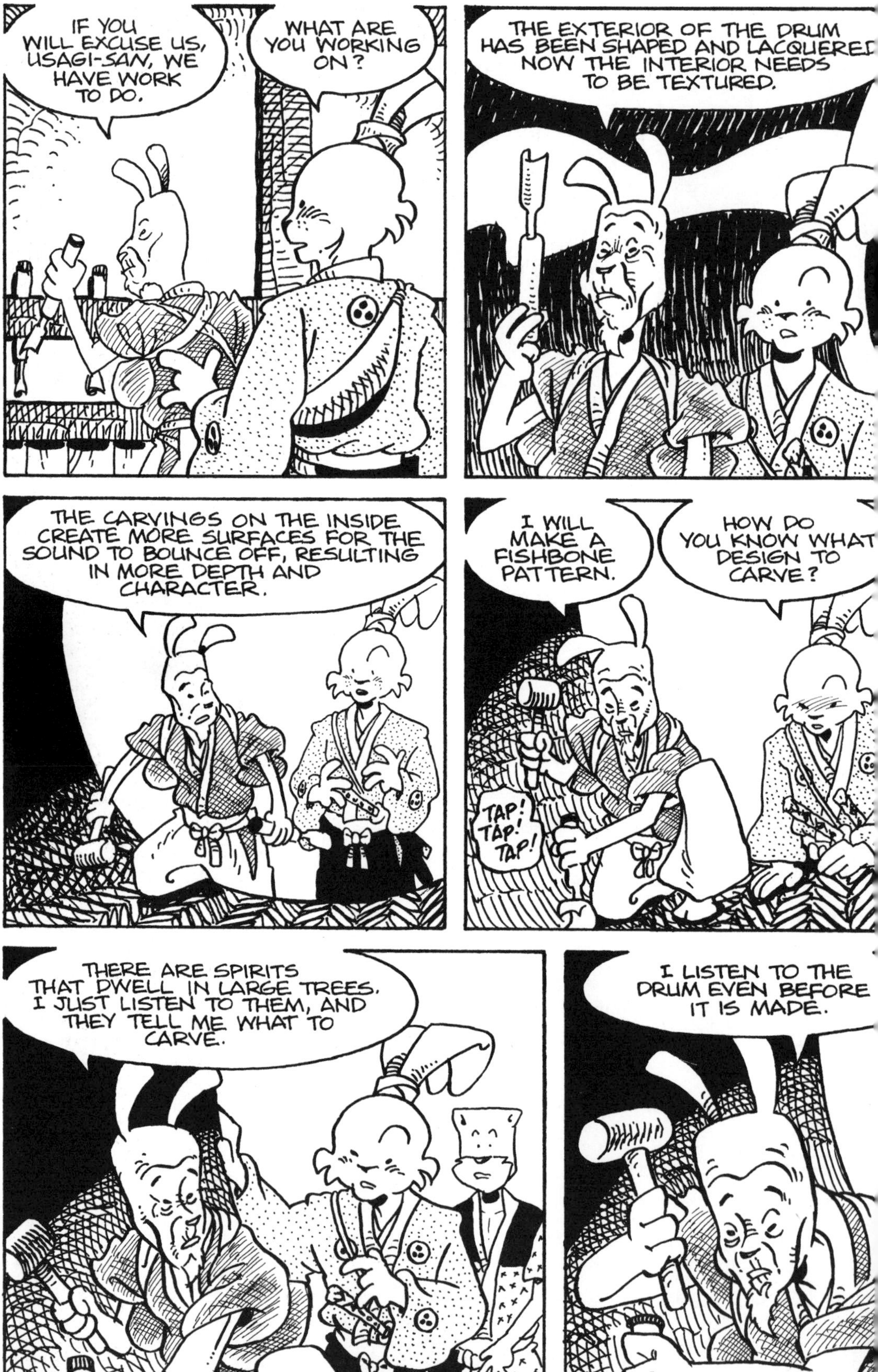
IF YOU WILL EXCUSE US, USAGI-SAN, WE HAVE WORK TO DO.
WHAT ARE YOU WORKING ON?
THE EXTERIOR OF THE DRUM HAS BEEN SHAPED AND LACQUERED. NOW THE INTERIOR NEEDS TO BE TEXTURED.
THE CARVINGS ON THE INSIDE CREATE MORE SURFACES FOR THE SOUND TO BOUNCE OFF, RESULTING IN MORE DEPTH AND CHARACTER.
I WILL MAKE A FISHBONE PATTERN.
HOW DO YOU KNOW WHAT DESIGN TO CARVE?
TAP! TAP! TAP!
THERE ARE SPIRITS THAT DWELL IN LARGE TREES. I JUST LISTEN TO THEM, AND THEY TELL ME WHAT TO CARVE.
I LISTEN TO THE DRUM EVEN BEFORE IT IS MADE.

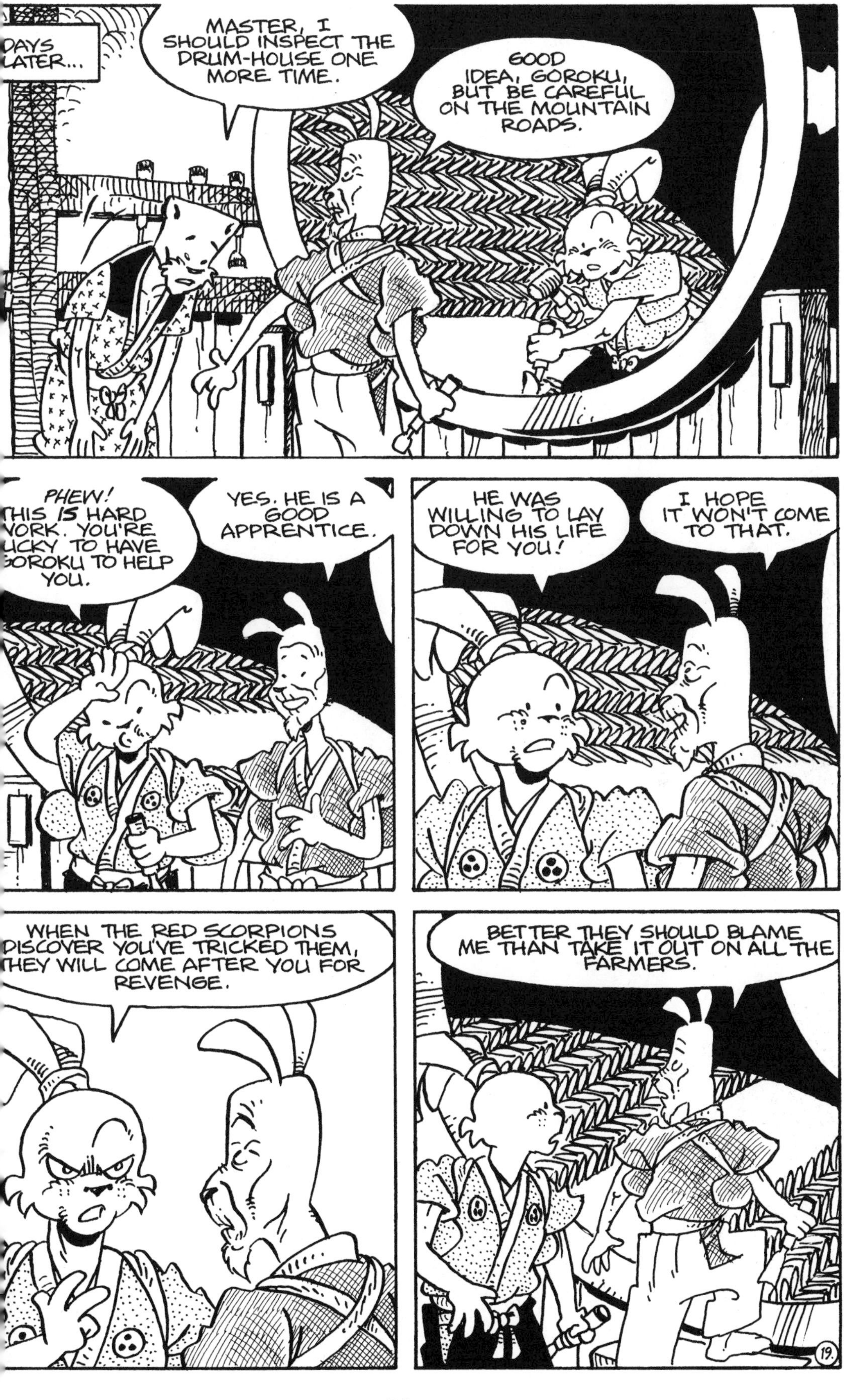
DAYS LATER...
MASTER, I SHOULD INSPECT THE DRUM-HOUSE ONE MORE TIME.
GOOD IDEA, GOROKU, BUT BE CAREFUL ON THE MOUNTAIN ROADS.
PHEW! THIS IS HARD WORK. YOU'RE LUCKY TO HAVE GOROKU TO HELP YOU.
YES. HE IS A GOOD APPRENTICE.
HE WAS WILLING TO LAY DOWN HIS LIFE FOR YOU!
I HOPE IT WON'T COME TO THAT.
WHEN THE RED SCORPIONS DISCOVER YOU'VE TRICKED THEM, THEY WILL COME AFTER YOU FOR REVENGE.
BETTER THEY SHOULD BLAME ME THAN TAKE IT OUT ON ALL THE FARMERS.
19.

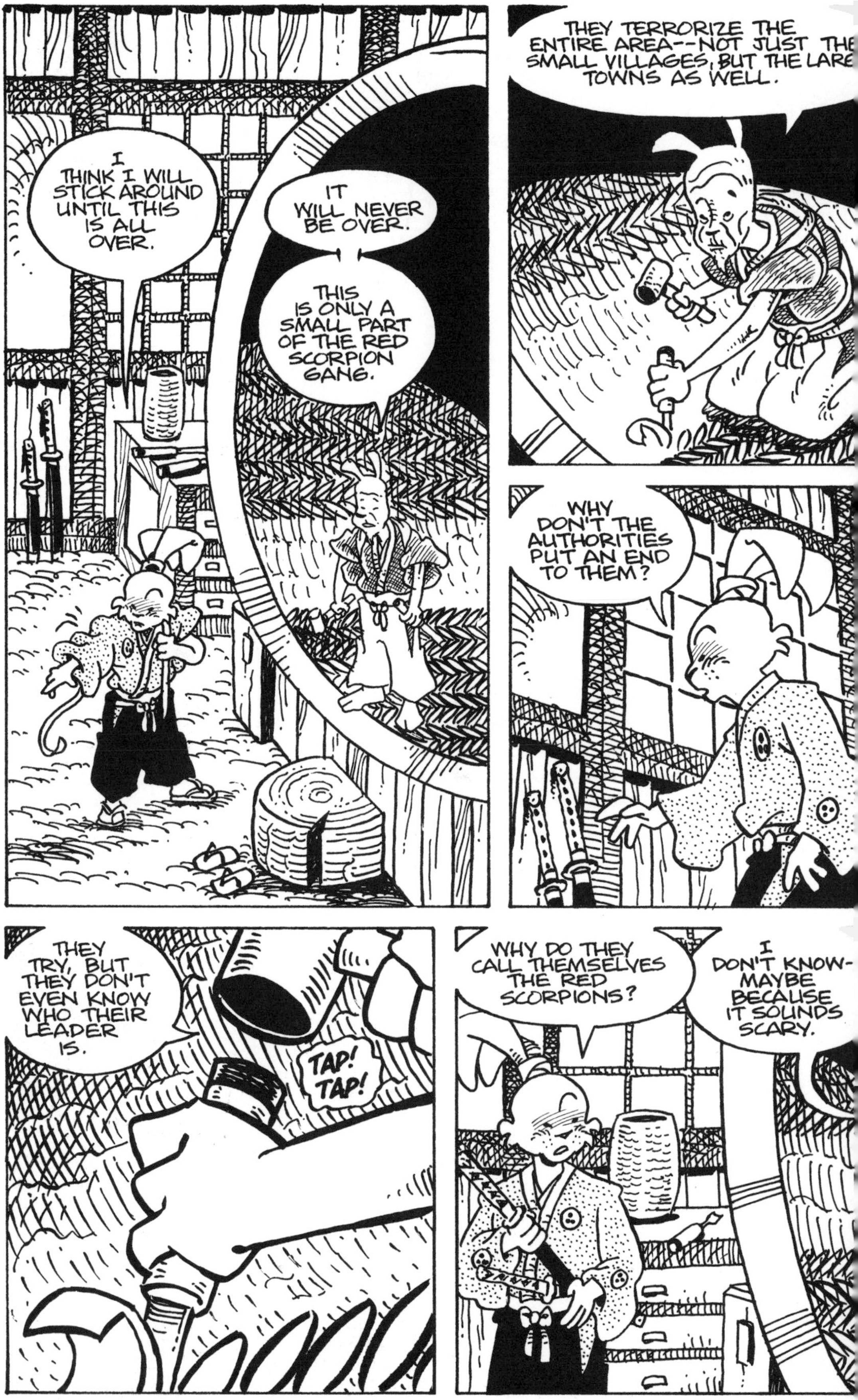
I THINK I WILL STICK AROUND UNTIL THIS IS ALL OVER.
IT WILL NEVER BE OVER.
THIS IS ONLY A SMALL PART OF THE RED SCORPION GANG.
THEY TERRORIZE THE ENTIRE AREA--NOT JUST THE SMALL VILLAGES, BUT THE LAR TOWNS AS WELL.
WHY DON'T THE AUTHORITIES PUT AN END TO THEM?
THEY TRY, BUT THEY DON'T EVEN KNOW WHO THEIR LEADER IS.
TAP! TAP!
WHY DO THEY CALL THEMSELVES THE RED SCORPIONS?
I DON'T KNOW-MAYBE BECAUSE IT SOUNDS SCARY.

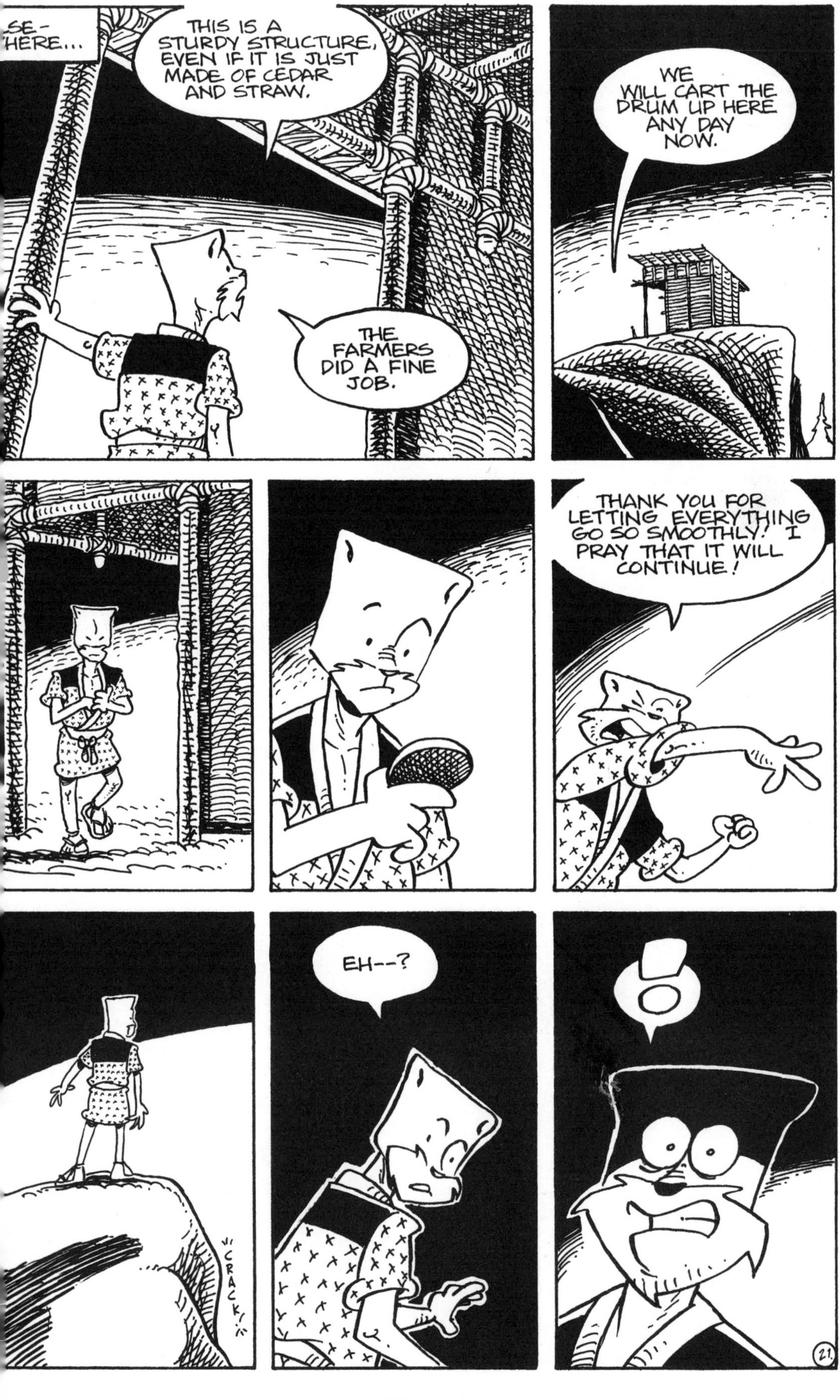
SE-
HERE...
THIS IS A STURDY STRUCTURE, EVEN IF IT IS JUST MADE OF CEDAR AND STRAW.
THE FARMERS DID A FINE JOB.
WE WILL CART THE DRUM UP HERE ANY DAY NOW.
THANK YOU FOR LETTING EVERYTHING GO SO SMOOTHLY! I PRAY THAT IT WILL CONTINUE!
CRACK!
EH--?
!
21.

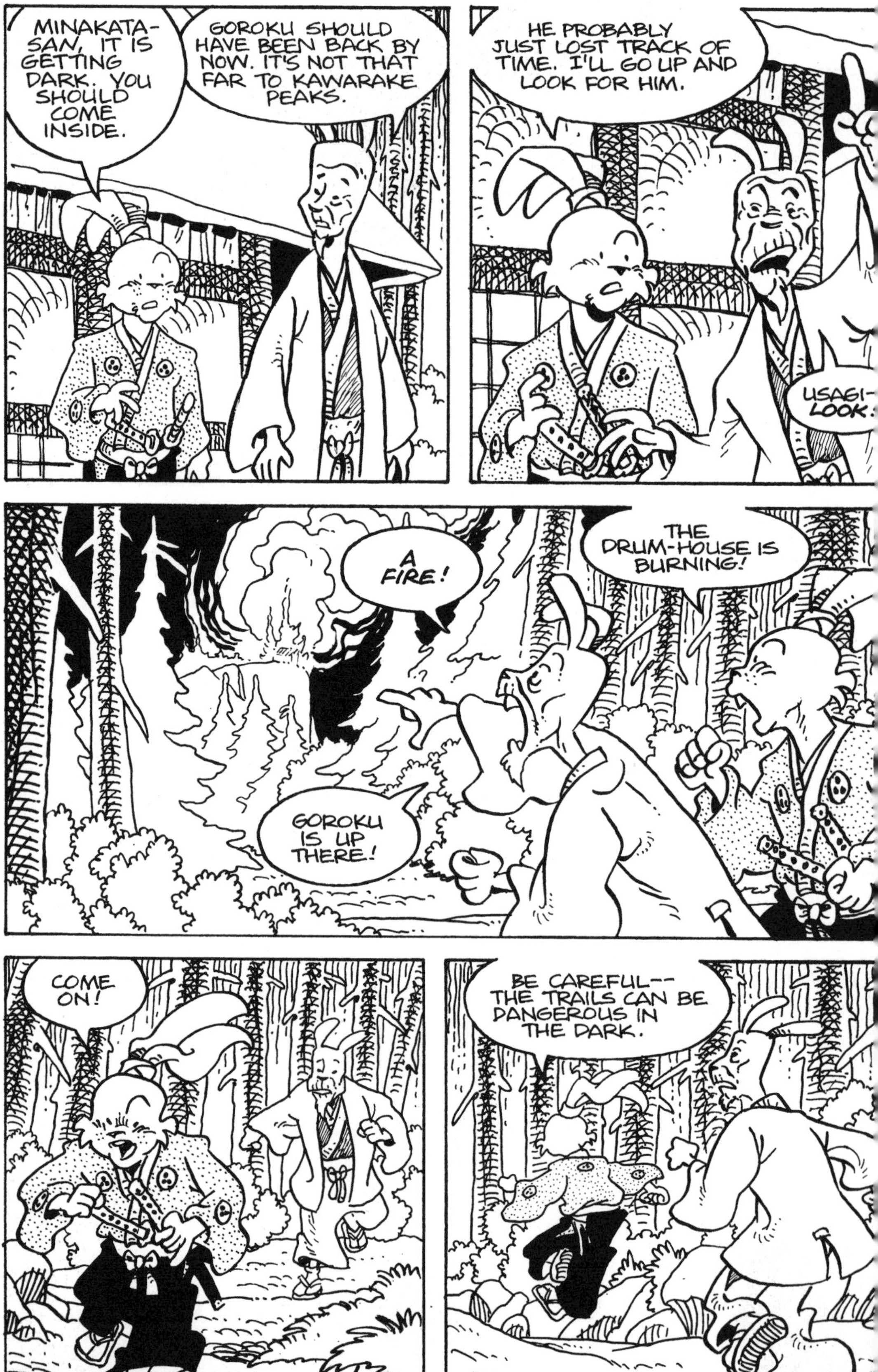
MINAKATA-SAN, IT IS GETTING DARK. YOU SHOULD COME INSIDE.
GOROKU SHOULD HAVE BEEN BACK BY NOW. IT'S NOT THAT FAR TO KAWARAKE PEAKS.
HE PROBABLY JUST LOST TRACK OF TIME. I'LL GO UP AND LOOK FOR HIM.
USAGI-LOOK!
A FIRE!
THE DRUM-HOUSE IS BURNING!
GOROKU IS UP THERE!
COME ON!
BE CAREFUL-- THE TRAILS CAN BE DANGEROUS IN THE DARK.

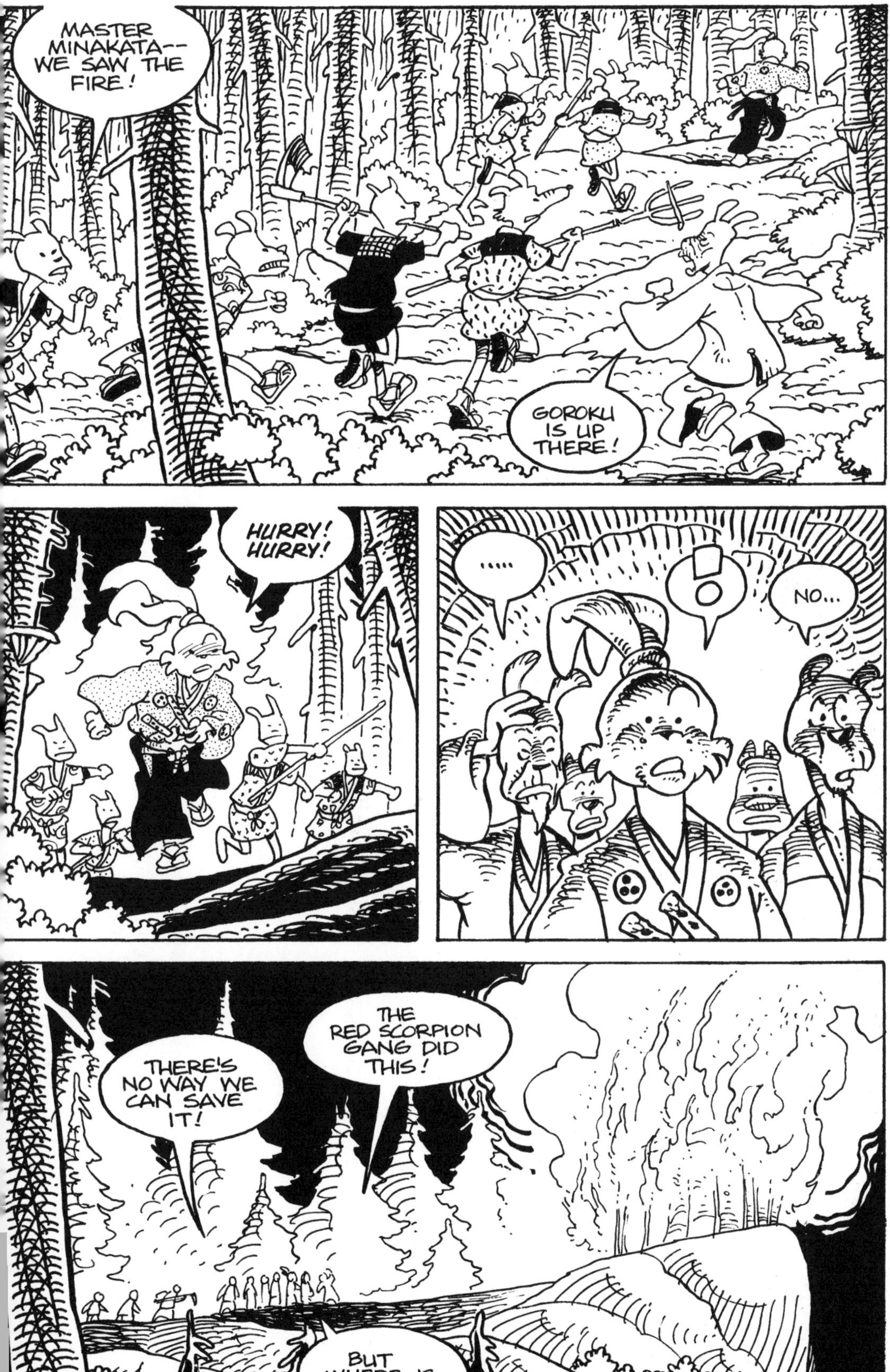
MASTER MINAKATA-- WE SAW THE FIRE!
GOROKU IS UP THERE!
HURRY! HURRY!
.....
!
NO...
THERE'S NO WAY WE CAN SAVE IT!
THE RED SCORPION GANG DID THIS!
BUT WHERE IS GOROKU?
23.

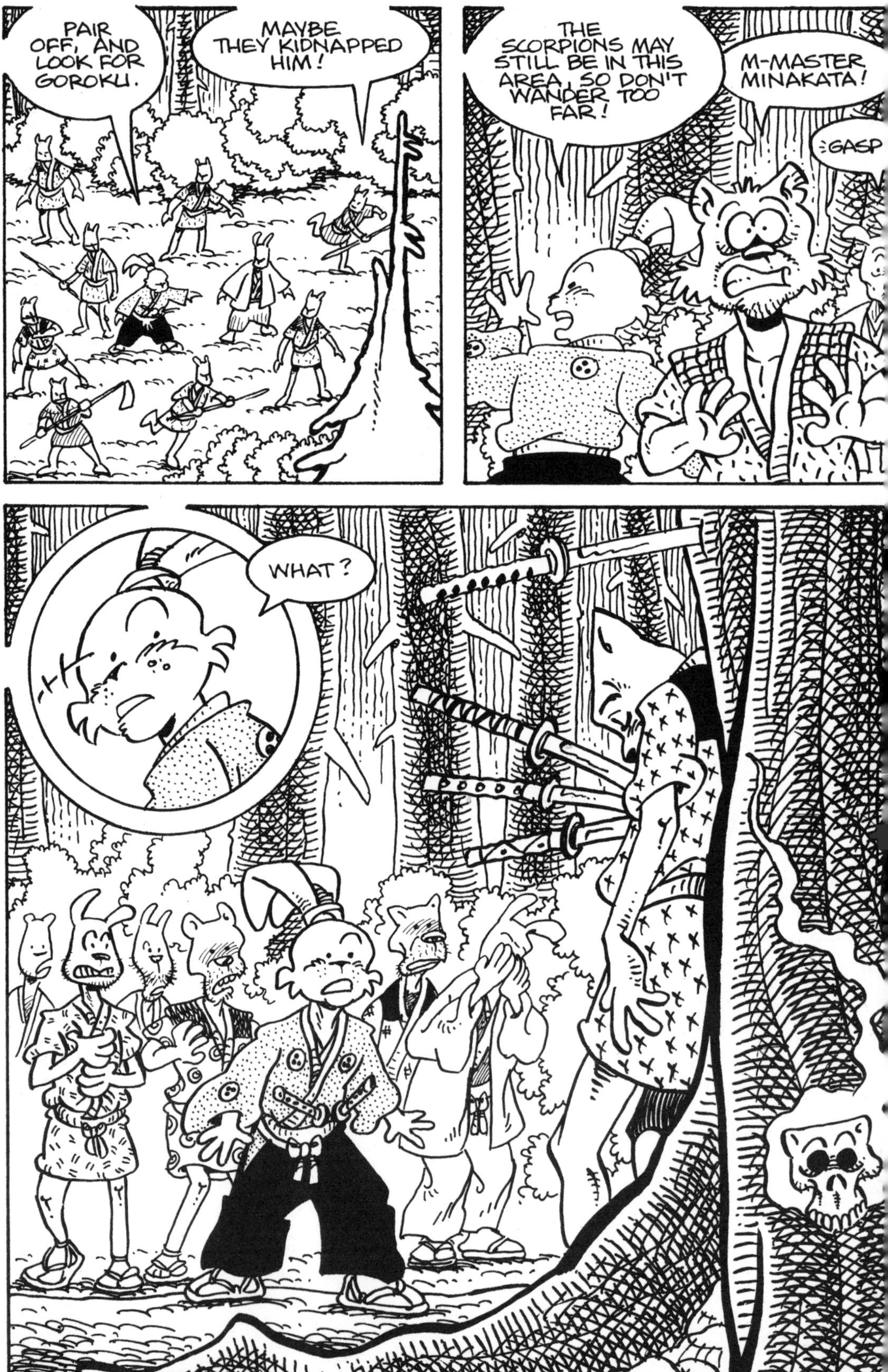
PAIR OFF, AND LOOK FOR GOROKU.
MAYBE THEY KIDNAPPED HIM!
THE SCORPIONS MAY STILL BE IN THIS AREA, SO DON'T WANDER TOO FAR!
M-MASTER MINAKATA!
GASP
WHAT?

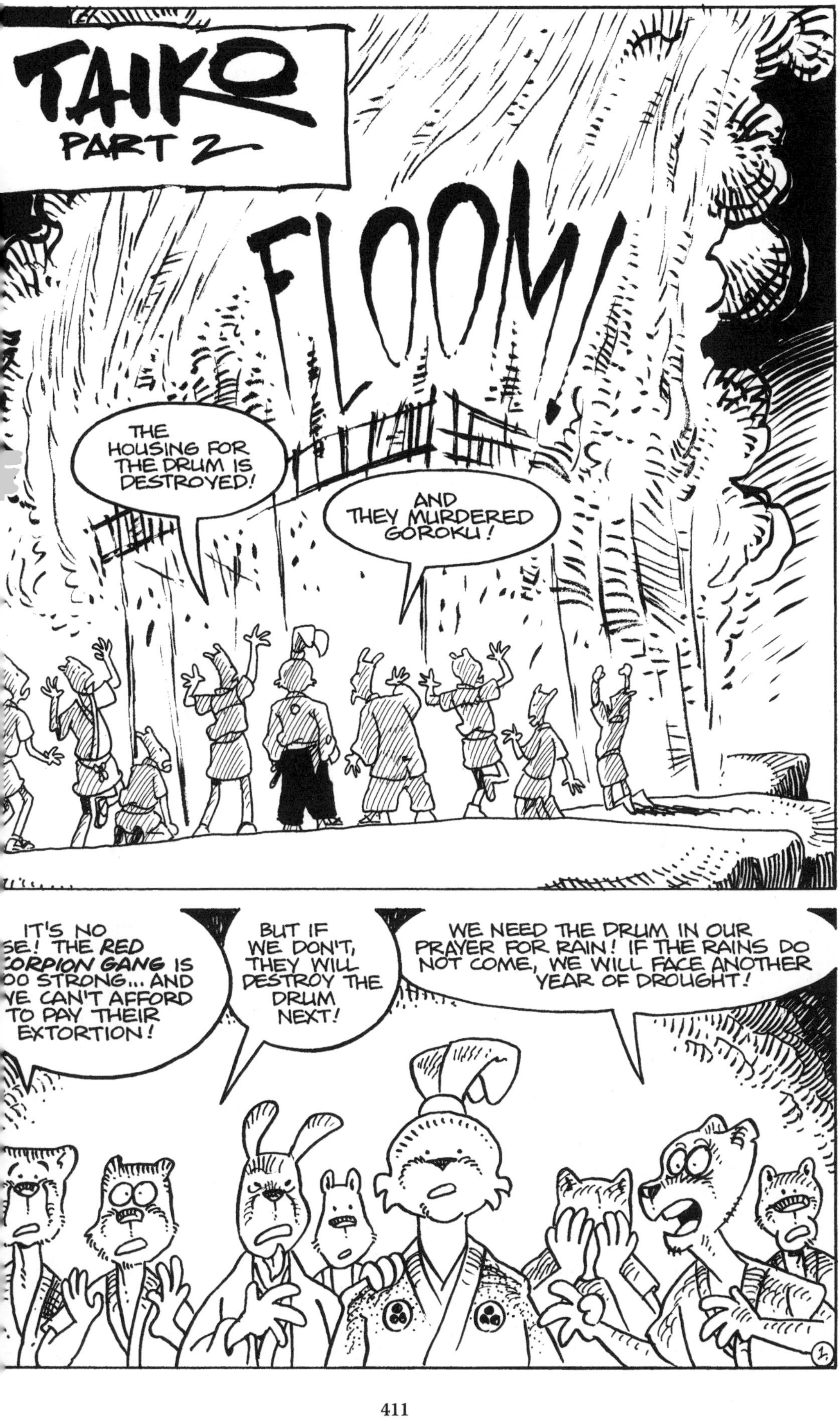
TAIKO
PART 2
FLOOM!
THE HOUSING FOR THE DRUM IS DESTROYED!
AND THEY MURDERED GOROKU!
IT'S NO SE! THE RED CORPION GANG IS OO STRONG... AND VE CAN'T AFFORD TO PAY THEIR EXTORTION!
BUT IF WE DON'T, THEY WILL DESTROY THE DRUM NEXT!
WE NEED THE DRUM IN OUR PRAYER FOR RAIN! IF THE RAINS DO NOT COME, WE WILL FACE ANOTHER YEAR OF DROUGHT!
1

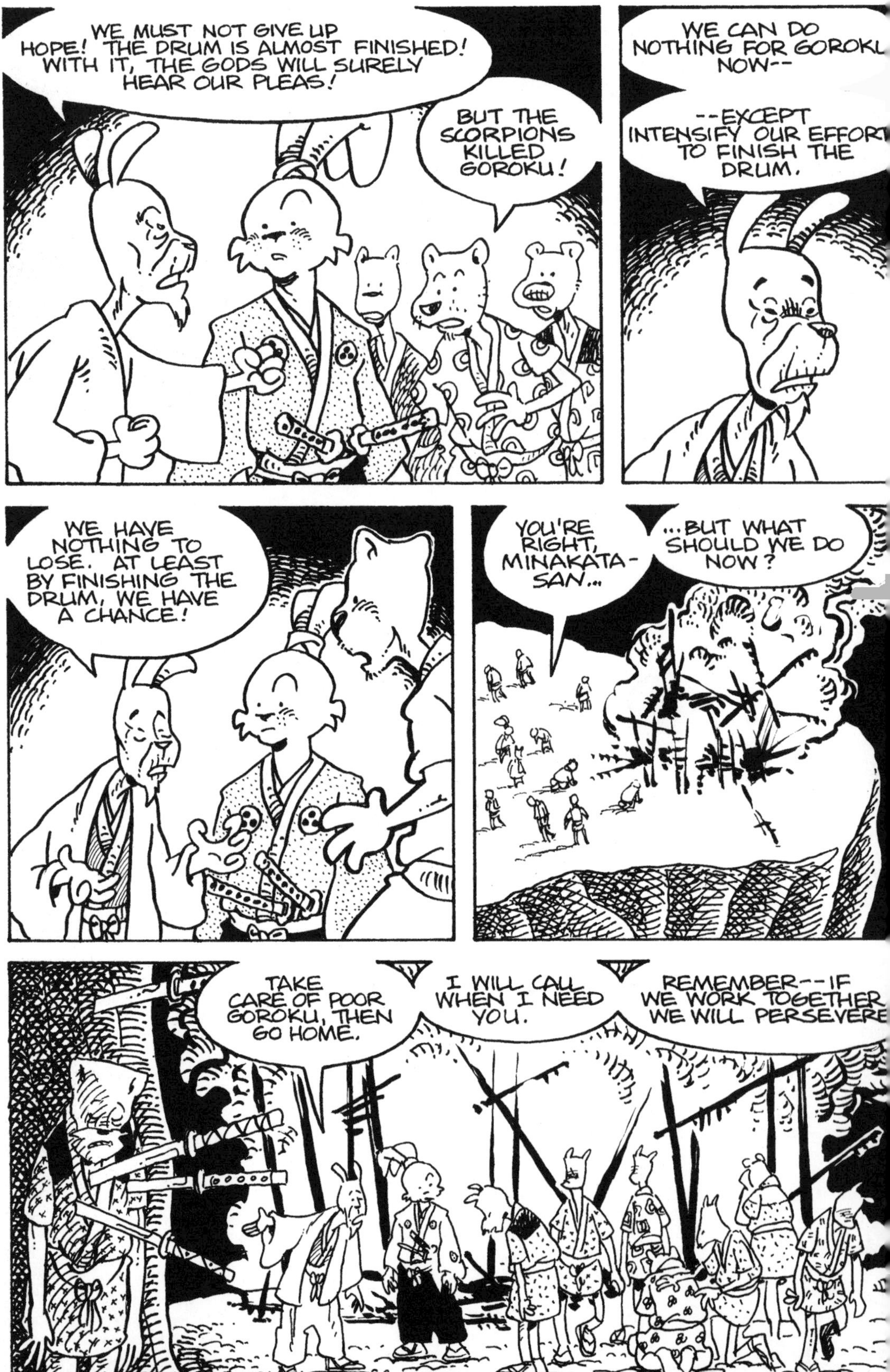
WE MUST NOT GIVE UP HOPE! THE DRUM IS ALMOST FINISHED! WITH IT, THE GODS WILL SURELY HEAR OUR PLEAS!
BUT THE SCORPIONS KILLED GOROKU!
WE CAN DO NOTHING FOR GOROKU NOW--
--EXCEPT INTENSIFY OUR EFFORT TO FINISH THE DRUM.
WE HAVE NOTHING TO LOSE. AT LEAST BY FINISHING THE DRUM, WE HAVE A CHANCE!
YOU'RE RIGHT, MINAKATA-SAN...
...BUT WHAT SHOULD WE DO NOW?
TAKE CARE OF POOR GOROKU, THEN GO HOME.
I WILL CALL WHEN I NEED YOU.
REMEMBER--IF WE WORK TOGETHER WE WILL PERSEVERE

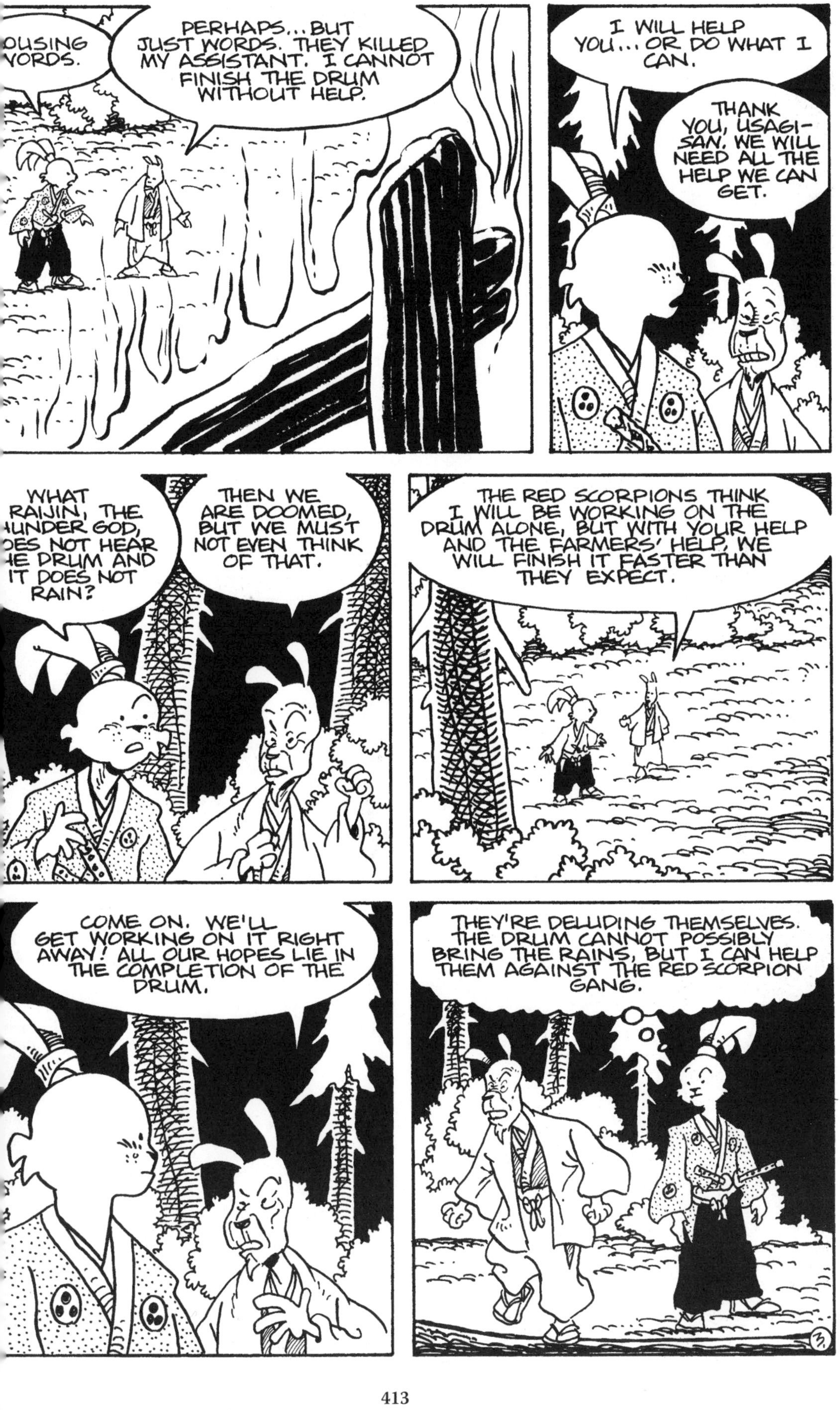
OUSING
VORDS.
PERHAPS... BUT JUST WORDS. THEY KILLED MY ASSISTANT. I CANNOT FINISH THE DRUM WITHOUT HELP.
I WILL HELP YOU... OR DO WHAT I CAN.
THANK YOU, USAGI-SAN. WE WILL NEED ALL THE HELP WE CAN GET.
WHAT
RAIJIN, THE
IUNDER GOD,
OES NOT HEAR
IE DRUM AND
IT DOES NOT
RAIN?
THEN WE ARE DOOMED, BUT WE MUST NOT EVEN THINK OF THAT.
THE RED SCORPIONS THINK I WILL BE WORKING ON THE DRUM ALONE, BUT WITH YOUR HELP AND THE FARMERS' HELP, WE WILL FINISH IT FASTER THAN THEY EXPECT.
COME ON. WE'LL GET WORKING ON IT RIGHT AWAY! ALL OUR HOPES LIE IN THE COMPLETION OF THE DRUM.
THEY'RE DELUDING THEMSELVES. THE DRUM CANNOT POSSIBLY BRING THE RAINS, BUT I CAN HELP THEM AGAINST THE RED SCORPION GANG.
3

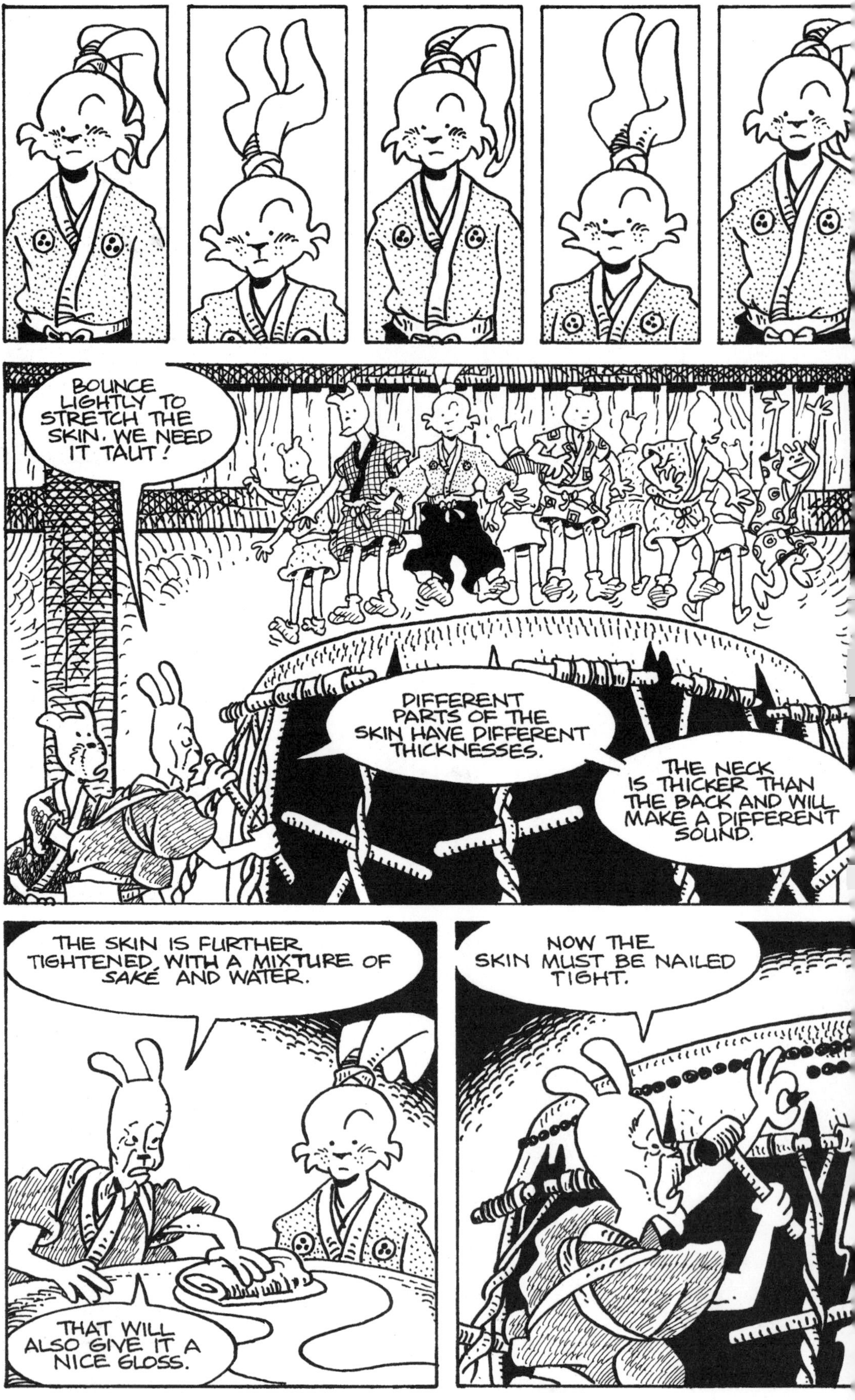
BOUNCE LIGHTLY TO STRETCH THE SKIN. WE NEED IT TAUT!
DIFFERENT PARTS OF THE SKIN HAVE DIFFERENT THICKNESSES.
THE NECK IS THICKER THAN THE BACK AND WILL MAKE A DIFFERENT SOUND.
THE SKIN IS FURTHER TIGHTENED WITH A MIXTURE OF *SAKÉ* AND WATER.
THAT WILL ALSO GIVE IT A NICE GLOSS.
NOW THE SKIN MUST BE NAILED TIGHT.

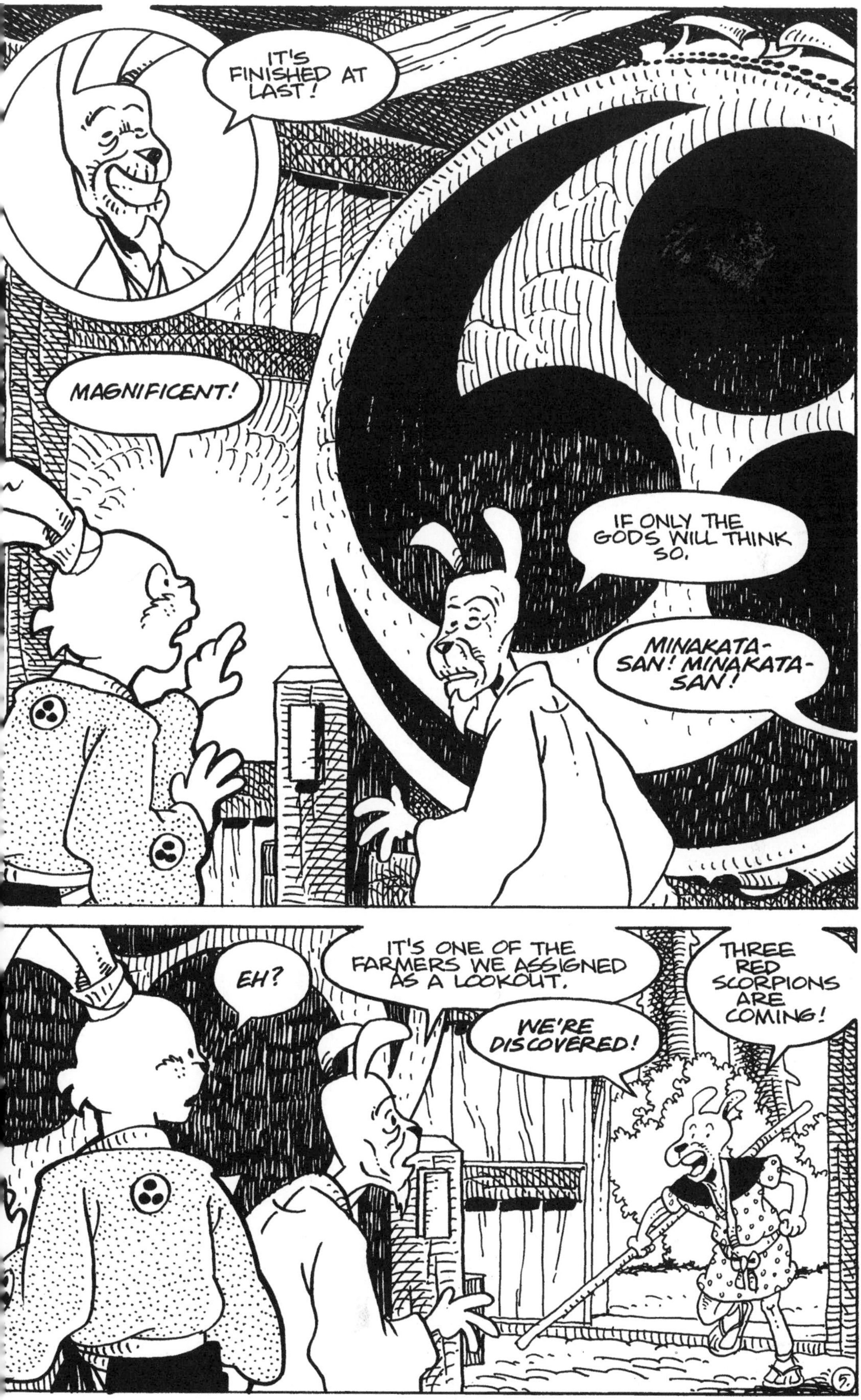
IT'S FINISHED AT LAST!
MAGNIFICENT!
IF ONLY THE GODS WILL THINK SO.
MINAKATA-SAN! MINAKATA-SAN!
EH?
IT'S ONE OF THE FARMERS WE ASSIGNED AS A LOOKOUT.
WE'RE DISCOVERED!
THREE RED SCORPIONS ARE COMING!

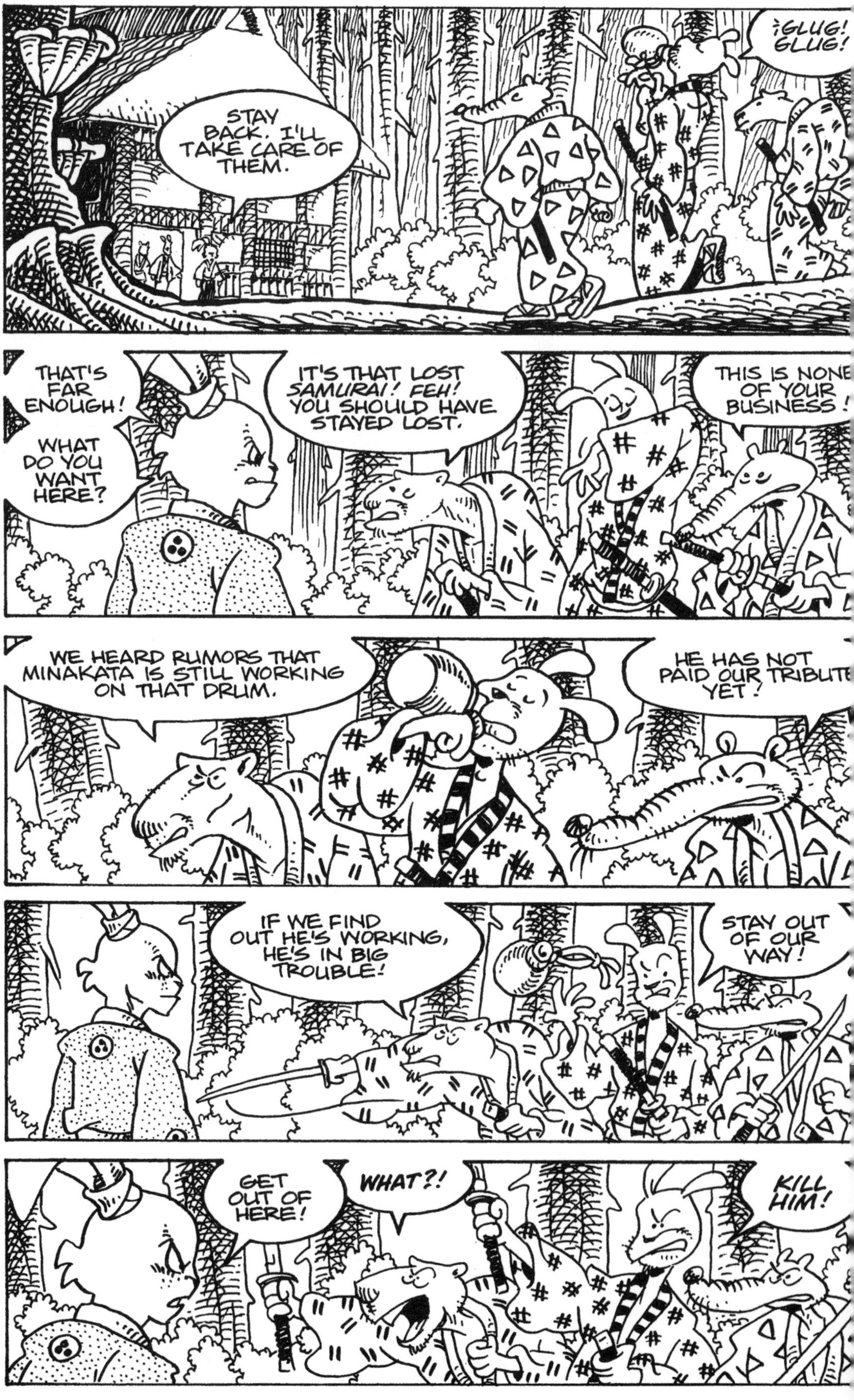
STAY BACK. I'LL TAKE CARE OF THEM.
¡GLUG! GLUG!
THAT'S FAR ENOUGH!
WHAT DO YOU WANT HERE?
IT'S THAT LOST SAMURAI! FEH! YOU SHOULD HAVE STAYED LOST.
THIS IS NONE OF YOUR BUSINESS!
WE HEARD RUMORS THAT MINAKATA IS STILL WORKING ON THAT DRUM.
HE HAS NOT PAID OUR TRIBUTE YET!
IF WE FIND OUT HE'S WORKING, HE'S IN BIG TROUBLE!
STAY OUT OF OUR WAY!
GET OUT OF HERE!
WHAT?!
KILL HIM!

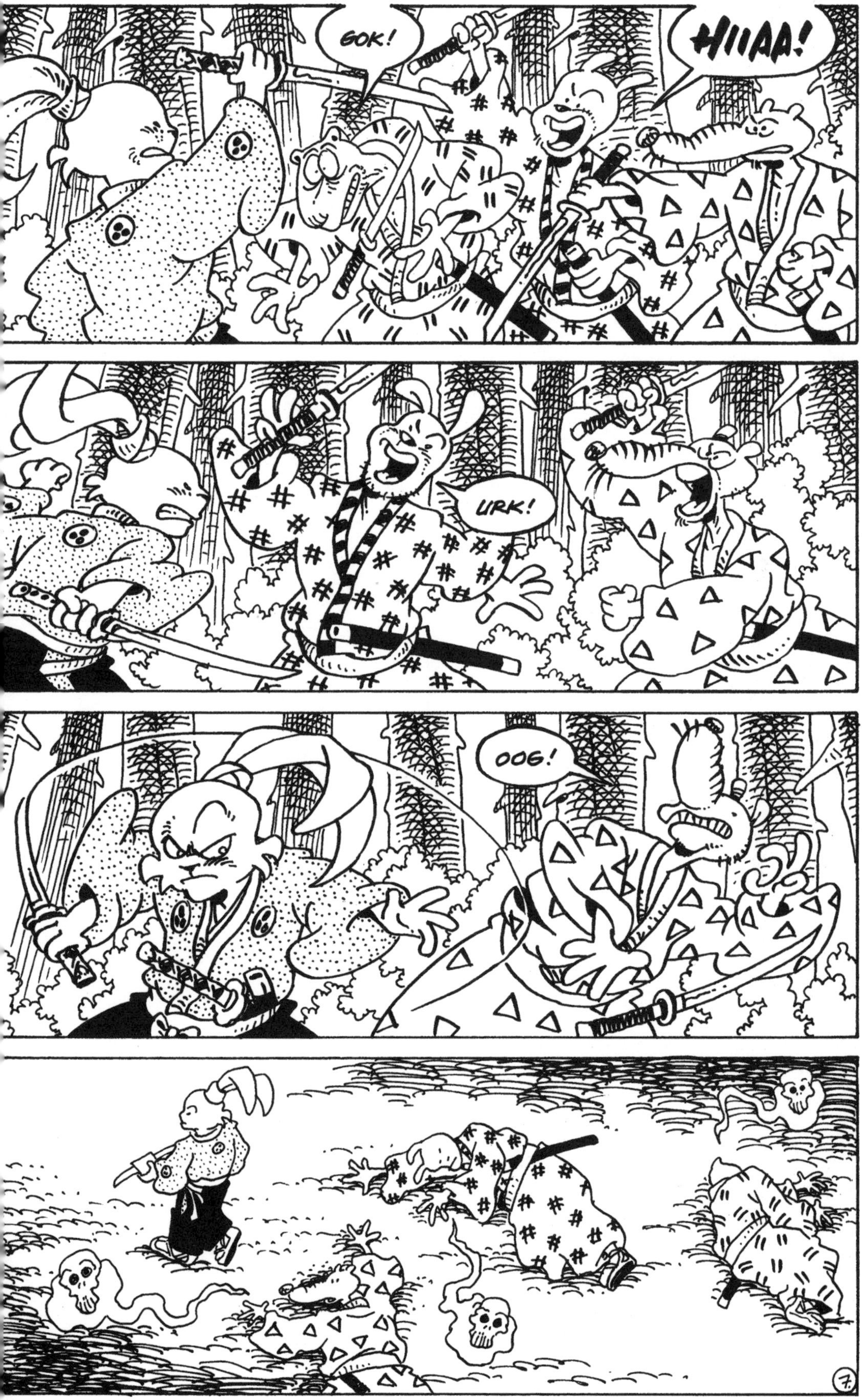
GOK!
HIIAA!
URK!
OOG!
7.

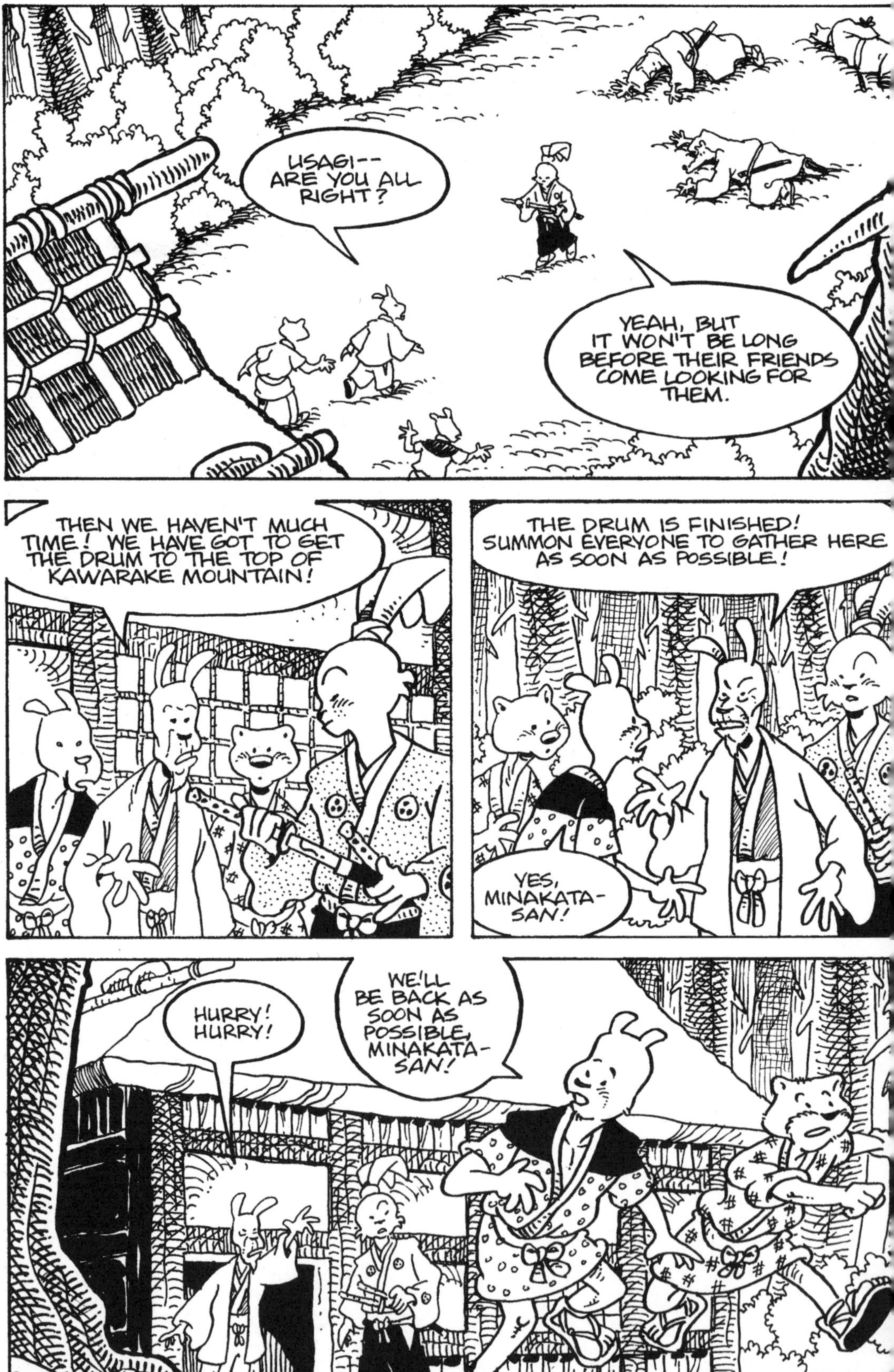
USAGI-- ARE YOU ALL RIGHT?
YEAH, BUT IT WON'T BE LONG BEFORE THEIR FRIENDS COME LOOKING FOR THEM.
THEN WE HAVEN'T MUCH TIME! WE HAVE GOT TO GET THE DRUM TO THE TOP OF KAWARAKE MOUNTAIN!
THE DRUM IS FINISHED! SUMMON EVERYONE TO GATHER HERE AS SOON AS POSSIBLE!
YES, MINAKATA-SAN!
HURRY! HURRY!
WE'LL BE BACK AS SOON AS POSSIBLE, MINAKATA-SAN!

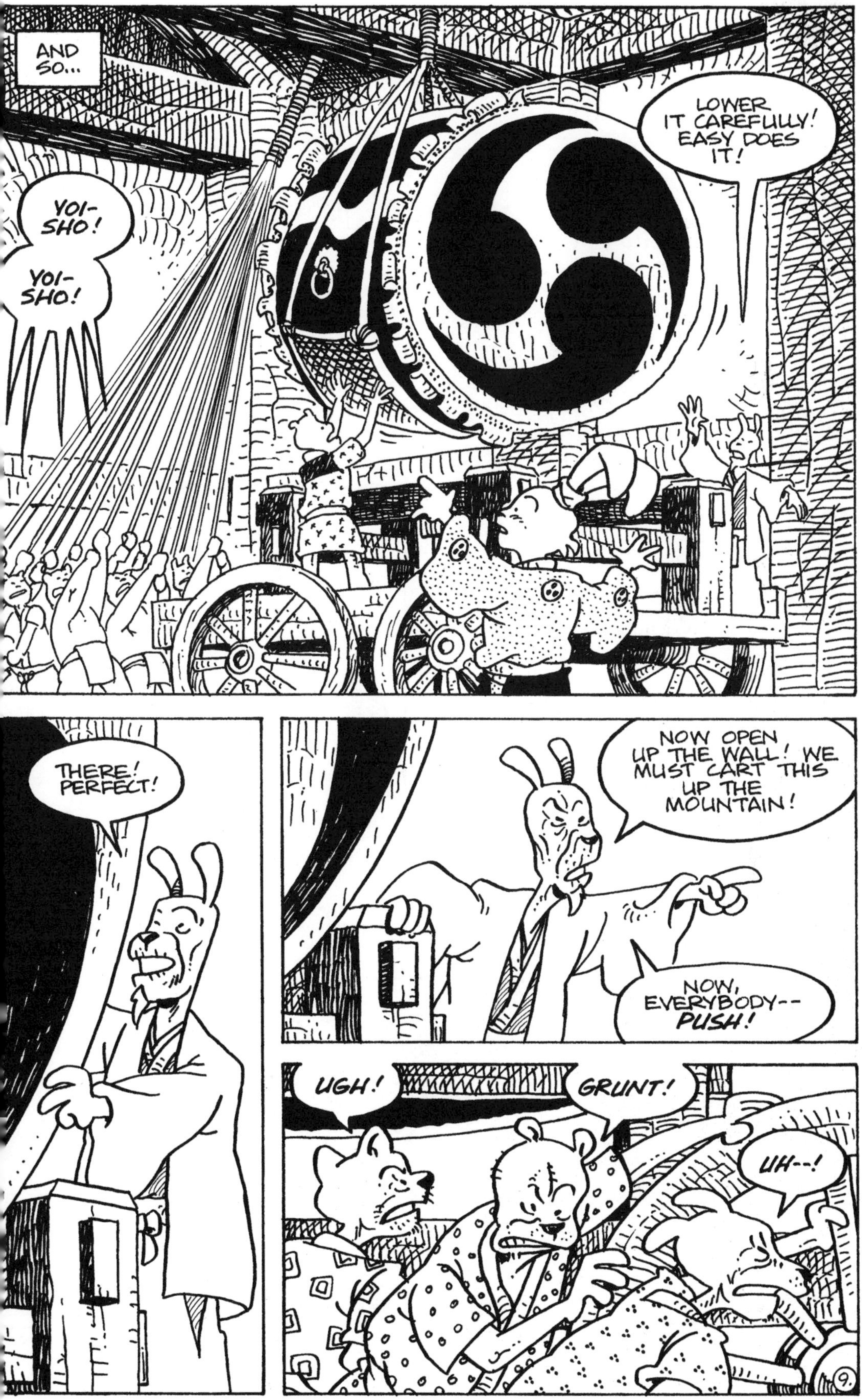
AND SO...
YOI-SHO!
YOI-SHO!
LOWER IT CAREFULLY! EASY DOES IT!
THERE! PERFECT!
NOW OPEN UP THE WALL! WE MUST CART THIS UP THE MOUNTAIN!
NOW, EVERYBODY-- PUSH!
UGH!
GRUNT!
UH--!
9.

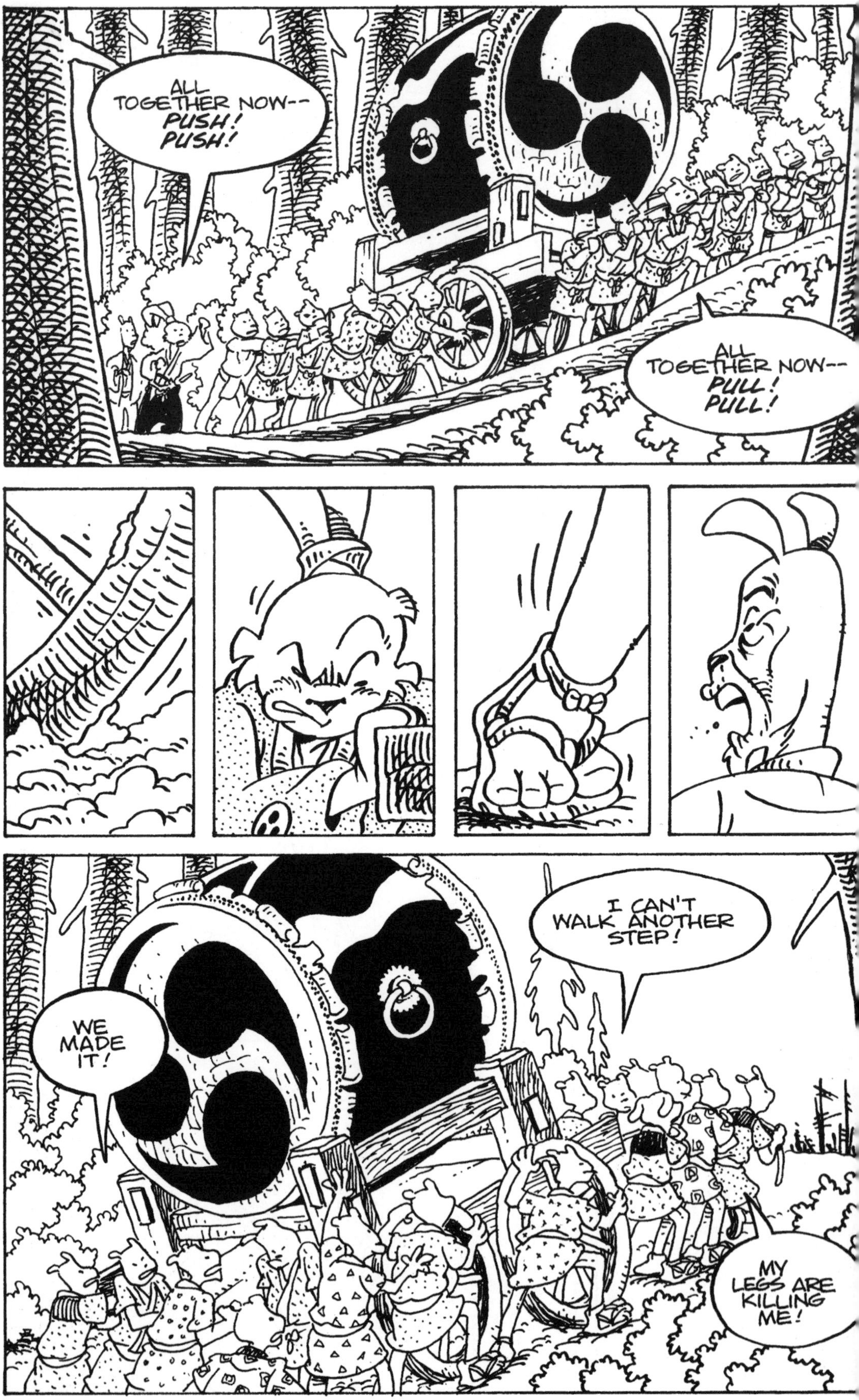
ALL TOGETHER NOW-- PUSH! PUSH!
ALL TOGETHER NOW-- PULL! PULL!
WE MADE IT!
I CAN'T WALK ANOTHER STEP!
MY LEGS ARE KILLING ME!

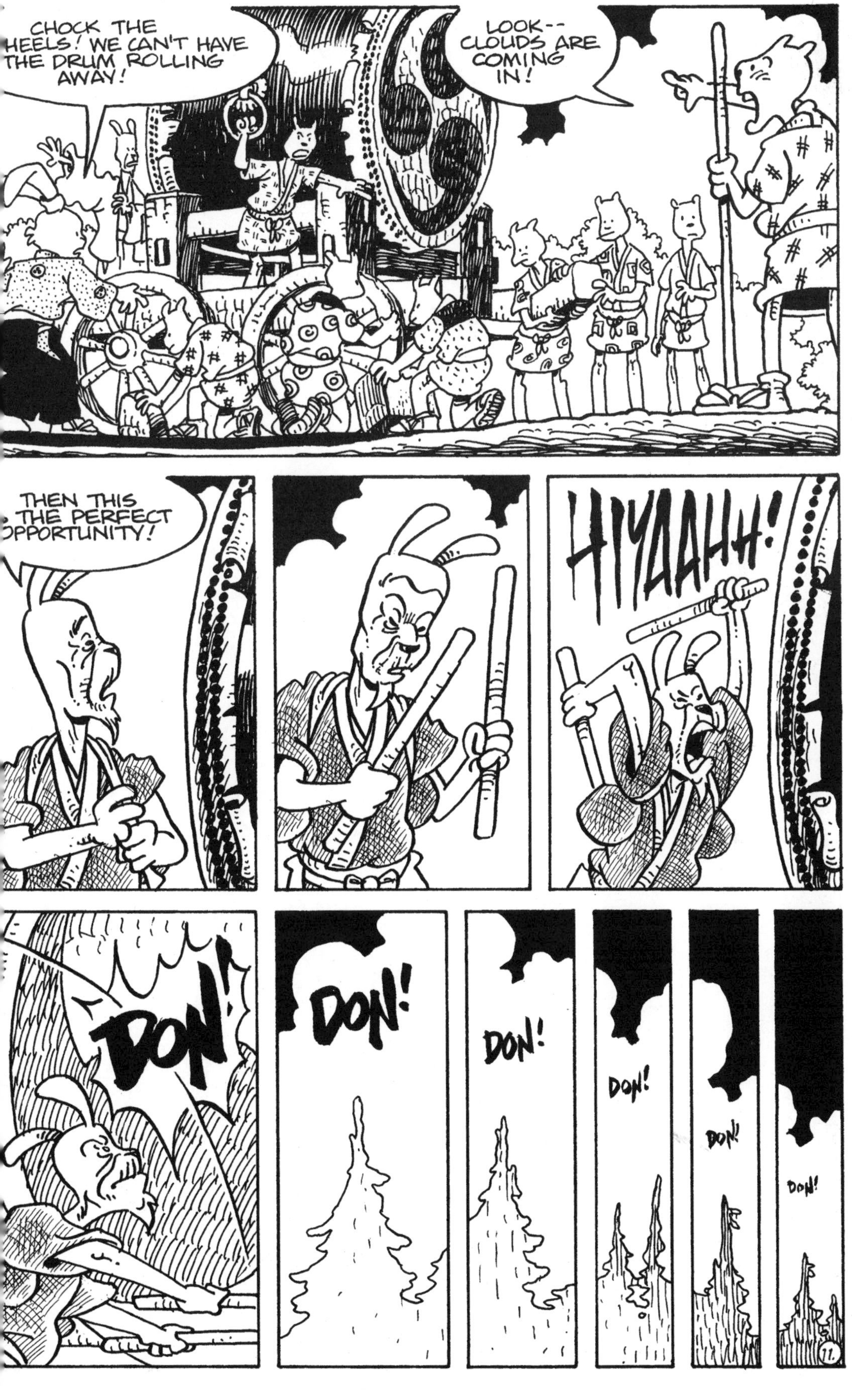
CHOCK THE
HEELS! WE CAN'T HAVE THE DRUM ROLLING AWAY!
LOOK-- CLOUDS ARE COMING IN!
THEN THIS
THE PERFECT
PPORTUNITY!
HIYAAHH!
DON!
DON!
DON!
DON!
DON!
DON!
11.

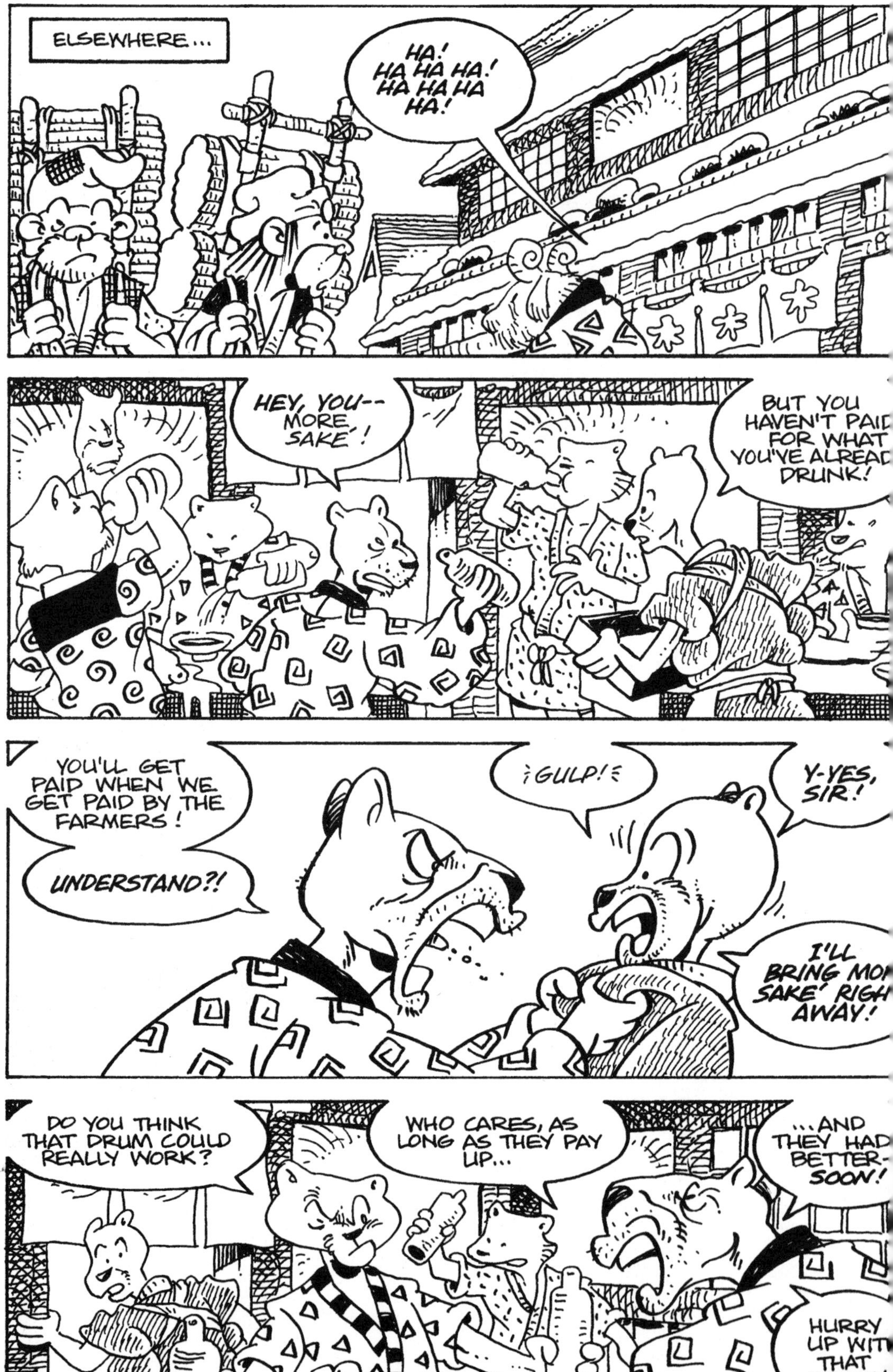
ELSEWHERE...
HA! HA HA HA! HA HA HA HA!
HEY, YOU-- MORE SAKE'!
BUT YOU HAVEN'T PAID FOR WHAT YOU'VE ALREAD DRUNK!
YOU'LL GET PAID WHEN WE GET PAID BY THE FARMERS!
UNDERSTAND?!
GULP!
Y-YES, SIR!
I'LL BRING MO SAKE' RIGH AWAY!
DO YOU THINK THAT DRUM COULD REALLY WORK?
WHO CARES, AS LONG AS THEY PAY UP...
...AND THEY HAD BETTER-- SOON!
HURRY UP WIT THAT DRINK!

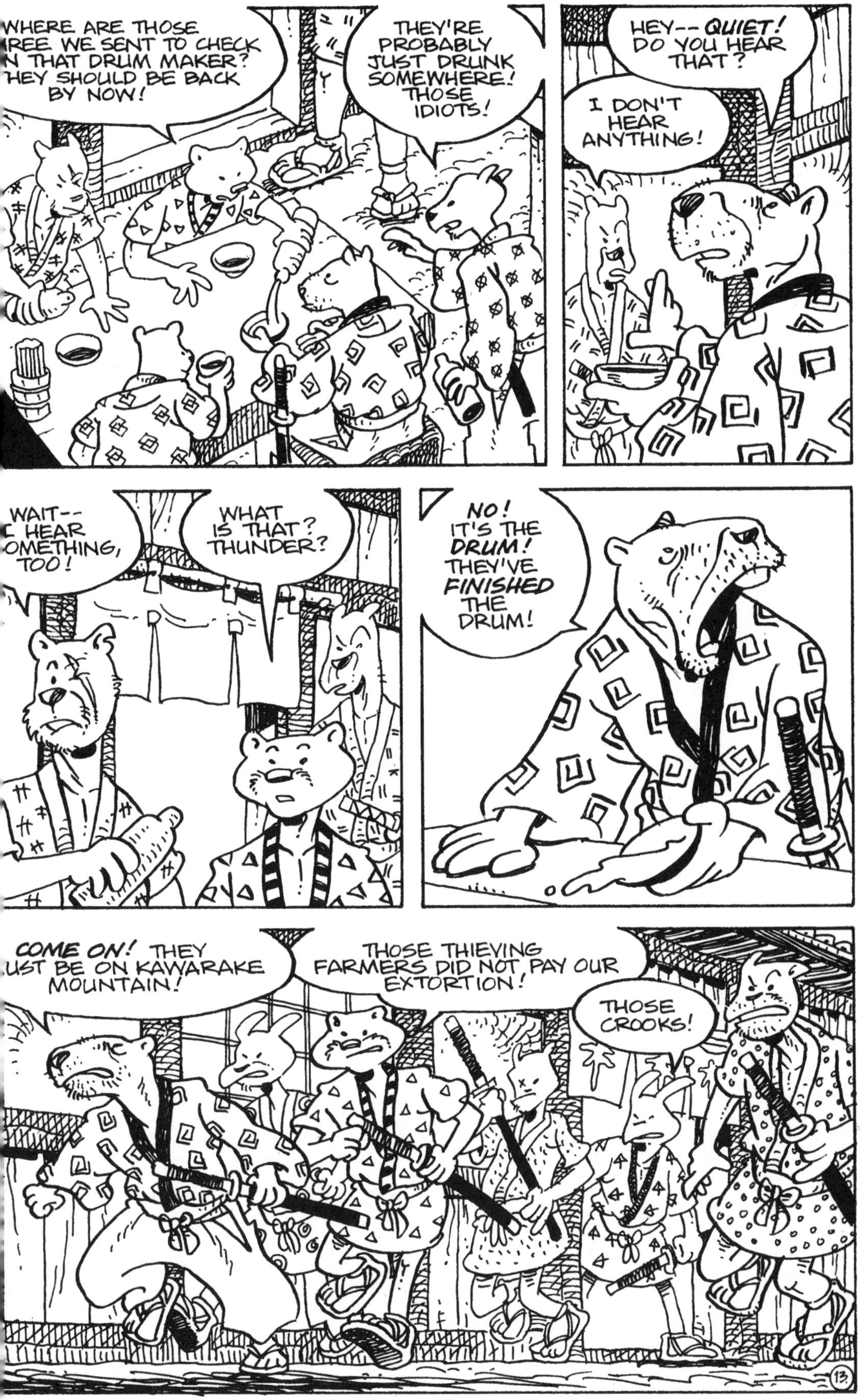
WHERE ARE THOSE REE WE SENT TO CHECK N THAT DRUM MAKER? HEY SHOULD BE BACK BY NOW!
THEY'RE PROBABLY JUST DRUNK SOMEWHERE! THOSE IDIOTS!
HEY-- QUIET! DO YOU HEAR THAT?
I DON'T HEAR ANYTHING!
WAIT-- HEAR OMETHING, TOO!
WHAT IS THAT? THUNDER?
NO! IT'S THE DRUM! THEY'VE FINISHED THE DRUM!
COME ON! THEY UST BE ON KAWARAKE MOUNTAIN!
THOSE THIEVING FARMERS DID NOT PAY OUR EXTORTION!
THOSE CROOKS!
13

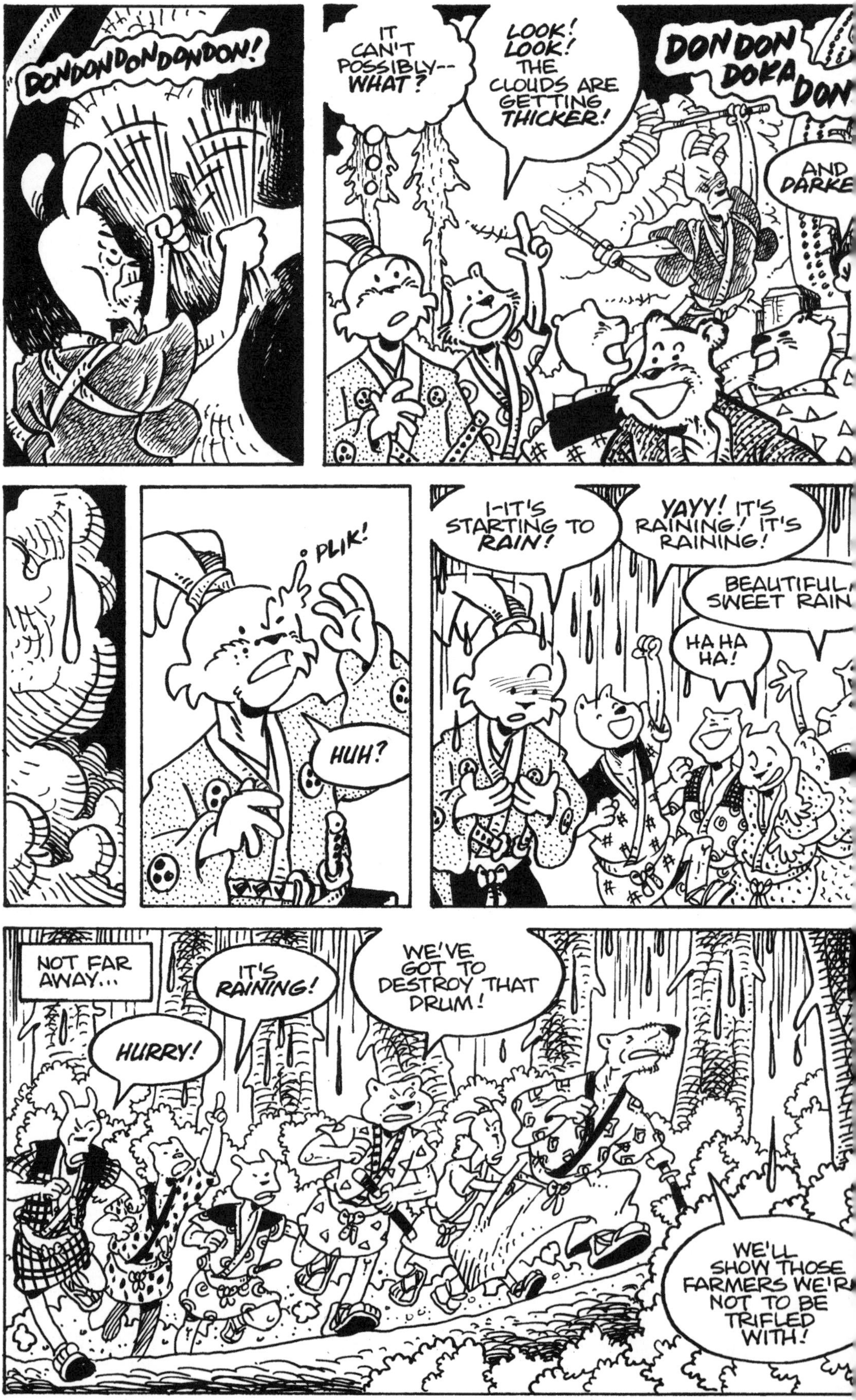
DONDONDONDONDON!
IT CAN'T POSSIBLY-- WHAT?
LOOK! LOOK! THE CLOUDS ARE GETTING THICKER!
DONDON DOKA DON
AND DARKE
PLIK!
HUH?
I-IT'S STARTING TO RAIN!
YAYY! IT'S RAINING! IT'S RAINING!
BEAUTIFUL, SWEET RAIN
HA HA HA!
NOT FAR AWAY...
HURRY!
IT'S RAINING!
WE'VE GOT TO DESTROY THAT DRUM!
WE'LL SHOW THOSE FARMERS WE'R NOT TO BE TRIFLED WITH!

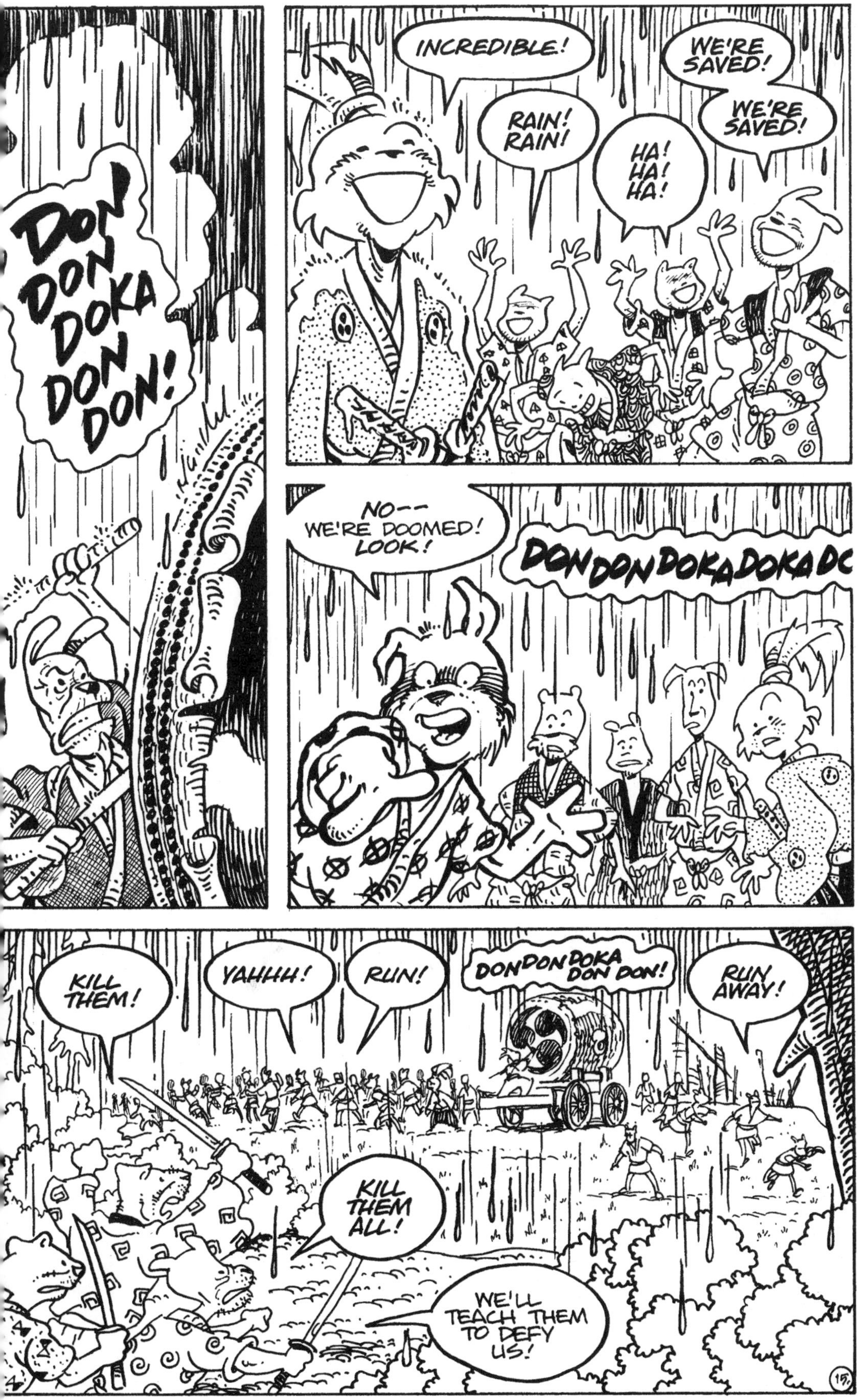
DON DON DOKA DOKA DON DON DON!
INCREDIBLE!
RAIN! RAIN!
HA! HA! HA!
WE'RE SAVED!
WE'RE SAVED!
NO-- WE'RE DOOMED! LOOK!
DONDONDOKADOKADO
KILL THEM!
YAHHH!
RUN!
DONDONDOKA DON DON!
RUN AWAY!
KILL THEM ALL!
WE'LL TEACH THEM TO DEFY US!
15

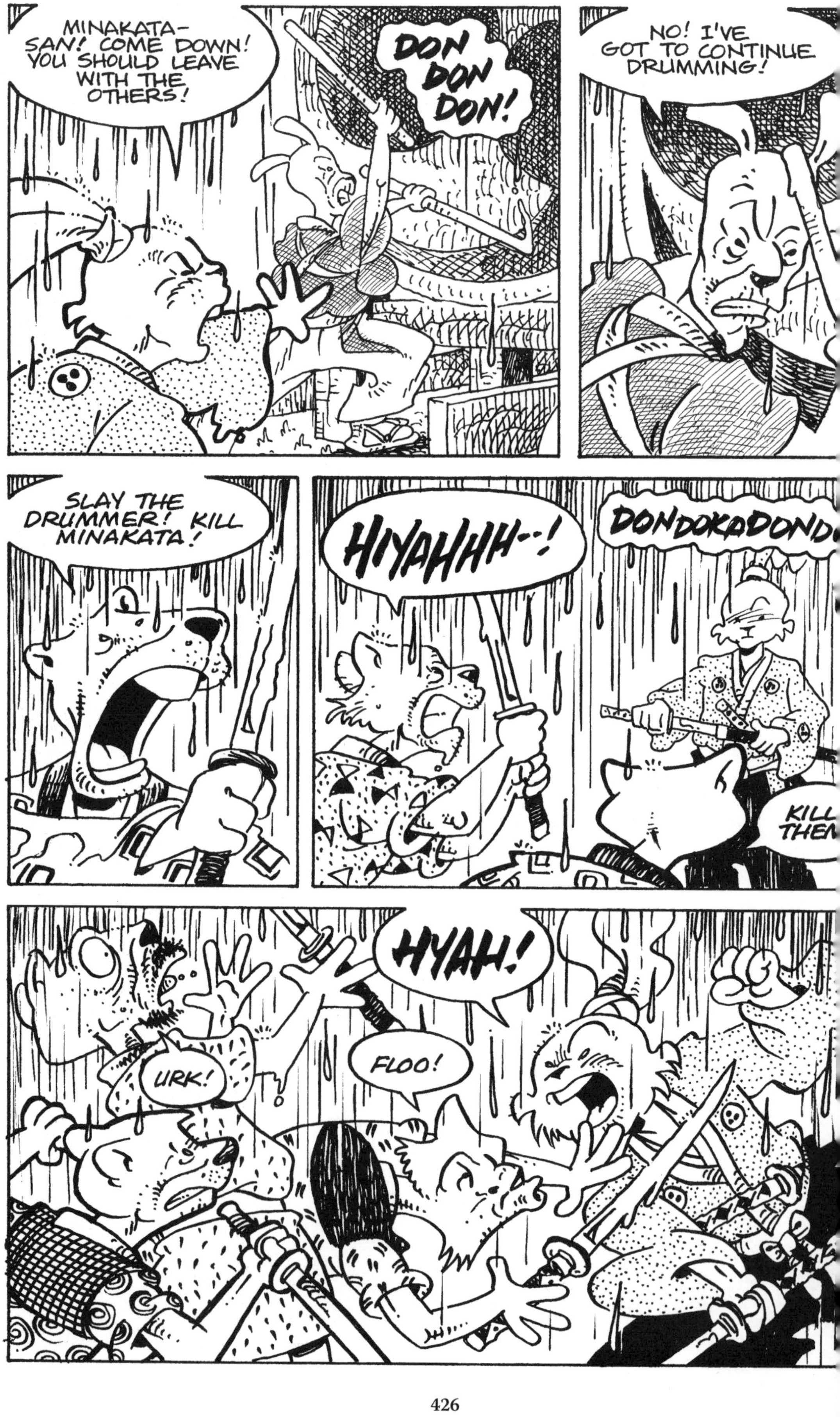
MINAKATA-SAN! COME DOWN! YOU SHOULD LEAVE WITH THE OTHERS!
DON DON DON!
NO! I'VE GOT TO CONTINUE DRUMMING!
SLAY THE DRUMMER! KILL MINAKATA!
HIYAHHH--!
DONDOKADOND
KILL THEM
HYAH!
URK!
FLOO!

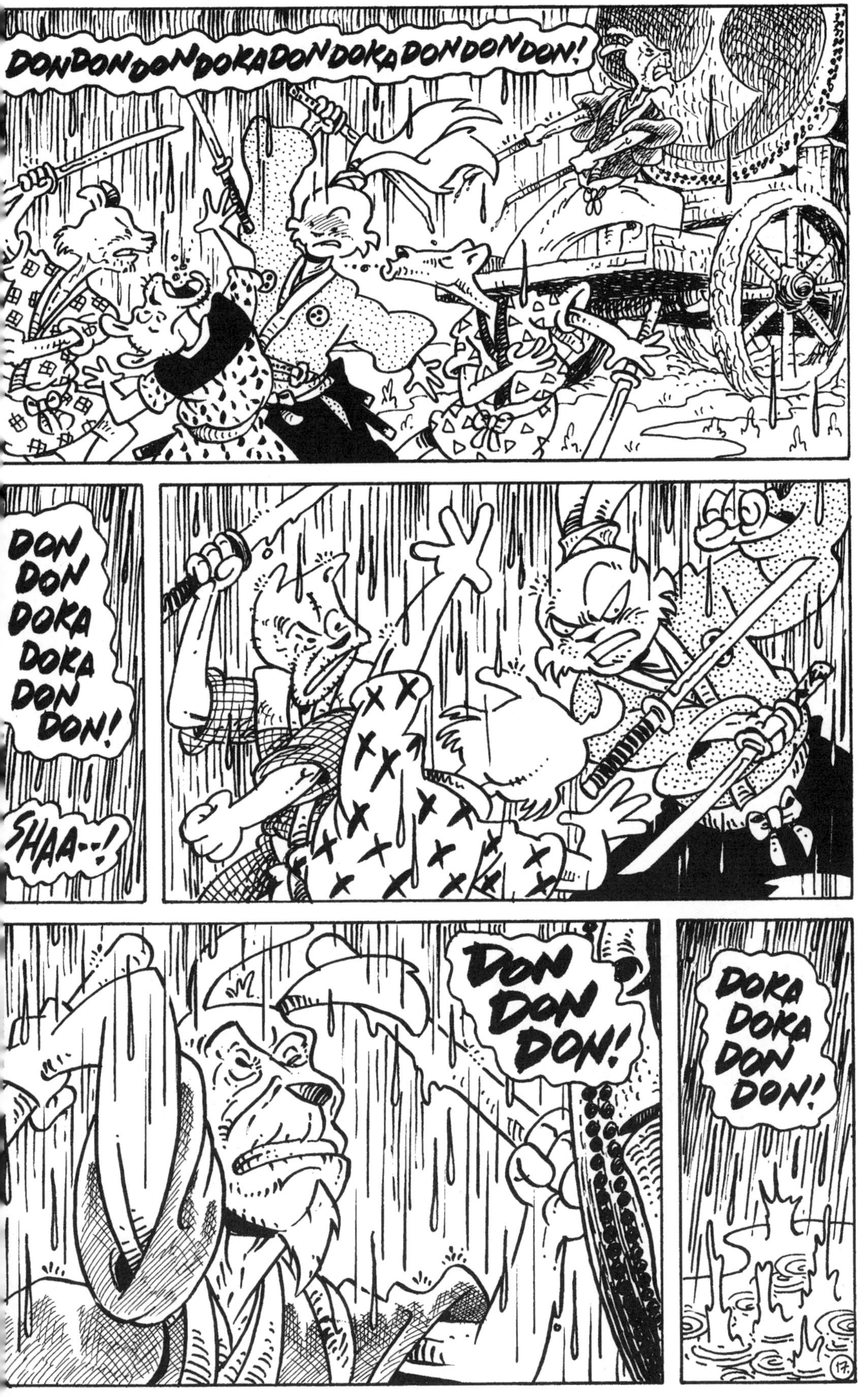
DONDONDONDOKADONDOKADONDONDON!
DON DON DOKA DOKA DON DON!
SHAA--!
DON DON DON!
DOKA DOKA DON DON!
17.

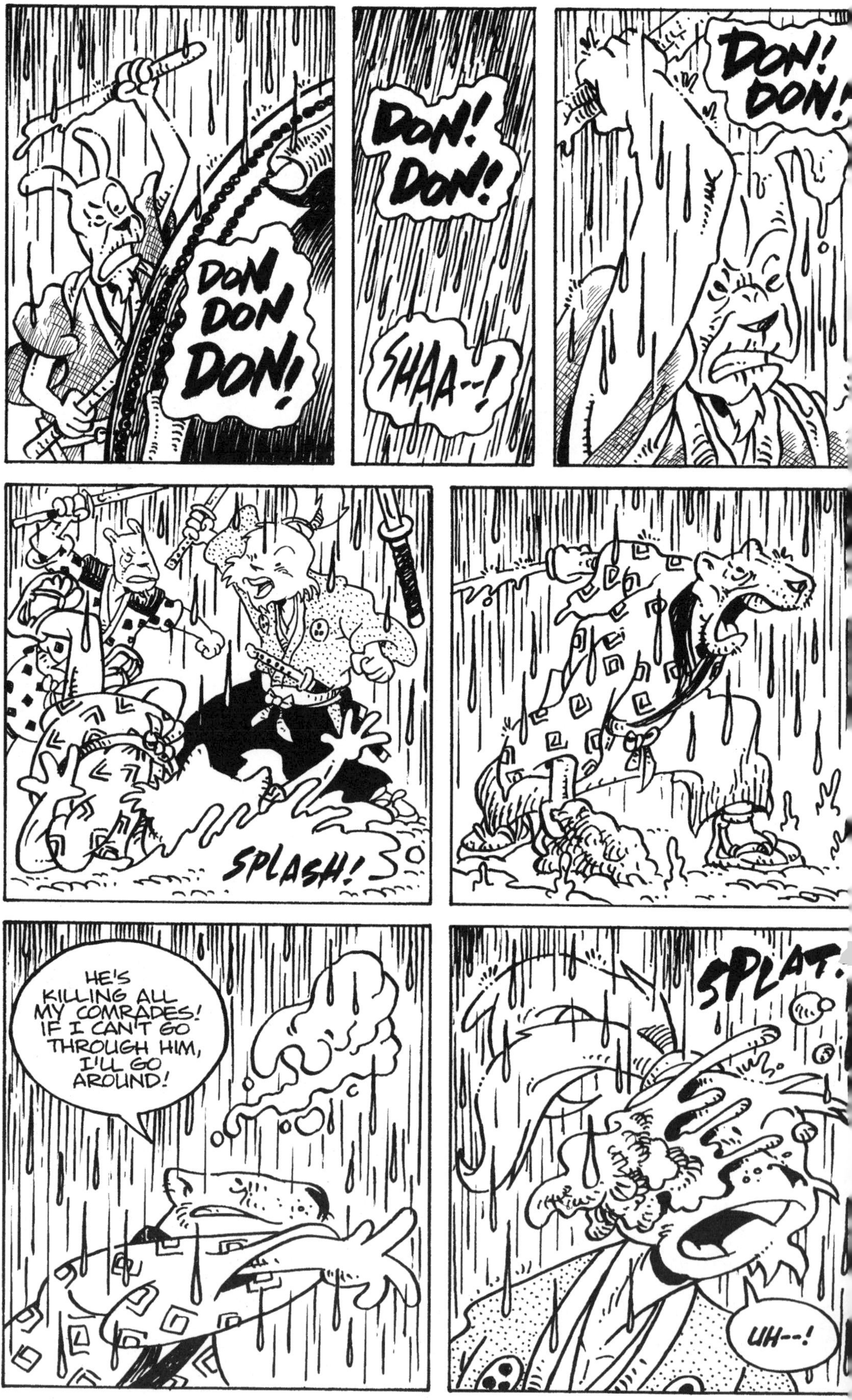
DON DON DON!
DON! DON!
SHAA--!
DON! DON!
SPLASH!
HE'S KILLING ALL MY COMRADES! IF I CAN'T GO THROUGH HIM, I'LL GO AROUND!
SPLAT!
UH--!

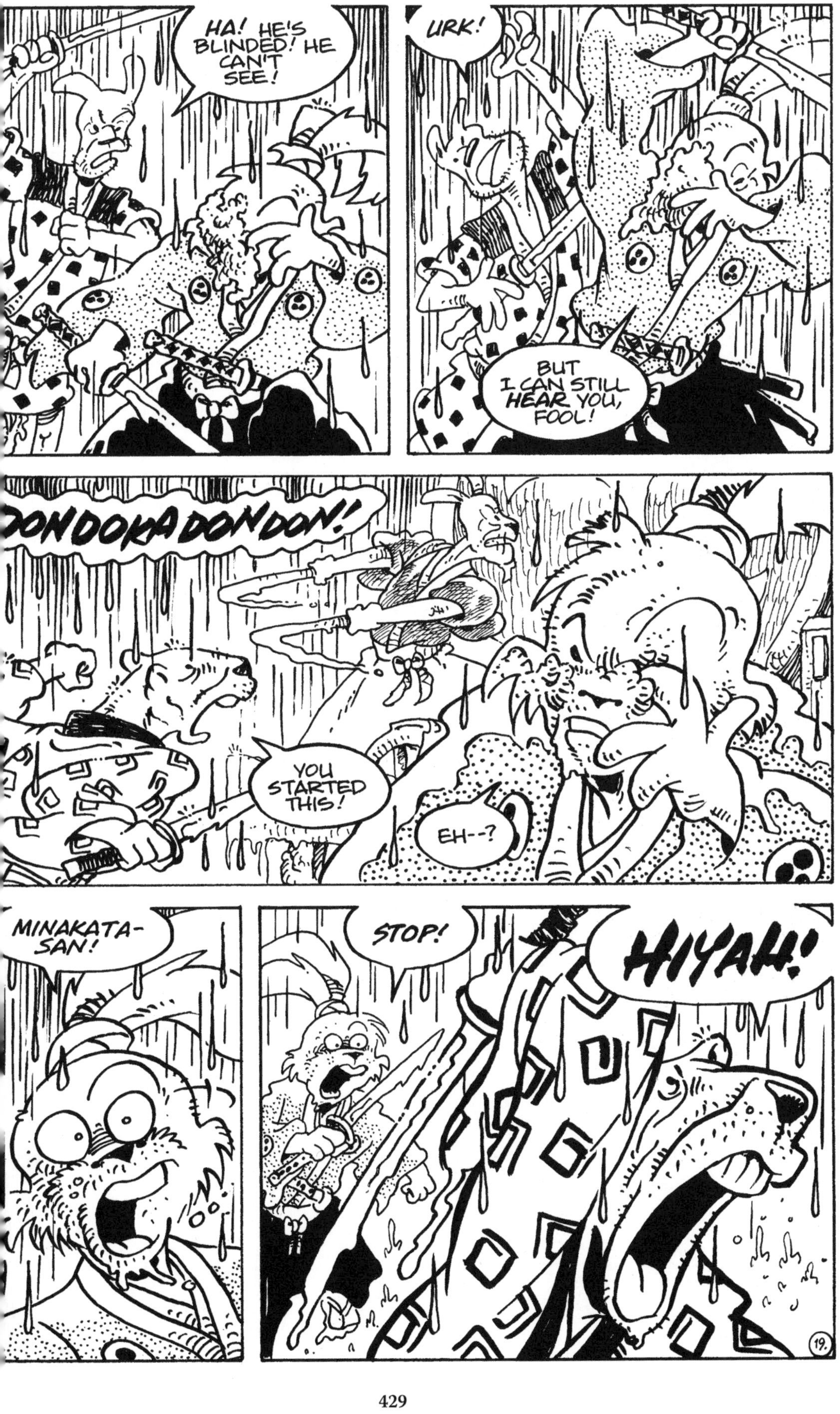
HA! HE'S BLINDED! HE CAN'T SEE!
URK!
BUT I CAN STILL HEAR YOU, FOOL!
DONDOKADONDON!
YOU STARTED THIS!
EH--?
MINAKATA-SAN!
STOP!
HIYAH!
19.

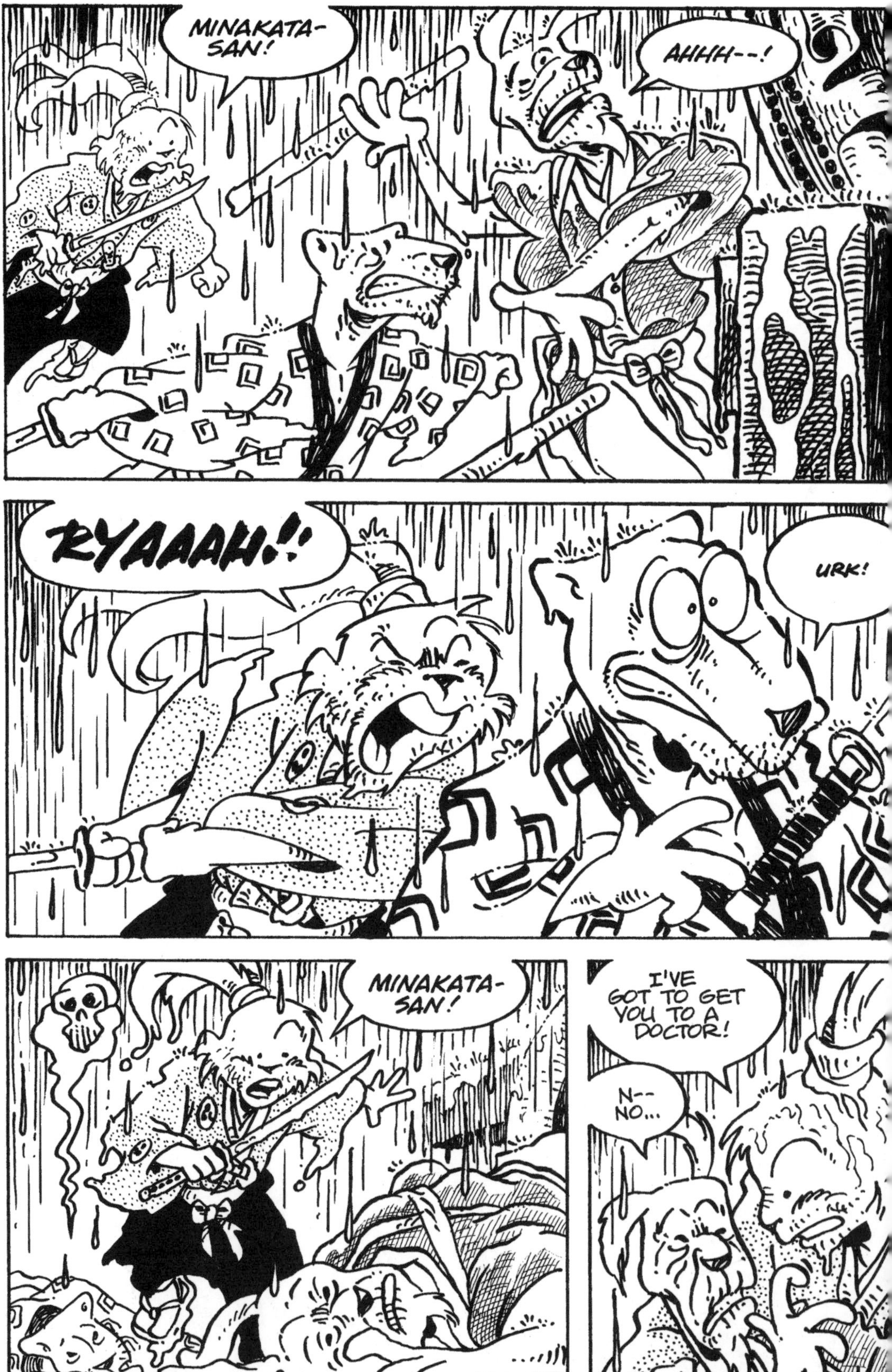
MINAKATA-SAN!
AHHH--!
RYAAAH!!
URK!
MINAKATA-SAN!
I'VE GOT TO GET YOU TO A DOCTOR!
N-- NO...

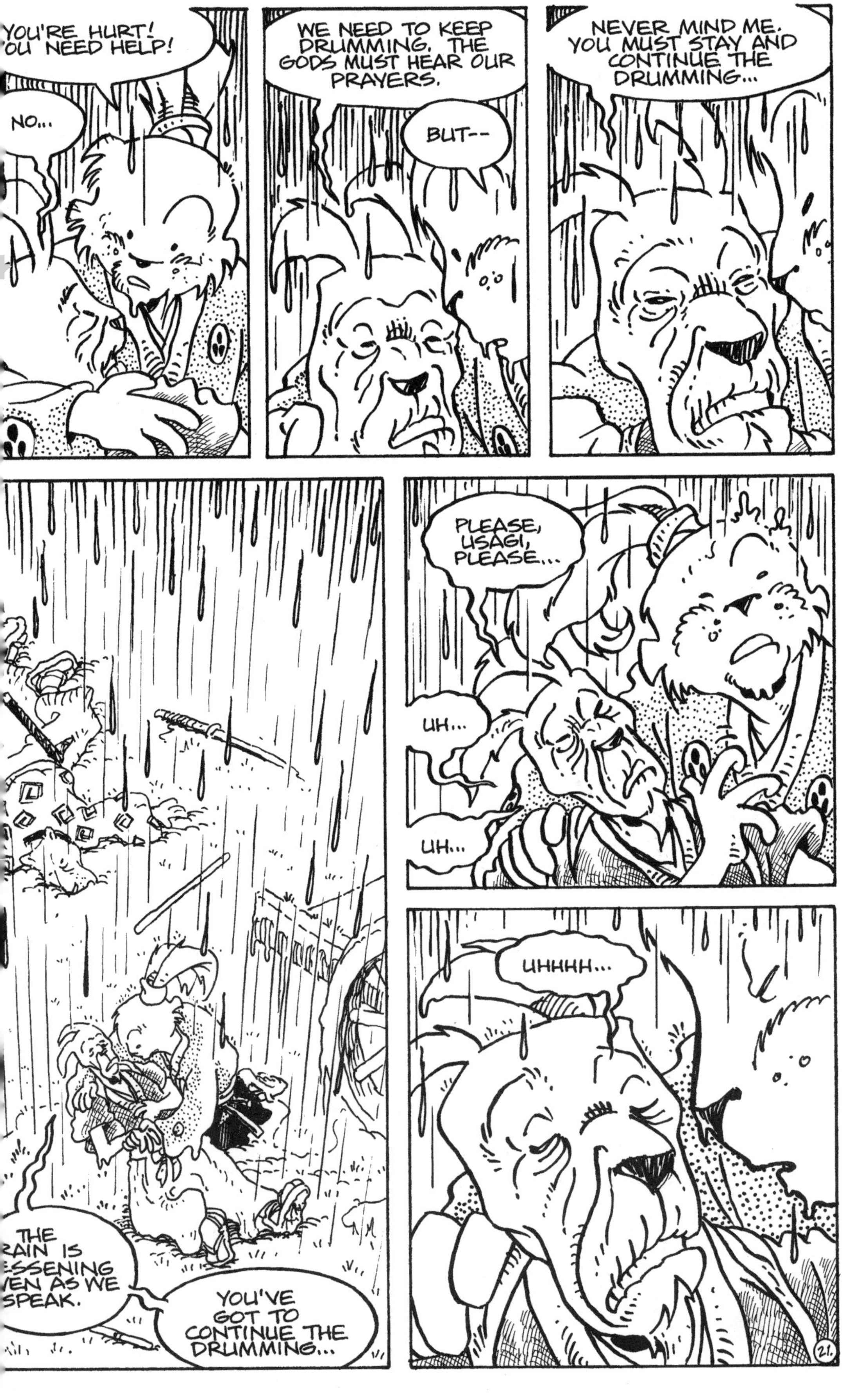
YOU'RE HURT! YOU NEED HELP!
NO...
WE NEED TO KEEP DRUMMING. THE GODS MUST HEAR OUR PRAYERS.
BUT--
NEVER MIND ME. YOU MUST STAY AND CONTINUE THE DRUMMING...
THE RAIN IS LESSENING EVEN AS WE SPEAK.
YOU'VE GOT TO CONTINUE THE DRUMMING...
PLEASE, USAGI, PLEASE...
UH...
UH...
UHHHH...
21.

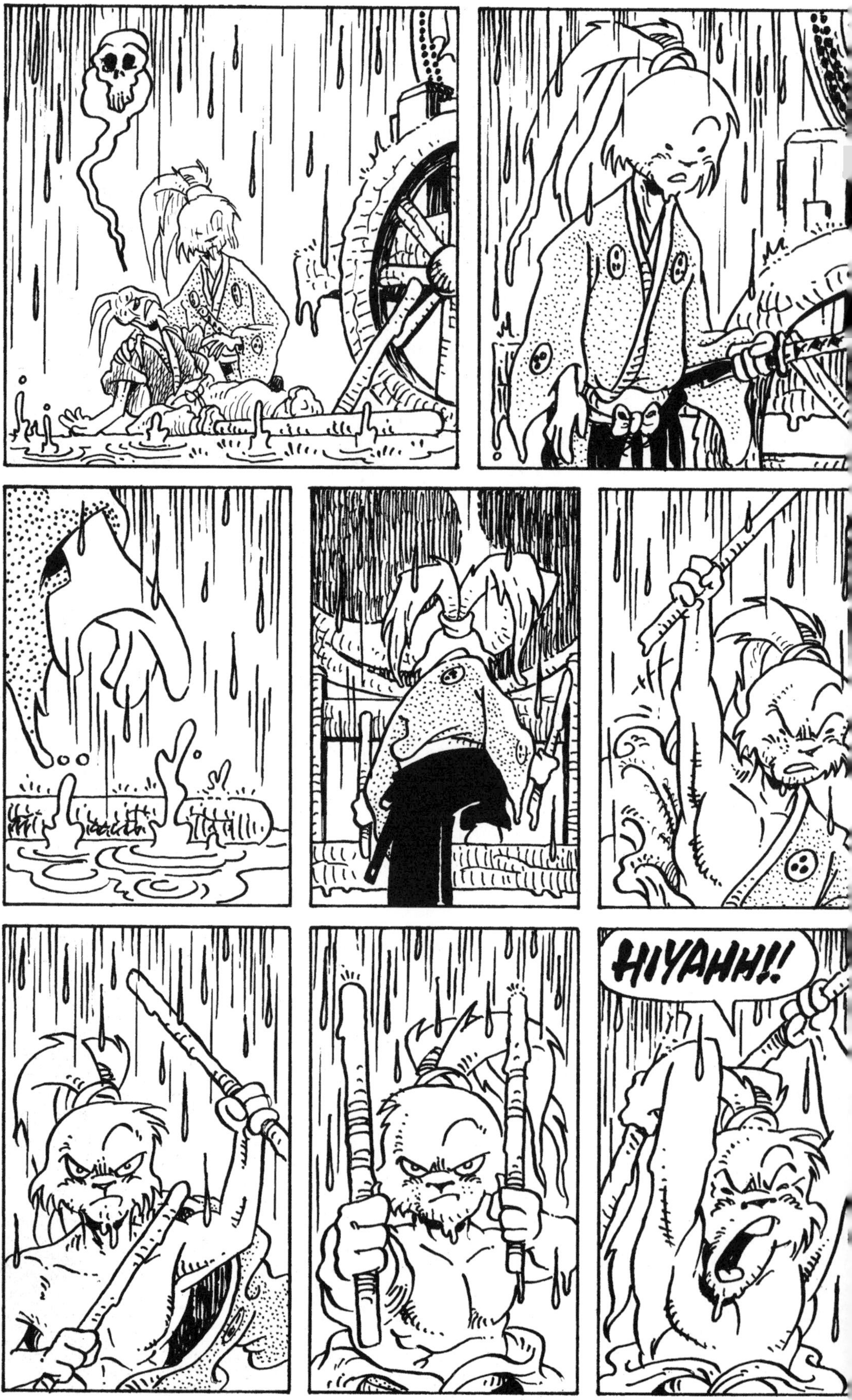
HIYAHH!!

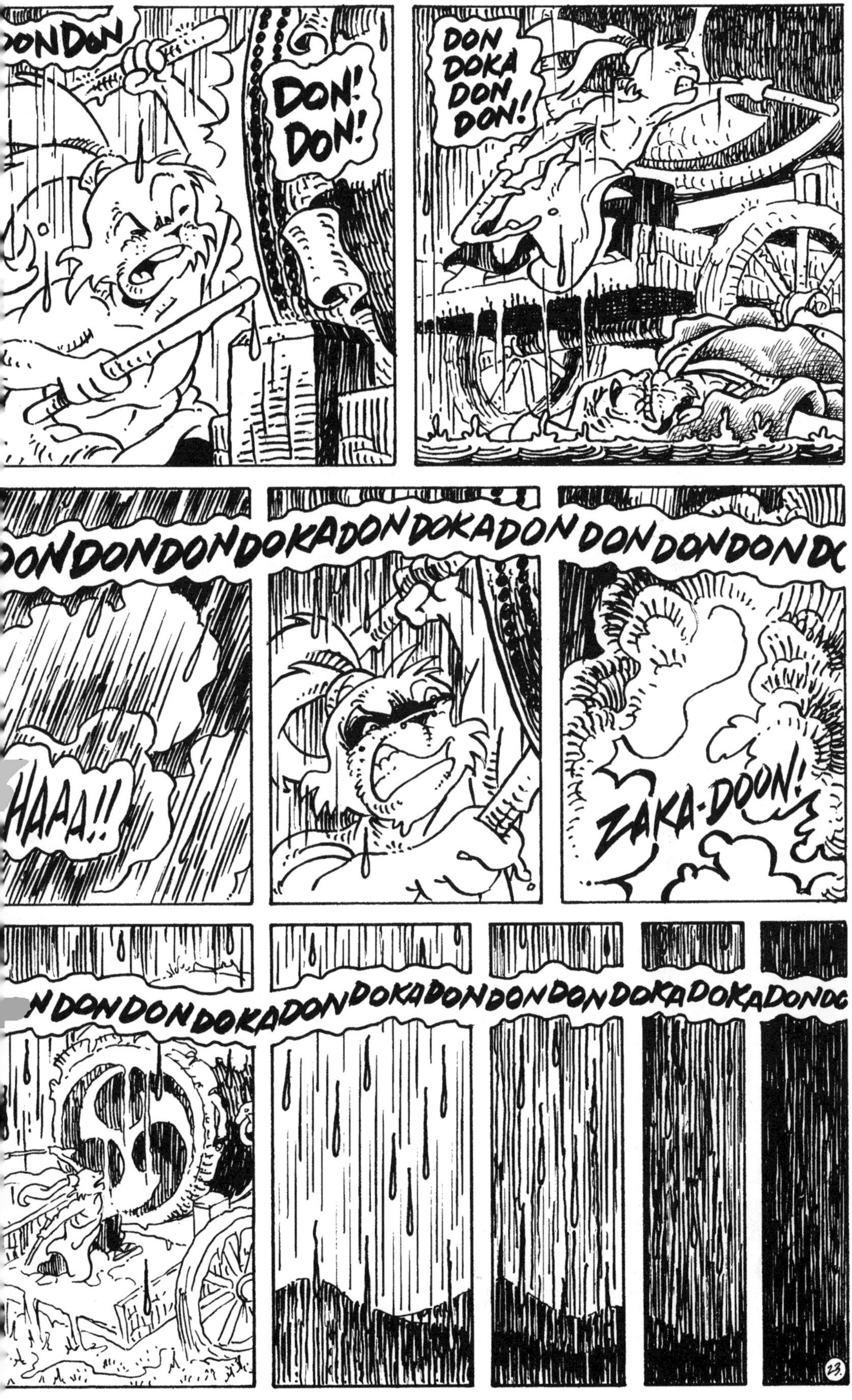
DONDON
DON! DON!
DON DOKA DON DON!
DONDONDONDOKADONDOKADON DON DONDONDC
HAAA!!
ZAKA-DOON!
NDONDONDOKADONDOKADONDONDONDOKADOKADOND
23

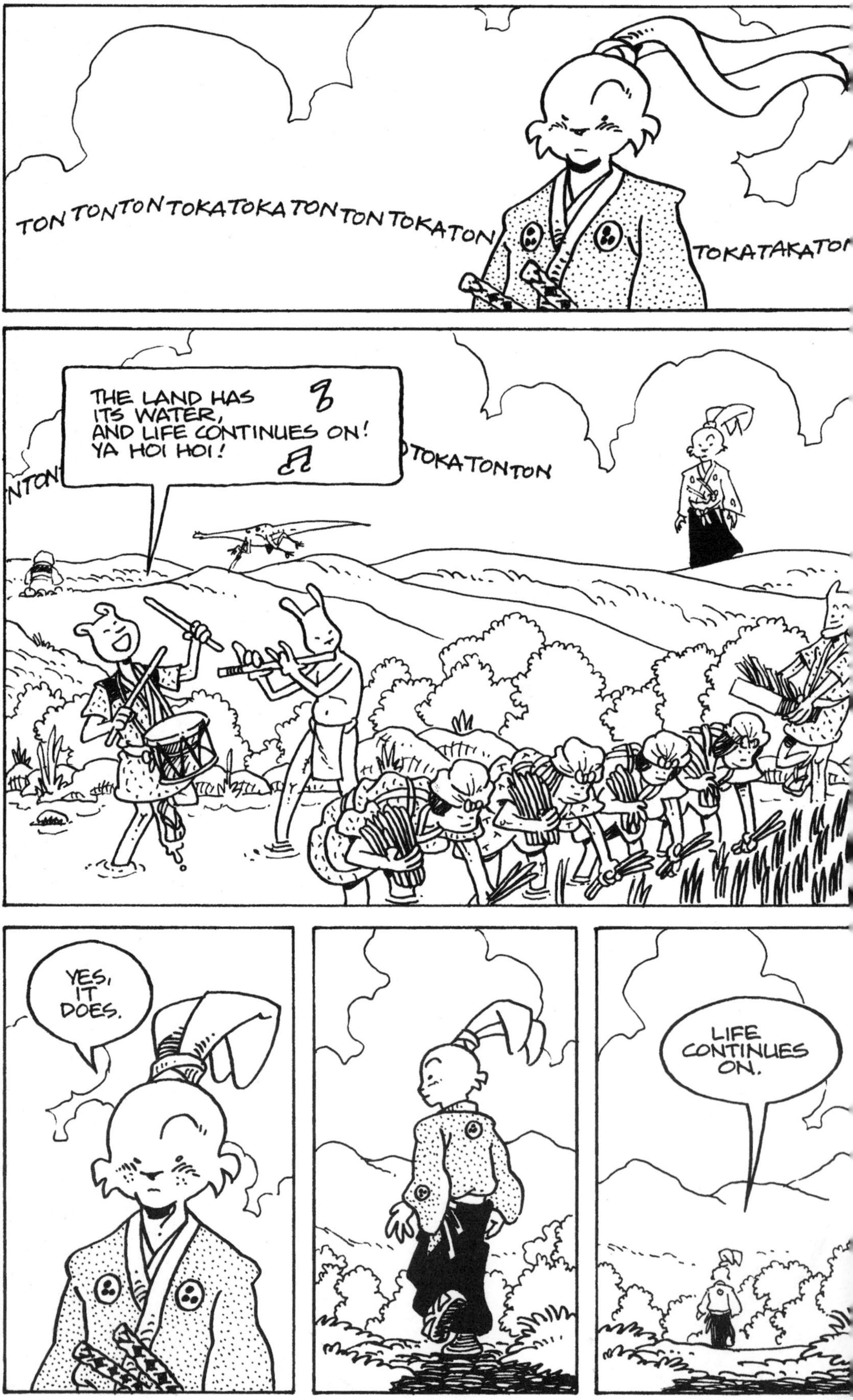
TON TONTON TOKATOKATON TON TOKATON
TOKATAKATON
NTON
THE LAND HAS ITS WATER, AND LIFE CONTINUES ON! YA HOI HOI!
TOKATONTON
YES, IT DOES.
LIFE CONTINUES ON.

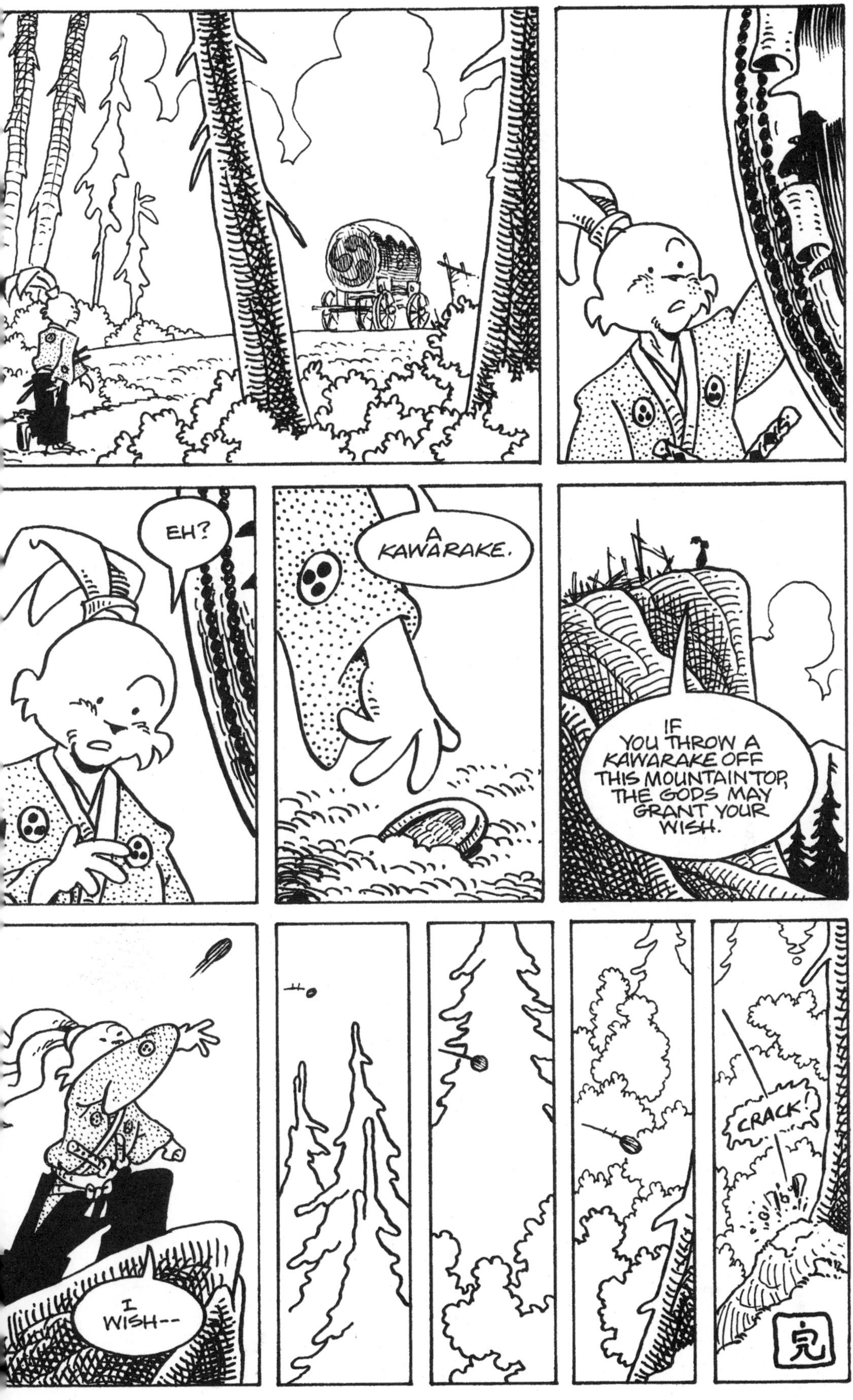
EH?
A KAWARAKE.
IF YOU THROW A KAWARAKE OFF THIS MOUNTAIN TOP, THE GODS MAY GRANT YOUR WISH.
I WISH--
CRACK!
完

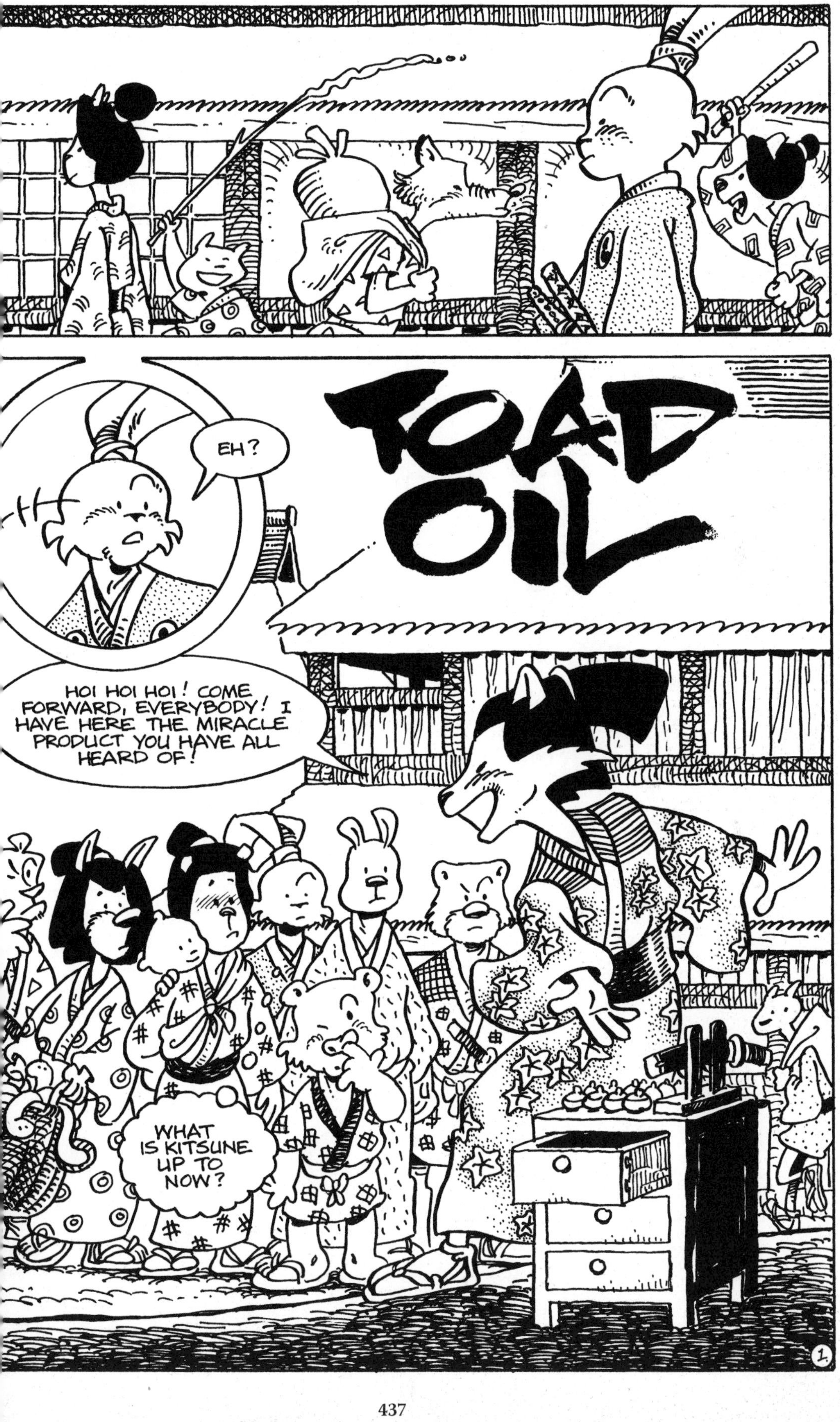
EH?
TOAD OIL
HOI HOI HOI! COME FORWARD, EVERYBODY! I HAVE HERE THE MIRACLE PRODUCT YOU HAVE ALL HEARD OF!
WHAT IS KITSUNE UP TO NOW?
1

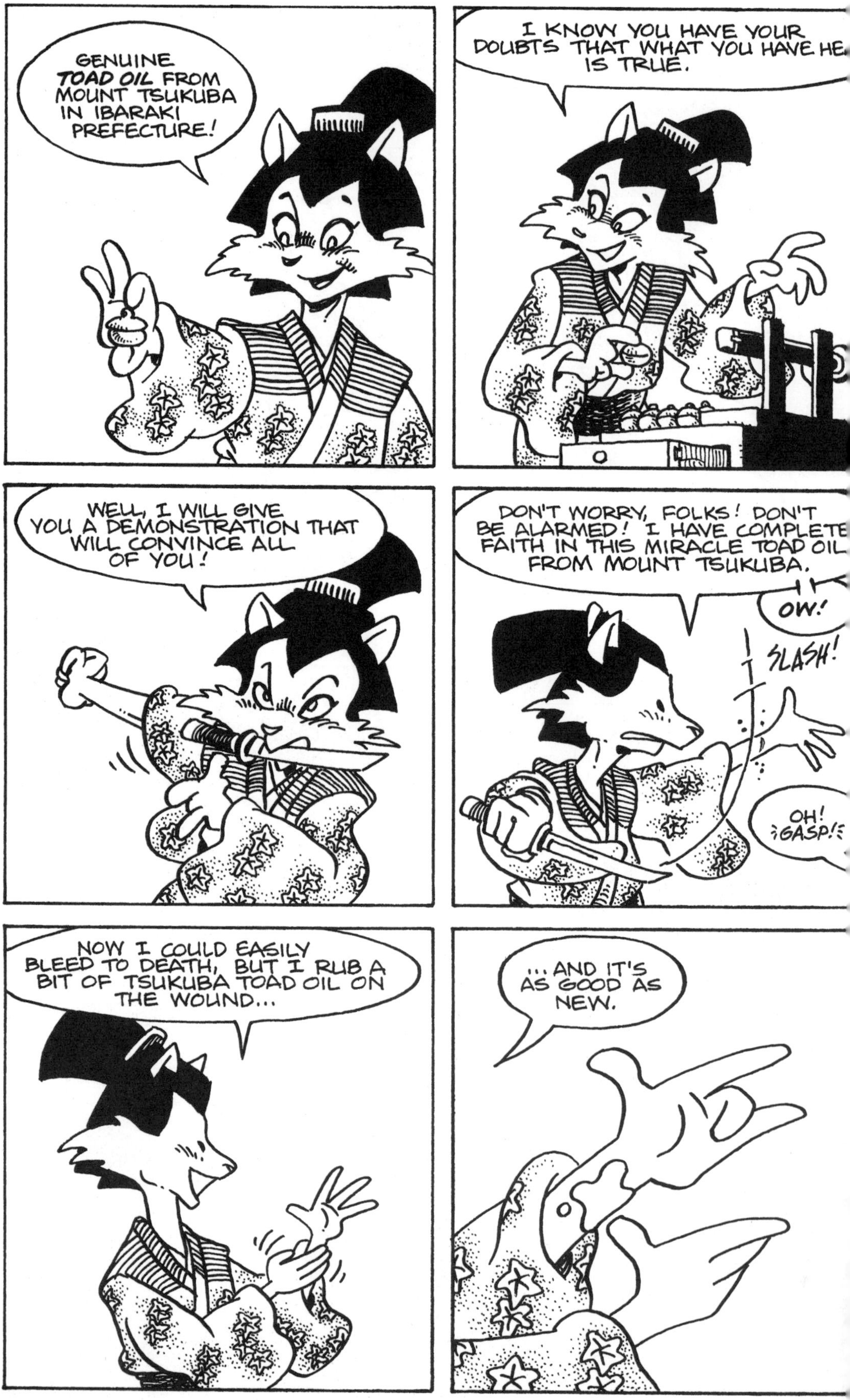

GENUINE TOAD OIL FROM MOUNT TSUKUBA IN IBARAKI PREFECTURE!
I KNOW YOU HAVE YOUR DOUBTS THAT WHAT YOU HAVE HE
IS TRUE.
WELL, I WILL GIVE YOU A DEMONSTRATION THAT WILL CONVINCE ALL OF YOU!
DON'T WORRY, FOLKS! DON'T BE ALARMED! I HAVE COMPLETE FAITH IN THIS MIRACLE TOAD OIL FROM MOUNT TSUKUBA.
OW!
SLASH!
OH! GASP!
NOW I COULD EASILY BLEED TO DEATH, BUT I RUB A BIT OF TSUKUBA TOAD OIL ON THE WOUND...
...AND IT'S AS GOOD AS NEW.

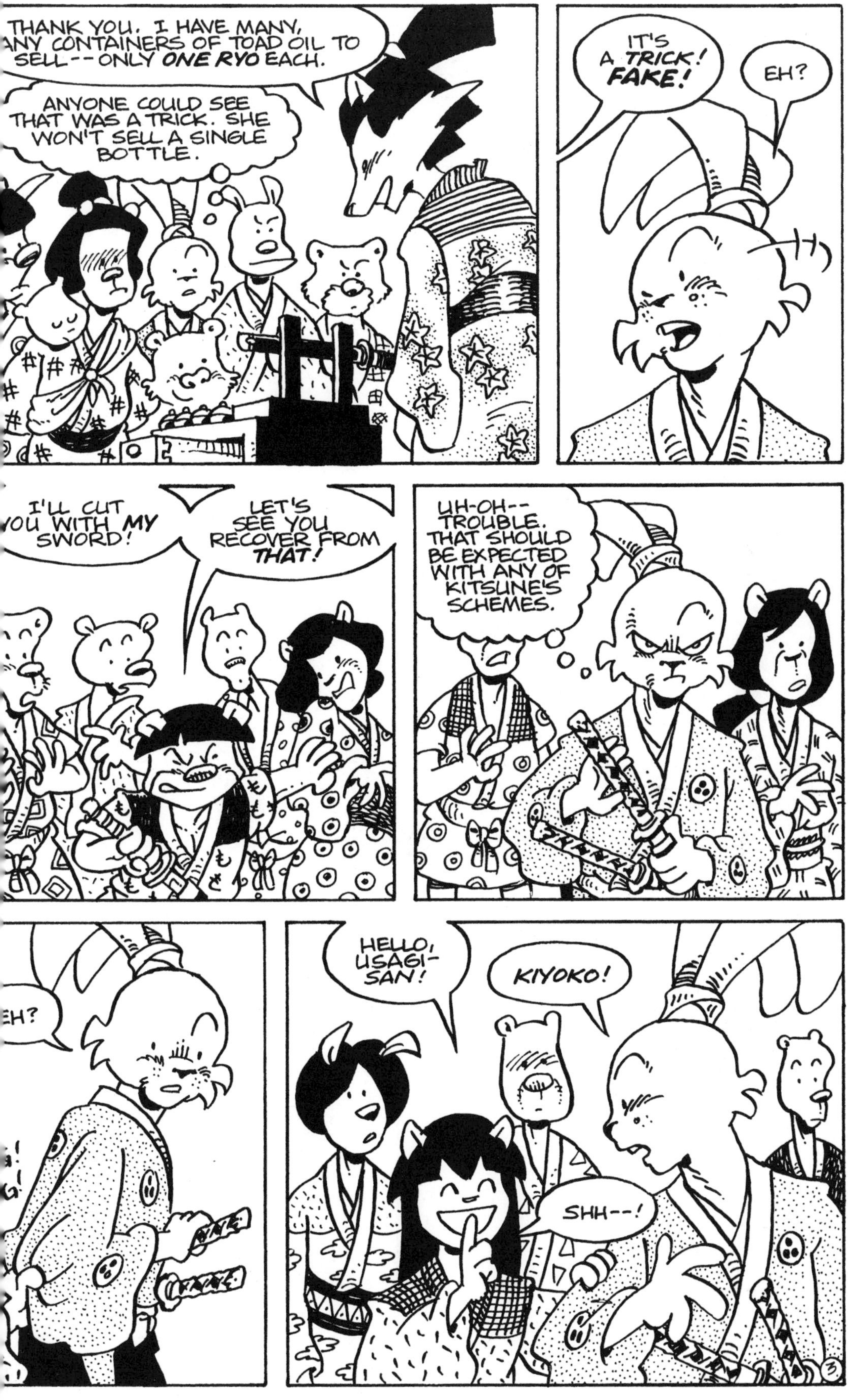
THANK YOU. I HAVE MANY, ANY CONTAINERS OF TOAD OIL TO SELL--ONLY ONE RYO EACH.
ANYONE COULD SEE THAT WAS A TRICK. SHE WON'T SELL A SINGLE BOTTLE.
IT'S A TRICK! FAKE!
EH?
I'LL CUT YOU WITH MY SWORD!
LET'S SEE YOU RECOVER FROM THAT!
UH-OH--TROUBLE. THAT SHOULD BE EXPECTED WITH ANY OF KITSUNE'S SCHEMES.
EH?
HELLO, USAGI-SAN!
KIYOKO!
SHH--!
3

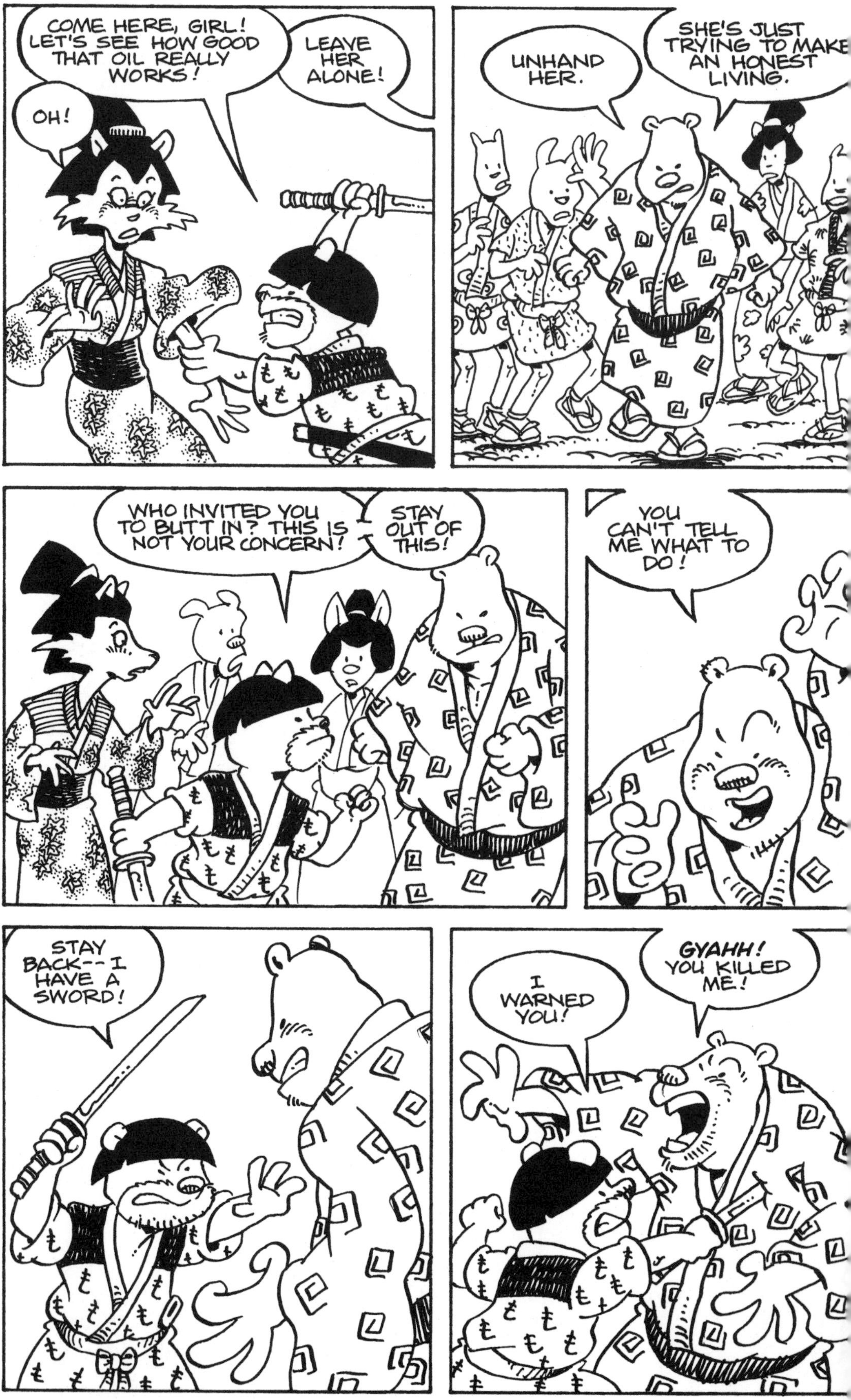
COME HERE, GIRL! LET'S SEE HOW GOOD THAT OIL REALLY WORKS!
OH!
LEAVE HER ALONE!
UNHAND HER.
SHE'S JUST TRYING TO MAKE AN HONEST LIVING.
WHO INVITED YOU TO BUTT IN? THIS IS NOT YOUR CONCERN!
STAY OUT OF THIS!
YOU CAN'T TELL ME WHAT TO DO!
STAY BACK-- I HAVE A SWORD!
I WARNED YOU!
GYAHH! YOU KILLED ME!

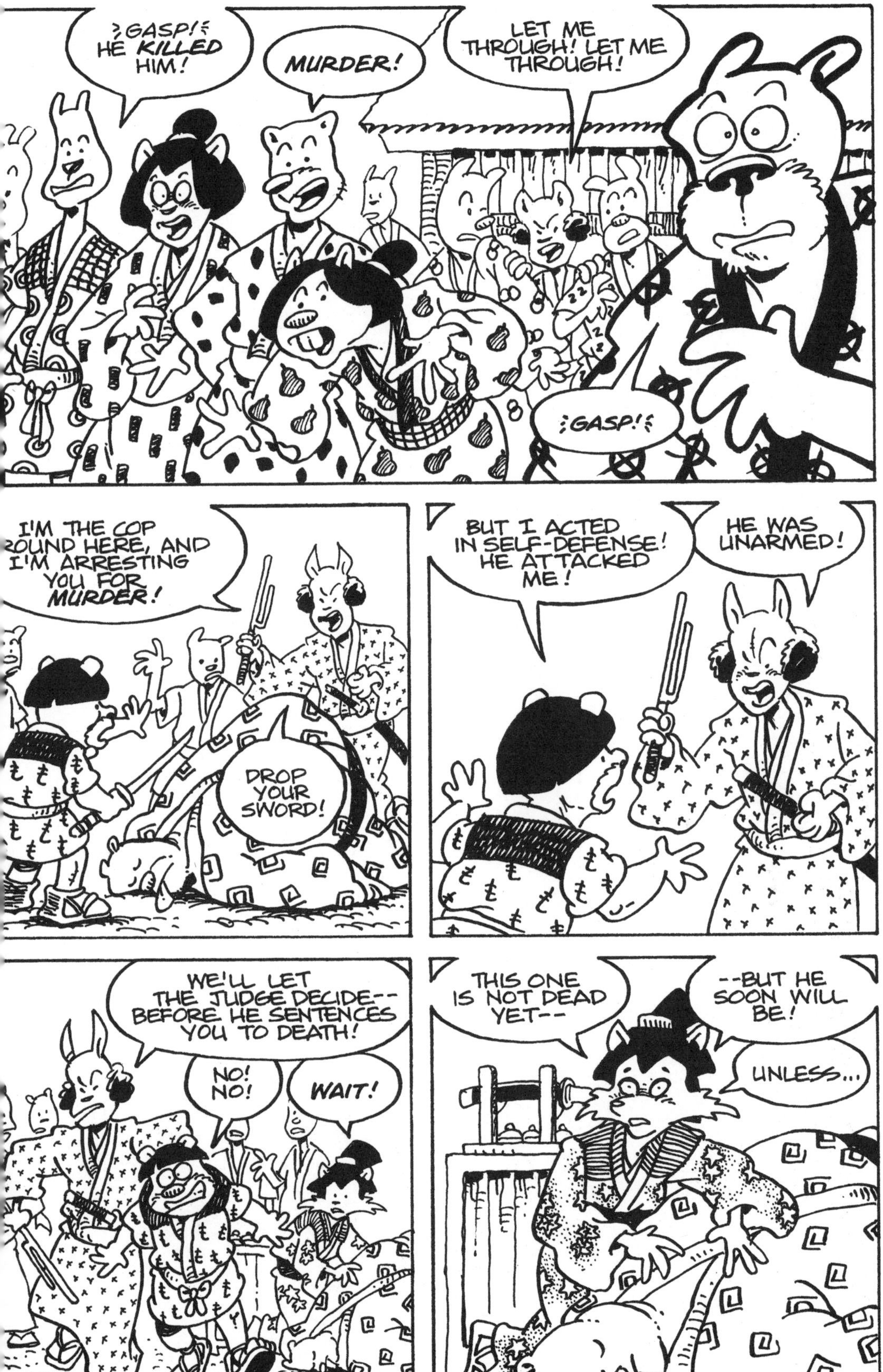

GASP! HE KILLED HIM!
MURDER!
LET ME THROUGH! LET ME THROUGH!
GASP!
I'M THE COP 'ROUND HERE, AND I'M ARRESTING YOU FOR MURDER!
DROP YOUR SWORD!
BUT I ACTED IN SELF-DEFENSE! HE ATTACKED ME!
HE WAS UNARMED!
WE'LL LET THE JUDGE DECIDE-- BEFORE HE SENTENCES YOU TO DEATH!
NO! NO!
WAIT!
THIS ONE IS NOT DEAD YET--
--BUT HE SOON WILL BE!
UNLESS...

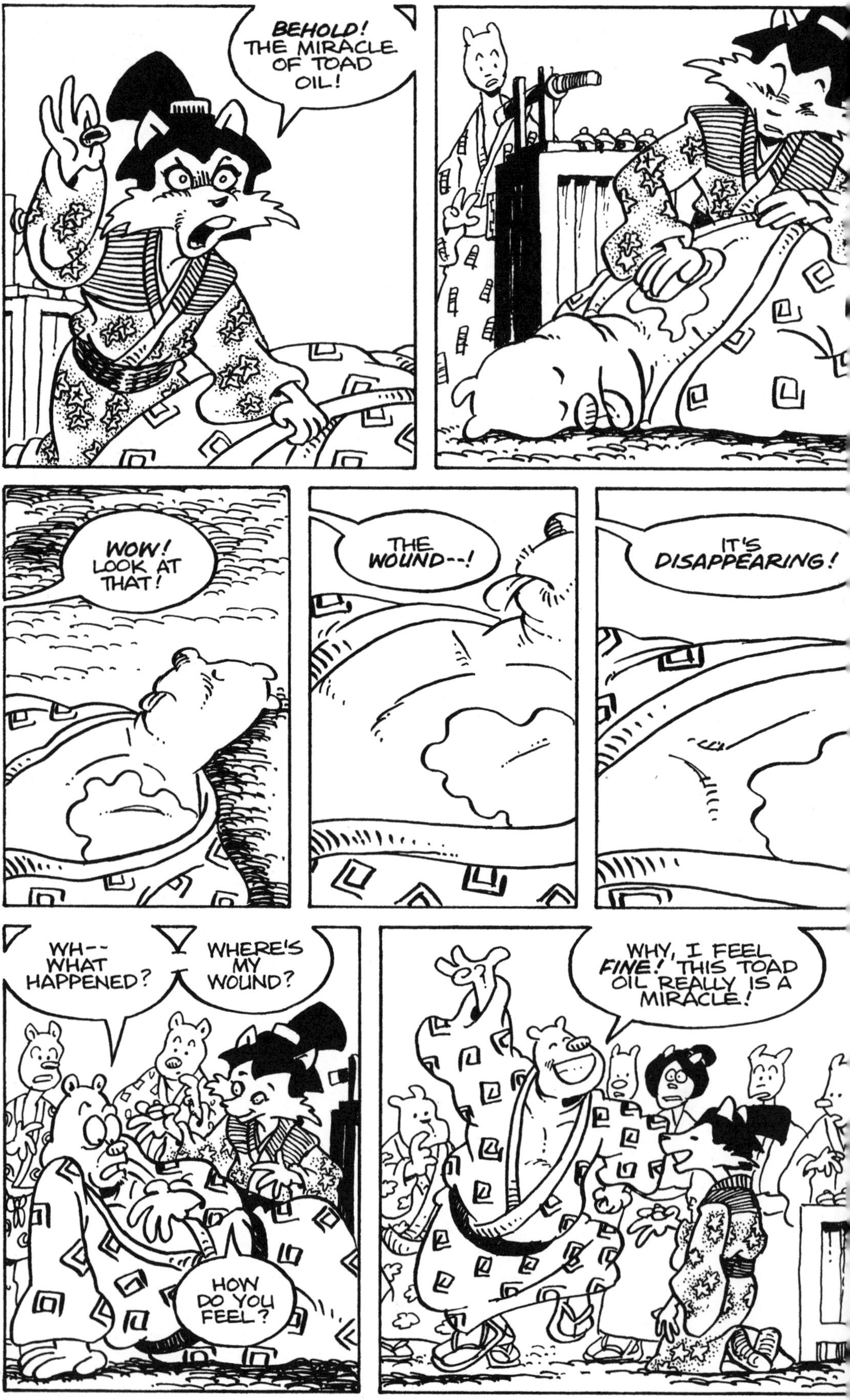
BEHOLD! THE MIRACLE OF TOAD OIL!
WOW! LOOK AT THAT!
THE WOUND--!
IT'S DISAPPEARING!
WH-- WHAT HAPPENED?
WHERE'S MY WOUND?
HOW DO YOU FEEL?
WHY, I FEEL FINE! THIS TOAD OIL REALLY IS A MIRACLE!

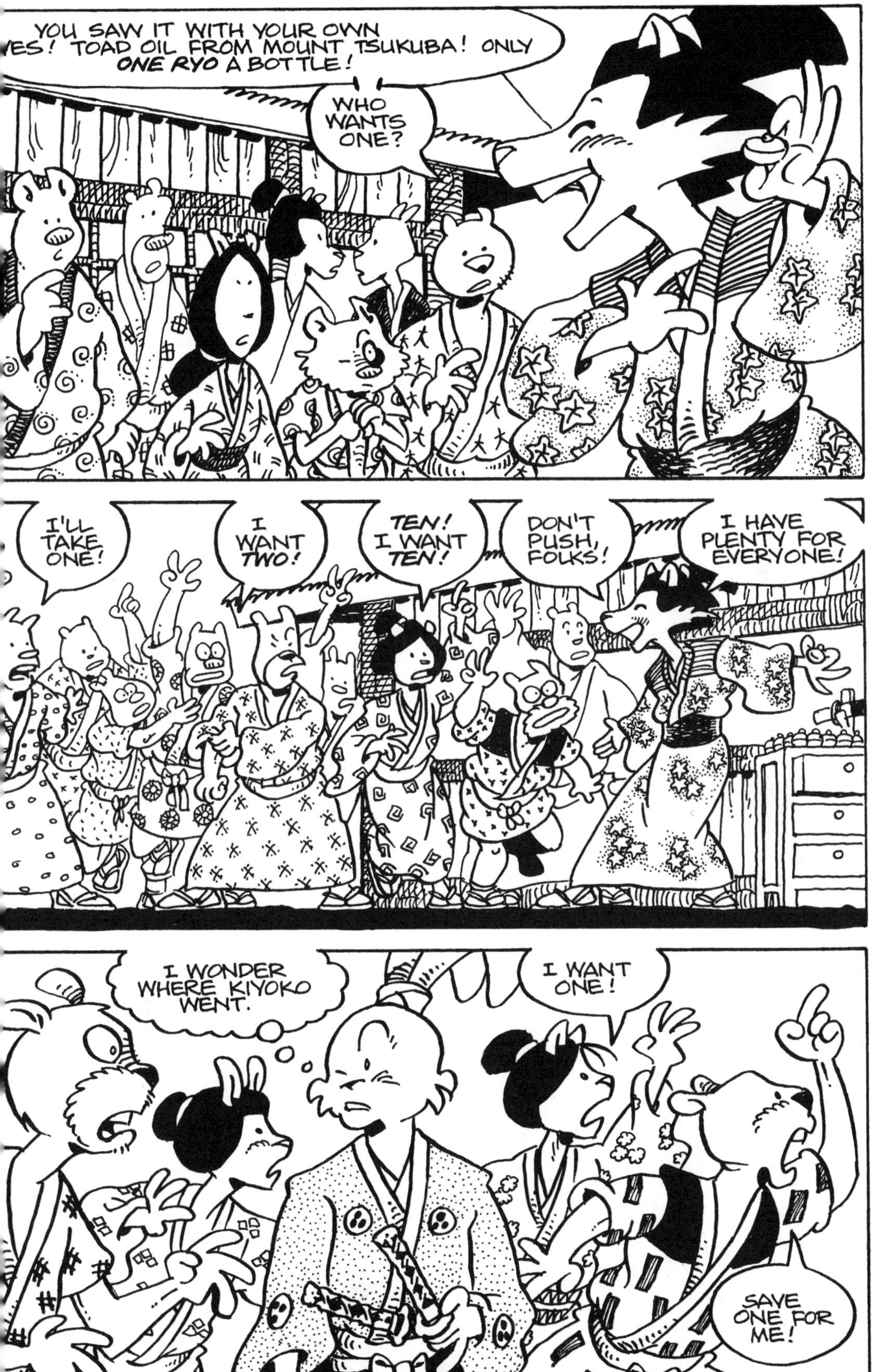
YOU SAW IT WITH YOUR OWN EYES! TOAD OIL FROM MOUNT TSUKUBA! ONLY ONE RYO A BOTTLE!
WHO WANTS ONE?
I'LL TAKE ONE!
I WANT TWO!
TEN! I WANT TEN!
DON'T PUSH, FOLKS!
I HAVE PLENTY FOR EVERYONE!
I WONDER WHERE KIYOKO WENT.
I WANT ONE!
SAVE ONE FOR ME!
7

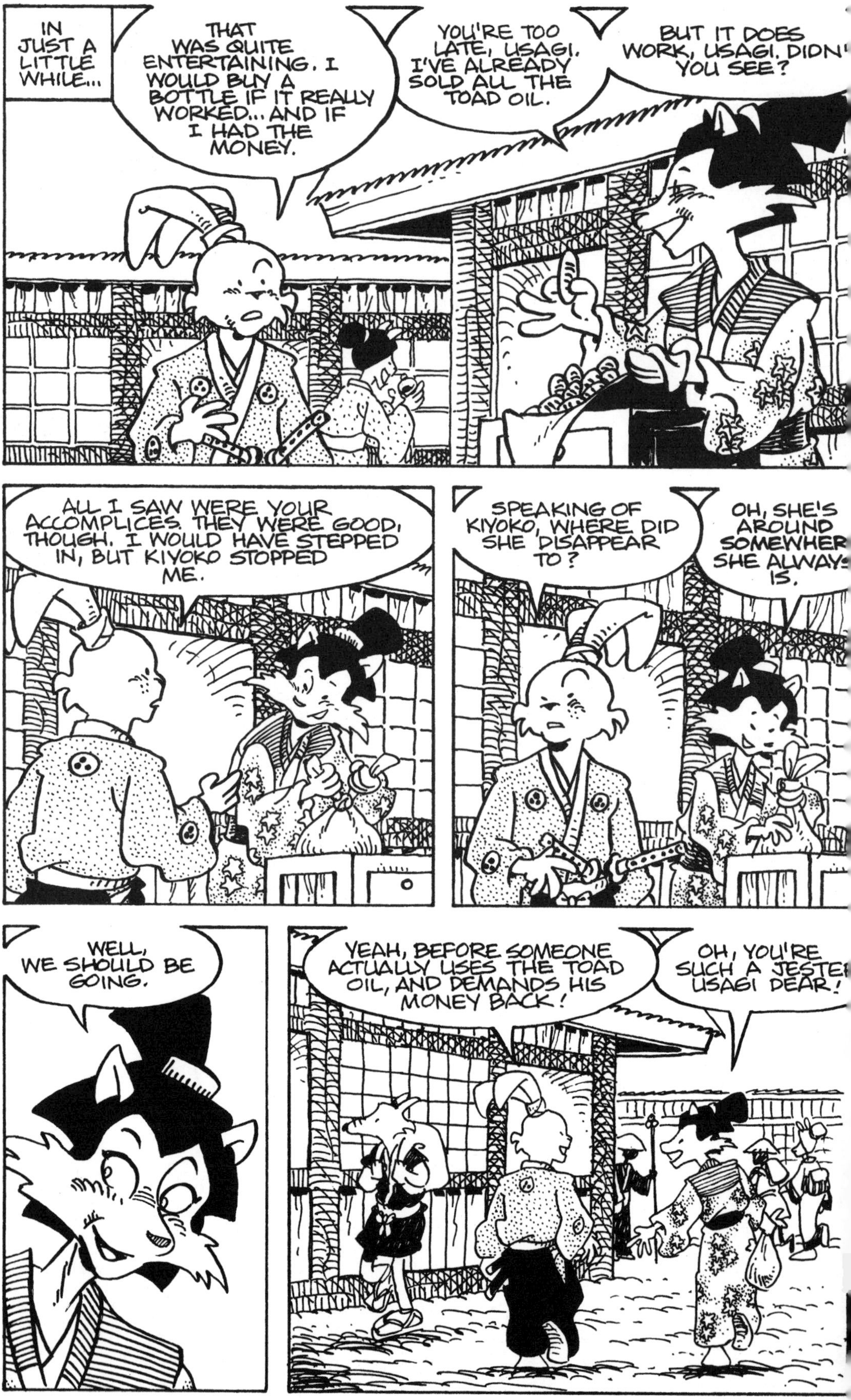
IN JUST A LITTLE WHILE...
THAT WAS QUITE ENTERTAINING. I WOULD BUY A BOTTLE IF IT REALLY WORKED... AND IF I HAD THE MONEY.
YOU'RE TOO LATE, USAGI. I'VE ALREADY SOLD ALL THE TOAD OIL.
BUT IT DOES WORK, USAGI. DIDN' YOU SEE?
ALL I SAW WERE YOUR ACCOMPLICES. THEY WERE GOOD, THOUGH. I WOULD HAVE STEPPED IN, BUT KIYOKO STOPPED ME.
SPEAKING OF KIYOKO, WHERE DID SHE DISAPPEAR TO?
OH, SHE'S AROUND SOMEWHER SHE ALWAYS IS.
WELL, WE SHOULD BE GOING.
YEAH, BEFORE SOMEONE ACTUALLY USES THE TOAD OIL, AND DEMANDS HIS MONEY BACK!
OH, YOU'RE SUCH A JESTER USAGI DEAR!

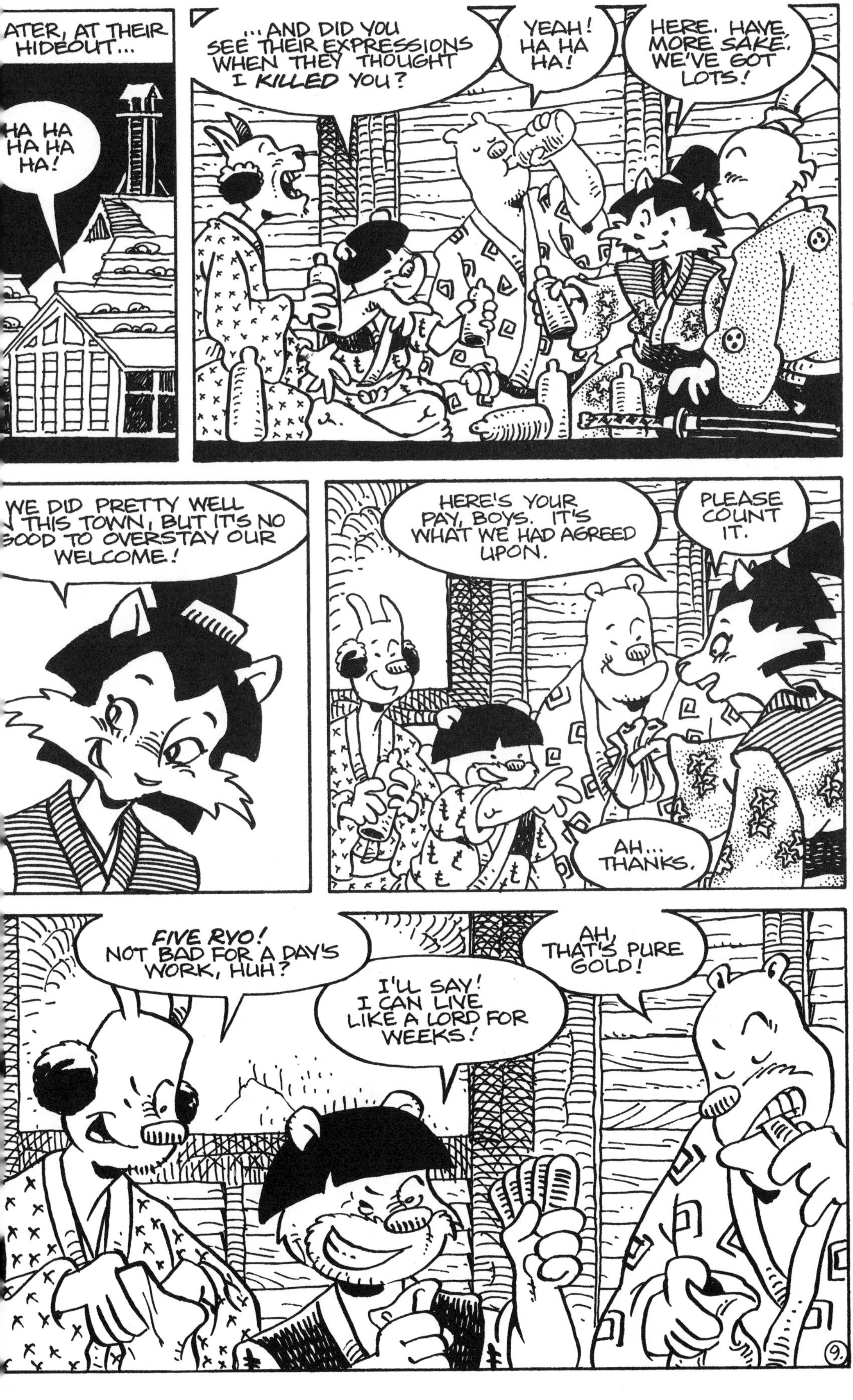
ATER, AT THEIR HIDEOUT...
HA HA HA HA HA!
...AND DID YOU SEE THEIR EXPRESSIONS WHEN THEY THOUGHT I KILLED YOU?
YEAH! HA HA HA!
HERE. HAVE MORE SAKE. WE'VE GOT LOTS!
WE DID PRETTY WELL N THIS TOWN, BUT IT'S NO GOOD TO OVERSTAY OUR WELCOME!
HERE'S YOUR PAY, BOYS. IT'S WHAT WE HAD AGREED UPON.
PLEASE COUNT IT.
AH... THANKS.
FIVE RYO! NOT BAD FOR A DAY'S WORK, HUH?
I'LL SAY! I CAN LIVE LIKE A LORD FOR WEEKS!
AH, THAT'S PURE GOLD!
9.

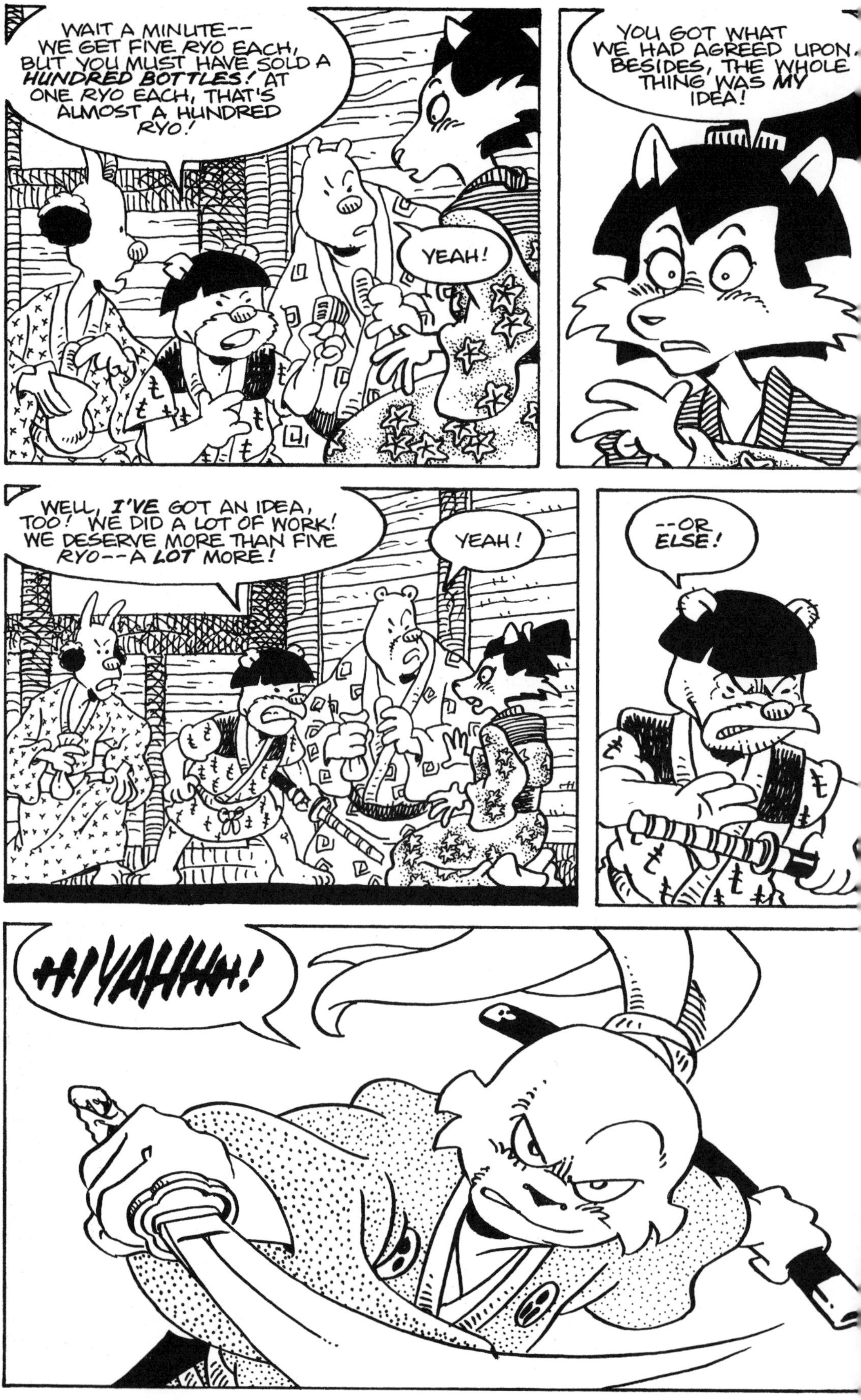
WAIT A MINUTE-- WE GET FIVE RYO EACH, BUT YOU MUST HAVE SOLD A HUNDRED BOTTLES! AT ONE RYO EACH, THAT'S ALMOST A HUNDRED RYO!
YEAH!
YOU GOT WHAT WE HAD AGREED UPON. BESIDES, THE WHOLE THING WAS MY IDEA!
WELL, I'VE GOT AN IDEA, TOO! WE DID A LOT OF WORK! WE DESERVE MORE THAN FIVE RYO--A LOT MORE!
YEAH!
--OR ELSE!
HIYAHHH!

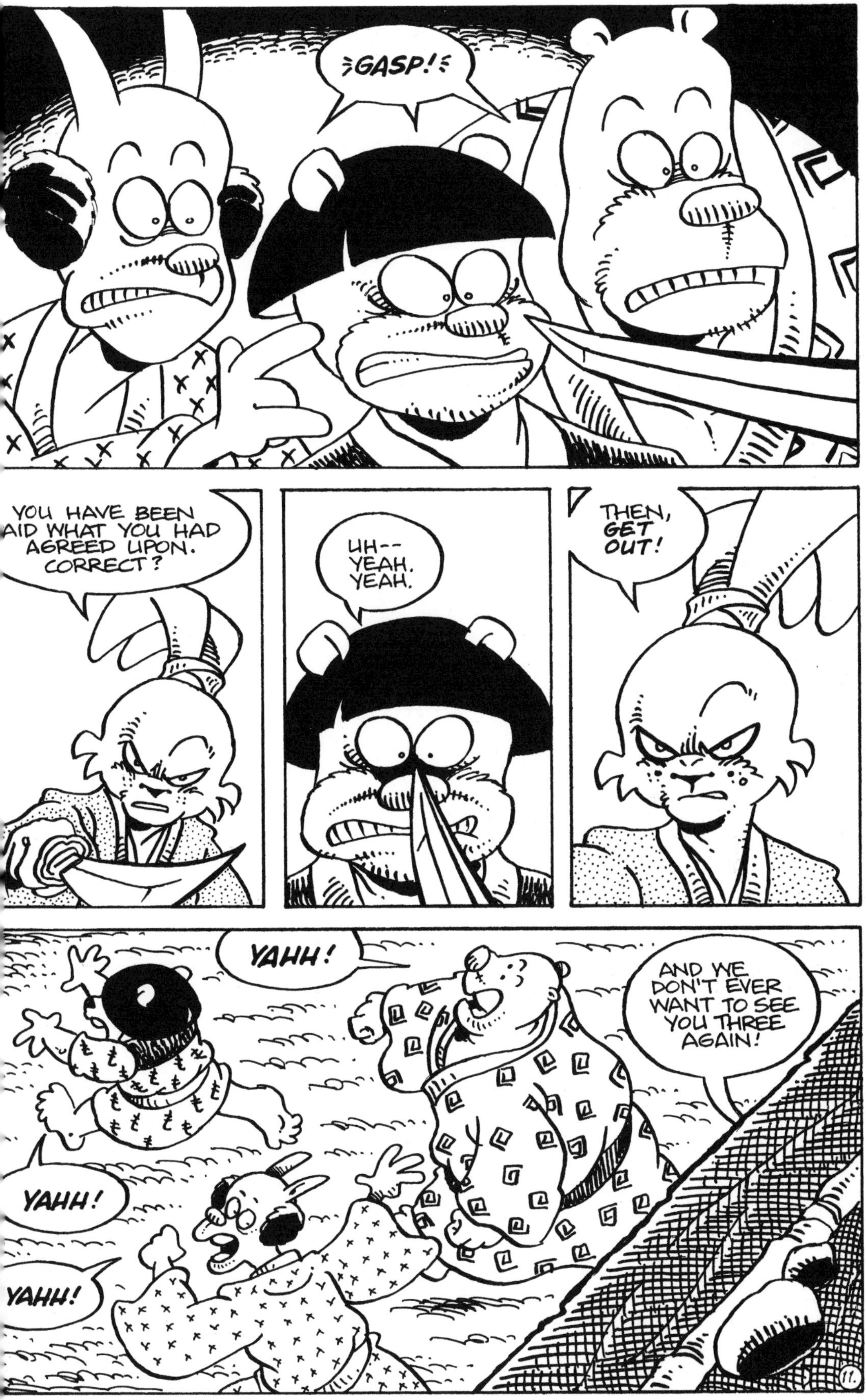
GASP!
YOU HAVE BEEN
AID WHAT YOU HAD
AGREED UPON.
CORRECT?
UH--
YEAH.
YEAH.
THEN,
GET
OUT!
YAHH!
AND WE
DON'T EVER
WANT TO SEE
YOU THREE
AGAIN!
YAHH!
YAHH!
11.

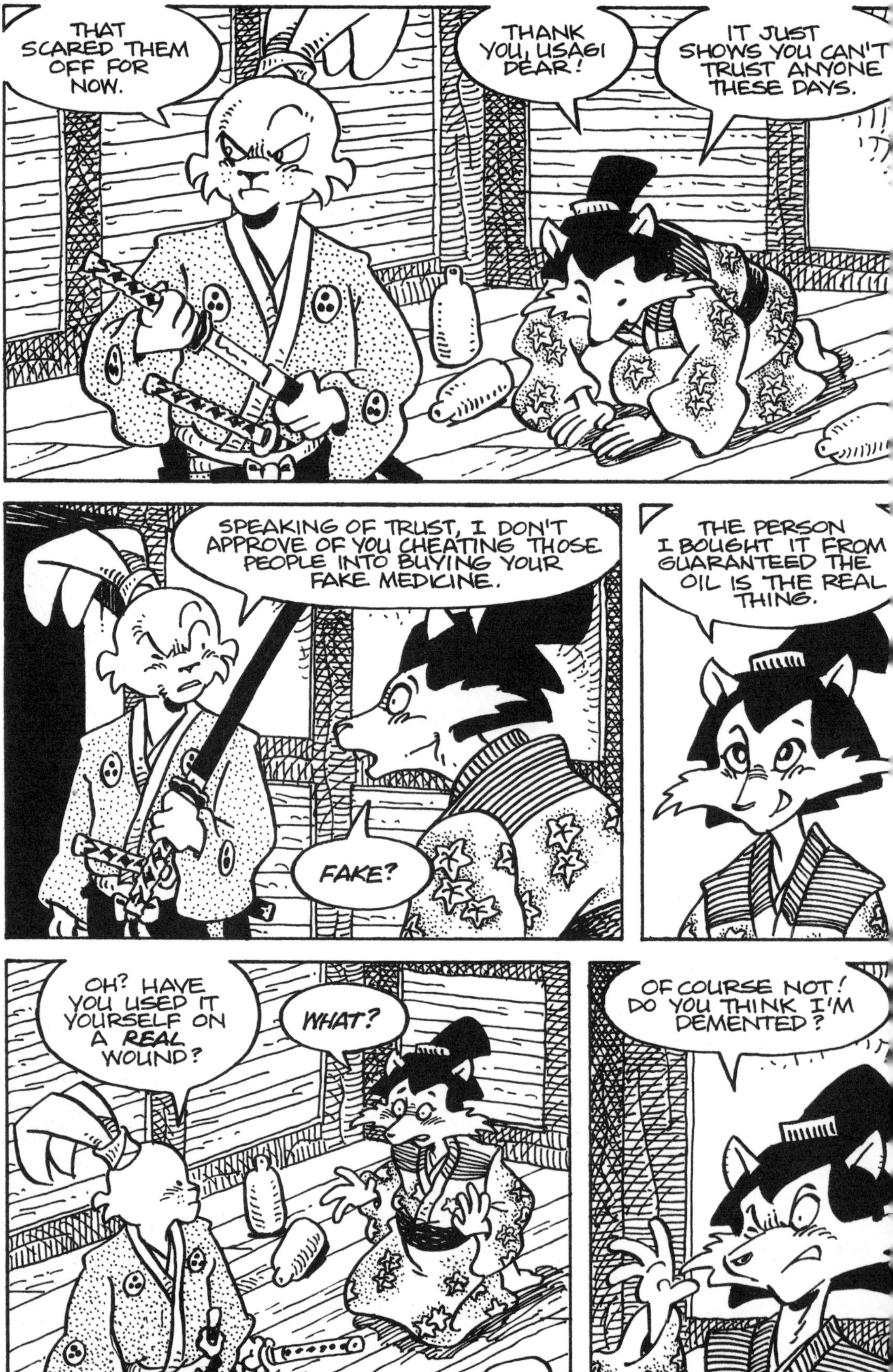
THAT SCARED THEM OFF FOR NOW.
THANK YOU, USAGI DEAR!
IT JUST SHOWS YOU CAN'T TRUST ANYONE THESE DAYS.
SPEAKING OF TRUST, I DON'T APPROVE OF YOU CHEATING THOSE PEOPLE INTO BUYING YOUR FAKE MEDICINE.
FAKE?
THE PERSON I BOUGHT IT FROM GUARANTEED THE OIL IS THE REAL THING.
OH? HAVE YOU USED IT YOURSELF ON A REAL WOUND?
WHAT?
OF COURSE NOT! DO YOU THINK I'M DEMENTED?

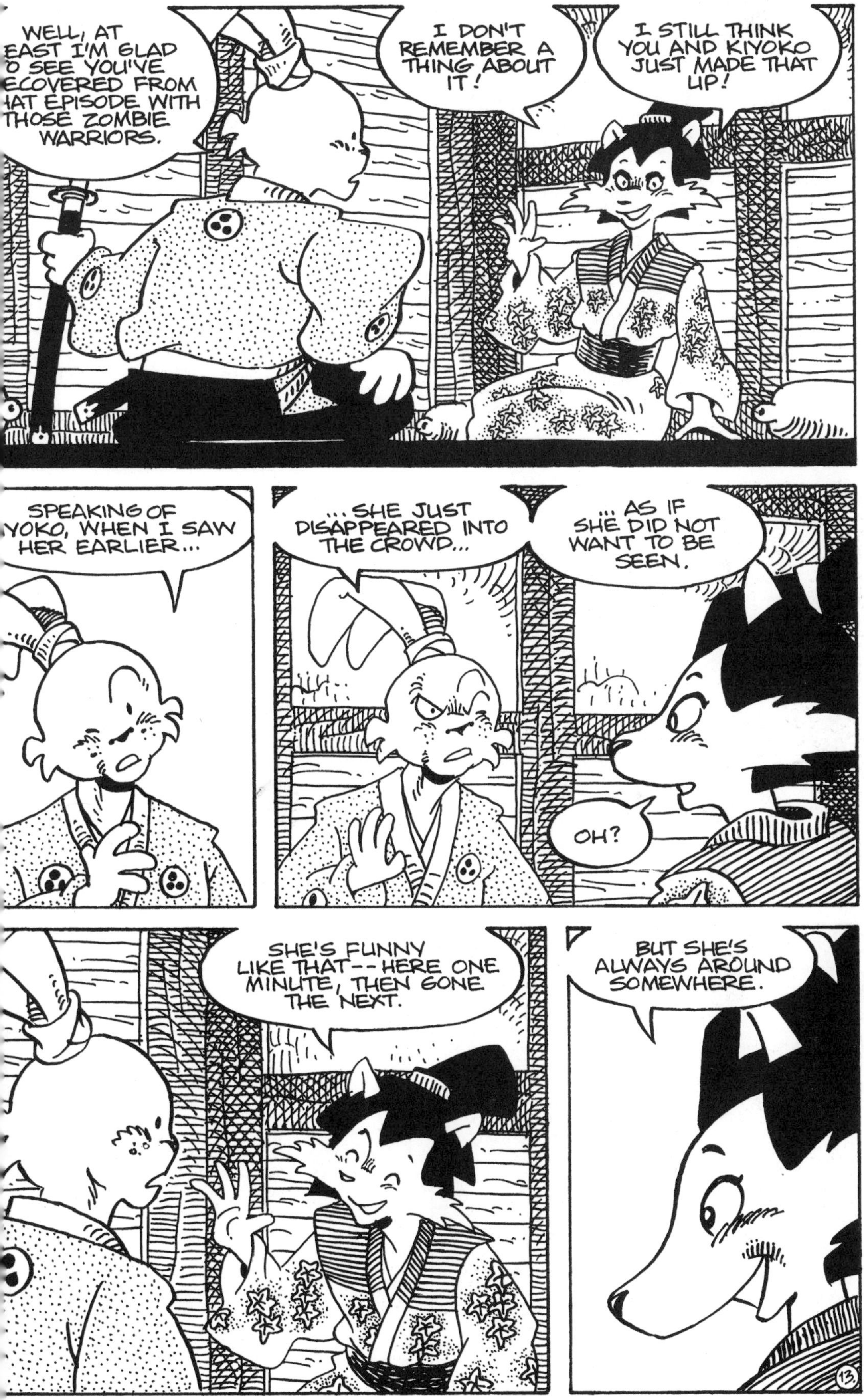
WELL, AT EAST I'M GLAD O SEE YOU'VE ECOVERED FROM HAT EPISODE WITH THOSE ZOMBIE WARRIORS.
I DON'T REMEMBER A THING ABOUT IT!
I STILL THINK YOU AND KIYOKO JUST MADE THAT UP!
SPEAKING OF YOKO, WHEN I SAW HER EARLIER...
...SHE JUST DISAPPEARED INTO THE CROWD...
...AS IF SHE DID NOT WANT TO BE SEEN.
OH?
SHE'S FUNNY LIKE THAT--HERE ONE MINUTE, THEN GONE THE NEXT.
BUT SHE'S ALWAYS AROUND SOMEWHERE.
13

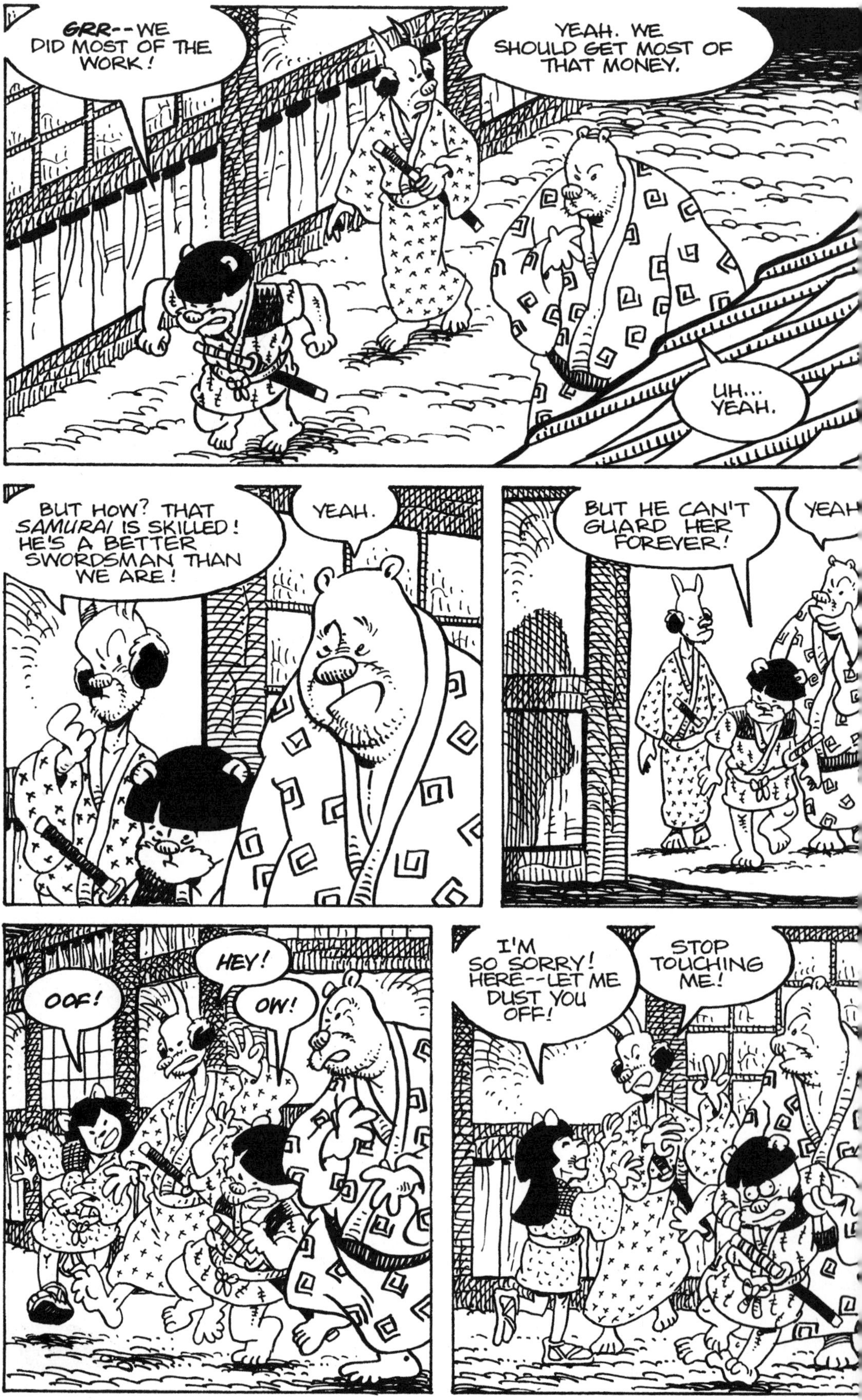
GRR--WE DID MOST OF THE WORK!
YEAH. WE SHOULD GET MOST OF THAT MONEY.
UH... YEAH.
BUT HOW? THAT SAMURAI IS SKILLED! HE'S A BETTER SWORDSMAN THAN WE ARE!
YEAH.
BUT HE CAN'T GUARD HER FOREVER!
YEAH
OOF!
HEY!
OW!
I'M SO SORRY! HERE--LET ME DUST YOU OFF!
STOP TOUCHING ME!

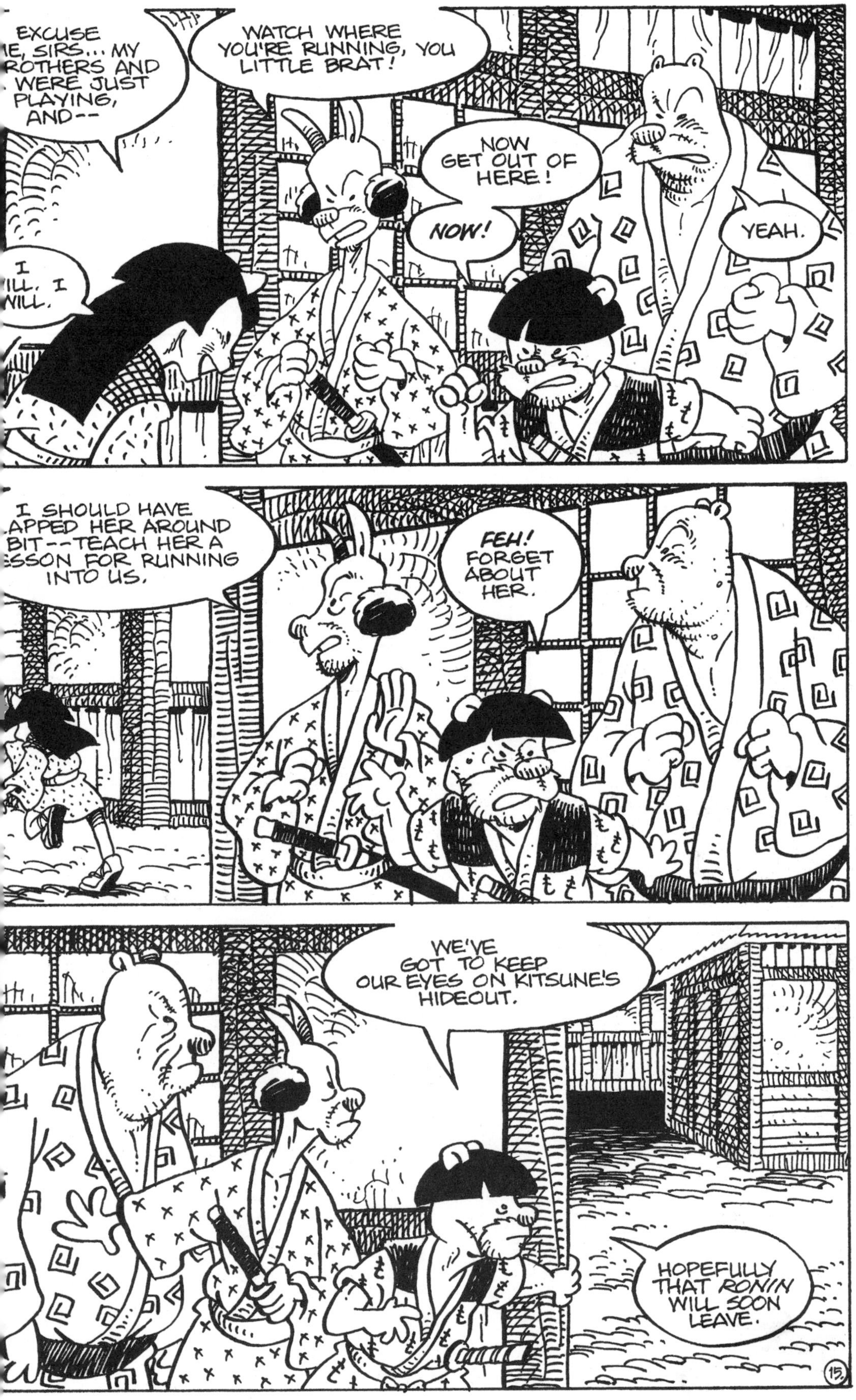
EXCUSE
E, SIRS... MY
ROTHERS AND
WERE JUST
PLAYING,
AND--
WATCH WHERE YOU'RE RUNNING, YOU LITTLE BRAT!
NOW GET OUT OF HERE!
NOW!
YEAH.
I
ILL. I
ILL.
I SHOULD HAVE
APPED HER AROUND
BIT--TEACH HER A
SSON FOR RUNNING
INTO US.
FEH! FORGET ABOUT HER.
WE'VE GOT TO KEEP OUR EYES ON KITSUNE'S HIDEOUT.
HOPEFULLY THAT RONIN WILL SOON LEAVE.
15

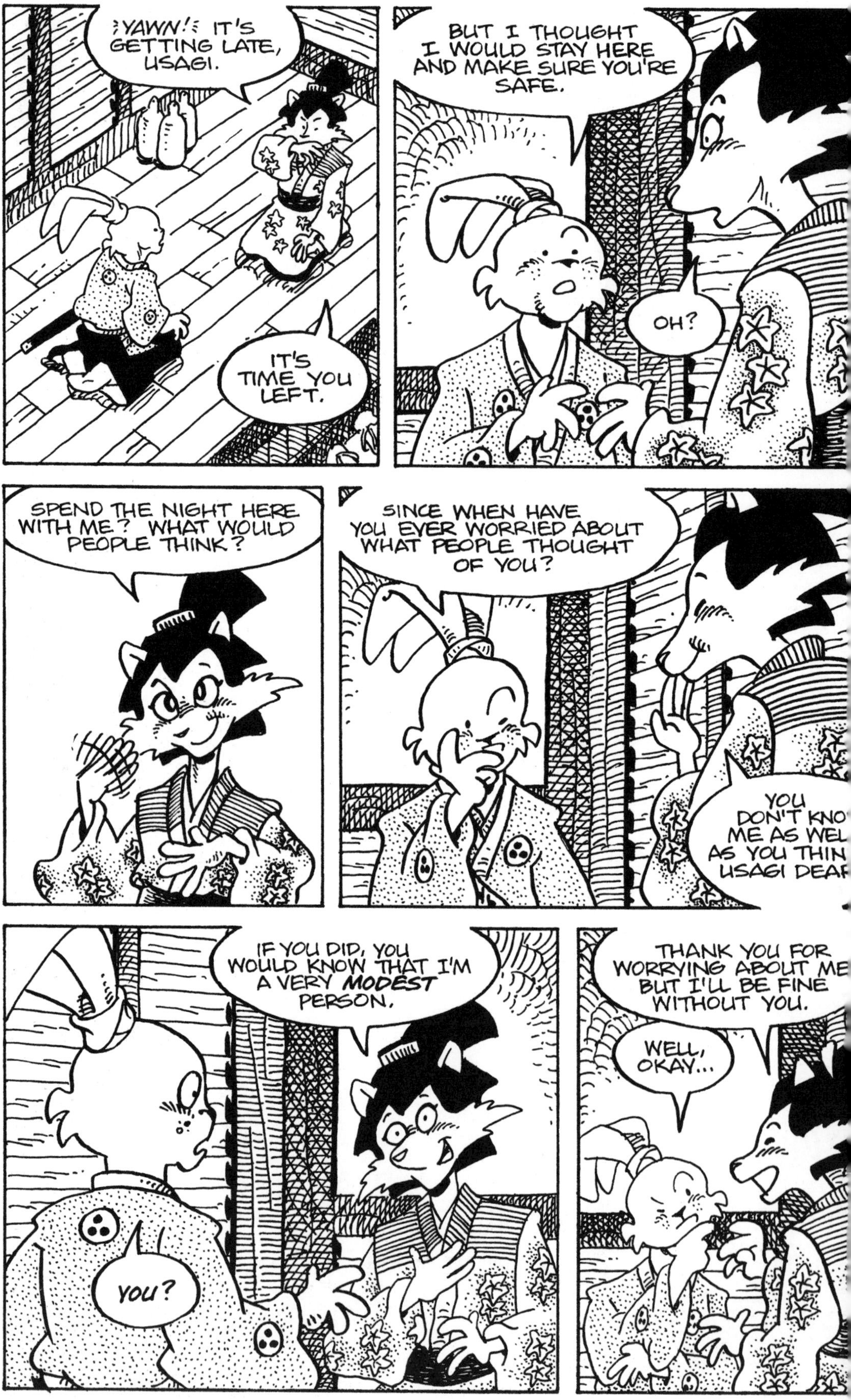

⸗YAWN!⸗ IT'S GETTING LATE, USAGI.
IT'S TIME YOU LEFT.
BUT I THOUGHT I WOULD STAY HERE AND MAKE SURE YOU'RE SAFE.
OH?
SPEND THE NIGHT HERE WITH ME? WHAT WOULD PEOPLE THINK?
SINCE WHEN HAVE YOU EVER WORRIED ABOUT WHAT PEOPLE THOUGHT OF YOU?
YOU DON'T KNO ME AS WEL AS YOU THIN USAGI DEAR
IF YOU DID, YOU WOULD KNOW THAT I'M A VERY ***MODEST*** PERSON.
YOU?
THANK YOU FOR WORRYING ABOUT ME BUT I'LL BE FINE WITHOUT YOU.
WELL, OKAY...

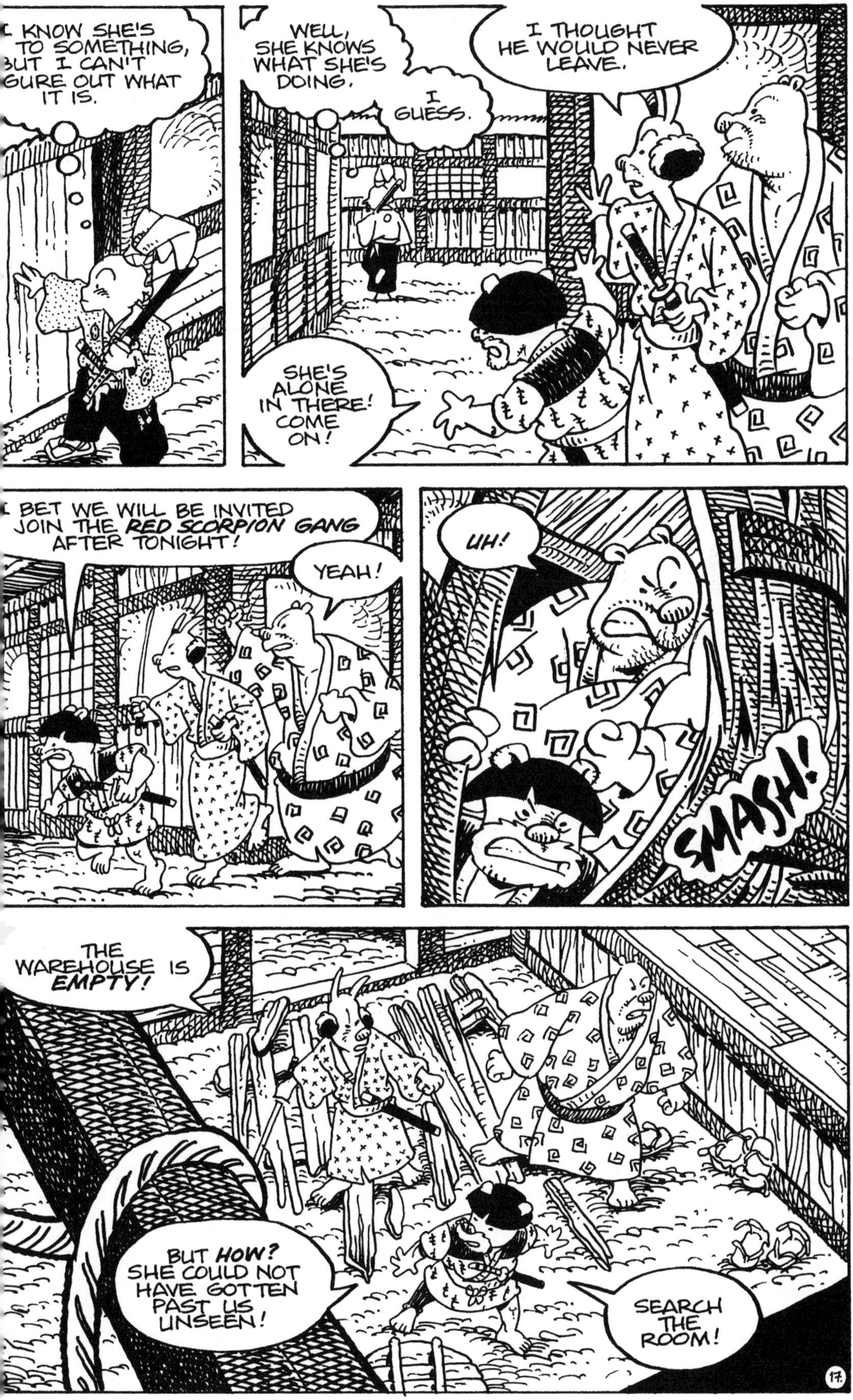
I KNOW SHE'S UP TO SOMETHING, BUT I CAN'T FIGURE OUT WHAT IT IS.
WELL, SHE KNOWS WHAT SHE'S DOING.
I GUESS.
I THOUGHT HE WOULD NEVER LEAVE.
SHE'S ALONE IN THERE! COME ON!
I BET WE WILL BE INVITED TO JOIN THE RED SCORPION GANG AFTER TONIGHT!
YEAH!
UH!
SMASH!
THE WAREHOUSE IS EMPTY!
BUT HOW? SHE COULD NOT HAVE GOTTEN PAST US UNSEEN!
SEARCH THE ROOM!
17.

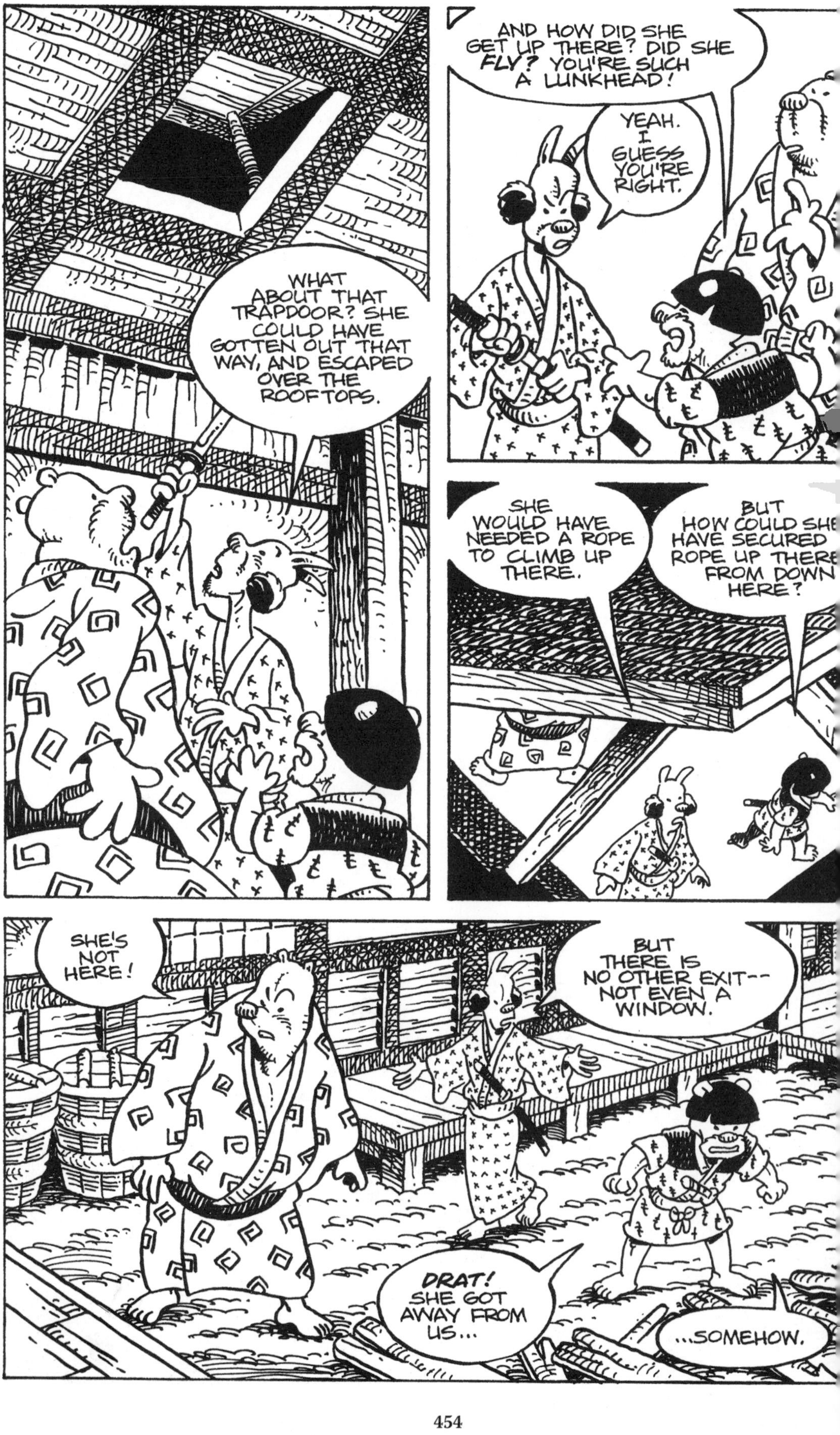
WHAT ABOUT THAT TRAPDOOR? SHE COULD HAVE GOTTEN OUT THAT WAY, AND ESCAPED OVER THE ROOFTOPS.
AND HOW DID SHE GET UP THERE? DID SHE FLY? YOU'RE SUCH A LUNKHEAD!
YEAH. I GUESS YOU'RE RIGHT.
SHE WOULD HAVE NEEDED A ROPE TO CLIMB UP THERE.
BUT HOW COULD SHE HAVE SECURED A ROPE UP THERE FROM DOWN HERE?
SHE'S NOT HERE!
BUT THERE IS NO OTHER EXIT-- NOT EVEN A WINDOW.
DRAT! SHE GOT AWAY FROM US...
...SOMEHOW.

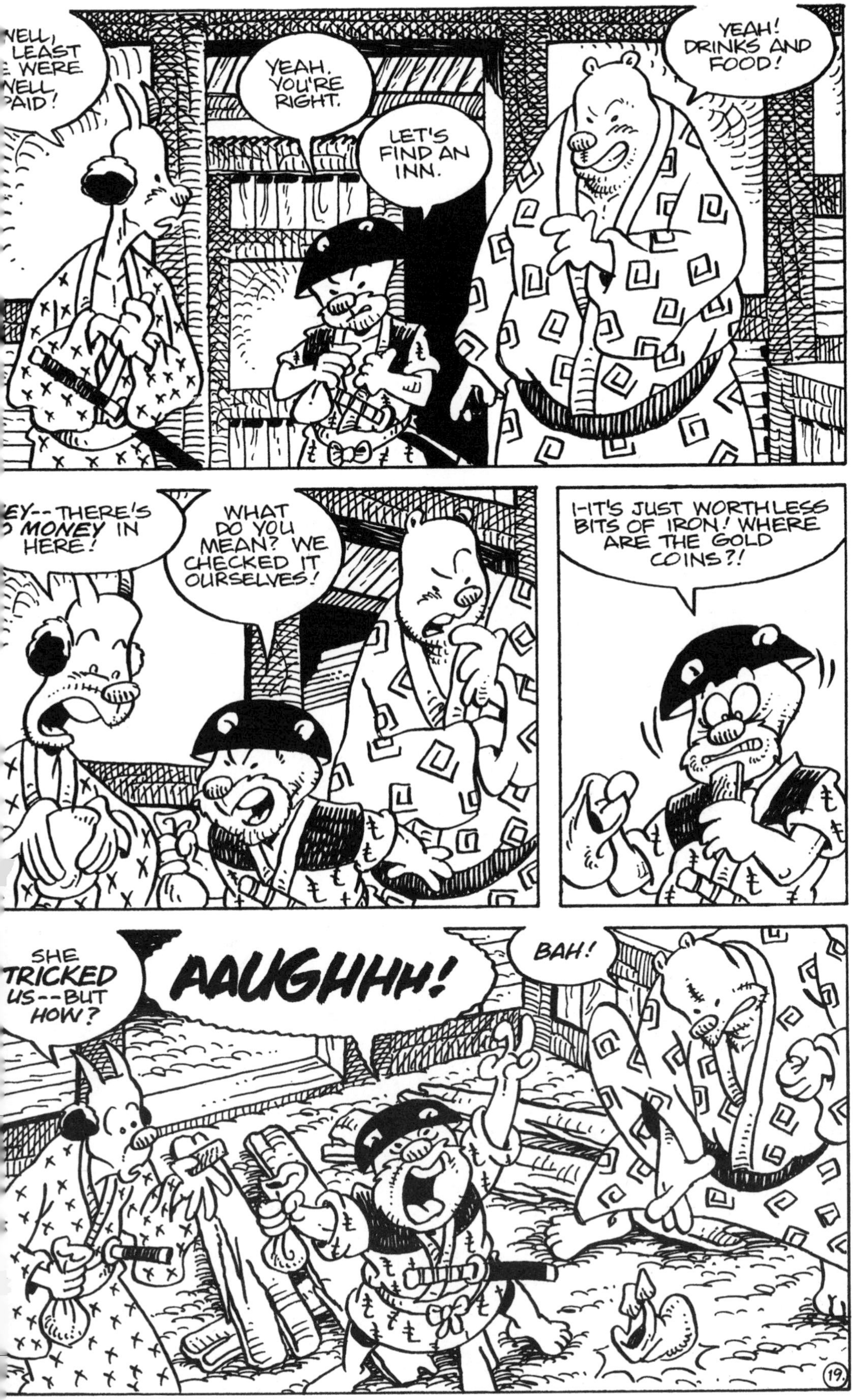
WELL, LEAST WERE WELL PAID!
YEAH. YOU'RE RIGHT.
LET'S FIND AN INN.
YEAH! DRINKS AND FOOD!
EY--THERE'S MONEY IN HERE!
WHAT DO YOU MEAN? WE CHECKED IT OURSELVES!
I-IT'S JUST WORTHLESS BITS OF IRON! WHERE ARE THE GOLD COINS?!
SHE TRICKED US--BUT HOW?
AAUGHHH!
BAH!
19

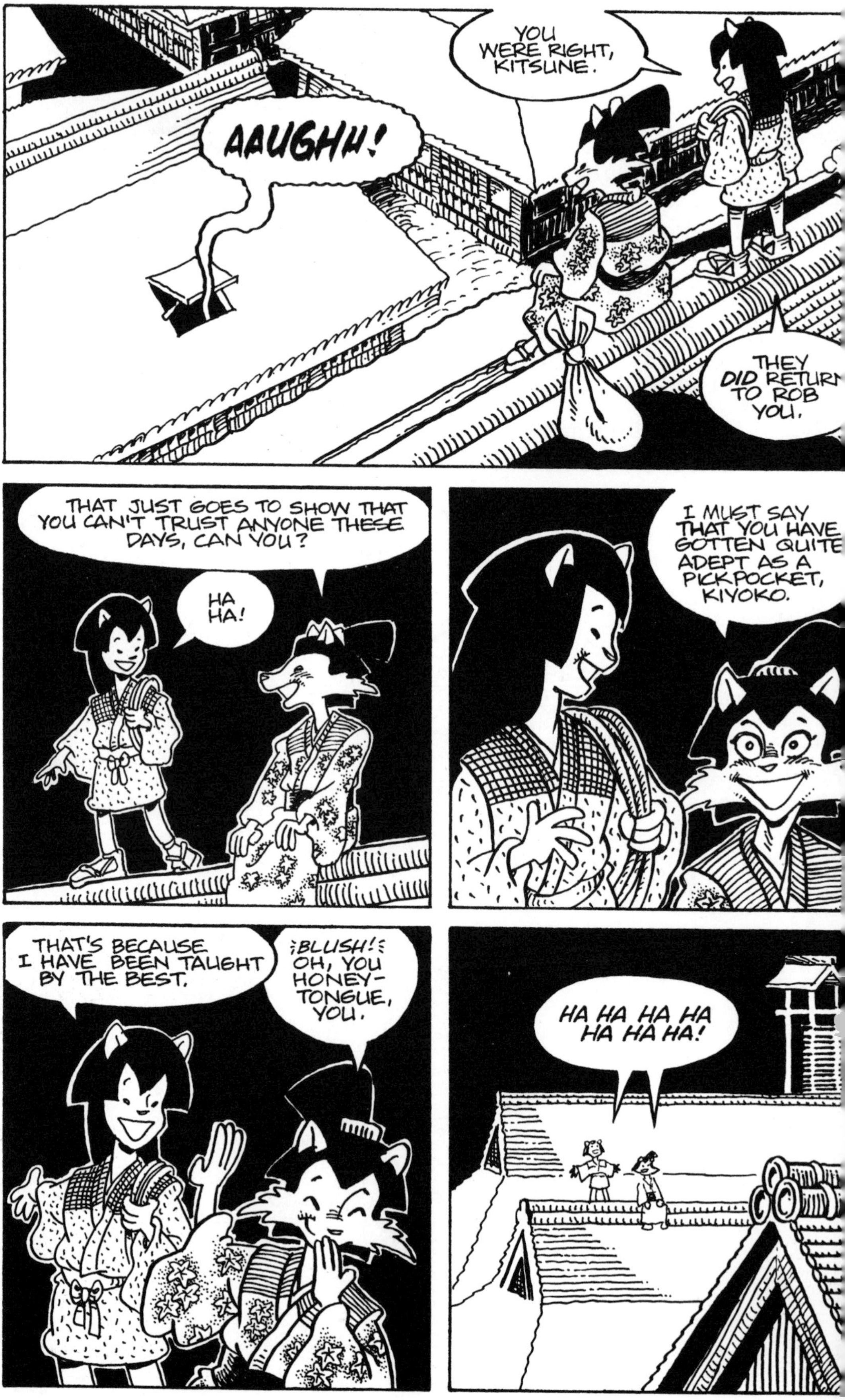
AAUGHH!
YOU WERE RIGHT, KITSUNE.
THEY DID RETURN TO ROB YOU.
THAT JUST GOES TO SHOW THAT YOU CAN'T TRUST ANYONE THESE DAYS, CAN YOU?
HA HA!
I MUST SAY THAT YOU HAVE GOTTEN QUITE ADEPT AS A PICKPOCKET, KIYOKO.
THAT'S BECAUSE I HAVE BEEN TAUGHT BY THE BEST.
BLUSH! OH, YOU HONEY-TONGUE, YOU.
HA HA HA HA HA HA HA!

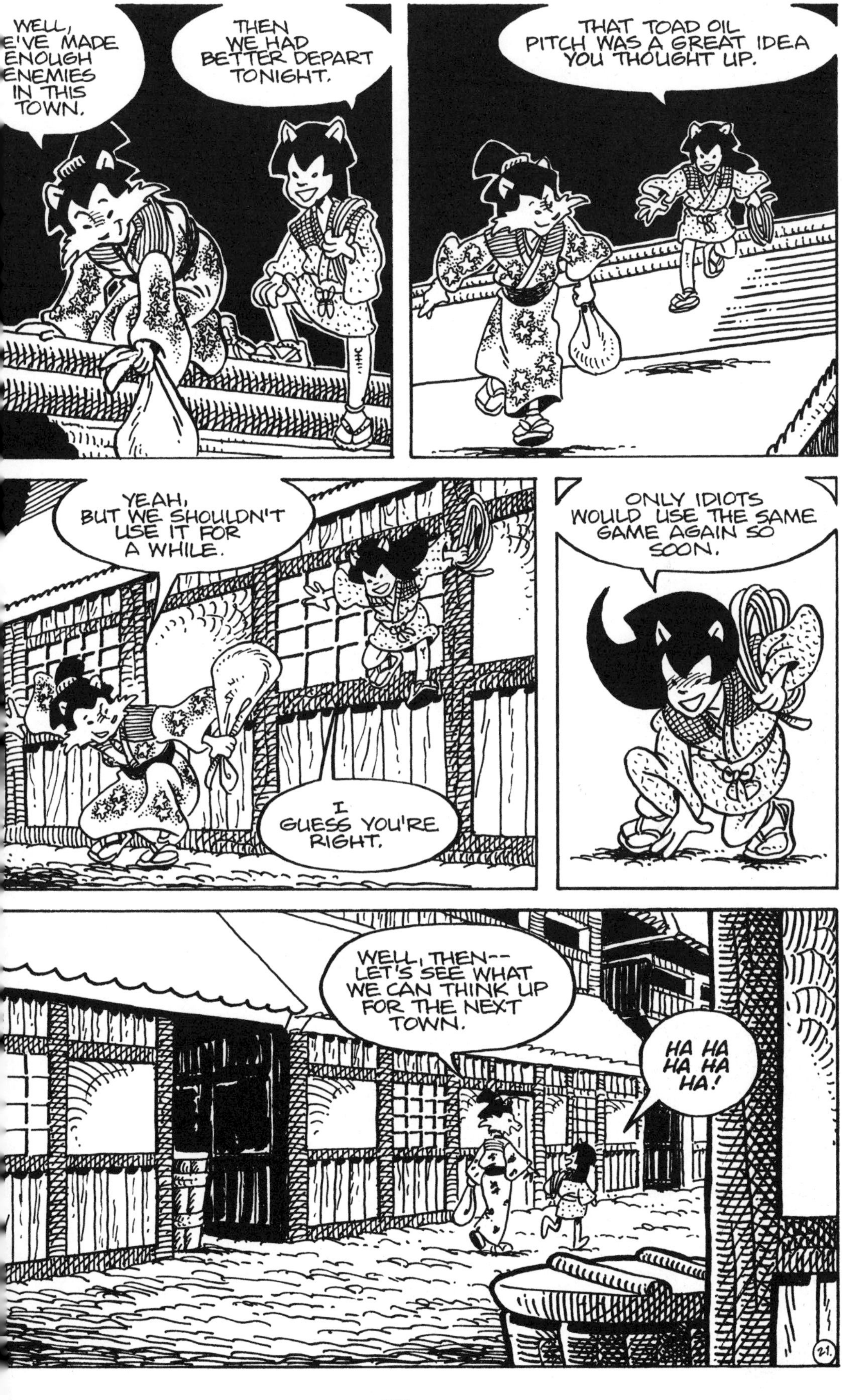
WELL, E'VE MADE ENOUGH ENEMIES IN THIS TOWN.
THEN WE HAD BETTER DEPART TONIGHT.
THAT TOAD OIL PITCH WAS A GREAT IDEA YOU THOUGHT UP.
YEAH, BUT WE SHOULDN'T USE IT FOR A WHILE.
I GUESS YOU'RE RIGHT.
ONLY IDIOTS WOULD USE THE SAME GAME AGAIN SO SOON.
WELL, THEN-- LET'S SEE WHAT WE CAN THINK UP FOR THE NEXT TOWN.
HA HA HA HA HA!
21.

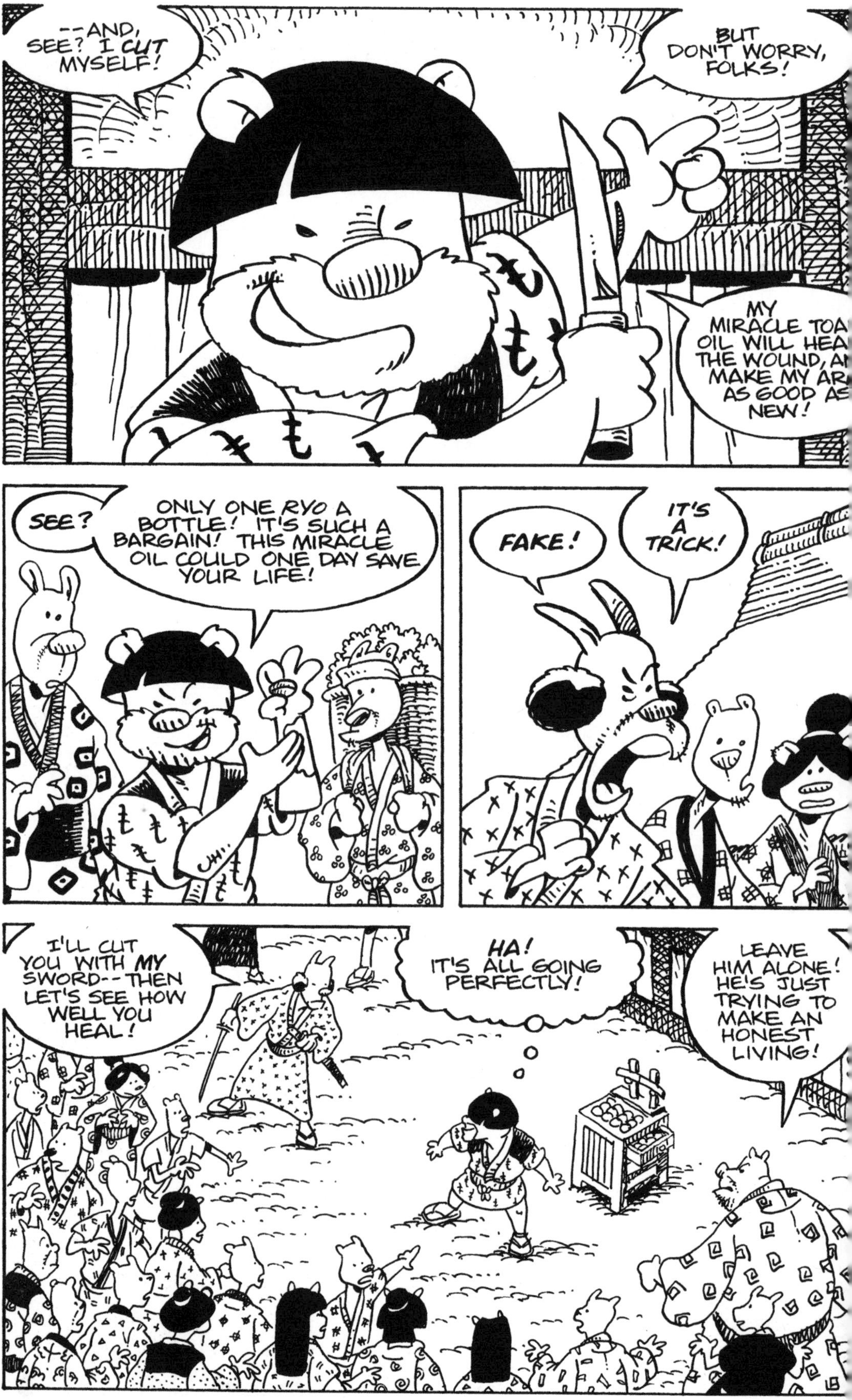
--AND, SEE? I CUT MYSELF!
BUT DON'T WORRY, FOLKS!
MY MIRACLE TOA OIL WILL HEA THE WOUND, AN MAKE MY AR AS GOOD AS NEW!
SEE?
ONLY ONE RYO A BOTTLE! IT'S SUCH A BARGAIN! THIS MIRACLE OIL COULD ONE DAY SAVE YOUR LIFE!
FAKE!
IT'S A TRICK!
I'LL CUT YOU WITH MY SWORD--THEN LET'S SEE HOW WELL YOU HEAL!
HA! IT'S ALL GOING PERFECTLY!
LEAVE HIM ALONE! HE'S JUST TRYING TO MAKE AN HONEST LIVING!

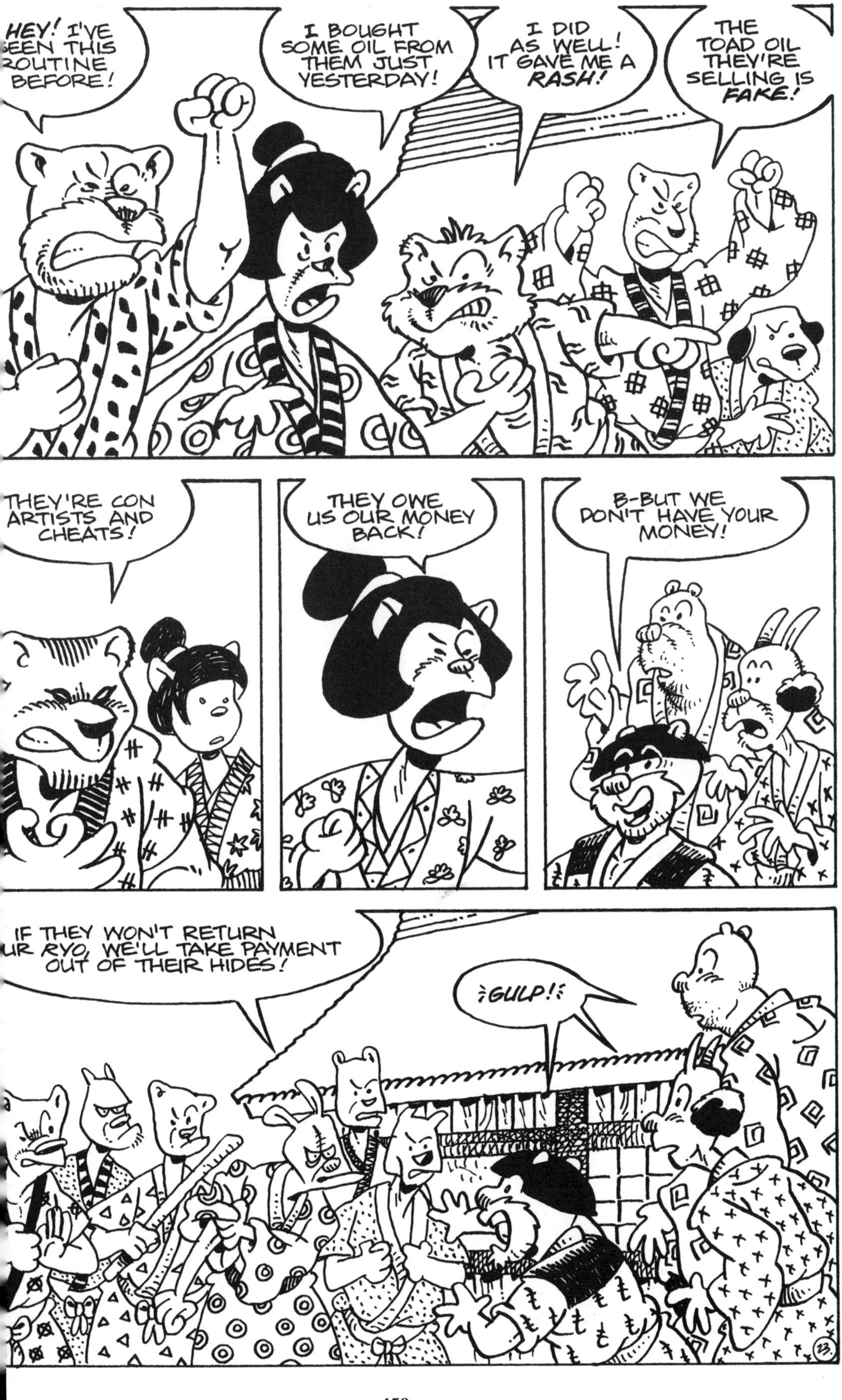
HEY! I'VE SEEN THIS ROUTINE BEFORE!
I BOUGHT SOME OIL FROM THEM JUST YESTERDAY!
I DID AS WELL! IT GAVE ME A RASH!
THE TOAD OIL THEY'RE SELLING IS FAKE!
THEY'RE CON ARTISTS AND CHEATS!
THEY OWE US OUR MONEY BACK!
B-BUT WE DON'T HAVE YOUR MONEY!
IF THEY WON'T RETURN UR RYO, WE'LL TAKE PAYMENT OUT OF THEIR HIDES!
GULP!
23.

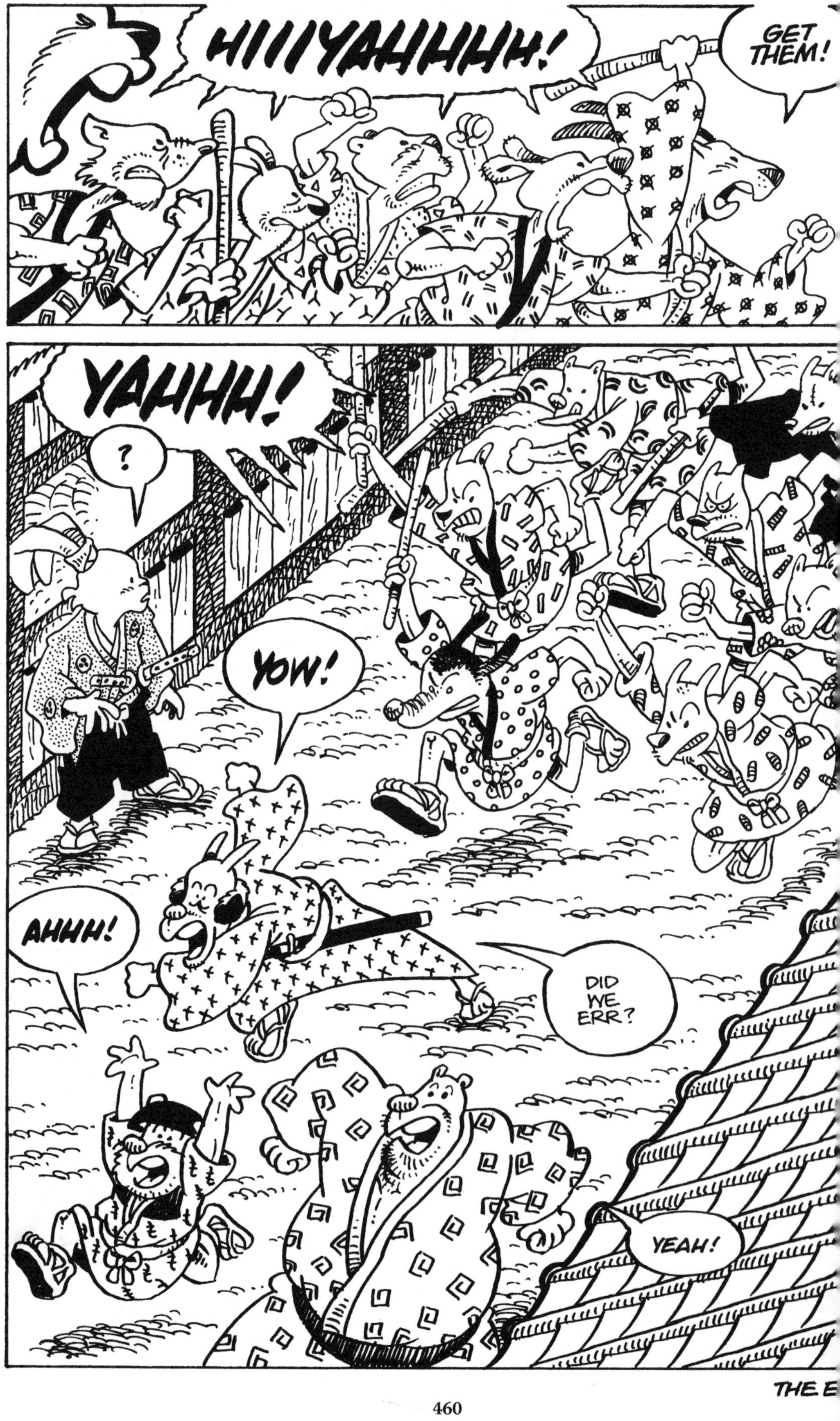
HIIIYAHHHH!
GET THEM!
YAHHH!
?
YOW!
AHHH!
DID WE ERR?
YEAH!
THE E

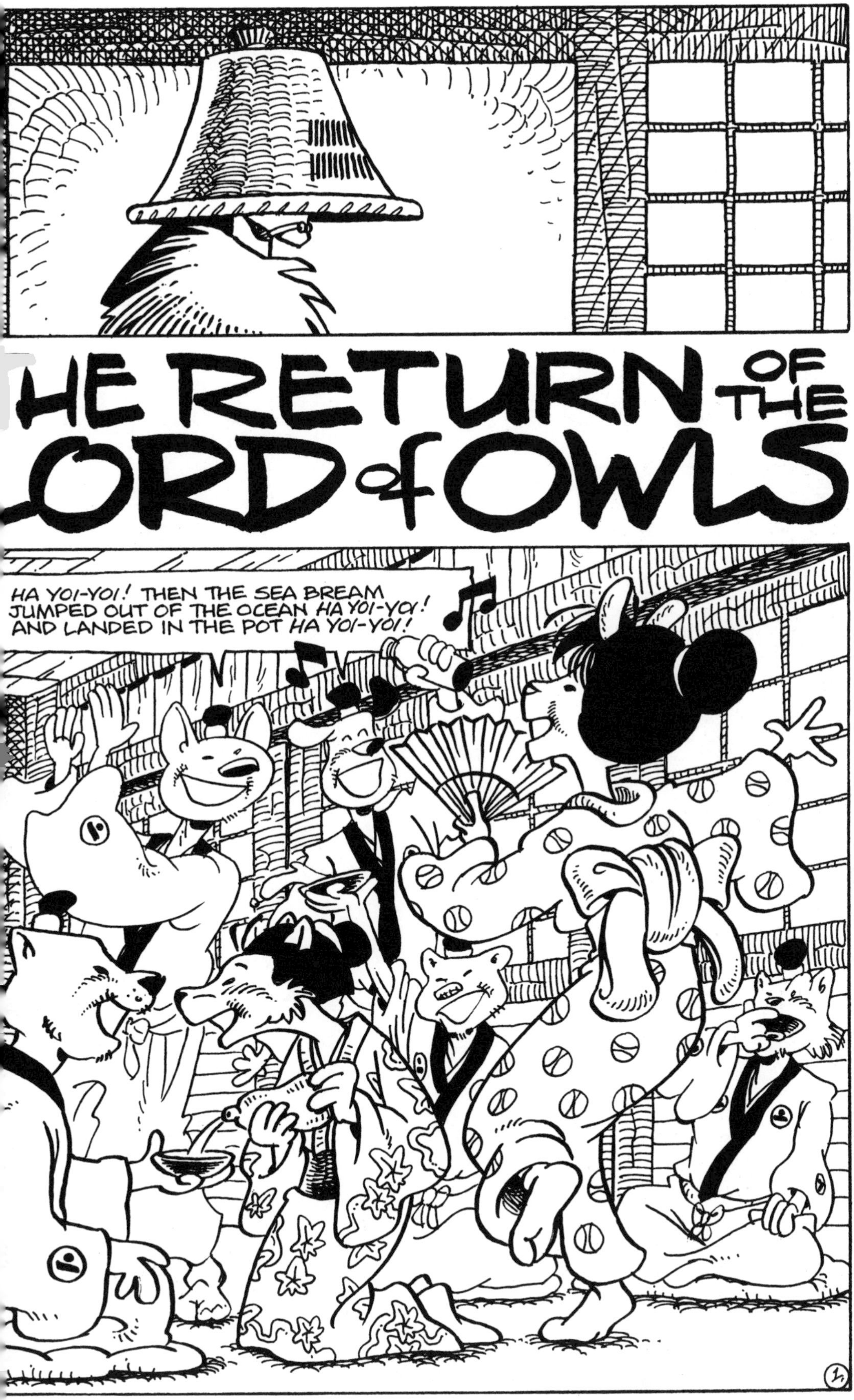
HE RETURN OF THE
ORD of OWLS
HA YOI-YOI! THEN THE SEA BREAM JUMPED OUT OF THE OCEAN HA YOI-YOI! AND LANDED IN THE POT HA YOI-YOI!

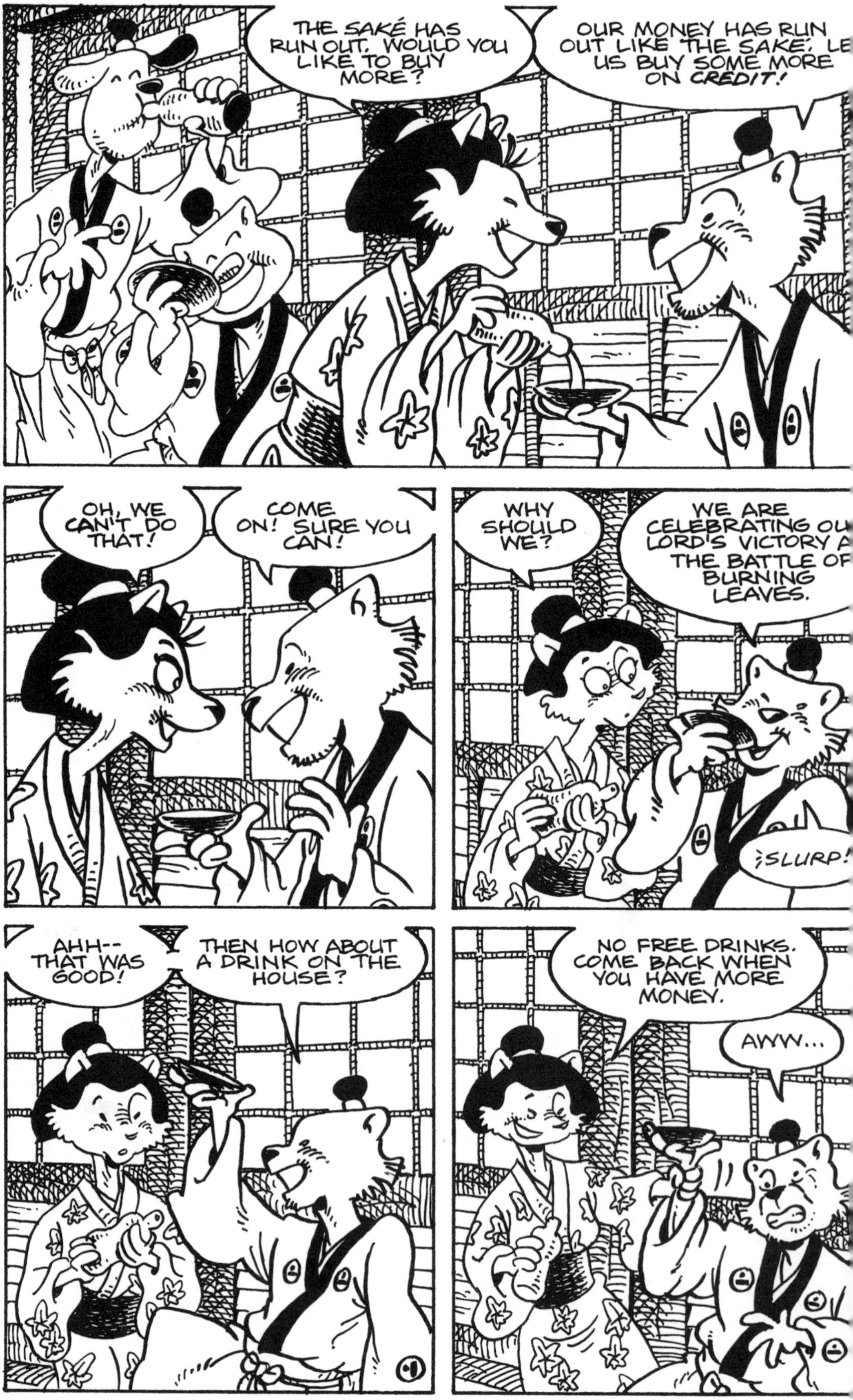
THE SAKÉ HAS RUN OUT. WOULD YOU LIKE TO BUY MORE?
OUR MONEY HAS RUN OUT LIKE THE SAKE! LE US BUY SOME MORE ON CREDIT!
OH, WE CAN'T DO THAT!
COME ON! SURE YOU CAN!
WHY SHOULD WE?
WE ARE CELEBRATING OU LORD'S VICTORY A THE BATTLE OF BURNING LEAVES.
SLURP!
AHH-- THAT WAS GOOD!
THEN HOW ABOUT A DRINK ON THE HOUSE?
NO FREE DRINKS. COME BACK WHEN YOU HAVE MORE MONEY.
AWW...

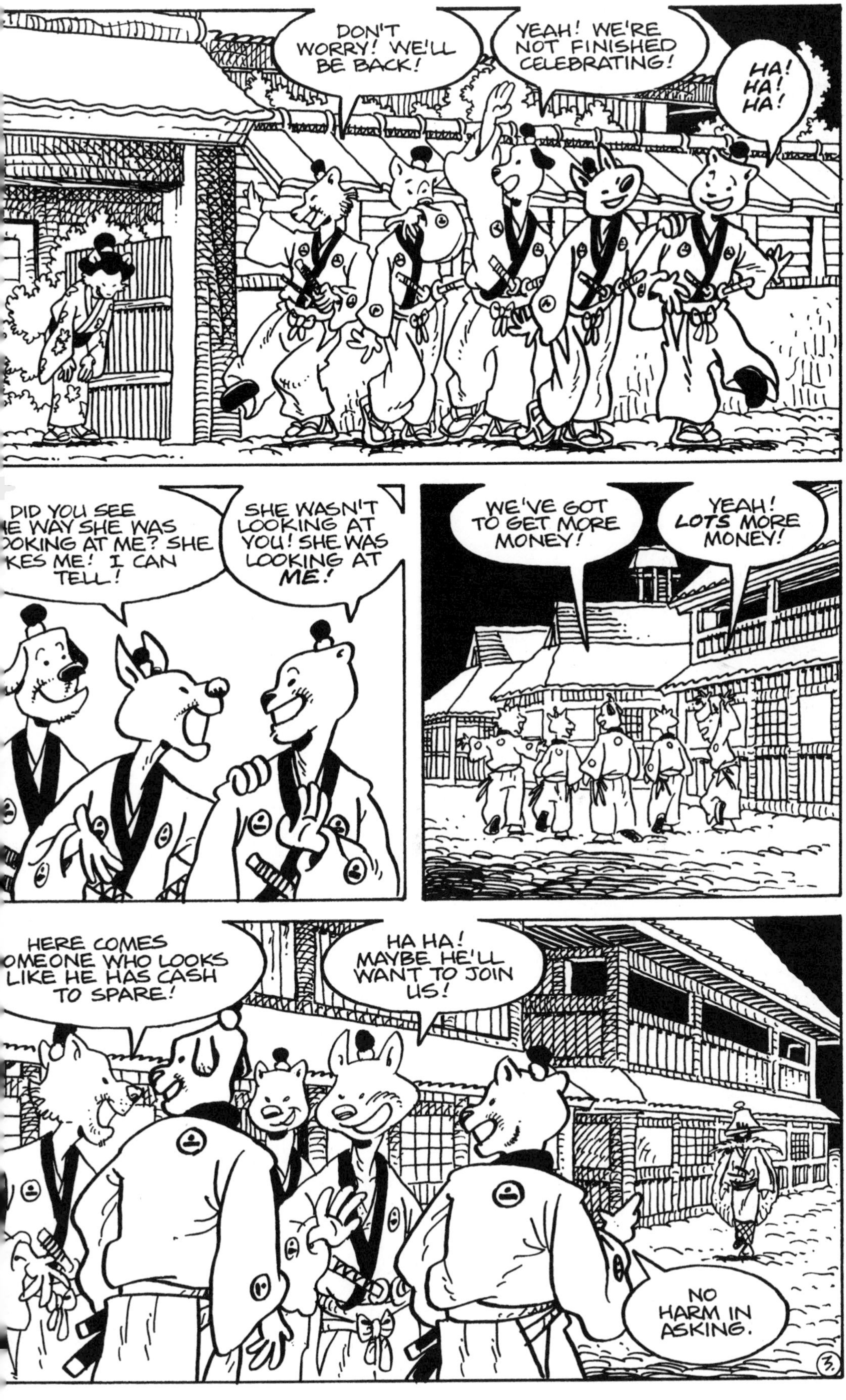
DON'T WORRY! WE'LL BE BACK!
YEAH! WE'RE NOT FINISHED CELEBRATING!
HA! HA! HA!
DID YOU SEE HE WAY SHE WAS OOKING AT ME? SHE KES ME! I CAN TELL!
SHE WASN'T LOOKING AT YOU! SHE WAS LOOKING AT ME!
WE'VE GOT TO GET MORE MONEY!
YEAH! LOTS MORE MONEY!
HERE COMES OMEONE WHO LOOKS LIKE HE HAS CASH TO SPARE!
HA HA! MAYBE HE'LL WANT TO JOIN US!
NO HARM IN ASKING.
3.

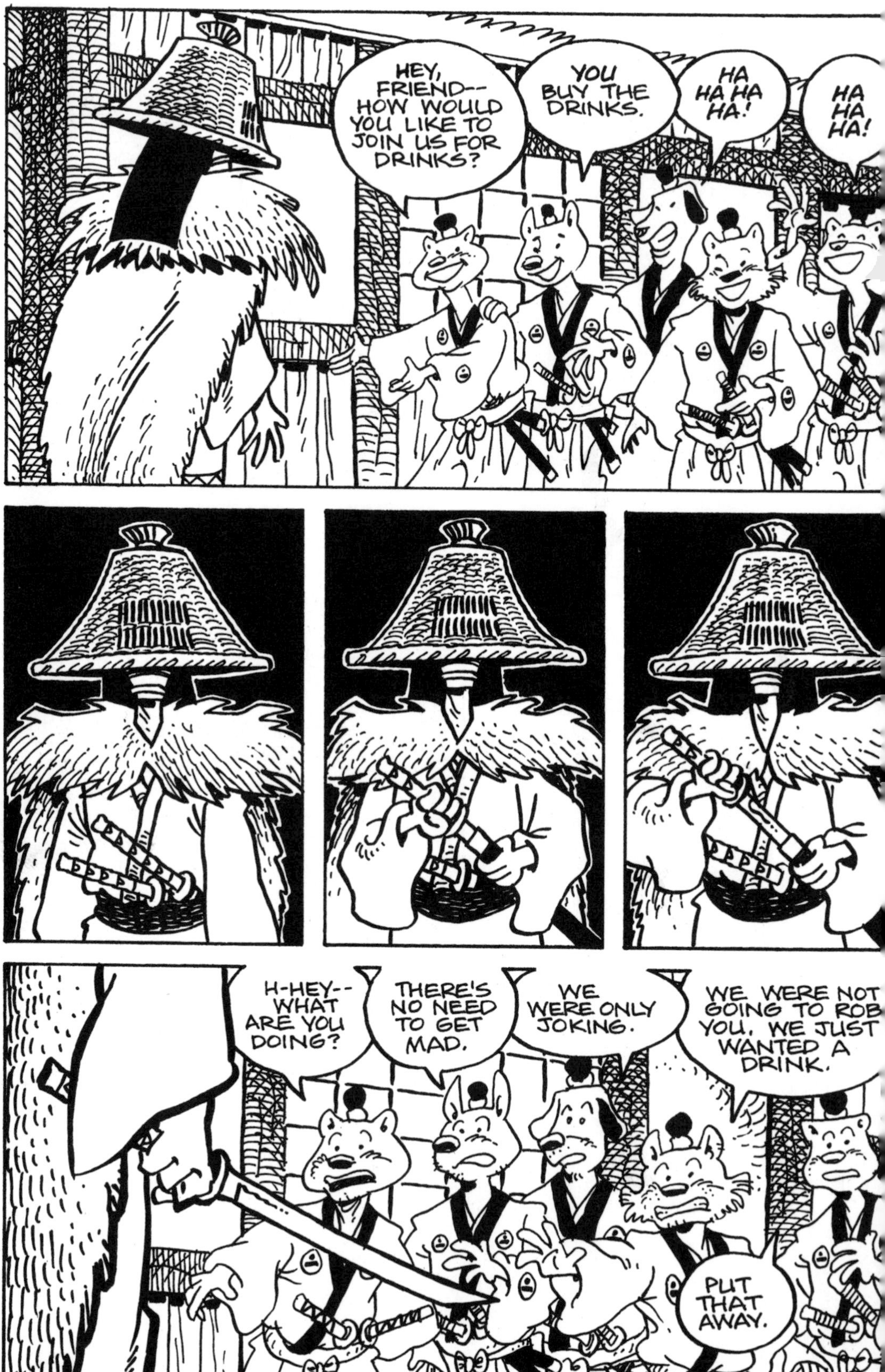
HEY, FRIEND-- HOW WOULD YOU LIKE TO JOIN US FOR DRINKS?
YOU BUY THE DRINKS.
HA HA HA HA!
HA HA HA!
H-HEY-- WHAT ARE YOU DOING?
THERE'S NO NEED TO GET MAD.
WE WERE ONLY JOKING.
WE WERE NOT GOING TO ROB YOU. WE JUST WANTED A DRINK.
PUT THAT AWAY.

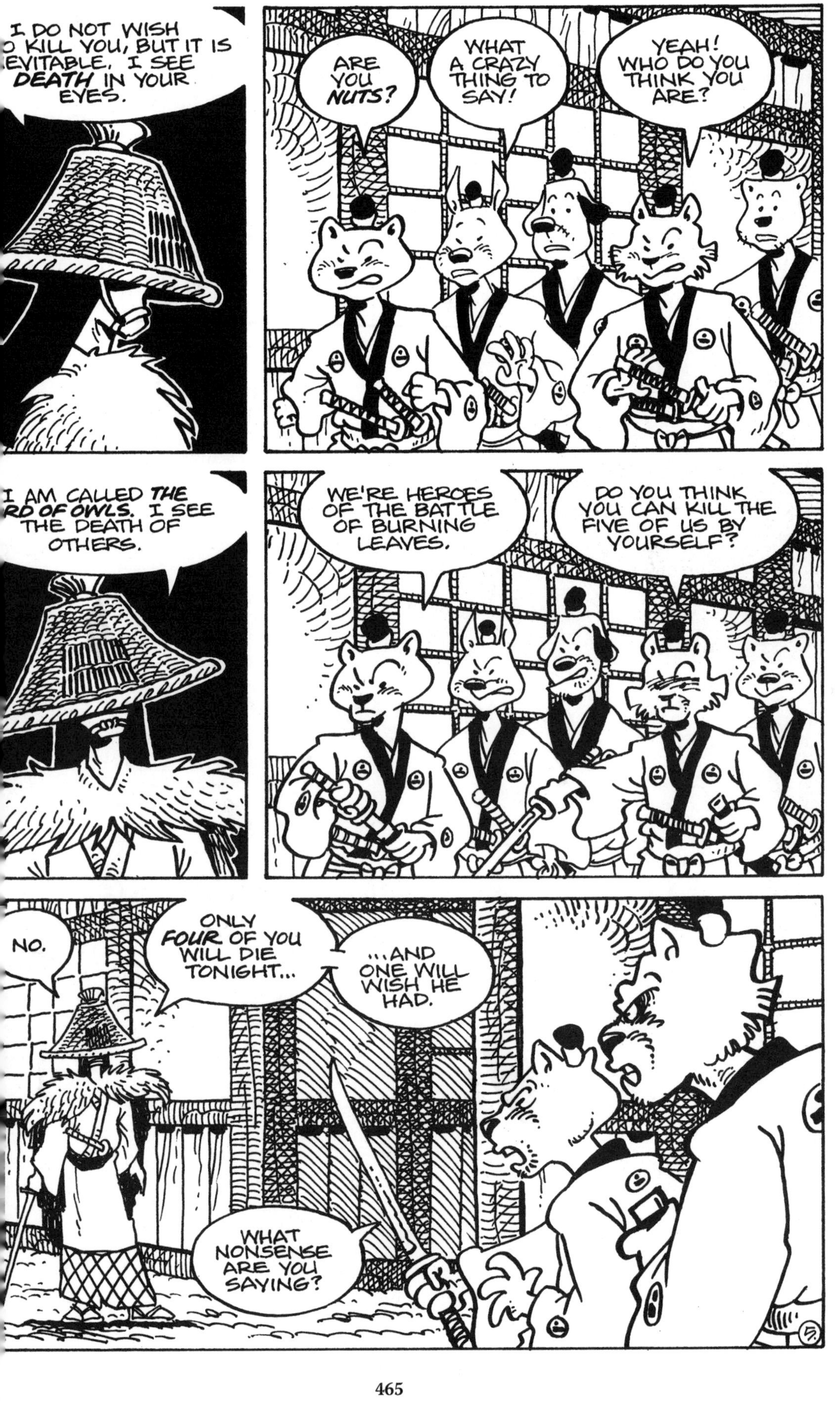
I DO NOT WISH O KILL YOU, BUT IT IS EVITABLE. I SEE *DEATH* IN YOUR EYES.
ARE YOU *NUTS*?
WHAT A CRAZY THING TO SAY!
YEAH! WHO DO YOU THINK YOU ARE?
I AM CALLED *THE RD OF OWLS*. I SEE THE DEATH OF OTHERS.
WE'RE HEROES OF THE BATTLE OF BURNING LEAVES.
DO YOU THINK YOU CAN KILL THE FIVE OF US BY YOURSELF?
NO.
ONLY *FOUR* OF YOU WILL DIE TONIGHT...
...AND ONE WILL WISH HE HAD.
WHAT NONSENSE ARE YOU SAYING?
5.

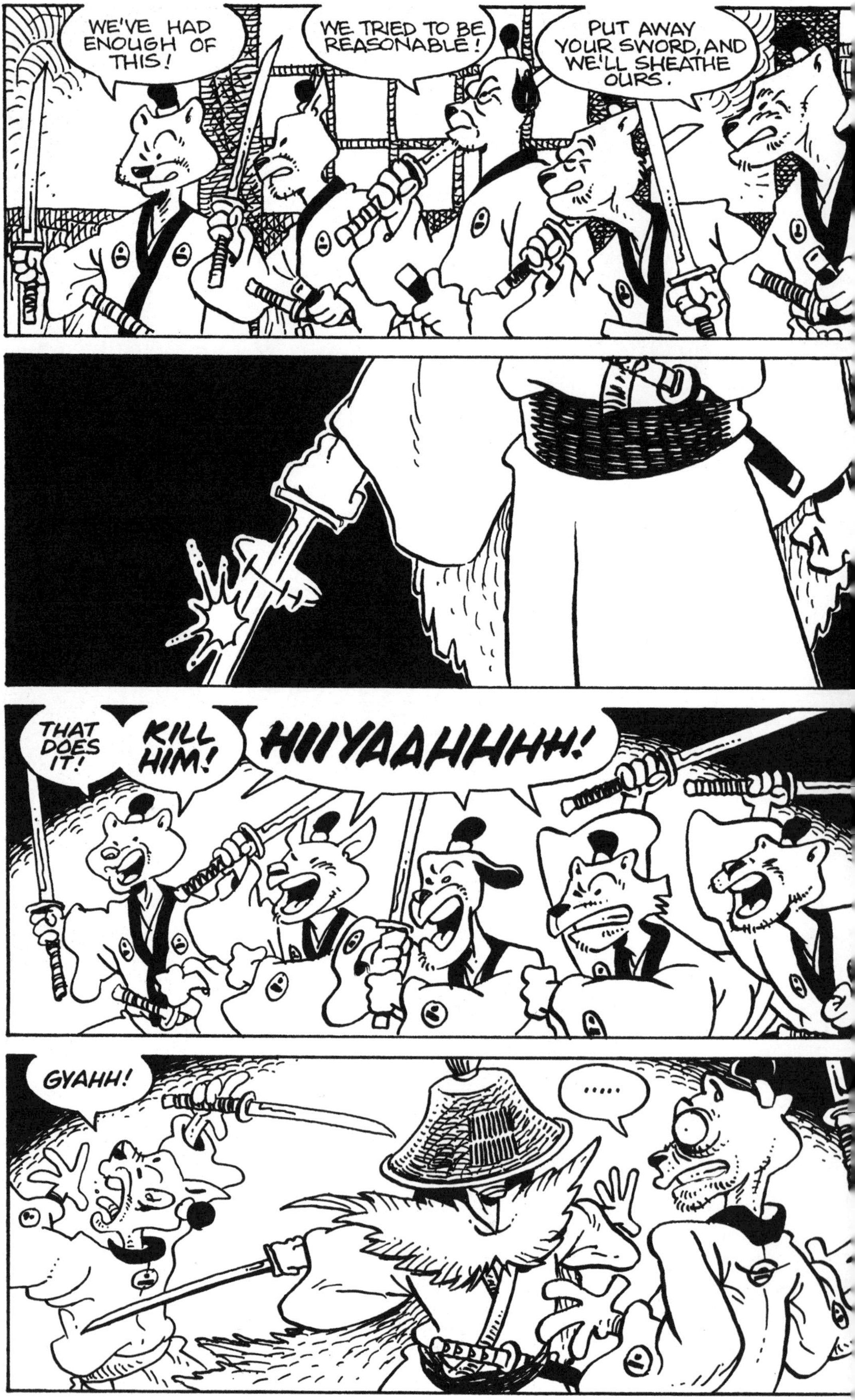
WE'VE HAD ENOUGH OF THIS!
WE TRIED TO BE REASONABLE!
PUT AWAY YOUR SWORD, AND WE'LL SHEATHE OURS.
THAT DOES IT!
KILL HIM!
HIIYAAHHHH!
GYAHH!
.....

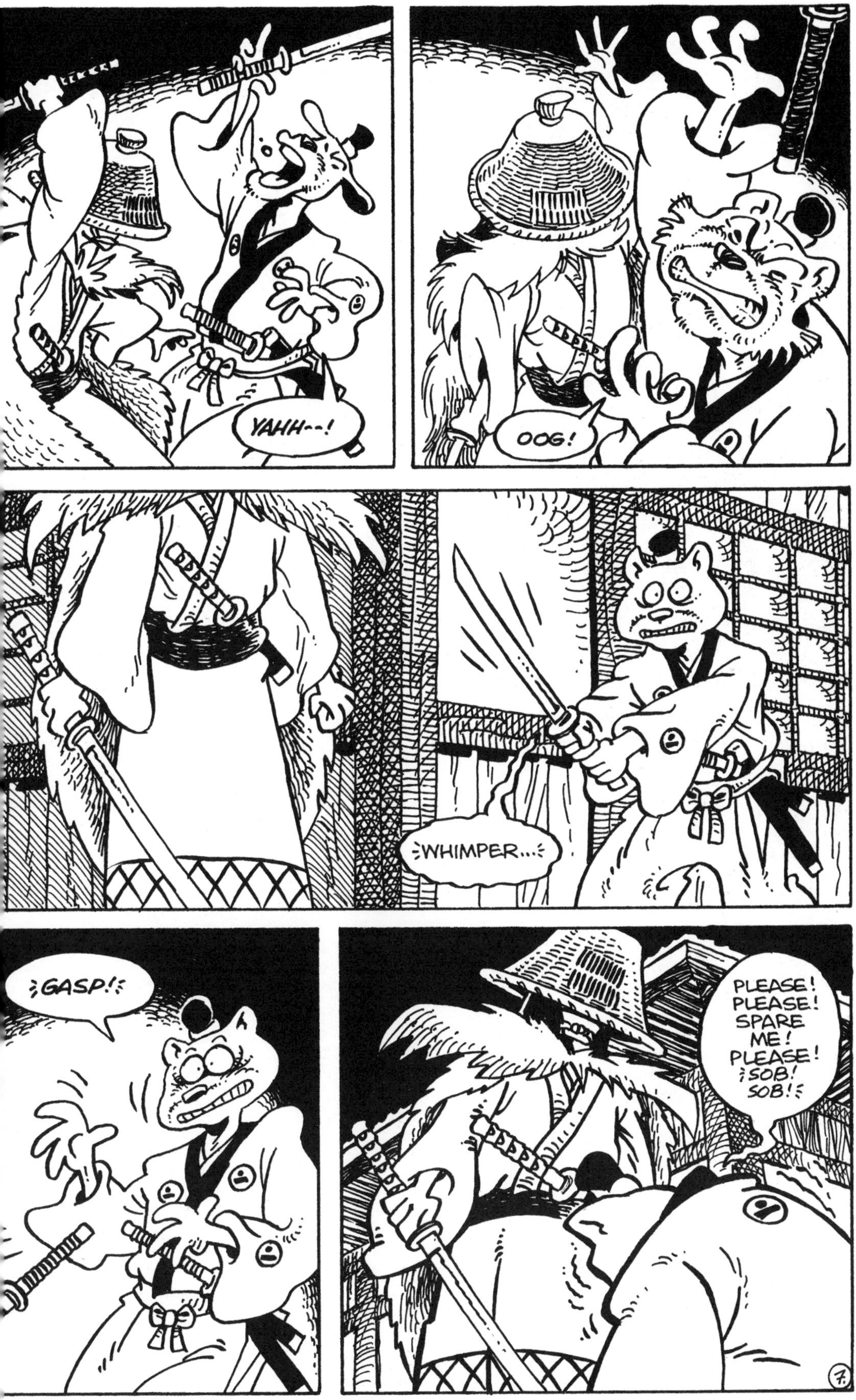
YAHH--!
OOG!
WHIMPER...
GASP!
PLEASE! PLEASE! SPARE ME! PLEASE! SOB! SOB!
7.

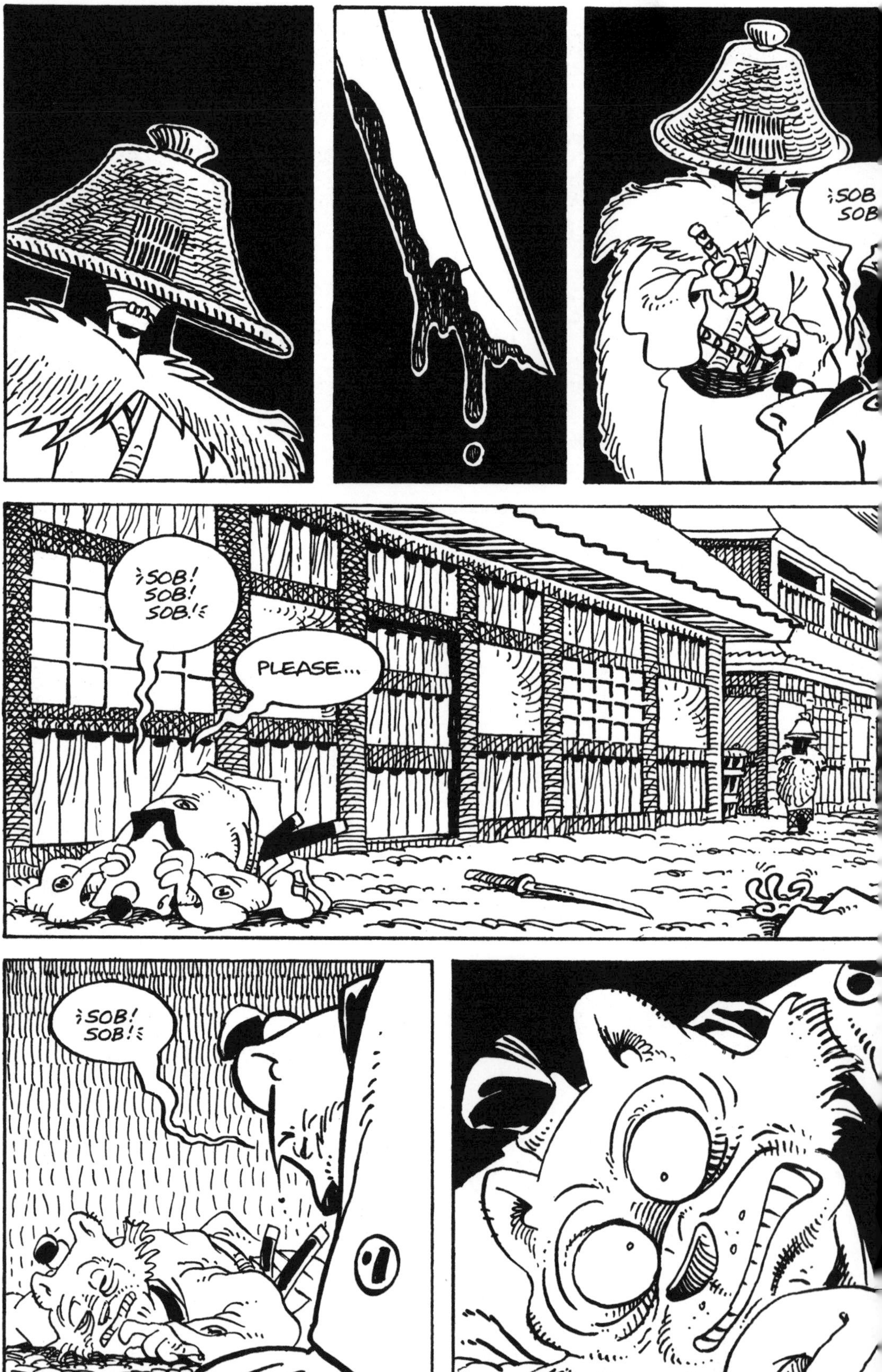
SOB
SOB
SOB! SOB! SOB!
PLEASE...
SOB! SOB!

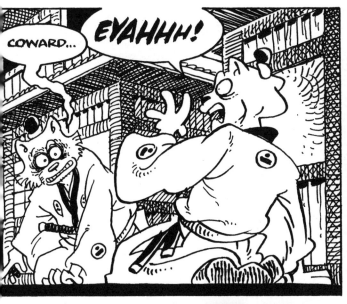

COWARD...

EYAHHH!

YOU WATCHED US--YOUR COMRADES--DIE, BUT YOU DID NOTHING TO HELP US...TO *AVENGE* US!

WORSE-- YOU THREW AWAY YOUR SWORD-- THE SYMBOL OF THE *SAMURAI*--YOU ARE A *DISGRACE!* I *CURSE YOU!*

I CURSE YOU!

CURSE YOU!

.....

CURSE YOU!

YAHHHH!

PLOP!

...AND THEY SAY HE RUNS STILL.

⑨

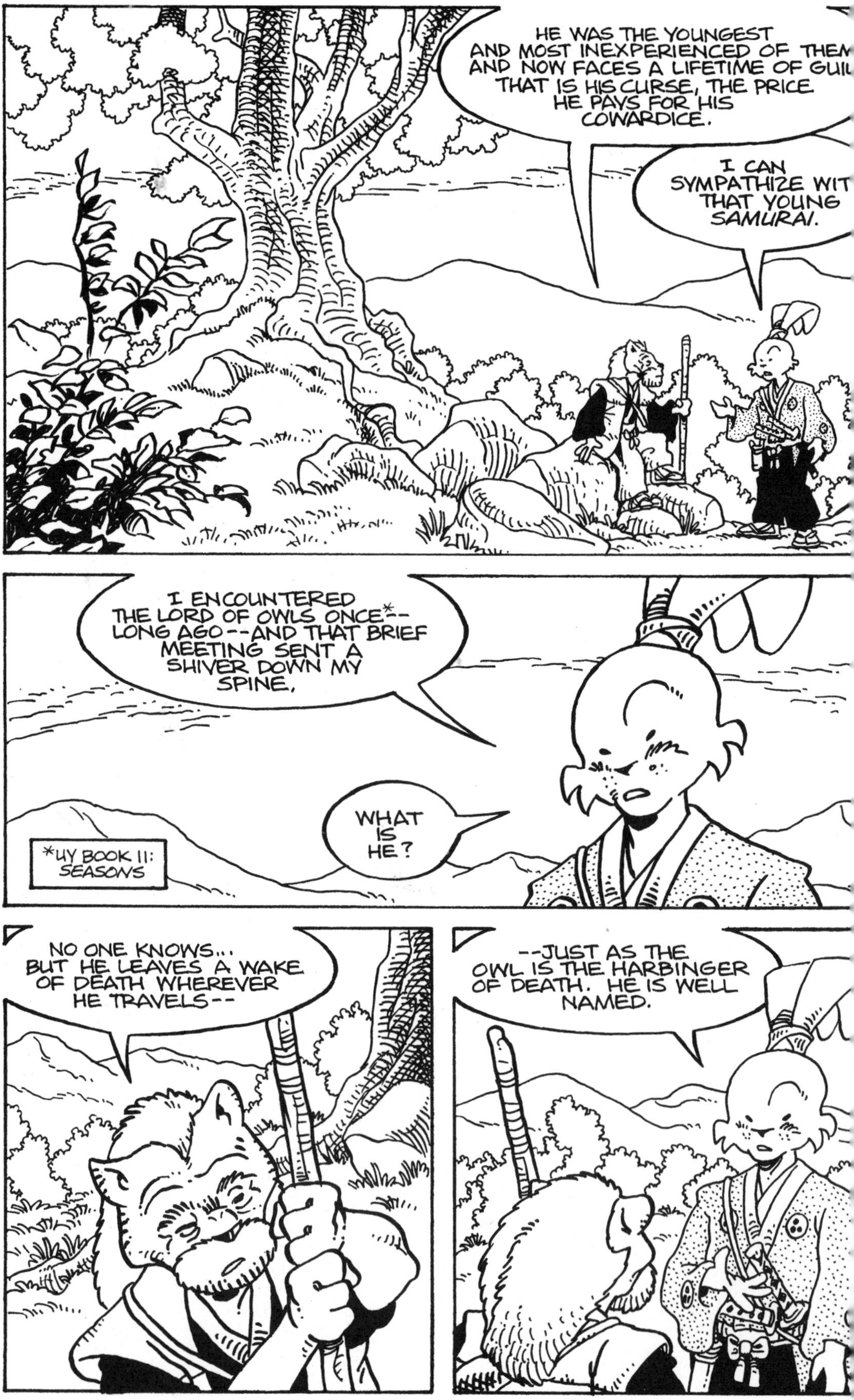
HE WAS THE YOUNGEST AND MOST INEXPERIENCED OF THEM AND NOW FACES A LIFETIME OF GUIL THAT IS HIS CURSE, THE PRICE HE PAYS FOR HIS COWARDICE.
I CAN SYMPATHIZE WIT THAT YOUNG SAMURAI.
I ENCOUNTERED THE LORD OF OWLS ONCE*-- LONG AGO--AND THAT BRIEF MEETING SENT A SHIVER DOWN MY SPINE.
*UY BOOK 11: SEASONS
WHAT IS HE?
NO ONE KNOWS... BUT HE LEAVES A WAKE OF DEATH WHEREVER HE TRAVELS--
--JUST AS THE OWL IS THE HARBINGER OF DEATH. HE IS WELL NAMED.

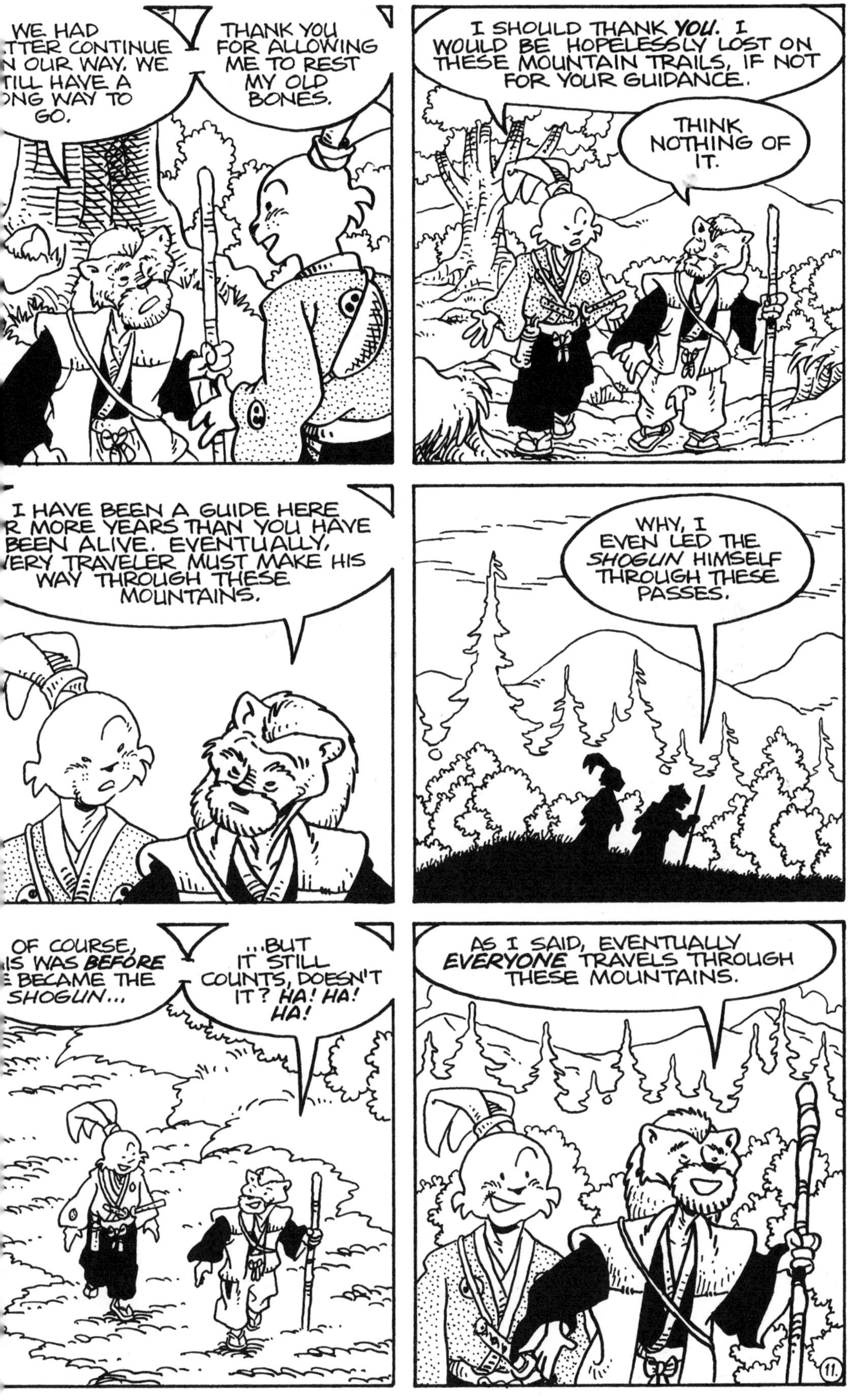
WE HAD
TTER CONTINUE
N OUR WAY. WE
TILL HAVE A
ONG WAY TO
GO.
THANK YOU
FOR ALLOWING
ME TO REST
MY OLD
BONES.
I SHOULD THANK *YOU*. I WOULD BE HOPELESSLY LOST ON THESE MOUNTAIN TRAILS, IF NOT FOR YOUR GUIDANCE.
THINK NOTHING OF IT.
I HAVE BEEN A GUIDE HERE
R MORE YEARS THAN YOU HAVE
BEEN ALIVE. EVENTUALLY,
/ERY TRAVELER MUST MAKE HIS
WAY THROUGH THESE
MOUNTAINS.
WHY, I EVEN LED THE *SHOGUN* HIMSELF THROUGH THESE PASSES.
OF COURSE,
IS WAS *BEFORE*
BECAME THE
*SHOGUN*...
...BUT IT STILL COUNTS, DOESN'T IT? *HA! HA! HA!*
AS I SAID, EVENTUALLY *EVERYONE* TRAVELS THROUGH THESE MOUNTAINS.
11.

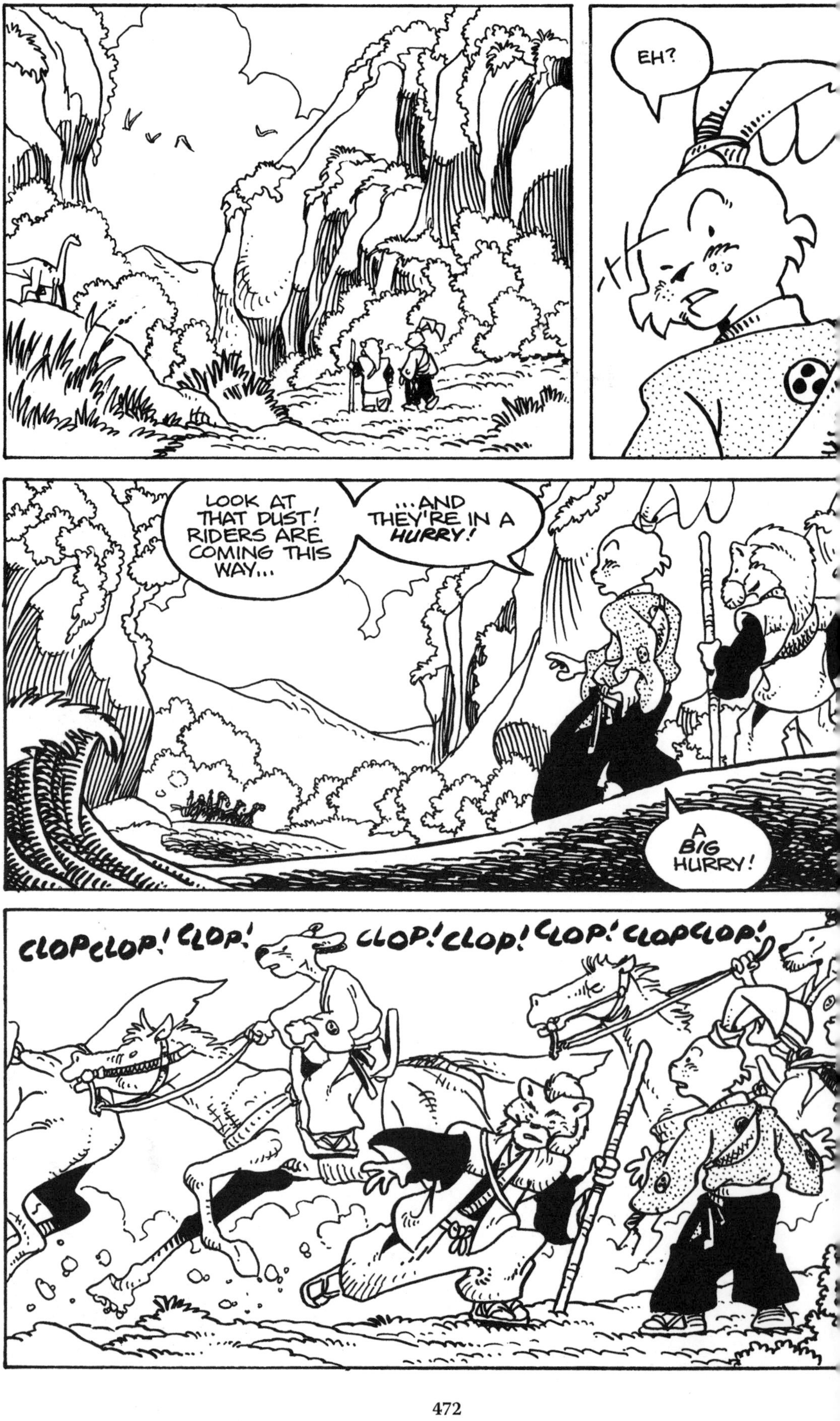
EH?
LOOK AT THAT DUST! RIDERS ARE COMING THIS WAY...
...AND THEY'RE IN A *HURRY!*
A *BIG* HURRY!
CLOPCLOP! CLOP! CLOP! CLOP! CLOP! CLOPCLOP!

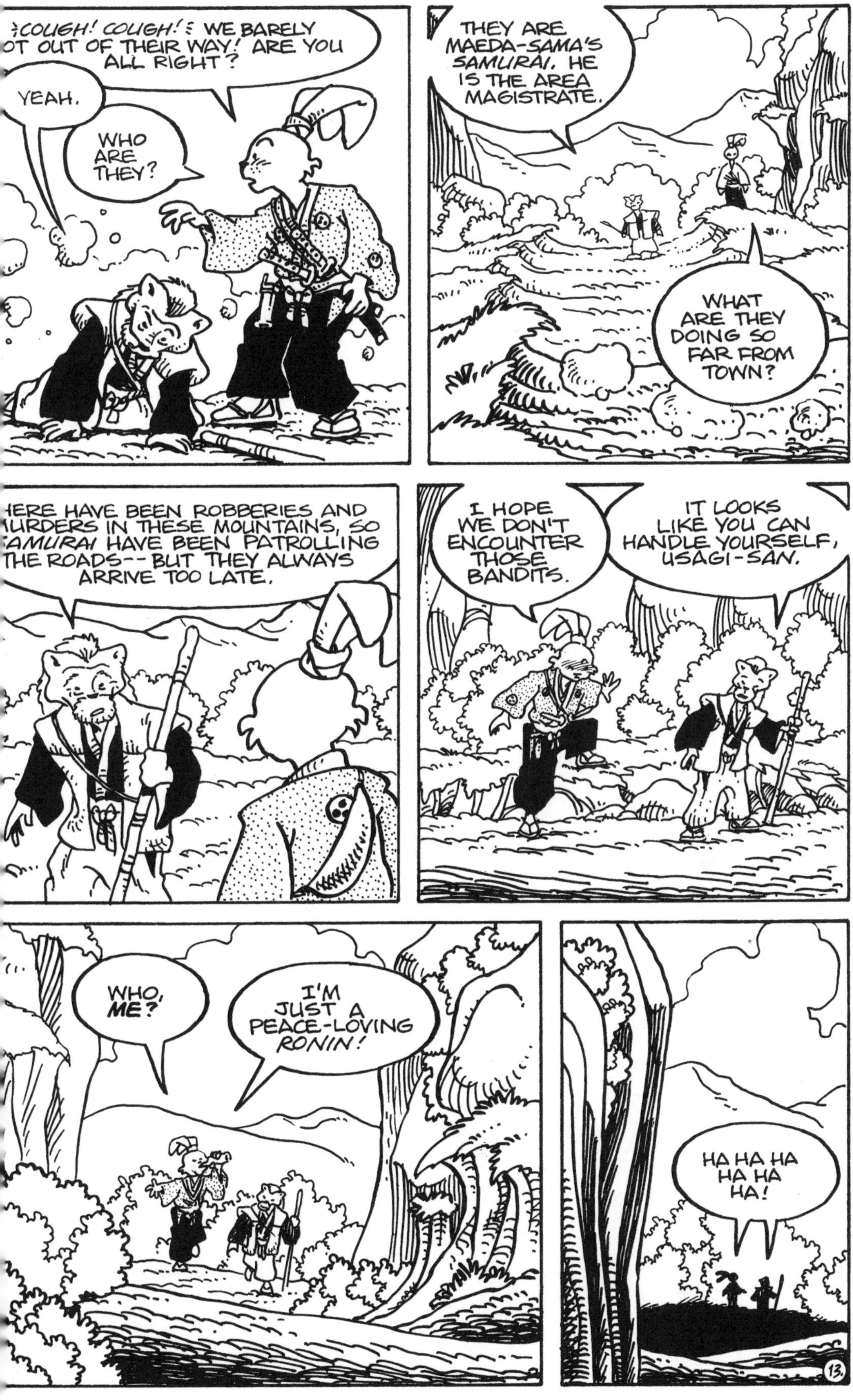
:COUGH! COUGH!: WE BARELY OT OUT OF THEIR WAY! ARE YOU ALL RIGHT?
YEAH.
WHO ARE THEY?
THEY ARE MAEDA-SAMA'S SAMURAI. HE IS THE AREA MAGISTRATE.
WHAT ARE THEY DOING SO FAR FROM TOWN?
HERE HAVE BEEN ROBBERIES AND IURDERS IN THESE MOUNTAINS, SO SAMURAI HAVE BEEN PATROLLING THE ROADS--BUT THEY ALWAYS ARRIVE TOO LATE.
I HOPE WE DON'T ENCOUNTER THOSE BANDITS.
IT LOOKS LIKE YOU CAN HANDLE YOURSELF, USAGI-SAN.
WHO, ME?
I'M JUST A PEACE-LOVING RONIN!
HA HA HA HA HA HA!
13.

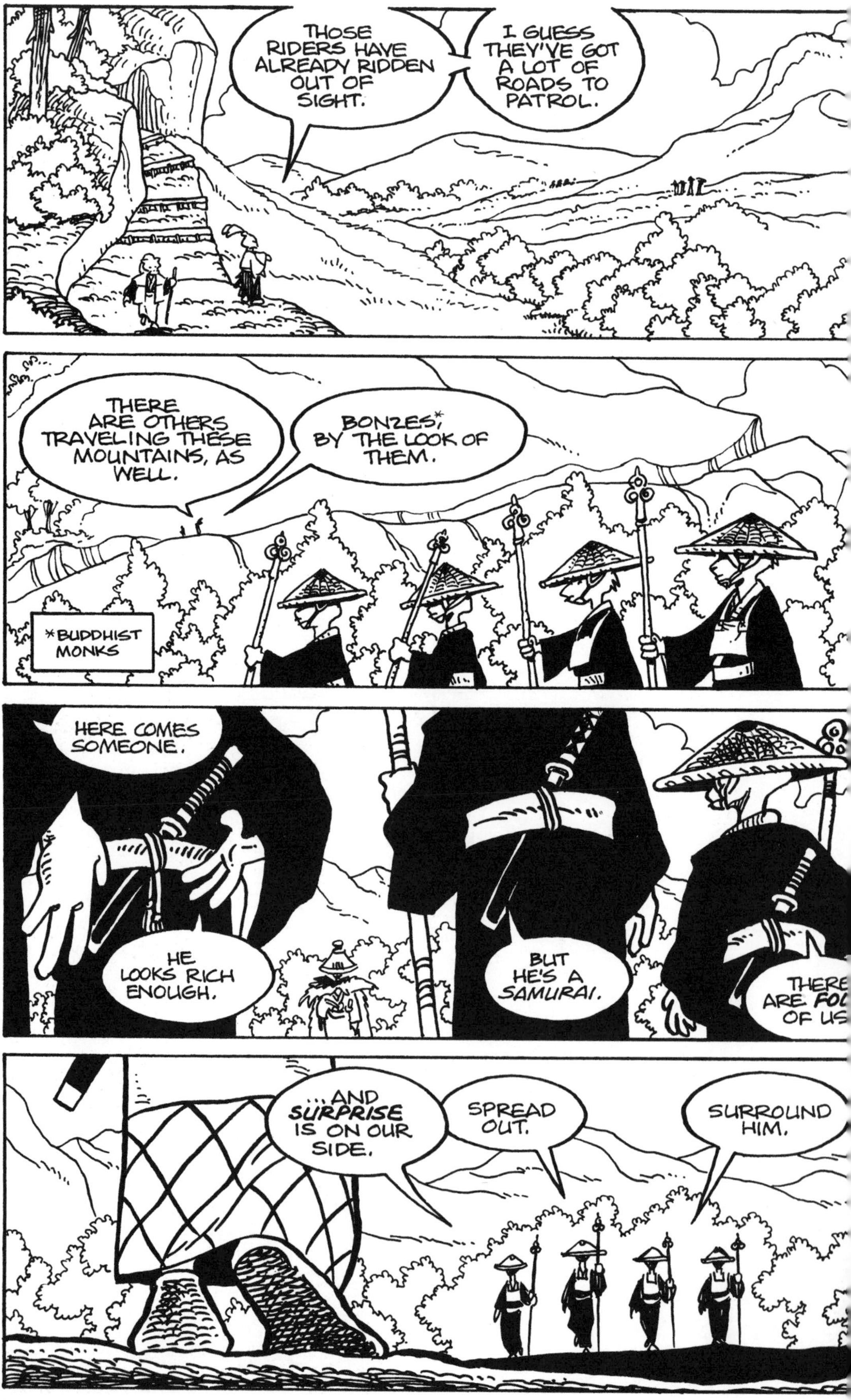
THOSE RIDERS HAVE ALREADY RIDDEN OUT OF SIGHT.
I GUESS THEY'VE GOT A LOT OF ROADS TO PATROL.
THERE ARE OTHERS TRAVELING THESE MOUNTAINS, AS WELL.
BONZES,* BY THE LOOK OF THEM.
*BUDDHIST MONKS
HERE COMES SOMEONE.
HE LOOKS RICH ENOUGH.
BUT HE'S A SAMURAI.
...AND SURPRISE IS ON OUR SIDE.
SPREAD OUT.
SURROUND HIM.

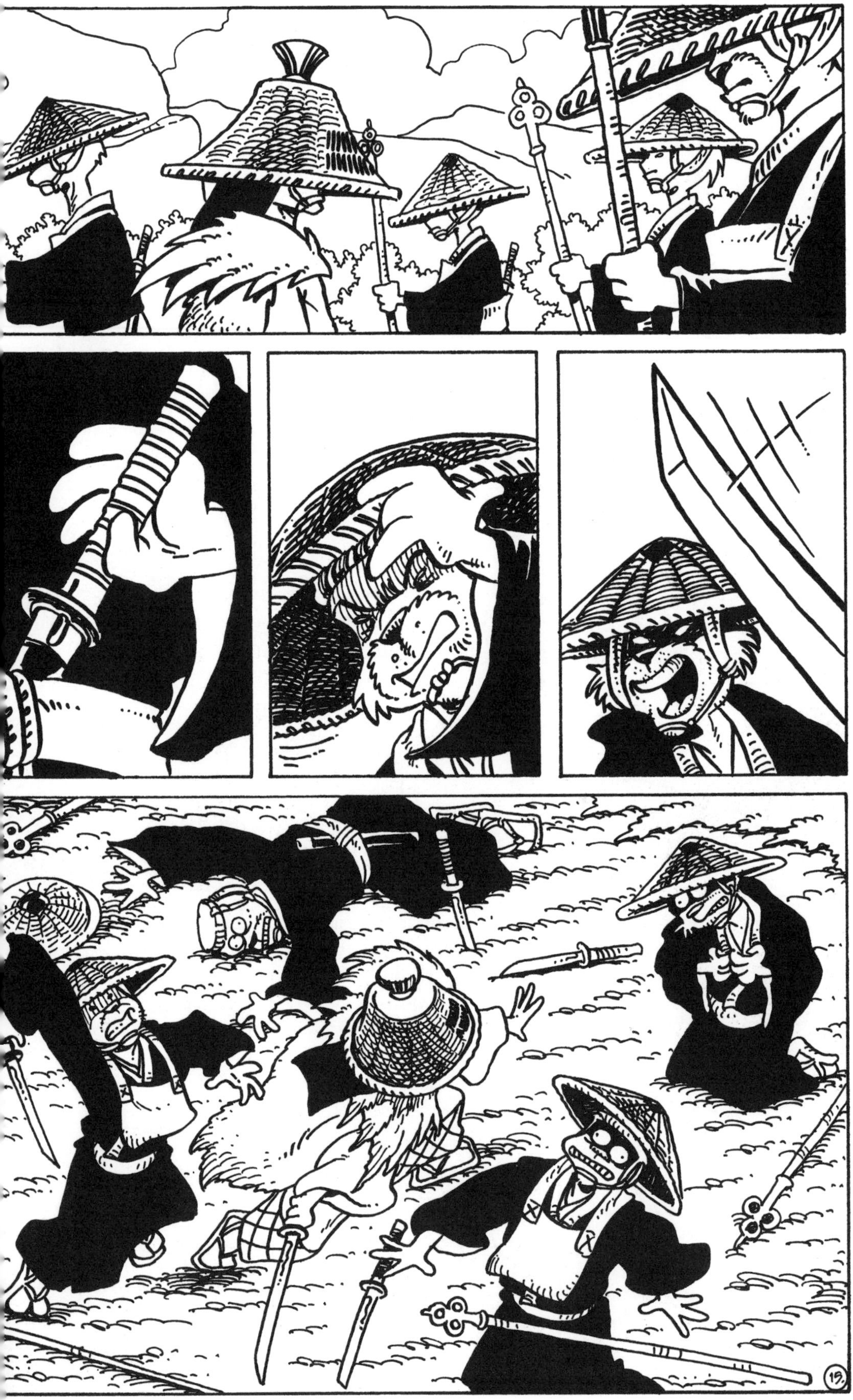
15

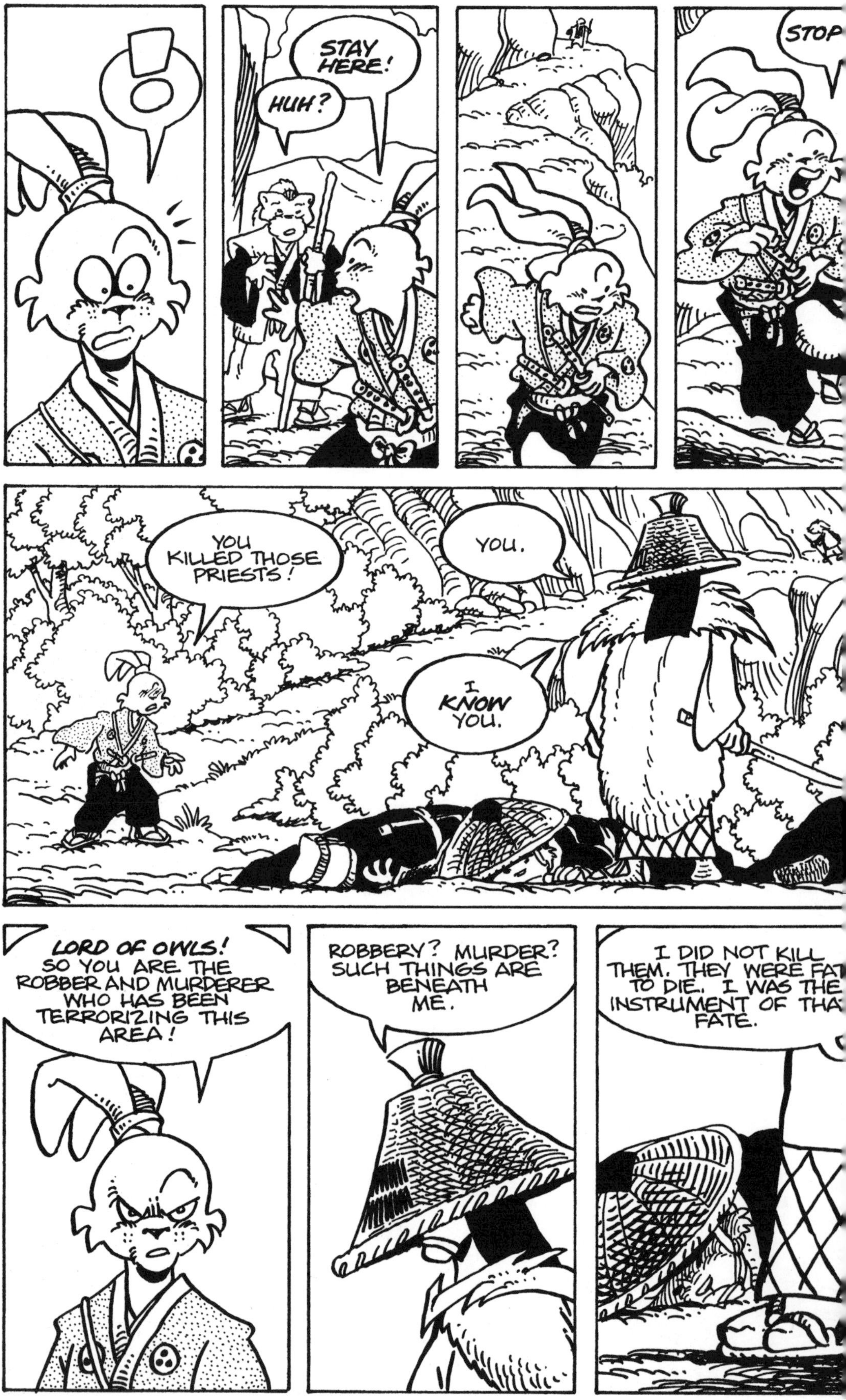
!
HUH?
STAY HERE!
STOP
YOU KILLED THOSE PRIESTS!
YOU.
I KNOW YOU.
LORD OF OWLS! SO YOU ARE THE ROBBER AND MURDERER WHO HAS BEEN TERRORIZING THIS AREA!
ROBBERY? MURDER? SUCH THINGS ARE BENEATH ME.
I DID NOT KILL THEM. THEY WERE FAT TO DIE. I WAS THE INSTRUMENT OF THA FATE.

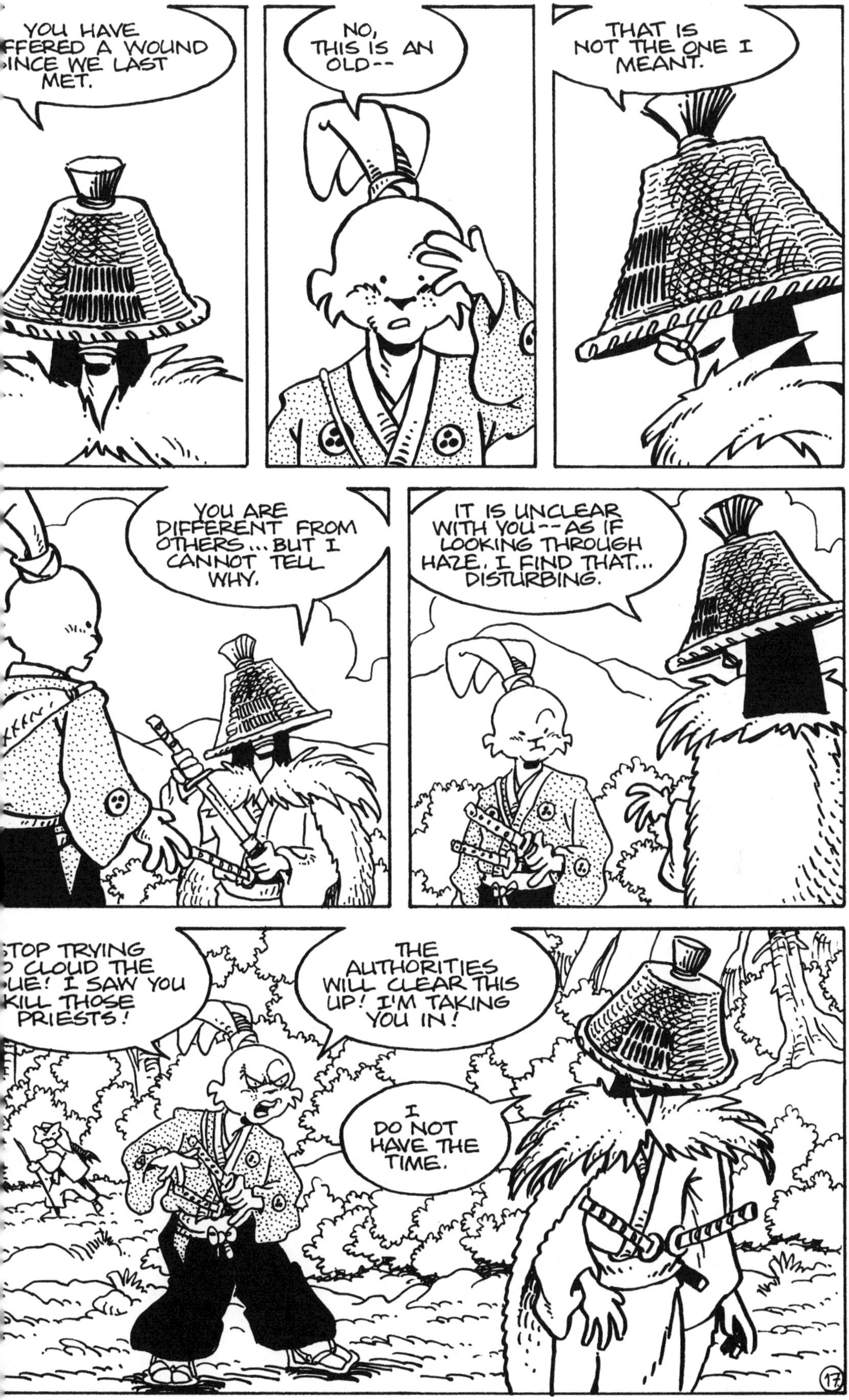
YOU HAVE
FFERED A WOUND
INCE WE LAST
MET.
NO,
THIS IS AN
OLD--
THAT IS
NOT THE ONE I
MEANT.
YOU ARE
DIFFERENT FROM
OTHERS... BUT I
CANNOT TELL
WHY.
IT IS UNCLEAR
WITH YOU--AS IF
LOOKING THROUGH
HAZE. I FIND THAT...
DISTURBING.
STOP TRYING
CLOUD THE
UE! I SAW YOU
KILL THOSE
PRIESTS!
THE
AUTHORITIES
WILL CLEAR THIS
UP! I'M TAKING
YOU IN!
I
DO NOT
HAVE THE
TIME.
17

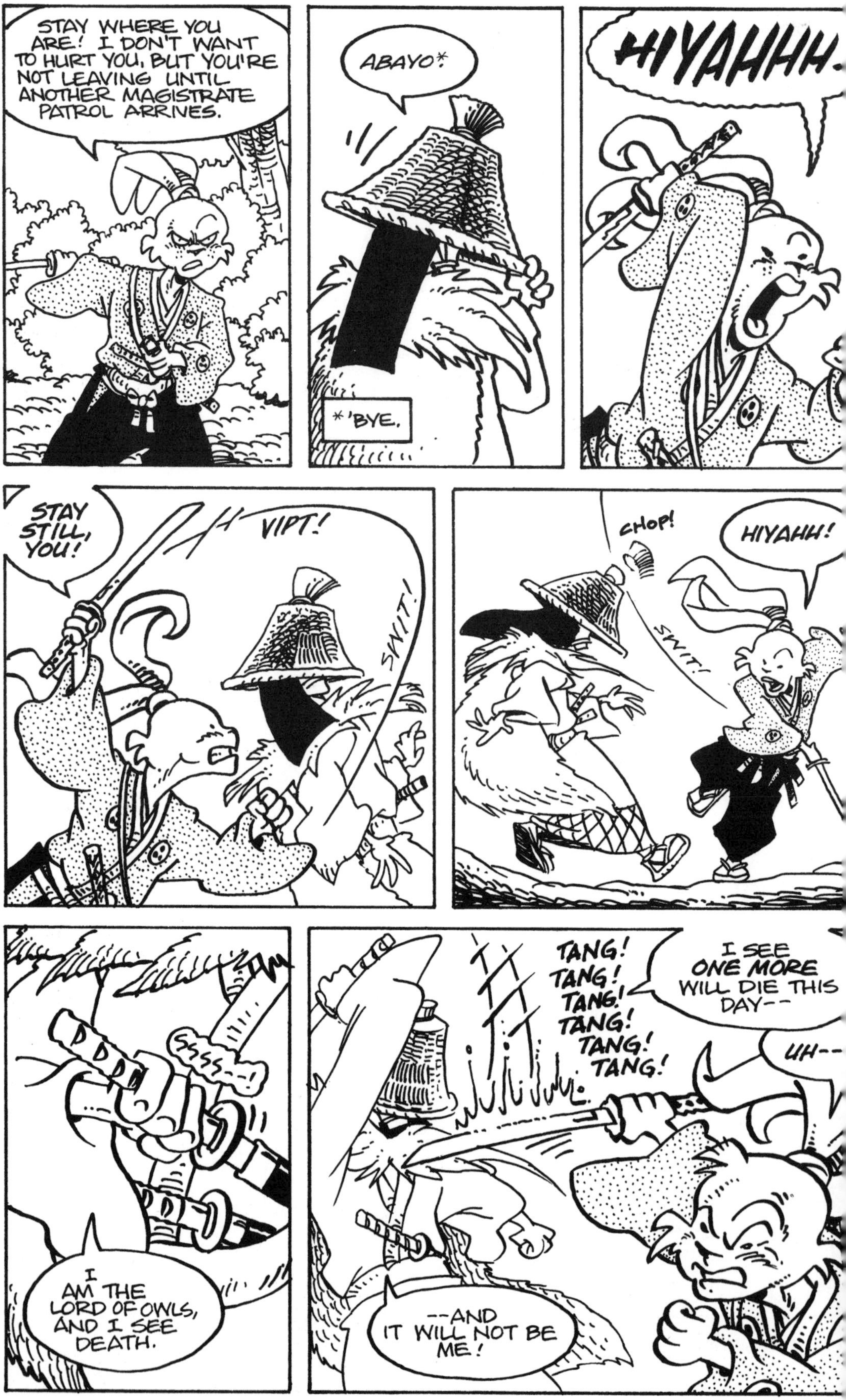
STAY WHERE YOU ARE! I DON'T WANT TO HURT YOU, BUT YOU'RE NOT LEAVING UNTIL ANOTHER MAGISTRATE PATROL ARRIVES.
ABAYO*
*'BYE.
HIYAHHH-
STAY STILL, YOU!
VIPT!
SWIT!
CHOP!
HIYAHH!
SWIT!
SSSS--!
I AM THE LORD OF OWLS, AND I SEE DEATH.
TANG! TANG! TANG! TANG! TANG! TANG!
I SEE ONE MORE WILL DIE THIS DAY--
UH--
--AND IT WILL NOT BE ME!

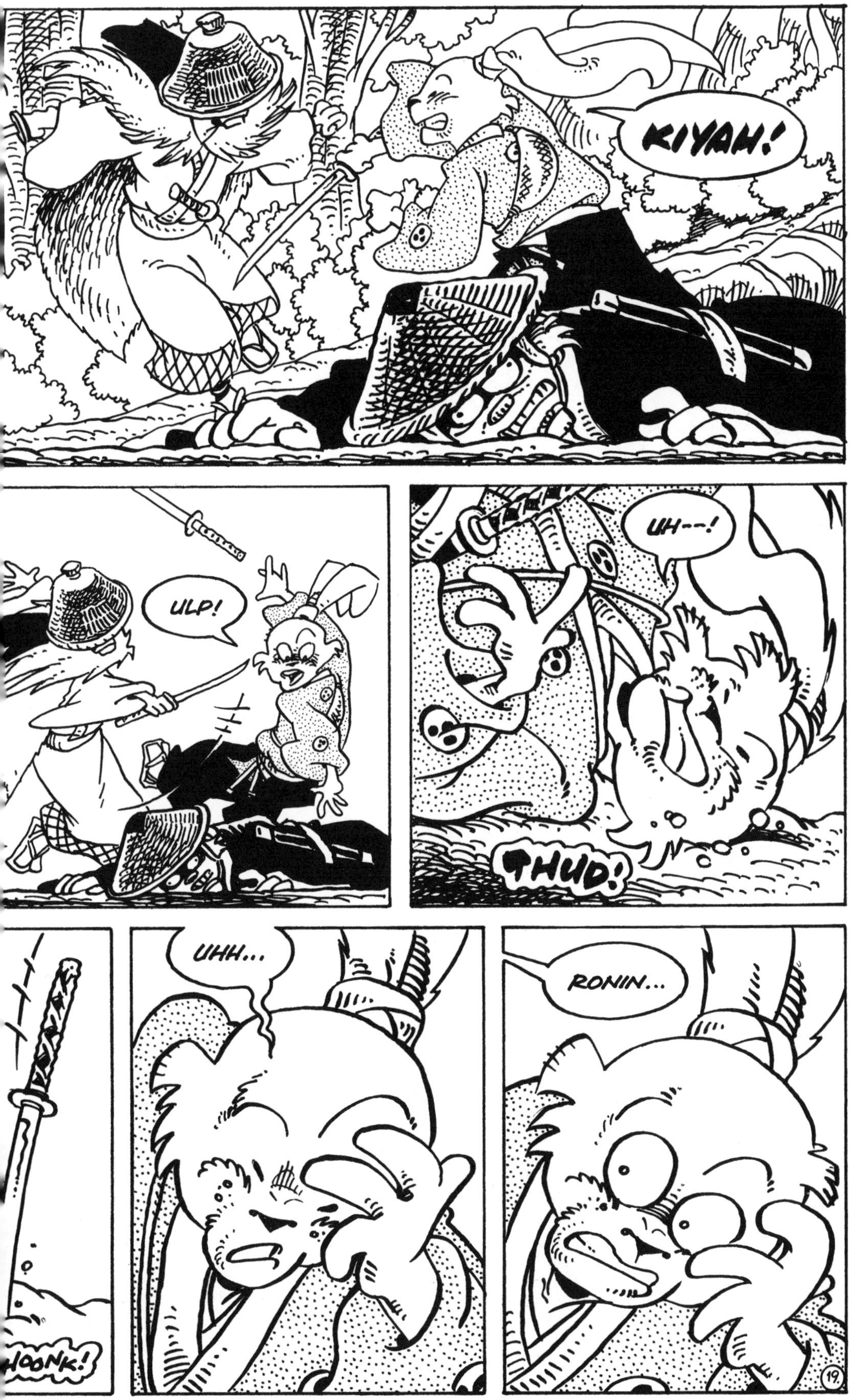
KIYAH!
ULP!
UH--!
THUD!
HOONK!
UHH...
RONIN...
19

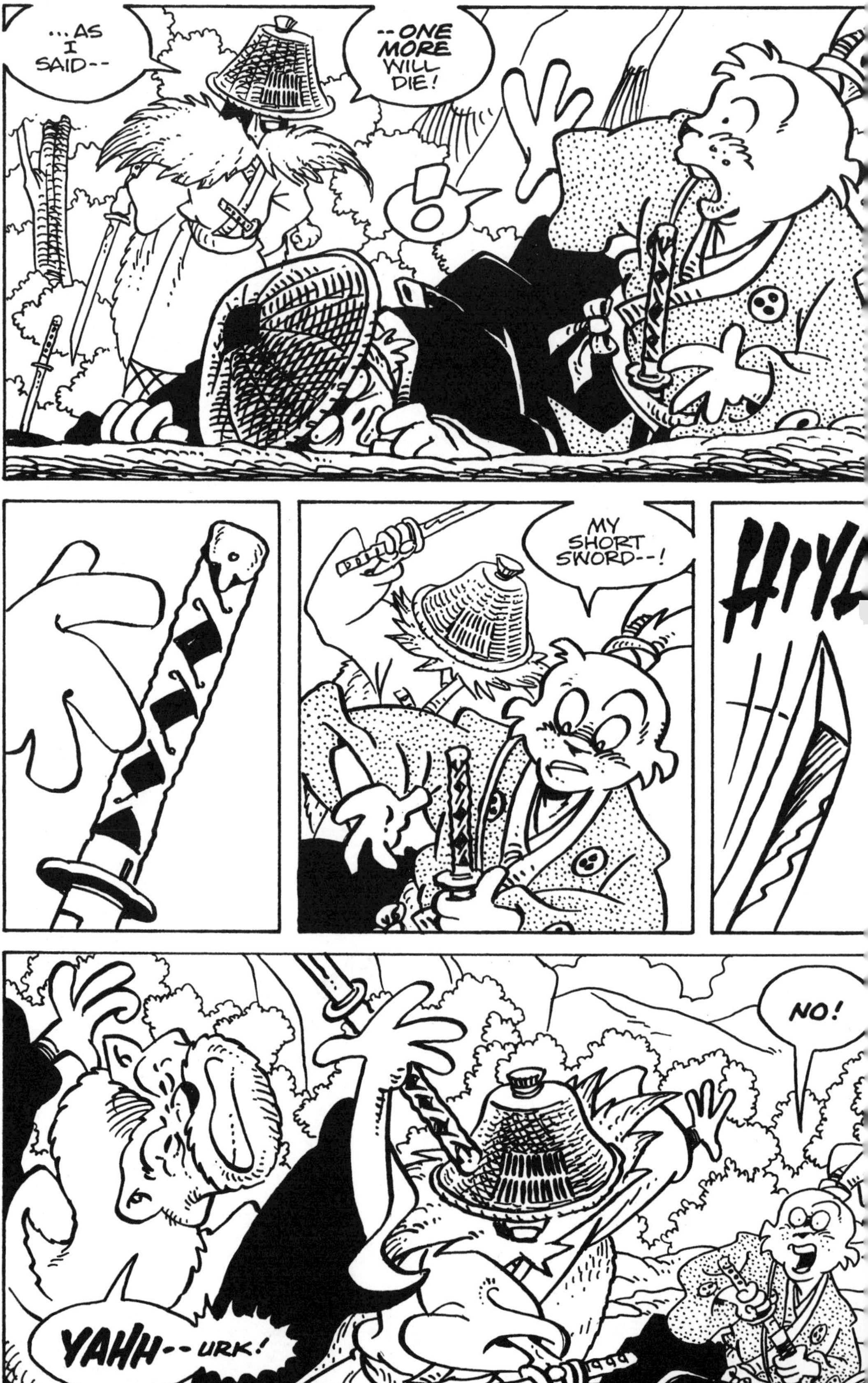
...AS I SAID--
--ONE MORE WILL DIE!
!
MY SHORT SWORD--!
YAHH--URK!
NO!

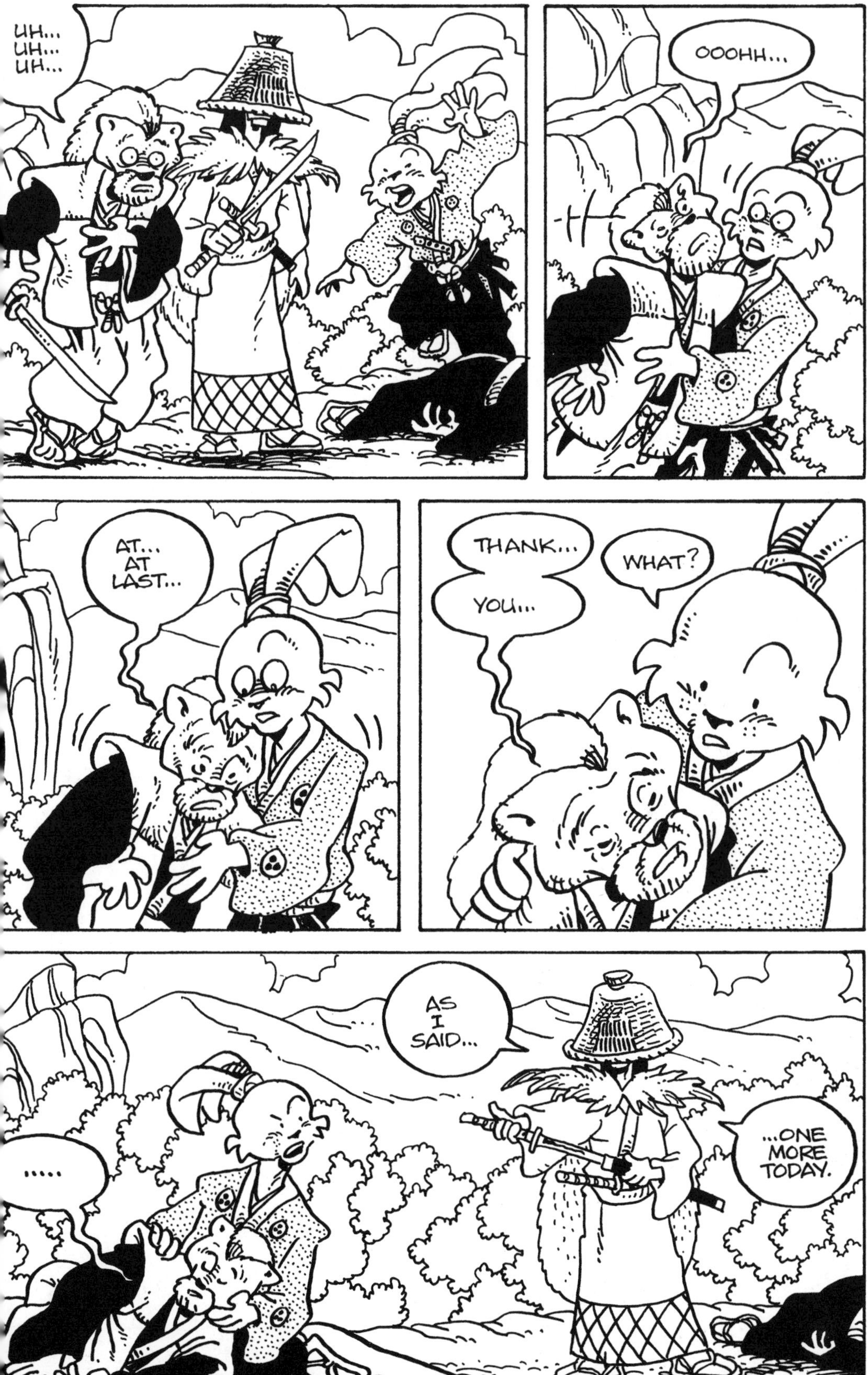
UH...
UH...
UH...
OOOHH...
AT...
AT
LAST...
THANK...
YOU...
WHAT?
AS
I
SAID...
.....
...ONE
MORE
TODAY.
21

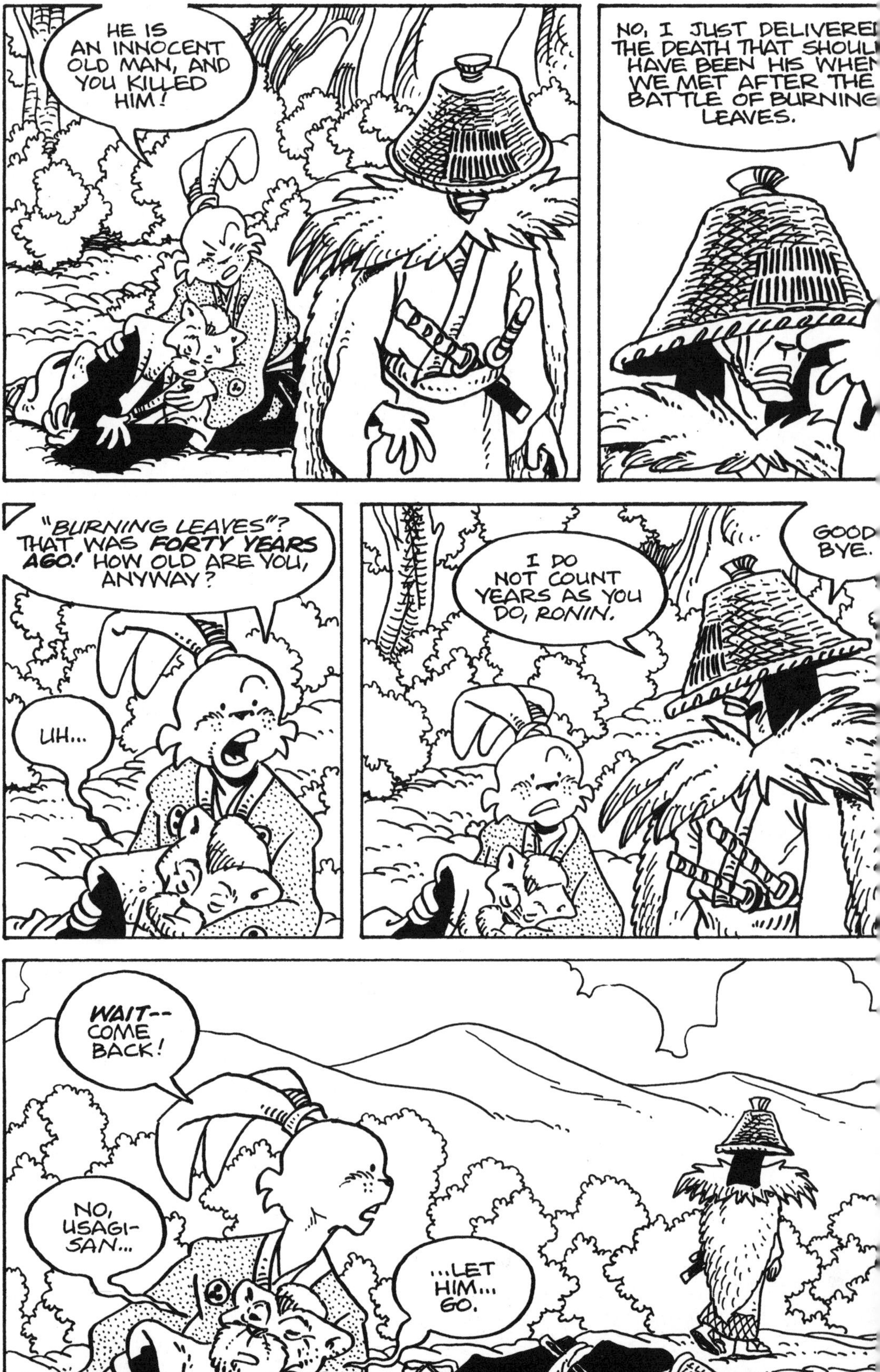
HE IS AN INNOCENT OLD MAN, AND YOU KILLED HIM!
NO, I JUST DELIVERED THE DEATH THAT SHOUL HAVE BEEN HIS WHEN WE MET AFTER THE BATTLE OF BURNING LEAVES.
"BURNING LEAVES"? THAT WAS FORTY YEARS AGO! HOW OLD ARE YOU, ANYWAY?
UH...
I DO NOT COUNT YEARS AS YOU DO, RONIN.
GOOD BYE.
WAIT-- COME BACK!
NO, USAGI-SAN...
...LET HIM... GO.

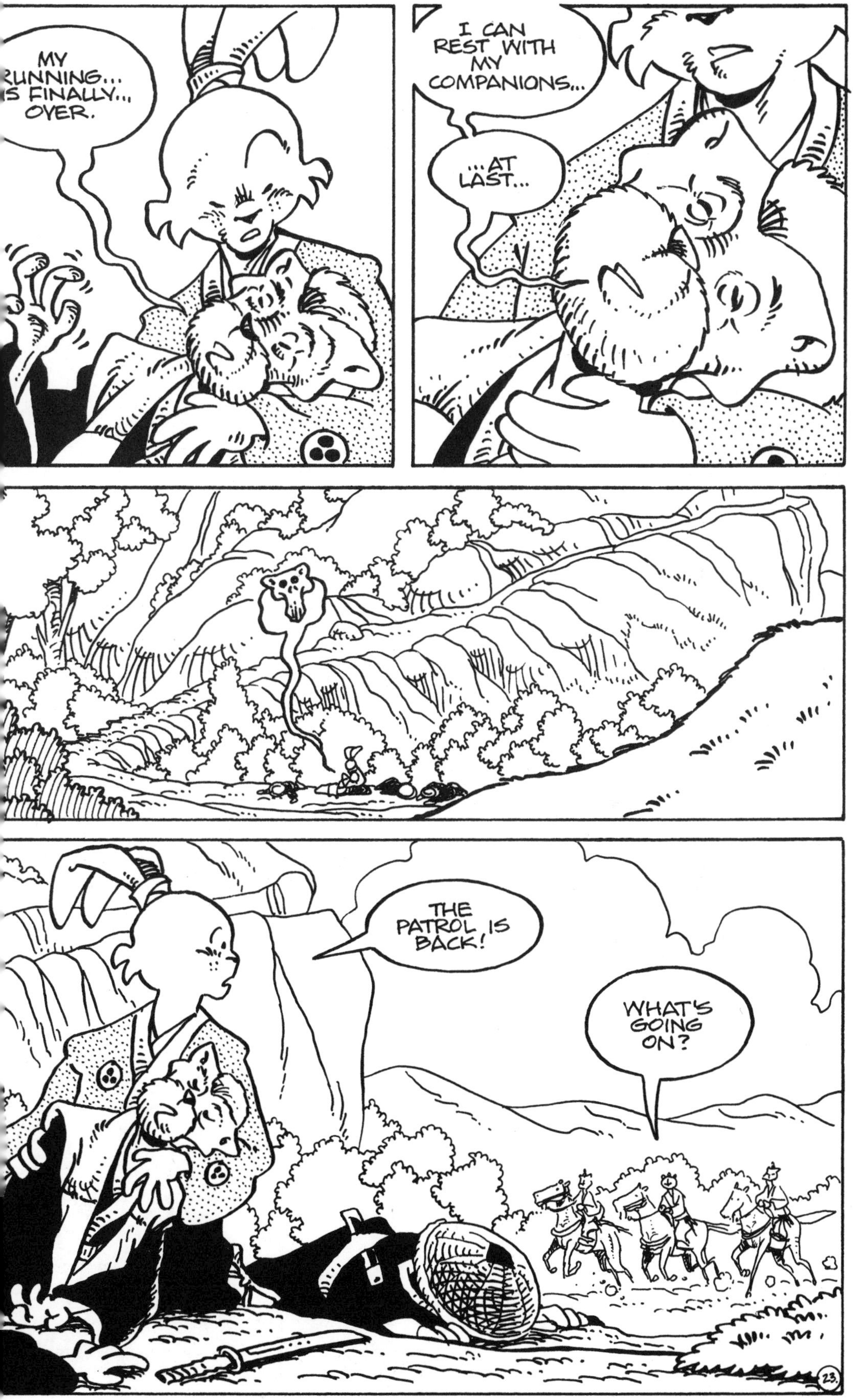
MY
RUNNING...
IS FINALLY...
OVER.
I CAN REST WITH MY COMPANIONS...
...AT LAST...
THE PATROL IS BACK!
WHAT'S GOING ON?
23.

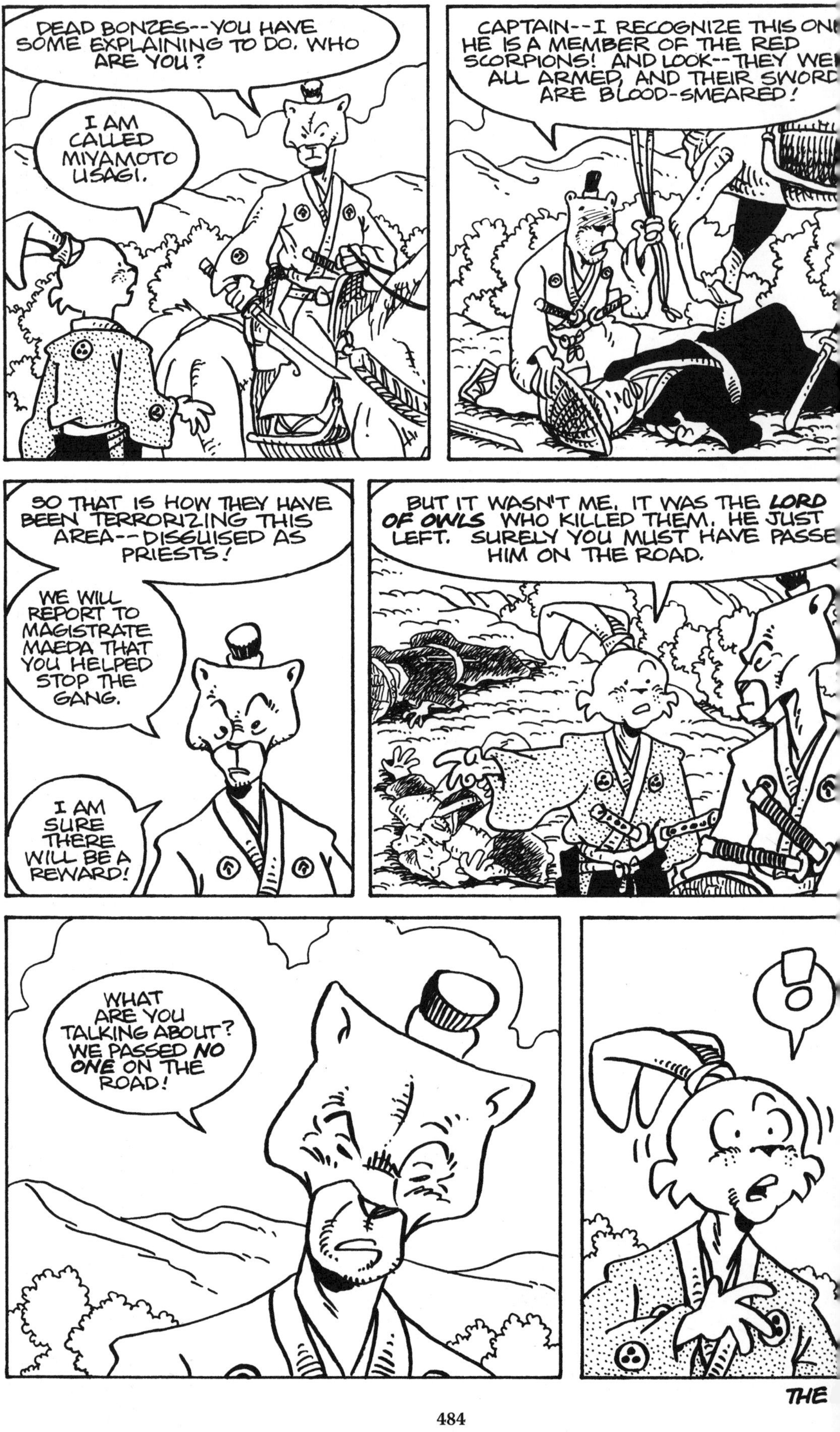
DEAD BONZES--YOU HAVE SOME EXPLAINING TO DO. WHO ARE YOU?
I AM CALLED MIYAMOTO USAGI.
CAPTAIN--I RECOGNIZE THIS ON
HE IS A MEMBER OF THE RED SCORPIONS! AND LOOK--THEY WE
ALL ARMED, AND THEIR SWORD
ARE BLOOD-SMEARED!
SO THAT IS HOW THEY HAVE BEEN TERRORIZING THIS AREA--DISGUISED AS PRIESTS!
WE WILL REPORT TO MAGISTRATE MAEDA THAT YOU HELPED STOP THE GANG.
I AM SURE THERE WILL BE A REWARD!
BUT IT WASN'T ME. IT WAS THE ***LORD OF OWLS*** WHO KILLED THEM. HE JUST LEFT. SURELY YOU MUST HAVE PASSE
HIM ON THE ROAD.
WHAT ARE YOU TALKING ABOUT? WE PASSED ***NO ONE*** ON THE ROAD!
!

**THE**

# HOSE WHO TREAD ON THE CORPION'S TAIL PART ONE

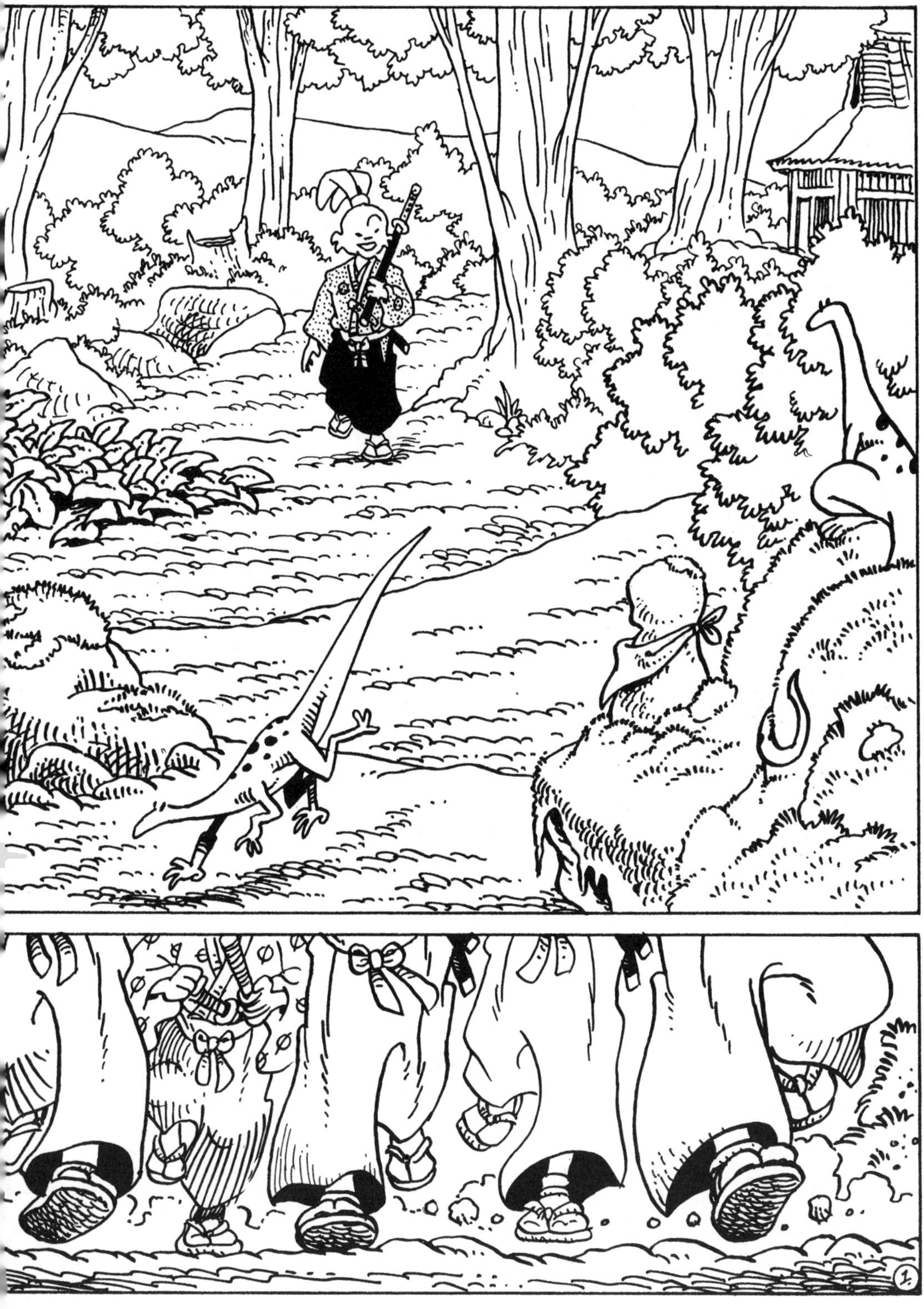

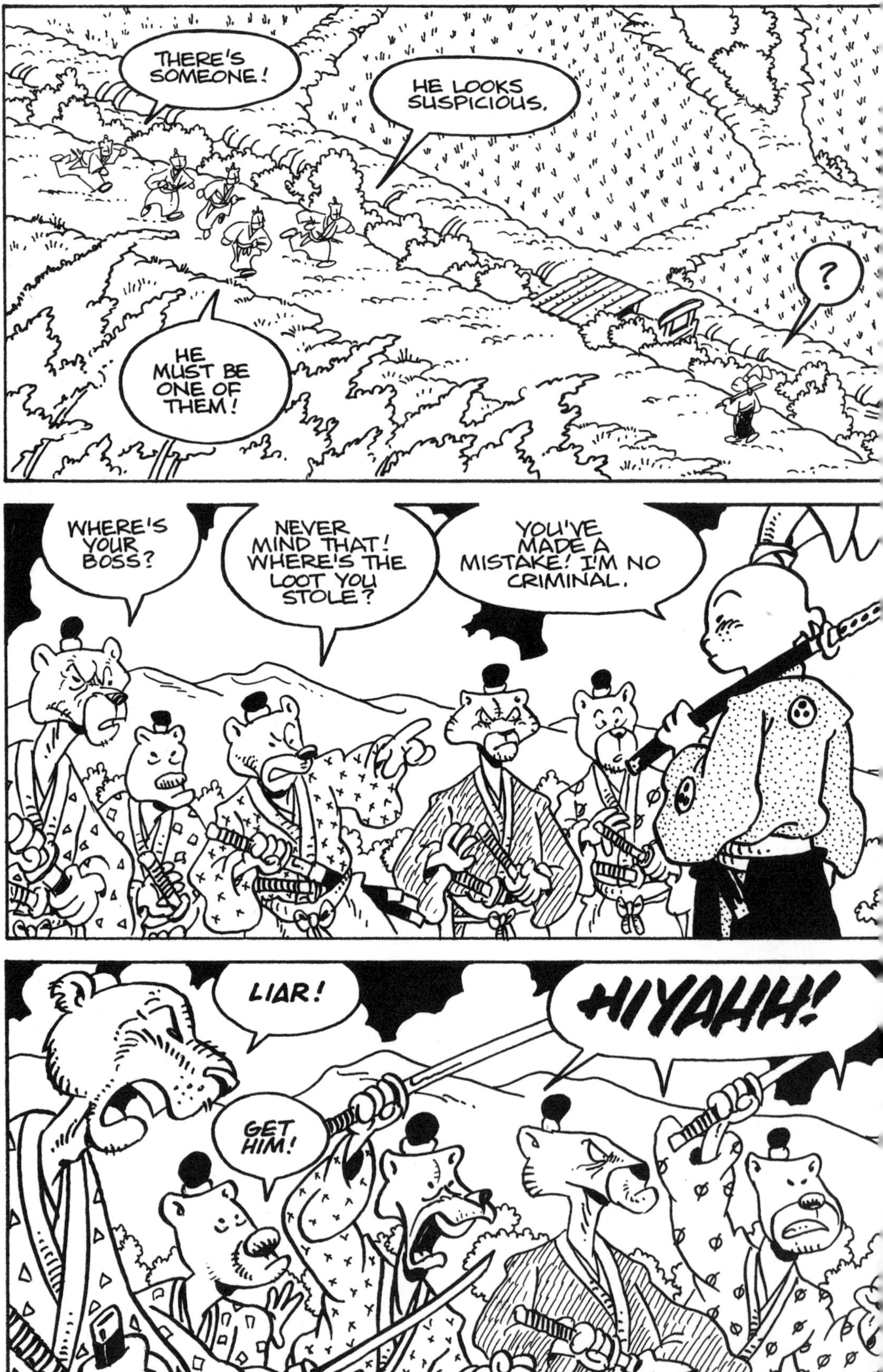
THERE'S SOMEONE!
HE LOOKS SUSPICIOUS.
HE MUST BE ONE OF THEM!
?
WHERE'S YOUR BOSS?
NEVER MIND THAT! WHERE'S THE LOOT YOU STOLE?
YOU'VE MADE A MISTAKE! I'M NO CRIMINAL.
LIAR!
GET HIM!
HIYAHH!

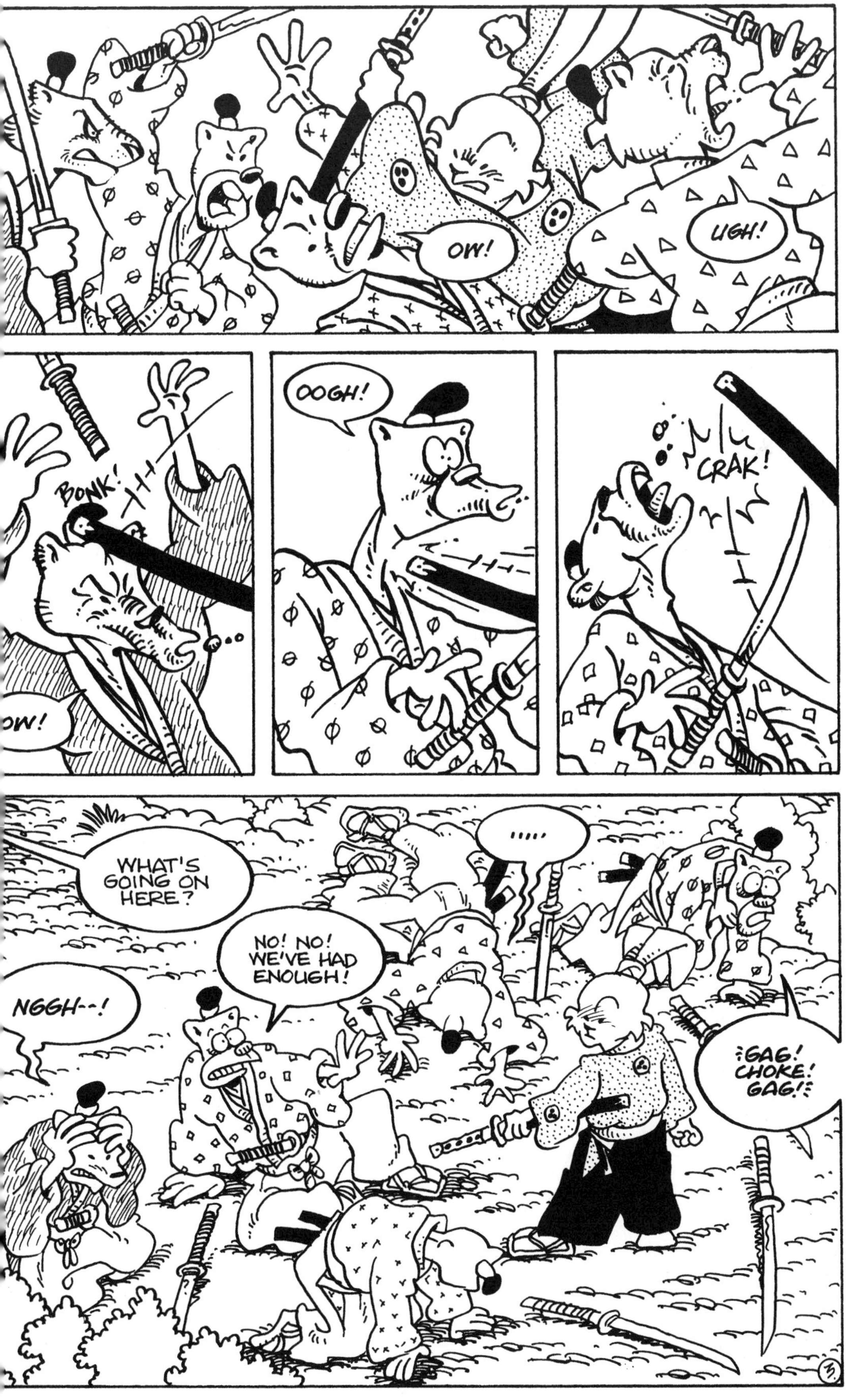
OW!
UGH!
BONK!
OW!
OOGH!
CRAK!
WHAT'S GOING ON HERE?
.....
NGGH--!
NO! NO! WE'VE HAD ENOUGH!
GAG! CHOKE! GAG!
3

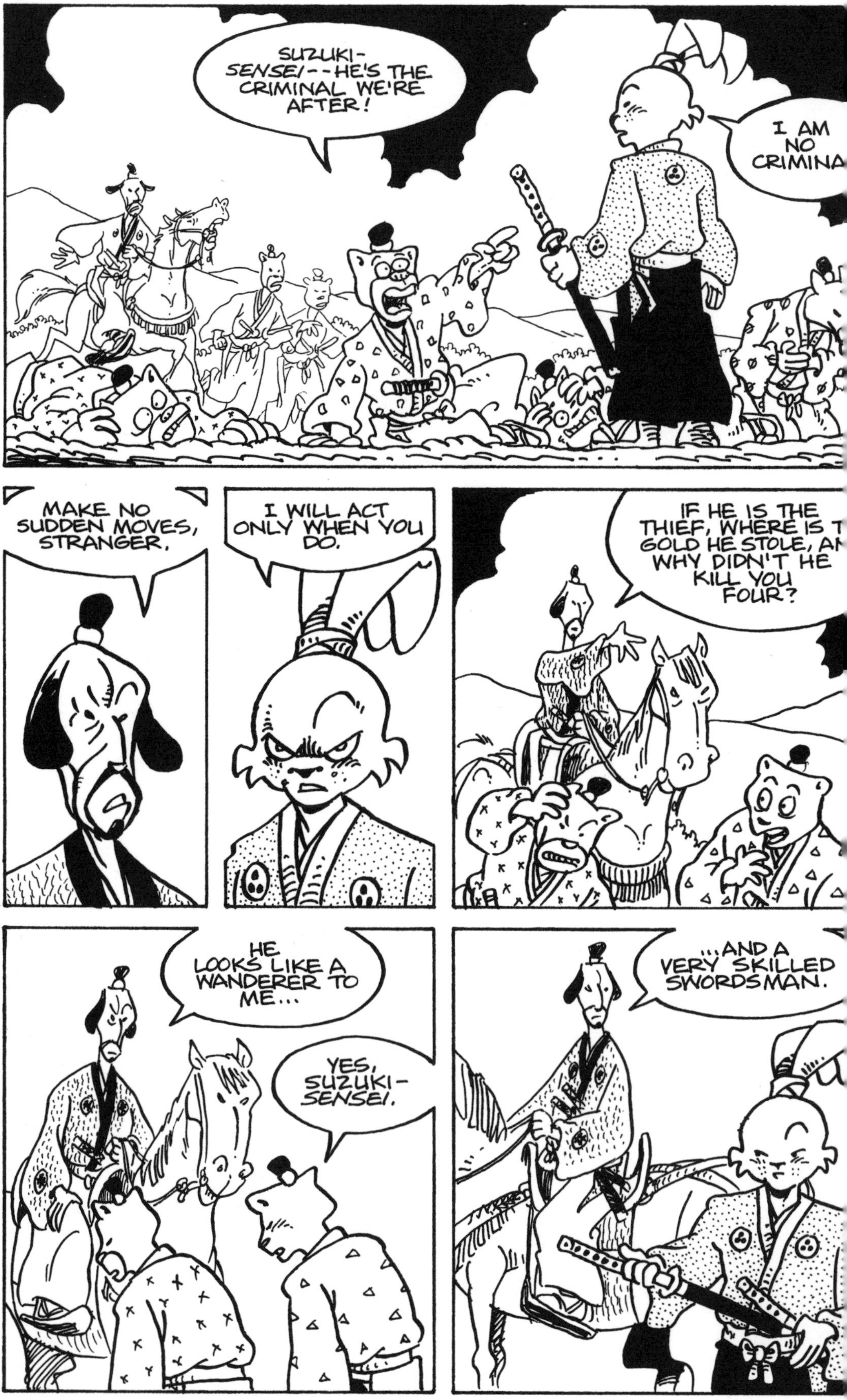
SUZUKI-SENSEI--HE'S THE CRIMINAL WE'RE AFTER!
I AM NO CRIMINA
MAKE NO SUDDEN MOVES, STRANGER.
I WILL ACT ONLY WHEN YOU DO.
IF HE IS THE THIEF, WHERE IS T GOLD HE STOLE, AN WHY DIDN'T HE KILL YOU FOUR?
HE LOOKS LIKE A WANDERER TO ME...
YES, SUZUKI-SENSEI.
...AND A VERY SKILLED SWORDSMAN.

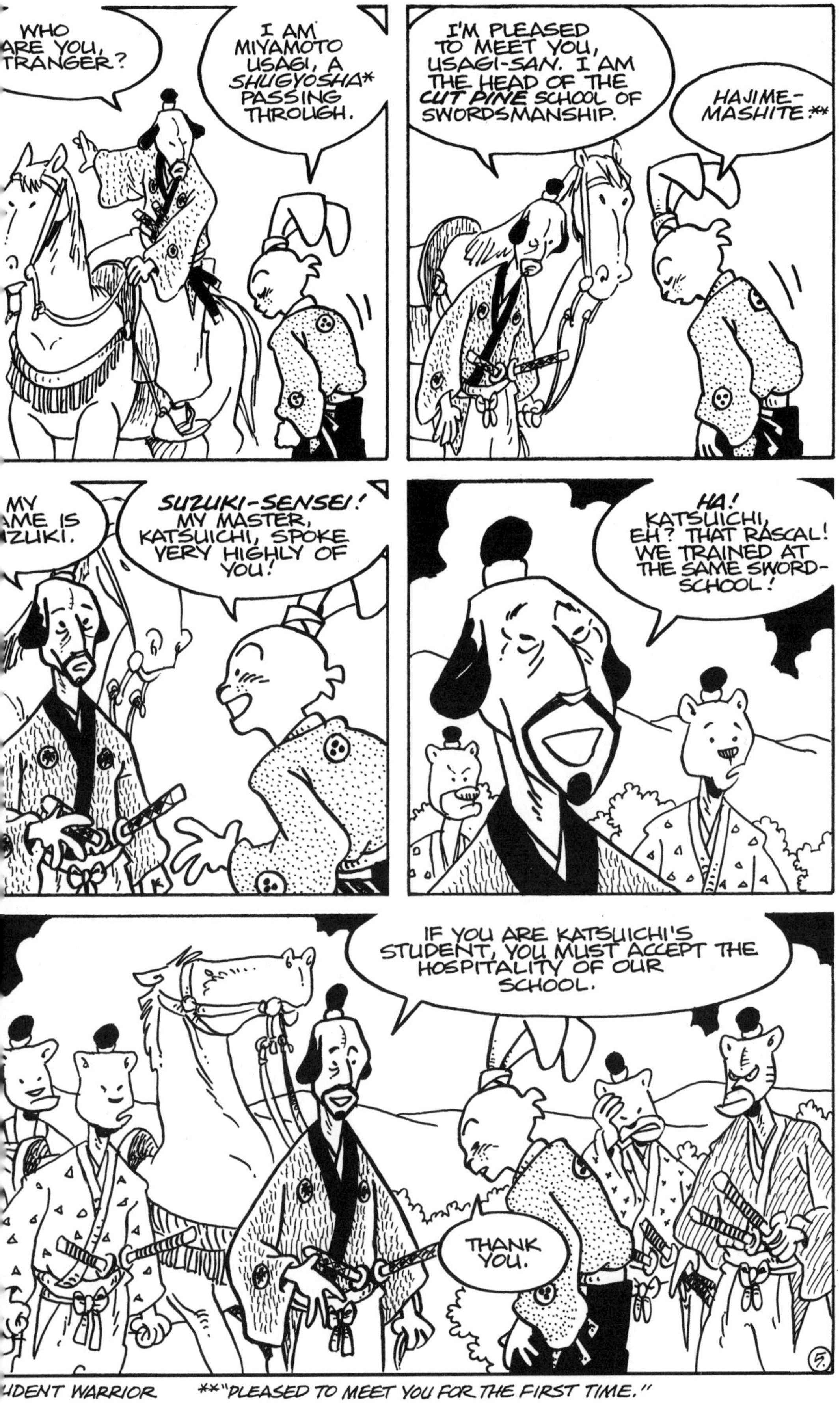
WHO ARE YOU, STRANGER?
I AM MIYAMOTO USAGI, A SHUGYOSHA* PASSING THROUGH.
I'M PLEASED TO MEET YOU, USAGI-SAN. I AM THE HEAD OF THE CUT PINE SCHOOL OF SWORDSMANSHIP.
HAJIME-MASHITE.**
MY NAME IS SUZUKI.
SUZUKI-SENSEI! MY MASTER, KATSUICHI, SPOKE VERY HIGHLY OF YOU!
HA! KATSUICHI, EH? THAT RASCAL! WE TRAINED AT THE SAME SWORD-SCHOOL!
IF YOU ARE KATSUICHI'S STUDENT, YOU MUST ACCEPT THE HOSPITALITY OF OUR SCHOOL.
THANK YOU.
5.

*STUDENT WARRIOR **"PLEASED TO MEET YOU FOR THE FIRST TIME."

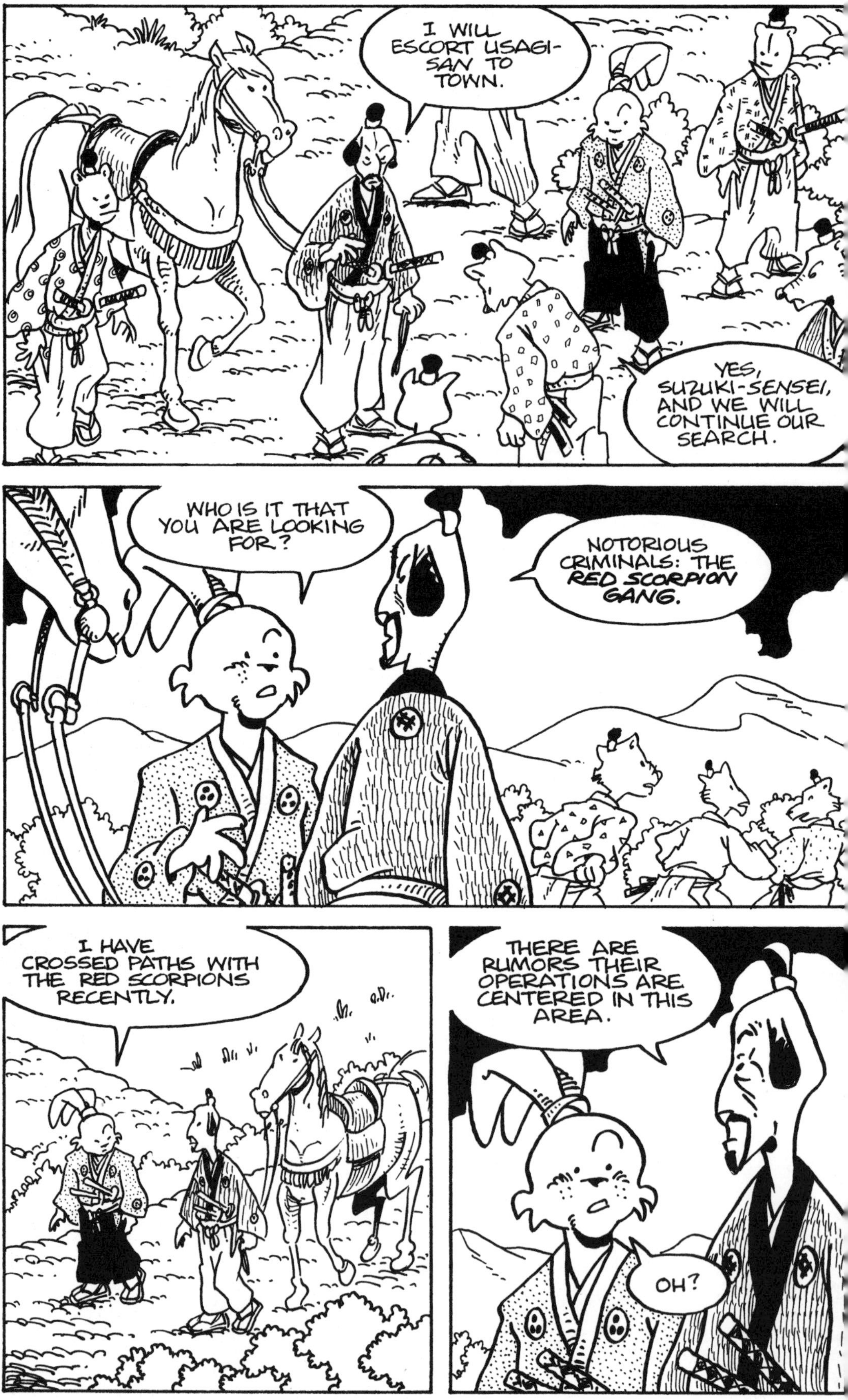
I WILL ESCORT USAGI-SAN TO TOWN.
YES, SUZUKI-SENSEI, AND WE WILL CONTINUE OUR SEARCH.
WHO IS IT THAT YOU ARE LOOKING FOR?
NOTORIOUS CRIMINALS: THE *RED SCORPION GANG*.
I HAVE CROSSED PATHS WITH THE RED SCORPIONS RECENTLY.
THERE ARE RUMORS THEIR OPERATIONS ARE CENTERED IN THIS AREA.
OH?

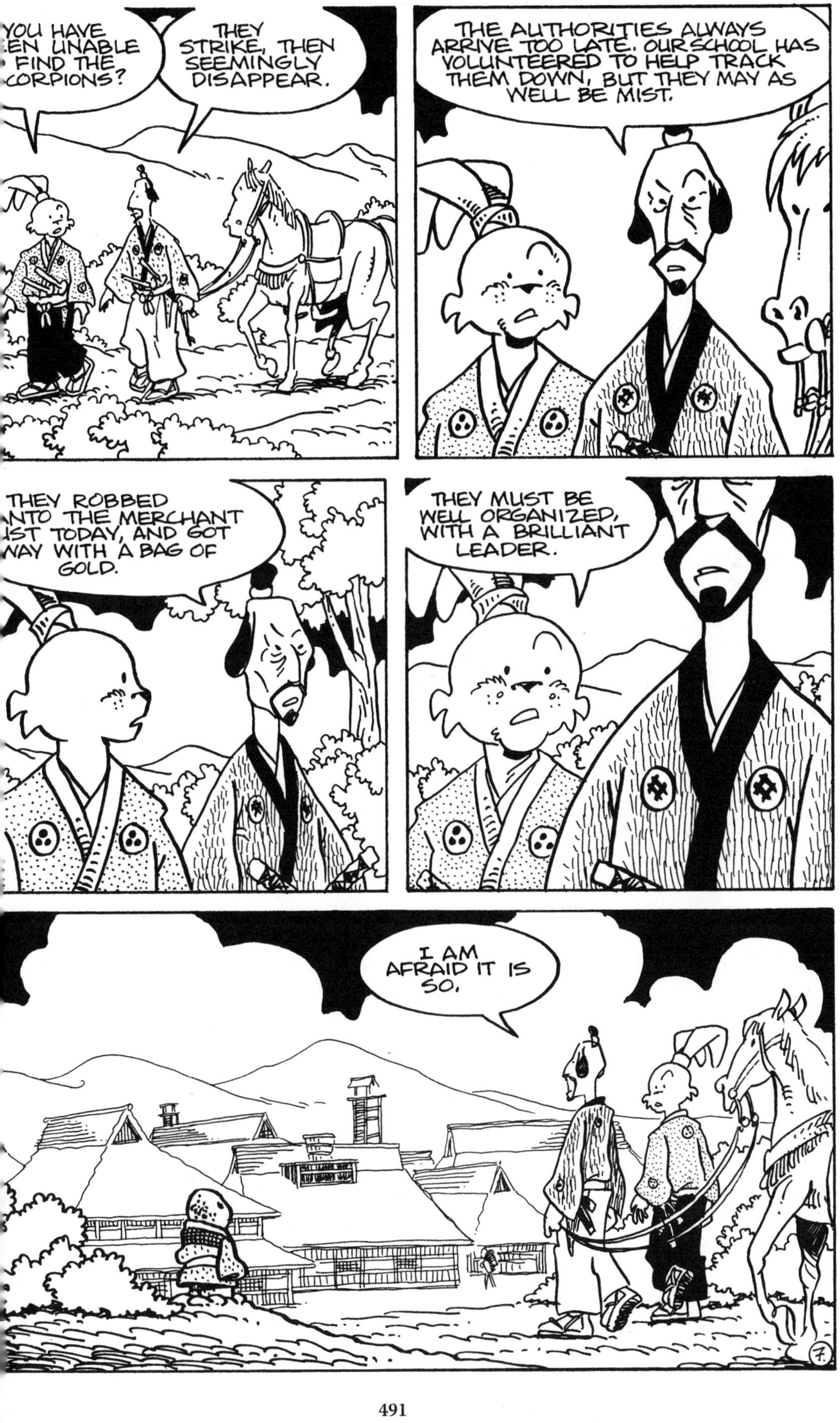

YOU HAVE EN UNABLE FIND THE CORPIONS?
THEY STRIKE, THEN SEEMINGLY DISAPPEAR.
THE AUTHORITIES ALWAYS ARRIVE TOO LATE. OUR SCHOOL HAS VOLUNTEERED TO HELP TRACK THEM DOWN, BUT THEY MAY AS WELL BE MIST.
THEY ROBBED NTO THE MERCHANT IST TODAY, AND GOT WAY WITH A BAG OF GOLD.
THEY MUST BE WELL ORGANIZED, WITH A BRILLIANT LEADER.
I AM AFRAID IT IS SO.
7.

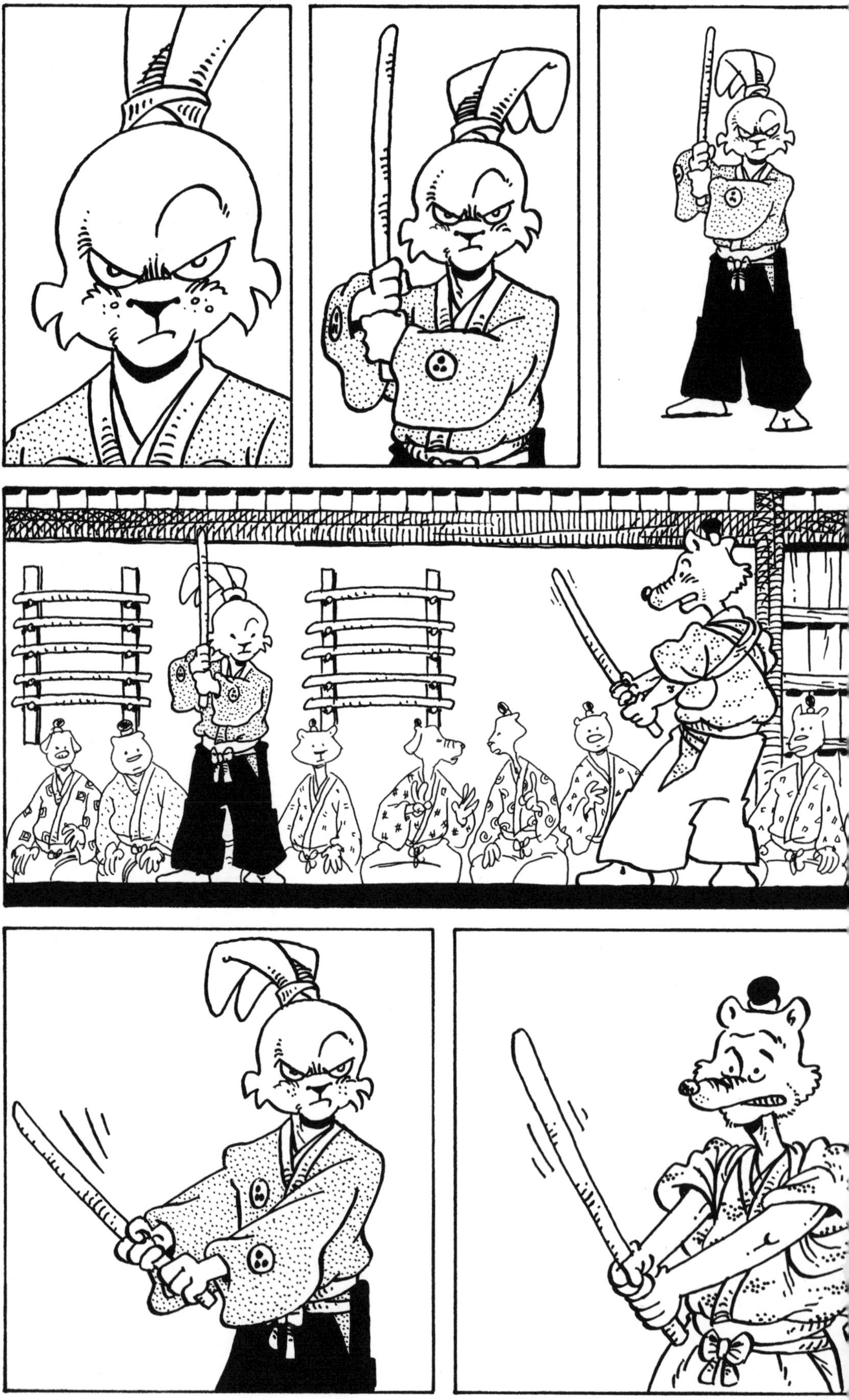

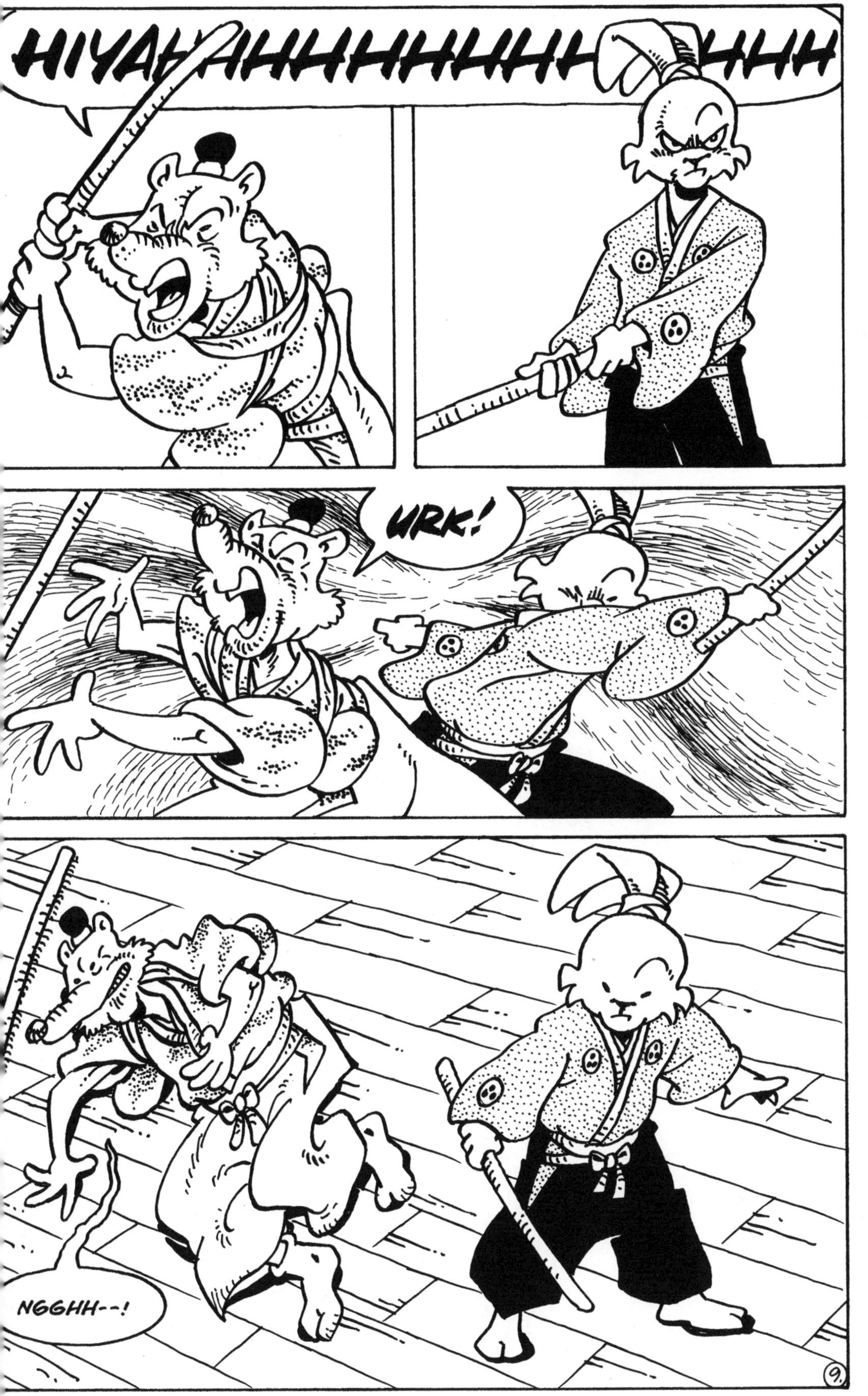
HIYAHAHHHHHHHHHHHHHHHH
URK!
NGGHH--!
9

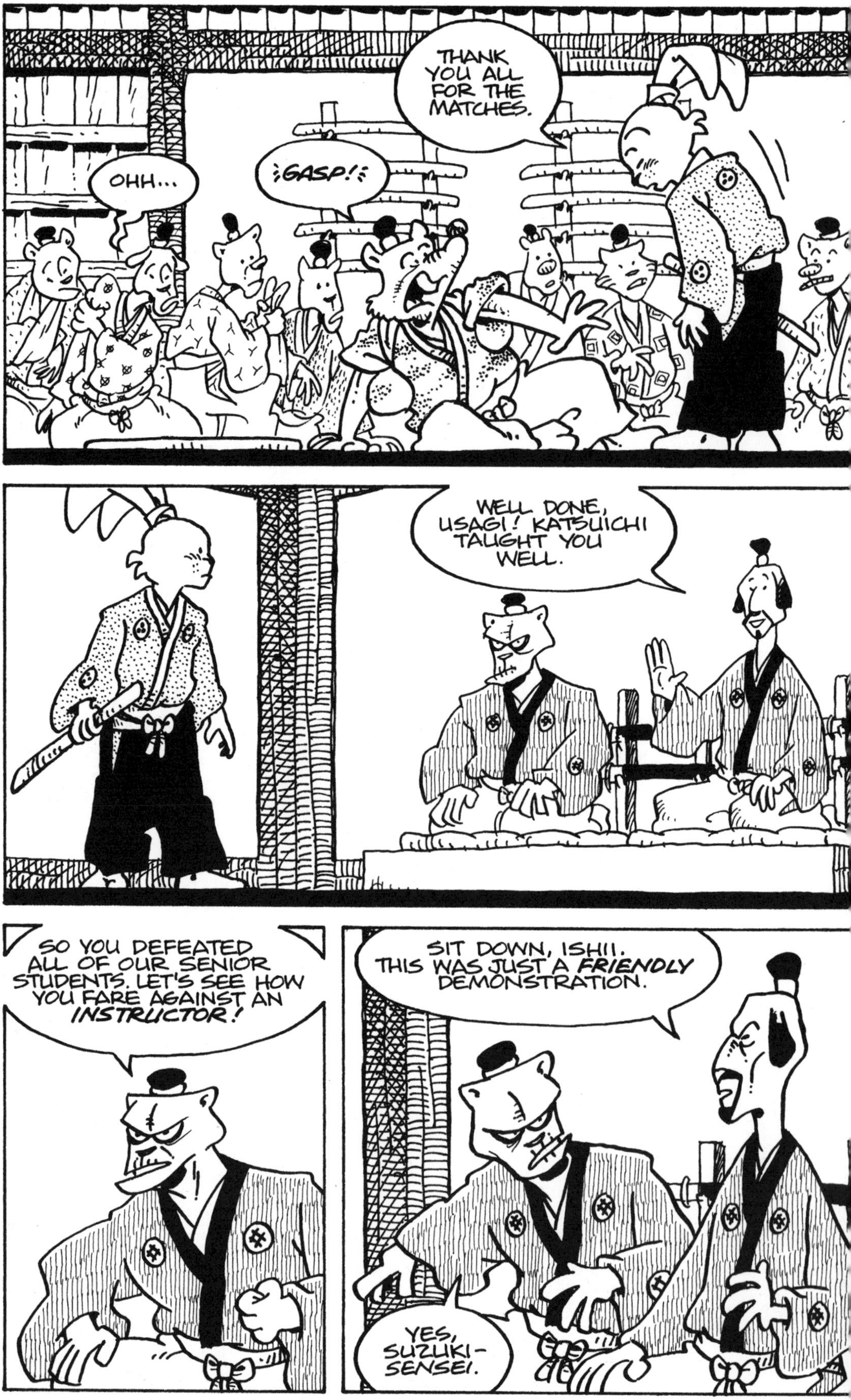

OHH...
GASP!
THANK YOU ALL FOR THE MATCHES.
WELL DONE, USAGI! KATSUICHI TAUGHT YOU WELL.
SO YOU DEFEATED ALL OF OUR SENIOR STUDENTS. LET'S SEE HOW YOU FARE AGAINST AN INSTRUCTOR!
SIT DOWN, ISHII. THIS WAS JUST A FRIENDLY DEMONSTRATION.
YES, SUZUKI-SENSEI.

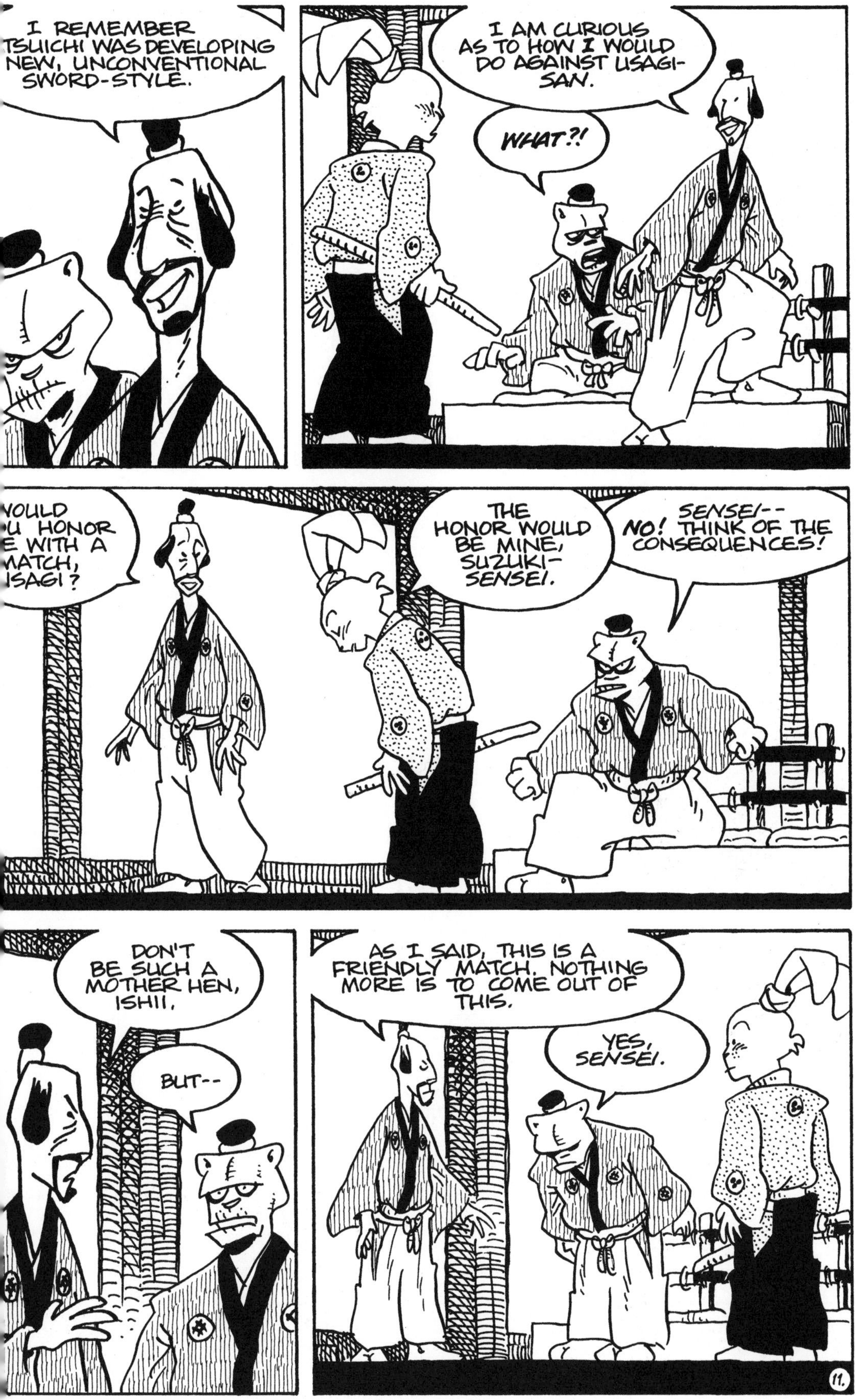
I REMEMBER TSUICHI WAS DEVELOPING NEW, UNCONVENTIONAL SWORD-STYLE.
I AM CURIOUS AS TO HOW I WOULD DO AGAINST USAGI-SAN.
WHAT?!
WOULD U HONOR E WITH A MATCH, USAGI?
THE HONOR WOULD BE MINE, SUZUKI-SENSEI.
SENSEI-- NO! THINK OF THE CONSEQUENCES!
DON'T BE SUCH A MOTHER HEN, ISHII.
BUT--
AS I SAID, THIS IS A FRIENDLY MATCH. NOTHING MORE IS TO COME OUT OF THIS.
YES, SENSEI.
11.

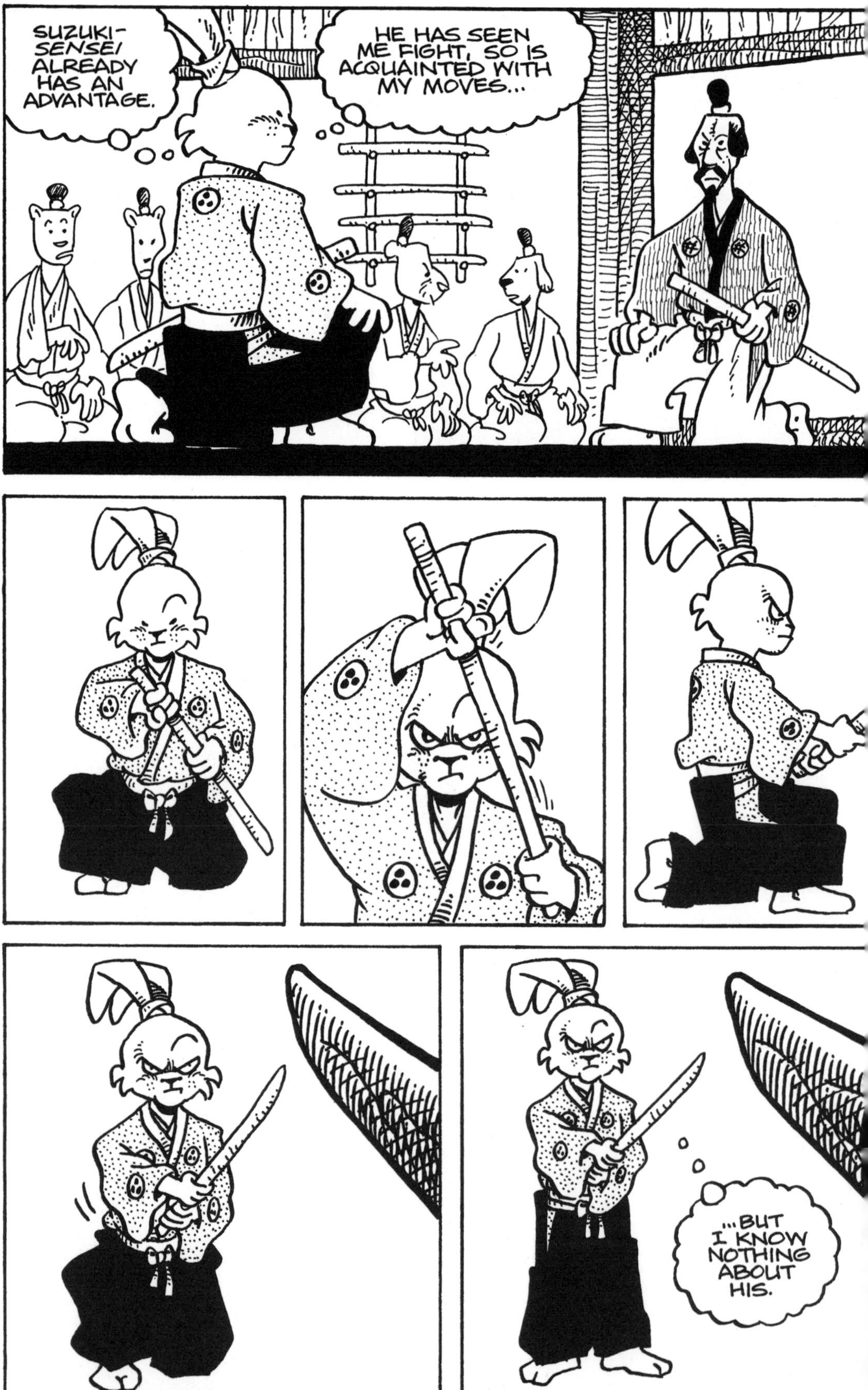
SUZUKI-SENSEI ALREADY HAS AN ADVANTAGE.
HE HAS SEEN ME FIGHT, SO IS ACQUAINTED WITH MY MOVES...
...BUT I KNOW NOTHING ABOUT HIS.

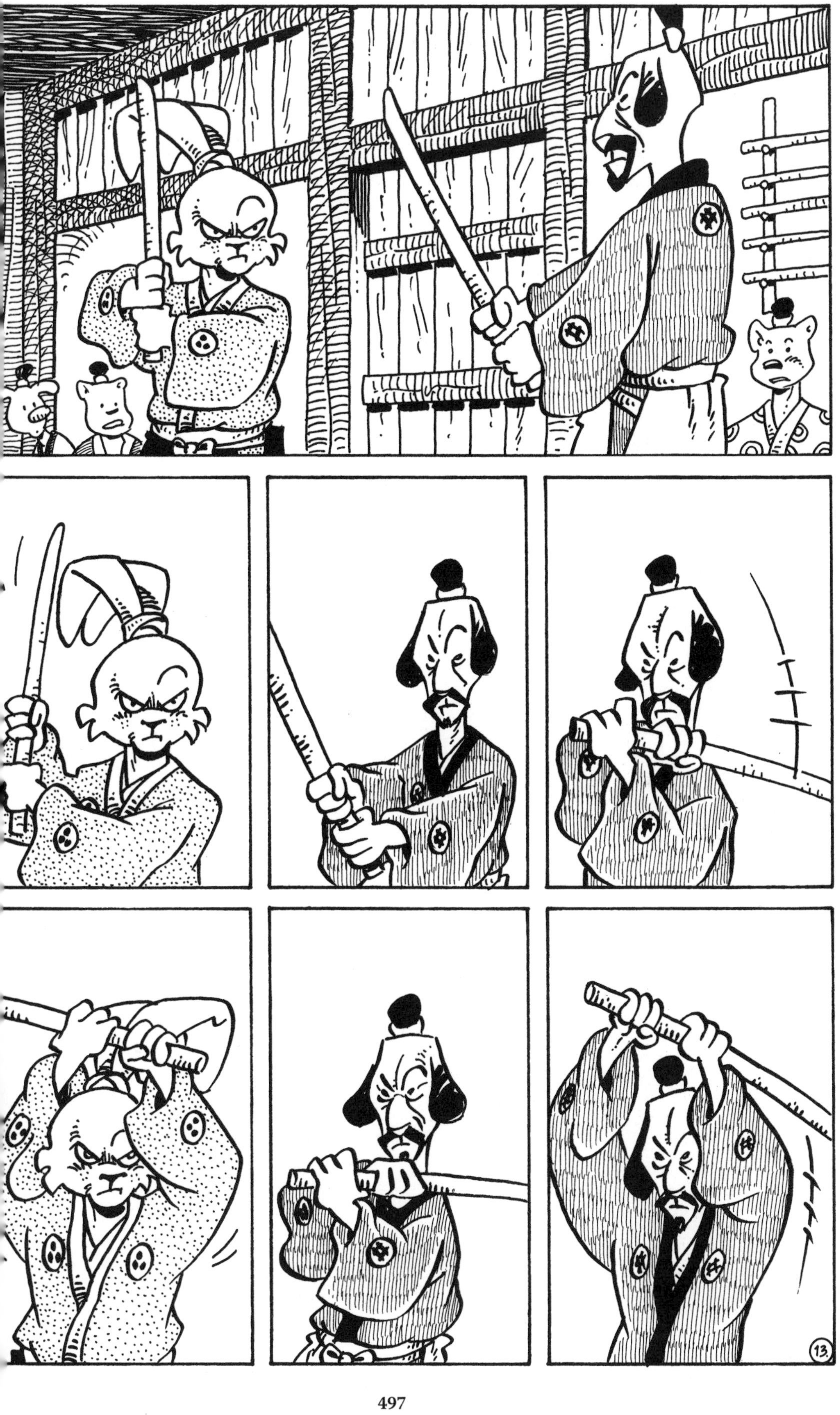
13

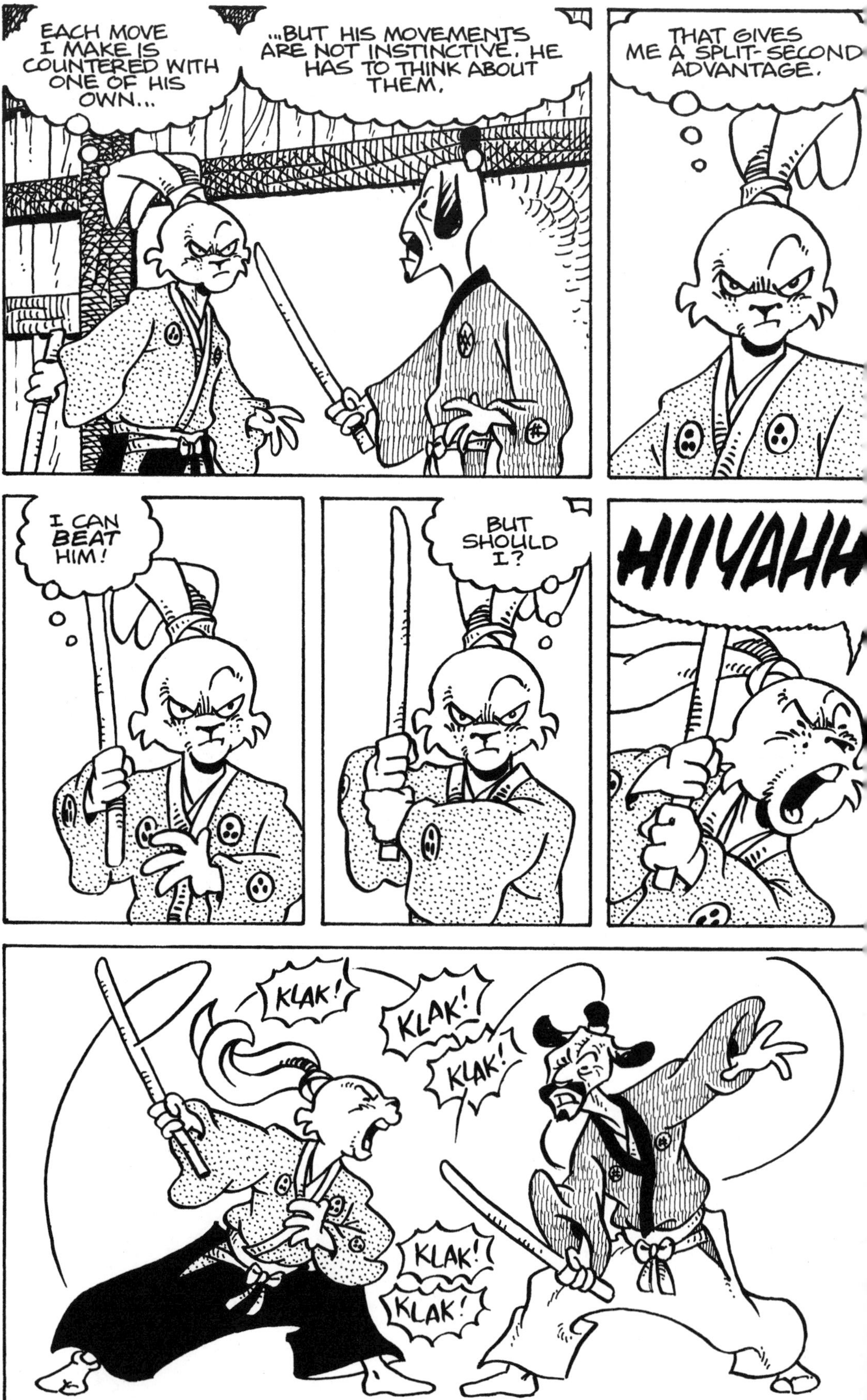
EACH MOVE I MAKE IS COUNTERED WITH ONE OF HIS OWN...
...BUT HIS MOVEMENTS ARE NOT INSTINCTIVE. HE HAS TO THINK ABOUT THEM.
THAT GIVES ME A SPLIT-SECOND ADVANTAGE.
I CAN BEAT HIM!
BUT SHOULD I?
HIIYAHH
KLAK!
KLAK!
KLAK!
KLAK!
KLAK!

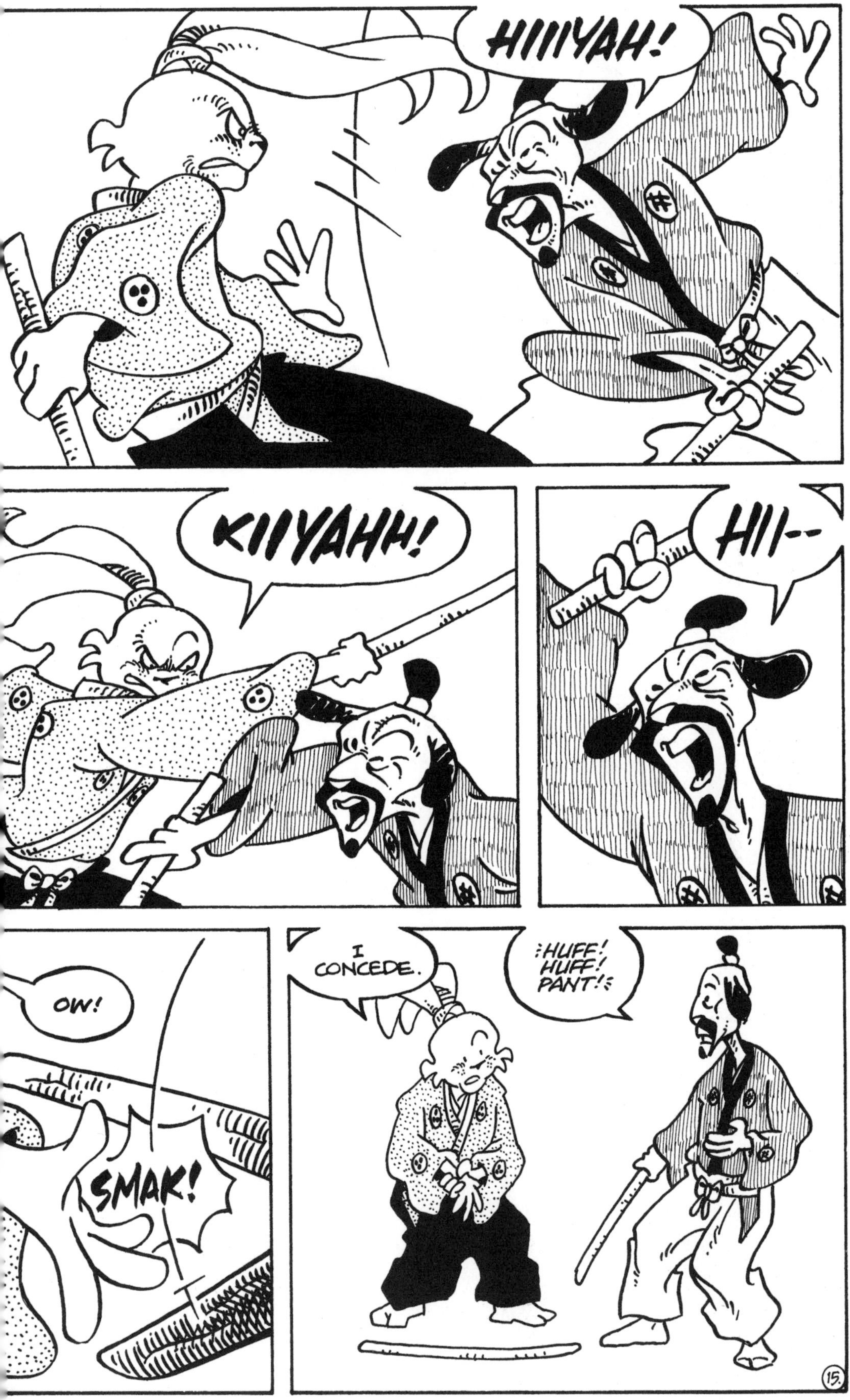
HIIIYAH!
KIIYAHH!
HII--
OW!
SMAK!
I CONCEDE.
HUFF! HUFF! PANT!
15.

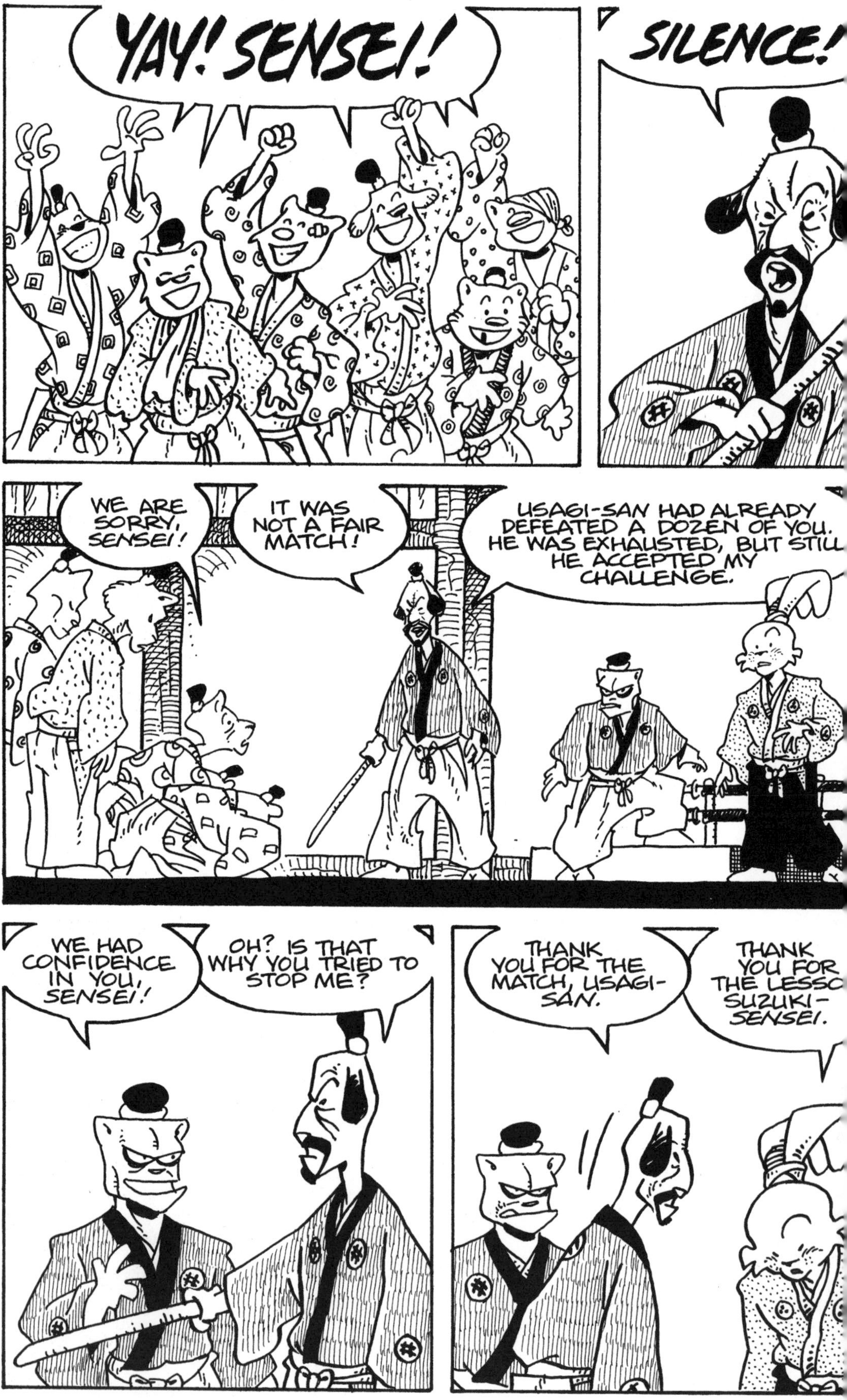

YAY! SENSEI!
SILENCE!
WE ARE SORRY, SENSEI!
IT WAS NOT A FAIR MATCH!
USAGI-SAN HAD ALREADY DEFEATED A DOZEN OF YOU. HE WAS EXHAUSTED, BUT STILL HE ACCEPTED MY CHALLENGE.
WE HAD CONFIDENCE IN YOU, SENSEI!
OH? IS THAT WHY YOU TRIED TO STOP ME?
THANK YOU FOR THE MATCH, USAGI-SAN.
THANK YOU FOR THE LESSO SUZUKI-SENSEI.

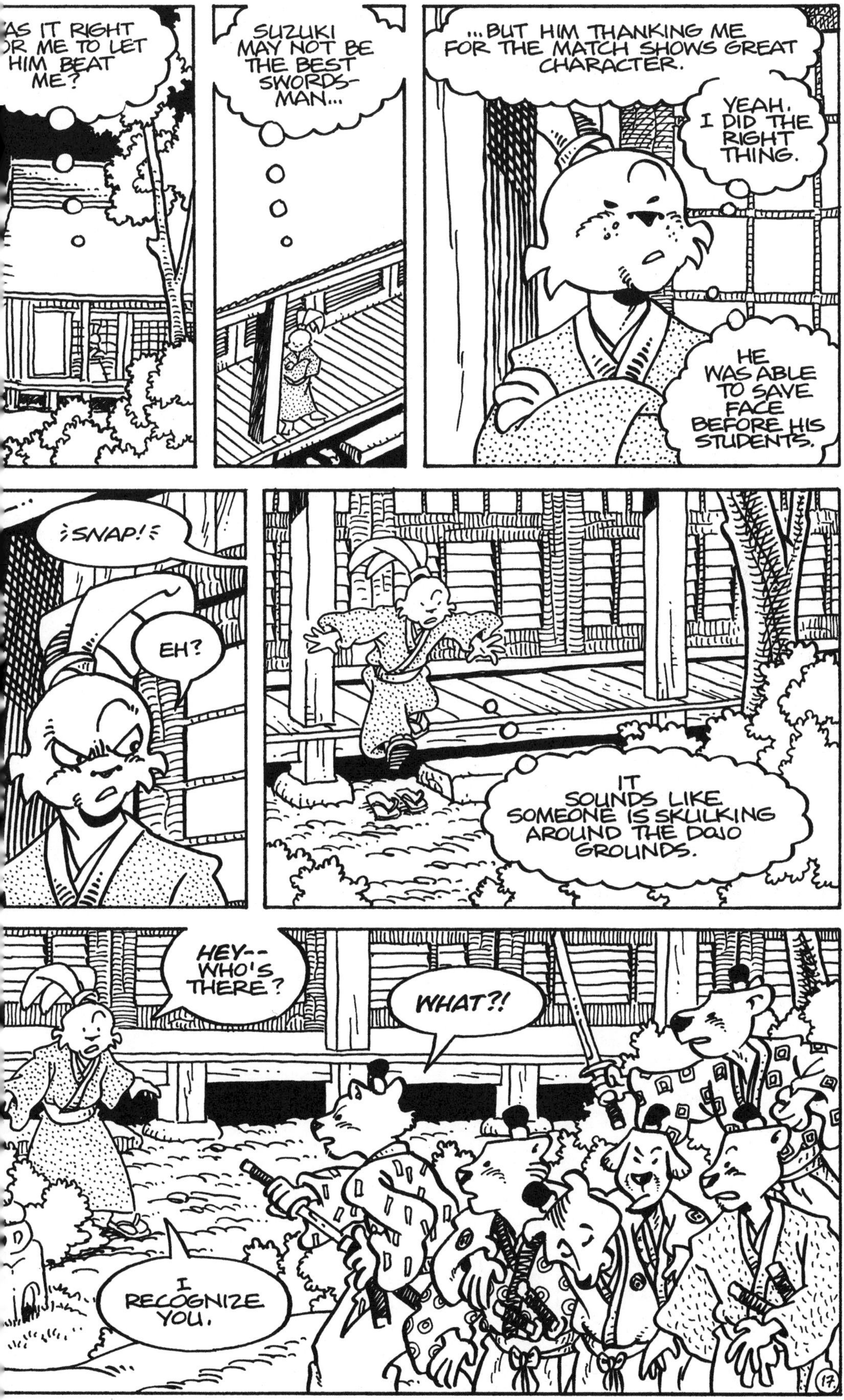
AS IT RIGHT OR ME TO LET HIM BEAT ME?
SUZUKI MAY NOT BE THE BEST SWORDS-MAN...
...BUT HIM THANKING ME FOR THE MATCH SHOWS GREAT CHARACTER.
YEAH. I DID THE RIGHT THING.
HE WAS ABLE TO SAVE FACE BEFORE HIS STUDENTS.
SNAP!
EH?
IT SOUNDS LIKE SOMEONE IS SKULKING AROUND THE DOJO GROUNDS.
HEY-- WHO'S THERE?
WHAT?!
I RECOGNIZE YOU.
17.

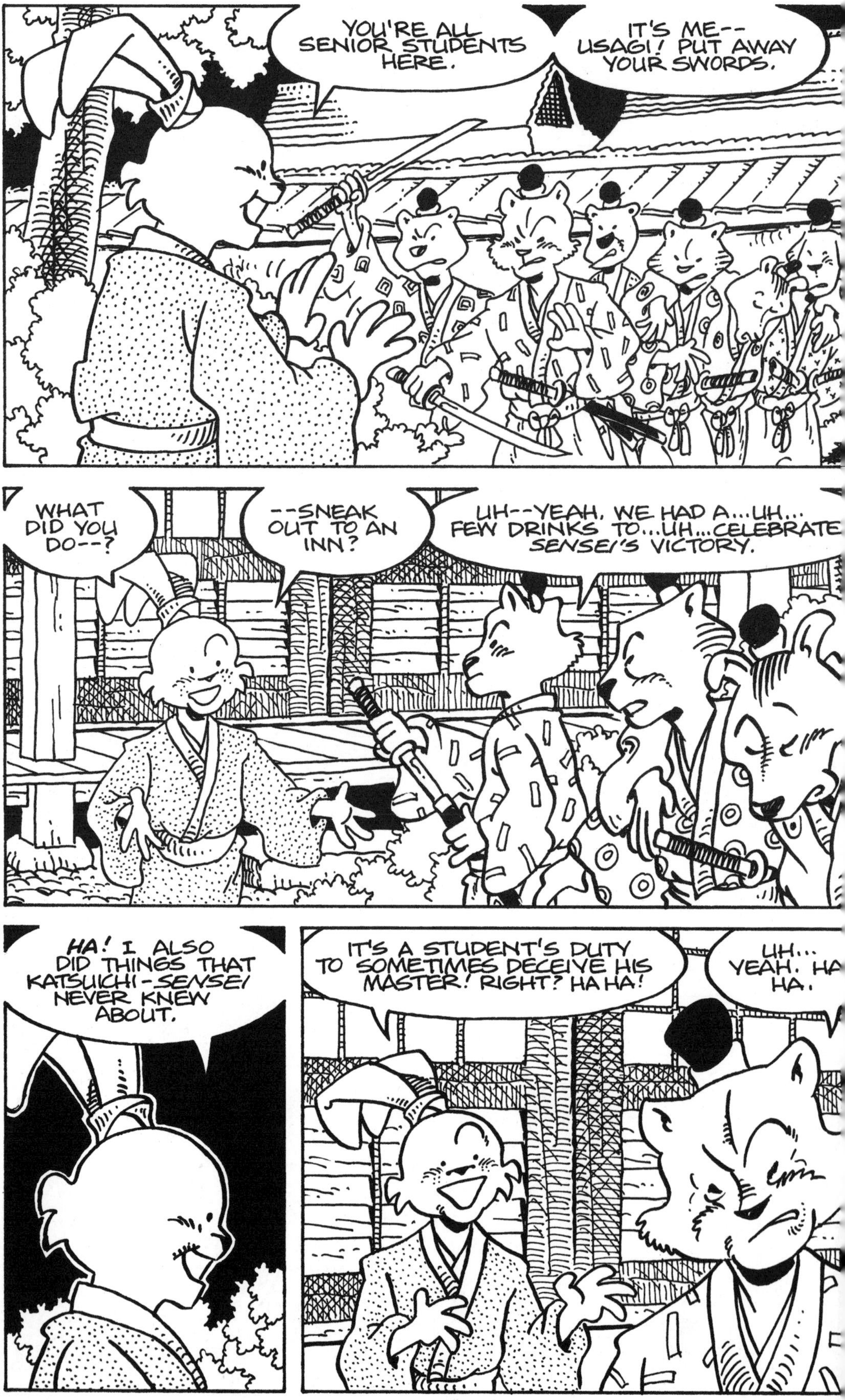
YOU'RE ALL SENIOR STUDENTS HERE.
IT'S ME-- USAGI! PUT AWAY YOUR SWORDS.
WHAT DID YOU DO--?
--SNEAK OUT TO AN INN?
UH--YEAH. WE HAD A...UH... FEW DRINKS TO...UH...CELEBRATE SENSEI'S VICTORY.
HA! I ALSO DID THINGS THAT KATSUICHI-SENSEI NEVER KNEW ABOUT.
IT'S A STUDENT'S DUTY TO SOMETIMES DECEIVE HIS MASTER! RIGHT? HA HA!
UH... YEAH. HA HA.

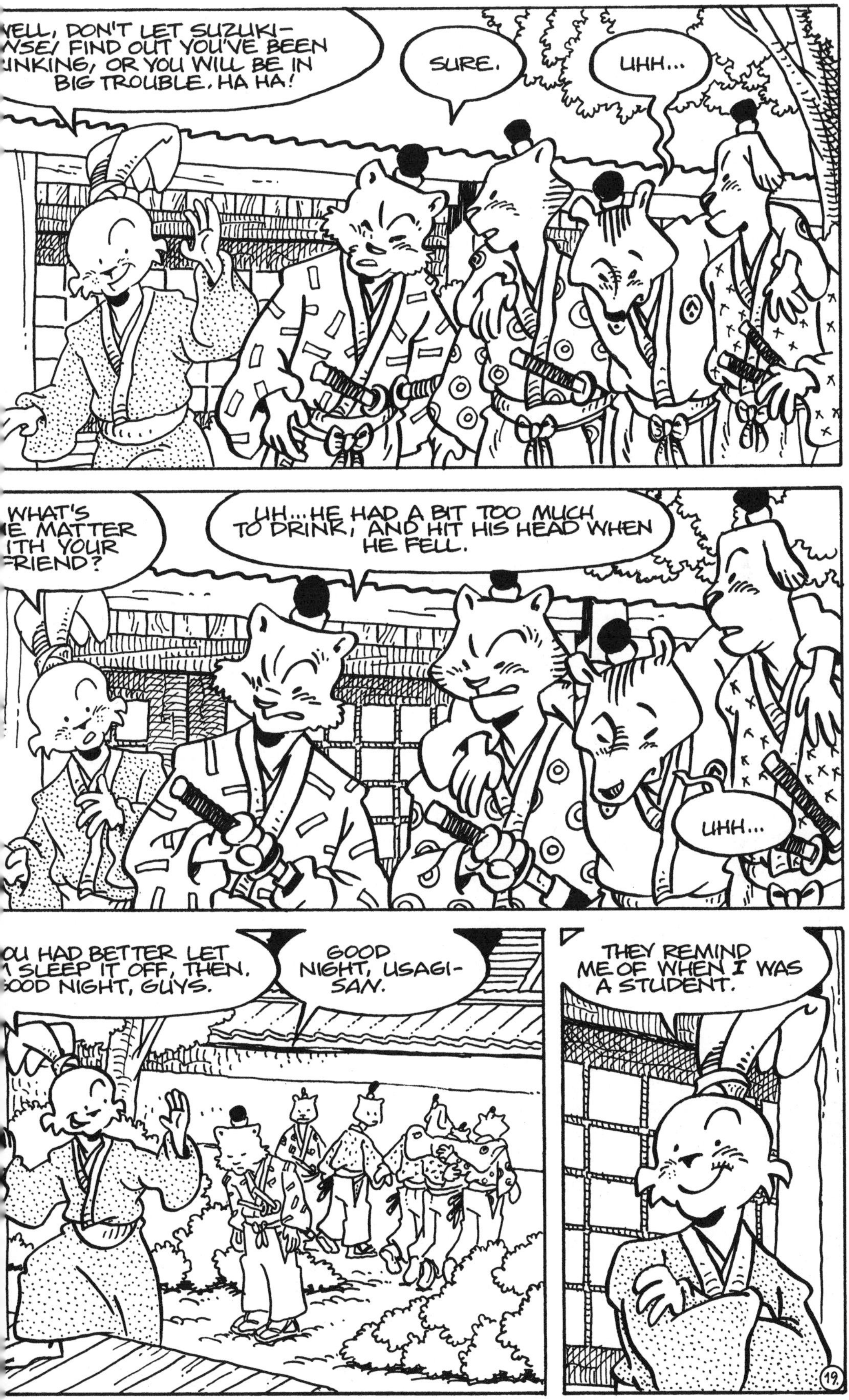
VELL, DON'T LET SUZUKI-
NSEI FIND OUT YOU'VE BEEN
INKING, OR YOU WILL BE IN
BIG TROUBLE. HA HA!
SURE.
UHH...
WHAT'S
E MATTER
ITH YOUR
RIEND?
UH...HE HAD A BIT TOO MUCH
TO DRINK, AND HIT HIS HEAD WHEN
HE FELL.
UHH...
OU HAD BETTER LET
I SLEEP IT OFF, THEN.
OOD NIGHT, GUYS.
GOOD
NIGHT, USAGI-
SAN.
THEY REMIND
ME OF WHEN I WAS
A STUDENT.
19.

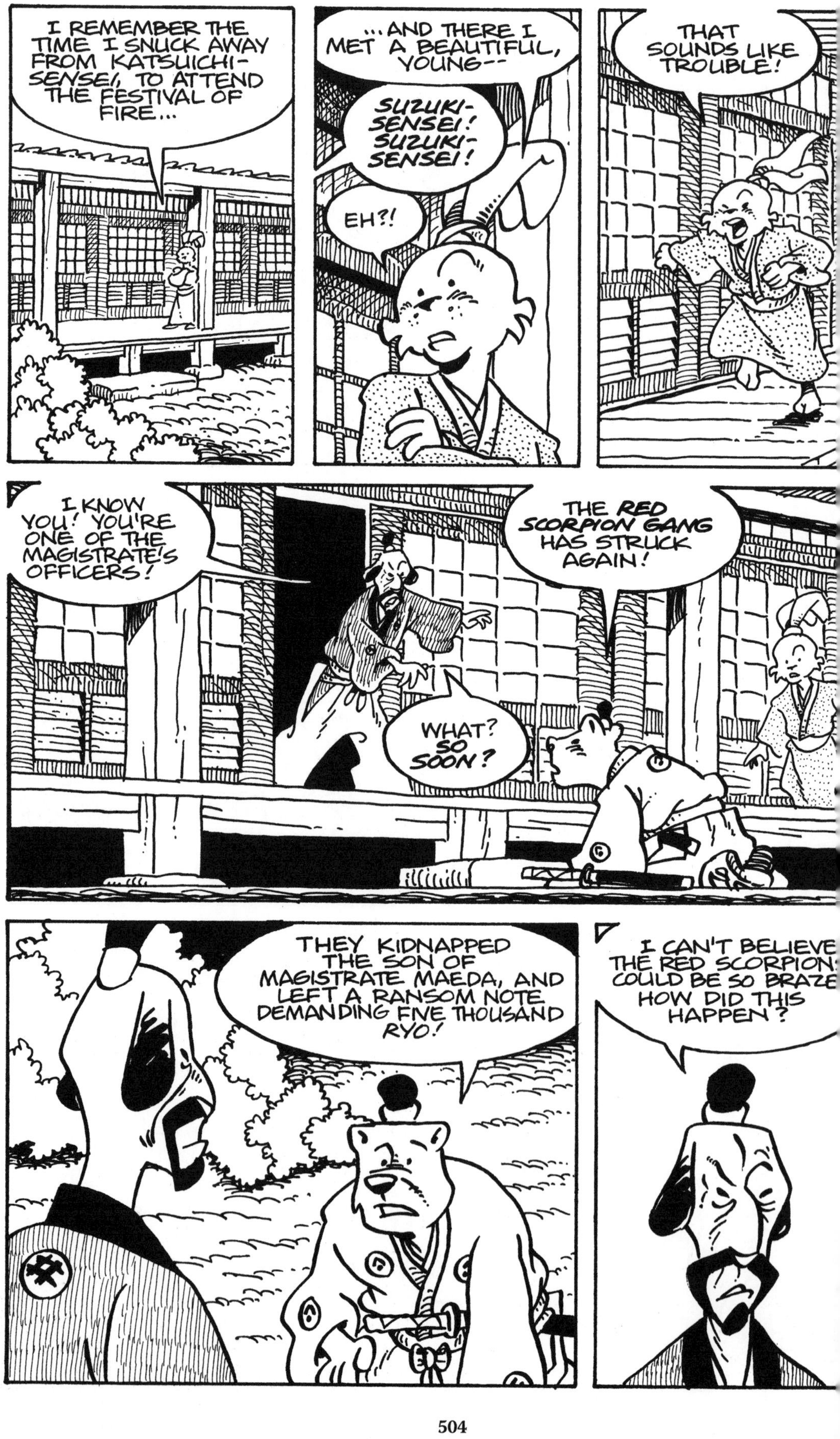
I REMEMBER THE TIME I SNUCK AWAY FROM KATSUICHI-SENSEI, TO ATTEND THE FESTIVAL OF FIRE...
...AND THERE I MET A BEAUTIFUL, YOUNG--
SUZUKI-SENSEI! SUZUKI-SENSEI!
EH?!
THAT SOUNDS LIKE TROUBLE!
I KNOW YOU! YOU'RE ONE OF THE MAGISTRATE'S OFFICERS!
THE RED SCORPION GANG HAS STRUCK AGAIN!
WHAT? SO SOON?
THEY KIDNAPPED THE SON OF MAGISTRATE MAEDA, AND LEFT A RANSOM NOTE DEMANDING FIVE THOUSAND RYO!
I CAN'T BELIEVE THE RED SCORPION COULD BE SO BRAZE HOW DID THIS HAPPEN?

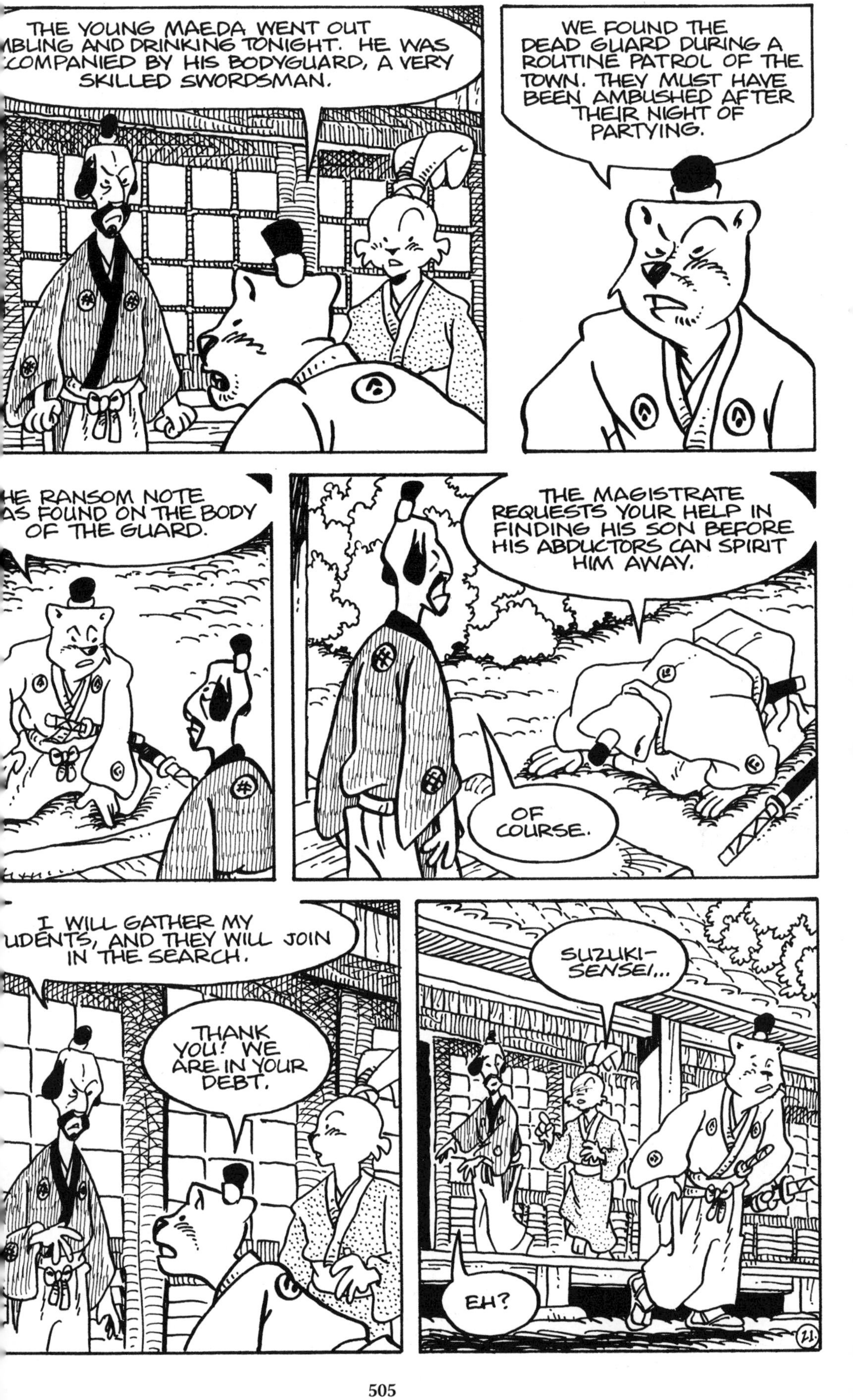
THE YOUNG MAEDA WENT OUT MBLING AND DRINKING TONIGHT. HE WAS COMPANIED BY HIS BODYGUARD, A VERY SKILLED SWORDSMAN.
WE FOUND THE DEAD GUARD DURING A ROUTINE PATROL OF THE TOWN. THEY MUST HAVE BEEN AMBUSHED AFTER THEIR NIGHT OF PARTYING.
HE RANSOM NOTE AS FOUND ON THE BODY OF THE GUARD.
THE MAGISTRATE REQUESTS YOUR HELP IN FINDING HIS SON BEFORE HIS ABDUCTORS CAN SPIRIT HIM AWAY.
OF COURSE.
I WILL GATHER MY UDENTS, AND THEY WILL JOIN IN THE SEARCH.
THANK YOU! WE ARE IN YOUR DEBT.
SUZUKI-SENSEI...
EH?
21.

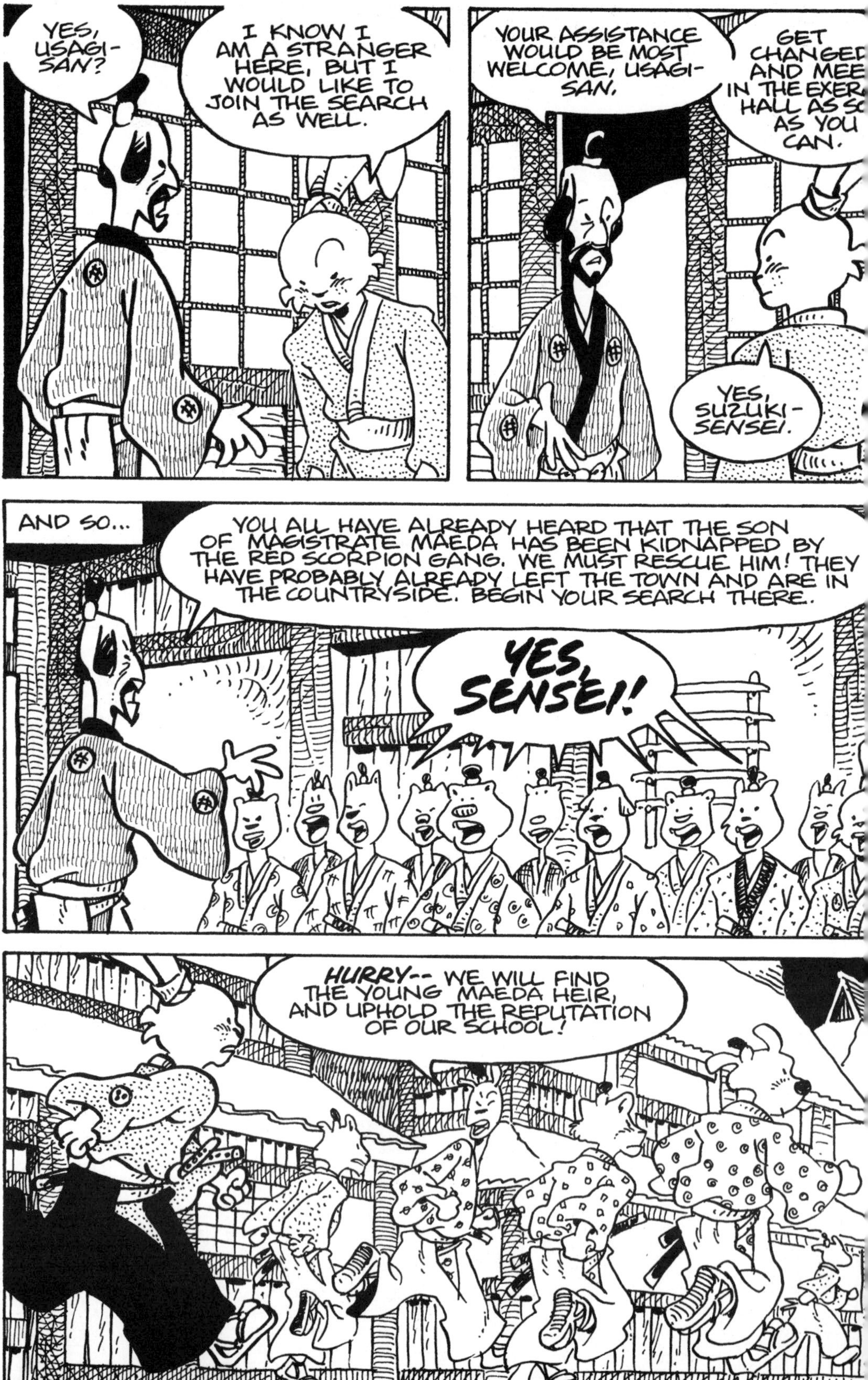
YES, USAGI-SAN?
I KNOW I AM A STRANGER HERE, BUT I WOULD LIKE TO JOIN THE SEARCH AS WELL.
YOUR ASSISTANCE WOULD BE MOST WELCOME, USAGI-SAN.
GET CHANGED AND MEE IN THE EXER HALL AS S AS YOU CAN.
YES, SUZUKI-SENSEI.
AND SO...
YOU ALL HAVE ALREADY HEARD THAT THE SON OF MAGISTRATE MAEDA HAS BEEN KIDNAPPED BY THE RED SCORPION GANG. WE MUST RESCUE HIM! THEY HAVE PROBABLY ALREADY LEFT THE TOWN AND ARE IN THE COUNTRYSIDE. BEGIN YOUR SEARCH THERE.
YES, SENSEI!
HURRY-- WE WILL FIND THE YOUNG MAEDA HEIR, AND UPHOLD THE REPUTATION OF OUR SCHOOL!

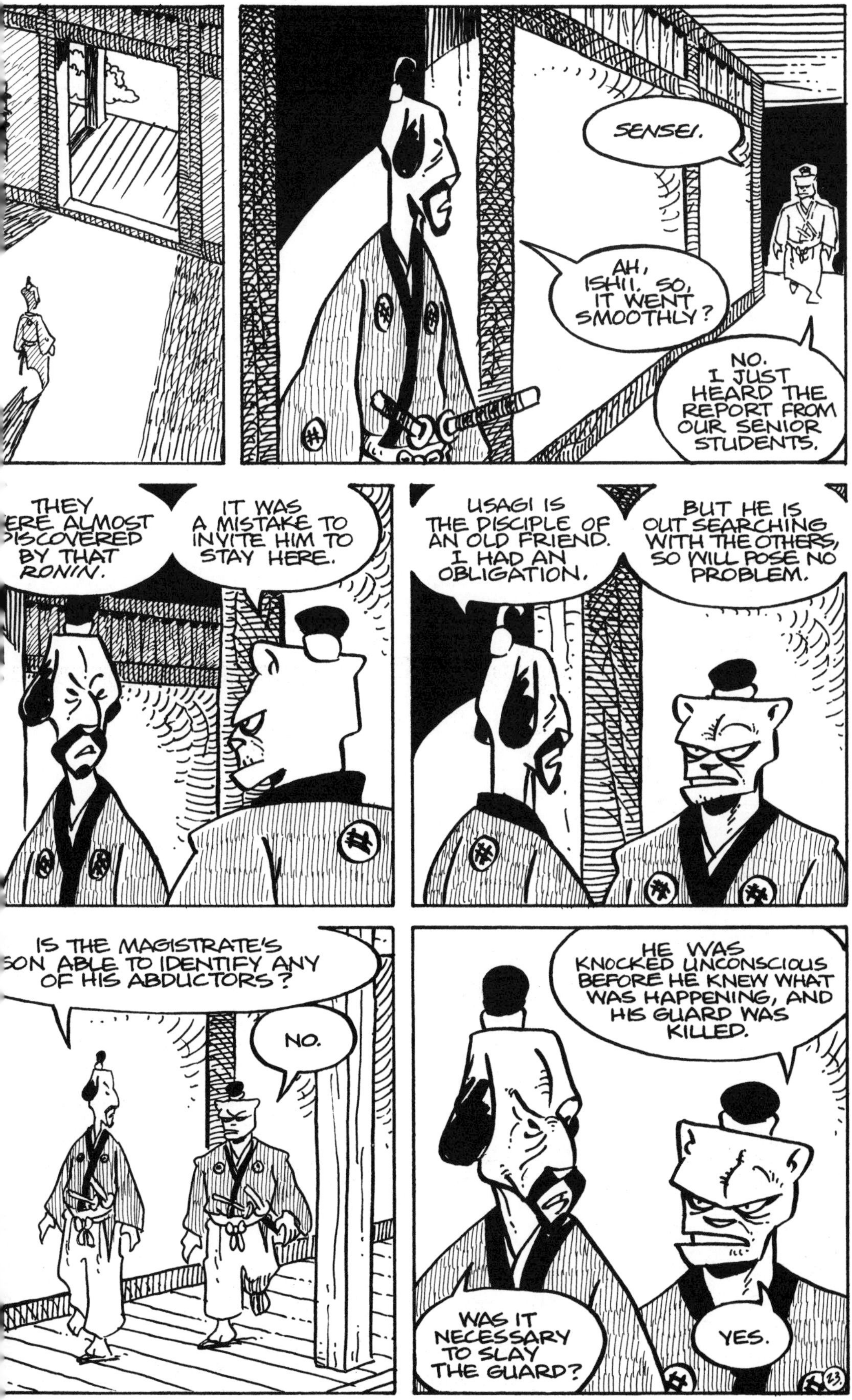
SENSEI.
AH, ISHII. SO, IT WENT SMOOTHLY?
NO. I JUST HEARD THE REPORT FROM OUR SENIOR STUDENTS.
THEY ERE ALMOST ISCOVERED BY THAT RONIN.
IT WAS A MISTAKE TO INVITE HIM TO STAY HERE.
USAGI IS THE DISCIPLE OF AN OLD FRIEND. I HAD AN OBLIGATION.
BUT HE IS OUT SEARCHING WITH THE OTHERS, SO WILL POSE NO PROBLEM.
IS THE MAGISTRATE'S SON ABLE TO IDENTIFY ANY OF HIS ABDUCTORS?
NO.
HE WAS KNOCKED UNCONSCIOUS BEFORE HE KNEW WHAT WAS HAPPENING, AND HIS GUARD WAS KILLED.
WAS IT NECESSARY TO SLAY THE GUARD?
YES.
23.

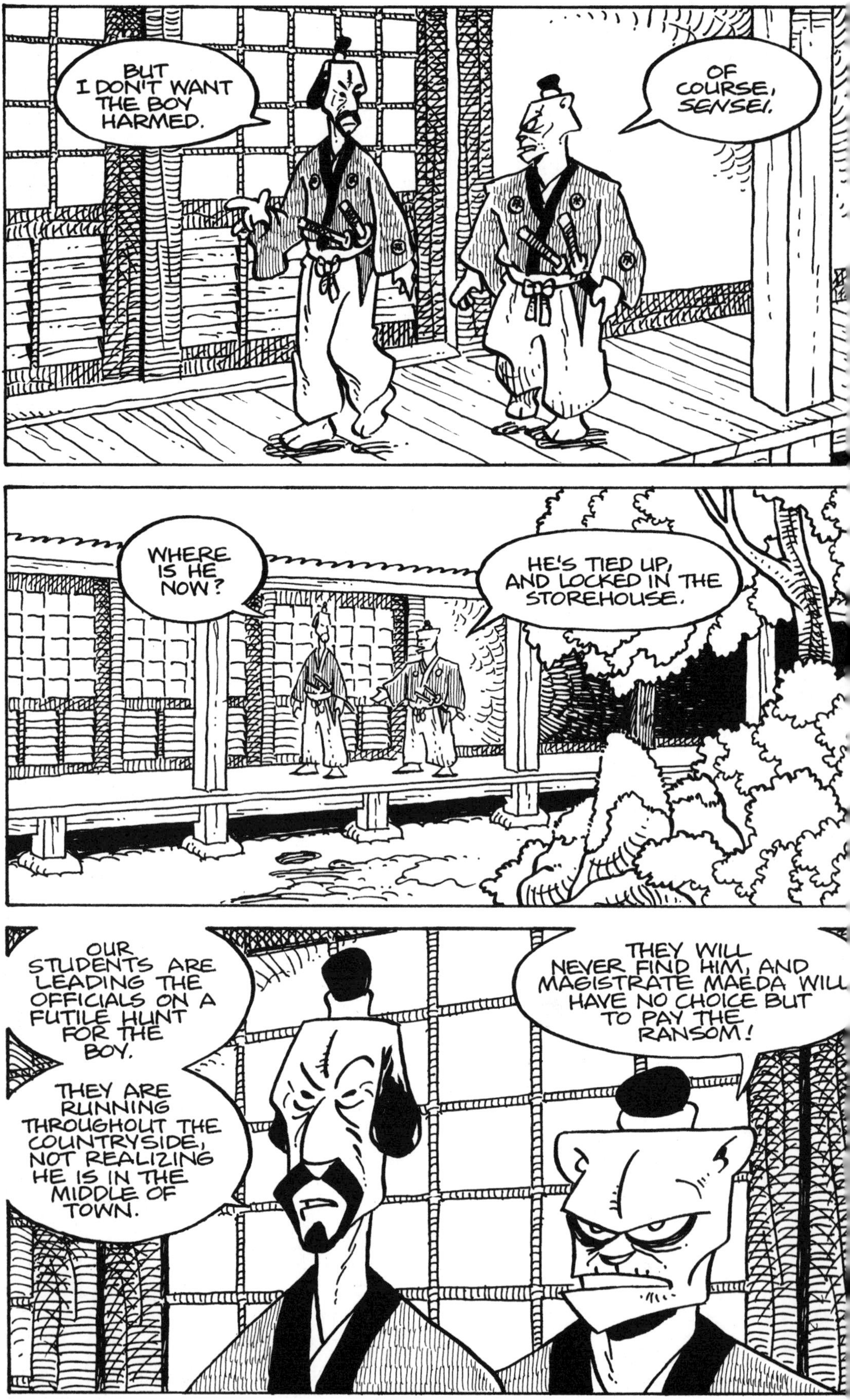
BUT I DON'T WANT THE BOY HARMED.
OF COURSE, SENSEI.
WHERE IS HE NOW?
HE'S TIED UP, AND LOCKED IN THE STOREHOUSE.
OUR STUDENTS ARE LEADING THE OFFICIALS ON A FUTILE HUNT FOR THE BOY.
THEY ARE RUNNING THROUGHOUT THE COUNTRYSIDE, NOT REALIZING HE IS IN THE MIDDLE OF TOWN.
THEY WILL NEVER FIND HIM, AND MAGISTRATE MAEDA WILL HAVE NO CHOICE BUT TO PAY THE RANSOM!

# HOSE WHO TREAD ON THE 'CORPION'S TAIL PART 2

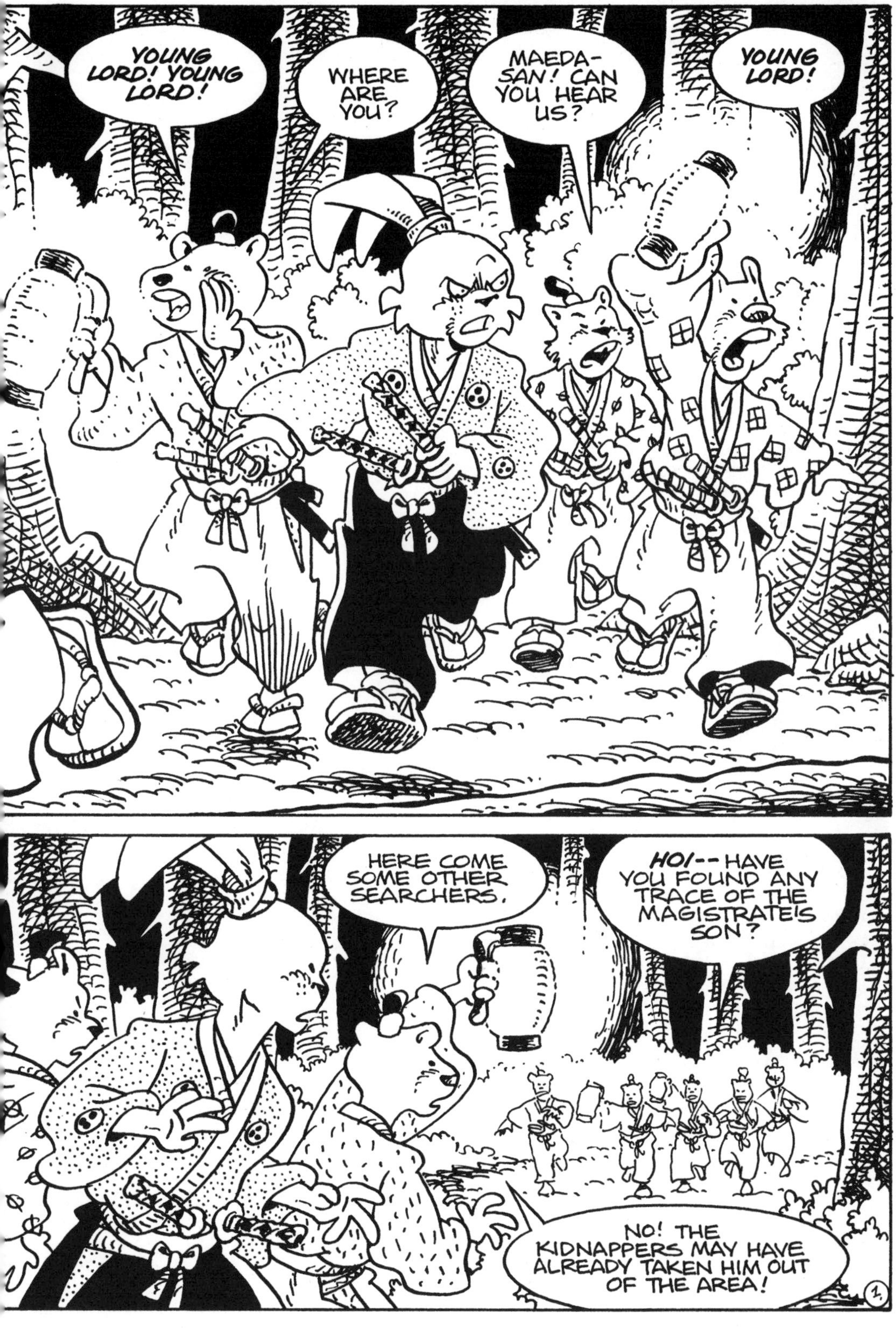
YOUNG LORD! YOUNG LORD!
WHERE ARE YOU?
MAEDA-SAN! CAN YOU HEAR US?
YOUNG LORD!
HERE COME SOME OTHER SEARCHERS.
HO! -- HAVE YOU FOUND ANY TRACE OF THE MAGISTRATE'S SON?
NO! THE KIDNAPPERS MAY HAVE ALREADY TAKEN HIM OUT OF THE AREA!
1.

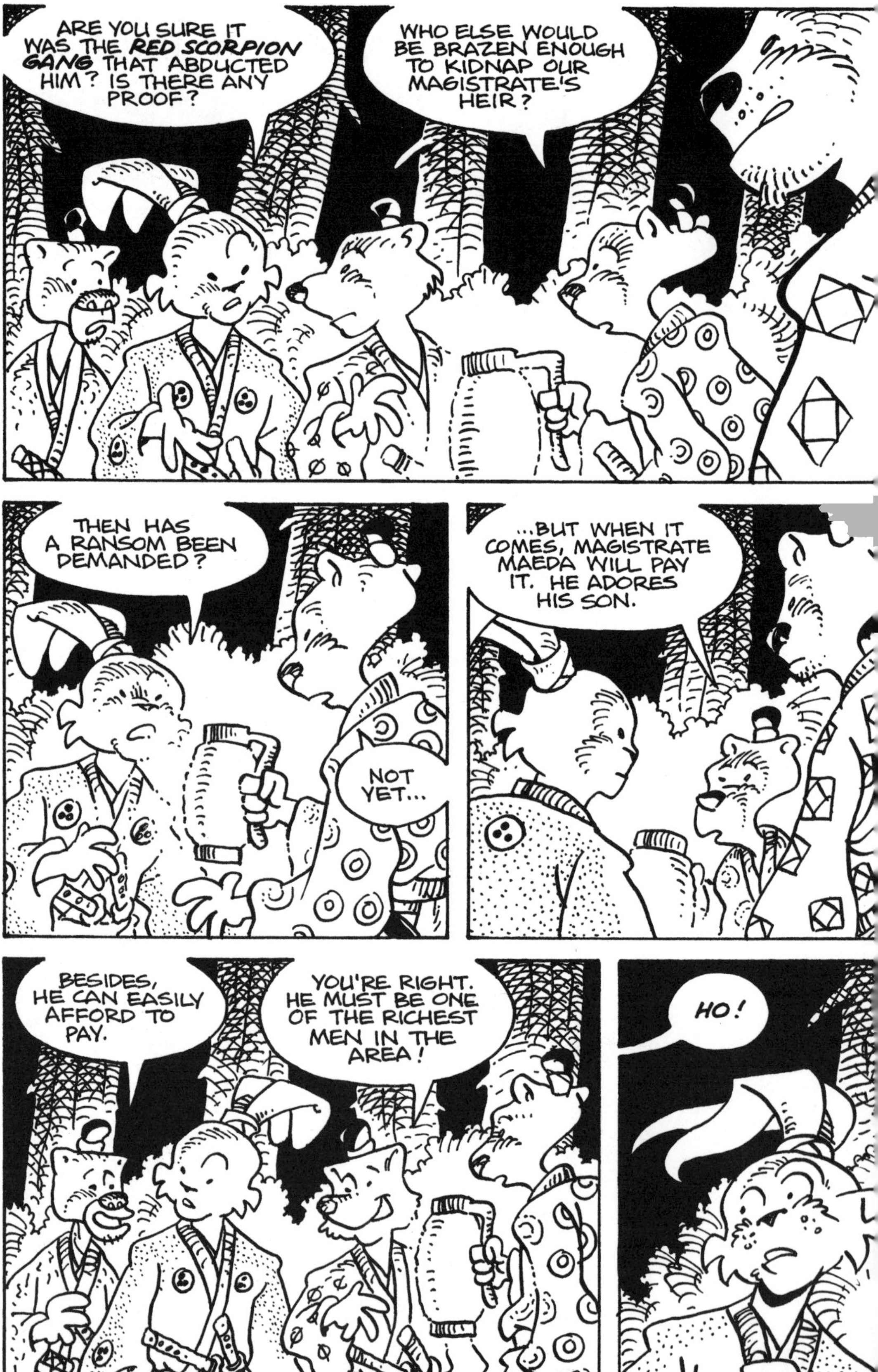
ARE YOU SURE IT WAS THE RED SCORPION GANG THAT ABDUCTED HIM? IS THERE ANY PROOF?
WHO ELSE WOULD BE BRAZEN ENOUGH TO KIDNAP OUR MAGISTRATE'S HEIR?
THEN HAS A RANSOM BEEN DEMANDED?
NOT YET...
...BUT WHEN IT COMES, MAGISTRATE MAEDA WILL PAY IT. HE ADORES HIS SON.
BESIDES, HE CAN EASILY AFFORD TO PAY.
YOU'RE RIGHT. HE MUST BE ONE OF THE RICHEST MEN IN THE AREA!
HO!

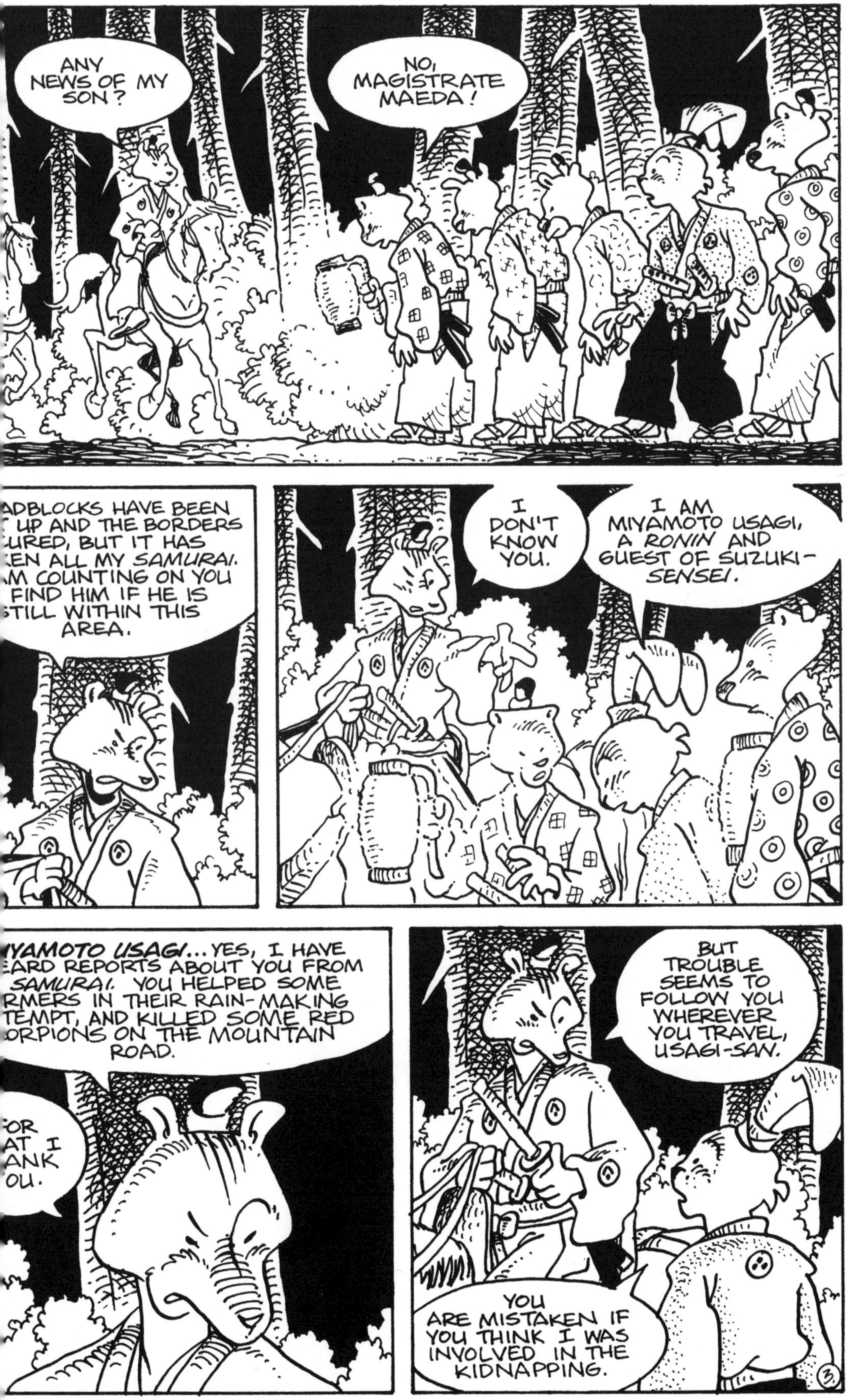
ANY NEWS OF MY SON?
NO, MAGISTRATE MAEDA!
ADBLOCKS HAVE BEEN T UP AND THE BORDERS CURED, BUT IT HAS EN ALL MY *SAMURAI*. M COUNTING ON YOU FIND HIM IF HE IS STILL WITHIN THIS AREA.
I DON'T KNOW YOU.
I AM MIYAMOTO USAGI, A *RONIN* AND GUEST OF SUZUKI-SENSEI.
IYAMOTO USAGI... YES, I HAVE EARD REPORTS ABOUT YOU FROM *SAMURAI*. YOU HELPED SOME RMERS IN THEIR RAIN-MAKING TEMPT, AND KILLED SOME RED ORPIONS ON THE MOUNTAIN ROAD.
FOR AT I ANK OU.
BUT TROUBLE SEEMS TO FOLLOW YOU WHEREVER YOU TRAVEL, USAGI-SAN.
YOU ARE MISTAKEN IF YOU THINK I WAS INVOLVED IN THE KIDNAPPING.
3

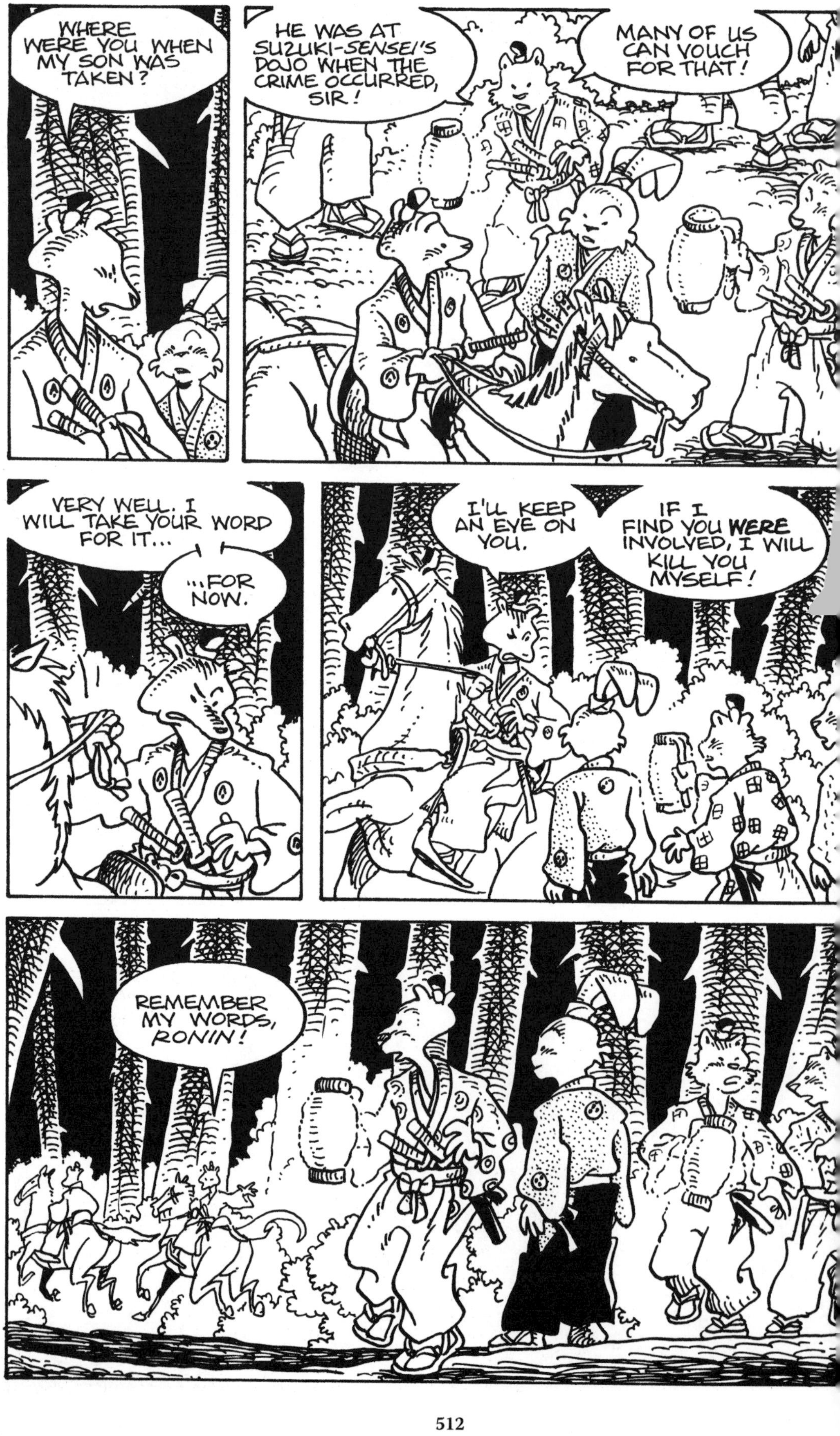
WHERE WERE YOU WHEN MY SON WAS TAKEN?
HE WAS AT SUZUKI-SENSEI'S DOJO WHEN THE CRIME OCCURRED, SIR!
MANY OF US CAN VOUCH FOR THAT!
VERY WELL. I WILL TAKE YOUR WORD FOR IT...
...FOR NOW.
I'LL KEEP AN EYE ON YOU.
IF I FIND YOU **WERE** INVOLVED, I WILL KILL YOU MYSELF!
REMEMBER MY WORDS, *RONIN!*

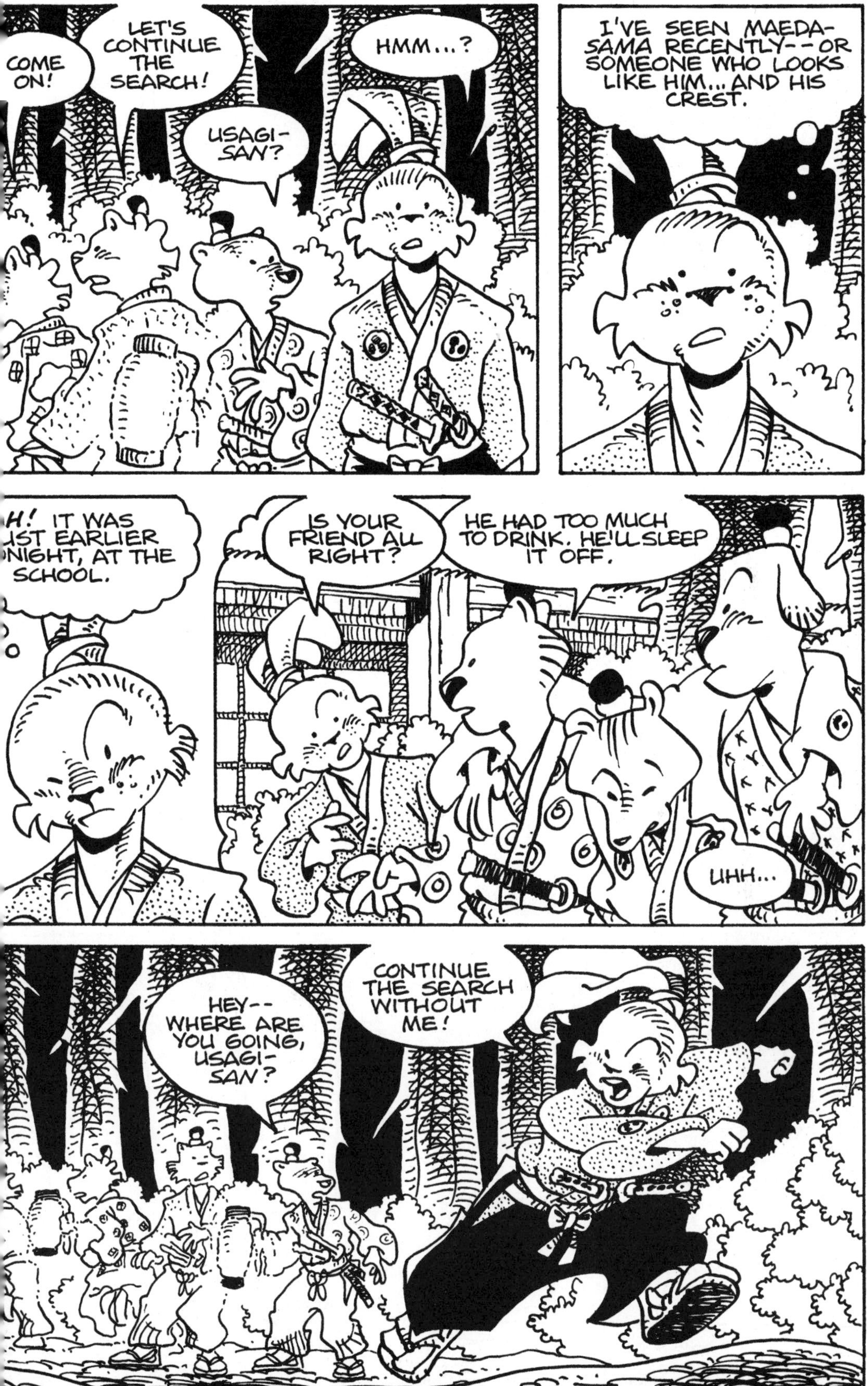
COME ON!
LET'S CONTINUE THE SEARCH!
USAGI-SAN?
HMM...?
I'VE SEEN MAEDA-SAMA RECENTLY--OR SOMEONE WHO LOOKS LIKE HIM... AND HIS CREST.
H! IT WAS UST EARLIER NIGHT, AT THE SCHOOL.
IS YOUR FRIEND ALL RIGHT?
HE HAD TOO MUCH TO DRINK. HE'LL SLEEP IT OFF.
UHH...
HEY-- WHERE ARE YOU GOING, USAGI-SAN?
CONTINUE THE SEARCH WITHOUT ME!
5

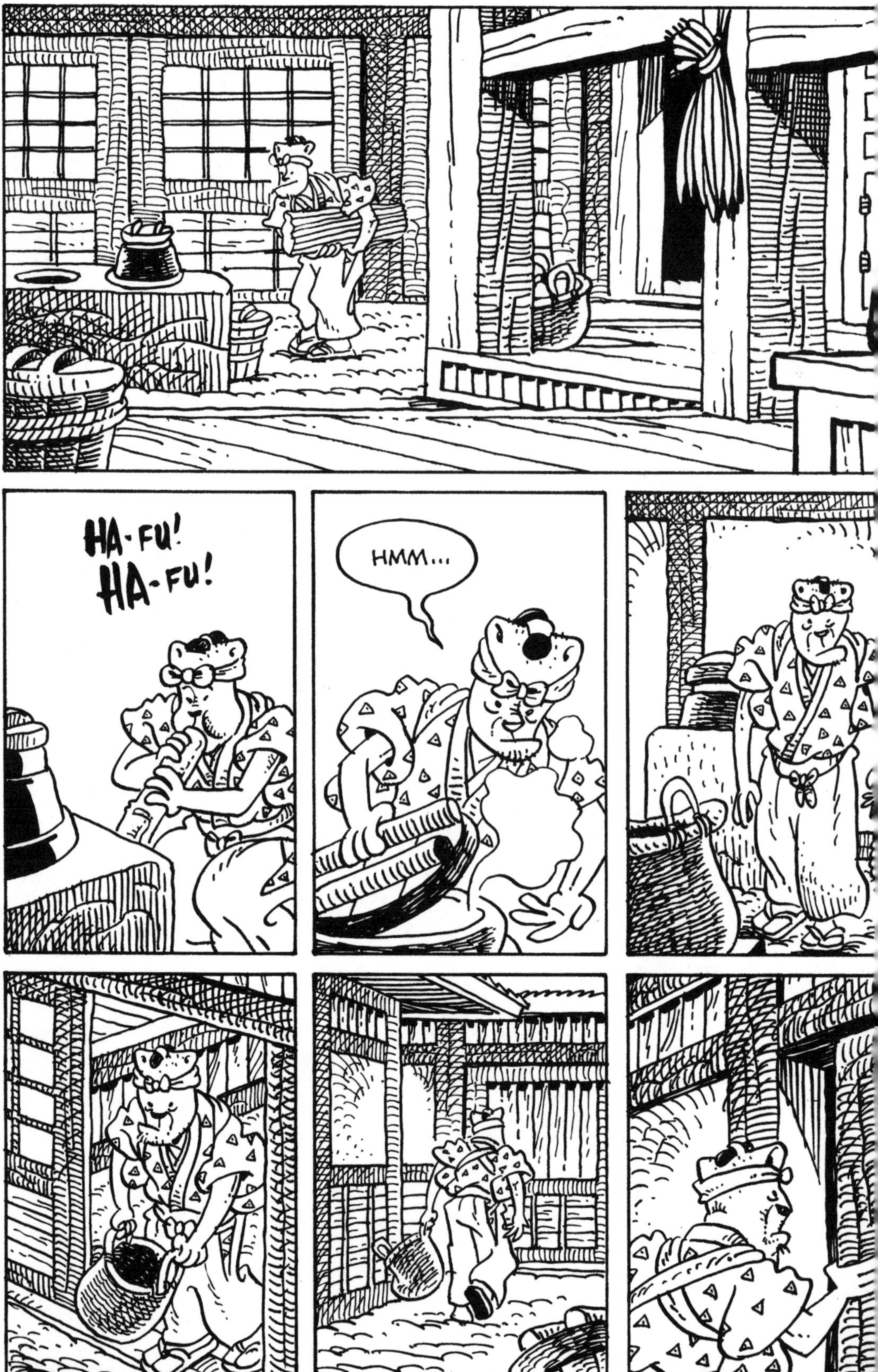
HA-FU!
HA-FU!
HMM...

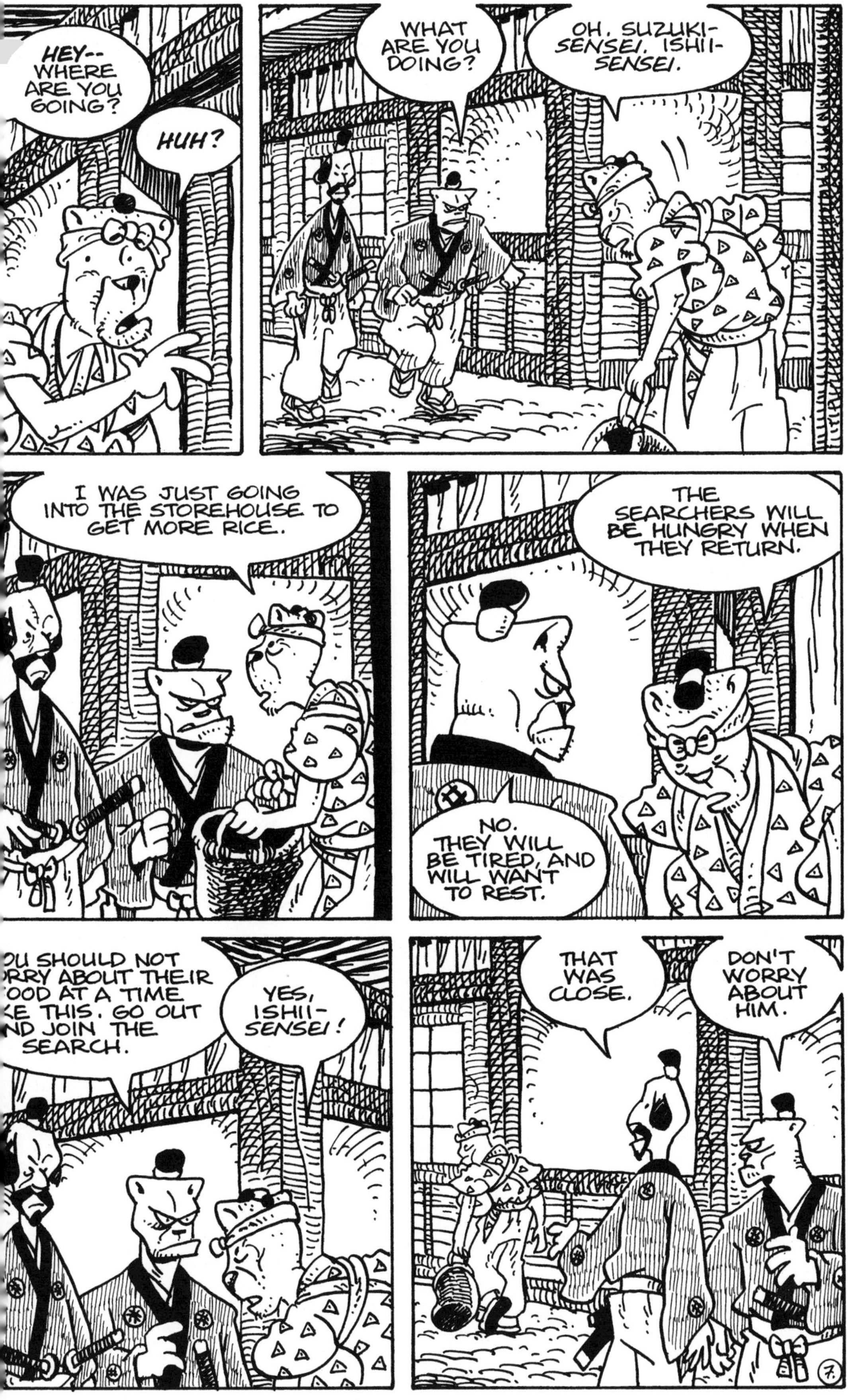
HEY-- WHERE ARE YOU GOING?
HUH?
WHAT ARE YOU DOING?
OH, SUZUKI-SENSEI, ISHII-SENSEI.
I WAS JUST GOING INTO THE STOREHOUSE TO GET MORE RICE.
THE SEARCHERS WILL BE HUNGRY WHEN THEY RETURN.
NO. THEY WILL BE TIRED, AND WILL WANT TO REST.
OU SHOULD NOT ORRY ABOUT THEIR OOD AT A TIME E THIS. GO OUT ND JOIN THE SEARCH.
YES, ISHII-SENSEI!
THAT WAS CLOSE.
DON'T WORRY ABOUT HIM.
7.

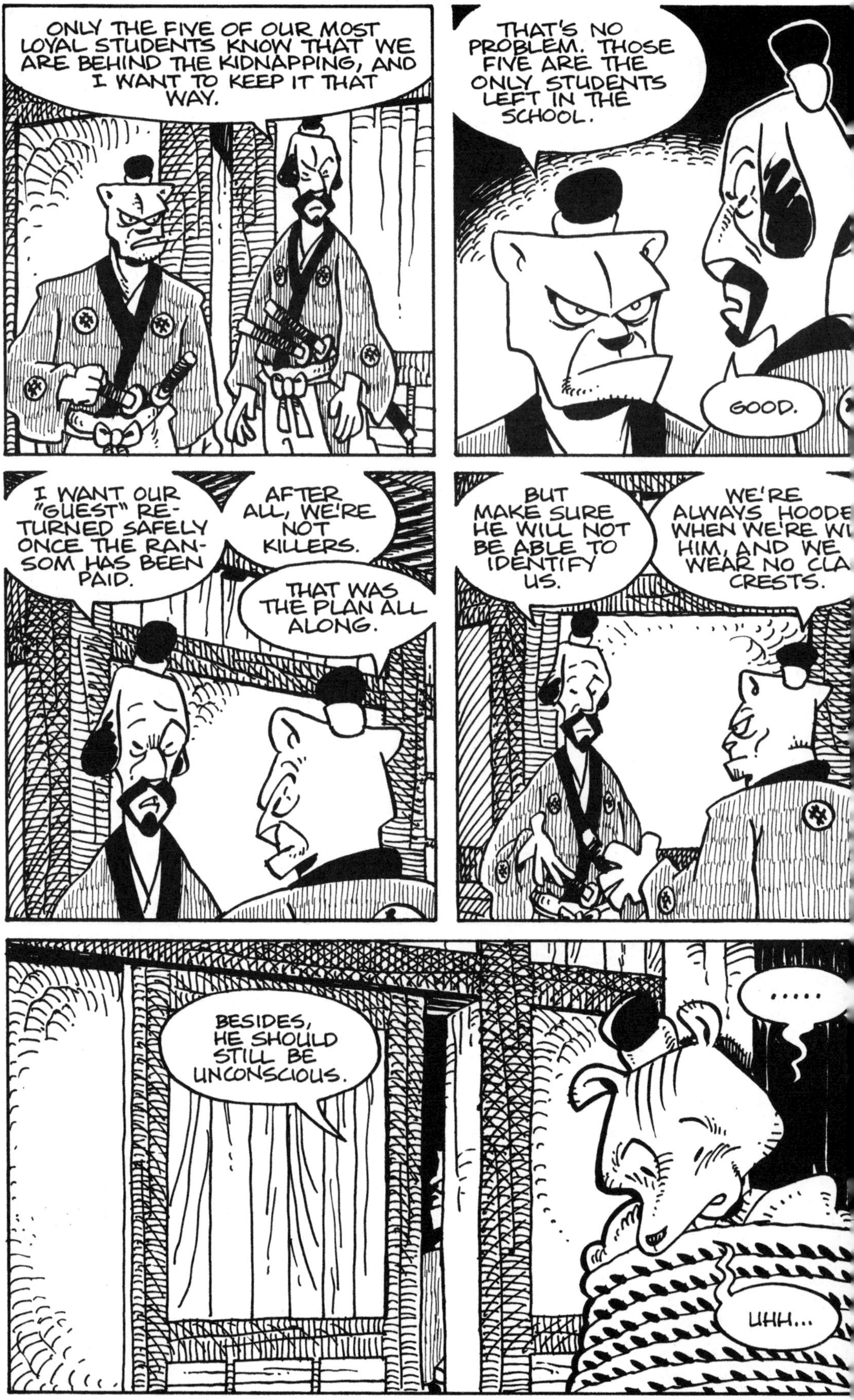
ONLY THE FIVE OF OUR MOST LOYAL STUDENTS KNOW THAT WE ARE BEHIND THE KIDNAPPING, AND I WANT TO KEEP IT THAT WAY.
THAT'S NO PROBLEM. THOSE FIVE ARE THE ONLY STUDENTS LEFT IN THE SCHOOL.
GOOD.
I WANT OUR "GUEST" RE-TURNED SAFELY ONCE THE RAN-SOM HAS BEEN PAID.
AFTER ALL, WE'RE NOT KILLERS.
THAT WAS THE PLAN ALL ALONG.
BUT MAKE SURE HE WILL NOT BE ABLE TO IDENTIFY US.
WE'RE ALWAYS HOODE WHEN WE'RE WI HIM, AND WE WEAR NO CLA CRESTS.
BESIDES, HE SHOULD STILL BE UNCONSCIOUS.
.....
UHH...

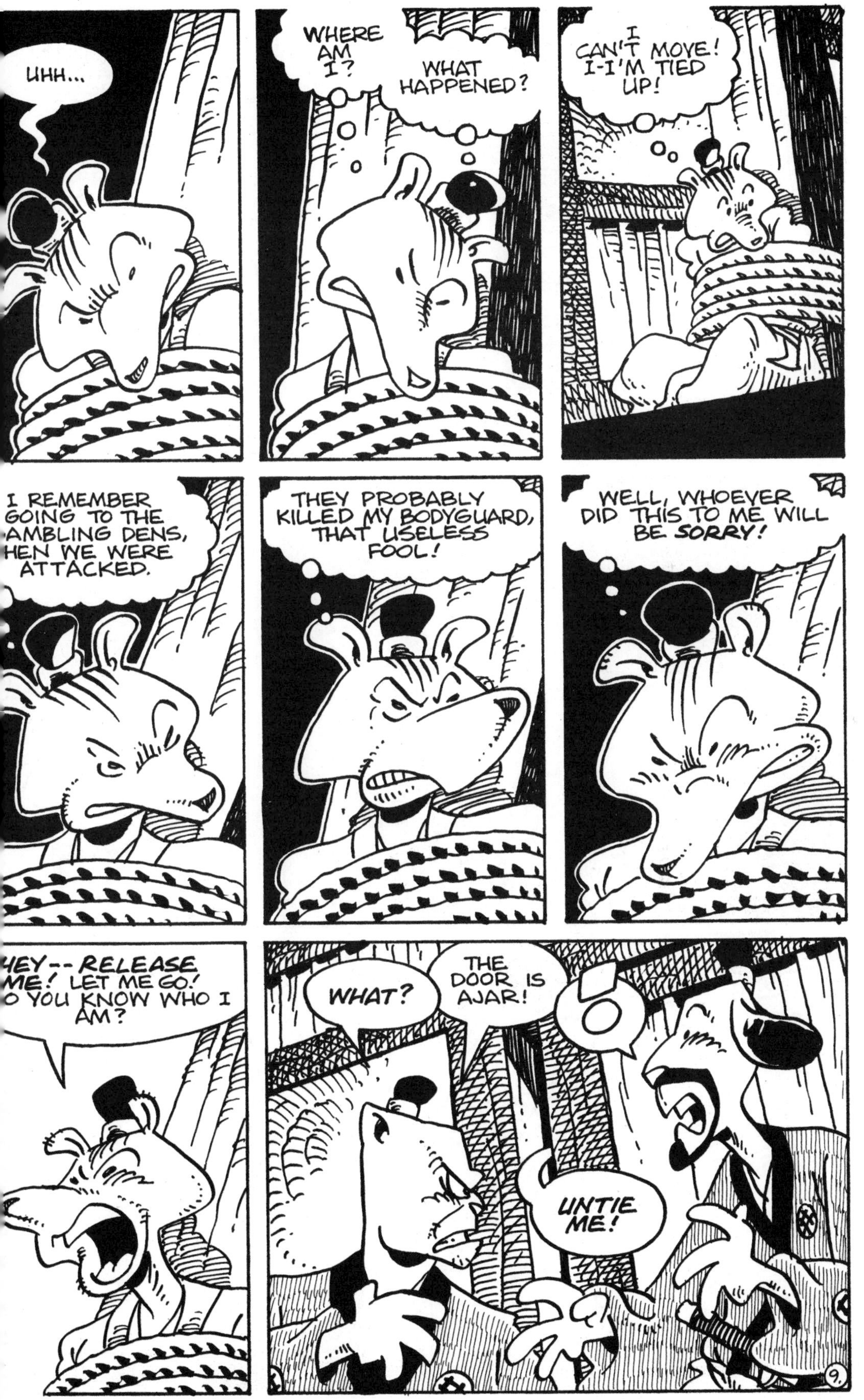

UHH...
WHERE AM I?
WHAT HAPPENED?
I CAN'T MOVE! I-I'M TIED UP!
I REMEMBER GOING TO THE AMBLING DENS, HEN WE WERE ATTACKED.
THEY PROBABLY KILLED MY BODYGUARD, THAT USELESS FOOL!
WELL, WHOEVER DID THIS TO ME WILL BE *SORRY!*
HEY-- *RELEASE ME!* LET ME GO! O YOU KNOW WHO I AM?
*WHAT?*
THE DOOR IS AJAR!
*UNTIE ME!*
9.

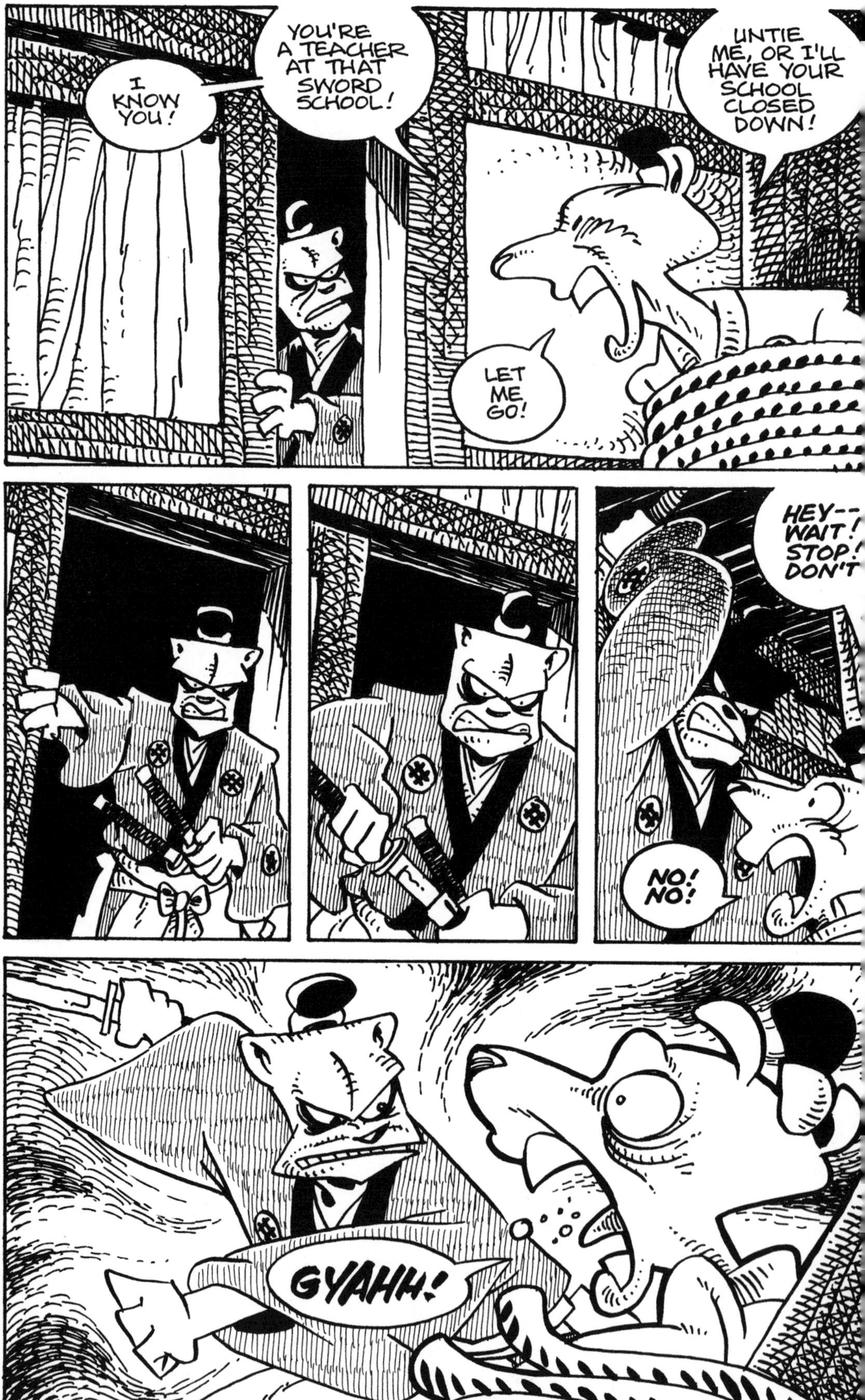
I KNOW YOU!
YOU'RE A TEACHER AT THAT SWORD SCHOOL!
UNTIE ME, OR I'LL HAVE YOUR SCHOOL CLOSED DOWN!
LET ME GO!
HEY-- WAIT! STOP! DON'T
NO! NO!
GYAHH!

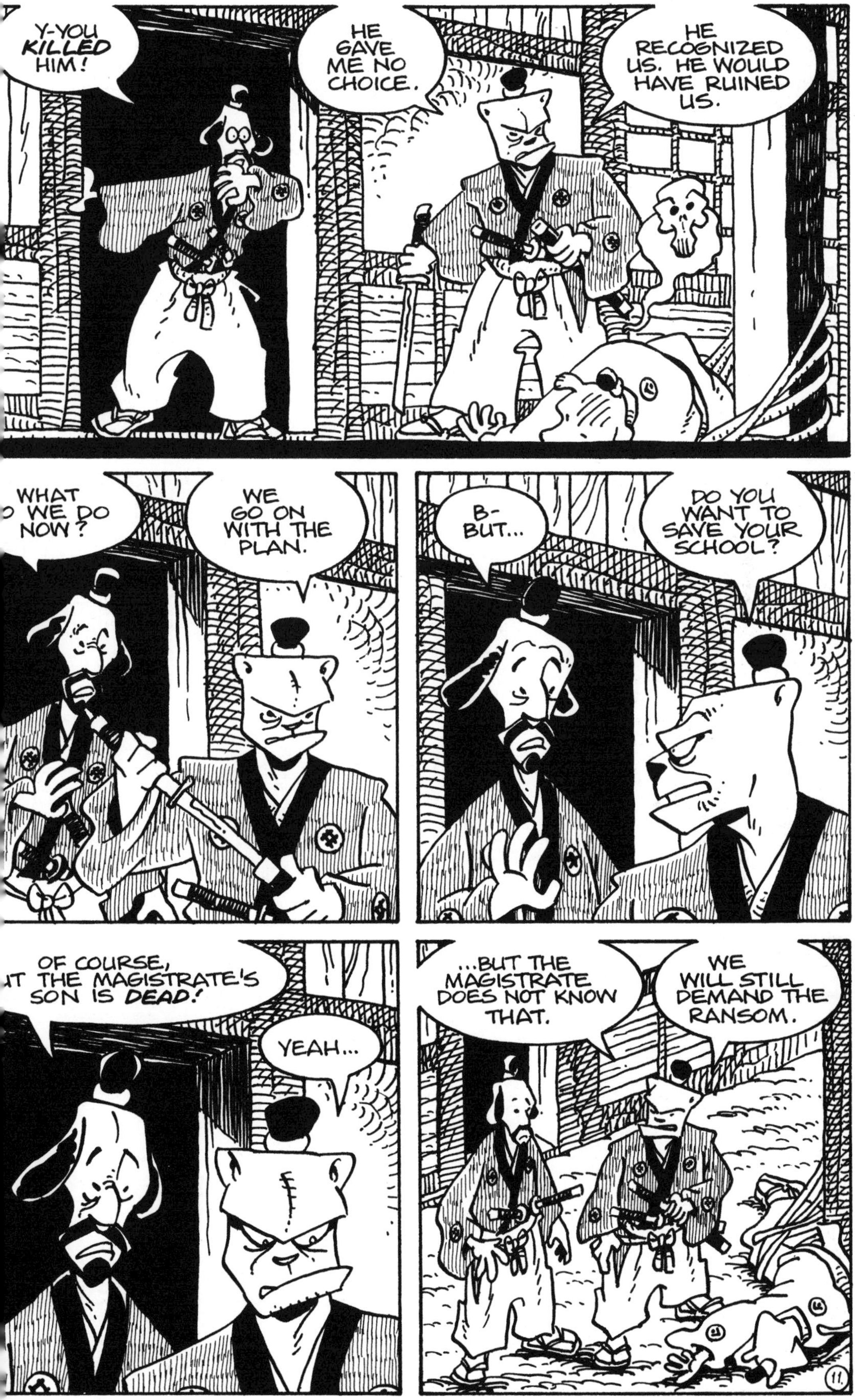
Y-YOU **KILLED** HIM!
HE GAVE ME NO CHOICE.
HE RECOGNIZED US. HE WOULD HAVE RUINED US.
WHAT O WE DO NOW?
WE GO ON WITH THE PLAN.
B-BUT...
DO YOU WANT TO SAVE YOUR SCHOOL?
OF COURSE, JT THE MAGISTRATE'S SON IS **DEAD!**
YEAH...
...BUT THE MAGISTRATE DOES NOT KNOW THAT.
WE WILL STILL DEMAND THE RANSOM.
11.

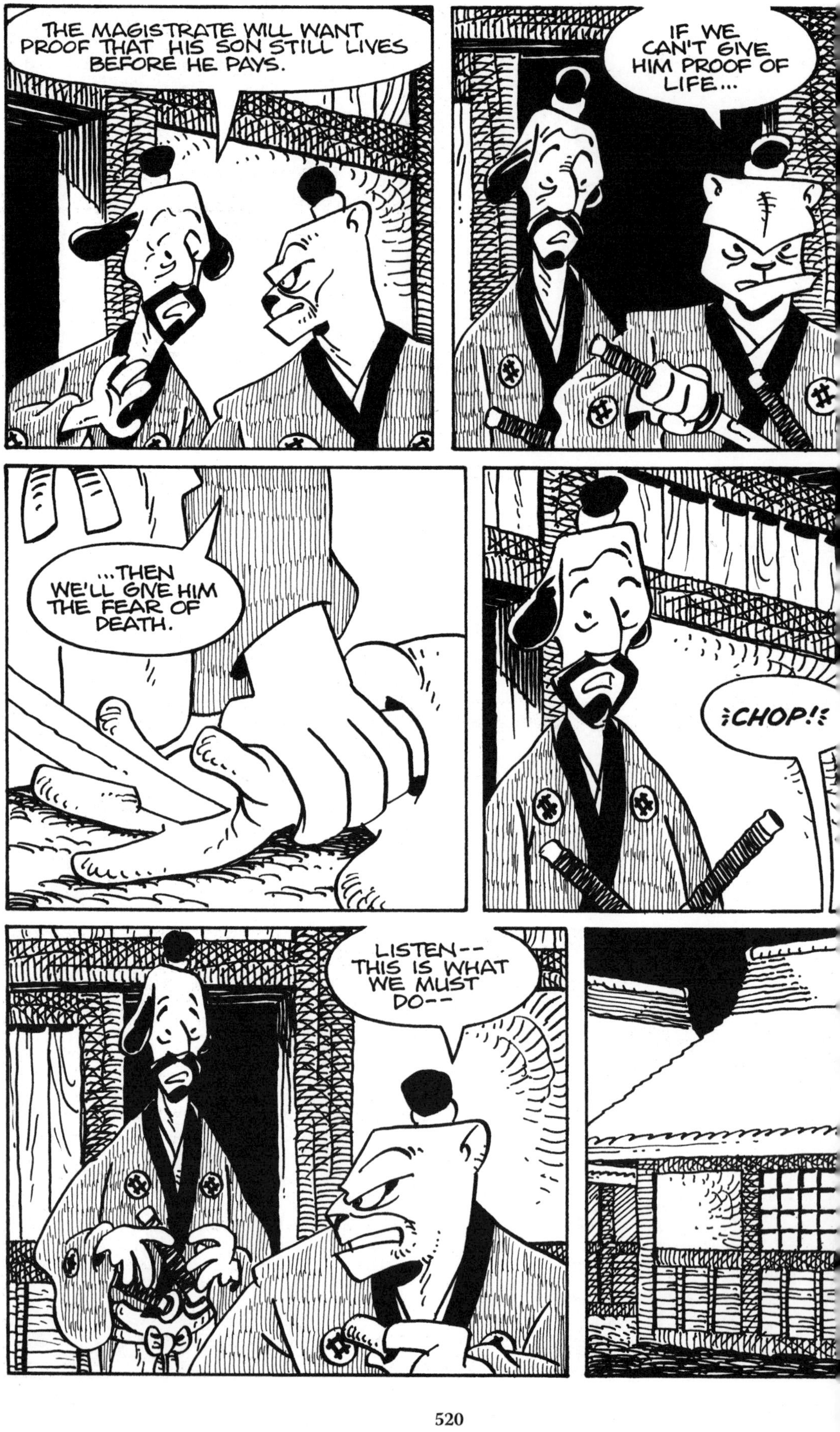
THE MAGISTRATE WILL WANT PROOF THAT HIS SON STILL LIVES BEFORE HE PAYS.
IF WE CAN'T GIVE HIM PROOF OF LIFE...
...THEN WE'LL GIVE HIM THE FEAR OF DEATH.
¡CHOP!¡
LISTEN-- THIS IS WHAT WE MUST DO--

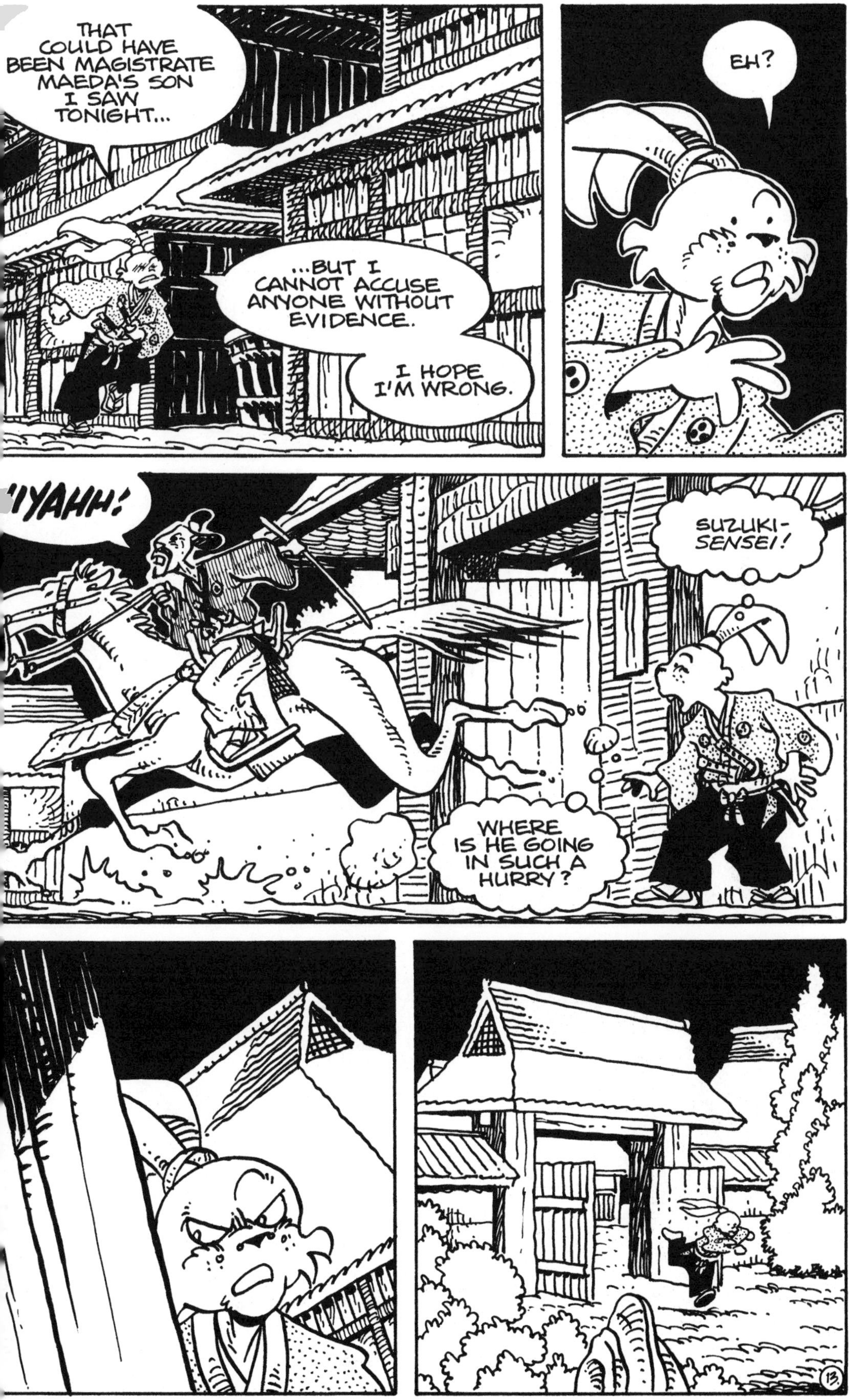
THAT COULD HAVE BEEN MAGISTRATE MAEDA'S SON I SAW TONIGHT...
...BUT I CANNOT ACCUSE ANYONE WITHOUT EVIDENCE.
I HOPE I'M WRONG.
EH?
IYAHH!
SUZUKI-SENSEI!
WHERE IS HE GOING IN SUCH A HURRY?
13

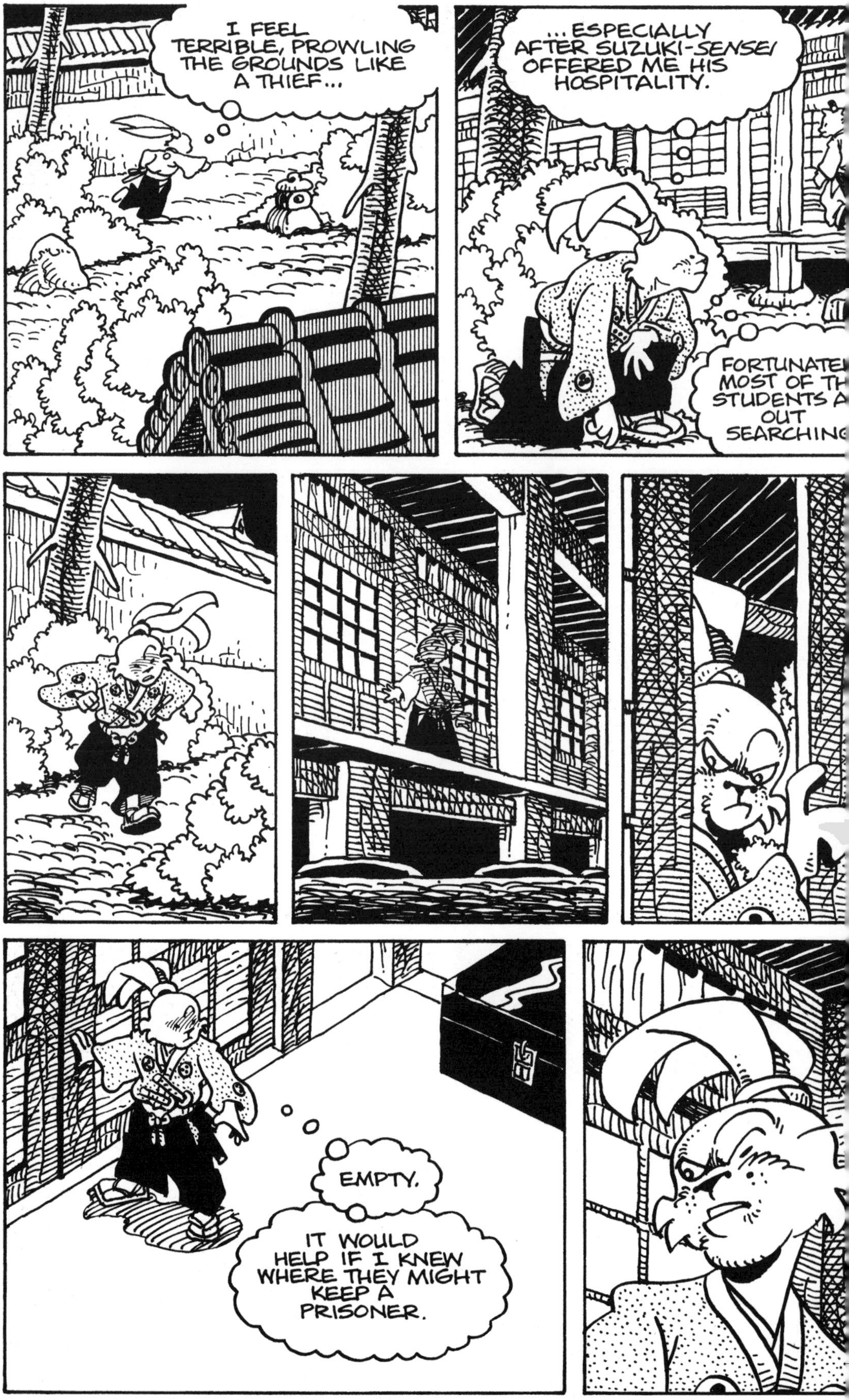
I FEEL TERRIBLE, PROWLING THE GROUNDS LIKE A THIEF...
...ESPECIALLY AFTER SUZUKI-SENSEI OFFERED ME HIS HOSPITALITY.
FORTUNATEL MOST OF TH STUDENTS A OUT SEARCHING
EMPTY.
IT WOULD HELP IF I KNEW WHERE THEY MIGHT KEEP A PRISONER.

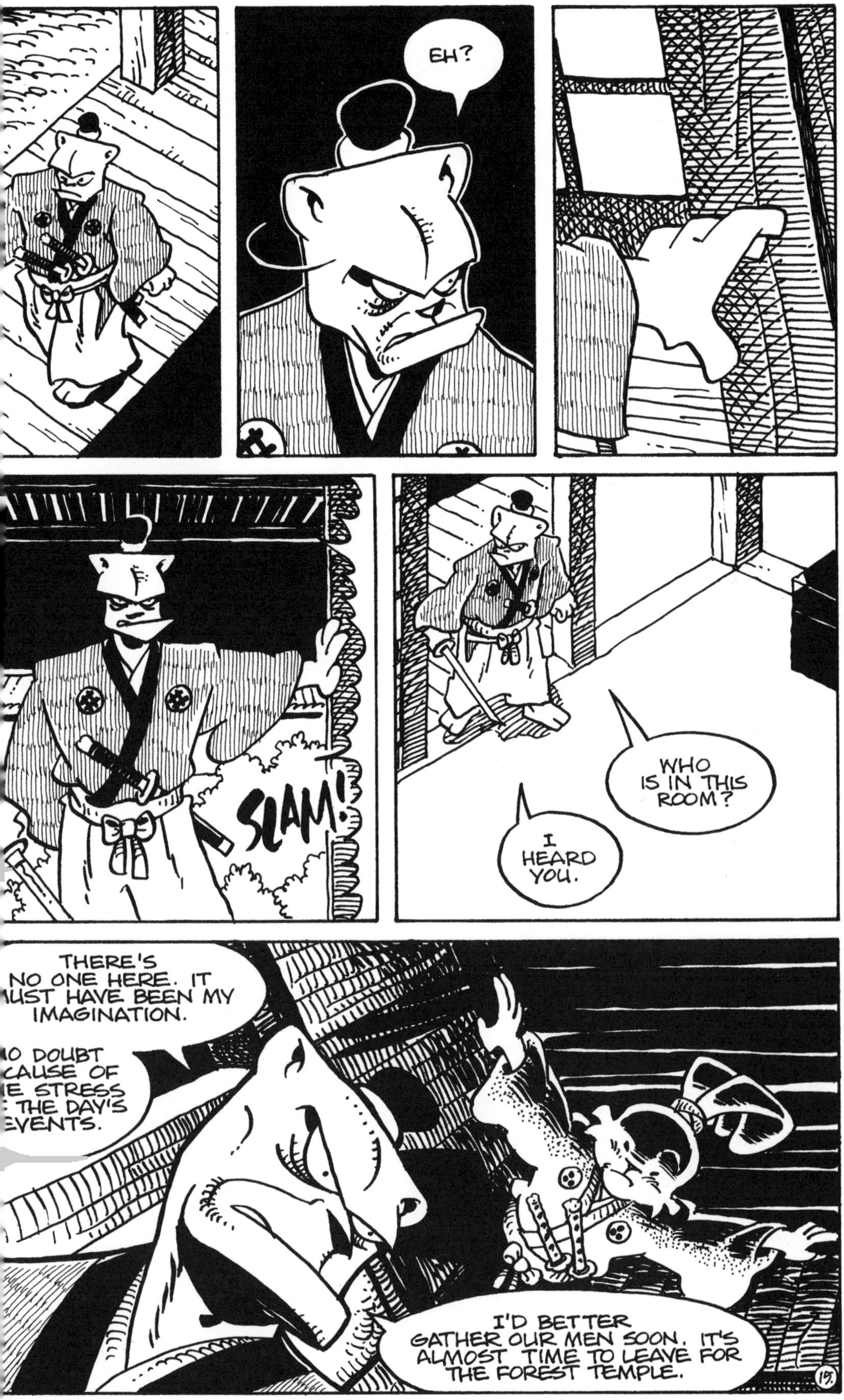
EH?
SLAM!
I HEARD YOU.
WHO IS IN THIS ROOM?
THERE'S NO ONE HERE. IT MUST HAVE BEEN MY IMAGINATION.
NO DOUBT BECAUSE OF THE STRESS OF THE DAY'S EVENTS.
I'D BETTER GATHER OUR MEN SOON. IT'S ALMOST TIME TO LEAVE FOR THE FOREST TEMPLE.
15.

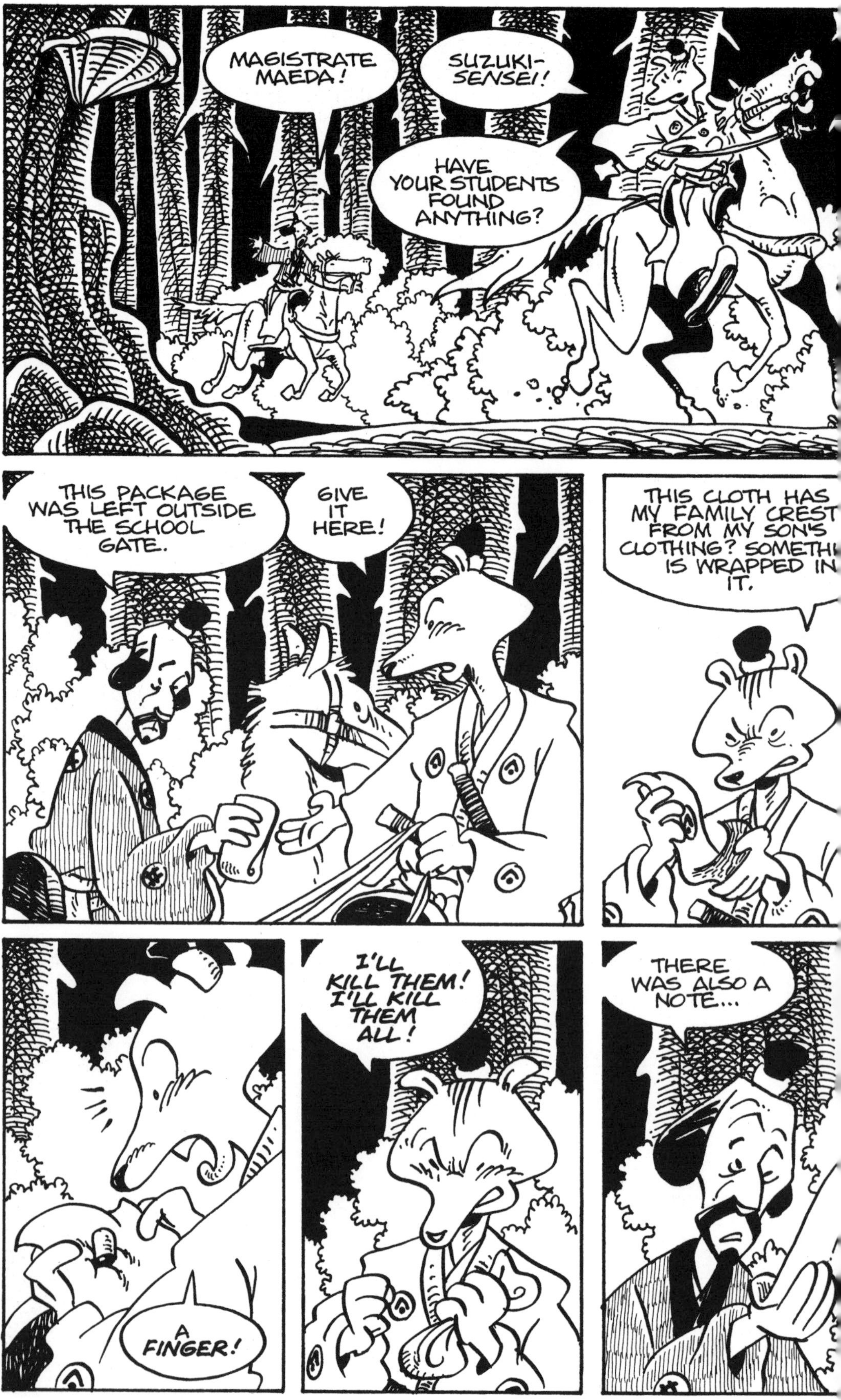
MAGISTRATE MAEDA!
SUZUKI-SENSEI!
HAVE YOUR STUDENTS FOUND ANYTHING?
THIS PACKAGE WAS LEFT OUTSIDE THE SCHOOL GATE.
GIVE IT HERE!
THIS CLOTH HAS MY FAMILY CREST FROM MY SON'S CLOTHING? SOMETHI IS WRAPPED IN IT.
A FINGER!
I'LL KILL THEM! I'LL KILL THEM ALL!
THERE WAS ALSO A NOTE...

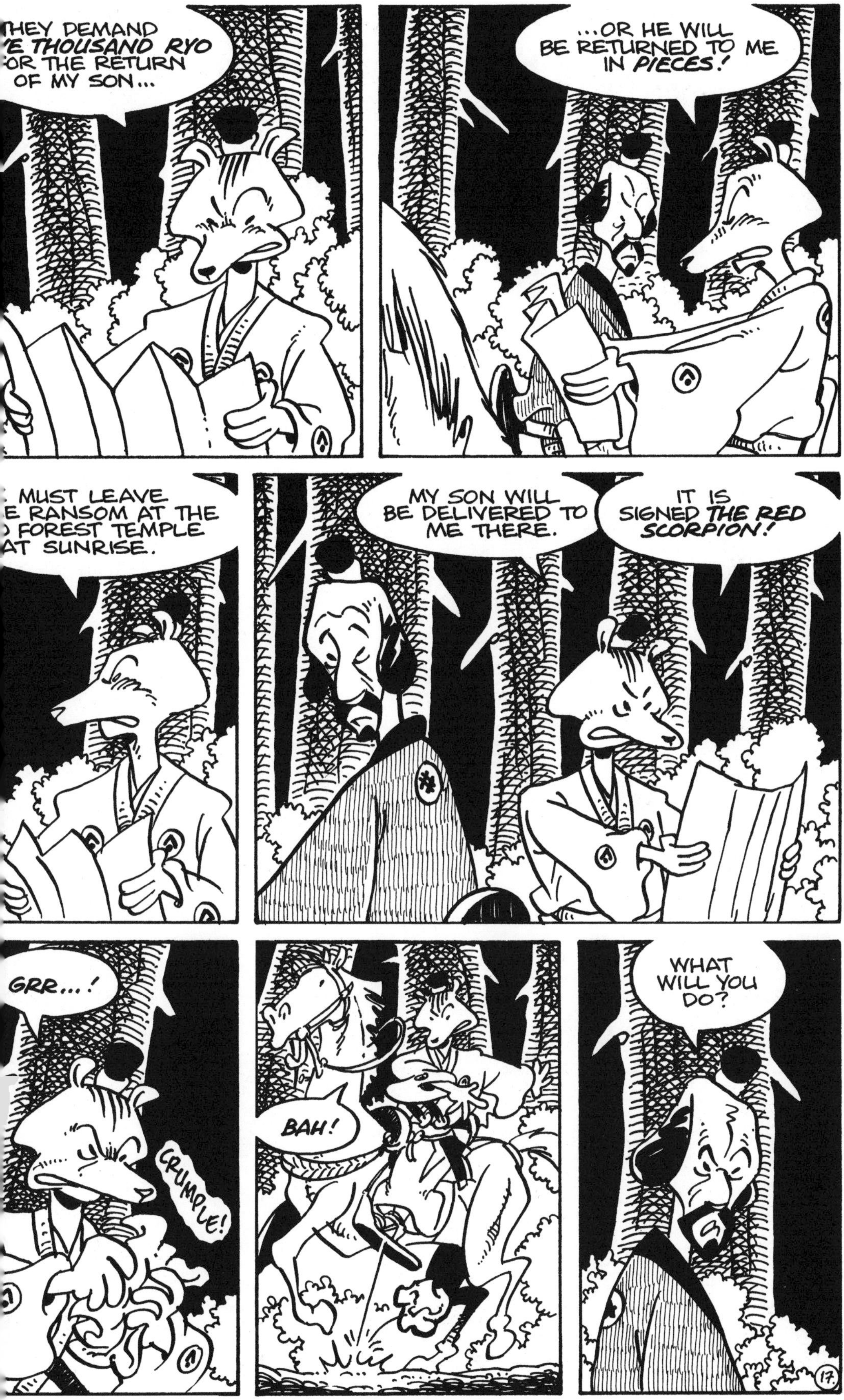
THEY DEMAND
E THOUSAND RYO
OR THE RETURN
OF MY SON...
...OR HE WILL
BE RETURNED TO ME
IN PIECES!
MUST LEAVE
E RANSOM AT THE
FOREST TEMPLE
AT SUNRISE.
MY SON WILL
BE DELIVERED TO
ME THERE.
IT IS
SIGNED THE RED
SCORPION!
GRR...!
CRUMPLE!
BAH!
WHAT
WILL YOU
DO?
17.

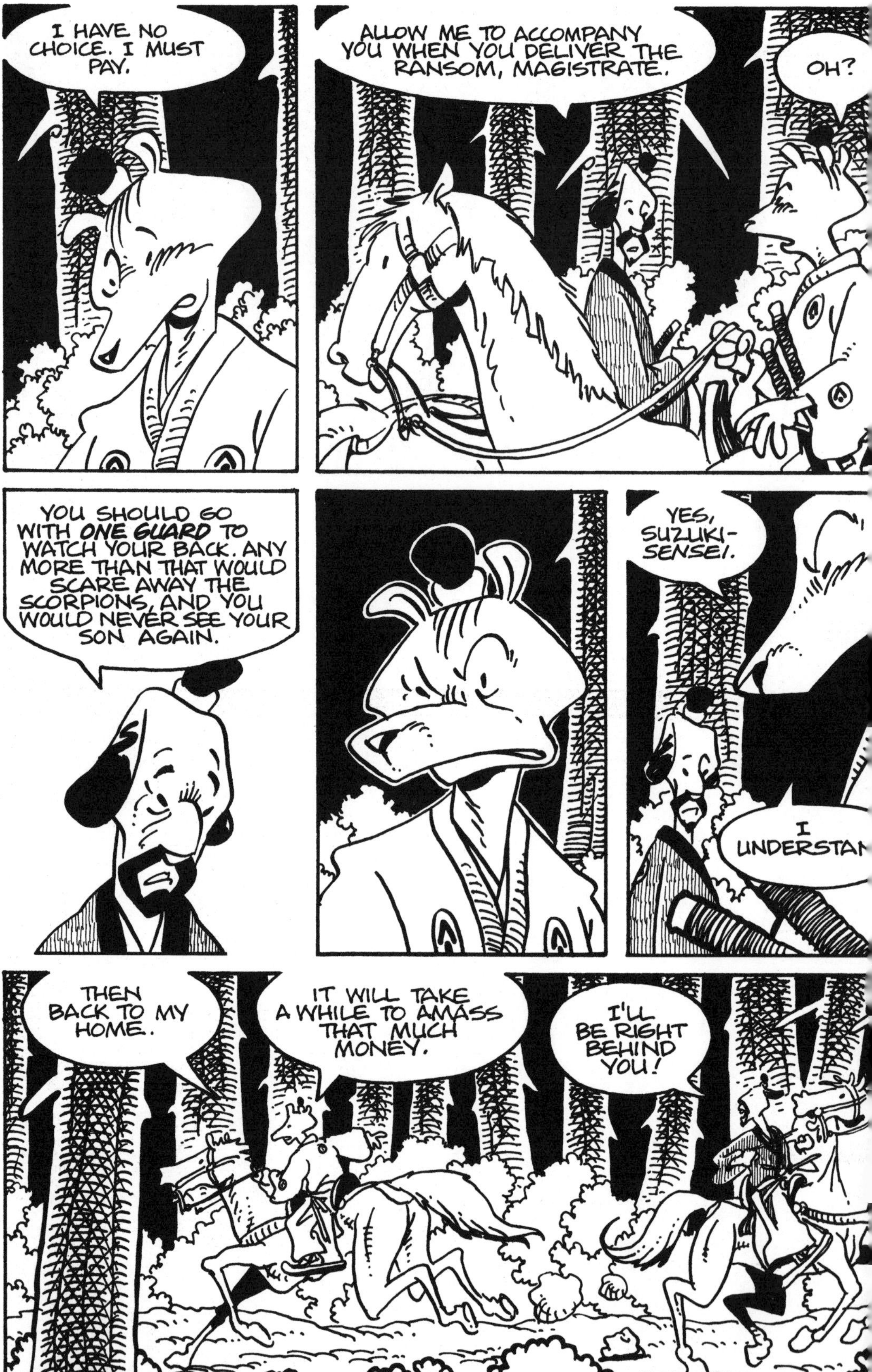
I HAVE NO CHOICE. I MUST PAY.
ALLOW ME TO ACCOMPANY YOU WHEN YOU DELIVER THE RANSOM, MAGISTRATE.
OH?
YOU SHOULD GO WITH ONE GUARD TO WATCH YOUR BACK. ANY MORE THAN THAT WOULD SCARE AWAY THE SCORPIONS, AND YOU WOULD NEVER SEE YOUR SON AGAIN.
YES, SUZUKI-SENSEI.
I UNDERSTAN
THEN BACK TO MY HOME.
IT WILL TAKE A WHILE TO AMASS THAT MUCH MONEY.
I'LL BE RIGHT BEHIND YOU!

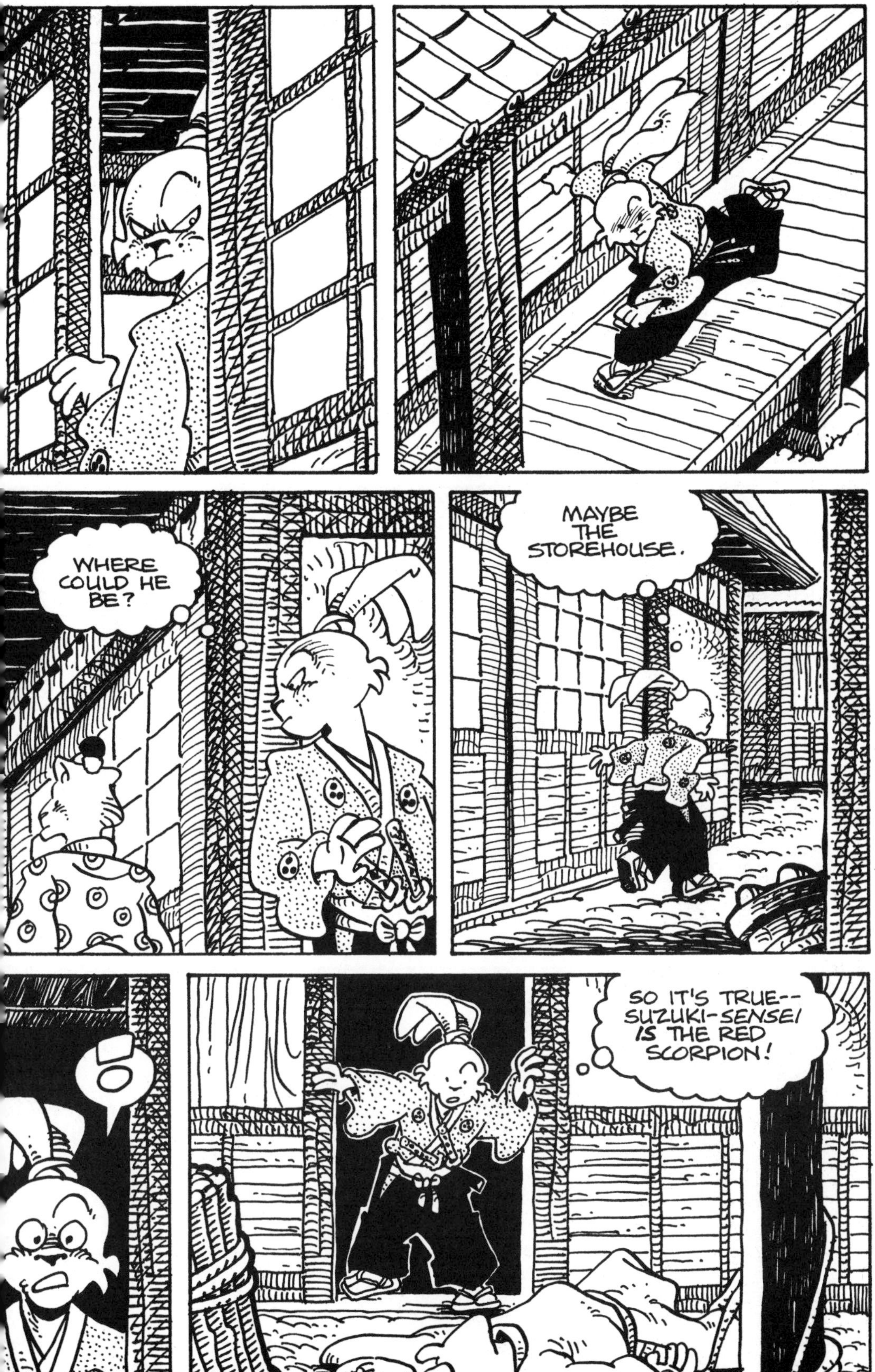
WHERE COULD HE BE?
MAYBE THE STOREHOUSE.
SO IT'S TRUE-- SUZUKI-SENSEI IS THE RED SCORPION!
19

HE HAS NOT BEEN DEAD LONG!

BUT WHY KILL HIM AT ALL?

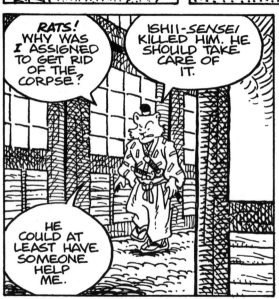
RATS! WHY WAS I ASSIGNED TO GET RID OF THE CORPSE?

ISHII-SENSEI KILLED HIM. HE SHOULD TAKE CARE OF IT.

HE COULD AT LEAST HAVE SOMEONE HELP ME.

AFTER ALL, WE HAVE GOT TO GET TO THE TEMPLE BEFORE SUZUKI-SENSEI AND THE MAGISTRATE GET THERE.

HUH?

INTRUDER! INTRUDER IN STOREHOUSE! HELP! HELP!

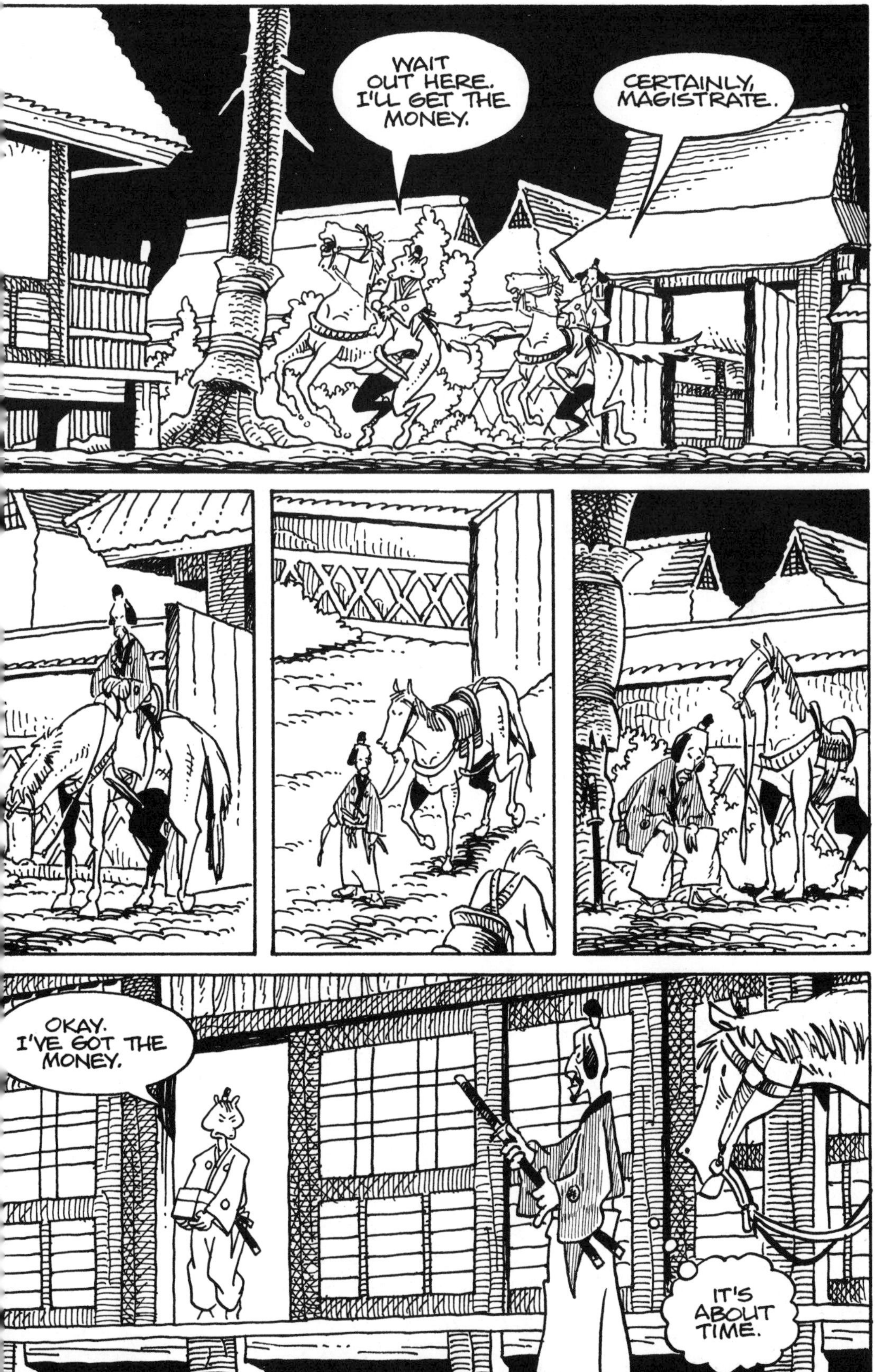
WAIT OUT HERE. I'LL GET THE MONEY.
CERTAINLY, MAGISTRATE.
OKAY. I'VE GOT THE MONEY.
IT'S ABOUT TIME.
21.

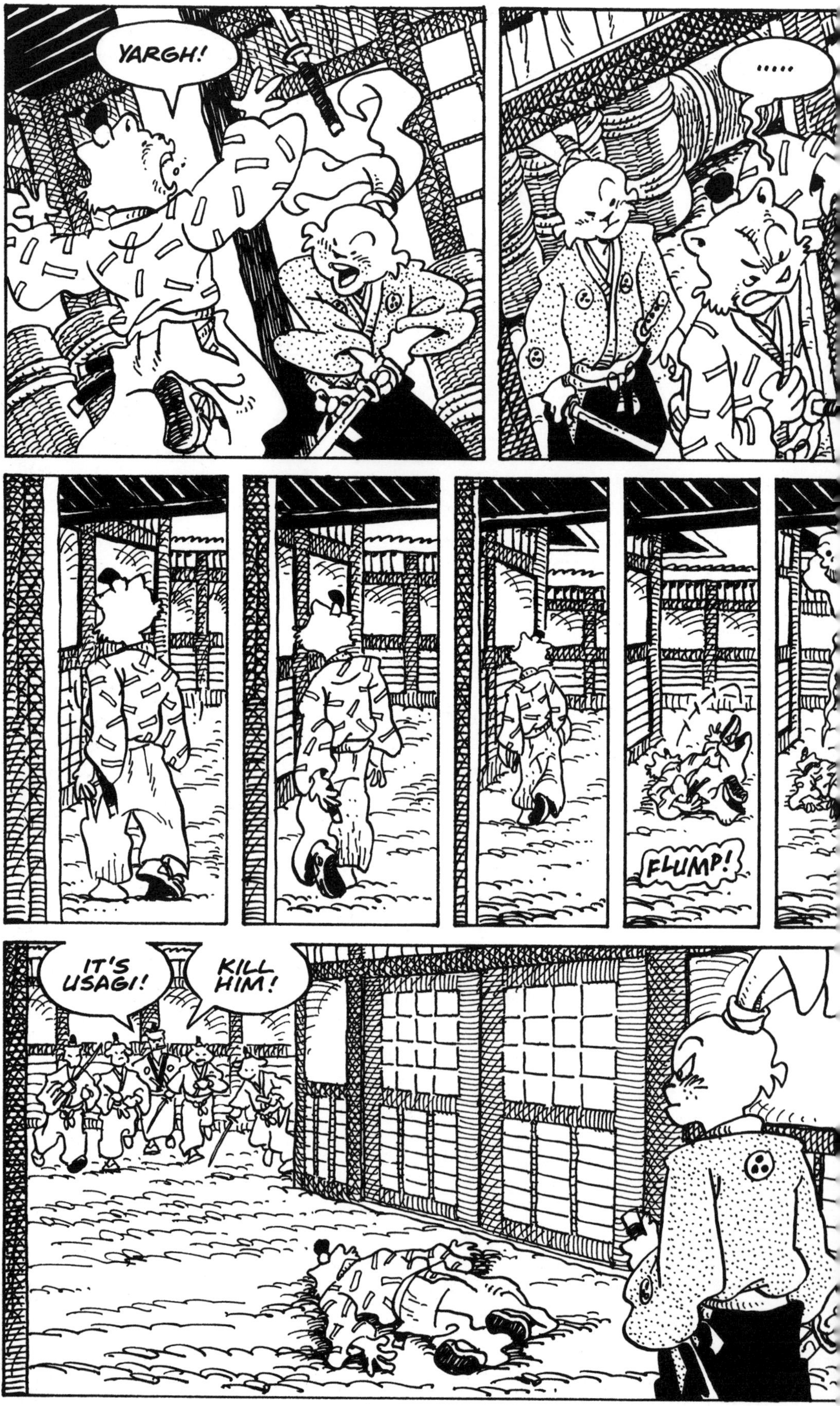
YARGH!
.....
FLUMP!
IT'S USAGI!
KILL HIM!

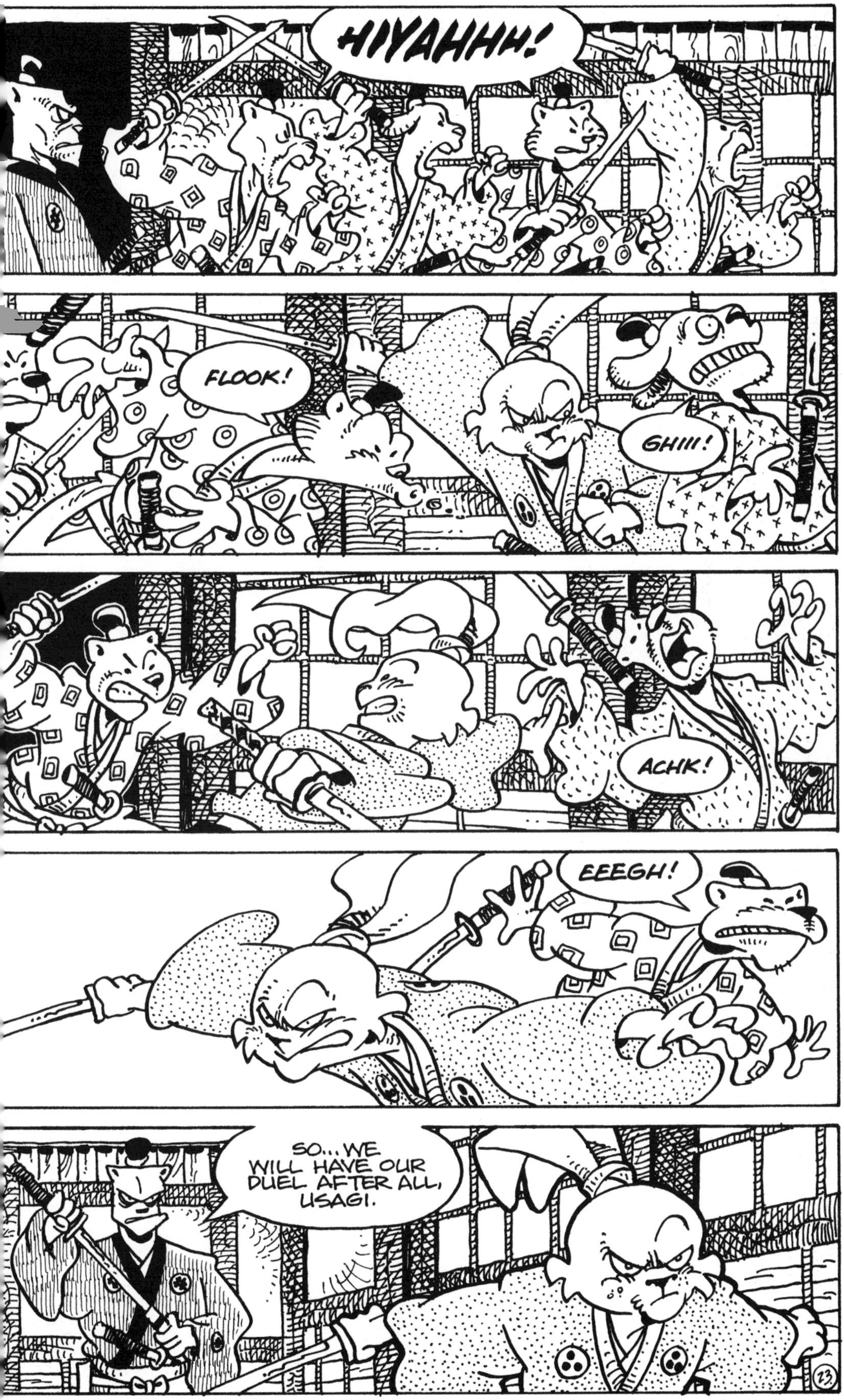
HIYAHHH!
FLOOK!
GHIII!
ACHK!
EEEGH!
SO... WE WILL HAVE OUR DUEL AFTER ALL, USAGI.
23

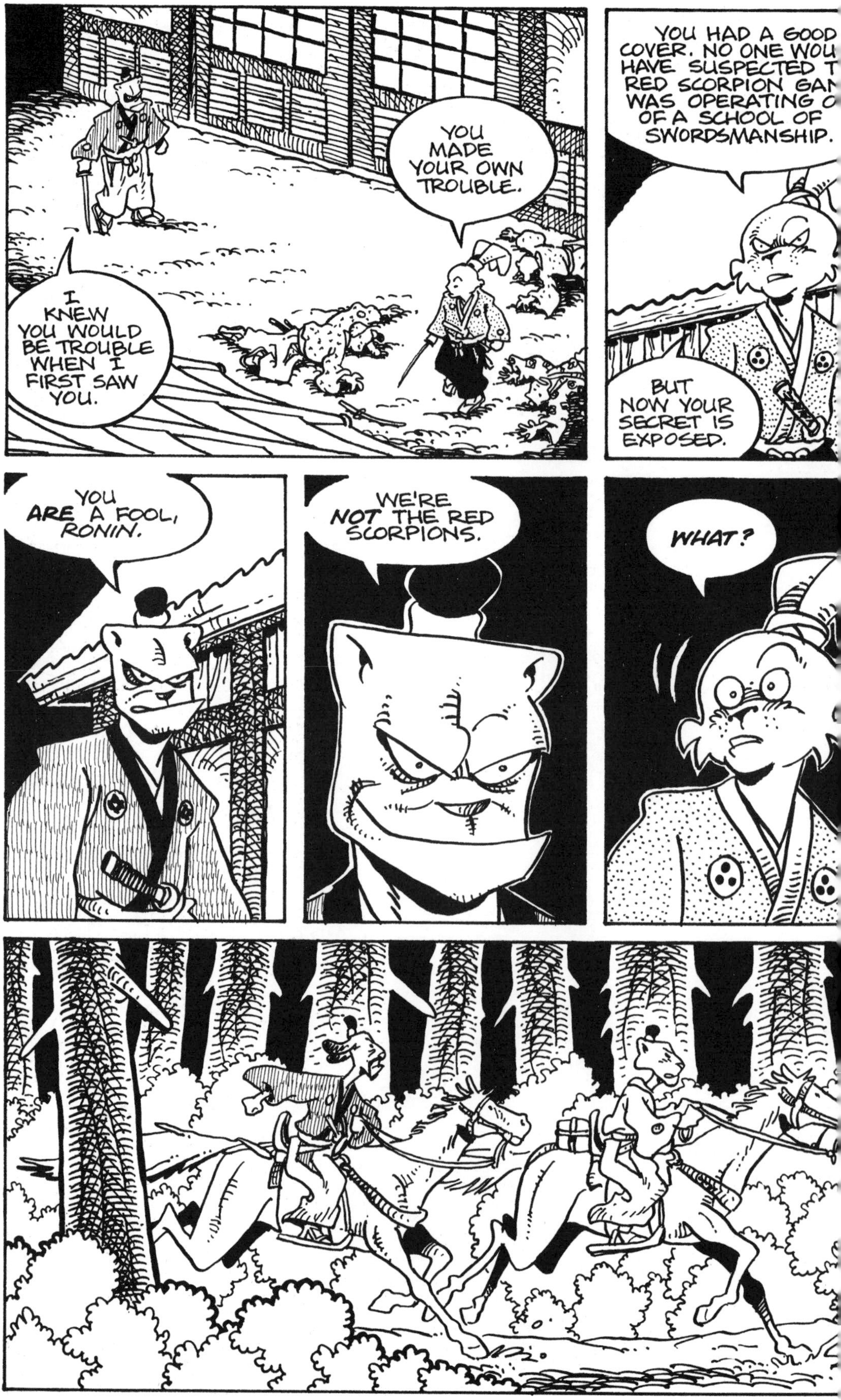
YOU MADE YOUR OWN TROUBLE.
I KNEW YOU WOULD BE TROUBLE WHEN I FIRST SAW YOU.
YOU HAD A GOOD COVER. NO ONE WOU HAVE SUSPECTED T RED SCORPION GAN WAS OPERATING O OF A SCHOOL OF SWORDSMANSHIP.
BUT NOW YOUR SECRET IS EXPOSED.
YOU **ARE** A FOOL, *RONIN.*
WE'RE ***NOT*** THE RED SCORPIONS.
***WHAT?***

# HOSE WHO TREAD ON THE CORPION'S TAIL PART THREE

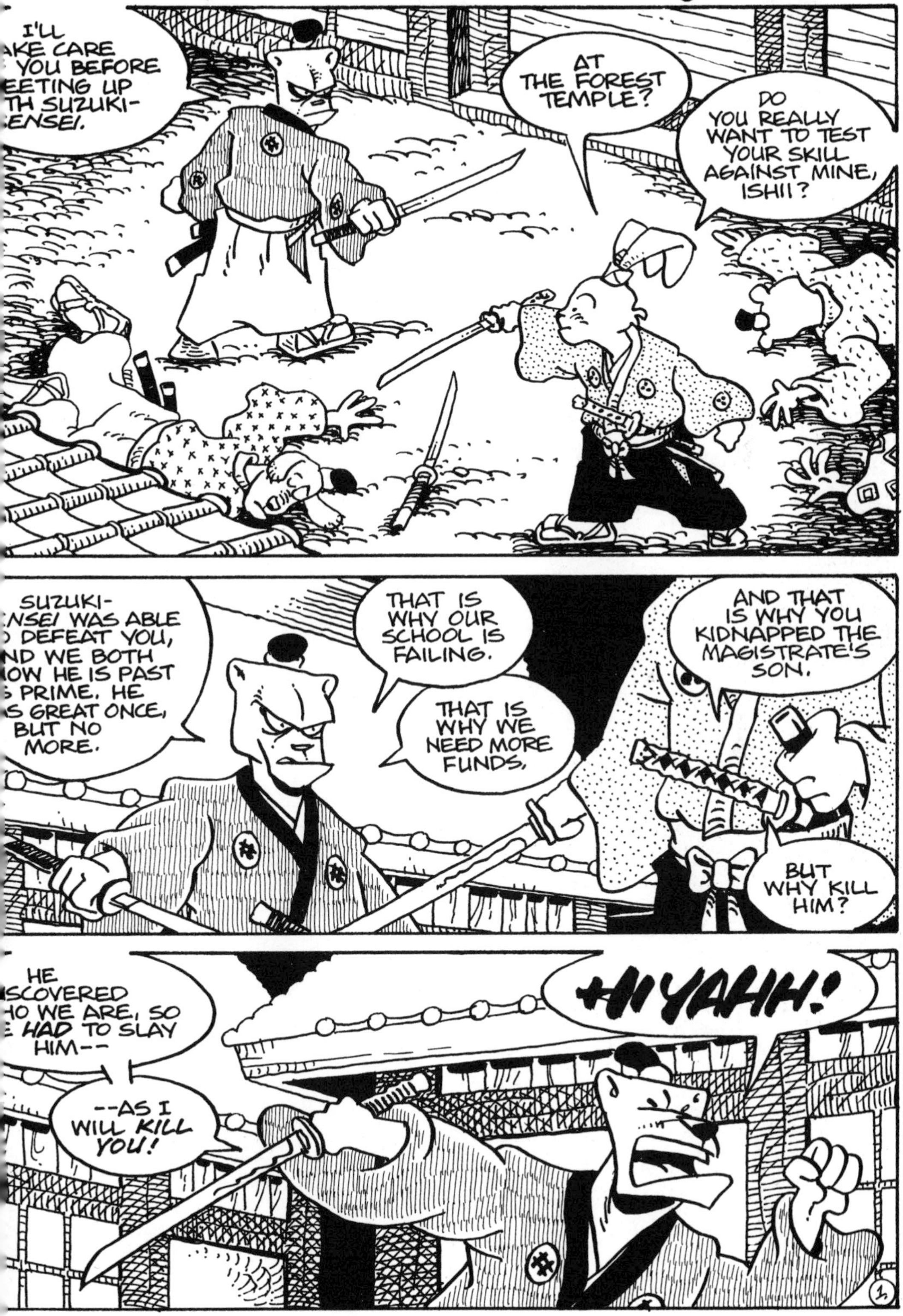
I'LL AKE CARE YOU BEFORE EETING UP TH SUZUKI- ENSEI.
AT THE FOREST TEMPLE?
DO YOU REALLY WANT TO TEST YOUR SKILL AGAINST MINE, ISHII?
SUZUKI- NSEI WAS ABLE DEFEAT YOU, ND WE BOTH OW HE IS PAST PRIME. HE S GREAT ONCE, BUT NO MORE.
THAT IS WHY OUR SCHOOL IS FAILING.
THAT IS WHY WE NEED MORE FUNDS,
AND THAT IS WHY YOU KIDNAPPED THE MAGISTRATE'S SON.
BUT WHY KILL HIM?
HE SCOVERED HO WE ARE, SO HAD TO SLAY HIM--
--AS I WILL KILL YOU!
HIIYAHH!
1

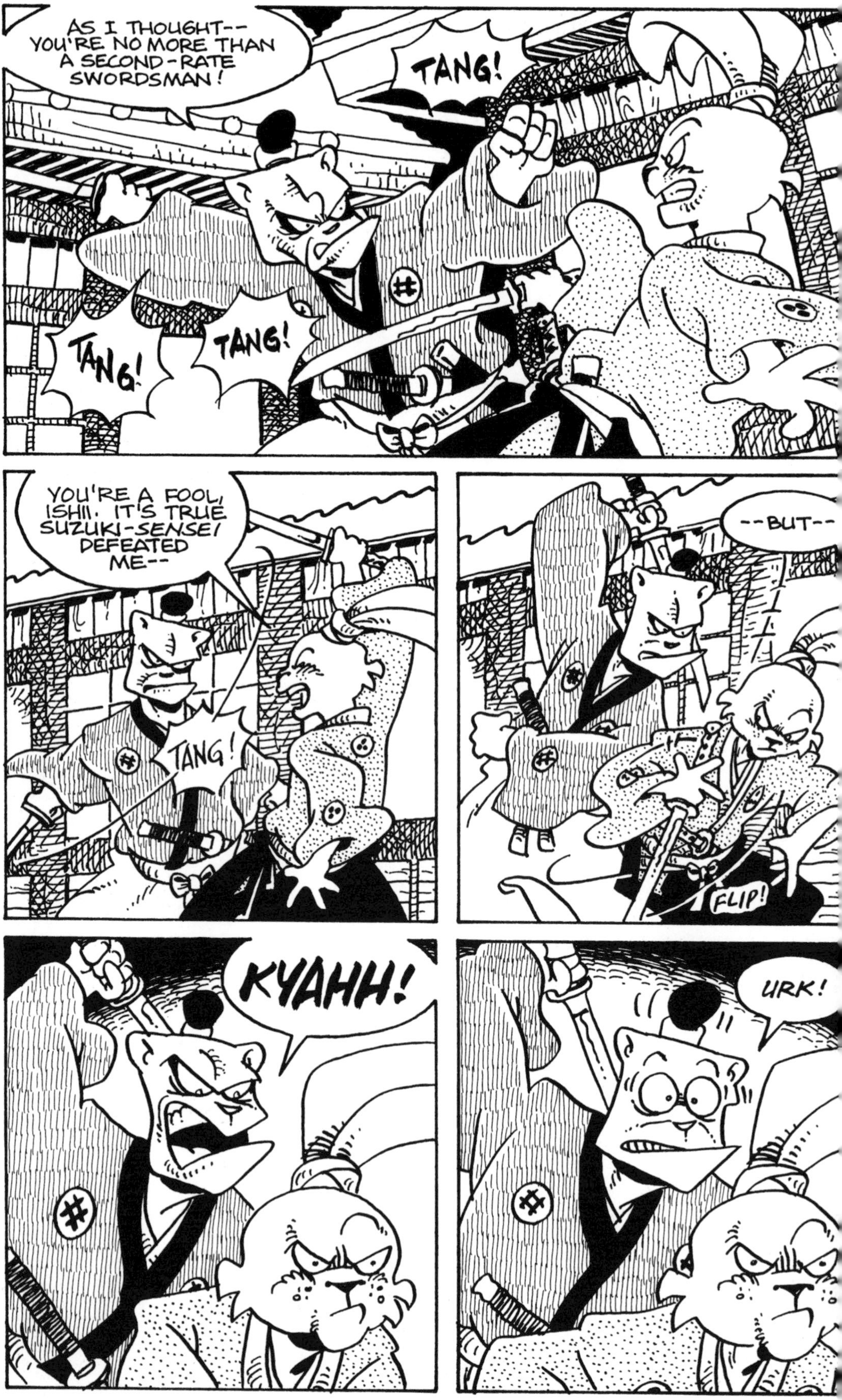
AS I THOUGHT-- YOU'RE NO MORE THAN A SECOND-RATE SWORDSMAN!
TANG!
TANG!
TANG!
YOU'RE A FOOL, ISHII. IT'S TRUE SUZUKI-SENSEI DEFEATED ME--
TANG!
--BUT--
FLIP!
KYAHH!
URK!

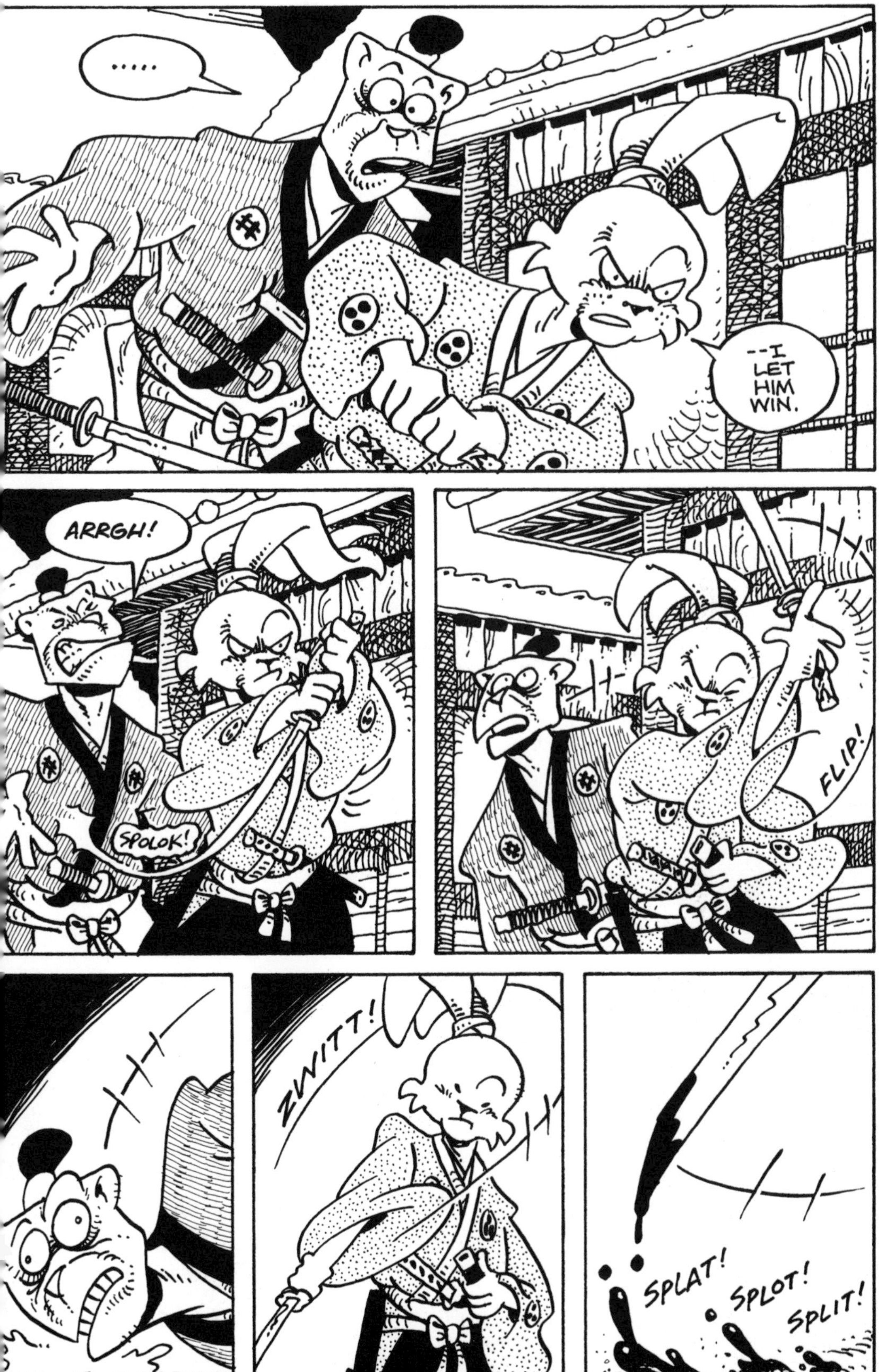
.....
--I LET HIM WIN.
ARRGH!
SPOLOK!
FLIP!
PLOP!
ZWITT!
SPLAT!
SPLOT!
SPLIT!
3

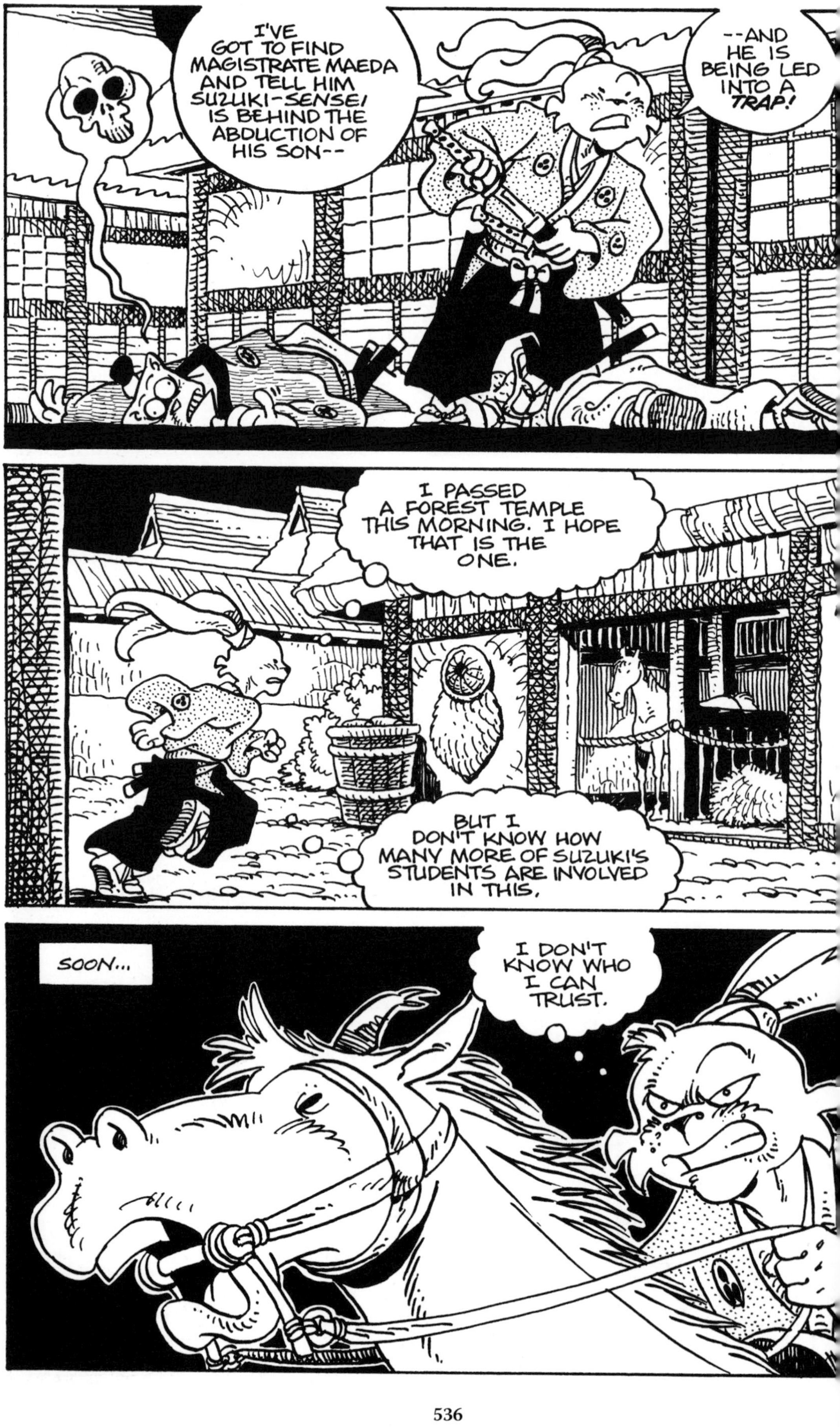
I'VE GOT TO FIND MAGISTRATE MAEDA AND TELL HIM SUZUKI-SENSEI IS BEHIND THE ABDUCTION OF HIS SON--
--AND HE IS BEING LED INTO A *TRAP!*
I PASSED A FOREST TEMPLE THIS MORNING. I HOPE THAT IS THE ONE.
BUT I DON'T KNOW HOW MANY MORE OF SUZUKI'S STUDENTS ARE INVOLVED IN THIS.
SOON...
I DON'T KNOW WHO I CAN TRUST.

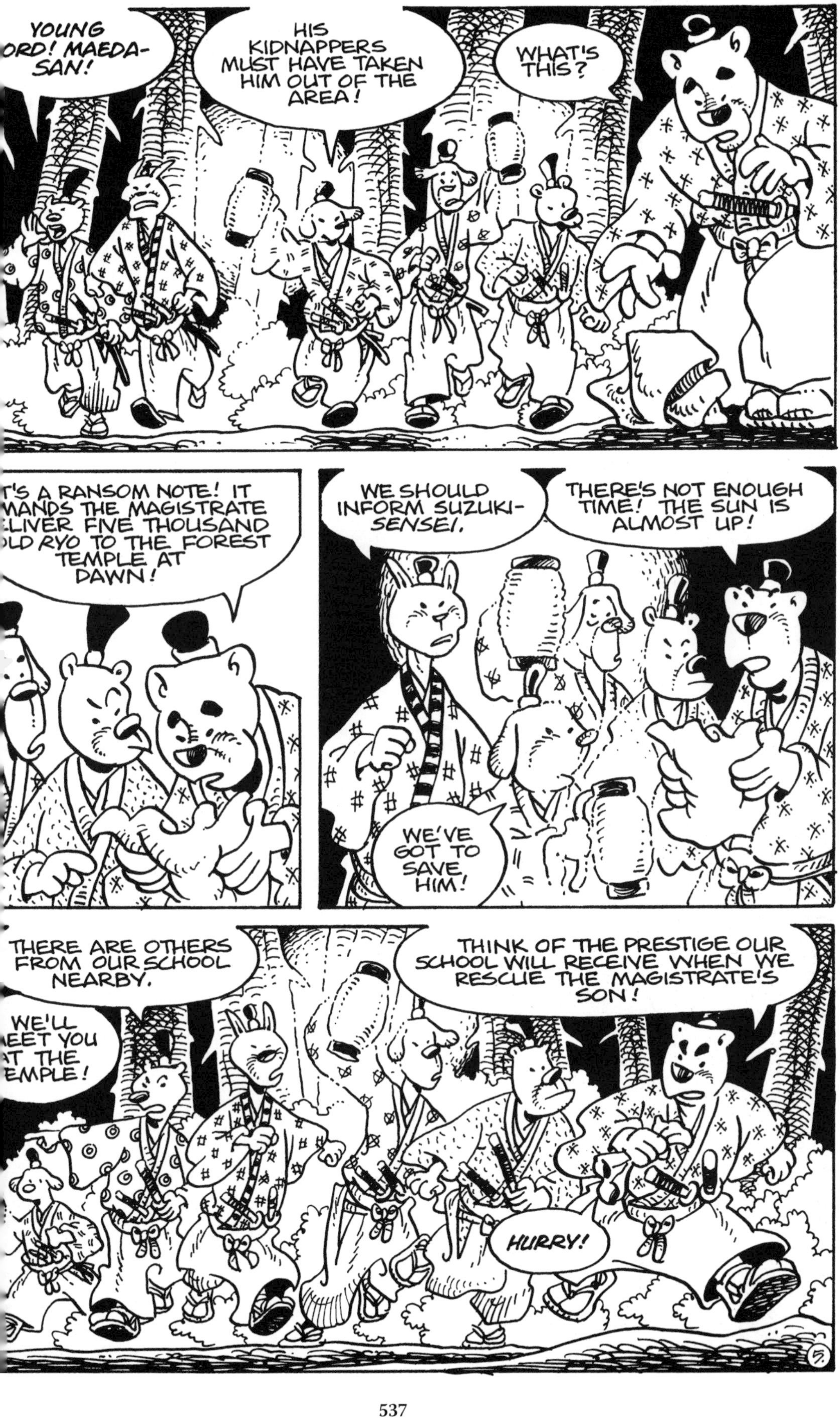
YOUNG ORD! MAEDA-SAN!
HIS KIDNAPPERS MUST HAVE TAKEN HIM OUT OF THE AREA!
WHAT'S THIS?
T'S A RANSOM NOTE! IT MANDS THE MAGISTRATE ELIVER FIVE THOUSAND OLD *RYO* TO THE FOREST TEMPLE AT DAWN!
WE SHOULD INFORM SUZUKI-SENSEI.
THERE'S NOT ENOUGH TIME! THE SUN IS ALMOST UP!
WE'VE GOT TO SAVE HIM!
THERE ARE OTHERS FROM OUR SCHOOL NEARBY.
WE'LL EET YOU T THE EMPLE!
THINK OF THE PRESTIGE OUR SCHOOL WILL RECEIVE WHEN WE RESCUE THE MAGISTRATE'S SON!
HURRY!

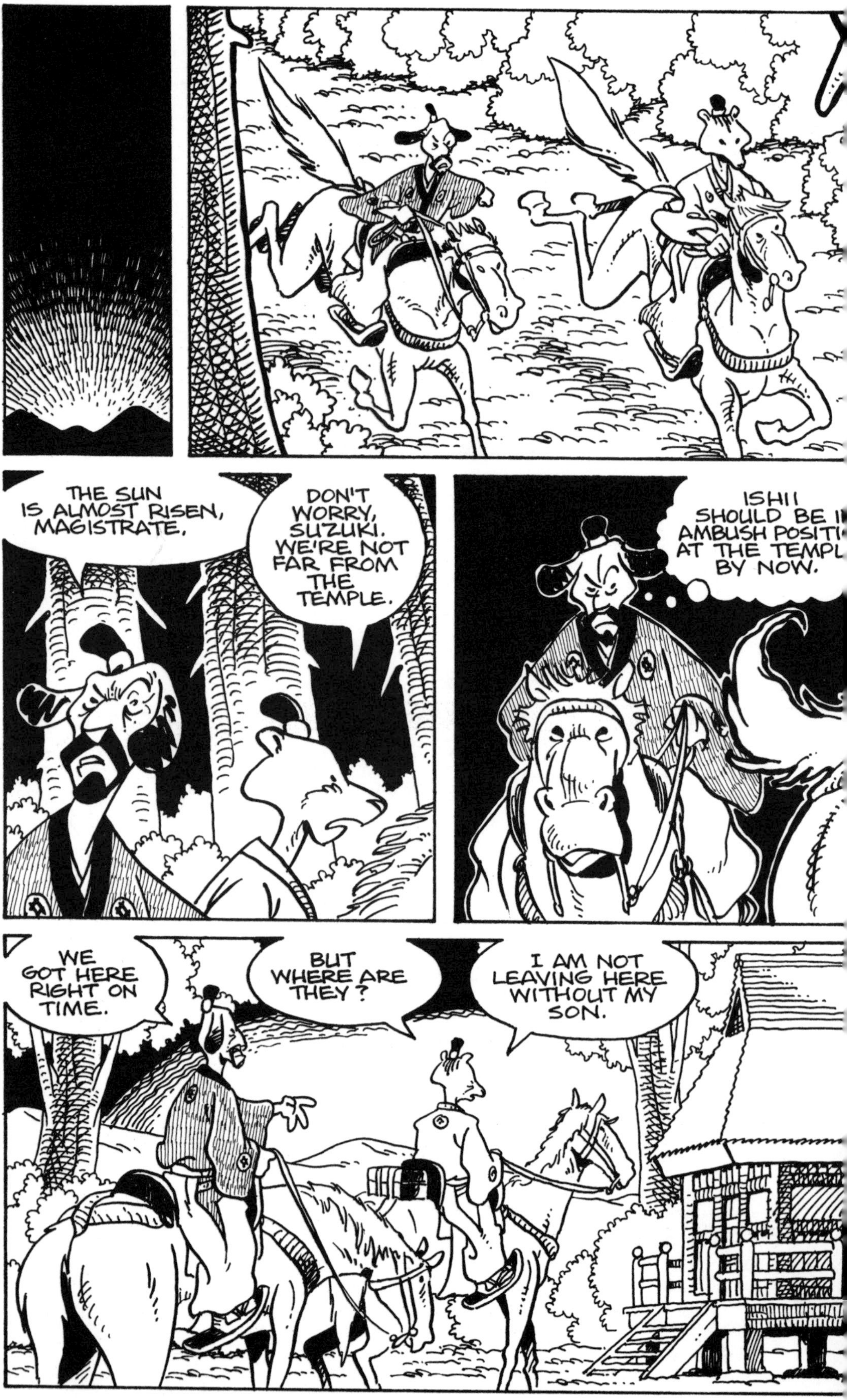
THE SUN IS ALMOST RISEN, MAGISTRATE.
DON'T WORRY, SUZUKI. WE'RE NOT FAR FROM THE TEMPLE.
ISHII SHOULD BE IN AMBUSH POSITION AT THE TEMPLE BY NOW.
WE GOT HERE RIGHT ON TIME.
BUT WHERE ARE THEY?
I AM NOT LEAVING HERE WITHOUT MY SON.

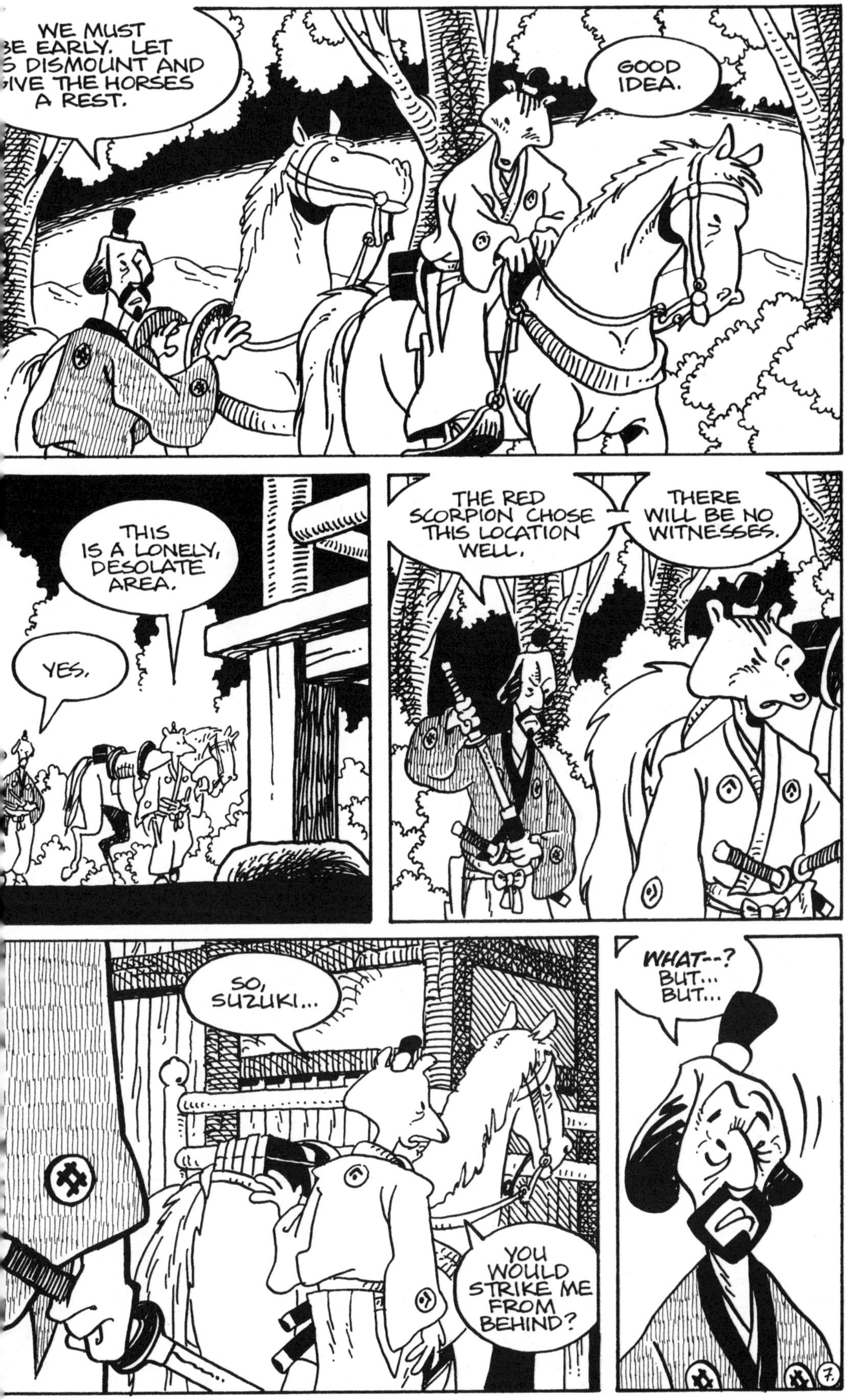
WE MUST BE EARLY. LET US DISMOUNT AND GIVE THE HORSES A REST.
GOOD IDEA.
THIS IS A LONELY, DESOLATE AREA.
YES.
THE RED SCORPION CHOSE THIS LOCATION WELL.
THERE WILL BE NO WITNESSES.
SO, SUZUKI...
YOU WOULD STRIKE ME FROM BEHIND?
WHAT--? BUT... BUT...
7.

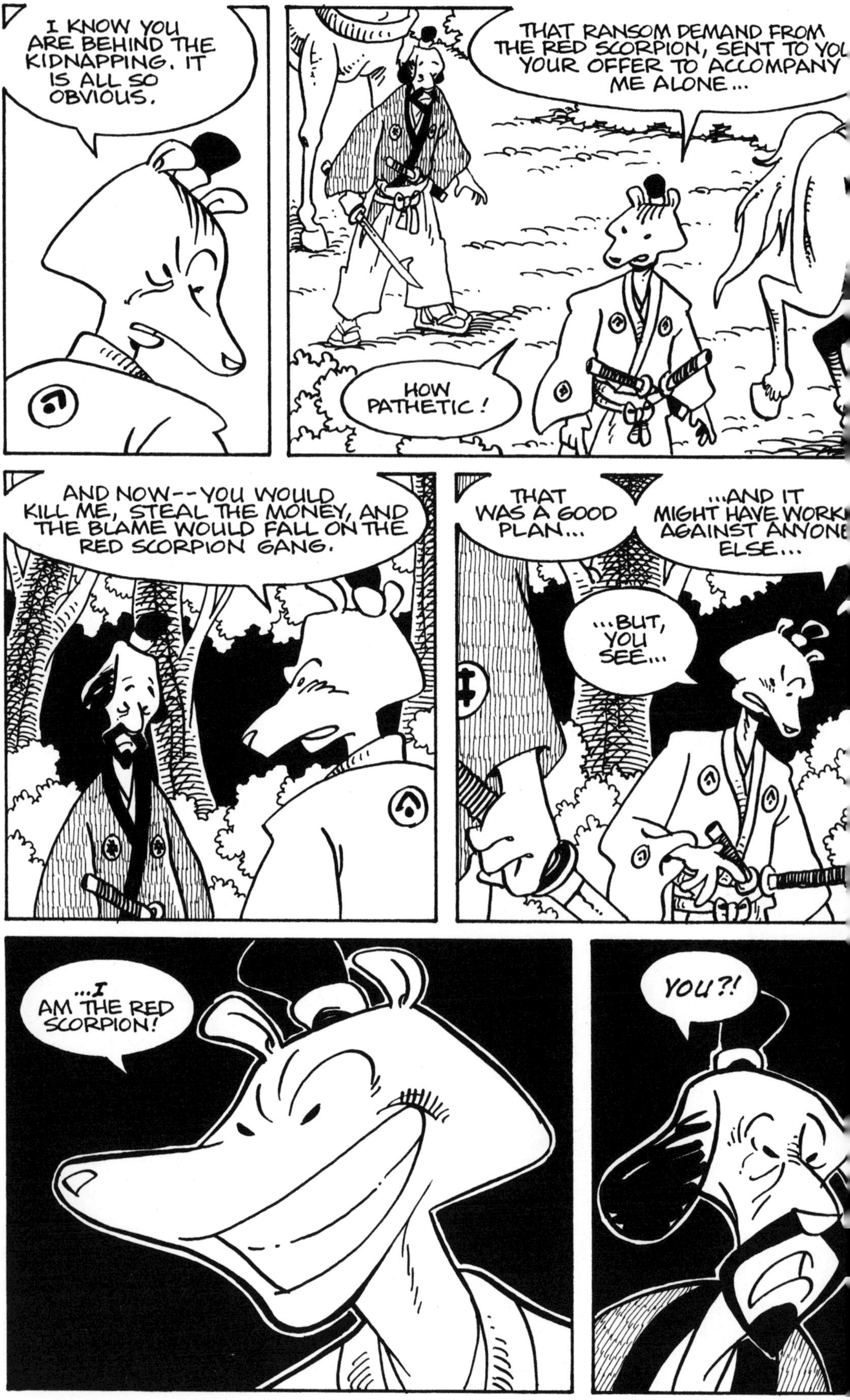
I KNOW YOU ARE BEHIND THE KIDNAPPING. IT IS ALL SO OBVIOUS.
THAT RANSOM DEMAND FROM THE RED SCORPION, SENT TO YOU YOUR OFFER TO ACCOMPANY ME ALONE...
HOW PATHETIC!
AND NOW--YOU WOULD KILL ME, STEAL THE MONEY, AND THE BLAME WOULD FALL ON THE RED SCORPION GANG.
THAT WAS A GOOD PLAN...
...AND IT MIGHT HAVE WORKED AGAINST ANYONE ELSE...
...BUT, YOU SEE...
...I AM THE RED SCORPION!
YOU?!

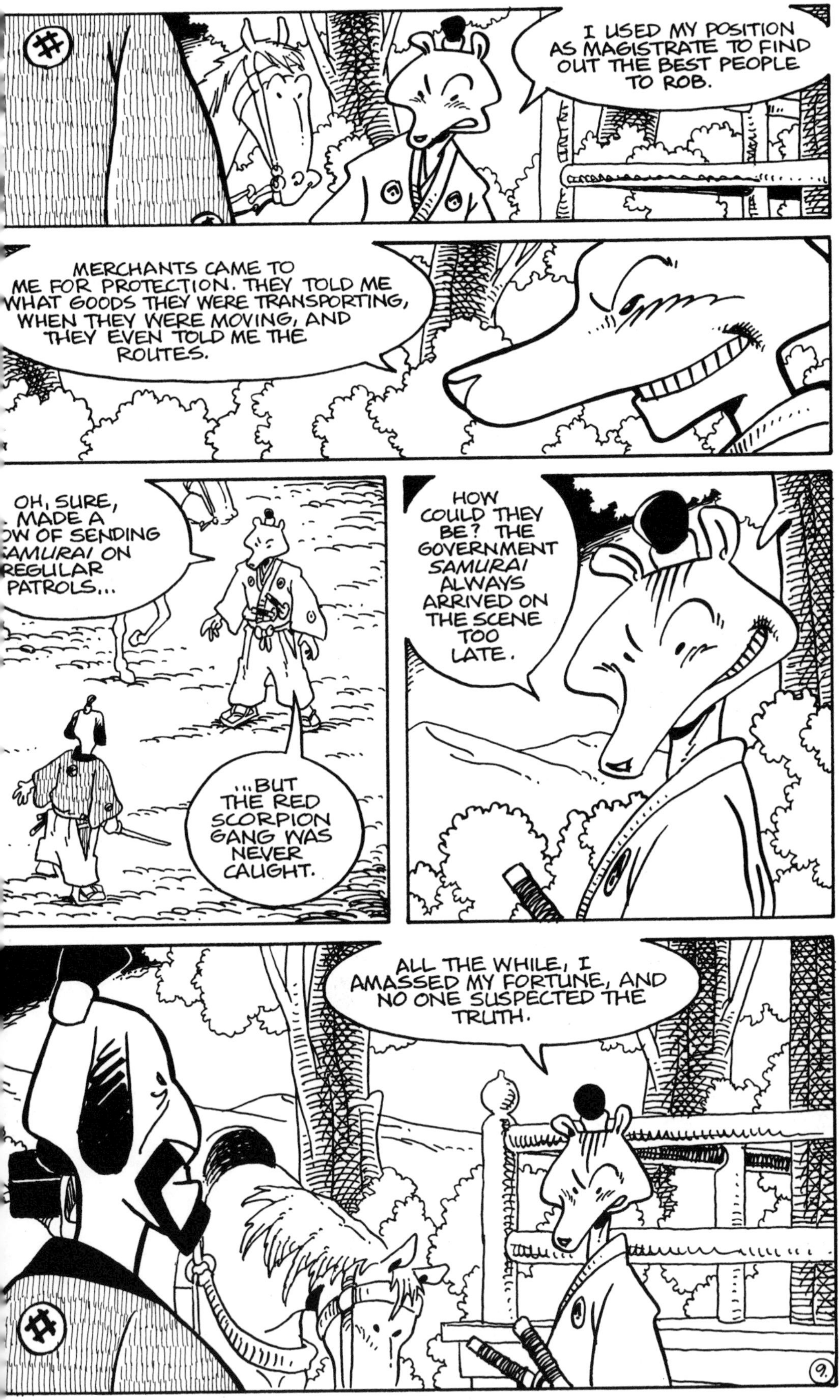
I USED MY POSITION AS MAGISTRATE TO FIND OUT THE BEST PEOPLE TO ROB.
MERCHANTS CAME TO ME FOR PROTECTION. THEY TOLD ME WHAT GOODS THEY WERE TRANSPORTING, WHEN THEY WERE MOVING, AND THEY EVEN TOLD ME THE ROUTES.
OH, SURE, MADE A OW OF SENDING SAMURAI ON REGULAR PATROLS...
...BUT THE RED SCORPION GANG WAS NEVER CAUGHT.
HOW COULD THEY BE? THE GOVERNMENT SAMURAI ALWAYS ARRIVED ON THE SCENE TOO LATE.
ALL THE WHILE, I AMASSED MY FORTUNE, AND NO ONE SUSPECTED THE TRUTH.
9.

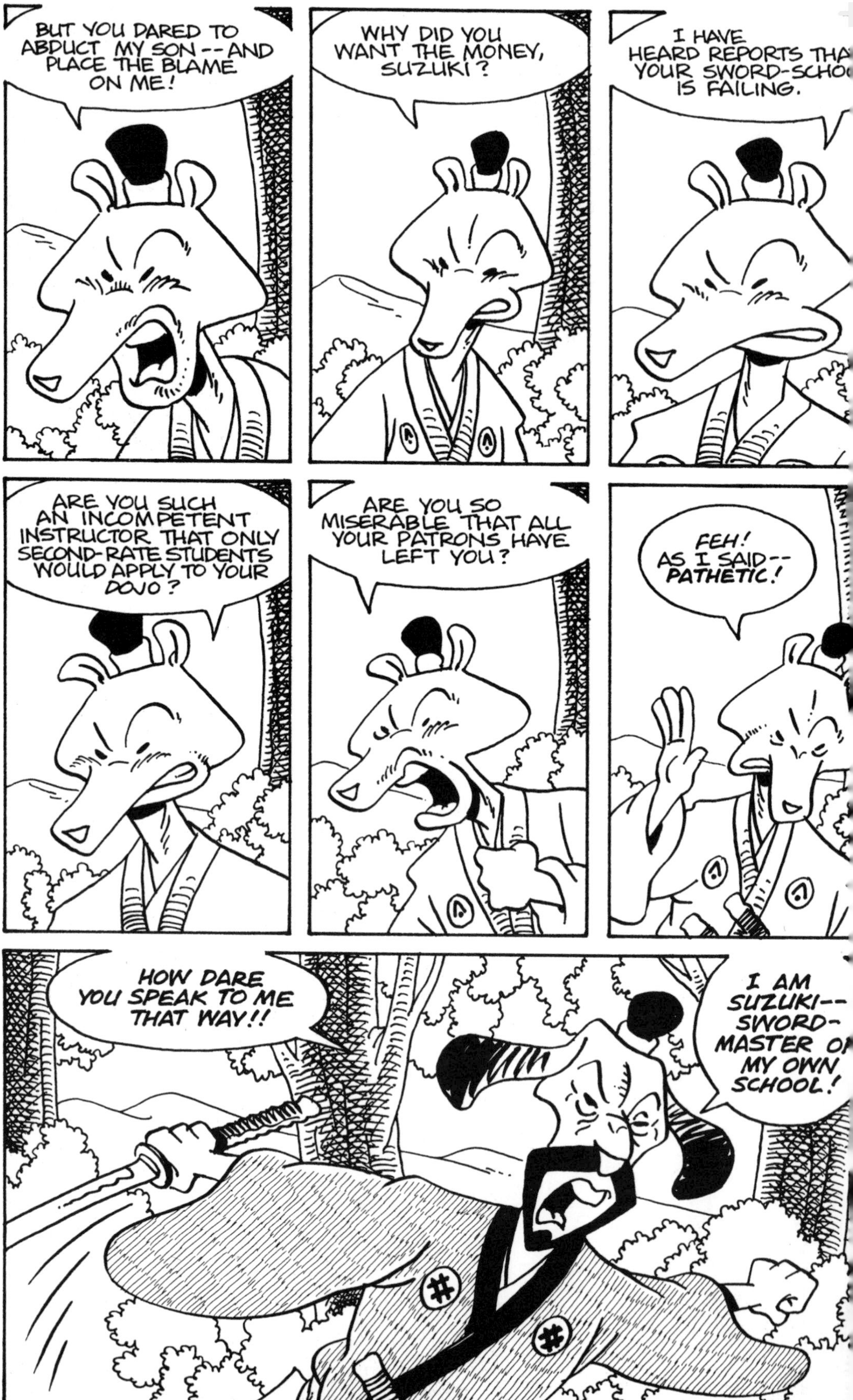
BUT YOU DARED TO ABDUCT MY SON --AND PLACE THE BLAME ON ME!
WHY DID YOU WANT THE MONEY, SUZUKI?
I HAVE HEARD REPORTS THA YOUR SWORD-SCHO IS FAILING.
ARE YOU SUCH AN INCOMPETENT INSTRUCTOR THAT ONLY SECOND-RATE STUDENTS WOULD APPLY TO YOUR DOJO?
ARE YOU SO MISERABLE THAT ALL YOUR PATRONS HAVE LEFT YOU?
FEH! AS I SAID-- PATHETIC!
HOW DARE YOU SPEAK TO ME THAT WAY!!
I AM SUZUKI-- SWORD-MASTER O MY OWN SCHOOL!

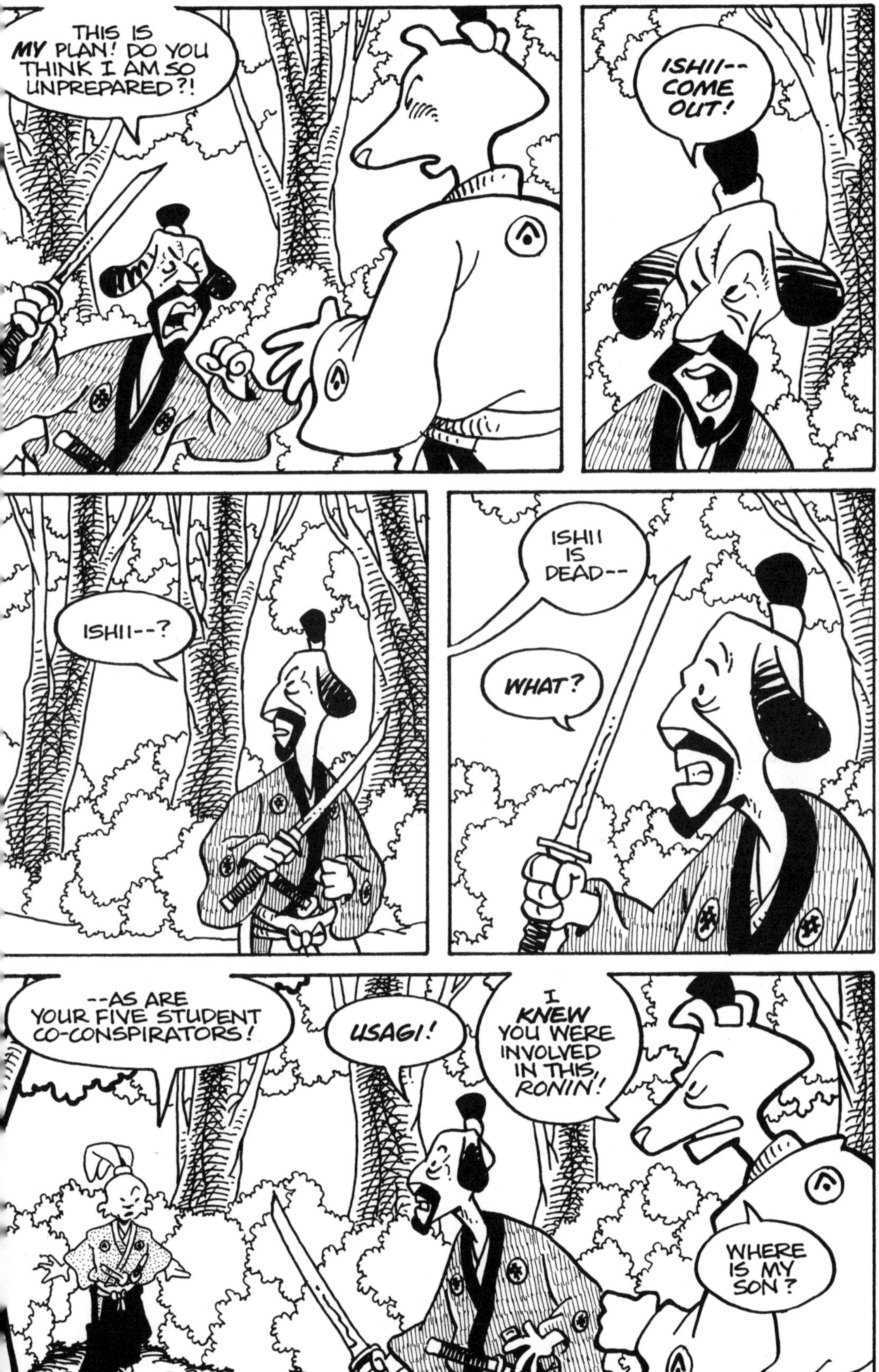
THIS IS MY PLAN! DO YOU THINK I AM SO UNPREPARED?!
ISHII--COME OUT!
ISHII--?
ISHII IS DEAD--
WHAT?
--AS ARE YOUR FIVE STUDENT CO-CONSPIRATORS!
USAGI!
I KNEW YOU WERE INVOLVED IN THIS, RONIN!
WHERE IS MY SON?
11.

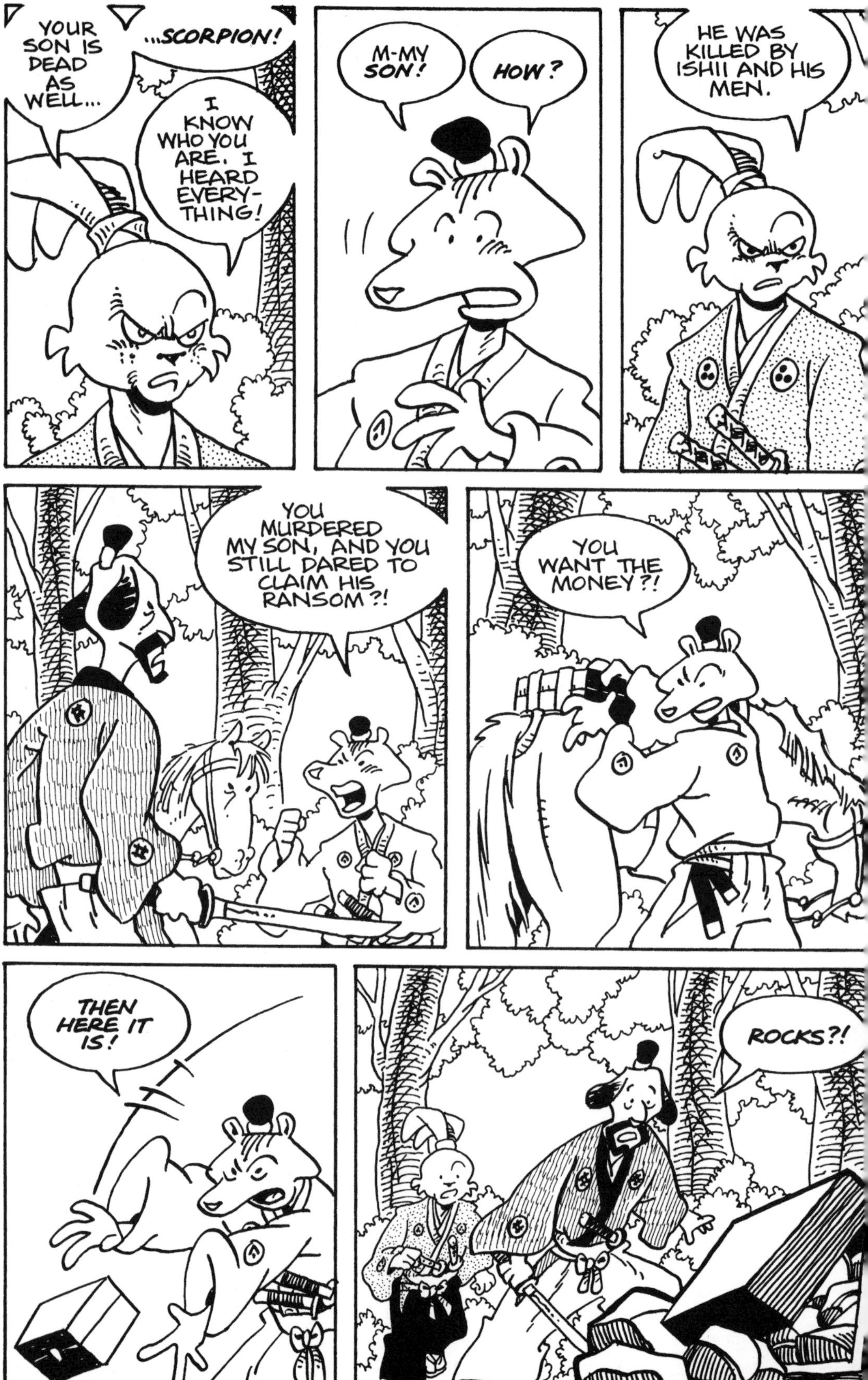
YOUR SON IS DEAD AS WELL...
...SCORPION!
I KNOW WHO YOU ARE. I HEARD EVERY-THING!
M-MY SON!
HOW?
HE WAS KILLED BY ISHII AND HIS MEN.
YOU MURDERED MY SON, AND YOU STILL DARED TO CLAIM HIS RANSOM?!
YOU WANT THE MONEY?!
THEN HERE IT IS!
ROCKS?!

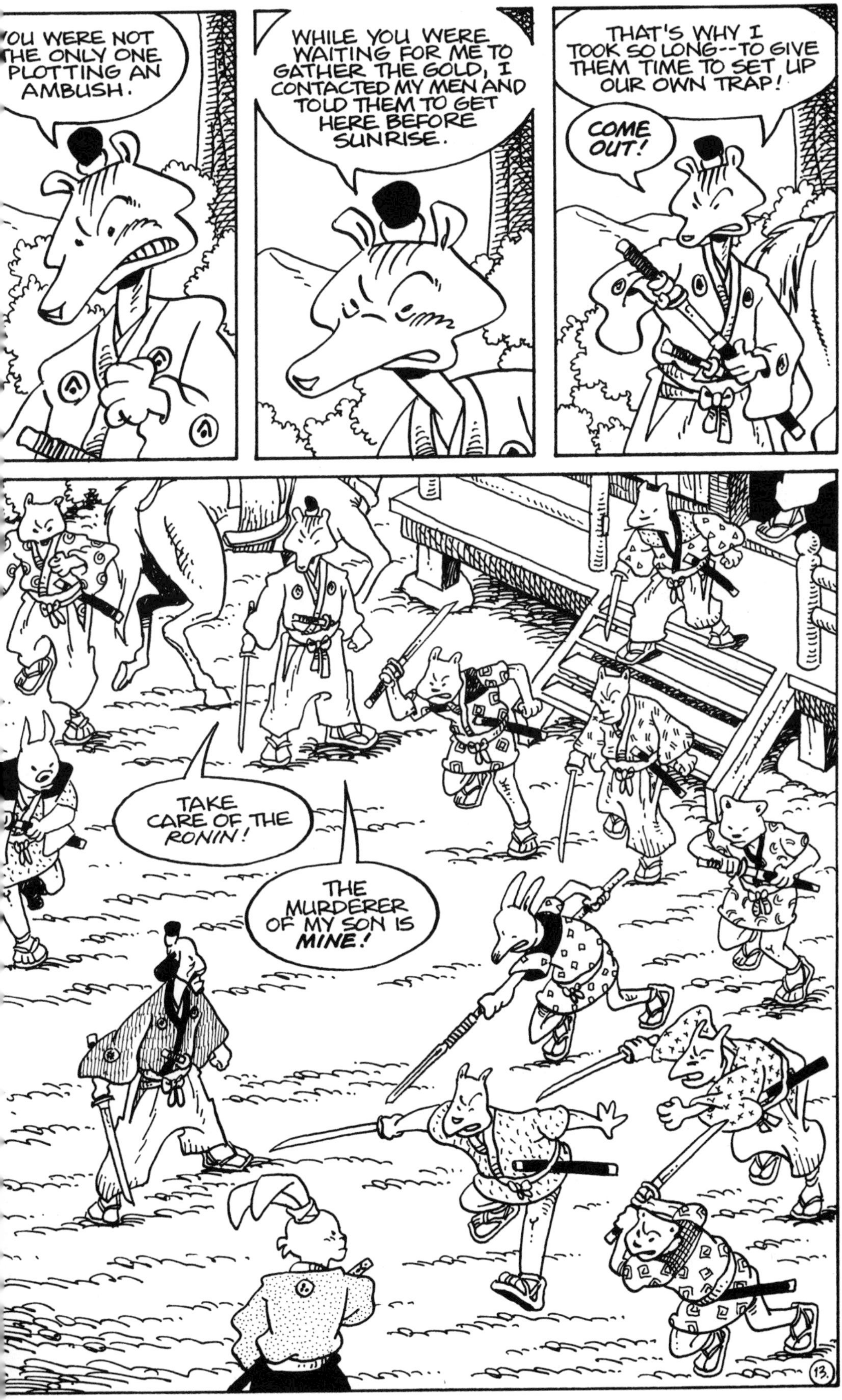
YOU WERE NOT THE ONLY ONE PLOTTING AN AMBUSH.
WHILE YOU WERE WAITING FOR ME TO GATHER THE GOLD, I CONTACTED MY MEN AND TOLD THEM TO GET HERE BEFORE SUNRISE.
THAT'S WHY I TOOK SO LONG--TO GIVE THEM TIME TO SET UP OUR OWN TRAP!
COME OUT!
TAKE CARE OF THE *RONIN*!
THE MURDERER OF MY SON IS ***MINE***!
13.

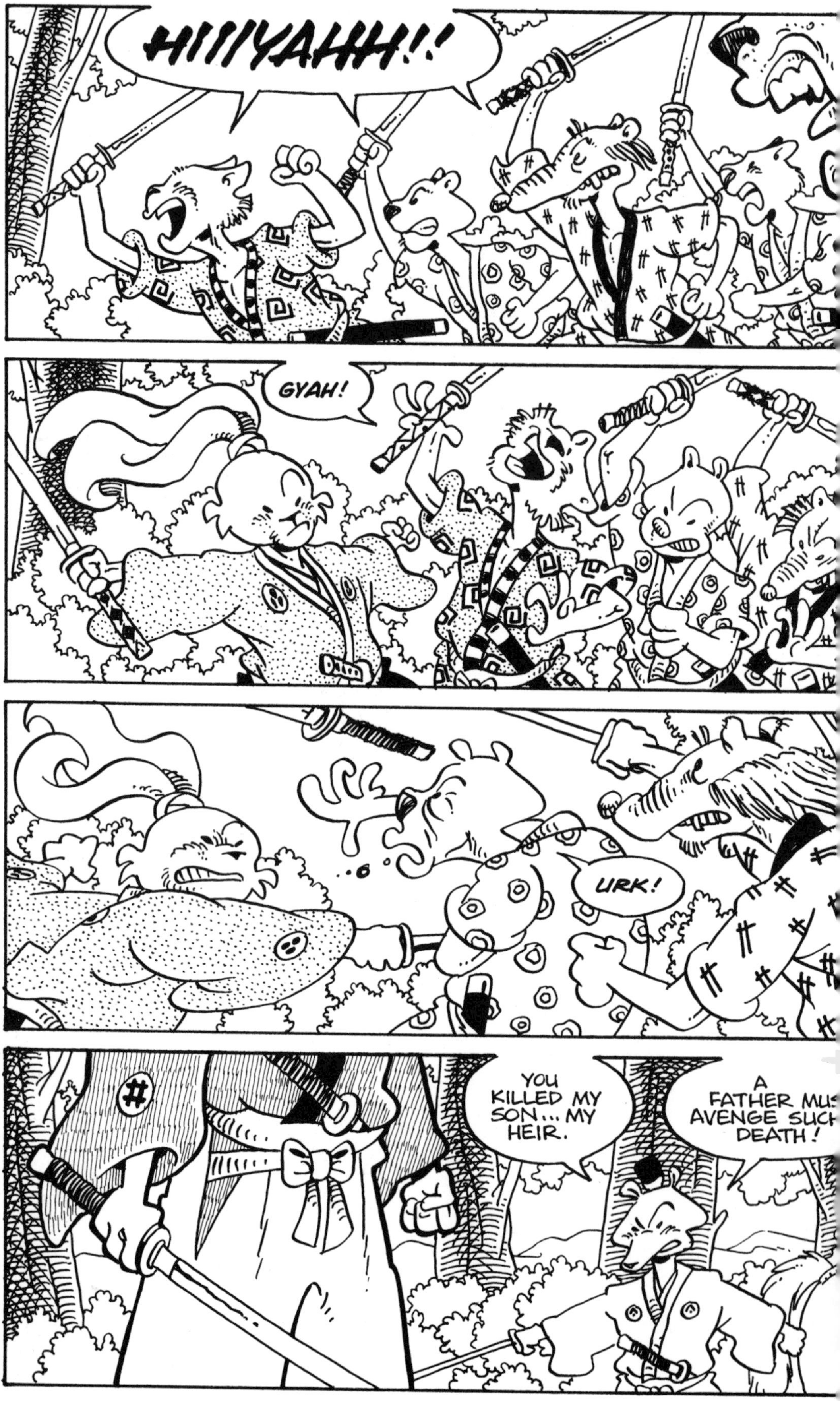
HIIIYAHHH!!
GYAH!
URK!
YOU KILLED MY SON... MY HEIR.
A FATHER MUS AVENGE SUCH DEATH!

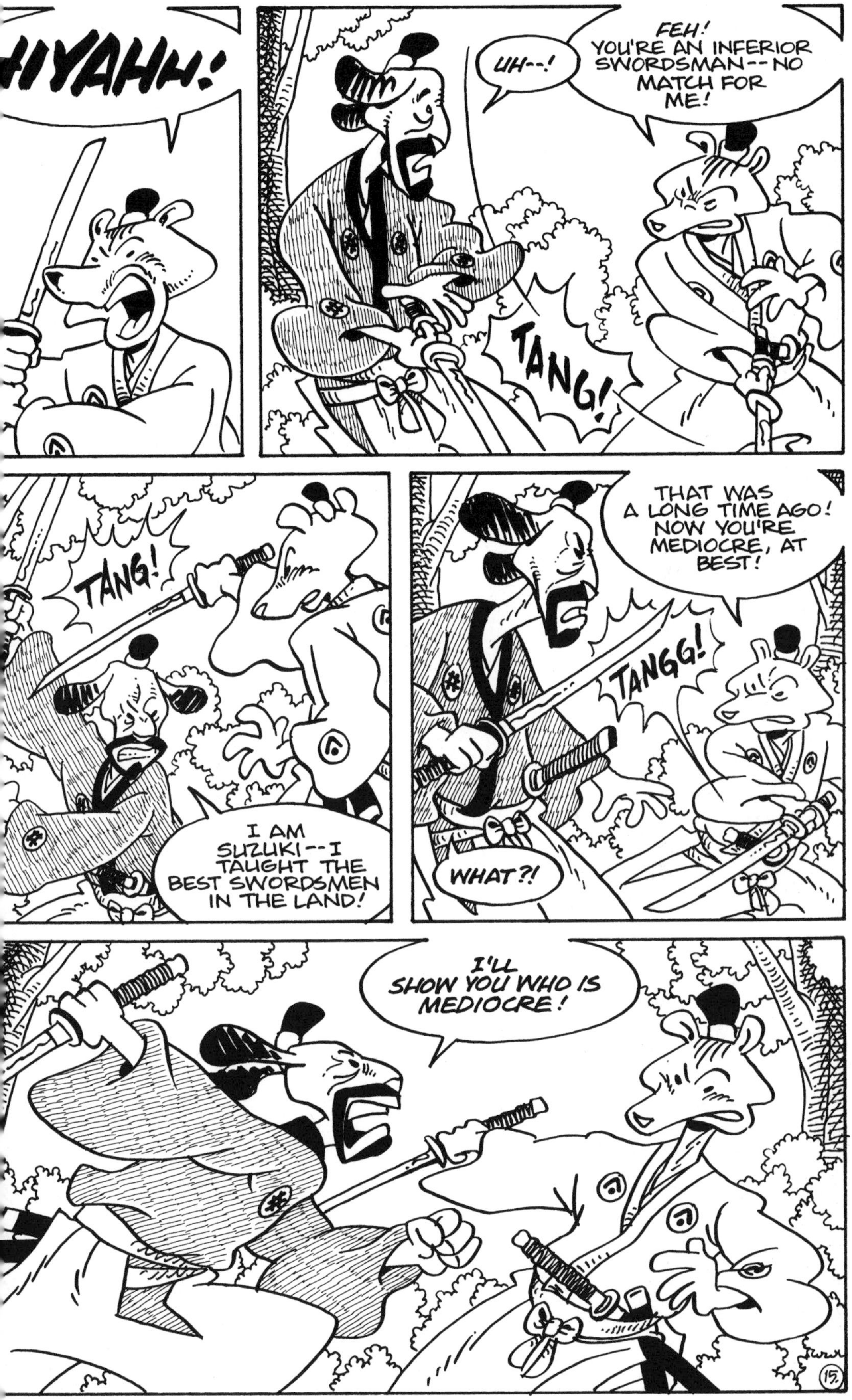
HIYAHH!
UH--!
FEH! YOU'RE AN INFERIOR SWORDSMAN--NO MATCH FOR ME!
TANG!
TANG!
I AM SUZUKI--I TAUGHT THE BEST SWORDSMEN IN THE LAND!
THAT WAS A LONG TIME AGO! NOW YOU'RE MEDIOCRE, AT BEST!
TANGG!
WHAT?!
I'LL SHOW YOU WHO IS MEDIOCRE!
15

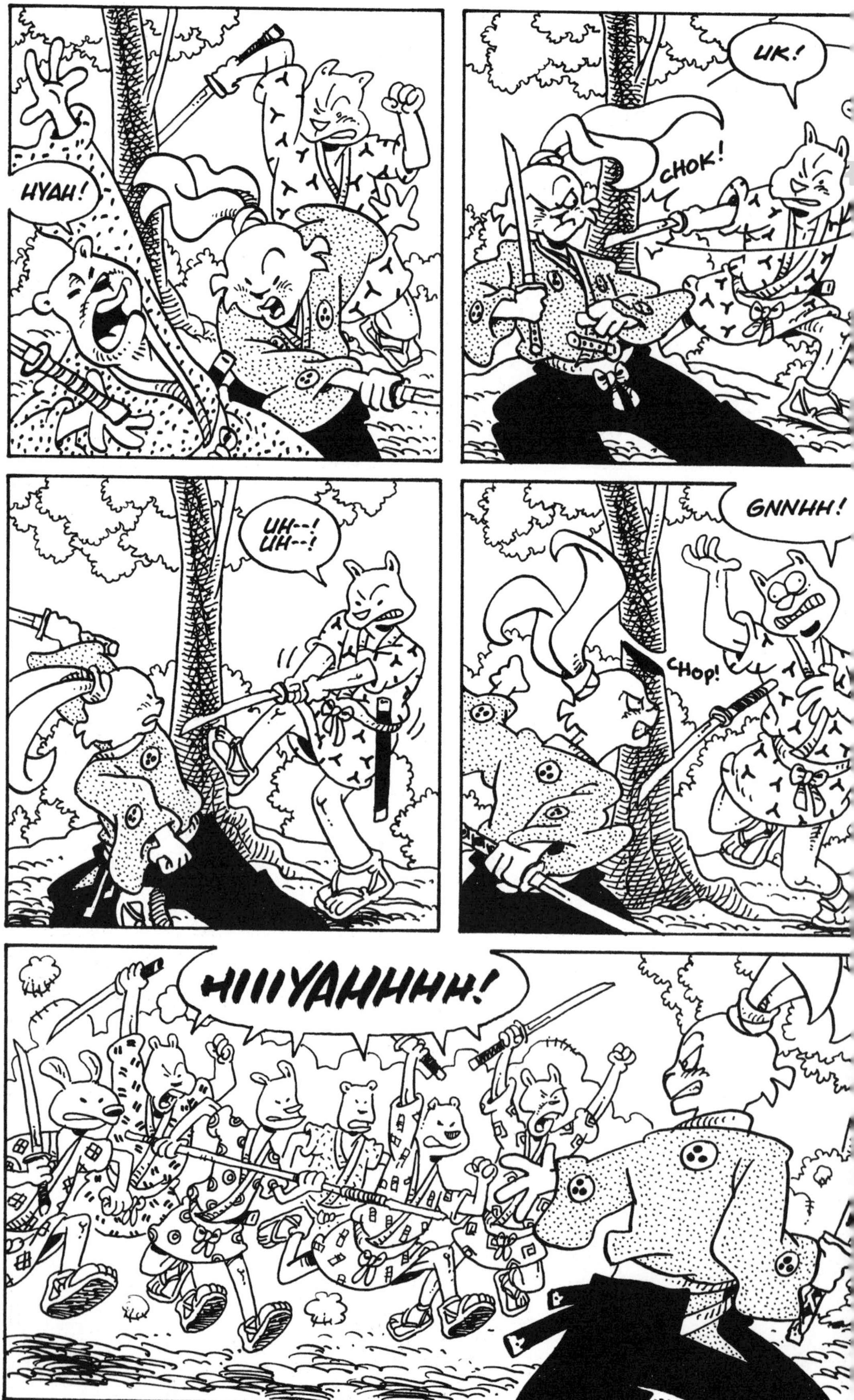
HYAH!
UK!
CHOK!
UH--!
UH--!
GNNHH!
CHOP!
HIIIYAHHHH!

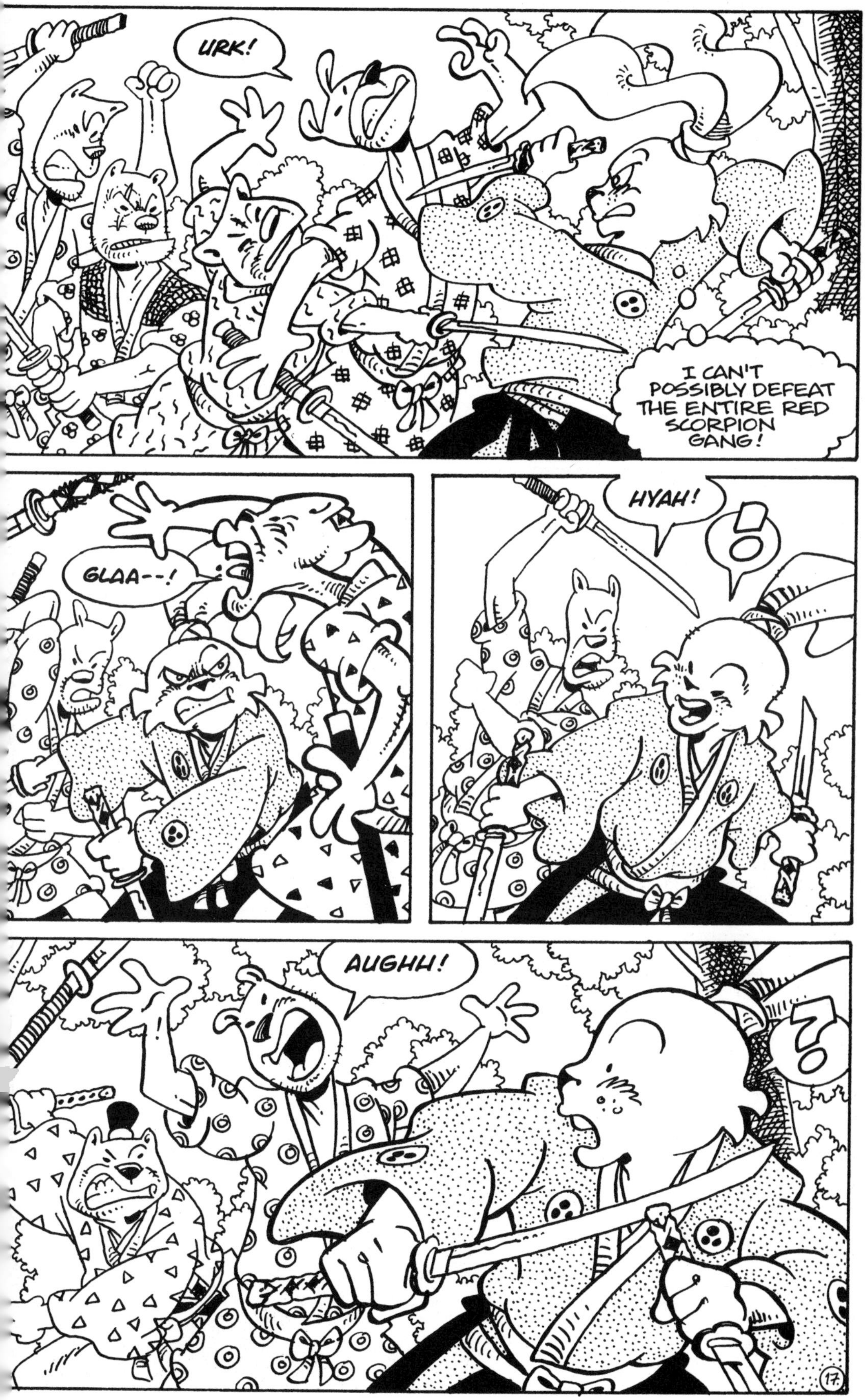
URK!
I CAN'T POSSIBLY DEFEAT THE ENTIRE RED SCORPION GANG!
GLAA--!
HYAH!
!
AUGHH!
?
17.

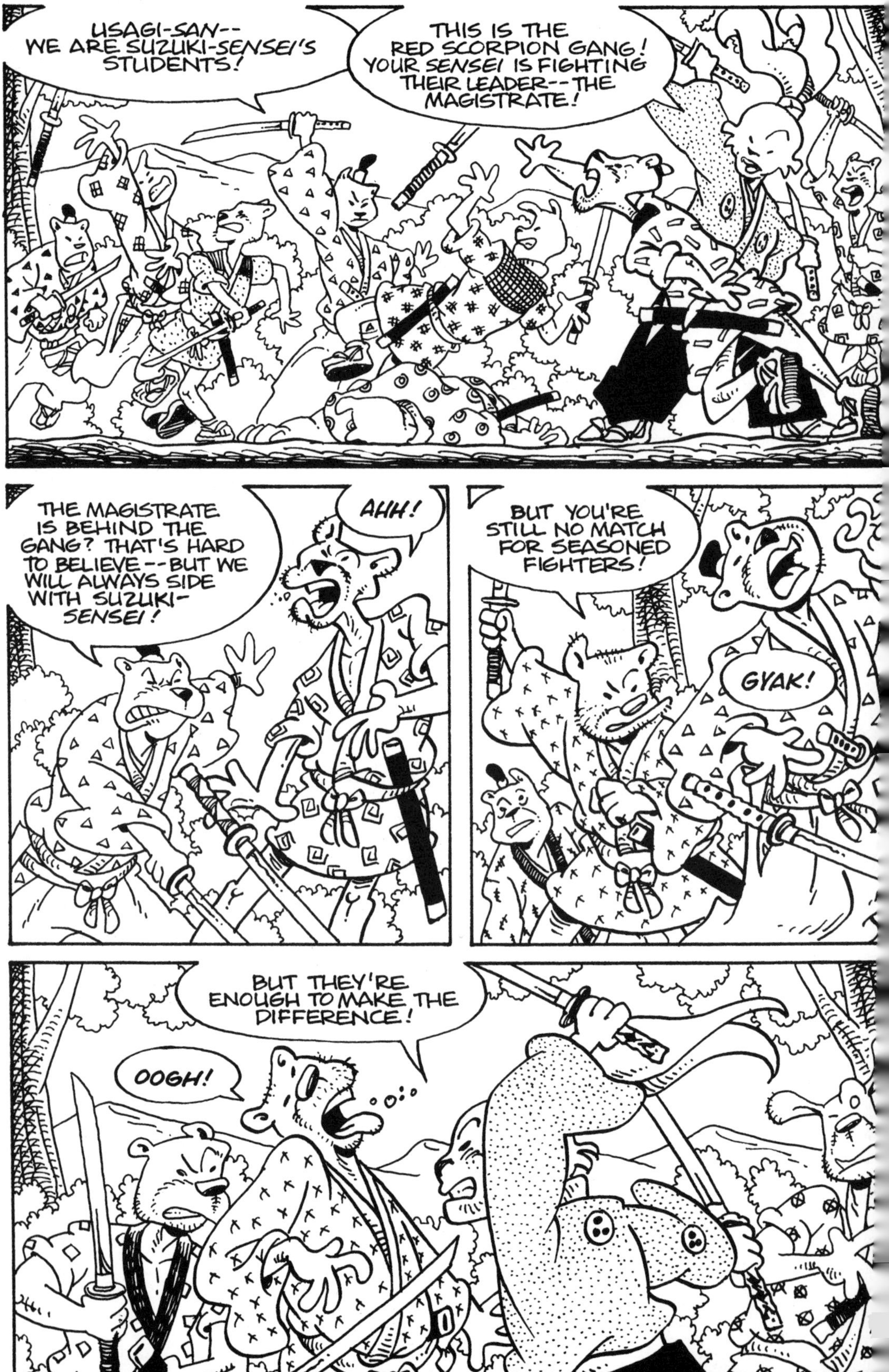
USAGI-SAN--
WE ARE SUZUKI-SENSEI'S STUDENTS!
THIS IS THE RED SCORPION GANG! YOUR SENSEI IS FIGHTING THEIR LEADER--THE MAGISTRATE!
THE MAGISTRATE IS BEHIND THE GANG? THAT'S HARD TO BELIEVE--BUT WE WILL ALWAYS SIDE WITH SUZUKI-SENSEI!
AHH!
BUT YOU'RE STILL NO MATCH FOR SEASONED FIGHTERS!
GYAK!
BUT THEY'RE ENOUGH TO MAKE THE DIFFERENCE!
OOGH!

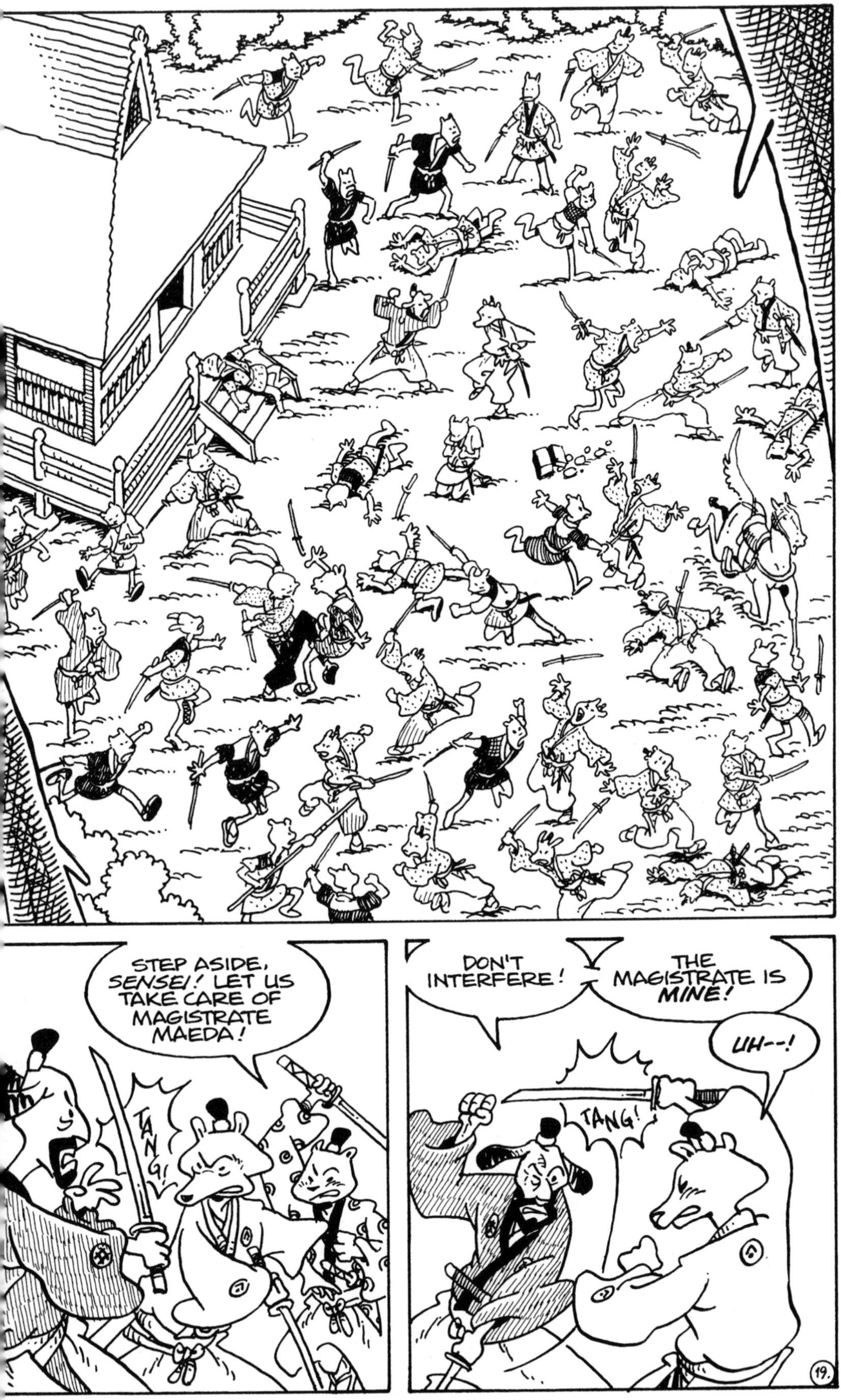
STEP ASIDE, SENSEI! LET US TAKE CARE OF MAGISTRATE MAEDA!
TANG!
DON'T INTERFERE!
THE MAGISTRATE IS MINE!
UH--!
TANG!
19.

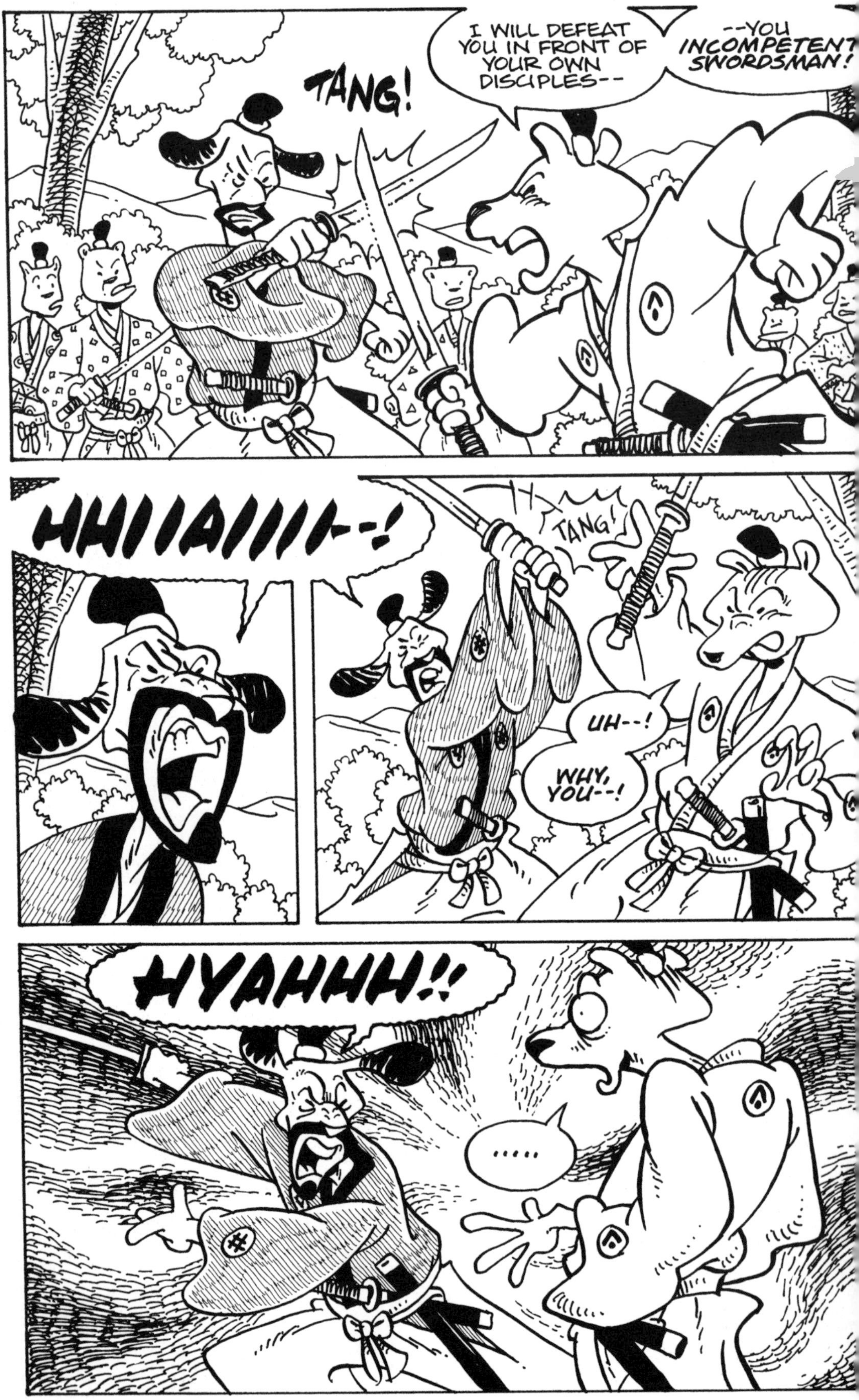
TANG!
I WILL DEFEAT YOU IN FRONT OF YOUR OWN DISCIPLES--
--YOU INCOMPETENT SWORDSMAN!
HHIIAIIII--!
TANG!
UH--!
WHY, YOU--!
HYAHHH!!
.....

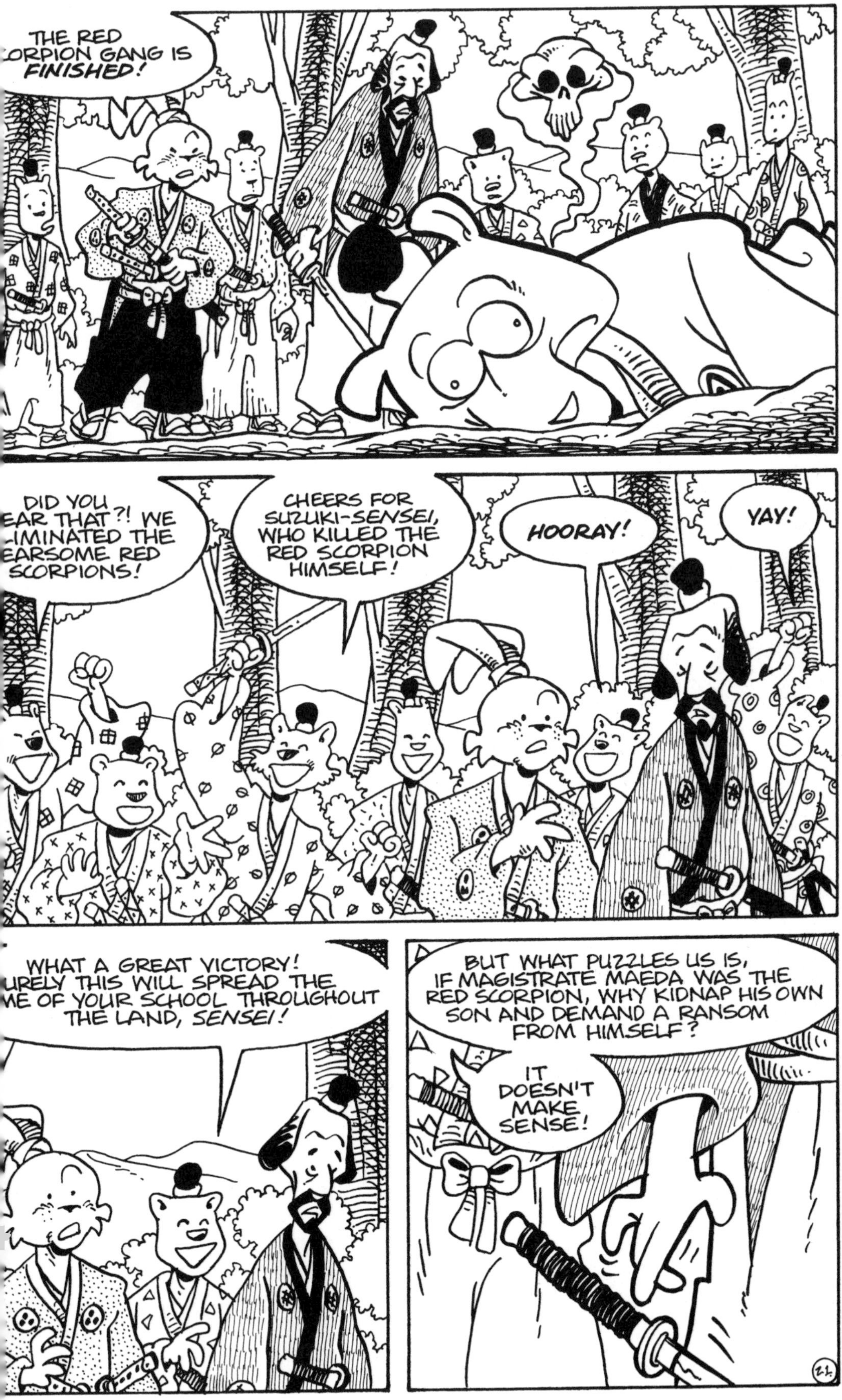
THE RED CORPION GANG IS FINISHED!
DID YOU EAR THAT?! WE LIMINATED THE EARSOME RED SCORPIONS!
CHEERS FOR SUZUKI-SENSEI, WHO KILLED THE RED SCORPION HIMSELF!
HOORAY!
YAY!
WHAT A GREAT VICTORY! URELY THIS WILL SPREAD THE ME OF YOUR SCHOOL THROUGHOUT THE LAND, SENSEI!
BUT WHAT PUZZLES US IS, IF MAGISTRATE MAEDA WAS THE RED SCORPION, WHY KIDNAP HIS OWN SON AND DEMAND A RANSOM FROM HIMSELF?
IT DOESN'T MAKE SENSE!
21.

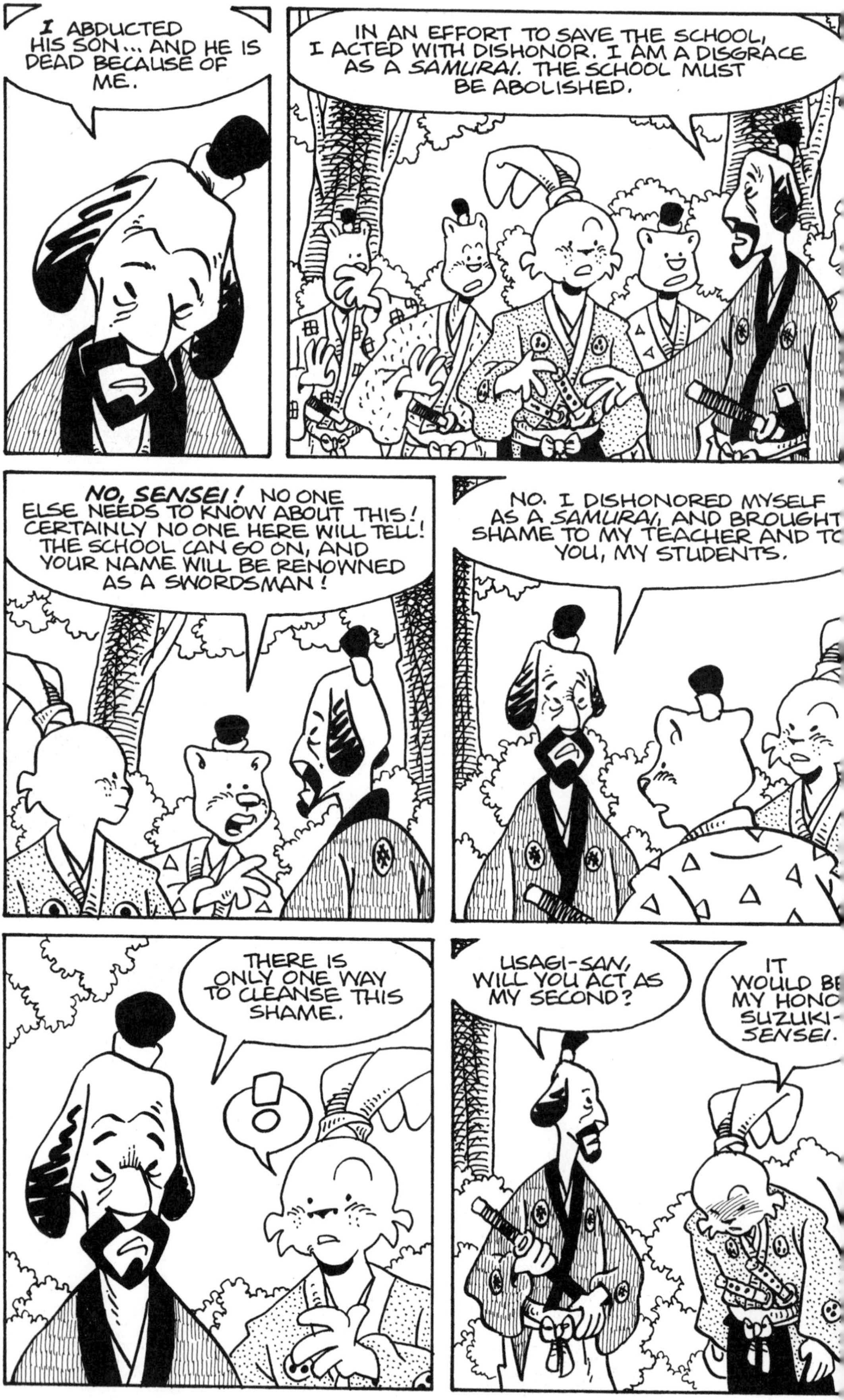
I ABDUCTED HIS SON... AND HE IS DEAD BECAUSE OF ME.
IN AN EFFORT TO SAVE THE SCHOOL, I ACTED WITH DISHONOR. I AM A DISGRACE AS A *SAMURAI*. THE SCHOOL MUST BE ABOLISHED.
*NO, SENSEI!* NO ONE ELSE NEEDS TO KNOW ABOUT THIS! CERTAINLY NO ONE HERE WILL TELL! THE SCHOOL CAN GO ON, AND YOUR NAME WILL BE RENOWNED AS A SWORDSMAN!
NO. I DISHONORED MYSELF AS A *SAMURAI*, AND BROUGHT SHAME TO MY TEACHER AND TO YOU, MY STUDENTS.
THERE IS ONLY ONE WAY TO CLEANSE THIS SHAME.
!
USAGI-SAN, WILL YOU ACT AS MY SECOND?
IT WOULD BE MY HONO SUZUKI-*SENSEI*.

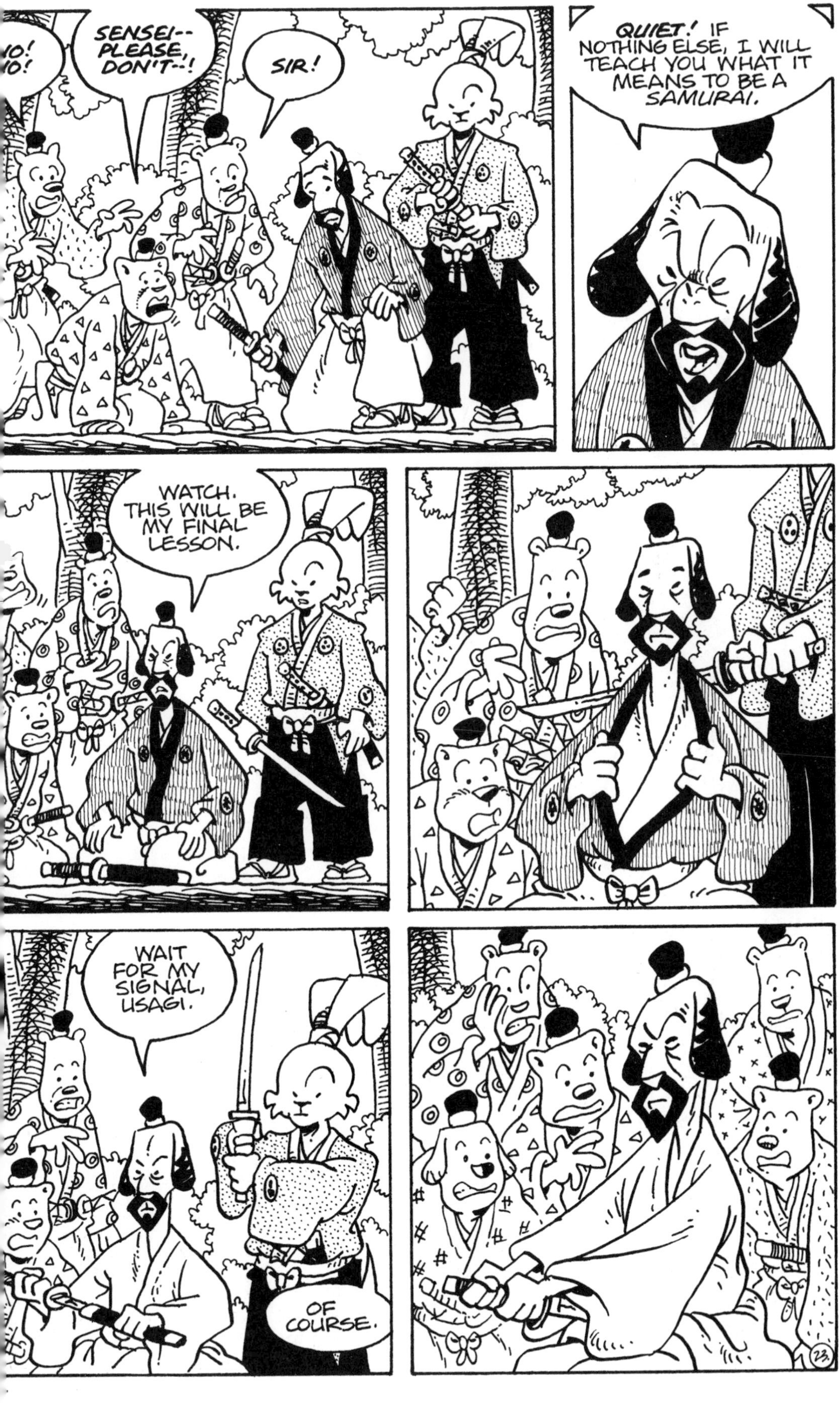
NO!
NO!
SENSEI-- PLEASE, DON'T--!
SIR!
QUIET! IF NOTHING ELSE, I WILL TEACH YOU WHAT IT MEANS TO BE A SAMURAI.
WATCH. THIS WILL BE MY FINAL LESSON.
WAIT FOR MY SIGNAL, USAGI.
OF COURSE.
23

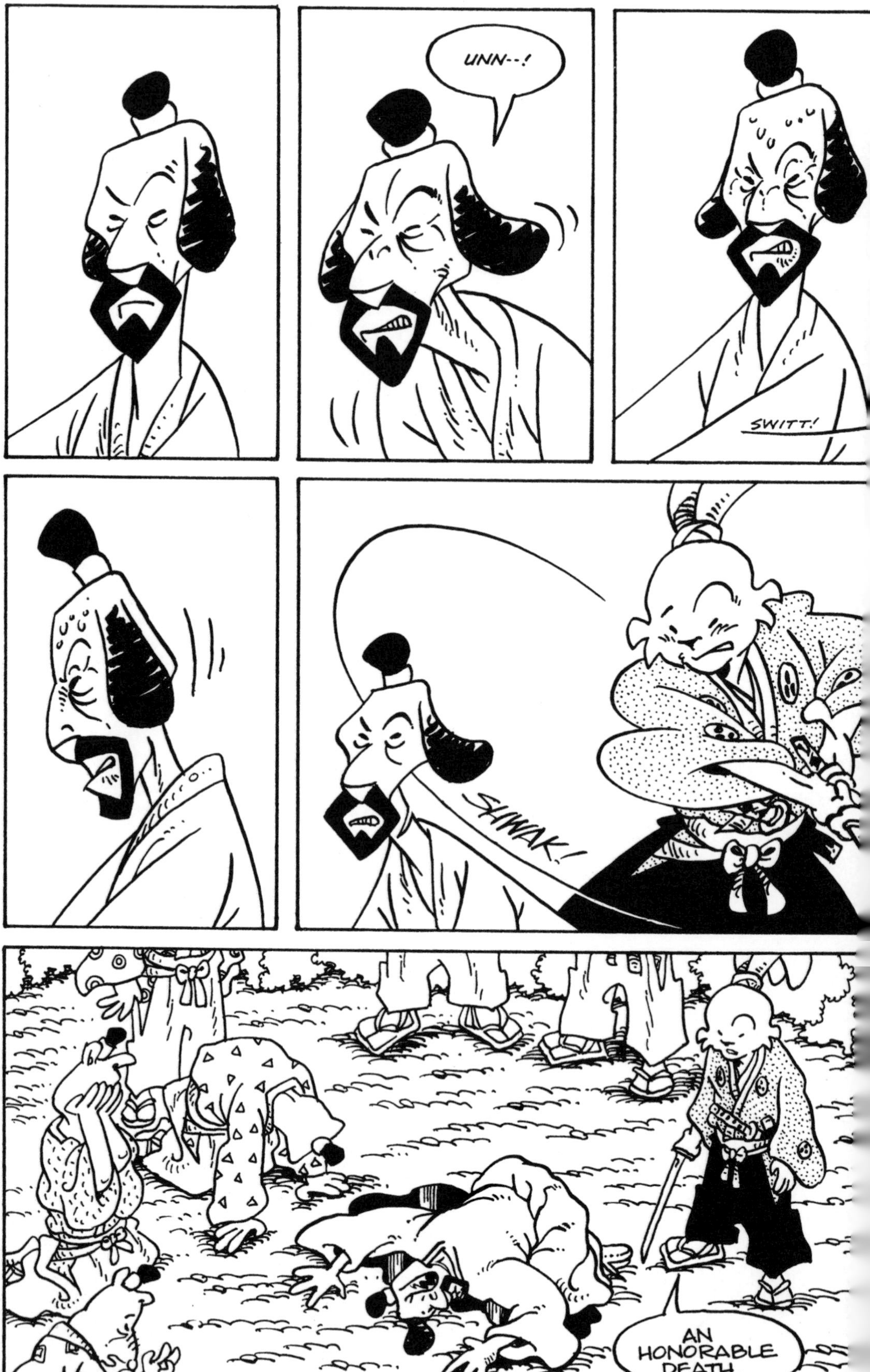
UNN--!
SWITT!
SHWAK!
AN HONORABLE DEATH.

# CUT the PLUM

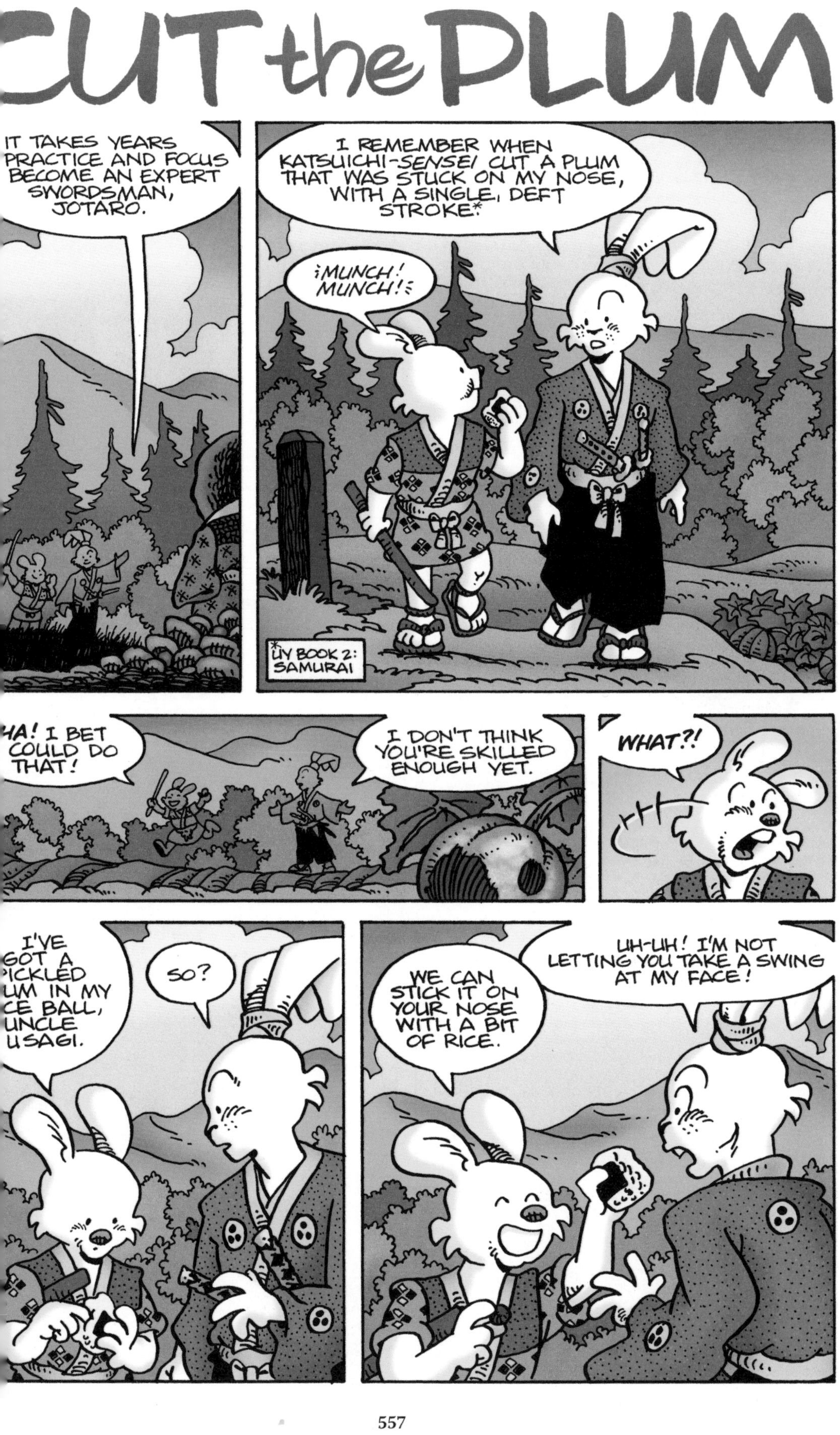
IT TAKES YEARS PRACTICE AND FOCUS BECOME AN EXPERT SWORDSMAN, JOTARO.
I REMEMBER WHEN KATSUICHI-SENSEI CUT A PLUM THAT WAS STUCK ON MY NOSE, WITH A SINGLE, DEFT STROKE*
¡MUNCH! MUNCH!
*UY BOOK 2: SAMURAI
HA! I BET COULD DO THAT!
I DON'T THINK YOU'RE SKILLED ENOUGH YET.
WHAT?!
I'VE GOT A PICKLED LUM IN MY CE BALL, UNCLE USAGI.
SO?
WE CAN STICK IT ON YOUR NOSE WITH A BIT OF RICE.
UH-UH! I'M NOT LETTING YOU TAKE A SWING AT MY FACE!

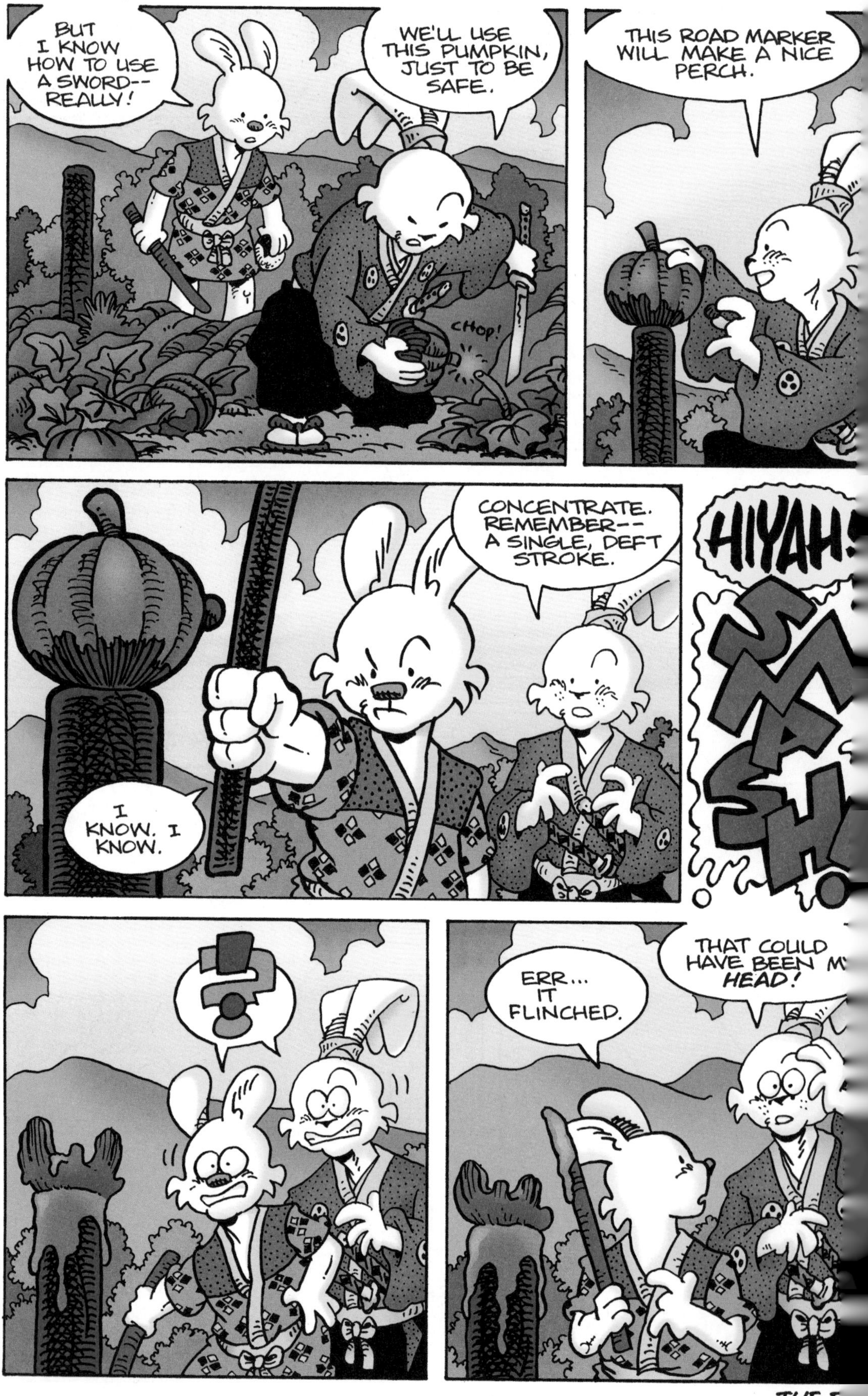
BUT I KNOW HOW TO USE A SWORD-- REALLY!
WE'LL USE THIS PUMPKIN, JUST TO BE SAFE.
CHOP!
THIS ROAD MARKER WILL MAKE A NICE PERCH.
CONCENTRATE. REMEMBER-- A SINGLE, DEFT STROKE.
I KNOW. I KNOW.
HIYAH
SMASH!
?!
ERR... IT FLINCHED.
THAT COULD HAVE BEEN M
HEAD!

THE E

## Traitors of the Earth

*Netsuke* are miniature sculptures, carved as toggles for pouches. (The word's literal meaning is "root for fastening.") They were used as early as the 1400s, but became popular in the seventeenth century. Japanese clothing has no pockets, so possessions were carried in small bags or boxes, which were hung on the *obi* (sash). These hanging containers were called *sagemono.* The *sagemono* were tied to the *obi* with a silken cord and secured with a *netsuke* that prevented the cord from slipping off. A bead, called an *ojime*, between the *netsuke* and *sagemono* could be slid to tighten or loosen the opening of the container.

The most commonly used material was ivory, but *netsuke* could also be made from bone, wood, stone, amber, bamboo, ceramics, or nuts. They could be carved in any variety of subjects: peasants in the field, samurai warriors, gods, animals, plants, and creatures from folklore. *Netsuke* also became status symbols, starting a new art form. The artists were called *netsukeshi.* Some were trained as painters or sculptors, but others were artisans, such as mask- or puppet-makers.

There are four categories of *netsuke*: the *katabori* are small and compact; the *sashi* are long, thin *netsuke*; the *kagamibuta* are shaped like a bowl with a lid; and the *manju* are round, flat, button-shaped *netsuke.*

With the Meiji Restoration in the nineteenth century, the Japanese adopted Western-style clothing and *netsuke* became obsolete.

*Netsuke* have become very collectible, especially in Europe and the US. Neither the materials used nor the existence of a signature has much bearing on the value of a piece. The determining factors are the quality of the carving, its originality, and its charm. A good source of information is the International Netsuke Society (netsuke.org).

My depiction of Shoki is based on a painting by Wu Tao-tzu (720–760), the greatest artist of the T'ang Dynasty. Emperor Ming-huang had a nightmare in which he was being tormented by a demon. Before he could summon his guards, a huge bearded giant appeared and seized the demon, gouged out its eyes, and ate it. The giant identified himself as Chung K'uei, a scholar who had failed the imperial examinations and killed himself in despair. The emperor at the time had nonetheless allowed him an official burial, and, in gratitude, Chung K'uei vowed to rid the world of demons. Emperor Ming-huang

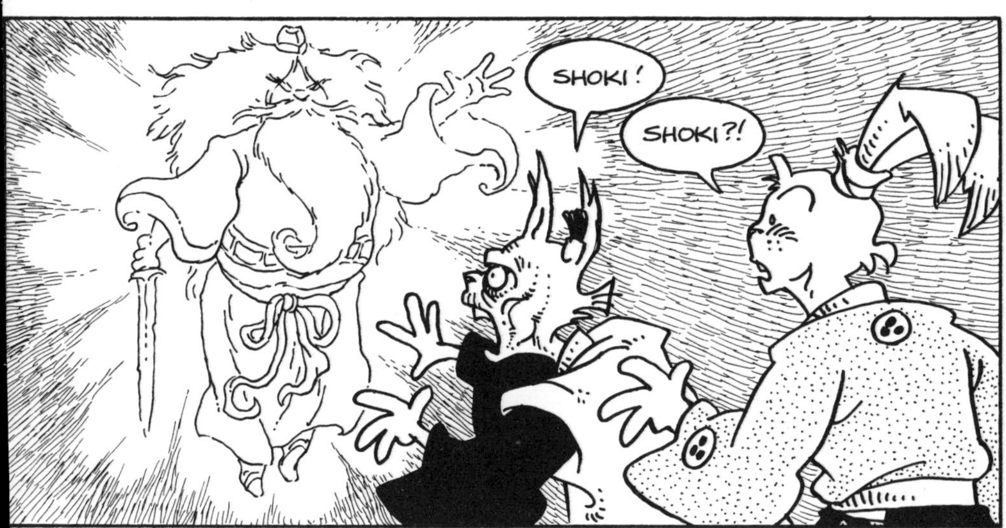
SHOKI!
SHOKI?!

commissioned Wu Tao-tzu to paint the image he had dreamed. The likeness was so striking that the emperor rewarded the artist with one hundred *taels* (an early Chinese currency) of gold. Stories of Chung K'uei became widespread, and Wu Tao-tzu's painting became the basis for his likeness. Eventually, the stories made their way to Japan and its folklore, and "Shoki" is the Japanese reading of the kanji characters that make up "Chung K'uei."

The *Komainu* are a pair of stone dogs that face each other either at the entrance to a Shinto shrine or at the approach to the oratory on the shrine grounds. They are usually carved from stone but are sometimes made of wood or metal. One dog, named A, breathes in with an open mouth, while his companion, Un, breathes out with his mouth closed, suggesting the inhalation and exhalation of heavenly forces and the balance of yin and yang. The phrase, *a-un-no-kokyu*, or "A-Un breathing," describes the relationship of people so close that they can communicate without speech. The two dogs protect the shrine against evil spirits with their fierce appearance.

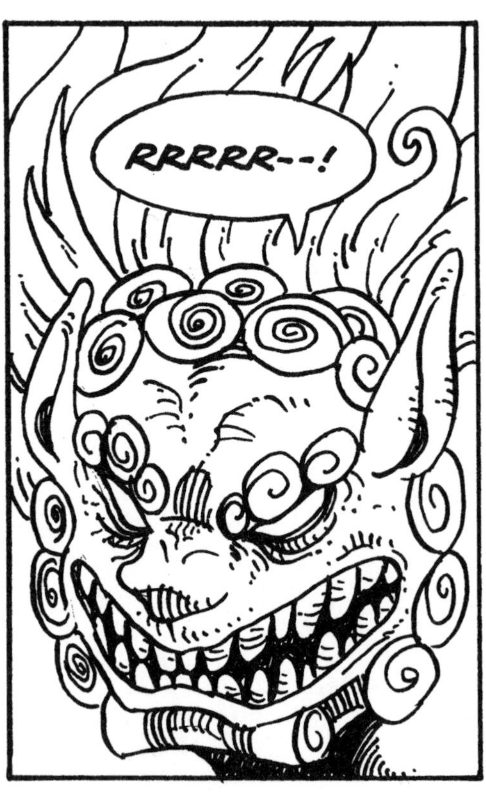
RRRRR--!

The *Komainu* can be traced to India and that culture's stylized representation of the lion. The Chinese adopted the lion and added attributes of their native tiger as well as the Pekinese dogs that were the pride of the Chinese Imperial family. That passed over to the Korean peninsula and on to Japan, where the lions were transformed into dogs. They are sometimes called *Karashishi* (Chinese lions). Okinawa has a similar creature called *Shissa*.

## What the Little Thief Heard

Pickled plums, or *umeboshi*, are reputed to have amazing medicinal properties, such as neutralizing fatigue, flushing out toxins, helping digestion, and providing an overall remedy for hangovers. Instead of an apple a day, the Japanese regard daily *umeboshi* as great preventative medicine.

The origin of the *umeboshi* in Japan is not really known. They probably came by way of China, where dried smoked plums, or *ubai*, are still used for a variety of medicinal purposes, including reducing nausea and fever. The oldest record of *umeboshi* as medicine dates from about a thousand years ago, when they were used to prevent fatigue as well as to cure food poisoning and other diseases.

*Umeboshi* were the samurai's most important field rations, and were used to flavor foods, cure fatigue, and increase endurance. Because of their high acid content, *umeboshi* were also used to purify water.

Plums (*ume*) are picked in late May or early June, when they are still green. They are layered in salt and weighed down with a heavy rock until late August, sun-dried on bamboo mats, then put in brine. Their red color comes from purplish *shiso* (perilla) leaves, which are pickled with the plums.

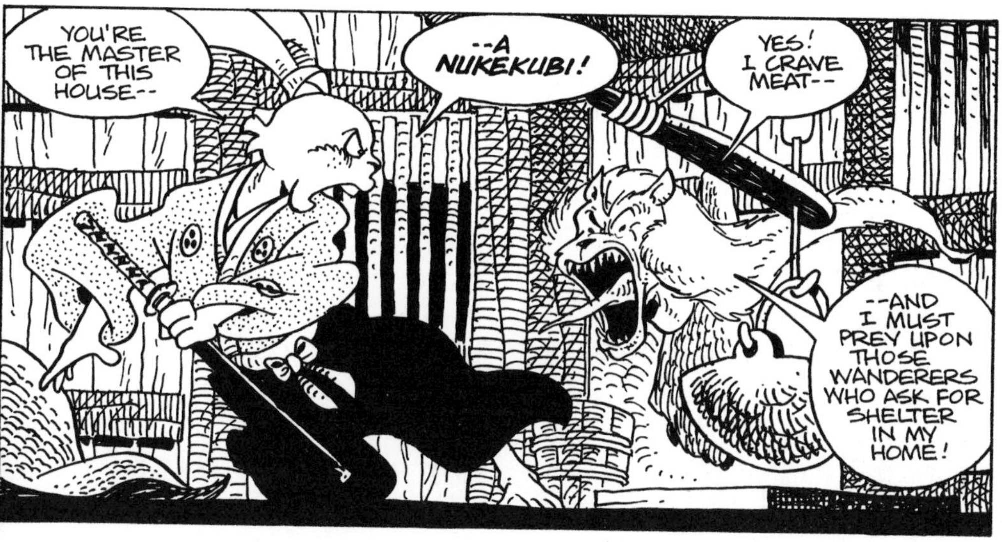
YOU'RE THE MASTER OF THIS HOUSE--
--A NUKEKUBI!
YES! I CRAVE MEAT--
--AND I MUST PREY UPON THOSE WANDERERS WHO ASK FOR SHELTER IN MY HOME!

*Fuku-ume* (*ume* of good fortune) are dropped in cups of tea and drunk on New Year's Day to ensure good health for the year ahead.

## Nukekubi

*Nukekubi* (literally "detachable neck") is a creature from Japanese folklore. It looks like a normal person during the day, but at night its head detaches from ts body and flies about in search of prey. The head screams as it attacks, frightening its victims before plunging its teeth into them. One way to identify a *nukekubi* is the line of red symbols around its neck where the head detaches, though the markings can be hidden under a neckerchief. While the head is away, he body remains inert. If the head does not reattach tself before sunrise, the *nukekubi* will die.

In his book *Kwaidan*, Lafcadio Hearn relates a priest's ncounter with five *nukekubi*, though the author mistakenly identifies them as *rokurokubi*, different monsters from folklore. The priest, Kwairyo, wandering alone in the mountains, accepts a woodcutter's invitation to spend the night with his family. Kwairyo awakens in the night, finding five headless bodies. He hides the bodies, and then follows the sound of voices into the forest, where the heads are planning how to devour the priest. The *nukekubi* discover their bodies are gone and attack Kwairyo, who fights them off with an uprooted tree. Four of them manage to flee, but Kwairyo kills the woodcutter's head.

## Toad Oil

Toad oil, or *gama no abura*, is the Japanese equivalent of Western "snake oil," an all-purpose remedy with often-questionable benefits, peddled by sometimes less-than-scrupulous salesmen.

Frogs and toads have held a special place in Japanese culture since rice was first cultivated (between 300 BC and AD 300). Besides controlling pests, they can be used to predict rain, as some species will "sing" in response to changes in humidity and air pressure. They have also been used in medicine, to cure everything from cancer to warts. Stone statues of them can be found in shrines and even some homes.

Ibaraki Prefecture is known for its frogs and toads. According to folklore, the toads of Mt. Tsukuba—*shiroku no gama*—produced an oily secretion that was highly effective on cuts, burns, and skin rashes.

The liquid was collected, made into an ointment, and then sold throughout Japan. You can still see toad-oil peddlers at Mt. Tsukuba, though their performances are now strictly for the tourist trade.

# THE RETURN OF THE LORD OF OWLS

The owl was regarded as a symbol of bad luck in Japanese folklore, and its cry was taken as an omen of death. It was thought that an owl would devour its own mother, and in a country where respect for parents and ancestors was stressed, ungrateful children were sometimes called "owls." The owl possessed the "evil eye," and so it was often depicted in traditional art with its back turned or its eyes closed.

The Ainu people of Hokkaido believed the eagle owl was a messenger of the gods and brought good luck during a hunt. The horned owl could discern a person's soul. If the owl narrowed its eyes when looking at someone, that person had a dark soul. If it stared with wide eyes, that person could be trusted.

In more recent times, however, the owl has come to be associated with good luck. The good luck stems from its name: *fukurou*. *Kurou* means "trouble" or "hardship," and *fu* can mean "no"—therefore, "no hardship." Ceramic owls might be given to newlyweds, or owl charms may be worn to ward off evil.

# THOSE WHO TREAD ON THE SCORPION'S TAIL

*Seppuku*, also called *hara-kiri*, is ritualized suicide by disembowelment. It literally means "stomach cutting." It was believed that a person's source of power was in his *hara* (lower abdomen). The samurai would take up his *tanto* (dagger) or *wakizashi* (short sword), plunge it into his abdomen, and then cut left to right, severing

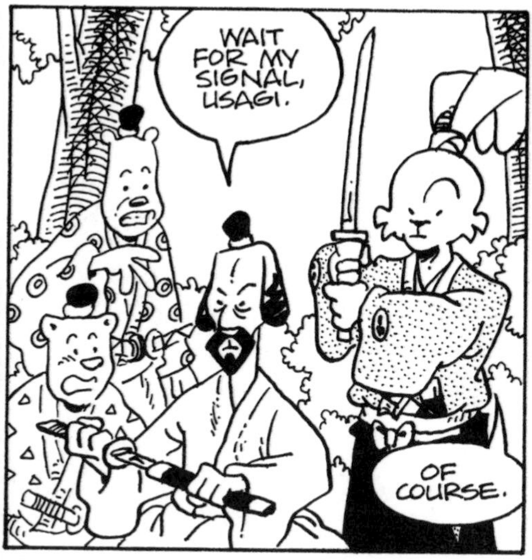
WAIT FOR MY SIGNAL, USAGI.
OF COURSE.

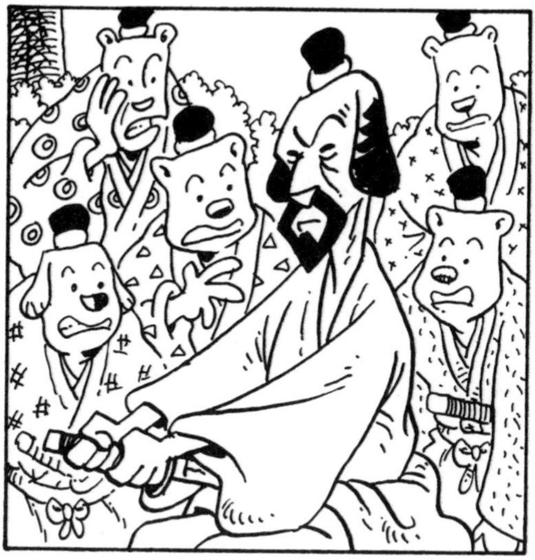

the spinal nerve centers. At a previously agreed-upon signal, a *kaishakunin* (second) would perform *daki-kubi* (decapitation), but would leave a small bit of flesh connecting the head to the neck so that the head would not tumble around. Sometimes the prearranged signal would come after a second cut was made, up from the abdomen toward the rib cage and on to the aorta. Grasping the *tanto* or *wakizashi* by the blade could also act as the trigger. Other times the ritual blade was replaced with a fan, and the act of touching the fan to the stomach would signal the fall of the real blade.

A woman in a samurai family was also expected to take her own life, if honor demanded it. Because the Japanese revere the womb as the place where life begins, a woman would instead cut her throat. She would sit with her legs tied together, in order to keep her modesty even in death. This form of suicide is called *jigai*.

The first recorded act of *seppuku* was committed by Minamoto no Yorimasa, a general in the Genpei War who was wounded in the leg and could no longer fight. Rather than surrender, he ordered his assistant, Watanabe Tonau, to cut off his head and hide it so that it would not be publicly displayed. Tonau refused, saying he could not carry out such an order while his master was still alive. Yorimasa wrote a poem, then cut his own stomach. As he had been instructed, Tonau severed his master's head and hid it away, thus keeping it from being defiled. After that, other samurai adopted the act as a way to avoid the disgrace of being captured by the enemy. Eventually, it evolved into a very detailed, stylized ritual performed before spectators. The samurai would bathe, dress in white robes, and might even write his own death poem.

There were many reasons for *seppuku*. *Oibara* was the act of committing *seppuku* to follow one's master after he had died. *Sokotsu-shi* was performed if a samurai had a feeling of guilt because of his actions or if he was unable to carry out a master's order. A samurai could kill himself as a form of public protest of unfair treatment—this was called *kanshi*, and might induce a master to reconsider a bad decision. If a samurai were unable to right a wrong, he would commit *munen-bara*. A strong lord might be ordered to die as part of a peace treaty, to weaken his clan. *Seppuku* could also be ordered if a retainer caused embarrassment or was a liability.

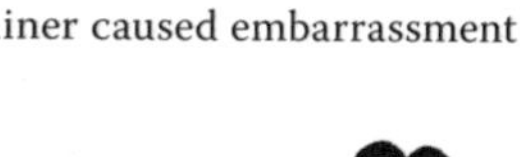

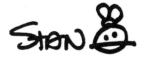

Colors by Tom Luth, except on Sakai's painted covers.

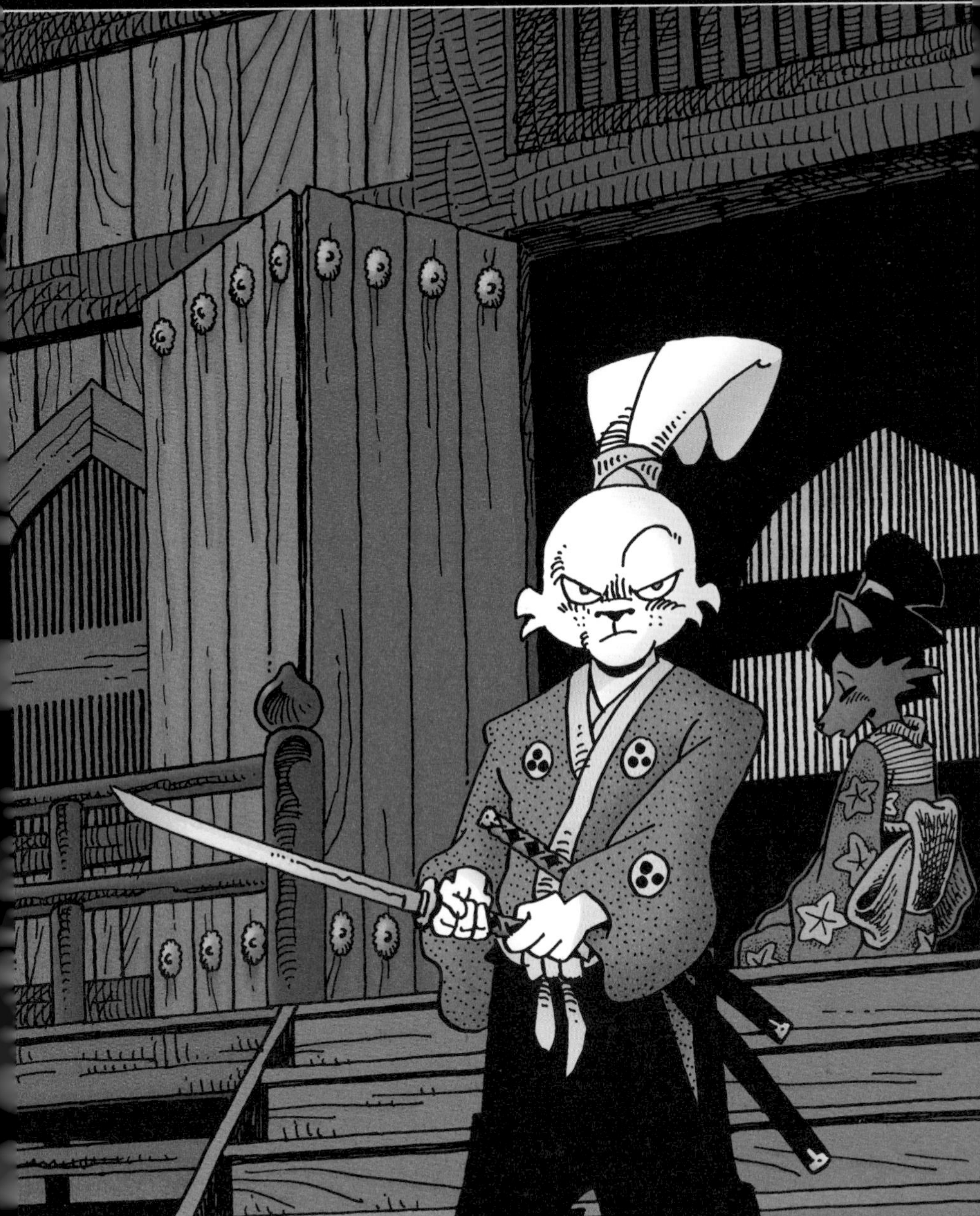
SAKAI
2008
LUTH

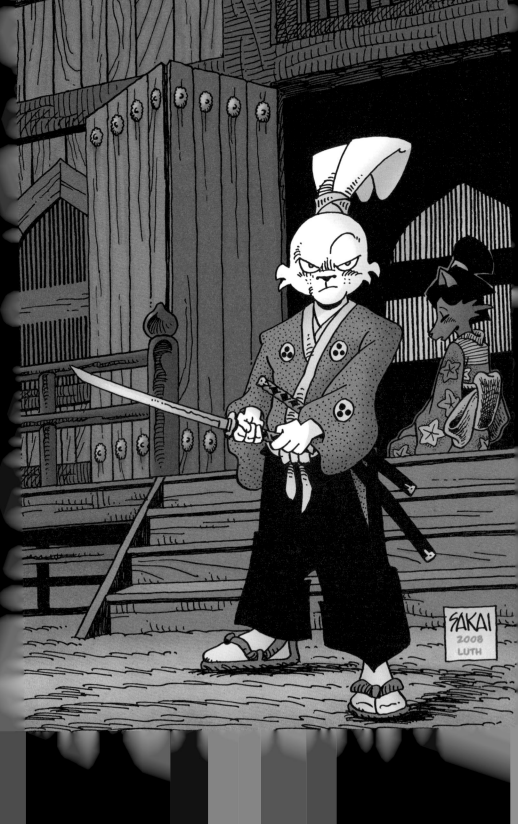

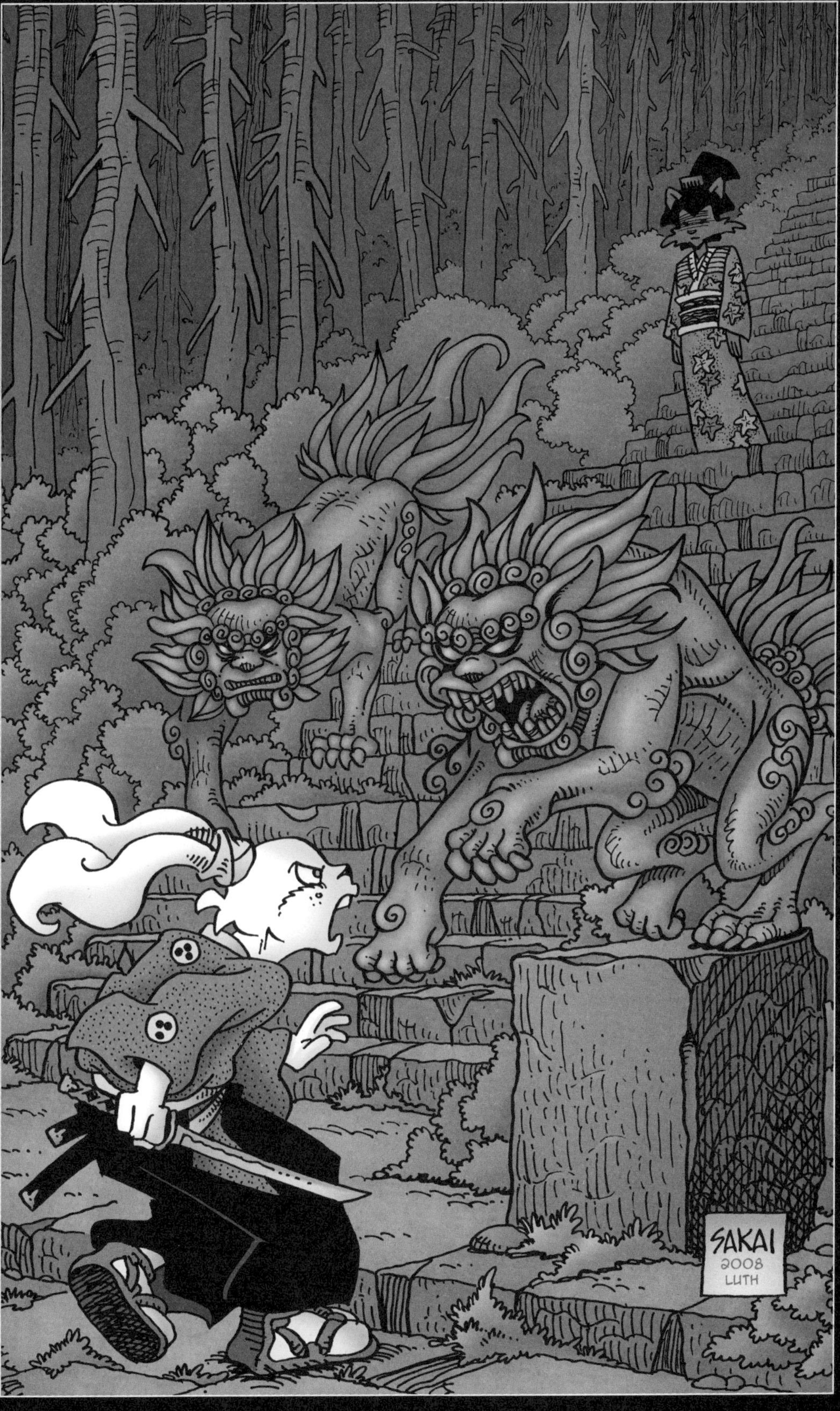
SAKAI
2008
LUTH

*Usagi Yojimbo Volume Three #118*

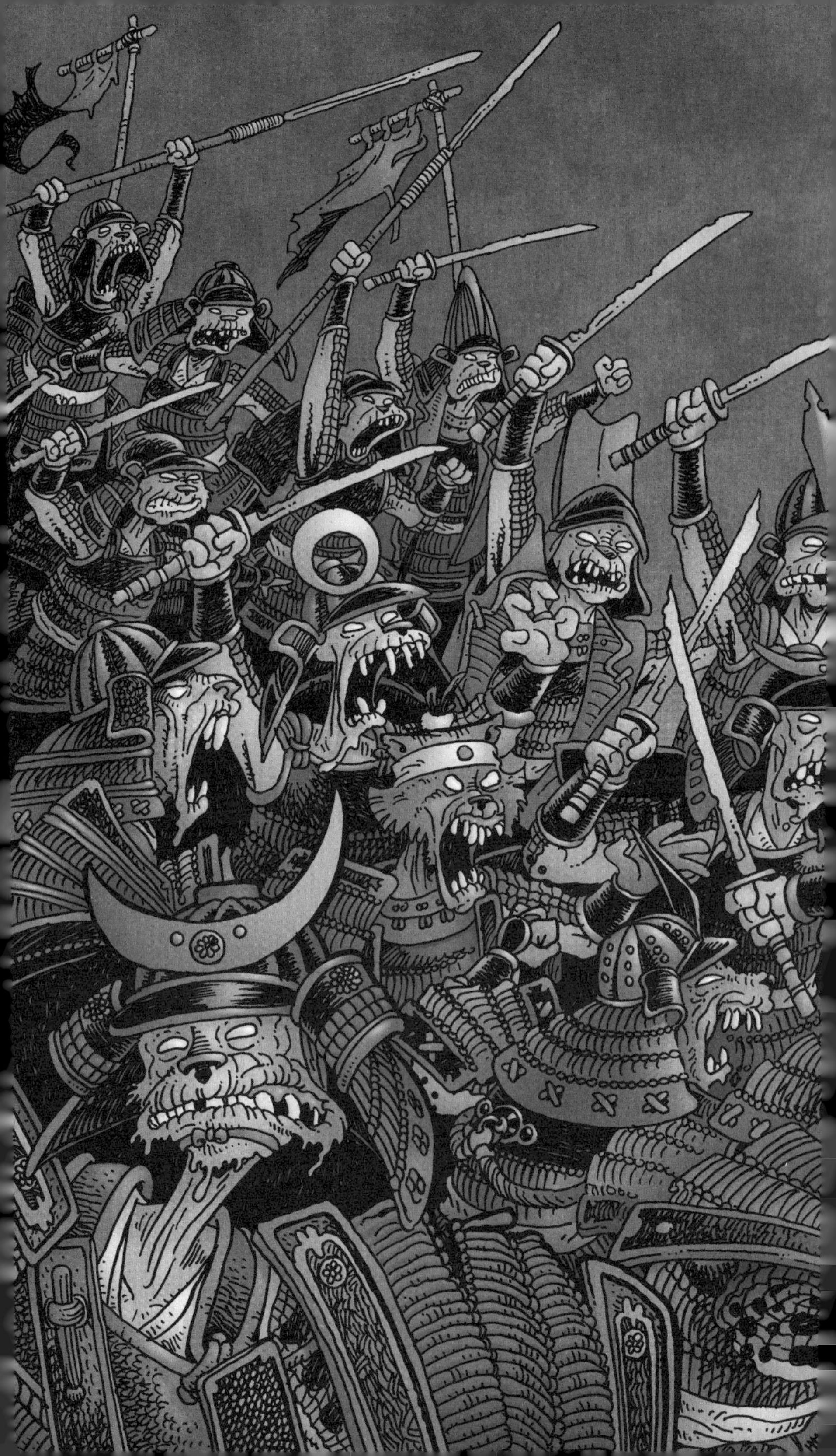

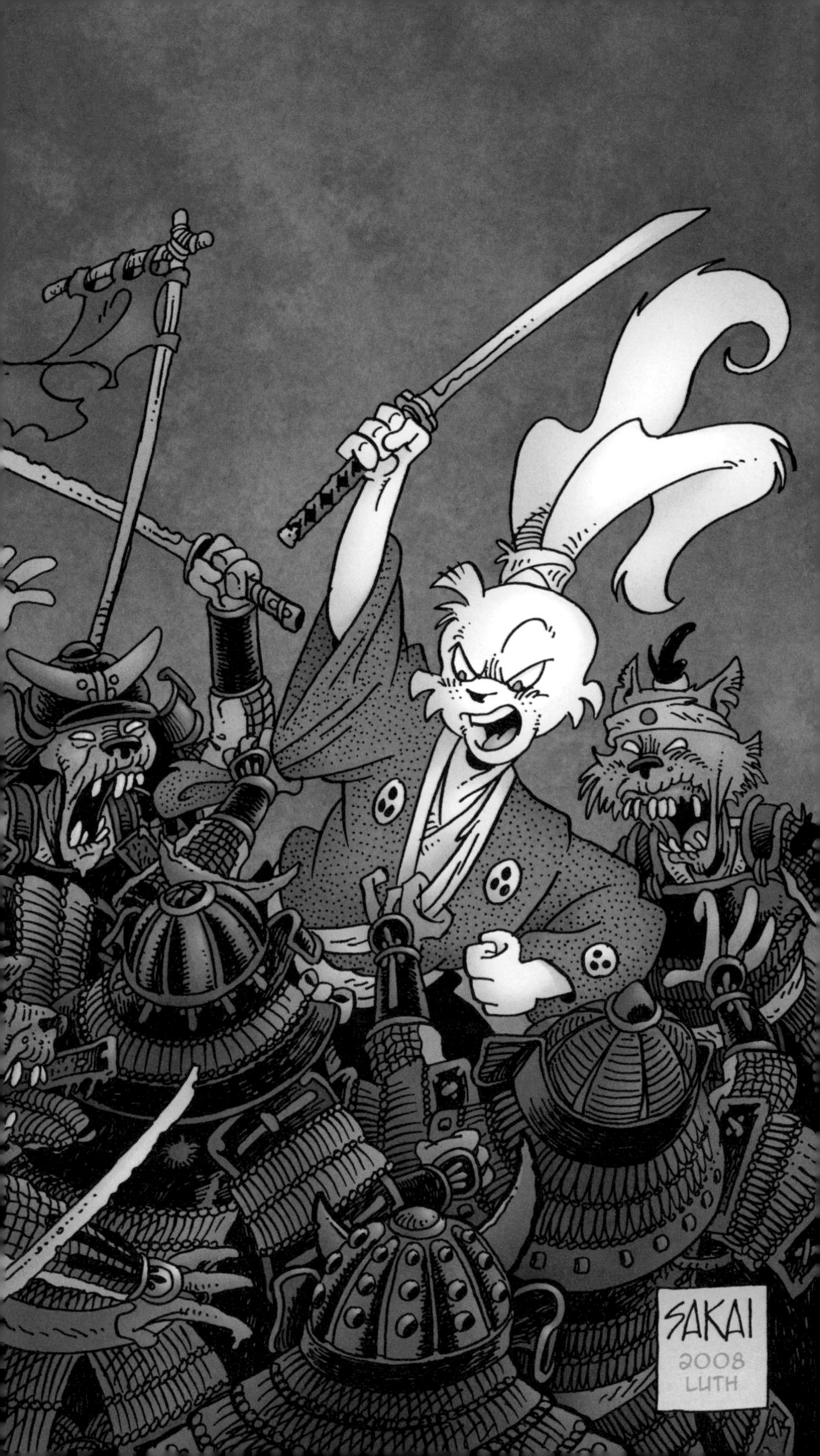
SAKAI
2008
LUTH

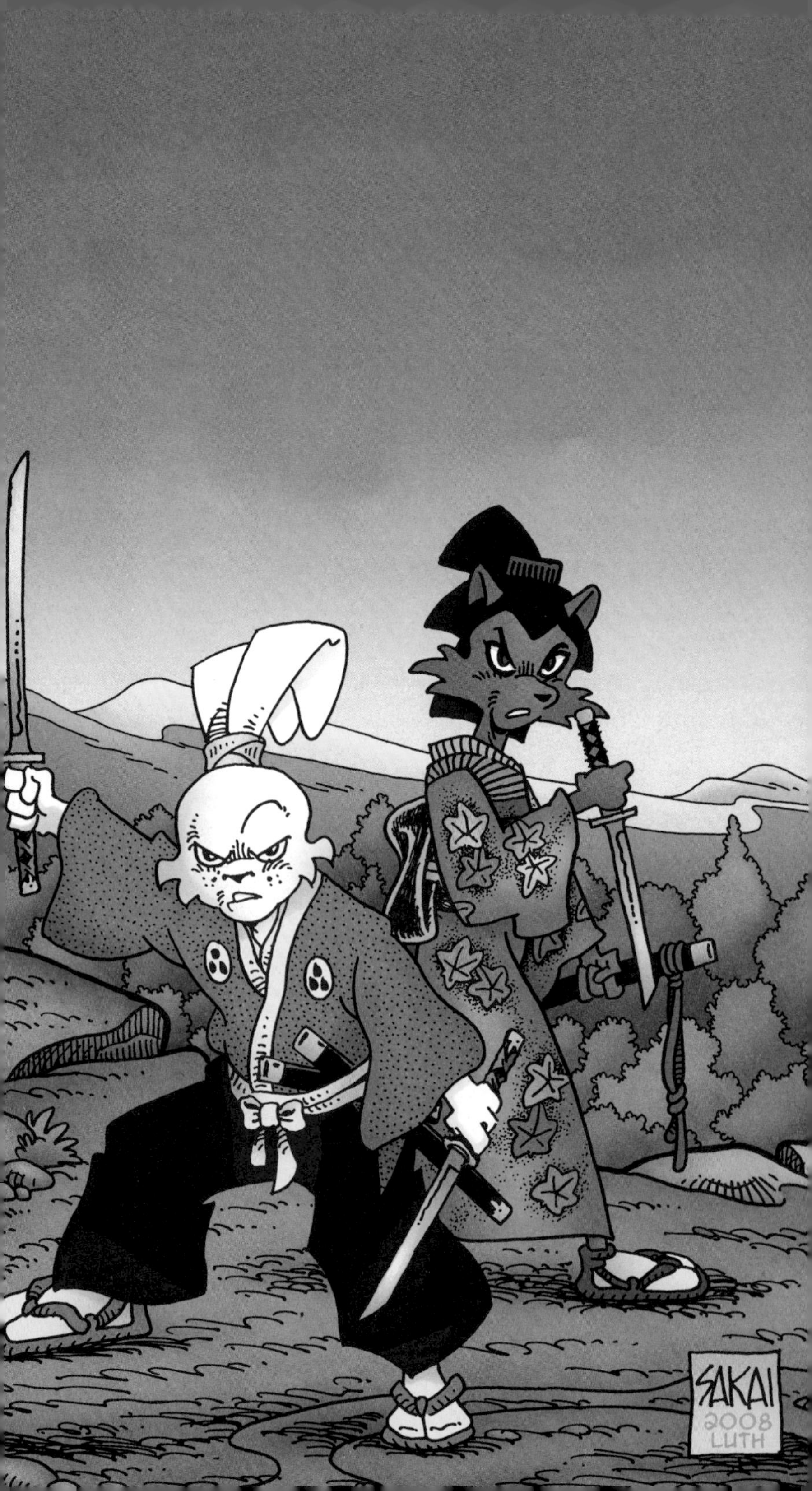
SAKAI
2008
LUTH

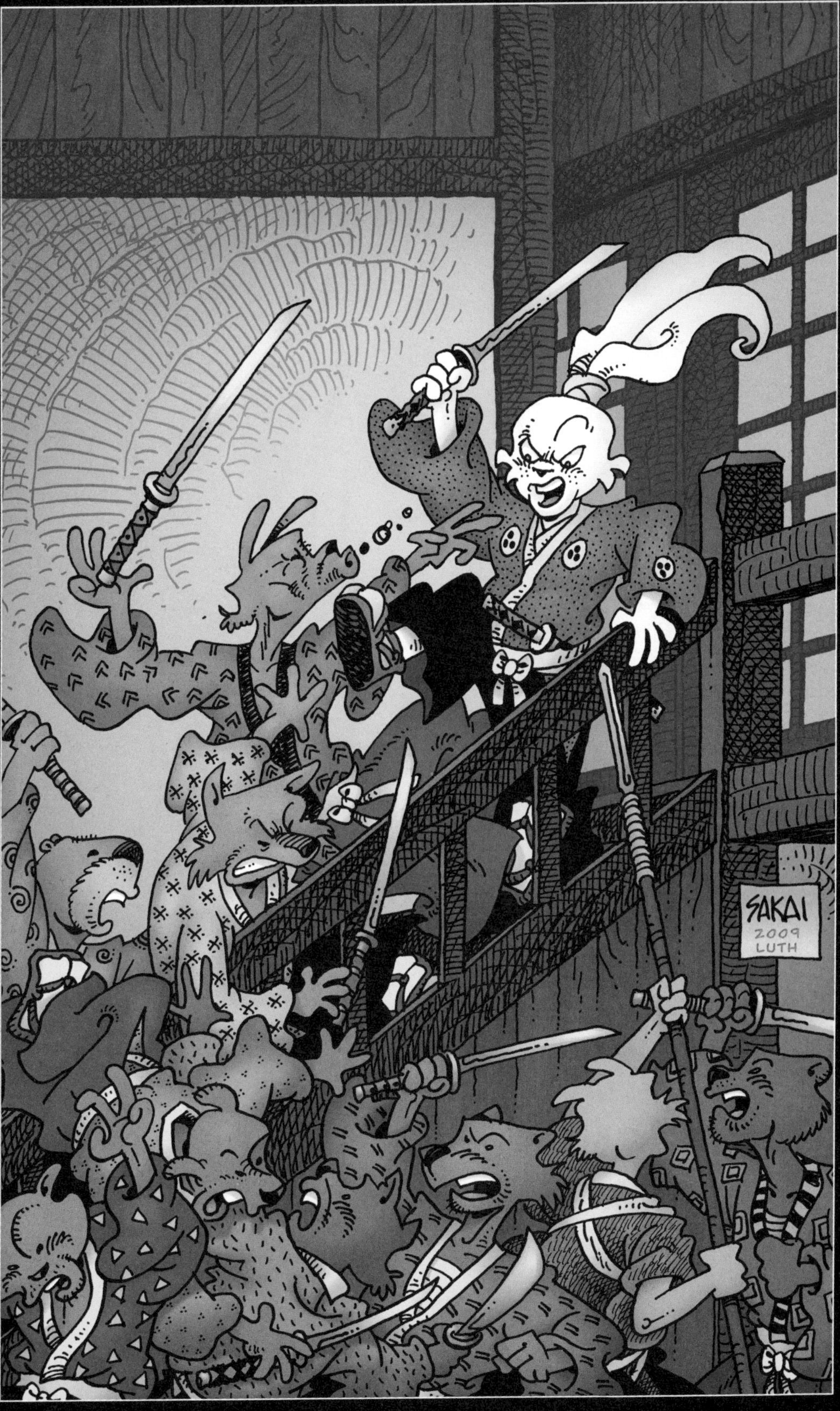
SAKAI
2009
LUTH

*Usagi Yojimbo Volume Three #121*

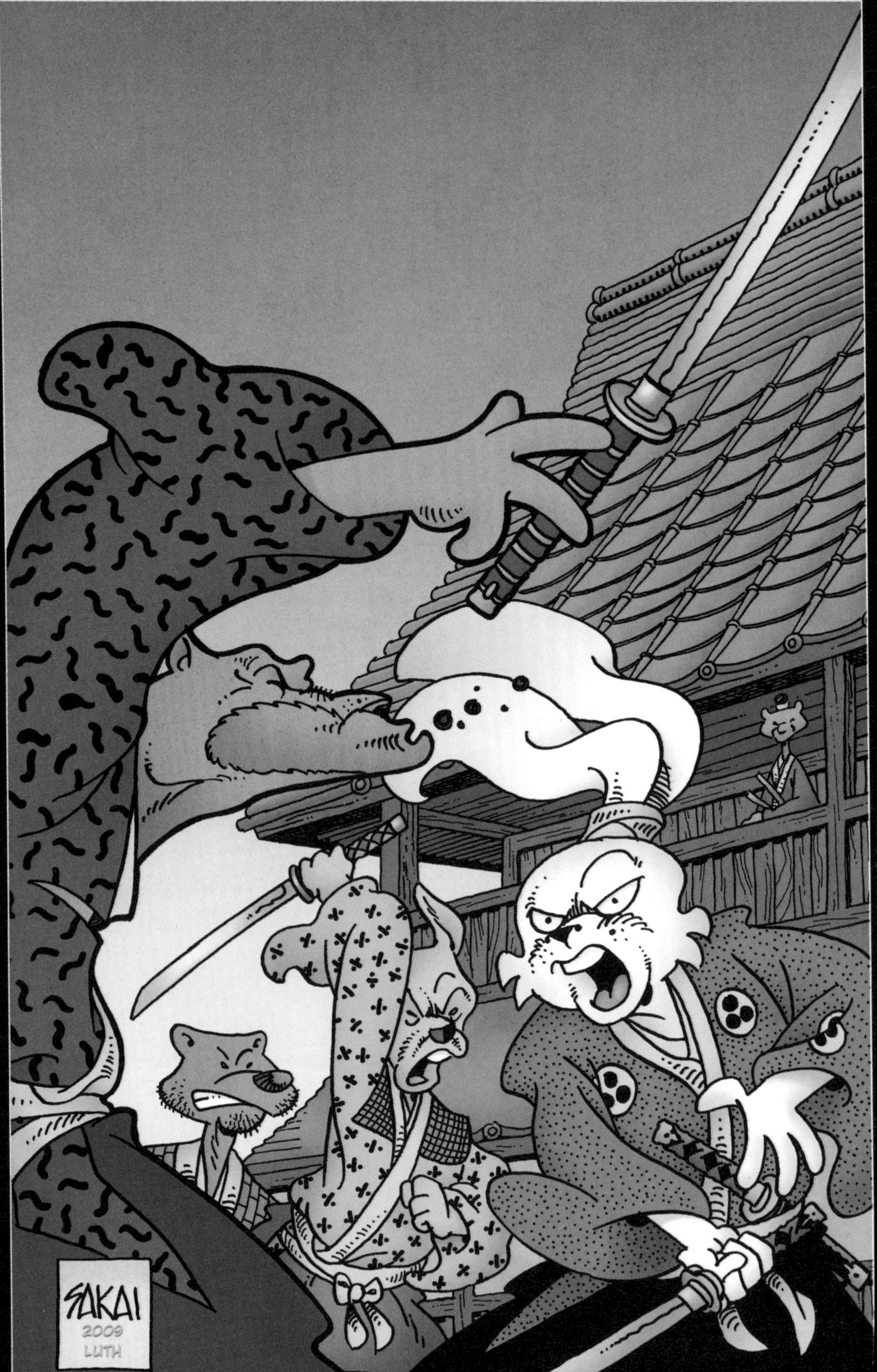
SAKAI
2009
LUTH

*Usagi Yojimbo Volume Three #122*

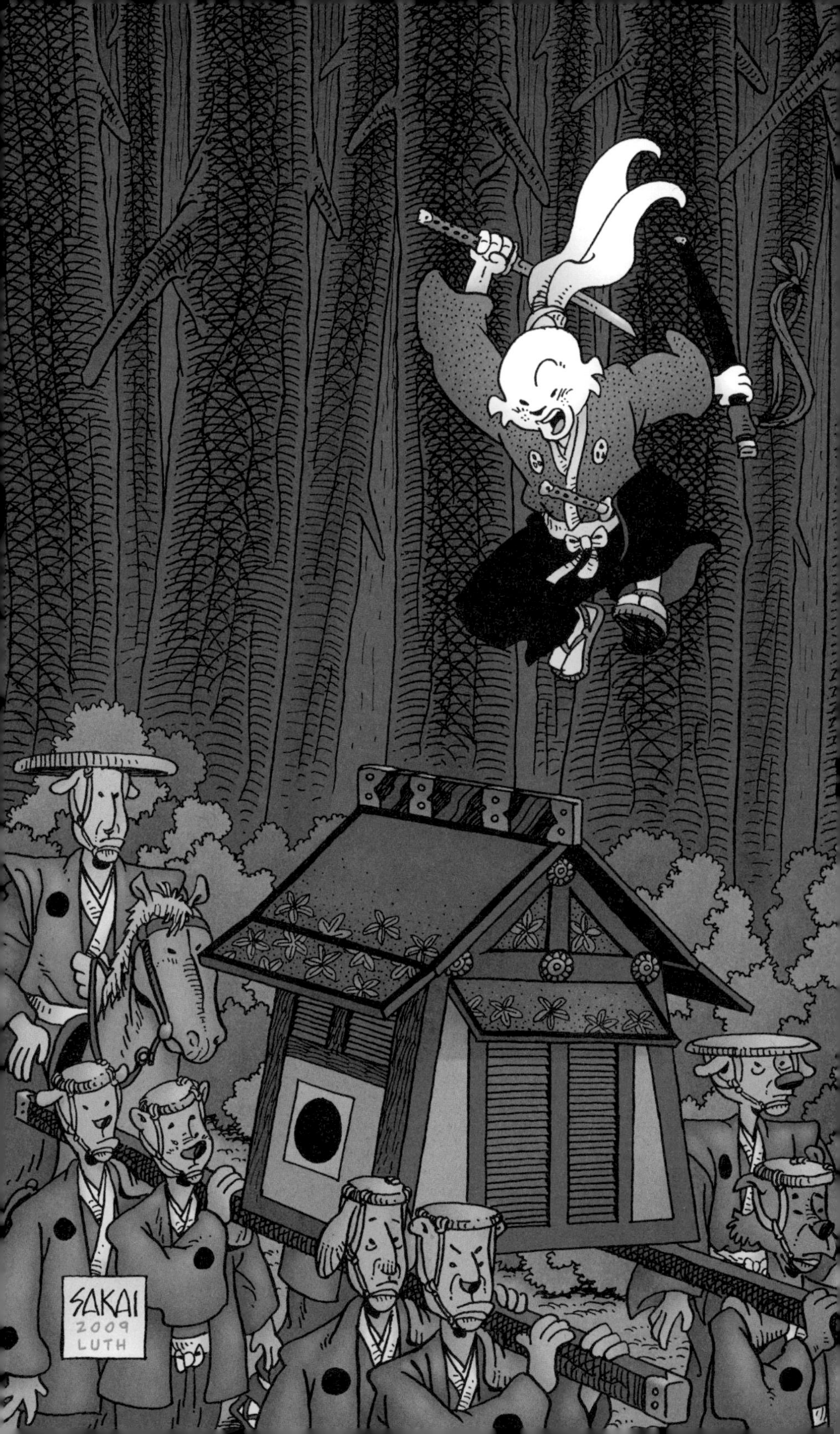
SAKAI
2009
LUTH

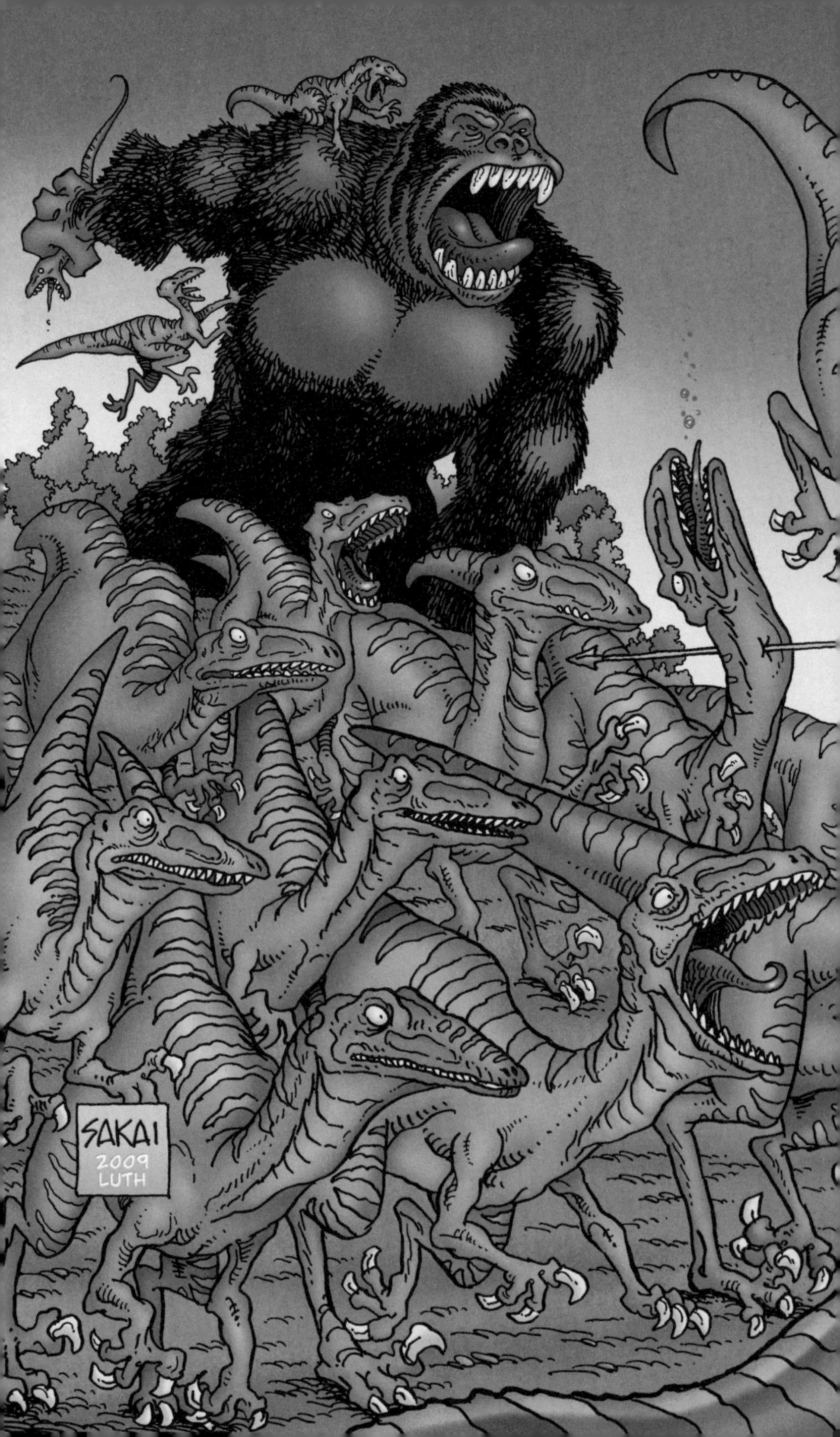
SAKAI
2009
LUTH

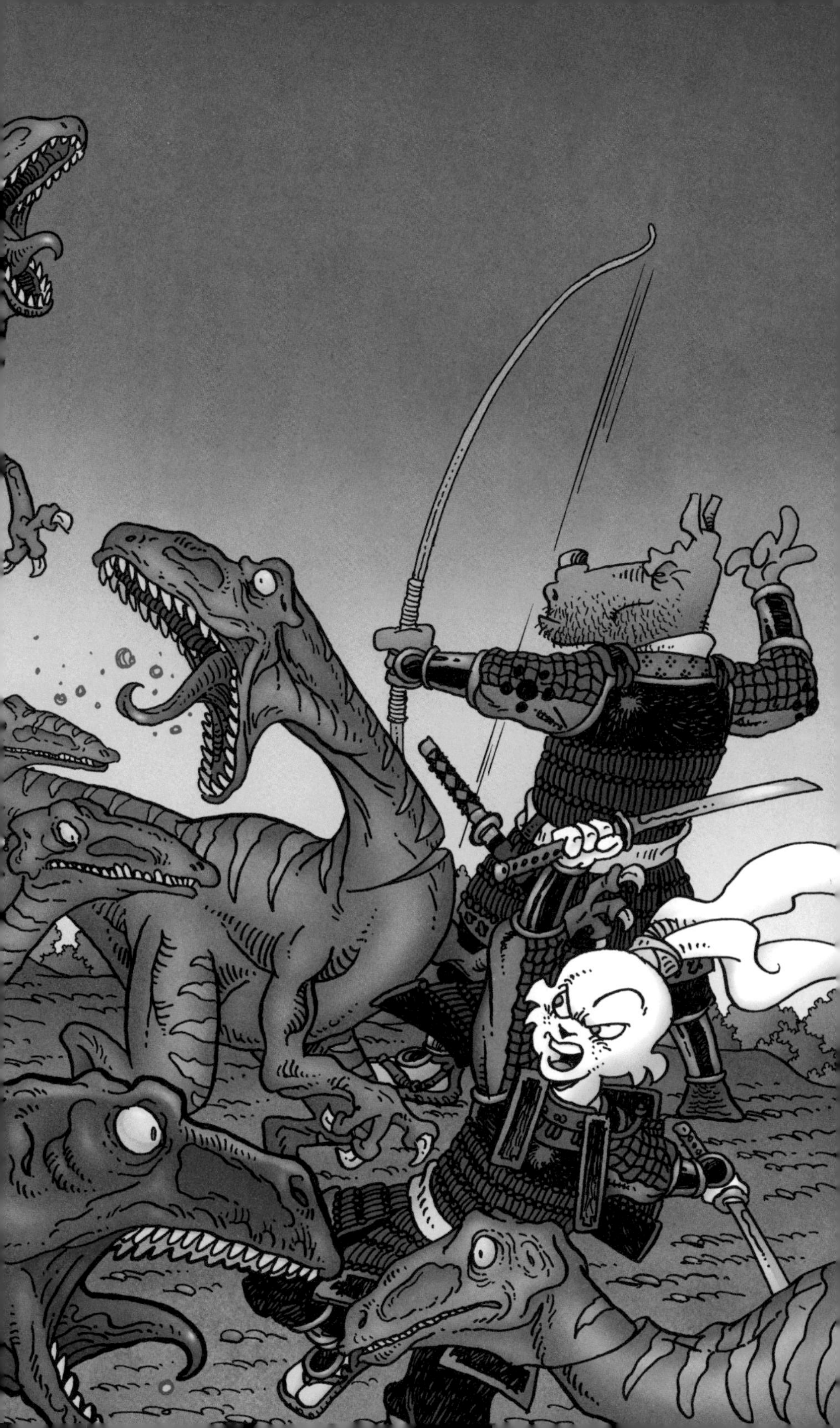

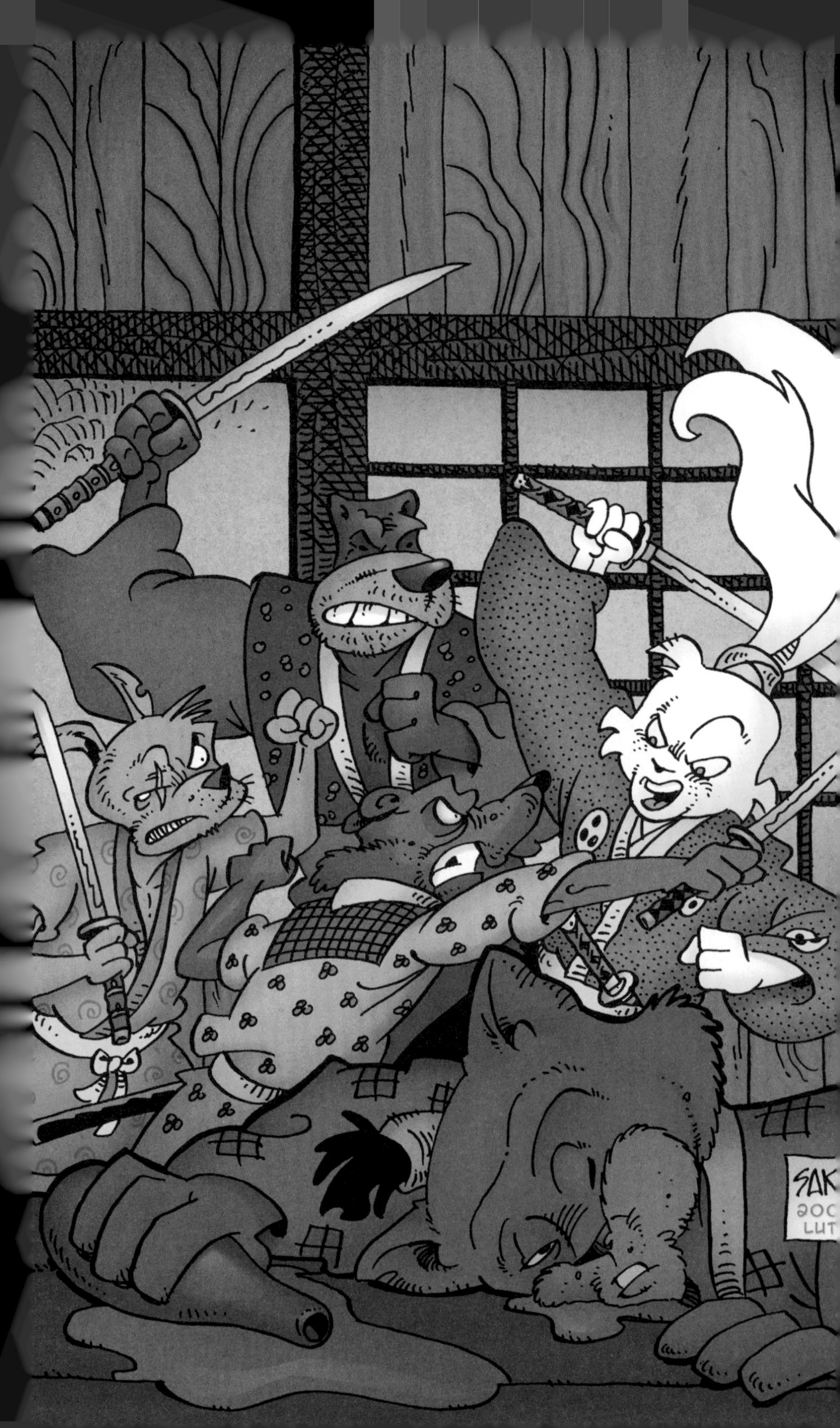

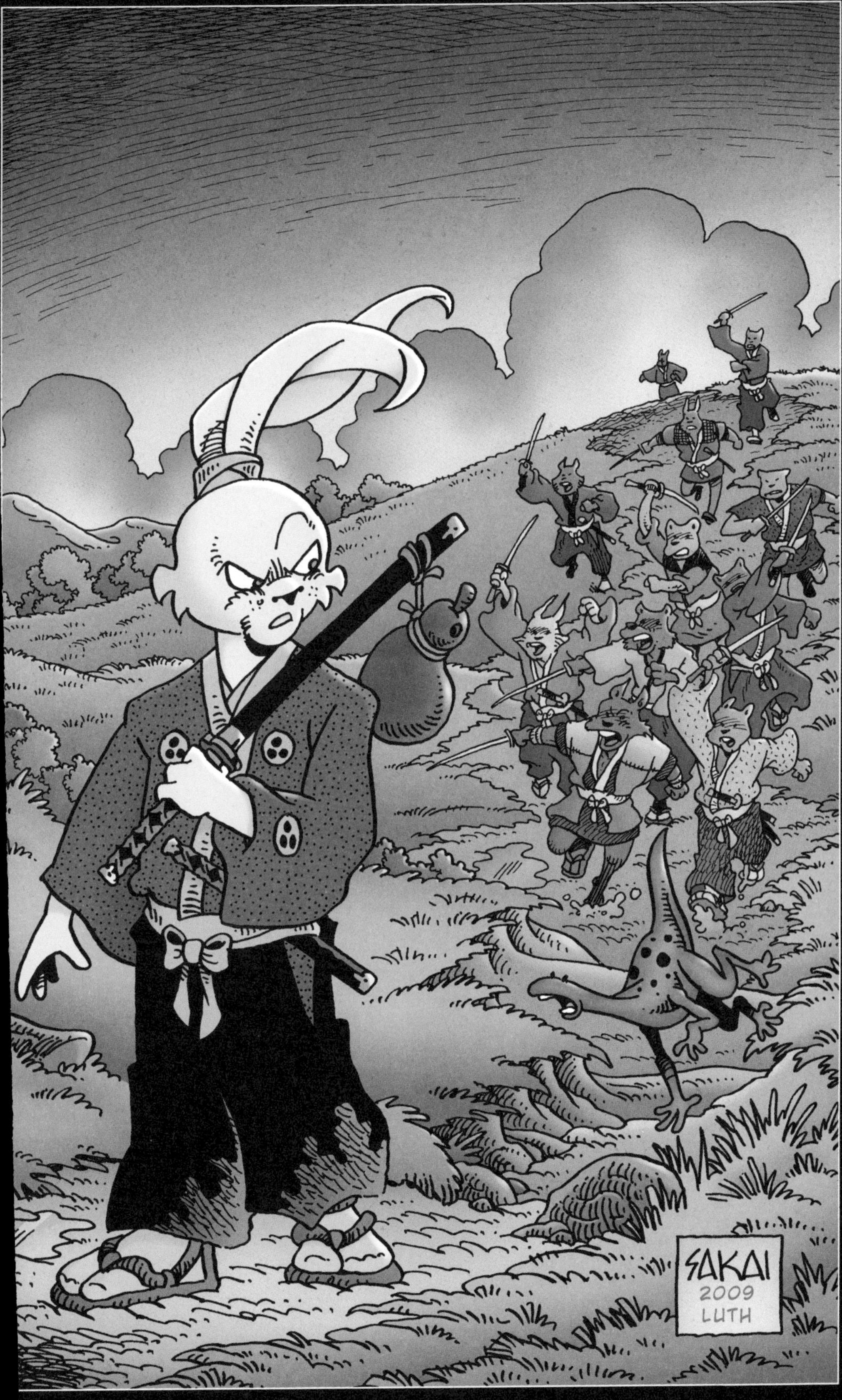
SAKAI
2009
LUTH

*Usagi Yojimbo Volume Three #125*

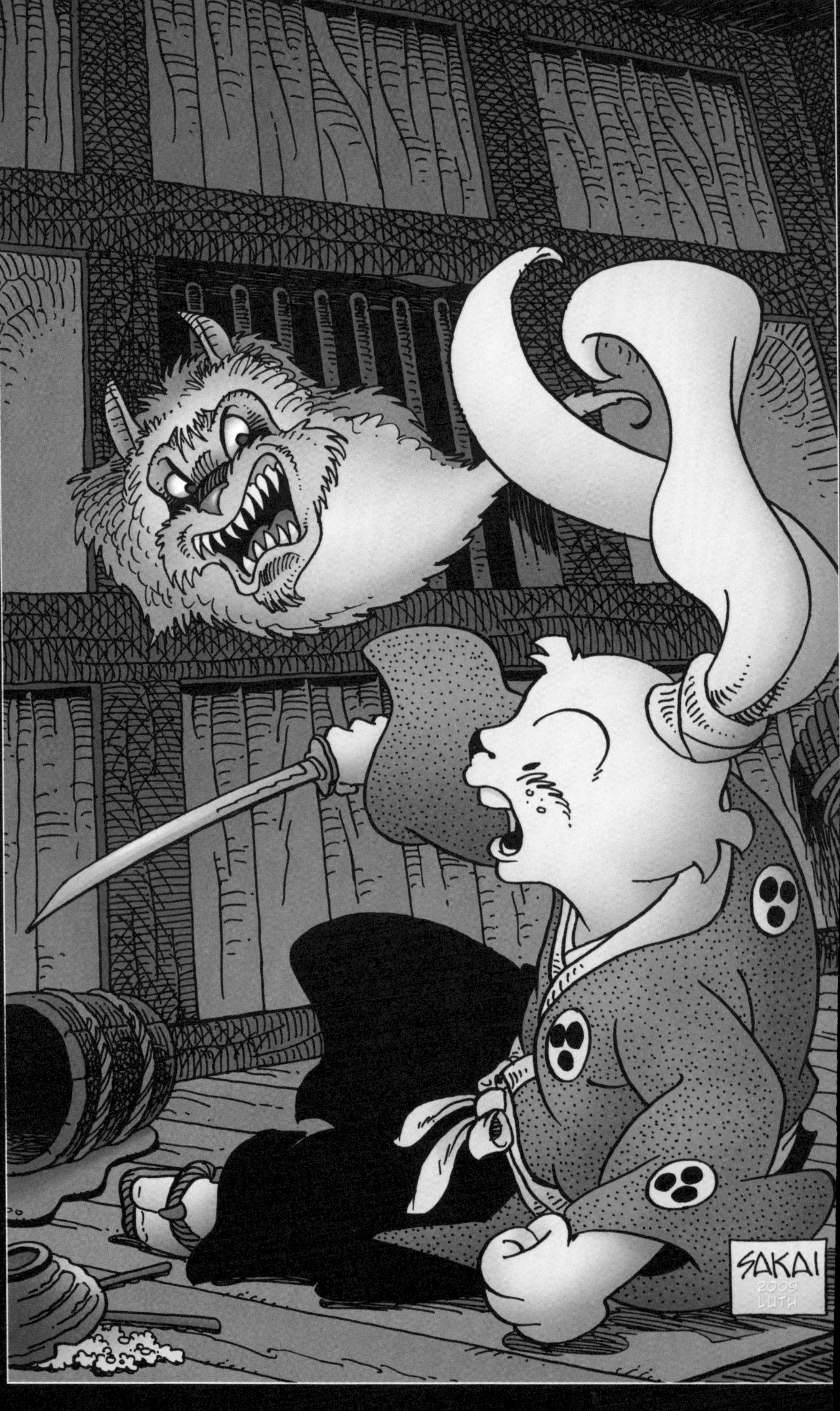
SAKAI
2009
LUTH

*Usagi Yojimbo Volume Three #126*

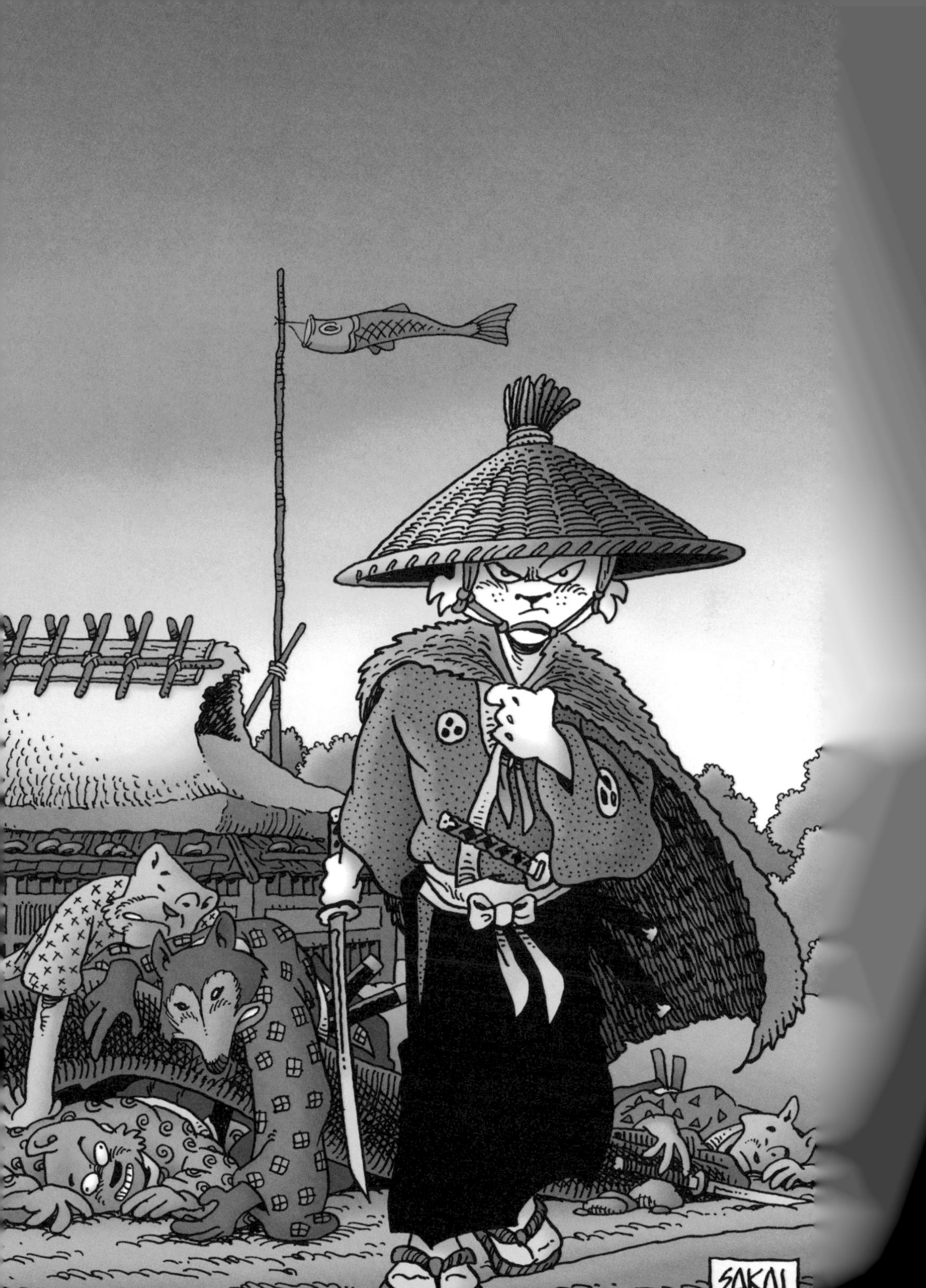
SAKAI
2009
LUTH

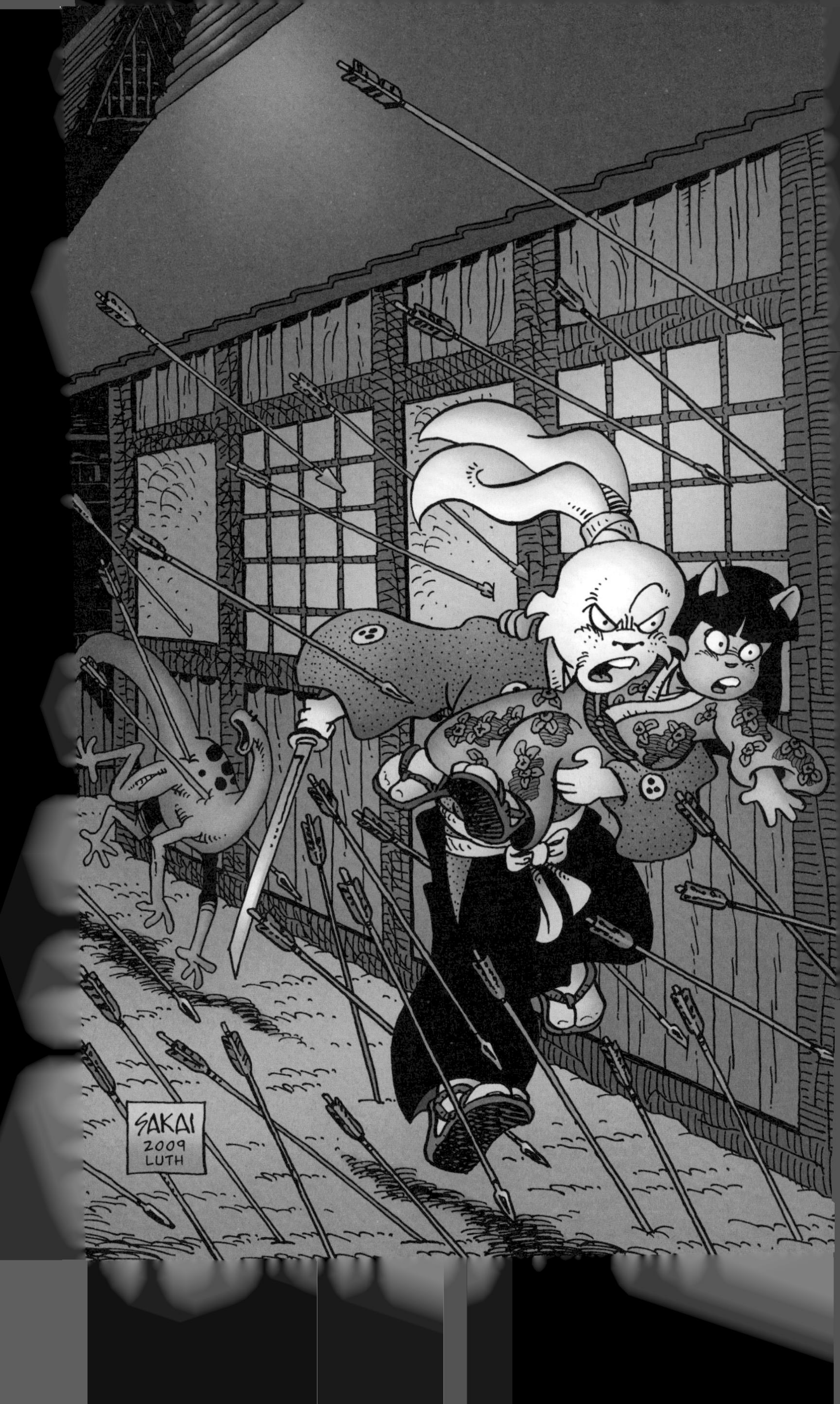
SAKAI
2009
LUTH

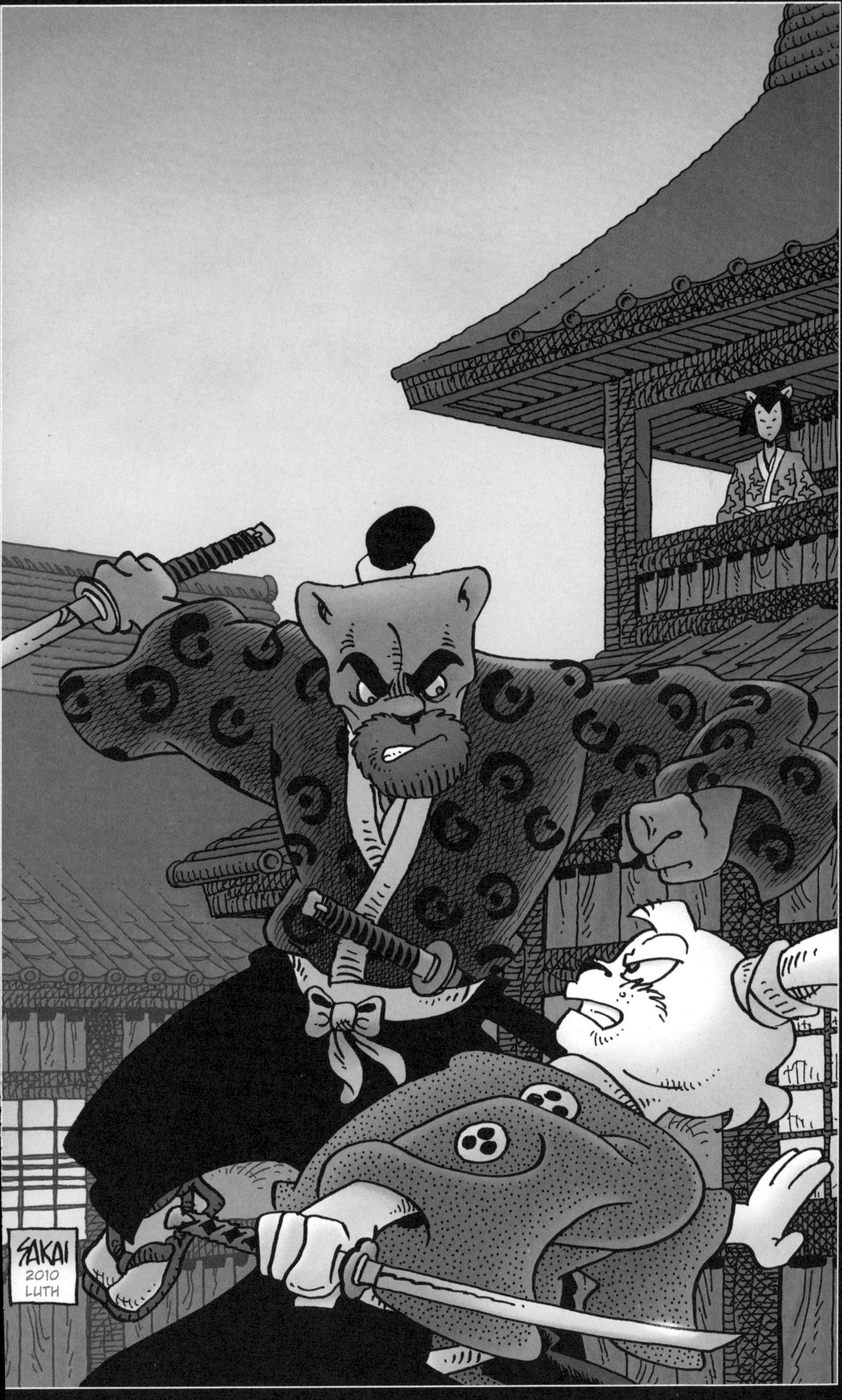
SAKAI
2010
LUTH

*Usagi Yojimbo Volume Three #129*

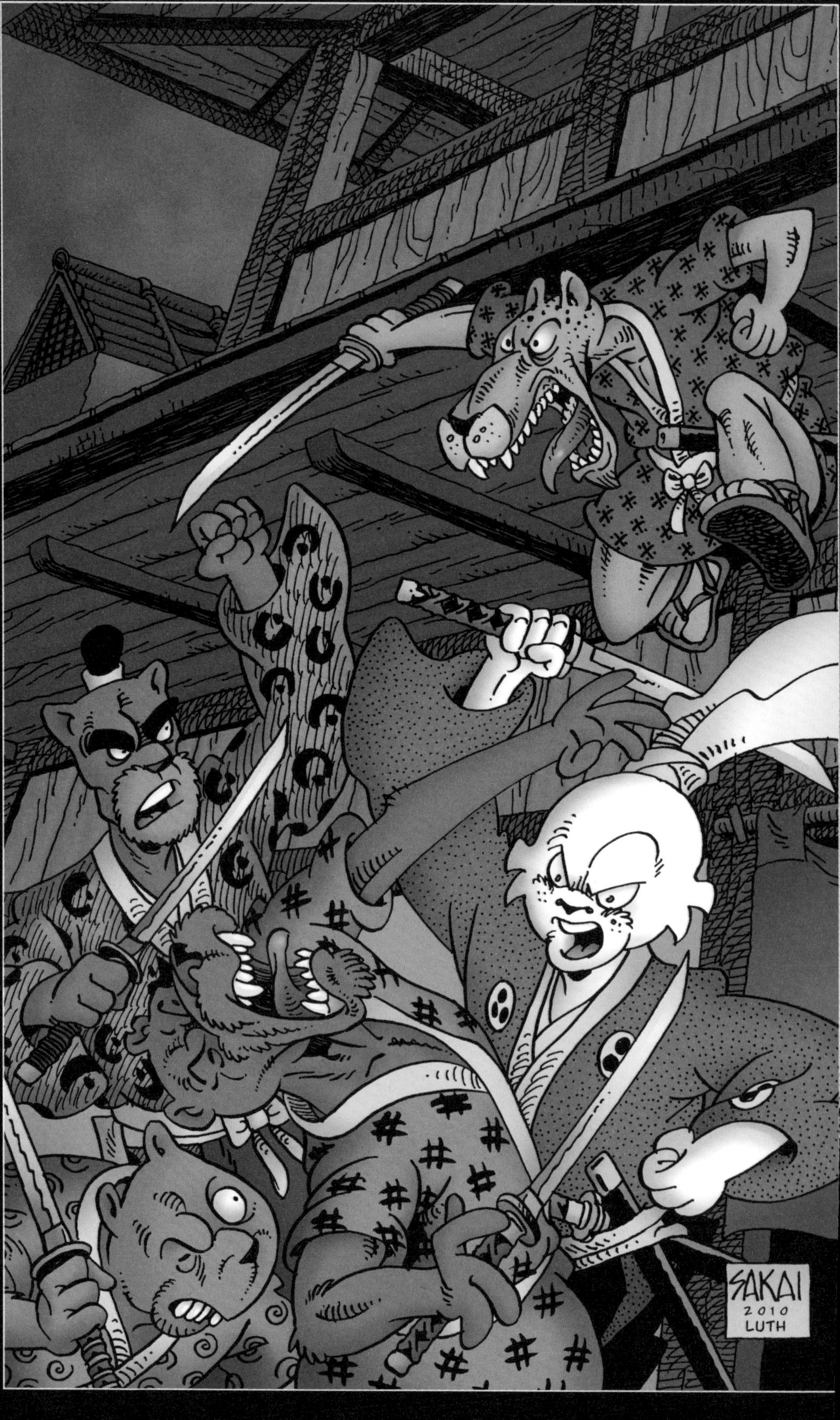
SAKAI
2010
LUTH

*Usagi Yojimbo Volume Three #130*

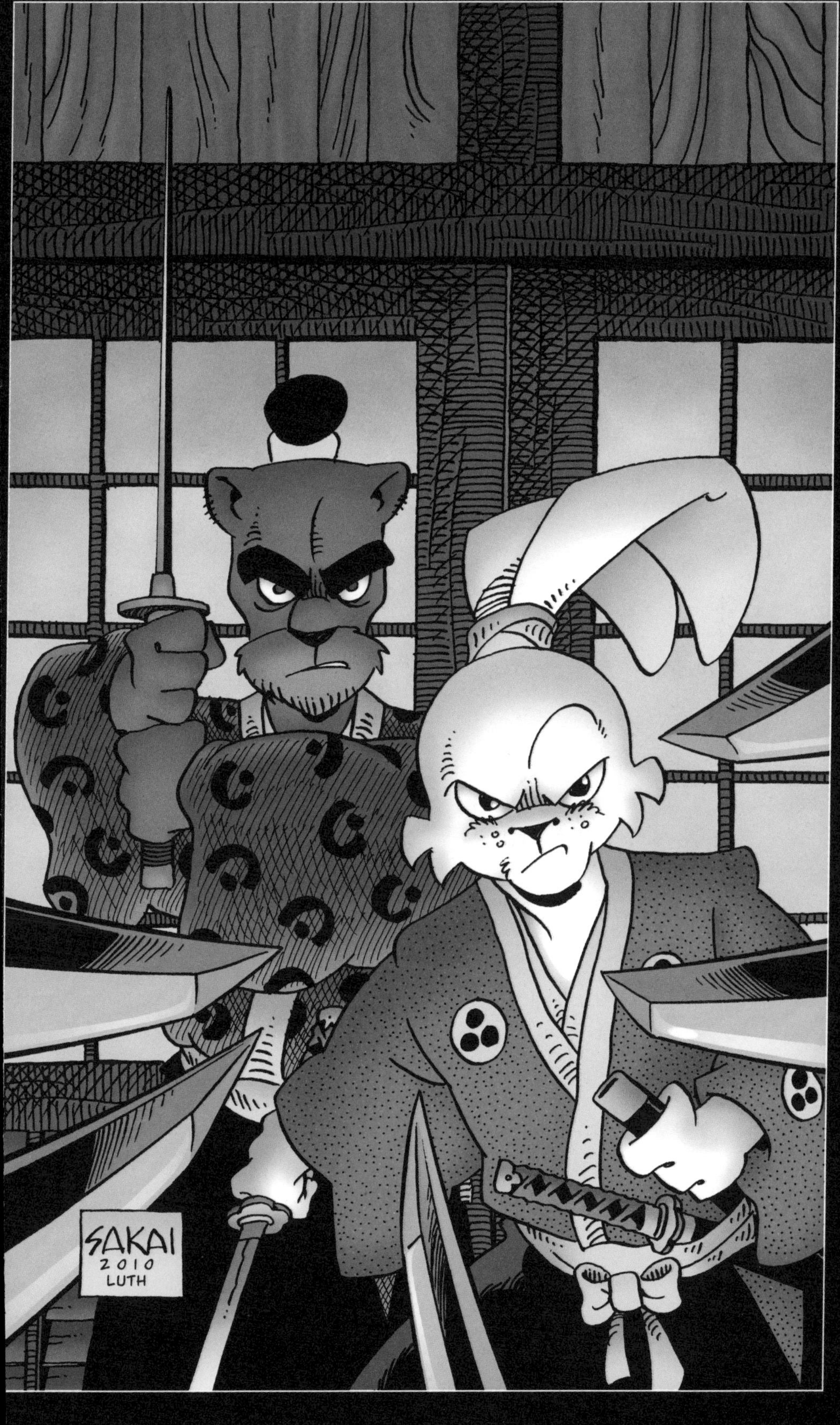
SAKAI
2010
LUTH
*Usagi Yojimbo Volume Three #131*

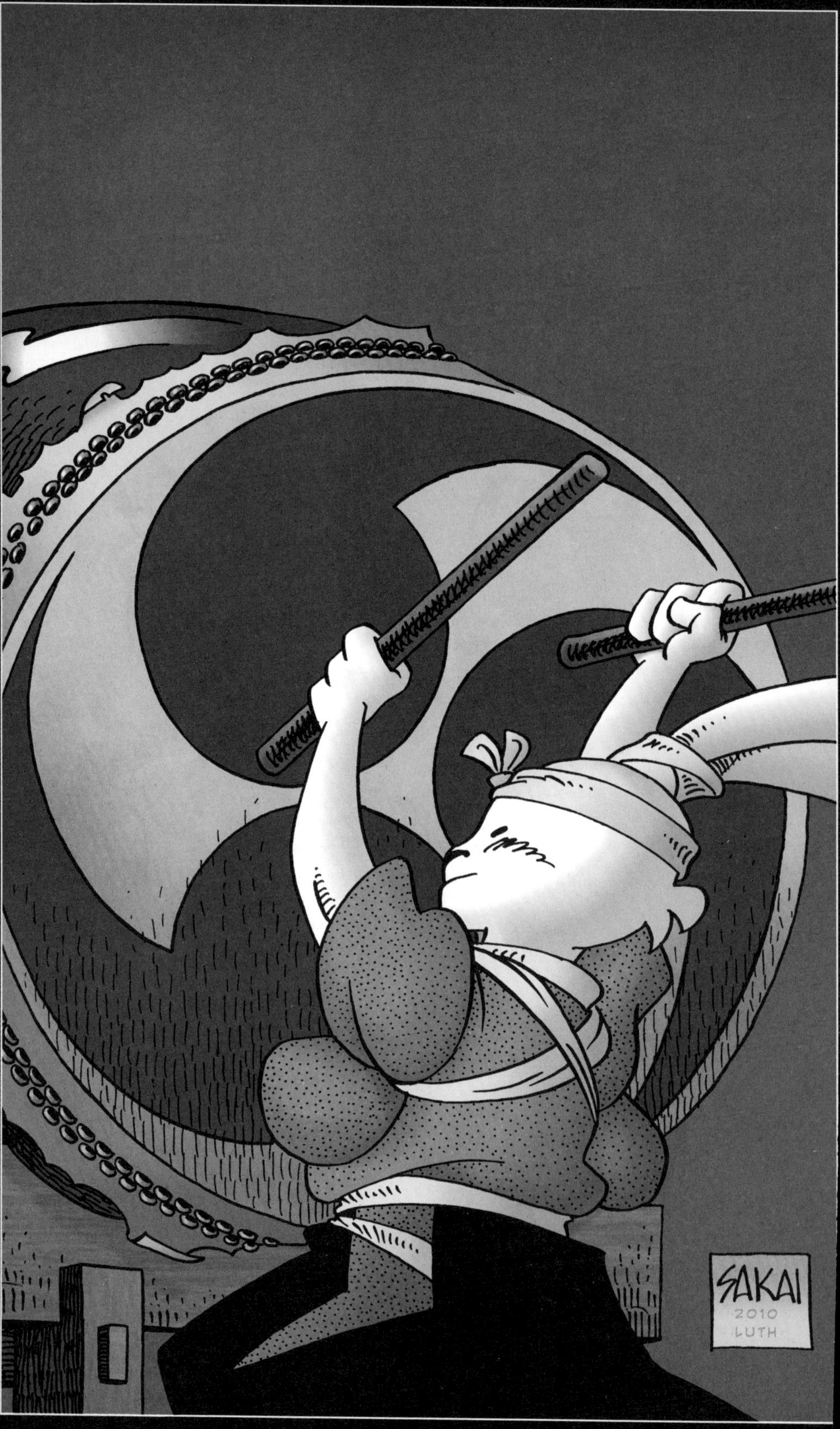
SAKAI
2010
LUTH

*Usagi Yojimbo Volume Three #132*

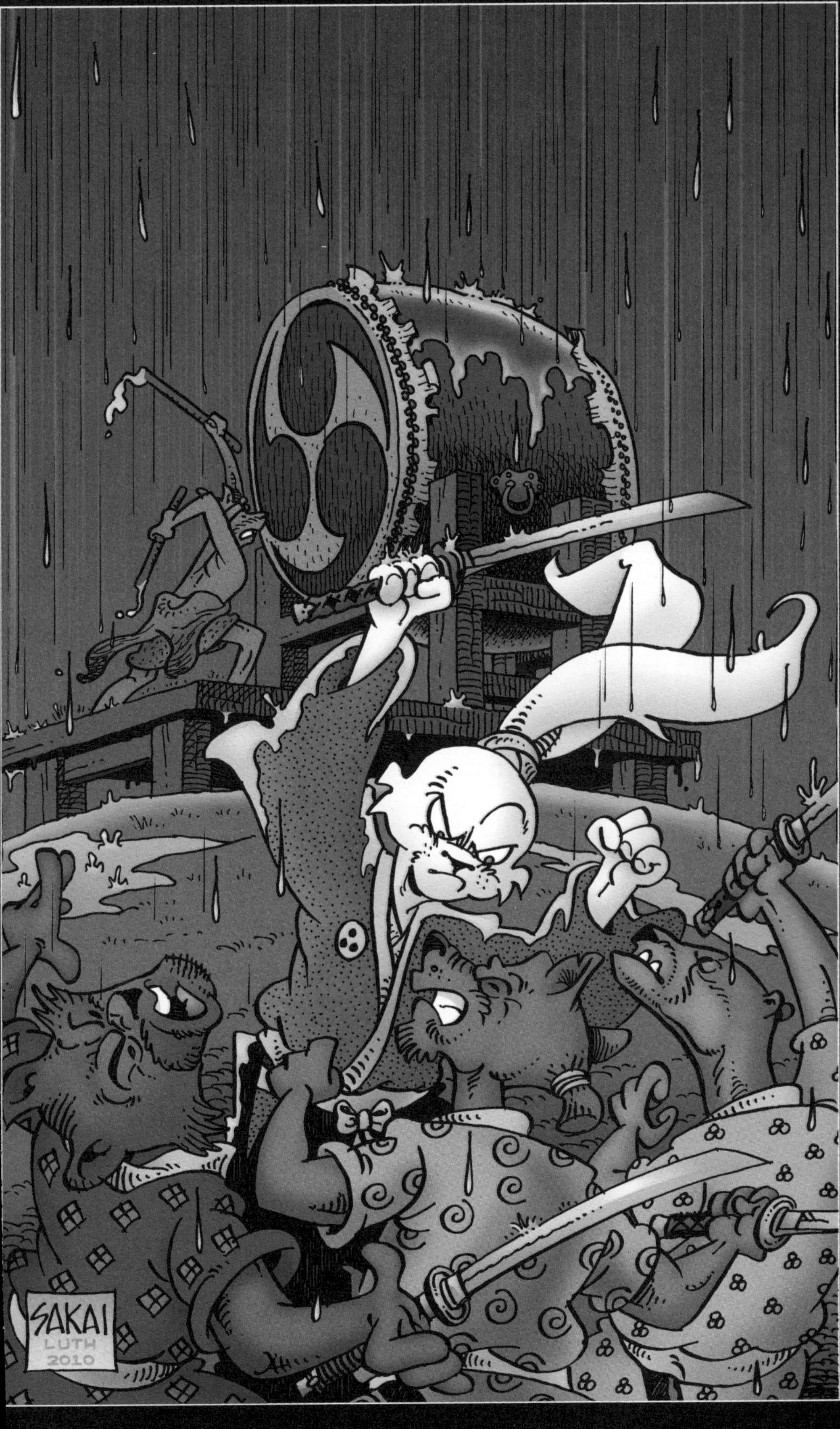
SAKAI
LUTH
2010

*Usagi Yojimbo Volume Three #133*

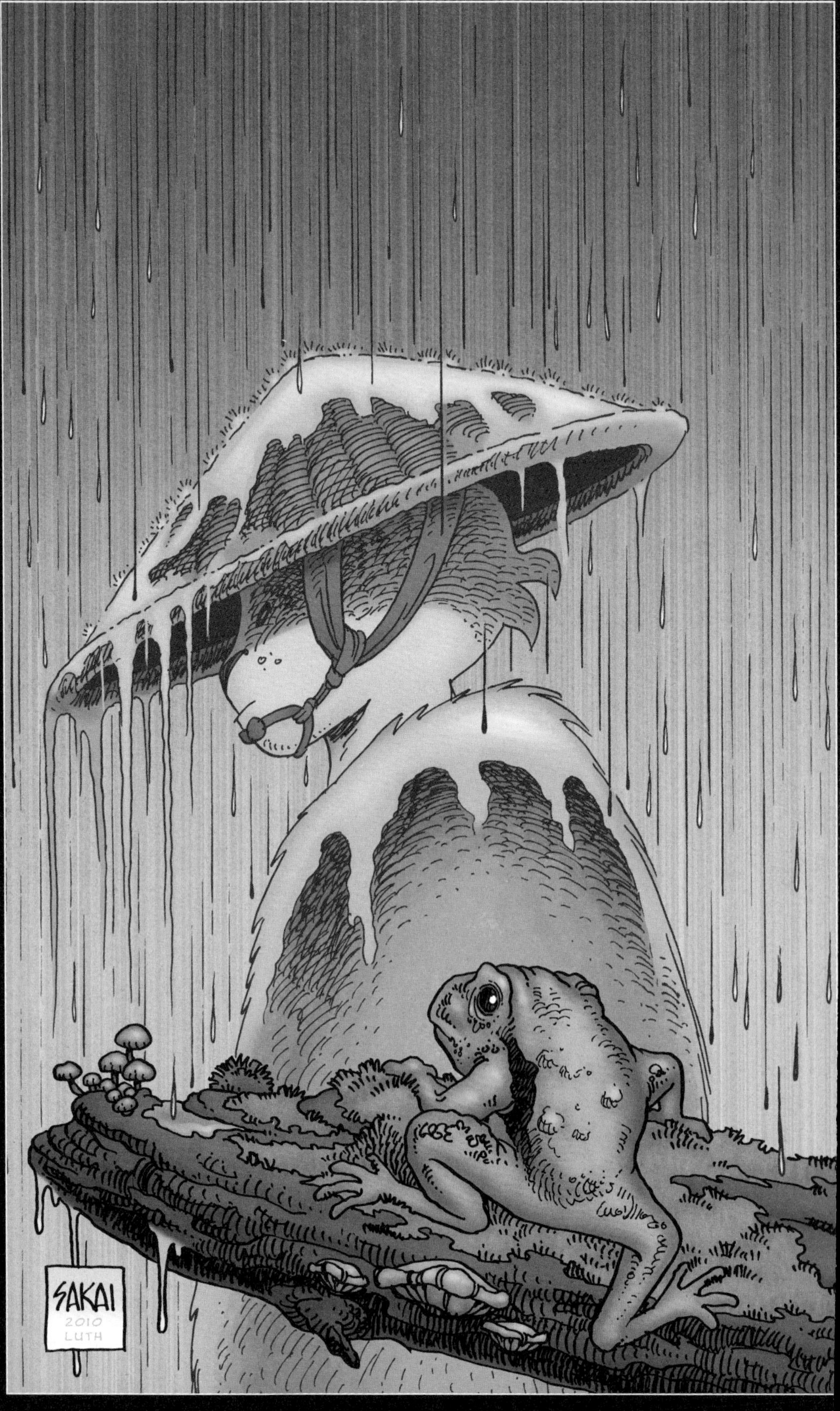
SAKAI
2010
LUTH

*Usagi Yojimbo Volume Three #134*

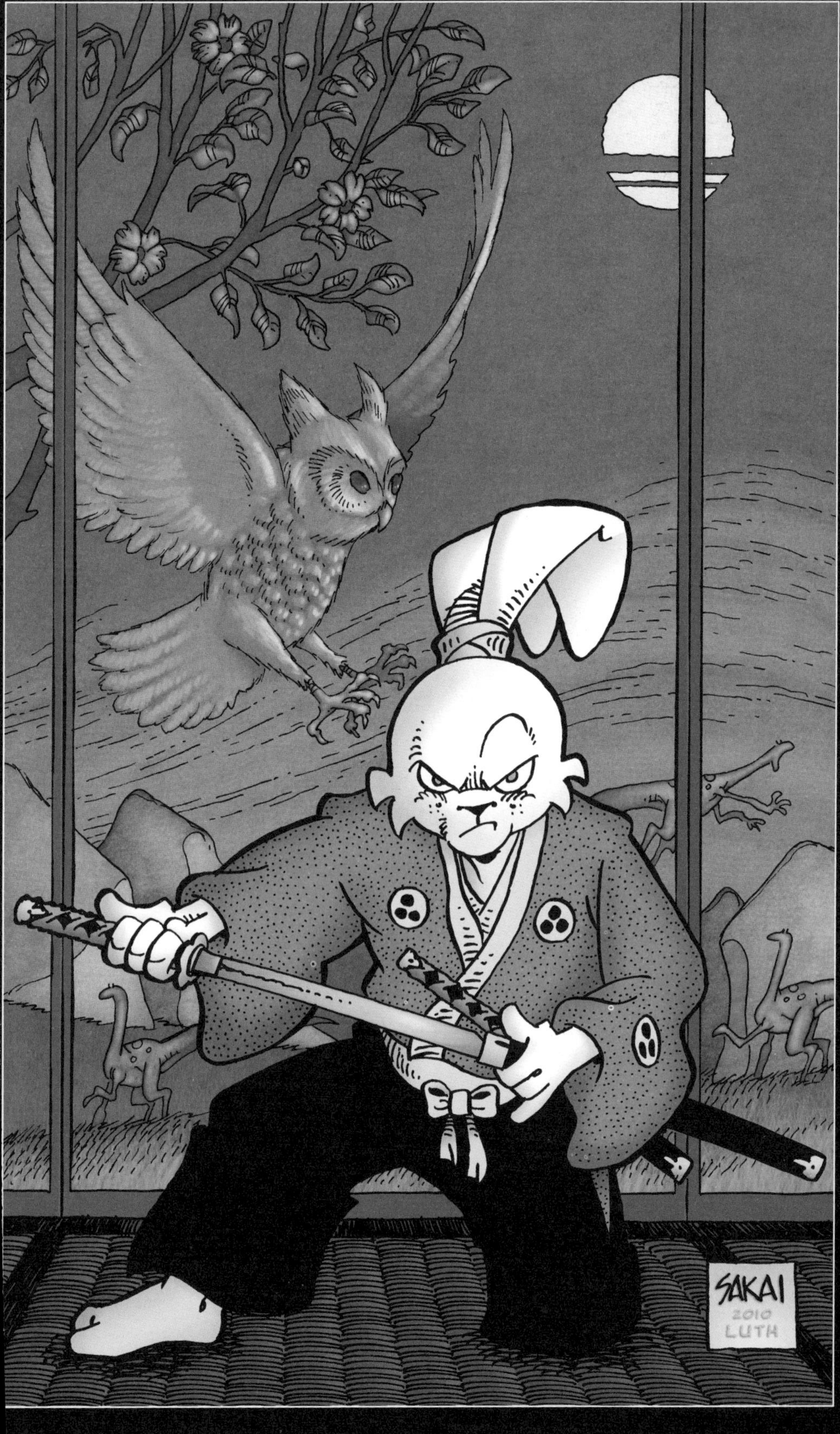
SAKAI
2010
LUTH

*Usagi Yojimbo Volume Three #135*

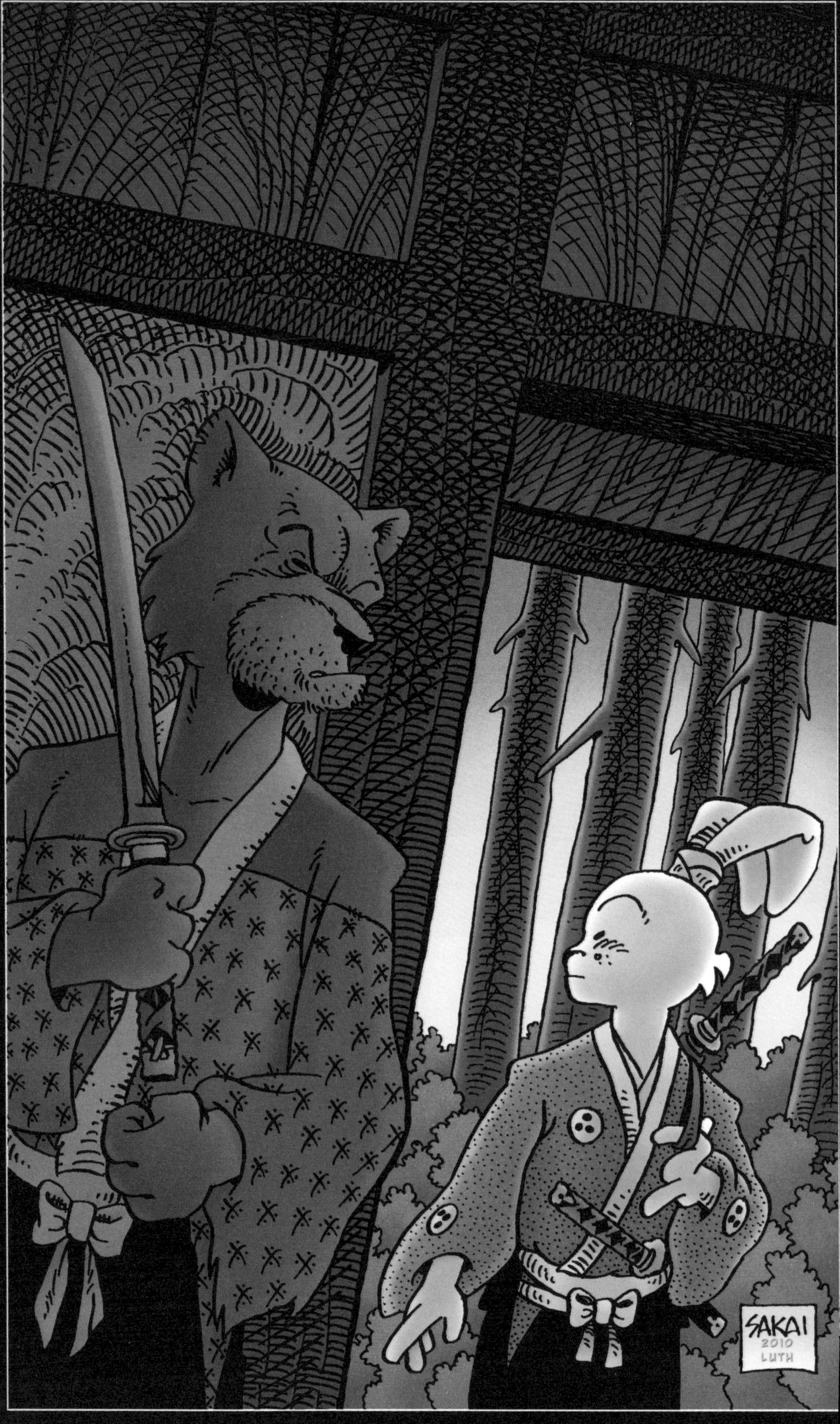
SAKAI
2010
LUTH

*Usagi Yojimbo Volume Three #136*

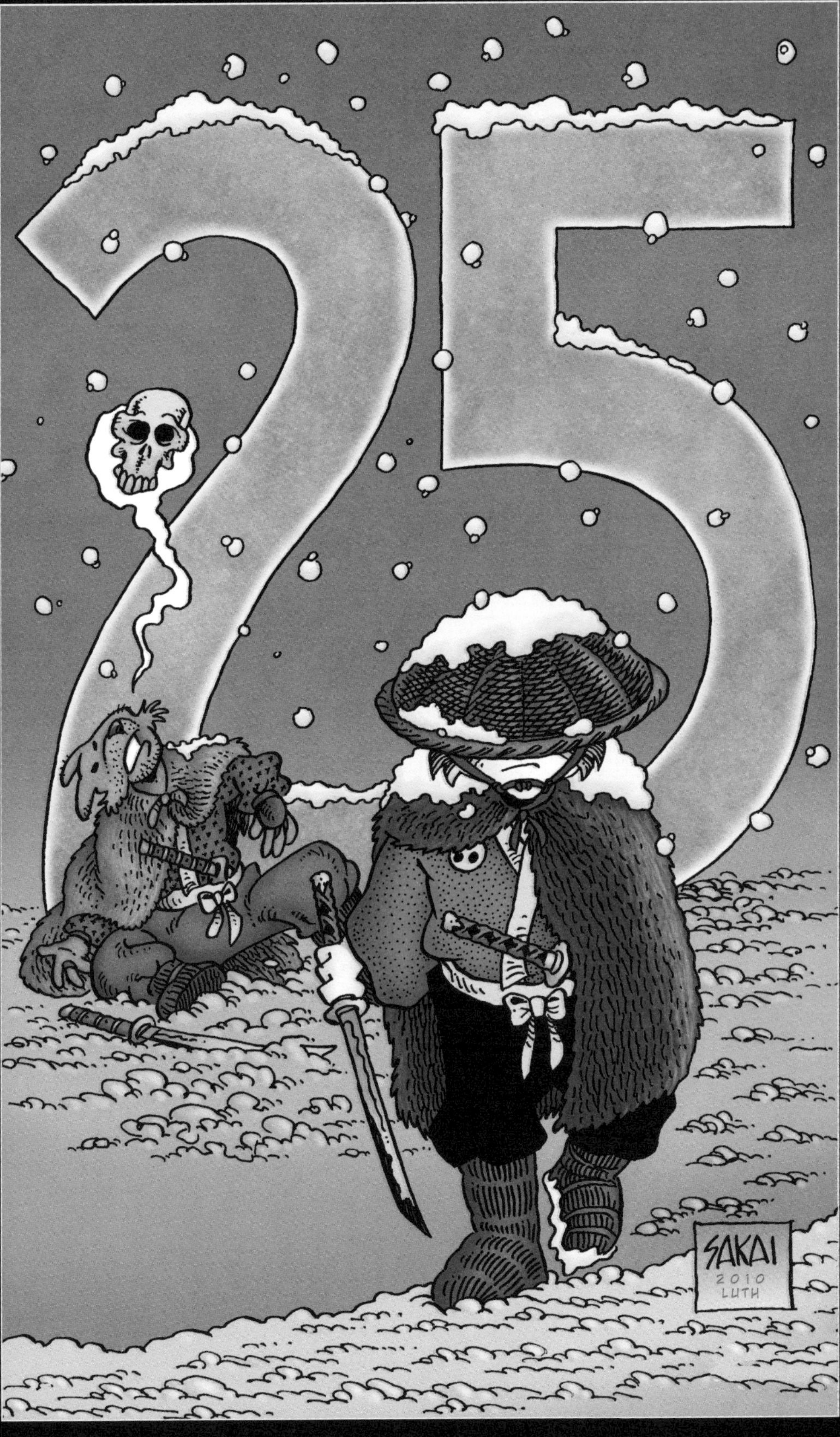
SAKAI
2010
LUTH

*Usagi Yojimbo Volume Three* #136, Dark Horse 25th Anniversary variant cover

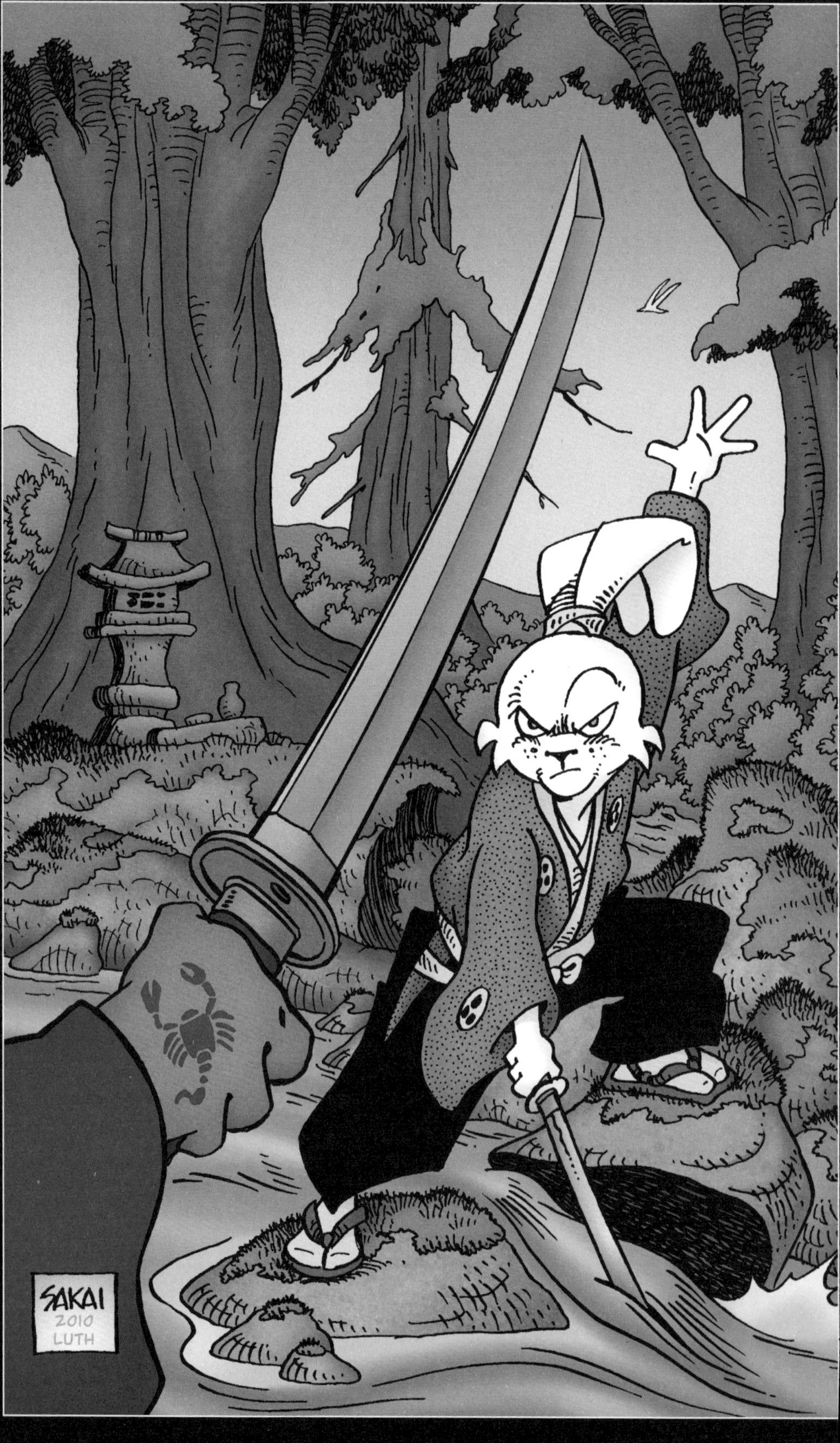
SAKAI
2010
LUTH
*Usagi Yojimbo Volume Three #137*

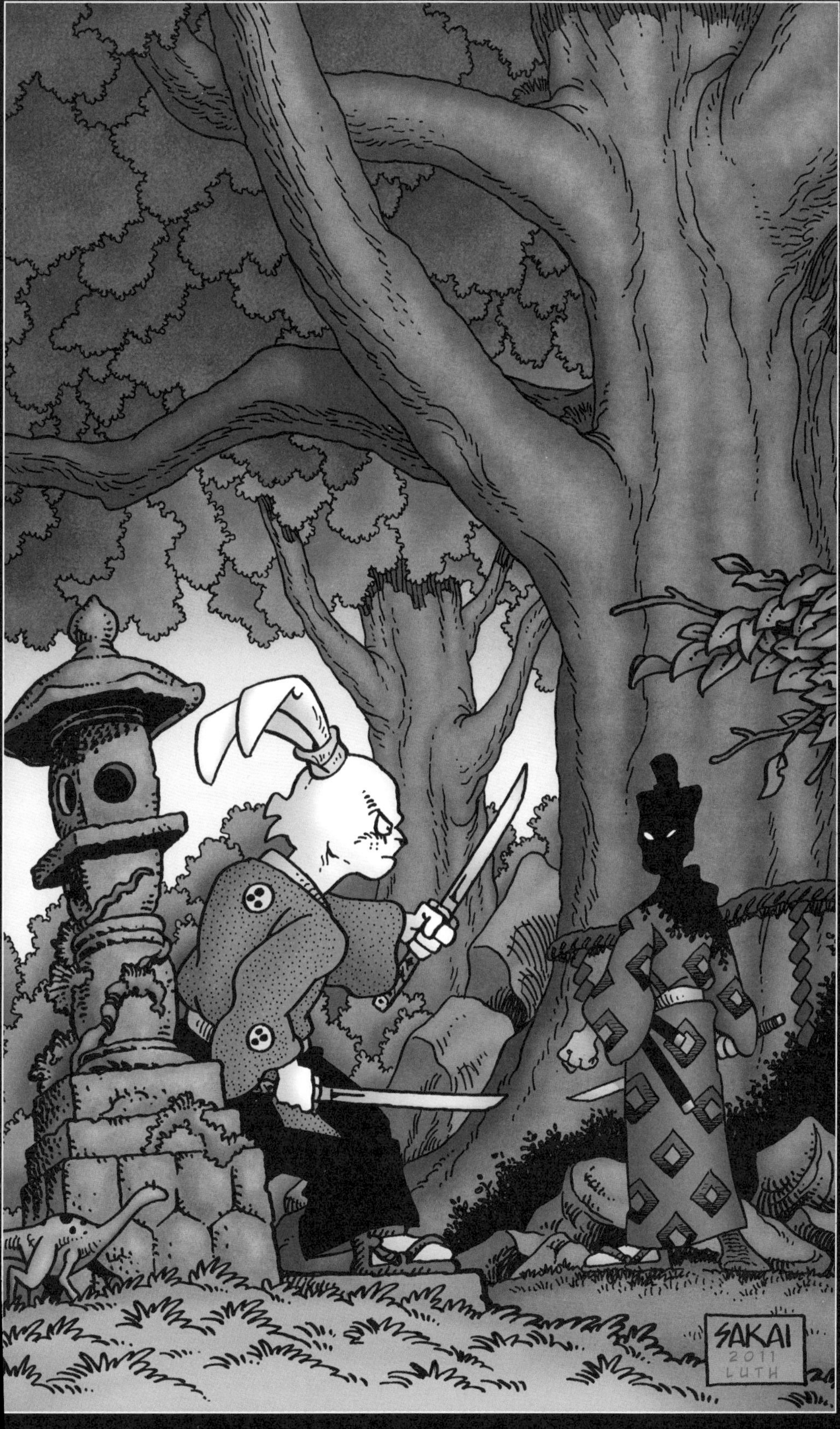
SAKAI
2011
LUTH
*Usagi Yojimbo Volume Three #138*

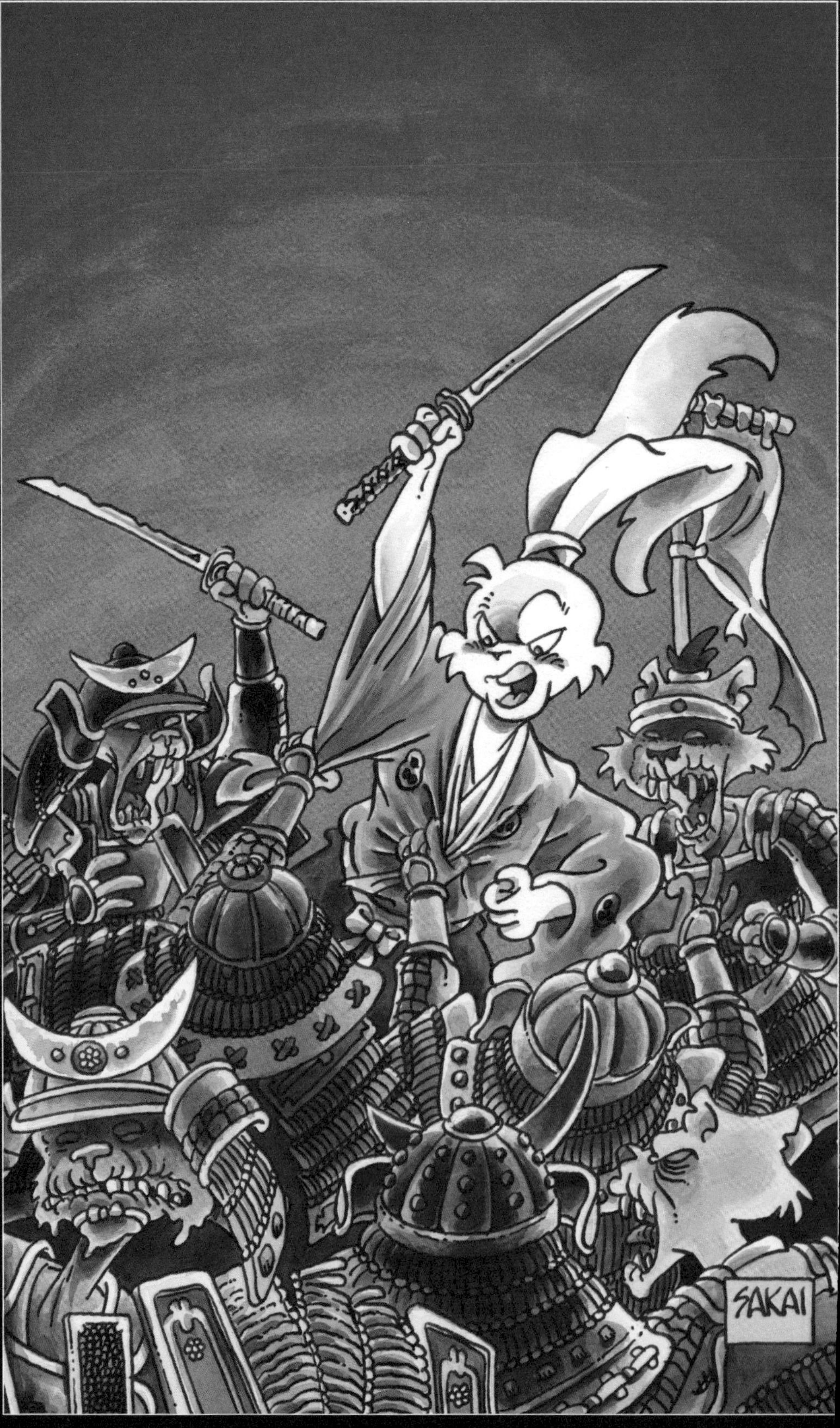
SAKAI

*Usagi Yojimbo* Book 26: *Traitors of the Earth*

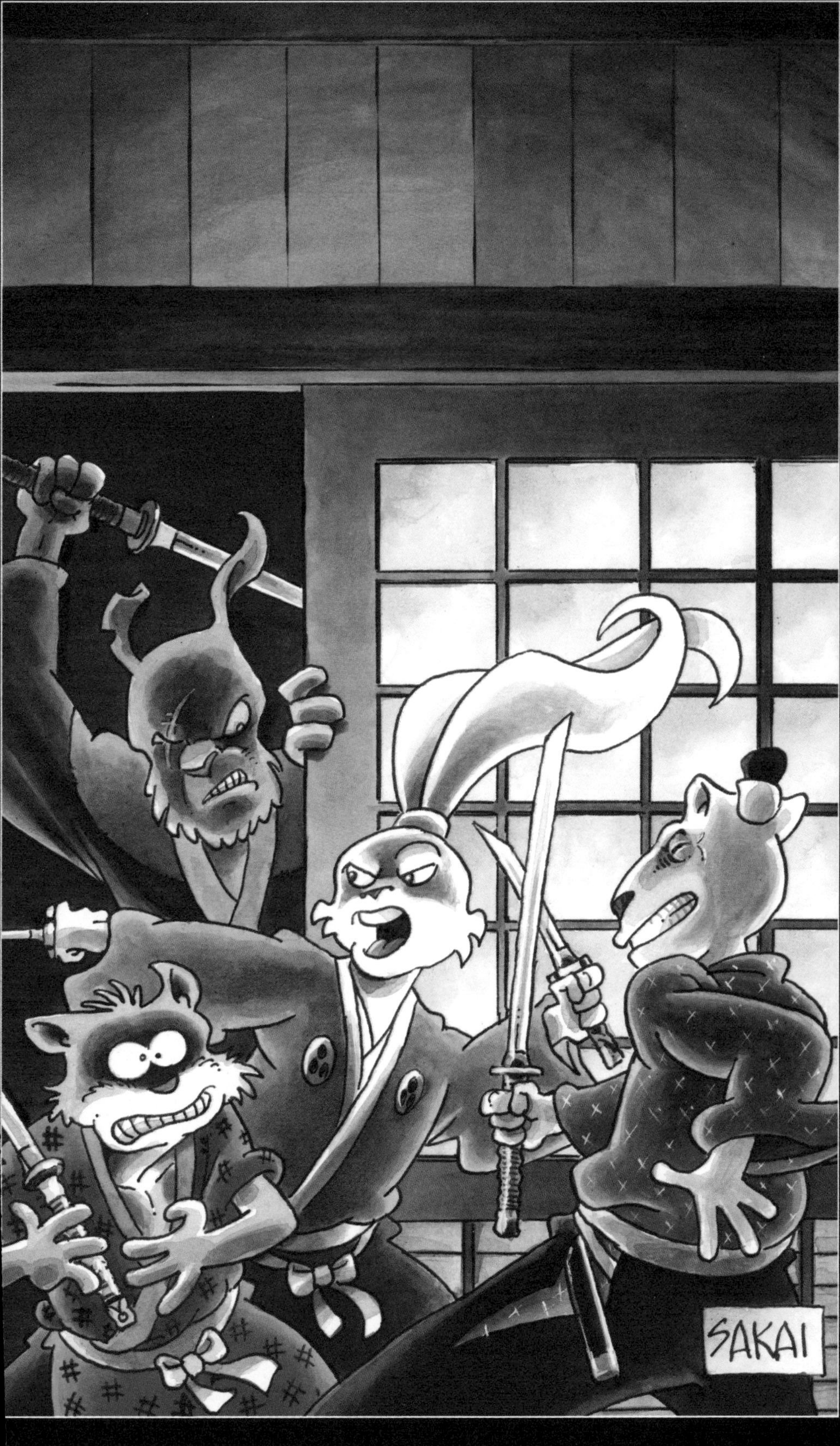
SAKAI

*Usagi Yojimbo* Book 27: *A Town Called Hell*

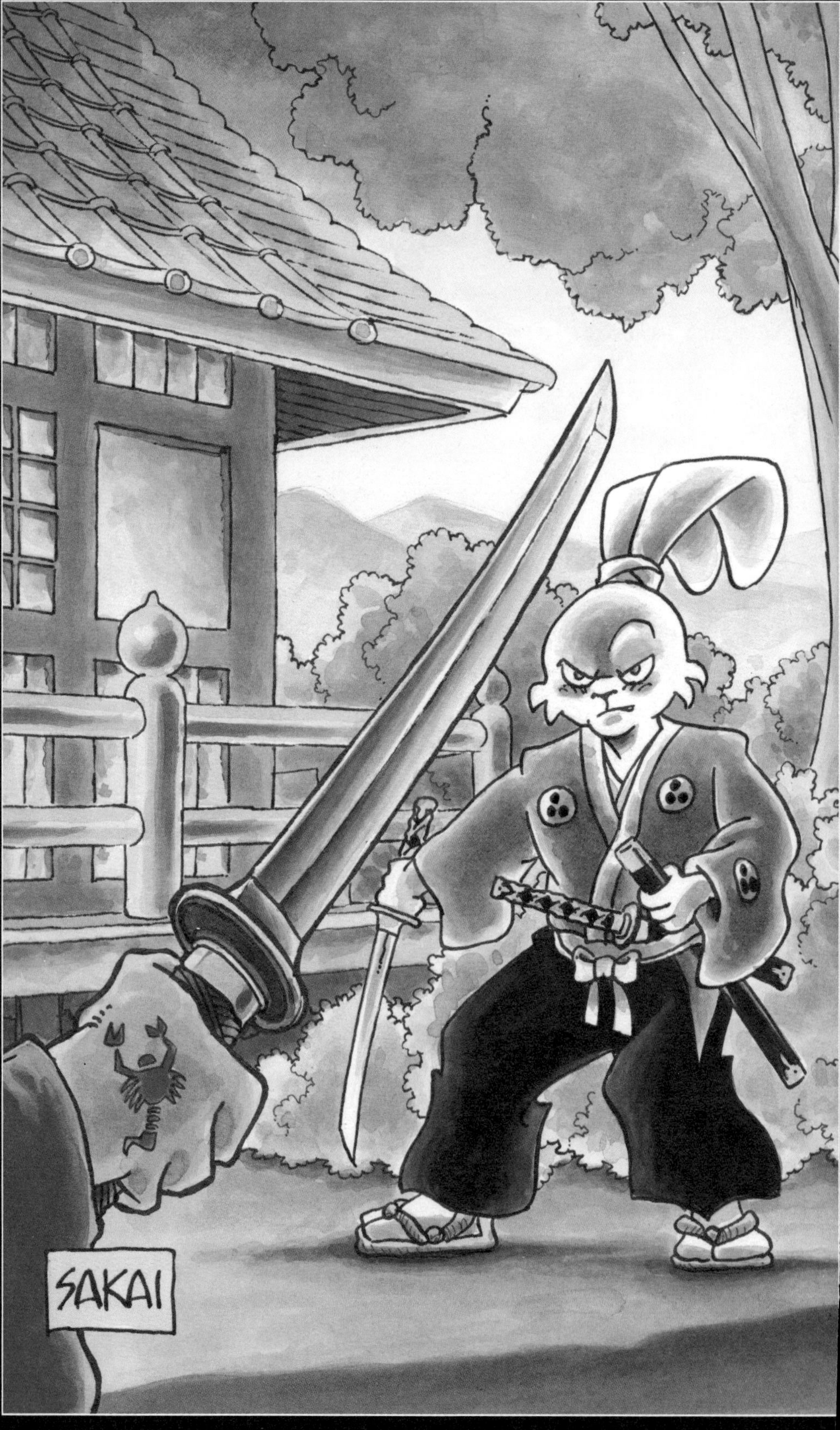
SAKAI
*Usagi Yojimbo* Book 28: *Red Scorpion*

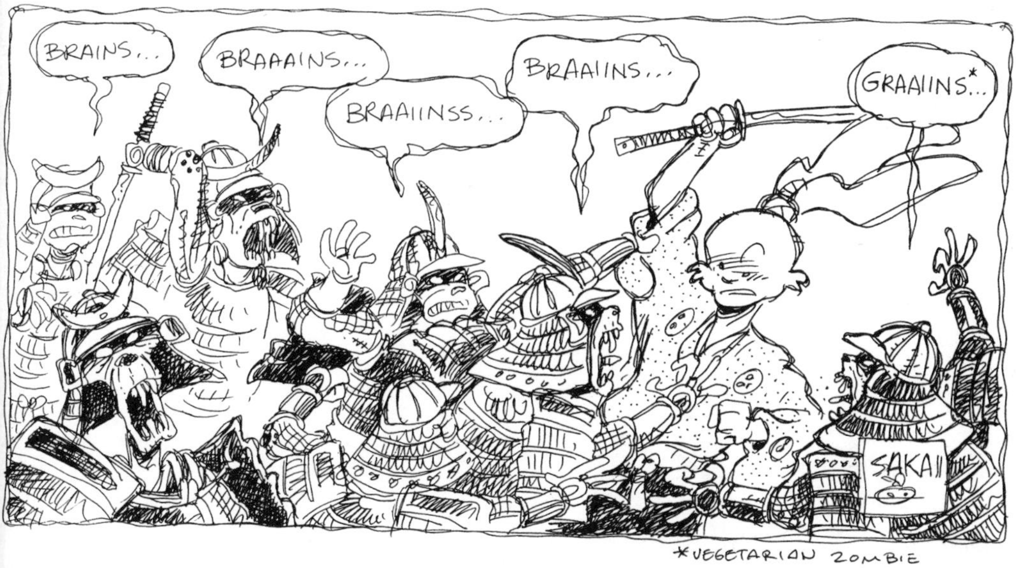
BRAINS...
BRAAAINS...
BRAAIINSS...
BRAAIINS...
GRAAIINS*...
SAKAI
*VEGETARIAN ZOMBIE

Stan's original concept art for *Usagi Yojimbo Volume Three* #119's wraparound cover, with dialogue added!

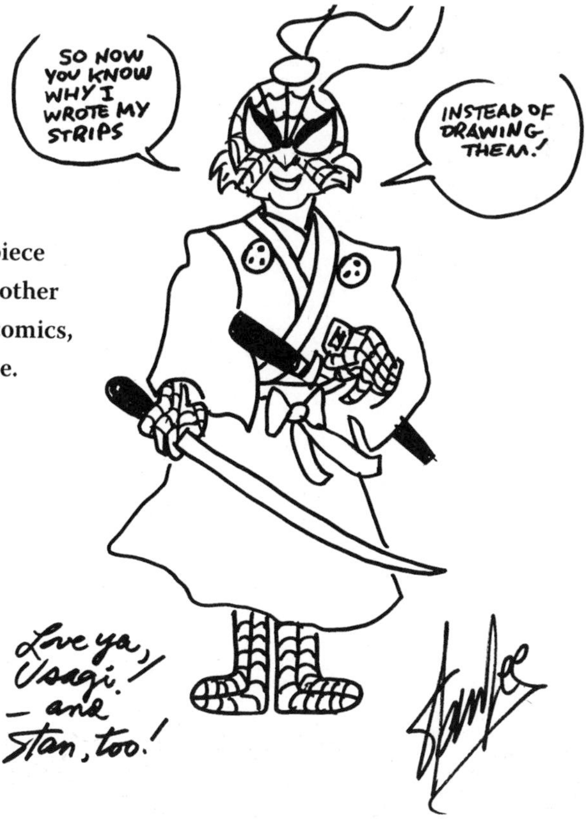
SO NOW YOU KNOW WHY I WROTE MY STRIPS
INSTEAD OF DRAWING THEM!
Love ya, Usagi! — and Stan, too!
Stan Lee

An amazing piece of fan art by another famous Stan in comics, Mr. Stan Lee.

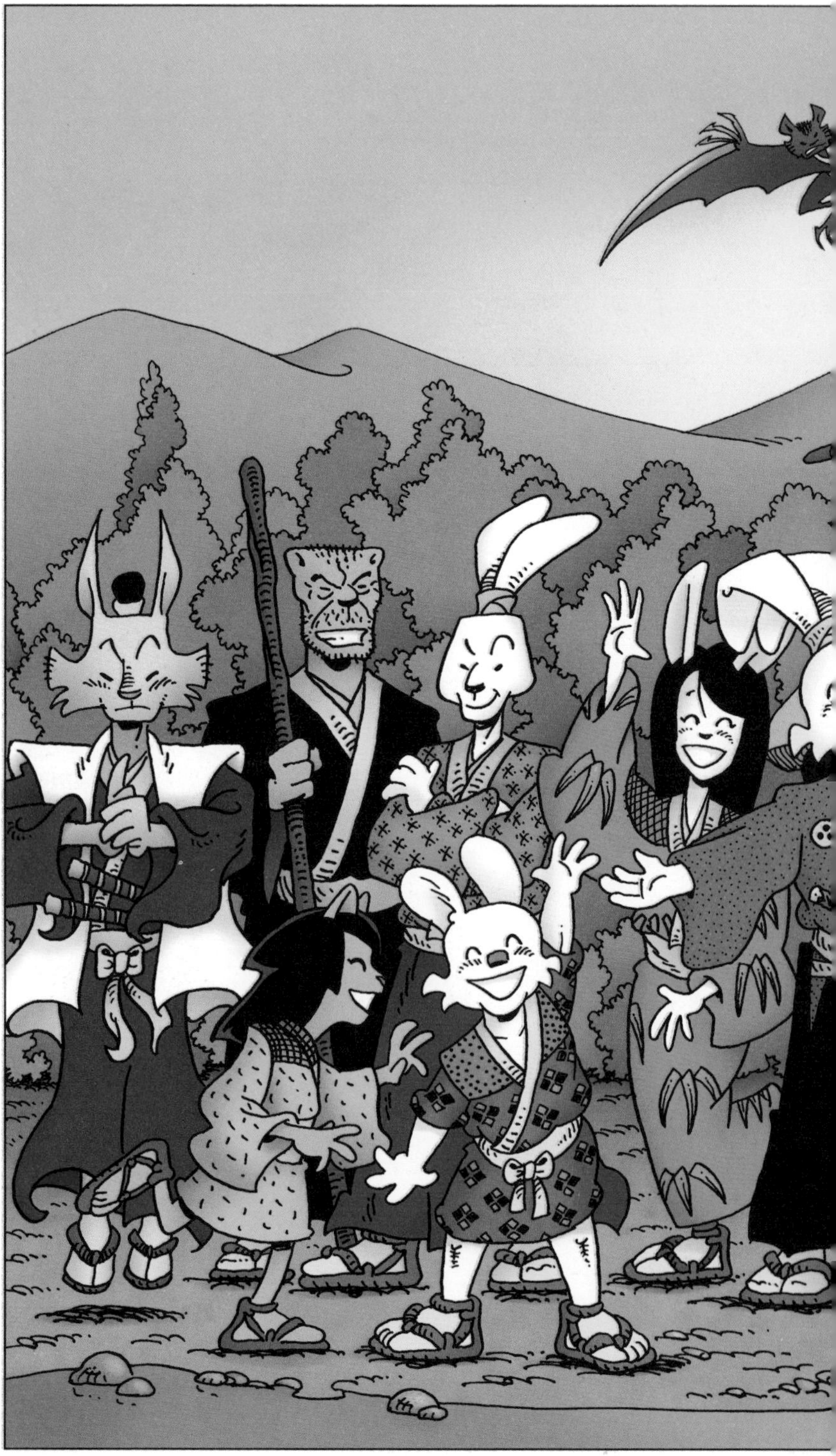

This poster art was created to commemorate *Usagi Yojimbo*'s twenty-fifth anniversary in 2009. Colors by Tom Luth.

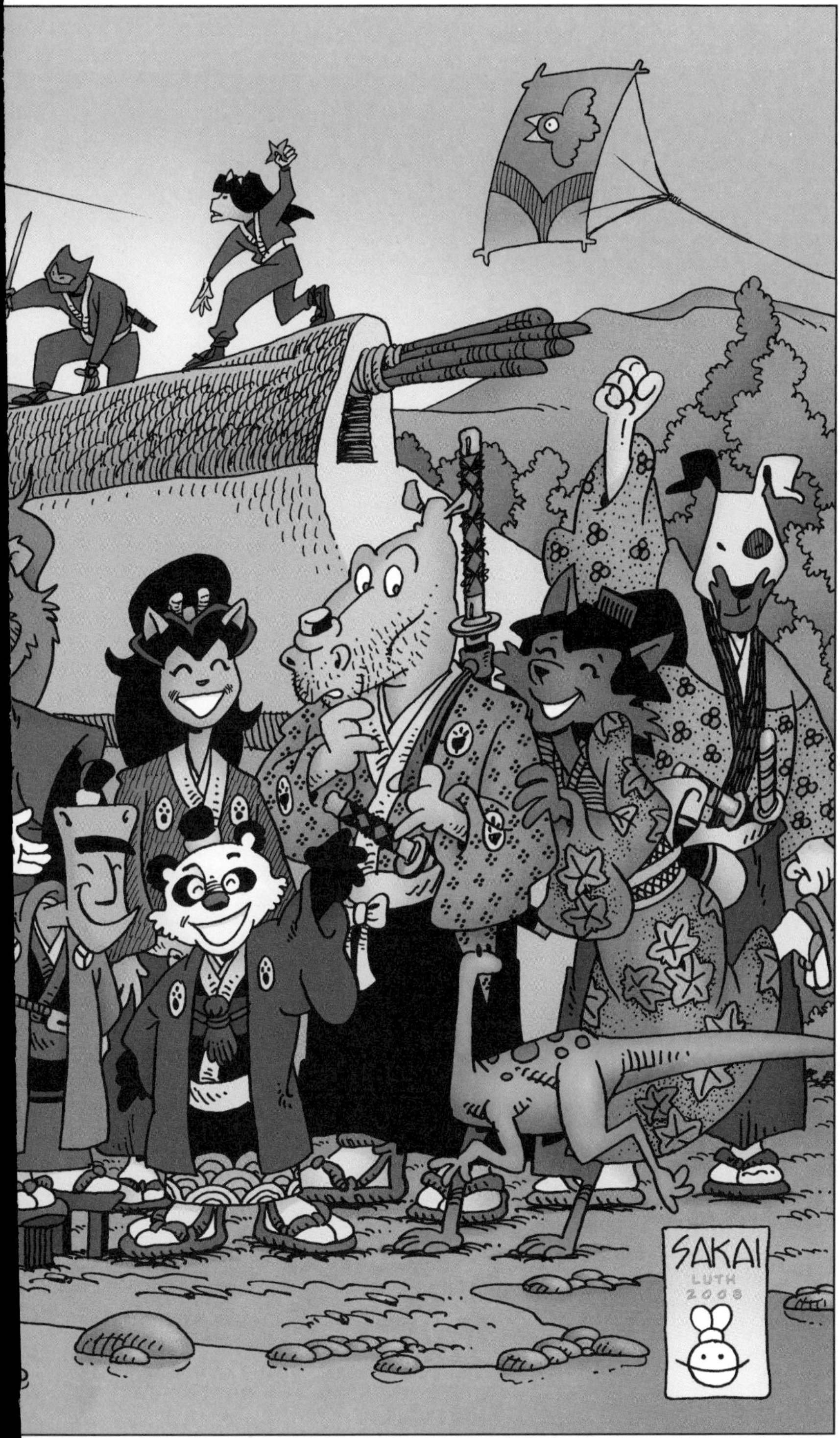
SAKAI
LUTH
2008

# 2009 SAN DIEGO COMIC-CON

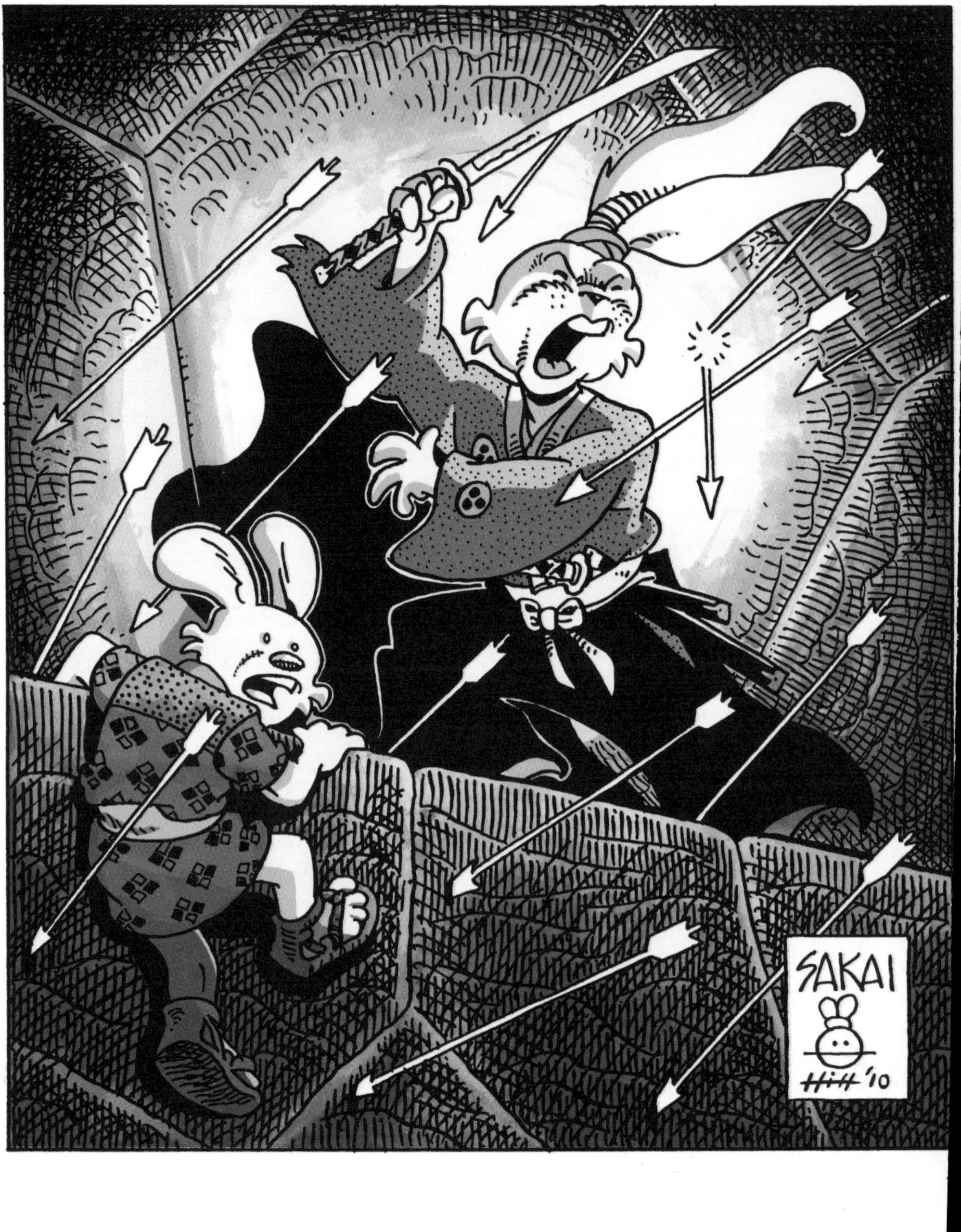
SAKAI
Hill '10

Art from Stan Sakai's 2009 San Diego Comic-Con signing card, created as a benefit for th
Comic Book Legal Defense Fund. Previously reprinted on the back cover of *Usagi Yojimb
Volume Three* #127. Colors by Ryan Hill.

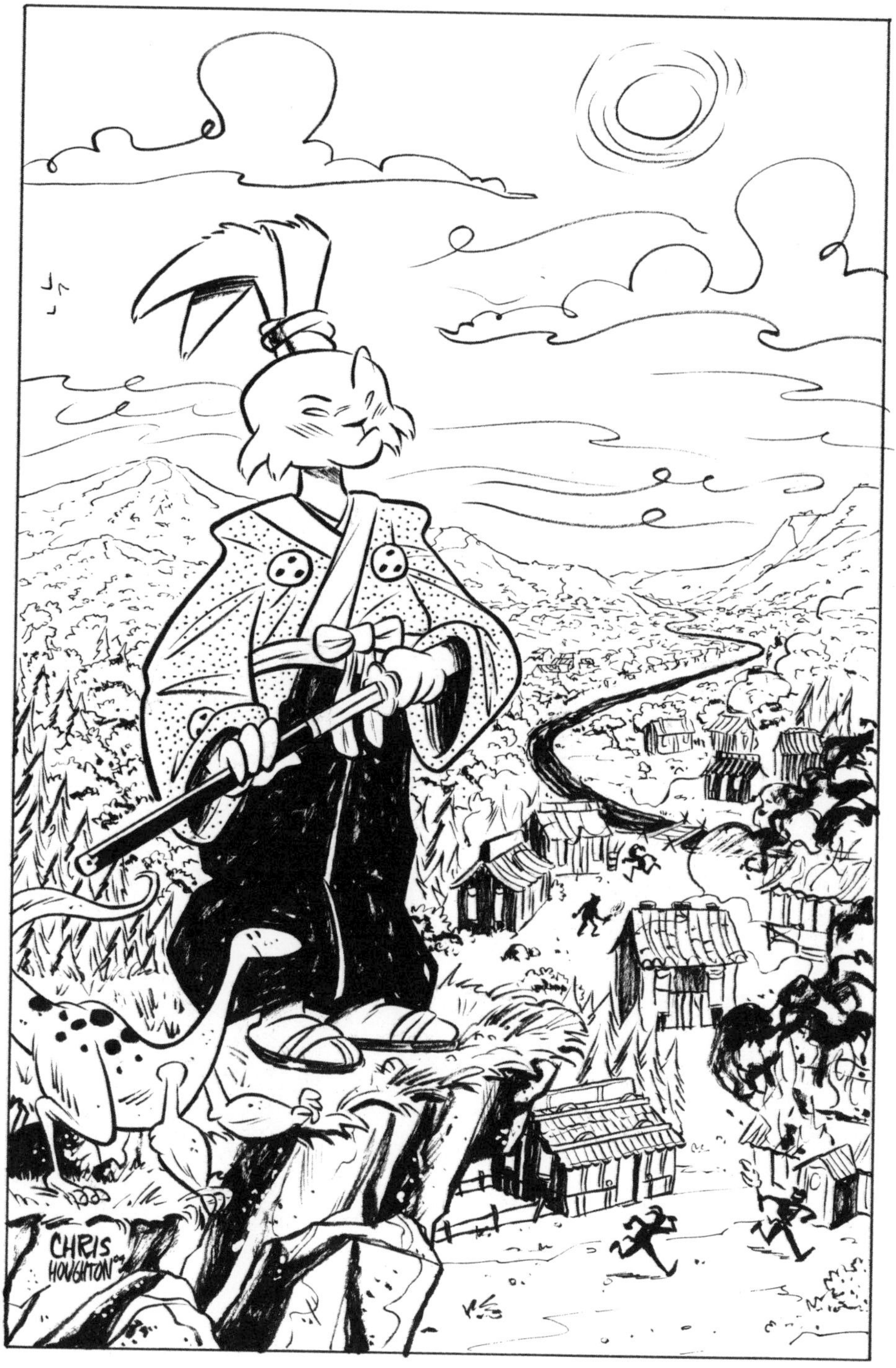
CHRIS HOUGHTON

Chris Houghton

*Stan in the Canadian Rockies at Lake Minnewanka, just outside of Banff, Alberta. Photo by Andy Runton.*

**STAN SAKAI** was born in Kyoto, Japan, grew up in Hawaii, and now lives in California with his wife, Julie. He has two children, Hannah and Matthew, and two stepchildren, Daniel and Emi. Stan received a fine arts degree from the University of Hawaii and furthered his studies at the Art Center College of Design in Pasadena, California.

Stan's creation *Usagi Yojimbo* first appeared in comics in 1984. Since then, Usagi has been on television as a guest of the Teenage Mutant Ninja Turtles and has been made into toys, seen on clothing, and featured in a series of graphic novel collections.

In 1991, Stan created *Space Usagi*, a series dealing with samurai in a futuristic setting, featuring the adventures of a descendant of the original Usagi.

Stan is also an award-winning letterer for his work on Sergio Aragonés's *Groo*, the *Spider-Man* Sunday newspaper strips, and *Usagi Yojimbo*.

Stan is the recipient of a Parents' Choice Award, an Inkpot Award, an American Library Association Award, a Harvey Award, five Spanish Haxtur Awards, several Eisner Awards, and an Inkwell Award. In 2003 he won the prestigious National Cartoonists Society Award in the Comic Book Division, and in 2011 Stan received the Cultural Ambassador Award from the Japanese American National Museum.

# USAGI™ YOJIMBO

## Created, Written, and Illustrated by Stan Sakai

AILABLE FROM
RK HORSE COMICS

*e Usagi Yojimbo Saga Book 1*
lects *Usagi Yojimbo* Books 8–10
.99 | ISBN 978-1-61655-609-9

*e Usagi Yojimbo Saga Book 2*
lects *Usagi Yojimbo* Books 11–13
.99 | ISBN 978-1-61655-610-5

*e Usagi Yojimbo Saga Book 3*
lects *Usagi Yojimbo* Books 14–16
.99 | ISBN 978-1-61655-611-2

*e Usagi Yojimbo Saga Book 4*
lects *Usagi Yojimbo* Books 17–19
.99 | ISBN 978-1-61655-612-9

*e Usagi Yojimbo Saga Book 5*
lects *Usagi Yojimbo* Books 20–22
.99 | ISBN 978-1-61655-613-6

*e Usagi Yojimbo Saga Book 6*
lects *Usagi Yojimbo* Books 23–25
.99 | ISBN 978-1-61655-614-3

*e Usagi Yojimbo Saga Book 7*
lects *Usagi Yojimbo* Books 26–28
.99 | ISBN 978-1-61655-615-0

*ok 29:*
*o Hundred Jizo*
.99 | ISBN 978-1-61655-840-6

*Book 30:*
*Thieves and Spies*
$17.99 | ISBN 978-1-50670-048-9

*Usagi Yojimbo: Yokai*
$14.99 | ISBN 978-1-59582-362-5

*Usagi Yojimbo: Senso*
$19.99 | ISBN 978-1-61655-709-6

*Space Usagi*
$17.99 | ISBN 978-1-56971-290-0

*The Art of Usagi Yojimbo*
$29.95 | ISBN 978-1-59307-493-7

*The Sakai Project:*
*Artists Celebrate Thirty*
*Years of Usagi Yojimbo*
$29.99 | ISBN 978-1-61655-556-6

*Gallery Edition Volume 1:*
*Samurai and Other Stories*
$125.00 | ISBN 978-1-61655-923-6

*Gallery Edition Volume 2:*
*The Artist and Other Stories*
$125.00 | ISBN 978-1-61655-924-3
**COMING OCTOBER 2016**

*47 Ronin*
Written by Mike Richardson
$19.99 | ISBN 978-1-59582-954-2

*The Adventures of Nilson*
*Groundthumper and Hermy*
$14.99 | ISBN 978-1-61655-341-8

AVAILABLE FROM
FANTAGRAPHICS BOOKS
*fantagraphics.com*

*Book 1: The Ronin*
*Book 2: Samurai*
*Book 3: The Wanderer's Road*
*Book 4: The Dragon Bellow Conspiracy*
*Book 5: Lone Goat and Kid*
*Book 6: Circles*
*Book 7: Gen's Story*

ZZZZ...
USAGI

AVAILABLE AT YOUR LOCAL COMICS SHOP OR BOOKSTORE
- To find a comics shop near your area, call 1-888-266-4226. For more information or to order direct:
- On the web: DarkHorse.com • E-mail: mailorder@darkhorse.com
- Phone: 1-800-862-0052 Mon.-Fri. 9 A.M. to 5 P.M. Pacific Time. *Prices and availability subject to change without notice.

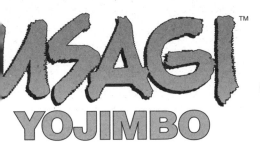

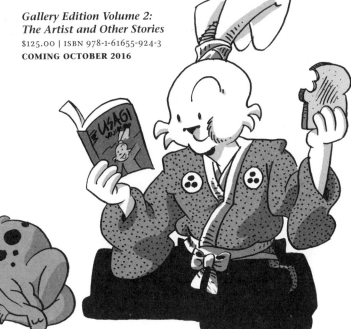

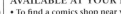

# Dark Horse Comics, Inc.

*President and Publisher* **MIKE RICHARDSON**

*Executive Vice President* **NEIL HANKERSON**

*Chief Financial Officer* **TOM WEDDLE**

*Vice President of Publishing* **RANDY STRADLEY**

*Vice President of Book Trade Sales* **MICHAEL MARTENS**

*Vice President of Marketing* **MATT PARKINSON**

*Vice President of Product Development* **DAVID SCROGGY**

*Vice President of Information Technology* **DALE LaFOUNTAIN**

*Vice President of Production and Scheduling* **CARA NIECE**

*Vice President of Media Licensing* **NICK McWHORTER**

*General Counsel* **KEN LIZZI**

*Editor in Chief* **DAVE MARSHALL**

*Editorial Director* **DAVEY ESTRADA**

*Executive Senior Editor* **SCOTT ALLIE**

*Senior Books Editor* **CHRIS WARNER**

*Director of Print and Development* **CARY GRAZZINI**

*Art Director* **LIA RIBACCHI**

*Director of Digital Publishing* **MARK BERNARDI**

*Director of International Publishing and Licensing* **MICHAEL GOMBOS**